Step 2 - Practice

Making it easy to learn new things!

ORION gives you feedback on your performance, and you pick where to practice or study.

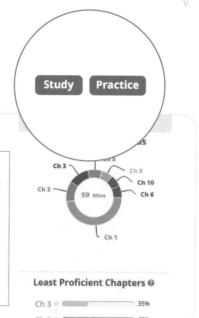

Ch 2: A Further Look at Financi... Practice	Proficiency	Performance
Identify the sections of a classified balance sheet.	41%	2/5
Identify tools for analyzing financial statements and ra...	65%	Study Practice
Explain the relationship between a retained earnings s...	47%	3/4
Identify and compute ratios for analyzing a company's ...	65%	5/5
Use the statement of cash flows to evaluate solvency.	31%	3/10
Explain the meaning of generally accepted accounting ...	56%	3/3
Discuss financial reporting concepts.	19%	1/7

Least Proficient Chapters

Ch 3 ○ ▬▬▬▬ 35%
Ch 1 ○ ▬▬▬▬ 45%

Step 3 - Maintain

Making it easy to remember everything you learn!

ORION provides a number of views into your overall proficiency so you can quickly review the things you might have forgotten before a quiz or exam.

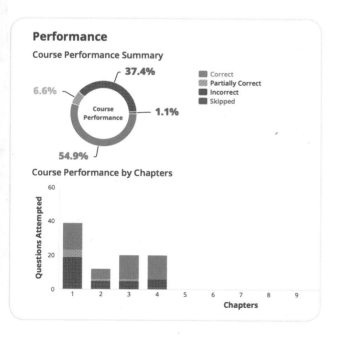

Performance

Course Performance Summary

37.4%
6.6%
Course Performance
1.1%
54.9%

- Correct
- Partially Correct
- Incorrect
- Skipped

Course Performance by Chapters

Metacognitive Report (Chapters)

Most Proficient

Least Confident — Most Confident

Least Proficient

RATIO SUMMARY
(Chapter 12)

	Ratio	Formula	Result	Chapter
Liquidity	Current Ratio	$\dfrac{\text{Current Assets}}{\text{Current Liabilities}}$	Ability to meet current obligations with current assets	6
	Quick Ratio	$\dfrac{\text{Current Assets} - \text{Inventory} - \text{Prepaid Expenses}}{\text{Current Liabilities}}$	Ability to meet current obligations with most liquid assets	6
Activity	Accounts Receivable Turnover	$\dfrac{\text{Credit Sales}}{\text{Average Accounts Receivable}}$	Efficiency of receivables collection	6
	Average Collection Period	$\dfrac{365 \text{ days}}{\text{Accounts Receivable Turnover}}$	Number of days to collect receivables	6
	Inventory Turnover	$\dfrac{\text{Cost of Goods Sold}}{\text{Average Inventory}}$	How frequently inventory is turned over during period	7
	Days to Sell Inventory	$\dfrac{365 \text{ days}}{\text{Inventory Turnover}}$	Number of days to sell through inventory	7
	Accounts Payable Turnover	$\dfrac{\text{Credit Purchases}}{\text{Average Accounts Payable}}$	How frequently creditors are paid	9
	Accounts Payable Payment Period	$\dfrac{365 \text{ days}}{\text{Accounts Payable Turnover}}$	Number of days to pay suppliers	9
Solvency	Debt to Equity	$\dfrac{\text{Net Debt}}{\text{Shareholders' Equity}}$	Amount of debt relative to shareholders' equity	10
	Net Debt as a Percentage of Total Capitalization	$\dfrac{\text{Net Debt}}{\text{Shareholders' Equity} + \text{Net Debt}}$	Portion of total financing represented by debt	10
	Interest Coverage	$\dfrac{\text{EBITDA (Earnings before Interest, Taxes, Depreciation, and Amortization)}}{\text{Interest Expense}}$	Ability to cover interest expense from earnings	10
	Cash Flows to Total Liabilities	$\dfrac{\text{Cash Flows from Operating Activities}}{\text{Total Liabilities}}$	Portion of total obligations that could be met with operating cash flows	5
Profitability	Gross Profit Margin	$\dfrac{\text{Gross Margin}}{\text{Sales Revenue}}$	Profit after product costs to cover other operating costs	7
	Net Profit Margin	$\dfrac{\text{Net Income}}{\text{Sales Revenue}}$	Net profit earned on each \$1 of sales	2
	Return on Equity	$\dfrac{\text{Net Income}}{\text{Average Total Shareholders' Equity}}$	Rate of return on resources provided by investors	2
	Return on Assets	$\dfrac{\text{Net Income}}{\text{Average Total Assets}}$	Rate of return on assets used	2
Equity Analysis	Basic Earnings per Share	$\dfrac{\text{Net Income} - \text{Preferred Dividends}}{\text{Weighted Average Number of Common Shares Outstanding}}$	Profit earned on each common share	4
	Price/Earnings	$\dfrac{\text{Market Price per Share}}{\text{Earnings per Share}}$	Multiple of EPS represented by current share price	11
	Dividend Payout	$\dfrac{\text{Dividends per Share}}{\text{Earnings per Share}}$	Proportion of income paid out as dividends	11
	Dividend Yield	$\dfrac{\text{Dividends per Share}}{\text{Price per Share}}$	Rate of return provided by dividends relative to current share price	11
	Net Free Cash Flow	Cash Flows from Operating Activities $-$ Net Capital Expenditures $-$ Dividends on Preferred Shares	Cash flow generated from operating activities that would be available to common shareholders	5

Note: Only 21 of the 24 ratios presented in the text are included in this table. The other three are unique to the analysis of property, plant, and equipment and do not fit within the five common categories. These are: Average Age, Average Age Percentage, and Fixed Asset Turnover, all from Chapter 8.

Understanding
FINANCIAL ACCOUNTING

Understanding
FINANCIAL
ACCOUNTING

CANADIAN EDITION

Christopher D. Burnley
Vancouver Island University

With contributions by
Julia A. Scott
McGill University

Peggy Wallace
Trent University

**Based on *Financial Accounting: A User Perspective*,
Sixth Canadian Edition**
Robert E. Hoskin
University of Connecticut

Maureen R. Fizzell
Simon Fraser University

Donald C. Cherry
Dalhousie University (Retired)

Library and Archives Canada Cataloguing in Publication

Burnley, Christopher D., 1966–, author
    Understanding financial accounting / Christopher D. Burnley,
Robert E. Hoskin, Maureen R. Fizzell, Donald C.
Cherry. — Canadian edition.

Issued in print and electronic formats.
ISBN 978-1-118-84938-5 (bound).—ISBN 978-1-119-04857-2
(loose-leaf).—ISBN 978-1-119-04855-8 (pdf)

    1. Accounting—Textbooks.   I. Fizzell, Maureen, author
II. Hoskin, Robert E., 1949–, author   III. Cherry, Donald C., author
IV. Title.

HF5636.B87 2014   657'.044   C2014-906821-2
                                           C2014-906822-0

Production Credits

Acquisitions Editor: Zoë Craig
Vice President and Publisher: Veronica Visentin
Director of Marketing: Joan Lewis-Milne
Marketing Manager: Anita Osborne
Editorial Manager: Karen Staudinger
Developmental Editor: Daleara Jamasji Hirjikaka
Media Editor: Luisa Begani
Editorial Assistant: Maureen Lau
Cover and Interior Design: Joanna Vieira
Cover Image: Christopher Burnley
Typesetting: Aptara®, Inc.

Printing & Binding: Quad/Graphics

Printed and bound in the United States of America
1 2 3 4 5 QG 18 17 16 15 14

John Wiley & Sons Canada, Ltd.
5353 Dundas Street West, Suite 400
Toronto, ON, M9B 6H8 Canada
Visit our website at: www.wiley.ca

Dedication

Dedicated with love and gratitude to my father, Donald Burnley, for being such a wonderful role model in all that is important in life and for guiding me down the accounting path.

ABOUT THE AUTHOR

Christopher Burnley, CPA/CA, is a professor in the Accounting Department at Vancouver Island University's Faculty of Management. Prior to his full-time academic career, Chris worked for 12 years in public practice and also audited federal government departments and United Nations agencies with the Office of the Auditor General of Canada. Chis also teaches in the CPA Professional Education Program for the CA School of Business.

At Vancouver Island University (VIU), Chris has developed a number of new courses, has served as departmental chair, and is in his second three-year term as an elected faculty representative on the university's board of governors. He is active internationally, teaching and delivering guest lectures at VIU's partner institutions in Europe, Asia, and the South Pacific. He has been awarded numerous internal and external grants in support of his academic work and has presented at national conferences.

Chris has received a number of awards from the Canadian Academic Accounting Association as a result of his academic work, including awards for case authoring and developing innovative ideas in accounting education.

Chris is active in the accounting profession, and chairs the board of the Chartered Accountants of British Columbia's Education Foundation. In 2007, Chris was awarded the Ritchie W. McCloy Award for CA Volunteerism.

PREFACE

The aim of *Understanding Financial Accounting* is to introduce students to the core concepts of financial accounting in a way that illustrates the relevance of the material to a wide variety of decision-making contexts. The focus is on providing students with the tools to help them understand the rationale behind the numbers. If students can develop an understanding of the language of accounting, grasp what the accounting information means, and appreciate what managers are saying when they present the financial information, they will have laid a foundation they can build upon in whatever position they hold in the future.

The text has been structured around a series of core questions, with the aim of making the material that follows each question more relevant to the students and to provide them with a clear picture of why they need to understand it. The text also walks students through the basic mechanical elements of accounting, because it is very difficult for students to understand the product of accounting if they lack an understanding of the system used to generate it. The material is written at a level meant to be understandable for all students who put the time into working through it. It is based on 15 years of teaching the material to thousands of students with a wide variety of backgrounds, the majority of whom have been non-accounting majors, but also to others who have gone on to medal on national professional accounting exams.

While *Understanding Financial Accounting* is in its first edition, it can also be viewed as a substantially renovated Hoskin's *Financial Accounting*: a renovation much like what you might undertake when you find a great old house in an excellent neighbourhood. The structure of the house and its solid foundation have been maintained. The new text continues to have 12 chapters, presenting material on key topics such as revenue recognition, cash flows, and financial statement analysis in the same order. One of the underlying strengths of the Hoskin text has been its end-of-chapter material, which is rich in both depth and breadth. Much of this material has been updated and supplemented. The rest of the house has largely been stripped back to its studs: all chapters have been rewritten, with significant additions of contextual material—largely excerpts from real financial statements—drawn from more than 50 Canadian public companies. With the renovations completed, it is hoped that this new text will continue to enhance the learning experience of students and that the builders of the original house will continue to feel pride when they see lights glowing in its windows.

Acknowledgements

The text's cover photo features the shoreline of the Georgia Strait, not far from my home on eastern Vancouver Island. It features a type of nurse log, which is common in the forests of coastal British Columbia. These trunks or stumps of trees, which were often giants in their time, provide the essence of new life for the seeds that germinate on them. The nurse log provides a wonderful metaphor for this book in a number of ways.

This first edition of *Understanding Financial Accounting* is rooted in the strength of the problem material from *Financial Accounting: A User Perspective*, and I am indebted to Maureen Fizzell, Donald Cherry, and Robert Hoskin for authoring such rich, diverse material. The Hoskin text was one of the books I used when I began teaching financial accounting and it helped inform and shape the way I continue to present this material. These teachings are reflected in this new text.

New growth also requires the right environmental conditions. I have been fortunate to work with a group of colleagues at Vancouver Island University who have supported my teaching and writing over the past 15 years. I have learned from each of them and would like to thank them, especially Gordon Holyer, Tracy Gillis, Colin Haime, Sameer Mustafa, Erin Egeland, Jeremy Clegg, Vanessa Oltmann, and Steve Purse. I have also been fortunate to work with three deans of the Faculty of Management: Ian Ross, Mike Mann, and David Twynam. Each created opportunities for me to grow and the space in which growth could occur. I am also grateful to Celia Sharp for the constant support and consistently wise counsel that she provides.

I am indebted to a number of accounting academics without whom I would never have considered authoring a text. The efforts of Sandy Hilton, especially at the Canadian Academic Accounting Association, to create venues to support teaching and learning for faculty made a significant difference to me. Sandy has also supported my case authoring efforts for years and provided excellent advice at the outset of this project. Peter Norwood has created numerous opportunities for me to broaden my participation in the academic community and also willingly shared wisdom garnered from his years as a successful author. Scott Sinclair provided feedback throughout the project that generated important momentum, especially at its outset, and resulted in a much improved text. I am also thankful for the advice and encouragement of Irene Gordon, Gary Spraakman, and Eldon Gardner in my earliest efforts as an author.

As a tree grows, new rings are added to its trunk. Many people have contributed growth rings to this text. Julia Scott and Peggy Wallace both made significant contributions to a number of chapters. I am also thankful for the excellent work of Katie Alahaivala, my research assistant on this project. Nickie Young made noteworthy contributions to a number of chapters and especially to much of the end-of-chapter material. Barb Trenholm, who inspired me as a student some 30 years ago, also provided valuable feedback. Laurel Hyatt's research work has made for interesting opening vignettes, while her talents as an editor greatly improved the readability of the text. The editorial contributions of Zofia Laubitz, Lindsay Humphreys, and Belle Wong are greatly appreciated. The typesetting expertise of Vishal Gaudhar and his team at Aptara is also greatly valued. I consider myself so fortunate to be part of the Wiley family. Their dedicated team provided outstanding support each step of the way. I am indebted to Zoë Craig for helping frame the initial vision and for her continuous encouragement throughout the process. The editorial talents of Dela Hirjikaka added much to the text and her efforts kept the project on track, bringing the numerous parts together in a seamless fashion. I am also thankful for the support of Luisa Begani, Deanna Durnford, Maureen Lau, Karen Staudinger, Anita Osborne, Maureen Talty, Joanna Vieira, and Veronica Visentin.

A number of faculty have also worked hard to develop the supplements that accompany this text:

Catherine Barrette
Angela Davis, *Booth University College*
Robert Ducharme, *University of Waterloo*
Cecile Laurin, *Algonquin College*
Rosalie Harms, *University of Winnipeg*

Kayla Levesque, *Cambrian College*
Sandy Qu, *York University*
Marie Sinnott, *College of New Caledonia*
Ruth Ann Strickland, *Western University*

Many other faculty reviewed parts of the text, providing advice and constructive criticism that resulted in a better book. I would like to thank:

Ibrahim Aly, *Concordia University*
George Boland, *Queen's University*
Else Grech, *Ryerson University*
Sohyung Kim, *Brock University*
Jennifer Li, *Brock University*
Anne Macdonald, *Simon Fraser University*
Robert Madden, *St. Francis Xavier University*

Julie McDonald, *Ryerson University*
Jaime Morales, *Trent University*
Peter Norwood, *Langara College*
Sandy Qu, *York University*
Scott Sinclair, *University of British Columbia*
Sara Wick, *University of Guelph*

I would also like to thank the following students from Vancouver Island University who gave me feedback on selected chapters of the book:

Alejandra Gómez Murcia
Tania Jacobs

Kaynon McDonald
Spencer Oberst

Just as trees use the magic of photosynthesis to transform light energy into chemical energy, a magical process takes place in classrooms at campuses the world over. Much of what is best about this book has resulted from such classroom interactions. The echoes of the hundreds of introductory accounting classes and seminars I have taught over the past 15 years can be heard throughout the pages of this text. So much of what I have learned about presenting this material is thanks to the thousands of students from these classes. I am so thankful for the shared learning experience.

The strength of a tree is provided by its heartwood, so it is no surprise that, for this text, this came from the people closest to my own heart. I am grateful for a wonderful collection of family and friends. Two key supports were my mother, Bernette, whose confidence that the book would eventually be completed never wavered, and my sister, Faith, whose early advice about the writing process and regular check-ins made a big difference for me. My children, Jacob and Erin, constantly encouraged their father to keep moving forward and patiently dealt with me disappearing into my office for long hours of writing. Erin, an author in her own right, was a great role model for her much older father. I am most indebted to my partner and best friend, Caroline. Throughout our 25-plus years together, she has always encouraged me to take on new challenges, providing constant and unwavering support. She was the initial editor for each chapter of the text and provided innumerable suggestions that improved the material. Caroline has inspired so much of what is wonderful in my life and this book is just another example of that.

I hope that the text is informative and that it assists you in your studies. Feedback and suggestions for improving future editions of the book are welcome. Please e-mail them to BurnleyAuthor@gmail.com.

Chris Burnley
Vancouver Island University
November 2014

A Closer Look at the Structure of the Text

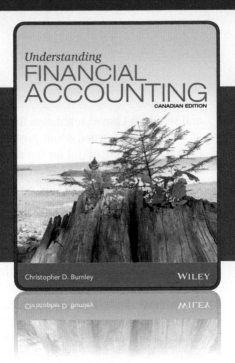

Understanding
FINANCIAL
ACCOUNTING
CANADIAN EDITION

Christopher D. Burnley   WILEY

Each chapter is based upon a series of **CORE QUESTIONS,** which, in turn, are linked to **LEARNING OBJECTIVES.** A variety of **TOOLS** are available to help your students master the content addressed by each **CORE QUESTION.** Using extracts from Chapter 8, Long-Term Assets, let's look at one of the core questions and see how the various pieces fit together . . .

STEP 1

Review the CORE QUESTIONS accompanying each learning objective.

Faculty could assign any number of core questions to students. The core questions break the chapter into manageable chunks of reading for students, enabling them to clearly link the material they are reading with the core question they are trying to address. Let's assume that you assign one core question as pre-reading for a class or seminar . . .

CORE QUESTIONS
If you are able to answer the following questions, then you have achieved the related learning objectives.

LEARNING OBJECTIVES
After studying this chapter, you should be able to:

●●● VALUATION OF PROPERTY, PLANT, AND EQUIPMENT

- At what amount are property, plant, and equipment reflected on the statement of financial position?
- What is included in "cost"?
- What happens when a company purchases multiple assets for a single price?
- How do we account for costs subsequent to purchase?

2 Describe the valuation methods for property, plant, and equipment, including identifying costs that are usually capitalized.

STEP 2

READ the relevant text and WATCH the related TAKE5 videos that explain the concept.

Students would READ the material in the text . . .

What happens when a company purchases multiple assets for a single price?

As you shop at the grocery store, you fill your cart or basket with a number of items. When you are finished shopping, you take it to the cash register where you pay a single price for all the goods in the basket. This same thing can occur when companies purchase PP&E. These kinds of purchases are called a **basket purchase** (or **lump-sum purchase**). The most common example is when a company purchases a warehouse or office building. At the same time, it would normally also acquire the land on which the building is situated. Just like at the grocery store, the warehouse purchase is completed for a single purchase price. It is important for the purchaser to be able to allocate this single purchase price between the building and the land because the building will need to be depreciated, while the land will not be.

The purchase price is allocated using the asset's **relative fair value** at the time of purchase, which can be determined in a number of ways. The most common way would be to have an appraisal completed that will provide the relative fair values of each asset. It is very common for the total purchase price and the total appraised value to differ. The purchaser may have received a good deal from a motivated seller or it may have paid a premium due to a number of factors such as superior location or the ability to complete the deal in a timely manner. It is important to remember that the company must record the purchase for what it paid, not what the appraised values are. Let's look at a simple example in Exhibit 8-3.

Exhibit 8-3 Example of Purchase Price Allocation

TAKE5

Assume that a company purchased a new warehouse for $2.4 million. As part of the purchase, it acquired the land that the warehouse was situated on, the warehouse building, some fencing around the property, and some storage racks. The company had an appraisal completed at the time of purchase that valued all components of the warehouse at $2.6 million. The buyer was able to negotiate a lower purchase price because the seller was in financial distress and was very motivated to sell. The appraisal provided the following values:

	Fair value	Percentage	Purchase price	Allocated cost
Land	$1,300,000	50%	$2,400,000	$1,200,000
Building	910,000	35%	$2,400,000	840,000
Storage racks	260,000	10%	$2,400,000	240,000

Basket purchase scenarios can occur in other situations, including the purchase of an airplane or cargo vessel. In both these situations, IFRS requires companies to determine if there are separate depreciable components within the asset. For an airplane, it may be necessary to depreciate the fuselage (or body of the plane) on a different basis than the engines. For a cargo ship, the company may depreciate the hull differently from the propulsion system.

WATCH THE TAKE5 VIDEOS

Each chapter includes a number of white-board screen capture videos that students can preview before coming to class or use for review after. These videos are a great tool for instructors who like to flip their classroom.

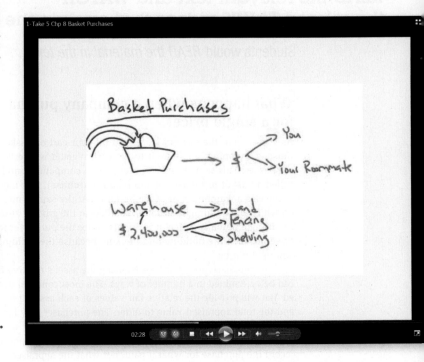

TAKE**5**

DISCUSS in class:

Each chapter of the text includes a number of features that can form the basis for classroom discussions. These include **Ethics in Accounting** features, **For Example** features and **Conceptual Framework** features . . .

 Ethics in Accounting

If management's bias was for a higher net income, this could motivate them to allocate more of the overall cost to the land, and less to the building and other depreciable assets. Why is this so?

Since land is not depreciated, the company would incur less depreciation expense each year if the portion of the purchase price allocated to land was maximized. Alternatively, if management was motivated to minimize net income in order to minimize income-based bonuses to employees, then they could allocate a smaller portion of the total cost to the land and a larger portion to the building and other depreciable assets.

STEP 3

Check your students' understanding with a variety of assignment material.

Each chapter includes a variety of assignment material, enabling faculty to choose the level of breadth and depth they want to assess the students at. This includes discussion questions, application problems, user perspective problems, reading and interpreting financial statement problems, and small cases.

ASSIGNMENT MATERIAL

Discussion Questions

DQ8-5 Why is it necessary to allocate the cost of a basket purchase to the individual assets included in the purchase price?

Application Problems

AP8-3 (Acquisition costs; basket purchase)

Matchett Machinery Ltd. acquired a new site for its manufacturing operations. The company was able to find the ideal location in terms of lot size and highway access. Matchett paid $3.2 million to acquire the site. The bank, which was providing Matchett with the financing for the purchase, required that an appraisal be completed of the property. The appraisal report came back with the following estimated market values: land $1,800,000, building $1,080,000, and land improvements $120,000. Matchett explained, to the bank's satisfaction, that it paid the $200,000 premium because of the savings it would realize from minimizing transportation distances given the site's superior highway access.

Required:
Allocate the $3.2-million purchase price to the land, building, and land improvements. Also explain why this allocation process is necessary.

User Perspective Problems

UP8-1 (Expensing versus capitalizing the cost of tools)

During the current year, a large chain of auto mechanic shops adopted the policy of expensing small tools costing less than $100 as soon as they are acquired. In previous years, the company had carried an asset account, Small Tools, which it had depreciated over the average expected useful lives of the tools. The balance in the Small Tools account represented about 1% of the company's total capital assets, and the depreciation expense on the tools was 0.3% of its sales revenues. It is expected that the average annual purchases of small tools will be approximately

Reading and Interpreting Published Financial Statements

RI8-1 (Financial statement analysis)

Reitmans (Canada) Limited is a leading Canadian retailer that operates more than 900 stores under the Reitmans, Smart Set, RW & Co., Thyme Maternity, Penningtons, and Addition Elle banners. The following information is an extract from Reitmans' annual report for its fiscal year ended February 1, 2014.

Cases

C8-1 Manuel Manufacturing Company

Maple Manufacturing Company recently purchased a property for use as a manufacturing facility. The company paid $850,000 for a building and four hectares of land. When recording the purchase, the company's accountant allocated $750,000 of the total cost to the building and the remaining $100,000 to the land.

After some investigation and an independent appraisal, you determine that the building is deemed to have a value of only $435,000. You also discover that the property is located near a major highway providing excellent access for shipping, and is therefore quite valuable. Similar properties in the area have been selling for $125,000 per hectare.

Maple Manufacturing is a very successful company and has traditionally reported very high net earnings. Last year, the company paid more than $200,000 in income taxes.

Required:
a. Determine the appropriate allocation between the buildings and land accounts for this basket purchase. (Remember that four hectares of land were purchased.)
b. Why would the company's accountant have wanted to allocate most of the purchase cost to the building rather than to the land?

ALSO, ENCOURAGE YOUR STUDENTS TO REVIEW THE OTHER INFORMATIVE FEATURES OF THE TEXT

READ ABOUT REAL-WORLD EXAMPLES.

For Example

When the **Port Authority** in Nanaimo, B.C., was looking for a container crane to use for loading barges several years ago, it was able to purchase an old crane from the Port of Vancouver for $1 (yes, $1). However, the Port Authority incurred costs in excess of $1 million to get the crane to Nanaimo and make it operational. This included transportation costs of $260,000 and installation costs of $750,000, which were capitalized as part of the cost of the crane. This illustrates how "cost" can be much more than just the purchase price of the asset.[2]

GET TO KNOW THE CONCEPTUAL FRAMEWORK OF ACCOUNTING.

The Conceptual Framework
CAPITALIZING VERSUS EXPENSING

Materiality is an element of the fundamental qualitative characteristic of **relevance**. Information is considered to be material if it would impact the decisions of a financial statement user. If it would not, it is considered to be immaterial and not relevant. If it would, then it is material and relevant. Materiality is considered by companies when they establish minimum thresholds for capitalizing PP&E. For example, companies often have policies that state that only PP&E with a cost in excess of $1,000 will be capitalized (that is, set up as an asset) and all purchases under that amount will be expensed as supplies because they are not material and therefore not relevant to financial statement users.

LOOK FOR THE KEY POINTS IN THE MARGIN.

KEY POINTS
Carrying amount is:
- the portion of the asset's cost that has yet to be expensed.
- *not* what the asset is worth.

SUM IT UP WITH CONCISE AND TO-THE-POINT CHAPTER-ENDING SUMMARIES.

3. **Explain why property, plant, and equipment assets are depreciated.**
   - Depreciating PP&E allocates a portion of the cost of each asset to each period in which the asset's economic benefits are being used up or consumed.
   - Only the depreciable amount (cost less estimated residual value) is expensed.
   - The depreciable amount is allocated or expensed over the asset's estimated useful life.

STUDY THE CHAPTER END REVIEW PROBLEMS WITH SOLUTIONS.

CHAPTER END REVIEW PROBLEM

Pete's Trucking Company has a fleet of large trucks that cost a total of $1.5 million. The trucks have an estimated useful life of five years and an estimated residual value of $150,000. The trucks are expected to be driven a total of 5 million kilometres during their lives.

Required:

   a. Calculate the annual straight-line depreciation that would be recorded over the lives of these trucks.

   b. Prepare a schedule showing depreciation on a units-of-production basis, if the following usage was expected.

Year 1	950,000 km
Year 2	1,050,000 km
Year 3	1,100,000 km
Year 4	1,000,000 km
Year 5	900,000 km

Suggested Solution to Chapter End Review Problem

a.

Straight-line method

$$\text{Depreciation Expense} = \frac{\text{Cost} - \text{Estimated Residual Value}}{\text{Estimated Useful Life}}$$

$$= \frac{\$1,500,000 - \$150,000}{5 \text{ years}} = \$270,000 \text{ per year}$$

b.

Units-of-production method

$$\text{Depreciation Expense} = \frac{\text{Cost} - \text{Estimated Residual Value}}{\text{Estimated Useful Life}}$$

$$= \frac{\$1,500,000 - \$150,000}{5,000,000 \text{ km}} = \$0.27 \text{ per km}$$

Depreciation Expense per Year

      Year 1: $0.27 per km ×   950,000 km = $256,500

      Year 2: $0.27 per km × 1,050,000 km = $283,500

      Year 3: $0.27 per km × 1,100,000 km = $297,000

      Year 4: $0.27 per km × 1,000,000 km = $270,000

      Year 5: $0.27 per km ×   900,000 km = $243,000

Practice Made Simple

Our focus is on helping students get the most out of their accounting course by **making practice simple**. Both in the printed text and the online environment of *WileyPLUS*, new opportunities for self-guided practice allow students to check their knowledge of accounting concepts, skills, and problem-solving techniques as they receive individual feedback at the question, learning objective, and course level.

Personalized Practice

Based on cognitive science, **WileyPLUS with ORION** is a personalized, adaptive learning experience that gives students the practice they need to build proficiency on topics while using their study time most effectively. The adaptive engine is powered by hundreds of unique questions per chapter, giving students endless opportunities for practice throughout the course.

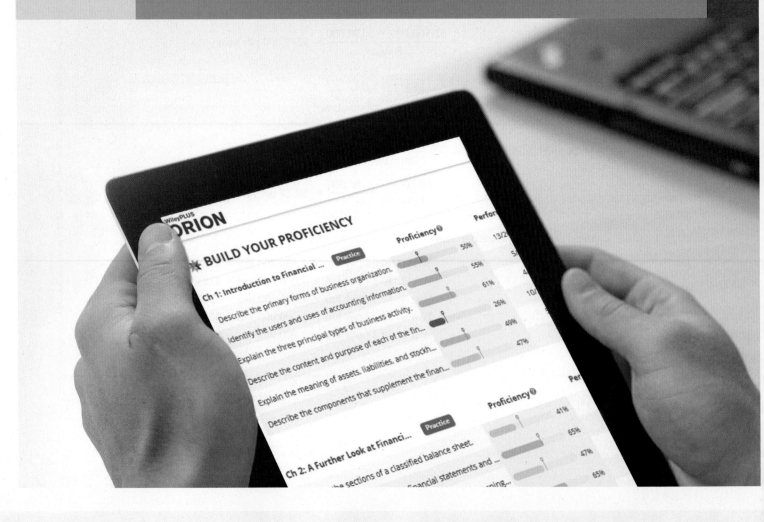

Streamlined Learning Objectives

Newly streamlined learning objectives help students make the best use of their time outside of class. Each learning objective contains a variety of practice and assessment questions, review material, and educational videos, so that no matter where students begin their work, the relevant resources and practice are readily accessible.

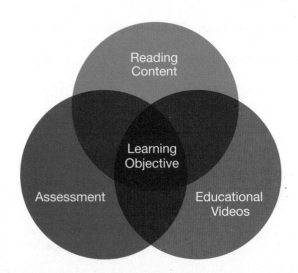

Review and Practice

Students have more opportunities for self-guided practice in the text and in WileyPLUS.

The text includes chapter end review problems with worked out solutions along with an action plan called Strategies for Success, plus:

- Core chapter questions
- Summary of learning objectives
- Glossary

Another exciting feature of this text is its companion material in WileyPLUS, an innovative, research-based on-line environment for effective teaching and learning.

WileyPLUS builds students' confidence because it takes the guesswork out of studying by providing students with a clear roadmap: what to do, how to do it, if they did it right. Students will take more initiative so you'll have greater impact on their achievement in the classroom and beyond.

For this text, WileyPLUS includes updated self-study assignments featuring problems and quizzes giving students the opportunity to check their work or see the answer and solution after their final attempt.

CHAPTER END REVIEW PROBLEM

Additional Practice Problems

Jonathan, Anthony, and Kendra operate a bicycle shop, The Silver Spoke Ltd. They sell assembled bicycles and bicycle accessories. They have a service bay in the back of the shop where Kendra repairs bicycles. Occasionally, they are awarded contracts to assemble 20 to 50 bicycles for a major retailer. Customers use either cash or credit cards when buying bicycles and accessories or paying for repairs. For minor repairs, the customer pays when the repairs are done. For major repairs, customers are required to make a down payment equal to 25% of the repair's estimated cost. The remaining 75% is paid when the work is complete. When the company assembles bicycles for retailers, it bills the retailers when the work is done. The company normally receives payment within 30 days of submitting the bill.

Required:
Based on the revenue recognition criteria, recommend when the company should recognize revenue for each of its various revenue-generating activities. Provide the rationale for each of your recommendations.

Suggested Solution to Chapter End Review Problem

1. **Sale of goods**
    Specific criteria:
    - Risks and rewards of ownership transferred
    - No continuing involvement
    - Revenue measurable
    - Probable economic benefits to seller
    - Costs can be reliably measured

    Sales of bicycles and bicycle accessories: The company should recognize revenue at the time of sale. Since the customer leaves with the merchandise, the risks and rewards of ownership have been transferred and the company's involvement with the goods also stops. The amount of revenue earned is also measurable and has been collected either in cash or through a credit card, so there are no issues regarding the flow of economic benefits. The costs associated with the sale are known as well.

2. **Provision of services**
    Specific criteria:
    - Revenue measurable
    - Probable economic benefits to seller
    - Costs can be reliably measured
    - Portion complete is measurable

    Minor repairs: The company should recognize revenue when the work is completed. Similar to the situation with the sale of bicycles, the company's work is complete and the customer has paid, so the amount of revenue can be measured reliably, and the costs associated with the repairs are also known.

    Major repairs: The company should recognize revenue when the work is completed. When the customer makes the 25% down payment, the work has not yet been started. As well, the total amount owed is still uncertain, although it has been estimated to determine the 25% down payment. There-

STRATEGIES FOR SUCCESS

- Start by identifying the various ways that the company generates revenue and then consider whether they relate to the sale of goods or the provision of services. This will help you identify the specific revenue recognition criteria that should be applied. Next, identify when the company has met these criteria: when the customer takes possession of the goods, when the services have been performed, when the related costs can be measured, when the amount earned can be measured, when the total of the costs associated with the revenue are known, or when it is probable that the economic benefits will flow to the seller.
- Remember to consider the time frame to complete the transaction. If the time frame is short, it is probably reasonable to recognize revenue at the time of sale or delivery of the goods. If the time frame to complete the transaction is long, you may need to consider whether to recognize revenue on a percentage basis as the work is completed or wait until the work is done to recognize it.
- Keeping these items in mind, go back through your notes to consider the specific revenue recognition criteria and apply the facts of the situation from each revenue stream.

BRIEF CONTENTS

CONTENTS

1 Overview of Corporate Financial Reporting

CORE QUESTIONS
If you are able to answer the following questions, then you have achieved the related learning objectives.

LEARNING OBJECTIVES
After studying this chapter, you should be able to:

●●● INTRODUCTION

- What is financial accounting?

1 Define financial accounting and understand its relationship to economic decision-making.

- Who needs to have an understanding of financial accounting and why?

2 Identify the main users of financial accounting information and explain how they use this information.

●●● FORMS OF BUSINESS ORGANIZATION

- What is a corporation?
- What differentiates a corporation from other forms of business?

3 Describe the major forms of business organization and explain the key distinctions between them.

●●● ACTIVITIES OF A BUSINESS

- What are the three categories of business activities?
- What are examples of financing activities?
- What are examples of investing activities?
- What are examples of operating activities?

4 Explain the three categories of business activities and identify examples of transactions related to each category.

●●● FINANCIAL REPORTING

- What information is included in a set of financial statements?
- What is the reporting objective of the statement of income? What does it include?
- What is the reporting objective of the statement of changes in equity? What does it include?
- What is the reporting objective of the statement of financial position? What does it include?
- What is the reporting objective of the statement of cash flows? What does it include?
- What type of information is in the notes to a company's financial statements?

5 Identify and explain the content and reporting objectives of the four basic financial statements and the notes to the financial statements.

●●● Are Higher Profits in the Bag?

Danier Leather Inc. was founded in 1972 as Royal Leather Goods Limited, and through the 1980s it amalgamated with various other leather manufacturers. Danier is now one of the largest publicly traded leather apparel retailers in the world. Headquartered in Toronto, Danier designs and manufactures women's and men's leather clothing, bags, and other goods. Some goods are manufactured in Canada while others are made overseas. Danier has more than 90 stores across Canada in malls, power centres ("big-box" stores), and streetfronts.

If you had a leather craft business and wanted to expand, you might finance this by using your savings or borrowing from family members. But how do large companies such as Danier finance growth? Like many companies that reach a certain size, Danier became a public company, issuing shares that trade on the Toronto Stock Exchange (TSX). The company's initial public offering, in 1998, raised $68 million, which was used to ramp up production and open new stores. In recent years, Danier seems to have taken a steady approach to growth, not needing to borrow to finance it. The company has had no long-term debt since 2007 and at the end of its 2014 fiscal year it had $13.5 million in cash.

Danier has been able to finance its growth through its operating profits and its cash reserves. Company management is continually looking for ways to increase sales, especially of those items that generate higher profits. A big focus for the company is to increase its higher-margin accessories business. Management believes that this focus on accessories will enable the company to attract new and younger customers, make sales less seasonal, generate higher margins, and reduce issues caused by needing to have the correct sizes on hand to fit customers.

One accessories area that Danier plans to expand is its handbag business. "Currently, we see a gap in the market for stylish leather handbags priced under $200," wrote Danier President and CEO Jeffery Wortsman in the company's 2013 annual report. "We believe there are tremendous opportunities for Danier in this under-served niche in the market."

Shareholders and others use a company's financial statements to see how the company has performed and what its future prospects might be. Shareholders use them to make informed decisions about things such as whether to sell their shares, hold onto them, or buy more. Creditors use financial statements to assess a company's ability to service its debts (pay interest and repay principal), while suppliers may use them to determine whether to allow the company to purchase on credit. Companies communicate all this information through financial reporting and the tool used to prepare financial information is accounting.

Whether or not Danier achieves the increased revenues and profits it hopes for by increasing its accessories business will be reported in the company's future financial statements. These financial statements will tell the story of whether higher profits for Danier really were "in the bag."[1]

INTRODUCTION

■ **LEARNING OBJECTIVE 1**
Define financial accounting and understand its relationship to economic decision-making.

The opening story describes how a large company grows and how accounting assists in that development. Whether a business is borrowing money for a start-up or expansion, restructuring the organization, or deciding to purchase or lease, it needs to have accounting information to make the best decisions. You, too, will use accounting information to help you make decisions, whether it's determining if you should buy a company's shares, apply for a job there, or make a large purchase from it.

What is financial accounting?

Financial accounting is the process by which information on the transactions of an organization is captured, analyzed, and used to report to decision makers outside of the organization's management team. These decision makers are often referred to as **financial statement users** and include the owners (normally referred to as **investors**) and those who have lent money to the organization (normally referred to as **creditors**). The primary purpose of financial accounting information is to aid these users in their economic decision-making relative to the organization. As these users are generally outside of the organization and are not involved in its day-to-day operations, the financial accounting information they receive is often their only "window" into the organization.

Users inside the organization (**management**) also use financial accounting information, but they generally require the information at a different level of detail. For example, managers in a national retail chain may need information for a particular store rather than for the organization as a whole. Managers may need different information altogether, such as information needed to develop forward-looking budgets rather than to report on past transactions. It is important to note that management has access to all of the organization's financial information, including information that is never shared outside of the organization. This information is known as **managerial accounting** and will be the basis for another course in your business studies.

Financial accounting, the focus of this textbook, can be as simple as determining the daily sales of a food truck or as complex as recording and reporting on the economic condition of your university, a multinational corporation, or the Government of Canada. All of these entities need to know economic information in order to continue to operate efficiently and effectively. Financial accounting provides the vital financial information that enables people and organizations to make decisions. Because it is very likely that you will be a financial statement user in some way, it is important that you have at least a basic understanding of what financial accounting is (and is not), what it is trying to accomplish, and how it does so.

The focus of this book is the financial accounting information produced by profit-oriented organizations, although we will occasionally refer to not-for-profit organizations or governments. We will concentrate mainly on the **financial statements**, which are management's reports to the company's owners that are produced at the end of each accounting period, such as every quarter or every year. They are included in the company's **annual report** together with **management's discussion and analysis (MD&A)** of the company's results for the year. The annual report is made available to the company's owners, but many other parties, such as lenders, financial analysts, credit-rating agencies, securities regulators, and taxing authorities, also use it.

■ **LEARNING OBJECTIVE 2**
Identify the main users of financial accounting information and explain how they use this information.

Who needs an understanding of financial accounting and why?

Before we answer these questions, let's take some time to think a little about the game of hockey. (Yes, hockey. After all, what's a Canadian textbook without a hockey reference?) Whether you have lived in Canada your whole life or you are here studying from some other part of the world, chances are good that you have seen a professional hockey game on television or perhaps even in person. During the game, the TV commentary or the conversations of those around you would have included terms like *icing*, *charging*, *slashing*, *five-hole*, *hash marks*, *neutral zone*, and so on. These would have been confusing terms the first time you heard them, but once they were explained to you, your ability to follow the game and understand it at a deeper level would have improved. This is the same with financial accounting. Through the text's 12 chapters we will learn the language of financial accounting and how to interpret financial accounting information so you can come away with a deeper understanding of the subject.

So, let's rephrase our opening question and think about "who needs to understand the rules of professional hockey?" Many groups likely come to mind fairly quickly, including:
- players (including their agents and players' union)
- coaches and general managers
- referees, linesmen, and off-ice officials
- fans
- TV commentators, arena announcers, and sports journalists
- league officials
- team owners
- suppliers, sponsors, and advertisers

We can call these people *stakeholders* because they have a stake in understanding hockey. Now, let's take this list of hockey stakeholders and find the parallel business stakeholders who would have a similar stake in a business, as shown in Exhibit 1-1.

Exhibit 1-1 Similarities between Hockey Stakeholders and Business Stakeholders

Hockey Stakeholders	Parallel Business Stakeholders
Players, including their agents and players' union	Employees, unions
Coaches and general managers	Management
Referees, linesmen, off-ice officials	Auditors, federal and provincial government departments, legislators
Fans	Potential investors, customers
Announcers, TV analysts, sports journalists	Stock analysts, brokers, financial advisors, business reporters
League officials	Stock exchange regulators
Team owners	Shareholders, board of directors
Suppliers, sponsors, advertisers	Creditors, suppliers

Now, let's consider some of the questions that each of the stakeholders in a business may be trying to answer about that business that would require an understanding of financial accounting, as shown in Exhibit 1-2.

Exhibit 1-2 Questions That Stakeholders in a Business May Be Asking

Business Stakeholders	Potential Questions They May Be Trying to Answer About the Business
Employees, unions	Is the business profitable? Will I earn a bonus this year? Could the company afford to negotiate increased wages? Is the company pension plan in decent shape?
Management	How do this year's sales compare with last year's? How do they compare with the budget? Are we maintaining our profit margins on certain product lines? How much do we owe our employees and suppliers?
Auditors, federal and provincial government departments, legislators	Has the company presented its financial information fairly? How does the company's financial information compare with the information submitted for taxation or payroll purposes?
Potential investors, customers	What are the long-term prospects for this company? Has the management team done a reasonable job? Will this company be around to honour its warranties?
Stock analysts, brokers, financial advisors, business reporters	What are the company's trends? What are the prospects for this company? How has this company performed relative to expectations?
Stock exchange regulators	Has the company complied with the financial reporting standards and listing requirements?
Shareholders, board of directors	Has the company generated a sufficient return on our investment? How effectively has management used the resources at their disposal? Does the company generate enough income to be able pay dividends?
Creditors, suppliers	Should we extend credit to this company? Is this a credible and successful company that we want to attach our brand to?

These groups of business stakeholders are often known as *financial statement users*. Throughout this book, we will be looking at the information needs of many of these users and discussing how they use financial accounting information in making a variety of decisions. The breadth of this list of users illustrates that no matter which path you take in your business studies, having a basic understanding of accounting information will be essential to business success or could be a job requirement. As we move through the chapters, try to see yourself in one or more of these roles and think about the ways in which you can make use of the accounting information that you will no doubt come across.

The primary goal of this book is to help you become an intelligent user of accounting information by enhancing your ability to read and understand corporate financial statements. You may become a manager, accountant, banker, or financial analyst, and even if you do not end up working directly in the finance industry, you will invest in the shares or bonds of a company at some point in your life. If you work in a company, whether in sales, human resources, or other areas, your decisions will likely have an impact on what is reported to owners. Whatever your business role, you will make decisions about companies, such as whether to invest in their shares, lend them money, or sell them goods or services on credit. In making these decisions, it will be important for you to understand the information that is presented in corporate financial statements. You must know not only what each piece of information tells you about the company, but also what it does not tell you. You should also have an understanding that some important information is not contained in the financial statements, yet could be useful in making certain decisions.

We have written this book for a broad readership, understanding that many of you will play multiple roles as owners (shareholders), creditors, and managers of companies. We have assumed that you know

little or nothing about accounting. We have not assumed that you are training to be an accountant, although that may be your objective. Therefore, this book does not emphasize accounting procedures. Instead, it emphasizes the underlying concepts of accounting and the analysis of financial statements. However, it is not really possible to have a knowledgeable understanding of the end result of the accounting process without first having an overall view of how the accounting system works. For this reason, the first three chapters present the basic mechanics of the accounting system. The remaining chapters are then devoted to more detailed accounting issues and concepts, and to a more in-depth analysis of financial statements.

We will now explore the financial statement users in more detail. Exhibit 1-3 lists the various financial statement users, categorizing them as either internal or external users.

Exhibit 1-3 Users of Financial Statement Information

Internal users:

Management

External users:

Shareholders, the board of directors, and potential investors

Creditors (for example, bankers and suppliers)

Regulators (for example, a stock exchange)

Taxing authorities (for example, the Canada Revenue Agency)

Other corporations, including competitors

Securities (stock) analysts

Credit-rating agencies

Labour unions

Journalists

Since the focus of financial accounting is reporting to external users, let's look at these users and their information needs in greater details.

Shareholders, the Board of Directors, and Potential Investors

A company is owned by its **shareholders**. There may be a single shareholder in the case of a **private company** or many thousands of shareholders in the case of a **public company**. We will discuss the distinctions between private and public companies a little later in the chapter, so for now it is just important to understand that companies are owned by their shareholder(s). In situations where there are numerous shareholders, they elect a **board of directors** to represent their interests. The board of directors is given the responsibility of overseeing the management team that has been hired to operate the company.

The board of directors, individual shareholders, and potential investors all require information to enable them to assess how well management has been running the company. Just like hockey fans look at the arena scoreboard to see how their team is doing in terms of the score, shots on goal, and so on, stakeholders in a business look at a company's financial reports to determine how it's doing in a number of areas. Business stakeholders want to make decisions about buying more shares or selling some or all of the shares they already own. (Similar to a hockey team's general manager deciding whether to acquire a star player or trade an underperforming one.) They will analyze the current share price (as reflected on the stock exchange) and compare it with the original price that they paid for the shares. Are the shares now worth more or less? They will also be comparing the share price with the company's underlying value, which is reflected in the financial statements and other sources of information they have about the company.

Individual shareholders will also want to assess whether the current board of directors have effectively carried out their oversight role. They will seek to answer questions such as:
- Is the company heading in the right direction (that is, has the strategic direction approved by the board resulted in increased sales, profits, and so on)?
- Is it making decisions that result in increased value to the shareholders?
- Is the company generating a sufficient return on the resources invested in it by the shareholders?

Creditors

Creditors are those who lend money or otherwise extend credit to a company rather than invest in it directly as investors do. There are two major groups of creditors:
1. Financial institutions and other lenders
2. Suppliers, employees, and the various levels of government

Financial institutions, such as banks and credit unions, lend money to companies. They do so seeking to generate a return on these loans in the form of **interest**. Of course, the lenders also want to ensure that the money they lend out will eventually be repaid (that is, they will get back their **principal**). The loans can either be short-term or extend over several years. These lenders need financial accounting information to assess the company's ability to service the loan. One of the ways this is done is by looking at the cash flows the company generates through its operations. They are also generally interested in the amount of the company's inventory, equipment, buildings, or land, because these may be pledged as security by the borrowing company in the event that it cannot repay the loan. Large companies enter into long-term borrowing arrangements by issuing corporate bonds. Rather than borrowing from a single lender, companies that issue bonds borrow from many lenders. Nevertheless, these lenders are also concerned about the company's ability to service the debt (pay interest and repay principal) over the term of the bond and their financial accounting information needs are similar to those of other lenders.

The other group of creditors includes suppliers, employees, and various levels of government. These groups often sell goods or provide services prior to receiving payment. For example, a supplier may agree to sell goods or provide services to a company and agree to wait 30 days for payment. Employees are another common creditor as they normally work for the company and then receive payment after the fact, such as at the end of every two weeks or at the end of a month. Different levels of government may also be creditors of a company as they wait to receive tax payments or payroll deduction amounts. These users normally focus on the short-term cash level in the company because they are concerned about being paid.

Regulators

The regulators who are interested in financial statements are numerous. For example, the federal and provincial governments have regulations related to how companies report their financial information and are interested in ensuring that these regulations are followed. The stock exchanges, on which the shares of public companies are traded, have regulations about the timing and format of information that companies must convey to them and to investors. Companies not complying with these regulations can be delisted, meaning their shares cease to trade on the exchange, which greatly affects their ability to raise capital.

Taxing Authorities

The **Canada Revenue Agency (CRA)** is the federal taxing authority in Canada and is responsible for federal tax collection. Corporate taxes are primarily based on taxable income, which is calculated based on accounting net income. As such, the CRA is another key user of a company's financial accounting information.

Other Users

Additional users of financial statement information include other companies, securities analysts, credit-rating agencies, labour unions, and journalists. Other companies may want information about the performance of a company if they are going to enter into contracts with it. If it is a direct competitor, they may seek information that will help assess the competitor's strength and future plans. Securities analysts and credit-rating agencies use the financial statements to provide information about the strengths and weaknesses of companies to people who want to invest. Labour unions need to understand the company's financial health in order to negotiate labour contracts with management. Companies often give journalists news releases that disclose financial information such as expected earnings. The journalists may refer to the actual financial statements to validate the information they were given and to supplement the original information.

It is important to understand that all of these users are using the same set of financial statements in spite of their various information needs. The bodies that establish the international and domestic standards for financial reporting are aware of all of these users, but have taken the position that they will emphasize the needs to investors and creditors in the determination of standards. As such, many pieces of information that particular users may want cannot be found in the financial statements and these users must look to other sources of information as well.

The types of financial information gathered and made available to stakeholders vary depending on the form of organization a business has, which we discuss next.

FORMS OF BUSINESS ORGANIZATION

■ LEARNING OBJECTIVE 3
Describe the major forms of business organization and explain the key distinctions between them.

What is a corporation?

Businesses can be operated in a number of different forms, including as a corporation, as a proprietorship, or as a partnership. Most businesses of any significant size operate as corporations and, as such, this text will focus on the accounting information related to that form of business. However, most of the accounting issues that we will identify in the text also apply in some degree to the other forms of business. If you have a good understanding of corporate accounting, it is not a big challenge to understand the nuances of accounting for proprietorships or partnerships.

As previously mentioned, corporations are owned by shareholders, with the initial shareholders having provided cash or other assets to a corporation in exchange for share certificates. These shares are called **common shares**. One of the key distinctions between corporations and other forms of business is that corporations are separate legal entities; that is, they are legally distinct from their owners. This is where the "Limited" or "Ltd." that you see in the names of many corporations comes from; it refers to the fact that the company has limited legal liability. Since the corporations are separate legal entities, they can enter into contracts and be sued. In the event the company fails, the liability of shareholders is limited to their investment in the corporation.

There are two main types of corporations: public companies (which are also known as *publicly traded companies*) and private companies (which are also known as *privately held companies*). The distinction between the two is that the shares of public companies trade on public stock exchanges such as the Toronto Stock Exchange (TSX) while the shares of private companies trade privately and are not available through public exchanges. The shares of public companies are often widely held, meaning that they are owned by a large number of individuals or entities. Some portion of their ownership will usually change hands every day. On the other hand, shares of a private company are often narrowly held, meaning that they are owned by a relatively small number of people. It is not as easy to transfer ownership in a private company.

Shareholders are not typically involved in the day-to-day operations, except in small private corporations. Given that public companies have a large number of shareholders who are not involved in day-to-day activities, the shareholders typically elect a board of directors to represent them. The board of directors has the authority to hire (and fire if necessary) the management team who will manage the company's day-to-day operations. These senior executives, along with the other managers they hire, are known as *management*. To keep shareholders informed of the performance of their investment in the company, management reports periodically to the shareholders. Financial statements are normally prepared for shareholders quarterly (every three months). Annual financial statements are also produced and are included in the company's annual report. It is these annual financial statements that we will be focusing on.

What differentiates a corporation from other forms of business?

There are a number of key distinctions between corporations and the other forms of business: partnerships and proprietorships. Exhibit 1-4 outlines a number of the key distinctions to help you understand them. It is important to be aware of these differences, but also to understand that there are circumstances in which it makes sense to organize a business using each one of these three main forms of business.

Exhibit 1-4 Key Distinctions between the Forms of Business

Distinguishing Feature	Corporation	Proprietorship	Partnership
Number of owners	Can be a single owner or multiple owners	Single owner	Multiple owners
Separate legal entity?	Yes, personal assets of shareholders *are not* at risk in the event of legal action against company	No, personal assets of owner *are* at risk in the event of legal action	No, partners' personal assets *are* at risk in the event of legal action
Owner(s) responsible for debts of the business?	Only to extent of investment	Yes	Yes
Taxed?	Yes, taxed separately	No, profits taxed in hands of owner	No, profits taxed in hands of owners
Costs to establish	Most expensive	Least expensive	Moderately expensive
Cost to maintain	Most expensive	Least expensive	Moderately expensive

ACTIVITIES OF A BUSINESS

What are the three categories of business activities?

To understand the information in financial statements, it is useful to think about the fundamental types of activities that all businesses engage in and report on. As illustrated in Exhibit 1-5, all of the activities of businesses can be grouped into three categories: (1) **financing activities**, (2) **investing activities**, and (3) **operating activities**. Each of these involves inflows and outflows of cash into and out of the company.

■ LEARNING OBJECTIVE 4
Explain the three categories of business activities and identify examples of transactions related to each category.

Exhibit 1-5 The Three Categories of Business Activities

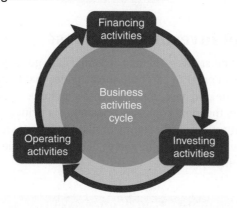

Now, let's explore each category.

What are examples of financing activities?

The first activities of all companies involve obtaining the funding (or *financing*) needed to purchase the equipment and/or buildings they require to start operations. At the outset of the business, funding may also be required to pay for things such as the initial purchase of goods for resale or to pay a landlord a deposit on rented space. While these activities are a necessity for new companies, they also continue as companies grow and expand. Companies obtain funding from two primary sources: (1) investors and (2) creditors.

Companies obtain funding from investors by issuing them shares (common shares) in the company in exchange for cash or other assets. These shares represent the investor's ownership interest in the company. For example, if the investor owns 10% of the shares issued by the company, they normally own 10% of the company. Since investors own shares in the company, we normally refer to them as *shareholders*. Shareholders purchase shares seeking to generate a return, which may be realized in two different ways. First, they hope to receive **dividends**. These are payments made by a company that distribute profits to shareholders. The other way shareholders seek to make a return is by being able to sell their shares to other investors for more than they paid for the shares. This gain or increase in value is known as **capital appreciation**. Of course, when the sale occurs, investors may also experience a loss if they receive less than the initial amount paid for the shares. The funds that flow into the company from its shareholders form part of what is called **shareholders' equity**.

Once a company has some shareholders' equity, it is then able to seek funding from the second primary financing source, creditors. Creditors are entities that lend money to a company rather than buying shares of the company. Banks are the most common example of a creditor. Creditors also seek a return from the money they lend to a company. This return is the interest they receive for the time they have allowed the company to use their money. Of course, creditors also expect to get their money back. This is known as a *return of principal*.

If a company is operating profitably, it has an internal source of new funding because those profits are not being paid out to shareholders as dividends. Any profits that are kept or retained by the company are known as **retained earnings**. If a company's retained earnings are less than the funding it requires to grow (such as purchasing additional equipment or carrying new lines of inventory), the only way it can expand is to obtain more funds from investors (existing shareholders or new investors) or to borrow from creditors. How much to borrow from creditors and how much funding to obtain from investors are important decisions that the company's management must make. Those decisions can determine whether a company grows, goes bankrupt, or is bought by another company. Examples of financing activities follow:

TYPICAL FINANCING ACTIVITIES
Inflows: Borrowing money
Issuing shares
Outflows: Repaying loan principal
Paying dividends

What are examples of investing activities?

Once a company obtains funds, it must invest them to accomplish its goals. Most companies make both long-term and short-term investments in order to carry out the activities that help them achieve their goals. Most short-term investments (such as the purchase of raw materials and inventories) are related to the day-to-day operations of the business and are therefore considered operating activities. Many long-term investments are related to the purchase of property, plant, and equipment that can be used to produce goods and services for sale. Companies can also consider investing in the shares of other companies either long-term or short-term.

Examples of investing activities follow:

TYPICAL INVESTING ACTIVITIES
Inflows: Proceeds from the sale of property, plant, and equipment
Proceeds from the sale of shares of other companies
Outflows: Purchase of property, plant, and equipment
Purchase of shares of other companies

What are examples of operating activities?

Operating activities are all of the activities associated with developing, producing, marketing, and selling the company's products and/or services. While financing and investing activities are necessary to conduct operations, they tend to occur on a more sporadic basis than operating activities. The day-to-day ongoing activities of a company are generally classified as operating activities.

Examples of operating activities follow:

TYPICAL OPERATING ACTIVITIES
Inflows: Sales to customers
Collections of amounts owed by customers
Outflows: Purchases of inventory
Payments of amounts owed to suppliers
Payments of expenses such as wages, rent, and interest
Payments of taxes owed to the government

Of the three categories of activities, operating activities are considered the most critical to the long-run success or failure of a company. If the company is not successful at generating cash flows from its operations, it will ultimately run out of cash as financing sources will dry up because it will be unable to attract new investors or lenders. It will have to sell the property, plant, and equipment it uses to generate its revenues.

Exhibit 1-6 illustrates the principal inflows and outflows associated with the three categories of business activities.

Exhibit 1-6 The Three Categories of Business Activities: Key Inflows and Outflows

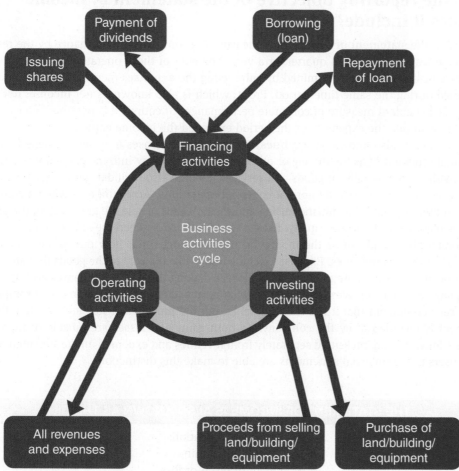

The financial statements provide information about a company's operating, financing, and investing activities. By the end of this book, you should be able to interpret financial statements as they relate to these activities. To help you become a successful user of financial statement information, in Appendix A at the back of the book, we present the financial statements of **Danier Leather Inc.**, which were included in the company's 2014 annual report. As noted in the feature story, Danier is a Canadian manufacturer and retailer of leather clothing and accessories. Let's walk through the various types of information contained in this part of Danier's annual report.

FINANCIAL REPORTING

■ LEARNING OBJECTIVE 5
Identify and explain the content and reporting objectives of the four basic financial statements and the notes to the financial statements.

What information is included in a set of financial statements?

The components of the financial statements are shown below.

COMPONENTS OF THE FINANCIAL STATEMENTS
Statement of income
Statement of changes in equity
Statement of financial position
Statement of cash flows
Notes to the financial statements

Let's look at each component of the financial statements in detail, including what it sets out to do and what information it includes.

What is the reporting objective of the statement of income? What does it include?

The objective of the **statement of income** is to measure the company's performance by the results of its operating activities for a month, a quarter, or a year. The sum of these operating activities is known as the company's **profit**, which is determined by subtracting the **expenses** incurred in the period from the **income** earned during the same time period. Profit, which is also known as **net income, net earnings**, or **earnings**, is a standard measure of corporate performance. Of course, it is possible to have a **net loss**, which would mean that the expenses for the period exceeded the income earned.

Income (which is also known as **revenues**) is defined as increases in economic benefits, but this is more commonly thought of as the money or other resources that flow into the company as a result of its ordinary activities, such as sales of goods and services. Income also includes **gains** that a company generates from sales that are outside its normal course of operations. An example is when a company sells some of its equipment that it has finished using and the proceeds of sale are greater than the amount the equipment is recorded at by the company. Expenses are defined as decreases in economic benefits, but are more commonly thought of as the money or other resources that flow out of the company in the course of it generating its revenues. Expenses include things like the cost of the goods that are sold in sale transactions or the wages that are paid to the employees making these sales. Expenses also include **losses** that a company can incur on sales that are outside its normal course of operations. An example is when a company sells equipment that it has finished using, but the proceeds of sale are less than the amount the equipment is recorded at by the company. As both gains and losses are outside of the company's normal operations, they are presented separately from revenues and expenses on the statement of income, so that the users of the financial statements are able to make this distinction.

THE STATEMENT OF INCOME IS ALSO KNOWN AS THE . . .
Statement of operations
Statement of earnings
Statement of profit or loss

Refer to the consolidated statements of earnings (loss) and comprehensive earnings (loss) for Danier in Appendix A. It is called a **consolidated financial statement** because it includes the financial information for the main or **parent company** plus the financial information of all the other companies that it controls (known as the **subsidiary companies**). The time period of the statement is indicated at the top, where it reads "Years Ended June 28, 2014 (52 weeks), and June 29, 2013 (52 weeks)." Companies are required to provide **comparative information** (the results of both the current period and preceding period) so that users can assess the changes from the previous period. As noted above, this statement reports on the company's operating performance for the year ended June 28, 2014. This period is also known as the company's **fiscal year**. You may be wondering why Danier's fiscal years ended on different days in 2014 and 2013 (that is, June 28 in 2014 and June 29 in 2013). This is because the company has established that its fiscal year ends on the last Saturday in June each year. Having a fiscal year end on a Saturday is common among retailers, but it means that every fifth or sixth year, the year includes 53 weeks rather than 52 weeks. Finally, it is also important to note that the numbers in the Danier financial statements are presented in thousands of Canadian dollars. Some Canadian companies, whose shares trade on U.S. stock exchanges, report in U.S. dollars instead of Canadian dollars.

Revenue

From the statement, we can see that Danier generated revenues of almost $142 million during its 2013 fiscal year. This would be the sales from all 90 stores that the company owns. From the comparative information, we can see that the company's sales decreased 8% over the prior period. This trend is negative, so we would need to read the management discussion and analysis (MD&A) section of the company's annual report to get additional details regarding the change in revenues. As the name implies, the MD&A section is where senior management discusses and analyzes its financial statements. (We will explore more aspects of an MD&A later in the chapter.) A look at Danier's MD&A tells us that 39% of the company's revenues resulted from sales of accessories and that the sales in the company's stores in all regions declined, with the decreases in Quebec and Atlantic Canada being the most significant. The MD&A also explains that the company's sales are very seasonal, with 44% of total sales occurring in the three-month period between October and December. As you can see, while the information presented in the statement of income is useful, it often needs to be supplemented with other information in order to carry out meaningful analysis.

Further down on the statement, we can see that the company earned interest income of $118,000 during the year. Since this income did not come from the sale of goods to customers, Danier has presented it separately from its revenues. This helps users of the financial statements to have a clearer picture of the results of the company's operations.

Expenses

Costs and expenses are also listed under various categories, including cost of goods sold (or cost of sales, or cost of merchandise sold); selling, general, and administrative expenses (or operating expenses); interest expense; and income tax expense (or provision for income taxes). As you would expect, cost of sales is a significant expense for a company like Danier. As a manufacturer, it purchases raw materials like leather from which it manufactures clothing to sell in its retail locations. The company also purchases finished goods, like the accessories it also sells in its stores. The other significant cost would be the wage costs for all of the company's employees, whether they work at the retail locations, manufacturing operations, or at the company's head office. These costs are included in selling, general, and administrative expenses. Danier provides some additional information on the makeup of cost of sales and selling, general, and administrative expenses in Notes 13, 21 and 22 to the financial statements. This is another example of providing information in addition to that presented in the statement itself so users can fully understand the financial information.

Gross Profit

Gross profit (or *gross margin*) is another very important number presented on the statement of income for all companies that sell goods. It is equal to the difference between the revenue received from the sale of the goods and the amount these goods cost the seller. From Danier's statement of income, we can see that this amounted to $68.2 million in 2014. It is often more meaningful to express gross profit as a percentage of revenue rather than as a dollar figure. For Danier, the gross profit percentage was 48.1% in 2014. This means that for every dollar in sales revenue, the company had just over $0.48 after paying for its products. This gross profit must then be used to cover the rest of the company's operating costs, such as wages, rent, and advertising. Another way of looking at this is to consider that Danier, on average, was able to sell its products for just about double the price they cost to manufacture or purchase.

Net Earnings

Net earnings (*net income* or *profit*) is the amount of the company's revenue that remains after all of its expenses, such as product costs, wages, rents, interest, and income taxes. In the case of Danier, the company had a net loss of $7,663,000 for 2013. If we reflect this as a percentage of sales, we can see that for every $1 in sales revenue, Danier lost about $0.05 in net earnings. In other words, all of Danier's expenses represented about $1.05 of every $1 in sales revenue.

Earnings per Share

At the bottom of the statement of income is an **earnings per share** disclosure. Basic earnings per share is the company's net income divided by the average number of common shares that are outstanding (owned by shareholders of the company) during the year. Shareholders find this calculation useful since it puts the performance of their investment into perspective. In other words, a shareholder who holds 10,000 shares of Danier can determine his or her share of the earnings during the period. In the fiscal year ending June 28, 2014, Danier's earnings per share was a loss of $2.00. Therefore, that investor's share of the loss for 2014 would be $20,000. The board of directors determines how much of the company's earnings, if any, will be paid to shareholders as dividends. Given the loss, no dividends were declared by Danier's board in 2014.

On some statements of income, there will also be a diluted earnings per share amount, which is normally lower than the basic earnings per share. Danier has indicated that its diluted earnings (loss) per share was $2.00. Diluted earnings per share reflects the earnings per share figure that would have been determined if all of the securities that can be converted into shares had actually been converted. More advanced financial accounting courses discuss diluted earnings per share in more detail.

Below is a list of some of the items you can expect to see on the statement of income.

COMMON STATEMENT OF INCOME ITEMS	
Sales revenues	The total amount of sales of goods and/or services for the period.
Other income	Various types of revenues or income to the company other than sales, including interest or rental income.
Cost of goods sold	The cost of the inventory that was sold during the period.
Selling, general, and administrative expense	The total amount of other expenses (such as salaries and rent) during the period that do not fit into any other category.
Depreciation expense (Amortization expense)	The allocation of part of the cost of long-lived items such as equipment or a patent.
Interest expense	The amount of interest incurred on the company's debt during the period.
Income tax expense (provision for taxes)	The taxes levied on the company's profits during the period.

 Ethics in Accounting

Accounting standards allow companies to choose among different measurement methods. These choices can impact the information on financial statements and provide management with the opportunity to select methods that can raise or lower income and report revenues and/or expenses at different times. When management selects accounting methods to achieve a specific reporting objective, it is called **earnings management**. Most times, managers will use earnings management legitimately, but as a user of the financial statement information, it is important that you recognize the circumstances that make it possible for earnings to be managed in an unethical way.

What is the reporting objective of the statement of changes in equity? What does it include?

The **statement of changes in equity** provides details on how each component of shareholders' equity changed during the period. As we begin thinking about the concept of **equity**, it can help to use the example of home ownership to illustrate that equity is a "net" number. For example, if we were trying to determine the equity that a person had in their home, we would calculate it as the value of their home (what they could sell it for) less the amount of any mortgage(s) that would have to be paid off if the home were sold. This difference would be the person's equity in the home, also known as homeowner's equity. Continuing with this example, we can see that the initial equity of the homeowner in the home would be equal to their down payment. We can also see that their equity would be increased by both increases in the value of the home and repayments of the mortgage. As the shareholders of a company are its owners, we can use a similar approach when thinking about their equity in the company. It includes the amount put into the company by shareholders when the company *initially* issued shares and any income generated by the company that has not been distributed to shareholders as dividends. We call these amounts **share capital** and retained earnings, which are the earnings or income that have been "retained" by the company and reinvested into the business. There are a couple of other components to equity that can appear in the statement of equity, including contributed surplus and accumulated other comprehensive income. We will ignore these in the early part of the book in order to concentrate on share capital and retained earnings. These other components will be discussed in later chapters.

THE STATEMENT OF CHANGES IN SHAREHOLDERS' EQUITY IS ALSO KNOWN AS THE . . .
Statement of shareholders' equity
Statement of changes in equity
Statement of equity

The objective of the statement of changes in equity is to illustrate the changes to a number of different components of equity. For example, this statement will explain changes to each class of shares issued by the company if the company issued additional shares during the year or repurchased and cancelled others. The statement will also explain the changes in the company's retained earnings during the year, which will be equal to the net income for the period less any dividends that the company's board of directors declared during the period; that is, the amount of earnings that have been retained rather than distributed.

If we refer to Danier's consolidated statements of changes in shareholders' equity in Appendix A, we can see the changes to the company's share capital. During the year ended June 28, 2014, the company received $350,000 when it issued shares as a result of stock options being exercised. We can also see that the company repurchased some of its shares during the year and cancelled them. The company had received $111,000 when it had initially issued the repurchased shares, so this amount was removed from share capital. The notes to the financial statements explained that 47,000 shares were issued during the year and 25,000 shares were repurchased and cancelled.

Looking at the changes to Danier's retained earnings, we can see that the company had a net loss of $7,663,000 during the most recent year, which we knew by looking at the company's statement of income. We can also see that the company did not declare any dividends during the year but did use some of its retained earnings when it repurchased and cancelled the 25,000 shares discussed above. When these shares were repurchased, the company paid the shareholders more than it received when the shares were initially issued. This difference, which is a distribution to shareholders, is treated like a dividend and is therefore reflected on the statement of changes in equity as a reduction to retained earnings. We will come back to the changes in retained earnings frequently throughout the book, so it will be important for you to understand that the retained earnings of a company are determined as follows:

RETAINED EARNINGS =
Opening Retained Earnings
+ Net Income
− Dividends Declared
Ending Retained Earnings

As previously mentioned, the two components of shareholders' equity that we will be focusing on throughout the early parts of the textbook are:

COMMON SHAREHOLDERS' EQUITY COMPONENTS	
Share capital	Represents the shares issued by the company, usually stated at an amount equal to what the company received from investors on the initial issuance of the shares. There can be different types of shares (common shares and preferred shares). There can also be different classes of shares; in other words, shares that have different rights and privileges.
Retained earnings	The company's earnings (as measured on the statement of income) that have been kept (retained) and not paid out as dividends.

What is the reporting objective of the statement of financial position? What does it include?

The **statement of financial position** is also known as the *balance sheet*. The term *financial position* indicates that this statement presents the company's financial status at a particular point in time. The consolidated statement of financial position for Danier is shown in Appendix A. In the case of Danier, the information presented is as at June 28, 2014, and June 29, 2013, which are the dates the company's fiscal year ended, also known as its *year end*. This means that the amounts in the statement are those that existed on those dates, which are considered to be the beginning and end points of the current accounting period. In the transition from one accounting period to the next, the ending balances of one accounting period become the beginning balances of the next accounting period. The statement of financial position is often described as a snapshot of a company's financial position at a particular point in time.

The format of this statement of financial position is known as a **classified statement of financial position** and is typical of most Canadian statements of financial position, which present information in order of **liquidity**. Liquidity refers to how soon something will be received, realized, or consumed, or else settled or paid. Canadian companies use a 12-month period to distinguish between items that are **current** and those that are **non-current**. Current items are those that will be received, realized, or consumed, or else settled or paid within 12 months from year end. Those are that are non-current will *not* be received, realized, consumed, or settled or paid within 12 months from the year end. It is important to note that other formats can be used to present a company's financial position, but all of them will reflect this notion of liquidity because it is critical for financial statement users to be able to assess a company's liquidity.

Throughout the book, we will learn about a number of ways that liquidity is commonly assessed. One of the most common measures of liquidity is **working capital**. This is quantified as the difference between a company's **current assets** (assets that are cash or will become cash within the next 12 months) and its **current liabilities** (liabilities that must be settled within the next 12 months). It measures a company's ability to meet its short-term obligations using its short-term assets. The working capital equation is shown below.

WORKING CAPITAL
Working Capital = Current Assets − Current Liabilities

So what makes up the company's financial position? Individuals, if asked about their own financial position, would probably start by listing what they own, such as a car, a computer, or a house, and then listing what they owe to others, such as bank loans and credit card balances. What is owned less what is owed would be a measure of an individual's net worth (wealth or equity) at a particular point in time. A company lists exactly the same types of things in its statement of financial position. They are referred to as **assets**, **liabilities**, and shareholders' equity. These are the three components of the **accounting equation**, which provides the structure to the statement of financial position:

THE ACCOUNTING EQUATION
Assets = Liabilities + Shareholders' Equity

Assets

When asked for a simple definition of an asset, many people reply that it is something of value that the company either owns or has the right to use. In fact, the accounting definition of an asset is very similar. Assets must meet three criteria, shown in the box below:

CHARACTERISTICS OF AN ASSET
1. It is a resource controlled by an entity. 2. The company expects future economic benefits from the use or sale of the resource. 3. The event that gave the company control of the resource has already happened.

The assets that Danier lists on its statement of financial position include:
- cash, accounts receivable, income taxes recoverable, inventories, and prepaid expenses
- property and equipment (often called *capital assets*)
- computer software (considered part of *intangible assets* as it lacks physical form)
- deferred income tax asset

While later chapters discuss in more detail how each of these assets meets the criteria of control and future economic benefits, we can look at Danier's inventory as an example for now. Control of the inventory is proven either by possession of the goods or by legal documentation. The inventory has future economic benefits because the company can later sell it and receive cash in the amount of the selling price. The presence of the inventory or the underlying documents of the purchase indicates that the event that gave the company control has already happened.

The total assets of Danier as at June 29, 2013, were $60,629 thousand. A list of assets normally found on a statement of financial position is below.

COMMON ASSETS	
Cash	The amount of currency that the company has, including amounts in bank accounts.
Short-term investments	Short-term investments in shares of other companies.
Accounts receivable	Amounts owed to the company by its customers as a result of credit sales.
Inventory	Goods held for resale to customers.
Prepaid expenses and deposits	Amounts that have been paid by the company but the underlying service has not yet been used. Common examples include insurance premiums or rent paid in advance.
Property, plant, and equipment	Land, buildings, equipment, vehicles, and so on that the company purchases to use to generate revenues in the future; they are *not* purchased to resell.
Intangible assets	Licences, patents, trademarks, copyrights, computer software, and other assets that lack physical form. These are also acquired to generate revenues in the future.
Goodwill	A premium that has been paid on the acquisition of another company related to factors such as management expertise and corporate reputation that will result in higher future earnings.

Liabilities

A simple definition of liabilities might be amounts that the company owes to others. (They are also known as *debt* and *obligations*.) The accounting definition of liabilities encompasses this concept and refers to items that will require the outflow or sacrifice of economic resources in the future to settle an obligation that exists as a result of a transaction that has already taken place. In most cases, the economic resource that will be sacrificed is cash, but a company can also settle liabilities by providing services or goods. For example, most of you will pay your university the full amount of the semester's tuition before or at the beginning of the semester. The university has a liability to you for this amount, which it will settle by providing the related course instruction over the semester. Alternatively, a warranty liability for a washing machine could be satisfied with a new part or by providing the services of a repair person. Liabilities must meet three criteria, as shown in the box below.

CHARACTERISTICS OF A LIABILITY
1.   It is a present obligation of the entity. 2.   The company expects to settle it through an outflow of resources that represent future economic benefits. 3.   The obligation results from an event that has already happened.

The liabilities that Danier lists on its statement of financial position include:
- payables and accruals (representing amounts owed to suppliers, unpaid wages, unpaid taxes, or estimates of warranty obligations)
- deferred revenue (often called *unearned revenue*, which represents customer *deposits* or amounts paid in advance of the company providing the related goods or service)
- sales return provision (representing an estimate of the sales to customers that may have to be negated as a result of the customer returning the purchased goods in accordance with the company's return policy)
- deferred lease inducements and rent liability (representing amounts received from landlords at some of the company's leased store locations that will be used to offset future rent expense)

The total liabilities of Danier as at June 28, 2014, were $12,222 thousand. The following list includes some of the more common liabilities found on the statement of financial position.

COMMON LIABILITIES	
Bank indebtedness	Amounts owed to the bank on short-term credit.
Accounts payable (Trade payables)	Amounts owed to suppliers from the purchase of goods on credit.
Deferred revenue (Unearned revenue)	Amounts owed to customers for advance payments until the related goods or services have been provided.
Dividends payable	Amounts owed to shareholders for dividends that have been declared by the board of directors.
Accrued liabilities	Amounts owed related to expenses that are not yet due, such as interest and warranty expense.
Income taxes payable	Amounts owed to taxing authorities.
Notes payable	Amounts owed to a creditor (bank or supplier) that are represented by a formal agreement called a *note* (sometimes called a *promissory note*). Notes payable often have an interest component, whereas accounts payable usually do not.
Long-term debt	Amounts owed to creditors due beyond one year.
Deferred income taxes	Amounts representing probable future taxes the company will have to pay.

Shareholders' Equity

The last major category in the statement of financial position is the section called *shareholders' equity*. This section captures the amount of the company's shareholders' interest in the assets of the company. Shareholders' equity is often referred to as the **net assets** of the company. This is the amount of assets that would remain after all of the company's liabilities were settled. If the accounting equation is rearranged, you can see that shareholders' equity is equal to the company's assets less its liabilities:

THE ACCOUNTING EQUATION (REARRANGED)
Assets − Liabilities = Shareholders' Equity (Net Assets)

It is important to understand that this amount is determined using the values of the assets and liabilities as they are reflected on the statement of financial position. These values will often differ from those in the current market. Throughout the text, we will explore the reasons why these values differ. For now, let's consider a company's inventory. It is reflected on the company's statement of financial position at its cost to the company, but this amount will differ from what the company would sell it for. The selling price would also differ if it were an urgent or distress sale (that is, if the company desperately had to sell the goods) rather than a sale in the ordinary course of its operations.

Based on Danier's statement of financial position, shareholders' equity at June 28, 2014, was $48,407 thousand.

$$\text{Assets} - \text{Liabilities} = \text{Shareholders' Equity}$$
$$\$60,629 \text{ thousand} - \$12,222 \text{ thousand} = \$48,407 \text{ thousand}$$

Note that the market value of the shares held by a company's shareholders is another measure of the shareholders' wealth in the company. By **market value**, we mean the price at which the shares are trading in the stock market. This value is likely very different from the book value of shareholders' equity because it reflects the market's expectations of future earnings and events.

One of the objectives of the statement of financial position is to enable financial statement users to assess the relative proportions of liabilities and shareholders' equity to better understand a company's financing strategy. For Danier as at June 28, 2014, total liabilities were $12,222 thousand and total shareholders' equity was $48,407 thousand, relative to total assets of $60,629 thousand. The proportion of liabilities is 20% ($12,222 ÷ $60,629), which is slightly less than one fifth of the total financing. This means that Danier has financed its assets using significantly more shareholders' equity than debt. Specifically, it gets about 80% of its financing from shareholders' equity. This low percentage of debt to equity demonstrates that the company has grown its operations using internal financing rather than through the use of debt. While the use of debt can be a good thing, generally the higher the proportion of debt to equity, the greater the financial risk facing the company. We will discuss the concept of leverage—using other people's money to make money—in a later chapter of the text.

As discussed in the section on the statement of changes in shareholders' equity, equity is usually composed of a number of components. For now, we will focus on two components: share capital and retained earnings. The first component, share capital (some companies use the term *common shares*), records the amount that the investors originally paid (invested) for the shares that the company issued. The second component, retained earnings, keeps track of the company's earnings less any amounts that the company pays to the shareholders in dividends. As mentioned previously, we will ignore the other components of shareholders' equity until later in the text.

Exhibit 1-7 illustrates how information flows between the first three financial statements. The statement of income is generally prepared first in order to determine net income. This statement is then used when preparing the statement of changes in equity. Finally, the share capital and retained earnings balances are used when preparing the statement of financial position.

Exhibit 1-7 Information Flows between the First Three Financial Statements

TAKE**5**

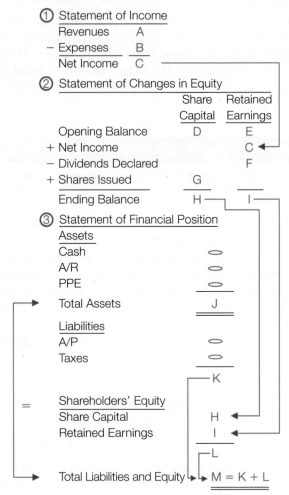

What is the reporting objective of the statement of cash flows? What does it include?

The **statement of cash flows** (sometimes called the *cash flow statement*) presents the flows of cash related to the three categories of business activities, which we discussed earlier in the chapter. The reporting objective of this statement is to enable financial statement users to assess the company's inflows and outflows of cash related to each of these activities, so they can see where the company's cash came from and how it was used.

Danier's consolidated statement of cash flow in Appendix A presents the company's inflows and outflows of cash for the years ending June 28, 2014, and June 29, 2013. This statement differs from the statement of income in that it measures cash flows during the period rather than the revenues and expenses for the period, which may not be received or paid in cash. Cash is very important to the company's operations and this statement is critical to a user's evaluation of a company. Given the importance of this statement, Chapter 5 of the text is focused on how the statement is prepared and used. For now, we will review the basic content of the statement.

The cash flow statement has three sections that report the sources and uses of cash and cash equivalents for the three categories of business activities described earlier: operating, financing, and investing.

SUBSECTIONS OF THE STATEMENT OF CASH FLOWS
Cash flow from operating activities
Cash flow from financing activities
Cash flow from investing activities

Operating activities include all inflows and outflows of cash related to the sale of goods and services. They are the activities that the company provides in its normal operations. The starting point in this section is frequently net earnings (or net income or profit) from the statement of income. There are adjustments to this number because the recognition (recording) of revenues and expenses does not necessarily coincide with the receipt and payment of cash, as we will see in future chapters. For instance, sales could be either cash sales or sales on account. That is, customers can pay at a later date, resulting in an account receivable rather than cash. Expenses may also be paid later if the company is given credit by its suppliers, which would result in an account payable. Because operating activities are the backbone of the company, a positive cash flow from operations is essential to the company's long-term health. Due to its loss in the current year, Danier had an out-flow of cash of $4,907 thousand from its operating activities in the fiscal year ending June 28, 2014, as compared to an in-flow of $6,752 thousand in the previous year.

Financing activities are transactions that either resulted from new funds being received from investors or creditors or from the return of funds to these two groups. Typical activities in this category are the issuance of shares, the proceeds of new borrowings, the repayment of debt, or the payment of dividends. Danier's cash flow from financing activities was an outflow of $48 thousand for the year ended June 28, 2014. We can see from this that the company did not obtain any new funding from either shareholders or creditors during the period and actually returned funds to shareholders through the repurchase of the company's shares from shareholders.

Investing activities generally involve the purchase and sale of long-term assets such as property, plant, and equipment, and investments in other companies. In the case of Danier, we can see the company purchased property, equipment, and computer software during the year ended June 28, 2014. It did not sell any long-term assets during the period. This resulted in cash outflows of $6,079 thousand for the period. Companies that are growing, and even those that are just maintaining their current operations, normally have negative cash flows from investing activities. This results from them spending more cash to purchase new long-term assets than they are receiving as proceeds from the sale of long-term assets that they have finished using in their operations.

Overall, we can see that Danier had a net decrease in cash of $11,034 million during the year ended June 28, 2014. This is the sum of the cash flows from the categories of business activities ($4,907 + $48 + $6,079 = −$11,034). This explains why the company's cash balance decreased from $24,541 thousand at the start of the year to $13,507 thousand at the end of the year.

SUMMARY OF THE FINANCIAL STATEMENTS	
Statement of income	Measures the operating performance of a company over a period of time.
Statement of changes in equity	Measures the changes in the equity of the company over a period of time, differentiating between changes that result from transactions with shareholders and those resulting from the company's operations.
Statement of financial position	Measures the resources controlled by a company (assets) and the claims on those resources (by creditors and investors) at a given point in time.
Statement of cash flows	Measures the change in cash flow through operating, financing, and investing activities over a period of time.

What type of information is in the notes to a company's financial statements?

You may have noticed that some of the items in the financial statements directed the user to specific notes. These **notes to the financial statements** are a critical part of the financial statements. In them, management gives more detail about specific items such as the various types of inventory held by the company and details on its long-term assets. By including additional explanations in notes rather than in the financial statements, management keeps the company's statements simple and uncluttered. Note disclosures help to increase the usefulness of the financial statements and enhance the user's understanding of the various components of the statements.

A full discussion of notes will be left to succeeding chapters, but some attention should be paid to two of the notes that normally appear at the beginning of the notes to the financial statements. These are the note explaining the basis on which the financial statements have been prepared and the note outlining the significant accounting policies used in the preparation of the statements. Danier presented this information in the second and third of 22 notes that were included with the company's financial statements.

From these two notes, we can see that Danier's financial statements were prepared using **International Financial Reporting Standards (IFRS)**, which are the accounting standards that must be followed by Canadian public companies. From these notes, we can also learn more about the choices and judgements made by management in applying these reporting standards. As you progress through the book, you will learn that these choices have important implications for how to interpret the statements. Comparing two companies that have made two different choices and judgements would pose difficulties. To help users compare various companies, management must therefore disclose in this note the major accounting principles that it uses.

While not part of the notes to the financial statements, all publicly traded companies are required to include a management discussion and analysis (MD&A) section in their annual reports. The MD&A section provides readers with senior management's perspective on the information contained in the financial statements. While it is not part of the financial statements, it provides very useful context for users of the financial statements.

In addition to management's perspectives on the company's financial results for the prior year, the MD&A also provides a discussion of the risks facing the company and information about future plans. Often information is presented from the perspective of the company's various divisions. It also includes information on significant events and about sales, profits, and cash flow during the year. The discussion focuses on the financial aspects of the business, including pricing strategies, expenses, earnings, liquidity, environmental and corporate social responsibility, expansion and future development, taxes, events after the end of the current year, and executive compensation policies.

 Ethics in Accounting

The management of a company, through the direction given to it by the board of directors, has both a moral and a legal obligation to safeguard the investment that shareholders have made in the company and entrusted to the care of management. To ensure that management fulfills this stewardship function over the company's resources, shareholders typically provide some incentives for and controls over management. You have probably heard about stock option plans and bonuses given to top management. These additional compensation arrangements are often tied to the company's financial performance and provide incentives for management to make decisions that are in the best interests of the shareholders. Danier has provided information about the remuneration, including salaries and share-based compensation, of senior executives and members of the board of directors in note 20 to the financial statements. This information is intended to show shareholders and others that the company is open and accountable for its decisions.

For a number of years, the Canadian Coalition for Good Governance, which represents institutional investors and asset managers, has been advocating for public companies to voluntarily implement annual shareholder "Say on Pay" votes. These votes involve shareholders approving the executive compensation programs implemented by the company's board of directors. These are non-binding votes (that is, the board is not required to make changes as a result of these votes) and are meant to advise the board on the perspective of shareholders. As of March 2014, 127 Canadian public companies had voluntarily adopted "Say on Pay" votes, including more than three quarters of the 60 largest companies listed on the TSX. This trend is not unique to Canada, as annual "Say on Pay" votes are required for public companies in the U.K. and Australia, while a vote must be held at least every three years for U.S. public companies.

To date, the vast majority of "Say on Pay" votes have indicated a high level of shareholder support for the executive compensation practices, with average overall support of close to 90%. Shareholders have only voted "no" at three Canadian companies. Barrick Gold Corporation was the largest of the three, with its institutional shareholders protesting the $17 million in compensation paid to the company's vice-chairman in 2012. In Barrick's case, only 15% of shareholders supported the company's "Say on Pay" vote.

The "Say on Pay" movement illustrates the importance of boards' ensuring that the executive compensation packages they approve are aligned with corporate performance. It also reflects the growing influence of institutional shareholders in overseeing governance of public companies.[2]

Now that you know what corporate financial reporting involves and what the main financial statements contain, in the next chapter we'll look at how users can analyze them.

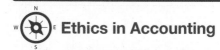

Ethics in Accounting

Shareholders hire an independent external **auditor** to review the financial statements presented to them by the company's management. The auditor must maintain their independence from the company's management team throughout the audit.

In order to ensure their independence and encourage ethical behaviour, the accounting profession has developed codes of professional conduct.

CHAPTER END REVIEW PROBLEM

The Chapter End Review Problems reinforce your understanding of major sections in the chapter. One or more questions have been created to illustrate the topics and demonstrate how you can use the information. Answers are provided so that you can check your knowledge. You can use these questions as examples when working on other questions assigned by your instructor.

The major financial statements of **High Liner Foods Incorporated** from its 2013 annual report are included in Exhibits 1-8 A, B, and C. Nova Scotia–based High Liner is a leading processor and marketer of frozen seafood. Note that its fiscal year is a 52-week period ended December 28, 2013. We will refer to these as the 2013 financial statements and use them to answer a series of questions.

Exhibit 1-8A High Liner Foods Incorporated's 2013 Consolidated Statement of Income

CONSOLIDATED STATEMENT OF INCOME

FINANCIAL STATEMENTS

		Fifty-two weeks ended	
(in thousands of U.S. dollars, except per share amounts)	Notes	**December 28, 2013**	December 29, 2012
Revenues		$ **947,301**	$ 942,631
Cost of sales		**731,884**	735,970
Gross profit		**215,417**	206,661
Distribution expenses		**53,368**	44,511
Selling, general and administrative expenses		**98,902**	100,862
Impairment of property, plant and equipment		**—**	13,230
Business acquisition, integration and other expenses		**3,256**	10,741
Results from operating activities		**59,891**	37,317
Finance costs		**16,329**	36,585
(Income) loss from equity accounted investee, net of income tax		**(86)**	196
Income before income taxes		**43,648**	536
Income taxes			
Current	20	**12,378**	5,442
Deferred	20	**(86)**	(7,109)
Total income tax expense (recovery)		**12,292**	(1,667)
Net income		$ **31,356**	$ 2,203
PER SHARE EARNINGS			
Earnings per common share			
Basic	17	$ **2.07**	$ 0.15
Diluted	17	$ **2.01**	$ 0.14
Weighted average number of shares outstanding			
Basic	17	**15,183,747**	15,118,752
Diluted	17	**15,593,166**	15,460,417

Exhibit 1-8B High Liner Foods Incorporated's 2013 Consolidated Statement of Financial Position

FINANCIAL
STATEMENTS

CONSOLIDATED STATEMENT OF FINANCIAL POSITION

(in thousands of U.S. dollars)	Notes	December 28, 2013	December 29, 2012
ASSETS			
Current:			
Cash		$ 1,206	$ 65
Accounts receivable	9	91,334	73,947
Income taxes receivable		3,509	5,145
Other financial assets	22	1,524	533
Inventories	8	254,072	222,313
Prepaid expenses		2,952	2,991
Total current assets		354,597	304,994
Non-current:			
Property, plant and equipment	6	97,503	89,268
Deferred income taxes	20	4,656	7,207
Other receivables and miscellaneous assets		1,906	2,035
Intangible assets	5	105,253	110,631
Goodwill	5	111,999	112,873
Total non-current assets		321,317	322,014
Assets classified as held for sale	7	542	4,819
Total assets		$ 676,456	$ 631,827
LIABILITIES AND SHAREHOLDERS' EQUITY			
Current:			
Bank loans	12	$ 97,227	$ 59,704
Accounts payable and accrued liabilities	10	103,215	101,441
Provisions	11	240	1,614
Other current financial liabilities	22	459	550
Income taxes payable		2,543	1,165
Current portion of long-term debt	13	—	34,237
Current portion of finance lease obligations	13	979	1,039
Total current liabilities		204,663	199,750
Non-current:			
Long-term debt	13	226,929	213,359
Other long-term financial liabilities	22	5,597	1,130
Other long-term liabilities		1,044	1,532
Long-term finance lease obligations	13	1,647	2,181
Deferred income taxes	20	43,998	45,126
Future employee benefits	14	7,929	13,791
Total non-current liabilities		287,144	277,119
Liabilities directly associated with the assets held for sale	7	—	1,604
Total liabilities		491,807	478,473
Shareholders' equity:			
Common shares	16	80,260	75,169
Contributed surplus		13,781	7,719
Retained earnings		90,792	66,373
Accumulated other comprehensive (loss) income		(184)	4,093
Total shareholders' equity		184,649	153,354
Total liabilities and shareholders' equity		$ 676,456	$ 631,827

Exhibit 1-8C High Liner Foods Incorporated's 2013 Consolidated Statement of Cash Flows

	Fifty-two weeks ended	
	December 28, 2013	December 29, 2012
(in thousands of U.S. dollars)		
Cash provided by (used in) operations:		
Net income for the period	**$ 31,356**	$ 2,203
Charges (credits) to income not involving cash from operations:		
Depreciation and amortization	**15,159**	19,381
Share-based payment expense	**6,704**	10,255
(Gain) loss on asset disposals, and impairment	**(126)**	13,589
Payments of future employee benefits in excess of expense	**(948)**	(1,728)
Finance costs	**16,329**	36,585
Income tax expense (recovery)	**12,292**	(1,667)
(Income) loss from equity accounted investee, net of income taxes	**(86)**	196
Unrealized foreign exchange loss	**700**	683
Cash flow provided by operations before changes in non-cash working capital, interest and income taxes paid:	**81,380**	79,497
Net change in non-cash working capital balances:		
Accounts receivable	**(15,157)**	4,958
Inventories	**(3,162)**	35,258
Prepaids	**841**	(423)
Provisions	**(1,237)**	904
Accounts payables and accrued liabilities	**(7,407)**	(14,535)
Net change in non-cash working capital balances	**(26,122)**	26,162
Interest paid	**(16,786)**	(19,145)
Income taxes paid	**(11,161)**	(7,530)
Net cash flows provided by operating activities	**27,311**	78,984
Cash provided by (used in) financing activities:		
Increase (decrease) in current working capital facilities	**37,771**	(59,673)
Repayment of finance lease obligations	**(1,052)**	(1,009)
Repayment of long-term debt	**(15,406)**	(1,875)
Finance costs	**(1,423)**	—
Common share dividends paid	**(10,305)**	(6,379)
Share repurchase	**—**	(497)
Stock options exercised	**1,395**	650
Net cash flows provided by (used in) financing activities	**10,980**	(68,783)
Cash provided by (used in) investing activities:		
Purchase of property, plant and equipment, net of investment tax credits (note 6)	**(14,734)**	(12,709)
Net proceeds on disposal of assets	**7,124**	232
Acquisition of business, net (note 4)	**(30,312)**	—
Change in other receivables and miscellaneous assets	**249**	(247)
Net cash flows used in investing activities	**(37,673)**	(12,724)
Foreign exchange (decrease) increase on cash	**(182)**	88
Change in cash during the period	**436**	(2,435)
Add-back: cash directly associated with assets held for sale (note 7)	**705**	(705)
Cash, beginning of period	**65**	3,205
Cash, end of period	**$ 1,206**	$ 65

STRATEGIES FOR SUCCESS

▶ Start by reviewing High Liner's three financial statements. Refresh your understanding of the kinds of information found in each statement.

▶ As you work through the list of items in question 1, try to remember which financial statement to look at by linking in your mind the name of the item identified and the financial statement on which it is included. As you work through more problems like this, you will become more familiar with what is on each statement.

▶ To answer question 2, first reread the section in the statement of financial position discussion in this chapter that explains shareholders' equity. The discussion of Danier's use of liabilities and shareholders' equity to finance its operations should be helpful.

Required:

1. Find the following amounts in the statements:
   a. Total revenues for fiscal year 2013
   b. Total cost of sales for fiscal year 2013
   c. Total selling, general, and administrative expenses for fiscal year 2013
   d. Finance costs for fiscal year 2013
   e. Income tax expense (recovery) (current and deferred) for fiscal year 2013
   f. Net income (earnings) for fiscal year 2013
   g. Inventories at the end of fiscal year 2013
   h. Accounts payable and accrued liabilities at the beginning of fiscal year 2013
   i. Shareholders' equity at the end of fiscal year 2013
   j. Retained earnings at the beginning of fiscal year 2013
   k. Cash provided from operating activities in fiscal year 2013
   l. Cash payments, net of investment tax credits, to acquire property, plant, and equipment in fiscal year 2013
   m. Cash used in the repayment of long-term debt in fiscal year 2013
   n. Cash used in the payment of dividends in fiscal year 2013
   o. Cash provided from (used for) investing activities in fiscal year 2013
2. Does High Liner Foods finance its business primarily with debt or with shareholders' equity? Support your answer with appropriate data.
3. List the two largest sources of cash and the two largest uses of cash in fiscal year 2013. (Consider operating activities to be a single source or use of cash.)
4. Does High Liner Foods use a classified statement of financial position? Explain.

Suggested Solution to the Chapter End Review Problem

To find the answers to the above questions, you will need to examine closely the three financial statements that have been provided.

1. The following answers are found on the financial statements included in Exhibits 1-8A, B, and C:
   a. Total revenues in 2013: $947,301 thousand. Revenues are reported on the statement of income.
   b. Total cost of sales in 2013: $731,884 thousand. The cost of sales is a type of expense. Expenses are reported on the statement of income.
   c. Total selling, general, and administrative expenses in 2013: $98,902 thousand. Expenses are reported on the statement of income.
   d. Finance costs in 2013: $16,329 thousand. Expenses are reported on the statement of income.
   e. Income tax expense (current and deferred) in 2013: $12,292 thousand ($12,378 + ($86)). Expenses are reported on the statement of income.
   f. Net income (earnings) in 2013: $31,356 thousand. The earnings are reported on the statement of income.
   g. Inventories at the end of 2013: $254,072 thousand. Inventories are assets, which are reported on the statement of financial position.
   h. Accounts payable and accrued liabilities at the beginning of 2013: $101,441 thousand (the end of 2012 is the same as the beginning of 2013). Liabilities are reported on the statement of financial position.
   i. Shareholders' equity at the end of 2013: $184,649 thousand. Shareholders' equity is reported on the statement of financial position.
   j. Retained earnings at the beginning of 2013: $66,373 thousand. (Again, you need to look to the end of 2012 to find the beginning of 2013.) The retained earnings are a part of shareholders' equity that is reported on the statement of financial position.
   k. Cash provided from operating activities in 2013: $27,311 thousand. The cash provided by various business activities is reported on the statement of cash flows. Operating activities are shown in the first section of this statement.
   l. Cash payments, net of investment tax credits, to acquire property, plant, and equipment in 2013: ($14,734 thousand). The net addition of capital assets is reported under the investing section on the statement of cash flows. Putting the amount in parentheses indicates that it is a negative number. In other words, cash was used.
   m. Cash used in the repayment of long-term debt in fiscal year 2013: ($15,406 thousand). The cash used for various business activities is reported on the statement of cash flows. The repayment of debt is a financing activity.

n. Cash used in the payment of dividends in 2013: ($10,305 thousand). The cash used for various business activities is reported on the statement of cash flows. Paying dividends is a financing activity.

o. Cash provided from (used for) investing activities in 2013: ($37,673 thousand). The cash provided by various business activities is reported on the statement of cash flows. Investing activities are one of the three main sections on this statement.

2. High Liner uses substantially more liabilities than shareholders' equity to finance its business. You can see this when you compare the total liabilities with the total liabilities plus shareholders' equity (on the statement of financial position as at December 28, 2013) as follows:

> Total liabilities: $491,807 thousand
> Total shareholders' equity: $184,649 thousand
> Total liabilities and shareholders' equity: $676,456 thousand

Total liabilities are, therefore, 73% (($491,807 ÷ $676,456) × 100) of High Liner's total sources of financing. Because debt must be repaid, it is important for users to understand how much of the company's activities are being financed by debt. The greater the percentage of debt to total liabilities and shareholders' equity, the more risk there is that the company may not be able to repay its debt when it comes due. At December 28, 2013, 73% of High Liner's financing was debt financing.

3. The two largest sources of cash are proceeds from the operating activities, $27,311 thousand, and the increase in current working capital facilities, $37,771 thousand. The two largest uses are the acquisition of business (net) ($30,312 thousand) and the repayment of long-term debt ($15,406 thousand).

4. High Liner does use a classified statement of financial position. It has labelled a section for current assets and current liabilities and for the non-current assets and non-current liabilities. It has included the non-current assets and non-current liabilities in separate sections after the totals of the current assets and current liabilities. It has also given you a separate total for the non-current assets and non-current liabilities.

SUMMARY

1. Define financial accounting and understand its relationship to economic decision-making.

- Financial accounting is the process by which information on the transactions of an organization is captured, analyzed, and reported to external decision makers.

- These decision makers are referred to as *financial statement users* and include investors and creditors.

- The primary purpose of financial accounting information is to aid these users in making economic decisions related to the reporting organization, such as whether to invest in it or lend it money.

2. Identify the main users of financial accounting information and explain how they use this information.

- The main users of financial accounting information include shareholders, the board of directors, potential investors, creditors (bankers and suppliers), regulators (stock exchanges), taxing authorities (governments), securities analysts, and others.

- Shareholders, the board of directors, and potential investors will use financial accounting information to enable them to assess how well management has run the company; determine whether they should buy, sell, or continue to hold shares in the company; assess the company's share price relative to the financial accounting information; and so on.

- Creditors will use financial accounting information to determine whether they should lend funds to the company, establish credit terms for it, assess a company's ability to meets its obligations, and so on.

- Regulators will use financial accounting information to determine whether a company has met its listing requirements.

- Taxing authorities will use this information in assessing the taxes owed by the organization.

3. Describe the major forms of business organization and explain the key distinctions between them.

- There are three major forms of business organization: (1) proprietorships, (2) partnerships, and (3) corporations.

- There are public corporations (whose shares trade on a public stock exchange and are widely held) and private corporations (whose shares do not trade on a public exchange and are generally owned by a small number of people).

- Corporations are separate legal entities, whereas proprietorships and partnerships are not. This means the personal assets of owners are protected in the event of legal action against corporations, whereas they are at risk in the case of proprietorships and partnerships. It also means corporations file separate tax returns, whereas the income from proprietorships and partnerships is reported on the personal tax returns of their owners.

4. **Explain the three categories of business activities and identify examples of transactions related to each category.**

   - The three categories of business activities are: (1) operating, (2) investing, and (3) financing activities.

   - Operating activities are related to the company's revenues and expenses, such as sales to customers, collections from customers, purchases of inventory, and payments of wages and other expenses.

   - Investing activities include buying and selling property, plant, and equipment and buying and selling the shares of other companies.

   - Financing activities include borrowing money, issuing shares, repaying loan principal, and paying dividends.

5. **Identify and explain the content and reporting objectives of the four basic financial statements and the notes to the financial statements.**

   - There are four basic financial statements: (1) the statement of income, (2) the statement of changes in equity, (3) the statement of financial position, and (4) the statement of cash flows.

   - The objective of the statement of income is to measure the company's operating performance (its profit) for a period of time. This is measured by subtracting the expenses incurred during the period from the income earned (revenues) in the same period.

   - The objective of the statement of changes in equity is to provide details on how each component of shareholders' equity changed during the period. The components of shareholders' equity include share capital (the shares issued by the company) and retained earnings (the company's earnings that have been kept and not distributed as dividends).

   - The objective of the statement of financial position is to present information on a company's assets, liabilities, and shareholders' equity at a specific date. Assets must be controlled by the company and embody a future benefit. Examples include cash; accounts receivable; inventory; property, plant, and equipment; land; and so on. Liabilities are obligations of a company that will result in an outflow of resources. Examples include accounts payable, deferred revenue, long-term debt, and so on. Shareholders' equity represents the shareholders' interest in the assets of the company and is referred to as *net assets*. Examples include common shares and retained earnings.

   - The objective of the statement of cash flows is to enable financial statement users to assess the company's inflows and outflows of cash related to its operating, investing, and financial activities for a period of time.

   - The notes to a company's financial statements are used to provide additional detail and context for items in the financial statements. They enable the financial statements themselves to remain uncluttered, while increasing their usefulness.

KEY TERMS

Accounting equation (16)
Annual report (4)
Assets (16)
Auditor (23)
Board of directors (6)
Canada Revenue Agency (CRA) (7)
Capital appreciation (10)
Classified statement of financial position (16)
Common shares (8)
Comparative information (13)
Consolidated financial statement (12)
Creditors (3)
Current (16)
Current assets (16)
Current liabilities (16)
Dividends (10)
Earnings (12)
Earnings management (14)
Earnings per share (14)
Expenses (12)
Equity (15)

Financial accounting (3)
Financial statement users (3)
Financial statements (4)
Financing activities (9)
Fiscal year (13)
Gains (12)
Gross profit (13)
Income (12)
Interest (7)
International Financial Reporting Standards (IFRS) (22)
Investing activities (9)
Investors (3)
Liabilities (16)
Liquidity (16)
Losses (12)
Management (3)
Management discussion and analysis (MD&A) (4)
Managerial accounting (3)
Market value (19)
Net assets (19)

Net earnings (12)
Net income (12)
Net loss (12)
Non-current (16)
Notes to the financial statements (21)
Operating activities (9)
Parent company (12)
Principal (7)
Private company (6)
Profit (12)
Public company (6)
Retained earnings (10)
Revenues (12)
Share capital (15)
Shareholders (6)
Shareholders' equity (10)
Statement of cash flows (20)
Statement of changes in equity (15)
Statement of financial position (16)
Statement of income (12)
Subsidiary companies (12)
Working capital (16)

ABBREVIATIONS USED

CRA   Canada Revenue Agency
IFRS   International Financial Reporting Standards
MD&A   Management discussion and analysis

SYNONYMS

Accounts payable | Trade payables
Depreciation | Amortization
Gross profit | Gross margin
Liabilities | Debt | Obligations
Net earnings | Net income | Net profit
Property, plant, and equipment | Capital assets
Share capital | Common shares
Shareholders | Investors
Shareholders' equity | Net assets

Statement of cash flows | Cash flow statement
Statement of changes in shareholders' equity | Statement
  of shareholders' equity | Statement of changes in
  equity | Statement of equity
Statement of income | Statement of operations |
  Statement of earnings | Statement of profit or loss |
  Statement of comprehensive income
Statement of financial position | Balance sheet
Unearned revenue | Deferred revenue | Deposits

ASSIGNMENT MATERIAL

Discussion Questions

DQ1-1 Describe the role that accounting plays in the management of a business.

DQ1-2 Describe the owner's legal liability and the taxation of income in the following forms of business: corporation, proprietorship and partnership.

DQ1-3 Explain the difference between a public corporation and a private corporation.

DQ1-4 Identify at least three major users of corporate financial statements, and briefly state how these users might use the information from the statements.

DQ1-5 Explain how investors expect to receive a return on the investment they make in a corporation.

DQ1-6 What is capital appreciation and how can an investor realize this type of return?

DQ1-7 Creditors are ultimately concerned with receiving two streams of cash in relation to the loans they make. Explain each of them.

DQ1-8 Describe and illustrate the three major types of activities in which all companies engage.

DQ1-9 Describe and illustrate the three major categories of items that appear in a typical statement of financial position.

DQ1-10 How do the activities that are considered to be operating activities differ from those considered to be investing activities?

DQ1-11 How do the activities that are considered to be operating activities differ from those considered to be financing activities?

DQ1-12 Would we normally expect a company to have an overall inflow or an overall outflow of cash from its operating activities? Explain why.

DQ1-13 Would we normally expect a company to have an overall inflow or an overall outflow of cash from its investing activities? Explain why.

DQ1-14 How is the statement of income related to the three major types of business activities?

DQ1-15 How does the statement of changes in equity relate to the statement of income? Which of these statements would need to be prepared first?

DQ1-16 Describe the purpose of the four main financial statements that are contained in annual reports.

DQ1-17 Explain the purpose behind the notes to the financial statements.

DQ1-18 What role does the management discussion and analysis section of an annual report play in informing users about a company?

Application Problems

AP1-1 (Characteristics of assets and liabilities)

Required:

Using the characteristics of assets and liabilities discussed in the chapter, explain whether the following items would be considered to be an asset or a liability. Be sure to apply the criteria in your response:

    a. A one-year insurance policy covering the company's delivery vehicles, paid in advance.

    b. Gift cards sold to customers.

AP1-2 (Identify financing, investing, and operating transactions)

Required:

For a company like **Canadian Tire Corporation**, provide two examples of transactions that you would classify as financing, investing, and operating activities.

AP1-3 (Identify financing, investing, and operating transactions)

Required:

For a company like **Hudson's Bay Company**, provide two examples of transactions that you would classify as financing, investing, and operating activities.

AP1-4 (Identify financing, investing, and operating transactions)

Required:

For a company like **Bank of Nova Scotia**, provide two examples of transactions that you would classify as financing, investing, and operating activities.

AP1-5 (Compare statement of income and statement of cash flows)

Required:

Compare and contrast the purpose of the statement of income and the purpose of the statement of cash flows. Outline how they are similar.

AP1-6 (Compare statement of income and statement of financial position accounts)

Required:
   a. On what financial statement would you expect to find sales revenue, and what does it represent?
   b. On what financial statement would you expect to find accounts receivable, and what does it represent?
   c. What is the connection between sales revenue and accounts receivable?

AP1-7 (Compare statement of income and statement of financial position accounts)

Required:
   a. On what financial statement would you expect to find wages payable, and what does it represent?
   b. On what financial statement would you expect to find wage expense, and what does it represent?
   c. What is the connection between wages payable and wage expense?

AP1-8 (Classify items on financial statements)

Use the following abbreviations to answer this question:

CA	Current assets
NCA	Non-current assets
CL	Current liabilities
NCL	Non-current liabilities
SC	Share capital
RE	Retained earnings
SI	Statement of income item
SCF	Statement of cash flows item
SCE	Statement of changes in equity item

Required:

Classify the following items according to where they would appear in the financial statements:
   a. Accounts payable
   b. Rent revenue
   c. Unearned revenue
   d. Property, plant, and equipment
   e. Short-term investment in the shares of another company
   f. Sales to customers
   g. Repayment of the principal of a loan owed to a financial institution
   h. Payment of interest on a loan owed to a financial institution
   i. Common shares
   j. Cash
   k. Loan payable (debt due in 10 years)

AP1-9 (Classify items on financial statements)

Use the same abbreviations as in AP1-8 to answer the following question.

Required:

Classify the following items according to where they would appear in the financial statements:
   a. Rent payable
   b. Amounts owed by customers of the company
   c. Administrative expense
   d. Proceeds received from taking out a long-term bank loan
   e. Office supplies
   f. Net earnings for the year
   g. Cash proceeds from the sale of old equipment
   h. Increase in the cash balance for the year
   i. Income taxes expense
   j. Cost to the company of inventory sold to customers this year
   k. Proceeds from issuing common shares during the year

AP1-10 (Classify items on financial statements)

Use the same abbreviations as in AP1-8 to answer the following question.

Required:

Classify the following items according to where they would appear in the financial statements:
   a. Intangible assets
   b. Interest revenue
   c. Cash collections from amounts owed by customers on account
   d. Cost of developing a new advertising campaign
   e. Earnings over the years that have not been paid to shareholders as dividends
   f. Revenue from the provision of services to customers
   g. Dividends paid
   h. Increase in a bank loan (additional borrowings)
   i. Supplies used this year
   j. An investment in the shares of another corporation (the intent is not to sell the investment in the near future)
   k. Amounts paid to repurchase shares from shareholders

AP1-11 (Classify items on statement of cash flows)

Use the following abbreviations to answer this question:

O	Operating activities item
I	Investing activities item
F	Financing activities item

Required:

Classify each of the following transactions according to whether they are operating, financing, or investing activities:
   a. Payment of employee wages
   b. Cash collected from customers for sales
   c. Payment of dividends
   d. Purchase of land for an office building
   e. Repayment of debt owed to a financial institution
   f. Purchase of shares of another company
   g. Cash received as rent payment from a tenant in a building owned by the company
   h. Issuance of shares

AP1-12 (Classify items on statement of cash flows)

Required:

Use the same abbreviations as in AP1-11 to classify each of the following transactions according to whether they are operating, financing, or investing activities:
   a. Proceeds from the sale of an investment in another company's shares
   b. Net income

c. Cash paid to suppliers of inventory
d. Acquisition of a long-term bank loan
e. Depreciation of the factory building
f. Purchase of a truck used for deliveries
g. Payment of dividends

AP1-13 (Identify items on statement of financial position and statement of income)

Required:

Indicate whether each of the following items will be reported on the statement of financial position (SFP), statement of income (SI), both the statement of financial position and statement of income (B), or neither statement (N)—for example, it might appear only on the statement of cash flows.

a. Cash
b. Land acquired four years ago
c. Prepaid rent
d. Interest revenue
e. Sales of goods and services
f. Dividends paid to shareholders
g. Rent expense
h. Sales anticipated next period
i. Payment made to reduce the principal amount of a bank loan
j. Common shares issued when the company was organized five years ago

AP1-14 (Identify items on statement of financial position and statement of income)

Required:

Indicate whether each of the following items will be reported on the statement of financial position (SFP), statement of income (SI), both the statement of financial position and statement of income (B), or neither statement (N)—for example, it might appear only on the statement of cash flows.

a. Notes receivable
b. Interest revenue from a short-term investment
c. Common shares
d. Accounts payable
e. Depreciation expense on a building
f. Interest expense
g. Cash from the issuance of shares
h. Wages payable
i. Interest expense on a bank loan
j. Retained earnings

AP1-15 (Relationship of statement of financial position and statement of income)

Required:

In question AP1-13 or AP1-14, did you identify any items that appeared on both the statement of financial position and statement of income? Would you expect to? Explain by describing the nature of each financial statement.

AP1-16 (Determine missing statement of financial position amounts)

Required:

Calculate the missing statement of financial position amounts in each of the following independent situations:

	A	B	C	D
Current assets	$?	$ 600,000	$180,000	$ 990,000
Non-current assets	780,000	?	390,000	?
Total assets	?	1,335,000	?	1,650,000
Current liabilities	375,000	345,000	135,000	390,000
Non-current liabilities	?	330,000	?	225,000
Shareholders' equity	638,000	?	330,000	?
Total liabilities and shareholders' equity	1,350,000	?	?	?

AP1-17 (Determine missing statement of financial position amounts)

Required:
Calculate the missing statement of financial position amounts in each of the following independent situations:

	A	B	C	D
Current assets	$ 650,000	$?	$150,000	$320,000
Non-current assets	?	380,000	?	760,000
Total assets	1,800,000	?	360,000	?
Current liabilities	750,000	170,000	50,000	410,000
Non-current liabilities	500,000	?	120,000	?
Shareholders' equity	?	425,000	?	400,000
Total liabilities and shareholders' equity	?	800,000	?	?

AP1-18 (Determine missing statement of changes in equity amounts of retained earnings)

The change in retained earnings from the beginning of the year to the end of the year is the result of net earnings minus dividends for the year. These changes are part of the information presented on the statement of changes in equity.

Required:
Calculate the missing amounts in the reconciliation of retained earnings in each of the following independent situations:

	A	B	C	D
Retained earnings, Dec. 31, 2015	$100,000	$420,000	$?	$ 930,000
Net earnings	40,000	?	550,000	290,000
Dividends declared and paid	10,000	50,000	225,000	?
Retained earnings, Dec. 31, 2016	?	530,000	1,800,000	1,080,000

AP1-19 (Prepare simple statement of income)

Jason Chan operates a takeout pizza business called A Slice of Life Ltd. During the month of November, the following things occurred:
1. He paid $7,692 for pizza ingredients, $1,200 for rent, $220 for the telephone system, and $1,090 for utilities.
2. He took in $23,870 from selling pizzas.
3. He used up $7,130 worth of ingredients to make the pizzas.
4. His employees earned and were paid wages totalling $5,120 for the month.

Required:
  a. Prepare a statement of income to determine how much A Slice of Life Ltd. earned in November.
  b. Are there any other costs that might have been incurred in November but are not listed?

AP1-20 (Prepare simple statement of income)

Lydia Cravette operates a florist shop called Scents Unlimited Ltd. During the month of May, the following things occurred:
1. She spent $160 on the telephone system, $370 on utilities, and $1,500 on rent.
2. She took in $24,730 from selling flowers and plants. All of the shop's sales were cash sales.
3. She spent $10,733 on flowers from a local grower, she paid $329 for gas and repairs to the delivery vehicle, and she paid her employees $7,000 for wages earned during the month.

Required:
  a. Prepare a statement of income to determine how much Scents Unlimited Ltd. earned in May.
  b. Are there any other costs that might have been incurred in May but are not listed?

AP1-21 (Prepare simple statement of income)

Michelle Fontaine runs an outdoor adventure company called Call of the Wild Ltd. Her busiest months are June through September, although, if the weather holds, she extends her excursions into October and November. For the month of July, she recorded the following items:
1. She paid $49,860 for employee wages and she spent $14,610 on advertising.
2. Customers paid her $171,430 for excursions that took place in July and $21,000 in deposits for trips scheduled in August and September.

3. She used supplies in July that cost $25,629.
4. She spent $1,532 on the utilities for the office and $3,460 on gas and repairs on the vehicles.

Required:
  a. Prepare a statement of income to determine how much Call of the Wild Ltd. earned in July.
  b. Are there any other costs that might have been incurred in July but were not listed?

AP1-22 (Prepare simple statement of financial position)

AP1-19 introduced Jason Chan and his pizza business, A Slice of Life Ltd. At the end of November, the following items were in his records:

Supply of ingredients	$ 670
Wages owed to employees	1,460
Loan owed to the bank	11,000
Cash held in a chequing account	3,490
Cost of ovens and refrigerators	14,300
Prepaid rent for December	1,200
Common shares	5,000
Retained earnings	2,200

Required:
  a. Identify each of the items in his records as an asset, liability, or shareholders' equity item.
  b. Prepare a statement of financial position for A Slice of Life Ltd. at the end of November.
  c. Jason Chan does not have accounts receivable in his records. Explain why it is unlikely that he will record accounts receivable. Under what business circumstances would it be necessary for him to record accounts receivable?

AP1-23 (Prepare simple statement of financial position)

AP1-20 introduced Lydia Cravette and her florist shop, Scents Unlimited Ltd. At the end of May, the following items were in her records:

Inventory	$ 1,100
Wages owed to employees	950
Loan owed to the bank	8,000
Cash held in a chequing account	8,361
Cost of refrigerator used to store the flowers	18,695
Prepaid rent for June	1,500
Common shares	18,000
Retained earnings	2,706

Required:
  a. Identify each of the items in her records as an asset, liability, or shareholders' equity item.
  b. Prepare a statement of financial position for Scents Unlimited Ltd. at the end of May.
  c. Lydia Cravette does not have accounts receivable in her records. Explain why it is unlikely that she will record accounts receivable. Under what business circumstances would it be necessary for her to record accounts receivable?

AP1-24 (Prepare statement of financial position)

AP1-21 introduced Michelle Fontaine and her outdoor adventure company, Call of the Wild Ltd. At the end of July, the following items were in her records:

Loan owed to the bank	$24,000
Supplies on hand to be used in August	13,420
Cash in bank accounts	33,670
Common shares	20,000
Cost of tents and rafts	34,100
Retained earnings	56,450
Amounts prepaid by customers for trips to be taken in August	19,140
Vehicles	38,400

Required:

    a. Identify each of the items in her records as an asset, liability, or shareholders' equity item.

    b. Prepare a statement of financial position for Call of the Wild Ltd. at the end of July.

    c. Does Michelle Fontaine have any inventory? Explain.

    d. Michelle Fontaine does not have accounts receivable in her records. Explain why it is unlikely that she will record accounts receivable. Under what business circumstances would it be necessary for her to record accounts receivable?

AP1-25 (Identify assets and liabilities)

Required:

For each of the following companies, list at least two types of assets and one type of liability that you would expect to find on its statement of financial position. Try to include at least one item for each company that is unique to its type of business.

    a. **Bombardier Inc.** This Quebec-based company manufactures transportation equipment and other industrial products.

    b. **Sobeys Inc.** This company operates grocery stores across Canada.

    c. **McCain Foods Limited.** This New Brunswick company prepares frozen vegetables.

    d. **Royal Bank of Canada.** This is a major commercial bank.

    e. **Suncor Energy Inc.** This is an energy company.

    f. **WestJet.** This is an airline company.

    g. **Danier Leather Inc.** This company designs and sells leather goods.

AP1-26 (Identify statement of income items)

Required:

For each of the companies listed in Problem AP1-25, list at least two line items that you would expect to find on its statement of income. Try to include at least one item for each company that is unique to its type of business.

AP1-27 (Identify statement of cash flows items)

Required:

For each of the companies listed in Problem AP1-25, list at least two line items that you would expect to find on its statement of cash flows. Try to include at least one item for each company that is unique to its type of business.

User Perspective Problems

UP1-1 (Information for decision-making)

Suppose that you started your own company that assembles and sells laptop computers. You do not manufacture any of the parts yourself. The computers are sold through orders received over the Internet and through mail orders.

Required:

Make a list of the information that would be relevant to running this business. Then discuss the information you would need to gather if you were going to approach a bank for a small business loan.

UP1-2 (Information for decision-making)

Suppose that you own and operate a company. You need to raise money to expand your operation, so you approach a bank for a loan. The loan officer has asked you for your company's financial statements.

Required:

    a. What items on your financial statements would be of the most interest to the loan officer?

    b. Develop four questions that you think the loan officer would be trying to answer by looking at your financial statements.

UP1-3 (Form of business)

Taylor Leblond just graduated from university and is planning to start a software development company to develop and market a mapping program he has developed. He is debating whether to operate the business as a proprietorship or incorporate.

Required:

    a. What advantages are there to operating as a proprietorship?

    b. What advantages are there to operating as a corporation?

    c. Which form of business organization would his customers likely prefer? Why?

d. Which form of business organization would his creditors likely prefer? Why?

e. Which form of business will be most advantageous to Taylor if he expects the business to grow rapidly? Why?

UP1-4 (Raising new capital)

Suppose that your best friend wants to start a new company that provides website development services to customers. Your friend has some savings to start the company but not enough to buy all the equipment that she thinks she needs. She has asked you for some advice about how to raise additional funds.

Required:
Give your friend at least two alternatives and provide the pros and cons for each alternative.

UP1-5 (Distribution of dividends to shareholders)

The board of directors of a public company is having its monthly meeting. One of the items on the agenda is the possible distribution of a cash dividend to shareholders. If the board decides to issue a cash dividend, the decision obliges the company to issue cash to shareholders based on the number of shares each shareholder owns.

Required:
Before making its decision, what information about the company should the board consider? Think of the items on the financial statements that you saw in this chapter.

Reading and Interpreting Published Financial Statements

RI1-1 (Financial statements of Dollarama)

Base your answers to the following questions on the financial statements for **Dollarama Inc.** in Exhibits 1-9A to D.

EXHIBIT 1-9A	DOLLARAMA INC.'S 2014 CONSOLIDATED STATEMENT OF FINANCIAL POSITION

Dollarama Inc.
Consolidated Statement of Financial Position as at
(Expressed in thousands of Canadian dollars)

	Note	February 2, 2014 $	February 3, 2013 $
Assets			
Current assets			
Cash and cash equivalents		71,470	52,566
Accounts receivable		5,963	5,798
Deposits and prepaid expenses		5,382	5,756
Merchandise inventories		364,680	338,385
Derivative financial instruments	15	11,455	3,710
		458,950	406,215
Non-current assets			
Property and equipment	7	250,612	197,494
Intangible assets	8	129,436	122,201
Goodwill	8	727,782	727,782
Total assets		1,566,780	1,453,692
Liabilities and shareholders' equity			
Current liabilities			
Accounts payable and accrued liabilities	9	128,857	101,286
Dividend payable		9,823	8,099
Income taxes payable		22,102	23,636
Derivative financial instruments	15	—	185
Current portion of finance lease obligations	11	1,022	604
Current portion of long-term debt	10	3,017	—
		164,821	133,810

continued

EXHIBIT 1-9A	DOLLARAMA INC.'S 2014 CONSOLIDATED STATEMENT OF FINANCIAL POSITION (continued)

	Note	February 2, 2014 $	February 3, 2013 $
Non-current liabilities			
Long-term debt	10	395,446	262,071
Finance lease obligations	11	1,484	—
Deferred rent and tenant inducements	12	51,592	45,327
Deferred income taxes	14	89,271	80,994
Total liabilities		702,614	522,202
Commitments	11		
Shareholders' equity			
Share capital	13	493,602	517,306
Contributed surplus		10,884	8,157
Retained earnings		346,478	403,266
Accumulated other comprehensive income	13	13,202	2,761
Total shareholders' equity		864,166	931,490
Total liabilities and shareholders' equity		1,566,780	1,453,692

EXHIBIT 1-9B	DOLLARAMA INC.'S 2014 CONSOLIDATED STATEMENT OF INCOME

Dollarama Inc.
Consolidated Statement of Net Earnings and Comprehensive Income for the years ended
(Expressed in thousands of Canadian dollars, except share and per share amounts)

	Note	52-weeks February 2, 2014 $	53-weeks February 3, 2013 $
Sales		2,064,676	1,858,818
Cost of sales		1,299,092	1,163,979
Gross profit		765,584	694,839
General, administrative and store operating expenses		363,182	339,662
Depreciation and amortization	18	47,898	39,284
Operating income		354,504	315,893
Net financing costs	18	11,673	10,839
Earnings before income taxes		342,831	305,054
Provision for income taxes	14	92,737	84,069
Net earnings for the year		250,094	220,985
Other comprehensive income			
Items to be reclassified subsequently to net earnings			
Unrealized gain on derivative financial instruments, net of reclassification adjustment		14,249	1,093
Income taxes relating to component of other comprehensive income		(3,808)	(308)
Total other comprehensive income, net of income taxes		10,441	785
Total comprehensive income for the year		260,535	221,770

EXHIBIT 1-9C   DOLLARAMA INC.'S 2014 CONSOLIDATED STATEMENT OF CASH FLOWS

Dollarama Inc.
Consolidated Statement of Cash Flows for the years ended
(Expressed in thousands of Canadian dollars)

	Note	52-weeks February 2, 2014 $	53-weeks February 3, 2013 $
Cash flows			
Operating activities			
Net earnings for the year		250,094	220,985
Adjustments for:			
Depreciation and amortization	18	47,898	39,284
Interest accrual long-term debt	10	3,017	(216)
Amortization of debt issue costs		592	1,133
Excess of receipts over amount recognized on derivative financial instruments	15	6,319	1,272
Recognition of deferred leasing costs		465	295
Recognition of deferred tenant allowances	12	(3,543)	(2,871)
Deferred lease inducements	12	3,750	5,328
Deferred tenant allowances	12	6,058	6,832
Share-based compensation	13	4,053	1,558
Deferred income taxes	14	4,469	6,921
Loss on disposal of assets		1,017	716
		324,189	281,237
Changes in non-cash working capital components	19	(15,811)	(24,198)
Net cash generated from operating activities		308,378	257,039
Investing activities			
Additions to property and equipment	7	(96,303)	(69,577)
Additions to intangible assets	8	(11,095)	(8,210)
Proceeds on disposal of property and equipment		552	256
Net cash used by investing activities		(106,846)	(77,531)
Financing activities			
Proceeds from senior unsecured notes	10	400,000	—
Disbursements on long-term debt		(264,420)	(10,361)
Proceeds from bank indebtedness		166,000	—
Repayment of bank indebtedness		(166,000)	—
Payment of debt issue costs		(2,797)	(837)
Repayment of finance leases		(985)	(695)
Dividends paid		(38,418)	(30,972)
Repurchase and cancellation of shares	13	(277,438)	(155,942)
Issuance of common shares		1,430	1,594
Net cash used by financing activities		(182,628)	(197,213)
Increase (decrease) in cash and cash equivalents		18,904	(17,705)
Cash and cash equivalents – Beginning of year		52,566	70,271
Cash and cash equivalents – End of year		71,470	52,566
Cash payment of interest		6,025	7,639
Cash payment of income taxes		89,801	75,090

EXHIBIT 1-9D — DOLLARAMA INC.'S 2014 CONSOLIDATED STATEMENTS OF CHANGES IN SHAREHOLDERS' EQUITY

Dollarama Inc.
Consolidated Statement of Changes in Shareholders' Equity for the years ended
(Expressed in thousands of Canadian dollars except share amounts)

	Note	Number of common shares	Share capital $	Contributed Surplus $	Retained earnings $	Accumulated other comprehensive income $	Total $
Balance – January 29, 2012		73,807,542	525,024	15,659	352,287	1,976	894,946
Net earnings for the year		—	—	—	220,985	—	220,985
Other comprehensive income Unrealized gain on derivative financial instruments, net of reclassification adjustment and income tax of $308	13	—	—	—	—	785	785
Repurchase and cancellation of shares	13	(2,583,264)	(18,372)	—	(137,570)	—	(155,942)
Dividends declared		—	—	—	(32,436)	—	(32,436)
Issuance of common shares	13	1,866,192	1,594	—	—	—	1,594
Share-based compensation	13	—	—	1,558	—	—	1,558
Reclassification related to exercise of stock options	13	—	9,060	(9,060)	—	—	—
Balance – February 3, 2013		73,090,470	517,306	8,157	403,266	2,761	931,490
Net earnings for the year		—	—	—	250,094	—	250,094
Other comprehensive income Unrealized gain on derivative financial instruments, net of reclassification adjustment and income tax of $3,808	13	—	—	—	—	10,441	10,441
Repurchase and cancellation of shares	13	(3,720,418)	(26,460)	—	(266,741)	—	(293,201)
Dividends declared		—	—	—	(40,141)	—	(40,141)
Issuance of common shares	13	108,817	1,430	—	—	—	1,430
Share-based compensation	13	—	—	4,053	—	—	4,053
Reclassification related to exercise of stock options	13	—	1,326	(1,326)	—	—	—
Balance – February 2, 2014		69,478,869	493,602	10,884	346,478	13,202	864,166

In the questions below, the year 2014 refers to Dollarama's fiscal year that ends February 2, 2014, and the year 2013 refers to the prior fiscal year ending February 3, 2013.

Required:

a. Determine the amount of dividends that Dollarama declared in 2014. On which financial statement(s) did you find this information?

b. Find the following amounts in the statements:
   i. Revenues from the sale of merchandise in 2014
   ii. Cost of sales and general, administrative, and store operating expenses in 2014
   iii. Net financing costs in 2014
   iv. Income tax expense in 2014
   v. Net earnings in 2013
   vi. Merchandise inventories at the end of 2013
   vii. Accounts payable and accrued liabilities at the beginning of the 2014 fiscal year
   viii. Retained earnings at the end of 2014
   ix. Long-term debt at the beginning of 2014 (include the current portion long-term debt)
   x. Cash flows generated from operating activities in 2014
   xi. Cash payments to purchase property, plant, and equipment in 2014
   xii. Cash proceeds from the issuance of common shares in 2014

xiii. Cash flows generated from (used for) financing activities in 2013

xiv. Cash payments to reduce long-term debt in 2014

c. List the two largest sources of cash and the two largest uses of cash in 2014. (Consider operations to be a single source or use of cash.)

d. Suggest two reasons why net earnings were $250,094 thousand in 2014, yet cash flows generated from operations were $308,378 thousand.

e. During 2014, total sales revenue was approximately $205,858 thousand higher than in 2013. However, net earnings in 2014 were only $29,109 thousand higher than in 2013. Examine the consolidated statement of net earnings and comprehensive income and explain where the additional revenue went.

RI1-2 (Financial statements of Le Château Inc.)

Base your answers to the following questions on the 2014 financial statements for **Le Château Inc.** in Exhibits 1-10A to C.

EXHIBIT 1-10A	LE CHÂTEAU INC.'S 2013 CONSOLIDATED BALANCE SHEETS

CONSOLIDATED BALANCE SHEETS
As at January 25, 2014 and January 26, 2013
[in thousands of Canadian dollars]

	2014 $	2013 $
ASSETS		
Current assets		
Cash	1,446	1,783
Accounts receivable [note 6]	1,476	1,906
Income taxes refundable	6,663	3,211
Derivative financial instruments	418	215
Inventories [notes 6 and 7]	124,878	123,218
Prepaid expenses	2,292	1,890
Total current assets	137,173	132,223
Property and equipment [notes 8 and 12]	69,870	83,315
Intangible assets [note 9]	3,815	4,672
	210,858	220,210
LIABILITIES AND SHAREHOLDERS' EQUITY		
Current liabilities		
Bank indebtedness [note 6]	30,767	13,034
Trade and other payables [note 10]	19,553	20,718
Deferred revenue	3,712	3,558
Current portion of provisions [note 11]	265	228
Current portion of long-term debt [note 12]	7,987	9,844
Total current liabilities	62,284	47,382
Long-term debt [note 12]	7,843	14,290
Provisions [note 11]	391	530
Deferred income taxes [note 14]	1,829	2,298
Deferred lease credits	13,412	15,912
Total liabilities	85,759	80,412
Shareholders' equity		
Share capital [note 13]	42,960	42,740
Contributed surplus	3,581	2,664
Retained earnings	78,253	94,239
Accumulated other comprehensive income	305	155
Total shareholders' equity	125,099	139,798
	210,858	220,210

EXHIBIT 1-10B   LE CHÂTEAU INC.'S 2013 CONSOLIDATED STATEMENTS OF LOSS

Years ended January 25, 2014 and January 26, 2013
[in thousands of Canadian dollars, except per share information]

	2014 $	2013 $
Sales [note 20]	274,840	274,827
Cost of sales and expenses		
Cost of sales [note 7]	101,770	92,565
Selling [note 8]	155,859	155,561
General and administrative [notes 8 and 9]	36,218	35,847
	293,847	283,973
Results from operating activities	(19,007)	(9,146)
Finance costs	2,714	3,063
Finance income	(13)	(23)
Loss before income taxes	(21,708)	(12,186)
Income tax recovery [note 14]	(5,722)	(3,469)
Net loss	(15,986)	(8,717)
Net loss per share [note 17]		
Basic	(0.59)	(0.34)
Diluted	(0.59)	(0.34)
Weighted average number of shares outstanding	27,288,766	25,658,585

EXHIBIT 1-10C   LE CHÂTEAU INC.'S 2013 CONSOLIDATED STATEMENTS OF CASH FLOWS

CONSOLIDATED STATEMENTS OF CASH FLOWS
Years ended January 25, 2014 and January 26, 2013
[in thousands of Canadian dollars]

	2014 $	2013 $
OPERATING ACTIVITIES		
Net loss	(15,986)	(8,717)
Adjustments to determine net cash from operating activities		
Depreciation and amortization [notes 8 and 9]	18,723	19,574
Write-off and net impairment of property and equipment and intangible assets [notes 8 and 9]	1,897	2,142
Loss on disposal of property and equipment [note 8]	—	108
Amortization of deferred lease credits	(2,539)	(1,285)
Deferred lease credits	39	1,088
Stock-based compensation	978	336
Provisions	(102)	338
Finance costs	2,714	3,063
Finance income	(13)	(23)
Interest paid	(2,436)	(2,863)
Interest received	13	28
Income tax recovery	(5,722)	(3,469)
	(2,434)	10,320

continued

EXHIBIT 1-10C	LE CHÂTEAU INC.'S 2013 CONSOLIDATED STATEMENTS OF CASH FLOWS (continued)		
		2014	2013
		$	$
Net change in non-cash working capital items related to operations *[note 21]*		(3,030)	(6,340)
		(5,464)	3,980
Income taxes refunded		2,108	2,056
Cash flows related to operating activities		(3,356)	6,036
FINANCING ACTIVITIES			
Increase in bank indebtedness		17,482	13,600
Repayment of long-term debt		(8,304)	(16,323)
Issue of share capital upon exercise of options		159	—
Cash flows related to financing activities		9,337	(2,723)
INVESTING ACTIVITIES			
Additions to property and equipment and intangible assets *[notes 8 and 9]*		(6,318)	(9,237)
Proceeds from disposal of property and equipment *[note 8]*		—	514
Cash flows related to investing activities		(6,318)	(8,723)
Decrease in cash		(337)	(5,410)
Cash, beginning of year		1,783	7,193
Cash, end of year		1,446	1,783

In the questions below, the year 2014 refers to Le Château's fiscal year ended January 25, 2014, and the year 2013 refers to the prior year ended January 26, 2013.

Required:

a. Le Château has issued consolidated financial statements. What does the word *consolidated* at the top of a financial statement tell you about the company's structure?

b. Le Château prepared a classified statement of financial position. Calculate the difference between current assets and current liabilities at the end of 2014, and at the end of 2013. This amount is referred to as *working capital*. Did the company's working capital improve in 2014? Explain.

c. Find the following amounts in Le Château's statements (note that the amounts are in thousands of Canadian dollars):

    i. Sales revenues in 2014
    ii. Cost of sales in 2014
    iii. Finance costs (cost of debt) in 2013
    iv. Income tax expense (recovery) in 2014
    v. Net income (loss) in 2013
    vi. Intangible assets at the end of 2014
    vii. Trade receivables (accounts receivable) at the beginning of 2014
    viii. Share capital at the end of 2014
    ix. Property, plant, and equipment at the end of 2014
    x. Cash flows from operating activities in 2014
    xi. Cash payments to acquire intangibles and property, plant, and equipment in 2013
    xii. Cash used for the payment of dividends in 2013
    xiii. Cash produced from or used for financing activities in 2014

d. Did Le Château finance the company's assets mainly from creditors (total liabilities) or from shareholders (shareholders' equity) in 2014? Support your answer with appropriate calculations.

e. List the two largest sources of cash and the two largest uses of cash in 2014. (Consider cash generated from operating activities to be a single source or use of cash.)

f. Suggest some reasons why there was a loss of approximately $15,986 thousand in 2014, yet cash generated from operating activities was only a negative (or outflow of) $3,356 thousand.

RI1-3 (Financial statements of Ten Peaks Coffee Company Inc.)

The major financial statements of **Ten Peaks Coffee Company Inc.** from its 2013 annual report are included in Exhibits 1-11A to C. Note that its fiscal year end is December 31, 2013.

EXHIBIT 1-11A	TEN PEAKS COFFEE COMPANY INC.'S 2013 CONSOLIDATED STATEMENTS OF FINANCIAL POSITION

TEN PEAKS COFFEE COMPANY INC.
CONSOLIDATED STATEMENTS OF FINANCIAL POSITION
(Tabular amounts in thousands of Canadian dollars, except per share and number of shares figures)

	December 31 2013	December 31 2012
Assets		
Current assets		
Inventories	$ 6,463	$ 9,494
Accounts receivable	4,972	3,962
Prepaid expenses and other receivables	236	169
Derivative assets	152	227
Cash	2,594	1,304
Total current assets	14,417	15,156
Non-current assets		
Plant and equipment	12,508	13,298
Intangible assets	2,465	2,724
Deferred tax assets	1,578	2,058
Derivative assets	—	37
Total non-current assets	16,551	18,117
Total assets	$ 30,968	$ 33,273
Liabilities and shareholders' equity		
Current liabilities		
Bank indebtedness	$ 4,786	$ 6,983
Accounts payable	916	1,559
Accrued liabilities	1,100	1,066
Dividend payable	417	417
Derivative liabilities	119	11
Current income tax liabilities	18	—
Current portion of other liabilities	219	—
Total current liabilities	7,575	10,036
Non-current liabilities		
Derivative liabilities	131	—
Other liabilities	28	69
Asset retirement obligation	725	705
Total non-current liabilities	884	774
Total liabilities	8,459	10,810
Shareholders' equity		
Share capital	24,631	24,631
Share-based compensation reserve	106	45
Deficit	(2,228)	(2,213)
Total equity	22,509	22,463
Total liabilities and shareholders' equity	$ 30,968	$ 33,273

EXHIBIT 1-11B TEN PEAKS COFFEE COMPANY INC.'S 2013 CONSOLIDATED STATEMENTS OF INCOME

TEN PEAKS COFFEE COMPANY INC.
CONSOLIDATED STATEMENTS OF INCOME AND COMPREHENSIVE INCOME
(Tabular amounts in thousands of Canadian dollars, except per share and number of shares figures)
for the years ended

	Note	December 31 2013	December 31 2012
Revenue		$ 53,873	$ 59,713
Cost of sales		(47,662)	(55,050)
Gross profit		6,211	4,663
Sales and marketing expenses		(1,415)	(1,292)
Occupancy expenses		(50)	(63)
Administration expenses		(3,034)	(2,847)
Finance income		92	117
Finance expenses		(149)	(258)
Realized gain on derivative financial instruments		1,614	1,678
Unrealized loss on derivative financial instruments		(1,045)	(197)
(Loss) gain on foreign exchange		(68)	223
Loss on disposal of plant and equipment		(4)	—
Income before tax		2,152	2,024
Income tax expense	11	(498)	(520)
Net income and comprehensive income for the year		$ 1,654	$ 1,504
Earnings per share			
Basic and Diluted (per share)	20	$ 0.25	$ 0.23

EXHIBIT 1-11C TEN PEAKS COFFEE COMPANY INC.'S 2013 CONSOLIDATED STATEMENTS OF CASH FLOWS

TEN PEAKS COFFEE COMPANY INC.
CONSOLIDATED STATEMENTS OF CASH FLOWS
(Tabular amounts in thousands of Canadian dollars, except per share and number of shares figures)
for the years ended

	December 31 2013	December 31 2012
Cash flows from operating activities		
Net income for the period	$ 1,654	$ 1,504
Items not affecting cash		
Depreciation and amortization	1,415	1,396
Unrealized loss on derivative financial instruments	1,045	197
Loss on disposal of plant and equipment	4	—
Share-based compensation	238	100
Foreign exchange gain on cash held	(102)	(149)
Foreign exchange loss on debt	315	—
Income taxes recognized in profit and loss	498	520
Finance income	(92)	(117)
Finance expenses	149	258
	5,124	3,709

continued

EXHIBIT 1-11C	TEN PEAKS COFFEE COMPANY INC.'S 2013 CONSOLIDATED STATEMENTS OF CASH FLOWS (continued)

	December 31 2013	December 31 2012
Movements in working capital:		
Accounts receivable	$ (1,010)	$ 236
Inventory	3,031	1,767
Prepaid expenses	(67)	(10)
Accounts payable and accrued liabilities	(608)	(396)
Derivative assets at fair value through profit or loss	112	(16)
Derivative liabilities at fair value through profit or loss	(806)	(315)
Change in non-cash working capital relating to operating activities	652	1,266
Cash generated from operations	5,776	4,975
Interest received	92	117
Interest paid	(129)	(240)
Net cash generated from operating activities	5,739	4,852
Cash flows from investing activities		
Additions to plant and equipment	(370)	(499)
Net cash used in investing activities	(370)	(499)
Cash flows from financing activities		
Dividends paid	(1,669)	(1,669)
Repayments of bank indebtedness	(2,512)	(2,029)
Net cash used in financing activities	(4,181)	(3,698)
Effects of foreign exchange rate changes on cash held	102	149
Net increase in cash	1,290	804
Cash, beginning of period	1,304	500
Cash, end of period	$ 2,594	$ 1,304

Required:
a. Find the following amounts in the statements:
   i. Total sales for fiscal year 2013
   ii. Total cost of sales for fiscal year 2013
   iii. Sales and marketing expenses for fiscal year 2012
   iv. Finance expenses for fiscal year 2013
   v. Income tax expense for fiscal year 2013
   vi. Net income for fiscal year 2013
   vii. Inventories at the end of fiscal year 2013
   viii. Accounts payable at the beginning of fiscal year 2013
   ix. Shareholders' equity at the end of fiscal year 2013
   x. Deficit at the beginning of fiscal year 2013
   xi. Cash provided from operating activities in fiscal year 2013
   xii. Cash payments to acquire plant and equipment in fiscal year 2013
   xiii. Cash used in the repayment of debt in fiscal year 2013
   xiv. Cash used to pay dividends in fiscal year 2013
b. Does Ten Peaks finance its business primarily with debt or with shareholders' equity? Support your answer with appropriate data.
c. Did Ten Peaks have a net inflow or a net outflow of cash from financing activities in 2013? What about from its investing activities?
d. Does Ten Peaks use a classified statement of financial position? Explain.

RI1-4 (Financial statements of Gildan Activewear Inc.)

Excerpts from the 2013 financial statements of **Gildan Activewear Inc.** are in Exhibits 1-12A to C.

EXHIBIT 1-12A	GILDAN ACTIVEWEAR INC.'S 2013 CONSOLIDATED STATEMENTS OF EARNINGS

GILDAN ACTIVEWEAR INC.
CONSOLIDATED STATEMENTS OF EARNINGS AND COMPREHENSIVE INCOME
Years ended September 29, 2013 and September 30, 2012
(in thousands of U.S. dollars, except per share data)

	2013	2012
Net sales	$2,184,303	$1,948,253
Cost of sales	1,550,266	1,552,128
Gross profit	634,037	396,125
Selling, general and administrative expenses (note 17(a))	282,563	226,035
Restructuring and acquisition-related costs (note 18)	8,788	14,962
Operating income	342,686	155,128
Financial expenses, net (note 15(c))	12,013	11,598
Equity earnings in investment in joint venture	(46)	(597)
Earnings before income taxes	330,719	144,127
Income tax expense (recovery) (note 19)	10,541	(4,337)
Net earnings	320,178	148,464
Other comprehensive income (loss), net of related income taxes (note 15(d)):		
Cash flow hedges	6,419	(6,399)
Actuarial gain on employee benefit obligations	436	323
	6,855	(6,076)
Comprehensive income	$ 327,033	$ 142,388

EXHIBIT 1-12B	GILDAN ACTIVEWEAR INC.'S 2013 CONSOLIDATED STATEMENTS OF FINANCIAL POSITION

GILDAN ACTIVEWEAR INC.
CONSOLIDATED STATEMENTS OF FINANCIAL POSITION
(in thousands of U.S. dollars)

	September 29, 2013	September 30, 2012
Current assets:		
Cash and cash equivalents (note 6)	$ 97,368	$ 70,410
Trade accounts receivable (note 7)	255,018	257,595
Income taxes receivable	700	353
Inventories (note 8)	595,794	553,068
Prepaid expenses and deposits	14,959	14,451
Assets held for sale (note 18)	5,839	8,029
Other current assets	11,034	8,694
Total current assets	980,712	912,600
Non-current assets:		
Property, plant and equipment (note 9)	655,869	552,437
Intangible assets (note 10)	247,537	259,981
Goodwill (note 10)	150,099	143,833
Investment in joint venture	—	12,126
Deferred income taxes (note 19)	1,443	4,471
Other non-current assets	7,991	10,989
Total non-current assets	1,062,939	983,837
Total assets	$2,043,651	$1,896,437
Current liabilities:		
Accounts payable and accrued liabilities	$ 289,414	$ 256,442
Total current liabilities	289,414	256,442

continued

EXHIBIT 1-12B	GILDAN ACTIVEWEAR INC.'S 2013 CONSOLIDATED STATEMENTS OF FINANCIAL POSITION (continued)

	September 29, 2013	September 30, 2012
Non-current liabilities:		
Long-term debt (note 11)	—	181,000
Employee benefit obligations (note 12)	18,486	19,612
Provisions (note 13)	16,325	13,042
Total non-current liabilities	34,811	213,654
Total liabilities	324,225	470,096
Commitments, guarantees and contingent liabilities (note 24)		
Equity:		
Share capital	107,867	101,113
Contributed surplus	28,869	25,579
Retained earnings	1,583,346	1,306,724
Accumulated other comprehensive income	(656)	(7,075)
Total equity attributable to shareholders of the Company	1,719,426	1,426,341
Total liabilities and equity	$2,043,651	$1,896,437

EXHIBIT 1-12C	GILDAN ACTIVEWEAR INC.'S 2013 CONSOLIDATED STATEMENTS OF CASH FLOWS

GILDAN ACTIVEWEAR INC.
CONSOLIDATED STATEMENTS OF CASH FLOWS
Years ended September 29, 2013 and September 30, 2012
(in thousands of U.S. dollars)

	2013	2012
Cash flows from (used in) operating activities:		
Net earnings	$ 320,178	$ 148,464
Adjustments to reconcile net earnings to cash flows from operating activities (note 22(a))	109,023	94,221
	429,201	242,685
Changes in non-cash working capital balances:		
Trade accounts receivable	2,986	(36,660)
Income taxes	(392)	2,440
Inventories	(38,092)	77,111
Prepaid expenses and deposits	(1,098)	(1,828)
Other current assets	(1,896)	(2,368)
Accounts payable and accrued liabilities	36,447	(61,798)
Cash flows from operating activities	427,156	219,582
Cash flows from (used in) investing activities:		
Purchase of property, plant and equipment	(162,643)	(71,316)
Purchase of intangible assets	(4,315)	(5,439)
Business acquisitions (note 5)	(8,027)	(87,373)
Proceeds on disposal of assets held for sale and property, plant and equipment	2,849	600
Dividend received from investment in joint venture	—	1,509
Cash flows used in investing activities	(172,136)	(162,019)
Cash flows from (used in) financing activities:		
Decrease in amounts drawn under revolving long-term bank credit facility	(181,000)	(28,000)
Dividends paid	(43,723)	(36,615)
Proceeds from the issuance of shares	6,014)	1,501
Share repurchases for future settlement of non-Treasury RSUs (note 14(e))	(9,621)	(5,990)
Cash flows used in financing activities	(228,330)	(69,104)
Effect of exchange rate changes on cash and cash equivalents denominated in foreign currencies	268	(74)
Net increase (decrease) in cash and cash equivalents during the year	26,958	(11,615)
Cash and cash equivalents, beginning of year	70,410	82,025
Cash and cash equivalents, end of year	$ 97,368	$ 70,410
Cash paid during the period (included in cash flows from operating activities):		
Interest	$ 4,278	$ 8,101
Income taxes	9,340	4,331

In the questions below, the year 2013 refers to Gildan's fiscal year ended September 29, 2013, and the year 2012 refers to the prior year ended September 30, 2012.

Required:
    a. Find the following amounts in the statements:
        i. Net sales in 2013
        ii. Total selling, general, and administrative expenses in 2013
        iii. Income tax expense (recovery) in 2012
        iv. Net income (earnings) in 2013
        v. Inventories at the beginning of 2013
        vi. Trade accounts receivable at the end of 2012
        vii. Retained earnings at the end of 2013
        viii. Long-term debt at the end of 2012
        ix. Cash flows from operating activities in 2013
        x. Cash payments to acquire property, plant, and equipment in 2013
        xi. Dividends paid in 2013
        xii. Cash produced or used for investing activities in 2013
    b. Did Gildan Activewear finance its business primarily from creditors (total liabilities) or from shareholders (shareholders' equity) in 2013? Support your answer with appropriate calculations.
    c. List the two largest sources of cash and the two largest uses of cash in 2013. (Consider operating activities to be a single source or use of cash.)
    d. Did Gildan Activewear prepare a classified statement of financial position? How can you tell?
    e. Calculate the difference between the current assets and current liabilities at the end of 2013, and at the end of 2012. This amount is referred to as *working capital*. Did the company's working capital improve in 2013? Explain.

RI1-5 (Use sources other than the textbook to find company information)

The SEDAR website (www.sedar.com) contains most securities-related information required by the Canadian securities regulatory authorities. It is probably your best source for financial statements of Canadian companies on the Internet. In addition, most companies that have a website have a section on investor information. In this section, they often include their most recent financial reports and news releases.

Required:
Choose a Canadian publicly traded company. Collect several articles about the company that cover the most recent two-year period. Try to find at least three longer articles. If the company has a website (most companies do), it will probably have useful news releases there. Finally, go to the SEDAR website and find the company's most recent financial statements filed there.
    Answer the following questions:
    a. What are the products (or product lines) and/or services that it sells? Be as specific as possible.
    b. Who are the company's customers?
    c. In what markets, domestic and global, does the company sell its products and/or services?
    d. Who are the company's major competitors?
    e. What are the major inputs that the company needs in order to produce its product? Who are the suppliers of these inputs?
    f. Are any of the items listed in the questions above changing substantially? Use a two-year time span to answer this question.

RI1-6 (Find information about a new company)

Required:
Go to a publicly traded company's website and find the company's most recent annual report. Answer the following questions:
    a. What are the major sections of the annual report?
    b. What are the three most important points in the letter to the shareholders?
    c. What are the titles of the major financial statements in the report?
    d. What are the company's total assets, total liabilities, and total shareholders' equity? What percentage of the company's total assets is financed through liabilities?
    e. Is the statement of financial position classified or unclassified? If it is classified, what are the major categories?
    f. What are the net sales in the most recent year? Are they up or down from the previous year? (Answer in both dollar and percentage amounts.)
    g. What is the net income and earnings per share in the most recent year? Are these amounts up or down from the previous year? (Answer in both dollar and percentage amounts.)
    h. What is the net cash provided (used) by operating, financing, and investing activities for the most recent year?
    i. What is the last day of the company's fiscal year?

Case

C1-1 Enticing Fashions Ltd.

Enticing Fashions Ltd. designs and manufactures upscale women's clothing. The company's early customers were small boutiques in Toronto, Montreal, and Vancouver. Customers liked the colours and fabrics used and enjoyed the unique styling of the garments. Demand for the company's clothing rose to the point where they are looking at opening a number of their own stores in various retail locations across Canada. The company has approached its bank seeking additional financing so that the company can proceed with its plan to develop retail locations and hire more people to assist with various aspects of the business. The bank wants to see the company's financial statements.

You are an accountant employed by a local accounting firm and Enticing Fashions Ltd. has been your client for several years. In previous years, you have prepared the company's financial statements and corporate tax returns. Enticing Fashion's CEO has approached you because he wants to have an understanding about how the bank may use the company's financial statements in determining whether or not to grant the loan.

Required:

Prepare a memo to Enticing Fashion's CEO addressing his question regarding how banks use financial statements to determine whether or not to grant loans to companies.

ENDNOTES

1. Ian McGugan, "Share Buybacks Put a Shine on Danier," *The Globe and Mail*, October 8, 2010; Danier Leather Inc. 2013 and 2014 annual reports; Danier corporate website, www.danier.com.
2. Canadian Coalition for Good Governance, *Model "Say on Pay" Policy for Issuers*, September 2010? www.ccgg.ca; Blakes Bulletin; *Say on Pay: Is the Canadian Future Voluntary?*; 03/27/2014; www.blakes.com; Theresa Tedesco, "Say-on-Pay Movement on the Rise in Canada, but Is It Changing Anything?", *The Financial Post*. March 12, 2014; Janet McFarland, "Shareholders Increasingly Draw Line in Sand on Executive Pay," *The Globe and Mail*, July 28, 2013.

(Amounts in millions)

Liabilities
Short-term borrowings:
Variable rate
Weighted-average interest rate
Long-term debt:
rate
average interest rate
rate

$6,805
0.1%

$4,542
3.9

$1,0

CHAPTER

2 | Analyzing Transactions and Their Effects on Financial Statements

CORE QUESTIONS
If you are able to answer the following questions, then you have achieved the related learning objectives.

LEARNING OBJECTIVES
After studying this chapter, you should be able to:

●●● INTRODUCTION
●●● ACCOUNTING STANDARDS

- What are accounting standards?
- Do all Canadian companies use the same accounting standards?
- Who sets the accounting standards used in Canada?

1 Identify the accounting standards used by Canadian companies.

●●● QUALITATIVE CHARACTERISTICS OF FINANCIAL INFORMATION

- How do the standard setters determine what constitutes useful financial information?

2 Identify and explain the qualitative characteristics of useful financial information and how the cost constraint affects these.

●●● TRANSACTION ANALYSIS AND THE ACCOUNTING EQUATION

- What is the difference between the cash basis of accounting and accrual basis of accounting?

3 Explain the difference between the cash basis of accounting and the accrual basis of accounting.

- How is the accounting equation used to analyze and record transactions?

4 Analyze basic transactions and record their effects on the accounting equation.

- What are the limitations of the accounting equation template approach?

5 Explain the limitations of using the accounting equation template approach to record transactions.

●●● FINANCIAL STATEMENTS

- How do we know if the company was profitable during the accounting period?
- How can we tell if the equity position of shareholders changed during the accounting period?
- How do we determine the company's financial position at the end of the accounting period?
- How can we tell if the company's cash position changed during the accounting period?

6 Summarize the effects of transactions on the accounting equation and prepare and interpret a simple set of financial statements.

CORE QUESTIONS (continued)

●●● **USING RATIOS TO ANALYZE FINANCIAL STATEMENTS**

- How do we determine the company's profit margin?
- How do we determine how effective the company has been at generating a return on shareholders' equity?
- How do we determine how effective the company has been at generating profits using its assets?

LEARNING OBJECTIVES (continued)

 Calculate and interpret three ratios used to assess the profitability of a company.

●●● Gearing Up for Financial Transparency

If you have ever shopped at Mountain Equipment Co-op (MEC), either on-line or in one of its 16 stores across Canada, then you're one of more than 3.5 million members of the outdoor gear co-operative. Co-operatives are founded on co-operation, not competition, and work to benefit members rather than to make profits.

MEC, founded in 1971 by six climbing enthusiasts in Vancouver who wanted to buy climbing gear, issues financial statements that follow Accounting Standards for Private Enterprises (ASPE). MEC is considered a private enterprise because it does not sell shares to the public on a stock market. But because it does sell shares to the public directly—via a $5 lifetime membership that gives members the right to elect directors to the board of directors—MEC commits to financial transparency, making its financial statements available on its website.

Even though MEC doesn't aim to maximize profit, "we operate in the same market environment as other businesses and must ensure we have a robust balance sheet and sufficient annual surplus to enable us to invest in the future," MEC pointed out in its 2012 annual report. "In key areas, our performance needs to be the same or better than our competitors."

Knowing that many members won't have the financial background to thoroughly understand the statements, MEC also produces an accountability report that includes easy-to-understand financial information presented in an uncommon manner.

MEC's simplified financial information consists of two statements: one called "What we were worth at year end" (which is the consolidated balance sheet in its

ASPE financial statements) and one called "What we sold, spent and saved" (which is the consolidated statement of earnings and surplus under ASPE).

On the "What we were worth at year end" statement, MEC refers to assets as "What we own." Those assets on the consolidated balance sheet known as "cash and cash equivalents," "inventory," "property and equipment", "accounts receivable," and "prepaids and deposits," are called "cash," "gear (product inventory)," "buildings, land and equipment to run our operations," and "other assets" in the simplified statements. The consolidated balance sheet section "Liabilities and members' equity" is known as "What we owe" in the simplified statements. Because co-operatives cannot make a profit, MEC has to return any surplus to members in what's called a "patronage return." In 2012, the board decided to retain this patronage return and invest it in capital projects. MEC's assets equalled its liabilities and members' equity in 2012, amounting to $222.4 million.

MEC's "What we sold, spent and saved" statement uses plain language to explain each item. For example, MEC takes the category of "Sales" from the ASPE earnings statement and calls it "We sold gear and provided services to our members" (which amounted to $302.0 million in 2012). The ASPE category of "Cost of sales" is called "We paid suppliers for gear-related costs."

There is a movement in Canada and other countries for publicly traded companies to make their financial statements easier to understand for potential investors and other users. But nothing can replace the rock-solid foundation that this accounting course will provide you in order to understand financial statements and make informed investing, business, and career decisions.[1]

INTRODUCTION

Mountain Equipment Co-op in our feature story uses a unique version of simplified financial statements to communicate its financial story to its members and other users. It presents the information in a way that mirrors the language of its members, reporting inventory as "gear" for example. Many organizations present simplified financial statements or summarized financial statement information in their annual reports, but all also present detailed financial statements that are prepared in accordance with financial accounting standards. This chapter will begin to show you how accounting information is obtained to create these financial statements, and how to start to interpret these statements.

ACCOUNTING STANDARDS

What are accounting standards?

When a company begins the task of measuring, collecting, recording, and reporting financial information for users, it needs some guidelines to follow so that the information is presented in a relatively standardized way. Accounting standards have been developed to provide companies with a broad set of rules to be followed when preparing their financial statements. These standards enhance the usefulness of financial information as they help to ensure that users can understand the information presented. They also enable users to evaluate the statements and compare them with those of other companies in order to make knowledgeable decisions.

■ **LEARNING OBJECTIVE 1**
Identify the accounting standards used by Canadian companies.

If there were no guidelines, each company would develop its own information reporting system, making financial statements difficult for users to understand and significantly impacting their ability to compare them.

Do all Canadian companies use the same accounting standards?

No. All Canadian public companies (those whose shares trade on a Canadian public stock exchange) are required to prepare their financial statements using **International Financial Reporting Standards (IFRS)**. Private companies generally follow **Accounting Standards for Private Enterprises (ASPE)**, but have the option of using IFRS if they wish. As the name implies, IFRS are international standards. They are being used in more than 100 countries around the world. Most public companies operate internationally and a significant number of them are also cross-listed, meaning that they are listed on stock exchanges both inside and outside of Canada. This common set of financial reporting standards was developed to minimize the differences in financial reporting across countries and to reduce the need for companies to generate different sets of financial information in each country in which they operate or raise funds. ASPE, on the other hand, represents a set of simplified standards that Canadian standard setters have established to reduce the financial reporting burden for private companies.

The objective of both IFRS and ASPE is to produce financial reporting that is useful to the financial statement users. Both IFRS and ASPE focus on the needs of shareholders (current and potential) and creditors in determining the financial information that would be useful. Specifically, the standards' aim is to provide financial information that assists these two user groups in making decisions about providing resources to the reporting company, such as whether they should buy or sell the reporting company's shares, and whether they should extend credit to the reporting company. The needs of these two user groups often correspond with the needs of other users, such as employees, unions, and governments, but they may not completely overlap.

Throughout this text, we will be concentrating on the reporting practices under IFRS because we will be focused on analyzing the financial statements of public companies. Because these companies are required to use IFRS, it is essential that we understand the requirements of these standards. In many cases, the financial reporting treatments under IFRS and ASPE are similar.

Who sets the accounting standards used in Canada?

The Canadian Accounting Standards Board (AcSB) is the body responsible for developing and establishing the accounting standards used by Canadian companies. The AcSB is responsible for the accounting standards for both public and private companies. It was the AcSB that made the decision that required Canadian public companies to adopt IFRS effective January 1, 2011. The responsibility for the ongoing development of IFRS belongs to the International Accounting Standards Board (IASB), but the AcSB retains ultimate responsibility for determining whether Canadian public companies continue to follow IFRS. In terms of ASPE, the AcSB is also the body responsible for the development and establishment of these standards for private companies.

QUALITATIVE CHARACTERISTICS OF FINANCIAL INFORMATION

■ LEARNING OBJECTIVE 2
Identify and explain the qualitative characteristics of useful financial information and how the cost constraint affects these.

How do the standard setters determine what constitutes useful financial information?

The objective of both IFRS and APSE is to produce financial information that is useful to financial statement users. In order to help users determine what is "useful," the IASB and the AcSB have each developed **conceptual frameworks** of financial reporting. A conceptual framework is an underlying set of objectives and concepts that guide accounting standard-setting bodies in justifying new standards and revising old ones.

The IASB's and AcSB's conceptual frameworks were developed with a number of objectives in mind:
- to assist the organizations as they develop new financial reporting standards;
- to assist accountants in determining how to account for items for which no specific accounting standards have been developed; and
- to assist users in their interpretation of the information contained in the financial statements.

The two conceptual frameworks have much in common, though they differ somewhat in both terminology and structure. Our discussion will focus on the IASB's conceptual framework because it serves as the basis for IFRS. According to this framework, useful financial information must be both **relevant** and **representationally faithful**. In other words, to be useful, the information must matter to users' decision-making and it must also represent events and transactions as they actually took place or are at present. Relevance and representational faithfulness are both considered to be **fundamental qualitative characteristics**. That means that they are essential if financial information is to be considered useful and, without them, the information is useless.

In addition to relevance and being representationally faithful, the IASB identified four other qualitative characteristics that increase the usefulness of financial information: **comparability**, **verifiability**, **timeliness**, and **understandability**. These are considered to be **enhancing qualitative characteristics**. In other words, on their own they cannot make useless information useful, but they can enhance the usefulness of useful information.

For Example

To help understand the conceptual framework of financial reporting, ask yourself this: Did you drive to the university or college today? If you did, how did you know how fast to drive?

We can draw a parallel between the conceptual framework of financial reporting and the framework used by governments to establish speed limits. Accounting standard setters developed the conceptual framework for financial reporting to help them determine the accounting treatment that should apply for specific types of transactions or the approach that should be taken in the absence of specific guidance.

This is similar to the process followed by governments when they establish speed limits for our roads and highways. Typically, their overriding concern is public safety, but rather than just post road signs that say "Drive Safe" and allow users to apply their own judgement about what this means, they post signs with maximum speeds that vary according to circumstance. The government uses characteristics to help it assess what it means to drive safely, factoring in things such as geography (steep hills, curvy roads, schools nearby), the type of road (divided, gravel), the volume of traffic, accident histories, and so on. Even when we are aware of what the maximum "safe" driving speed is, many of us will drive slower (or perhaps faster) than this based on our judgement about whether or not it is safe to do so. Our judgement is informed by the framework that has been established by government. For example, in British Columbia, the speed limit in school zones is 30 km/h and generally 50 km/h in other urban areas. However, many drivers will consider it unsafe to drive faster than 30 km/h if small children are present on and around the road even if they are outside of a school zone and the posted speed limit is higher.

This is the same way that the conceptual framework of accounting is used. It provides us with a framework for understanding why standard setters consider certain types of financial information to be useful and for determining what this means in the absence of specific standards.[2]

Let's explore the qualitative characteristics in a bit more depth.

To be relevant, financial information must matter to users. In assessing this, standard setters consider whether the information has **predictive value** or **confirmatory value**. Predictive information is information that users can use as the basis for developing expectations about the company's future. For example, based on the changes in sales this year, what might next year's sales be? Information has a confirmatory value if it provides feedback to users on their previous assessments of the company. For example, analysts may have projected that a company would achieve a certain revenue target and the actual revenues for that period allow them to assess this. Some financial information may reflect both predictive and confirmatory value.

The concept of **materiality** must also be considered in determining whether or not financial information is relevant. Information is considered to be material if it, or its absence, would impact the decisions of a financial statement user. Information that is critical to user decision-making is considered to be **material**, and therefore relevant, while information that would not affect the user's decisions is considered to be **immaterial**. The concept of materiality is company-specific. In other words, something may be material to the users of one company that is immaterial to the users of another company. Materiality is also assessed from a quantitative perspective (it can be measured in dollars) *and* a qualitative perspective (it can be assessed in context). Normally, the greater the dollar value of an item, the more material it is considered to be, although some small dollar items may also be qualitatively material, such as payments to senior management.

Standard setters have also determined that useful financial information must be representationally faithful. In other words, it must present the company's transactions in a manner that reflects what actually happened. To be representationally faithful information, it must be **complete, neutral,** and **free from error**.

Completeness is related to providing users with all of the information needed to understand what is being presented in the financial statements, including any necessary explanations. Neutral financial information is unbiased: it is neither optimistic nor overly conservative. Information is free from error if it has been determined based on the best information available, using the correct process and with an adequate explanation provided.

Enhancing qualitative characteristics can increase the usefulness of financial information. In situations where there are alternative methods of accounting for a transaction that are considered to be relevant and representationally faithful, the enhancing qualitative characteristics can be used to determine which treatment should be used. Comparability refers to the need for users to be able to compare the financial information of two companies, especially if they are in the same industry, or the need to be able to compare financial information for the same company across multiple periods. In either case, the goal is that the users are able to compare "apples to apples" rather than "apples to bananas." Verifiability is achieved if a third party, with sufficient understanding, would arrive at a similar result to that used by the company. Information must be timely if it is to be useful. Generally, the older the financial information is, the less useful it is considered to be. Finally, to be useful, financial information must be understandable to users. This is achieved when the information is presented in as clear and concise a manner as is possible given its complexity.

In addition to the qualitative characteristics, there is an overriding constraint that must be kept in mind. This is the **cost constraint**, which is applied to all financial information. It recognizes that capturing and reporting financial information is costly for companies. According to this constraint, the benefits of reporting financial information must exceed the costs of doing so. If they do not, then the financial information should not be captured and reported in the financial statements.

Exhibit 2-1 summarizes our discussion of the characteristics and constraints of the IFRS conceptual framework.

Exhibit 2-1 Characteristics and Constraints of Accounting Information According to the IFRS Conceptual Framework

Fundamental Qualitative Characteristics	**Enhancing Qualitative Characteristics**
Relevance	Comparability
Predictive value	Verifiability
Confirmatory value	Timeliness
Materiality	Understandability
Faithful representation	**Constraints**
Completeness	Cost constraint
Neutrality	
Freedom from error	

The conceptual framework's qualitative characteristics create a flow of useful financial information. We can picture this like a series of rivers, shown in Exhibit 2-2. Every major river has tributaries, such as smaller rivers, streams, and creeks, that flow into it to increase its volume. Think of useful financial information as a major river, established when its two main tributaries (relevance and faithful representation) flow together. At this confluence, a major river begins: useful financial information is created.

Each of these major tributaries has three minor tributaries, but they all contribute to the downstream flow; that is, they all add to usefulness. Without the two major tributatries, there would be no significant river, or no useful financial information.

There are also four minor tributaries that flow into the river below the confluence. While these add to the flow of the river (to usefulness), they would not, on their own, have created a major river.

Exhibit 2-2 How the Qualitative Characteristics Create a Flow of Useful Financial Information

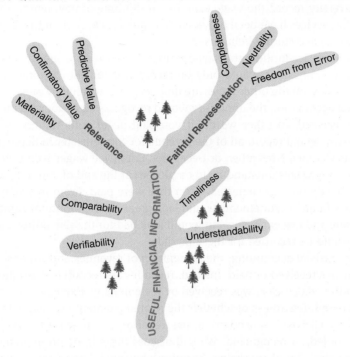

 The Conceptual Framework

Throughout the text, we will refer back to the conceptual framework and consider its impact on the accounting treatment used for different items. Text boxes such as this will be used to highlight these references for you.

By the end of the text, you will have seen that the framework's qualitative characteristics permeate financial statements.

TRANSACTION ANALYSIS AND THE ACCOUNTING EQUATION

What is the difference between the cash basis of accounting and accrual basis of accounting?

Before transactions can be analyzed and recorded, it is important for you to understand the difference between the **cash basis of accounting** and the **accrual basis of accounting**. Accounting standard setters have concluded that the financial information that results from accrual accounting is more useful to users than the information that results from the cash basis. Under the accrual basis of accounting, transactions are recorded in the period in which they occur, regardless of when the cash related to these transactions flowed into or out of the company. Under the cash basis of accounting, transactions are only recorded when the cash is actually received or paid by the company.

■ **LEARNING OBJECTIVE 3**
Explain the difference between the cash basis of accounting and the accrual basis of accounting.

To help you understand the distinction between the cash and accrual bases of accounting, let's look at a couple of simple examples. Most universities and colleges require students to pay their tuition before the semester starts or within the first few weeks of the semester. Is this tuition revenue to the university at the time of payment or is the revenue earned over the course of the semester? Alternatively, the university has faculty and staff who work to provide you with instruction and related services. These people are all employees of the university and are typically paid after they have provided their services. They are normally paid every two weeks for the services they provided in the preceding two-week period. When should the university record the wage expense: at the time of payment to the employees or over the period in which the services have been provided? The answers to both of these questions are different depending on the basis of accounting being used.

Under the cash basis of accounting, transactions are only recorded when cash flows into or out of the company. In other words, revenues would only be recorded when the customer or client pays for the goods or services. Expenses, on the other hand, are only recorded when they are paid for by the company. Under the cash basis of accounting, the university would recognize all of your tuition payment as revenue in the month it was received. In other words, if you paid all of your tuition for the fall semester in September, the university would record all of the revenue for the semester in September. There would be no revenue recorded in October, November, or December. Employee wages would only be recorded when they are paid. As such, any wages outstanding to employees at the end of a month or semester would not be recorded until the next month or semester, when they were paid. From this simple example, you can see that the university's financial statements would look great for the month of September, because there would be lots of revenue and few expenses, but would look bad for the remaining months of the semester because no revenue would be recorded for these periods.

Under the accrual basis of accounting, the recognition of revenues and expenses is *not* a function of when the related cash was received or paid. Instead, revenues are recorded when they have been **earned,** regardless of whether the related cash was received by the company. Expenses are recorded in the period in which they are **incurred**, regardless of whether the related payment was made by the company. Organizations using the accrual basis of accounting use **revenue recognition criteria** to determine when revenue should be recorded, or recognized. We will discuss these in depth in chapter 4. For now, focus on the fact that companies should recognize revenues when they have been earned (that is, when the company has provided the goods or services to its customers).

Under the accrual basis of accounting, the university would recognize a portion of your tuition payment as revenue in each month of the semester in which it is delivering your courses to you. In other words, if you paid all of your tuition for a 15-week fall semester in September, the university would record 4/15 of the revenue in September (because it would have provided 4 of the 15 weeks of instruction), 4/15 in October, and so on. Employee wages would be recorded in the period in which the faculty and staff provided their services, rather than when the wages were paid. As such, even if wages were outstanding to employees at the end of a month or semester, they would be recorded in the month the work was provided. From this simple example, you can see that the university's financial statements would be much more reflective of actual events because the revenues and related expenses would be shown in the periods in which they were earned or incurred.

Ethics in Accounting

If financial information is prepared on the cash basis of accounting, it is much easier for management to manipulate the revenues and expenses being reported in a given accounting period. **Why?**

Under the cash basis of accounting, revenues and expenses are only recognized when cash flows into or out of a company rather than when they are actually earned or incurred. Management would just have to get customers to make deposits before the end of an accounting period (which could then be recognized as revenue) or delay paying suppliers or employees until the next accounting period (which would delay the recording of these as expenses until that time).

The Conceptual Framework
THE ACCRUAL BASIS

Accounting standard setters have concluded that financial information prepared on the accrual basis provides users with information that is more relevant and representationally faithful than the information that results from the cash basis of accounting. In the IFRS conceptual framework, they state that information prepared under accrual accounting "provides a better basis for assessing the entity's past and future performance than information solely about cash receipts and payments during that period."[3]

How is the accounting equation used to analyze and record transactions?

■ **LEARNING OBJECTIVE 4**
Analyze basic transactions and record their effects on the accounting equation.

If financial information is to be useful, it must be understandable. Understanding financial information is significantly enhanced if the user has a basic knowledge of the accounting system: how to analyze transactions, how they are measured and recorded (or not recorded), and how financial statements are generated from the recorded data. Without that knowledge, users will have difficulty understanding the importance and relevance of accounting reports, and may not be able to use them effectively to support their decisions. Chapter 1 provided an overview of the types of information that are presented in financial statements. The next part of this chapter and a significant portion of the next chapter explain how accountants collect and classify the information used to build the financial statements.

Initially, we will use the accounting equation as the framework for our transaction analysis and recording. This approach is known as the **template approach** or **synoptic approach** and is the most basic of accounting systems. It is an approach that some very small businesses use as their accounting system, but most quickly outgrow it as they require financial information that is not readily available from the template. We will discuss more about the limitations of this approach in the next section, but for now let's focus on learning how it works. If you can develop a solid understanding of the mechanics of the template approach, making the next step to the **double-entry accounting system** used by most companies is much easier.

In Chapter 1, we learned about the accounting equation, which was as follows:

ACCOUNTING EQUATION
Assets = Liabilities + Shareholders' Equity

We then went on to learn about what an asset was and discussed some common assets. We did the same thing for liabilities and shareholders' equity. As part of our discussion of shareholders' equity, we discussed how retained earnings was determined. It is useful to review this quickly as it will affect the way in which we record certain transactions within the accounting equation. Retained earnings represents the company's profits (revenues less expenses) that have been reinvested in the business rather than being distributed to the shareholders as dividends. It is determined as follows:

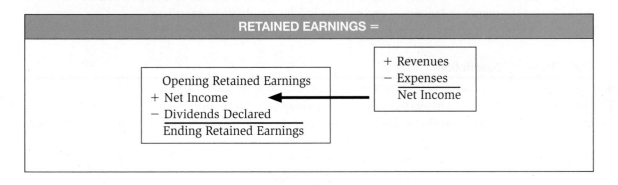

The transactions involving assets, liabilities, and shareholders' equity are recorded in a company's books in various **accounts**. Each account groups transactions of a similar nature and is given a title, such as Cash, Equipment, or Retained Earnings and we will show account titles in capital letters. We will learn more about accounts in the next chapter. In this chapter, we will focus on how these accounts fit within an expanded accounting equation. This expanded equation will provide the framework within which we will analyze and record transactions. Each of the various asset, liability, and shareholders' equity accounts will have its own column in the template. We will call these *accounts*, as in "Cash is an asset account." We also have a column in which to record the transaction date and another in which we will record the effect, if any, that the transaction has on retained earnings. The template will be set up as follows:

	ASSETS						=	LIABILITIES		+	S/H EQUITY		
Date	Cash	A/R	Inv.	Prepaid Ins.	Equip.	Land	A/P	Interest Payable	Bank Loan Payable	Common Shares	Retained Earnings	R/E/ DD

The template uses the following abbreviations:
- "A/R" for accounts receivable
- "Inv." for inventory
- "Prepaid ins." for prepaid insurance
- "Equip." for equipment
- "A/P" for accounts payable
- "S/H Equity" for shareholders' equity

The abbreviations in the final column are explained below.

When recording transactions within the template, we will follow a few basic rules:
1. Every transaction must affect *at least two* accounts.
2. The accounting equation must remain in balance with each transaction; that is, assets must constantly equal the sum of liabilities and shareholders' equity.
3. Nothing can be recorded in the Retained Earnings account without an explanation of the nature of that transaction being recorded in the final column, stating whether it is due to a revenue, an expense, or a dividend declared.

The third rule is to help you understand the links between the financial statements, because we will see that the information in the Retained Earnings account is a "bridge" between the financial statements. We will use the following abbreviations in the final column:
- "R" for revenues (which will increase retained earnings)
- "E" for expenses (which will decrease retained earnings)
- "DD" for dividends declared (which also decrease retained earnings)

The basic accounting equation will now be used to illustrate the fundamentals of the accounting system and the preparation of financial statements. We will use typical transactions for a retail sales company to demonstrate the analysis of transactions and how they affect the financial statements.

Assume that a business, called Sample Company Ltd. (SCL), is formed as a corporation on January 1, 2016. During the month of January, it engages in the following basic transactions:

TAKE5

#	Date	Description
1	Jan. 1	SCL issued 10,000 common shares in exchange for $250,000 cash.
2	Jan. 1	To raise additional financing, SCL borrowed $100,000 from its bank. The loan principal is due in three years, while the interest rate on the loan is 6% per year. The interest is payable every three months.
3	Jan. 1	The company rented a retail location, paying $1,100 in rent for the month of January.
4	Jan. 1	The company paid $65,000 to purchase equipment.

#	Date	Description
5	Jan. 1	SCL paid $1,800 cash for a one-year insurance policy covering the new equipment for the period January 1 to December 31.
6	Jan. 6	SCL purchased some land for $180,000 on which it plans to build a warehouse in the future.
7	Jan. 10	The company bought $23,000 of inventory from suppliers on account. (This means that SCL will pay for the goods at a later date.)
8	Jan. 12	SCL sold products to customers for $34,000, of which $21,000 was received in cash and the balance was on account. (SCL's customers will pay at a later date.) The products that were sold had cost SCL $17,000.
9	Jan. 20	SCL received $11,000 from its customers as payments on their accounts that originated from the sale on January 12.
10	Jan. 22	The company made payments of $13,500 to its suppliers, settling part of the account that originated from the purchase on January 10.
11	Jan. 25	SCL paid monthly utility costs of $1,900.
12	Jan. 26	SCL paid advertising costs for the month of $2,200.
13	Jan. 28	SCL paid $2,900 in wages to its employees for the month of January.
14	Jan. 31	Dividends in the amount of $400 were declared by SCL's board of directors and paid.
15	Jan. 31	SCL's accountant determined that the depreciation expense on the company's equipment was $850 per month.
16	Jan. 31	SCL's insurance expense was recorded for January.
17	Jan. 31	SCL recorded the interest expense on the bank loan for the month. Although the principal of the loan does not have to be repaid for three years, the company is incurring interest expense each month that the loan is outstanding.

Let's analyze each of these transactions in detail and show its effects on the basic accounting equation.

Transaction 1: Issuance of Shares for Cash

SCL issued 10,000 common shares in exchange for $250,000 cash.

ANALYSIS   SCL's shareholders invested $250,000 in the company, in exchange for ownership rights represented by share certificates that indicate ownership of 10,000 common shares. The issuance of shares is the first transaction for a new company because it is part of the process of establishing the company, which is known as **incorporation**. Companies also issue shares subsequent to incorporation as a means of raising capital. This is a common financing transaction.

KEY POINT
When analyzing transactions, it is often helpful to think first about the effect, if any, the transaction had on the Cash account.

All companies issue common shares. Many have other classes and types of shares, which we will discuss further in Chapter 11. For now, we will assume that the company has a single class of common shares and that each share entitles its owner to a single vote when electing the company's board of directors. The number of shares issued does *not* affect the accounting entry, but will matter when it comes to votes or the payment of dividends. We will also see information on the number of issued shares in the statement of changes in equity. The cash received by SCL is recorded as an asset (cash) and represents an increase in shareholders' equity (common shares).

The analysis of this transaction and its effects on the basic accounting equation are summarized below:

ANALYSIS OF TRANSACTION
Assets (specifically, Cash) **increased** by $250,000
Shareholders' Equity (specifically, Common Shares) **increased** by $250,000

Note: These entries keep the two sides of the basic accounting equation in balance; that is, Assets = Liabilities + Shareholders' Equity.

EARNINGS EFFECT   It is important to note that the issuance of shares is not considered revenue to a company. This is not what the company is in the business of doing. In other words, it is not related to the sale of goods or services to customers. As such, this transaction will have no effect on the company's earnings.

	ASSETS						=	LIABILITIES		+	S/H EQUITY		
Date	Cash	A/R	Inv.	Prepaid Ins.	Equip.	Land		A/P	Interest Payable	Bank Loan Payable	Common Shares	Retained Earnings	R/E/ DD
Jan. 1	250,000										250,000		

Transaction 2: Taking Out a Bank Loan

To raise additional financing, SCL borrowed $100,000 from its bank. The loan principal is due in three years, while the interest rate on the loan is 6% per year. The interest is payable every three months.

ANALYSIS   SCL borrowed $100,000 by taking out a bank loan. This is also a very common financing transaction. At the time the loan is taken out, we only account for the principal and not the interest. This is because the interest expense on the loan will be incurred with the passage of time. At the date the loan is taken out, no interest has been incurred, but with each day that passes, interest expense is being incurred. Interest costs are normally recorded at the end of each month. SCL does this at the end of January in transaction #17, which we will get to later. For now, we only need to record the initial receipt of the loan principal.

The analysis of this transaction and its effects on the basic accounting equation are summarized below:

ANALYSIS OF TRANSACTION
Assets (specifically, Cash) **increased** by $100,000
Liabilities (specifically, Bank Loan Payable) **increased** by $100,000

EARNINGS EFFECT   It is important to note that taking out a loan is not considered revenue to a company. Just like with issuing shares, taking out a loan is not what the company is in the business of doing; it is not related to the sale of goods or services to customers. As such, this transaction will have no effect on the company's earnings.

	ASSETS						=	LIABILITIES		+	S/H EQUITY		
Date	Cash	A/R	Inv.	Prepaid Ins.	Equip.	Land		A/P	Interest Payable	Bank Loan Payable	Common Shares	Retained Earnings	R/E/ DD
Jan. 1	100,000									100,000			

Transaction 3: Paying Rent for the Month

The company rented a retail location, paying $1,100 in rent for the month of January.

ANALYSIS   SCL paid rent of $1,100 to its landlord (the owner of the building where its retail operation is located). Rent is a common expense for many companies. In this case, the rent is only for the month of January, so all of it will be an expense for the month. Sometimes, companies prepay their rent or are required to pay a deposit to the landlord. In these cases, the advance payments are not an expense. We will see examples of these in subsequent chapters. The current month's rent is an expense to SCL. As we have discussed, expenses reduce retained earnings.

The analysis of this transaction and its effects on the basic accounting equation are summarized below:

ANALYSIS OF TRANSACTION
Assets (specifically, Cash) **decreased** by $1,100
Shareholders' Equity (specifically, Retained Earnings) **decreased** by $1,100

EARNINGS EFFECT   Note that we record an "E" in the final column of the template so that user can clearly see the reason that Retained Earnings decreased: the company incurred an expense. Each time we enter an amount into the Retained Earnings account, we will indicate the rationale for the change in the final column.

	ASSETS						=	LIABILITIES		+	S/H EQUITY		
Date	**Cash**	**A/R**	**Inv.**	**Prepaid Ins.**	**Equip.**	**Land**		**A/P**	**Interest Payable**	**Bank Loan Payable**	**Common Shares**	**Retained Earnings**	**R/E/ DD**
Jan. 1	(1,100)											(1,100)	E

Transaction 4: Purchasing Equipment

The company paid $65,000 to purchase equipment.

ANALYSIS   SCL paid $65,000 to purchase equipment. The company will use this equipment in its operations to generate revenues. Equipment is part of a group of assets known as property, plant, and equipment (PP&E). These assets are purchased to use in the business and not with the intent of being resold. If they were being purchased for resale, they would be part of the company's inventory. This does not mean that they can't be sold when the company has finished using them in the business. The purchase of PP&E is a common investing activity of all companies. Companies "invest" in these assets to help them generate revenues.

The analysis of this transaction and its effects on the basic accounting equation are summarized below:

ANALYSIS OF TRANSACTION
Assets (specifically, Cash) **decreased** by $65,000
Assets (specifically, Equipment) **increased** by $65,000

EARNINGS EFFECT   The equipment is an asset at the time of acquisition. In a subsequent transaction, we will learn that the cost of the equipment will be allocated and expensed in each period in which it generates revenues, but at this point there are no effects on the company's earnings.

Note that both of these entries are being made on the left side of the accounting equation. Since they offset each other (one increased assets, while the other decreased assets), the accounting equation remained in balance.

	ASSETS						=	LIABILITIES		+	S/H EQUITY		
Date	**Cash**	**A/R**	**Inv.**	**Prepaid Ins.**	**Equip.**	**Land**		**A/P**	**Interest Payable**	**Bank Loan Payable**	**Common Shares**	**Retained Earnings**	**R/E/ DD**
Jan. 1	(65,000)				65,000								

Transaction 5: Purchasing Insurance Coverage

SCL paid $1,800 cash for a one-year insurance policy covering the new equipment for the period January 1 to December 31.

ANALYSIS   SCL paid $1,800 for a one-year insurance policy covering the new equipment. The company benefits from this insurance coverage in each month of the policy. For example, if the equipment was stolen or damaged in a fire, the insurance company would replace or cover the costs of repairing it no matter when it happened. We will see in a subsequent transaction that, as each month of the policy passes, the company will expense 1/12 of the policy costs. These transactions are normally recorded at the end of the month, after the company has benefited from the coverage.

     The analysis of this transaction and its effects on the basic accounting equation are summarized below:

ANALYSIS OF TRANSACTION
Assets (specifically, Cash) **decreased** by $1,800
Assets (specifically, Prepaid Insurance) **increased** by $1,800

EARNINGS EFFECT   The insurance is an asset at the time of acquisition. In a subsequent transaction, we will learn that the insurance will be allocated and expensed in each period as the company benefits from the insurance coverage, but at this point there are no effects on the company's earnings.

	ASSETS						=	LIABILITIES			+	S/H EQUITY		
Date	Cash	A/R	Inv.	Prepaid Ins.	Equip.	Land		A/P	Interest Payable	Bank Loan Payable		Common Shares	Retained Earnings	R/E/ DD
Jan. 1	(1,800)			1,800										

Transaction 6: Purchasing Land

SCL purchased some land for $180,000 on which it plans to build a warehouse in the future.

ANALYSIS   SCL paid $180,000 to purchase a piece of land on which the company hopes to construct a warehouse in the future. The land is an asset for the company because it hopes to use it to generate revenues in the future and it could sell it if needed. The purchase of land is a common investing activity of all companies. Companies "invest" in PP&E to help them generate revenues.

     The analysis of this transaction and its effects on the basic accounting equation are summarized below:

ANALYSIS OF TRANSACTION
Assets (specifically, Cash) **decreased** by $180,000
Assets (specifically, Land) **increased** by $180,000

EARNINGS EFFECT   The land is an asset at the time of acquisition. Land is not expensed because the economic benefits it embodies are not being used up. Therefore, there are no effects on the company's earnings as a result of this transaction.

	ASSETS						=	LIABILITIES			+	S/H EQUITY		
Date	Cash	A/R	Inv.	Prepaid Ins.	Equip.	Land		A/P	Interest Payable	Bank Loan Payable		Common Shares	Retained Earnings	R/E/ DD
Jan. 6	(180,000)					180,000								

Transaction 7: Purchasing Inventory

The company bought $23,000 of inventory from suppliers on account. (SCL will pay for the goods at a later date.)

ANALYSIS   SCL purchased goods to resell to its customers. The goods cost $23,000, but SCL's supplier agreed that the company could pay for them at a later date. This is known as purchasing **on account** (also known as a **credit sale**) and results in a liability being created on SCL's records because it owes the supplier for those goods.

The analysis of this transaction and its effects on the basic accounting equation are summarized below:

ANALYSIS OF TRANSACTION
Assets (specifically, Inventory) **increased** by $23,000
Liabilities (specifically, Accounts Payable) **increased** by $23,000

EARNINGS EFFECT   These goods, which will be sold to customers in the future, are an asset at the time of acquisition. Until they are sold, there are no effects on the company's earnings.

	ASSETS						=	LIABILITIES		+	S/H EQUITY		
Date	Cash	A/R	Inv.	Prepaid Ins.	Equip.	Land		A/P	Interest Payable	Bank Loan Payable	Common Shares	Retained Earnings	R/E/ DD
Jan. 10			23,000					23,000					

Transaction 8: Selling Products

SCL sold products to customers for $34,000, of which $21,000 was received in cash and the balance was on account. (SCL's customers will pay it at a later date.) The products that were sold had cost SCL $17,000.

ANALYSIS   When a company sells products to a customer, it is useful to separate the transaction into two parts. Part one is to account for the sales revenue and the cash or accounts receivable that flow into the company as a result. Part two is to account for the inventory that has been provided to the client and has become an expense (known as **cost of goods sold**) to the company.

Part one of the sales transactions will always be known because companies always know the price at which goods are being sold. Part two of the sales transaction will not always be known at the time of sale because it requires that the company know how much the goods being sold cost it when they were acquired. Some inventory systems constantly provide this information, while under other systems this information will only be known when inventory has been counted, such as at the end of a month, quarter, or year. We will discuss inventory systems in Chapter 7. For now, it is important that you understand that the information needed to record the second part of a sales transaction may not always be available at the time of sale. If this information is not available, then the company would not record part two of the sales transaction until the information is available at the end of the month, quarter, or year.

With part one of the sales transaction, it is often easiest to think first about the cash effects, if any. Often sales are made on account or partially on account, meaning that the customer is not required to pay the entire purchase price at the time of sale. Regardless of whether or not the customer has paid the full amount, if the company has provided the customer with the goods, it has earned sales revenue. As we discussed earlier in the chapter, revenues increase net income, which ultimately increases Retained Earnings. Accordingly, we will record an increase in Retained Earnings and indicate the reason for that change by noting an "R" for revenue in the adjacent column.

KEY POINT

When analyzing transactions involving the sale of goods, think "two parts."
- Part 1 accounts for the sales revenue and cash/ accounts receivable.
- Part 2 accounts for the inventory that has become cost of goods sold.

In part two of the sales transaction, we need to recognize that goods have been provided to the customer and are no longer in the company's inventory. The goods, which have been recorded in inventory at the amount they cost the company when they were initially purchased, must be removed from inventory. The cost of these goods becomes an expense to the company, which is called cost of goods sold. As discussed earlier in the chapter, expenses decrease net income, which means they ultimately also decrease Retained Earnings. Accordingly, we will record a decrease in Retained Earnings and indicate the reason for that change by noting an "E" for expense in the adjacent column. The difference between the selling price of the goods in part one and the cost of goods sold in part two represents the company's gross profit on the sale. As discussed previously, this amount will be seen on the company's statement of income.

The analysis of this transaction and its effects on the basic accounting equation are summarized below:

ANALYSIS OF TRANSACTION
Part 1   **Assets** (specifically, Cash and Accounts Receivable) **increased** by $34,000
Shareholders' Equity (specifically, Retained Earnings) **increased** by $34,000
Part 2   **Assets** (specifically, Inventory) **decreased** by $17,000
Shareholders' Equity (specifically, Retained Earnings) **decreased** by $17,000

EARNINGS EFFECT

Part 1: The sale of goods to a customer results in revenue to the company and increases the company's earnings.

Part 2: The cost of goods sold to the customer results in an expense to the company, decreasing the company's earnings.

			ASSETS				=		LIABILITIES	+		S/H EQUITY	
Date	**Cash**	**A/R**	**Inv.**	**Prepaid Ins.**	**Equip.**	**Land**		**A/P**	**Interest Payable**	**Bank Loan Payable**	**Common Shares**	**Retained Earnings**	**R/E/ DD**
Jan. 12: 1	21,000	13,000										34,000	R
Jan. 12: 2			(17,000)									(17,000)	E

Transaction 9: Receiving Payments from Customers

SCL received $11,000 from its customers as payments on their accounts that originated from the sale on January 12.

ANALYSIS   In this transaction, SCL is receiving payments from customers who owe the company money as a result of a previous transaction. SCL had sold them goods and the customers agreed to pay for them at a later date. In this transaction, the customers are following through on this agreement.

The analysis of this transaction and its effects on the basic accounting equation are summarized below:

ANALYSIS OF TRANSACTION
Assets (specifically, Cash) **increased** by $11,000
Assets (specifically, Accounts Receivable) **decreased** by $11,000

EARNINGS EFFECT   The transaction involves the company collecting from its customers for sales made previously. This does not involve a new sale being made; therefore, there are no effects on the company's earnings as a result of this transaction.

	ASSETS						=	LIABILITIES		+		S/H EQUITY		
Date	Cash	A/R	Inv.	Prepaid Ins.	Equip.	Land		A/P	Interest Payable	Bank Loan Payable		Common Shares	Retained Earnings	R/E/ DD
Jan. 20	11,000	(11,000)												

Transaction 10: Making Payments to Suppliers

The company made payments of $13,500 to its suppliers, settling part of the account that originated from the purchase on January 10.

ANALYSIS   When SCL purchased goods from one of its suppliers, the supplier agreed to let SCL pay it at a later date. In this transaction, SCL is making part of that payment. The company is not receiving additional goods in this transaction; it is simply paying for goods it received previously. The company is settling or extinguishing part of its liability to its supplier.

The analysis of this transaction and its effects on the basic accounting equation are summarized below:

ANALYSIS OF TRANSACTION
Assets (specifically, Cash) **decreased** by $13,500
Liabilities (specifically, Accounts Payable) **decreased** by $13,500

EARNINGS EFFECT   No new goods are received in this transaction. SCL is settling part of its liability to its supplier (an *account payable*) by paying the supplier cash. There are no effects on the company's earnings as a result of this transaction.

	ASSETS						=	LIABILITIES		+		S/H EQUITY		
Date	Cash	A/R	Inv.	Prepaid Ins.	Equip.	Land		A/P	Interest Payable	Bank Loan Payable		Common Shares	Retained Earnings	R/E/ DD
Jan. 22	(13,500)							(13,500)						

Transaction 11: Paying Utility Costs

SCL paid monthly utility costs of $1,900.

ANALYSIS   In this transaction, SCL is paying for the costs of utilities (such as electricity, natural gas, and water) it used during the month. These costs are expenses to SCL. As noted previously, expenses reduce Retained Earnings and we will record an "E" in the final column to indicate that Retained Earnings has been reduced as a result of an expense.

The analysis of this transaction and its effects on the basic accounting equation are summarized below:

ANALYSIS OF TRANSACTION
Assets (specifically, Cash) **decreased** by $1,900
Shareholders' Equity (specifically, Retained Earnings) **decreased** by $1,900

EARNINGS EFFECT   The utility costs have been incurred by SCL. The company has used the electricity, natural gas, and so on provided by the utility companies. These costs are an expense incurred by SCL to generate revenue. Expenses decrease net income (reduce earnings).

	ASSETS						=	LIABILITIES		+	S/H EQUITY		
Date	Cash	A/R	Inv.	Prepaid Ins.	Equip.	Land		A/P	Interest Payable	Bank Loan Payable	Common Shares	Retained Earnings	R/E/ DD
Jan. 25	(1,900)											(1,900)	E

Transaction 12: Paying Advertising Costs

SCL paid advertising costs for the month of $2,200.

ANALYSIS   In this transaction, SCL is paying the costs of its monthly advertising. These costs are an expense to SCL. As noted previously, expenses reduce Retained Earnings and we will record an "E" in the final column to indicate that Retained Earnings has been reduced as a result of an expense.
The analysis of this transaction and its effects on the basic accounting equation are summarized below:

ANALYSIS OF TRANSACTION
Assets (specifically, Cash) **decreased** by $2,200
Shareholders' Equity (specifically, Retained Earnings) **decreased** by $2,200

EARNINGS EFFECT   These advertising costs have been incurred by SCL to generate revenue. The purpose of the advertising was to increase sales. Expenses decrease net income (reduce earnings).

	ASSETS						=	LIABILITIES		+	S/H EQUITY		
Date	Cash	A/R	Inv.	Prepaid Ins.	Equip.	Land		A/P	Interest Payable	Bank Loan Payable	Common Shares	Retained Earnings	R/E/ DD
Jan. 26	(2,200)											(2,200)	E

Transaction 13: Paying Wages

SCL paid $2,900 in wages to its employees for the month of January.

ANALYSIS   SCL hires employees to help the company generate revenue either directly or indirectly. In this transaction, the employees have worked (provided their services) and SCL is paying them. As noted previously, expenses reduce Retained Earnings and we will record an "E" in the final column to indicate that Retained Earnings has been reduced as a result of an expense.

The analysis of this transaction and its effects on the basic accounting equation are summarized below:

ANALYSIS OF TRANSACTION
Assets (specifically, Cash) **decreased** by $2,900
Shareholders' Equity (specifically, Retained Earnings) **decreased** by $2,900

EARNINGS EFFECT   The wage costs have been incurred by SCL because the employees have worked. Wage costs are an expense to SCL. Expenses decrease net income (reduce earnings).

	ASSETS						=	LIABILITIES		+	S/H EQUITY		
Date	Cash	A/R	Inv.	Prepaid Ins.	Equip.	Land		A/P	Interest Payable	Bank Loan Payable	Common Shares	Retained Earnings	R/E/ DD
Jan. 28	(2,900)											(2,900)	E

Transaction 14: Declaring and Paying Dividends

Dividends in the amount of $400 were declared by SCL's board of directors and paid.

ANALYSIS   Dividends are a distribution of a company's profits to its shareholders. They are declared by the company's board of directors. In this case, SCL's board declared and paid dividends of $400. As noted previously, the declaration of dividends reduces Retained Earnings because the dividends are actually a distribution of retained earnings. We will record a "DD" in the final column to indicate that Retained Earnings has been reduced as a result of dividends being declared. When dividends are declared by a company's board, they become a liability. In this case, the dividends that were declared by the board of directors were paid immediately, so we reduce Cash rather than recording a liability. We will see situations later in this text where dividends are declared, but paid at a later date.

The analysis of this transaction and its effects on the basic accounting equation are summarized below:

ANALYSIS OF TRANSACTION
Assets (specifically, Cash) **decreased** by $400
Shareholders' Equity (specifically, Retained Earnings) **decreased** by $400

EARNINGS EFFECT   Dividends are a distribution of a company's profits (or earnings) to its shareholders. They have no effect on a company's earnings because they are not an expense incurred to generate revenues. Therefore, there are no effects on the company's earnings as a result of this transaction.

	ASSETS						=	LIABILITIES		+	S/H EQUITY		
Date	Cash	A/R	Inv.	Prepaid Ins.	Equip.	Land		A/P	Interest Payable	Bank Loan Payable	Common Shares	Retained Earnings	R/E/ DD
Jan. 31	(400)											(400)	DD

Transaction 15: Recording Depreciation Expense on Equipment

SCL's accountant determined that the depreciation expense on the company's equipment was $850 per month.

KEY POINT
To depreciate property, plant, and equipment, we need to know four things:
1. the pattern in which the asset is expected to generate revenues
2. the asset's cost
3. the asset's estimated residual value
4. the asset's estimated useful life

ANALYSIS   In transaction 4, SCL purchased equipment costing $65,000. The company purchased this equipment to help it generate revenue for a number of years. Since the equipment was expected to generate these future economic benefits, it was recorded as an asset at the time of purchase. These future economic benefits will be realized over a fixed period of time (the **useful life** of the equipment). Therefore, the cost of the equipment (less any amount the company estimates it may be able to recover from the disposition of the asset when it has finished using it) must be allocated to those periods. The process of cost allocation is known as **depreciation**. The amount the company estimates it may be able to recover from the disposal of the asset when the company is finished using it is known as the **estimated residual value**. It is equal to the estimate of the amount that the company would receive today if it disposed of the asset in the age and condition it is expected to be in at the time of disposal. The amount of time a company estimates an asset will be used to generate revenue is its **estimated useful life**.

There are a number of different ways that the cost of property, plant, and equipment can be allocated or depreciated. These are based on the manner in which the property, plant, and equipment is expected to generate revenues for the company. We will discuss a number of these in depth in Chapter 8. For now, we will assume that the equipment is expected to generate revenues evenly over the course of its useful life. As such, we will allocate a consistent portion of the asset's cost to each of these periods. This approach is known as **straight-line depreciation**, because the amount of depreciation expense is constant each year and would form a straight line if shown graphically.

The straight-line method of depreciation determines the portion of an asset's cost that should be expensed each year as follows:

$$\text{Straight-Line Depreciation Expense} = \frac{\text{Original Cost} - \text{Estimated Residual Value}}{\text{Estimated Useful Life}}$$

This formula is used to determine the annual depreciation expense. This must be prorated for periods of less than 12 months. That is, the monthly depreciation expense can be determined by dividing the annual amount by 12. It is also important to note that the formula includes two estimated amounts. These amounts are estimated by the company's management. In the case of SCL, let's assume that management has estimated that the equipment will have a useful life of six years and a residual value of $3,800. Based on these estimates, the company's accountant would have determined the monthly depreciation expense as follows:

$$= \frac{65,000 - 3,800}{6 \text{ years}} = 10,200 \text{ per year}$$

The monthly depreciation expense would be:

$$= 10,200/12 = 850 \text{ per month}$$

We will record a reduction in the Equipment account to reflect the fact that a portion of the asset's cost has been expensed. We will also reduce Retained Earnings because expenses have this effect. We will record an "E" in the final column to indicate that Retained Earnings has been reduced as a result of an expense. It should be noted that recording depreciation as a reduction directly to the Equipment account is something that we will only be doing when we are using the template method. In the next chapter, we will learn that companies follow a slightly different approach in practice. The net effect of both approaches is the same, but having an awareness that the approach to recording the transaction will change in future chapters will help you when we get to that material.

The analysis of this transaction and its effects on the basic accounting equation are summarized below:

ANALYSIS OF TRANSACTION
Assets (specifically, Equipment) **decreased** by $850
Shareholders' Equity (specifically, Retained Earnings) **decreased** by $850

EARNINGS EFFECT   The depreciation expense will decrease net income (reduce earnings).

| | ASSETS | | | | | | = | | LIABILITIES | + | S/H EQUITY | | |
Date	Cash	A/R	Inv.	Prepaid Ins.	Equip.	Land		A/P	Interest Payable	Bank Loan Payable	Common Shares	Retained Earnings	R/E/ DD
Jan. 31					(850)							(850)	E

Transaction 16: Recording Insurance Expense

SCL's insurance expense was recorded for January.

ANALYSIS   In transaction 5, SCL paid $1,800 for a one-year insurance policy covering the company's new equipment. The term of the policy was from January 1 to December 31. On January 1, when the policy was taken out, SCL accounted for it as an asset, Prepaid Insurance. We also noted that SCL would expense 1/12 of the cost of the policy each month as the company benefits from that month's coverage. The monthly insurance cost is an expense, which reduces Retained Earnings. We will record an "E" in the final column to indicate that Retained Earnings has been reduced as a result of an expense. The asset, Prepaid Insurance, will also be reduced by the amount that has been expensed for the month.

The analysis of this transaction and its effects on the basic accounting equation are summarized below:

ANALYSIS OF TRANSACTION
Assets (specifically, Prepaid Insurance) **decreased** by $150
Shareholders' Equity (specifically, Retained Earnings) **decreased** by $150

EARNINGS EFFECT   The monthly insurance cost of $150 ($1,800 $\times$ 1/12) is an expense, which decreases net income.

| | ASSETS | | | | | | = | | LIABILITIES | + | S/H EQUITY | | |
Date	Cash	A/R	Inv.	Prepaid Ins.	Equip.	Land		A/P	Interest Payable	Bank Loan Payable	Common Shares	Retained Earnings	R/E/ DD
Jan. 31				(150)								(150)	E

Transaction 17: Recording Interest Expense

SCL recorded the interest expense on the bank loan for the month. Although the *principal* of the loan does not have to be repaid for three years, the company is incurring *interest* expense each month that the loan is outstanding.

ANALYSIS   In transaction #2, SCL borrowed $100,000 from the bank. The loan, which bears interest at 6% per year, is to be repaid in three years and the interest on the loan must be paid to the bank every three months. The loan interest is an expense to SCL and is a function of the amount of time that SCL has borrowed the money. As such, the company's interest expense grows each day that the borrowed funds are outstanding. SCL will quantify its monthly interest expense as follows:

Loan Principal Outstanding $\times$ Interest Rate $\times$ 1/12
= $100,000 $\times$ 6% $\times$ 1/12
= $500 per month

Any unpaid interest on the loan is a liability to SCL because it will involve an outflow of economic benefits. That is, it will be paid in cash every three months.

The analysis of this transaction and its effects on the basic accounting equation are summarized below:

ANALYSIS OF TRANSACTION
Liabilities (specifically, Interest Payable) **increased** by $500
Shareholders' Equity (specifically, Retained Earnings) **decreased** by $500

EARNINGS EFFECT   The monthly interest cost is an expense, which decreases net income.

	ASSETS						=	LIABILITIES		+		S/H EQUITY	
Date	**Cash**	**A/R**	**Inv.**	**Prepaid Ins.**	**Equip.**	**Land**	**A/P**	**Interest Payable**	**Bank Loan Payable**	**Common Shares**	**Retained Earnings**	**R/E/ DD**
Jan. 31								500			(500)	E

TAKE**5**

Exhibit 2-3 is a summary of all of the individual transactions we have analyzed. It provides enough information for the owners of a small business to prepare a set of financial statements for SCL, but it does have some limitations, which we'll see in the next section.

Exhibit 2-3 Accounting Equation Template

	ASSETS							LIABILITIES		+	S/H EQUITY		
Date	**Cash**	**A/R**	**Inv.**	**Prepaid Ins.**	**Equip.**	**Land**	**A/P**	**Interest Payable**	**Bank Loan Payable**	**Common Shares**	**Retained Earnings**	**R/E/ DD**
Jan. 1	250,000									250,000		
Jan. 1	100,000								100,000			
Jan. 1	(1,100)										(1,100)	E
Jan. 1	(65,000)				65,000							
Jan. 1	(1,800)			1,800								
Jan. 6	(180,000)					180,000						
Jan. 10			23,000				23,000					
Jan. 12: 1	21,000	13,000									34,000	R
Jan. 12: 2			(17,000)								(17,000)	E
Jan. 20	11,000	(11,000)										
Jan. 22	(13,500)						(13,500)					
Jan. 25	(1,900)										(1,900)	E
Jan. 26	(2,200)										(2,200)	E
Jan. 28	(2,900)										(2,900)	E
Jan. 31	(400)										(400)	DD
Jan. 31				(850)							(850)	E
Jan. 31			(150)								(150)	E
Jan. 31								500			(500)	E
	113,200	2,000	6,000	1,650	64,150	180,000	9,500	500	100,000	250,000	7,000	
	367,000						367,000					

What are the limitations of the accounting equation template approach?

■ **LEARNING OBJECTIVE 5**
Explain the limitations of using the accounting equation template approach to record transactions.

The template method is an acceptable method for recording financial information and is simple and easy to understand. However, it is normally only used by very small businesses due to a number of limitations. Before we discuss a few of these limitations, it is important to note that having a solid understanding of how transactions are analyzed and recorded within the template method is important. This understanding will make it much easier for you to move to the system of transaction analysis and recording that is used by the vast majority of companies and that we will learn about in the next chapter.

One of the main limitations of the template method is the number of columns that can be included within the template. Having many columns is not a problem when the user is working on a computer where there are no limitations to the width of the spreadsheet, but it is a real challenge when printing out reports. You will see from the templates used throughout the chapter that the number of accounts is limited and may not provide sufficient detail for management or users. For example, a company may have many different types of inventory or capital assets that it would like to account for separately, but it would be unable to do so within this method.

Another significant limitation of the template method is the lack of specific revenue, expense, and dividends declared accounts. Instead, these transactions are recorded directly to Retained Earnings. While this accounting treatment is ultimately correct, it makes it difficult and time-consuming for business owners to quantify revenue and expense information. If they were wondering about their sales for a given period, they would have to go through the retained earnings column and pull out all of the transactions with an "R" indicated in the adjacent column. If they were wondering about wage expense for a period, they would need to identify all of the transactions in the retained earnings column with an "E" in the adjacent column and then determine which of those were related to wages rather than other expenses. This may not be a significant limitation for companies with only a few transactions each period, but it certainly is for those with significant transaction volumes.

Now that we are aware of a few of the limitations of this method, let's have a look at the financial statements that can be developed for SCL using the information recorded in the template.

FINANCIAL STATEMENTS

How do we know if the company was profitable during the accounting period?

■ **LEARNING OBJECTIVE 6**
Summarize the effects of transactions on the accounting equation and prepare and interpret a simple set of financial statements.

In Chapter 1, we learned that the statement of income was the first financial statement that should be prepared for a company due to the fact that the net income figure provided by this statement is needed for all of the other financial statements. We also learned that the statement of income included information about the revenues and expenses of a company. Refer back to Chapter 1 if you need to review the contents of this statement.

The statement of income can be constructed from the information recorded in the retained earnings column in Exhibit 2-3. Since we labelled each of the amounts that affected retained earnings with an R to indicate revenues, an E to indicate expenses, or a DD to indicate dividends declared, this will be an easy task. Each of the revenue and expense items in the retained earnings column of Exhibit 2-3 has to be reported on the statement of income.

In its simplest form, the statement of income would be presented as shown in Exhibit 2-4. While it would normally be prepared on a comparative basis, because this is SCL's first month of operations, there are no figures from previous periods for comparison.

We can see from the statement of income that SCL was profitable during the month of January. The company's net income for the month was $7,400 because the revenues earned during the month exceeded the expenses incurred. We can also see that SCL's gross profit percentage was 50% (i.e. $17,000/$34,000), meaning that for every $1 in sales, the company had profits after cost of goods sold of $0.50. It is important to remember that the dividends declared do not appear on the statement of income. As they are a distribution of earnings, they will appear on the statement of changes in equity instead.

Exhibit 2-4 Statement of Income

SAMPLE COMPANY LIMITED	
Statement of Income	
For the month ended January 31, 2016	
Sales revenue	$34,000
Cost of goods sold	17,000
Gross profit	17,000
Wage expense	2,900
Utilities expense	1,900
Rent expense	1,100
Advertising expense	2,200
Insurance expense	150
Depreciation expense	850
Interest expense	500
Net income	$ 7,400

How can we tell if the equity position of shareholders changed during the accounting period?

In Chapter 1, we learned about two components of shareholders' equity: share capital and retained earnings. The statement of changes in equity reflects all of the information recorded in the common shares and retained earnings columns of the template. From the template, we know that the balance in SCL's Common Shares account was $250,000 at the end of the month, while the company's Retained Earnings balance was $7,000. In Exhibit 2-5, we can see how we arrive at these numbers using a statement of changes in equity.

Exhibit 2-5 Statement of Changes in Equity

SAMPLE COMPANY LIMITED				
Statement of Changes in Equity				
For the month ended January 31, 2016				
	Number of Common Shares	Share Capital— Common Shares	Retained Earnings	Total
Balance, Jan. 1	-	$ -	$ -	$ -
Net income	-	-	7,400	7,400
Declaration of dividends	-	-	(400)	(400)
Issuance of common shares	10,000	250,000	-	250,000
Balance, Jan. 31	10,000	$250,000	$7,000	$257,000

From the statement of changes in equity, we can see that SCL started the month with no equity (because it was a new company) and ended the month with total shareholders' equity of $257,000. We can see that of the company's earnings of $7,400, dividends totalling $400 were distributed to shareholders. Finally, we can also see that the company had 10,000 common shares outstanding at the end of the month. From this we can determine that a dividend of $0.04 ($400/10,000 common shares) was paid to the owner of each of SCL's common shares.

How do we determine the company's financial position at the end of the accounting period?

The last two rows of Exhibit 2-3 present the net results of SCL's January transactions. As both the template and the statement of financial position are based on the accounting equation, the totals for each of the accounts on the template are the figures that appear on the company's statement of financial position at the end of the month. We can also see from the final row of Exhibit 2-3 that the accounting equation was in balance at the end of the month. In other words, SCL's total assets ($367,000) equalled the sum of the company's liabilities and shareholders' equity ($367,000); therefore, the statement of financial position was balanced!

We can use the totals from each account determined using the template to prepare the company's statement of financial position, as shown in Exhibit 2-6. We will group certain accounts and build in subtotals as a means of enhancing the usefulness of the information presented on the statement. The groupings will be based on the concept of liquidity that we learned about in Chapter 1. The company's current assets will be grouped separately from the non-current assets and the current liabilities will be grouped separately from the non-current liabilities. This enables users to determine the company's working capital and assess its ability to meet those obligations coming due within the next 12 months. This presentation is known as a **classified statement of financial position**.

Exhibit 2-6 Statement of Financial Position

TAKE**5**

SAMPLE COMPANY LIMITED
Statement of Financial Position
As at January 31, 2016

ASSETS		
Current assets		
Cash	$113,200	
Accounts receivable	2,000	
Inventory	6,000	
Prepaid insurance	1,650	
		$122,850
Non-current assets		
Equipment		64,150
Land		180,000
		244,150
Total assets		$367,000
LIABILITIES		
Current liabilities		
Accounts payable	$ 9,500	
Interest payable	500	
		$ 10,000
Non-current liabilities		
Bank loan payable		100,000
Total liabilities		110,000
SHAREHOLDERS' EQUITY		
Common shares		250,000
Retained earnings		7,000
Total shareholders' equity		257,000
Total liabilities and shareholders' equity		$367,000

From SCL's statement of financial position, we can see that the company had working capital of $112,850 (current assets of $122,850 – current liabilities of $10,000) and has a strong liquidity position. The company will have no difficulty meeting its current liabilities because it has more than enough current assets. We can also see that 70% of the company's assets have been financed by shareholders' equity ($257,000/$367,000), while 30% have been financed by creditors ($110,000/$367,000).

We can also see that SCL's equipment is presented on the statement of financial position at $64,150. We know this equipment cost SCL $65,000 and that the company recorded $850 in depreciation expense related to it for the month. This left the carrying amount of $64,150 that we see on the statement of financial position. This **carrying amount** is also known as the **net book value** of the equipment. It represents the portion of the equipment's cost that has yet to be expensed.

How can we tell if the company's cash position changed during the accounting period?

In Chapter 1, we learned that there are three categories of business activities: operating, financing, and investing. Operating activities include all inflows of cash related to the sale of goods and services to customers and the outflows related to the payment of expenses. Investing activities generally involve the purchase and sale of long-term assets such as property, plant, and equipment, and investments in other companies. Finally, financing activities are transactions that either resulted from new funds being received from investors or creditors or from the return of funds to these two groups.

In order to understand how the company's cash position changed during the month, let's review how each of the transactions recorded during the month affected the Cash account, as shown in Exhibit 2-7.

Exhibit 2-7 Analysis of SCL's Cash Account

Date	Cash	Description	Operating Activities	Investing Activities	Financing Activities
Jan. 1	250,000	Issued common shares			250,000
Jan. 1	100,000	Took out bank loan			100,000
Jan. 1	(1,100)	Paid rent	(1,100)		
Jan. 1	(65,000)	Purchased equipment		(65,000)	
Jan. 1	(1,800)	Purchased insurance policy	(1,800)		
Jan. 6	(180,000)	Purchased land		(180,000)	
Jan. 10		No cash effect			
Jan. 12: 1	21,000	Made sales to customers	21,000		
Jan. 12: 2		No cash effect			
Jan. 20	11,000	Collected from customers	11,000		
Jan. 22	(13,500)	Paid suppliers	(13,500)		
Jan. 25	(1,900)	Paid utility costs	(1,900)		
Jan. 26	(2,200)	Paid advertising costs	(2,200)		
Jan. 28	(2,900)	Paid wages	(2,900)		
Jan. 31	(400)	Paid dividends			(400)
Jan. 31		No cash effect			
Jan. 31		No cash effect			
Jan. 31		No cash effect			
	113,200		8,600	(245,000)	349,600

While any of the three categories of business activities could have a net cash inflow or outflow depending upon the company's transactions, we would normally expect the following pattern:

- Operating activities are normally expected to result in a net inflow of cash (and therefore have a *positive* effect on cash) because companies would be expected to collect more cash from customers than they spend to generate these sales. This may not be the case for new businesses.

- Investing activities are normally expected to result in a net outflow of cash (and therefore have a *negative* effect on cash) because companies would be expected to spend more purchasing new property, plant, and equipment than they would receive from selling the property, plant, and equipment that they have finished using.

- Financing activities are normally expected to result in a net inflow of cash (and therefore have a *positive* effect on cash) because companies are generally borrowing and issuing shares to finance their growth. Mature companies may not fit this pattern because they are often able to finance new assets through operating activities, while returning some profits to shareholders as dividends or repaying debt.

We will discuss cash flow patterns further in Chapter 5. For now, we can see that SCL fits this normal + / − / + (Operating / Investing / Financing) cash flow pattern. The company's statement of cash flows would be as shown in Exhibit 2-8.

Exhibit 2-8 Statement of Cash Flows

TAKE5

	SAMPLE COMPANY LIMITED Statement of Cash Flows For the month ended January 31, 2016	
Cash flows from operating activities		
Cash received from customers	$ 32,000	
Cash paid for rent	(1,100)	
Cash paid for insurance	(1,800)	
Cash paid for inventory	(13,500)	
Cash paid for utilities	(1,900)	
Cash paid for advertising	(2,200)	
Cash paid for wages	(2,900)	
Total cash flows from operating activities	8,600	A
Cash flows from investing activities		
Cash paid to purchase equipment	(65,000)	
Cash paid to purchase land	(180,000)	
Total cash flows from investing activities	(245,000)	B
Cash flows from financing activities		
Cash received from issuance of shares	250,000	
Cash received from bank loan	100,000	
Cash paid for dividends	(400)	
Total cash flows from financing activities	349,600	C
Net change in cash during the period	113,200	= A + B + C
Cash balance on January 1, 2016	0	
Cash balance on January 31, 2016	$ 113,200	

USING RATIOS TO ANALYZE FINANCIAL STATEMENTS

■ LEARNING OBJECTIVE 7
Calculate and interpret three ratios used to assess the profitability of a company.

Ratios allow users to compare companies of different sizes, or to compare the same company's situation at various times. Ratio analysis can be used to assess things such as profitability, the effectiveness of management, and the company's ability to meet debt obligations. In Chapter 1, we discussed how the ratio of a company's total liabilities to its total liabilities plus shareholders' equity could be used to indicate how much a company relies on debt financing. As we introduce new topics, we will present and discuss additional ratios that can help users understand and evaluate a set of financial statements. In addition to this, Chapter 12 presents a complete discussion of these ratios.

We will now use SCL's financial statements to examine *profitability ratios*. Profitability ratios are usually constructed by comparing some measure of the company's profit (net income or earnings) with the amount invested, or by comparing the profit with the company's revenues. We will calculate three such measures.

How do we determine the company's profit margin?

The **profit margin ratio** is calculated by dividing the company's profit (or net income) by the revenues that produced the profit. For SCL, this ratio is calculated by dividing its net income of $7,400 by its sales revenue of $34,000, giving a result of 0.217. This means that SCL's profit was 21.7% of sales revenue. In other words, for every $1 in sales, SCL has profits after all expenses of $0.217.

$$\text{Profit Margin} = \text{Net Income/Sales Revenue}$$
$$= 7,400/34,000$$
$$= 0.217 \text{ or } 21.7\%$$

A higher profit margin is considered to be better than a lower one. These profits can be retained and reinvested in the company, distributed to shareholders as dividends, or a combination of the two.

For Example

The profit margins for **Danier Leather Inc.** in 2014 and 2013 were as follows (amounts in thousands of Canadian dollars):

	2014	**2013**
Profit Margin =	(7,663)/141,930	= 1,411/154,999
	= (0.054) or (5.4%)	= 0.009 or 0.9%

From this analysis, we can see that Danier went from being slightly profitable in 2013 to being unprofitable in 2014 and that the company's profit margin fell by 6.3% in 2014.

How do we determine how effective the company has been at generating a return on shareholders' equity?

The **return on equity** ratio compares the profit (or net income) earned relative to the amount invested by the shareholders (represented by the total shareholders' equity). Again, we would normally calculate the *average* shareholders' equity. However, an average amount would not be very meaningful for the month of January, because it was the company's first period of operations and the beginning balances were zero. Therefore, we will simply use the amount for total shareholders' equity at the end of January.

For SCL, this ratio is calculated by dividing its net income of $7,400 by shareholders' equity of $257,000, giving a result of 0.0288, or 2.88%. This measure shows that in the month of January, SCL's shareholders earned a 2.88% return on their investment in the company. It also means that during its first month of operations, the company earned profit at the rate of $0.0288 for each $1.00 that was invested by the owners.

Return on Equity = Net Income / Average Total Shareholders' Equity
= 7,400/257,000*
= 0.0288 or 2.88%

*In this case, SCL's shareholders' equity was not averaged because there was no opening balance.

Again, a higher return on equity is considered to be better than a lower one. Shareholders can compare this return with other investment alternatives to help them assess whether they should invest, stay invested, or move their resources to other alternatives.

For Example

Danier Leather Inc.'s return on shareholders' equity ratios for 2014 and 2013 were as follows:

	2014	2013
Return on Shareholders' Equity =	(7,663)/((55,909 + 48,407)/2)	1,411/((65,491 + 55,909)/2)
	= (0.1469) or (14.69%)	= 0.0232 or 2.32%

From this analysis, we can see that the return that Danier shareholders realized on their equity investment decreased significantly in 2014. In 2013 it was 2.32%, but the return decreased to a negative 14.69% in 2014.

How do we determine how effective the company has been at generating profits using its assets?

The **return on assets** is another measure of profitability. It is calculated by dividing the company's profit (or net income) by its average total assets.

Like all the amounts on the statement of financial position, the amount for total assets is determined at a particular point in time. For SCL, the relevant points in time are January 1 and January 31, 2016 (that is, the beginning and end of the current accounting period). To get a measure of the total assets during the period *between* these two dates, we would normally calculate the *average*. However, since SCL had no beginning balances for January, the average amount would not be very meaningful in this situation. Therefore, we will simply use the amount for total assets at the end of the period.

In January 2016, SCL's return on assets was its net income of $7,400 divided by its total assets of $367,000, giving a result of 0.020 or 2.0%. Remember that a company acquires assets to use them to generate profits. SCL's return on assets of 2.0% means that during its first month of operations, it earned profit at the rate of $0.02 for each $1 that was invested in its assets.

Return on Assets = Net Income/Average Total Assets
= 7,400/367,000*
= 0.020 or 2.0%

*In this case, SCL's total assets were not averaged because there was no opening balance.

Again, a higher return on assets is considered to be better than a lower one. It shows that the company is using its assets effectively to generate profits.

> ### For Example
>
> Danier Leather Inc.'s return on asset ratios for 2014 and 2013 were as follows:
>
> | 2014 | 2013 |
> | --- | --- |
>
> Return on Assets $= (7,663)/((69,049 + 60,629)/2) = 1,411/((78,612 + 69,049)/2)$
>
> $\qquad\qquad\qquad = (0.118)$ or (11.8%) $\qquad\quad = 0.019$ or 1.9%
>
> From this analysis, we can see that Danier did a better job of using its assets to generate profits in 2013. In 2014, the company had a negative return on assets ratio of 11.8%, indicating that it was unable to generate a profit from use of its assets.

Now that you know how users can analyze financial statements, in the next chapter, we'll look in more detail at transactions and how they are recorded and used to create financial statements.

SUMMARY

1. **Identify the accounting standards used by Canadian companies.**

   - Canadian public companies (those whose shares trade on a public stock exchange) are required to prepare their financial statements using International Financial Reporting Standards (IFRS).

   - Private companies in Canada generally follow Accounting Standards for Private Enterprises (ASPE), but have the option of following IFRS.

2. **Identify and explain the qualitative characteristics of useful financial information and how the cost constraint affects these.**

   - Standard setters have developed conceptual frameworks (one for IFRS and another for ASPE) to assist them in determining what "useful information" is.

   - Useful information has two fundamental qualitative characteristics. It must be relevant (it must matter to users' decision-making) and it must be representationally faithful (it must represent transactions and balances as they took place or are at present).

   - To be relevant, the information must be material and have a predictive value or a confirmatory value.

   - To be representationally faithful, the information must be complete, neutral, and free from error.

   - Four other enhancing qualitative characteristics have been identified that can increase the usefulness of financial information. These are comparability, verifiability, timeliness, and understandability. These characteristics increase usefulness, but they cannot make useless information useful.

3. **Explain the difference between the cash basis of accounting and the accrual basis of accounting.**

   - Under the cash basis of accounting, revenues are only recorded when cash is received and expenses are recorded when cash is paid out.

   - Under the accrual basis of accounting, revenues are recorded when they are earned and expenses are recorded when they are incurred.

   - Accounting standard setters have determined that financial information prepared using the accrual basis of accounting is more useful than that resulting9 from the use of the cash basis.

4. **Analyze basic transactions and record their effects on the accounting equation.**

   - Every transaction must affect at least two accounts when it is recorded.

   - The accounting equation must remain in balance as transactions are recorded; total assets must equal the sum of total liabilities plus shareholders' equity.

   - Transactions affecting the Retained Earnings account (revenues, expenses, and the declaration of dividends) should be referenced to indicate the nature of the transaction.

   - Revenues increase Retained Earnings, while expenses and the declaration of dividends decrease Retained Earnings.

5. **Explain the limitations of using the accounting equation template approach to record transactions.**

   - One of the main limitations of the accounting equation template method is that the number of columns that can be used is limited, which means that the number of accounts is also limited. The information resulting from this system may lack the level of detail required by management and other users.

   - The other main limitation of the accounting equation template method is the lack of specific accounts for recording revenues, expenses, and dividends declared. Instead, these are recorded in the Retained Earnings account. This makes it difficult and time-consuming for management to quantify revenue and expense information, which is critical for managing any business.

6. **Summarize the effects of transactions on the accounting equation and prepare and interpret a simple set of financial statements.**

   - The statement of income is normally the first financial statement prepared. This statement, which includes all revenues and expenses, provides the net income figure that is required for all of the other financial statements.

- The statement of changes in equity is the next financial statement prepared. It illustrates any changes in the number of shares, changes in the dollar value of share capital, and changes to the Retained Earnings account (due to net income or loss or the declaration of dividends).

- The statement of financial position is a vertical presentation of the accounting equation. It includes all assets, liabilities, and shareholders' equity accounts. It is often prepared on a classified basis, meaning that asset and liability accounts are presented in order of liquidity. Current assets are presented separately from non-current assets, while current liabilities are presented separately from non-current liabilities.

- All assets expected to be received, realized, or consumed within the next 12 months are considered to be current assets. All liabilities expected to be settled or paid within the next 12 months are considered to be current liabilities.

- The final financial statement to be prepared is the statement of cash flows. This statement categorizes all transactions of a business that affect cash into three categories: operating activities, investing activities, and financing activities.

7. **Calculate and interpret three ratios used to assess the profitability of a company.**

- The profit margin ratio is calculated by dividing net income by sales revenue. It indicates the percentage of sales revenue that remains after all expenses, including income taxes, have been recorded.

- The return on equity ratio is calculated by dividing net income by average shareholders' equity. It compares profit relative to the amount invested by shareholders. It provides shareholders with a sense of the returns being generated on their equity in the company.

- The return on assets ratio is calculated by dividing net income by average total assets. It provides an indication of how effective management has been at generating a return given the assets at their disposal.

KEY TERMS

Accounting Standards for Private Enterprises (ASPE) (52)
Accounts (58)
Accrual basis of accounting (55)
Carrying amount (74)
Cash basis of accounting (55)
Classified statement of financial position (73)
Complete (54)
Comparability (53)
Conceptual frameworks (52)
Confirmatory value (53)
Cost constraint (54)
Cost of goods sold (63)
Credit sale (63)
Depreciation (68)
Double-entry accounting system (57)

Earned (56)
Enhancing qualitative characteristics (53)
Estimated residual value (68)
Estimated useful life (68)
Free from error (54)
Fundamental qualitative characteristics (53)
Immaterial (53)
Incorporation (59)
Incurred (56)
International Financial Reporting Standards (IFRS) (52)
Material (53)
Materiality (53)
Net book value (74)
Neutral (54)

On account (63)
Predictive value (53)
Profit margin ratio (76)
Relevant (53)
Representationally faithful (53)
Return on assets (77)
Return on equity (76)
Revenue recognition criteria (56)
Straight-line depreciation (68)
Synoptic approach (57)
Template approach (57)
Timeliness (53)
Understandability (53)
Useful life (68)
Verifiability (53)

ABBREVIATIONS USED

AcSB	Canadian Accounting Standards Board
ASPE	Accounting Standards for Private Enterprises
IASB	International Accounting Standards Board
IFRS	International Financial Reporting Standards
PP&E	Property, plant, and equipment

SYNONYMS

Sale on account | Credit sale
Template approach | Synoptic approach

CHAPTER END REVIEW PROBLEM

Doing this problem will reinforce and extend what you have learned in this chapter. You should carefully work through the following problem, and then check your work against the suggested solution.

Exhibit 2-9 shows the statement of financial position of Alahai Ltd. at December 31, 2016. Note that the company has a December 31 year end and that these balances will be opening balances for the company's accounts at January 1, 2016.

STRATEGIES FOR SUCCESS

▶ Start by setting up a table, such as the one that was constructed in Exhibit 2-3 of this chapter. Use the account titles from Alahai's statement of financial position (given in Exhibit 2-9) as the column headings. Enter the beginning balances as the first line of data in the table.

▶ Begin your analysis of each transaction by thinking about what items are affected by it, bearing in mind that there must be at least two. Then determine whether each of those items is increasing or decreasing, and enter the effects in the table.

▶ As you enter the effects of each transaction, ensure that the basic accounting equation remains balanced (that is, Assets = Liabilities + Shareholders' Equity).

▶ Watch for key words such as *collected*, *received*, or *paid*, indicating that cash has increased or decreased. On the other hand, *on account* means that the collection, receipt, or payment will occur later; in the meantime, an account receivable or account payable will exist.

▶ Remember that revenues have to be *earned* by selling goods or services. Issuing shares in the company does not generate revenue, because the money that comes in has not been earned by operating the business; it has simply been invested by the owners. Similarly, collecting accounts receivable from customers does not generate revenue. The revenue is earned and recorded when the goods are sold, not when the accounts are collected.

▶ Be careful to distinguish between expenses and assets. Expenses are costs that have been used up or consumed in the process of operating the business and generating revenues. Assets are costs that have not yet been consumed and can be used to operate the business and generate revenues in the future.

| EXHIBIT 2-9 | ALAHAI LIMITED'S STATEMENT OF FINANCIAL POSITION |

ALAHAI LIMITED
Statement of Financial Position
As at December 31, 2015

ASSETS		
Current assets		
Cash	$4,500	
Accounts receivable	2,500	
Inventory	7,500	
Prepaid rent	1,000	
		$15,500
Non-current assets		
Equipment		9,500
TOTAL ASSETS		$25,000
LIABILITIES		
Current liabilities		
Accounts payable	$3,100	
Wages payable	1,300	
		$ 4,400
Non-current liabilities		
Bank loan payable		3,500
TOTAL LIABILITIES		7,900
SHAREHOLDERS' EQUITY		
Common shares		10,600
Retained earnings		6,500
TOTAL SHAREHOLDERS' EQUITY		17,100
TOTAL LIABILITIES AND SHAREHOLDERS' EQUITY		$25,000

The following transactions occurred during 2016:
1. Additional inventory was purchased for $39,700 on account.
2. Goods with selling prices totalling $80,000 were sold, all on account. These goods had cost Alahai Ltd. $38,200.
3. The company received $78,400 from customers as payments on accounts receivable.
4. The company paid $37,300 to suppliers on its accounts payable.
5. The company issued 10,000 common shares to investors for $20,000 cash. This brought the total number of issued common shares to 20,600.
6. New equipment was purchased for $15,000 cash during the year.
7. Dividends of $1,500 were declared and paid during the year.
8. Employees earned salaries for the year totalling $20,500. (Hint: The next transaction deals with the *payment* of salaries. Therefore, at this point the salaries should be recorded as *payable*.)
9. Cash payments for salaries during the year totalled $20,800.
10. The rent for each month was prepaid on the last day of the previous month. Accordingly, a payment of $1,000 had been made on December 31, 2015, for the rent for the month of January 2016. The rent payments during 2016 were $1,000 per month from January 31 through November 30, and $1,200 on December 31 (because the rent was increased for 2016). (Hint: Record the payments as *prepaid rent*, initially; then, as a separate transaction, transfer the cost for the year 2016 to rent *expense*.)
11. Interest on the bank loan, at 8%, was paid on December 31, 2016. At the same time, $400 of the loan principal was repaid.
12. Depreciation expense on the company's equipment totalled $2,000 for the year.

Required:

    a. Analyze and record the effects of each transaction on the company's accounts using the template approach (as illustrated in this chapter).

    b. Use your answer for part "a" of this problem to prepare a statement of income, a statement of changes in equity, a statement of financial position, and statement of cash flows.

    c. Calculate the following ratios for the year 2016:

        i. Profit margin ratio

        ii. Return on assets

        iii. Return on equity

Suggested Solution to Chapter End Review Problem

The template analysis (part "a" of the problem) is shown in Exhibit 2-10. The entries are numbered to match the transaction numbers in the problem. The financial statements (required for part "b") are shown in Exhibits 2-11, 2-12, 2-13, 2-14, and 2-15. Following these, the ratios (required for part "c") are presented.

Part (a)

EXHIBIT 2-10   **ANALYSIS OF TRANSACTIONS: ALAHAI LTD.**

	ASSETS						LIABILITIES		+	S/H EQUITY		
Trans. #	Cash	A/R	Inv.	Prepaid Rent	Equip.	A/P	Wages Payable	Bank Loan Payable		Common Shares	Retained Earnings	R/E/ DD
Opening Balances	4,500	2,500	7,500	1,000	9,500	3,100	1,300	3,500		10,600	6,500	
1			39,700			39,700						
2: 1		80,000									80,000	R
2: 2			(38,200)								(38,200)	E
3	78,400	(78,400)										
4	(37,300)					= (37,300)						
5	20,000									20,000		
6	(15,000)				15,000							
7	(1,500)										(1,500)	DD
8							20,500				(20,500)	E
9	(20,800)						(20,800)					
10: 1	(12,200)			12,200								
10: 2				(12,000)							(12,000)	E
11	(680)							(400)			(280)	E
12					(2,000)						(2,000)	E
	15,420	4,100	9,000	1,200	22,500	5,500	1,000	3,100		30,600	12,020	
			52,220							52,220		

Explanations follow for *selected* transactions.

Transactions 8 and 9: Salaries

The company's wage expense for the period should be the amount of salaries *earned* by employees during that period. This may be different than the amounts actually *paid* to employees for wages during the same period. The two amounts may differ due to payments being made for wages owing at the beginning of the year (the opening balance in Wages Payable) or because some of the wages earned by the employees during the period remain unpaid at the end of it. (These would be the amount of wages payable at the end of the period.)

Transaction 10: Rent

There were 12 rent *payments* during 2016:

- 11 × $1,000   = $11,000 (these were related to the rent for February to December 2016)
- 1 × $1,200   = $ 1,200 (this was related to the rent for January 2017)

    $12,200

However, the rent *expense* for 2016 is equal:

- 1 × $1,000   = $ 1,000 (the rent for January 2016 had been prepaid in December 2015)
- 11 × $1,000   = $ 11,000 (the rent for February to December 2016)

    = $12,000

The final payment of $1,200 on December 31, 2016, is the rent for January 2017. It is an *asset* at the end of 2016 and is recorded as prepaid rent.

Transaction 11: Loan Interest and Principal Repayment

During 2016, Alahai Ltd. incurred and paid interest of $280 on its bank loan, which was determined as follows:

$$= \text{Loan Principal} \times \text{Annual Interest Rate} \times (\text{number of months outstanding} /12)$$
$$= \$3,500 \times 8\% \times 12/12$$
$$= \$280$$

This interest is an expense to the company. Alahai Ltd. also repaid $400 in loan principal at the end of the year. Repaying the principal of a loan does not create an expense; it simply reduces the loan liability.

Part (b)

EXHIBIT 2-11	STATEMENT OF INCOME

ALAHAI LIMITED
Statement of income
For the year ended December 31, 2016

Sales revenue	$80,000
Cost of goods sold	38,200
Gross profit	41,800
Wage expense	20,500
Rent expense	12,000
Depreciation expense	2,000
Interest expense	280
Net income	$ 7,020

EXHIBIT 2-12	STATEMENT OF CHANGES IN EQUITY

ALAHAI LIMITED
Statement of Changes in Equity
For the year ended December 31, 2016

	Number of Common Shares	Share Capital—Common Shares	Retained Earnings	Total
Balance, Jan. 1	10,600	$10,600	$ 6,500	$17,100
Net income	-	-	7,020	7,020
Declaration of dividends	-	-	(1,500)	(1,500)
Issuance of common shares	10,000	20,000	-	20,000
Balance, Dec. 31	20,600	$30,600	$12,020	$42,620

EXHIBIT 2-13   STATEMENT OF FINANCIAL POSITION

ALAHAI LIMITED
Statement of Financial Position
As at December 31, 2016

ASSETS
  Current assets
    Cash ... $15,420
    Accounts receivable ... 4,100
    Inventory ... 9,000
    Prepaid rent ... 1,200
      ... $29,720
  Non-current assets
    Equipment ... 22,500
  TOTAL ASSETS ... $52,220

LIABILITIES
  Current liabilities
    Accounts payable ... $ 5,500
    Wages payable ... 1,000
      ... $ 6,500
  Non-current liabilities
    Bank loan payable ... 3,100
  TOTAL LIABILITIES ... 9,600

SHAREHOLDERS' EQUITY
  Common shares ... 30,600
  Retained earnings ... 12,020
  TOTAL SHAREHOLDERS' EQUITY ... 42,620

TOTAL LIABILITIES AND SHAREHOLDERS' EQUITY ... $52,220

EXHIBIT 2-14   ANALYSIS OF ALAHAI LTD.'S CASH ACCOUNT

Date	Cash	Description	Operating Activity	Investing Activity	Financing Activity
1		No cash effect			
2: 1		No cash effect			
2: 2		No cash effect			
3	78,400	Collected from customers	78,400		
4	(37,300)	Paid suppliers	(37,300)		
5	20,000	Issued common shares			20,000
6	(15,000)	Purchased equipment		(15,000)	
7	(1,500)	Paid dividends			(1,500)
8		No cash effect			
9	(20,800)	Paid wages	(20,800)		
10: 1	(12,200)	Paid rent	(12,200)		
10: 2		No cash effect			
11	(680)	Paid loan principal and interest	(280)		(400)
12		No cash effect			
	10,920		7,820	(15,000)	18,100

EXHIBIT 2-15	STATEMENT OF CASH FLOWS

ALAHAI LIMITED
Statement of Cash Flows
For the year ended December 31, 2016

Cash flows from operating activities		
Cash received from customers	$78,400	
Cash paid for inventory	(37,300)	
Cash paid for wages	(20,800)	
Cash paid for rent	(12,200)	
Cash paid for interest	(280)	
Total cash flows from operating activities	7,820	A
Cash flows from investing activities		
Cash paid to purchase equipment	(15,000)	
Total cash flows from investing activities	(15,000)	B
Cash flows from financing activities		
Cash received from issuance of shares	20,000	
Cash payments of dividends	(1,500)	
Cash repayments of bank loan principal	(400)	
Total cash flows from financing activities	18,100	C
Net change in cash during the period	10,920	= A + B + C
Cash balance on January 1, 2016	4,500	
Cash balance on December 31, 2016	$15,420	

Part (c)

$$\text{Profit Margin} = \text{Net Income/Sales Revenue}$$
$$= 7,020/80,000$$
$$= 0.0878 \text{ or } 8.78\%$$

$$\text{Return on Equity} = \text{Net Income/Average Total Shareholders' Equity}$$
$$= 7,020/((17,100 + 42,620)/2)$$
$$= 7,020/29,860$$
$$= 0.235 \text{ or } 23.5\%$$

$$\text{Return on Assets} = \text{Net Income/Average Total Assets}$$
$$= 7,020/((25,000 + 52,200)/2)$$
$$= 7,020/38,610$$
$$= 0.182 \text{ or } 18.2\%$$

ASSIGNMENT MATERIAL

Discussion Questions

DQ2-1 Explain the difference between a fundamental qualitative characteristic and an enhancing qualitative characteristic.

DQ2-2 Explain how the fundamental qualitative characteristics of relevance and representational faithfulness may be in conflict when deciding the value at which land is carried on a company's statement of financial position.

DQ2-3 Explain how the conceptual framework is useful in situations where there is no specific accounting standard for a particular transaction.

DQ2-4 In your own words, define *materiality* and identify the fundamental qualitative characteristic that it is related to.

DQ2-5 Describe how the basic accounting equation (or *statement of financial position equation*) is used to analyze how transactions are recorded in the template system.

DQ2-6 Discuss why dividends do not appear on the statement of income but do appear on the statement of cash flows.

DQ2-7 Explain, in your own words, the difference between the cash basis of accounting and the accrual basis of accounting.

DQ2-8 What are the advantages and disadvantages of using the accrual basis of accounting rather than the cash basis?

DQ2-9 Identify the three major sections in the statement of cash flows, and briefly describe the nature of the items that appear in each section.

DQ2-10 In the first two chapters, we have discussed financing, investing, and operating activities in the business cycle (or statement of cash flows). Identify one example of a financing activity that would result in an outflow of cash and one example of an investing activity that would result in an inflow of cash.

DQ2-11 In the first two chapters, we have discussed financing, investing, and operating activities in the business cycle (or statement of cash flows). Identify one example of a financing activity that would result in an inflow of cash and one example of an investing activity that would result in an outflow of cash.

DQ2-12 Indicate whether each of the following statements is true or false:
   a. The cash basis of accounting recognizes revenues when they are received.
   b. In the cash basis of accounting, there is no such thing as a prepaid rent account.
   c. In the accrual basis of accounting, paying an account payable creates an expense.
   d. In the accrual basis of accounting, interest should be recognized only when it is paid.
   e. Cash receipts from customers increase accounts receivable.
   f. Expenses decrease shareholders' equity.
   g. Dividends are an expense of doing business and should appear on the statement of income.
   h. Interest paid on bank loans is reported in the operating activities section of the statement of cash flows.

DQ2-13 Explain, in your own words, why the normal cash flow pattern is generally + / − / + (operating, investing, financing).

DQ2-14 Under the accrual basis of accounting when would your university or college bookstore recognize revenue from the sale of textbooks? What about from the sale of a parking pass for the semester that is paid for at the beginning of the semester? How would this change under the cash basis of accounting?

DQ2-15 Explain how a prepaid expense (such as rent) is handled under accrual basis accounting.

DQ2-16 Explain how an accrued expense (such as interest) is handled under accrual basis accounting.

DQ2-17 Explain what *depreciation* is, and how it is calculated using the straight-line method.

DQ2-18 Briefly explain why it is necessary to prepare the statement of income before preparing the statement of changes in shareholders' equity.

DQ2-19 Explain why companies depreciate their buildings and equipment.

DQ2-20 Explain what is meant by *estimated residual value*. Why is it subtracted from the asset's cost when calculating depreciation under the straight-line method?

Application Problems

AP2-1 (Qualitative characteristics of the conceptual framework)

Required:

Identify the following qualitative characteristics as F (fundamental) or E (enhancing):
   a. Understandability
   b. Faithful representation
   c. Timeliness
   d. Comparability
   e. Verifiability
   f. Relevance

AP2-2 (Qualitative characteristics of the conceptual framework)

Required:

Identify which of the fundamental qualitative characteristics each of the following traits are related to: R (relevance) or F (faithful representation):
   a. Confirmatory value
   b. Neutrality
   c. Completeness
   d. Predictive value
   e. Materiality
   f. Freedom from error

AP2-3 (Transaction analysis and the basic accounting equation)

Required:

For each of the following transactions, indicate the effect on the basic accounting equation (Assets = Liabilities + Shareholders' Equity):

a. Issuance of shares for cash
b. Purchase of land for cash
c. Sale of services to a customer on credit
d. Receipt of cash from customers as payments on their accounts
e. Payment of cash to shareholders as a distribution of earnings
f. Receipt of a loan from a bank
g. Payment of interest on the bank loan
h. Purchase of inventory on credit
i. Payment of an account payable
j. Payment to a courier company for delivering goods to a customer
k. Payment of an insurance premium to cover the following year
l. Depreciation of equipment

AP2-4 (Transaction analysis)

Required:

For each of the transactions below, indicate which accounts are affected and whether they are increased or decreased:

a. Sold shares for cash.
b. Borrowed money from a bank.
c. Bought equipment from a supplier on credit.
d. Bought inventory from a supplier, partly for cash and partly on account.
e. Sold inventory to a customer on account. (Hint: Your answer should deal with both the revenue and the related expense.)
f. Made a payment on an account owing to a supplier.
g. Received a payment from a customer on account.
h. Bought supplies for cash.
i. Declared and paid a dividend.
j. Accrued the interest on the money that was borrowed in transaction "b" (that is, recognized the interest but did not pay it).
k. Paid for the equipment that was purchased on credit in transaction "c."
l. Used some of the supplies that were purchased in transaction "h."

AP2-5 (Transaction analysis and the basic accounting equation)

Required:

Using the template below, record the following transactions for Jared's Appliances Ltd. (JAL):

Sept. 9	JAL made sales of $19,500, of which $11,000 was on account. The appliances sold had cost JAL $11,200 when they were originally purchased from Samsung.
Sept. 11	JAL collected $6,200 from customers making payments on their accounts.
Sept. 18	JAL purchased dishwashers with a cost of $7,800 on account.

	Assets			Liabilities		S/H Equity		
Date	Cash	A/R	Inventory	A/P	Loan Payable	Common Shares	Retained Earnings	R/E/DD

AP2-6 (Transaction analysis and the basic accounting equation)

Bounce House Party Supply Ltd. rents bouncy castles and inflatable slides for parties, school fairs, and company picnics. The company also sells party supplies such as balloons, streamers, and piñatas. The company started business in September 2016 and had the following transactions in its first month:

Date:

Sept. 1	Bounce House Party Supply Ltd. issued 40,000 common shares for $260,000 cash.
1	The company took out a $160,000 bank loan with an interest rate of 6%. The loan terms require that Bounce repay $3,000 in principal on the last day of each month plus interest.
3	Bounce purchased 10 inflatable slides and bouncy castles at a cost of $140,000. The company paid $100,000 at the time of purchase and the balance is due in 30 days.
8	Bounce purchased balloons and other party supplies costing $6,600 on account.
11	A major local company paid Bounce a $2,500 deposit to reserve all of Bounce's inflatables for a grand opening function that is scheduled for the second week in October.
15	Bounce recorded its party supply sales of the first two weeks of the month. Total sales (half in cash and half on account) amounted to $8,600 and the inventory related to these sales was determined to have a cost of $5,700.
19	Bounce paid the suppliers $1,700 for goods previously purchased on account.
23	Collections from customers on account totalled $3,400.
31	Bounce made the loan payment required under the terms of the borrowing agreement.

Required:

Analyze and record these transactions using the template method.

	ASSETS					LIABILITIES			S/H EQUITY		
Date/ Ref.	Cash	A/R	Inv.	Inflatable Equip.		A/P	Unearned Revenue	Loan Payable	Common Shares	Retained Earnings	R/E/ DD

AP2-7 (Transaction analysis and the basic accounting equation)

The following transactions of Carswell Wholesale Inc. occurred in the month of September 2016:

Date:

Sept. 1	Issued 200 common shares for $20,000.
4	To raise additional capital, Carswell borrowed $10,000 from the bank on a long-term loan.
7	Purchased equipment for $4,500.
9	Purchased inventory costing $2,500 on account.
15	Sold units from inventory to customers, on account, for $4,000.
19	Purchased additional inventory, on credit, at a cost of $2,100 to replace the units sold.
20	Made payments of $2,700 on its accounts payable.
21	Purchased a used delivery van for $15,000.
28	At month end, counted inventory and determined that the cost of the units sold on September 15 totalled $1,800.
28	Paid employee wages of $700 for the month.
29	Received an invoice from the local newspaper for $400 for advertising run during the month of September. The invoice is due on October 15.
30	Paid utilities costs of $150 for the month.
30	During the month, Carswell received $2,200 from customers as payments on their accounts.

Required:

Analyze and record these transactions using the template method.

	ASSETS					LIABILITIES		S/H EQUITY		
Date/Ref.	Cash	A/R	Inv.	Equip.	Delivery Van	A/P	Bank Loan Payable	Common Shares	R/E	R/E/DD

AP2-8 (Transaction analysis and the basic accounting equation)

The following transactions of Jaker Ltd. occurred in the month of January 2016:

Date:

1	Borrowed $12,500 from the bank.
3	Issued 2,200 common shares for $22,000.
5	Purchased inventory on account totalling $24,700.
9	Bought computer equipment costing $8,000 for $4,000 cash and the balance on account.
15	Made sales totalling $25,000, of which $9,000 were on account. The cost of the products sold from inventory was $14,000.
19	Made payments to suppliers totalling $15,000.
25	Collected on account from customers totalling $7,800.
27	Made sales totalling $10,500, all on account. The cost of the products sold from inventory was $7,600.
28	Employees earned wages of $2,400 during the month, of which $2,200 was paid.
28	Incurred $800 of utilities expenses during the month.

Required:
Analyze and record these transactions using the template method.

	ASSETS					LIABILITIES			S/H EQUITY		
Date/Ref.	Cash	A/R	Inv.	Equip.	A/P	Wages Payable	Loan Payable	Common Shares	R/E	R/E/DD

AP2-9 (Transaction analysis and the basic accounting equation)

Primrose Beauty Supplies Ltd. was incorporated in January 2016. Primrose had the following transactions in its first month:

Date:

Jan. 1	Received $150,000 in exchange for issuing 15,000 common shares.
1	Borrowed $100,000 from the local bank at 9%. The terms of the borrowing agreement state that the loan is to be repaid at the end of each month in the amount of $5,000 per month plus interest.
2	Leased a commercial warehouse, paying $8,000, of which $5,000 represented a damage deposit and $3,000 was the rent for January.
8	Purchased nail art kits, one of Primrose's best-selling product lines, costing $26,200 on account.
12	A chain of beauty salons paid Primrose a deposit of $6,500 related to a special order of hair products that were to be custom packaged under the salon's logo. Primrose agreed to deliver these products on February 15.
16	Recorded its sales of the first two weeks of the month. Total sales (half in cash and half on account) amounted to $18,200 and the inventory related to these sales was determined to have a cost of $9,200.
19	Paid the suppliers $7,000 for goods previously purchased on account.
25	Collections from customers on account totalled $7,100.
31	Made the loan payment required under the terms of the borrowing agreement.

Required:
Analyze and record these transactions using the template method.

	ASSETS					LIABILITIES			S/H EQUITY		
Date/Ref.	Cash	A/R	Inv.	Prepaid Rent	A/P	Unearned Revenue	Loan Payable	Common Shares	R/E	R/E/DD

AP2-10 (Transaction analysis and the basic accounting equation)

Required:

For each of the following transactions, indicate how (i) net earnings and (ii) cash flows are affected. For each, state whether there will be an increase, a decrease, or no effect, and the amount (if any):

a. Issued shares to investors for $60,000.

b. Purchased inventory from suppliers for $2,500, on account.

c. Sold a unit of inventory for $500, on account. The unit had cost $300 and was already in inventory prior to its sale.

d. Purchased equipment for $10,000 cash.

e. Made a payment of $1,000 on accounts payable.

f. Used $300 of supplies. The supplies were purchased for cash in an earlier period.

g. Received a payment of $700 from a customer for inventory previously sold on account.

h. Declared (but did not yet pay) a dividend of $2,000.

i. Paid the $2,000 dividend that was declared above.

j. Depreciated equipment by $500.

AP2-11 (Transaction analysis and the basic accounting equation)

Required:

Analyze the following transactions and show their effects on the basic accounting equation, by preparing a table like the one in Exhibit 2-3:

a. Received $150,000 from investors buying shares in the company.

b. Bought land for $50,000. Paid half in cash, with the remainder to be paid in six months.

c. Bought inventory costing $45,000, on account.

d. Sold inventory costing $35,000 to customers, on account, for $52,000.

e. Paid $1,000 of taxes that were owed from the previous period.

f. Borrowed $25,000 from a bank. The interest on the loan is 6% per year.

g. Depreciated equipment by $1,200.

h. Paid $750 for supplies to be used in the future.

i. Paid $250 to the power company for electricity used during the period.

j. Declared and paid dividends of $8,000.

AP2-12 (Transaction analysis and the basic accounting equation)

Dr. Walter Wong completed the following business transactions during the month of November:

1. Incorporated a veterinary practice by investing (a) $30,000 in cash and (b) equipment worth $20,000.
2. Rented a furnished office and clinic, and paid $1,500 in rent for the month of November.
3. Purchased medical supplies on account, $850.
4. Performed veterinary services and immediately collected $2,400 for the work.
5. Paid for the medical supplies that were purchased in transaction "3."
6. Provided $700 of additional veterinary services, on account.
7. Used $350 of the medical supplies that were purchased in transaction "3."
8. Received $500 in partial payment for the services that were provided in transaction "6."
9. Paid the November telephone bill for the office, $75.
10. Received a bill of $250 for advertising that took place in November, but decided not to pay it until next month when it was due.
11. Paid rent on the office for the months of December and January, totalling $3,200.

Required:

Analyze these transactions and show their effects on the basic accounting equation for November, by preparing a table like the one in Exhibit 2-3.

AP2-13 (Transaction analysis and the basic accounting equation)

Required:

Show how each of the following transactions affects the basic accounting equation by preparing a table like the one in Exhibit 2-3, and identify the ones that have an immediate impact on the statement of income and/or the statement of cash flows:

a. Bought parts inventory for $15,000, on account. (The company repairs and services vehicles, and will use these parts for repairs.)

b. Paid $12,000 to suppliers as partial payment for the purchases that were made in transaction "a."

c. Received $20,000 in cash for repairing and servicing vehicles; another $5,000 of work was done on account.

d. Collected $3,000 from customers for the work that was done on account in transaction "c." The balance remains outstanding.

e. In the repair work done in transaction "c," $10,000 of the parts and supplies inventory was used.

f. The owners of the company invested a further $25,000 in the business, and 10,000 additional common shares were issued to them.

g. Received utility (electricity, water, and telephone) bills for the month that totalled $600. Paid all these bills except for $100 that will be paid next month.

h. Borrowed $50,000 from the bank.

i. Bought a vehicle hoist for $45,000.

j. Paid the employees their wages for the month, $9,000.

k. Recorded accrued interest of $200 on the bank loan. The interest will be paid when the loan is due, in one year.

AP2-14 (Transaction analysis and the basic accounting equation)

Required:

For each of the following transactions, explain what the immediate effect will be on the basic accounting equation.

a. Sold inventory to customers for cash.

b. Sold inventory to customers on account.

c. Collected cash from customers as payments on their accounts.

d. Purchased inventory on account.

e. Paid suppliers for goods purchased on account.

f. Purchased production equipment for cash.

g. Paid for a one-year insurance policy on an office building.

h. Borrowed money from the bank.

i. Made a loan payment, which included interest expense and repayment of principal.

AP2-15 (Transaction analysis and the basic accounting equation)

Required:

Show the effect of each of the following transactions on the basic accounting equation, by preparing a table like the one in Exhibit 2-3. The company's fiscal year end is December 31.

a. On January 1, 2016, the company borrowed $15,000 from the bank.

b. On December 31, 2016, the company paid the interest on the bank loan in transaction "a." The interest rate is 6%.

c. On January 1, 2016, the company bought equipment for $10,000 cash.

d. On December 31, 2016, the company recorded depreciation on the equipment, using the straight-line method. The equipment has an estimated useful life of six years and an estimated residual value of $1,000.

e. Purchases of inventory on account during the year totalled $87,500.

f. Sales for the year totalled $147,500, of which $17,500 was for cash and the remainder was on account.

g. The cost of the products sold from inventory during the year in transaction (e) was $85,000.

h. Payments to suppliers for inventory purchases totalled $73,000 during the year.

i. Collections on account from customers totalled $116,000 for the year.

j. Employees earned wages of $48,400 during the year, which were recorded as Wages Payable.

k. All employee wages were paid by the end of the year except the wages for the last week in December, which totalled $1,200.

l. Dividends were declared and paid in the amount of $1,000.

AP2-16 (Transaction analysis and the basic accounting equation)

Required:

Show the effect of each of the following transactions on the basic accounting equation, by preparing a table like the one in Exhibit 2-3. The fiscal year end of the company (which has been operating for several years) is December 31.

a. Purchased equipment costing $10,000, paying cash.

b. Purchased $42,000 of inventory on account during the year.

c. Made sales of $60,000 during the year, of which $24,000 were cash sales.

d. Paid $36,000 owed to suppliers on accounts payable. (This included some amounts owed from the previous year.)

e. Collected $34,000 due from customers on accounts receivable. (This included some amounts due from the previous year.)

f. Paid an insurance premium of $900 on March 31 that provides coverage for the 12-month period starting April 1. The company had no insurance prior to this.

g. Determined that the cost of the inventory sold during the year was $39,000. (This included some inventory purchased the previous year.)

h. Paid $7,000 for utilities expenses during the year.

i. On December 31, the company recognized the amount of insurance expense incurred during the period. (Refer to transaction "f.")

j. Recorded $3,600 of depreciation for the year on the company's equipment.

k. Declared (but did not immediately pay) dividends of $400 each quarter, for a total of $1,600.

l. By the end of the year, $1,200 of the dividends were paid.

AP2-17 (Determine amounts using the basic accounting equation)

Ballentine Company Ltd. has assets of $100,000, liabilities of $40,000, and shareholders' equity of $60,000.

Required:

Refer to the basic accounting equation (Assets = Liabilities + Shareholders' Equity) to answer each of the following independent questions:

a. At what amount will assets be stated if total liabilities decrease by $5,000 and shareholders' equity remains unchanged?

b. Go back to the original data. At what amount will assets be stated if total liabilities increase by $3,000 and shareholders' equity increases by $4,000?

c. Go back to the original data. At what amount will shareholders' equity be stated if the company pays $7,000 of its liabilities?

d. Go back to the original data. At what amount will liabilities be stated if total assets decrease by $7,000 and shareholders' equity increases by $2,000?

e. Go back to the original data. At what amount will shareholders' equity be stated if the company declares a $1,000 dividend but does not pay it?

AP2-18 (Determine the missing amounts using financial statement relationships)

Required:

For the two independent cases that follow, determine the missing amount for each letter. (Hint: You might not be able to calculate them in the order in which they appear.)

	Case 1	Case 2
Revenues	$ A	$29,000
Expenses	17,000	25,000
Net earnings	2,000	F
Dividends declared	500	G
Retained earnings:		
Beginning of year	6,000	10,000
End of year	B	11,000
Total assets:		
Beginning of year	C	H
End of year	28,000	I
Total liabilities:		
Beginning of year	9,000	10,500
End of year	D	9,500
Common shares:		
Beginning of year	1,000	J
End of year	E	8,500
Additional common shares issued during the year	4,000	3,500

AP2-19 (Determine net earnings or loss from statement of financial position changes)

The following are from a company's statements of financial position:

	Dec. 31, 2015	Dec. 31, 2016
Total assets	$110,000	$125,000
Total liabilities	$80,000	$85,000

During 2016, the company issued additional shares for $7,000 and declared dividends of $4,000.

Required:

Calculate what the company's net income or loss must have been for the year 2016. Be sure to indicate whether your answer represents net earnings or a net loss.

AP2-20 (Determine revenues, expenses, and dividends)

The following information for the current year was obtained from the accounting records of Safari Supplies Corporation:

Retained earnings, beginning	$ 96,000
Retained earnings, ending	105,600
Sales	448,800
Cost of goods sold	272,000
Selling expenses	63,300
General and administrative expenses	38,800
Dividend revenue	4,800
Interest revenue	2,200
Interest expense	1,200
Income taxes expense	26,400

Required:

Calculate the following items:
a. Total revenues
b. Total expenses
c. Net earnings
d. Dividends declared

AP2-21 (Determine statement of income and statement of financial position amounts)

Rhaman Company had the following transactions in its first month of operations:
1. On incorporation, the company had issued 11,000 common shares in exchange for $10,000 cash and office furniture and equipment worth $1,000.
2. Additional equipment costing $4,000 was purchased for cash.
3. Supplies costing $500 were purchased for cash.
4. Inventory costing $5,000 was acquired on account. Later in the month, the company paid half of the amount owed. It will pay the remainder next month.
5. The entire inventory was sold to customers for $8,000. The company received half of this amount in cash and will receive the remainder next month.
6. By the end of the month, $400 of the supplies were used up.
7. The equipment was depreciated $100 for the month.
8. Operating expenses paid in cash during the month were $1,900.
9. Dividends of $200 were declared and paid during the month.

Required:
a. Calculate the following amounts for the month:
    i. Sales revenue
    ii. Cost of goods sold
    iii. Total expenses other than cost of goods sold
    iv. Net earnings or loss
b. Calculate the following amounts as at the end of the month:
    i. Cash on hand
    ii. Total assets other than cash
    iii. Total liabilities
    iv. Share capital
    v. Retained earnings

AP2-22 (Cash basis versus accrual basis)

Required:

Based on the following transactions, calculate the revenues, expenses and net income that would be reported (a) on the cash basis and (b) on the accrual basis:
    i. Credit sales to customers totalled $35,000.
    ii. Cash sales totalled $115,000.

iii. Cash collections on account from customers totalled $30,000.

iv. Cost of goods sold during the period was $85,000.

v. Payments made to suppliers of inventory totalled $75,000.

vi. Wages of $32,500 were paid during the year. In addition, wages of $2,500 remained unpaid at year end; there were no wages unpaid at the beginning of the year.

vii. Halfway through the year, a one-year insurance policy was purchased at a cost of $1,000.

AP2-23 (Cash basis versus accrual basis)

Required:

Based on the following transactions, calculate the revenues, expenses, and net income that would be reported on (a) the cash basis and (b) the accrual basis:

i. Inventory costing $70,000 was purchased on account.

ii. Inventory costing $60,000 was sold for $100,000. Eighty percent of the sales were for cash.

iii. Cash collected from credit customers (those who bought on account) totalled $20,000.

iv. A lease was signed at the beginning of the year, requiring monthly payments of $1,000. The rent for the first month was paid when the lease was signed. After that, the $1,000 rent was paid on the last day of each month, to cover the following month.

v. Supplies costing $5,500 were purchased for cash. At the end of the year, $500 of the supplies were still unused.

vi. Wages of $37,500 were paid during the year. Also, wages of $500 remained unpaid at year end.

AP2-24 (Nature of retained earnings)

Required:

Explain why you agree or disagree with the following statement: "Retained earnings are like money in the bank. If you are running out of cash, you can always use some of your retained earnings to pay your bills."

AP2-25 (Statement of income and statement of cash flows)

Required:

Compare and contrast the purpose of the statement of income and the statement of cash flows. Outline how they differ, and briefly describe their relationship to the statement of financial position.

AP2-26 (Prepare a statement of income)

Sara's Bakery had the following account balances at the end of 2016:

Supplies	$ 4,000
Wage expense	42,000
Sales	178,000
Cash	24,000
Supplies expense	14,000
Accounts payable	8,000
Rent expense	12,000
Common shares	90,000
Accounts receivable	10,000
Cost of goods sold	101,000
Equipment	87,500
Depreciation expense	2,500
Retained earnings	22,500
Dividends declared	2,000
Prepaid rent	1,000
Wages payable	1,500

Required:

a. Prepare a statement of income for the year ended December 31, 2016.

b. In answering part "a," you did not need to use all the accounts provided. For each item that you did not use, explain why you did not include it on the statement of income.

AP2-27 (Prepare a statement of income)

The Garment Tree Ltd. sells clothing. At the end of 2016, it had the following account balances:

Accounts receivable	$ 9,000
Rent expense	12,000
Inventory	18,000
Retained earnings	11,000
Advertising expense	5,000
Cash	6,000
Wage expense	32,000
Dividends declared	1,000
Miscellaneous expense	3,000
Wages payable	2,000
Common shares	15,000
Prepaid rent	1,000
Cost of goods sold	57,000
Accounts payable	6,000
Sales	110,000

Required:
   a. Prepare a statement of income for the year ended December 31, 2016.
   b. In answering part "a," you did not need to use all the accounts provided. For each item that you did not use, explain why you did not include it on the statement of income.

AP2-28 (Prepare a statement of financial position)

Tree Top Restaurants Ltd., a chain that has several restaurants in cities across Canada, had the following account balances at December 31, 2016:

Retained earnings	$ 60,000
Wages payable	10,000
Accounts receivable	90,000
Bank loan payable (due in five years)	250,000
Buildings	230,000
Accounts payable	82,000
Prepaid insurance	8,000
Common shares	200,000
Cash	53,000
Land	100,000
Income taxes payable	5,000
Inventory	46,000
Equipment	80,000

Required:
Prepare a classified statement of financial position for Tree Top Restaurants Ltd. for December 31, 2016.

AP2-29 (Calculate net income and retained earnings; prepare statement of financial position)

Little Tots Ltd. sells children's clothing. At the end of December 2016 (its first year of operations), it had the following account balances:

Accounts receivable	$ 2,500
Rent expense	3,600
Cash	3,500
Wages payable	400
Equipment	5,000
Depreciation expense	500
Wage expense	26,000
Prepaid rent	300
Cost of goods sold	34,900
Sales revenue	69,900
Bank loan payable (due in two years)	4,800
Advertising expense	800
Accounts payable	2,000
Utilities expense	300
Dividends declared	1,200
Common shares	10,000
Interest expense	100
Inventory	8,000
Miscellaneous expenses	400
Retained earnings	?

Required:
a. Calculate the net income for the year by adding the revenue and deducting all the expenses.
b. Calculate the retained earnings by following the process outlined below:

Balance in retained earnings at the beginning of the year	$ 0*
Add: Net income for the year	?
Deduct: Dividends declared during the year	
Balance in Retained Earnings at the end of the year	?

*The beginning balance is zero because this was the company's first year of operations.

c. Prepare a classified statement of financial position.

AP2-30 (Calculate net income and retained earnings; prepare statement of financial position)

On December 31, 2016 (the end of its first year of operations), Minute Print Company had the following account balances:

Bank loan payable (due in three years)	$ 40,000
Wage expense	93,000
Supplies	68,000
Dividends payable	1,500
Sales	486,000
Cash	24,000
Supplies expense	214,500
Wages payable	4,500
Prepaid rent	2,000
Interest expense	2,500
Rent expense	12,000
Dividends declared	3,000

Accounts payable	$ 8,000
Common shares	30,000
Accounts receivable	30,000
Miscellaneous expenses	9,000
Equipment	$112,000
Retained earnings	?

Required:

a. Identify the accounts that would appear on the statement of income, and use them to calculate the net earnings for the year.

b. Find the amount of retained earnings at December 31, 2016, by subtracting the dividends declared from the net earnings you calculated in part "a."

c. Prepare a classified statement of financial position for December 31, 2016. Use the retained earnings amount calculated in part "b."

AP2-31 (Prepare statement of income and statement of financial position)

The Wizard's Corner, a company that sells video games and related items, had the following account balances at the end of June 2016:

Cost of goods sold	$103,000
Common shares	33,000
Advertising expense	6,000
Equipment	11,000
Depreciation expense	2,000
Dividends declared	3,000
Accounts payable	11,000
Inventory	28,000
Wage expense	36,000
Sales	160,000
Accounts receivable	15,000
Rent expense	12,000
Cash	10,000
Prepaid rent	1,000
Wages payable	2,000
Retained earnings (as at July 1, 2015)	21,000

Required:

a. Prepare a statement of income for the year ended June 30, 2016.

b. Calculate the amount of retained earnings as at June 30, 2016.

c. Prepare a statement of financial position as at June 30, 2016.

AP2-32 (Transaction analysis and financial statement preparation)

Singh Company started business on January 1, 2016. The following transactions occurred in 2016:

1. On January 1, the company issued 10,000 common shares for $250,000.
2. On January 2, the company borrowed $50,000 from the bank.
3. On January 3, the company purchased land and a building for a total of $200,000 cash. The land was recently appraised at a fair market value of $60,000. (Note: Because the building will be depreciated in the future and the land will not, these two assets should be recorded in separate accounts.)
4. Inventory costing $130,000 was purchased on account.
5. Sales to customers totalled $205,000. Of these, $175,000 were sales on account.
6. The cost of the inventory that was sold to customers in transaction 5 was $120,000.
7. Payments to suppliers on account totalled $115,000.
8. Collections from customers on account totalled $155,000.
9. Payments to employees for wages were $55,000. In addition, there was $2,000 of unpaid wages at year end.
10. The interest on the bank loan was recognized and paid for the year. The interest rate on the loan was 6%.

11. The building was estimated to have a useful life of 30 years and a residual value of $20,000. The company uses the straight-line method of depreciation.
12. The company declared dividends of $7,000 on December 15, 2016, to be paid on January 15, 2017.

Required:

a. Analyze the effects of each of the transactions on the basic accounting equation, using a table like the one in Exhibit 2-3.
b. Prepare a statement of income, a statement of changes in equity, a statement of financial position (unclassified), and a statement of cash flows for 2016.

AP2-33 (Transaction analysis and financial statement presentation)

The Hughes Tools Company started business on October 1, 2015. Its fiscal year runs through to September 30 the following year. The following transactions occurred in the fiscal year that started on October 1, 2015, and ended on September 30, 2016.

1. On October 1, 2015, Jill Hughes invested $175,000 to start the business. Hughes is the only owner. She was issued 10,000 common shares.
2. On October 1, Hughes Tools borrowed $225,000 from a venture capitalist (a lender who specializes in start-up companies) and signed a note payable.
3. On October 1, the company rented a building. The rental agreement was a two-year contract requiring quarterly rental payments (every three months) of $15,000, payable in advance. The first payment was made on October 1, 2015 (covering the period from October 1 to December 31). Thereafter, payments were due on December 31, March 31, June 30, and September 30 for each three-month period that followed. All the rental payments were made as specified in the agreement.
4. On October 1, the company purchased equipment costing $220,000 for cash.
5. Initial inventory was purchased for $90,000 cash.
6. Additional purchases of inventory during the year totalled $570,000, all on account.
7. Sales during the year totalled $800,000, of which $720,000 were on account.
8. Collections from customers on account totalled $650,000.
9. Payments to suppliers on account totalled $510,000.
10. The cost of the inventory that was sold during the year was $560,000.
11. Selling and administrative expenses totalled $86,500 for the year. Of this amount, $4,000 was unpaid at year end.
12. Interest on the note payable from the venture capitalist was paid at year end (September 30, 2016). The interest rate on the note is 10%. In addition, $25,000 of the note principal was repaid at that time.
13. The equipment was depreciated based on an estimated useful life of 10 years and a residual value of $20,000.
14. The company declared and paid a dividend of $7,000.

Required:

a. Show the effects of the transactions on the basic accounting equation, by preparing a table like the one in Exhibit 2-3.
b. Prepare a statement of income, statement of changes in equity, statement of financial position, and statement of cash flows for the year.
c. Comment on the results of the company's first year of operations.

AP2-34 (Transaction analysis and financial statement preparation)

A. J. Smith Company started business on January 1, 2016, and the following transactions occurred in its first year:

1. On January 1, the company issued 12,000 common shares at $25 per share.
2. On January 1, the company purchased land and a building from another company in exchange for $80,000 cash and 6,000 shares. The land's value is approximately one quarter of the total value of the transaction. (Hint: You need to determine a value for the shares using the information given in transaction 1, and the land and building should be recorded in separate accounts.)
3. On March 31, the company rented out a portion of its building to Frantek Company. Frantek is required to make quarterly payments of $7,500 on March 31, June 30, September 30, and December 31 of each year. The first payment, covering the period from April 1 to June 30, was received on March 31, and the other payments were all received as scheduled.
4. Equipment worth $120,000 was purchased on July 1, in exchange for $60,000 cash and a one-year note with a principal amount of $60,000 and an interest rate of 10%. No principal or interest payments were made during the year.
5. Inventory costing $250,000 was purchased on account.
6. Sales were $300,000, of which credit sales were $250,000.
7. The inventory sold had a cost of $190,000.
8. Payments to suppliers totalled $205,000.
9. Accounts receivable totalling $200,000 were collected.

10. Operating expenses amounted to $50,000, all of which were paid in cash.
11. The building purchased in transaction 2 is depreciated using the straight-line method, with an estimated useful life of 20 years and an estimated residual value of $30,000.
12. The equipment purchased in transaction 4 is depreciated using the straight-line method, with an estimated useful life of 10 years and an estimated residual value of $5,000. Because the equipment was purchased on July 1, only a half year of depreciation is recognized in 2016.
13. Dividends of $20,000 were declared during the year, of which $5,000 remained unpaid at year end.
14. Interest expense on the note payable from transaction 4 was recorded.

Required:
   a. Show the effects of the transactions on the basic accounting equation, by preparing a table like the one in Exhibit 2-3.
   b. Prepare a statement of income, statement of changes in equity, statement of financial position (unclassified), and statement of cash flows for 2016.
   c. Comment on the company's results for its first year of operations.

AP2-35 (Transaction analysis from both parties' perspectives)

Most transactions take place between two independent entities. How you record a particular transaction depends on whose perspective you take.

Required:
For each of the following transactions, explain how it would affect the basic accounting equation of each entity.
   a. Loan from a bank: from the borrower's and the bank's perspectives
   b. Cash sales from the provision of services: from the seller's and the customer's perspectives
   c. Investment made by Company A in shares of Company B, with the shares being obtained directly from Company B: from Company A's and Company B's perspectives
   d. Investment made by Company A in shares of Company B, with the shares being purchased through the Toronto Stock Exchange; that is, the shares had previously been issued by Company B and now trade in the stock market: from Company A's and Company B's perspectives
   e. Purchase of inventory on account: from the buyer's and the seller's perspectives

User Perspective Problems

UP2-1 (Accounting standards)

Required:
Assume that you are a member of the Canadian Accounting Standards Board (AcSB) and are a guest speaker at a commercial lender. You have been asked to explain why the board concluded that it would be useful to have a different set of accounting standards for privately held companies than those used by public companies. Prepare your remarks.

UP2-2 (Areas of risk in a new company)

Required:
Assume that you are a commercial loan officer for a bank and are preparing to meet with a corporate client. The client has approached you seeking an increase in the loan it has with the bank. Prepare a list of things that you would want to know about the company's operations before you decide whether to approve the increase in the loan.

UP2-3 (Cash basis of accounting)

Under the cash basis of accounting, the purchase of a new piece of equipment for cash would be treated as an expense of the accounting period when the purchase occurred.

Required:
   a. If you were a shareholder, how would this treatment affect your assessment of the company's earnings and financial position?
   b. If you were a prospective buyer of the company (someone who wanted to purchase all the company's shares), how would this treatment affect your assessment of the company as a potential acquisition?

UP2-4 (Accrual basis of accounting and revenue recognition)

Required:
Assume that all of the students of your university or college registering in courses offered in the fall semester had to pay their tuition fees by August 31. These courses begin on September 4 and run for 13 weeks. Assuming that your university or college follows the accrual basis of accounting, explain when it should recognize this tuition revenue.

UP2-5 (Accrual basis of accounting versus cash basis of accounting)

Required:

You have been asked to give a presentation to your colleagues in the commercial lending unit of a bank explaining why it is important to request both a statement of cash flows and a statement of income, along with a statement of financial position, from clients seeking loans. Many of your colleagues think that a statement of income and a statement of financial position are sufficient. Prepare your remarks.

UP2-6 (Cash flow patterns)

A friend came to you to discuss a potential investment she was considering making. A quick look at the company's statement of cash flows shows the company had a − / + / + (operating / investing / financing) cash flow pattern.

Required:

What does this tell you about the company? What would you advise your friend to do?

Reading and Interpreting Published Financial Statements

RI2-1 (Determination of items from a North American company's financial statements)

Winnipeg-based **New Flyer Industries Inc.** is one of North America's largest manufacturers of heavy-duty transit buses. Excerpts from its 2013 financial statements are in Exhibits 2-16A and B.

EXHIBIT 2-16A	NEW FLYER INDUSTRIES INC.'S 2013 CONSOLIDATED STATEMENTS OF NET EARNINGS AND COMPREHENSIVE INCOME

NEW FLYER INDUSTRIES INC.
CONSOLIDATED STATEMENTS OF NET EARNINGS AND COMPREHENSIVE INCOME
52 weeks ended December 29, 2013 ("Fiscal 2013") and 52 weeks ended December 30, 2012 ("Fiscal 2012")
(in thousands of U.S. dollars except per share figures)

	Fiscal 2013	Fiscal 2012 Restated (notes 2.5, 2.23)
Revenue (note 20)	$1,199,424	$865,250
Cost of sales (note 4, 25)	1,078,657	791,480
Gross profit	120,767	73,770
Sales, general and administration costs and other operating expenses (note 25)	69,540	43,091
Foreign exchange loss (gain) (note 19c)	118	(2,812)
Earnings from operations	51,109	33,491
Unrealized foreign exchange loss on non-current monetary items	2,146	1,403
Loss on exercise of redemption right	—	5,530
Fair value adjustment to embedded derivatives	—	1,395
Earnings before finance costs and income taxes	48,963	25,163
Finance costs		
Interest on long-term debt and convertible debentures	8,749	11,852
Accretion in carrying value of long-term debt and convertible debentures	2,208	1,432
Other interest and bank charges	2,857	2,701
Fair market value adjustment on interest rate swap	532	(835)
	14,346	15,150
Earnings before income tax expense	34,617	10,013
Income tax expense (note 7)		
Current income taxes	23,849	12,809
Deferred income taxes recovered	(15,993)	(12,086)
	7,856	723
Net earnings for the period	$ 26,761	$ 9,290

EXHIBIT 2-16B   **NEW FLYER INDUSTRIES INC.'S 2013 CONSOLIDATED STATEMENTS OF FINANCIAL POSITION**

NEW FLYER INDUSTRIES INC.
CONSOLIDATED STATEMENTS OF FINANCIAL POSITION
As at December 29, 2013 and December 30, 2012
(in thousands of U.S. dollars)

	December 29, 2013	December 30, 2012 Restated (notes 2.5, 24)
Assets		
Current		
Cash	$ 11,896	$ 11,182
Accounts receivable (note 3, 19c)	230,315	113,460
Inventories (note 4)	183,338	124,712
Derivative financial instruments	—	—
Prepaid expenses and deposits	7,658	4,724
	433,207	254,078
Property, plant and equipment (note 5)	64,832	42,024
Embedded derivative instruments	—	—
Unused investment tax credits (note 7)	13,659	23,262
Deferred tax assets (note 7)	55,290	49,332
Goodwill and intangible assets (note 6)	568,864	528,528
	$1,135,852	$897,224
Liabilities		
Current		
Accounts payable and accrued liabilities	$ 212,938	$150,828
Income taxes payable	504	6,756
Current portion of deferred revenue (note 13)	57,614	23,430
Provision for warranty costs (note 24)	26,102	7,472
Current portion of long-term debt (note 10)	35,000	40,035
Derivative financial instruments (note 19 b,c)	740	14
Current portion of deferred compensation obligation (note 9)	258	—
Current portion of obligations under finance leases (note 8)	1,283	1,857
	334,439	230,392
Accrued benefit liability (note 17)	228	8,973
Obligations under finance leases (note 8)	1,770	2,314
Deferred compensation obligation (note 9)	1,663	1,233
Deferred revenue (note 13)	17,382	8,394
Other long-term liabilities	9,303	—
Deferred tax liabilities (note 7)	114,816	122,244
Long-term debt (note 10)	140,241	120,950
Convertible debentures (note 11)	58,322	56,760
Derivative financial instruments (note 19 b, c)	2,508	1,976
	680,672	553,236
Commitments and contingencies (note 22)		
Shareholders' equity		
Share capital (note 14)	589,208	476,918
Stock option reserve (note 12)	299	—
Equity component of convertible debentures (note 11)	3,841	3,841
Accumulated other comprehensive loss	(5,001)	(6,490)
Deficit	(133,167)	(130,281)
	455,180	343,988
	$1,135,852	$897,224

Required:

Use the financial statements to answer the following questions.

    a. Calculate the growth in the following accounts from 2012 to 2013:

        i. Revenue

        ii. Cost of Sales

        iii. Net Earnings

        iv. Total Assets

        v. Total Equity

        Would you expect each of these accounts to grow at the same rate? Why or why not? Comment on the growth rates you calculated.

    b. Based on your analysis from part "a," did the equity investors finance more of the company in 2013 than they did in 2012?

    c. Calculate the following ratios for each of the two years presented. (Note that, in order to be able to calculate these ratios for each of the years, you will have to use the total assets for each year and the total shareholders' equity for each year in your ratios, rather than average total assets and average shareholders' equity.)

        i. Profit margin ratio

        ii. Return on assets

        iii. Return on equity

        Comment on your results. Do the results from part "a" help you interpret the changes in these ratios? Why or why not?

RI2-2 (Determination of items from a Canadian company's financial statements)

Excerpts from the 2013 statement of income, statement of operations, and notes to the financial statements of **High Liner Foods Inc.** are in Exhibits 2-17A to C. Although it is a Canadian company based in Lunenburg, Nova Scotia, High Liner prepares its financial statements in U.S. dollars. However, the general format and accounting policies are similar to the financial statements you have seen so far.

EXHIBIT 2-17A	HIGH LINER FOODS INCORPORATED'S 2013 CONSOLIDATED STATEMENT OF INCOME

CONSOLIDATED STATEMENT OF INCOME

(in thousands of U.S. dollars, except per share amounts)	Notes	December 28, 2013	Fifty-two weeks ended December 29, 2012
Revenues		$ 947,301	$ 942,631
Cost of sales		731,884	735,970
Gross profit		215,417	206,661
Distribution expenses		53,368	44,511
Selling, general and administrative expenses		98,902	100,862
Impairment of property, plant and equipment		—	13,230
Business acquisition, integration and other expenses		3,256	10,741
Results from operating activities		59,891	37,317
Finance costs		16,329	36,585
(Income) loss from equity accounted investee, net of income tax		(86)	196
Income before income taxes		43,648	536
Income taxes			
Current	20	12,378	5,442
Deferred	20	(86)	(7,109)
Total income tax expense (recovery)		12,292	(1,667)
Net income		$ 31,356	$ 2,203
PER SHARE EARNINGS			
Earnings per common share			
Basic	17	$ 2.07	$ 0.15
Diluted	17	$ 2.01	$ 0.14
Weighted average number of shares outstanding			
Basic	17	15,183,747	15,118,752
Diluted	17	15,593,166	15,460,417

EXHIBIT 2-17B   HIGH LINER FOODS INCORPORATED'S 2013 CONSOLIDATED STATEMENT OF FINANCIAL POSITION

CONSOLIDATED STATEMENT OF FINANCIAL POSITION

(in thousands of U.S. dollars)	Notes	December 28, 2013	December 29, 2012
ASSETS			*(note 27)*
Current:			
Cash		$ 1,206	$ 65
Accounts receivable	9	91,334	73,947
Income taxes receivable		3,509	5,145
Other financial assets	22	1,524	533
Inventories	8	254,072	222,313
Prepaid expenses		2,952	2,991
Total current assets		354,597	304,994
Non-current:			
Property, plant and equipment	6	97,503	89,268
Deferred income taxes	20	4,656	7,207
Other receivables and miscellaneous assets		1,906	2,035
Intangible assets	5	105,253	110,631
Goodwill	5	111,999	112,873
Total non-current assets		321,317	322,014
Assets classified as held for sale	7	542	4,819
Total assets		$676,456	$631,827
LIABILITIES AND SHAREHOLDERS' EQUITY			
Current:			
Bank loans	12	$ 97,227	$ 59,704
Accounts payable and accrued liabilities	10	103,215	101,441
Provisions	11	240	1,614
Other current financial liabilities	22	459	550
Income taxes payable		2,543	1,165
Current portion of long-term debt	13	—	34,237
Current portion of finance lease obligations	13	979	1,039
Total current liabilities		204,663	199,750
Non-current:			
Long-term debt	13	226,929	213,359
Other long-term financial liabilities	22	5,597	1,130
Other long-term liabilities		1,044	1,532
Long-term finance lease obligations	13	1,647	2,181
Deferred income taxes	20	43,998	45,126
Future employee benefits	14	7,929	13,791
Total non-current liabilities		287,144	277,119
Liabilities directly associated with the assets held for sale	7	—	1,604
Total liabilities		491,807	478,473
Shareholders' equity:			
Common shares	16	80,260	75,169
Contributed surplus		13,781	7,719
Retained earnings		90,792	66,373
Accumulated other comprehensive (loss) income		(184)	4,093
Total shareholders' equity		184,649	153,354
Total liabilities and shareholders' equity		$676,456	$631,827

EXHIBIT 2-17C **EXCERPT FROM HIGH LINER FOODS INCORPORATED'S 2013 ANNUAL REPORT**

NOTE 19 Operating segment information

The Company operates in one dominant industry segment, the manufacturing and marketing of prepared and packaged frozen seafood. The Company evaluates performance of the reportable segments on a geographical basis using net income before financing and taxes from continuing operations. Transfer prices between operating segments are on an arm's length basis in a manner similar to transactions with third parties. Operations and identifiable assets and liabilities by reporting segment are as follows:

(Amounts in $000s)	December 28, 2013			December 29, 2012		
	Canada	U.S.	Total	Canada	U.S.	Total
Sales within geographic region [1]	$303,589	$642,938	$946,527	$312,884	$627,039	$939,923
Sales outside of geographic region [1]	38,277	13,753	52,030	8,130	14,474	22,604
	341,866	656,691	998,557	321,014	641,513	962,527
Intercompany sales outside of geographic region [1]	(38,277)	(12,979)	(51,256)	(8,130)	(11,773)	(19,903)
Revenue (excluding intercompany sales)	303,589	643,712	947,301	312,884	629,747	942,631
Cost of sales (excluding intercompany sales)	230,399	501,485	731,884	243,670	492,300	735,970
Gross profit	73,190	142,227	215,417	69,214	137,447	206,661
Distribution expenses	14,352	39,016	53,368	14,588	29,923	44,511
Selling, general and administrative expenses	36,047	62,855	98,902	38,354	62,508	100,862
Impairment of property plant and equipment	—	—	—	4,407	8,823	13,230
Business acquisition integration and other expenses	29	3,227	3,256	2,321	8,420	10,741
Financing costs	1,234	15,095	16,329	1,512	35,073	36,585
(Loss) income from equity accounted investee	(43)	(43)	(86)	98	98	196
Income (loss) before income tax	21,571	22,077	43,648	7,934	(7,398)	536
Income tax expense (recovery)	7,651	4,641	12,292	3,668	(5,335)	(1,667)
Net income (loss)	$13,920	$17,436	$31,356	$4,266	$(2,063)	$2,203
Add back:						
Depreciation included in:						
Cost of sales	1,761	5,219	6,980	2,363	9,110	11,473
Distribution	161	1,170	1,331	171	469	640
Selling, general and administrative expenses	1,407	183	1,590	1,303	414	1,717
Total depreciation	3,329	6,572	9,901	3,837	9,993	13,830
Amortization included in:						
Cost of sales	—	3	3	—	33	33
Selling, general and administrative expenses	553	4,702	5,255	190	5,328	5,518
Total amortization	553	4,705	5,258	190	5,361	5,551
Total depreciation and amortization	3,882	11,277	15,159	4,027	15,354	19,381
Financing costs	1,234	15,095	16,329	1,512	35,073	36,585
Income tax expense (recovery)	7,651	4,641	12,292	3,668	(5,335)	(1,667)
Income before depreciation, amortization, financing and income taxes	$26,687	$48,449	$75,136	$13,473	$43,029	$56,502

(1) Geographic regions include Canada, U.S., and Mexico, where Mexico is presented as part of the U.S. segment.

Required:
Use the exhibits to answer the following questions.
  a. In the shareholders' equity section, what does the $80,260 thousand in common shares represent?
  b. In the shareholders' equity section, what does the $90,792 thousand in retained earnings represent?
  c. What percentage of High Liner's assets was financed by liabilities? Has this percentage increased or decreased from 2012?
  d. How much did total assets increase in 2013 over 2012? What were the major areas (or accounts) that accounted for the increase?
  e. If High Liner were to pay the income taxes payable, in the current liabilities section, what would be the effect on the basic accounting equation?
  f. What was High Liner's gross profit as percentage of revenues in 2013? How did this compare with 2012?

g. In the accompanying notes to the financial statements, High Liner discloses separately the revenues and cost of sales for its two business segments: Canadian and U.S. Calculate gross profit for each business segment as a percentage of revenues. Are the segments more or less profitable in 2013 than in 2012? Which segment is more profitable? Base your answers on High Liner's note 19, Operating Segment Information (Exhibit 2-17C).

RI2-3 (Determination of items from a Canadian company's financial statements)

DHX Media Inc. is a Halifax-based developer, producer, and distributor of films and television programs. Excerpts from the company's financial statements for the year ended June 30, 2013, are in Exhibits 2-18A to C.

EXHIBIT 2-18A **DHX MEDIA LTD.'S 2013 CONSOLIDATED BALANCE SHEETS**

DHX Media Ltd.
Consolidated Balance Sheets
As at June 30, 2013 and June 30, 2012

(expressed in thousands of Canadian dollars)

	June 30, 2013 $	June 30, 2012 $
Assets		
Current assets		
Cash	12,640	19,166
Short-term investments (note 6)	—	3,323
Restricted cash (note 13)	1,278	—
Amounts receivable (note 7)	72,849	41,823
Prepaid expenses and deposits	2,763	1,581
Investment in film and television programs (note 8)	116,994	44,163
	206,524	110,056
Investment in associates (note 9)	—	1,541
Long-term amounts receivable	3,177	—
Deferred financing fees	684	—
Property and equipment (note 10)	4,924	8,520
Long-term investment	330	330
Intangible assets (note 11)	27,956	2,714
Goodwill (note 12)	80,802	11,800
	324,397	134,961
Liabilities		
Current liabilities		
Bank indebtedness (note 13)	5,000	2,665
Accounts payable and accrued liabilities (note 14)	45,095	14,019
Deferred revenue	19,753	10,647
Other liability	445	—
Interim production financing (note 13)	37,676	21,177
Current portion of long-term debt and obligations under capital lease (note 13)	3,977	1,948
	111,946	50,456
Other liability	—	1,319
Long-term debt and obligations under capital lease (note 13)	45,466	3,845
Long-term deferred revenue	707	—
Deferred income taxes (note 17)	3,403	441
	161,522	56,061
Shareholders' Equity (note 15)	162,875	78,900
	324,397	134,961

EXHIBIT 2-18B   DHX MEDIA LTD.'S 2013 CONSOLIDATED STATEMENTS OF INCOME

DHX Media Ltd.
Consolidated Statements of Income
For the years ended June 30, 2013 and 2012

(expressed in thousands of Canadian dollars, except for amounts per share)

	2013 $	2012 $
Revenues (note 25)	97,263	72,647
Operating expenses (income)		
Direct production costs and expense of film and television programs produced	45,117	47,928
Expense of acquired libraries	6,313	617
Acquisition costs	1,696	—
Amortization of property and equipment and intangible assets	4,583	2,538
Development expenses and other	3,055	773
Write-down of investment in film and television programs	608	515
Selling, general and administrative	31,886	16,077
Share of loss of associates	172	146
Realized loss (gain) on disposals of short-term investment and property and equipment	(1,419)	224
Finance expense (income), net (note 18)	1,948	(151)
	93,959	68,667
Income before income taxes	3,304	3,980
Provision for (recovery of) income taxes (note 17)		
Current income taxes	1,468	147
Deferred income taxes	(24)	786
	1,444	933
Net income for the years	1,860	3,047

EXHIBIT 2-18C   DHX MEDIA LTD.'S 2013 CONSOLIDATED STATEMENTS OF CASH FLOWS

DHX Media Ltd.
Consolidated Statements of Cash Flows
For the years ended June 30, 2013 and 2012

(expressed in thousands of Canadian dollars)

	2013 $	2012 $
Cash provided by (used in)		
Operating activities		
Net income for the years	1,860	3,047
Charges (credits) to income not involving cash		
Amortization of property and equipment	1,937	1,700
Amortization of intangible assets	2,646	838
Unrealized foreign exchange loss	2,905	57
Write-down of investment in film and television programs	608	515
Realized loss (gain) on sale of property and equipment and short-term investment	(1,419)	80
Share of loss of associates	172	146
Share-based compensation and warrant expense	1,347	492
Interest on promissory notes	1	3
Deferred tax expense (recovery)	(24)	786
	10,033	7,664
Net change investment in film and television programs	(9,652)	(5,494)
Net change in other non-cash working capital balances related to operations (note 24)	(10,382)	12,084
Cash provided by (used in) operating activities	(10,001)	14,254

continued

| EXHIBIT 2-18C | DHX MEDIA LTD.'S 2013 CONSOLIDATED STATEMENTS OF CASH FLOWS (continued) |

	2013 $	2012 $
Financing activities		
Proceeds from issuance of common shares, net of issuance costs	16,745	—
Dividends paid	(1,535)	—
Proceeds from issuance of common shares related to employee share purchase plan	314	9
Proceeds from repayment of employee share purchase loan	2	5
Common shares repurchased and cancelled	—	(6,193)
Change in long-term receivables and payables	(401)	—
Increase in deferred financing fees	(684)	—
Proceeds from (repayment of) bank indebtedness	2,335	(2,535)
Decrease in long-term deferred revenue	(1,492)	—
Proceeds from (repayment of) interim production financing	9,608	(10,227)
Proceeds from long-term debt, net of transaction costs	48,292	4,000
Increase in restricted cash	(1,278)	—
Repayment of other liabilities	(874)	—
Repayment of long-term debt and obligations under capital lease	(64,695)	(1,478)
Repayment of shareholder debt assumed on acquisition	(8,665)	—
Cash provided by (used in) financing activities	(2,328)	(16,419)
Investing activities		
Business acquisitions, net of cash acquired	(2,191)	—
Acquisitions of short-term investments	—	(7,185)
Proceeds on sale of long-term investment	1,352	—
Proceeds on disposal of short-term investments	3,294	10,009
Proceeds on sale of property and equipment	5,214	—
Acquisition of property and equipment	(1,455)	(1,053)
Cost of internally generated intangible assets	(478)	—
Cash provided by investing activities	5,736	1,771
Effect of foreign exchange rate changes on cash	67	35
Net change in cash during the years	(6,526)	(359)
Cash - Beginning of years	19,166	19,525
Cash - End of years	12,640	19,166

Required:

a. How much cash did DHX have available to use at the end of fiscal 2013?

b. What percentage of DHX's assets were financed by shareholders in 2013? Did this represent an increase or decrease relative to 2012? What does this change mean?

c. How much did DHX's accounts receivable increase from 2012 to 2013? How did this compare with the change in revenues during the same period? What does this tell you?

d. Determine direct production costs and expense of film and television programs produced as a percentage of DHX's revenues in 2013. How did this compare with 2012? Do the same analysis for selling, general, and administrative expenses. Comment on what these trends tell you about the company.

e. Did the company pay dividends during fiscal 2013? How did you determine this?

f. How much property and equipment did DHX acquire in 2013? How did this compare with the proceeds it received from the sale of property and equipment during the year?

g. Calculate the following ratios for fiscal 2013 and 2012. (Note that, in order to be able to calculate these ratios for each of the years, you will have to use the total assets for each year and the total shareholders' equity for each year in your ratios, rather than average total assets and average shareholders' equity.)

   i. Profit margin ratio

   ii. Return on assets

   iii. Return on equity

h. Comment on your results in part "g."

RI2-4 (Determination of items from a Canadian company's financial statements)

Calgary-based **WestJet Airlines Ltd.** provides services throughout Canada and to some international destinations. Excerpts from its 2013 financial statements are in Exhibits 2-19A to C.

EXHIBIT 2-19A   **WESTJET AIRLINES LTD.'S 2013 CONSOLIDATED STATEMENT OF EARNINGS**

Consolidated Statement of Earnings
For the years ended December 31
(Stated in thousands of Canadian dollars, except per share amounts)

	Note	2013	2012
Revenue:			
Guest		3,337,569	3,133,492
Other		324,628	293,917
		3,662,197	3,427,409
Operating expenses:			
Aircraft fuel		1,039,448	992,787
Airport operations		459,465	424,911
Flight operations and navigational charges		410,052	376,050
Sales and distribution		356,988	333,106
Marketing, general and administration		222,567	202,398
Depreciation and amortization		200,840	185,401
Inflight		176,907	162,633
Aircraft leasing		175,646	173,412
Maintenance		169,197	154,406
Employee profit share		51,577	46,585
		3,262,687	3,051,689
Earnings from operations		399,510	375,720
Non-operating income (expense):			
Finance income	15	17,848	18,391
Finance cost	15	(43,447)	(48,900)
Gain on foreign exchange		1,136	1,061
Gain (loss) on disposal of property and equipment		(2,962)	469
Loss on fuel derivatives		–	(6,512)
		(27,425)	(35,491)
Earnings before income tax		372,085	340,229
Income tax expense (recovery):			
Current		154,964	66,230
Deferred		(51,601)	31,607
	11	103,363	97,837
Net earnings		268,722	242,392

EXHIBIT 2-19B   **WESTJET AIRLINES LTD.'S 2013 CONSOLIDATED STATEMENT OF FINANCIAL POSITION**

Consolidated Statement of Financial Position
At December 31
(Stated in thousands of Canadian dollars)

	Note	2013	2012
Assets			
Current assets:			
Cash and cash equivalents	5	1,256,005	1,408,199
Restricted cash	6	58,106	51,623
Accounts receivable	19	42,164	37,576
Prepaid expenses, deposits and other	19	133,263	101,802
Inventory	19	36,722	35,595
		1,526,260	1,634,795

continued

EXHIBIT 2-19B **WESTJET AIRLINES LTD.'S 2013 CONSOLIDATED STATEMENT OF FINANCIAL POSITION (continued)**

	Note	2013	2012
Non-current assets:			
Property and equipment	7	2,487,734	1,985,599
Intangible assets	8	58,691	50,808
Other assets	19	70,778	75,413
Total assets		4,143,463	3,746,615
Liabilities and Shareholders' Equity			
Current liabilities:			
Accounts payable and accrued liabilities	19	543,167	460,003
Advance ticket sales	19	551,022	480,947
Non-refundable guest credits	19	46,975	47,859
Current portion of maintenance provisions	9	76,105	34,135
Current portion of long-term debt	10	189,191	164,909
		1,406,460	1,187,853
Non-current liabilities:			
Maintenance provisions	9	142,411	145,656
Long-term debt	10	689,204	574,139
Other liabilities	19	8,834	9,914
Deferred income tax	11	306,714	356,748
Total liabilities		2,553,623	2,274,310
Shareholders' equity			
Share capital	12	603,861	614,899
Equity reserves		69,079	69,856
Hedge reserves		105	(5,746)
Retained earnings		916,795	793,296
Total shareholders' equity		1,589,840	1,472,305
Total liabilities and shareholders' equity		4,143,463	3,746,615

EXHIBIT 2-19C **WESTJET AIRLINES LTD.'S 2013 CONSOLIDATED STATEMENT OF CASH FLOWS**

Consolidated Statement of Cash Flows
For the years ended December 31
(Stated in thousands of Canadian dollars)

	Note	2013	2012
Operating activities:			
Net earnings		**268,722**	242,392
Items not involving cash:			
Depreciation and amortization		**200,840**	185,401
Change in maintenance provisions		**26,610**	31,378
Change in other liabilities		**1,782**	(383)
Amortization of hedge settlements		**1,400**	1,400
Loss on fuel derivatives		**—**	6,512
(Gain) loss on disposal of property and equipment		**2,962**	(469)
Share-based payment expense	12	**14,533**	12,815
Deferred income tax expense (recovery)		**(51,601)**	31,607
Unrealized foreign exchange gain		**(12,020)**	(1,487)
Change in non-cash working capital		**298,697**	208,110
Change in restricted cash		**(6,484)**	(3,282)
Change in other assets		**(1,374)**	(6,894)
Cash interest received		**19,079**	17,780
Cash taxes paid		**(147,868)**	(950)
Purchase of shares pursuant to compensation plans		**(7,131)**	(1,306)
		608,147	722,624

continued

EXHIBIT 2-19C	WESTJET AIRLINES LTD.'S 2013 CONSOLIDATED STATEMENT OF CASH (continued)

	Note	2013	2012
Investing activities:			
Aircraft additions		**(639,592)**	(218,116)
Other property and equipment and intangible additions		**(75,580)**	(51,191)
		(715,172)	(269,307)
Financing activities:			
Increase in long-term debt		**318,075**	72,995
Repayment of long-term debt		**(178,647)**	(162,678)
Decrease in obligations under finance leases		**—**	(75)
Shares repurchased	12	**(112,362)**	(112,065)
Dividends paid	13	**(52,188)**	(37,549)
Issuance of shares pursuant to compensation plans		**106**	198
Cash interest paid		**(36,677)**	(43,055)
Change in non-cash working capital		**146**	(6,815)
		(61,547)	(289,044)
Cash flow from operating, investing and financing activities		**(168,572)**	164,273
Effect of foreign exchange on cash and cash equivalents		**16,378**	321
Net change in cash and cash equivalents		**(152,194)**	164,594
Cash and cash equivalents, beginning of year		**1,408,199**	1,243,605
Cash and cash equivalents, end of year	5	**1,256,005**	1,408,199

Required:
  a. Assuming that all the sales were on account, determine the amount of cash that was collected from customers in 2013.
  b. Why do you think WestJet does not report a Cost of Goods Sold account on its statement of income?
  c. Explain what the item *advance ticket sales* in the current liabilities section of the statement of financial position represents. What type of transaction gave rise to this liability? What will cause this liability to decrease?
  d. How much money did WestJet use in 2013 to repurchase shares? Assuming the shares were all repurchased using cash, what was the effect on the accounting equation of the share repurchase?
  e. How much did WestJet spend on acquiring new aircraft in 2013? If it financed the acquisitions with long-term debt, what was the effect on the accounting equation?

RI2-5 (Determination of items from a Canadian company's financial statements)

Required:
Base your answers to the following questions on the financial statements of WestJet Airlines Ltd. in Exhibit 2-19.
  a. Calculate the following ratios for each of the two years presented. (Note that, in order to be able to calculate these ratios for each of the years, you will have to use the total assets for each year and the total shareholders' equity for each year in your ratios, rather than average total assets and average shareholders' equity.)
    i. Profit margin ratio (use total revenues)
    ii. Return on assets
    iii. Return on equity
  b. Comment on WestJet's profitability during 2012 and 2013.

RI2-6 (Determination of items from a company's financial statements)

Cineplex Inc. is currently Canada's largest film exhibition organization, with theatres in six provinces. Excerpts from its 2013 financial statements are in Exhibits 2-20A to E.

EXHIBIT 2-20A   **CINEPLEX INC.'S 2013 CONSOLIDATED BALANCE SHEETS**

Consolidated Balance Sheets

(expressed in thousands of Canadian dollars)	December 31, 2013	December 31, 2012 (note 2)
Assets		
Current assets		
Cash and cash equivalents (note 6)	$ 44,140	$ 48,665
Trade and other receivables (note 7)	100,891	77,278
Inventories (note 8)	7,234	5,193
Prepaid expenses and other current assets	6,838	3,047
	159,103	134,183
Non-current assets		
Property, equipment and leaseholds (note 9)	459,112	418,498
Deferred income taxes (note 10)	17,635	53,528
Fair value of interest rate swap agreements (note 4)	92	—
Interests in joint ventures (note 11)	44,359	41,623
Intangible assets (note 12)	113,601	78,460
Goodwill (note 13)	797,476	608,929
	$1,591,378	$1,335,221
Liabilities		
Current liabilities		
Accounts payable and accrued expenses (note 14)	$ 157,333	$ 129,499
Share-based compensation (note 15)	12,151	—
Dividends payable (note 16)	7,552	7,063
Income taxes payable (note 10)	2,656	13,654
Deferred revenue	136,373	106,253
Finance lease obligations (note 18)	2,394	2,222
Fair value of interest rate swap agreements (note 4)	635	513
Convertible debentures (note 21)	—	—
	319,094	259,204
Non-current liabilities		
Share-based compensation (note 15)	15,622	12,223
Long-term debt (note 17)	217,151	148,066
Fair value of interest rate swap agreements (note 4)	—	273
Finance lease obligations (note 18)	17,722	20,548
Post-employment benefit obligations (note 19)	6,522	6,274
Other liabilities (note 20)	170,125	141,319
Convertible debentures (note 21)	96,870	—
	524,012	328,703
Total liabilities	843,106	587,907
Equity		
Share capital (note 22)	853,411	847,235
Deficit	(107,323)	(102,547)
Accumulated other comprehensive loss	(1,715)	(1,142)
Contributed surplus	3,899	3,768
	748,272	747,314
	$1,591,378	$1,335,221

EXHIBIT 2-20B   **CINEPLEX INC.'S 2013 CONSOLIDATED STATEMENTS OF CASH FLOWS**

Consolidated Statements of Cash Flows
For the years ended December 31, 2013 and 2012

(expressed in thousands of Canadian dollars)	2013	2012 (note 2)
Cash provided by (used in)		
Operating activities		
Net income	$ 83,557	$ 120,484
Adjustments to reconcile net income to net cash provided by operating activities Depreciation and amortization of property, equipment and leaseholds, and intangible assets	70,890	62,163
Amortization of tenant inducements, rent averaging liabilities and fair value lease contract liabilities	(6,735)	(5,033)
Accretion of debt issuance costs and other non-cash interest	2,001	562
Loss (gain) on disposal of assets	4,372	(2,352)
(Gain) on acquisition of business	—	(24,752)
Deferred income taxes	29,369	1,189
Interest rate swap agreements - non-cash interest	(939)	1,485
Non-cash share-based compensation	1,826	2,108
Accretion of convertible debentures	274	323
Net change in interests in joint ventures	(2,686)	4,356
Tenant inducements	5,417	7,615
Changes in operating assets and liabilities (note 26)	37,302	7,486
Net cash provided by operating activities	224,648	175,634
Investing activities		
Proceeds from sale of assets	3,573	3,683
Purchases of property, equipment and leaseholds	(62,410)	(72,242)
Acquisition of business, net of cash acquired (note 3)	(238,338)	(2,811)
Net cash invested in CDCP	(50)	(438)
Net cash used in investing activities	(297,225)	(71,808)
Financing activities		
Dividends paid	(88,130)	(80,794)
Borrowings (repayments) under credit facility, net	70,000	(20,000)
Repayment of debt acquired with business (note 3)	(12,875)	—
Payments under finance leases	(2,277)	(2,104)
Proceeds from issuance of shares	—	501
Net proceeds from issuance of convertible debentures (note 21)	103,469	—
Deferred financing fees (notes 17 and 21)	(2,135)	—
Shares repurchased and cancelled	—	(1,786)
Repayment of convertible debentures at maturity	—	(1,123)
Net cash provided by (used in) financing activities	68,052	(105,306)
Decrease in cash and cash equivalents	(4,525)	(1,480)
Cash and cash equivalents - Beginning of year	48,665	50,145
Cash and cash equivalents - End of year	$ 44,140	$ 48,665
Supplemental information		
Cash paid for interest	$ 9,421	$ 10,293
Cash paid for income taxes	$ 14,148	$ 35,268

EXHIBIT 2-20C   CINEPLEX INC.'S 2013 CONSOLIDATED STATEMENTS OF OPERATIONS

Consolidated Statements of Operations
For the years ended December 31, 2013 and 2012

(expressed in thousands of Canadian dollars, except per share amounts)

	2013	2012 (note 2)
Revenues		
Box office	$ 665,306	$ 638,296
Concessions	350,353	329,332
Other	155,608	124,873
	1,171,267	1,092,501
Expenses		
Film cost	346,373	331,281
Cost of concessions	74,693	68,398
Depreciation and amortization	70,890	62,163
Loss (gain) on disposal of assets	4,372	(2,352)
(Gain) on acquisition of business (note 3 d)	—	(24,752)
Other costs (note 23)	551,819	495,537
Share of income of joint ventures	(3,850)	(3,263)
Interest expense	10,743	12,585
Interest income	(307)	(205)
	1,054,733	939,392
Income before income taxes	116,534	153,109
Provision for income taxes		
Current (note 10)	3,608	31,436
Deferred (note 10)	29,369	1,189
	32,977	32,625
Net income	$ 83,557	$ 120,484

EXHIBIT 2-20D   CINEPLEX INC.'S 2013 CONSOLIDATED STATEMENTS OF CHANGES IN EQUITY

Consolidated statements of changes in equity
For the years ended December 31, 2013 and 2012

(expressed in thousands of Canadian dollars)

	Share Capital (note 22)	Contributed Surplus (note 15)	Accumulated Other Comprehensive Loss	Deficit	Total
Balance - January 1, 2013	$ 847,235	$ 3,768	$ (1,142)	$ (102,547)	$ 747,314
Net income	—	—	—	83,557	83,557
Other comprehensive income (page 4)	—	—	(573)	286	(287)
Total comprehensive income			(573)	83,843	83,270
Dividends declared (note 16)	—	—	—	(88,619)	(88,619)
Long-term incentive plan obligation	248	—	—	—	248
Issuance of convertible debentures	4,471	—	—	—	4,471
Share option expense	—	1,588	—	—	1,588
Issuance of shares on exercise of options	1,457	(1,457)	—	—	—
Balance - December 31, 2013	$ 853,411	$ 3,899	$ (1,715)	$ (107,323)	$ 748,272

continued

EXHIBIT 2-20D CINEPLEX INC.'S 2013 CONSOLIDATED STATEMENTS OF CHANGES IN EQUITY (continued)

	Share Capital (note 22)	Contributed Surplus (note 15)	Accumulated Other Comprehensive Loss	Deficit	Total
Balance - January 1, 2012	$ 764,801	$ —	$ (2,723)	$ (140,469)	$ 621,609
Share option liabilities reclassified	—	6,850	—	—	6,850
Net income	—	—	—	120,484	120,484
Other comprehensive income (page 4)	—	—	1,581	(140)	1,441
Total comprehensive income			1,581	120,344	121,925
Dividends declared (note 16)	—	—	—	(81,572)	(81,572)
Long-term incentive plan obligation	(4,818)	—	—	—	(4,818)
Long-term incentive plan shares	6,471	—	—	—	6,471
Share option expense	—	2,071	—	—	2,071
Issuance of shares on exercise of options	5,873	(5,372)	—	—	501
Issuance of shares on conversion of debentures	75,844	219	—	—	76,063
Shares repurchased and cancelled	(936)	—	—	(850)	(1,786)
Balance - December 31, 2012	$847,235	$3,768	$(1,142)	$ (102,547)	$ 747,314

EXHIBIT 2-20E EXCERPT FROM CINEPLEX INC.'S 2013 ANNUAL REPORT

23. Other costs

	2013	2012 (note 2)
Employee salaries and benefits	$191,286	$169,304
Rent	127,745	117,840
Realty and occupancy taxes and maintenance fees	61,448	56,212
Utilities	25,423	22,941
Purchased services	41,191	35,225
Other inventories consumed	11,969	11,005
Repairs and maintenance	19,157	17,620
Office and operating supplies	13,026	10,739
Licences and franchise fees	12,937	9,237
Insurance	2,380	2,112
Advertising and promotion	24,256	23,374
Professional and consulting fees	4,088	5,191
Telecommunications and data	4,204	3,801
Bad debts	403	513
Equipment rental	2,569	2,058
Other costs	9,737	8,365
	$551,819	$495,537

Required:
a. Determine the amount of dividends *declared* during fiscal 2013. Where did you find this information?
b. How does the declaration of dividends affect the accounting equation?
c. Determine the amount of dividends *paid* during fiscal 2013. Where did you find this information?
d. How does the payment of dividends affect the accounting equation?
e. Given Cineplex Inc.'s cost of goods sold of $74,693 in 2013 and $68,398 in 2012, determine the gross margin on concession sales for the two years. Explain the results of your gross margin calculations.
f. What was Cineplex's cash flow pattern in 2013? Did it fit the "normal" pattern discussed in the chapter?
g. Refer to Cineplex Inc.'s "Other Costs" note 23. What are the largest two expenses? Why would these costs be expected in this line of business?

RI2-7 (Determination of items from a company's financial statements)

Required:

Find the annual report of a Canadian company in the retailing business and answer the following questions:

- a. How important is inventory relative to the other assets on the company's statement of financial position (or balance sheet)?
- b. Does the company finance its business primarily with debt (funds borrowed from creditors) or with equity (funds invested by owners)?
- c. Read through the management discussion and analysis (which was covered in Chapter 1) and determine whether there is any information there that is not included in the financial statements. If you were a shareholder, would you think the extra information is important? Why or why not?
- d. How many directors does the company have? What positions do they hold? Are any of them directors of other companies?

Cases

C2-1 Wroad Wrunner Courier Service

At the end of her first year of university, Nola Lam decided that she should start a business to help finance her education, so she set up her own courier service. She invested savings of $1,800 in the company, which she called Wroad Wrunner Ltd. In addition, her parents loaned the company $3,000 to help it get started. Since this was a business venture, Nola insisted on paying interest on this loan and her parents agreed to charge a rate of 6% per year.

Nola then negotiated the purchase of a used car for the business for $8,000. The company made a down payment of $3,000 on the car, and financed the remainder of the purchase price at an interest rate of 9% per year. Due to all of the kilometres that would be put on the car while it was used in the courier business, Nola estimated that the car could be sold at the end of the summer for $6,000.

Wroad Wrunner began operations on May 1, and continued until August 31. Although she did not keep any formal accounting records, at the end of the summer Nola put together the following additional information related to the business:

- 1. During the summer, the company made payments of $623 on the car, which included interest of $123 and principal of $500.
- 2. No payments (of either interest or principal) were made on the loan from her parents.
- 3. Nola paid herself a salary of $1,500 per month for the four months that the business operated.
- 4. Payments for other operating costs (including advertising, insurance, and gas) totalled $9,600. In addition, there were unpaid bills totalling $100 at the end of August.
- 5. Courier charges collected from customers totalled $19,200. In addition, customers still owed $300 for services performed in the last two weeks of August.
- 6. After the close of business on August 31, there was a balance of $4,694 in the company's bank account, plus a "float" of $83 in the car.

Required:

- a. Analyze the transactions that affected the business during the summer. Prepare a statement of income for Wroad Wrunner for the four-month period ending on August 31, and a statement of financial position on that date.
- b. Comment on the profitability of the business during its four-month period of operations. How much did Nola make from her venture during the summer?
- c. Comment on the financial position of the company on August 31. If Nola dissolves the business before she returns to university, will there be enough cash to pay off the liabilities?

C2-2 Daisy-Fresh Dry Cleaning

Daisy-Fresh Dry Cleaning is in the process of preparing its annual financial statements. The owner of the business, Petr Radmanovich, is not an accountant, but likes to prepare the financial statements himself. Most of the business transactions are straightforward and can be easily recorded; however, Petr is having trouble determining how to account for the following events that occurred during the year:

- 1. On January 1, the company purchased a three-year insurance policy for $3,000. Because the entire amount had to be paid when the policy took effect, Petr charged $3,000 to expense in the current year.
- 2. On July 1, the company bought a new dry-cleaning machine for $10,000. Although it is expected to have a five-year life, Petr thinks he would only get $2,000 for it if he sold it now, so he recorded an asset of $2,000 and an expense of $8,000.
- 3. On October 31, the company borrowed $10,000 from a bank. Since the loan does not have to be repaid until four years later, Petr does not think it should be reported as a payable on this year's statement of financial position.

4. No interest has to be paid on the loan until October 31 of next year, so Petr did not record any interest this year.

5. On December 31, the company declared and paid a dividend of $10,000. Petr recorded this payment as an expense.

Required:
Advise Petr as to how the above transactions should be recorded and reported in the financial statements for the current year.

C2-3 Mega Manufacturing

Mega Manufacturing has calculated the following financial ratios, based on the company's comparative financial statements for 2016 and 2015:

	2016	2015	Industry Average
Profit margin ratio	18%	20%	16%
Return on assets	10%	8%	12%
Return on equity	12%	10%	14%

Required:
Briefly explain what each of the ratios indicates, and comment on the company's performance during this two-year period.

C2-4 Canadian Cookies and Cakes Ltd.

One of the shareholders of the Canadian Cookies and Cakes Ltd. is considering selling her shares, which represent one-third of the company's outstanding shares. The company is preparing its financial statements, which will be used by the shareholder to help determine the value of her shares. The following transactions have occurred since the shop started operations at the beginning of this year:

1. The company borrowed $30,000 from the bank to help get the business started, and repaid $10,000 of this before year end. Shareholders also paid $30,000 for their shares when the company started.

2. Ingredients costing $42,000 were purchased on account, and 80% of these ingredients were used in goods that were baked and sold during the year. Before the end of the year, payments of $37,000 were made for these ingredients.

3. Baking ovens were rented for $12,000 cash, paid at the rate of $1,000 per month. At the end of the year, the company purchased its own ovens for $46,000 cash.

4. Employees earned wages of $30,000 during the year. The company withheld income taxes of $3,000 from their paycheques, which it will forward to the Canada Revenue Agency (CRA) early next year. In other words, although the employees' wages were $30,000, the company deducted income taxes and paid only the remaining $27,000 net amount to the employees; it will pay the $3,000 of income taxes directly to the CRA. (Note that these income taxes relate to the *employees'* earnings, not the company's earnings. Consequently, they are recorded as part of the company's wage expense, not as income taxes expense.)

5. Interest on the bank loan for the year totalled $1,600, but has not yet been paid.

6. Various other expenses totalled $15,000 for the year, but only $13,500 of this amount was paid before the end of the year.

7. After $98,000 was collected from the sale of goods (which was the full sales amount), the cash balance at the end of the year was $12,500, and net income of $5,800 was reported.

Required:
a. Show calculations to prove that the ending cash balance was $12,500 and the net income for the year was $5,800.

b. Prepare a statement of financial position for the Canadian Cookies and Cakes Ltd. as at the end of the year.

c. If the shareholder sells her one-third ownership interest in the company, what does the foregoing tell you regarding how much she should expect to get for her shares?

ENDNOTES

1. MEC 2012 Annual Report; MEC 2012 Accountability Report; Chris Strashok, "Mountain Equipment Co-op: A Co-operative Business Model," Community Research Connections, May 13, 2011.

2. Analogy shared by Professor Gordon Holyer, Vancouver Island University.

3. CPA Standards and Guidance Collection; Part 1 – International Financial Reporting Standards; The Conceptual Framework.

HUDSON'S BAY CO.
SINCE 1670 DEPUIS

CHAPTER

3 Double-Entry Accounting and The Accounting Cycle

CORE QUESTIONS
If you are able to answer the following questions, then you have achieved the related learning objectives.

LEARNING OBJECTIVES
After studying this chapter, you should be able to:

●●○ INTRODUCTION

- How does the double-entry accounting system work and how does it overcome the limitations of the template method?

1 Explain how the double-entry accounting system works, including how it overcomes the limitations of the template approach.

- What is the normal balance concept and how is it used?

2 Explain the normal balance concept and how it is used within the double-entry accounting system.

●●○ UNDERSTANDING THE ACCOUNTING CYCLE

- What are the steps in the accounting cycle?

3 Identify and explain the steps in the accounting cycle.

●●○ THE CHART OF ACCOUNTS

- What is the chart of accounts?
- Can companies change their chart of accounts and what are the implications if they do?

4 Explain the significance of a company's decisions regarding its chart of accounts and the implications of subsequent changes.

●●○ OPENING BALANCES

- What is the difference between permanent and temporary accounts?

5 Explain the difference between permanent and temporary accounts.

●●○ TRANSACTION ANALYSIS AND RECORDING

- How are transactions identified?
- How are transactions recorded in the general journal?
- Why are transactions also recorded in the general ledger?
- What is the purpose of preparing a trial balance?

6 Identify and record transactions in the general journal and general ledger.

●●○ ADJUSTING ENTRIES

- What are adjusting entries and why are they necessary?
- What is the purpose of preparing an adjusted trial balance?

7 Explain why adjusting entries are necessary and prepare them.

●●○ PREPARING FINANCIAL STATEMENTS AND CLOSING ENTRIES

- What are closing entries and why are they necessary?

8 Explain why closing entries are necessary and prepare them.

●●● Balancing the Books when Bartering

When the Hudson's Bay Company (HBC) was established under a royal charter from King Charles II in 1670, it had 18 shareholders who invested a total of £10,500. The company's fur-trading operations, which would eventually span the upper half of North America, were complicated by the lack of any monetary system. Instead, the company largely worked by bartering, trading things like blankets and kettles for furs.

For over 150 years, HBC valued items in units equivalent to one prime beaver pelt, called a "made beaver" (MB), and this became the standard of currency used in trading. For example, trappers could trade 11 MB for a gun, 3 MB for a yard of cloth, and 6 MB for a 3-gallon kettle. Even other furs were translated into MB. An otter or a fox pelt was worth two MB, whereas a marten was worth one third of an MB.

HBC required its chief factors, who commanded the company's trading posts, to record these transactions and maintain a complete set of accounts. Across the various trading posts, the company used standardized accounting practices, many of which are similar to those still in use 350 years later. The company required a journal and a ledger to be maintained at each post, together with inventory records and a reconciliation between the goods traded and the MBs received in exchange. These records were sent to HBC's London headquarters for review and to inform the company's decision-making for the next trading period.

Coming back to the company's earlier practice of bartering, it is worth noting that barter transactions should not result in profits, because goods of equivalent values are being exchanged. In spite of this, the accounting records of virtually all of HBC's trading posts reported an amount known as "overplus." This represented profits that resulted from traders altering the standard of trade in the company's favour, such as requiring 8 MB in exchange for a kettle rather than 6 MB. Overplus added to the company's profits from the eventual sale of the furs. Between 1670 and 1857, HBC produced profits of at least £20 million, some of which it returned to shareholders. While those initial 18 shareholders had to wait 15 years for their first dividend, on the strength of its profits, HBC paid dividends in 249 of the 314 years between its inception in 1670 and 1984!

HBC is the world's oldest commercial enterprise that still carries on its original line of business, operating over 300 stores under banners such as Hudson's Bay, Saks Fifth Avenue, Lord & Taylor, and Home Outfitters in Canada and the United States. Its sales in 2013 were $5.2 billion—equal to an untold number of made beavers. You can bet that keeping good accounting records has contributed to its success over nearly 350 years.[1]

INTRODUCTION

Now that you understand the basic accounting equation and can work through the analysis of some transactions, we are going to take you further into the practical side of accounting. We are going to show you how data are recorded in an accounting system so that organizations can easily extract information and summarize it into financial statements and other reports. Of course, today's technology makes financial record-keeping far easier than in the early days of the **Hudson's Bay Company**.

■ **LEARNING OBJECTIVE 1**
Explain how the double-entry accounting system works, including how it overcomes the limitations of the template approach.

How does the double-entry accounting system work and how does it overcome the limitations of the template method?

As we discussed in Chapter 2, recording transactions in a template or spreadsheet, with columns reflecting the basic accounting equation, is adequate for small entities with few transactions to record. However, it is cumbersome when large numbers of accounts and transactions are involved. To address this, accountants developed the **double-entry accounting system**. It is called this because it requires that each transaction be recorded in a way that affects at least two accounts, with the transaction amount recorded in *each* account. (In other words, the transaction amount is recorded twice, which is the "double" in the term *double-entry accounting*.) The total effects of these entries will be equal and offsetting. This is similar to what we did in the template method, which required that each line balance.

The most significant limitation of the template method is the number of columns that can be manageably used. This significantly limits the information that management can capture and analyze in managing the business. For example, an organization may have multiple types of inventory that it wishes to track and would need specific accounts (or columns) for each. Think of the bookstore at your university or college. At a minimum, management would want to track the major categories of inventory separately (such as new textbooks, digital textbooks, used textbooks, clothing, office supplies, and information technology). They may also want some of this information further broken down by program or faculty. Obviously, the number of accounts (or columns) would quickly become too large for a workable spreadsheet.

The double-entry accounting system overcomes this limitation by enabling companies to uses hundreds or even thousands of accounts to capture information at the level of detail required to manage the business effectively. It enables businesses to capture transaction details while making it easy to summarize information by account.

For Example
The level of detail required to manage the operations of a major Canadian university is significant. According to the director of financial services at Vancouver-based Simon Fraser University, the university has "8,500 cost centres that have detailed object accounts below them, so that translates into more than 100,000 general ledger accounts." Imagine trying to work with a spreadsheet having 100,000 columns![2]

■ LEARNING OBJECTIVE 2
Explain the normal balance concept and how it is used within the double-entry accounting system.

What is the normal balance concept and how is it used?

Before discussing the double-entry accounting system further, we have to learn about the **normal balance** concept. First, picture yourself as a crew member on a sailboat out on a local lake or bay. Your duties include working with the sails, hoisting them up and down and moving them from one side of the boat to the other. Your friend, the captain, loves to shout out orders referring to "port" or "starboard." If you aren't a regular sailor, you would likely be confused by these terms. Is the captain referring to the left side of the boat or the right side? If you don't understand, you probably can't follow the captain's orders and may even get knocked out of the boat by a sail boom that you had no idea was coming!

Just as sailors have invented their own terms for left (*port*) and right (*starboard*), so have accountants. Understanding what these mean is one of the keys to the double-entry accounting system. While you will not literally get hit by a sail boom while working with accounting information, it may feel as though you have been figuratively knocked overboard if you don't understand what the terms *debit* and *credit* mean.

While these terms are the accounting equivalent of left and right, you are likely wondering "left and right of what?" The easiest way to explain this is to revisit the accounting equation, through which we will draw a big "T" to divide it in half as follows:

TAKE**5**

ASSETS	LIABILITIES + SHAREHOLDERS' EQUITY
"LEFT"	"RIGHT"
DEBIT	CREDIT
DR	CR

KEY POINTS
- Asset accounts normally have a debit balance.
- Liabilities and shareholders' equity accounts normally have a credit balance.

This illustrates the normal balance concept. Basically, accountants say that accounts on the left side of the T (asset accounts) *normally* have a **debit** balance, while accounts on the right side of the T (liabilities and shareholders' equity accounts) *normally* have a **credit** balance.˙

Using the normal balance concept, we can determine whether an account normally has a debit or a credit balance. Once we know this, we will use the account's normal balance to increase it and do the opposite to decrease it. Let's look at a couple of examples.

- Cash is an asset. It is on the left side of the T and, therefore, it normally has a debit balance. Therefore, to record an increase in the Cash account, we would debit it. To record a decrease, we would do the opposite: we would credit it. At the end of a period, when we tally up the debits and credits, we would expect there to be more debits than credits, because this account normally has a debit balance.

- Accounts payable is a liability. It is on right side of the T and, therefore, it normally has a credit balance. Therefore, to record an increase in the Accounts Payable account, we would credit it. To record a decrease, we would do the opposite: we would debit it. At the end of a period, when we tally up the debits and credits, we would expect there to be more credits than debits, because this account normally has a credit balance.

Under the template system, each account had its own column in which the transactions affecting it were recorded. These columns were organized just like the accounting equation; that is, asset accounts came first, then the liability accounts, and finally the shareholders' equity accounts. When thinking about the structure of the double-entry accounting system further, it helps to picture a box of playing cards, organized by suit (hearts, clubs, spades, and diamonds) and order (such as 2, 3, 4, 5 or Jack, Queen, King, Ace). If you were looking for a specific card, say the 8 of clubs, it is easy to find it within the organized box

˙Accountants use *DR* to abbreviate for debit and *CR* to abbreviate for credit. These abbreviations stem from the first and last letters of the old English terms *debitor* and *creditor* (much like *Mr.* is used as an abbreviation for *Mister*). While the term *debitor* is seldom used any more, *creditor* is still commonly used, as are the abbreviations for both.

of cards. Continuing with this analogy, picture each account in the double-entry accounting system having its own card, with the box of cards organized by type of account; that is, asset cards coming first, followed by the cards for the liability accounts and then the cards for the shareholders' equity accounts. Within each type of account, the cards will also be in order of **liquidity**. That is, the most current assets will come before the non-current assets and the current liabilities will come before the non-current liabilities. Just as with the deck of cards, if we know which account we are looking for, it is easy to find it within the box of cards. The box of cards is known as the **general ledger** (or **G/L**), so each account is referred to as a **general ledger account**. Each card will have the account name written on top of a big T as follows:

All of the transactions affecting that account are recorded as debits or credits on that particular card. For example, since cash is an asset that normally has a debit balance, transactions increasing the account are recorded on the debit side (or left side), while transactions that decrease the account are recorded on the credit side (or right side). After all of the transactions for the period are recorded, each side is totalled, but the account is expected to end up with a net debit balance (that is, with more debits than credits).

Another key difference between the template method and the double-entry accounting system is that there are cards for revenue accounts, expense accounts, and the Dividends Declared account. You will recall that transactions affecting these accounts were recorded in the retained earnings column in the template method. This is not the case under the double-entry accounting system. Instead, we will use specific accounts for them. At the end of each accounting period, we will transfer the balances of the Revenues, Expenses, and Dividends Declared accounts to the Retained Earnings account. This is the closing entry process, which we will discuss later in the chapter. For now, it is important to understand that we can no longer make entries directly to the Retained Earnings account. The ability to easily track revenues and expenses is essential for managing any business and this is one of the significant advantages of the double-entry accounting system.

Given that each revenue account, expense account, and dividends declared account will have its own card, it is important to understand what their normal balances are. The easiest way to think of this is to reflect on the impact each of these has on retained earnings. In Chapter 2, we discussed the following:

From this we can deduce the following:
- Revenues ultimately increase Retained Earnings because they increase net income, which increases retained earnings.
- Expenses ultimately decrease Retained Earnings because they decrease net income and a lower net income means lower retained earnings.
- Dividends declared decrease Retained Earnings because they are a distribution of retained earnings.

If we know the above and we know that Retained Earnings normally has a credit balance (that is, it is on the right side of the "T"), then we also know the following.
- Revenue accounts will normally have a credit balance. This is because revenue accounts increase Retained Earnings and Retained Earnings normally has a credit balance, so it must be credited to increase it.
- Expense accounts will normally have a debit balance. This is because expense accounts decrease Retained Earnings and Retained Earnings normally has a credit balance, so it must be debited to decrease it.
- Dividends Declared will normally have a debit balance. This is because Dividends Declared decreases Retained Earnings and Retained Earnings normally has a credit balance, so it must be debited to decrease it.

Exhibit 3-1 presents a visual summary of the normal balance rules.

HELPFUL HINT
Remember that increases in accounts *are recorded in the same way as the account balances:*
- Asset accounts normally have debit balances; increases in assets are also recorded as debits.
- Liability and shareholders' equity accounts normally have credit balances; increases in liabilities and shareholders' equity are also recorded as credits.

KEY POINTS
- Revenue accounts normally have a credit balance.
- Expense accounts normally have a debit balance.
- The Dividends Declared account normally has a debit balance.

Exhibit 3-1 Normal Balance Illustration

TAKE**5**

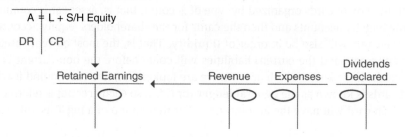

Exhibit 3-2 presents an expanded version of the normal balance illustration, with the specific rules for each type of account, including Revenues, Expenses, and Dividends Declared.

Exhibit 3-2 Expanded Normal Balance Illustration

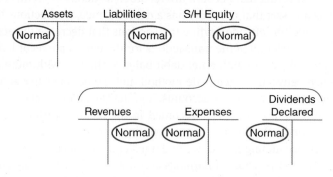

UNDERSTANDING THE ACCOUNTING CYCLE

■ **LEARNING OBJECTIVE 3**
Identify and explain
the steps in the
accounting cycle.

What are the steps in the accounting cycle?

We are now ready to look at the whole system by which transactions are first measured, recorded, and summarized, and then communicated to users through financial statements. This system is called the **accounting cycle** because it is repeated each accounting period.

Exhibit 3-3 illustrates the complete cycle. Each of the steps will be discussed in the subsections that follow.

Exhibit 3-3 The Accounting Cycle

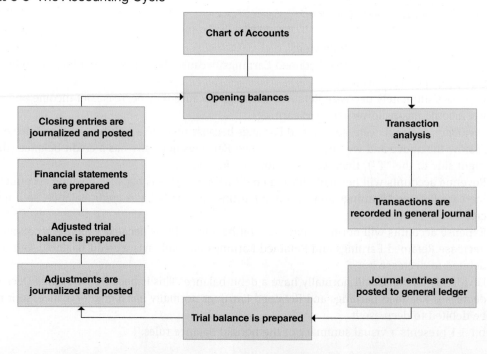

As we proceed through a discussion of the accounting cycle, we will demonstrate each stage by revisiting the Sample Company Ltd. ("SCL") example that we used in Chapter 2. In that chapter, we analyzed and recorded SCL's January transactions using the template method and then prepared the company's financial statements for the month of January. In this chapter, we will use these same transactions to explain how they are recorded within the double-entry accounting system and to illustrate each of the steps in the accounting cycle. You can refer back to the transaction analysis in Chapter 2 for any of the transactions if needed as we learn how to record them within the double-entry accounting system.

A system for maintaining accounting records can be as simple as a notebook, in which everything is processed by hand, or as sophisticated as a computerized system. We will use a simple manual system to illustrate the accounting cycle. However, the same underlying processes apply to any accounting system, no matter how simple or sophisticated it is.

THE CHART OF ACCOUNTS

What is the chart of accounts?

Accounting systems are information systems. When a company is formed, one of the most critical initial decisions management makes as they set up the accounting system is to determine what information they need to manage the business. They would ask themselves the following questions:

■ **LEARNING OBJECTIVE 4**
Explain the significance of a company's decisions regarding its chart of accounts and the implications of subsequent changes.

- What information is needed to make well-informed decisions?
- What information is needed by outside users?
- What information is needed to satisfy the applicable financial reporting standards?

The information needs of managers differ, so companies in the same type of business will develop their own unique information systems and capture different information or summarize information in different ways.

Each type of information that management wishes to capture requires its own account in which it can be recorded. In Chapter 2, each column within the template was considered an account and all of the transactions affecting that account were recorded in that column. As we discussed above, the double-entry accounting system also uses accounts, but rather than columns, there are cards (although they are generally virtual), one for each account.

The list of all of a company's accounts is known as its **chart of accounts**. Establishing the chart of accounts is the starting point for a company's initial accounting cycle. However, the chart of accounts is dynamic and can be changed. As a company grows, management may need to add different types of accounts, such as when different types of property, plant, and equipment are purchased or when new types of products and services are offered to customers. Although there are certain account titles that are commonly used, an account can be given any name that makes sense to the company and describes the account's purpose. In most accounting systems, each of the accounts in the chart of accounts would also be identified by a number that indicates the sequence of the accounts and makes it easier to record transactions. In this textbook, accounts are designated by their names and not by account numbers.

Exhibit 3-4 shows the chart of accounts for Sample Company Ltd. It consists of all the accounts that were used to record SCL's transactions in Chapter 2. There is an account for each column that was used in the template method. There are also accounts for Revenues, Expenses, and Dividends Declared because transactions affecting these accounts will no longer be recorded directly to Retained Earnings.

Notice that the accounts are listed in the chart of accounts in the order in which they will appear on the financial statements. Accounts are kept in this order so that it is easy to locate them in the general ledger and easier to prepare the financial statements. If account numbers are assigned to the accounts, a different set of account numbers will usually be assigned to each section of the financial statements. For example, many companies using four-digit account numbers will assign numbers between 1000 and 1999 to assets, 2000–2999 to liabilities, 3000–3999 to shareholders' equity, 4000–4999 to revenues, 5000–5999 to expenses, and so on.

Exhibit 3-4 Sample Company Limited's Chart of Accounts

Assets

Cash

Accounts Receivable

Inventory

Prepaid Expenses

Equipment

Land

Liabilities

Accounts Payable

Interest Payable

Bank Loan Payable

Shareholders' Equity

Common Shares

Retained Earnings

Revenues

Sales Revenue

Expenses

Cost of Goods Sold

Wages Expense

Rent Expense

Utilities Expense

Depreciation Expense

Insurance Expense

Interest Expense

Dividends Declared

Can companies change their chart of accounts and what are the implications if they do?

Yes, companies can and do make changes to their chart of accounts. Companies can add new accounts when they enter into new types of operations, open new locations, wish to capture information at a different level of detail, and so on. They can also delete accounts that are no longer required. Changes to permanent accounts (assets, liabilities, and shareholders' equity accounts) within the chart of accounts can be made anytime. However, changes to temporary accounts (revenue and expense accounts) are generally made only at the beginning of an accounting period. This is because management normally wants to capture annual data related to the company's revenues and expenses. Introducing new revenue and expense accounts during a cycle would require the company to go back and adjust the accounting for any such revenues or expenses already recorded in the period or else it would have incomplete information. Of course, if the revenue or expense account being added is related to a new activity, this is not a problem.

OPENING BALANCES

■ LEARNING OBJECTIVE 5
Explain the difference between permanent and temporary accounts.

What is the difference between permanent and temporary accounts?

When a company begins operations, none of its accounts will have an opening balance. This will not be the case once a company completes its first accounting cycle because all of the accounts on its statement of financial position (its assets, liabilities, and shareholders' equity) will have balances at the end of the cycle. These ending balances will become the opening balances for the next cycle; that is, the cash that the company had at the end of its accounting cycle will be the cash it begins the next cycle with. Accounts with balances that carry over from one period to the next are known as **permanent accounts**.

Management normally wants to track its revenues and expenses each period (such as each year) in order to assess things such as the profitability of operations and the outcome of their decisions. They are less interested in cumulative numbers, such as sales revenues earned or total wages paid during the life of the company. As a result, it is necessary for the balances in all the accounts that appear on the statement of income (that is, all revenues and expenses) to be "reset" at the end of each accounting cycle or period. Accounts with balances that are closed at the end of each accounting period are known as **temporary accounts**. The amount of dividends declared is also tracked period to period and the Dividends Declared account is also a temporary account. The balance in each temporary account is transferred

KEY POINTS

- Asset, liabilities, and shareholders' equity accounts are permanent accounts.
- Revenue, expense, and dividends declared accounts are temporary accounts.

to retained earnings, so that it starts each accounting cycle with zero or nil balances. This transfer/reset process is accomplished through closing entries. These entries are discussed a little later in the chapter.

TRANSACTION ANALYSIS AND RECORDING

How are transactions identified?

■ **LEARNING OBJECTIVE 6**
Identify and record transactions in the general journal and general ledger.

The next step in the accounting cycle is transaction analysis. This involves identifying whether an event or transaction has occurred and, if so, determining its effects on the company's accounts.

Evidence of a transaction or event is usually some sort of "source document"—a document that is received or created by the company indicating that a transaction that needs to be recorded has happened. Examples of source documents include invoices, cheques, cash register tapes, bank deposit slips, and shipping documents.

When a transaction or event has occurred, the accountant must analyze it to determine what accounts have been affected and how the transaction should be recorded in the accounting system. We introduced this phase of the process in Chapter 2, where we analyzed the effects of various transactions on the basic accounting equation and recorded the results by entering positive and negative amounts in the template columns. In this chapter—and throughout the remainder of this book—we will analyze the effects of transactions to see how they should be recorded as debits and credits in a company's accounts.

How are transactions recorded in the general journal?

After an accountant has decided how to record transactions, appropriate entries must be made in the accounting system. The initial entries are usually made in the **general journal**. The journal is a chronological listing of all the events that are recorded in the accounting system. It is similar to the diary or travel journal that many people keep of their daily life or travels. A journal could be as simple as a book in which a chronological list of transactions is recorded, but most organizations' journals are computerized. Each entry in the journal shows the effects of a transaction on the company's accounts and is called a **journal entry**.

Journal entries are always dated and are normally numbered sequentially. Then, the names of the accounts affected by the transaction, and the amounts involved, are listed. The accounts being debited are listed first, followed by the accounts being credited. The credit portions are indented. Finally, an explanation of the transaction is generally included for future reference.

In this book, we will not include explanations with each journal entry because they would just repeat the wording in the question. As such, the format we will use to record journal entries is:

KEY POINTS
• Transactions are initially recorded in the general journal.
• Subsequently, they are posted to the general ledger.

BASIC JOURNAL ENTRY FORMAT		
Date and/or	DR Name of Account	Amount debited
entry number	CR Name of Account	Amount credited

As illustrated above, when journal entries are made, the customary practice is to list the accounts that are being debited before the accounts that are being credited, and to indent the accounts that are being credited. Of course, each journal entry must keep the accounting system balanced. As such, the total debits must equal the total credits. Also, the dollar signs are omitted from journal entries; in this text, assume all amounts in journal entries are in dollars.

We will now illustrate the process of analyzing transactions and recording them as journal entries by working through SCL's January transactions (see Exhibit 3-5). Each transaction will be presented and analyzed to determine what accounts are affected and whether they should be debited or credited. Then the journal entry to record the transaction will be presented. You should study this material carefully to ensure that you understand how debits and credits are applied and how journal entries are used to record transactions in an accounting system.

Exhibit 3-5 SCL's Transactions for January 2016

#	Date	Description
1	Jan. 1	SCL issued 10,000 common shares in exchange for $250,000 cash.
2	Jan. 1	To raise additional financing, SCL borrowed $100,000 from its bank. The loan principal is due in three years, while the interest rate on the loan is 6% per year. The interest is payable every three months.
3	Jan. 1	The company rented a retail location, paying $1,100 in rent for the month of January.
4	Jan. 1	The company paid $65,000 to purchase equipment.
5	Jan. 1	SCL paid $1,800 cash for a one-year insurance policy covering the new equipment for the period January 1–December 31.
6	Jan. 6	SCL purchased some land for $180,000 on which it plans to build a warehouse in the future.
7	Jan. 10	The company bought $23,000 of inventory from suppliers on account. (That is, SCL will pay for the goods at a later date.)
8	Jan. 12	SCL sold products to customers for $34,000, of which $21,000 was received in cash and the balance was on account. (That is, SCL's customers will pay at a later date.) The products that were sold had cost SCL $17,000.
9	Jan. 20	SCL received $11,000 from its customers as payments on their accounts that originated from the sale on January 12.
10	Jan. 22	The company made payments of $13,500 to its suppliers, settling part of the account that originated from the purchase on January 10.
11	Jan. 25	SCL paid monthly utility costs of $1,900.
12	Jan. 26	SCL paid advertising costs for the month of $2,200.
13	Jan. 28	SCL paid $2,900 in wages to its employees for the month of January.
14	Jan. 31	Dividends in the amount of $400 were declared by SCL's board of directors and paid.
15	Jan. 31	SCL's accountant determined that the depreciation expense on the company's equipment was $850 per month.
16	Jan. 31	SCL's insurance expense was recorded for January.
17	Jan. 31	SCL recorded the interest expense on the bank loan for the month. Although the principal of the loan does not have to be repaid for three years, the company is incurring interest expense each month that the loan is outstanding.

Transaction 1: Issuing Shares for Cash

SCL issued 10,000 common shares in exchange for $250,000 cash.

ANALYSIS OF TRANSACTION
Assets (specifically, Cash) **increased** by $250,000
Shareholders' Equity (specifically, Common Shares) **increased** by $250,000

This analysis must be translated into debits and credits. As we have learned, asset accounts normally have a debit balance; therefore, an increase to the Cash account is recorded as a debit. Shareholders' equity accounts normally have a credit balance; therefore, the increase to the Common Shares account is recorded as a credit.

Jan. 1	DR Cash	250,000	
	CR Common Shares		250,000

From this transaction, we can see that the total amount debited in the transaction equals the total amount credited. This is required in order to keep the accounting records in balance.

Transaction 2: Taking Out a Bank Loan

To raise additional financing, SCL borrowed $100,000 from its bank. The loan principal is due in three years, while the interest rate on the loan is 6% per year. The interest is payable every three months.

ANALYSIS OF TRANSACTION
Assets (specifically, Cash) **increased** by $100,000
Liabilities (specifically, Bank Loan Payable) **increased** by $100,000

As asset accounts normally have a debit balance, the increase to the Cash account is recorded as a debit. Liability accounts normally have a credit balance; therefore, the increase to the Bank Loan Payable account is recorded as a credit.

| Jan. 1 | DR Cash | 100,000 | |
| | CR Bank Loan Payable | | 100,000 |

Transaction 3: Paying Rent for the Month

The company rented a retail location, paying $1,100 in rent for the month of January.

ANALYSIS OF TRANSACTION
Assets (specifically, Cash) **decreased** by $1,100
Expenses (specifically, Rent Expense) **increased** by $1,100

As asset accounts normally have a debit balance, a decrease to the Cash account is recorded as a credit. Since they ultimately reduce retained earnings, expense accounts normally have a debit balance. Therefore, the increase to the Rent Expense account is recorded as a debit.

| Jan. 1 | DR Rent Expense | 1,100 | |
| | CR Cash | | 1,100 |

Transaction 4: Purchasing Equipment

The company paid $65,000 to purchase equipment.

ANALYSIS OF TRANSACTION
Assets (specifically, Equipment) **increased** by $65,000
Assets (specifically, Cash) **decreased** by $65,000

Asset accounts normally have a debit balance. Therefore, the Equipment account must be debited to record the increase (the new equipment) and the Cash account must be credited (that is, the opposite of its normal balance) to record the decrease.

| Jan. 1 | DR Equipment | 65,000 | |
| | CR Cash | | 65,000 |

Transaction 5: Purchasing Insurance Coverage

SCL paid $1,800 cash for a one-year insurance policy covering the new equipment for the period January 1 to December 31.

ANALYSIS OF TRANSACTION
Assets (specifically, Cash) **decreased** by $1,800
Assets (specifically, Prepaid Expenses) **increased** by $1,800

Asset accounts normally have a debit balance. Therefore, the Prepaid Expenses account must be debited to record the increase and the Cash account must be credited (that is, the opposite of its normal balance) to record the decrease.

Jan. 1	DR Prepaid Expenses	1,800	
	CR Cash		1,800

Transaction 6: Purchasing Land

SCL purchased some land for $180,000 on which it plans to build a warehouse in the future.

ANALYSIS OF TRANSACTION
Assets (specifically, Cash) **decreased** by $180,000
Assets (specifically, Land) **increased** by $180,000

Asset accounts normally have a debit balance. Therefore, the Land account must be debited to record the increase (the new land) and the Cash account must be credited (that is, the opposite of its normal balance) to record the decrease.

Jan. 6	DR Land	180,000	
	CR Cash		180,000

Transaction 7: Purchasing Inventory

The company bought $23,000 of inventory from suppliers on account. (That is, SCL will pay for the goods at a later date.)

ANALYSIS OF TRANSACTION
Assets (specifically, Inventory) **increased** by $23,000
Liabilities (specifically, Accounts Payable) **increased** by $23,000

Asset accounts normally have a debit balance. Therefore, the Inventory account must be debited to record the increase (the additional inventory). Liabilities normally have a credit balance. Therefore, the Accounts Payable account must be credited to record the increase.

Jan. 6	DR Inventory	23,000	
	CR Accounts Payable		23,000

Transaction 8: Selling Products to Customers

SCL sold products to customers for $34,000, of which $21,000 was received in cash and the balance was on account. (That is, SCL's customers will pay at a later date.) The products that were sold had cost SCL $17,000.

ANALYSIS OF TRANSACTION	
Part 1	**Assets** (specifically, Cash and Accounts Receivable) **increased** by $34,000
	Revenues (specifically, Sales Revenue) **increased** by $34,000
Part 2	**Assets** (specifically, Inventory) **decreased** by $17,000
	Expenses (specifically, Cost of Goods Sold) **increased** by $17,000

As discussed in Chapter 2, when a company sells products to customers, it is useful to separate the transaction into two parts. Part one is to account for the sales revenue and the cash and/or accounts receivable that flow into the company as a result. Part two is to account for the inventory that has been provided to the customer and has become an expense (known as cost of goods sold) to the company.

For part one, because asset accounts normally have a debit balance, the Cash and Accounts Receivable accounts must each be debited to record the increases in both accounts. Revenue accounts normally have a credit balance because they ultimately increase retained earnings. Therefore, the Sales Revenue account must be credited.

For part two, expense accounts, like Cost of Goods Sold, normally have a debit balance because they ultimately reduce retained earnings. Asset accounts like Inventory normally have a debit balance, so this account must be credited to reduce it to reflect the cost of the goods that have been removed from inventory and provided to customers.

Jan. 6	DR Cash	21,000	
	DR Accounts Receivable	13,000	
	CR Sales Revenue		34,000
Jan. 6	DR Cost of Goods Sold	17,000	
	CR Inventory		17,000

Notice that the journal entry for part one affects three accounts. However, the total of the two debits (21,000 and 13,000) is equal to the amount of the credit entry (34,000), so the entry as a whole balances. This illustrates the fact that, although every journal entry must have at least one debit and one credit, a journal entry can have any number of debit and credit parts, as long as the sum of the amounts debited is equal to the sum of the amounts credited. The term **compound journal entry** is used for a journal entry that affects more than two accounts.

Transaction 9: Collecting Payments from Customers

SCL received $11,000 from its customers as payments on their accounts that originated from the sale on January 12.

ANALYSIS OF TRANSACTION
Assets (specifically, Cash) **increased** by $11,000
Assets (specifically, Accounts Receivable) **decreased** by $11,000

Asset accounts normally have a debit balance. Therefore, the Cash account must be debited to record the increase. The opposite must be done to the Accounts Receivable account to reduce it. Therefore, the account must be credited.

| Jan. 12 | DR Cash | 11,000 | |
| | CR Accounts Receivable | | 11,000 |

Transaction 10: Paying Suppliers

The company made payments of $13,500 to its suppliers, settling part of the account that originated from the purchase on January 10.

ANALYSIS OF TRANSACTION
Assets (specifically, Cash) **decreased** by $13,500
Liabilities (specifically, Accounts Payable) **decreased** by $13,500

Asset accounts normally have a debit balance. Therefore, to reduce the Cash account, it must be credited to record the decrease. Liabilities normally have a credit balance, so the opposite must be done to the Accounts Payable account to reduce it. Therefore, the account must be debited.

Jan. 22	DR Accounts Payable	13,500	
	CR Cash		13,500

Transaction 11: Paying Utility Costs

SCL paid monthly utility costs of $1,900.

ANALYSIS OF TRANSACTION
Assets (specifically, Cash) **decreased** by $1,900
Expenses (specifically, Utilities Expense) **increased** by $1,900

Asset accounts normally have a debit balance. Therefore, to reduce the Cash account, it must be credited to record the decrease. Expenses normally have a debit balance because they reduce retained earnings. As such, the Utilities Expense account must be debited.

Jan. 25	DR Utilities Expense	1,900	
	CR Cash		1,900

Transaction 12: Paying Advertising Costs

SCL paid advertising costs for the month of $2,200.

ANALYSIS OF TRANSACTION
Assets (specifically, Cash) **decreased** by $2,200
Expenses (specifically, Advertising Expense) **increased** by $2,200

Asset accounts normally have a debit balance. Therefore, to reduce the Cash account, it must be credited to record the decrease. Expenses normally have a debit balance because they reduce retained earnings. As such, the Advertising Expense account must be debited.

Jan. 26	DR Advertising Expense	2,200	
	CR Cash		2,200

Transaction 13: Paying Wages to Employees

SCL paid $2,900 in wages to its employees for the month of January.

ANALYSIS OF TRANSACTION
Assets (specifically, Cash) **decreased** by $2,900
Expenses (specifically, Wages Expense) **increased** by $2,900

Asset accounts normally have a debit balance. Therefore, to reduce the Cash account, it must be credited to record the decrease. Expenses normally have a debit balance because they reduce retained earnings. As such, the Wages Expense account must be debited.

| Jan. 28 | DR Wages Expense | 2,200 | |
| | CR Cash | | 2,200 |

Transaction 14: Declaring and Paying Dividends

Dividends in the amount of $400 were declared by SCL's board of directors and paid.

ANALYSIS OF TRANSACTION
Assets (specifically, Cash) **decreased** by $400
Shareholders' Equity (specifically, Dividends Declared) **decreased** by $400

Asset accounts normally have a debit balance. Therefore, to reduce the Cash account, it must be credited to record the decrease. The declaration of dividends reduces retained earnings, so this account normally has a debit balance. As such, the Dividends Declared account must be debited.

| Jan. 31 | DR Dividends Declared | 400 | |
| | CR Cash | | 400 |

Transaction 15: Recording Depreciation of Equipment

SCL's accountant determined that the depreciation expense on the company's equipment was $850 per month.

ANALYSIS OF TRANSACTION
Contra-asset accounts (specifically, Accumulated Depreciation, Equipment) **increased** by $850
Expenses (specifically, Depreciation Expense) **increased** by $850

As discussed in the previous chapter, companies allocate the cost of property, plant, and equipment to those periods in which the asset is expected to help generate revenues. We learned about the straight-line depreciation method, which allocates a consistent portion of the asset's cost each period. In Chapter 2, the depreciation expense for the period was recorded directly to the Equipment account as a reduction in that column. While the net effect of doing this is correct, it is not what is done in practice. Instead of reducing the Equipment account, accountants use an account called **Accumulated Depreciation**. This is a **contra-asset account**, which is an asset account, but its normal balance is contrary or opposite to what an asset account would normally have. As such, a contra-asset account normally has a credit balance rather than a debit balance. Using this account to record the cumulative portion of the asset's costs that have been expensed allows accountants to leave the asset's original cost intact in the Equipment account. This enables financial statement users to assess the relative age of a company's property, plant, and equipment by comparing the asset's costs with the amount recorded in its related contra-asset account. We will explore this concept further in Chapter 8. For now, it is important to know that we will make entries in a property, plant, and equipment account only when an asset is purchased or sold, but not when recording depreciation.

Property, plant, and equipment are carried on the statement of financial position at their **carrying amount**. Carrying amount is the cost of the property, plant, and equipment less the accumulated depreciation on that asset. It represents the portion of the asset's cost that has yet to be expensed. It does *not* represent the asset's market value (the amount for which it could be sold). It is useful to view carrying amount as shown in Exhibit 3-6.

KEY POINTS
- Accumulated Depreciation is a contra-asset account.
- Its normal balance is credit.
- The carrying amount of property, plant, and equipment is its cost less accumulated depreciation.

Exhibit 3-6 Carrying Amount

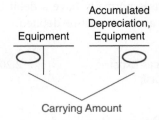

Carrying Amount

In terms of recording the journal entry for depreciation expense, we will debit the Depreciation Expense account because expense accounts normally have a debit balance. The normal balance of a contra-asset account is a credit, so we will credit the Accumulated Depreciation, Equipment account.

| Jan. 31 | DR Depreciation Expense | 850 | |
| | CR Accumulated Depreciation, Equipment | | 850 |

Transaction 16: Recording Insurance Expense

SCL's insurance expense was recorded for January.

ANALYSIS OF TRANSACTION
Assets (specifically, Prepaid Expenses) **decreased** by $150
Expenses (specifically, Insurance Expense) **decreased** by $150

Asset accounts normally have a debit balance. Therefore, to reduce the Prepaid Expenses account, it must be credited. Expenses normally have a debit balance because they reduce retained earnings. As such, the Insurance Expense account must be debited.

| Jan. 31 | DR Insurance Expense | 150 | |
| | CR Prepaid Expenses | | 150 |

Transaction 17: Recording Interest Expense

SCL recorded the interest expense on the bank loan for the month. Although the principal of the loan does not have to be repaid for three years, the company is incurring interest expense each month that the loan is outstanding.

ANALYSIS OF TRANSACTION
Liabilities (specifically, Interest Payable) **increased** by $500
Expenses (specifically, Interest Expense) **decreased** by $500

Liabilities normally have a credit balance. Therefore, to increase the Interest Payable account, it must be credited. Expenses normally have a debit balance because they reduce retained earnings. As such, the Interest Expense account must be debited.

| Jan. 31 | DR Interest Expense | 500 | |
| | CR Interest Payable | | 500 |

This completes the journal entries required to record SCL's transactions for January 2015 in the company's general journal. These journal entries are an example of how companies initially record their transactions. While companies need the detailed information that is captured in the general journal, they also require information at a summary level.

Let's continue to think of a company's general journal as being similar to a tourist's travel journal. We can visualize how the entries in the travel journal would provide the details of each art gallery or museum visited

during the trip. However, if the traveller wanted to know how many galleries or museums they had visited during their trip, they would need to flip through the journal and count up the number of entries in which visits to galleries and museums were recorded. This may not be too difficult on a short trip, but the longer their travels, the longer it would take to obtain the information. This is exactly the same for companies when they require summary information. For example, while they want to record the details of each individual sale, they also want to know their total sales number. Summarizing the information from the general journal is known as posting to the general ledger (or *posting*) and is the next step in the accounting cycle.

Why are transactions also recorded in the general ledger?

While the general journal provides an important chronological record of the effects of each transaction, companies require summarized information. For example, if a manager wanted to know the balance in the Cash account, the accountant would have to take the beginning balance of Cash and add or subtract all the journal entries that affected Cash. To prepare financial statements, the accountant would have to go through this process for all of the accounts in order to determine their ending balances. If the company had hundreds or thousands of journal entries, this would be extremely time-consuming and inefficient. Therefore, to provide more efficient access to information about the cumulative effects of transactions on individual accounts, the next step in the accounting cycle transfers or posts the data in the journal to the accounts in the general ledger.

Earlier in the chapter, we discussed using the analogy of a box of cards for the general ledger. We noted that each account would have its own card and that the debits and credits affecting an account would be recorded on its card. These would then be totalled at the end of each period and an ending debit or credit balance would be determined for each account. The process of transferring the information from the journal entries to the ledger accounts is known as **posting**.

Each account in the ledger represents a separate, specific T account, and includes the account name (and its number, if applicable), its beginning balance, all of the postings that affected the account during the period, and its ending balance. Each posting includes the transaction date and number, as well as the amount debited or credited. Including the date and transaction number enables users to trace the amount posted to the related journal entry and, thus, to the transaction details.

The posting process itself is very mechanical and, while we will not focus on it, it is important that you have a basic understanding of it. As such, let's look at how the January transactions affecting SCL's Cash account are posted to the company's Cash account. This is shown in Exhibit 3-7.

Exhibit 3-7 SCL's Cash Account after the January Transactions have been Posted

Cash

Opening Bal.	Jan. 1	-			
Entry #1	Jan. 1	250,000			
Entry #2	Jan. 1	100,000			
			1,100	Jan. 1	Entry #3
			65,000	Jan. 1	Entry #4
			1,800	Jan. 1	Entry #5
			180,000	Jan. 6	Entry #6
Entry #8a	Jan. 12	21,000			
Entry #9	Jan. 20	11,000			
			13,500	Jan. 22	Entry #10
			1,900	Jan. 25	Entry #11
			2,200	Jan. 26	Entry #12
			2,900	Jan. 28	Entry #13
			400	Jan. 31	Entry #14
Ending Bal.		113,200			

As Cash is an asset, it normally has a debit balance. To determine the ending balance of the Cash account, we would add all of the debits posted to the account to its opening balance and subtract all of the credits posted to the account. Because SCL began operations in January, the account had no opening balance. The total debits posted to the account amounted to $382,000, while the total credits posted to the account amounted to $268,800. The difference between these two amounts gives us the account's ending balance of $113,200.

As a result of the posting references, a user can determine the details for any of the postings to the account. For example, if they want to determine what the $180,000 cash payment on January 6 was related to, they can go to the general journal and look at entry 6. Then they can see the cash was spent to purchase land.

Posting to the ledger can be done daily, weekly, monthly, or at any frequency desired. The timing of the postings is determined to some extent by management's (or the shareholders') need for up-to-date information. If managers need to know the balance in a particular account, say Cash, on a daily basis, then the postings have to be done at least daily. If management needs to know the amount of cash available on an hourly basis, then the postings have to be done at least hourly. Computerized accounting systems can post journal entries instantly, so that the information in the company's general ledger is always up to date. Other computer systems collect journal entries in batches and post them all at the same time (for example, twice a day, after they have been reviewed by management).

At this point, it is important to note that a system consisting only of journal entries would make it difficult for managers to know the balances in the accounts. On the other hand, a system of only ledger accounts, without the original journal entries, would make it difficult to understand the sources of the amounts in the accounts. Accounting systems need both journal entries and ledger accounts in order to collect information in a way that makes it readily accessible and as useful as possible.

HELPFUL HINT

Do not confuse a *trial balance* with a *statement of financial position*. A trial balance lists the balances in *all* the accounts, while a statement of financial position (balance sheet) includes only the asset, liability, and shareholders' equity accounts.

What is the purpose of preparing a trial balance?

The **trial balance** is a listing of all the account balances in the general ledger at a specific point in time. The final balances of each account are listed, with the accounts having final debit balances in one column and accounts having final credit balances in another. A check can then be done to ensure that the total of all accounts with debit balances equals the total of all accounts with credit balances. If these amounts are not equal, an error has been made in the journal entries or the posting process. It must be found and corrected before proceeding.

SCL's trial balance as at January 31, 2016, is presented in Exhibit 3-8.

Exhibit 3-8 SCL's Trial Balance as at January 31, 2016

Account Names	Debit Balances	Credit Balances
Cash	$113,200	
Accounts receivable	2,000	
Inventory	6,000	
Prepaid expenses	1,650	
Equipment	65,000	
Accumulated depreciation, equipment		$ 850
Land	180,000	
Accounts payable		9,500
Interest payable		500
Bank loan payable		100,000
Common shares		250,000
Retained earnings		0
Dividends declared	400	
Sales revenue		34,000
Cost of goods sold	17,000	
Wages expense	2,900	
Utilities expense	1,900	
Rent expense	1,100	
Advertising expense	2,200	
Insurance expense	150	
Depreciation expense	850	
Interest expense	500	
Totals	$394,850	$394,850

Notice that the accounts are presented in the trial balance in the same order that they appear in the ledger. The permanent accounts are presented first (in the same order as they will appear on the statement of financial position), followed by the temporary accounts (the dividends declared, revenues, and expenses). This makes it easier to prepare the financial statements.

The purpose of a trial balance is to assist in detecting errors that may have been made in the recording process. Something is wrong if the ledger does not balance; that is, if the total of all the accounts with debit balances does not equal the total of all the accounts with credit balances. In such cases, there is no point in proceeding until the errors have been found and corrected. This makes the preparation of a trial balance a useful step in the accounting cycle. However, it is important to realize that, because a trial balance only checks whether the total of the debit balances in the ledger accounts equals the total of the credit balances, it cannot detect all types of errors. For example:

- The trial balance will still balance if the correct amount was debited or credited, but to the wrong account. An example is if a purchase of equipment was debited to the Inventory account, rather than to the Equipment account.
- The trial balance will still balance if an incorrect amount was recorded. An example is if a $450 transaction was recorded as a $540 transaction, for both the debit and credit portions of the entry.
- The trial balance will also not detect the complete omission of an entire journal entry. If neither the debit nor the credit portions of a journal entry were posted, the totals on the trial balance will still be equal.

Despite these limitations, preparing a trial balance is very helpful in detecting many other types of common errors in the recording process, and is an important step in the accounting cycle.

ADJUSTING ENTRIES

What are adjusting entries and why are they necessary?

Most of a company's transactions are easy to identify because there are obvious indications that a transaction has taken place. For example, cash is received or paid, receipts are issued, invoices are received, and so on. However, there are other events that lack any obvious indications that a transaction has taken place. At the end of each accounting period, a number of additional journal entries are normally required to adjust the company's accounts to reflect these transactions. These entries are known as **adjusting entries** and are classified into two broad categories: accruals and deferrals.

Accruals are required when a company needs to recognize a revenue or expense *before* the receipt or payment of cash. A common example of an adjusting entry for an accrued revenue is where a company has made interest-bearing loans to a customer or an employee that involve the interest being paid sometime in the future. Each month, the company would need to accrue the interest revenue earned on these loans. Common examples of adjusting entries for accrued expenses are the entry to recognize the wages expense for employees who have worked but have not yet been paid or the entry to record interest expense that had been incurred during the period on borrowed funds.

Deferrals are required when a company needs to recognize a revenue or expense in an accounting period *after* the cash has been received or paid. For example, when a customer or client has prepaid for goods or services, a deferral adjusting entry is required to recognize the revenue that had been earned during the period between prepayment and the end of the accounting period. For example, your university or college would normally require you to prepay tuition for your semester within the first few weeks of the term. At that time, the institution would record the receipt of cash and a related liability (unearned revenue). Over the course of the semester, the institution would use adjusting entries each month to recognize the revenues earned in that period and the reduction of the unearned revenue liability. An example of a deferral adjusting entry related to expenses is the entries necessary to recognize insurance or rent expense. Both of these are normally paid in advance (that is, they are prepaids) and an adjusting entry is required each month to recognize rent expense or insurance expense and reduce the amount of the prepaid expense. Another example of a deferral adjusting entry related to expenses is the depreciation of property, plant, and equipment. These assets may be paid for years before the accounting period in which they are depreciated (expensed). Some accountants consider depreciation entries to be a third category of adjusting entries. However, as they are really a form of deferral, we will consider them to be part of that category of adjusting entries.

It is important to understand that adjusting entries *never* involve cash. This is because whenever cash is paid or received, companies would account for it at that time. They would not wait until the end of the accounting period, which is when adjusting entries are made. Notice also that the types of items that need to be adjusted generally relate to the passage of time: the depreciation of property, plant, and equipment, the expiration of prepaid expenses, the accrual of interest, and the consumption of supplies all occur daily. However, they are typically updated only at the end of the accounting period, through adjusting entries. In most situations, there is no external transaction at the end of a period to signal that an adjustment needs to be made. Only the passage of time triggers an adjustment. As a result, the ending balances in the accounts have to be carefully reviewed to determine those that need to be adjusted.

The Conceptual Framework
COMPARABILITY AND ADJUSTING ENTRIES

Comparability is one of the enhancing qualitative characteristics included in the conceptual framework. Accounting standard setters have concluded that financial information is more useful when it can be compared with financial information from a previous period prepared on a comparable basis. Preparing adjusting entries each period to accrue expenses such as interest and wages helps to enhance the period-to-period comparability of financial information.[3]

Adjusting entries are very important. They ensure that all events and transactions related to the period have been accounted for, and thus make the financial statements as accurate as possible. While we did not initially identify them as adjusting entries, transactions 15, 16, and 17 for SCL were just that. Transaction 15 recorded the depreciation of SCL's equipment for the month of January and transaction 16 was the recognition of the company's monthly insurance expense for which premiums for one year's coverage had been paid in advance. These transactions were both examples of deferral entries. Transaction 17 recorded SCL's interest expense on its bank loan for the month of January. This was an example of an accrual entry.

The next step in the accounting cycle is the preparation of another trial balance. This one includes the effects of posting all of the adjusting entries to the related accounts.

 ### Ethics in Accounting

Many adjusting entries require management to make estimates and exercise judgement, providing opportunities for managers to manipulate earnings or balances on the statement of financial position. For other adjusting entries, there is no obvious evidence that a transaction has taken place and should be recorded.

For example, suppose that you, as an accountant for a company, are asked by your manager to postpone making the adjusting entry to accrue the interest on a company bank loan. Your manager has proposed this because it will increase net income, enabling the company to meet the earnings target it had forecast. The manager has said that the underaccrual of interest can be corrected in the next period and no one will be harmed by your actions. What should you do?

As you consider your response to this, or any, ethical question, it is sometimes helpful to think about who will be affected by your decision (including yourself), and how it will help or hurt them. Particularly, think of who the users or potential users of the financial statements are, and how they might be affected by your action or inaction. This should help you better understand the situation and make an ethical decision.

It is essential that financial statements not be presented in a way that could mislead, or potentially harm, a user—such as creditors and investors, in this case.

What is the purpose of preparing an adjusted trial balance?

After all the adjusting entries have been recorded and posted, an **adjusted trial balance** is prepared. This is done to ensure that the total debits in the accounts still equal the total credits. Any imbalance must be corrected before the financial statements are prepared. Since we had already included the effects of SCL's three adjusting entries (transactions 15, 16, and 17) in the company's trial balance (Exhibit 3-8), the adjusted trial balance in Exhibit 3-9 is exactly the same.

Exhibit 3-9 SCL's Adjusted Trial Balance as at January 31, 2016

Account Names	Debit Balances	Credit Balances
Cash	$113,200	
Accounts receivable	2,000	
Inventory	6,000	
Prepaid expenses	1,650	
Equipment	65,000	
Accumulated depreciation, equipment		$ 850
Land	180,000	
Accounts payable		9,500
Interest payable		500
Bank loan payable		100,000
Common shares		250,000
Retained earnings		0
Dividends declared	400	
Sales revenue		34,000
Cost of goods sold	17,000	
Wages expense	2,900	
Utilities expense	1,900	
Rent expense	1,100	
Advertising expense	2,200	
Insurance expense	150	
Depreciation expense	850	
Interest expense	500	
Totals	$394,850	$394,850

PREPARING FINANCIAL STATEMENTS AND CLOSING ENTRIES

What are closing entries and why are they necessary?

■ **LEARNING OBJECTIVE 8**
Explain why closing entries are necessary and prepare them.

After the adjusted trial balance has been prepared, the financial statements for the period can be prepared. As discussed in Chapters 1 and 2, the statement of income (Exhibit 3-10) is the first statement prepared, using the information related to the revenue and expense accounts in the adjusted trial balance. The next statement is

Exhibit 3-10 Statement of Income

SAMPLE COMPANY LIMITED		
Statement of Income		
For the month ended January 31, 2016		
Sales revenue		$34,000
Cost of goods sold		17,000
Gross profit		17,000
	Wages expense	2,900
	Utilities expense	1,900
	Rent expense	1,100
	Advertising expense	2,200
	Insurance expense	150
	Depreciation expense	850
	Interest expense	500
Net income		$ 7,400

the statement of changes in equity (Exhibit 3-11) and then the statement of financial position (Exhibit 3-12). The final major financial statement to be prepared is the statement of cash flows. However, because we prepared the statement of cash flows for SCL in Chapter 2 and because Chapter 5 is devoted entirely to this topic, we will defer any further discussion of the statement until Chapter 5.

Exhibit 3-11 Statement of Changes in Equity

	Number of Common Shares	Share Capital— Common Shares	Retained Earnings	Total
SAMPLE COMPANY LIMITED				
Statement of Changes in Equity				
For the month ended January 31, 2016				
Balance - Jan. 1	–	$ –	$ –	$ –
Net income	–	–	7,400	7,400
Declaration of dividends	–	–	(400)	(400)
Issuance of common shares	10,000	250,000	–	250,000
Balance - Jan. 31	10,000	$250,000	$ 7,000	$257,000

Exhibit 3-12 Statement of Financial Position

SAMPLE COMPANY LIMITED
Statement of Financial Position
As at January 31, 2016

ASSETS		
Current assets		
Cash	$113,200	
Accounts receivable	2,000	
Inventory	6,000	
Prepaid expenses	1,650	
		$122,850
Non-current assets		
Equipment (net)		64,150
Land		180,000
		244,150
Total assets		$367,000
LIABILITIES		
Current liabilities		
Accounts payable	$ 9,500	
Interest payable	500	
		$ 10,000
Non-current liabilities		
Bank loan payable		100,000
Total liabilities		110,000
SHAREHOLDERS' EQUITY		
Common shares		250,000
Retained earnings		7,000
Total shareholders' equity		257,000
Total liabilities and shareholders' equity		$367,000

You will recall from Chapter 2 that dividends declared are reflected on the statement of changes in equity as a reduction to retained earnings. The sum of opening retained earnings plus net income less dividends declared gives us the company's ending retained earnings balance. This amount must be determined before preparing the company's statement of financial position.

As discussed earlier in the chapter, all of the accounts on a company's statement of financial position are permanent accounts. That is, their balances carry over from one period to the next. Meanwhile, all of the accounts on a company's statement of income are temporary. That is, the balance in each of these accounts is transferred to the Retained Earnings account at the end of each year, so that the temporary accounts start each accounting period with a nil balance. Dividends Declared is also a temporary account and its balance is also transferred to Retained Earnings at the end of each accounting period.

Once the financial statements have been prepared, the balances in the temporary accounts must be transferred to the Retained Earnings account. This resets these accounts so that they have a nil balance to start the next year. This is referred to as *closing the accounts* and the required entries are known as *closing entries*.

Closing entries are required to transfer the balances in the temporary accounts (revenues, expenses, and Dividends Declared) to retained earnings. By doing this, the temporary accounts will start each year with nil balances. Companies are then able to measure their revenues, expenses, and dividends declared for each year rather than having cumulative balances for multiple years. It is much more relevant for financial statement users to know the revenues or expenses of a period, so that this amount can be compared with prior periods, budgets, forecasts, and so on. Preparing closing entries is the last stage of the accounting cycle.

There are a few different ways to prepare closing entries. Some accountants use a two-entry approach, some use three entries, while others use four entries. Some accountants even prepare individual closing entries—one for each temporary account—which could mean hundreds of closing entries. We will use four closing entries to close the temporary accounts because this method most closely replicates the format used to show the changes to a company's retained earnings on the statement of changes in equity. On the statement of changes in equity, a company's ending retained earnings balance is determined as:

$$= \text{Beginning Retained Earnings} + \text{Net Income} - \text{Dividends Declared}$$

The first three closing entries will close the revenue and expense accounts while determining net income and transferring it to the Retained Earnings account. The fourth will close the Dividends Declared account. Therefore, the four closing entries are as follows:

1. Close all revenue accounts to the Income Summary account.
2. Close all expense accounts to the Income Summary account.
3. Close the Income Summary account to Retained Earnings.
4. Close the Dividends Declared account to Retained Earnings.

The first closing entry will close all revenue accounts to the Income Summary account. The **Income Summary account** is a temporary account that is opened and closed on the last day of a company's fiscal year. It is used only to determine the amount of the company's net income, which is then transferred to Retained Earnings. Using the Income Summary account minimizes the number of entries flowing through the Retained Earnings account. Because revenue accounts normally have a credit balance, a debit for the total account balance has to be made to each revenue account to reset the account balances to zero and a credit is made to the Income Summary account for the total revenue amount. If there were 100 revenue accounts, closing entry 1 would have 100 debits, but only a single credit transferring total revenues to the Income Summary account.

In the case of SCL, there was only a single revenue account, Sales Revenue, so closing entry 1 is:

Closing Entry 1

| Year-end date | DR Sales Revenue | 34,000 | |
| | CR Income Summary | | 34,000 |

The second closing entry will close all expense accounts to the Income Summary account. Because expense accounts normally have a debit balance, a credit for the total account balance has to be made to each expense account to reset the account balances to zero and a debit is made to the income summary account for the total expense amount. Again, if there were 100 expense accounts, closing entry 2 would have 100 credits, but only a single debit transferring total expenses to the Income Summary account.

In the case of SCL, there were eight expense accounts, so closing entry 2 is:

Closing Entry 2

	DR Income Summary	26,600	
	CR Cost of Goods Sold		17,000
	CR Wages Expense		2,900
	CR Utilities Expense		1,900
Year-end date	CR Rent Expense		1,100
	CR Advertising Expense		2,200
	CR Insurance Expense		150
	CR Depreciation Expense		850
	CR Interest Expense		500

Preparing a T account for Income Summary after the first two closing entries enables us to easily determine net income:

INCOME SUMMARY			
		34,000	Closing Entry #1
Closing Entry #2	26,600		
		7,400	Net Income

It is also worth noting that, if a temporary account had a debit or a credit prior to the closing entries, it remains the same way in the Income Summary account. As such, the total revenue amount is reflected as a credit balance in the Income Summary account and the total expense amount is reflected as a debit balance in the Income Summary account. Because revenues normally exceed expenses for most companies, we would normally expect to have a net credit balance in the Income Summary account, meaning that the company has net income. It is possible to have a net debit balance in the Income Summary account if the company has a net loss for the period; that is, expenses exceed revenues. In the case of SCL, the company was profitable. We know that net income ultimately increases retained earnings. This is what is accomplished through closing entry 3, which in the case of SCL is:

Closing Entry 3

Year-end date	DR Income Summary	7,400	
	CR Retained Earnings		7,400

The final closing entry is required to close the Dividends Declared account to Retained Earnings. We know that dividends are a distribution to shareholders of retained earnings—a company's profits from current and prior years. If a company declared dividends in the year, then Retained Earnings must be reduced accordingly. The Dividends Declared account normally has a debit balance, so the account must be credited to close it. Retained Earnings, which normally has a credit balance, is debited to reflect the reduction in the account balance resulting from the declaration of dividends. In the case of SCL, the company declared dividends of $400 during the year, so closing entry 4 is as follows:

Closing Entry 4

Year-end date	DR Retained Earnings	400	
	CR Dividends Declared		400

If we prepared a T account for the Retained Earnings account after the four closing entries, it would be as follows:

RETAINED EARNINGS			
	–	Opening Balance	
	7,400	Net Income – Closing Entry #3	
Closing Entry #4 – Dividends Declared	400		
	7,000	Ending Balance	

This ending retained earnings balance equals the amount of retained earnings on SCL's statement of changes in equity (Exhibit 3-11) and the company's statement of financial position (Exhibit 3-12).

Exhibit 3-13 provides an overview of the four closing entries, including their effects on the Income Summary and Retained Earnings accounts.

Exhibit 3-13 Overview of Closing Entry Process

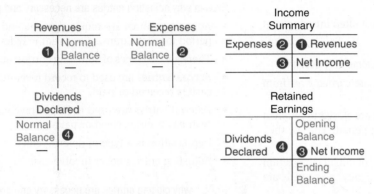

TAKE**5**

The closing entry process has achieved two key objectives:

- The balance in the Retained Earnings account has been brought up to date by adding the net income for the period and deducting the dividends declared during the period.
- The balances in all of the temporary accounts have been reset to zero, so that the accounts are ready to use at the start of the next accounting period.

This completes our review of the accounting cycle. As with any cycle, the end of one cycle is the beginning of the next. With the exception of the closing entry process, which happens only once a year, most companies will have monthly cycles, meaning they will prepare adjusting entries and financial statements at the end of each month.

KEY POINTS
Closing entries:
- transfer the balances in all temporary accounts to Retained Earnings.
- reset all temporary account balances to zero.
- are made at the end of each year.

SUMMARY

1. **Explain how the double-entry accounting system works, including how it overcomes the limitations of the template approach.**

   - Every transaction must be recorded in a way that affects at least two accounts, with the effects of these entries being equal and offsetting.

   - The double-entry accounting system enables the use of a huge number of accounts and is not limited to a fixed number of columns as is the case with the template approach. This allows the company to capture information at the level of detail required to manage the business, yet make it easy to summarize the information for reporting purposes.

2. **Explain the normal balance concept and how it is used within the double-entry accounting system.**

   - The normal balance concept is used to determine whether an account *normally* has a debit or credit balance.

   - To determine an account's normal balance, a "T" is drawn through the middle of the accounting equation. Accounts on the

   left side of the "T" (assets) normally have a debit (DR) balance, while accounts on the right side of the "T" (liabilities and shareholders' equity) normally have a credit (CR) balance.

   - An account's normal balance illustrates what needs to be done to increase that account. The opposite is done to decrease it.

   - As Retained Earnings is a shareholders' equity account, it normally has a credit balance. Therefore, to increase it, we would credit it, and to decrease it, we would debit it.

   - Following this, revenue accounts, which ultimately increase retained earnings, normally have a credit balance. Expense and dividends declared accounts, which ultimately decrease retained earnings, normally have a debit balance.

3. **Identify and explain the steps in the accounting cycle.**

   - The steps in the accounting cycle are: (1) start with opening balances, (2) complete transaction analysis, (3) record transactions in the general journal, (4) post transactions to the general ledger, (5) prepare a trial balance, (6) record and post adjusting entries, (7) prepare an adjusted trial balance, (8) prepare financial statements, and (9) prepare closing entries.

- At a minimum, this cycle is repeated annually, but parts of it repeat much more frequently (quarterly, monthly, weekly, or even daily).

4. **Explain the significance of a company's decisions regarding its chart of accounts and the implications of subsequent changes.**

- The chart of accounts outlines the type of information management wishes to capture to assist them in managing the business.
- The chart of accounts is dynamic and can be changed when the company enters into new types of operations, opens new locations, requires more detailed information, or requires less detailed information.
- Changes to the chart of accounts are most often introduced at the beginning of a fiscal year.

5. **Explain the difference between permanent and temporary accounts.**

- Permanent accounts have balances that are carried over from one accounting period to the next.
- Temporary accounts have balances that are closed to retained earnings at the end of each accounting period. That is, they are reset to zero.
- All of the accounts on the statement of financial position (assets, liabilities, and shareholders' equity accounts) are permanent accounts.
- All of the accounts on the statement of income (revenues and expenses) and Dividends Declared are temporary accounts.

6. **Identify and record transactions in the general journal and general ledger.**

- The general journal is a chronological listing of all transactions. It contains detailed information on each transaction.

- Each journal entry must affect two or more accounts and the total dollar amount of debits in the entry must be equal to the total dollar amount of credits. In other words, total DR = total CR.
- On a periodic basis (such as daily, weekly, or monthly), the information recorded in the general journal is posted to the general ledger.
- The general ledger is used to prepare summary information for each account. The detail from each journal entry affecting a specific account is recorded in the general ledger account for that specific account.
- A trial balance is prepared to ensure that the total of all debits posted to the general ledger is equal to the total credits posted.

7. **Explain why adjusting entries are necessary and prepare them.**

- Adjusting entries are required at the end of each accounting period to record transactions that may have been missed.
- There are two types of adjusting entries: accruals and deferrals.
- Accrual entries are used to record revenues or expenses before cash is received or paid.
- Deferral entries are used to record revenues or expenses after cash has been received or paid.
- Depreciation is a type of deferral entry.
- Adjusting entries never involve cash.

8. **Explain why closing entries are necessary and prepare them.**

- Closing entries are used to close temporary accounts and transfer the balances in these accounts to Retained Earnings.
- There are four closing entries: (1) close all revenue accounts to the Income Summary account, (2) close all expense accounts to the Income Summary account, (3) close the Income Summary Account to Retained Earnings, and (4) close Dividends Declared to Retained Earnings.

KEY TERMS

Accounting cycle (120)	Contra-asset account (129)	Income Summary account (137)
Accruals (133)	Credit (118)	Journal entry (123)
Accumulated depreciation (129)	Debit (118)	Liquidity (119)
Adjusted trial balance (134)	Deferrals (133)	Normal balance (118)
Adjusting entries (133)	Double-entry accounting	Permanent accounts (122)
Carrying amount (129)	system (117)	Posting (131)
Chart of accounts (121)	General journal (123)	Temporary accounts (122)
Closing entries (137)	General ledger (G/L) (119)	Trial balance (132)
Compound journal entry (127)	General ledger account (119)	

ABBREVIATIONS USED

CR	Credit
DR	Debit
G/L	General ledger

SYNONYMS

Carrying Amount | Net Book Value

CHAPTER END REVIEW PROBLEM 1

This problem will reinforce and extend what you have learned in this chapter about transaction analysis, journal entries, and adjusting entries. You should carefully work through the following problem and then check your work against the suggested solution.

Exhibit 3-14 shows the trial balance of Matchett Manufacturing Ltd. ("MML") at November 30, 2016.

EXHIBIT 3-14   MML'S TRIAL BALANCE

MATCHETT MANUFACTURING LIMITED
Trial Balance
As at November 30, 2016

Account	Debit (DR)	Credit (CR)
Cash	$ 37,000	
Accounts receivable	298,900	
Inventory	108,000	
Prepaid expenses	8,400	
Equipment	76,000	
Accumulated depreciation, equipment		$ 16,000
Building	500,000	
Accumulated depreciation, building		75,200
Land	385,000	
Accounts payable		145,000
Wages payable		23,000
Bank loan payable		400,000
Common shares		250,000
Retained earnings		230,800
Dividends declared	30,000	
Sales revenue		1,650,000
Cost of goods sold	908,000	
Wages expense	375,000	
Insurance expense	12,000	
Depreciation expense	29,700	
Interest expense	22,000	
	$2,790,000	$2,790,000

MML has a December 31 year end and had the following transactions in December 2016:
1. Sales for the month totalled $155,000, all on account. The inventory sold had cost MML $70,000.
2. Payments received from customers during the month in relation to their accounts receivable were $215,900.
3. The company's employees earned wages of $37,300 during the month.
4. The company made wage payments of $41,700 to its employees during the month.
5. Purchases of inventory, all on account, amounted to $125,000.
6. During the month, the company made payments to suppliers totalling $98,000.
7. The company declared dividends of $10,000 on its 100,000 common shares. MML had a policy of declaring quarterly dividends of this amount. The dividends from the first three quarters had been paid on April 15, 2016; July 15, 2016; and October 15, 2016. The dividends from the last quarter will be paid on January 15, 2017.

MML also prepared adjusting entries for the following transactions:
A1. Interest on the company's bank loan was recorded for the month of December. The interest rate on the loan was 6% per year and was payable on the first day of each month. (That is, the interest for December 2016 will be paid on January 1, 2017.)

A2. Depreciation expense for the month of December was recorded on MML's equipment. The equipment, which had been purchased on January 1, 2015, for $76,000, was estimated to have a useful life of five years and a residual value of $10,000. MML uses the straight-line method to depreciate its equipment.

A3. Depreciation expense for the month of December was recorded on MML's building. The building had been purchased on January 1, 2013, at a cost of $500,000. Company management had determined that it had a useful life of 25 years and a residual value of $20,000. MML uses the straight-line method to depreciate the building.

A4. Insurance expense for the month of December was recorded. The company had renewed insurance coverage on its equipment and building on July 1, 2016, when its previous policy ended. The annual premiums of $14,400 were paid at that time.

Required:

a. Prepare journal entries for transactions 1 to 7.

b. Prepare adjusting entries for transactions A1 to A4.

CHAPTER END REVIEW PROBLEM 2

This problem will reinforce and extend what you have learned in this chapter about closing entries. After the journal entries and adjusting entries for MML had been posted, the company prepared an adjusted trial balance (see Exhibit 3-15).

EXHIBIT 3-15   MML'S ADJUSTED TRIAL BALANCE

MATCHETT MANUFACTURING LIMITED Adjusted Trial Balance As at December 31, 2016		
Account	Debit (DR)	Credit (CR)
Cash	$ 113,200	
Accounts receivable	238,000	
Inventory	163,000	
Prepaid expenses	7,200	
Equipment	76,000	
Accumulated depreciation, equipment		$ 17,100
Building	500,000	
Accumulated depreciation, building		76,800
Land	385,000	
Accounts payable		172,000
Wages payable		18,600
Dividends payable		10,000
Interest payable		2,000
Bank loan payable		400,000
Common shares		250,000
Retained earnings		230,800
Dividends declared	40,000	
Sales revenue		1,805,000
Cost of goods sold	978,000	
Wages expense	412,300	
Insurance expense	13,200	
Depreciation expense	32,400	
Interest expense	24,000	
	$2,982,300	$2,982,300

Required:
   a. Prepare a statement of income for 2016, a statement of changes in equity, and a classified statement of financial position.
   b. Prepare the closing entries required to ready MML's accounts for the beginning of 2017.

Suggested Solution To Chapter End Review Problem 1

The journal entries and adjusting entries for MML are shown in Exhibit 3-16. Extended explanations are provided for transaction 1 and the four adjusting entries because they are the more complex transactions.

EXHIBIT 3-16	MML'S JOURNAL ENTRIES AND ADJUSTING ENTRIES FOR DECEMBER 2016		
Journal Entries:			
1a.	Accounts Receivable	155,000	
	Sales Revenue		155,000
1b.	Cost of Goods Sold	70,000	
	Inventory		70,000
2.	Cash	215,900	
	Accounts Receivable		215,900
3.	Wages Expense	37,300	
	Wages Payable		37,300
4.	Wages Payable	41,700	
	Cash		41,700
5.	Inventory	125,000	
	Accounts Payable		125,000
6.	Accounts Payable	98,000	
	Cash		98,000
7.	Dividends Declared	10,000	
	Dividends Payable		10,000
Adjusting entries:			
A1.	Interest Expense	2,000	
	Interest Payable		2,000
A2.	Depreciation Expense	1,100	
	Accumulated Depreciation, Equipment		1,100
A3.	Depreciation Expense	1,600	
	Accumulated Depreciation, Building		1,600
A4.	Insurance Expense	1,200	
	Prepaid Expenses		1,200

Transaction 1: Sale of Goods

As we discussed in Chapter 2, when you see the word *sale,* you should think "two parts." Part 1 is to account for the sale and the related cash and accounts receivable. Part 2 is to account for the cost of goods sold and inventory. The information to prepare part 1 will always be provided because a company knows its selling price and whether the sale was for cash or on account. The information for part 2 may not be available, because some companies may not know the cost of the products being sold at the time of sale.

Adjusting Entry 1: Interest

MML has had an outstanding bank loan for the entire month. Even though the interest will not be paid until January 1, the expense was incurred in December. The interest rate on the loan is 6% and it is important to remember that interest rates are stated in annual terms. As such, the interest rate must be prorated to determine the monthly interest expense. The interest expense for the month is determined as follows:

$$\$400,000 \times 6\% \times 1/12 = \$2,000$$

Adjusting Entry 2: Depreciation Expense (Equipment)

Depreciation expense must be recorded to allocate a portion of the equipment's cost to each period in which it is being used to generate revenue. As we have discussed, there are a number of different methods that can be used to depreciate property, plant, and equipment, but for now, we will assume that companies use the straight-line method. This method allocates a consistent amount of the asset's cost each period. Most companies use a single account to record depreciation expense, because it is usually a single line on the statement of income. However, companies use separate accumulated depreciation accounts for each asset, because separate contra-asset accounts are required to report the carrying amount of each asset category on the statement of financial position.

As we have discussed, an accumulated depreciation account is referred to as a contra-asset because its normal balance is contrary or opposite to the normal balance for that category of accounts. Assets normally have a debit balance, so a contra-asset account will normally have a credit balance. The balance in this account represents the portion of the asset's cost that has been expensed to date.

MML's depreciation expense on its equipment for the month of December is determined as follows:

$$\frac{\$76,000 - \$10,000}{5 \text{ years}} = \$13,200 \text{ per year}/12 = \$1,100 \text{ per month}$$

Adjusting Entry 3: Depreciation Expense, Building

MML's depreciation expense on its building for the month of December is determined as follows:

$$\frac{\$500,000 - \$20,000}{25 \text{ years}} = \$19,200 \text{ per year}/12 = \$1,600 \text{ per month}$$

Adjusting Entry 4: Insurance Expense

MML had purchased a one-year insurance policy covering its equipment and building on July 1, 2015. The total premiums of $14,400 were paid at that time and would have been recorded as an asset, Prepaid Expenses, at that time. With each month, the coverage is being used up and the monthly insurance expense must be recorded. The amount of the expense for December is as follows:

$$\$14,400/12 = \$1,200$$

Suggested Solution To Chapter End Review Problem 2

EXHIBIT 3-17	STATEMENT OF INCOME

MATCHETT MANUFACTURING LIMITED
Statement of Income
For the year ended December 31, 2016

Sales revenue	$1,805,000
Cost of goods sold	978,000
Gross profit	827,000
Wages expense	412,300
Insurance expense	13,200
Depreciation expense	32,400
Interest expense	24,000
Net income	$ 345,100

EXHIBIT 3-18   STATEMENT OF CHANGES IN EQUITY

MATCHETT MANUFACTURING LIMITED
Statement of Changes in Equity
For the year ended December 31, 2016

	Number of Common Shares	Share Capital, Common Shares	Retained Earnings	Total
Balance - Jan. 1	10,000	$250,000	$230,800	$480,800
Net income	–	–	345,100	345,100
Declaration of dividends	–	–	(40,000)	(40,000)
Issuance of common shares	–	–	–	–
Balance - Dec. 31	10,000	$250,000	$535,900	$785,900

EXHIBIT 3-19   STATEMENT OF FINANCIAL POSITION

MATCHETT MANUFACTURING LIMITED
Statement of Financial Position
As at December 31, 2016

ASSETS		
Current assets		
Cash	$113,200	
Accounts receivable	238,000	
Inventory	163,000	
Prepaid expenses	7,200	
		$ 521,400
Non-current assets		
Equipment (net)		58,900
Building (net)		423,200
Land		385,000
		867,100
TOTAL ASSETS		$1,388,500
LIABILITIES		
Current liabilities		
Accounts payable	$172,000	
Wages payable	18,600	
Dividends payable	10,000	
Interest payable	2,000	
		$ 202,600
Non-current liabilities		
Bank loan payable		400,000
TOTAL LIABILITIES		602,600
SHAREHOLDERS' EQUITY		
Common shares		250,000
Retained earnings		535,900
TOTAL SHAREHOLDERS' EQUITY		785,900
TOTAL LIABILITIES AND SHAREHOLDERS' EQUITY		$1,388,500

EXHIBIT 3-20	MML'S CLOSING ENTRIES

C1. Close all revenue accounts to the Income Summary account.

Sales Revenue	1,805,000	
Income Summary		1,805,000

C2. Close all expense accounts to the Income Summary account.

Income Summary	1,459,900	
Cost of Goods Sold		978,000
Wages Expense		412,300
Insurance Expense		13,200
Depreciation Expense		32,400
Interest Expense		24,000

C3. Close the Income Summary account to Retained Earnings.

Income Summary	345,100	
Retained Earnings		345,100

C4. Close the Dividends Declared account to Retained Earnings.

Retained Earnings	40,000	
Dividends Declared		40,000

Income Summary			Retained Earnings	
C2 1,459,900	1,805,000 **C1**			230,800 Opening Balance
	345,100 Net Income	**C4** Dividends Declared 40,000		345,100 Net Income **C3**
C3 345,100				
	-			535,900 Ending Balance

Note that, after posting the closing entries, all the revenue and expense accounts and the Dividends Declared account have zero balances. They are now ready to start the new accounting cycle for 2017. Also, the Retained Earnings account has been updated to reflect the cumulative amount as at the end of 2016.

ASSIGNMENT MATERIAL

Discussion Questions

DQ3-1 In general terms, explain the role of each of the two main financial statements for a business enterprise: the statement of income and the statement of financial position. Outline the type of information that each statement presents, and the basic difference between the types of items that appear on the statement of income versus those that appear on the statement of financial position.

DQ3-2 Indicate whether each of the following statements is true or false:
a. Under the accrual basis of accounting, when cash is collected on accounts receivable, revenue is recorded.
b. Cash receipts from customers are debited to Accounts Receivable.
c. The cash basis of accounting recognizes expenses when they are incurred.
d. Under the cash basis of accounting, there is no such thing as a Prepaid Expenses account.
e. Asset accounts and expense accounts normally have debit balances.

f. Credits increase asset accounts.
g. Revenues are recorded with credit entries.
h. Dividends are an expense of doing business and should appear on the statement of income.

DQ3-3 Indicate whether each of the following accounts normally has a debit balance or a credit balance:
a. Sales Revenue
b. Rent Expense
c. Prepaid Expenses
d. Bank Loan Payable
e. Common Shares
f. Accounts Receivable
g. Accounts Payable
h. Retained Earnings
i. Dividends Declared
j. Dividends Payable
k. Depreciation Expense

DQ3-4 Indicate whether each of the following accounts normally has a debit balance or a credit balance:
   a. Inventory
   b. Cost of Goods Sold
   c. Prepaid Expenses
   d. Wages Expense
   e. Wages Payable
   f. Interest Revenue
   g. Equipment
   h. Accumulated Depreciation, Equipment
   i. Notes Payable
   j. Common Shares
   k. Cash

DQ3-5 The Retained Earnings account has a credit balance and credit entries are used to record increases in this account. Why do expense accounts, which are transferred to Retained Earnings when they are closed, have debit balances? Why are debit entries used to record increases in these accounts?

DQ3-6 List the steps in the accounting cycle, and briefly explain each step.

DQ3-7 In the adjusted trial balance part of the accounting cycle, the Retained Earnings account has its beginning-of-period balance, whereas the rest of the permanent accounts have their end-of-period balances. Explain why this is so.

DQ3-8 Explain what is meant by the term *prepaid expense*, including how a prepaid expense arises and where it is reported in the financial statements.

DQ3-9 Explain what is meant by the term *accrued expense*, including how an accrued expense arises and where it is reported in the financial statements.

DQ3-10 Explain how a prepaid expense differs from an accrued expense.

DQ3-11 If a company fails to record an accrued expense at the end of an accounting period, what effect will this omission have on the current period's financial statements? On the next period's financial statements?

DQ3-12 Explain the meaning of *depreciation expense* and *accumulated depreciation*. How do they differ? Where does each of these items appear in the financial statements?

DQ3-13 Explain why closing entries are made. What are the two objectives that are accomplished by making closing entries?

DQ3-14 Discuss why one company might close its books monthly and another might close them quarterly.

Application Problems

AP3-1 (Determine effects of transactions on statement of financial position accounts)

Ann and Greg Fenway run a small art gallery and custom framing business.

Required:
Explain how the basic statement of financial position accounts of assets, liabilities, and shareholders' equity would be affected by each of the following transactions and activities:
   a. Framing materials are purchased on credit.
   b. Payment is made for the framing materials that were purchased previously.
   c. Wages are paid to their assistant in the shop.
   d. Pictures are purchased by the gallery for cash.
   e. A picture is sold for cash, at a profit.
   f. A receivable is collected on a framing project that was completed for a customer last month.
   g. A loan from the bank is repaid, with interest.
   h. Depreciation on the equipment is recognized.

AP3-2 (Determine effects of transactions on statement of financial position accounts)

Gagnon's Autobody Ltd. repairs and paints automobiles after accidents.

Required:
Explain how the basic statement of financial position accounts of assets, liabilities, and shareholders' equity would be affected by each of the following transactions and activities:
   a. Gagnon's Autobody purchases new spray-painting equipment. The supplier gives the company 60 days to pay.
   b. The company pays for the spray-painting equipment that was purchased above.
   c. Supplies such as paint and putty are purchased for cash.
   d. The company pays for a one-year liability insurance policy.
   e. The company pays its employees for work done.
   f. A car is repaired and repainted. The customer pays the deductible required by her insurance policy, and the remainder of the bill is sent to her insurance company.
   g. Cash is collected from the customer's insurance company.

AP3-3 (Prepare journal entries)

Required:
For each of the following transactions, construct journal entries:
- a. Inventory costing $3,100 was purchased on account.
- b. A payment of $3,000 was made on accounts payable.
- c. Inventory costing $1,800 was sold on account for $2,700. (Hint: Two journal entries are required.)
- d. Accounts receivable of $2,000 were collected.
- e. Supplies costing $1,400 were purchased on account.
- f. Supplies costing $500 were consumed during the period.
- g. New equipment costing $7,500 was purchased for cash.
- h. The company borrowed $12,000 from a bank.
- i. The company issued common shares for $20,000.
- j. Wages totalling $6,300 were earned by employees and paid to them.
- k. The company paid $2,000 on its bank loan, which included $150 of interest.
- l. The company paid $2,500 for the monthly rent on its leased premises.
- m. Land costing $23,000 was purchased. The company paid $3,000 in cash and the remainder was financed with a mortgage (a long-term loan).

AP3-4 (Prepare journal entries)

Chapati Company started business on January 1, 2016. Some of the events that occurred in its first year of operations follow:
1. An insurance policy was purchased on February 28 for $1,800.
2. During the year, inventory costing $140,000 was purchased, all on account.
3. Sales to customers totalled $200,000. Of these, $40,000 were cash sales.
4. Payments to suppliers for inventory that had been purchased earlier totalled $110,000.
5. Collections from customers on account during the year totalled $140,000.
6. Customers paid $25,000 in advance payments for goods that will be delivered later.
7. Equipment that cost $140,000 was purchased on October 1 for $40,000 cash plus a two-year, 10% note with a principal amount of $100,000.
8. Wages totalling $44,000 were paid to employees during the year.
9. The board of directors declared dividends of $12,000 in December 2016, to be paid in January 2017.
10. A year-end review revealed that the insurance policy (in item 1) was for one year of coverage that began on March 1, 2016.
11. The equipment that was purchased (in item 7) on October 1, 2016, is to be depreciated using the straight-line method, with an estimated useful life of 10 years and an estimated residual value of $20,000.
12. No interest was paid on the note during the year.
13. A physical count at year end revealed $20,000 of unsold inventory still on hand.
14. It was determined that 80% of the goods that were paid for in advance (in item 6) had been delivered to the customers by the end of the year.
15. In addition to the wages that were paid during the year, wages of $4,000 remained unpaid at the end of the year.

Required:
Prepare journal entries for each of the above transactions and adjustments.

AP3-5 (Prepare journal entries)

Le Petit Croissant Ltd. ("LPC") is a wholesale bakery that supplies flash frozen croissants to restaurants, hotels, and other commercial customers. LPC began operating in August 2016 and had the following transactions in its first month:

Aug. 1	LPC issued 30,000 common shares to its two founding shareholders in exchange for $250,000 in cash and equipment valued at $50,000.
1	The company borrowed $100,000 from the Commercial Bank at an interest rate of 6%. The borrowing agreement terms state that the loan is to be repaid at the end of each month in the amount of $2,500 per month plus interest.
3	In order to access a commercial kitchen, LPC leased the site of a former restaurant, paying $6,000, of which $3,000 represented the rent for August and the balance was a damage deposit.
8	LPC purchased flour and other ingredients costing $32,800 on account.
12	LPC paid $6,800 to a local marketing company for its logo design and media planning services.

14	LPC recorded its sales of the first two weeks of the month. Total sales (half in cash and half on account) amounted to $50,200 and the inventory related to these sales was determined to have a cost of $17,100.
19	Paid the suppliers $25,000 for goods previously purchased on account.
25	Collections from customers on account totalled $22,600.
26	LPC purchased additional inventory (flour and so on) on account for $23,000.
29	LPC received an invoice from its natural gas supplier for $2,700, which is payable on September 14.
31	LPC recorded the sales for the balance of the month. Sales for this period totalled $60,800, of which $20,000 was on account. The cost of the ingredients from inventory related to these sales amounted to $20,700.
31	LPC's six full-time employees were paid $3,900 each in wages for the month.
31	LPC made the loan payment required under the terms of the borrowing agreement.
31	LPC's board of directors declared a dividend of $1.00 per share to the holders of the company's common shares.

Required:
Prepare all necessary journal entries related to the above transactions.

AP3-6 (Journalize, post, and prepare trial balance)

Sweet Dreams Chocolatiers Ltd. began operations on January 1, 2016. During its first year, the following transactions occurred:
1. Issued common shares for $200,000 cash.
2. Purchased $475,000 of inventory on account.
3. Sold inventory on account for $640,000. The original cost of the inventory that was sold was $380,000.
4. Collected $580,000 from customers on account.
5. Paid $430,000 to suppliers for the inventory previously purchased on account.
6. Bought a delivery vehicle for $36,000 cash.
7. Paid $26,000 for rent, including $2,000 related to the next year.
8. Incurred $20,000 of operating expenses, of which $18,000 was paid.
9. Recorded $2,000 of depreciation on the vehicle.
10. Declared and paid dividends of $6,000.

Required:
a. Prepare journal entries to record each of the above transactions.
b. Create T accounts and post the journal entries to the T accounts.
c. Prepare a December 31, 2016, trial balance.

AP3-7 (Journalize, post, and prepare trial balance)

Sparkling Clean Dry Cleaners Inc. began operations on January 1, 2016. In its first year, the following transactions occurred:
1. Issued common shares for $150,000 cash.
2. Purchased dry cleaning equipment for $75,000 cash.
3. Purchased cleaning supplies, on account, for $9,600.
4. Used $8,400 of the supplies in cleaning operations.
5. Collected $124,000 from customers for dry cleaning services provided.
6. Borrowed $15,000 from the bank on July 1, 2015, at an interest rate of 8% per year.
7. Paid wages of $49,000 to employees. In addition to this, $1,000 of wages were owed to employees at the end of the year.
8. Depreciated the equipment by $3,000 for the year.
9. Paid $22,000 for utilities (telephone, electricity, and water).
10. On December 31, paid interest on the bank loan described in transaction 6.

Required:
a. Prepare journal entries to record each of the above transactions.
b. Create T accounts and post the journal entries to the T accounts.
c. Prepare a December 31, 2016, trial balance.

AP3-8 (Journal entries and adjusting entries)

Offcopy Ltd. ("OL") is an office supply company that also sells and services commercial office copiers. OL was founded in 2012 and has seen significant growth since then. OL's bookkeeper retired in August and her replacement has asked for your assistance in recording the following transactions from the month of September 2016:

Regular entries:

Sept. 1	OL purchased a new delivery truck for $80,000, paying $30,000 cash and financing the balance using a note payable at 9% per annum. The note payable is due in 12 months, and interest on the note must be paid on the first day of every month, beginning on October 1, 2016. OL's management has determined that the truck will have a useful life of six years and a residual value of $8,000.
1	OL paid $2,400 for an insurance policy on the new truck for the period September 1, 2016, to August 31, 2017.
5	The company purchased inventory on credit at a cost of $13,000.
12	Pinamalas University, one of OL's largest customers, signed a photocopy service contract with OL. The contract runs from October 1, 2016, to September 30, 2017, and will mean that OL services all of the university's photocopiers. In accordance with the contact terms, Pinamalas paid OL $7,500, representing the first month's service revenue under the contract.
18	OL sold $16,000 of office supplies, of which one quarter was on account and the balance was cash. The cost to OL of the products sold was $10,500.
30	OL paid dividends in the amount of $15,000, which had been declared by the board (and recorded) in August 2016.

Adjusting entries:

Sept. 30	OL made the necessary month-end adjusting entry related to the depreciation of the new delivery truck.
30	OL made the necessary month-end adjusting entry related to the interest on the note payable.
30	OL made the necessary month-end adjusting entry related to the insurance policy.

Required:
Prepare the journal entries for the above transactions.

AP3-9 (Journal entries and adjusting entries)

Aquarium World Ltd. ("AWL") was incorporated in 2013 and imports fish tanks and related supplies for the salt-water aquarium market. AWL primarily imports from Asian suppliers and is a wholesaler supplying independent retailers in Western Canada.

During the month of January 2016, AWL had the following transactions:

Regular entries:

Jan. 1	In order to better service its growing business and manage its inventory more effectively, AWL purchased new computer equipment to run its inventory system for $145,000, paying cash. AWL's management determined that the new computer equipment would have a useful life of five years and have a residual value of $10,000.
1	AWL also entered into an agreement to lease a warehouse. This would allow the company to import larger shipments from its Asian suppliers and reduce the impact of the long shipping times. In accordance with the lease terms, AWL paid $14,400, which represented the first six months' rent in advance.
13	A major hotel contacted AWL about supplying it with an 8-metre saltwater aquarium for the lobby. AWL agreed to this and received a $50,000 payment from the hotel. AWL ordered the tank the same day and it was scheduled to arrive on February 25. AWL has guaranteed that it will be installed before the end of February.
14	AWL paid its employees $9,000 for wages earned during the first two weeks of January.
15	AWL's board of directors declared dividends in the amount of $20,000, which will be paid on February 15.
19	AWL made sales totalling $62,000. Of this, half was cash and the balance was on account. The cost to AWL of the products sold was $36,000.

Adjusting entries:

Jan. 31	The company recorded the $9,000 in wages earned by employees during the last two weeks of the month. These wages will be paid on February 1, 2016.
31	AWL recorded the adjusting entry to depreciate the new computer equipment.
31	AWL recorded the adjusting entry for the warehouse lease.

Required:
Prepare the journal entries and adjusting entries for January 2016 based on the above transactions.

AP3-10 (Closing entries and ending retained earnings balance)

Presented below are the balances from Elsie's Electronics Ltd.'s general ledger as at September 30, 2016:

	DR	CR
Cash	28,000	
Accounts receivable	35,000	
Inventory	65,000	
Equipment	331,000	
Accumulated depreciation, equipment		150,000
Accounts payable		120,000
Bank loan payable		70,000
Unearned revenue		22,000
Common shares		10,000
Retained earnings		70,000
Dividends declared	18,000	
Sales revenue		488,000
Interest revenue		2,000
Cost of goods sold	316,000	
Wages expense	70,000	
Rent expense	26,000	
Depreciation expense	43,000	

Required:
a. Prepare the necessary closing entries for Elsie's Electronics at September 30.
b. Determine the closing Retained Earnings account balance.

AP3-11 (Closing entries and ending Retained Earnings balance)

Presented below are the balances from Zoë Developments Ltd.'s general ledger as at January 31, 2016:

	DR	CR
Cash	56,000	
Accounts receivable	135,000	
Inventory	124,000	
Prepaid expenses	5,000	
Equipment	361,000	
Accumulated depreciation, equipment		120,000
Accounts payable		32,000
Unearned revenue		5,000
Wages payable		11,000
Common shares		103,000
Retained earnings		88,000
Dividends declared	21,000	
Sales revenue		956,000
Interest revenue		19,000
Cost of goods sold	560,000	
Depreciation expense	10,000	
Wages expense	41,000	
Utilities expense	9,000	
Insurance expense	12,000	

Required:
    a. Prepare the necessary closing entries for Zoë Developments at January 31.
    b. Determine the ending Retained Earnings account balance.

AP3-12 (Journalize, post, and prepare trial balance and closing entries)

Singh Company started business on January 1, 2015. The following transactions occurred in 2015:
    1. On January 1, the company issued 10,000 common shares for $250,000.
    2. On January 2, the company borrowed $50,000 from the bank.
    3. On January 3, the company purchased land and a building for a total of $200,000 cash. The land was recently appraised at a fair market value of $60,000. (Note: As the building will be depreciated in the future and the land will not, these two assets should be recorded in separate accounts.)
    4. Inventory costing $130,000 was purchased on account.
    5. Sales to customers totalled $205,000. Of these, $175,000 were sales on account.
    6. The cost of the inventory that was sold to customers in transaction 5 was $120,000.
    7. Payments to suppliers on account totalled $115,000.
    8. Collections from customers on account totalled $155,000.
    9. Payments to employees for salaries were $55,000. In addition, there was $2,000 of unpaid salaries at year end.
    10. The interest on the bank loan was recognized and paid. The interest rate on the loan was 6%.
    11. The building was estimated to have a useful life of 30 years and a residual value of $20,000. The company uses the straight-line method of depreciation.
    12. The company declared dividends of $7,000 on December 15, 2015, to be paid on January 15, 2016.

Required:
    a. Prepare journal entries for each of the transactions and adjustments listed in the problem.
    b. Prepare the necessary T accounts and post the journal entries to them.
    c. Prepare an adjusted trial balance.
    d. Prepare the closing entries and post them to the T accounts.

AP3-13 (Journalize, post, and prepare trial balance and closing entries)

The Hughes Tools Company started business on October 1, 2015. Its fiscal year runs through to September 30 the following year. The following transactions occurred in the fiscal year that started on October 1, 2015, and ended on September 30, 2016.
    1. On October 1, 2015, Jill Hughes invested $175,000 to start the business. Hughes is the only owner. She was issued 10,000 common shares.
    2. On October 1, Hughes Tools borrowed $225,000 from a venture capitalist (a lender who specializes in start-up companies).
    3. On October 1, the company rented a building. The rental agreement was a two-year contract requiring quarterly rental payments (every three months) of $15,000, payable in advance. The first payment was made on October 1, 2015 (covering the period from October 1 to December 31). Thereafter, payments were due on December 31, March 31, June 30, and September 30 for each three-month period that followed. All the rental payments were made as specified in the agreement.
    4. On October 1, the company purchased equipment costing $220,000 for cash.
    5. Initial inventory was purchased for $90,000 cash.
    6. Additional purchases of inventory during the year totalled $570,000, all on account.
    7. Sales during the year totalled $800,000, of which $720,000 was on account.
    8. Collections from customers on account totalled $650,000.
    9. Payments to suppliers on account totalled $510,000.
    10. The cost of the inventory that was sold during the year was $560,000.
    11. Selling and administrative expenses totalled $86,500 for the year. Of this amount, $4,000 was unpaid at year end.
    12. Interest on the loan from the venture capitalist was paid at year end (September 30, 2016). The interest rate on the loan is 10%. In addition, $25,000 of the loan principal was repaid at that time.
    13. The equipment was depreciated based on an estimated useful life of 10 years and a residual value of $20,000.
    14. The company declared and paid a dividend of $7,000.

Required:
    a. Prepare journal entries for each of the transactions and adjustments listed in the problem.
    b. Prepare the necessary T accounts and post the journal entries to them.
    c. Prepare an adjusted trial balance.
    d. Prepare the closing entries and post them to the T accounts.

AP3-14 (Journalize, post, and prepare trial balance and closing entries)

A.J. Smith Company started business on January 1, 2015, and the following transactions occurred in its first year:

1. On January 1, the company issued 12,000 common shares at $25 per share.
2. On January 1, the company purchased land and a building from another company in exchange for $80,000 cash and 6,000 shares. The land's value is approximately one quarter of the total value of the transaction. (Hint: You need to determine a value for the shares using the information given in transaction 1, and the land and building should be recorded in separate accounts.)
3. On March 31, the company rented out a portion of its building to Frantek Company. Frantek is required to make quarterly payments of $7,500 on March 31, June 30, September 30, and December 31 of each year. The first payment, covering the period from April 1 to June 30, was received on March 31, and the other payments were all received as scheduled.
4. Equipment worth $120,000 was purchased on July 1, in exchange for $60,000 cash and a one-year note with a principal amount of $60,000 and an interest rate of 10%. No principal or interest payments were made during the year.
5. Inventory costing $250,000 was purchased on account.
6. Sales were $300,000, of which credit sales were $250,000.
7. The inventory sold had a cost of $190,000.
8. Payments to suppliers totalled $205,000.
9. Accounts receivable totalling $200,000 were collected.
10. Operating expenses amounted to $50,000, all of which were paid in cash.
11. The building purchased in transaction 2 is depreciated using the straight-line method, with an estimated useful life of 20 years and an estimated residual value of $30,000.
12. The equipment purchased in transaction 4 is depreciated using the straight-line method, with an estimated useful life of 10 years and an estimated residual value of $5,000. Because the equipment was purchased on July 1, only a half year of depreciation is recognized in 2015.
13. Dividends of $20,000 were declared during the year, of which $5,000 remained unpaid at year end.

Required:
a. Prepare journal entries for each of the transactions and adjustments listed in the problem.
b. Prepare the necessary T accounts and post the journal entries to them.
c. Prepare an adjusted trial balance.
d. Prepare the closing entries and post them to the T accounts.

AP3-15 (Determine statement of income amounts)

Jake Fromowitz owns and operates a tire and auto repair shop named Jake's Jack'em and Fix'em Shop. During the current month, the following activities occurred:
1. The shop charged $8,500 for repair work done during the month. All but one of Jake's customers paid in full. The one customer who had not yet paid owed Jake $500. Jake still has the car in the shop's parking lot and he intends to keep it until the customer pays the bill. The $500 is included in the $8,500.
2. The total cost of parts and oil purchased during the month was $2,900. Jake pays for the parts with cash, but the oil is purchased in bulk from a supplier on 30 days' credit. At the end of the month, he still owes $400 to this supplier.
3. The cost of the parts that were used in repair work during the month was $2,600.
4. Jake paid $750 monthly rent on the repair shop on the first day of the month, and since he had extra cash on hand at the end of the month, he paid another $750 to cover the next month's rent.
5. On the 10th of the month, Jake paid the previous month's utility bills of $250. At the end of the month, he received this month's utility bills, totalling $230, which he intends to pay on the 10th of next month.
6. Jake paid a friend $500 for helping him in the repair shop, and also gave him a new set of tires from the shop's stockroom. These tires had cost Jake $300, and could have been sold to customers for $400.
7. Utilities expenses related to operating the repair shop for the month totalled $875. All of these were paid during the month, as well as $125 that was owed from the previous month.
8. During the last week of the month, a customer dropped off her vehicle for repair work. Jake set aside $600 of parts to be used in these repairs, but he has not yet had time to do any work on this job.

Required:
Referring to the concepts discussed so far in this textbook:
a. Determine the amounts that would properly be reported in the statement of income for Jake's shop this month. If an item is excluded, explain why.
b. Calculate the net income for the month.

AP3-16 (Determine statement of income amounts)

Jan Wei owns a cycle store that sells equipment, clothing, and other accessories. During the month of June, the following activities occurred:
1. The business earned $30,000 from the sale of bicycles, clothing, and accessories. Half the sales were for cash and the other half was on account.
2. The merchandise that was sold originally cost $17,400.

3. Jan purchased additional merchandise on credit for $20,800.
4. Jan paid $18,000 to the suppliers of the merchandise purchased above.
5. The telephone, electricity, and water bills for the month came to $430. All but one of these bills, for $130, was paid by the end of the month.
6. Additional expenses for the month, including depreciation expense of $600, totalled $2,100. They were all paid in cash, except the depreciation expense, and were for repairs and maintenance done to the store.
7. At the end of May, Jan had an 8% loan for $5,000 outstanding with the bank. On the last day of June, Jan paid the monthly interest that was owed on the loan, and also paid $500 on the loan principal.
8. On the last day of June, a customer ordered a $1,300 bicycle. Jan did not have it in stock, so it was ordered and will be delivered in July. Since it was a special order, the customer paid a $300 deposit on it.

Required:
Referring to the concepts discussed so far in this textbook:
   a. Determine the amounts that would properly be reported in the June statement of income for Jan's shop. If an item is excluded, explain why.
   b. Calculate the net income for the month.

AP3-17 (Determine expenses)

The following are activities in a three-month period for Basiliadis Company:
   1. A new lease for the business premises goes into effect on October 1 and increases the rent from $1,000 to $1,150 per month. The rent for the next month is always prepaid on the last day of the current month. Accordingly, rent of $1,000 was paid on August 31, and $1,150 was paid on September 30 and October 31.
   2. The company borrowed $12,000 on September 1. The interest rate on the loan is 10% per year and interest is to be repaid quarterly.
   3. Basiliadis Company purchased a large supply of lubricant for $2,000 on September 1. The lubricant is to be used in the company's operations and is expected to last for four months.
   4. Employees work Monday through Friday and are paid each Monday for the previous week's work. The payroll for the week of Monday, September 29, to Friday, October 3 (paid on October 6), is $10,000. The payroll for the week of Monday, October 27, to Friday, October 31 (paid on November 3), is $10,500.

Required:
For each of the above independent cases, determine how much of the cost should be recognized as expense in each of the months of September, October, and November.

AP3-18 (Determine previous account balances)

Puzzle-Solver Consulting Services Ltd. has a December 31 year end. Selected items from the company's adjusted trial balance as at January 31, 2016, follow:

Partial Adjusted Trial Balance as at January 31, 2016		
	Debit balances	**Credit balances**
Supplies	$ 800	
Prepaid expenses	2,400	
Wages payable		$2,600
Unearned revenue		1,000
Service revenue		7,000
Wages expense	4,100	
Insurance expense	400	
Supplies expense	300	

Required:
   a. If supplies costing $1,000 were purchased in January, determine what the balance in the Supplies account must have been at the beginning of the month.
   b. If the Prepaid Expenses and Insurance Expense amounts relate to an insurance policy with an original term of one year, determine the total premium that was paid and the date on which the policy was purchased.
   c. If the amount paid for wages during the month was $3,000, determine what the balance in the Wages Payable account must have been at the beginning of the month.
   d. If there are no accounts receivable, and the amount of fee payments received during the month was $3,000, determine what the balance in the Unearned Revenue account must have been at the beginning of the month. (Note: Customers are required to prepay for all services.)

AP3-19 (Journalize, post, prepare statement of income and statement of financial position, and prepare closing entries)

On December 31, 2015, Clean and White Linen Supplies Ltd. had the following account balances:

Cash	$ 90,000	Accumulated Depreciation, Equipment	$ 90,000
Accounts Receivable	96,000	Accounts Payable	60,000
Inventory	60,000	Wages Payable	8,000
Supplies	2,000	Bank Loan Payable	150,000
Long-Term Investment	80,000	Common Shares	250,000
Equipment	330,000	Retained Earnings	100,000

In 2016, the following transactions occurred:
1. On January 1, paid $3,900 for a three-year fire insurance policy.
2. Purchased additional uniform inventory on credit for $120,000.
3. Sold uniforms for $180,000 on account. The inventory that was sold had been purchased for $100,000.
4. Performed cleaning services for customers for $520,000. One quarter of this amount was paid in cash and the remainder was on account.
5. Paid $130,000 to suppliers to settle some of the accounts payable.
6. Received $246,000 from customers to settle amounts owed to the company.
7. Paid $12,000 for advertising.
8. At the end of 2016, paid the interest on the bank loan for the year at the rate of 7%, as well as $30,000 on the principal. The remaining principal balance is due in three years.
9. Received a $3,000 dividend from the long-term investment.
10. Paid $15,000 for utilities for the year.
11. Declared and paid dividends of $12,000 at the end of the year.
12. Paid $102,000 for wages during the year. At year end, the company still owed $2,000 to the employees for the last week of work in December.
13. Depreciated the equipment for the year. The company had bought its equipment at the beginning of 2013, and it was expected to last 10 years and have a residual value of $30,000.
14. Made an adjustment for the cost of the insurance that expired in 2016.

Required:
a. Prepare journal entries to record each of the above transactions and adjustments.
b. Create T accounts. Enter the beginning balances from 2015, post the 2016 journal entries, and determine the ending balances for 2016.
c. Prepare an adjusted trial balance, and ensure that the total of the debit balances is equal to the total of the credit balances.
d. Prepare a statement of income for 2016.
e. Prepare the closing entries and post them to the T accounts.
f. Prepare a statement of financial position for 2016.

AP3-20 (Prepare journal entries, trial balances, and closing entries)

Evergreen Retail Company, whose fiscal year end is December 31, had the following transactions in its first year of operations:
1. Issued common shares for $65,000 cash on January 1, 2016.
2. Borrowed $15,000 of additional financing from the bank on January 1, 2016.
3. Bought equipment for $25,000 cash, also on January 1, 2016.
4. Made $60,000 of inventory purchases on account.
5. Had total sales of $92,000, of which $28,000 were on account. The cost of the products sold was $44,000.
6. Bought supplies for $800 cash.
7. Collected payments of $24,000 from customers on their accounts.
8. Paid suppliers $25,000 for the inventory that had been purchased on account.
9. Paid employees $36,200.
10. Paid the interest on the bank loan on December 31, 2016. The interest rate was 8%.
11. Declared dividends of $2,000, which will be paid in 2017.
Information for adjusting entries:
12. The equipment purchased on January 1 has an estimated useful life of eight years and an estimated residual value of $1,000 at the end of its life.
13. Supplies costing $200 were still on hand at the end of the year.
14. Wages in the amount of $800 were owed to employees at the end of the year. These will be paid early in 2017.

Required:
  a. Prepare journal entries for transactions 1 through 11.
  b. Prepare adjusting journal entries for adjustments 12 to 14.
  c. Set up T accounts, post the 2016 entries, and calculate the balance in each account.
  d. Prepare a trial balance, and ensure that the total of the debit balances is equal to the total of the credit balances.
  e. Prepare the closing entries, post them to the T accounts, and calculate the final balance in each account.

AP3-21 (Journalize, post, prepare statement of income and statement of financial position, and prepare closing entries)

Perfect Pizza had the following account balances at December 31, 2015:

Cash	$ 33,000	Vehicles	80,000
Accounts Receivable	15,000	Accumulated Depreciation, Vehicles	36,000
Inventory	10,000	Accounts Payable	7,000
Prepaid Expenses	3,000	Wages Payable	2,000
Equipment	60,000	Common Shares	110,000
Accumulated Depreciation, Equipment	30,000	Retained Earnings	16,000

During 2016, the following transactions occurred:
  1. Purchases of ingredients and supplies (inventory) were $230,000, all on account.
  2. Sales of pizzas for cash were $510,000, and sales of pizzas on account were $40,000.
  3. The company paid $105,000 for wages and $25,000 for utilities expenses.
  4. Payments for ingredients and supplies purchased on account totalled $220,000.
  5. Collections from customers for sales on account totalled $50,000.
  6. Ingredients and supplies valued at $225,000 were used in making pizzas.
  7. A dividend of $15,000 was declared and paid at the end of the year.
Information for adjusting entries:
  8. At the end of 2016, the amount of rent paid in advance was $1,500.
  9. Wages owed to employees at the end of 2016 were $2,500.
  10. The equipment had an estimated useful life of eight years, with no residual value.
  11. The delivery vehicles had an estimated useful life of six years with a residual value of $8,000.

Required:
  a. Prepare journal entries for transactions 1 through 7. Create new accounts as necessary.
  b. Prepare adjusting journal entries for adjustments 8 to 11.
  c. Set up T accounts, enter the beginning balances from 2015, post the 2016 entries, and calculate the balance in each account.
  d. Prepare a trial balance, and ensure that the total of the debit balances is equal to the total of the credit balances.
  e. Prepare a statement of income for 2016.
  f. Prepare the closing entries, post them to the T accounts, and calculate the final balance in each account.
  g. Prepare a statement of financial position for 2016.

AP3-22 (Prepare journal entries, trial balances, and closing entries)

Genesis Sportswear Ltd. is a wholesale company that buys sports clothing from manufacturers and sells it to retail stores. It had the following transactions in its first year of operations. The company's fiscal year end is December 31.
  1. Common shares were issued for $60,000.
  2. An insurance premium that provides coverage for the 12-month period starting March 1 was bought for $1,200 on February 15.
  3. Clothing was purchased for $75,000 on account.
  4. Employees were paid $46,900 in wages.
  5. Utilities expenses totalled $10,000. Of this amount, $9,000 was paid during the year; the remainder was due to be paid early in the next year.
  6. Sales recorded for the period totalled $105,000, all on credit.
  7. The cost of the inventory sold during the year was $62,000.

8. Cash collections on customer accounts totalled $96,000.
9. Payments to suppliers for clothing purchased totalled $54,000.
10. New equipment was purchased for $15,000 cash.

Adjusting entries: (Hint: You may need to use information recorded in the first 10 transactions.)

11. Recognized the amount of insurance expense that was incurred during the period.
12. Recorded depreciation of $2,000 on the equipment.

Required:
    a. Prepare journal entries to record transactions 1 through 10.
    b. Prepare adjusting journal entries for adjustments 11 and 12.
    c. Set up T accounts, post the 2016 entries, and calculate the balance in each account.
    d. Prepare a trial balance, and ensure that the total of the debit balances is equal to the total of the credit balances.
    e. Prepare the closing entries, post them to the T accounts, and calculate the final balance in each account.

AP3-23 (Determine amounts to appear in financial statements)

The following is the final trial balance (after the adjusting and closing entries had been made) for Hartman Company as at August 31, 2016. Hartman adjusts and closes its books at the end of each month.

	Debit balances	Credit balances
Cash	$ 6,000	
Accounts receivable	40,000	
Inventory	90,000	
Prepaid expenses	8,000	
Equipment	18,000	
Accumulated depreciation, equipment		$ 3,000
Accounts payable		32,000
Note payable		30,000
Interest payable		1,500
Common shares		50,000
Retained earnings		45,500
	$162,000	$162,000

Hartman's transactions in September 2016 and all relevant data for month-end adjustments follow:

1. Sales on account were $41,000.
2. Payments of $37,000 were collected from customers on their accounts.
3. Cash sales were $50,000.
4. Merchandise was purchased for $39,000 on account.
5. The cost of merchandise sold in September was $59,000.
6. Payments of $33,000 were made to suppliers for accounts owing.
7. Advertising costs of $3,000 were paid.
8. Employees were paid $15,000 in wages.
9. Wages of $1,000 were earned by employees but not yet paid.
10. Miscellaneous expenses of $9,000 were paid in cash.
11. The prepaid expense balance represented the rent paid in advance for the period from September 1 to December 31, 2016.
12. The equipment was purchased on September 1, 2015 (one year before the start of the current month), and is expected to have a total useful life of six years.
13. The note payable was dated March 1, 2015, and the principal is due to be repaid in two equal instalments on March 1, 2016 and 2017. Interest on the note, at a rate of 10% per year, is also to be paid on March 1, 2016 and 2017.

Required:
Based on the above information, answer the following questions:
    a. What amount should Hartman report as revenue for September?
    b. What amount should Hartman report as wages expense for September?
    c. What amount should Hartman report as rent expense for September?

    d. What amount should Hartman report as interest expense for September?

    e. As at the end of September, what should the balance in Hartman's cash account be?

    f. As at the end of September, what is the amount of Hartman's accounts receivable?

    g. As at the end of September, what should the balance in Hartman's merchandise inventory account be?

    h. As at the end of September, what is the amount of Hartman's accounts payable?

    i. Is the equipment expected to have any value at the end of its useful life? If so, how much?

    j. As at September 30, 2016, what is the carrying value of Hartman's equipment?

    k. What amount should be shown under long-term liabilities on Hartman's statement of financial position as at September 30, 2016?

AP3-24 (Prepare adjusting entries)

The trial balance for Cozy Fireplaces Inc. for December 31, 2016, follows:

	Debit balances	Credit balances
Cash	$ 89,000	
Accounts receivable	38,000	
Inventory	95,000	
Supplies	5,000	
Prepaid expenses	46,000	
Land	80,000	
Building	150,000	
Accumulated depreciation, building		$ 19,500
Accounts payable		21,400
Salaries and wages payable		0
Interest payable		0
Income tax payable		0
Unearned revenue		12,400
Bank loan payable		40,000
Common shares		150,000
Retained earnings		16,700
Sales revenue		840,000
Cost of goods sold	482,000	
Wages expense	95,000	
Rent expense	0	
Supplies expense	0	
Depreciation expense	0	
Interest expense	0	
Miscellaneous expense	14,000	
Income tax expense	0	
Dividends declared	6,000	
Totals	$1,100,000	$1,100,000

Additional information for adjusting entries:

    1. The deposits from customers were for future deliveries. As at December 31, three quarters of these goods had been delivered.

    2. There is $2,000 in salaries and wages owed at year end.

    3. Rent is paid in advance on the last day of each month. There was a balance of $3,000 in the Prepaid Expenses account on January 1, 2016. At the end of January, $3,000 was paid for the February rent and was debited to the Prepaid Expenses account. All the rent payments during the year were treated the same way. The rent for July to December increased to $4,000 per month. (Hint: Determine the amount of rent expense for 2016, as well as the correct amount that has been prepaid for 2017, and make an adjustment that will bring both these accounts to the correct balances.)

4. A count of the supplies at year end revealed that $500 of supplies were still on hand.
5. The building is being depreciated over 20 years with a residual value of $20,000.
6. The bank loan was taken out on April 1, 2016. The first interest payment is due on April 1, 2017. The interest rate is 9%.
7. Income tax for the year should be calculated using a tax rate of 30%. (Hint: After you finish the other adjusting entries, you will have to determine the *income before income tax* and then calculate the tax as 30% of this amount.)

Required:
Prepare the adjusting entries for the year 2016.

AP3-25 (Prepare adjusting entries)

The following trial balance before adjustments is for Snowcrest Ltd. on December 31, 2016:

	Debits	Credits
Cash	$ 10,000	
Inventory	24,000	
Advances to employees	2,000	
Supplies	3,000	
Equipment	56,000	
Accumulated depreciation, equipment		$ 4,000
Unearned revenue		6,000
Bank loan payable		20,000
Common shares		40,000
Retained earnings		9,000
Sales revenue		230,000
Cost of goods sold	130,000	
Wages expense	34,000	
Repairs and maintenance expense	25,000	
Rent expense	6,600	
Miscellaneous expense	15,000	
Dividends declared	3,400	
Totals	$309,000	$309,000

Data for adjusting entries:
1. As at December 31, 2016, 80% of the wages that had been paid in advance to the salespeople had been earned.
2. A count of the supplies at year end revealed that $600 of supplies were still on hand.
3. Depreciation on the equipment for 2016 was $1,000.
4. The unearned revenue was advance receipts for future deliveries of goods. By December 31, 2016, two thirds of these deliveries had been made.
5. The bank loan was a six-month loan taken out on October 1, 2016. The interest rate on the loan is 9%, but the interest is not due to be paid until the note is repaid on April 1, 2017.
6. Salaries owed at year end and not yet recorded were $500.
7. The rent expense figure includes $600 paid in advance for January 2017.
8. Income tax for the year should be calculated using a tax rate of 25%. (Hint: After you finish the other adjusting entries, determine the *income before income tax* and then calculate the tax as 25% of this amount.)

Required:
Prepare the adjusting entries for the year 2016.

AP3-26 (Determine statement of income and statement of financial position values)

The following information was available for Brilliant Consulting Company at its year end, December 31, 2016:
1. During the year, the company agreed to provide certain consulting services to a client for a fee of $10,000, which was received in advance. At the end of the year, it was estimated that 85% of the services had been provided.
2. The Supplies account had a balance of $350 at the beginning of the year and additional supplies costing $950 were purchased during the year. At the end of the year, a count of the supplies indicated that supplies costing $250 remained on hand.

3. A new "business occupancy" tax was introduced by the municipal government in 2016. The company was required to pay $1,800 to cover the period from April 1, 2016, to March 31, 2017. (Hint: Use the Property Tax Expense account.)

4. The company rents some surplus space in its building to a tenant for $1,500 per quarter, payable in advance. The agreement began on September 1, 2016, and the tenant paid $1,500 on that date and an additional $1,500 on December 1.

5. Another tenant rents space in the company's building for $750 per month, due on the first day of each month. The agreement began several years ago and the tenant has paid the rent as scheduled every month, except for the most recent one. At year end, the rent for December 2016 was still outstanding.

6. During the year, the company used an advertising agency and paid $3,000 for its services. In addition to this, there were unpaid advertising bills at year end totalling $450; these are due in January 2017.

Required:
For each of the items above, indicate what should appear on the statement of income for the year ended December 31, 2016, and on the statement of financial position as at that date.

AP3-27 (Determine statement of income and statement of financial position values)

The Great Graphics Group began operations on January 1, 2015. At the end of its *second* year of operations, and before any adjustments had been made, the trial balance was as follows:

	Debit balances	Credit balances
Cash	$ 8,600	
Accounts receivable	13,500	
Prepaid expenses	1,800	
Equipment	48,000	
Accumulated depreciation, equipment		$ 3,300
Accounts payable		11,000
Unearned revenue		7,500
Notes payable		18,000
Common shares		22,000
Retained earnings		7,200
Service revenue		45,500
Wages expense	33,000	
Supplies expense	3,300	
Advertising expense	1,700	
Rent expense	2,700	
Utilities expense	1,900	
	$114,500	$114,500

Analysis reveals the following additional data for adjustments to be made:

1. There were $2,000 of supplies on hand at year end.

2. The note payable was issued on October 1, 2016. It is a nine-month note, with an interest rate of 9% per year. The interest does not have to be paid until July 1, 2017, when the note is due to be repaid.

3. The balance in the Prepaid Expenses account is the insurance premium paid for a one-year policy that began March 1, 2016.

4. By year-end $4,500 of the amount recorded in the Unearned Revenue account had been earned. In addition, $3,000 of additional service fees had been earned, but not yet billed or recorded. The work was completed in December 2016, and the clients will pay for it in January 2017.

5. The equipment was acquired on April 1, 2015, and is being depreciated at a rate of $4,400 per year.

Required:
Calculate the amount that should appear (after adjustments) on the December 31, 2016, financial statements for each of the following items:

a. On the statement of income, related to supplies

b. On the statement of financial position, related to interest

c. On the statement of financial position, related to insurance

d. On the statement of income, related to service

e. On the statement of financial position, as the carrying value of the equipment

AP3-28 (Determine effects of omitted adjustment)

When it was preparing its financial statements for the year ended December 31, 2016, D'Amelio Ltd. failed to record $3,000 of accrued salaries. These salaries were paid, and recorded as an expense, in 2017.

Required:

State the effect (if any) that this error will have on each of the following financial statement items:

a. Net income for 2016

b. Total assets on December 31, 2016

c. Total liabilities on December 31, 2016

d. Total shareholders' equity on December 31, 2016

e. Net income for 2017

f. Total assets on December 31, 2017

g. Total liabilities on December 31, 2017

h. Total shareholders' equity on December 31, 2017

AP3-29 (Determine adjusted balances; prepare statement of income and statement of financial position)

On December 31, 2016, Information Inc. completed its third year of operations. Abdul Mukhtar is a student working part-time in the company's business office while taking his first accounting course. Abdul assembled the following list of account balances, which are not arranged in any particular order:

Accounts Receivable	$150,000	Advertising Expense	$ 76,000
Interest Expense	2,000	Cash	20,000
Notes Receivable	26,000	Inventory	140,000
Cost of Goods Sold	590,000	Dividends Declared	12,000
Common Shares	570,000	Unearned Revenue	6,000
Building	360,000	Insurance Expense	6,300
Accumulated Depreciation, Equipment	20,000	Retained Earnings (as at January 1, 2016)	177,000
Land	160,000	Equipment	200,000
Accumulated Depreciation, Building	40,000	Miscellaneous Expense	5,200
Sales	963,000	Accounts Payable	72,700
Utilities Expense	2,500	Wages Expense	125,000
Notes Payable	30,000	Supplies	3,700

These account amounts are correct, but Abdul did not consider the following information:

1. The amount shown as insurance expense includes $900 for coverage during the first two months of 2017.

2. The note receivable is a six-month note that has been outstanding for four months. The interest rate is 10% per year. The interest will be received by the company when the note becomes due at the end of February 2017.

3. As at December 31, 2016, the supplies still on hand had a cost of $600.

4. On November 1, 2016, the company rented surplus space in its building to a tenant for $1,000 per month. The tenant paid for six months in advance.

5. Depreciation for 2016 is $10,000 on the building and $20,000 on the equipment.

6. Employees earned $3,000 of salaries in December 2016 that will not be paid until the first scheduled payday in 2017.

7. Additional dividends of $50,000 were declared in December 2016, but will not be paid until January 2017.

Required:

a. Determine the amounts that would appear in an adjusted trial balance for Information Inc. as at December 31, 2016.

b. Prepare a statement of income for the year ended December 31, 2016.

    c. Calculate the amount of retained earnings as at December 31, 2016.
    d. Prepare a classified statement of financial position as at December 31, 2016.

AP3-30 (Calculate income and retained earnings; prepare statement of financial position)

Little Lads and Ladies Ltd. sells children's clothing. At the end of December 2016, it had the following adjusted account balances, which are listed in random order:

Cash	$ 3,000	Utilities Expense	$ 600
Wages Payable	500	Dividends Declared	1,200
Supplies Expense	4,200	Depreciation Expense	500
Equipment	23,000	Common Shares	20,000
Wages Expense	25,000	Telephone Expense	200
Prepaid Expenses	400	Interest Expense	300
Cost of Goods Sold	32,000	Accumulated Depreciation, Equipment	1,500
Sales Revenue	66,450	Retained Earnings	17,600
Accounts Receivable	10,000	Inventory	8,000
Rent Expense	4,800	Repairs and Maintenance Expenses	400
Bank Loan Payable	3,800	Supplies	800
Advertising Expense	750	Interest Payable	300
Accounts Payable	5,000		

Required:
    a. Identify the statement of income accounts and calculate the net income (or loss) for the year.
    b. Determine the amount of retained earnings at the end of 2016.
    c. Prepare a classified statement of financial position as at December 31, 2016.

AP3-31 (Calculate income and retained earnings; prepare statement of financial position)

Your assistant prepared the following adjusted trial balance data for Commerce Company on December 31, 2016. The accounts are arranged in alphabetical order.

Accounts Payable	$ 36,000	Land	$ 70,000
Accounts Receivable	67,000	Long-Term Investment	12,000
Accumulated Depreciation, Buildings	20,000	Miscellaneous Expenses	13,000
Buildings	72,000	Mortgage Payable	48,000
Cash	24,000	Notes Payable	15,000
Common Shares	85,000	Prepaid Expenses	500
Cost of Goods Sold	110,000	Retained Earnings	31,500
Depreciation Expense	4,500	Sales Revenue	179,800
Dividends Declared	12,400	Selling Expenses	27,000
Dividends Payable	4,000	Service Revenue	93,100
Income Tax Expense	8,000	Supplies	800
Income Tax Payable	2,000	Supplies Expense	2,200
Insurance Expense	1,400	Unearned Revenue	1,200
Interest Expense	1,700	Utilities Expense	2,400
Interest Payable	300	Wages Expense	60,000
Inventory	30,000	Wages Payable	3,000

Required:
a. Calculate the net income for the year ended December 31, 2016.
b. Determine the Retained Earnings balance as at the end of the year.
c. Prepare a classified statement of financial position as at December 31, 2016. The note payable is due in 6 months.

AP3-32 (Prepare statement of financial position—manufacturing company)

The following adjusted trial balance data are for Novasco Manufacturing Corporation as at December 31, 2016. (Note: The accounts are listed in alphabetical order, first for debit balances, then for credit balances.)

	Debit balances	Credit balances
Accounts receivable	$ 77,000	
Administrative expenses	75,000	
Cash	30,000	
Cost of goods sold	430,000	
Dividends declared	35,000	
Equipment	280,000	
Income tax expense	21,700	
Interest expense	25,000	
Inventory	290,000	
Prepaid expenses	3,000	
Selling expenses	95,300	
Short-term investments	65,000	
Accounts payable		$ 65,000
Accumulated depreciation, equipment		65,000
Common shares		150,000
Dividends payable		7,000
Income tax payable		13,000
Interest revenue		10,000
Notes payable (current portion)		85,000
Notes payable (non-current portion)		250,000
Retained earnings		114,000
Sales revenue		650,000
Unearned revenue		18,000
	$1,427,000	$1,427,000

Required:
Prepare a classified statement of financial position for Novasco Manufacturing Corporation as at December 31, 2016.

AP3-33 (Determine missing amounts in financial statements)

Lee's Enterprises Ltd. suffered serious flood damage that destroyed most of its accounting records. The statements shown here were reconstructed from the records that were recovered, but many of the amounts are missing.

The following information is also available, to help you determine the missing amounts:
1. The company's Retained Earnings balance at the end of 2014 was $10,000.
2. The company's profit margin ratio was 15% in 2015 and 10% in 2016.
3. In both 2015 and 2016, the company's current assets were twice the amount of the current liabilities.

	2015	2016
Statement of Income		
Revenues	A	200,000
Expenses	B	K
Net income	15,000	L
Retained Earnings		
Opening balance	C	M
Net income	D	20,000
Dividends	5,000	N
Ending balance	E	O
Statement of Financial Position		
Current assets	F	30,000
Other assets	54,000	P
Total assets	G	80,000
Current liabilities	10,000	Q
Long-term liabilities	H	10,000
Total liabilities	40,000	R
Common shares	I	20,000
Retained earnings	20,000	S
Total shareholders' equity	34,000	55,000
Total equity and liabilities	J	T

Required:
For each of the letters above, determine the missing dollar amount that will complete the financial statements. (Hint: It might not be possible to find all the missing amounts in the order they are presented in. You may have to skip over some, initially, and come back to them after you have determined other items.)

AP3-34 (Determine missing amounts in financial statements)

Rao's Recycling Centre suffered a serious fire that destroyed most of the firm's accounting records. The following statements were reconstructed from the records that were recovered, but many of the amounts are missing:

	2015	2016
Statement of Income		
Revenues	A	180,000
Expenses	B	K
Net income	14,000	L
Retained Earnings		
Opening balance	C	M
Net income	D	18,000
Dividends	5,000	N
Ending balance	20,000	O
Statement of Financial Position		
Current assets	E	30,000
Other assets	54,000	P
Total assets	F	90,000
Current liabilities	10,000	Q
Long-term liabilities	G	20,000
Total liabilities	40,000	R
Common shares	H	25,000
Retained earnings	I	S
Total shareholders' equity	J	55,000
Total equity and liabilities	74,000	T

The following information is also available, to help you determine the missing amounts:
1. The company's profit margin ratio was 10% in both 2015 and 2016.
2. In both 2015 and 2016, the company's current assets were twice the amount of the current liabilities.

Required:
For each of the letters above, determine the missing dollar amount that will complete the financial statements. (Hint: It might not be possible to find all the missing amounts in the order they are presented in.)

User Perspective Problems

UP3-1 (Differences between the adjusted trial balance and a set of financial statements)

Assume that you are part of a commercial lending team for a bank. As part of the loan terms, one of the bank's clients must submit monthly financial statements for review. The client has just phoned and left your boss a message asking if it would be enough to just provide the bank with an adjusted trial balance. Your boss has asked you to prepare a brief memo outlining any differences between the information that would be provided by the financial statements and that provided by the adjusted trial balance. Your boss has also asked that you recommend the position the bank should take regarding this request.

Required:
Respond to your boss's requests.

UP3-2 (Purpose of closing entries)

A friend came to ask you a question about accounting for a small business she started at the beginning of the year. She said that her accounting software had a "closing entry" option. She was uncertain what this meant, when she should select it, and what impact it would have on her company's accounting records.

Required:
Prepare a response to your friend's questions.

UP3-3 (Importance of the chart of accounts)

You have been asked to give a brief presentation to members of your local chamber of commerce regarding the importance of the chart of accounts in relation to managing their business.

Required:
Prepare an overview of the key points you plan to address in your presentation.

UP3-4 (Normal balances)

One of your friends, who is also a classmate, came to you in the library and asked if you can explain the concept of normal balances to her. She was busy on social media during part of the class in which this topic was discussed.

Required:
Prepare your response.

Reading and Interpreting Published Financial Statements

RI3-1 (Closing entries, unearned revenue and prepaid expenses)

Le Château Inc. is a leading Canadian specialty retailer offering contemporary fashion apparel, accessories, and footwear to women and men. Exhibits 3-21 and 3-22 contain excerpts from the company's consolidated financial statements dated January 25, 2014.

EXHIBIT 3-21	EXCERPT FROM LE CHÂTEAU'S CONSOLIDATED STATEMENTS OF CHANGES IN SHAREHOLDERS' EQUITY

(in thousands of Canadian dollars)

RETAINED EARNINGS	2014	2013
Balance, beginning of year	94,239	102,956
Net Loss	(15,986)	(8,717)
Dividends Declared	-	-
Balance, end of year	78,253	94,239

EXHIBIT 3-22   **EXCERPT FROM NOTE 3**

"Gift cards or gift certificates [collectively referred to as "gift cards"] sold are recorded as deferred revenue and revenue is recognized at the time of redemption or in accordance with the Company's accounting policy or breakage. Breakage income represents estimated value of gift cards that is not expected to be redeemed by customers and is estimated based on historical redemption patterns."

Required:
    a. Prepare the closing entries that would have been required to close the Income Summary and Dividends Declared accounts. Refer to Exhibit 3-21.
    b. The company has deferred revenues of $3,712 thousand as at January 25, 2014. Refer to Exhibit 3-22 and explain the note in your own words.
    c. The company has prepaid expenses of $2,292 thousand as at January 25, 2014. Identify two of Le Château's likely prepaid expenses and when they would be expensed.

RI3-2 (Retained earnings, depreciation and prepaid expenses)

High Liner Foods Inc. operates in the North American packaged foods industry and primarily processes and markets frozen seafood and distributes products to retail and food service customers. Exhibit 3-23 contains selected financial information for 2013.

EXHIBIT 3-23   **SELECTED 2013 FINANCIAL INFORMATION FOR HIGH LINER FOODS**

(in thousands of U.S. dollars)

Net Income	34,724
Retained Earnings, opening balance	66,373
Dividends Declared	10,305

Required:
    a. Determine the company's ending Retained Earnings balance. Refer to Exhibit 3-23.
    b. Identify three things that we know about the company because it has an opening balance in Retained Earnings.
    c. During the year ended December 28, 2013, High Liner Foods had depreciation expense of $6,006 thousand on its production equipment, $213 thousand on its building structures, and $816 thousand on its computer hardware and peripherals. Prepare the adjusting entry that would have been required if the company recorded all of its depreciation in a single entry.
    d. The company had prepaid expenses of $2,952 thousand as at December 28, 2013. Identify two types of likely prepaid expenses and explain when they would be expensed.

RI3-3 (Retained earnings, accrued liabilities and carrying value)

North West Company Inc. is a leading retailer to underserved rural communities and urban markets in northern and Western Canada and internationally. Its stores offer a broad range of products and services with an emphasis on food. Exhibit 3-24 contains an excerpt from the company's consolidated financial statements for the year ended January 31, 2014.

EXHIBIT 3-24   **EXCERPT FROM NORTH WEST COMPANY'S 2014 FINANCIAL STATEMENTS**

(in thousands of dollars)

Net Income	71,767
Retained Earnings, opening balance	128,224
Dividends Declared	54,229

Required:
a. Determine the company's ending retained earnings balance. Refer to Exhibit 3-24.
b. Identify three things that we know about the company because it has an opening balance in Retained Earnings.
c. The company had accounts payable and accrued liabilities of $128,999 thousand at January 31, 2014. Identify two possible liabilities the company may have had as part of this balance.
d. Based on the information below (given in thousands of dollars), determine the carrying value of the North West Company's building and computer equipment. Comment on how old or new these capital assets are and how you determined this.

	Cost	Accumulated Depreciation
Building	350,921	191,439
Fixtures & equipment	245,863	171,321

RI3-4 (Retained earnings, prepaid expenses and dividends)

Big Rock Brewery Inc. is a regional producer of premium craft beers and cider, which are sold across Canada. Exhibit 3-25 contains an excerpt from the company's consolidated financial statements for the year ended December 31, 2013.

EXHIBIT 3-25   EXCERPT FROM BIG ROCK'S 2013 FINANCIAL STATEMENTS

(in thousands of Canadian dollars)

Net Income	2,551
Deficit, Opening Balance	(68,739)
Dividends Declared	4,855

Required:
a. Determine the company's Retained Earnings (Deficit) balance using the information from Exhibit 3-25.
b. Identify three things that we know about the company because it has an opening deficit balance.
c. The company had $84,000 in prepaid insurance premiums at December 31, 2013. Which financial statement would this be presented on? When would the premiums be expensed?
d. On December 18, 2013, Big Rock's directors declared dividends of $0.20 per share on the company's 6,070,000 common shares. The dividend was paid on January 15, 2014. Prepare the journal entries necessary to record the declaration and payment of these dividends.

RI3-5 (Examine financial statement disclosures)
Required:
Find the annual report of a Canadian company that is listed on a Canadian stock exchange, and answer the following questions about it:
a. Has the company prepared a classified statement of financial position (balance sheet)? If not, look for an explanation and state it briefly.
b. Referring to items in the statement of financial position, explain what liquidity is and how it is reflected in the statement of financial position.
c. Discuss how important inventory is compared with the other assets on the company's statement of financial position. Also address how important capital assets (property, plant, and equipment) are to the company.
d. Does the company rely more heavily on debt financing or equity financing?

RI3-6 (Find additional information about a company)
Required:
For the company you selected in RI3-5, find at least three articles in the financial media that discuss the nature of this company's markets, and that forecast what the future may be for this sector of the economy. Write a one-page summary of your findings.

Cases

C3-1 Al's Gourmet Fish

Leadfoot Al decided to retire from a successful career in stock car racing and invest all his winnings in a fish farm. He had majored in genetics in university, and he experimented with many different species of fish before coming up with a catfish that had the texture and taste of ocean trout. After incorporating Al's Gourmet Fish Company and operating for two years, he decided to explore expansion possibilities. He talked with his banker about getting a loan and presented a statement of income for the current year, based strictly on cash flows, as follows:

Cash collected from sale of fish		$520,000
Less: Feed purchases	$460,000	
Purchase of new fish tank	40,000	
Wages paid	80,000	
Other operating expenses paid	20,000	600,000
Operating loss		(80,000)
Plus: Proceeds from sale of land		130,000
Net income		$ 50,000

From discussions with Al, the banker learned the following:
1. Of the cash collected in the current period from sales of fish, $120,000 was for shipments delivered to customers last year. All the sales made this year were collected before the end of the year.
2. The fish feed can be stored indefinitely, and about 40% of this year's feed purchases were still on hand at year end.
3. Two fish tanks were purchased last year at a total cost of $80,000. These tanks, along with the one purchased at the beginning of this year, were used all year. Each tank is expected to last five years.
4. The amount for wages includes $60,000 paid to Al, as compensation for his time devoted to the business.
5. There was a total of $1,000 in bills for other operating expenses for the current year that had not been recorded or paid by year end.
6. The land that was sold for $130,000 had been purchased two years ago for $90,000.

Required:
Provide Al and his banker with answers to the following questions:
a. What amount of revenue from the sale of merchandise should be reported in this period?
b. What amount of expense for fish food should be reported in this period? How should the remainder of the food be reported?
c. Should some amount for the fish tanks be included in calculating the income for the current period? If so, how much?
d. Is it all right for Al's company to pay him wages? Why or why not?
e. What amount for "other operating expenses" should be included in calculating the earnings for the current period?
f. The land was sold for more than its original purchase price. The difference between the selling price and the purchase price of a capital asset is called a gain, and is included on the statement of income in the period of the sale. What amount should be included in the company's earnings as the gain on the sale of the land?
g. How much did Al earn from his business this year?
h. Comment on whether you think Al should stay in the fish business or go back to auto racing. In addition to financial factors, briefly describe several non-financial considerations that would be relevant to this decision.

C3-2 Sentry Security Services

Samir Sarkov incorporated Sentry Security Services and began operations on January 1, 2016. After a busy year, Samir thinks his business has done well, at least in terms of the volume of work done. However, he has asked for your help in determining the financial results.

The company's accounting records, such as they are, have been kept by Samir's son. Although he kept good records of all the cash received and spent by the business during the year, he has no formal training in accounting. At the end of the year, he prepared the following statement:

SENTRY SECURITY SERVICES Statement of Cash Receipts and Disbursements For the Year Ended December 31, 2016		
Cash Receipts:		
Invested in the business by the Sarkov family	$ 25,000	
Received from customers for services provided	75,000	
Borrowed from the Provincial Bank	15,000	
		$115,000
Cash Disbursements:		
Paid to the Provincial Bank	6,500	
Rent paid	6,500	
Security equipment purchased	18,000	
Wages paid	37,000	
Security services truck payments made	25,000	
Insurance premiums paid	2,000	
Security system parts and supplies purchased	15,000	110,000
Cash remaining (equals the bank balance)		$ 5,000

After reviewing the records, you confirm that the amounts are correct, and you also discover these additional facts:
1. The business does most of its work for cash, but at the end of the year customers owe $5,000 for security services that were provided on account.
2. The amount borrowed from the Provincial Bank is a three-year loan, with an interest rate of 10% per year.
3. The amount paid to the bank during the year includes $1,500 of interest on the loan and $5,000 of principal.
4. The rental contract for the company's space covers a two-year period and requires payments of $500 per month, paid at the beginning of each month. In addition, the last month's rent had to be paid in advance. All the required payments have been made as scheduled.
5. The security equipment was purchased at the beginning of the year and has an estimated five-year lifespan, after which it will be worthless.
6. In addition to the wages that were paid during 2016, $250 is owed to employees for overtime that was worked during the last few days of the year. This will be paid early in 2017.
7. The security services truck payments consist of $21,000 paid to purchase the truck at the beginning of the year plus $4,000 paid for gas, oil, and repairs during the year. Samir Sarkov expects to use the truck for four years, after which he thinks he should be able to get about $1,000 for it as a trade-in on a new truck.
8. The $2,000 for insurance resulted from paying premiums on two policies at the beginning of the year. One policy cost $700 for one year of insurance coverage; the other policy cost $1,300 for two years of coverage.
9. In addition to the $15,000 of parts and supplies that were purchased and paid for during the year, creditors have billed the business $500 for parts and supplies that were purchased and delivered but not paid for.
10. A count at the end of the year shows that $1,750 of unused parts and supplies were still on hand.

Required:
a. Prepare an accrual-basis statement of income for the year ended December 31, 2016, and a classified statement of financial position for Sentry Security Services at the end of the year.
b. Comment on the company's performance during its first year of operations, and its financial position at the end of the year.

C3-3 Shirley's Snack Shop

Shirley Sze incorporated Shirley's Snack Shop on April 30, 2016, by investing $5,000 in cash. The following is a summary of the other events affecting the business during its first eight months of operations:
1. On May 1, Shirley acquired a licence from the municipality at a cost of $150. The licence allows her to operate the snack shop for a period of one year.
2. On May 2, she borrowed $10,000 from the bank and used most of it to buy equipment costing $9,600. The interest rate on the loan is 10%, and the interest is to be paid annually (each May). The entire principal

amount is repayable at the end of three years. Shirley estimates that the equipment will last 10 years, after which it will be scrapped. On December 31, 2016, she estimated that the equipment could have been sold for $9,200.

3. At the beginning of September, Shirley realized that she should have liability insurance and purchased a one-year policy effective immediately. The premium paid was $750.

4. Her business is located in a small shop near the university campus. The rental cost is $900 per month and she has paid nine months of rent thus far.

5. Shirley paid herself a salary of $1,000 a month, and a part-time assistant earned wages of $350 each month. However, she has not yet paid her assistant his wages for December.

6. Shirley's purchases of food supplies, on account, cost a total of $22,500. All but $4,500 of this has been used, and she still owes the supplier $4,000. Of the food supplies that have been used, most went into snacks that were sold to customers; however, Shirley ate some of them herself, as on-the-job meals. She estimates that the snacks she consumed were purchased from the supplier at a cost of approximately $200, and were priced to sell to her customers for approximately $400.

7. According to her bank records, Shirley received $42,300 from her customers and deposited this in the bank during the period. However, a customer still owes her $500 for snacks provided for a company party held shortly before the end of the year. The balance in her bank account on December 31 is $9,750.

8. Shirley thinks that she has had fairly successful operations since opening the business. However, she has no idea how to calculate its net income or determine its financial position.

Required:

a. Provide Shirley with a statement of income for the eight-month period ended December 31, 2016, and a statement of financial position as at that date.

b. Comment on the snack shop's performance during its first eight months of operations, and its financial standing as at December 31, 2016.

C3-4 Mbeke's Hardware Store

In the middle of January 2017, Mark Mbeke, the owner of Mbeke's Hardware Store, decided to expand the business by buying out a local lumberyard. To finance the purchase, Mark had to obtain financing from a local bank. The bank asked Mark to provide financial statements for the year ended December 31, 2016, as support for the loan application.

Over the last year, Mark was so busy managing the store that he had no time to review the financial aspects of its operations. However, when the company's bookkeeper provided him with a set of hastily prepared financial statements for 2016, Mark was pleasantly surprised to see that the hardware store's net income had increased from $60,000 in 2015 to $90,000 in 2016. He commented, "With financial results like these—a 50% increase in income during the past year—we should have no trouble getting the loan." However, further investigation revealed the following:

1. On January 2, 2017, the company repaid a $140,000 loan in full, including interest. The loan was a one-year, 10% term loan. No interest expense was recorded in 2016.

2. On January 3, 2017, wages of $10,000 were paid. A review of the time cards shows that these wages relate to work done in the last week of 2016.

3. Goods that originally cost $11,000 and were sold in December 2016 for $15,000 were returned by the customer on January 4, 2017. Accompanying the goods was a letter that stated, "As we agreed on December 30, 2016, these goods are not what we had ordered and are therefore being returned for full credit."

4. Mbeke's Hardware received bills totalling $2,000 in the first week of January 2017 for utilities and other operating costs incurred in 2016. They were immediately recorded as accounts payable when they were received.

Mark is concerned that some of these transactions may affect the company's financial statements for the year 2016, and therefore its ability to obtain the necessary bank financing.

Required:

a. Calculate the effect of each of these items on the store's net income for 2016.

b. By what percentage did the store's net income increase (or decrease) over the last year?

c. In light of this information, how should Mark proceed?

d. What should the bank do to ensure that it is receiving accurate financial information?

C3-5 Downunder Company

You have been retained by Downunder Company to straighten out its accounting records. The company's trusted accountant for the past 25 years suddenly retired to a tropical island in the South Pacific and, in his rush to get away, he seems to have misplaced the company's accounting records. Now the bank has asked for the latest financial statements, so it can determine whether to renew the company's loan. Luckily, you managed to find the following listing of accounts and their balances, in alphabetical order, written on the back of one of the accountant's travel brochures.

Accumulated Depreciation, Equipment	$ 4,000	Equipment (original cost)	51,500
Common Shares	20,000	Interest Expense	500
Accounts Receivable	20,200	Bank Loan Payable	15,000
Accounts Payable	13,000	Miscellaneous Expenses	8,000
Cash (in bank account and in cash box)	1,100	Sales to Customers	93,600
Cost of Goods Sold	41,000	Wages Expense	27,500
Inventory	7,900	Wages Payable	1,200
Depreciation Expense	2,000		

Required:

a. Based on the information available, prepare a statement of income for the year 2016 and a statement of financial position as at December 31, 2016. Note that there is no amount available for Retained Earnings, so you will have to enter whatever amount is required to make the statement of financial position balance.

b. Identify several additional pieces of information that would be needed for preparing more complete and accurate financial statements. (Hint: Think in terms of the types of adjustments that would normally be made.)

ENDNOTES

1. Gary P. Spraakman, "Management Accounting at the Historical Hudson's Bay Company: A Comparison to 20th Century Practices," *Accounting Historians Journal*, Vol. 26, No. 2, December 1999; Arthur J. Ray, *Give Us Good Measure*, University of Toronto Press, 1978; HBC 2013 annual report; HBC Heritage website, www.hbcheritage.ca/.
2. Yan Barcelo, "Devil in the Details," *CA Magazine*, January/February 2013.
3. CPA Standards and Guidance Collection; Part 1 — International Financial Reporting Standards; The Conceptual Framework.

4 Revenue Recognition and the Statement of Income

CORE QUESTIONS

If you are able to answer the following questions, then you have achieved the related learning objectives.

LEARNING OBJECTIVES

After studying this chapter, you should be able to:

●●● INTRODUCTION

- What is revenue and why is it of significance to users?
- Why are a company's revenue recognition policies of significance to users?

1 Explain the nature of revenue and why revenue is of significance to users.

●●● REVENUE RECOGNITION

- When are revenues recognized?

2 Identify and explain the general criteria for revenue recognition and the specific revenue recognition criteria related to the sale of goods, the provision of services, and the receipt of interest, royalties, and dividends.

●●● MEASUREMENT

- How is the amount of revenue measured?
- How do sales discounts and sales returns affect revenue recognition?

3 Explain how revenues are measured.

●●● STATEMENT OF INCOME AND COMPREHENSIVE INCOME

- How does a single-step statement of income differ from a multi-step statement of income?

4 Understand the difference between a single-step statement of income and a multi-step statement of income.

- What is comprehensive income and how does it differ from net income?

5 Understand the difference between comprehensive income and net income.

- How does a statement of income presenting expenses by function differ from one presenting expenses by nature of the items?

6 Understand the difference between presenting expenses by function or by nature of the item on the statement of income.

●●● FINANCIAL STATEMENT ANALYSIS

- What is meant by earnings per share and how is it calculated?

7 Calculate and interpret a company's basic earnings per share.

●●● Expanding the Cast to Bring in the Cash

Selling popcorn and other snacks doesn't add up to peanuts. Just look at Cineplex Inc., Canada's largest movie chain, with more than 160 theatres and 1,600 screens from coast to coast. In 2013, for every $1 in box office revenues, Cineplex earned $0.53 in concession revenues. Its total box office take was $665.3 million, while it earned $350.4 million from its concession stands. Even more significantly, in 2013, Cineplex earned a gross profit of $0.48 on each $1 of box office revenue, but earned a gross profit of $0.79 on each $1 of concession sales!

Movie tickets and snacks are part of Cineplex's revenue model—how it earns cash. Most movie theatres sell snacks because moviegoers want them and they're profitable. For example, guests at Cineplex theatres spent an average of $4.82 on concessions during each visit in 2013. But Cineplex has expanded the "cast of characters" in its revenue model partly because movie attendance ebbs and flows with the seasons and with the popularity of blockbusters. On the movie side, it's added Hindi and Punjabi films along with videos from live opera and theatre productions.

On the food side, Cineplex has launched its own branded Outtakes bistros and leased space for Tim Hortons and Pizza Pizza outlets. It moved beyond its theatres by acquiring a 50% stake in 2013 of YoYo's Yogurt Café, an Ontario-based self-serve frozen yogurt chain. "We believe Cineplex's proprietary food service brands represent an opportunity to grow our merchandising business outside the walls of our theatres," said Cineplex President and CEO Ellis Jacob in the company's 2013 annual report to shareholders.

Cineplex's revenue model grows even larger with its gaming business. It operates 10 XSCAPE Entertainment Centres in its theatres, offering video and interactive games with prizes and even a licensed lounge.

The company has varied operations in what it calls the "high-margin media business." Its Cineplex Media division shows advertising on its screens before showtime, as well as digital ads on signs inside the theatre, on its mobile apps, and other locations that are seen by its 80 million customers a year. Cineplex Digital Solutions provides digital signs, mobile advertising, and social media in stores such as Holt Renfrew and The Beer Store. In 2013, Cineplex bought EK3 Technologies (which it renamed Cineplex Digital Media), which provides in-store digital signs for clients such as McDonald's and Walmart. "We see a bright future for Cineplex in the digital signage space in North America," said Mr. Jacob.

Cineplex's main revenue sources and expenses are presented on its consolidated statements of operations. In 2013, Cineplex's total revenues were $1,171.3 million, which included $665.3 million in box office revenues, $350.4 million in concession revenues, and $155.6 million in other revenue from its various media businesses. After deducting expenses and income taxes, Cineplex had net income of almost $83.6 million—a happy ending for the company's shareholders![1]

INTRODUCTION

In Chapters 1 through 3, four basic financial statements were described, and we saw that two of these, the statement of income and the statement of cash flows, measure the company's performance across a time period. This chapter discusses the accounting concepts and guidelines for the recognition of income, provides more detail about the statement of income, and considers some of the challenges that are inherent in performance measurement.

■ **LEARNING OBJECTIVE 1**
Explain the nature of revenue and why revenue is of significance to users.

What is revenue and why is it of significance to users?

Revenues are defined as inflows of economic benefits from a company's ordinary **operating activities**. In other words, revenues result in inflows such as cash or accounts receivable and are generated by the transactions a company normally has with its customers, selling them products and/or providing services. There is a huge range of transactions that can be considered normal operating activities because there are so many different types of businesses. For example, the ordinary operating activities for clothing retailers include the sale of clothing and accessories, while the provision of air travel and vacation packages is a normal operating activity for airline companies. Your university or college has a range of activities considered normal operating activities. These include tuition revenues from providing educational services, the sale of goods in its bookstore or cafeteria, the sale of parking passes, and rental revenues from its student residences.

As we discussed in Chapter 2, there does not have to be a receipt of cash in order for a company to recognize revenue. This is why the term *economic benefit* is used when defining revenue. While the economic benefit will ultimately be an inflow of cash, the sale and the receipt of cash do not have to occur at the same time. In this chapter, we will see examples of revenue transactions for which the cash is received prior to the sale, at the time of sale, or subsequent to the sale.

The amount of revenue (or sales) is one of the most significant amounts reported in the financial statements. For a company to be successful, it must be able to generate revenues from what it is in the business of doing. A company's total revenues must be greater than the expenses incurred to generate them. When total revenues exceed total expenses, a company reports net income. Financial statement users see this as a sign that the company is viable, has the ability to sustain itself or grow, and has the ability to declare dividends. On the other hand, if total expenses exceed total revenues, a company reports a net loss. A user may see a loss as a signal that all is not well with the company. When losses occur, it is important for management and users to evaluate both the size and cause of the loss.

When assessing revenues, financial statement users evaluate both quantity and quality. Quantity refers to the amount of revenue and whether or not the trend shows an increase or decrease over a number of accounting periods. Quality refers to the source(s) of revenue and the company's ability to sustain the revenue over the longer term. For example, retail stores often report a key measure: same-store sales. This helps users to determine whether revenue growth is from new locations or increased sales at existing locations. If sales at established stores are increasing year over year, it suggests a high quality of earnings. If, on the other hand, a retailer reports a decrease in same-store sales, this may signal an issue with the quality of earnings.

> ### For Example
>
> **Canadian Tire Corporation** reported the following same-store sales growth for the various segments of its operations:
>
> | | 2013 | 2012 |
> | ----------------------------------- | ---- | ---- |
> | Canadian Tire retail stores | 1.8% | 0.3% |
> | Mark's/Mark's Work Wearhouse stores | 4.6% | 3.7% |
> | FGL Sports stores | 7.7% | 4.2% |
>
> From this we can see that, on a percentage basis, the company experienced sales growth in each of its segments in 2013, with the greatest sales growth at its FGL Sports stores.[2]

As we learned in Chapter 2, companies use the accrual basis of accounting. Under the accrual basis, accounting revenues are recognized when they are earned regardless of whether the related cash was received by the company. However, revenues must, at some point, be collected in cash. Cash is essential to a company's ultimate survival. Another way the quality of earnings is measured is to compare the cash flow from operations (from the statement of cash flows) with net income (or net earnings). If these two amounts are moving together (both up or both down) and if the cash flow from operating activities is greater than the net income, we consider the earnings to be of higher quality. If the two amounts do not move together and if the cash flow from operating activities is less than the net income, we consider the earnings to be of lower quality.

Why are a company's revenue recognition policies of significance to users?

Users need to be aware of the company's revenue recognition policies so that they can make informed judgements about reported revenues. Accounting standards outline principles for revenue recognition rather than providing specific rules, so it is possible that different companies have different revenue recognition policies. Therefore, when comparing companies, a user must understand which revenue recognition policies each company is using. Some companies have multiple business activities. For example, **Rogers Communications** sells Internet services, owns a Major League Baseball team, and publishes several magazines. Rogers uses different revenue recognition policies for each of its business activities. When analyzing such companies, it is important for users to understand the various revenue recognition policies in use.

Financial statement users can find information about a company's revenue recognition policies in the notes to its financial statements. Accounting standards require companies to disclose this information. These standards also require companies to disclose the amount of revenues for each significant category or stream of revenue.

REVENUE RECOGNITION

When are revenues recognized?

Determining when a company has earned revenue is one of the most critical accounting decisions. We learned in Chapter 2 that, under the accrual basis of accounting, revenues are recognized when they have been earned. Accounting standard setters have developed two **general revenue recognition criteria** to help management and other financial statement users determine when revenue is earned. The two general revenue recognition criteria state that revenue is earned when:

1. It is probable that economic benefits will flow to the company.
2. The amount of these benefits can be reliably measured.

In other words, a company has earned revenue when it is likely that a sales transaction will result in the company receiving an economic benefit (such as cash or accounts receivable), the amount of which can be reliably measured. While this can be relatively straightforward for many sales transactions, there are others for which professional judgement is required. To assist with this process, standard setters have established **specific revenue recognition criteria** for three common categories of revenue-generating activities:

1. the sale of goods;
2. the provision of services; and
3. the receipt of interest, royalties, and dividends.

Exhibit 4-1 presents the specific criteria applicable to each category. As you can see, the two general revenue recognition criteria (numbers 3 and 4) are common to all three categories of revenue-generating activities. One of the other specific criteria (criterion 5) is common to two of the categories, while the others are unique to one specific category.

Exhibit 4-1 Revenue Recognition Criteria by Category of Revenue-Generating Activity[3]

Criteria	Revenue is earned from the:		
	Sale of Goods	Provision of Services	Receipt of Interest, Royalties, and Dividends
1. The significant risks and rewards of ownership of the goods have been transferred to the buyer.	Yes	Not applicable	Not applicable
2. The seller has no continuing involvement or control over the goods.	Yes	Not applicable	Not applicable
3. The amount of the revenue can be reliably measured.	Yes	Yes	Yes
4. It is probable that the economic benefits from the transaction will flow to the seller.	Yes	Yes	Yes
5. The costs incurred or that will be incurred to complete the transaction can be reliably measured.	Yes	Yes	Not applicable
6. The portion of the total services completed can be reliably measured (if services are ongoing).	Not applicable	Yes	Not applicable

Let's look at each category of revenue-generating activity in a little more detail.

Sale of Goods

Accounting standards identify five revenue recognition criteria that must be met before a company selling goods can recognize revenue. Applying these criteria to sales transactions can result in the recognition of revenue at different times. In most cases, revenue is recognized at the time of sale (when the buyer takes possession of the goods), but there are situations where it may be appropriate to recognize revenue at times other than the time of sale. These can include recognizing revenue at the time of production or at the time of collection. These situations are relatively rare in practice or are limited to a few specialized industries. As such, they are beyond the scope of an introductory accounting course, so we will focus only on recognizing revenues at the time of sale.

Exhibit 4-2 outlines how each of the five specific criteria is applied when determining when revenue from the sale of goods can be recognized.

HELPFUL HINT
Regardless of the nature of a company's revenues (sales of goods, provision of services, and so on), they can only be recognized if the two general revenue recognition criteria are met (that is, it must be probable that economic benefits will flow to the seller and the amount of revenue must be reliably measurable). It can be helpful to check whether these two criteria have been met prior to considering the other specific criteria.

Exhibit 4-2 Specific Revenue Recognition Criteria for the Sale of Goods

Criterion	How Applied
1. The significant risks and rewards of ownership of the goods have been transferred to the buyer.	Recognizing revenues at the time of sale is the most common revenue recognition point in relation to the sale of goods. At this point, the selling company has normally completed everything it has to do in relation to the transaction and the customer either takes the goods away or the goods are shipped to it. When the title to the goods has been transferred to the customer, the risks and rewards of ownership of the goods has also been shifted.
2. The seller has no continuing involvement or control over the goods.	When the customer takes the goods away or the goods have been shipped to the customer, the selling company no longer has control over the goods.
3. The amount of the revenue can be reliably measured.	At the time of sale, the selling price has normally been agreed to by the seller and buyer, so the selling company can quantify the amount of the economic benefits that will flow to it in relation to the transaction.
4. It is probable that the economic benefits from the transaction will flow to the seller.	Often the customer will pay cash, which provides immediate economic benefits to the seller. If the company sells the goods on credit, the amount of the receivable is also a measurable economic benefit. Most companies will not sell on credit if they have doubts about their ability to collect from the customer in the future. That is, credit will not be granted unless the selling company considers it probable that the customer will pay in the future.
5. The costs incurred or that will be incurred to complete the transaction can be reliably measured.	Generally, the selling company has incurred all of the costs related to the transaction by the time the goods are sold. That is, the costs of the goods, including transportation and selling costs, have been incurred. However, there may be other costs associated with completing the sale of the goods that will be incurred in the future. The most common example is bad debts related to selling on account: situations in which customers who purchased on account may not pay. These costs can normally be estimated using either historical data (the selling company's previous collections experience) or industry data (the collection experience of other companies in the industry). If the selling company can do this, then the final criterion is met.

FINANCIAL STATEMENTS

For Example

The revenue recognition policy of Canadian retailer **Dollarama Inc.** is typical of many retailers. The company recognizes revenue from the sale of goods at the time the customer pays for the goods and takes possession of them (at the cash register). The company's revenue recognition policy is included in the significant accounting policies note to the financial statements and is as follows:[4]

Revenue recognition

The Corporation recognizes revenues at the time the customer tenders payment for and takes possession of the merchandise. All sales are final. Revenue is shown net of sales tax, rebates and discounts. Gift cards sold are recorded as a liability, and revenue is recognized when gift cards are redeemed.

For Example

Rogers Sugar Inc. is headquartered in Vancouver, but has operations in Alberta, Ontario, Quebec, and New Brunswick. The company is the largest producer of refined sugar in Canada and also packages and markets sugar products. The company's revenue recognition policy, presented below, explains that the company recognizes revenue from the sale of goods at the time of shipment, net of estimated returns and allowances. The company's revenue recognition policy also explains how the company estimates these allowances, which are primarily volume rebates.[5]

(continued)

For Example (continued)

Revenue recognition

Revenue is measured at the fair value of the consideration received or receivable and recognized at the time sugar products are shipped to customers, at which time significant risks and rewards of ownership are transferred to the customers. Revenue is recorded net of all returns and allowances, and excludes sales taxes.

Sales incentives, including volume rebates provided to customers are estimated based on contractual agreements and historical trends and are recognized at the time of sale as a reduction in revenue. Such rebates are primarily based on a combination of volume purchases and achievement of specified volume levels.

Provision of Services

Companies that earn revenue from the delivery of services are a growing sector of the economy. Examples of service revenues include:

- subscriber fees related to cell phones (including data or roaming services), television, or Internet services;
- guest, charter, and cargo revenues when airlines provide flight services to their customers;
- service and maintenance revenues provided by equipment and vehicle manufacturers; and
- tuition revenues when universities and colleges provide educational services.

Accounting standards identify four revenue recognition criteria that must be met before a company selling services can recognize revenue. Exhibit 4-3 outlines how each of the four specific criteria is applied when determining when revenue from the provision of services can be recognized.

Exhibit 4-3 Specific Revenue Recognition Criteria for the Provision of Services

Criterion	How Applied
1. The amount of the revenue can be reliably measured.	At the time of entering into an agreement to sell/purchase services, the price is normally agreed to by the seller and buyer. As such, the selling company can normally quantify the amount of revenue related to the transaction.
2. It is probable that the economic benefits from the transaction will flow to the seller.	If the customer pays cash, there are no concerns regarding the probability that the economic benefits will flow to the seller. Most companies will not sell on credit if they have doubts about their ability to collect from the customer in the future. That is, credit will not be granted unless the selling company considers it probable that the customer will pay in the future.
3. The costs incurred or that will be incurred to complete the transaction can be reliably measured.	The seller must be able to estimate the total costs that will be incurred to provide the contracted services. Normally, the seller will be able to determine this with sufficient reliability because these estimates would have been prepared prior to the company entering into the contract.
4. The portion of the total services completed can be reliably measured (if services are ongoing).	Many service contracts require the seller to provide services for multiple periods; for example, student tuitions require universities or colleges to provide classes over a number of months. Other service contracts require the seller to provide services by completing a project that will take multiple accounting periods to complete; for example, construction management or engineering services in relation to the construction of a building. In both these situations, the seller must be able to reliably quantify the proportion of the services that has been provided in a specific accounting period. This is known as recognizing revenue using the **percentage of completion method**. This can be done as a percentage of total services. For example, 4 weeks completed of a 13-week semester in the case of a university or college would result in a 30.8% completion percentage. Instead, revenue can be recognized as costs to date relative to the total expected costs or based on a survey (such as an engineering analysis) of the work completed.

The application of these criteria normally results in revenue from the provision of services being recognized in the period in which the services are performed.

FINANCIAL STATEMENTS

For Example

The revenue recognition policy of **Air Canada** illustrates how the revenue recognition criteria related to the provision of services are applied. For example, revenues related to providing flights to passengers or cargo services are recognized when the flights occur; that is, when the services are provided. The company also sells flight passes that enable customers to take unlimited flights during the period of the pass. In this case, Air Canada recognizes the revenues from the sale of the pass evenly over the period for which the pass is valid, which is consistent with the fourth criterion related to the provision of services. The company's revenue recognition policy is included in the significant accounting policies note to the financial statements and is as follows:[6]

C) PASSENGER AND CARGO REVENUES

Passenger and cargo revenues are recognized when the transportation is provided, except for revenue in unlimited flight passes which is recognized on a straight-line basis over the period during which the travel pass is valid. The Corporation has formed alliances with other airlines encompassing loyalty program participation, code sharing and coordination of services including reservations, baggage handling and flight schedules. Revenues are allocated based upon formulas specified in the agreements and are recognized as transportation is provided. Passenger revenue also includes certain fees and surcharges and revenues from passenger-related services such as ticket changes, seat selection, and excess baggage which are recognized as the services are provided.

Receipt of Interest, Royalties, and Dividends

Accounting standards identify two revenue recognition criteria that must be met before a company can recognize revenues related to interest, royalties, or dividends. Exhibit 4-4 outlines how each of the specific criteria is applied when determining when revenue from the receipt of interest, royalties, or dividends can be recognized.

Exhibit 4-4 Specific Revenue Recognition Criteria for the Receipt of Interest, Royalties, and Dividends

Criterion	How Applied
• The amount of the revenue can be reliably measured.	The amount of revenue can generally be measured because companies will know: • the interest rate and outstanding principal, • the royalty rate and the base to which it is applied, or • the dividend rate and number of shares held.
• It is probable that the economic benefits from the transaction will flow to the company.	The company will consider the likelihood that the interest, royalties, or dividends will be paid when determining whether revenue has been earned. For example, generally a company would only lend funds to a borrower it has assessed as creditworthy and may have taken security over assets of the borrower that could be drawn upon in the event the borrower failed to repay the outstanding principal and interest. Likewise, companies would assess the creditworthiness of a company with which they entered into royalty agreements. Normally, a company must have a sufficient cash balance available to meet any dividends it declares.

For Example

The Second Cup Limited is a specialty coffee franchisor. There are 356 cafés operating in Canada under the Second Cup trade name, of which 10 are company-owned stores. The remaining 346 stores are franchises that pay royalties to the Second Cup Limited. For 2013, the company's effective royalty rate was 7.6% of franchised café sales. The company recognizes these royalties as products are sold in accordance with the revenue recognition policy presented below.[7]

p. Revenue recognition
Revenue is recognized when it is probable the economic benefits will flow to the Company and delivery has occurred, the sales price is fixed or determinable, and collectability is reasonably assured. Revenue is measured at the fair value of the consideration received or receivable. Revenue is reduced for estimated customer returns, rebates and other revenue related concessions.

(i) Royalties
Royalty revenue from franchised cafés is recognized as the products are sold based on agreed percentage royalty rates as a function of the franchise location sales. Revenue is recognized on an accrual basis in accordance with the substance of the relevant agreement, provided that it is probable that the economic benefits will flow to the Company and the amount of revenue can be measured reliably.

(ii) Sale of goods
Revenue from the sale of goods from Company-operated cafés and from the sale of products through the e-commerce channel is recognized as the products are delivered to customers.

MEASUREMENT

How is the amount of revenue measured?

Whether they are selling goods, providing services, or earning interest, royalties, or dividends, companies must be able to reliably measure the amount of revenue if they are to meet the revenue recognition criteria. Accounting standards state that revenue should be measured at the **fair value** of the consideration received or receivable. Fair value is the price of a product or service that both the buyer and seller agree to at the time of the transaction. In many transactions, the consideration is cash, which makes the measurement of the fair value of revenue relatively simple, because the amount of revenue equals the amount of cash received from the buyer. It is important to note that the amount of revenue is not determined using the listed or posted price, but rather the price actually agreed to by the buyer and seller. As such, the fair value is determined *after* any **trade discount** (a negotiated or posted reduction to the selling price) or any **quantity discount** (a discount offered to a customer purchasing large quantities of goods).

For example, assume you purchased a pair of shoes at a shoe store in the mall. The posted price (or regular price) of the shoes was $125. However, the shoes were on sale for 20% off, meaning that you were able to purchase them for $100 ($125 × 80%). You paid the store with cash or a credit card and left with your shoes. In this example, the store can reliably measure the amount of revenue ($100). The store has also met the other criteria related to the sale of goods: the risks and rewards of ownership have transferred, the store has no continuing involvement with the shoes, the economic benefits have flowed to the seller, and the costs of the transaction are known. As such, the shoe store can recognize $100 of revenue from the sale of the shoes immediately. The trade discount of $25 would not be recorded.

The measurement of revenue is not always as simple as the example above suggests. For example, companies such as Rogers Communications Inc. and Telus sell products (smart phones) and services (data access) together for one price. This is known as **bundling**. In transactions like this, if you agree to pay a monthly fee for phone and data services, you may receive a phone at no apparent cost. Accounting standards require these transactions to be accounted for as separate components (the sale of services and the sale of the smart phone). These companies will need to estimate a fair value for each component. They will then recognize the appropriate revenue as each component is earned.

■ LEARNING OBJECTIVE 3
Explain how revenues are measured.

KEY POINT
Revenue is measured using the fair value of the consideration received or receivable, after any trade or quantity discounts.

Transactions involving bundled sales are beyond the scope of introductory accounting. However, they are one example of sales transactions for which the measurement of revenues is complex. There are numerous other examples that will be discussed in more advanced accounting courses. For now, it is important that you be aware that determining the amount of revenue can be more complicated than simply looking at the amount of cash received or receivable in the future.

How do sales discounts and sales returns affect revenue recognition?

There are two common commercial practices that can affect the amount of revenue reported by a company. These are the use of **sales discounts** and the effect of **sales returns**.

TAKE**5**

When a company makes sales on account, it generally gives customers 30 days (or more), interest-free, to pay their account. To stimulate these customers to pay their accounts more quickly, some companies provide terms, known as sales discounts, which provide the customer with a discount off the purchase price if they pay within a shorter period of time. A typical sales discount is "2/10, n/30," which means that the customer could take a 2% discount if they paid within 10 days of purchase or, if this was not done, the net (or full) amount of the account would be due within 30 days. If a customer took advantage of a sales discount, then the seller would only receive 98% of the selling price when the customer paid their account. Companies offering sales discounts do not normally adjust the original amount of the sales revenue recognized, but instead record sales discounts in a **contra revenue account** (meaning it will normally have a debit balance). The sales discounts are then subtracted from sales revenue, with only the resulting **net sales** amount reported on the statement of income (also known as the statement of earnings or income statement). Using a contra revenue account enables the seller to track the use of sales discounts by its customers. This information allows the company to assess the effectiveness of the technique and the costs associated with it. This information would not be available if the sales discounts were accounted for by a direct reduction in sales revenue. The accounting for a sales discount is presented in Exhibit 4-5.

Exhibit 4-5 Accounting for a Sales Discount

On April 7, Talty Engineering Ltd. (TEL) recorded $25,000 in revenues related to a project it was working on for Gillis Developments Ltd. (GDL). The terms were 2/10, n/30.

If GDL paid on April 11, the journal entries for the sale and payment transactions would be as follows:

April 7	Accounts Receivable	25,000	
	Sales Revenue		25,000
April 11	Cash[1]	24,500	
	Sales Discounts[2]	500	
	Accounts Receivable		25,000

[1]Cash = $25,000 × 98% = $24,500
[2]Sales Discount = $25,000 × 2% = $500

In April, TEL would report net sales revenues of $24,500 (sales revenue of $25,000 – sales discounts of $500).

The other common commercial practice that has an impact on the amount of revenue reported is sales returns. Many companies provide a period in which customers can return goods for a variety of reasons (such as they were the wrong goods or they arrived damaged). When a customer returns goods, the seller may offer a refund (either in cash or as a reduction of accounts receivable, if the customer's payment is still outstanding). It may also replace the product or offer the customer a reduction in the sales price, which is known as an allowance, if they are willing to keep the goods. Being able to assess the extent of sales returns and allowances is important information for management because it helps them evaluate product quality, either the quality of goods purchased from suppliers or the quality of the company's own manufacturing process. Just as was done with sales discounts, companies normally use a contra revenue account to track this information. The account is normally called **sales returns and allowances** and is subtracted from sales revenue when determining the net sales amount to be reported on the statement of income. The accounting for sales returns and allowances is presented in Exhibit 4-6.

Exhibit 4-6 Accounting for Sales Returns and Allowances

On October 12, Visinet Ltd. (VL) sold products to one of its customers for $50,000 on account. Five days later, the customer contacted VL to report that a few of the goods were not the colour that they had ordered. VL's sales manager negotiated with the customer and agreed to reduce the sales price by $400 if the customer agreed to keep all of the products. The customer paid the account on October 28.

The journal entries for the sale and payment transactions would be as follows:

October 12	Accounts Receivable	50,000	
	Sales Revenue		50,000
October 17	Sales Returns and Allowance	400	
	Accounts Receivable[1]		400
October 28	Cash	49,600	
	Accounts Receivable		49,600

In October, VL would report net sales revenues of $49,600 (sales revenue of $50,000 – sales returns and allowances of $400).

[1]If the customer had already paid for the goods, then the credit could have been to cash (if a refund was provided), credit notes payable (if a credit note to be used against future purchases was provided), or inventory (if replacement goods were provided).

Companies must estimate possible sales returns when recognizing revenue; otherwise, sales revenue and, in turn, net income may be overstated. This is required by the fifth revenue recognition criterion related to the sale of goods. It requires that companies estimate the costs that will be incurred to complete the transaction.

For Example

Canadian Tire's return policy, which is detailed on the company's website, is as follows:

"Unopened items in original packaging returned with a receipt within 90 days of purchase will receive a refund to the original method of payment or will receive an exchange. Items that are opened, damaged and/or not in resalable condition may not be eligible for a refund or exchange."

The company accounts for sales and warranty returns in accordance with the following accounting policy:[8]

Sales and warranty returns
The provision for sales and warranty returns relates to the Company's obligation for defective goods in current store inventories and defective goods sold to customers that have yet to be returned, as well as after sales service for replacement parts. Accruals for sales and warranty returns are estimated on the basis of historical returns and are recorded so as to allocate them to the same period the corresponding revenue is recognized. These accruals are reviewed regularly and updated to reflect management's best estimate; however, actual returns could vary from these estimates.

FINANCIAL
STATEMENTS

We can see from the Canadian Tire example that the company estimates the amount of expected sales returns using historical results. The estimated returns are recorded in the same period as the related sales, which ensures that the company's net sales revenues are fairly stated.

STATEMENT OF INCOME AND COMPREHENSIVE INCOME

In Chapter 1, we learned that the objective of the statement of income was to measure the company's performance in terms of the results of its operating activities for a month, quarter, or year. A company's income was the difference between the revenues it earned during the period and the expenses incurred during the same period to earn that revenue. In this chapter, we have expanded upon the revenue recognition criteria to help give us a better understanding of when revenues are earned and can be reported on the statement of income. In this part of the chapter, we will revisit the statement of income and discuss a couple of the different formats used to prepare it. Understanding the way in which information is presented in these formats will help you to interpret the information presented.

How does a single-step statement of income differ from a multi-step statement of income?

There are two main formats that can be used to prepare a statement of income: the single-step format and the multi-step format. When a company uses a **single-step statement of income**, all items of revenue are presented first regardless of the source, together with a total revenue amount. This is followed by a list of all expense items, including income taxes, together with a total expense amount. The total expense amount is subtracted from the total revenue amount to calculate net income or loss for the period. In other words, one arithmetic step is required to arrive at net income (loss).

Exhibit 4-7 illustrates the format of a single-step statement of income.

Exhibit 4-7 Single-Step Statement of Income Format

SHARP LTD.	
Statement of Income	
For the year ended December 31, 2016	
Revenue	
Sales	$500,000
Interest income	25,000
Total revenue	525,000
Expenses	
Cost of goods sold	415,000
Salaries expense	30,000
Rent expense	9,000
Utilities expense	7,000
Depreciation expense	6,000
Interest expense	4,000
Income tax expense	10,800
Total expenses	481,800
Net income	$ 43,200

While the single-step statement presents all of the required information, it presents it in a way that requires users to complete their own analysis to determine important measures such as gross profit (or gross margin) or net income from operating activities (net income without incidental revenues such as interest or dividend income). These issues are alleviated when a multi-step statement of income is prepared.

As the name suggests, the **multi-step statement of income** requires several steps to reach a company's net profit or loss. The results of each step provide the user with a key piece of information. A typical multi-step statement includes the following five steps:

1. Sales Revenue (or Revenue)	The revenues reported in this step are the revenues earned by the company from its operating activities—what the company is in the business of doing. Operating activities can be the sale of goods or services. The sales revenue figure is generally presented on a net basis, after sales discounts and sales returns and allowances.
2. Gross Profit (or Gross Margin)	As discussed in Chapter 1, this is the difference between sales revenue and the cost of goods sold. This step is required for retail companies, but not for companies selling services because they do not have any cost of goods sold.
	Gross profit is a key performance measure for retail companies. Dividing gross profit by net sales revenue results in the gross profit margin percentage. You can use the gross profit and gross profit margin percentage to evaluate a company's performance over time or compare it with other companies in the same industry.
3. Profit from Operations (or Operating Income)	This is the difference between gross profit and the company's operating expenses. Operating expenses, such as advertising, depreciation, rent, and salaries, are subtracted from gross profit (retail company) or from revenues (service company).
4. Profit Before Income Tax Expense (or Income Before Income Taxes)	This step factors in all of the company's non-operating activities. This includes activities that a company engaged in during the year that are not part of its normal operating activities. This includes revenues such as interest earned on employee loans or dividends received from short-term investments and expenses such as interest paid on loans. Incidental revenues are added to profit from operations, while any incidental expenses are subtracted, to determine profit before income tax expense.
5. Net Income (Loss) (or Profit)	This is the final step in preparing a multi-step statement of income. Income tax expense (or the provision for income taxes) is subtracted from profit before income tax to arrive at the net income (loss) for the accounting period.

Exhibit 4-8 illustrates the format of a multi-step statement of income.

Exhibit 4-8 Multi-Step Statement of Income Format

TAKE**5**

SHARP LTD. Statement of Income For the year ended December 31, 2016	
Sales revenue	$500,000
Cost of goods sold	415,000
Gross profit	85,000
Operating expenses	
Salaries expense	30,000
Rent expense	9,000
Utilities expense	7,000
Depreciation	6,000
Total operating expenses	52,000
Profit from operations	33,000
Other revenues and expenses	
Interest revenue	25,000
Interest expense	(4,000)
Profit before income tax	54,000
Income tax expense	10,800
Net income	$ 43,200

KEY POINTS
Statements of income prepared using a multi-step format present key measures, including gross profit and profit from operating activities, making analysis easier for decision makers.

As you can see from Exhibits 4-7 and 4-8, the choice of format has no effect on the revenues, expenses, and net income amounts reported. Each presents information on the company's performance in different ways, which can have an impact on the understanding of those results. The benefit of a multi-step statement of income is that it allows the reader to easily identify gross profit and profits earned from operating activities separately from other revenues and expenses related to non-operating activities. This can be important information for decision-makers such as shareholders, potential investors, and creditors.

Exhibits 4-7 and 4-8 are illustrations of the single-step and multi-step formats, but in practice, companies are free to use hybrid formats in which some parts of the statement follow a single-step format, while other parts follow a multi-step format. There is nothing in the accounting standards that prohibits a company from using whatever model it believes presents its financial performance in the most relevant way for the financial statement users.

■ LEARNING OBJECTIVE 5
Understand the difference between comprehensive income and net income.

What is comprehensive income and how does it differ from net income?

In addition to reporting net income, public companies must report comprehensive income in their financial statements. **Comprehensive income** is defined as the total change in the shareholders' equity (or net assets) of the enterprise from non-owner sources. It is equal to net income plus **other comprehensive income**. Accounting standards require that certain gains and losses be reported as other comprehensive income rather than being included in net income. These gains and losses normally arise when certain financial statement items are revalued, either to fair value or as a result of changes in foreign currency exchange rates. As these revaluation transactions are not with third parties, they are considered to be unrealized. They are excluded from net income, but are included in other comprehensive income. These revaluation transactions are beyond the scope of an introductory accounting course, but it is important that you have a basic understanding of the difference between net income and total comprehensive income. Other comprehensive income is added to net income to arrive at the total comprehensive income. Comprehensive income and its components are an integral part of the financial statements. The items that make up other comprehensive income can either be presented on the statement of income, immediately below net income, or in a separate **statement of comprehensive income**. The starting point for this statement is net income. In either case, the final total is the total comprehensive income for the period. To illustrate, Exhibit 4-9 presents **Loblaw Companies Limited**'s consolidated statements of earnings, while Exhibit 4-10 presents the company's separate consolidated statements of comprehensive income.

KEY POINTS
- Comprehensive income includes gains and losses from revaluing financial statement items to fair value or from changes in foreign exchange rates.
- These transactions are not included in net income as they are not transactions with third parties, but they are included in comprehensive income.

FINANCIAL STATEMENTS

Exhibit 4-9 Loblaw Companies Limited's 2013 Consolidated Statements of Earnings

Consolidated Statements of Earnings

For the years ended December 28, 2013 and December 29, 2012
(millions of Canadian dollars except where otherwise indicated)

	2013	2012
Revenue	$ 32,371	$ 31,604
Cost of Merchandise Inventories Sold (note 12)	24,696	24,185
Selling, General and Administrative Expenses	6,349	6,224
Operating Income	$ 1,326	$ 1,195
Net interest expense and other financing charges (note 6)	468	351
Earnings Before Income Taxes	$ 858	$ 844
Income taxes (note 7)	228	210
Net Earnings	$ 630	$ 634
Net Earnings per Common Share ($) (note 8)		
Basic	$ 2.24	$ 2.25
Diluted	$ 2.22	$ 2.23

Exhibit 4-10 Loblaw Companies Limited's 2013 Consolidated Statements of Comprehensive Income

FINANCIAL STATEMENTS

Consolidated Statements of Comprehensive Income

For the years ended December 28, 2013 and December 29, 2012

(millions of Canadian dollars)

	2013	2012
Net earnings	**$ 630**	$ 634
Other comprehensive income (loss), net of taxes		
Items reclassified to profit or loss:		
Gain on derecognized derivative instrument (note 30)	**$ (5)**	$ —
Items that will not be reclassified to profit or loss:		
Net defined benefit plan actuarial gain (loss) (note 27)	**234**	(6)
Other comprehensive income (loss)	**$ 229**	$ (6)
Total Comprehensive Income	**$ 859**	$ 628

How does a statement of income presenting expenses by function differ from one presenting expenses by nature of the items?

■ **LEARNING OBJECTIVE 6**
Understand the difference between presenting expenses by function or by nature of the item on the statement of income.

Accounting standards offer companies the choice of presenting their expenses by **function** or by **nature** when preparing their statements of income. Function refers to what functional area of the business the expenses were related to. Examples of functional areas are cost of sales, administrative activities, or selling and distribution activities. The nature of the expense refers to what the expense actually was, rather than the purpose for which it was incurred. Statements of income presenting expenses by nature include expense items such as employee wages, depreciation expense, cost of goods sold, advertising expenses, and rent expense. So far in the text, we have generally been preparing statements of income by the nature of the expenses by simply listing the various expense account balances.

The choice of presenting expenses based on their nature or function rests with management. Accounting standard setters have taken the position that management should use whichever method they believe presents the most reliable and relevant information. Note that preparing statements of income by function requires management to exercise judgement in terms of which expenses are allocated to which function. For example, wages must be allocated to the various functions. No such judgement is required when the statement of income is prepared by nature of the expenses. For example, wages are simply presented as "wage expense." Standard setters stipulate that companies that prepare their statements of income on a functional basis must also present information on the nature of the expenses in the notes to the company's financial statements. Specifically, companies must provide information on depreciation and amortization expenses and employee benefits expenses.

Exhibit 4-11 is the consolidated statements of comprehensive income for **Big Rock Brewery Inc.**, a Calgary-based producer of premium craft beers and ciders sold in nine provinces and the three territories. It is an example of a statement of income that presents expenses by function.

With this presentation, users can assess the expenses related to different functions. For example, we can see that the company's selling expenses decreased by $1.077 million from 2012 to 2013, but that they remained a consistent percentage of sales (around 31%). Similar analysis could be done for other functional areas. However, with this presentation format, it is not possible to determine the amount incurred for specific expenses, such as the company's total wage expense. For this information, it would be necessary to look at the notes to the company's financial statements. (See Exhibit 4-12, which presents the notes to Big Rock Brewery's financial statements that disclose the company's expense information by nature of the expense.)

Exhibit 4-11 Big Rock Brewery Inc.'s 2013 Consolidated Statements of Comprehensive Income

BIG ROCK BREWERY INC.

Consolidated Statements of Comprehensive Income
(In thousands of Canadian dollars, except per share amounts)

	Year ended	
	December 30, 2013	**December 30, 2012**
Net revenue (Notes 3.2 and 4)	**$ 41,587**	$ 46,057
Cost of sales (Notes 5 and 24)	**20,260**	21,149
Gross profit	**21,327**	24,908
Expenses		
Selling expenses (Notes 6 and 23)	**12,910**	13,987
General and administrative (Notes 7 and 24)	**4,821**	4,945
Depreciation and amortization	**314**	358
Operating expenses	**18,045**	19,290
Operating profit	**3,282**	5,618
Finance costs (Note 8)	**9**	93
Other income	**286**	351
Other expenses	**109**	147
Income before income taxes	**3,450**	5,729
Current income tax expense (Note 9)	**2,485**	426
Deferred income tax expense (recovery) (Note 9)	**(1,586)**	1,168
Net income and comprehensive income for the period	**$ 2,551**	$ 4,135

Exhibit 4-12 Excerpt from Big Rock Brewery Inc.'s Notes to the 2013 Consolidated Financial Statements

Notes to the Consolidated Financial Statements
(In thousands of Canadian dollars, unless otherwise stated)

5. COST OF SALES

The cost of sales of the Corporation is broken down into its cash and non-cash components as follows:

	Year ended	
	Dec. 30, 2013	Dec. 30, 2012
Operating expenses	**$ 17,417**	$ 18,279
Depreciation and amortization	**2,843**	2,870
Cost of sales	**$ 20,260**	$ 21,149

6. SELLING EXPENSES

The selling expenses for the Corporation are broken down as follows:

	Year ended	
	Dec. 30, 2013	Dec. 30, 2012
Delivery and distribution costs	**$ 3,314**	$ 3,870
Salaries and benefits	**3,739**	3,640
Trade marketing	**1,158**	1,078
Regional sales	**3,740**	4,636
Community sponsorship and other	**959**	763
Selling expenses	**$12,910**	$13,987

continued

Exhibit 4-12 Excerpt from Big Rock Brewery Inc.'s Notes to the 2013 Consolidated
Financial Statements (continued)

7. GENERAL AND ADMINISTRATIVE EXPENSES

The general and administrative expenses for the Corporation are broken down as follows:

	Year ended	
	Dec. 30, 2013	Dec. 30, 2012
Salaries and benefits [(1)]	**$ 2,813**	$ 2,844
Professional fees	**658**	706
Reporting and filing fees	**105**	82
Insurance	**210**	211
Building maintenance and taxes	**506**	572
Bank charges	**26**	71
Office, administrative and other	**503**	459
General and administrative expenses	**$ 4,821**	$ 4,945

(1) Salaries and benefits included stock option expense of $191 (2012 – $208) and stock appreciation right expense (non-cash charges) of $449 (2012 – $238).

The Conceptual Framework
RELEVANCE, FAITHFUL REPRESENTATION, AND THE STATEMENT OF INCOME

Relevance is a fundamental qualitative characteristic in the conceptual framework. According to this characteristic, to be useful, financial information must matter to financial statement users. This is one of the factors that management must consider when deciding whether to present the statements of income by function or by nature of the items. In some cases, it may be more meaningful to users to present the company's expenses by function (such as sales and marketing costs, administration costs, and distribution expenses), while in other cases it may be more meaningful to report by nature of the expenses (such as wage expense, advertising expense, and rent expense). As noted previously, when companies present their statement of income by function, they must use judgement to allocate costs to the various functions. In doing so, they must also ensure that these allocations are representationally faithful, meaning that the expenses are allocated to functions in a manner that is consistent with where these expenses were actually incurred.

As an example, some universities present their expenses by function (such as academic, student services, and administration). When doing so, they would need to make decisions about how to allocate costs such as the salaries of department heads, faculty deans, and so on. They would need to consider whether these costs were related to academic activities or if they were administrative costs. Perhaps a case could be made that a portion should be allocated to each function. As a student, you might want to assess how much your institution spends on academic activities relative to administration. In doing so, these types of allocation decisions made by management will be relevant to you.[9]

FINANCIAL STATEMENT ANALYSIS

Now that you have an understanding of the various ways that revenue can be recognized and the components of the statement of income, let's use that information to have a closer look at how we can measure performance. Most financial statement users are interested in the company's performance. Senior management can receive bonuses based on the company meeting earnings targets, specified as either overall amounts or percentage increases. Creditors such as banks are interested because profitable companies are able to service their debt (pay interest and repay loans principal). Common shareholders (investors) want to know how well the company they have invested in is performing and whether there are sufficient earnings to pay dividends. Potential investors use earnings numbers when assessing whether shares of the company could be a good investment. In the next section, we will discuss earnings per share, one of the primary earnings-based measures that provides users with information about a company's performance.

■ **LEARNING OBJECTIVE 7**
Calculate and interpret a company's basic earnings per share.

What is meant by earnings per share and how is it calculated?

Earnings per share (EPS) is a measure used by many financial statement users. The earnings per share figure expresses net income, after deducting preferred dividends, on a per-share basis. (As such, this figure presents total earnings on a per-share basis.) It is one of the most frequently cited financial measures, appearing in company news releases and the business media, as a key measure of a company's performance. Accounting standards require that EPS be reported either on the statement of income or in a note accompanying the financial statements.

There are a couple of variations of the earnings per share ratio. For now, we will focus on the **basic earnings per share** ratio. This ratio is determined as follows.

$$\text{Basic earnings per share} = \frac{\text{Net income} - \text{Preferred dividends}}{\text{Weighted average number of common shares outstanding}^1}$$

[1] If the number of issued common shares changes during the year (because new shares were issued or previously issued shares were repurchased by the company), then this must be factored into the calculation.

Exhibit 4-13 illustrates the EPS calculation when there has been no change in the number of common shares during the period.

Exhibit 4-13 Basic EPS Calculation (When No Change in Numbers of Common Shares)

Montgomery Ltd. reported net income of $625,000 for the year ended December 31, 2016. During the year, the company also declared and paid dividends of $30,000 on the company's preferred shares. At the beginning of the year, Montgomery had 250,000 common shares outstanding. No shares were issued or repurchased during the year.

$$\text{Basic earnings per share} = \frac{\text{Net income} - \text{Preferred dividends}}{\text{Weighted average number of common shares outstanding}}$$

$$= \frac{\$625,000 - \$30,000}{250,000} = \$2.38$$

This EPS amount could be compared with the EPS of prior periods to determine whether earnings had improved on a per-share basis over prior periods or with the EPS results of other companies to compare relative per-share profitability, which can be used to assess share prices. Typically, a higher EPS will result in a higher share price.

Exhibit 4-14 illustrates the basic EPS calculation when there has been a change in the number of common shares during the period. When this happens, a weighted average number of shares must be used. A weighted average calculation is demonstrated below using the Montgomery example from Exhibit 4-13, except that the company issued 50,000 common shares at the beginning of April 2016.

Exhibit 4-14 Basic EPS Calculation (When Number of Common Shares Changes)

Before we can calculate basic EPS, we must determine the weighted average number of shares outstanding as follows:

$$
\begin{array}{rcl}
250,000 \text{ shares} \times 3/12^1 & = & 62,500 \text{ shares} \\
300,000 \text{ shares} \times 9/12^2 & = & 225,000 \text{ shares} \\
\hline
\text{Weighted-average} & = & 287,500 \text{ shares}
\end{array}
$$

continued

Exhibit 4-14 Basic EPS Calculation (When Number of Common Shares Changes) (Continued)

$$\text{Basic earnings per share} = \frac{\text{Net income} - \text{Preferred dividends}}{\text{Weighted average number of common shares outstanding}}$$

$$= \frac{\$625,000 - \$30,000}{287,500} = \$2.07$$

Again, this EPS amount could be compared with the EPS of prior periods to determine whether earnings had improved on a per-share basis over prior periods or with the EPS results of other companies to compare relative per-share profitability.

[1] January to March = 3 months
[2] April to December = 9 months

For Example

The 2013 and 2012 basic EPS results for three of Canada's largest food retailers were as follows:

	2013*	2012*
Loblaw Companies Limited	$2.24	$2.25
Metro Inc.	$7.46	$4.88
Empire Company Limited	$2.94	$5.59

These results show us that in 2013, Metro Inc. achieved the highest EPS, which was more than three times higher than that of Loblaw. Metro also achieved the greatest year-over-year increase in its basic EPS.[10]

* Note that all three companies have different year ends, so these EPS numbers cover different 12-month periods. For example, Loblaw's fiscal year ends on the Saturday closest to December 31, while Metro's fiscal year ends on the last Saturday in September and Empire's fiscal year ends on the first Saturday in May. The EPS figures for Loblaw and Metro are for periods ending in 2013 and 2012, while those for Empire are for the period ending in May 2014 and 2013.

As you learned in this chapter, the statement of income shows how much income was earned in a period using the accrual basis of accounting. In the next chapter we'll look at the statement of cash flows, which uses the cash basis of accounting to show the various inflows and outflows of cash.

SUMMARY

1. **Explain the nature of revenue and why revenue is of significance to users.**

   - Revenues are inflows of economic benefits from a company's ordinary operating activities (the transactions a company normally has with its customers in relation to the sale of goods or services).

   - Revenues are not tied to the receipt of cash because other economic benefits such as accounts receivable can result.

   - For a company to be successful, it must generate revenues in excess of the expenses it incurs doing so.

   - Users assess the quantity of revenues (changes in the amount of revenues) and the quality of revenues (the source of any growth and how closely any change in revenues corresponds with changes in cash flows from operating activities).

2. **Identify and explain the general criteria for revenue recognition and the specific revenue recognition criteria related to the sale of goods, the provision of services, and the receipt of interest, royalties, and dividends.**

   - Accounting standards outline principles for revenue recognition rather than specific rules.

   - There are two general revenue recognition criteria that are used to determine when revenue has been earned. Revenue is considered to have been earned when: (1) it is probable that economic benefits will flow to the company and (2) the amount of these benefits can be measured reliably.

   - When considering whether revenue has been earned from the sale of goods, three additional criteria are considered together with the two general criteria. The three additional criteria are: (1) the significant risks and rewards of ownership of the goods have been transferred, (2) there is no continuing involvement with the goods, and (3) the costs to be incurred to complete the transaction can be reliably measured.

- When considering whether revenue has been earned from the sale of services, two additional criteria are considered together with the two general criteria. The two additional criteria are: (1) the costs to be incurred to complete the transaction can be reliably measured and (2) the portion of the total services provided can be reliably measured (if the services are ongoing).

- When considering whether revenue has been earned from the receipt of interest, royalties, or dividends, the two general criteria are used.

3. Explain how revenues are measured.

- Revenues are measured using the fair value of the consideration received or receivable from the customer.

- This amount is reduced by any trade discounts (negotiated or posted reductions in the selling price) or quantity discounts (discounts offered for purchasing large quantities).

- If sales discounts (such as 2/10, n/30) are offered to stimulate customers to pay their accounts before the payment deadline, then these discounts are normally recorded in a separate contra revenue account so that management is able to quantify the amounts of sales discounts taken. Sales revenue is reported net of these discounts on the statement of income.

- Companies also estimate and record the amount of expected sales returns and allowances. Sales revenues are also reported net of this amount.

4. Understand the difference between a single-step statement of income and a multi-step statement of income.

- A single-step statement of income has two parts. All revenues are reported together in one section and all expenses are reported together in another section. The source of the revenues and the nature of the expenses are not considered.

- On a multi-step statement of income, the revenues earned from operations are presented separately from incidental revenues such as interest or dividends. Some expenses, such as cost of goods sold, are presented separately from other expenses.

Multi-step statements of income also provide users with key measures such as gross profit and income from operations.

- Users of a single-step statement of income can determine measures such as gross margin and income from operations, but they are not presented on the statement itself.

5. Understand the difference between comprehensive income and net income.

- Companies are required to report net income and comprehensive income.

- Comprehensive income is equal to net income plus other comprehensive income.

- Other comprehensive income includes gains and losses resulting from the revaluation of certain financial statement items to fair value or as a result of changes in foreign currency exchange rates. As these revaluation transactions are not transactions with third parties, they are not included in net income but are included in other comprehensive income.

6. Understand the difference between presenting expenses by function or by nature of the item on the statement of income.

- Companies can present their expenses by function or by nature on the statement of income. Function refers to the functional area of the business (such as sales, distribution, and administration), while nature refers to the type of expense (such as wages, rent, and insurance).

- Management can choose which method to use. If they choose to present expenses by function, then they must disclose information on the nature of the expenses in the notes to the company's financial statements.

7. Calculate and interpret a company's basic earnings per share.

- The *earnings per share ratio* can be determined by dividing net income less preferred dividends by the weighted average number of common shares outstanding.

- EPS expresses net income, after preferred dividends, on a per-share basis.

- EPS is one of the most commonly cited financial measures and companies are required to report their EPS on the statement of income or disclose it in the notes to their financial statements.

KEY TERMS

Basic earnings per share (188)	Multi-step statement of income (182)	Sales returns (180)
Bundling (179)	Nature (185)	Sales returns and allowances (181)
Comprehensive income (184)	Net sales (180)	Single-step statement of income (182)
Contra revenue account (180)	Operating activities (173)	Specific revenue recognition
Earnings per share (EPS) (188)	Other comprehensive income (184)	criteria (175)
Fair value (179)	Percentage of completion	Statement of comprehensive
Function (185)	method (177)	income (184)
General revenue recognition	Quantity discount (179)	Trade discount (179)
criteria (174)	Sales discounts (180)	

ABBREVIATIONS USED

EPS   Earnings per share

SYNONYMS

Gross profit | Gross margin
Net income | Net earnings
Statement of income | Statement of earnings | Income statement

CHAPTER END REVIEW PROBLEM

Additional Practice Problems

Jonathan, Anthony, and Kendra operate a bicycle shop, The Silver Spoke Ltd. They sell assembled bicycles and bicycle accessories. They have a service bay in the back of the shop where Kendra repairs bicycles. Occasionally, they are awarded contracts to assemble 20 to 50 bicycles for a major retailer. Customers use either cash or credit cards when buying bicycles and accessories or paying for repairs. For minor repairs, the customer pays when the repairs are done. For major repairs, customers are required to make a down payment equal to 25% of the repair's estimated cost. The remaining 75% is paid when the work is complete. When the company assembles bicycles for retailers, it bills the retailers when the work is done. The company normally receives payment within 30 days of submitting the bill.

Required:
Based on the revenue recognition criteria, recommend when the company should recognize revenue for each of its various revenue-generating activities. Provide the rationale for each of your recommendations.

Suggested Solution to Chapter End Review Problem

1. **Sale of goods**

Specific criteria:
- Risks and rewards of ownership transferred
- No continuing involvement
- Revenue measurable
- Probable economic benefits to seller
- Costs can be reliably measured

Sales of bicycles and bicycle accessories: The company should recognize revenue at the time of sale. Since the customer leaves with the merchandise, the risks and rewards of ownership have been transferred and the company's involvement with the goods also stops. The amount of revenue earned is also measurable and has been collected either in cash or through a credit card, so there are no issues regarding the flow of economic benefits. The costs associated with the sale are known as well.

2. **Provision of services**

Specific criteria:
- Revenue measurable
- Probable economic benefits to seller
- Costs can be reliably measured
- Portion complete is measurable

Minor repairs: The company should recognize revenue when the work is completed. Similar to the situation with the sale of bicycles, the company's work is complete and the customer has paid, so the amount of revenue can be measured reliably, and the costs associated with the repairs are also known.

Major repairs: The company should recognize revenue when the work is completed. When the customer makes the 25% down payment, the work has not yet been started. As well, the total amount owed is still uncertain, although it has been estimated to determine the 25% down payment. Therefore, the revenue cannot be measured reliably. The costs associated with the work are also uncertain. The company should record the down payment as unearned revenue. When the repairs are done, the company will have completed the work (therefore earned the revenue) and the total amount owed is known. The customer pays for the work with cash or a credit card so the collectibility is assured. All of the costs associated with the work are also known. At this time, revenue recognition criteria have been met. Although it is a major repair, the work will likely be completed in a reasonably short time, which means the delay in revenue recognition will not be very long.

Assembly contract: The company should recognize revenue when the assembly work is complete. At the time of the contract signing, although the company knows how much it will receive and is confident that it will receive that amount, it has not yet assembled any bicycles. Because a substantial amount of work remains to be done, the company has not earned the revenue. When the work is complete, the amount earned is known and it is reasonable to assume that the company will collect the amount owed. As well, the costs associated with the assembly of the bicycles are also known. At this time, the revenue recognition criteria have been met and revenue should be recognized.

ASSIGNMENT MATERIAL

Discussion Questions

DQ4-1 Identify and explain the two general revenue recognition criteria.

DQ4-2 What are the three main types of revenue-generating activities that are typical of most companies?

DQ4-3 Explain the five specific criteria used for determining when revenue should be recognized from the sale of goods.

DQ4-4 Explain the meaning of "significant risks and rewards of ownership."

DQ4-5 What is the most common point at which revenue is recognized for the sale of goods? How does this point meet the five criteria for revenue recognition?

DQ4-6 Explain the four specific criteria used for determining when revenue should be recognized from the provision of services.

DQ4-7 Explain how the percentage of completion method is used to recognize revenue from the provision of services.

DQ4-8 Describe the accounting treatment for a deposit made by a customer for the future delivery of goods. Using the specific revenue recognition criteria, explain the rationale for this treatment.

DQ4-9 Explain the difference between a trade discount and a sales discount and whether either of them is recorded in a company's accounting records.

DQ4-10 Contra revenue accounts are used for both sales discounts and sales returns and allowances. Explain the advantages of this approach.

DQ4-11 Explain why a multi-step statement of income provides users with better information than a single-step statement of income does. Identify some of this information.

DQ4-12 Identify and briefly describe the major sections of a multi-step statement of income.

DQ4-13 How does the single-step statement of income differ from the multi-step statement of income? Do they produce different net income amounts? Explain.

DQ4-14 What kinds of items are included on the statement of comprehensive income?

DQ4-15 Explain the difference between a statement of income with expenses presented by nature and one with expenses presented by function. Does one require more judgement on the part of management? Why or why not?

DQ4-16 Explain what the basic earnings per share ratio tells users, including why net income is reduced by preferred dividends as part of the ratio calculation.

Application Problems

AP4-1 (Revenue recognition criteria)

The following independent situations require judgement to determine when revenue should be recognized.

Required:
Identify when the company providing the goods or services should recognize revenue. Use the revenue recognition criteria to support your answers.

a. The insurance policy on your car starts February 1, 2016, and covers one year. You paid the insurance company $1,800 on January 28, 2016.

b. Porter Airlines sold you a non-refundable one-way ticket in October 2016 for your flight home at Christmas. The cost of the ticket was $398.

c. You went for your annual dental checkup on April 5, 2016. The fees were $125 and the dentist's office requires payment within 30 days of the visit. You paid the bill on April 30, 2016.

d. The Winnipeg Jets sell season tickets in one section of the arena for $6,087 per seat. The season begins in September, ends in March, and covers 41 games. You paid for the tickets in July 2016 for the 2016–17 season.

e. You bought a printer from Best Buy's on-line site and paid with your credit card on June 14, 2016. The printer was delivered on June 18. You paid the credit card balance on July 15.

f. You bought furniture from Leon's in December 2016 during a promotion. The selling price of the furniture was $1,100 and the first payment is due January 2, 2018.

g. On December 20, 2016, you borrowed $1,100 from TD Canada Trust. The loan plus interest of 5% is due in full on February 28, 2017.

h. You decide you need a new smart phone. You can purchase an iPhone from Rogers Communications. The current promotion indicates there is no cost for the phone if you sign up for a two-year phone and data plan at $65 per month.

AP4-2 (Revenue recognition and statement of income)

Vanessa Simon and Juan Cassetto started a landscaping company as a way of earning money for the summer. They purchased two lawn mowers for $250 each, a leaf blower for $59, and various smaller items, such as rakes, a shovel, canvas, clippers, and pails, which cost them $63. Vanessa and Juan figured that the lawn mowers and all of the equipment would have no resale value after being used throughout the summer. Vanessa rented her father's van for $100 per month. They began work in May and worked through to the end of September. They had several regular customers who paid them for managing their yards either once or twice a week. These customers paid them at the end of each week. They did the landscaping for three malls, watering and planting flowers and trimming hedges. They left an invoice with the mall manager every two weeks and received a cheque for the work the following week. They set up a separate bank account for their company and deposited money when they were paid. On September 30, they tallied up what they had earned over the summer. They had deposited $14,350 in the bank account, which represented the amount received from customers. One customer still owed them $150 for work and had promised to pay them on October 5. The final cheque from the mall manager for $136 had not arrived yet.

In addition to the original amount spent at the beginning of summer, they paid for the following items: $100 per month for their two cell phones, $450 for gas and $39 for an oil change for the van, $20 for sunscreen, $250 for gas and oil for the lawn mowers, and $600 to rent a trailer to carry their equipment. Vanessa still owes her father for renting the van for September.

Required:

Prepare as much of the statement of income for Vanessa and Juan as you can, showing the proper amount of revenue and any expenses that should be included. Show all calculations. Using the revenue recognition criteria, justify the revenue recognition method you selected. Do you have a cost of goods sold? Why or why not? What other expenses do you think they would probably have?

AP4-3 (Revenue recognition and statement of income)

Dimitri Chekhov owns a medium-sized Russian restaurant called The Steppes. Most of his business is from customers who enjoy in-restaurant lunches and dinners and pay before they leave. He also provides catered food for functions outside of the restaurant. Because he needs to prepare the food in large quantities and transport it to the venue, he requires these customers to make a 40% deposit at the time of booking the event. The remaining 60% is due on the day of the function.

During 2016, the restaurant took in $736,432 from restaurant and catered sales. At year end, December 31, 2016, the catered sales amount included $12,678 for a convention scheduled for January 12, 2017. Dimitri paid $198,108 for food supplies during the year and $248,572 for wages for the chefs and other restaurant staff. The restaurant owed $6,161 in wages to its staff at year end, which will be paid on January 4, 2017, as part of the normal weekly pay schedule.

Required:

Prepare as much of the statement of income for The Steppes as you can, showing the amount of sales and any other amounts that should be included. Show all calculations. Using the revenue recognition criteria, justify the revenue recognition method you selected. Do you have a cost of goods sold? Why or why not? What other expenses do you think the restaurant probably has?

AP4-4 (Revenue recognition and statement of income)

The Warm as Toast Company installs furnaces and fireplaces in homes and businesses. Each furnace and fireplace carries a four-year warranty. During 2016, the company had sales of $835,000. Customers paid half of the sales price when they arranged for an installation and the other half when the furnace or fireplace was installed. At year end, $76,000 of the sales amount represented amounts paid for furnaces or fireplaces that were not yet installed and for which the second half of the payment had not yet been received. The cost associated with the sales was $407,000 for the furnaces and fireplaces that had been installed that year. An additional cost of $198,000 was incurred for the labour associated with the installation. The accountant estimated that total future warranty costs associated with the installed items would likely be $46,000 over the next five years.

Required:

Prepare as much of the statement of income for The Warm as Toast Company for 2016 as you can, showing the proper amount of sales, cost of goods sold, gross profit, and any other amounts that can be included. Show all calculations. What other expenses do you think the company would probably have?

AP4-5 (Revenue recognition on a layaway sale)

Enchanted Brides Ltd. sells complete bridal ensembles. The most expensive part of the ensemble is the wedding gown. Recognizing that some of its customers may not have enough immediate funds to purchase one of its gowns, the store provides a layaway plan. The customer selects a gown and the store agrees to hold the gown until it is paid for. The store sets up a monthly payment schedule for the customer, extending the payment time over six months to a year. The store charges an additional $35 layaway application fee and $100 in possible default charges. If all payments are made on schedule, the default charge reduces the final payment. If the customer defaults, the $100 is not refunded.

Required:

Using the revenue recognition criteria, explain how the store should account for the monthly payments from the customer. Should the $35 storage fee be treated as revenue? Why or why not? Should the $100 default charge be treated as revenue? Why or why not? When should the store recognize the original cost of the wedding gown?

AP4-6 (Revenue recognition on gift cards)

The Carrot Top Ltd. is a trendy clothing store that is very popular with young teens. Because it is difficult to select clothes that young people might wear, the store offers gift cards to parents, friends, and relatives. The cards are very popular, particularly for birthdays. When a card is purchased, the cashier identifies the purchase as a gift card and activates the card so that it can be used within 24 hours. There is no time limit on when the card must be used.

Required:
Using the revenue recognition criteria, explain how the store should account for the purchase of a gift card. Discuss how the store could account for gift cards that are not used. Is there a time when the store can assume that the card will not be used?

AP4-7 (Revenue recognition decision)

After graduating with a degree in computer systems and design, Terry Park set up a company to design and produce computer games for arcades. Terry hired two other designers because of the anticipated volume of business. One designer, Kim, is paid an hourly wage. The second, Marie-Hélène, is paid 50% of the revenue received by Terry on the games designed or redesigned by Marie-Hélène. Terry rents an office where they all work and provides all the necessary equipment, supplies, and other items. Terry is not paid a wage but keeps all of the profits earned.

Terry realized there were two kinds of business: speculative design and custom design. For the speculative designs, Terry or one of the designers would think of a new game and then design, program, and test it. Terry would then try to sell it to a distribution company, for either a fixed price or a percentage (which ranges from 10% to 25%) of the total revenues earned by the game. To date, Terry has sold three of the four games produced. He is currently negotiating the sale of the fourth game.

For the custom design business, Terry would receive an order from a distribution company for either the design of a new game or the redesign of an existing game (which occurs frequently because games have a useful life of only six months as players quickly get bored with them). Terry negotiates either a fixed fee payable upon completion, or an hourly rate based on the estimated length of time it should take to redesign the game. Terry sets the hourly rate based on the perceived difficulty of the project, but the rate is always at least triple the amount paid to Kim. For the hourly rate contracts, Terry submits monthly invoices showing the number of hours worked on the project.

Required:
    a. What revenue recognition options are open to Terry? Which one(s) would you recommend and why?
    b. Using your recommended revenue recognition policy, how would you account for all of the costs incurred by Terry?

AP4-8 (Revenue recognition decision)

Javier Hernandez had seen many signs advertising house painters during the previous summers. Between his third and fourth year of university, he decided that he would start a painting company so that he could earn enough money to pay his tuition in the fall. He talked with a fellow student who ran a business like this the previous summer and knew the rates that he could charge. He made the following decisions: When he had a customer sign a contract for the inside or outside painting of a house, he would ask for a 20% down payment. The remainder of the contract price would be required when the job was completed. He made a deal with a local paint supplier for a discount on paint and other supplies. He assumed that most of the brushes and other painting supplies would be worth very little by summer's end, but he would sell off other supplies, such as ladders, when summer ended. If he needed a piece of equipment to do a job that he would likely not need again, he would rent it. His parents provided him with $500 in start-up money that needed to be repaid when he closed his business.

Required:
    a. What revenue recognition options are open to Javier? Which one would you recommend and why?
    b. Using your recommended revenue recognition policy, how would Javier account for all the costs for his various contracts?
    c. How should he account for the original loan that he received from his parents?

AP4-9 (Revenue recognition decision)

Sonya's Christmas Tree Company began operations on April 1, 2016, when Sonya bought a parcel of land on which she intended to grow Christmas trees. The normal growth time for a Christmas tree is approximately six years, so she divided her land into seven plots. In 2016, she planted the first plot with trees and watered, cultivated, and fertilized her trees all summer. In 2017, she planted her second plot with trees and watered, cultivated, and fertilized both planted plots. She continued with her plantings and cultivation every year through 2022, when she planted the last plot. In November 2022, she harvested the first plot of trees that she had planted in 2016. In 2023, she replanted the first plot.

Required:

   a. Explain when the company should be recognizing revenue. Why is this the case?
   b. Using your recommended revenue recognition policy, how would Sonya account for all her costs for growing the trees?

AP4-10 (Revenue recognition decision)

Sparkling Cleaners Ltd. operated six outlets in the city. At each outlet, customers could drop off clothes to be either dry cleaned or laundered. Clothes were normally ready for pickup within one to three days, and customers paid with cash, debit, or credit when they picked them up. Sparkling Cleaners had a central facility at which the clothing was cleaned. The company also had large contracts with hospitals and hotels. Under these contracts, laundry was picked up daily, cleaned, and returned the following day, and the customer was sent a weekly invoice for the laundry cleaned that week. Payment was due before the next invoice was sent out. Whenever a payment had not yet been received by the time that the next invoice needed to be sent, the unpaid amount was added to the new invoice.

Required:

What should Sparkling recognize as revenue with respect to its two types of customers? Why is this the case?

AP4-11 (Revenue recognition decision)

Carolina Dubasov enjoyed working with wood. She had a workshop set up in her backyard where she built articles of furniture, including tables, chairs, chests of drawers, end tables, and desks. Every Saturday, she opened her workshop to the public and sold items of furniture that she had completed. Customers paid with cash or credit card. Sometimes customers asked her to make specific articles such as a table and six chairs or a bedroom suite. For these customers, she would draw up the plans. When the customer agrees to the design and the wood, she draws up a contract and receives a 30% down payment. When the furniture is 60% complete, she shows it to the customer and collects another 30%. She collects the final 40% of the contract price when the furniture is completed.

Required:

   a. What revenue recognition options are open to Carolina? Which one(s) would you recommend and why?
   b. Using your recommended revenue recognition policy, how would you account for all the costs incurred by Carolina?
   c. If a customer had signed a contract for a roll-top desk, paid the 30% down payment, and then decided he did not want the desk, should Carolina return the 30% down payment? Why or why not? How can she protect her business from this possibility?

AP4-12 (Statement of income presentation)

The following account balances are taken from Sherwood Ltd.'s adjusted trial balance at June 30, 2016:

	Debit	Credit
Sales		$1,250,000
Sales returns	$125,000	
Cost of goods sold	596,000	
General expenses	40,000	
Selling expenses	75,000	
Depreciation expense	70,000	
Interest expense	37,000	
Interest revenue		44,000
Income tax expense	10,700	
Utilities expense	106,000	
Salaries expense	165,000	

Required:

   a. Prepare a single-step statement of income for the year ended June 30, 2016.
   b. Prepare a multi-step statement of income for the year ended June 30, 2016.
   c. Compare the two statements and comment on the usefulness of each one.

AP4-13 (Statement of income presentation: basic EPS)

The following information was taken from Riddell Ltd.'s adjusted trial balance as at April 30, 2016:

Sales revenue	$1,045,800
Interest revenue	7,200
Sales returns and allowances	24,000
Sales discounts	6,000
Cost of goods sold	396,000
Distribution expenses	230,250
Administration expenses	90,250
Depreciation expense	81,000
Interest expense	16,500
Income tax expense	56,700
Dividends declared—Common shares	15,000
Dividends declared—Preferred shares	20,000

Required:
   a. Prepare a single-step statement of income for the year ended April 30, 2016.
   b. Prepare a multi-step statement of income for the year ended April 30, 2016.
   c. Determine Riddell's gross margin percentage for the year.
   d. If Riddell had 35,000 common shares outstanding throughout the year, determine the company's basic earnings per share.

AP4-14 (Statement of income presentation: basic EPS)

The following information was taken from Egeland Ltd.'s adjusted trial balance as at July 31, 2016:

Sales revenue	$2,788,800
Interest expense	44,000
Cost of goods sold	1,556,000
Sales discounts	16,000
Depreciation expense	216,000
Distribution expenses	414,000
Administration expenses	279,000
Sales returns and allowances	64,000
Interest revenue	19,200
Income tax expense	44,000
Dividends declared—Common shares	30,000
Dividends declared—Preferred shares	15,000

Required:
   a. Prepare a single-step statement of income for the year ended July 31, 2016.
   b. Prepare a multi-step statement of income for the year ended July 31, 2016.
   c. Determine Egeland's gross margin percentage for the year.
   d. If Egeland had 80,000 common shares outstanding throughout the year, determine the company's basic earnings per share.

User Perspective Problems

UP4-1 (Revenue recognition and earnings)

Financial analysts frequently refer to the quality of a company's earnings. By quality, they mean that the earnings are showing growth and are good predictors of future earnings.

Required:
If you were looking for evidence of a company's quality of earnings, what would you look for on the financial statements?

UP4-2 (Revenue recognition)

Suppose that your company sells appliances to customers under sales contracts that require them to pay for the appliance in monthly payments over one year.

Required:
a. Describe a revenue recognition policy that would be appropriate for this type of sale.
b. How should the company account for the fact that some customers might not make the payments as required?

UP4-3 (Revenue recognition policy and management performance measurement)

Suppose that you are the sales manager of a company with an incentive plan that provides bonuses based on meeting sales targets.

Required:
Explain how meeting your sales target is affected by the company's revenue recognition policies.

UP4-4 (Revenue recognition policy and sales targets)

Suppose that you are the vice-president in charge of marketing and sales in a large company. You want to boost sales, so you have developed an incentive plan that will provide a bonus to the salespeople based on the revenue they generate.

Required:
At what point would you recommend that the company count a sale: when the salesperson generates a purchase order, when the company ships the goods, or when the company receives payment for the goods? Explain.

UP4-5 (Revenue recognition policy and return policies)

In the toy manufacturing industry, it is common to allow customers (retail stores) to return unsold toys within a specified period of time. Suppose that a toy manufacturer's year end is December 31 and that the majority of its products are shipped to customers during the last quarter of the year (October to December) in anticipation of the holiday season.

Required:
Is it appropriate for the company to recognize revenue upon shipment of the product? Refer to revenue recognition criteria to support your answer.

UP4-6 (Revenue recognition for car leases)

Suppose that you are the owner of a car dealership that sells and leases cars. When customers lease a vehicle, they are required to sign a three-year or five-year lease. A lease is a contract whereby the customer agrees to make monthly payments for the duration of the lease period. There are penalties if the customer decides to return the vehicle before the end of the lease. During the lease, the customer is required to keep the vehicle in good condition with respect to mechanical operations and appearance. When the customer returns the vehicle at the end of the lease, it is inspected for damage. The customer is often expected to pay for mechanical work or repainting that is required.

Required:
a. Using revenue recognition criteria, explain when you would recognize the revenue from the monthly lease payments.
b. How is your decision affected by your awareness that the customers pay a penalty if they return the vehicle early and that they pay for any damages at the end of the lease term?

UP4-7 (Advertising revenue recognition)

Suppose the sports channel on television sells $10 million in advertising slots to be aired during the games that it broadcasts during the FIFA World Cup. Suppose also that these slots are contracted out during the month of October with a down payment of $2 million. The ads will be aired in June and July of the following year.

Required:
If the sports channel's fiscal year end is December 31, how should it recognize this revenue in its financial statements?

UP4-8 (Revenue recognition for gift certificates)

Suppose that a national clothing retailer sells gift cards for merchandise. During the Christmas holiday period, it issues $500,000 in gift cards.

Required:
If the company's fiscal year end is December 31, how should it recognize the issuance of these gift cards in its financial statements at year end? Explain your answer in relation to the revenue recognition criteria.

UP4-9 (Revenue recognition on software sales)

Suppose that Solution Software Company produces inventory-tracking software that it sells to retail companies. The software keeps track of what inventory is on hand and where it is located. It automatically adjusts the information when items are sold and alerts the company when new inventory needs to be ordered. The software package sells for $100,000 and the company agrees to customize it to the buyer's operations, which can take several months.

Required:
If the fiscal year end is September 30 and the company sells 10 software units in August, how should it recognize these sales in the financial statements at year end? Use the revenue recognition criteria to support your answer.

UP4-10 (Statement of income: expense presentation)

You are a member of the executive of the students' union at your university. As one of the few executive members with some knowledge of financial accounting, you have been tasked with responding to a request from the office of the university's vice-president of finance. She has asked the student union to provide its thoughts on the university's move to present the expenses on its statement of operation (statement of income) by function rather than by nature. The VP is proposing two functions: (1) instruction/student support and (2) ancillary.

Required:
   a. What concerns might the student union have with this proposal?
   b. What recommendation(s) would you suggest the student union make in relation to the proposal?

Reading and Interpreting Published Financial Statements

Financial Analysis Assignments

RI4-1 (Revenue recognition and statement of income presentation)

Ten Peaks Coffee Company Inc. is a Burnaby, British Columbia–based specialty coffee company. The company provides green coffee decaffeination services as well as green coffee handling and storage services. Exhibits 4-15A and B contain excerpts from Ten Peaks' 2013 annual report.

EXHIBIT 4-15A	TEN PEAKS COFFEE COMPANY INC.'S 2013 CONSOLIDATED STATEMENTS OF INCOME AND COMPREHENSIVE INCOME

CONSOLIDATED STATEMENTS OF INCOME AND COMPREHENSIVE INCOME

(Tabular amounts in thousands of Canadian dollars, except per share and number of shares figures)
for the years ended

	Note	December 31 2013	December 31 2012
Revenue		$ 53,873	$ 59,713
Cost of sales		(47,662)	(55,050)
Gross profit		6,211	4,663
Sales and marketing expenses		(1,415)	(1,292)
Occupancy expenses		(50)	(63)
Administration expenses		(3,034)	(2,847)
Finance income		92	117
Finance expenses		(149)	(258)
Realized gain on derivative financial instruments		1,614	1,678
Unrealized loss on derivative financial instruments		(1,045)	(197)
(Loss) gain on foreign exchange		(68)	223
Loss on disposal of plant and equipment		(4)	–
Income before tax		2,152	2,024
Income tax expense	11	(498)	(520)
Net income and comprehensive income for the year		$ 1,654	$ 1,504
Earnings per share			
Basic and Diluted (per share)	20	$ 0.25	$ 0.23

EXHIBIT 4-15B   EXCERPT FROM TEN PEAKS COFFEE COMPANY INC.'S 2013 ANNUAL REPORT

3.13 Revenue recognition

Revenue is measured at the fair value of the consideration received or receivable. Revenue is reduced for estimated customer returns, rebates and other similar allowances.

Revenue is recognized when all the following conditions are satisfied:

1) a persuasive evidence of arrangement exists;
2) the goods are shipped;
3) title has passed to the customer;
4) the price has been substantively determined; and
5) collection is reasonably assured.

Required:

a. Calculate Ten Peaks' gross profit percentage for 2013 and 2012. Has it improved?
b. Does Ten Peaks prepare its consolidated income statement using a single-step or a multi-step approach?
c. Does Ten Peaks present its expenses by function or by nature? Does this approach require a higher level of management judgement when preparing the statement?
d. Is the revenue reported on Ten Peaks' statements of income and comprehensive income net of estimated customer returns, rebates, and allowances?
e. Compare the five conditions for revenue recognition identified by Ten Peaks with the five revenue recognition criteria outlined in Exhibit 4-2. Are they consistent? Are there any significant differences?

RI4-2 (Revenue recognition and statement of income presentation)

Gildan Activewear Inc. is a Montreal-based company that manufactures and sells activewear, socks, and underwear. The company's brands include Gildan, Gold Toe, and Anvil. The company also manufactures products through licensing arrangements with Under Armour and New Balance brands. Exhibit 4-16A presents the company's consolidated statements of earnings and comprehensive income for the years ended September 29, 2013, and September 30, 2012. Exhibit 4-16B is an extract from the company's significant accounting policies note that outlines its revenue recognition policy.

EXHIBIT 4-16A   GILDAN ACTIVEWEAR INC.'S 2013 CONSOLIDATED STATEMENTS OF EARNINGS AND COMPREHENSIVE INCOME

GILDAN ACTIVEWEAR INC.
CONSOLIDATED STATEMENTS OF EARNINGS AND COMPREHENSIVE INCOME
Years ended September 29, 2013 and September 30, 2012
(in thousands of U.S. dollars, except per share data)

	2013	2012
Net sales	$ 2,184,303	$ 1,948,253
Cost of sales	1,550,266	1,552,128
Gross profit	634,037	396,125
Selling, general and administrative expenses (note 17(a))	282,563	226,035
Restructuring and acquisition-related costs (note 18)	8,788	14,962
Operating income	342,686	155,128
Financial expenses, net (note 15(c))	12,013	11,598
Equity earnings in investment in joint venture	(46)	(597)
Earnings before income taxes	330,719	144,127
Income tax expense (recovery) (note 19)	10,541	(4,337)
Net earnings	320,178	148,464
Other comprehensive income (loss), net of related income taxes (note 15(d)):		
Cash flow hedges	6,419	(6,399)
Actuarial gain on employee benefit obligations	436	323
	6,855	(6,076)
Comprehensive income	$ 327,033	$ 142,388
Earnings per share:		
Basic (note 20)	$ 2.64	$ 1.22
Diluted (note 20)	$ 2.61	$ 1.22

EXHIBIT 4-16B   EXCERPT FROM GILDAN ACTIVEWEAR INC.'S 2013 ANNUAL REPORT

(s) Revenue recognition:

Revenue is recognized upon shipment of products to customers, since title passes upon shipment, and to the extent that the selling price is fixed or determinable. At the time of sale, estimates are made for customer price discounts and volume rebates based on the terms of existing programs. Sales are recorded net of these program costs and estimated sales returns, which are based on historical experience, current trends and other known factors, and exclude sales taxes. New sales incentive programs which relate to prior sales are recognized at the time the new program is introduced.

Required:

a. Gildan reports "net sales" on its consolidated statements of earnings. Explain what this means.
b. Calculate the amount of Gildan's gross profit percentage for 2013 and 2012. Has it improved?
c. Does Gildan prepare its consolidated statements of earnings using a single-step or a multi-step approach?
d. Does Gildan present its expenses by function or by nature? Does this approach require a higher level of management judgement when preparing the statement?
e. Explain Gildan's revenue recognition policy in your own words.

RI4-3 (Revenue recognition and statement of income presentation)

RONA Inc. is a major Canadian retailer of hardware, building supplies, and home renovation products. The company's headquarters are in Boucherville, Quebec, and approximately 25,000 employees work in the network of 530 corporate, franchise, and affiliate stores across Canada. Exhibit 4-17A presents an extract from the company's consolidated statements of income and statements of other comprehensive income. Exhibit 4-17B presents supplemental note disclosure related to the consolidated statement of income, while Exhibit 4-17C presents note disclosure related to the company's revenue recognition policies.

EXHIBIT 4-17A   RONA INC.'S 2013 CONSOLIDATED STATEMENTS OF INCOME AND STATEMENTS OF OTHER COMPREHENSIVE INCOME (PARTIAL)

RONA Inc.
Consolidated Statements of Income and Statements of Other Comprehensive Income
Years ended December 29, 2013 and December 30, 2012
(in thousands of Canadian dollars, except per share amounts)

Consolidated Statements of Income

	2013	2012
		Restated (Notes 10 and 32)
Continuing operations		
Revenues (Note 4)	$ 4,192,192	$ 4,444,175
Earnings before interest, taxes, depreciation, amortization, impairment of non-financial assets, restructuring costs and other charges (Note 5.1)	162,088	188,654
Restructuring costs and other charges (Note 5.4)	(82,879)	(37,261)
Depreciation, amortization and impairment of non-financial assets (Note 5.2)	(113,850)	(107,261)
Operating (loss) income	(34,641)	44,132
Finance costs (Note 26)	(14,000)	(12,462)
(Loss) income before income taxes	(48,641)	31,670
Income tax recovery (expense) (Note 7)	13,044	(8,281)
Net (loss) income from continuing operations	(35,597)	23,389

EXHIBIT 4-17B   **EXCERPT FROM RONA INC.'S 2013 ANNUAL REPORT**

5. Supplemental information on consolidated statement of income

5.1 Earnings before interest, taxes, depreciation, amortization, impairment of non-financial assets, restructuring costs and other charges

	2013	2012
		Restated (Notes 10 and 32)
Revenues	$ 4,192,192	$ 4,444,175
Cost of sales (Note 6)	(3,094,856)	(3,244,870)
Gross profit	1,097,336	1,199,305
Selling, general and administrative expenses		
Employee benefits expense (Note 5.3)	(529,271)	(557,654)
Rent and occupancy costs	(223,971)	(234,431)
Net gain on disposal of assets	4,640	3,973
Share of income of equity-accounted investees	1,599	1,570
Finance income (Note 26)	5,665	5,305
Other income	12,069	10,486
Other(a)	(205,979)	(239,900)
	(935,248)	(1,010,651)
Earnings before interest, taxes, depreciation, amortization, impairment of non-financial assets, restructuring costs and other charges	$ 162,088	$ 188,654

(a) Other includes advertising and selling expenses, information technology expenses and professional fees.

EXHIBIT 4-17C   **EXCERPT FROM RONA INC.'S 2013 ANNUAL REPORT**

(c) Revenue

Revenue from the sale of goods is measured at the fair value of the consideration received or receivable, net of returns, rebates and trade and quantity discounts. The Corporation recognizes revenue at the time of sale in stores or upon delivery of the merchandise, when the sale is accepted by the customer and when collection is reasonably assured.

Revenue also includes various services provided by the Corporation, such as product installation and delivery. Revenue from the rendering of services is measured at the fair value of the consideration received or receivable. The Corporation recognizes revenue when the commercial obligations have been fulfilled, the services have been accepted by the customer and collection is reasonably assured.

Revenue also includes royalties received from franchised stores. Royalties are measured as a percentage of revenue and are recognized as earned and when collection is reasonably assured.

Interest income relating to trade and other receivables and loans and advances are reported on an accrual basis using the effective interest method.

Required:

a. RONA's consolidated statements of income present revenue information followed immediately by earnings information. The statement does not contain any information on the company's expenses for the period. Financial statement users can obtain this information in note 5.1 to the financial statements. Comment on your perspective of this approach, including identifying any advantages and disadvantages with it.

b. Calculate RONA's gross profit percentage for 2013 and 2012. Has it improved?

c. Does RONA present its expenses by function or by nature? Does this approach require a higher level of management judgement when preparing the statement?

d. Explain RONA's revenue recognition policies in your own words.

RI4-4 (Revenue recognition and statement of income presentation)

Maple Leaf Foods Inc. produces value-added meat, meal, and bakery products for customers across North America, the United Kingdom, and Japan. Exhibit 4-18A presents the company's consolidated statements of earnings for the years ended December 31, 2013 and 2012. Exhibit 4-18B is an extract from the notes to the company's financial statements presenting its revenue recognition policies.

EXHIBIT 4-18A   MAPLE LEAF FOODS INC.'S 2013 CONSOLIDATED STATEMENTS OF EARNINGS

Consolidated Statements of Earnings

Years ended December 31,
(In thousands of Canadian dollars, except share amounts)

	2013	2012
		(Restated) (Note 22, 32)
Sales	$ 4,406,448	$ 4,551,828
Cost of goods sold	3,920,652	3,878,219
Gross margin	$ 485,796	$ 673,609
Selling, general, and administrative expenses	484,192	508,356
Earnings from continuing operations before the following:	$ 1,604	$ 165,253
Restructuring and other related costs *(Note 17)*	(93,164)	(47,511)
Change in fair value of non-designated interest rate swaps	2,022	7,297
Other income (expense) *(Note 19)*	77,995	8,640
Earnings (loss) before interest expense, other financing costs, and income taxes from continuing operations	$ (11,543)	$ 133,679
Interest expense and other financing costs *(Note 20)*	69,842	71,707
Earnings (loss) before income taxes from continuing operations	$ (81,385)	$ 61,972
Income taxes *(Note 21)*	(22,842)	20,005
Net earnings (loss) from continuing operations	$ (58,543)	$ 41,967
Net earnings and gain on disposal of discontinued operations *(Note 22)*	570,706	54,595
Net earnings	$ 512,163	$ 96,562

EXHIBIT 4-18B   EXCERPT FROM MAPLE LEAF FOODS INC.'S 2013 ANNUAL REPORT

(r) Revenue Recognition

The majority of the Company's revenue is derived from the sale of product to retail and foodservice customers, as well as the sale of rendering products and by-products to industrial and agricultural customers. The Company recognizes revenue from product sales at the fair value of the consideration received or receivable, net of estimated returns, and an estimate of sales incentives provided to customers. Revenue is recognized when the customer takes ownership of the product, title has transferred, all the risks and rewards of ownership have transferred to the customer, recovery of the consideration is probable, the Company has satisfied its performance obligations under the arrangement, and has no ongoing involvement with the sold product. The value of sales incentives provided to customers are estimated using historical trends and are recognized at the time of sale as a reduction of revenue. Sales incentives include rebate and promotional programs provided to the Company's customers. These rebates are based on achievement of specified volume or growth in volume levels and other agreed promotional activities. In subsequent periods, the Company monitors the performance of customers against agreed upon obligations related to sales incentive programs and makes any adjustments to both revenue and sales incentive accruals as required.

Except for fresh bread, the Company generally does not accept returns of spoiled products from customers. For product that may not be returned, the Company, in certain cases, provides customers with allowances to cover any damage or spoilage, and such allowances are deducted from sales at the time of revenue recognition. In the case of fresh bread, customer returns are deducted from revenue.

Required:

a. Calculate Maple Leaf's gross profit percentage for 2013 and 2012. Has it improved?

b. Does Maple Leaf present its expenses by function or by nature? Does this approach require a higher level of management judgement when preparing the statement?

c. Explain Maple Leaf's revenue recognition policies in your own words.

RI4-5 (Revenue recognition and statement of income presentation)

Dollarama Inc. is Canada's largest operator of dollar stores, with more than 800 stores and operations across the country. The company's headquarters, distribution centre, and warehouses are located in Montreal, Quebec. Exhibit 4-19A presents the company's consolidated statement of net earnings and comprehensive income for the years ended February 2, 2014, and February 3, 2013. Exhibit 4-19B is an extract from the notes to the company's financial statements presenting expenses by nature.

EXHIBIT 4-19A	DOLLARAMA INC.'S 2014 CONSOLIDATED STATEMENT OF NET EARNINGS AND COMPREHENSIVE INCOME

Dollarama Inc.
Consolidated Statement of Net Earnings and Comprehensive Income for the years ended
(Expressed in thousands of Canadian dollars, except share and per share amounts)

		52-weeks	53-weeks
		February 2,	February 3,
	Note	2014	2013
		$	$
Sales		2,064,676	1,858,818
Cost of sales		1,299,092	1,163,979
Gross profit		765,584	694,839
General, administrative and store operating expenses		363,182	339,662
Depreciation and amortization	18	47,898	39,284
Operating income		354,504	315,893
Net financing costs	18	11,673	10,839
Earnings before income taxes		342,831	305,054
Provision for income taxes	14	92,737	84,069
Net earnings for the year		250,094	220,985
Other comprehensive income			
Items to be reclassified subsequently to net earnings			
Unrealized gain on derivative financial instruments, net of reclassification adjustment		14,249	1,093
Income taxes relating to component of other comprehensive income		(3,808)	(308)
Total other comprehensive income, net of income taxes		10,441	785
Total comprehensive income for the year		260,535	221,770
Earnings per share			
Basic net earnings per common share	17	$3.48	$3.00

The accompanying notes are an integral part of these consolidated financial statements.

EXHIBIT 4-19B   EXCERPT FROM DOLLARAMA INC.'S 2013 ANNUAL REPORT

18 Expenses by nature included in the consolidated statement of net earnings

	52-weeks February 2, 2014 $	53-weeks February 3, 2013 $
Depreciation and amortization:		
Depreciation of property and equipment (Note 7)	44,503	37,443
Amortization of intangible assets (Note 8)	3,395	3,121
Amortization of unfavourable lease rights (Note 8)	–	(1,280)
Total depreciation and amortization	47,898	39,284
Employee benefits:		
Remuneration for services rendered	262,015	249,380
Share options granted to directors and employees (Note 13)	4,053	1,558
Defined contribution plan	1,591	1,491
Total employee benefit expense	267,659	252,429
Net financing costs:		
Interest expense and banking fees	11,081	9,706
Amortization of debt issue costs	592	1,133
Total net financing costs	11,673	10,839

Required:

a. Calculate Dollarama's gross profit percentage for 2014 and 2013. Has it improved? What does this figure tell us about each $1-priced item on Dollarama's shelves?

b. Dollarama presents its expenses by function and then discloses depreciation, employee benefits, and financing costs in a note to its financial statements. Comment on why this additional expense information is useful or relevant to users of the company's financial statements.

c. Identify other expenses not currently disclosed by nature that might be relevant to users of the company's financial statements.

RI4-6 (Revenue recognition and statement of income presentation)

High Liner Foods Inc. processes and markets seafood products throughout Canada, the United States, and Mexico under the High Liner and Fisher Boy brands. It also produces private label products and supplies restaurants and institutions. Exhibit 4-20A presents High Liner Foods' consolidated statements of income for 2013 and 2012, while Exhibit 4-20B is an extract from the notes to the company's financial statements outlining its revenue recognition policy.

EXHIBIT 4-20A   HIGH LINER FOODS INCORPORATED'S 2013 CONSOLIDATED STATEMENT OF INCOME

		Fifty-two weeks ended	
(in thousands of U.S. dollars, except per share amounts)	**Notes**	**December 28, 2013**	**December 29, 2012**
Revenues		$ 947,301	$ 942,631
Cost of sales		731,884	735,970
Gross profit		215,417	206,661

continued

| EXHIBIT 4-20A | HIGH LINER FOODS INCORPORATED'S 2013 CONSOLIDATED STATEMENT OF INCOME (continued) |

| | | Fifty-two weeks ended | |
| | | December 28, | December 29, |
(in thousands of U.S. dollars, except per share amounts)	Notes	2013	2012
Distribution expenses		53,368	44,511
Selling, general and administrative expenses		98,902	100,862
Impairment of property, plant and equipment		–	13,230
Business acquisition, integration and other expenses		3,256	10,741
Results from operating activities		59,891	37,317
Finance costs		16,329	36,585
(Income) loss from equity accounted investee, net of income tax		(86)	196
Income before income taxes		43,648	536
Income taxes			
Current	20	12,378	5,442
Deferred	20	(86)	(7,109)
Total income tax expense (recovery)		12,292	(1,667)
Net income		$ 31,356	$ 2,203
PER SHARE EARNINGS			
Earnings per common share			
Basic	17	$ 2.07	$ 0.15

| EXHIBIT 4-20B | EXCERPT FROM HIGH LINER FOODS INCORPORATED'S 2013 ANNUAL REPORT |

Revenue recognition

The Company recognizes sales in income when the risks and rewards of the underlying products have been substantially transferred to the customer, usually on delivery of the goods. The Company experiences very few product returns and collectability of its invoices is consistently high.

Marketing programs provided to customers and operators including volume rebates, cooperative advertising and other trade marketing programs are all customer specific programs to promote the Company's products. Consequently, sales are recorded net of these estimated sales and marketing costs, which are recognized as incurred at the time of sale. Consumer coupons used to encourage consumers to purchase the Company's products through the Company's customers are recognized as a reduction to sales when the coupons are issued. Certain customers require the payment of one-time listing allowances (slotting fees) in order to obtain space for a new product on its shelves. These fees are recognized as reductions of revenue at the earlier of the date the fees are paid in cash or on which a liability to the customer is created (usually on shipment of the new product). All other non-customer specific marketing costs (general advertising), are expensed as incurred as selling, general and administrative expense.

Required:

a. Has High Liner Foods used a single-step or a multi-step income statement? What aspects of the statement influenced your answer?

b. Calculate High Liner Foods' gross profit percentage for 2013 and 2012. Did the company's gross profit, as a percentage of its revenue, increase or decrease?

c. Calculate High Liner Foods' net profit rate (net earnings divided by net sales) for 2013 and 2012. Did the company's net profit, as a percentage of its revenue, increase or decrease?

d. High Liner Foods' revenue recognition policy outlines the company's accounting treatment for both coupons and slotting fees. In your own words, explain what slotting fees are and how they are accounted for. Is this treatment consistent with how the company accounts for coupons?

Cases

C4-1 Quebec Supercheese Company

Quebec Supercheese Company (QSC) produces many varieties of cheese that are sold in every province in Canada, mainly through large grocery stores and specialty cheese shops. The cheese is produced at its factory in Montreal and shipped across Canada using commercial refrigerated trucks that pick up the cheese at the factory loading dock. The purchasers pay for the trucking and assume responsibility for the cheese as soon as the trucks pick it up at the factory. In accordance with IFRS, QSC recognizes the sale as soon as the trucks load the cheese, because the purchasers have title and responsibility for the cheese at this point.

QSC is not happy with these arrangements because it has received many complaints from purchasers about spoilage. Even though the purchasers and their truckers have full responsibility for this spoilage, many disputes have occurred because the truckers insist the cheese is spoiled when they pick it up. QSC is considering setting up its own fleet of trucks to deliver its cheese across Canada. It estimates that the additional freight costs can be regained through the higher prices it would charge for including shipping in the price.

If the company makes the deliveries, the title to the cheese will not transfer until the cheese is delivered. QSC's president was not happy when she learned that sales would be recognized and recorded only upon delivery to the customer, since she knew that an average of five days' sales are in transit at all times because of the distances involved. One day's sales total approximately $100,000 on average. The effect of this change would be an apparent drop in sales of $500,000 and a $50,000 decrease in net income in the year of the change.

Required:

Respond to the president's concerns about the impact of changing the point at which the company recognizes revenue.

C4-2 Mountainside Appliances

Danielle Madison owns a store called Mountainside Appliances Ltd. that sells several different brands of refrigerators, stoves, dishwashers, washers, and dryers. Each of the appliances comes with a factory warranty on parts and labour that is usually one to three years. For an additional charge, Danielle offers customers more extended warranties. These extended warranties come into effect after the manufacturers' warranties end.

Required:

Using the revenue recognition criteria, discuss how Danielle should account for the revenue from the extended warranties.

C4-3 Furniture Land Inc.

Furniture Land Inc. is a producer and retailer of high-end custom-designed furniture. The company produces only to special order and requires a one-third down payment before any work begins. The customer is then required to pay one third at the time of delivery and the balance within 30 days after delivery.

It is now February 1, 2016, and Furniture Land has just accepted $3,000 as a down payment from H. Gooding, a wealthy stockbroker. Per the contract, Furniture Land is to deliver the custom furniture to Gooding's residence by June 15, 2016. Gooding is an excellent customer and has always abided by the contract terms in the past. If Furniture Land cannot make the delivery by June 15, the contract terms state that Gooding has the option of cancelling the sale and receiving a full reimbursement of any down payment.

Required:

As Furniture Land's accountant, describe what revenue recognition policy the company should be using. Prepare all journal entries related to the sale in a manner that supports the revenue recognition policy you chose.

ENDNOTES

1. Charlie Smith, "Cineplex Entertainment Forges Ahead while Other Movie Theatres Falter," Straight.com, May 28, 2014; Dave Friend, The Canadian Press, "Return of the Arcade? Cineplex Wants to Expand Past Movie Theatres," CTV Kitchener online, May 14, 2014; Cineplex Inc. 2013 annual report.
2. Canadian Tire Corporation, Limited 2013 annual report.
3. IAS 18 *Revenue*.
4. Dollarama Inc. 2014 annual report, Note 3.
5. Rogers Sugar Inc. 2013 annual report.
6. Air Canada 2013 annual report, Note 2(c).
7. The Second Cup Limited 2013 annual report, Note 2.
8. Canadian Tire Corporation, Limited 2013 annual report, Note 3.
9. IFRS Conceptual Framework.
10. Loblaw Companies Limited 2013 annual report; Metro Inc. 2013 annual report; Empire Company Limited 2014 annual report.

5 The Statement of Cash Flows

CORE QUESTIONS

If you are able to answer the following questions, then you have achieved the related learning objectives.

LEARNING OBJECTIVES

After studying this chapter, you should be able to:

●●● INTRODUCTION

- Why is the statement of cash flows of significance to users?

1 Understand and explain why the statement of cash flows is of significance to users.

●●● DISCUSS THE DIFFERENCES BETWEEN THE STATEMENTS OF CASH FLOWS AND INCOME

- How does the statement of cash flows differ from the statement of income?

2 Explain how the statement of cash flows and the statement of income differ.

●●● UNDERSTANDING THE STATEMENT OF CASH FLOWS

- What are the categories of cash flows presented in the statement of cash flows and what are typical transactions included in each category?
- Why is so much significance placed on cash flows from operating activities?

3 Identify the three major types of activities that are presented in a statement of cash flows and describe some of the typical transactions included in each category of activity.

●●● PREPARING THE STATEMENT OF CASH FLOWS

- How is "cash" defined?
- How is a statement of cash flows prepared?
- What is the difference between the direct and indirect methods of preparing cash flows from operating activities?
- Are there investing and financing activities that do not appear on the statement of cash flows?

4 Prepare a statement of cash flows using a comparative statement of financial position, a statement of income, and some additional information.

●●● INTERPRETING CASH FLOW INFORMATION

- How can the information presented in a statement of cash flows be used to manage a company?
- What can cash flow patterns tell us?

5 Interpret a statement of cash flows and develop potential solutions to any cash flow challenges identified.

●●● FINANCIAL STATEMENT ANALYSIS

- How do we determine what portion of a company's liabilities could be met with cash flows from operating activities?
- How do we determine how much net free cash flow a company generates?

6 Calculate and interpret a company's cash flows to total liabilities ratio and determine the amount of net free cash flow being generated.

●●● The Dash for Cash

When Joseph-Armand Bombardier created a gas-powered "snow vehicle" in 1937, he probably could never have imagined the company he founded would one day be the third-largest civil aviation manufacturer in the world. It's also unique because it manufactures trains in addition to planes.

Montreal-based Bombardier, maker of such products as the iconic Dash 8 turboprop, had $18.2 billion in revenues in its year ended December 31, 2013. But as you would expect from a company that develops and manufactures aircraft and rail equipment that cost millions of dollars each, Bombardier requires a lot of cash to finance its operations. The company's CSeries smaller passenger jets are an example of where significant research and development costs are incurred long before the products are sold. When significant costs are incurred before collecting sales receipts or deposits from customers, companies like Bombardier can have cash flow problems.

In the first quarter of 2014, Bombardier had an outflow of $915 million in cash, meaning it paid out nearly $1 billion more than it brought in during that period. After these results were announced, the company's stock price dropped 6%. Investors must consider the risks related to businesses with high costs and long cash-to-cash cycles: the time it takes from when raw materials are purchased until the customer pays for the manufactured item. Companies try to shorten their cash-to-cash cycles, but it's difficult for Bombardier because planes and trains have multi-year development and manufacturing cycles.

Part of Bombardier's 2014 cash flow problem was a delay in the rollout of its CSeries planes, originally expected for late 2013 but pushed back to 2015, delaying the inflow of cash from operating activities (sales). Meanwhile, the planes' development costs increased from a planned $3.4 billion to $4.4 billion.

One of the ways companies like Bombardier address their long cash-to-cash cycles is to borrow the required funds, such as by issuing bonds. For example, Bombardier issued $2.0 billion in bonds during 2013 and another $1.8 billion in April 2014.

When assessing a company's liquidity—its ability to meet its short-term obligations—investors and creditors look at the company's cash balances. In spite of a $915-million outflow of cash, Bombardier assured investors that its liquidity was fine. It said its cash outflow would decrease in the rest of 2014 and pointed to its backlog of $69.7 million in unfilled product orders as at the end of 2013 as a future source of cash inflow. The company stated it would not need to issue more bonds in the near future to increase cash inflows. "We don't anticipate to go back to any sources to increase our liquidity. We have ample liquidity to meet our plans," said Chief Financial Officer Pierre Alary.[1]

INTRODUCTION

Many users consider the **statement of cash flows** to be the most important financial statement in determining a company's future prospects. As we saw in the feature story on **Bombardier Inc.**, investors keep a close eye on whether cash is flowing into and out of a company. This information is presented in the the statement of cash flows, which categorizes the inflows and outflows of cash into operating, investing, and financing activities.

■ LEARNING OBJECTIVE 1
Understand and explain why the statement of cash flows is of significance to users.

Why is the statement of cash flows of significance to users?

In Chapter 4, the basic revenue recognition criteria and the measurement of income were discussed. Although this is a very important perspective on a company's performance, other aspects that affect the company's overall health are not adequately captured by the statement of income. For example, creditors want to be able to assess a company's ability to generate sufficient cash to service its debts (to pay interest and repay the principal as it comes due). The use of accrual accounting means that the revenues and expenses on the statement of income do not correspond to the company's **cash flows**—inflows and outflows of cash—and therefore do not provide all of the information that creditors need. Aside from assessing profitability, creditors and other outside users of financial information need some way to assess an organization's cash flows and predict its future cash position. The statement of cash flows provides this perspective on an organization's performance, by summarizing its cash inflows and outflows and highlighting the activities that resulted in the net change in its cash position during the period.

Having an understanding of how cash flows into and out of a company is critical for users. The information presented in this statement enables users to:

- Assess the company's ability to generate cash flows from its core operations.
- Evaluate the cash flows the company has been able to obtain from investors (through the issuance of new shares) and creditors (through new borrowings).
- Assess the extent to which the company has invested cash to replace or add revenue-generating assets such as property, plant, and equipment.
- Determine the amount of cash that the company has used to repay debt.
- Evaluate the amount of cash dividends distributed to shareholders, together with the sources of that cash.

All of the uses noted above provide financial statement users with an historical perspective—how the company performed in prior periods. It is important to note that the information in the statement of cash flows is also used on a predictive basis—what a user can expect in the future. Specifically, information on a company's cash flows is used to:

- Estimate the value of the company, because a number of commonly used business valuation techniques are based on estimated future cash flows.
- Assess the company's ability to repay debt in the future.
- Evaluate the potential for the company to be able to pay dividends in the future.
- Estimate the company's future cash requirements and assess these needs relative to the company's existing cash and short-term investment balances, together with the company's access to funding that has already been secured (that is, existing operating lines of credit).

The statement of cash flows also serves as a key tool for financial statement users because it illustrates the relationships between the other statements. For example, while the statement of financial position shows the net change in property, plant, and equipment, and the statement of income shows the amount of any gain or loss on the sale of property, plant, and equipment, only the statement of cash flows will explain these amounts by presenting the amount of property, plant, and equipment purchased during the period along with the proceeds received from any disposals of these assets.

The statement of cash flows also explains the changes in key account balances. For example, while the statement of financial position may indicate the net change in a company's long-term debt (an increase or decrease), the statement of cash flows will explain the change. It will indicate how much the company has borrowed and how much principal it repaid during the year.

In Chapters 1 and 2, we discussed how the statement of cash flows summarizes a company's cash inflows and outflows by the three categories of business activities: operating activities, investing activities, and financing activities. Understanding what is included in each of these categories assists financial statement users in assessing the significance of the cash flows reported for each.

The primary focus of most financial statement users will be on the company's **operating activities**. These are the lifeblood of any company and should generate a positive cash flow (an inflow of cash). After all, the operating activities include all of the inflows and outflows related to the sale of goods and services—the activities that the company provides in its normal operations. A positive cash flow from operating activities indicates that a company's core business operations are generating more cash than it is using. This net inflow of cash may then be used for other activities, such as purchasing new capital assets, repaying debts, or paying dividends to shareholders. A negative cash flow from operations indicates that a company's regular operating activities required more cash than they generated. This may suggest that investments or capital assets may have to be sold and/or external sources of financing have to be found in order to offset this cash outflow and enable the company to continue to operate.

Assessing a company's cash flows from **investing activities** enables users to examine a company's decisions regarding the purchase or sale of property, plant, and equipment. If the company has made any long-term investments in other companies or disposed of ones made previously, the cash flows related to these transactions will also be reflected in this cash flow category. This information enables users to assess the company's strategy when it comes to replacing the property, plant, and equipment required to continue operations or whether additional assets are being acquired to provide the capacity to grow the company's operations.

Users will also examine a company's **financing activities** to assess the decisions made by management and/or the board of directors in relation to the company's debt and equity. They will determine whether the company incurred more debt or repaid principal during the period. They will also assess whether new shares were issued and whether any dividends were declared and paid. This information enables users to evaluate the company's financial strength and strategy, as well as to estimate its reliance on debt versus equity financing in the future.

Even those users who consider the statement of income to be the most important statement will examine it together with the statement of cash flows and statement of financial position to more fully understand and analyze a company. As a future user of financial information, it is important that you know what to look for on the statement of cash flows and understand what the amounts in its various categories mean. For this reason, we are going to show you how the statement is developed and how you can analyze it.

For Example

> **Canadian Tire Corporation, Limited** began its 2013 fiscal year with $1,015.5 million in cash and cash equivalents and ended the year with $643.2 million. Users of the Company's financial statements would want to determine the reasons behind this $372.3-million decrease in cash and cash equivalents. Did it result from challenges with the company's retail operations? Is it because the company repaid debt? Is it because the company purchased significant amounts of property, plant, and equipment during the year? Being able to determine the answers to questions like these is critical for users, and the statement of cash flows provides them with the answers.[2]

DISCUSS THE DIFFERENCES BETWEEN THE STATEMENT OF CASH FLOWS AND THE STATEMENT OF INCOME

How does the statement of cash flows differ from the statement of income?

In each of the preceding chapters, we have discussed how financial statements, including the statement of income, are prepared using the accrual basis of accounting rather than the cash basis of accounting. As such, revenues are recognized on the statement of income when they have been earned rather than when cash is received from customers. In fact, as we saw in Chapter 4, determining when revenue has been earned has nothing to do with the receipt of cash. In terms of expenses, we have learned that these are recognized when they have been incurred under the accrual basis of accounting. Again, there are often differences between when an expense is incurred and when it is paid in cash.

As a result, the statement of income measures a company's performance for a period (usually a month, quarter, or year) on an accrual basis. While the revenue, expense, and net income amounts presented on this statement are very important, they do not represent cash flowing into and out of the business during that same period. If management is only paying attention to the statement of income and not to cash flows, they may think that all is well with the company, in spite of a looming cash shortfall. For example, if a significant portion of a company's sales are on account and customers are not paying these accounts on a timely basis, the company may be running short of cash in spite of an increase in sales. Alternatively, if a company's suppliers require it to pay for goods in advance or to make upfront deposits, the company may be paying out cash well in advance of these items becoming expenses; the payments would be accounted for as inventory or prepaid expenses. In this case, in spite of a statement of income that portrays the company as profitable, the company could also be running short of cash due to these payments. In other cases, companies can have significant non-cash expenses, such as depreciation and amortization. While these reduce net income, they have no impact on the amount of cash a company is able to generate from its operations.

Another key difference between the two statements has to do with the fact that the statement of income focuses only on the operating activities of a company. It reflects the profit or earnings generated from the company's sales to its customers less the expenses the company incurred to generate them. The statement of income does not reflect many of the transactions a company has with its creditors (such as borrowing funds or repaying principal) or shareholders (such as the proceeds of issuing shares or the payment of dividends). As such, even if there was little difference in the timing of revenues and expenses being recorded and their receipt and payment in cash, the statement of income would tell users only part of the story.

Information related to a company's cash payments for the purchase of property, plant, and equipment or the cash receipts from their sale is also not included on a company's statement of income. These cash flows related to a company's investing activities can be very significant and would not be apparent to financial statement users relying solely on the statement of income.

■ LEARNING OBJECTIVE 2
Explain how the statement of cash flows and the statement of income differ.

KEY POINTS
The statement of cash flows differs from the statement of income because it:
- reflects the cash basis rather than the accrual basis of accounting, and
- focuses on more than just operating activities (it includes investing and financing activities).

For Example

One of Canada's leading retailers of women's fashion, **Reitmans (Canada) Limited**, had net earnings of $10.8 million during the year ended February 1, 2014, yet it purchased more than $34.5 million in property, equipment, and intangible assets, and paid $41.9 million in dividends during the year. It did all of this without borrowing any money. A quick review of the company's statement of cash flows, specifically the company's cash flows from operating activities, illustrates how this was possible. It turns out that Reitmans had depreciation and amortization expenses and impairment losses of $63.7 million. While these expenses and losses reduced net income, they were non-cash charges. In fact, the company's cash flow from operating activities was an inflow of $84.716 million—an amount significantly different from net earnings. This example illustrates why it is important for financial statement users to consider both the statement of income and the statement of cash flows when assessing corporate performance.[3]

As its name implies, the statement of cash flows reports all transactions involving the receipt or payment of cash. This is not restricted to those resulting from a company's operating activities, but includes those related to its investing activities (from the purchase and sale of capital assets) and its financing activities (the transactions a company has with its creditors and investors).

UNDERSTANDING THE STATEMENT OF CASH FLOWS

■ **LEARNING OBJECTIVE 3**
Identify the three major types of activities that are presented in a statement of cash flows and describe some of the typical transactions included in each category of activity.

What are the categories of cash flows presented in the statement of cash flows and what are typical transactions included in each category?

In Chapter 1, we discussed how all of the activities that companies engage in can be grouped in to three categories: operating activities, investing activities, and financing activities. We also discussed how these categories provided the structure for the statement of cash flows. As such, we will not repeat that discussion here. It is beneficial, however, to review examples of the typical transactions included in each category of cash flows. This information is presented in Exhibit 5-1.

Exhibit 5-1 Typical Transactions for Each Category of Cash Flows

Typical Operating Activities	Inflows:	• Cash sales to customers • Collections of amounts owed by customers
	Outflows:	• Purchases of inventory • Payments of amounts owed to suppliers • Payments of expenses such as wages, rent, and interest • Payments of taxes owed to the government
Typical Investing Activities	Inflows:	• Proceeds from the sale of property, plant, and equipment • Proceeds from the sale of shares of other companies
	Outflows:	• Purchases of property, plant, and equipment • Purchases of shares of other companies
Typical Financing Activities	Inflows:	• Borrowing money • Issuing shares
	Outflows:	• Repaying loan principal • Paying dividends

KEY POINTS
Cash flows from operating activities are key because they:
• result from what the company is in the business of doing,
• are the source for future debt repayments,
• are the source for future dividends payments.

In terms of the order in which the three categories of cash flows are presented on the statement of cash flows, all companies present cash flows from operating activities first. Some companies then present cash flows from investing activities, while others present cash flows from financing activities. This is something to watch for when reviewing statements of cash flows. In this chapter, cash flows from investing activities will be presented after cash flows from operating activities, followed by cash flows from financing activities.

Why is so much significance placed on cash flows from operating activities?

As previously noted, cash flows from operating activities normally receive the greatest scrutiny from financial statement users. The cash flows in this category result from the company's normal activities: the sale of goods and services to customers. In other words, these cash flows are generated from what the company is in the business of doing. As such, it is natural that users focus on how successful the company has been at doing so. Since these cash flows are generated by the company's operations, they are considered to be internally generated, as opposed to cash flows that come from sources outside the company, such as from investors or creditors. It will be these operating cash flows that can be reinvested to grow the company, to repay debt, or to fund dividends.

The Conceptual Framework
FAITHFUL REPRESENTATION AND THE STATEMENT OF CASH FLOWS

The conceptual framework notes that "information about cash flows helps users understand a (company's) operations, evaluate its financing and investing activities, assess its liquidity or solvency and interpret other information about its performance." Given the emphasis placed on the various cash flow categories, it is essential that management faithfully represent these by presenting them in the appropriate category. For example, prior to adopting IFRS, **Sino-Forest Corporation**, which traded on the TSX, treated timber sales as cash flows from operating activities but timber purchases as investing activities.

This resulted in the company having positive operating cash flows and negative investing cash flows, the normal pattern for a successful, growing company. When it restated its results under IFRS for the first quarter of 2010, timber sales and timber purchases were both included in cash flows from operating activities. This changed cash flows from operating activities from a positive U.S. $51.4 million to a negative U.S. $122 million. This significant change would have given the users of the company's financial statements a very different perspective on the company's operations and future prospects.[4]

Without operating cash flows, the company's ability to continue would depend upon it being able to attract new capital by issuing additional shares or securing new loans. Neither of these is a likely possibility if investors or creditors are not confident in the company's ability to generate the operating cash flows that could be used to pay dividends, grow the company, make interest payments, or repay loan principal. Without operating cash flows or financing cash flows, the only cash inflows available would come from the company selling some of its property, plant, and equipment. They would, in effect, be "cannibalizing the company" by selling its cash-generating assets. Obviously, this would not be a sustainable strategy.

PREPARING THE STATEMENT OF CASH FLOWS

How is "cash" defined?

The statement of cash flows explains the net change in a company's cash position during an accounting period. While it may sound simple, having an understanding about how "cash" is defined for purposes of this statement is important. Cash normally includes both **cash** and **cash equivalents**. As you would expect, cash includes amounts the company has on hand, together with balances in **demand deposits** (chequing and savings accounts) with banks and other financial institutions. Cash equivalents include short-term, highly liquid investments. They must be convertible into known amounts of cash and be maturing within the next three months, meaning that there is little risk of a change in their value, due to changes in interest rates or other economic factors. Investments in money market funds, short-term deposits, and Government of Canada treasury bills are examples of cash equivalents.

HELPFUL HINT
If a company is able to generate positive cash flows from operating activities, you know that it will likely succeed and will continue to operate in the future. An inability to generate operating cash flows means that the company will face significant challenges in continuing to operate.

■ **LEARNING OBJECTIVE 4**
Prepare a statement of cash flows using a comparative statement of financial position, a statement of income, and some additional information.

Bank borrowings and repayments are normally considered to be cash inflows and outflows from financing activities. However, it is possible for certain borrowings to be considered as cash equivalents. For example, if a company has used a **bank overdraft facility** or has drawn on a **line of credit** from its bank, then the amount of the borrowing can be considered "negative cash" and included in the determination of the company's cash and cash equivalents. This is normally done when the overdraft facility or line of credit is used as part of the company's normal cash management strategy. In other words, the company regularly draws on these, but then repays these borrowings as cash is collected from customers.

FINANCIAL STATEMENTS

For Example

Reitmans (Canada) Limited reported the following cash and cash equivalents at February 1, 2014, and February 2, 2013:[5]

(amounts in thousands of dollars)

5. CASH AND CASH EQUIVALENTS

	February 1, 2014	February 2, 2013
Cash on hand and with banks	$ 19,224	$ 9,248
Short-term deposits, bearing interest at 0.9% (February 2, 2013 – 0.6%)	103,131	88,378
	$122,355	$97,626

How is a statement of cash flows prepared?

As was discussed in Chapter 1, the statement of cash flows is the final financial statement prepared. This is because information from the statement of income, the statement of financial position, and the statement of changes in equity is required in order to complete the statement of cash flows. As such, these other statements, together with some additional information, will be provided as the basis for preparing the statement of cash flows. Additional information is often provided related to the company's purchases and sales of property, plant, and equipment or the extent of bank borrowings or principal repayments during the period.

Prior to preparing the statement of cash flows, companies have to make a decision regarding which method they will use for determining cash flows from operating activities. Accounting standard setters have identified two acceptable methods: the **direct method** and the **indirect method**. It is important to note that the total cash flows from operating activities are exactly the same regardless of the method; the only difference is in how the amount is determined. The choice of method has no impact on the other two categories of cash flow activities.

While standard setters have encouraged companies to use the direct method, the vast majority of public companies use the indirect method. This is because it is considered simpler to prepare and it uses information that is easily obtained within most accounting systems. Given the prevalence of the indirect method, we will use this method as we discuss the preparation of the statement of cash flows. We will review the direct method later in the chapter, so you can understand how it differs from the indirect method.

The indirect method is also known as the *reconciliation method*. This is because when using the indirect method to determine cash flows from operating activities, the starting point is net income. Since net income is determined using the accrual basis of accounting, a reconciliation is required to adjust it to a cash basis. This reconciliation is a strength of the indirect method, in that it makes the linkage between net income and cash flows from operating activities very clear.

There are a number of different methods that can be used to prepare the statement of cash flows. These include the T account and worksheet methods. Both of these are very mechanical and do not promote a deeper understanding of the concepts underlying the statement of cash flows. We will illustrate the preparation of the statement of cash flows using a hybrid approach, which is based on a structured framework involving some T account analysis, but that also involves analyzing the information in the financial statements to logically determine the related cash flows. An overview of this methodical approach to preparing the statement of cash flows is presented in Exhibit 5-2.

Next, we will discuss how to apply this framework to the financial statements of a hypothetical company. The statement of financial position and statement of income for Matchett Manufacturing Ltd.

(MML) are presented in Exhibits 5-3 and 5-4. Additional information on the company's investing and financing activities is presented in Exhibit 5-5. The information provided, while typical of many small companies, has been simplified for illustrative purposes.

Exhibit 5-2 Steps for the Preparation of the Statement of Cash Flows

General

1. Determine the net change in cash during the period.

2. Read any additional information provided and cross-reference it to the related statement of financial position accounts.

Cash Flows from Operating Activities

3. Using the statement of income, record net income and adjust it for any non-cash items included on the statement (such as depreciation and amortization expense) and/or items that do not involve operating activities (such as gains and losses from the sale of property, plant, and equipment or investments).

4. Determine the net change in each current asset and current liability account (except for the Cash and the Dividends Payable accounts) and record the impact that these changes had on cash.

Cash Flows from Investing Activities

5. Determine and record the cash proceeds received from selling property, plant, and equipment and the cost of property, plant, and equipment purchased with cash during the period.

6. Determine and record the cash proceeds from the sale of shares of other companies (from the sale of investments) and the cost of any investments in other companies purchased with cash during the period.

Cash Flows from Financing Activities

7. Determine the amount of cash dividends paid during the period.

8. Determine and record the amount of cash received from borrowings made during the year (new loans or increases to existing loans) and the amount of cash principal repaid on loans during the period.

9. Determine the cash received from shares issued during the period.

General

10. Calculate the sum of the cash flows from operating, investing, and financing activities and agree it to the net change in cash for the period as determined in Step 1.

Exhibit 5-3 Matchett Manufacturing Ltd. Statement of Financial Position

MATCHETT MANUFACTURING LTD.
Statement of Financial Position
As at October 31, 2016

ASSETS	2016	2015
Current assets		
Cash	$ 19,050	$ 11,250
Accounts receivable	45,200	57,700
Inventories	76,500	49,000
Total current assets	140,750	117,950
Equipment	127,000	62,000
Accumulated depreciation, equipment	(25,200)	(35,000)
	$242,550	$144,950
LIABILITIES AND SHAREHOLDERS' EQUITY		
Current liabilities		
Accounts payable	$ 38,600	$ 36,200
Income taxes payable	1,200	3,800
Dividends payable	3,200	5,200
Total current liabilities	43,000	45,200
Loans payable	43,000	36,000
Common shares	50,000	40,000
Retained earnings	106,550	23,750
	$242,550	$144,950

Exhibit 5-4 Matchett Manufacturing Ltd. Statement of Income

MATCHETT MANUFACTURING LTD.
Statement of Income
For the Year Ending October 31, 2016

Sales revenue	$480,000
Cost of goods sold	305,000
Gross profit	175,000
Expenses	
Wage expense	53,900
Rent expense	13,250
Utilities expense	7,600
Depreciation expense	10,200
Interest expense	2,970
Income tax expense	4,980
Income from operations	82,100
Gain on sale of equipment	3,900
Net income	$ 86,000

Exhibit 5-5 Matchett Manufacturing Ltd. Additional Information

The following additional information was gathered in relation to the company's investing and financing activities:

a. Equipment that had originally cost $25,000 and had a net carrying amount of $5,000 was sold for $8,900 during the year.
b. No principal repayments were made on the loan during the year.

The completed statement of cash flows for MML Manufacturing Ltd. is presented in Exhibit 5-6, with each line item referenced to the related step from the suggested framework.

Exhibit 5-6 Matchett Manufacturing Ltd. Statement of Cash Flows

MATCHETT MANUFACTURING LTD.
Statement of Cash Flows
For the year ended October 31, 2016

Cash flows from operating activities		
Net income	$86,000	Step 3
Add: Depreciation expense	10,200	Step 3
Less: Gain on sale of equipment	(3,900)	Step 3
Add: Decrease in accounts receivable	12,500	Step 4
Less: Increase in inventory	(27,500)	Step 4
Add: Increase in accounts payable	2,400	Step 4
Less: Decrease in income taxes payable	(2,600)	Step 4
Net cash provided by operating activities	77,100	

continued

Exhibit 5-6 Matchett Manufacturing Ltd. Statement of Cash Flows (continued)

Cash flows from investing activities		
Add: Proceeds from the sale of equipment	8,900	Step 5
Less: Purchase of equipment	(90,000)	Step 5
Net cash used in investing activities	(81,100)	
Cash flows from financing activities		
Less: Payment of dividends	(5,200)	Step 7
Add: Proceeds of borrowing—loan payable	7,000	Step 8
Add: Proceeds from issuing common shares	10,000	Step 9
Net cash provided by financing activities	11,800	
Ending cash	19,050	Step 1
Opening cash	11,250	Step 1
Net change in cash	$7,800	Steps 1 and 10
Supplementary disclosures:		
Cash paid for interest	$2,970	
Cash paid for income tax	$7,580	

We will now review each line item from MML's statement of cash flows in greater detail. The first two steps are general steps, which are required to set up the statement of cash flows.

Step 1 – Determine the net change in cash during the period.

This can be determined by subtracting the balance of cash and cash equivalents at the beginning of the accounting period from the balance of cash and cash equivalents at the end of the accounting period. MML began the year with $11,250 in cash and cash equivalents and ended the year with $19,050. We can quickly see that the company's cash balance increased by $7,800 during the year. The statement of cash flows will explain how the company's various activities resulted in this increased cash balance.

Step 2 – Read any additional information provided and cross-reference it to the related statement of financial position accounts.

This step, which may seem overly simplistic, will help to ensure that you remember to take the additional information into account when you are analyzing the related account(s). Without this step, many students forget to use these pieces of additional information, so give it a try and see if it helps you. In this case, item "a" from Exhibit 5-5, which relates to the sale of equipment, should be cross-referenced to the equipment account on the statement of financial position. Cross-referencing just means that the letter "a" should be added beside "Equipment" on the statement of financial position. Item "b" relates to the company's loans, so the letter "b" should be added next to "Loans payable."

As previously noted, the first section of the statement of cash flows to be prepared is the cash flows from operating activities. This section determines what the company's net income would have been if the cash basis of accounting had been used rather than the accrual basis. The calculation starts with net income, with two types of adjustments made to this amount. The first type of adjustment removes the effects of non-cash items that appear on most statements of income. The most common non-cash item is depreciation and amortization expense. The adjustments also adjust for items on the statement of income that are not operating activities. The most common adjustment involves gains and losses from the sale of property, plant, and equipment. The second type of adjustment removes the income effects of accrual accounting. Net income is reduced by the amount of accrued revenues (as no cash has been collected in relation to them) and increased by the amount of accrued expenses (as no cash has been paid in relation to them). This is done by calculating the changes in the company's current asset and current liability accounts. These two types of adjustments are the next two steps in the process.

HELPFUL HINT

It can be helpful to cross out the statement of income once you have determined net income, the amount of any non-cash items, and the amount of any gains or losses from investing activities. This ensures that you will not be tempted to go back and try to use any additional information from the statement of income.

Step 3 – Using the statement of income, record net income and adjust it for any non-cash items included on the statement (such as depreciation and amortization expense) and/or items that do not involve operating activities (such as gains and losses from the sale of property, plant, and equipment or investments).

From MML's statement of earnings, we can see that the company's net income for the year was $86,000. We can also see that the company reported $10,200 in depreciation expense. As an expense, it reduced net income for the period, but because it did not involve cash, we add it back in order to determine what net income would have been without this amount. Amortization expense is treated the same way.

MML also reported a gain of $3,900 from the sale of equipment during the year. Since this transaction involved the sale of property, plant, and equipment, it is considered to be an investing activity and does not belong in the operating activities section. Because the gain increased net income, it has to be subtracted in order to eliminate it; that is, to determine what net income would have been without it. If there had been a loss on the sale, the opposite would have been done. Because losses reduce net income, they are added back to net income in order to eliminate them. Gains and losses from the sale of investments in other companies are treated the same way, as they are also investing rather than operating activities.

Step 4 – Determine the net change in each current asset and current liability account (except for the Cash and the Dividends Payable accounts) and record the impact that these changes had on cash.

In this step, net income is adjusted to remove the effects of accrual accounting. This is done by calculating the change in each of the company's current asset and current liability accounts, with the exception of the Cash account (because this was done in Step 1) and the Dividends Payable account (because the payment of dividends is a financing activity rather than an operating activity). Once the amount of the change has been determined, it is analyzed to determine whether it resulted in cash flowing into or out of the company. For example, a net increase in the Inventory account would indicate that goods had been purchased, resulting in an outflow of cash. Alternatively, a decrease in Accounts Receivable would indicate that customers paid their accounts, resulting in an inflow of cash.

From MML's statement of financial position, we can see that:

- Accounts Receivable decreased by $12,500; the company began the year with receivables of $57,700 and ended with $45,200. This means that the company's customers paid their accounts, resulting in a cash inflow (an increase in cash flows from operating activities).
- Inventory increased by $27,500; the company began the year with $49,000 in inventory and ended with $76,500. This means that the company purchased goods, resulting in a cash outflow (a decrease in cash flows from operating activities).
- Accounts Payable increased by $2,400; the company owed its suppliers $36,200 at the start of the year and ended owing them $38,600. This tells us that some of the expenses on the statement of income have not yet been paid, so we need to add them back to determine what net income would have been without them. Sometimes it can help to think about what the cash flow impact would have been if the opposite had happened. In this case, if Accounts Payable had decreased, it would be clear that the company paid some of its accounts, resulting in a cash outflow. Since the Accounts Payable increased, we do the opposite and treat it as a cash inflow by adding the amount back to net income.
- Income Taxes payable decreased by $2,600; the company owed the government $3,800 at the beginning of the year, but only $1,200 at the end of the year. This means that the company paid the government, resulting in a cash outflow (a decrease in cash flows from operating activities).

From the above, you can see that when determining cash flow from operations, *increases* in current assets have to be *subtracted* from net income on the statement of cash flows, while *decreases* in current assets have to be *added*. We do the opposite for current liabilities: increases have to be *added* to net income on the statement of cash flows, while decreases in current liabilities have to be *subtracted*. Exhibit 5-7 presents this in a tabular format. It can be useful to use this to support your analysis.

Exhibit 5-7 Cash Flow Impact of Changes in Current Assets and Current Liabilities

	Increase	Decrease
Current Asset	–	+
Current Liability	+	–

Once we have completed Step 4, we can determine the cash flows from operating activities for the period. From Exhibit 5-6, we can see that MML's cash flows from operating activities totalled $77,100. As previously discussed, we would normally expect cash flows from operating activities to be positive, meaning that the company generated a net inflow of cash from its operations.

Once cash flows from operating activities have been determined, we will then calculate cash flows from investing activities. The process for doing this is outlined in steps 5 and 6. In Step 5, the extent of the company's cash investments in long-term revenue-generating assets is calculated, together with the cash proceeds received from the sale of these assets. Step 6 involves determining the cash outflows related to long-term investments in other companies. This includes outflows related to purchasing shares of other companies, together with the proceeds from disposing of these investments. It is important to note that some companies may not make investments in the shares of other companies. As this is the case with MML, Step 6 would not be required. This is discussed further below.

Step 5 – Determine and record the cash proceeds received from selling property, plant, and equipment and the cost of property, plant, and equipment purchased with cash during the period.

When beginning our analysis of the Equipment account, the note we added in Step 2 would remind us that we were provided with the following additional information:

TAKE**5**

a. Equipment that had originally cost $25,000 and had a net carrying amount of $5,000 was sold for $8,900 during the year.

The sale of this equipment would be the first investing activity reported in MML's cash flows from investing activities. Since cash was received, this would increase the company's cash flows from investing activities.

Notice that the equipment that was sold had an original cost of $25,000 and a net carrying amount of $5,000. Since the term *net carrying amount* is equal to the original cost minus the accumulated depreciation, this is an indirect way of telling us that the accumulated depreciation on the equipment was $20,000 ($25,000 − $5,000).

Considerable detail is often provided about disposals of property, plant, and equipment such as this. However, you should bear in mind that, for purposes of the statement of cash flows, what really matters is the amount of cash that was received from the sale. In this case, the amount of cash is given, $8,900, so it can be entered directly into the statement of cash flows.

MML's Equipment account had a balance of $62,000 at the beginning of the period (from Exhibit 5-3). Remember that this amount reflects the original *cost* of the equipment purchased by the company. We also know, from the preceding step, that equipment with a cost of $25,000 was sold during the year. When the disposal was recorded, the cost of the equipment sold would have been removed from the Equipment account, bringing its balance down to $37,000. Since the balance at the end of the period was $127,000 (from Exhibit 5-3), we can deduce that additional equipment costing $90,000 must have been purchased during the period. The purchase, which would have resulted in an outflow of cash, would be recorded as a negative amount under cash flows from investing activities.

Our analysis of the Equipment account is sufficient to identify all of MML's investing activities related to equipment and there is no need to analyze the company's Accumulated Depreciation account. It represents the cumulative depreciation expense related to all of the company's equipment, but as we have discussed, depreciation is a non-cash transaction. As such, changes in this account balance do not impact cash flows. In more advanced accounting courses, it is possible that you will need to analyze this account if the selling price of any dispositions of property, plant, and equipment is not provided, but this is beyond the scope of an introductory accounting course.

When an account such as Equipment is affected by more than one transaction during the period, you may find it helpful to use a T account to organize the known data and determine any missing amount. For example, here is how a T account could be used to determine how much equipment MML purchased in 2015:

Equipment			
Beginning balance (from Exhibit 5-3)	62,000		
		25,000	Cost of equipment sold (given)
Balance after sale of equipment	37,000		
Cost of equipment purchased	**90,000**	←	**This is the missing amount, which will produce the ending balance.**
Ending balance (from Exhibit 5-3)	127,000		

Step 6 – Determine and record the cash proceeds from the sale of shares of other companies (the sale of investments) and the cost of any investments in other companies purchased with cash during the period.

From the assets section of MML's statement of financial position, we can see that the company had no investments in the shares of other companies at either the beginning or end of the year. As such, no further analysis is required to complete this step. When preparing the statement of cash flows for companies that have invested in other companies, any proceeds received from the sale of these shares during the period are treated as cash inflows from investing activities, while the cost of any shares purchased during the period is treated as an outflow of cash from investing activities.

Once a company's long-term asset accounts have been analyzed, the cash flows from investing activities are complete. We can then move on to determine the company's cash flows from financing activities. Steps 7, 8, and 9 outline how this is done. Financing activities generally involve changes to long-term liabilities and shareholders' equity accounts. However, they can also involve a few *current* liabilities. For example, in Step 4 of this analysis, we found that MML had one current liability, Dividends Payable, which was related to financing activities. Accordingly, the changes in this current liability account, as well as the changes in each long-term liability and shareholders' equity account, will be analyzed to determine the cash flows from financing activities.

Step 7 – Determine the amount of cash dividends paid during the period.

TAKE**5**

From Exhibit 5-3, we can see that MML began the year with dividends payable of $5,200 and ended the year with a balance of $3,200. Recall that in Chapter 1, we learned that dividends were a distribution of a company's retained earnings to its shareholders. As such, our analysis of the changes in the Dividends Payable account must be done in conjunction with an analysis of the Retained Earnings account. From Exhibit 5-3, we see that MML's Retained Earnings account had a balance of $23,750 at the beginning of the period and an ending balance of $106,550. The key to analyzing this $82,800 increase in Retained Earnings is to remember what affects this account. Each period, it is increased by net income (or decreased by a net loss) and decreased by any dividends declared. Because MML had net income of $86,000 in 2015, we would have expected the company's Retained Earnings balance to increase by this amount. Since it only increased by $82,800, we can deduce that dividends of $3,200 must have been *declared* during the year. However, the payment of dividends can take place weeks after they have been declared. As such, it is possible that dividends that have been declared near the end of an accounting period remain unpaid. An analysis of the Dividends Payable account will enable us to determine the amount of dividends that have been paid. If MML began the year with dividends payable of $5,200 and dividends of $3,200 were *declared* during the year, the company would have had a dividends payable balance of $8,400. As the company's ending balance in its Dividends Payable account was $3,200, we know that dividends of $5,200 were *paid* during the year. The payment of these dividends would be an outflow of cash and reported as a negative cash flow from financing activities.

Here is another example of how a T account can help you organize the known data and determine a missing amount. It shows how the Dividends Payable and Retained Earnings accounts can be used to determine the amount of dividends that MML declared and paid during the year:

Retained Earnings		
	23,750	Beginning balance (from Exhibit 5-3)
	86,000	Net earnings for 2016 (given)
	109,750	Balance after earnings added
Dividends declared during year 3,200	←	This is the missing amount, which will produce the ending balance
	106,550	Ending balance (from Exhibit 5-3)

Dividends Payable		
	5,200	Beginning balance (from Exhibit 5-3)
	3,200	Dividends declared (determined above)
	8,400	Balance
Dividends paid during year 5,200	←	This is the missing amount, which will produce the ending balance
	3,200	Ending balance (from Exhibit 5-3)

Step 8 – Determine and record the amount of cash received from borrowings (new loans or increases to existing loans) made during the year and the amount of cash principal repaid on loans during the period.

When beginning our analysis of the Loans Payable account, the note we added in Step 2 would remind us that we were provided with the following additional information:

b.   No principal repayments were made on the loan during the period.

From this note, we know that MML had no cash outflows related to the repayment of principal on its loan payable during the year.

By looking at the Loans Payable account on MML's statement of financial position (Exhibit 5-3), we can see that the account increased by $7,000 during the year. The Loans Payable account had a balance of $36,000 at the beginning of the period and an ending balance of $43,000. From this, we know that the company must have borrowed at least $7,000 during the period. Since we know that the company repaid no principal on its loans during the year, we can deduce that this increase represents all of the company's borrowings. That is, there are no principal repayments netted against it. These new borrowings would have resulted in an inflow of cash and would be recorded as a positive amount under cash flows from financing activities.

Here is another example of how a T account can help you organize the known data and determine a missing amount. It shows how the Loans Payable account can be used to determine the principal repayments that MML made during 2015:

Loans Payable			
Loan principal repaid during year (given)	–	36,000	Beginning balance (from Exhibit 5-3)
		36,000	Balance after principal repayments
This is the missing amount, which will ➝ **produce the ending balance.**		**7,000**	**New borrowings**
		43,000	Ending balance (from Exhibit 5-3)

Step 9 – Determine the cash received from shares issued during the period.

From Exhibit 5-3, we can see that MML's Common Shares account increased by $10,000 during the year. The account balance was $40,000 at the beginning of the year and $50,000 at the end. This tells us that that company must have issued new common shares during the year and received proceeds of $10,000. The issuance of shares is a financing activity and the proceeds would be recorded as a cash inflow.

Step 10 – Calculate the sum of the cash flows from operating, investing, and financing activities and agree it to the net change in cash for the period as determined in Step 1.

We can now complete MML's statement of cash flows by simply entering a subtotal for each of the three sections, and then combining these into an overall net change in cash for the period. This has been done in Exhibit 5-6. We then check that the total of the cash flows determined for the three categories add up to the overall change in cash for the period that was determined in Step 1. In Step 1, we determined that MML's cash balance had increased by $7,800 during the period. This is equal to the total of cash flows from operating activities (an inflow of $77,100), cash flows from investing activities (an outflow of $71,100), and cash flows from financing activities (an inflow of $1,800).

Finally, to assist users in their analysis of cash flows, standard setters require a few additional pieces of cash flow-related information to be disclosed. Specifically, companies are required to disclose the amount of:

- interest paid and received during the period,
- dividends paid and received during the period, and
- income taxes paid during the period.

These disclosures can be presented at the end of the statement of cash flows or in the notes to the financial statements. MML has included the amount of dividends paid in its cash flows from financing activities, so no additional disclosure is required. The company's interest expense for the period was $2,970 (per Exhibit 5-4) and the company had no Interest Payable account. As such, this amount represents the interest paid by the company during the year. The company's income tax expense for the period was $4,980 (per Exhibit 5-4), but, as we saw in Step 4, the company also paid $2,600 in taxes owing at the beginning of the period. As such, the company's total payments related to income taxes were $7,580 and this is disclosed at the bottom of the statement of cash flows (Exhibit 5-6). No information is provided regarding any interest or dividends received by MML, so we will assume that there were none during the period.

As an alternative to presenting the supplementary disclosures (about the amount of cash used for interest and income tax) on the statement of cash flows, this information may be provided in the notes accompanying the financial statements.

What is the difference between the direct and indirect methods of preparing cash flows from operating activities?

The direct method of preparing cash flows from operating activities only differs from the indirect method in how the operating cash flows are determined and presented, but total cash flows from operating activities are the same under either method.

Rather than reconciling net income from the accrual basis of accounting to the cash basis, the direct method directly presents a company's operating cash flows by major category of cash receipts and payments. These categories commonly include:

- Receipts from customers
- Payments to suppliers
- Payments to employees
- Payments of interest
- Payments of income taxes

Essentially, the company is adjusting each line of the statement of income (sales revenue, cost of goods sold, wage expense, and so on) from the accrual basis to the cash basis, rather than just the bottom line (net income). For example, to determine its receipts from customers, a company will start with the sales revenue reported on the statement of income and then adjust it to remove the amount of sales made on account that have yet to be collected and increase it by collections on customer receivables outstanding from prior periods. Similar steps will be taken to adjust the expenses presented on the statement of income. For example, to determine its payments to employees, a company will start with the wage expense reported on the statement of income and then adjust it to remove the wages that remain unpaid and increase it for any payments made to employees of wages owing from prior periods.

Exhibit 5-8 illustrates how each of the common categories of cash receipts and payments can be determined.

Exhibit 5-8 Direct Method – Determining Cash Receipts/Payments from Common Categories

Category	Starting Point (from Statement of Income)	Adjustments (from Statement of Financial Position)
Receipts from Customers	Sales Revenue	+/– Change in Accounts Receivable
Payments to Suppliers	Expenses other than:	+/– Change in Inventory
	• Wage Expense	+/– Change in Prepaid Expenses
	• Interest Expense	+/– Change in Accounts Payable
	• Income Tax Expense	
	• Depreciation and Amortization Expense	
Payments to Employees	Wage Expense	+/– Change in Wages Payable
Payment of Interest	Interest Expense	+/– Change in Interest Payable
Payment of Income Taxes	Income Tax Expense	+/– Change in Income Taxes Payable

We can apply these steps to the information from Exhibits 5-3 and 5-4 to determine the cash flows from operating activities for Matchett Manufacturing Ltd. using the direct method, as shown in Exhibit 5-9.

Exhibit 5-9 Cash Flow from Operating Activities: Direct Method

Category	Starting Point (from Statement of Income)		Adjustments (from Statement of Financial Position)		Total
		A		B	= A + B
Receipts from Customers	Sales Revenue	480,000	Change in Accounts Receivable	12,500	492,500
Payments to Suppliers	Cost of Goods Sold	(305,000)	Change in Inventory	(27,500)	
	Rent Expense	(13,250)	Change in Prepaid Expenses	N/A	
	Utilities Expense	(7,600)	Change in Accounts Payable	2,400	(350,950)
Payments to Employees	Wage Expense	(53,900)	Change in Wages Payable	N/A	(53,900)
Payment of Interest	Interest Expense	(2,970)	Change in Interest Payable	N/A	(2,970)
Payment of Income Taxes	Income Tax Expense	(4,980)	Change in Income Taxes Payable	(2,600)	(7,580)
			CASH FLOWS FROM OPERATING ACTIVITIES		77,100

Notice that the total cash flows from operating activities is $77,100, the same amount that was determined using the indirect method. Also notice that Column B reflects the exact same analysis that was required in Step 4 of the indirect method. Finally, note that it is not necessary to have an adjustment for depreciation and amortization expenses (because these are non-cash transactions), nor for any gains and losses (because these are related to investing activities), as we are not starting our analysis with net income.

Other categories can be used under the direct method. Some companies separate payments to suppliers and payment of other operating expenses. Also, if a company has earned interest income, it would have a category presenting the receipts of interest.

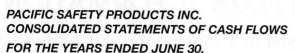
For Example

FINANCIAL STATEMENTS

Pacific Safety Products Inc. is headquartered in Arnprior, Ontario, and its shares trade on the TSX Venture Exchange. The company manufactures and sells a line of protective products for the defence and security markets. The company prepares its statement of cash flows using the direct method for determining cash flows from operating activities. The company's statements of cash flows for the years ended June 30, 2013 and 2012, were as follows:[6]

PACIFIC SAFETY PRODUCTS INC.
CONSOLIDATED STATEMENTS OF CASH FLOWS
FOR THE YEARS ENDED JUNE 30,

	2013	2012
CASH FLOW FROM OPERATING ACTIVITIES		
Cash receipts from customers	$ 13,758,593	$ 15,813,155
Cash paid to suppliers and employees	(13,342,225)	(16,370,981)
Interest paid	(116, 635)	(92,119)
Interest received	8,774	12,493
Investment tax credits recovered	16,036	—
Income taxes recovered	—	6,319
Income taxes paid	—	(102,509)
CASH FLOW FROM (USED IN) OPERATING ACTIVITIES	**324,543**	**(733,642)**

(continued)

For Example (continued)

	2013	2012
CASH FLOW FROM INVESTING ACTIVITIES		
Purchase of property and equipment	**(44,019)**	(64,037)
Investment in intangible assets	**–**	(133,999)
CASH FLOW USED IN INVESTING ACTIVITIES	**(44,019)**	(198,036)
CASH FLOW FROM FINANCING ACTIVITIES		
Repayment of long-term debt	**(214,320)**	(214,320)
CASH FLOW USED IN FINANCING ACTIVITIES	**(214,320)**	(214,320)
INCREASE (DECREASE) IN CASH AND CASH EQUIVALENTS	**66,204**	(1,146,002)*
CASH AND CASH EQUIVALENTS, NET OF BANK INDEBTEDNESS, BEGINNING OF YEAR	**1,087,219**	2,204,709
Effect of exchange rate fluctuations on cash held	**27,486**	28,508
CASH AND CASH EQUIVALENTS, NET OF BANK INDEBTEDNESS, END OF YEAR (note 7)	**$ 1,180,909**	$ 1,087,219

There was a $4 rounding difference in the company's published financial statements.

Are there investing and financing activities that do not appear on the statement of cash flows?

Yes, it is possible for a company to have investing and financing activities that do not appear on the statement of cash flows. This would be the case if any of the following occurred:
- The company purchased property, plant, and equipment, by assuming debt or issuing shares rather than paying cash.
- The company acquired the shares of another company by assuming debt or issuing shares rather than paying cash.
- The company repaid debt by issuing shares rather than paying cash.

As these transactions did not involve the inflow or outflow of cash, they would not be presented on the statement of cash flows. Instead, they would be disclosed in the notes to the company's financial statements so that financial statement users were made aware of them.

INTERPRETING CASH FLOW INFORMATION

How can the information presented in a statement of cash flows be used to manage a company?

■ **LEARNING OBJECTIVE 5**
Interpret a statement of cash flows and develop potential solutions to any cash flow challenges identified.

Managing cash flows is a key challenge for most companies. It is essential that management have information on the cash flows from the company's operating, investing, and financing activities. This information can then be analyzed to determine whether there may be opportunities to enhance cash inflows and/or minimize cash outflows. The causes of cash flow challenges can be found in the statement of cash flows and management can then develop strategies to address them. Common cash flow challenges include:
- significant increases in sales volumes,
- lengthy cash-to-cash cycles, and
- undercapitalization (or inadequate financing).

We will look at each of these challenges in more detail.

While significant increases in sales volumes are a positive sign for a company, this can lead to cash flow challenges. These increased sales require companies to purchase or produce more and more inventory, as well as to expand their storage and operating capacity. Purchasing additional inventory and/or expanding production and storage capacity requires cash. This challenge is very common among start-up companies, which can often experience rapid growth of sales. Without adequate cash flow, these companies can "grow" themselves out of business.

Compounding the growth problem is the presence of a lengthy **cash-to-cash cycle**. As illustrated in Exhibit 5-10, this cycle is the time between when a company pays out cash to purchase goods or raw materials for manufacturing products until those goods are ultimately paid for by the customer. The longer the cash-to-cash cycle, the greater the company's cash requirements, and this issue is magnified in periods of high sales growth. Again, start-up companies often face challenges in this area because suppliers require them to pay for goods and raw materials up front, but it may take weeks or months before the start-up is able to sell the product and collect from customers. As we saw in our feature story on Bombardier Inc., lengthy cash-to-cash cycles for manufacturing multi-million-dollar items like planes and trains can also place pressure on cash flow.

KEY POINT
The longer a company's cash-to-cash cycle, the more pressure is placed on cash flow.

Exhibit 5-10 The Cash-to-Cash Cycle

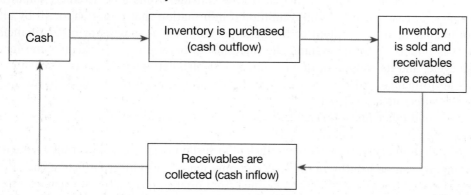

Finally, companies, especially start-ups, can be undercapitalized; that is, they are not sufficiently financed. It is common for companies to begin operations without a large enough pool of cash. This may be due to borrowing limitations or an inability to raise cash through the issuance of shares. When the company faces the need for a large amount of cash due to rapid growth, a lengthy cash-to-cash cycle, or the need to purchase capital assets, it may not have sufficient cash reserves to get through prolonged periods of net cash outflows.

Each of these challenges would be evident on the company's statement of cash flows. For example, significant cash outflows to purchase inventory, payments to suppliers and employees, or increases in accounts receivable would be reported in the company's cash flows from operating activities. Significant cash payments for property, plant, and equipment would be reflected in the company's cash flows from investing activities, while a lack of cash inflows from financing activities could also be observed.

Companies can resolve the common cash flow challenges by taking the following measures.

1. *Alleviate cash flow problems by reducing the rate of growth.*
   One way to solve cash flow challenges is to slow down the sales growth rate. However, reducing the growth rate may not be the best response because it will reduce net income and may hurt the company in the long run, as it attempts to develop a strong customer base. Limiting the growth in sales may divert customers to competing companies and, if these customers develop loyalties to the competitors, a company's long-term potential may be reduced. Regardless of these concerns, it may be a necessary step for companies facing cash flow challenges related to growth.

2. *Alleviate cash flow problems by shortening the cash-to-cash cycle.*
   Shortening the company's cash-to-cash cycle is another way to improve cash flow. There are many ways to do this. For example, increasing the amount of cash sales, accepting credit cards, or reducing the credit period for customers who buy on account would all reduce the cash-to-cash cycle. Alternatively, negotiating with suppliers to be able to purchase on credit would also reduce the cash-to-cash cycle; however, this generally requires the company to have established its creditworthiness to suppliers, which takes time.

Companies have to carefully consider the sales terms they provide their customers. Customers may not be happy with having to pay cash or with reduced credit periods and may be able to

get better terms from competitors. While accepting credit cards would enable the company to collect its receivables more quickly, credit card companies charge fees and these additional costs will affect overall profitability.

3. *Alleviate cash flow problems by increasing the amount of capitalization.*
    Another way to solve the cash flow concerns is to address any undercapitalization problem; that is, to raise additional cash through financing activities. Two typical ways of doing this are to issue additional shares (equity financing) or to borrow the cash (debt financing). If additional shares are issued, it may dilute the ownership interest of existing shareholders, so this may be an unpopular decision. If the company enters into new borrowing arrangements, the company will have to service this debt by paying interest and repaying principal in future periods. Therefore, this may only be a short-term solution to the company's cash flow problems.

It should now be clear to you that (1) cash flow considerations are extremely important, and (2) the statement of cash flows provides additional information that is not captured by either the statement of income or the statement of financial position. For managers or other financial statement users, it is important to understand the relationship between the company's net income, its cash-to-cash cycle, and its statement of cash flows. It is also extremely important when evaluating a company's performance and cash position to understand how its receivables, payables, and inventory policies affect its cash flows.

Management and other financial statement users can also use three basic questions as a starting point for analyzing the statement of cash flows:

1. Is the cash from operating activities sufficient to sustain the company over the long term?
    A company can be healthy in the long run only when it produces sufficient cash from its operations. Although cash can be obtained from financing activities (issuance of new debt or shares) and from investing activities (the sale of investments or capital assets), there is a limit to the cash inflows that can be achieved from financing and investing activities. Financing inflows are limited by the willingness of lenders and shareholders to invest their money in the company. As the level of debt rises, so does the risk; consequently, the interest rate that must be paid will also increase. At some level of debt, the company becomes so risky that lenders will simply not lend more. Investing inflows are limited by amount of property, plant, and equipment that the company can dispose of and still remain in operation or the extent of any investments it has in the shares of other companies that can be sold. When the inflows from financing and investing are limited, if a company is to remain in business, it must generate sufficient cash inflows from operating activities to make the principal, interest, and dividend payments associated with the financing activities, and to continue investing at appropriate levels in property, plant, and equipment and other long-term assets.

2. Do any of the items on the statement of cash flows suggest that the business may be having problems?
    For example, a large increase in accounts receivable may indicate that the company is having difficulties collecting its receivables. A large increase in inventories may indicate that it is having trouble selling its products. A large increase in accounts payable may indicate that the company is having difficulty paying its bills. Large disposals of property, plant, and equipment may indicate that it is contracting, rather than expanding.

3. Of the sources and uses of cash, which ones are related to items or activities that will continue from period to period, and which are sporadic or non-continuing?
    A large source or use of cash in one period may not have long-term implications if it will not continue in the future. To address this question, the historical trend in the cash flow data must be considered. While some users will be interested in what has happened to cash in the current period, most are likely to be more interested in predicting the company's future cash flows. For example, a bank loan officer wants assurance that, if money is loaned to the company, the company will be able to pay it back. A stock analyst, on the

other hand, will want to know what cash flows can be expected over a long period of time, to ensure an adequate return on an investment in the company's shares. Users interested in the company's future will analyze this statement to try to decide which cash flows will continue in the future and which will not.

 Ethics in Accounting

There are a number of actions that management can take that improve a company's cash flow from operating activities in the short term, but that may be detrimental to the company over the long term. For example, delaying payments to suppliers and employees would improve operating cash flows, but may jeopardize relationships with suppliers and upset employees. Delaying inventory purchases would also improve operating cash flows, but could result in lost sales due to stockouts.

What can cash flow patterns tell us?

A company's **cash flow pattern** is the direction (positive or negative) of its cash flows in the three categories: operating, investing, and financing. Given the three categories and that each could be positive (a net inflow of cash) or negative (a net outflow of cash), there are eight possible cash flow patterns. These are presented in Exhibit 5-11. Reviewing a company's cash flow pattern can provide financial statement users with quick means of initially assessing its financial condition. Of course, the dollar amount of each category is also critical, but the pattern helps users to quickly identify situations where more in-depth analysis would be required.

While it is possible to find companies that fit into each of the patterns, the majority of public companies fit into pattern 3 (+ / − / +) or 4 (+ / − / −). These companies are generating positive cash flows from their operating activities and are continuing to grow and replace property, plant, and equipment, which means negative cash flows from investing activities. They are either able to attract new debt or investors to finance part of this growth, which means positive cash flows from financing activities, or are repaying debt and paying dividends, which means negative cash flows from financing activities.

KEY POINT
The most common cash flow patterns are: (Operating / Investing / Financing)
+ / − / +
+ / − / −

For Example

Groupe Bikini Village Inc. is a public company, headquartered in Sainte-Julie, Quebec, which operates 53 stores across Eastern Canada selling swimwear, travel clothing, and accessories. The company's cash flow patterns for the years ended February 1, 2014, and February 2, 2013, were as follows:

	Operating	Investing	Financing
2014	+	−	−
2013	−	−	−

These basic patterns can quickly tell you a lot about the company. We can see that the company has struggled to generate cash flow from its operations, has repaid more capital than it has attracted, yet has continued to expand its operations. Of course, it would be important to analyze the cash flow results in more detail as well as to consider the dollar amounts of each cash flow, but this analysis would confirm the initial understanding provided by the cash flow pattern.[7]

Exhibit 5-11 outlines the profile of the company that would fit within each cash flow pattern. Being able to link the profile with the cash flow patterns enables financial statement users to develop expectations in terms of cash flows for companies they are analyzing. Cases in which the actual pattern differs from the expected pattern highlight the need for additional analysis.

Exhibit 5-11 Cash Flow Patterns[8]

Cash Flow from Operating Activities	Cash Flow from Investing Activities	Cash Flow from Financing Activities	Pattern Number and Company Profile
+	+	+	1. Successful, but actively repositioning or relocating using financing from operations together with cash from creditors and shareholders
+	+	−	2. Successful, mature company that is downsizing and returning capital to shareholders or repaying debt
+	−	+	3. Successful and growing, with growth partially financed by creditors and shareholders
+	−	−	4. Successful, with operating activities providing sufficient cash to finance growth and repay debt or pay dividends
−	+	+	5. Struggling, but using cash inflows from the sale of property, plant, and equipment and new borrowings to remain in operation
−	+	−	6. Struggling and using cash from the sale of property, plant, and equipment to repay creditors
−	−	+	7. A start-up or a struggling company that is able to attract financing for growth or reorganization
−	−	−	8. Struggling, but using existing cash balances to cover losses, purchase property, plant, and equipment, and repay creditors

FINANCIAL STATEMENT ANALYSIS

■ LEARNING OBJECTIVE 6
Calculate and interpret a company's cash flows to total liabilities ratio and determine the amount of net free cash flow being generated.

How do we determine what portion of a company's liabilities could be met with cash flows from operating activities?

Companies must be able to generate cash from their operating activities that is sufficient to repay their current and long-term liabilities. There are a number of cash flow ratios that are used to assess a company's ability to meet its liabilities through its operating cash flows. We will focus on one of these ratios, the **cash flows to total liabilities ratio**. This ratio is determined as follows:

$$\text{Cash flows to total liabilities} = \frac{\text{Cash flows from operating activities}}{\text{Total liabilities}}$$

This ratio measures the percentage of a company's total liabilities that could be met with one year's operating cash flows. It is important to note that total liabilities include both current and non-current liabilities and that only the current liabilities are due within the next year. In addition, some of the liabilities will not be paid in cash. For example, unearned revenues are often settled by providing services to customers. Also, the company may have other assets that could be used to settle liabilities, such as investments in the shares of other companies. As such, this ratio can be safely less than 1. Rather than using total liabilities, some analysts will calculate this ratio using long-term debt (including the current portion). This enables them to assess the company's ability to repay its debt using its operating cash flows. We will use the cash flows to total liabilities ratio as it is simple and the information necessary to calculate it is readily available for all financial statements.

The cash flows to total liabilities ratio for **Danier Leather Inc.** for the years ended June 28, 2014, and June 29, 2013, would be as follows:

$$\text{Cash flows to total liabilities} = \begin{array}{cc} \underline{2014} & \underline{2013} \\ \frac{(\$4,907)}{\$12,222} = (0.40) & \frac{\$6,752}{\$13,140} = 0.51 \end{array}$$

($ in thousands)

From this, we can see that because Danier's cash flows from operating activities were negative in 2014, they could not cover any of the company's liabilities. This was a significant change from 2013, when it was able to cover 51% of its liabilities with its operating cash flows. While this trend is not positive, the company had cash reserves of more than $13.5 million at June 28, 2014, which would be more than enough to settle all of the company's liabilities if necessary.

How do we determine how much net free cash flow a company generates?

Free cash flow is a commonly used measure in the **management discussion and analysis (MD&A)** section of annual reports. The concept of free cash flow is to measure the amount of cash that a company generates from its operations that is in excess of the cash required to maintain the company's productive capacity. The term *free cash flow* is not a measure that has been defined by accounting standard setters. As such, it is often referred to as a **non-IFRS financial measure**. The implications of this are that there is no standardized definition for determining the measure. In practice, a variety of different definitions are used for this measure, making it a challenge for users to understand and interpret it.

Canadian accounting standard setters have attempted to address this by introducing **net free cash flow** as a standardized measure with a consistent definition. They have defined net free cash flow as follows:

$$\text{Net free cash flow} = \begin{array}{ccc} \text{Cash flows from} & - & \text{Net capital} & - & \text{Dividends on} \\ \text{operating activities} & & \text{expenditures}^1 & & \text{preferred shares} \end{array}$$

[1]Net capital expenditures are equal to the total purchases of property, plant, and equipment less the proceeds from the sale of property, plant, and equipment.

Net free cash flow is considered to be the cash flow generated from a company's operating activities that would be available to the company's common shareholders. While management has discretion with respect to the use of these cash flows, it is unlikely that the entire amount would be distributed to common shareholders. Instead, portions of these cash flows are likely to be used to repay debt, finance expansion plans, repurchase company shares, or make investments in other companies.

While a positive net free cash flow is considered to be a good thing, it is also important to consider why a company may have a negative free cash flow amount. It may be due to the company having made significant capital expenditures, such as buying property, plant, and equipment, during the period. If this is the case, then this is also positive, because these assets will be available to generate revenues for the company in future periods.

Cash Flow

The net free cash flow for Danier Leather Inc. for the years ended June 28, 2014, and June 29, 2013, would be as follows:

($ in thousands)

$$\text{Net free cash flow} = \begin{array}{ccc} \text{Cash flows from} & - & \text{Net capital} & - & \text{Dividends on} \\ \text{operating activities} & & \text{expenditures} & & \text{preferred shares} \end{array}$$

$$2014 = (\$4,907) - \$6,079 - \$0$$
$$= (\$10,986)$$
$$2013 = \$6,752 - \$5,327 - \$0$$
$$= \$1,425$$

From this we can see that there was a significant decrease in the net free cash flow the company was able to generate from 2013 to 2014. We can see that the company went from having a free cash flow of $1.4 million to having a negative free cash flow of $11 million. This means that the company would need cash from its cash reserves or from other sources to continue operating. While this trend is not positive, Danier had a cash balance of $13.5 million at June 28, 2014, so the company had significant cash reserves available to support its operations.

Now that you know how a statement of cash flows is created, in the next chapter we'll take a closer look at cash and at another significant liquid asset: accounts receivable.

SUMMARY

1. **Understand and explain why the statement of cash flows is of significance to users.**

   - The statement of cash flows enables users to assess the cash generated from core operations, the cash that has been obtained from investors and creditors, the extent of new investment in capital assets, the cash available to repay debt, and the amount of cash distributed to shareholders as dividends.

   - The statement of cash flows also provides a basis for estimating the value of a company and predicting its ability to service its debt and pay dividends.

2. **Explain how the statement of cash flows and the statement of income differ.**

   - The statement of cash flows uses the cash basis of accounting, whereas the statement of income is prepared using the accrual basis.

   - The statement of income focuses only on a company's operating activities (its revenues and expenses). The statement of cash flows includes cash flows from operating activities, but it also includes cash flows related to investing and financing activities.

3. **Identify the three major types of activities that are presented in a statement of cash flows and describe some of the typical transactions included in each category of activity.**

   - The statement of cash flows categorizes a company's cash-related transactions into three categories: operating activities, investing activities, and financing activities.

   - Typical operating activities include cash sales to customers, collections of customer receivables, purchases of inventory, payments to suppliers, payments of wages, and payments of taxes.

   - Typical investing activities include cash purchases of property, plant, and equipment; purchases of shares of other companies; sales of property, plant, and equipment; and sales of shares in other companies.

   - Typical financing activities include the proceeds from issuing shares, the proceeds received from new loans, repayments of loan principal, and payments of cash dividends.

   - Cash flows from operating activities normally receive the greatest scrutiny as these are the cash flows that result from what the company is in the business of doing and are a key source for financing future growth. They are also the source for future debt repayments and/or dividend payments.

4. **Prepare a statement of cash flows using a comparative statement of financial position, a statement of income, and some additional information.**

   - Cash includes cash on hand, bank deposits, and cash equivalents (which are short-term, highly liquid investments with little risk of a change in their value).

   - There are two methods of preparing the statement of cash flows: the direct method and indirect method. The only difference between the two methods is how cash flows from operating activities is determined. Total operating cash flows are the same under both methods and the choice of method has no effect on cash flows from investing or financing activities.

   - The indirect method is simpler to prepare, uses information available in most accounting systems, and provides a linkage between net income and cash flows from operating activities.

   - To determine cash flows from operating activities under the indirect method, net income is adjusted for any non-cash expenses (depreciation and amortization), any gains or losses from investing activities, and changes in current asset and liability accounts (except for the Cash and Dividends Payable accounts).

   - To determine cash flows from operating activities under the direct method, cash flows are aggregated into categories that commonly include receipts from customers, payments to suppliers, payments to employees, payments of interest, and payments of income taxes. Each category is calculated using the relevant revenue or expense account(s) and adjusted for changes in the related current asset or current liability account.

   - Cash flows from investing activities are equal to the cash payments to purchase property, plant, and equipment less any cash receipts from sales of property, plant, and equipment. The amount of cash payments to purchase the shares of other companies and any proceeds from the sale of such shares are also included.

   - Cash flows from financing activities are equal to the cash received from issuing shares or the proceeds from any new loans less any principal repayments or dividends paid during the period.

   - The sum of the three cash flows should be equal to the net change in cash and cash equivalents for the period.

   - Companies are also required to disclose the amount of interest paid and received, the amount of dividends paid and received, and the amount of income taxes paid.

   - Any non-cash investing and financing activities should also be disclosed.

5. **Interpret a statement of cash flows and develop potential solutions to any cash flow challenges identified.**

   - Information from the statement of cash flows can help to identify challenges related to significant increases in sales volumes, lengthy cash-to-cash cycles, and undercapitalization.

   - The cash-to-cash cycle is the time between a company paying out cash to purchase goods and when those goods are ultimately paid for by customers. The longer the cycle, the more pressure is placed on cash flow.

   - When assessing a company's cash flows, users will consider whether the cash flows from operating activities are sufficient to sustain the company over time. They will also look for indications of concern related to the collection of receivables; excess inventories; an inability to settle payables; or significant sales of property, plant, and equipment.

   - A company's cash flow pattern is the direction (positive or negative) of its cash flows from operating, investing, and financing activities. Reviewing a company's cash flow pattern can provide users with a quick means of initially assessing its financial condition. The most common cash flow patterns are positive operating cash flows, negative investing cash flows, and either positive or negative financing cash flows.

6. **Calculate and interpret a company's cash flows to total liabilities ratio and determine the amount of net free cash flow being generated.**

   - The *cash flows to total liabilities ratio* can be determined by dividing cash flows from operating activities by total liabilities.

   - It measures the percentage of a company's total liabilities that could be met with one year's operating cash flows. When interpreting this ratio, it is important to remember that only a company's current liabilities must be settled within the next year.

- *Net free cash flow* is equal to cash flows from operating activities less net capital expenditures and any dividends on preferred shares. Net capital expenditures equal the total purchases of property, plant, and equipment less the proceeds from the sale of property, plant, and equipment.

- It is considered to be the cash flow generated from operations that would be available to the company's common shareholders. It would be reinvested in the company to grow the business, while a portion may be distributed to shareholders as dividends.

KEY TERMS

Bank overdraft facility (214)
Cash (213)
Cash equivalents (213)
Cash flow (209)
Cash flow pattern (227)
Cash flows to total liabilities ratio (228)
Cash-to-cash cycle (225)

Demand deposits (213)
Direct method (214)
Financing activities (210)
Free cash flow (229)
Indirect method (214)
Investing activities (210)
Line of credit (214)

Management discussion and
   analysis (MD&A) (229)
Net free cash flow (229)
Non-IFRS financial measure (229)
Operating activities (210)
Statement of cash flows (209)

ABBREVIATIONS USED

IFRS   International Financial Reporting Standards
MD&A   Management discussion and analysis

SYNONYMS

Indirect method | Reconciliation method

CHAPTER END REVIEW PROBLEM 1

The 2016 statement of financial position and statement of income of Beaman Industries Ltd. are presented in Exhibit 5-12. Beaman manufactures and distributes a broad range of electrical equipment to contractors and home renovation stores.

STRATEGIES FOR SUCCESS

▶ Start by setting up the outline of the statement of cash flows, with three sections labelled Operating Activities, Investing Activities, and Financing Activities. Leave a lot of space for the Operating Activities, as this is usually the biggest section.

▶ Follow the 10 steps from Exhibit 5-2.

EXHIBIT 5-12	SELECTED FINANCIAL STATEMENTS FOR BEAMAN INDUSTRIES LTD.

BEAMAN INDUSTRIES LTD.
Statement of Financial Position
As at March 31

	2016	2015
Assets		
Current assets:		
Cash	$ 32,970	$ 45,900
Accounts receivable	62,000	105,000
Inventory	91,000	55,200
Total current assets	185,970	206,100
Equipment	307,800	297,000
Accumulated depreciation, equipment	(128,520)	(111,420)
	$365,250	$391,680
Liabilities and Shareholders' Equity		
Current liabilities:		
Accounts payable	$ 74,900	$122,680
Total current liabilities	74,900	122,680
Bank loan payable	95,050	80,000
Common shares	180,000	180,000
Retained earnings	15,300	9,000
	$365,250	$391,680

BEAMAN INDUSTRIES LTD.
Statement of Income
For the year ended March 31, 2016

Sales revenue		$333,900
Cost of goods sold		157,500
Gross profit		176,400
Expenses		
Wages expense	$86,400	
Interest expense	14,400	
Depreciation expense	25,000	
Loss on sale of equipment	9,000	
Income tax expense	17,300	152,100
Net income		$ 24,300

Additional information:
1. During the year, equipment costing $63,000 was sold for $46,100.
2. The company made no principal repayments on its loans during the year.

Required:
Prepare the statement of cash flows for Beaman for the year ended March 31, 2016. Use the indirect method for determining cash flows from operating activities.

CHAPTER END REVIEW PROBLEM 2

The statement of cash flows for Pomeroy Distributors Ltd. for 2014 to 2016 is presented in Exhibit 5-13.

EXHIBIT 5-13	POMEROY DISTRIBUTORS LTD. STATEMENT OF CASH FLOWS

POMEROY DISTRIBUTORS LTD.
Statement of Cash Flows
(in thousands)
For the year ended May 31

	2016	2015	2014
Operating Activities:			
Net income	$10,575	$19,202	$19,786
Adjustments to convert net income to net cash from operating activities:			
Depreciation expense	7,805	7,040	6,457
(Gain) loss on sale of property, plant, and equipment	1,070	488	(212)
(Increase) decrease in:			
Receivables	(8,797)	(7,072)	(935)
Inventories	(23,513)	(11,872)	(18,687)
Prepaid expenses	660	(652)	(2,363)
(Decrease) increase in:			
Accounts payable	9,308	10,120	(3,734)
Accrued interest	(1,058)	1,458	646
Other accrued expenses	(2,332)	970	432
Income tax payable	(620)	–	(402)
Net cash provided (used) by operating activities	(6,902)	19,682	988
Investing Activities:			
Paid for purchase of property, plant, and equipment	(18,130)	(9,395)	(8,550)
Proceeds from sale of property, plant, and equipment	2,722	415	2,324
Net cash used by investing activities	(15,408)	(8,980)	(6,226)
Financing Activities:			
Additions to short-term borrowings	4,000	1,000	18,500
Repayments of long-term debt	–	(4,913)	(14,734)
Additions to long-term debt	22,000	–	5,000
Paid to purchase and retire shares		(1,885)	(2,448)
Received from the issuance of shares	678	–	–
Paid for dividends	(6,470)	(5,956)	(5,486)
Net cash provided (used) by financing activities	20,208	(11,754)	832
Net change in cash during period	(2,102)	(1,052)	(4,406)
Cash at beginning of period	3,226	4,278	8,684
Cash at end of period	$ 1,124	$ 3,226	$ 4,278

Required:

a. Consider Pomeroy's cash flow patterns from 2014 to 2016. What profile do these provide of the company?

b. Explain why so much cash was consumed by the company's operations in fiscal 2016.

c. dentify the two most significant recurring non-operating cash outflows over the last three years and comment on how the company has met these needs. Does this analysis support your initial assessment from part "a"?

Suggested Solution to Chapter End Review Problem 1

The completed statement of cash flows for Beaman Industries Ltd. for the year ended March 31, 2016, is shown below. Explanations for certain items follow the statement.

BEAMAN INDUSTRIES LTD. Statement of Cash Flows For the year ended March 31, 2016	
Cash flows from operating activities:	
Net income	$24,300
add: Depreciation expense	25,000
add: Loss on sale of equipment	9,000
add: Decrease in accounts receivable	43,000
less: Increase in inventory	(35,800)
less: Decrease in accounts payable	(47,780)
Cash provided by operating activities	17,720
Cash flows from investing activities:	
add: Proceeds from sale of equipment	46,100
less: Purchase of equipment	(73,800)
Cash used for investing activities	(27,700)
Cash flows from financing activities:	
less: Payment of dividends	(18,000)
add: Proceeds of borrowing—loan payable	15,050
Cash used for financing activities	(2,950)
	(12,930)
Ending cash	32,970
Opening cash	45,900
Net change in cash	($12,930)

a. Because both depreciation expense and the loss on sale of equipment reduced net income, they are added back in order to eliminate the effect they had on net income. Depreciation is a non-cash expense and the loss on sale is related to an investing activity.

b. The following T accounts illustrate how the amount of equipment purchased and the dividends paid during the year were determined.

Equipment	
297,000	
	63,000
73,800	
307,800	

Retained Earnings	
	9,000
	24,300
18,000	
	15,300

Dividends Payable	
	—
	18,000
18,000	
	—

Suggested Solution to Chapter End Review Problem 2

a. Pomeroy's cash flow patterns over the past three years were as follows:

2014:	+ / − / +	The company was successful and growing, with growth financed by operations and also from financing provided by creditors and shareholders.
2015:	+ / − / −	The company was successful, with operating activities providing sufficient cash to finance growth and repay debt or pay dividends.
2016:	− / − / +	The company struggled operationally, but was able to attract financing to fund the acquisition of capital assets and the cash deficiency resulting from its operating activities.

A quick analysis of Pomeroy's cash flow patterns illustrates that the company began to struggle operationally in 2016. In 2014 and 2015, the company was able to generate cash from its operating activities, with almost $20 million generated from operations in 2015. The company has continued to increase its property, plant, and equipment each year, though some of these acquisitions were asset replacements (that is, replacements of the property, plant, and equipment sold during the period). In 2016, Pomeroy paid just over $18 million to acquire property, plant, and equipment, while receiving just under $3 million from the sale of property, plant, and equipment the company had finished using. In spite of its operational challenges in 2016, the company was able to attract new financing, receiving $22 million from new long-term borrowings and another $4 million from additional short-term borrowings. We would want to assess the company's operational challenges in greater depth to get a sense of where the difficulties were. For example, were they a result of declining sales, growth in inventory or receivables, or a reduction in the payment periods offered by suppliers?

b. In analyzing the company's cash flows from operating activities for 2016, it is clear that the biggest outflow was related to the increase in inventory. This resulted in cash outflows of more than $23 million during the year. This was a continuation of a trend that has seen the company's inventory levels increase significantly over the past three years, resulting in cash outflows of $54 million over the period. It would be important to know why the levels of inventories have increased so much. These changes in inventory level should also be compared with changes in sales revenues over the same period.

Accounts receivable have also been steadily increasing over the three-year period, with significant increases in 2015 and 2016. Again, this growth in receivables should be compared with the change in the sales revenues to determine if it is the growth in sales that is driving the increase in receivables. We should also determine if the company lengthened its credit terms. If increased sales and changes in credit terms do not explain the increase in receivables, it would indicate that Pomeroy is having trouble collecting from its customers.

A portion of the increased inventory levels was offset by financing provided by the company's suppliers through increased accounts payable. This covered all of the inventory increase in 2015, but only 40% of the increase in 2016. While the increase in accounts payable helps the company's cash flow situation, it may also indicate that Pomeroy is having trouble paying its bills and is therefore slowing down its payments to suppliers.

The fact that the company's net income fell by 45% in 2016 had a significant impact on its cash flow from operating activities for that year. In 2014 and 2015, Pomeroy was able to generate a net income of approximately $19 million and the company had positive cash flows from operations in both years. The significant decrease in net income in 2016 was one of the reasons the company's operating cash flows were negative in that year.

Overall, the biggest concern is likely the increase in inventory levels. The reason for the very large growth in inventories, particularly in 2016, should definitely be investigated.

c. Pomeroy's two most significant recurring cash outflows in the three years between 2014 and 2016 were related to the purchase of property, plant, and equipment, and the payment of dividends. Pomeroy's cash outflows to acquire property, plant, and equipment, net of the proceeds received from the sale of property, plant, and equipment, were over $30 million. Dividend payments during the three-year period resulted in cash outflows of almost $18 million.

The company met these cash needs though increased borrowings (short-term and long-term debt), cash flows from operations (in 2014 and 2015), and a drawdown of its existing cash balances. Pomeroy increased its debt by almost $31 million, net of repayments, during the three-year period. This was the largest source of cash inflows for the company, surpassing the net inflows of $14 million generated by the company's operating activities. The company's cash balances also decreased by more than $7 million between 2014 and 2016.

Pomeroy's operating activities produced a net inflow of cash in both 2014 and 2015, while there was a negative cash flow from operations in 2016. Between 2015 and 2016, cash flow from operations swung from close to a $20-million inflow to a $7-million outflow. This is consistent with the + / + / – pattern we observed for operating activities in part "a."

The net increase in property, plant, and equipment is consistent with the – / – / – pattern we observed in part "a" for investing activities. This, coupled with the increase in inventory levels noted in part "b," would be indicative of the company expanding its current operation (that is, increasing its warehouse and increasing the quantity and range of goods carried in inventory) or opening new locations and acquiring the inventory to stock them. We would want to investigate to determine which, if either, of these is the case. If one of these scenarios reflects the company's actions, it could be that cash is being spent up front to expand its current operation or establish the new locations, while these new products or new locations have yet to generate the expected cash flows through sales revenues.

This detailed analysis supports the assessment from part "a" that was based on an initial analysis of the company's cash flow patterns. This illustrates the usefulness of cash flow pattern analysis.

ASSIGNMENT MATERIAL

Discussion Questions

DQ5-1 Discuss why, in addition to preparing a statement of income, it is important for companies to also prepare a statement of cash flows.

DQ5-2 Discuss how a company's policies regarding receivables, inventory, and payables affect its cash flows relative to the income generated in a given period.

DQ5-3 In terms of cash flows, what is meant by the cash-to-cash cycle?

DQ5-4 For a company with a cash flow problem related to the length of its cash-to-cash cycle, list at least three potential reasons for the problem and suggest a possible solution for each.

DQ5-5 Describe the three major categories of activities that are shown on the statement of cash flows.

DQ5-6 Discuss the major difference between the direct method and the indirect method for presenting the operating section of a statement of cash flows.

DQ5-7 Explain why the indirect method of preparing cash flows from operating activities is also known as the *reconciliation method*.

DQ5-8 Explain why it is important to a company's financial health to have a positive cash flow from operations.

DQ5-9 Explain why, under the indirect method, depreciation is added to the net income to calculate the cash flow from operations. Is depreciation a source of cash, as this treatment seems to suggest?

DQ5-10 Explain what the outcome will be if a company increases its depreciation charges in an attempt to increase its cash flow from operations.

DQ5-11 Explain why the net cash flow from investing activities is usually a negative amount.

DQ5-12 Explain how the net cash flow from financing activities could be a negative amount.

DQ5-13 Explain how a gain on the sale of equipment would be treated in the operating activities section of a statement of cash flows prepared using the indirect method.

DQ5-14 Explain what it means if the net cash flow from investing activities is a positive amount.

DQ5-15 Explain how the net cash flow from financing activities could be a positive amount.

DQ5-16 Explain why a high sales growth rate can create significant cash flow problems for a company.

DQ5-17 Explain how the timing of cash flows relates to the purchase, use, and ultimate disposal of property, plant, and equipment.

DQ5-18 Explain why it is common for companies to have positive cash flows from operating activities and negative cash flows from investing activities.

DQ5-19 Explain how net free cash flow is determined and what it represents.

DQ5-20 When analyzing the statement of cash flows, explain why it is important to compare the current year's amounts with those of prior years.

Application Problems

AP5-1 (Classification of activities)

Required:
In what section of the statement of cash flows (operating, financing, or investing) would each of the following items appear?

a. Issuance of common shares to investors
b. Payment of dividends to shareholders
c. Purchase of new property, plant, and equipment
d. Proceeds from the sale of old property, plant, and equipment
e. Gain or loss on the sale of property, plant, and equipment
f. Net income
g. Proceeds from a bank loan
h. Retirement of debt
i. Proceeds from the sale of a long-term investment in another company
j. Net change in inventory

AP5-2 (Classification of activities)

Required:
Indicate whether each of the following items should be classified as an operating, investing, or financing activity on the statement of cash flows. If an item does not belong on the statement, indicate why.

a. Declaration of dividends on common shares, to be paid later
b. Payment of dividends on common shares
c. Purchase of equipment
d. Receipt of cash from the sale of a warehouse
e. Receipt of cash through a long-term bank loan
f. Interest payments on a long-term bank loan
g. Acquisition of land for cash
h. Investment in another company by purchasing some of its shares
i. Net decrease in accounts payable

AP5-3 (Effect of transactions on cash flows)

Required:
Classify each of the following transactions as increasing, decreasing, or having no effect on cash flows:

a. Purchasing inventory from a supplier on account
b. Purchasing office supplies and writing a cheque to cover the amount
c. Selling inventory to a customer on account
d. Buying a building by making a down payment and taking out a mortgage for the balance of the amount owed
e. Depreciating capital assets
f. Making a payment on a bank loan, where the amount paid includes interest and a portion of the principal
g. Issuing common shares
h. Declaring and paying dividends to shareholders
i. Paying wages owed to employees
j. Receiving interest owed from a customer

AP5-4 (Effect of transactions on cash flows)

Required:
Classify each of the following transactions as increasing, decreasing, or having no effect on cash flows:

a. Prepaying rent for the month
b. Accruing the wages owed to employees at the end of the month, to be paid on the first payday of the next month
c. Selling bonds to investors
d. Buying the company's own shares on the stock market
e. Selling merchandise to a customer who uses a debit card to pay for the purchase
f. Paying for inventory purchased earlier on account
g. Buying new equipment for cash
h. Selling surplus equipment at a loss
i. Paying the interest owed on a bank loan
j. Paying the income taxes owed for the year

AP5-5 (Effect of transactions on cash flows)

The following transactions occurred for Dussault Ltd.
1. Annual interest of 6% is paid on $500,000 of bonds payable that were issued last year.
2. A truck was purchased for $50,000 at the beginning of this year. The truck is being depreciated over five years at a rate of $10,000 per year.
3. Old equipment is sold for $40,000. The asset originally cost $160,000 and has accumulated depreciation of $125,000.
4. New equipment is purchased for $200,000. A cash payment of $50,000 is made and a long-term note payable for $150,000 is issued for the remainder.
5. A deposit of $2,000 is received in advance from a customer for goods to be delivered at a later date.
6. Income tax expense for the year is $85,000; $70,000 of this amount was paid during the year and the remainder will be paid next year.

Required:

For each of the above items:
a. Identify the accounts affected and give the amounts by which they would be increased or decreased.
b. State the amount of any cash flow and whether cash is increased or decreased.
c. Identify how each item would be reported in Dussault's statement of cash flows.

AP5-6 (Effect of transactions on cash flows)

The following transactions occurred for Mouawad Inc.
1. Inventory costing $300,000 was purchased on account.
2. A new vehicle costing $30,000 was purchased. Mouawad paid $5,000 as a down payment and the remaining $25,000 was financed through a bank loan.
3. Surplus land was sold for $80,000, which was $20,000 more than its original cost.
4. During the year, the company made a payment of $20,000 on its mortgage payable; $2,500 of this amount was for the interest on the debt.
5. Wages of $45,000 were charged to expense as they were incurred. No wages were owing to the employees at the end of the year.
6. The company declared and paid dividends of $30,000.

Required:

For each of the above items:
a. Identify the accounts affected and give the amounts by which they would be increased or decreased.
b. State the amount of any cash flow and whether cash is increased or decreased.
c. Identify how each item would be reported in Mouawad's statement of cash flows.

AP5-7 (Cash flow from operations)

Required:

For each of the following companies, calculate the cash flow from operations:

	NuVu Ltd.	ABC Inc.	Akhtar Ltd.
Sales revenue	$380,000	$575,000	$936,000
Cost of goods sold	210,000	330,000	620,000
Selling and administrative expenses	65,000	95,000	105,000
Depreciation expense	7,000	18,000	28,000
Interest expense	3,000	1,000	2,000
Income tax expense	18,000	35,000	45,000
Dividends paid	7,000	5,000	25,000
Increase/(Decrease) in			
Accounts receivable	(2,500)	5,000	(8,500)
Inventory	4,000	(8,000)	14,000
Property, plant, and equipment	50,000	(10,000)	60,000
Accounts payable	3,500	(6,500)	4,200
Interest payable	(1,500)	1,200	(500)
Income tax payable	2,500	(1,500)	6,500
Mortgage payable	20,000	(40,000)	10,000
Common shares	30,000	(5,000)	(80,000)

AP5-8 (Cash flow from operations)

Required:

For each of the following companies, calculate the cash flow from operations using the indirect method:

	Kotei & Sons Ltd.	SaskCo.	Movilla Ltd.
Sales revenue	$453,000	$790,000	$960,000
Cost of goods sold	235,000	420,000	550,000
Depreciation expense	40,000	70,000	80,000
Other operating expenses	50,000	60,000	70,000
Interest expense	15,000	20,000	35,000
Gain (loss) on sale of equipment	9,000	(15,000)	(14,000)
Dividends paid	6,000	10,000	12,000
Increase/(Decrease) in			
Accounts receivable	14,000	(16,000)	15,000
Inventory	(20,000)	25,000	(30,000)
Prepaid expenses	1,000	(2,400)	(2,600)
Property, plant, and equipment	220,000	(70,000)	150,000
Accounts payable	(8,000)	12,000	(8,000)
Interest payable	3,000	(8,000)	5,000
Bonds payable	(20,000)	50,000	60,000
Common shares	70,000	(10,000)	120,000

AP5-9 (Prepare statement of cash flows)

Organic Developments Ltd. (ODL) is an importer of organic produce from California. The company has been experiencing significant growth and is preparing to approach the bank for a loan to acquire additional capital assets. As CFO, you are tasked with preparing the statement of cash flows that is required as part of the loan application. You have the statement of financial position and the statement of income to help you prepare the statement of cash flows. In addition you also have the following information:

1. During the year, the company borrowed $14,000 by increasing its bank loan payable.
2. In September, ODL sold equipment for $6,000 cash. The equipment had originally cost $134,000 and had a net carrying amount of $14,000 at the time of sale.
3. In June, ODL acquired land with a value of $120,000 by issuing common shares with an equivalent value. The land is to be used as a site for a warehouse it hopes to construct in the next year.

ORGANIC DEVELOPMENTS LTD.
Statement of Financial Position
As at October 31

Assets	2016	2015
Current assets:		
Cash	$ 48,000	$ 36,000
Accounts receivable	58,000	68,000
Inventory	180,000	160,000
Total current assets	286,000	264,000
Equipment	620,000	540,000
Accumulated depreciation, equipment	(300,000)	(360,000)
Land	120,000	—
	$ 726,000	$ 444,000
Liabilities and Shareholders' Equity		
Current liabilities		
Accounts payable	$ 82,000	$ 40,000
Dividends payable	30,000	36,000
Total current liabilities	112,000	76,000
Bank loan payable	74,000	120,000
Common shares	300,000	180,000
Retained earnings	240,000	68,000
	$726,000	$444,000

ORGANIC DEVELOPMENTS LTD.
Statement of Income
For the year ended October 31, 2016

Sales revenue		$1,040,000
Cost of goods sold		520,000
Gross margin		520,000
Expenses		
Advertising expense	$ 30,000	
Wage expense	144,000	
Utilities expense	12,000	
Depreciation expense	60,000	
Rent expense	26,000	272,000
Net income from operations		248,000
Loss on sale of equipment		8,000
Net income		$240,000

Required:

a. Using the information, prepare the statement of cash flows for Organic Developments Ltd. for the year ended October 31, 2016.

b. Determine the cash flows from operating activities using the direct method.

AP5-10 (Prepare statement of cash flows)

Whiskey Industries Ltd., a Nanaimo, British Columbia–based company, has a December 31 year end. The company's comparative statement of financial position and its statement of income for the most recent fiscal year are presented here along with some additional information:

1. During the year, Whiskey Industries sold, for $500 cash, equipment that had an original cost of $1,000 and a net carrying amount of $200.
2. Whiskey Industries borrowed an additional $8,000 by issuing notes payable in 2016.
3. During the year, the company purchased a piece of land for a future manufacturing site for $200,000. The land was purchased with no money down and the company entered into a mortgage payable for the full amount.

WHISKEY INDUSTRIES LTD.
Statement of Financial Position
As at December 31, 2016

	2016	2015
Assets		
Current assets		
Cash	$ 6,050	$ 19,500
Accounts receivable	10,000	20,000
Prepaid rent	600	500
Inventory	40,000	30,000
Total current assets	56,650	70,000
Manufacturing equipment	159,000	100,000
Accumulated depreciation, manufacturing equipment	(69,200)	(50,000)
Land	200,000	0
Total Assets	$346,450	$120,000
Liabilities and Shareholders' Equity		
Current liabilities		
Accounts payable	$ 11,000	$ 6,000
Wages payable	600	400
Dividends payable	470	300
Total current liabilities	12,070	6,700
Mortgage payable	200,000	0
Notes payable	46,000	40,000
Common shares	29,000	25,000
Retained earnings	59,380	48,300
Total Liabilities and Shareholders' Equity	$346,450	$120,000

WHISKEY INDUSTRIES LTD.
Statement of Income
For the Year Ending December 31, 2016

Sales	$130,000
Cost of goods sold	80,000
Gross margin	50,000
Expenses	
Rent expense	7,100
Wage expense	9,600
Depreciation expense	20,000
Interest expense	600
Income tax expense	520
Income from operations	12,180
Gain on sale of equipment	300
Net income	$ 12,480

Required:
   a. Using the information above, prepare the statement of cash flows for Whiskey Industries Ltd. for the year ended December 31, 2016, using the indirect method.
   b. Determine the cash flows from operating activities using the direct method.

AP5-11 (Prepare statement of cash flows)

Required:
Using the following information, prepare the statement of cash flows for Harley Holdings Ltd. for the year ended January 31, 2016, using either method.

HARLEY HOLDINGS LTD.
Statement of Financial Position
As at January 31

	2016	2015
Assets		
Current assets:		
Cash	$ 50,000	$ 36,500
Accounts receivable	86,800	55,000
Inventory	95,600	101,700
Total current assets	232,400	193,200
Equipment	175,000	145,000
Accumulated depreciation, equipment	(43,500)	(39,000)
Land	120,000	170,000
	$ 483,900	$469,200
Liabilities and Shareholders' Equity		
Current liabilities:		
Accounts payable	$ 45,300	$ 62,200
Dividends payable	13,000	5,000
Total current liabilities	58,300	67,200
Bank loan payable	100,000	140,000
Common shares	150,000	130,000
Retained earnings	175,600	132,000
	$ 483,900	$469,200

HARLEY HOLDINGS LTD.
Statement of Income
For the year ended January 31, 2016

Sales revenue		$435,000
Cost of goods sold		295,000
Gross profit		140,000
Expenses		
Wages expense	$15,200	
Depreciation expense	26,500	
Rent expense	15,100	
Income tax expense	14,700	71,500
Operation income		68,500
Gain on sale of equipment		1,000
Net income		$ 69,500

Additional information:
1. Equipment costing $35,000 was sold for $14,000.
2. Land was sold at cost and none was purchased during the year.

AP5-12 (Prepare statement of cash flows)

Financial statement data for Metro Moving Company for 2016 follow.

METRO MOVING COMPANY Comparative Statement of Financial Position		
	Dec. 31, 2016	Dec. 31, 2015
Assets		
Cash	$ 68,600	$ 49,100
Accounts receivable	95,000	59,400
Prepaid insurance	30,000	20,000
Total current assets	193,600	128,500
Property, equipment, and vehicles	400,000	345,000
Accumulated depreciation	(110,400)	(105,900)
Total non-current assets	289,600	239,100
Total assets	$ 483,200	$ 367,600
Liabilities and shareholders' equity		
Accounts payable	$ 21,500	$ 18,600
Wages payable	3,000	4,000
Total current liabilities	24,500	22,600
Bank loan	50,000	60,000
Total liabilities	74,500	82,600
Common shares	200,000	200,000
Retained earnings	208,700	85,000
Total shareholders' equity	408,700	285,000
Total liabilities and shareholders' equity	$ 483,200	$ 367,600

METRO MOVING COMPANY Statement of Income For the year ended December 31, 2016		
Moving revenue		$450,000
Gain on sale of vehicles		4,000
		454,000
Expenses		
Vehicle operating expenses	$102,400	
Wages expense	134,000	
Depreciation expense	59,500	
Interest expense	5,400	
Total expenses		301,300
Net income		$152,700

Additional information:
1. Vehicles that cost $65,000 and had a net carrying amount of $10,000 were sold for $14,000.
2. A cash payment was made to reduce the bank loan.
3. Dividends were declared and paid during the year.

Required:
a. Prepare a statement of cash flows for Metro Moving Company for the year ended December 31, 2016, using the indirect method.
b. Determine the cash flows from operating activities using the direct method.

AP5-13 (Prepare statement of cash flows)

Financial statement data for Gibbons Electronics Company for 2016 follow.

GIBBONS ELECTRONICS COMPANY Comparative Statement of Financial Position		
	Dec. 31, 2016	Dec. 31, 2015
Assets		
Cash	$ 285,000	$ 295,000
Accounts receivable	334,000	384,000
Inventory	311,000	266,000
Prepaid insurance	50,000	35,000
Total current assets	980,000	980,000
Property, plant, and equipment	650,000	590,000
Accumulated depreciation	(165,000)	(130,000)
Net capital assets	485,000	460,000
Total assets	$1,465,000	$1,440,000
Liabilities and shareholders' equity		
Accounts payable	$ 60,000	$ 50,000
Wages payable	15,000	10,000
Unearned revenue	50,000	35,000
Income taxes payable	55,000	45,000
Total current liabilities	180,000	140,000
Bonds payable	490,000	575,000
Total liabilities	670,000	715,000
Common shares	350,000	285,000
Retained earnings	445,000	440,000
Total shareholders' equity	795,000	725,000
Total liabilities and shareholders' equity	$1,465,000	$1,440,000

GIBBONS ELECTRONICS COMPANY Statement of Income For the year ended December 31, 2016		
Sales revenue		$ 3,855,000
Gain on sale of equipment		10,000
		3,865,000
Expenses		
Cost of goods sold	$ 2,105,000	
Wages expense	353,000	
Depreciation expense	95,000	
Other operating expenses	555,000	
Interest expense	60,000	
Income taxes	345,000	
Total expenses		3,513,000
Net income		$ 352,000

Additional information:
1. Equipment that cost $100,000 and had a net carrying amount of $40,000 was sold for $50,000.
2. Dividends were declared and paid during the year.

Required:

    a. Prepare a statement of cash flows for Gibbons Electronic Company for the year ended December 31, 2016. Include supplementary information to disclose the amounts paid for interest and income taxes using the indirect method.

    b. Determine the cash flows from operating activities using the direct method.

AP5-14 (Prepare statement of cash flows)

Marchant Ltd. reported the following abbreviated statement of financial position and statement of earnings for 2016.

MARCHANT LTD. Comparative Statement of Financial Position		
	Dec. 31, 2016	**Dec. 31, 2015**
Cash	$ 60,000	$ 70,000
Accounts receivable	120,000	140,000
Inventory	320,000	280,000
Property, plant, and equipment	700,000	650,000
Less: Accumulated depreciation	(260,000)	(230,000)
Total assets	$ 940,000	$ 910,000
Accounts payable	$ 82,000	$ 85,000
Wages payable	8,000	10,000
Loan payable	350,000	400,000
Common shares	200,000	150,000
Retained earnings	300,000	265,000
Total liabilities and shareholders' equity	$ 940,000	$ 910,000

MARCHANT LTD. Statement of Income For the year ended December 31, 2016		
Sales		$450,000
Cost of goods sold		240,000
Gross profit		210,000
Other expenses:		
Supplies expense	$ 15,000	
Depreciation expense	30,000	
Wages expense	100,000	
Other operating expenses	5,000	
Interest expense	24,000	174,000
		36,000
Other income		8,000
Net income		$ 44,000

Required:

    a. Prepare a statement of cash flows for Marchant Ltd. for the year ended December 31, 2016, using the indirect method.

    b. Determine the cash flows from operating activities using the direct method.

    c. Was the cash flow generated by the company's operating activities during the year larger or smaller than the net income? Should these two amounts be the same? Explain.

    d. Was the change in the amount of working capital during the year the same amount as cash from operating activities? Should these two amounts be the same? Explain. (Hint: Working capital = current assets − current liabilities.)

AP5-15 (Prepare statement of cash flows)

The comparative statement of financial position and statement of income for NextWave Company follow.

NEXTWAVE COMPANY
Comparative Statement of Financial Position

	Dec. 31, 2016	Dec. 31, 2015
Assets		
Cash	$ 66,700	$ 47,250
Accounts receivable	76,800	57,000
Inventory	121,900	92,650
Long-term investments	84,500	97,000
Property, plant, and equipment	280,000	235,000
Accumulated depreciation	(79,500)	(70,000)
	$550,400	$458,900
Liabilities and shareholders' equity		
Accounts payable	$ 52,700	$ 49,200
Income taxes payable	12,000	18,000
Bonds payable	100,000	70,000
Common shares	230,000	200,000
Retained earnings	155,700	121,700
	$550,400	$458,900

NEXTWAVE COMPANY
Statement of Income
For the year ended December 31, 2016

Sales revenue		$437,500
Gain on sale of equipment		3,700
		441,200
Expenses		
Cost of goods sold	$200,500	
Operating expenses (excluding depreciation)	63,800	
Depreciation expense	49,700	
Income tax expense	40,000	354,000
Net income		$ 87,200

Additional information:
1. Some of the long-term investments were sold at their carrying value. As a result, there was no gain or loss on this transaction.
2. Equipment costing $47,000 was sold for $10,500, which was $3,700 more than its net carrying amount at the time of disposal.

Required:
a. Prepare the company's statement of cash flows for 2016 using the indirect method.
b. Calculate the amount of cash that was paid for income taxes during 2016.
c. Determine the cash flows from operating activities using the direct method.

AP5-16 (Prepare statement of cash flows)

A comparative statement of financial position and a statement of earnings for Standard Card Company follow.

STANDARD CARD COMPANY Statement of Financial Position		
	Dec. 31, 2016	Dec. 31, 2015
Assets		
Current assets		
Cash	$134,000	$ 111,000
Accounts receivable	83,000	78,000
Inventory	200,000	110,000
Prepaid insurance	10,000	20,000
Total current assets	427,000	319,000
Non-current assets		
Equipment	305,000	350,000
Accumulated depreciation	(67,000)	(75,000)
Total non-current assets	238,000	275,000
Total assets	$665,000	$594,000
Liabilities		
Current liabilities		
Accounts payable	$ 88,000	$ 83,000
Interest payable	3,000	4,000
Unearned revenue	13,000	18,000
Total current liabilities	104,000	105,000
Long-term debt	100,000	150,000
Total liabilities	204,000	255,000
Shareholders' equity		
Common shares	200,000	115,000
Retained earnings	261,000	224,000
Total shareholders' equity	461,000	339,000
Total liabilities and shareholders' equity	$665,000	$594,000

STANDARD CARD COMPANY Statement of Income For the year ended December 31, 2016		
Sales		$207,000
Expenses		
Cost of goods sold	$97,000	
Depreciation expense	12,000	
Insurance expense	10,000	
Interest expense	8,000	
Loss on sale of equipment	13,000	
Income tax	23,000	
Total expenses		163,000
Net income		$ 44,000

Additional information:

The loss on the sale of equipment occurred when a relatively new machine with a cost of $100,000 and accumulated depreciation of $20,000 was sold because a technological change had made it obsolete.

Required:

    a. Prepare a statement of cash flows for the year ended December 31, 2016, using the indirect method.

    b. Determine the cash flows from operating activities using the direct method.

AP5-17 (Prepare statement of cash flows)

Digiread Technologies Ltd. (DTL) is a privately held distributor of e-readers and tablets. The Calgary-based company is well established and is currently managed by its founder, Erin Jacobs. The company's financial statements are presented below, together with some additional information.

DIGIREAD TECHNOLOGIES LTD.
Statement of Income
As at December 31, 2016

Sales	$ 50,500,000
Cost of goods sold	34,400,000
Gross profit	16,100,000
Wage expense	4,000,000
Depreciation expense	1,200,000
Interest expense	1,900,000
Income tax expense	1,600,000
Net income from operations	7,400,000
Gain on sale of equipment	600,000
Net income	$ 8,000,000

DIGIREAD TECHNOLOGIES LTD.
Statement of Financial Position
As at December 31

	2016	2015
Assets		
Current assets:		
Cash	$15,500,000	$ 8,500,000
Accounts receivable (net)	11,500,000	15,500,000
Inventory	16,900,000	19,000,000
Total current assets	43,900,000	43,000,000
Equipment	39,400,000	30,000,000
Accumulated depreciation, equipment	(6,600,000)	(6,400,000)
Total Assets	$76,700,000	$66,600,000
Liabilities and Shareholders' Equity		
Current liabilities:		
Accounts payable	$11,900,000	$ 7,000,000
Wages payable	1,200,000	1,000,000
Total current liabilities	13,100,000	8,000,000
Bonds payable	21,000,000	26,000,000
Common shares	14,000,000	9,000,000
Retained earnings	28,600,000	23,600,000
Total Liabilities and Shareholders' Equity	$76,700,000	$66,600,000

DIGIREAD TECHNOLOGIES LTD.
Other Selected Financial Information for the Year Ended December 31, 2016

1. Total sales in 2016 were consistent with the prior year's and the company's dividend policy has remained consistent for the past five years.

2. During 2016, DTL sold a piece of equipment for $2.1 million. The equipment had originally cost $2.5 million and had a net carrying amount of $1.5 million at the time of sale.

3. On August 1, 2016, DTL's board of directors approved the retirement of bonds with a face value of $5 million through the issuance of common shares.

Required:
DTL's management shareholders have asked you to prepare the statement of cash flows for DTL using either the direct or indirect method for determining cash flows from operating activities. Prepare the statement for them.

AP5-18 (Prepare statement of cash flows)

Tangent Controls Ltd. is a manufacturer of crash-protected event recorders that are used in railway systems around the world to record event data. These data can be retrieved and analyzed to monitor and improve operations, but also to provide diagnostic data in the event of rail crashes. The small Ottawa-based company has customers across the world, but its largest market is North America. The company has been hurt by the U.S. economy, seeing a 12% decline in sales over the prior year. The company is hoping that the latest industry developments, which call for a significant increase in the shipment of oil by railcar, will mean an increase in sales. In the meantime, the company has been seeking new investors and has approached a leading Canadian venture capital firm to see if it might be interested in investing. As part of its approach, Tangent has provided the following financial information for the most recent fiscal year.

TANGENT CONTROLS LTD.		
Statement of Financial Position		
As at September 30		
	2016	**2015**
Assets		
Current assets:		
Cash	$ –	$ 72,000
Accounts receivable (net)	601,000	378,000
Inventory	760,000	594,000
Total current assets	1,361,000	1,044,000
Equipment	1,608,000	1,908,000
Accumulated depreciation, equipment	(1,425,000)	(1,440,000)
Total Assets	$1,544,000	$1,512,000
Liabilities and Shareholders' Equity		
Current liabilities:		
Bank indebtedness	$ 22,000	$ –
Accounts payable	260,000	252,000
Total current liabilities	282,000	252,000
Bank loan payable	152,000	144,000
Common shares	900,000	900,000
Retained earnings	210,000	216,000
Total Liabilities and Shareholders' Equity	$1,544,000	$1,512,000

TANGENT CONTROLS LTD. Statement of Income For the year ended September 30, 2016	
Sales revenue	$6,070,000
Cost of goods sold	3,875,000
Gross profit	2,195,000
Wages expense	1,580,000
Utilities expense	290,000
Depreciation expense	225,000
Rent expense	79,000
Interest expense	47,000
Loss from operations	(26,000)
Gain on sale of equipment	40,000
Earnings before income tax	14,000
Income tax expense	3,000
Net income	$ 11,000

Additional information:
1. During the year, the company repaid principal of $30,000 on its loan payable.
2. During the year, equipment with a net carrying amount of $60,000 was sold.
3. No equipment was purchased during the year.

Required:
 a. You work for the venture capital firm and have been tasked with preparing the statement of cash flows for Tangent using either the direct or indirect method for determining cash flows from operating activities. Prepare the statement.
 b. Discuss significant observations from the statement of cash flows that your firm would want to consider.

AP5-19 (Determine cash collected from customers and paid to suppliers)

Southbend Company had sales of $734,000 for the year. The company reported accounts receivable of $54,000 at the end of last year and $60,000 at the end of this year. Southbend's cost of goods sold this year was $440,000. In last year's statement of financial position, the company reported inventory of $62,000 and accounts payable of $32,000. In this year's statement of financial position, Southbend reported inventory of $66,000 and accounts payable of $38,000.

Required:
 i. Calculate the amount of cash that Southbend Company collected from its customers during the year.
 ii. Calculate the amount of cash that Southbend paid to its suppliers for inventory during the year.

AP5-20 (Determine cash collected from customers and paid to suppliers)

Practical Company had sales of $315,000 for the year. The company reported accounts receivable of $30,000 at the end of last year and $34,000 at the end of this year. Practical's cost of goods sold this year was $246,000. In last year's statement of financial position, the company reported inventory of $49,000 and accounts payable of $33,000. In this year's statement of financial position, Practical reported inventory of $43,000 and accounts payable of $37,000.

Required:
 i. Calculate the amount of cash that Practical Company collected from customers during the year.
 ii. Calculate the amount of cash that Practical paid to suppliers for inventory during the year.

AP5-21 (Interpret statement of cash flows)

The following are the comparative statements of cash flows for Yellow Spruce Incorporated.

YELLOW SPRUCE INCORPORATED Statements of Cash Flows (in millions)			
	2016	2015	2014
Operating activities			
Net income	$ 57	$ 86	$ 98
Add back:			
Depreciation expense	82	75	65
Loss (gain) on sale of investments	2	–	(11)
Effect of changes in working capital items:			
Accounts receivable	(38)	30	(39)
Inventory	(21)	(17)	(21)
Prepaid expenses	4	13	(9)
Accounts payable	27	(12)	35
Net cash inflow from operations	113	175	118
Investing activities			
Acquisition of property, plant, and equipment	(154)	(161)	(152)
Acquisition of investments	(23)	(51)	(72)
Proceeds from sale of property, plant, and equipment	16	11	27
Net cash outflow for investing activities	(161)	(201)	(197)
Financing activities			
Issuance of long-term debt	213	156	332
Repayment of long-term debt	(131)	(72)	(93)
Issuance of shares	12	–	–
Repurchase of shares	–	(38)	(84)
Dividends paid	(16)	(14)	(15)
Net cash inflow from financing activities	78	32	140
Overall increase in cash	30	6	61
Cash position at beginning of year	100	94	33
Cash position at end of year	$ 130	$ 100	$ 94

Required:
a. Discuss the company's ability to meet its non-operating needs for cash over these three years, and comment on the continuing nature of the major items that have appeared over this time period.
b. Comment on the changes in Yellow Spruce's accounts receivable, accounts payable, and inventory levels over these three years.
c. How did Yellow Spruce finance its repayment of long-term debt and its acquisition of property, plant, and equipment and investments in 2016?
d. Describe how the company's mix of long-term financing has changed during this three-year period, in terms of the proportion of debt versus equity. (Hint: Start by calculating the total amount of the increase or decrease in long-term debt, and comparing it with the total amount of the increase or decrease in shareholders' equity.)

AP5-22 (Cash flow patterns)

Urban Eats Ltd. (UEL) has been successfully operating upscale supermarkets in the Lower Mainland of British Columbia as well as a profitable on-line market through which customers place orders for home delivery by UEL. In the current year, UEL sold one of its warehouses while no new stores were acquired or opened. However, UEL's management team completed a successful bond issuance in order to position the company to be able to make a bid to acquire one of its competitors early in the next fiscal year.

Required:
Determine the cash flow pattern that you expect UEL to have and explain your rationale.

AP5-23 (Cash flow patterns)

Crafty Resources Ltd. is a new creator and publisher of children's craft kit books. It has created kits for dolls, twirled paper crafts, paper doll clothes, and so on. The publishing industry is characterized by lengthy credit periods for bookstores and a lack of credit granting on the part of paper suppliers and commercial grade copy and binding machine manufacturers.

Required:
Determine the cash flow pattern that you expect Crafty Resources to have in its first year of operation and explain your rationale.

User Perspective Problems

UP5-1 (Cash flows from operations)

In this chapter, we have emphasized the importance of carefully analyzing the operating section of the statement of cash flows. In fact, the operating activities section is always the first one listed on the statement.

Required:
From a user perspective, explain why this section is so important for understanding a company's financial health.

UP5-2 (Cash flow and compensation plans)

Required:
If you were the owner of a company and wanted to establish a management compensation plan to motivate your top managers, would you want to base your performance targets on cash flows from operations or on income from operations? Discuss the pros and cons of using these two measures of performance.

UP5-3 (Format of the statement of cash flows from a lender's perspective)

Required:
As a lender, discuss whether you would be satisfied with the current method of classifying cash flows into only three categories. In addition, discuss the normal treatment of interest expense within the statement of cash flows relative to the treatment of dividends and whether you think there are any problems with this.

UP5-4 (Statement of cash flows and lending decisions)

Required:
From the perspective of a bank loan officer, discuss why the statement of cash flows may or may not be more important than the statement of income when you are analyzing a company that is applying for a loan.

UP5-5 (Accrual accounting and cash flows)

Loan officer Han Blackford once commented that cash flow analysis has risen in importance due to a "trend over the past 20 years toward capitalizing costs and deferring more and more expenses. Although the practice may be better in terms of reporting expenses in the same period as the revenues they generated, it has also made it harder to find the available cash in a company, and easier for lenders to wind up with a loss." He further noted that recessions, and the bankruptcies that often result, draw attention to the need for better warning signals of the sort that cash flow analysis could provide.

Required:
   a. Why would the process of capitalizing costs (recording them as assets to be depreciated over future periods) be better in terms of reporting expenses in the same period as the revenues they generated, yet make it harder to find the cash available in a company?
   b. Explain why unexpected bankruptcies would draw attention to cash flow analysis. Your response should include a discussion of why the statements of income and financial position might not adequately alert users to impending bankruptcies.

UP5-6 (Statement of cash flows and investing decisions)

Required:
From the perspective of a stock analyst, discuss why the statement of cash flows may or may not be more important than the statement of income when analyzing a company to make a recommendation about investing in its shares.

UP5-7 (Analyze investment decision)

Jacques Rousseau is considering investing in Health Life Ltd., a pharmaceutical company. He read in the paper that this company is doing cancer research and is close to a breakthrough in developing a new drug that will be effective against bone cancer. The author of the article said that this was a good time to buy because, once the breakthrough happens, the share price is going to rise very rapidly. Jacques therefore decided to look at the company's most recent financial statements.

On the statement of financial position, he saw that the company had a significant amount of cash and short-term investments. It had some assets listed as "buildings and equipment under capital lease," which he interpreted to mean that the company was leasing its buildings and equipment rather than owning them. When he looked at the statement of income, he saw that there was no revenue. By far the largest expense was for research and development. The company had a loss during the current year, and the company reported a deficit on the statement of financial position. He thought that this made sense, because the company had yet to make its first medical breakthrough. The company had little debt, and its shares were recorded at approximately $35 million. When he looked at the notes, he saw that there were about 7 million shares issued. In fact, 1 million of those shares had been issued during the current year.

Required:

Help Jacques with his decision by answering the following questions:

    a. Do you think that investing in this company would be risky? Explain.

    b. Does the fact that Health Life is holding a large amount of cash and short-term investments mean that management is doing a good job? Explain in detail.

    c. Is it possible for Jacques to make a rough estimate of how much longer the cash and short-term investments will last, assuming that the company does not get its breakthrough? What information would help him make this estimate?

    d. Based on the number of shares that have been issued and the amount that is recorded in the share capital account, it is obvious that many investors have concluded that this is a good investment. Think carefully about this, and then list three or four advantages and disadvantages of buying shares in Health Life at this time.

UP5-8 (Interpret statement of cash flows data)

The 2016 financial statements of Green Company include the following statement of cash flows:

GREEN COMPANY Statement of Cash Flows For the year ended December 31, 2016		
Operating:		
Net income	$ 644,000	
Adjustments to convert to cash:		
Depreciation expense	230,000	
Gain on sale of operating assets	(14,000)	
Change in current assets other than cash	(120,000)	
Change in current liabilities	80,000	
Cash provided by operations		$820,000
Investing:		
Purchase of property, plant, and equipment	(1,200,000)	
Proceeds from the sale of property, plant, and equipment	400,000	
Cash used for investing		(800,000)
Financing:		
Issuance of shares	1,000,000	
Retirement of bonds	(1,300,000)	
Dividends paid	(250,000)	
Cash used for financing		(550,000)
Decrease in cash		$(530,000)

Required:
   a. Did Green Company increase or decrease its current assets, other than cash, during 2016? Is this change consistent with an increase in sales, or a decrease in sales, during the period? Explain.
   b. From an investor's point of view, has Green Company become more risky or less risky in 2016? Explain.
   c. Does Green Company appear to be expanding or contracting its operations? How can you tell? What other financial statement information might you examine to determine whether the company is expanding or contracting its operations?
   d. Does Green appear to be able to maintain its productive capacity without additional financing? Explain.

UP5-9 (Interpret operating section)

The operating activities section of Johann Manufacturing Ltd.'s statement of cash flows is shown below. In answering the questions after the statement, assume that the net cash flows from Johann's investing and financing activities were zero; that is, that the cash inflows within the investing and financing sections were offset by the cash outflows.

JOHANN MANUFACTURING LTD. **Statement of Cash Flows** **For the year ended December 31, 2016**		
Cash flows from operations:		
Net income		$ 632,000
Adjustments to convert earnings to cash flows:		
Depreciation expense	$110,000	
Loss on sale of investments	50,000	160,000
Change in current items other than cash:		
Accounts receivable	$ (80,000)	
Inventory	20,000	
Prepaid expenses	(45,000)	
Accounts payable	75,000	
Income tax payable	(14,000)	(44,000)
Cash provided by operations		748,000
Cash balance, January 1		566,000
Cash balance, December 31		$1,314,000

Required:
Use the preceding information to answer the following questions. If a question cannot be answered based on the information given, indicate why.
   a. Have the accounts receivable increased or decreased this year? Explain briefly.
   b. Has the inventory increased or decreased this year? Explain how this affects cash.
   c. Did the amount of expenses prepaid by the company increase or decrease during the year? Does this help or hurt its cash position? Explain briefly.
   d. Compared with last year, does the company seem to be relying more heavily, or less heavily, on trade credit to finance its activities? Explain briefly.
   e. If you were a potential creditor, would you see any warning signs in the statement of cash flows that you would want to investigate before lending money to Johann Manufacturing? Explain briefly.
   f. Johann Manufacturing has $2 million of bonds maturing in January 2017. Do you think the company will be able to meet its obligation to pay off the bonds, without obtaining additional long-term financing? Explain briefly.

UP5-10 (Net free cash flow)

Required:
As a lender, discuss why you might be interested in knowing a company's net free cash flow. How might it be factored into a lending decision?

UP5-11 (Net free cash flow)

Required:
As a shareholder or potential investor, discuss why you might be interested in knowing a company's net free cash flow. Comment on whether this measure is of more use than cash flows from operating activities.

Reading and Interpreting Published Financial Statements

RI5-1 (Analyze a company's statement of cash flows)

Exhibits 5-14A and B contain the consolidated statements of cash flows and related note disclosure for **The Second Cup Ltd.**

EXHIBIT 5-14A	THE SECOND CUP LTD.'S 2013 STATEMENTS OF CASH FLOWS

STATEMENTS OF CASH FLOWS
For the periods ended December 28, 2013 and December 29, 2012
(Expressed in thousands of Canadian dollars)

	2013	2012
CASH PROVIDED BY (USED IN)		
Operating activities		
Loss for the period	$ (7,369)	$ (9,404)
Items not involving cash		
Depreciation of property and equipment	749	716
Amortization of intangible assets	502	451
Impairment charges	13,552	15,656
Amortization of deferred financing charges	38	82
Amortization of provisions	(116)	(89)
Amortization of leasehold inducements	69	26
Deferred income taxes	(1,772)	(993)
(Gain) Loss on disposal of capital related items	(197)	70
Movement in fair value of interest rate swap	44	(206)
Changes in non-cash working capital (note 21)	2,178	(1,159)
Cash provided by operating activities	7,678	5,150
Investing activities		
Proceeds from disposal of capital related items	1,240	350
Cash payments for capital expenditures (note 21)	(2,904)	(1,938)
Proceeds from repayment of leases receivable	—	36
Proceeds from repayment of notes receivable	13	185
Investment in notes receivable	(10)	—
Cash used by investing activities	(1,661)	(1,367)
Financing activities		
Dividends paid to shareholders	(3,367)	(5,298)
Repayment of note payable	—	(18)
Deferred financing charges	(29)	(50)
Payments on long-term lease	—	(2)
Cash used by financing activities	(3,396)	(5,368)
Increase (decrease) in cash and cash equivalents during the period	2,621	(1,585)
Cash and cash equivalents – Beginning of the period	3,880	5,465
Cash and cash equivalents – End of the period	$ 6,501	$ 3,880

Supplemental cash flow information is provided in note 21
See accompanying notes to the financial statements.

EXHIBIT 5-14B	EXCERPT FROM THE SECOND CUP LTD.'S 2013 ANNUAL REPORT

21. SUPPLEMENTAL CASH FLOW INFORMATION

	2013	2012
Changes in non-cash working capital (inflow (outflow)):		
Trade and other receivables	$ 248	$ 722
Notes and leases receivable	248	(400)
Inventories	14	(58)
Prepaid expenses and other assets	505	(501)
Accounts payable and accrued liabilities	1,463	(780)
Provisions	1,212	349
Other liabilities	(65)	46
Gift card liability	(665)	207
Deposits from franchise partners	(602)	447
Income taxes	(180)	(1,191)
	$ 2,178	$(1,159)
Cash payments for capital expenditures		
Purchase of property and equipment	$(2,117)	$(1,758)
Purchase of intangible assets	(787)	(180)
	$(2,904)	$(1,938)
Supplementary information		
Interest paid	$ 522	$ 689
Income taxes paid	$ 1,687	$ 2,835

Required:

a. In total, how much did Second Cup's cash and cash equivalents change during 2013? Was this an increase or a decrease? How did this compare with the previous year?

b. Did Second Cup have net income or a net loss in 2013? How did this compare with the cash flows from operating activities? What was the largest difference between these two amounts?

c. What effect did the change in the company's accounts payable and accrued liabilities have on cash flows from operating activities in 2013? What does this tell you about the balance owed to these creditors?

d. Did the balance of outstanding gift cards increase or decrease during 2013? Was this considered to be an inflow or an outflow of cash?

e. Did Second Cup purchase property, plant, and equipment during 2013? Did the company receive any proceeds from the sale of property, plant, and equipment during the period?

f. Calculate Second Cup's net free cash flow for 2013 and 2012. Is the trend positive or negative?

g. Second Cup's total liabilities were $31,376 at December 28, 2013, and $31,980 at December 29, 2012. Determine the company's cash flows to total liabilities ratio. Comment on the change year over year.

h. If you were a user of Second Cup's financial statements—a banker or an investor—how would you interpret the company's cash flow pattern? How would you assess the risk of a loan to or an investment in Second Cup? Do you think the company is growing rapidly?

RI5-2 (Analyze a company's statement of cash flows)

Exhibits 5-15A and B show the consolidated statement of cash flows of **Dollarama Inc.** for the years ended February 2, 2014, and February 3, 2013, along with related note disclosure.

| EXHIBIT 5-15A | DOLLARAMA INC.'S 2014 CONSOLIDATED STATEMENT OF CASH FLOWS |

	Note	52-weeks February 2, 2014 $	53-weeks February 3, 2013 $
Cash flows			
Operating activities			
Net earnings for the year		250,094	220,985
Adjustments for:			
Depreciation and amortization	18	47,898	39,284
Interest accrual long-term debt	10	3,017	(216)
Amortization of debt issue costs		592	1,133
Excess of receipts over amount recognized on derivative financial instruments	15	6,319	1,272
Recognition of deferred leasing costs		465	295
Recognition of deferred tenant allowances	12	(3,543)	(2,871)
Deferred lease inducements	12	3,750	5,328
Deferred tenant allowances	12	6,058	6,832
Share-based compensation	13	4,053	1,558
Deferred income taxes	14	4,469	6,921
Loss on disposal of assets		1,017	716
		324,189	281,237
Changes in non-cash working capital components	19	(15,811)	(24,198)
Net cash generated from operating activities		308,378	257,039
Investing activities			
Additions to property and equipment	7	(96,303)	(69,577)
Additions to intangible assets	8	(11,095)	(8,210)
Proceeds on disposal of property and equipment		552	256
Net cash used by investing activities		(106,846)	(77,531)
Financing activities			
Proceeds from senior unsecured notes	10	400,000	—
Disbursements on long-term debt		(264,420)	(10,361)
Proceeds from bank indebtedness		166,000	—
Repayment of bank indebtedness		(166,000)	—
Payment of debt issue costs		(2,797)	(837)
Repayment of finance leases		(985)	(695)
Dividends paid		(38,418)	(30,972)
Repurchase and cancellation of shares	13	(277,438)	(155,942)
Issuance of common shares		1,430	1,594
Net cash used by financing activities		(182,628)	(197,213)
Increase (decrease) in cash and cash equivalents		18,904	(17,705)
Cash and cash equivalents – Beginning of year		52,566	70,271
Cash and cash equivalents – End of year		71,470	52,566
Cash payment of interest		6,025	7,639
Cash payment of income taxes		89,801	75,090

EXHIBIT 5-15B   **EXCERPT FROM DOLLARAMA INC.'S 2014 ANNUAL REPORT**

19. CONSOLIDATED STATEMENT OF CASH FLOWS INFORMATION

The changes in non-cash working capital components are as follows:

	February 2, 2014	February 3, 2013
	$	$
Accounts receivable	(165)	(3,954)
Deposits and prepaid expenses	374	(1,320)
Merchandise inventories	(26,295)	(22,512)
Accounts payable and accrued liabilities	11,809	587
Income taxes payable	(1,534)	3,001
	(15,811)	(24,198)

Required:

a. How did Dollarama's net income in 2014 compare with the cash flows from operating activities? What was the largest difference between these two amounts?

b. Did Dollarama increase or decrease the amount of inventory in its stores between 2013 and 2014? Is this consistent with the nature of the changes reflected in the company's cash flows from investing activities?

c. What effect did the change in the company's accounts payable and accrued liabilities have on cash flows from operating activities in 2014? What does this tell you about the balance owed to these creditors?

d. Examine the financing activities section of Dollarama's statement of cash flows and comment on the main differences between 2014 and 2013.

e. Dollarama's total liabilities were $702,614 at February 2, 2014, and $522,202 at February 3, 2013. Calculate the company's cash flows to total liabilities ratio and comment on whether this has improved or worsened from 2013 to 2014.

f. Calculate Dollarama's net free cash flow and discuss the company's ability to generate the cash required to continue to grow the company's operations and repay its debt.

RI5-3 (Analyze a company's statement of cash flows)

The consolidated statements of cash flows and related note disclosure for **Sirius XM Canada Holdings Inc.** are in Exhibits 5-16A and B. Sirius broadcasts satellite radio channels to subscribers.

EXHIBIT 5-16A   **SIRIUS XM CANADA HOLDINGS INC.'S 2013 CONSOLIDATED STATEMENTS OF CASH FLOWS**

CONSOLIDATED STATEMENTS OF CASH FLOWS

For the year ended August 31

(Canadian dollars)	Notes	2013	2012
Cash provided by (used in)			
OPERATING ACTIVITIES			
Net income (loss) for the year		12,190,542	(4,178,816)
Add (deduct) items not involving cash			
Amortization of intangible assets	6	33,167,880	36,899,668
Depreciation of property and equipment	5	2,407,716	2,789,385
Loss on disposal of property and equipment	5	11,109	—
Deferred tax recovery	7	5,374,778	(8,312,710)
Stock-based compensation	13	2,257,295	1,493,400
Accrued interest		—	(5,088)
Interest accretion	10	954,375	950,583
Revaluation of derivatives	10	(2,291,378)	(1,213,473)
Foreign exchange losses		769,540	3,010
Net change in non-cash working capital and deferred revenue related to operations	18	5,409,419	12,649,125
Cash provided by operating activities		60,251,276	41,075,084

continued

EXHIBIT 5-16A | **SIRIUS XM CANADA HOLDINGS INC.'S 2013 CONSOLIDATED STATEMENTS OF CASH FLOWS (continued)**

For the year ended August 31
(Canadian dollars)

	Notes	2013	2012
INVESTING ACTIVITIES			
Purchase of property and equipment	5	(753,788)	(728,425)
Purchase of intangible assets	6	(7,624,829)	(3,700,491)
Prepayment of property and equipment		(2,240,000)	—
Purchase of short-term investments	14	(5,306,295)	—
Interest received on short-term investments	14	176,649	—
Cash (used in) investing activities		(15,748,263)	(4,428,916)
FINANCING ACTIVITIES			
Payment of dividends	12	(53,706,925)	—
Proceeds from exercise of stock options	13	2,247,747	464,132
Repayments of debt	10	—	(917,700)
Payment of related party promissory notes	9	—	(11,173,290)
Cash (used in) financing activities		(51,459,178)	(11,626,858)
Net (decrease) increase in cash and cash equivalents during the year		(6,956,165)	25,019,310
Cash and cash equivalents, beginning of year		51,034,749	26,015,439
Cash and cash equivalents, end of year		44,078,584	51,034,749

EXHIBIT 5-16B | **EXCERPT FROM SIRIUS XM CANADA HOLDINGS INC.'S 2013 ANNUAL REPORT**

18. SUPPLEMENTAL CASH FLOW DISCLOSURE

The net change in non-cash working capital balances related to operations consists of the following:

For the year ended August 31	**2013**	**2012**
Decrease (increase) in assets		
Accounts receivable	(1,226,308)	(1,414,462)
Prepaid expenses	(1,226,187)	48,441
Inventory	89,967	1,941,122
Increase (decrease) in liabilities		
Trade, other payables and provisions	5,582,248	2,334,378
Due to related parties	4,027,425	745,399
Deferred revenue	3,416,582	11,493,635
Long-term liabilities	(5,254,308)	(2,499,388)
Net change in non-cash working capital related to operations	5,409,419	12,649,125

Operating activities include the following payments and receipts:

For the year ended August 31	**2013**	**2012**
Interest income received	646,678	360,906
Interest paid	14,350,173	14,429,138
Taxes paid	—	—

Required:

a. In total, how much did Sirius's cash and cash equivalents change during 2013? Was this an increase or a decrease? How did this compare with the previous year?

b. Did Sirius have net income or a net loss in 2013? How did this compare with the cash flows from operating activities? What was the largest difference between these two amounts?

c. What effect did the change in the company's trade, other payables, and provisions have on cash flows from operating activities in 2013? What does this tell you about the balance owed to these creditors?

d. Did the balance of deferred revenue increase or decrease during 2013? Was this considered to be an inflow or an outflow of cash? What does this tell you about the trend in the amount of the customers' prepaid subscription fees?

e. Calculate Sirius's net free cash flow for 2013 and 2012. Is the trend positive or negative?

f. Sirius's total liabilities were $370,878,874 at August 31, 2013, and $361,872,956 at August 31, 2012. Determine the company's cash flows to total liabilities ratio. Comment on the change year over year. Would your perspective on the results of this ratio calculation change if you were advised that approximately 40% of Sirius's liabilities were related to deferred revenue?

g. How did the dividends paid by Sirius to its shareholders compare with the company's net income and cash flows from operating activities?

RI5-4 (Analyze a company's statement of cash flows)

The consolidated statements of cash flows and related note disclosure for **Big Rock Brewery Inc.** are in Exhibits 5-17A and B.

EXHIBIT 5-17A	BIG ROCK BREWERY INC.'S 2013 CONSOLIDATED STATEMENTS OF CASH FLOWS

BIG ROCK BREWERY INC.
Consolidated Statements of Cash Flows
(In thousands of Canadian dollars)

	Year ended	
	December 30, 2013	December 30, 2012
OPERATING ACTIVITIES		
Net income for the period	$ 2,551	$ 4,135
Items not affecting cash:		
Depreciation and amortization	3,157	3,228
Gain on sale of assets	(13)	(19)
Stock-based compensation	640	446
Deferred income tax expense (recovery)	(1,586)	1,168
Net change in non-cash working capital related to operations (note 25)	3,148	1,496
Cash provided by operating activities	7,897	10,454
FINANCING ACTIVITIES		
Dividend payments	(4,855)	(4,850)
Principal repayments of long-term debt	(2,042)	(641)
Cash received on exercise of options	—	131
Cash used in financing activities	(6,897)	(5,360)

continued

EXHIBIT 5-17A	BIG ROCK BREWERY INC.'S 2013 CONSOLIDATED STATEMENTS OF CASH FLOWS (continued)

	December 30, 2013	December 30, 2012
INVESTING ACTIVITIES		
Purchase of property, plant and equipment	(2,992)	(1,487)
Purchase of intangibles	(6)	—
Proceeds from sale of equipment	34	19
Cash used in investing activities	(2,964)	(1,468)
Net increase (decrease) in cash	(1,964)	3,626
Cash, beginning of year	4,281	655
Cash, end of year	$ 2,317	$ 4,281
Supplemental cash-flow information		
Cash interest paid	$ 52	$ 103
Cash taxes paid	958	—

EXHIBIT 5-17B	EXCERPT FROM BIG ROCK BREWERY INC.'S 2013 ANNUAL REPORT

25. CHANGE IN NON-CASH WORKING CAPITAL

	Year ended	
	December 30, 2013	December 30, 2012
Accounts payable and accrued liabilities	$ 1,649	$ 741
Inventory	884	472
Accounts receivable	1,005	430
Prepaid expenses	(390)	(147)
Total change in non-cash working capital	$ 3,148	$ 1,496

Required:

a. In total, how much did Big Rock's cash and cash equivalents change during 2013? Was this an increase or a decrease? How did this compare with the previous year?

b. How did Big Rock's net income in 2013 compare with the cash flows from operating activities? What was the largest difference between these two amounts?

c. What effect did the change in the company's accounts receivable have on cash flows from operating activities in 2013? What does this tell you about the balance owed by the company's customers?

d. What effect did the change in the company's accounts payable and accrued liabilities have on cash flows from operating activities in 2013? What does this tell you about the balance owed to these creditors?

e. Calculate Big Rock's net free cash flow for 2013 and 2012. Is the trend positive or negative?

f. How did the dividends paid by Big Rock to its shareholders compare with the company's net income and cash flows from operating activities?

g. If you were a user of Big Rock's financial statements—a banker or an investor—how would you interpret the company's cash flow pattern? How would you assess the risk of a loan to or an investment in Big Rock? Do you think the company is growing rapidly?

RI5-5 (Analyze a company's statement of cash flows)

The consolidated statements of cash flows and related note disclosure for **Le Château Inc.** are in Exhibits 5-18A and B.

EXHIBIT 5-18A   LE CHATEAU INC.'S 2014 CONSOLIDATED STATEMENTS OF CASH FLOWS

Le Château Inc.

CONSOLIDATED STATEMENTS OF CASH FLOWS

Years ended January 25, 2014 and January 26, 2013
(In thousands of Canadian dollars)

	2014 $	2013 $
OPERATING ACTIVITIES		
Net loss	(15,986)	(8,717)
Adjustments to determine net cash from operating activities		
Depreciation and amortization [notes 8 and 9]	18,723	19,574
Write-off and net impairment of property and equipment and intangible assets [notes 8 and 9]	1,897	2,142
Loss on disposal of property and equipment [note 8]	–	108
Amortization of deferred lease credits	(2,539)	(1,285)
Deferred lease credits	39	1,088
Stock-based compensation	978	336
Provisions	(102)	338
Finance costs	2,714	3,063
Finance income	(13)	(23)
Interest paid	(2,436)	(2,863)
Interest received	13	28
Income tax recovery	(5,722)	(3,469)
	(2,434)	10,320
Net change in non-cash working capital items related to operations [note 21]	(3,030)	(6,340)
	(5,464)	3,980
Income taxes refunded	2,108	2,056
Cash flows related to operating activities	(3,356)	6,036
FINANCING ACTIVITIES		
Increase in bank indebtedness	17,482	13,600
Repayment of long-term debt	(8,304)	(16,323)
Issue of share capital upon exercise of options	159	–
Cash flows related to financing activities	9,337	(2,723)
INVESTING ACTIVITIES		
Additions to property and equipment and intangible assets [notes 8 and 9]	(6,318)	(9,237)
Proceeds from disposal of property and equipment [note 8]	–	514
Cash flows related to investing activities	(6,318)	(8,723)
Decrease in cash	(337)	(5,410)
Cash, beginning of year	1,783	7,193
Cash, end of year	1,446	1,783

EXHIBIT 5-18B   EXCERPT FROM LE CHATEAU INC.'S 2013 ANNUAL REPORT

21. CHANGES IN NON-CASH WORKING CAPITAL

The cash generated from (used for) non-cash working capital items is made up of changes related to operations in the following accounts:

	January 25, 2014 $	January 26, 2013 $
Accounts receivable	430	447
Income taxes refundable	(360)	(340)
Inventories	(1,660)	(3,893)
Prepaid expenses	(402)	(326)
Deferred finance costs	–	(755)
Trade and other payables	(1,192)	(1,113)
Deferred revenue	154	(360)
Net change in non-cash working capital items related to operations	**(3,030)**	**(6,340)**

Required:

a. Determine the cash flow patterns for Le Château. In total, how much did Le Château's cash and cash equivalents change during 2014? Was this an increase or a decrease? How did this compare with the previous year?

b. How did Le Château's net loss in 2014 compare with the cash flows from operating activities? What was the largest difference between these two amounts?

c. What effect did the change in the company's inventory balance have on cash flows from operating activities in 2014? What does this tell you about the company's inventory balances? Does this cause any particular concerns given the nature of the company's operations?

d. What effect did the change in the company's trade and other payables have on cash flows from operating activities in 2014? What does this tell you about the balance owed to these creditors?

e. Calculate Le Château's net free cash flow for 2014 and 2013. Is the trend positive or negative?

f. If you were a user of Le Château's financial statements—a banker or an investor—how would you interpret the company's cash flow pattern? How would you assess the risk of a loan to or an investment in Le Château?

RI5-6 (Analyze a statement of cash flows)

Required:

For a company of your own choosing, answer the following questions based on its statement of cash flows:

a. Summarize the results for cash from operating, investing, and financing activities over the last two years.

b. Explain any significant changes in the items listed in part "a," from last year to this year.

c. Treating operations as a single source, what were the three most significant (largest) sources of cash in the most recent year?

d. Within the investing and financing sections, what were the four most significant (largest) uses of cash in the most recent year?

e. How has the company been financing its investing activities—through operating activities, financing activities, or both? Support your answer with numbers from the statement of cash flows.

Cases

C5-1 Atlantic Service Company

Atlantic Service Company was established in Moncton, New Brunswick, five years ago to provide services to the home construction industry. It has been very successful, with assets, sales, and profits increasing each year. However, Atlantic is experiencing serious cash shortages and is in danger of going into bankruptcy, because it cannot pay its suppliers and already has a very substantial overdraft at its bank. The president has asked you to analyze the statement of cash flows for the years 2016 and 2015, which appears below.

ATLANTIC SERVICE COMPANY
Statement of Cash Flows
As of December 31

	2016	2015
Operating activities:		
Net income	$200,000	$185,000
Adjustments to convert earnings to cash flows:		
Depreciation expense	25,000	20,000
Gain on sale of investments	3,000	2,000
Changes in non-cash working capital:		
Increase in accounts receivable	(35,000)	(25,000)
Increase in inventory	(30,000)	(20,000)
Increase in prepaid expenses	(5,000)	(4,000)
Increase in accounts payable	52,000	43,000
Net cash provided by operating activities	210,000	201,000
Financing activities:		
Repayment of short-term bank loan	(100,000)	(60,000)
Renewal of short-term bank loan	180,000	100,000
Dividends paid	(15,000)	(10,000)
Net cash provided by financing activities	65,000	30,000
Investing activities:		
Purchase of equipment	(300,000)	(250,000)
Net cash used by investing activities	(300,000)	(250,000)
Net decrease in cash during year	(25,000)	(19,000)
Cash position (bank overdraft) at beginning of year	(29,000)	(10,000)
Cash position (bank overdraft) at end of year	$ (54,000)	$ (29,000)

Required:
Write a memo that:
   a. explains what appears to be causing the cash shortage and
   b. recommends a plan to save the company from bankruptcy.

C5-2 Robertson Furniture Ltd.

Kayla Martchenko has just received a small inheritance from her grandparents' estate. She would like to invest the money and is currently reviewing several opportunities. A friend has given her the financial statements of Robertson Furniture Ltd., a company she found on the Internet. Kayla has reviewed the financial statements and is ready to invest in Robertson Furniture.

Before she invests, Kayla comes to you for some financial advice, because she knows you are taking an accounting course and may be able to give her some insights into the financial statements. She is convinced that this company will be a profitable investment because the statement of financial position indicates that the company's cash balances have been increasing very rapidly, from only $8,000 two years ago to $354,000 now.

Kayla has copied Robertson's statement of cash flows for you, so that you can see how much cash the company has been able to generate each year.

ROBERTSON FURNITURE LTD.
Statement of Cash Flows
As of December 31

	2016	2015
Operating activities:		
Net income (loss)	$ (4,000)	$ 12,000
Add back items not representing cash flows:		
Depreciation expense	20,000	40,000
Loss on disposal of property, plant, and equipment	12,000	10,000
Loss on sale of investments	4,000	3,000

continued

	2016	2015
Adjustment for working capital items:		
Increase in accounts receivable	(40,000)	(36,000)
Increase in inventory	(54,000)	(42,000)
Decrease in prepaid insurance	8,000	2,000
Increase in accounts payable	45,000	28,000
Cash flow from operating activities	(9,000)	17,000
Financing activities:		
Issuance of bonds payable	100,000	20,000
Issuance of shares	50,000	30,000
Payment of dividends	(2,000)	(20,000)
Cash flow from financing activities	148,000	30,000
Investing activities		
Sale of property, plant, and equipment	70,000	22,000
Sale of investments	50,000	20,000
Cash flow from investing activities	120,000	42,000
Overall increase in cash during year	259,000	89,000
Cash—beginning of year	97,000	8,000
Cash—end of year	$356,000	$ 97,000

Required:

   a. Comment on Robertson Furniture's statement of cash flows and address Kayla's opinion that, in light of the amount of cash it has generated, the company must be a good investment.
   b. Based on the results of your analysis of Robertson's statement of cash flows, outline several points that Kayla should investigate about this company before investing her inheritance in it.

C5-3 Ridlow Shipping Ltd.

Jim Shea is an accountant at King and Associates, which is an accounting firm based in Halifax, Nova Scotia. The firm specializes in dealing with small business clients who generally are very successful business people but have limited accounting knowledge.

   Owen Ridlow is a client and the sole owner of Ridlow Shipping Ltd. He recently called Jim with some questions about the financial statements prepared for the year ended December 31, 2016. During the conversation, Owen made the following comment: "Jim, I am wondering why I have to pay you guys to prepare a statement of cash flows. I understand the importance of the statement of financial position and the statement of income, but since I always know how much cash I have in the bank and I reconcile my bank accounts regularly, why do I need a statement of cash flows? It seems to me that paying to have this statement prepared is an unnecessary expense."

Required:

Do you think Owen is at all justified in making this comment? Outline several points that Jim should raise in his discussion with Owen to explain the importance of the statement of cash flows and justify the need for it. Support your answer by referring to Ridlow Shipping's most recent statement of cash flows, which follows.

RIDLOW SHIPPING LTD. Statement of Cash Flows As of December 31		
	2016	2015
Operating activities:		
Net income	$206,250	$254,500
Add back items not representing cash flows:		
Depreciation	40,000	50,000
Loss on sale of investments	6,000	2,000

continued

Adjustment for working capital items:		
Decrease (increase) in accounts receivable	(40,000)	16,000
Increase in inventory	(5,000)	(2,000)
Decrease in prepaid rent	750	500
Increase (decrease) in accounts payable	45,000	(28,000)
Net cash provided by operating activities	253,000	293,000
Financing activities:		
Repayment of bonds	(100,000)	–
Issuance of shares	50,000	–
Payment of dividends	(75,000)	(75,000)
Net cash consumed by financing activities	(125,000)	(75,000)
Investing activities:		
Sale of investments	50,000	20,000
Purchase of capital assets	(215,000)	(197,000)
Net cash consumed by investing activities	(165,000)	(177,000)
Overall increase (decrease) in cash during year	(37,000)	41,000
Cash balance at beginning of year	50,000	9,000
Cash balance at end of year	$ 13,000	$ 50,000

C5-4 Jones Printing

Ben Jones would like to expand his small printing business to include a new computerized colour printing system. To finance the purchase of this equipment, Ben has applied for a loan from a government venture capital agency. The agency requires a complete set of financial statements before it can approve any loan application, and assigns an employee to each applicant to help prepare the necessary financial statements.

You have been assigned to assist Ben with his application, and he has provided you with a statement of income and a statement of financial position for his business. You explain to Ben that a complete set of financial statements includes a statement of cash flows, and that one will have to be prepared for his company before the loan application can be processed. Ben does not understand the purpose of the statement of cash flows and what types of information he will have to gather in order to have one prepared for his business.

Required:
Prepare a brief memo to Ben explaining the purpose and structure of the statement of cash flows and outlining any additional information, beyond the statement of income and statement of financial position, that he will have to provide to enable you to prepare a statement of cash flows for his business.

C5-5 Kralovec Company

As discussed in the chapter, there are two methods for presenting the information in the operating activities section of the statement of cash flows: the direct method and the indirect method. Accounting standards generally express a preference for the direct method but allow the indirect method. The vast majority of companies prepare their statements of cash flows using the indirect method of presentation.

Presented below are two statements of cash flows for Kralovec Company. In the first one, the operating activities section is presented using the direct method; in the second statement, the indirect method is used.

KRALOVEC COMPANY Statement of Cash Flows For the year ended December 31, 2016	
1. Direct Method	
Cash flows from operating activities	
Cash collections from customers	$ 6,446,000
Cash payments for operating expenses	(4,883,000)
Cash payments for interest	(80,000)
Cash payments for income taxes	(313,000)
Net cash provided by operating activities	1,170,000

continued

Cash flows from investing activities		
Sale of machinery	$ 140,000	
Purchase of machinery	(750,000)	
Net cash used by investing activities		(610,000)
Cash flows from financing activities		
Retirement of bonds	(100,000)	
Payment of dividends	(200,000)	
Net cash used by financing activities		(300,000)
Net increase in cash during year		260,000
Cash at beginning of year		130,000
Cash at end of year		$ 390,000

2. Indirect Method

Cash flows from operating activities		
Net income		$ 705,000
Adjustments to convert net earnings to net cash provided by operating activities:		
Depreciation expense	$ 470,000	
Loss on sale of machinery	34,000	
Increase in accounts receivable	(100,000)	
Decrease in inventory	35,000	
Increase in accounts payable	21,000	
Decrease in interest payable	(5,000)	
Increase in taxes payable	10,000	465,000
Net cash provided by operating activities		1,170,000
Cash flows from investing activities		
Sale of machinery	140,000	
Purchase of machinery	(750,000)	
Net cash used by investing activities		(610,000)
Cash flows from financing activities		
Retirement of bonds	(100,000)	
Payment of dividends	(200,000)	
Net cash used by financing activities		(300,000)
Net increase in cash during year		260,000
Cash at beginning of year		130,000
Cash at end of year		$ 390,000

Required:

a. As discussed in Chapter 2, understandability is an important qualitative characteristic of financial statements. With this in mind, compare the two statements above and comment on the understandability of the direct versus the indirect method of presentation in the operating activities section. Which approach do you think most users of financial statements would prefer?

b. Looking only at the first statement (presented using the direct method), analyze the cash flow data for Kralovec Company and note any significant points that can be observed from it regarding the company's operations during the year. Then repeat this process, looking only at the second statement (presented using the indirect method).

c. Based on your experience in working through part "b," which method of presentation do you find more useful (i.e. more relevant) for analyzing the cash flow data, understanding the company's operations, and identifying points to be investigated further? Explain why.

ENDNOTES

1. Solarina Ho, "Bombardier Results Raise Cash Burn Concerns, Hurt Stock," Reuters, May 1, 2014; Bertrand Marotte, "Investor Concern over Bombardier Spending Pushes Shares Lower," *The Globe and Mail*, May 1, 2014; David Parkinson, "Bombardier Cash Flow Needs to Reverse Course Soon," *The Globe and Mail*, May 1, 2014; Frederic Tomesco, "Bombardier Tumbles as Cash Usage Pace Nearly Doubles," Bloomberg, May 1, 2014; Bombardier 2013 Annual Report; Bombardier corporate website, www.bombardier.com.

2. Canadian Tire Corporation, Limited's 2013 annual report.

3. Reitmans (Canada) Limited's 2014 annual report.

4. IFRS – Conceptual Framework, OB20; Jeff Gray and Andy Hoffman, "Report Alleges Possibility Sino-Forest 'An Accounting Fiction,'" *The Globe and Mail*, April 15, 2012; Al and Mark Rosen, "Don't Be Suckered by Cash Flow Statements," Advisor.ca, August 1, 2011.

5. Reitmans (Canada) Limited's 2014 annual report.

6. Pacific Safety Products Inc.'s 2013 annual report.

7. Groupe Bikini Village's 2013 annual report.

8. Dugan, M., Gup. B., and Samson, W. (1999, Vol. 9). "Teaching the Statement of Cash Flows," *Journal of Accounting Education*, pp. 33–52.

6 | Cash and Accounts Receivable

CORE QUESTIONS
If you are able to answer the following questions, then you have achieved the related learning objectives.

LEARNING OBJECTIVES
After studying this chapter, you should be able to:

●●● INTRODUCTION

- Why are cash and accounts receivable of significance to users?

1 Explain why cash and accounts receivable are of significance to users.

●●● CASH

- What is included in the definition of "cash"?
- At what amount is cash reflected on the statement of financial position?

2 Describe the valuation methods for cash.

●●● INTERNAL CONTROL

- What are the main principles of internal control?

3 Explain the main principles of internal control.

●●● BANK RECONCILIATION

- What is the purpose of a bank reconciliation and why must it be prepared?
- How is a bank reconciliation prepared?

4 Explain the purpose of bank reconciliations, including their preparation and the treatment of related adjustments.

●●● ACCOUNTS RECEIVABLE

- What are accounts receivable?
- Why do companies sell on account?
- Are there any additional costs from selling on account?

5 Explain why companies sell on account and identify the additional costs that result from this decision.

●●● BAD DEBTS

- At what amount are accounts receivable reflected on the statement of financial position?

6 Describe the valuation methods for accounts receivable.

- What is the allowance method of accounting for bad debts?

7 Explain the allowance method of accounting for bad debts.

- How are bad debts estimated under the allowance method?

8 Identify the two methods of estimating bad debts under the allowance method and describe the circumstances for using each method.

- What is the direct writeoff method and when is it acceptable to use it?

9 Explain the direct writeoff method of accounting for bad debts and when it is acceptable to use it.

- How do companies shorten their cash-to-cash cycle?

10 Explain alternative ways in which companies shorten their cash-to-cash cycle.

●●● FINANCIAL STATEMENT ANALYSIS

- What is liquidity and how is it assessed?
- How effective has the company been at collecting its accounts receivable?

11 Explain the concept of liquidity. Calculate the current ratio, quick ratio, accounts receivable turnover ratio, and average collection period ratio and assess the results.

●●● Will That Be Cash or Credit?

If you had a summer lawn-mowing business, would you want customers to pay you in cash every time or would you accept an IOU for them to pay you later? If you allowed them to pay later, how much time would you give them before you came to collect your money?

If you were a company in the wholesale apparel business, like Montreal-based Gildan Activewear Inc., your credit policy would have to follow certain industry practices but not be too restrictive, or you could lose out on sales, and not be too loose, or you could end up with bad debts.

Gildan, which makes and markets family apparel such as underwear, fleece, and blank T-shirts ready for screen printing, invoices most sales with payment terms of 30 to 60 days. The company notes that it is industry practice that sales to wholesale distributors of seasonal products, especially in the last six months of the year, to be given extended payment terms, usually up to four months.

Among the credit risks Gildan faces is that its sales are concentrated: its 10 largest customers accounted for 53% of trade receivables in 2013. Many of those customers are highly leveraged, such as having bank loans for which their inventory is pledged as collateral. If a customer can't pay off its loan or obtain additional financing, it could result in Gildan having an uncollectible account receivable from that customer. "Future credit losses relating to any one of our top ten customers could be material and could result in a material charge to earnings," the company's credit risk note in its 2013 annual report states. At its fiscal year end of September 29, 2013, Gildan had U.S. $255 million in trade receivables (outstanding invoices, also known as accounts receivable), while its sales that fiscal year were almost U.S. $2.2 billion.

Gildan tries to reduce its credit risk. "The Company's extension of credit to customers involves considerable judgment and is based on an evaluation of each customer's financial condition and payment history. The Company has established various internal controls designed to mitigate credit risk, including a dedicated credit function which recommends customer credit limits and payment terms that are reviewed and approved on a quarterly basis by senior management," its annual report states. "Where available, the Company's credit departments periodically review external ratings and customer financial statements, and in some cases obtain bank and other references. New customers are subject to a specific validation and pre-approval process." Sometimes, Gildan will require riskier customers to pay up front, just like a lawn-mowing business might do with a new neighbour.

In 2014, Gildan announced it was buying Montreal-based Doris Inc., which makes women's hosiery, giving it access to Canadian retailers such as Shoppers Drug Mart and Hudson's Bay. Gildan will certainly monitor its credit practices with these new customers.[1]

INTRODUCTION

Our opening story talks about an apparel company's efforts to control its accounts receivable and limit the number of uncollectible accounts, or bad debts. Determining the value of the accounts receivable and estimating the amount that will be collected in cash is important for both external financial reporting and sound internal financial management. This chapter discusses accounting and management control issues related to an organization's most liquid assets: its cash and its receivables.

Why are cash and accounts receivable of significance to users?

Cash and **accounts receivable** are a company's most liquid assets. These items, together with inventory (which will be discussed in Chapter 7), give the company the resources necessary to meet its immediate, short-term financial obligations. Users therefore need to have a good understanding of these items. For example, while cash seems to be straightforward, in reality it constitutes a number of things, including money physically on hand, amounts in bank accounts, and cheques held for deposit. Accounts receivable (also known as trade receivables) are amounts due from customers as a result of sales of goods or services and are typically due within 30 days. In some industries, this credit period may extend up to 180 days. (As we saw in the opening story, **Gildan Activewear Inc.** grants credit up to four months, or 120 days.) As a user, you need to know how much credit a company has extended to its customers and be aware of the potential for **uncollectible accounts**, also known as doubtful accounts or bad debts, that will never be paid by customers. You should also be able to assess how well the company has done historically at collecting its receivables.

Presenting cash and accounts receivable separately on the financial statements helps users evaluate a company's **liquidity**, or its ability to meet its obligations in the short term. In other words, users can assess how well positioned the company is in terms of having sufficient cash or current assets that will become cash (when the receivables are collected) to pay the company's current liabilities (such as accounts payable and wages payable) as they come due.

■ **LEARNING OBJECTIVE 1**
Explain why cash and accounts receivable are of significance to users.

CASH

What is included in the definition of "cash"?

As noted above, cash includes the cash physically on hand at a company, such as the cash in the cash register drawers or in the company's safe. Cash also includes the cash represented by the customers' cheques held by the company for deposit and the cash held on deposit in the company's accounts at

■ **LEARNING OBJECTIVE 2**
Describe the valuation methods for cash.

financial institutions (banks, credit unions, and so on). Cash also includes amounts known as **cash equivalents**. These are amounts that can be easily converted into known amounts of cash; that is, there is no doubt about the amount of cash that will be received when they mature. Cash equivalents also have short maturity dates (within three months of the date of acquisition). An example of a cash equivalent is a government treasury bill.

It is also possible for a company to have a negative cash balance. This would be the case if the company has a line of credit or overdraft facility and has drawn on it. We will discuss this situation in Chapter 9 on current liabilities.

At what amount is cash reflected on the statement of financial position?

The amount of cash and cash equivalents is presented on the statement of financial position. Cash is measured at its face value at the reporting date—the date that the statement of financial position is being prepared at. Cash may also be held in foreign currencies, such as U.S. dollars or euros. If this is the case, then these amounts are translated or converted into Canadian dollars using the rate of exchange at the statement of financial position date.

Companies normally prepare their financial statements using the currency of the country in which they are headquartered. Canadian companies typically prepare their financial statements in Canadian dollars, U.S. companies prepare their financial statements in U.S. dollars, and so on. It is possible for Canadian companies that are also listed on U.S. stock exchanges and file their financial statements in the United States to prepare their financial statements in U.S. dollars rather than Canadian dollars. We will see excerpts in this textbook from the financial statements of several Canadian companies that report in U.S. dollars.

INTERNAL CONTROL

■ **LEARNING OBJECTIVE 3**
Explain the main principles of internal control.

What are the main principles of internal control?

One of management's key responsibilities is to safeguard the company's assets. This includes ensuring that the company's assets are used effectively within the business and are not lost or stolen. All assets, including cash, inventory, and equipment, are common targets of theft either internally (by management or employees) or externally (by customers, delivery companies, and so on). To fulfill their responsibility to safeguard assets, management establishes a system of internal controls that are then continually monitored. Generally, cash is the asset most susceptible to theft and we will use it as an example to explain the elements of an internal control system.

The key elements of an effective **internal control system** include:

KEY POINT

An internal control system includes:
- physical controls
- assignment of responsibilities
- separation of duties
- independent verification
- documentation

1. **Physical Controls**

   These controls are designed to protect assets from theft, diversion, damage, or destruction. Management protects assets by ensuring that premises and resources are secure through the use of such things as locks, alarms, and fencing. In the case of cash, regular bank deposits should be made and any cash on hand should be securely stored in cash registers and safes.

2. **Assignment of Responsibilities**

   An essential characteristic of internal control is the assignment of responsibility to specific individuals. Control is most effective when only one person is responsible for each task. To illustrate, assume that at the end of the day the cash in the cash register drawer is less than the amount of cash sales rung up on the cash register. If only one person has operated the register, responsibility for the shortage can be determined immediately. If more than one individual has worked the register, it may be impossible to determine who is responsible for the shortage, unless each person is assigned a separate cash drawer.

KEY POINT

Where possible, the following duties should be separated:
- transaction authorization
- recording of transactions
- asset custody

3. **Separation of Duties**

   Separation of duties involves ensuring that individual employees cannot authorize transactions, record them, and have custody of the related assets. If these responsibilities are assigned to separate employees, no single employee will have the opportunity to defraud a company and conceal the theft while performing the duties associated with their position. If duties are effectively separated, the only way for a theft or fraud to occur is through **collusion**, where two or more employees work together to commit the theft and conceal it.

For cash, separation of duties means that one person receives cash, another is authorized to sign cheques, and a third records the receipts or payments of cash in the accounting records. Personnel who receive, disburse, or otherwise handle cash should not maintain, or even have access to, the cash records. Bear in mind that "cash" transactions can occur in many forms. In addition to currency and cheques, cash transactions include credit card and debit card transactions, and other direct payments such as **electronic funds transfers (EFTs)** to and from the company.

4. **Independent Verification**

These controls involve one person checking the work of another. The independent verification can be internal, such as one employee checking the work of another, or external, such as an external auditor verifying transactions. When one person is responsible for verifying the work of another, behaving dishonestly without being detected would also require collusion.

In small companies, achieving the appropriate level of separation of duties and independent verification is more difficult because there is a limited number of employees. In this case, the owners or senior management must sometimes perform some of the key tasks and periodically verify the work of employees. When dealing with cash, independent verification may involve having the store manager double check the cash counts made by the store cashiers.

5. **Documentation**

Documents provide evidence that transactions and events have occurred, as well as an **audit trail** by which transactions can be traced back to source documents, if necessary. For example, the cash register tape is documentation for the amount of revenue earned and cash received. Similarly, a shipping document indicates that the goods have been shipped, and a sales invoice indicates that the customer has been billed for the goods. By adding a signature (or initials) to the documents, the individual responsible for the transaction or event can be identified. Whenever possible, documents should be prenumbered and used sequentially. This allows the company to verify that all of the documents used have been accounted for.

The main issues with cash are the control of cash to ensure that it is not lost or stolen, and the management of cash balances. Proper control of cash includes policies such as ensuring that all cash is deposited into bank accounts daily (or even more frequently), using secure safes and cash registers to hold cash until it is deposited, writing cheques or using debit or credit cards instead of using cash to pay expenses, and keeping as little cash on hand as possible.

BANK RECONCILIATION

What is the purpose of a bank reconciliation and why must it be prepared?

An important internal control procedure that is used by almost every company is the **bank reconciliation**. This ensures that any differences between the accounting records for cash and the bank statement received from the bank are identified, explained, and recorded where necessary. By doing this, business owners and managers have assurance that:

1. Every transaction recorded by the bank has also been recorded by the company or the reason why not has been explained.
2. Every transaction recorded by the company in its cash account(s) has also been recorded by the bank or the reason why not has been explained.

There are many reasons why a transaction may have been reflected in the company's accounting records but not by the bank or vice versa. Some common differences include:

- A cheque has been written and mailed out by the company but has yet to be deposited by the recipient. Until it is deposited, there is no way that the company's bank could be aware of it.

■ **LEARNING OBJECTIVE 4**
Explain the purpose of bank reconciliations, including their preparation and the treatment of related adjustments.

- The bank has charged service fees to the company's account. The company will not be aware of the fees until it receives the bank statement at the end of the month.
- The company has made a deposit on the last day of the month after the bank closed for business, by using the night deposit slot. The bank will credit the company's account for this deposit on the first business day of the new month.
- A company has deposited a cheque from one of its customers that is not honoured by the customer's bank because there are insufficient funds in the account to cover the cheque. The company will not be aware of this until the cheque is returned with the bank statement at the end of the month.

Bank reconciliations should be prepared for each bank account maintained by a company and this should be done at least monthly. If a company's cash position is very tight, then reconciliations may need to be prepared even more frequently.

 Ethics in Accounting

There are numerous unethical ways that accounting records can be manipulated. Many transactions ultimately impact the cash account, including cash sales, collection of receivables, payment of expenses, settlement of payables, asset purchases, and so on. Ensuring the accuracy of the cash account minimizes the risk of fraudulent cash transactions being reflected in a company's accounts. Cash is either in the bank account or it is not, and bank reconciliations are a key control to assess this.

How is a bank reconciliation prepared?

The process of preparing a bank reconciliation is quite straightforward, if you bear in mind that the objective is to determine what the cash balance would be if the same items were recorded in both sets of records (the company's and the bank's). Accordingly, when an item is identified as being recorded in one set of records but not in the other, or recorded differently in one set of records than in the other, that item has to be included in the reconciliation. Whether it is added or deducted depends on whatever needs to be done with it, logically, to determine what the correct cash balance would be if each item were recorded correctly in both sets of records.

When reconciling the bank balance and general ledger (G/L) balance for an account, one of the simplest ways of thinking about the reconciliation is to split it in two. One side will be the "bank side," while the other side will be the "G/L side." The reconciling items on the bank side will be all those items that the company knows about, but the bank does not. The reconciling items on the G/L side will be all those items that the bank knows about, but the company does not until it receives the bank statement for the account at the end of the month.

Exhibit 6-1 illustrates the format of a bank reconciliation and identifies common items that require reconciliation.

Exhibit 6-1 The Format of a Bank Reconciliation

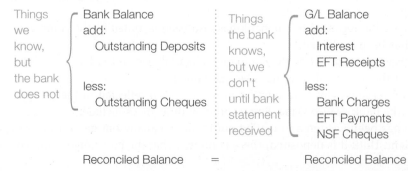

The following information about Gelardi Company will illustrate the process of preparing a bank reconciliation. As you consider each of the items that follow, refer to Exhibit 6-1 to see how the item is treated on the bank reconciliation.

- According to the bank statement received for the month of October 2016, the balance in Gelardi's bank account on October 31 was $8,916.39. This is the starting point for the bank portion of the reconciliation, labelled "Bank Balance."
- The balance in the company's Cash account in the general ledger on October 31, 2016, was $9,770.44. This is the starting point for the company portion of the bank reconciliation, labelled "G/L Balance."

Gelardi's accountant reviewed the bank statement, comparing the transactions recorded on it with the transactions recorded in the ledger account, and discovered the following differences:

Item	Which side of reconciliation?	How handled on bank reconciliation
1. The last deposit of the month, for $1,035.62, was made as a night deposit on October 31 and therefore was not recorded by the bank until the beginning of November. Consequently, it did not appear on the October bank statement.	Company knows, but bank does not. Therefore, adjust bank side.	Since this deposit has been added to Gelardi's ledger account but not to its bank account, it is listed as an addition in the bank portion of the reconciliation. The bank will record the addition to Gelardi's account on the first business day of November when it records the night deposits.
2. One of Gelardi's customers paid its account by making an electronic transfer from its bank into Gelardi's bank account. The amount appeared on the bank statement as an EFT deposit in the amount of $312.98. Until the bank statement was reviewed, Gelardi was not aware that this payment had been received.	Bank knows but company does not. Therefore, adjust company side.	Since this transaction has been recorded by the bank but not by Gelardi, an adjustment has to be made in the company portion of the reconciliation. As the item is a cash receipt, this amount has to be added to the G/L balance.
3. The bank subtracted a service charge of $25.75 from the company's bank account for October, but Gelardi's accountant had not yet recorded it in the company's books. Typically, a company only becomes aware of these charges when the bank statement is reviewed.	Bank knows but company does not. Therefore, adjust company side.	Since this charge has been deducted from the bank account but not from Gelardi's ledger, it is deducted on the company portion of the reconciliation, to reduce the G/L balance by the amount of the charge.
4. Cheque number 873 for $262.89, cheque number 891 for $200.00, and cheque number 892 for $65.78 were still outstanding at the end of October. That is, they had been mailed to suppliers, but had not yet cleared the bank. The cheques may still be in the mail or the recipients have yet to deposit them.	Company knows but bank does not. Therefore, adjust bank side.	Since these cheques have been deducted from Gelardi's ledger account but not from its bank account, they are deducted from the bank portion of the reconciliation to reflect the reduced cash balance that will be available when they eventually clear the bank.
5. The bank statement showed that $500.00 was deducted from Gelardi's account by the bank as payment of loan principal. The payment was not recorded in the company's ledger at the time of payment.	Bank knows but company does not. Therefore, adjust company side.	Since this payment has been deducted from the bank account but not recorded in Gelardi's ledger, it is deducted from the company portion of the reconciliation, reducing the G/L balance by the amount of the payment.

6. The bank returned a cheque from one of Gelardi's customers marked *NSF* (non-sufficient funds). This was a cheque for $186.80 that a customer used to pay off his account. Gelardi had deposited it and the bank had increased Gelardi's account balance to reflect this deposit. However, when Gelardi's bank sent the cheque to the customer's bank for payment, it was informed that the customer did not have enough money in his account to cover the cheque. Consequently, Gelardi's bank removed the amount from Gelardi's account and returned the cheque to Gelardi with the bank statement.

Bank knows but company does not.

Therefore, adjust company side.

NSF cheques are also known as *bounced cheques*. Once the bank became aware of the NSF cheque, it adjusted Gelardi's account to reflect it. Gelardi was not aware of the NSF cheque until it was returned by the bank. Since Gelardi recorded an increase to cash when it originally received the cheque from the customer, it must now reduce cash in the G/L to reflect that the amount was never actually received and is still owing by the customer. It will be deducted from the company portion of the reconciliation. We will assume that there were no bank service charges related to the returned cheque.

7. The bank statement showed that cheque number 885 (which Gelardi had issued to pay for an advertising expense) was recorded by the bank as $246.81, while the company recorded this cheque as $426.81. A review of the cancelled cheques accompanying the bank statement showed that the amount recorded by the bank was correct.

Error! Made by company.

Therefore, adjust company side.

As this was an error made by the company, an adjustment has to be made to the G/L balance. The amount of the error was $180 ($426.81 − $246.81). Since the company reduced its cash balance by $180.00 too much when it recorded this cheque, this amount needs to be added back to get the correct balance.

8. The bank deducted a cheque written by Gardeli Company (a different company) from Gelardi Company's account. The amount of the cheque was $127.53.

Error! Made by bank.

Therefore, adjust bank side.

Since this was an error made by the bank, an adjustment has to be made to the bank balance. Since $127.53 was mistakenly taken out of Gelardi's bank account, this amount has to be added back to get the correct balance. Gelardi will need to inform the bank of the error.

Using the above information, the accountant would prepare the bank reconciliation as shown in Exhibit 6-2.

Exhibit 6-2 Gelardi Company Bank Reconciliation as at October 31, 2016

Bank Balance		$8,916.39	G/L Balance		$9,770.44
Add:	Outstanding deposit	1,035.62	Add:	EFT receipts	312.98
	Correction of error made by the bank	127.53		Correction of error made by the company	180.00
Deduct:	Outstanding cheques		Deduct:	Bank charges	(25.75)
	#873	(262.89)		Automatic deduction for loan payment	(500.00)
	#891	(200.00)		NSF cheque	(186.80)
	#892	(65.78)			
Reconciled Balance		$9,550.87	**Reconciled Balance**		$9,550.87

Once all of the differences between the bank's records and the company's records have been dealt with, the bank reconciliation is complete. The reconciliation shows that the actual amount of cash available at the end of October is $9,550.87, which is not the balance per the bank statement nor the balance in the general ledger prior to the reconciliation being completed. At this point, the company's records (the general ledger) still reflect a balance in the cash account of $9,770.44. To adjust this to the correct balance, the accountant needs to make journal entries for all of the adjustments on the G/L side of the bank reconciliation. These entries would be as shown in Exhibit 6-3.

Exhibit 6-3 Journal Entries from the Bank Reconciliation

Cash	312.98	
Accounts Receivable		312.98
Cash	180.00	
Advertising Expense		180.00
Bank Charges Expense	25.75	
Cash		25.75
Bank Loan Payable	500.00	
Cash		500.00
Accounts Receivable	186.80	
Cash		186.80

Notice that the bank reconciliation gives you half of each journal entry before you start. All of the adjustments that were additions to the G/L balance are debits to cash, while all of the deductions are credits to the cash account.

Bank reconciliations are an important control procedure. They ensure that all transactions affecting the bank account have been properly recorded, providing the company with the correct balance of cash that it has available. They are normally made each month for every bank account, as soon as the bank statements are received. Practically, this means that bank reconciliations are always prepared effective the last day of the month, but are completed early in the subsequent month when the bank statement is received.

As previously stated, duties must be separated appropriately for effective internal control. In terms of the bank reconciliation, this means that the person who reconciles the bank account should not be the person who is responsible for either doing the banking or maintaining the accounting records. This will ensure that any errors or discrepancies will be found and properly corrected. This also ensures that no individual has an opportunity to misappropriate cash and then change the accounting records to cover the fraud.

The other issue associated with cash is cash management. Proper cash management involves maintaining sufficient cash in readily accessible bank accounts to be able to make payments when the need arises, while at the same time not keeping excessive amounts of cash. Because cash is an inactive asset—it does not earn a return except possibly a small amount of interest—companies usually try to keep as much of their cash invested in income-earning assets as they safely can. A company's cash management policies are critical for effectively managing its cash position and maximizing its total earnings. Advanced cash management techniques are not discussed in this book, but are a very important aspect of financial management for the company's shareholders and other stakeholders.

ACCOUNTS RECEIVABLE

What are accounts receivable?

Accounts receivable are amounts owed to a company by its customers. They arise as a result of normal business transactions, the sale of goods and services, that have been made on credit. Receivables may be supported by a written contract, but normally the arrangement is less formal, with only a sales

HELPFUL HINT
The main objective of a bank reconciliation is to determine the correct cash balance. Therefore, items that the bank has not yet recorded must be added to, or deducted from, the balance shown on the bank statement, while items that the company has not yet recorded must be added to, or deducted from, the balance shown in the company's cash account.

HELPFUL HINT
When correcting errors, the first thing to do is to determine who made the error (the bank or the company). This tells us which side of the bank reconciliation that the error will appear on. If the bank made the error, then it must be corrected on the bank side of the reconciliation and vice versa. The second thing to determine is whether the error resulted in the cash amount being too high or too low. If it is too high, then the error should be subtracted on the reconciliation. If it is too low, then the error should be added on the reconciliation.

■ **LEARNING OBJECTIVE 5**
Explain why companies sell on account and identify the additional costs that result from this decision.

invoice as supporting documentation. The outstanding amounts are normally non–interest-bearing for a 30-day period, though this may be longer depending upon the industry, customer relationship, and so on.

Why do companies sell on account?

Companies sell on account for a number of reasons. The most obvious reason is that selling on account increases overall sales. Most of us have purchased something on credit that we did not have the money for at the time of purchase. If companies required their customers to purchase with cash, many sales would never be made. Also, if a company's competitors sell on account, then the company must also do so if it wishes to remain competitive. While it may seem odd, selling on account can actually result in increased revenue. This can happen if the company's customers are unable to pay within the credit period. After this period, the receivable normally becomes interest-bearing and this interest can be a significant additional revenue stream for the company.

For Example

Canadian Tire Corporation is an excellent example of a company that has used its credit function to increase overall profits. In fact, the company even has its own federally regulated bank, the Canadian Tire Bank. In fiscal 2013, Canadian Tire's retail segment (the company's Canadian Tire, Mark's, SportChek, and other retail stores) had total revenues of $10,690.2 million, from which the company realized income before taxes of $463.4 million. In the same period, the company's financial services segment (such as the bank, Canadian Tire MasterCard, home and auto insurance sales, and in-store instant credit program) had total revenues of $1,025.9 million, from which the company realized income before taxes of $320.0 million. In other words, of the company's $784.6 million net income before taxes, approximately 40.8% of Canadian Tire's income before taxes comes from financial services rather than retail sales. The company financial statements also indicate that 72.1% of its financial services revenue is interest income. Clearly, this is a significant stream of additional revenues and profits for the company.[2]

Are there any additional costs from selling on account?

Yes! Companies incur a number of costs when they make the decision to sell on account. There are additional staff costs related to the credit-granting function. Companies will have to have employees who are responsible for authorizing customers to be able to purchase on account. They will need to take steps such as assessing the credit histories of customers seeking credit. There will also be staff costs related to the credit follow-up and collection functions. Employees will be needed who are responsible for sending statements to customers with outstanding accounts and for following up by mail or phone with those customers who do not pay their accounts by the due dates. The most significant cost from selling on account is likely to be the bad debts associated with those customers who fail to pay their accounts, known as **bad debts expense** (or doubtful accounts expense).

For Example

Winnipeg-based **New Flyer Industries Inc.**, which manufactures heavy-duty transit buses, has assessed that its risk of bad debts is mitigated, or lessened, by the fact that a "significant portion" of its customers are "well established transit authorities," which can usually pay their bills in full. "Historically, the Company has experienced nominal bad debts as a result of the customer base being principally comprised of municipal and other local transit authorities," New Flyer says in its 2013 annual report. Many of its customers are in the United States, where the U.S. federal government typically pays up to 80% of the capital costs of transit systems acquiring new buses, with the remaining 20% coming from state and municipal sources.[3]

The likelihood that a customer will default on payments depends on the customer's creditworthiness. A company can improve its chances of receiving payments by performing credit checks on its customers before granting them credit. Gildan Activewear in the opening story does this. However, a company must balance its desire to sell its products to the customer with the risk that the customer will not pay. Too strict a credit policy will mean that many customers will be denied credit and may therefore purchase their goods from other suppliers. Too loose a credit policy, and the company may lose more money from bad debts than it gains from additional sales. The company should do a cost-benefit analysis when determining its credit policies.

The company must also stay aware of changes in its industry and changes in the economy in general. Changes in interest rates, a downturn in the global economy, legislative changes, or adverse industry conditions can all impact a customer's credit status.

FINANCIAL STATEMENTS

For Example

Canadian mining company **PotashCorp.** included this information about the company's credit-granting policies in its 2013 consolidated financial statements:

> The company seeks to manage the credit risk relating to its trade receivables through a credit management program. Credit approval policies and procedures are in place to guide the granting of credit to new customers as well as its continued expansion to existing customers. Existing customer accounts are reviewed every 12–18 months. Credit is extended to international customers based upon an evaluation of both customer and country risk. The company uses credit agency reports where available, and an assessment of other relevant information such as current financial statements and/or credit references before assigning credit limits to customers. Those that fail to meet specified benchmark creditworthiness may transact with the company on a prepayment basis or provide another form of credit support that it approves.

From this, we can see examples of the types of costs that are part of the company's credit management program and result from the company's decision to extend credit to its customers.[4]

BAD DEBTS

At what amount are accounts receivable reflected on the statement of financial position?

Accounts receivable are reflected on the statement of financial position at their **carrying amount**, which is the full value of all the company's accounts receivable less the **allowance for doubtful accounts**. This is also known as the *allowance for credit losses*. Allowance for doubtful accounts is a contra-asset account. This means that it is associated with another asset account but its normal balance is contrary or opposite of what we would normally expect for an asset account. It represents management's best estimate of the total accounts receivable that it does not expect to be able to collect. The net amount is called the *carrying amount* and is what is normally presented on the statement of financial position.

When companies use the allowance for doubtful accounts, they are using the **allowance method**. Under this method, management estimates the amount of receivables that it expects it will be unable to collect and accounts for the related bad debts expense in the same period as the credit sales were reported. The company does not wait until some time in future, when some customers fail to pay, to record the bad debts expense.

It is important to understand that Accounts Receivable is a **control account**. This means that a **subledger** (or **subsidiary**) **ledger** is used to manage all of the details in the account. In the case of accounts receivable (A/R), the A/R subledger is used to manage the individual account details of each of the company's customers. This detail is of critical importance and would be lost within the Accounts Receivable account. In simple terms, if a customer phones the company's A/R clerk to inquire about their outstanding balance, the clerk needs to have the customer's individual details readily at hand. This is the detail that would be found in the A/R subledger. If there were no subledger, then the A/R clerk would need to work through all of the detail in the Accounts Receivable account trying to pull out the information related to that particular customer. While this may not be a big deal for a company with only a few significant customers, for those with thousands of customers, it would not be practical.

■ **LEARNING OBJECTIVE 6**
Describe the valuation methods for accounts receivable.

KEY POINTS
- No entry can be made to the Accounts Receivable (A/R) account if an entry cannot be made to the A/R subledger. That is, you must know which customer's account is affected.
- Total A/R = Total in A/R subledger.

Another critical thing to understand is that the total of all the accounts in the A/R subledger must equal the total of the Accounts Receivable account. In other words, the control account must always equal the total of the related subledger. This also means that an entry cannot be made to one if it cannot be made to the other. That is, we cannot record an entry in Accounts Receivable if we cannot make the same entry to one of the customer accounts in the A/R subledger. The A/R subledger should be regularly reconciled to the Accounts Receivable account to ensure the two remain in balance. This is normally done monthly.

Exhibit 6-4 shows how the Accounts Receivable account is related to the accounts receivable subledger and how the carrying amount of accounts receivable is determined.

Exhibit 6-4 Accounts Receivable and Allowance for Doubtful Accounts

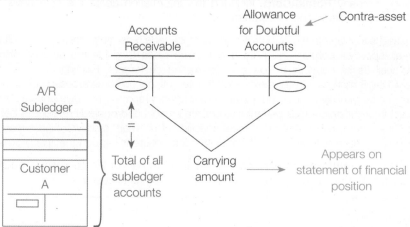

While all Canadian companies present trade receivables at their carrying amount (net of the allowance for doubtful accounts), the level of detail regarding the amount of the allowance for doubtful accounts varies. Bad debts expense is generally included as part of selling, general, and administrative expenses, rather than being separately disclosed. However, companies following IFRS must disclose changes in the allowance for doubtful accounts balance in the notes to the financial statements. The annual bad debts expense is presented as part of this note.

FINANCIAL STATEMENTS

For Example

RONA Inc.'s 2013 annual report included the following note disclosure related to the company's accounts receivable and allowance for doubtful accounts (amounts in thousands of Canadian dollars):

The aging of trade accounts receivable is as follows:

	As at December 29, 2013	As at December 30, 2012
		Restated (Note 32)
Current	$155,031	$246,988
Past due 0–30 days	38,650	49,470
Past due 31–120 days	22,473	38,033
Past due over 121 days	36,163	34,675
Trade receivables	252,317	369,166
Less: allowance for doubtful accounts	12,231	14,748
Balance, end of year	$240,086	$354,418

(continued)

For Example (continued)

The allowance for doubtful accounts is mainly for customer accounts over 121 days past due.
The following table provides the change in allowance for doubtful accounts for trade receivables:

	2013	2012
		Restated (Note 32)
Balance, beginning of year	$ 14,748	$ 15,827
Doubtful accounts (recovery) expense	(2,517)	(1,079)
Balance, end of year	$ 12,231	$ 14,748

In the consolidated income statement, the doubtful accounts expense is recorded in selling, general and administrative expenses.

From this we can see that Rona expected that $12,231 or 4.85% of its receivables would be uncollectible as at December 31, 2013, which was a slight increase from the 3.99% expected at the end of the preceding year.[5]

What is the allowance method of accounting for bad debts?

■ **LEARNING OBJECTIVE 7**
Explain the allowance method of accounting for bad debts.

TAKE**5**

Each period, management estimates the amount of accounts receivable that it does not expect to be able to collect in the future. The company establishes an allowance for these doubtful accounts and records the bads debts expense in the same period in which the credit sales have been recorded. This is known as the allowance method. In this section, we will review the three key transactions that may occur under the allowance method. These are:

1. *Establishing the allowance and recording the bad debts expense. This is called the allowance entry.*
   At the end of each accounting period, management will use one of two methods (which are discussed later in the chapter) to estimate the amount of accounts receivable they do not expect to be able to collect. An allowance for doubtful accounts will be established to reduce the carrying amount accordingly. The journal entry for this transaction is:

Bad Debts Expense	XXX	
Allowance for Doubtful Accounts		XXX

   It is important to understand that, at this point, management does not know which specific customers will not pay their accounts. Instead, they are simply using historical or industry averages to make an estimate. Since they do not know which specific customers will not be paying, they cannot make any entries in the A/R subledger and, therefore, they cannot make any entries in the Accounts Receivable control account. The contra-asset account, Allowance for Doubtful Accounts, is used instead.

   This entry effects both the statement of income, by increasing expenses, and the statement of financial position, by reducing the carrying amount of accounts receivable.

2. *Writing off a specific receivable. This is called the writeoff entry.*
   Companies establish policies for when accounts are to be written off. A **writeoff** is the process of removing a specific customer's account receivable from a company's books when the account is deemed uncollectible. Some companies' writeoff policies may use timelines, such as writing off an account once it is more than 180 days overdue. Other companies may wait for specific indications, such as being notified of a customer's bankruptcy, before writing off an account. Once the specific customer account has been identified, entries can be made to both the A/R subledger and Accounts Receivable to reflect the writeoff. The journal entry for this transaction is:

Allowance for Doubtful Accounts	XXX	
Accounts Receivable		XXX

It may be helpful to view this entry as the company using up some of the allowance that had been previously established for accounts like this. It is also important to know that, even after a customer's account has been written off for accounting purposes, the company generally continues to try to collect the account. The company may do this itself or it may use a collection agency.

Note that this entry has no effect on the statement of income, nor does it change the carrying amount of receivables, because it has offsetting effects on the two accounts making up this amount.

3. **Recovery of a specific receivable that has been previously written off. This is called a recovery entry.** As previously mentioned, companies continue to pursue collection efforts even after accounts have been written off. If these efforts are successful and the customer makes full or partial payment on its account, this is considered a **recovery**. If an account receivable is recovered, the company's accounting records would show the customer as owing nothing because their account had previously been written off. As such, the company must first reverse the writeoff and then record the cash collection as it ordinarily does. The journal entries for this transaction are:

Accounts Receivable	XXX	
Allowance for Doubtful Accounts		XXX
Cash	XXX	
Accounts Receivable		XXX

It may be helpful to view this entry as the company re-establishing an allowance taken previously that it did not end up needing. It is important to note that by re-establishing the receivable and the allowance, the company has a complete history of its credit experience with that customer. In the A/R subledger, the company can see the sales to the customer, the account being written off, the reversal of the writeoff, and the eventual payment. This kind of detail will be important information for making future credit decisions regarding the customer.

This entry has no effect on the statement of income. However, it does affect the statement of financial position by increasing cash and decreasing the carrying amount of accounts receivable.

Let's review these entries using a numerical example in Exhibit 6-5.

Exhibit 6-5 The Allowance Method of Accounting for Bad Debts

Assume the following:
- The company began the year with $21,000 of accounts receivable and an allowance for doubtful accounts of $1,100.
- Total sales for the year were $140,000, of which 80% were on account.
- During the year, the company collected $101,000 of its accounts receivable.
- Historically, the company's bad debts have been approximately 4.5% of credit sales.
- The company's policy is to write off accounts that have been outstanding more than 180 days. The company uses a collection agency to try to collect accounts that have been written off. During the year, accounts with a value of $3,200 reached the 180-day mark and were written off. The collection agency was able to collect $1,800 from customers whose accounts have been written off.

Based on the above information, the journal entries related to bad debt and the allowance for doubtful accounts would be as follows:

1. Allowance entry:

Bad Debts Expense	5,040	
Allowance for Doubtful Accounts		5,040
($140,000 × 80%) × 4.5% = $5,040		

2. Writeoff entry:

Allowance for Doubtful Accounts	3,200	
Accounts Receivable		3,200

3. Recovery entries:		
Accounts Receivable	1,800	
Allowance for Doubtful Accounts		1,800
Cash	1,800	
Accounts Receivable		1,800

Now, let's look at the impact of these entries on the related accounts. The T account information for the above scenario is shown in Exhibit 6-6.

Exhibit 6-6 The Allowance Method: T Accounts

STATEMENT OF FINANCIAL
POSITION ACCOUNTS

STATEMENT OF
INCOME ACCOUNTS

Accounts Receivable

Beginning balance	21,000		
Credit sales	112,000		
		101,000	Collections
		3,200	Writeoff
Recovery	1,800		
		1,800	Recovery
Ending balance	28,800		

Sales Revenue

	140,000

Allowance for Doubtful Accounts

		1,100	Beginning balance
		5,040	Allowance
Writeoff	3,200		
		1,800	Recovery
		4,740	Ending balance

Bad Debts Expense

5,040	

Based on the above transactions, accounts receivable would be presented as follows:

Accounts receivable (gross)	$28,800
Less: Allowance for doubtful accounts	4,740
Accounts receivable (net)	$24,060 → Carrying amount

The Conceptual Framework
ACCOUNTS RECEIVABLE AND FAITHFUL REPRESENTATION

Using the allowance for doubtful accounts ensures that accounts receivable are not overstated on the statement of financial position. The carrying amount of accounts receivable (that is, accounts receivable net of the allowance for doubtful accounts) represents management's best estimate of what it expects will be realized when these accounts are collected. As such, this treatment means that the asset, accounts receivable, is presented at the amount of cash flows expected to be realized from it.

HELPFUL HINT
The Allowance for Doubtful Accounts is a contra asset, and therefore it is a permanent account whose balance is cumulative and carried forward from one period to another. However, Bad Debts Expense (like all expenses) is a temporary account and therefore begins each period with a zero balance.

As noted previously, there are two methods used to estimate the amount of receivables that will not be collectible. These are the **percentage of credit sales method** and the **aging of accounts receivable method**. Each of these methods will be discussed in the following sections.

■ **LEARNING OBJECTIVE 8**
Identify the two methods of
estimating bad debts under
the allowance method and
describe the circumstances
for using each method.

How are bad debts estimated under the allowance method?

In order to use the allowance method of accounting for bad debts, companies must estimate the amount of bad debts expense at the end of each period. There are two methods that can be used to determine this amount:

1. **Percentage of credit sales method:** This method uses sales on account as the basis for the estimate. It is also known as the *statement of income method* because it is based on information from the statement of income.

2. **Aging of accounts receivable method:** This method uses an aging of the various receivables as the basis for the estimate. It is also known as the *statement of financial position method* because it is based on information from the statement of financial position.

Both are acceptable methods, so the choice is a management decision. It depends on whether management wishes to focus on income measurement (by matching expenses and revenues) or on asset valuation (by determining the net realizable value of the accounts receivable). It is also possible for companies to use a combination of the two methods. Some companies use the percentage of credit sales method when preparing their interim financial statements because it is quick and simple to apply and then use the aging method for their year-end financial statements because it involves a more thorough analysis of the company's accounts at year end.

Percentage of Credit Sales Method

The percentage of credit sales method of estimating bad debts is based on the assumption that the amount of bad debts expense is a function of the total sales made on credit. Bad debts expense is estimated by multiplying the credit sales for the period by the percentage that management estimates will be uncollectible. This percentage is normally based on the company's past collection experiences. In other words, historically, bad debts have averaged X% of credit sales. New businesses do not have this data and use industry data, such as data from Statistics Canada, or advice from an accounting firm to make their estimate.

Under this method:

$$\text{Bad Debts Expense} = \text{Sales on Account} \times \text{Historic \%}$$

As you can see, determining bad debts expense under this method is simple and quick, making it easy for companies to use. Exhibit 6-5 above illustrates this method, using a historical level of bad debts of 4.5% of credit sales.

Companies must adjust their percentage estimates to reflect the company's recent collection experience and changes in general economic conditions. If the company is experiencing more writeoffs than were estimated, the percentage should be increased for the next accounting period. Companies do not go back to prior periods to adjust the percentage or recalculate the bad debts expense. Therefore, an overestimate or underestimate in one period will be corrected by an adjustment to the percentage used in a subsequent period.

As mentioned at the beginning of this discussion, this basis of estimating bad debts emphasizes the matching of expenses with revenues. Accordingly, because the focus is on the amount of the expense rather than on the amount of the allowance, when the adjusting entry is made to record the bad debts expense and increase the allowance for doubtful accounts, *the existing balance in the allowance account is not considered*. The ending balance in the Allowance for Doubtful Accounts is therefore simply the net total of the various entries in that account. There is thus no predetermined percentage relationship between the ending balance in the allowance account and the related Accounts Receivable account, and it has nothing directly to do with the percentage that is used to estimate the bad debts expense.

Aging of Accounts Receivable Method

The aging of accounts receivable method uses a review of the length of time that the receivables have been outstanding as the basis for determining bad debts expense. As you might expect, the longer a receivable goes without being collected, generally the less likely it is to be collected. Just as companies have historic or industry data on the percentage of their credit sales that normally remain uncollected, they also have data on the collection experience for receivables of a certain age; that is, the percentage of customers who default on their accounts at each age threshold or grouping. These thresholds are determined by management, but the most common involve aging receivables into the following groupings (which are all based on the length of time that has transpired since the initial sale):

- Less than 30 days
- 31–60 days
- 61–90 days
- Greater than 90 days

Generally, the older the receivable, the higher the likelihood the company will be unable to collect it. Under this method, management looks at each customer's account balance and the individual sales that comprise each. The details of individual customer balances are found in the A/R subledger. Using this information, each customer's receivables balance is allocated to the various age groupings. For example, part of the balance may be from a recent sale, say, less than 30 days ago, while another portion of the balance may have been outstanding for 70 days.

Once all of the receivables in the A/R subledger have been allocated to the various age groupings, the total receivables balance for each age grouping is determined. The historical default rates for each age grouping are then applied to the related receivables balance. These amounts are added together, giving the company the total allowance for doubtful accounts, which should be established against the receivables balance. The bad debts expense for the period is then determined as the difference between the balance in the Allowance for Doubtful Accounts account before this analysis is prepared and the ending balance determined as a result of the analysis.

Let's look at an example of the aging of accounts receivable method, shown in Exhibit 6-7.

Exhibit 6-7 The Aging of Accounts Receivable Method

Assume that:
- The company has $12,000 in Accounts Receivable.
- The company's Allowance for Doubtful Accounts balance before the aging analysis is $800.

TAKE**5**

| | Customer's name | Total balance | Number of days the account receivable has been outstanding | | | | |
			1–30	31–60	61–90	91–120	121–180
Step 1: Prepare aging analysis using information from the A/R subledger.	T. E. Bansal	$2,700	$2,700				
	R. C. Lortz	3,000	1,850	$1,150			
	I. M. Owen	1,700		900	$800		
	A. Rashad	1,100				$1,100	
	O. L. Su	2,500	950	1,550			
	T. Woznow	1,000					$1,000
		$12,000	**$5,500**	**$3,600**	**$800**	**$1,100**	**$1,000**
Step 2: Apply historic rates for each age grouping. (Note how rates increase with age of A/R.)	Estimated percentage uncollectible			1%	5%	15%	35%	65%
	Total estimated writeoffs	**$1,390**	$55	$180	$120	$385	$650

Step 3: Total the amounts determined for each age grouping; the total is the required allowance for doubtful accounts.

Step 4: Determine the bad debts expense for the period. This is the amount that needs to be added to the balance in the Allowance for Doubtful Accounts account prior to the aging analysis to equal the amount determined in Step 3.

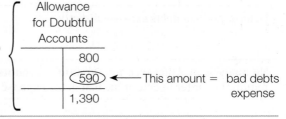

The allowance entry that would result from this example would be:

Bad Debts Expense	590	
Allowance for Doubtful Accounts		590

As it is a contra-asset account, Allowance for Doubtful Accounts would normally be expected to have a credit balance. However, it is possible for the account to have a debit balance during the year and it is important to be able to understand what could cause this and what it would tell us about the prior year's financial statements. Of the three key transactions discussed earlier in the chapter, only the writeoff entry results in a debit being recorded in Allowance for Doubtful Accounts. So, for there to be an overall debit balance in this account, a company would have had to write off more accounts than it had previously allowed for. In other words, writeoffs exceeded the amount of the allowance that had been established for doubtful accounts. If this was the case, then we know two things about the prior year's financial statements:

1. The bad debts expense for that year was understated (an insufficient allowance was established) and, therefore, net income was overstated.
2. The carrying amount of accounts receivable on the statement of financial position was overstated because an insufficient allowance was established.

Because bad debts expense is an accounting estimate, changes to it are treated prospectively; that is, going forward. Changes are not treated retrospectively; that is, changes are not made to the prior year's financial statements. If there is a debit balance in Allowance for Doubtful Accounts prior to the aging analysis, then you have to add that amount to the required ending balance (which will always be a credit) in order to get the bad debts expense for the period. However, if the balance before the aging analysis is a credit, you have to subtract that amount from the required ending balance (also a credit) in order to determine the amount of bad debts expense for the period. In either case, the end result is the same: the final balance in the Allowance for Doubtful Accounts is adjusted to the amount that the aging schedule indicates as the amount of accounts receivable that are expected to be written off as bad debts in the future.

If it is based on a careful aging analysis, the aging of accounts receivable method will normally result in a better approximation of the net realizable value of the receivables than the percentage of credit sales method. However, the matching of expenses with revenues may not be as good if significant amounts of customers' accounts have been outstanding for more than a year. This is because, under these circumstances, the bad debts expense for the current year will include amounts applicable to the sales of prior years.

The following table summarizes the key differences between the methods:

Percentage of Credit Sales Method	Aging of Accounts Receivable Method
Focuses on income measurement by using credit sales revenue as the basis for calculating the bad debts expense.	**Focuses on asset valuation** by using accounts receivable as the basis for calculating the allowance for doubtful accounts.
Emphasizes statement of income relationships by ensuring that the amount of expense is logically related to the amount of revenue.	**Emphasizes statement of financial position relationships** by ensuring that the balance in the contra-asset account is logically related to the balance in the asset account.
Determines bad debts expense directly.	**Determines the ending Allowance for Doubtful Accounts balance; then bad debts expense can be determined.**
No analysis of Allowance for Doubtful Accounts required in order to determine bad debts expense.	**Analysis of Allowance for Doubtful Accounts required in order to determine bad debts expense.**

What is the direct writeoff method and when is it acceptable to use it?

■ LEARNING OBJECTIVE 9
Explain the direct writeoff method of accounting for bad debts and when it is acceptable to use it.

As its name implies, the **direct writeoff method** involves companies recognizing bad debts expense only when they can directly write off a specific customer's account; that is, only when they know which customer is not going to pay. This means that companies must wait until an account has reached the age when the company's policy states that it should be written off (such as 180 days overdue) or when there is a specific indication (such as notification of a customer bankruptcy). Rather than recognizing an estimated amount for bad debts expense in the period of the sale and providing an allowance for future writeoffs, the direct writeoff method waits to recognize bad debts expense in the period in which the account is, in fact, uncollectible.

The direct writeoff method is often used by companies with an insignificant amount of bad debts. In this case, there would not be a significant or material (as discussed in Chapter 2) difference in the amount of bad debts expense regardless of which method is used.

Under the direct writeoff method, there is only a single journal entry. This is made when an account is written off and is as follows:

| Bad Debts Expense | XXX | |
| Accounts Receivable | | XXX |

Note that *no allowance for doubtful accounts is used with the direct writeoff method*, and the debit to Bad Debts Expense reduces net income in the period in which the writeoff occurs.

HELPFUL HINT
There are two main methods for dealing with bad debts: the allowance method and the direct writeoff method. If the allowance method is used, which it should be whenever bad debts are significant, there are two alternative approaches to estimating the amount of bad debts: the aging of accounts receivable method and the percentage of credit sales method.

The direct writeoff method is a simple way to account for bad debts. The company makes every reasonable effort to collect the account and, when it finally decides that an account is uncollectible, it records the entry to remove it from the accounting system. The problem with this method is that it results in the revenue being recognized in one accounting period and the associated bad debts expense being recorded in a later period. If bad debts are not significant, this mismatching will not be material and can be ignored. If bad debts are significant, however, this mismatching can distort the measurement of income enough for the direct writeoff method to be unacceptable. The appropriate method to use when bad debts are significant is the allowance method.

Finally, note that bad debts expense is somewhat different from other expenses. It is more like a reduction in a revenue account, since it represents revenue the company will never receive. In recognition of this, a few companies report it as a direct reduction of the sales revenue amount on the statement of income. The majority of companies, however, show bad debts as an operating expense rather than as a reduction of revenues.

 Ethics in Accounting

We have seen that bad debts expense is a function of management estimates. Management determines the percentages used to calculate bad debts expense under both the aging and percentage of credit sales methods. This provides management with an opportunity to manage earnings. They could minimize bad debts expense if they were motivated to maximize earnings or they could overstate the percentages used if they were motivated to minimize earnings. Bad debts expense is normally not significant relative to total revenues, so any manipulations would not have a large effect on net income. Nevertheless, it is an area of concern. The Canada Revenue Agency does not allow companies to deduct bad debts calculated using the allowance method. It essentially requires companies to follow the direct writeoff method for tax purposes. You will learn more about this in taxation courses you may take in the future.

■ LEARNING OBJECTIVE 10
Explain alternative ways in
which companies shorten
their cash-to-cash cycle.

How do companies shorten their cash-to-cash cycle?

As discussed in Chapter 5, companies are always looking for ways to shorten their cash-to-cash cycle. This cycle is the time between when companies pay out the cash to purchase goods or raw materials for manufacturing products until those goods are ultimately paid for by the customer. Selling to customers on account, as opposed to cash sales, actually lengthens this cycle because companies normally provide these customers with a 30-day credit period. During this time, the receivable is an inactive asset in that the company is not generating any return on it.

Exhibit 6-8 illustrates the cash-to-cash cycle.

Exhibit 6-8 The Cash-to-Cash Cycle

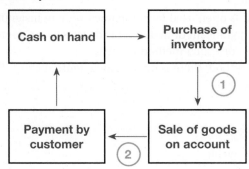

① Goods may be on hand for 30–90 days

② Customer may have 30 or more days of free credit

Companies look for ways to shorten the cash-to-cash cycle while still enjoying the benefits of selling on account, such as increasing sales and remaining competitive. One of the ways that they do this is to accept credit card purchases. By doing this, it is the credit card companies (financial institutions) that have to wait the 30 days to be paid, not the company making the sale. The sellers are usually paid within a day or two, depending upon their arrangements with the credit card company. These arrangements also result in the credit card company being responsible for many of the costs associated with credit sales, including credit granting, collections, and bad debts. In exchange for absorbing these costs, the credit card companies charge a fee to the merchants making the sales. This fee varies depending upon a number of factors, including transaction volume, but it is normally between 1% and 5%. The fee is known as the **credit card discount**. These fees are the reason why many smaller merchants have a minimum sales amount before they allow customers to use a credit card and why some smaller merchants don't accept credit cards at all.

Let's look at an example of how a company would record a credit card transaction, including the related fee. If a company made a $3,500 credit card sale and the credit card discount was 3%, the journal entry would be as follows:

Accounts Receivable—Credit Card Company	3,395	
Credit Card Expense	105	
Sales Revenue		3,500

Then, when the company receives payment from the credit card company a day or two later, the entry is the normal cash collection entry. If the company has an arrangement whereby the credit card sales are paid within the same day, then the debit to Accounts Receivable would be replaced with a debit to Cash.

Another way that companies try to shorten the cash-to-cash cycle is to motivate their customers to pay their accounts receivable before the end of the 30-day credit period. They often do this by offering a **sales discount**. While these vary across industries, a fairly typical one is illustrated in Exhibit 6-9, which uses the common shorthand for sales terms, including "n" for *net*.

Exhibit 6-9 Sales Discounts

2% discount   if you pay within 10 days, then take a   otherwise, the net amount is due within 30 days

Companies looking to shorten their cash-to-cash cycle can also sell their accounts receivable to another company, typically a financial institution. This process is known as **factoring** and is becoming increasingly common in Canada. While the journal entries for factoring are beyond the scope of an introductory accounting course, it is important that you understand some of the terms related to factoring transactions. The company purchasing the accounts receivable is known as the **factor** and it may purchase the receivable **with recourse** or **without recourse**. If the receivables are purchased with recourse, then the factor is able to come back to the seller for payment if it is unable to collect the receivable. If the receivables are purchased without recourse, then the factor will bear the loss of any receivable it is unable to collect. Obviously, the factor will pay less than face value for the receivables, because the difference is how it makes its money on the transaction. The factor would also pay less if the transaction was on a without recourse basis than if it was on a with recourse basis.

For Example

According to its 2013 annual report, Canadian food processor **Maple Leaf Foods Inc.** uses "very limited recourse accounts receivable securitization programs as (an) additional source of financing." At December 31, 2013, the company had $166.4 million in trade receivables being serviced under these programs. "In return for the sale of its trade receivables, the company will receive cash of $50.9 million and notes receivable (non-interest bearing) in the amount of $115.5 million." These arrangements enabled the company to receive approximately 30% of the cash value of these receivables sooner than if it had waited to collect them.

FINANCIAL STATEMENT ANALYSIS

What is liquidity and how is it assessed?

As discussed in Chapter 1, and earlier in this chapter, liquidity refers to the company's ability to convert assets into cash so that liabilities can be paid. An important part of the analysis of short-term liquidity comes from considering the short-term assets on the statement of financial position. There are two very common ratios that provide quantitative measures of short-term liquidity: the current ratio and the quick ratio.

■ LEARNING OBJECTIVE 11
Explain the concept of liquidity. Calculate the current ratio, quick ratio, accounts receivable turnover ratio, and average collection period ratio and assess the results.

Current Ratio

The **current ratio**, which is also known as the **working capital ratio**, is measured by comparing the current assets with the current liabilities. It is calculated as follows:

$$\text{Current ratio} = \frac{\text{Current assets}}{\text{Current liabilities}}$$

Remember that current assets are those that are going to be converted into cash within the next year or operating cycle, and that current liabilities are going to require the use of cash within the next year or operating cycle. As such, if this ratio is greater than 1, then it means that the company has more than $1 in current assets for every $1 of current liabilities. As such, it indicates that the company should be able to meet its expected obligations over the coming year. This ratio can vary significantly, depending on the type of industry and the types of assets and liabilities that are considered current. As such, comparing current ratios across industries may not be relevant, whereas comparing the ratio year to year for the same company would be relevant. For effective analysis, it is important to be aware of industry norms and to analyze data across multiple periods.

We can calculate the current ratios for **Danier Leather** and **Le Château** as follows.

Danier's Current Ratio:

$$= \frac{39,970}{10,790} = 3.70$$

Le Château's Current Ratio:

$$= \frac{137,173}{62,284} = 2.20$$

This tells us that Danier had $3.70 in current assets for every $1 in current liabilities, while Le Château had $2.20 in current assets for every $1 of current liabilities. Both companies appear to be well positioned to meet their liabilities as they come due over the next year. In terms of which company is in better position, the answer is not as simple as looking at which company has the highest ratio. If the ratio is too high, then the company may not be managing its assets effectively: it may have too much cash on hand, significant receivables, or overly high levels of inventory. Answering this question requires an analysis of the company's specific current assets.

Quick Ratio

One problem with using the current ratio as a measure of short-term liquidity is that some current assets may be much less liquid than others. In other words, they may take considerable time to become cash. An example is inventory, some of which may be on hand for a number of months before it can be sold and then it may take another month or more before the related receivable is collected. Some current assets may never become cash, such as prepaid expenses. In the case of manufacturing companies, the inventory may be even less liquid as it will often include raw materials or partially manufactured goods. As a result, if a company has significant levels of inventory requiring lengthy sales periods, then the current ratio will not adequately measure the company's short-term liquidity.

Another ratio, the **quick ratio** (also known as the **acid test ratio**), can be used to assess short-term liquidity. It differs from the current ratio because the numerator only includes the **quick assets**, which are the company's current assets less inventory and prepaid expenses. The quick ratio takes into account the shortcomings of the current ratio. The quick ratio is calculated as follows:

$$\text{Quick ratio} = \frac{\text{Current assets} - \text{Inventory} - \text{Prepaid expenses}}{\text{Current liabilities}}$$

As with the current ratio, the quick ratio gives the user the number of dollars of quick assets that the company has with which to pay each dollar of its current liabilities. Again, this ratio can vary significantly depending on the type of industry. Just as with the current ratio, the quick ratio can vary significantly across industries. Also, analyzing the ratio across multiple periods provides the most meaningful context for interpreting changes.

Let's again compare the results of Danier Leather with Le Château; this time, to get a better understanding of the quick ratio.

Danier's Quick Ratio:

$$= \frac{39,970 - 21,721 - 643}{10,790} = 1.63$$

Le Château's Quick Ratio:

$$= \frac{137,173 - 124,878 - 2,292}{62,284} = 0.16$$

This tells us that Danier had $1.63 in quick assets for every $1 in current liabilities, while Le Château had only $0.16 in quick assets for every $1 of current liabilties. As such, Danier is well positioned to meet its liabilities as they come due over the next year, whereas Le Château would only be able to meet just over a quarter of its liabilities over the next year based on its quick assets. This would mean that it is critical that Le Château be able to sell through its inventory and collect these sales in a timely manner (which would normally not be an issue in a retail environment). If this is the case, there are no issues, as we have seen from the current ratio that the company would be able to meet its short-term obligations.

Again, it may be that Danier's solid quick ratio is the result of the company having too much cash on hand or too high a level of receivables. An analysis of the company's specific quick assets would be needed to determine if there were any issues related to company's asset management.

The current and quick ratios are two of the ratios that are often analyzed by the company's lenders, such as banks. Lenders are understandably concerned with the borrower's ability to service their debt, including repaying the portion of the loan due within the next year. The current and quick ratios allow lenders to assess debt-servicing ability. Lenders will often build current ratio and quick ratio–related **covenants** into their lending agreements. Covenants will be discussed in greater detail in Chapter 10, but they are essentially minimum conditions set by the lender which, if not met, can trigger immediate repayment of the loan. Lenders may set minimum current and quick ratios that must be met and it is important for financial statement users to be aware of this.

 ## Ethics in Accounting

Because ratios can be critical, especially if related covenants are in place in lending agreements, there is the potential for them to be manipulated by management. For example, it is possible for a company to manipulate the current ratio at year end.

For example, consider a company that has $10,000 in current assets (consisting of $3,000 in cash and $7,000 in inventory) and $5,000 in current liabilities just before the end of the year. Its current ratio would be 2 ($10,000 ÷ $5,000). Suppose that the company uses all its $3,000 in cash to pay off $3,000 worth of current liabilities at year end. This greatly improves the current ratio, increasing it to 3.5 ($7,000 ÷ $2,000), and the company looks more liquid. Notice, however, that the company is actually less liquid. In fact, it is very illiquid in the short term because it has no cash, and must sell its inventory and wait until it collects on those sales before it will have any cash to pay its bills. In this case, the current ratio is deceptive. This shows how important it is to analyze multiple ratios. In this case, looking at a second short-term liquidity ratio, the quick ratio, would provide more insight into the company's liquidity.

How effective has the company been at collecting its accounts receivable?

Accounts Receivable Turnover Ratio

As previously mentioned, accounts receivable are generally non–interest-bearing for at least 30 days. During this period, the asset is essentially inactive: it is not generating any return for the company. As discussed, to lessen the impacts of this inactivity, companies take various steps to shorten their cash-to-cash cycle; that is, reducing the length of time it takes until cash returns to the company in the form of customer payments. The sooner a company can collect its receivables, the sooner the cash can be used in the business to settle payables, purchase inventory, and so on. The effectiveness with which these collection efforts are taking place can be assessed using the **accounts receivable turnover ratio**. This ratio is calculated by dividing the credit sales (because cash sales do not give rise to receivables) for the period by the average accounts receivable, as follows:

$$\text{Accounts receivable turnover ratio} = \frac{\text{Credit sales}}{\text{Average accounts receivable*}}$$

*Average accounts receivable = (Accounts receivable at the beginning of the year + Accounts receivable at the end of the year)/2

In this context, *turnover* means how often the accounts receivable are turned over, or how often they are collected in full and replaced by new accounts. This is the first of the asset turnover ratios we will explore in the text. A good rule of thumb when thinking about asset turnover is that a higher number is better than a lower number. In other words, we would consider a company that collects its receivables more frequently than another to be doing a better job.

Calculating this ratio from financial statement data usually requires you to assume that all the sales are credit sales. If the analyst has more detailed information about the composition of sales, then some adjustment can be made in the numerator to include only the sales on account. In addition, information in the financial statements may indicate that not all receivables are from customers. Therefore, a more sophisticated calculation would include only customer receivables in the denominator, as only these relate to the credit sales figure in the numerator.

Average Collection Period

Once you have determined the accounts receivable turnover ratio for a company, it is a simple step to calculate the average length of time, in days, that it takes the company to collect its receivables. This is known as the **average collection period** and is determined as follows:

$$\text{Average collection period} = \frac{365 \text{ days}}{\text{Accounts receivable turnover}}$$

Retailers like Danier Leather and Le Château typically have very low levels of receivables because they accept credit card payments rather than granting credit to their customers directly. As such, we will look at the results of **Ten Peaks Coffee Company Inc.**, a British Columbia–based specialty coffee company, to get a better understanding of the accounts receivable turnover and average collection period ratios. Ten Peaks is a premium green coffee decaffeinator and also provides a range of green coffee handling and storage services. The company sells its products to retail coffee houses. Like Gildan Activewear, Ten Peaks is therefore a wholesaler, not a retailer, so its accounts receivable are with businesses, not consumers. Let's look at Ten Peaks' A/R turnover ratio and average collection period ratio.

2013 A/R Turnover Ratio:

$$= \frac{53,873}{(3,962 + 4,972)/2} = 12.1$$

2012 A/R Turnover Ratio:

$$= \frac{59,301}{(4,198 + 3,962)/2} = 14.5$$

2013 Average Collection Period Ratio:

$= 365/12.1 = 30.2$ days

2012 Average Collection Period Ratio:

$= 365/14.6 = 25.2$ days

From this we can see that Ten Peaks' receivables turn over just about monthly, which tells us that the company's receivables are not outstanding for long. In fact, the company's average collection period in 2013 was 30.2 days. On a comparative basis, we can see that the time taken to collect its receivables has increased by 5 days from 2012, thereby extending the company's cash-to-cash cycle.

Another way to analyze the performance of accounts receivable collection is to compare a company's average collection period with the company's normal credit terms. If the company's normal credit terms are 30 days, then you would expect that the average collection period would be 30 days or fewer. This analysis is only possible if the details of a company's normal credit terms are known. This is not something that is generally disclosed in the financial statements or annual report.

SUMMARY

1. **Explain why cash and accounts receivable are of significance to users.**

   - As a company's most liquid assets, cash and accounts receivable provide the resources necessary to meet immediate, short-term financial obligations.

   - Knowing a company's cash and receivables balances enables users to assess a company's liquidity (its ability to meet its obligations in the short term).

2. **Describe the valuation methods for cash.**

   - Cash includes the cash physically on hand, on deposit at financial institutions, and any cash equivalents.

   - Cash equivalents are amounts that can be converted into known amounts of cash and must be maturing within three months of the acquisition date.

   - Cash is measured at its face value at the reporting date, with any foreign currency translated into Canadian dollars using the rate of exchange at the statement of financial position date.

3. **Explain the main principles of internal control.**

   - An internal control system includes (1) physical controls (locks, alarms, cash registers); (2) assignment of responsibilities (making one person responsible for each task); (3) separation of duties (separation of transaction authorization, recording, and asset custody); (4) independent verification (either internal or external); and (5) documentation (receipts, invoices, and so on).

4. **Explain the purpose of bank reconciliations, including their preparation and the treatment of related adjustments.**

   - A bank reconciliation ensures that any differences between the accounting records for cash and the bank statement are identified and explained.

   - The reconciliation adjusts the bank balance for items that the company is aware of but the bank is not (outstanding cheques and outstanding deposits). It also adjusts the company's cash balance for items that appear on the bank statement that have not yet been reflected in the company's records (such as bank charges, interest, and cheque returns due to non-sufficient funds).

   - Journal entries must be made for each adjustment required to the company's cash balance in order to adjust the cash balance in the general ledger.

5. **Explain why companies sell on account and identify the additional costs that result from this decision.**

   - Companies sell on account to increase total sales, remain competitive, and generate additional revenue (interest).

   - When selling on account, companies incur additional costs, including wages for the credit-granting function, wages for the collections function, and bad debts expense.

6. **Describe the valuation methods for accounts receivable.**

   - Accounts receivable are reflected on the statement of financial position at their carrying amount, which is equal to the full amount of all receivables less the allowance for doubtful accounts.

   - The allowance for doubtful accounts represents management's best estimate of the total accounts receivable that it expects it will be unable to collect.

7. **Explain the allowance method of accounting for bad debts.**

   - The allowance method involves management estimating the amount of receivables that they expect they will be unable to collect. The estimated bad debts expense is recorded in the same period in which the credit sales were reported rather than waiting to record the bad debt until the customers fail to pay.

   - Since the specific customers who will not pay are unknown at the time the bad debts expense is estimated, no adjustment can be made to the Accounts Receivable account. Instead, the amount is recorded in Allowance for Doubtful Accounts, a contra-asset account.

   - Under the allowance method, journal entries are required to initially record the bad debts expense, to record the writeoff of specific receivables once they are known, and to record the recovery of any receivables that have previously been written off.

8. **Identify the two methods of estimating bad debts under the allowance method and describe the circumstances for using each method.**

   - The two methods of estimating bad debts under the allowance method are: the percentage of credit sales method and the aging of accounts receivable method.

   - With the percentage of credit sales, the estimated bad debts expense is determined using a percentage (historic or industry average) of credit sales revenue. No analysis of the allowance for doubtful accounts is required to determine bad debts expense.

   - With the aging of accounts receivable method, an estimate of uncollectible accounts is made using a percentage (historic or industry average), with bad debts expense equal to the amount required to adjust the Allowance for Doubtful Accounts balance to this estimated total. An analysis of allowance for doubtful accounts is required to determine bad debts expense.

9. **Explain the direct writeoff method of accounting for bad debts and when it is acceptable to use it.**

   - Under the direct writeoff method, there is no accounting for bad debts expense until a specific customer's account is written off. As such, an allowance for doubtful accounts is not needed.

   - This method is not acceptable under accounting standards in Canada, but it is sometimes used by companies with an insignificant amount of bad debts because the difference between it and the allowance method would not result in material differences.

10. **Explain alternative ways in which companies shorten their cash-to-cash cycle.**

    - One way that companies shorten their cash-to-cash cycle is to accept credit cards rather than offering their customers credit directly. The company is able to collect much more quickly from the credit card companies than it would from customers.

    - Another way that companies shorten the cash-to-cash cycle is to offer sales discounts to encourage customers who have purchased on account to pay their accounts early. A common sales discount is "2/10, n/30," which entitles customers to a 2% discount if they pay they account within 10 days; otherwise, the net amount is due within 30 days.

    - Some companies also factor (sell) their accounts receivable to a financial institution (known as a *factor*) in order to shorten their cash-to-cash cycle. The receivables may be sold with recourse (the company remains responsible for their ultimate collection) or without recourse (the factor assumes collection responsibility).

11. **Explain the concept of liquidity. Calculate the current ratio, quick ratio, accounts receivable turnover ratio, and average collection period ratio and assess the results.**

    - Liquidity refers to a company's ability to convert assets into cash so that liabilities can be paid.

    - The current ratio is equal to current assets divided by current liabilities and is a measure of the amount of current assets the company has relative to each dollar of current liabilities.

    - The quick ratio is a stricter measure of liquidity than the current ratio. This is because it is determined without including inventory and prepaid expenses. Specifically, the ratio is equal to current assets less inventory and prepaids divided by current liabilities.

    - The accounts receivable turnover ratio is equal to credit sales divided by average accounts receivable. It measures how often accounts receivable are collected in full during the period.

    - The average collection period is the average length of time, in days, that it takes a company to collect its receivables. It is calculated by dividing 365 by the accounts receivable turnover ratio.

KEY TERMS

Accounts receivable (269)
Accounts receivable turnover
  ratio (289)
Acid test ratio (288)
Aging of accounts receivable
  method (281)
Allowance for doubtful accounts (277)
Allowance method (277)
Audit trail (271)
Average collection period (290)
Bad debts expense (276)
Bank reconciliation (271)
Carrying amount (277)

Cash (269)
Cash equivalent (270)
Collusion (271)
Control account (277)
Covenant (289)
Credit card discount (286)
Current ratio (287)
Direct writeoff method (285)
Electronic funds transfer (EFT) (271)
Factor (287)
Factoring (287)
Internal control system (270)
Liquidity (269)

Percentage of credit sales
  method (281)
Quick assets (288)
Quick ratio (288)
Recovery (280)
Sales discount (286)
Subledger (277)
Uncollectible accounts (269)
With recourse (287)
Without recourse (287)
Working capital ratio (287)
Writeoff (279)

ABBREVIATIONS USED

A/R   Accounts Receivable
EFT   Electronic funds transfer
G/L   General ledger

SYNONYMS

Accounts receivable | Trade receivables
Aging of accounts receivable method | Statement of
  financial position method
Bad debts expense | Doubtful accounts expense
Current ratio | Working capital ratio
Percentage of credit sales method | Statement of
  income method
Quick ratio | Acid test ratio
Subledger | Subsidiary ledger
Uncollectible accounts | Doubtful accounts | Bad debts

CHAPTER END REVIEW PROBLEM 1

During 2016, Kumar Company sold $150,000 of goods on credit and collected $135,000 from its customers on account. The company started the period with a balance of $15,000 in Accounts Receivable and a balance in the Allowance for Doubtful Accounts of $450. During 2016, Kumar wrote off $2,725 of accounts receivable. Kumar estimates that 2% of its credit sales will ultimately be uncollectible.

Required:
  a. Show the journal entries that would be made during the year that affect Accounts Receivable and the Allowance for Doubtful Accounts. Then, calculate the amount of bad debts expense for 2016 and make the journal entry to record it.
  b. What amount(s) would be reported on the statement of financial position at the end of 2016 regarding accounts receivable?
  c. Now assume that, instead of using the percentage of credit sales method to estimate its bad debts expense, Kumar Company performed an aging analysis of its accounts receivable at the end of 2016 and determined that it should have an allowance for doubtful accounts of $1,000. How would this affect your answers to parts "a" and "b" above?

CHAPTER END REVIEW PROBLEM 2

Big Rock Brewery Inc. is a Calgary-based producer of all-natural craft beers and cider that are sold in nine provinces and three territories in Canada. Exhibits 6-10A and 6-10B contain excerpts from the company's 2013 financial statements.

Required:
Using the information in the exhibits, calculate the following ratios for 2013 and 2012 and briefly comment on whether these ratios have improved or worsened:
  a. Current ratio
  b. Quick ratio
  c. Accounts receivable turnover ratio (Note: Assume all sales were on account. Also, at December 30, 2011, the company's accounts receivable were $2,788 thousand.)
  d. Average collection period

STRATEGIES FOR SUCCESS

▶ Bear in mind that the allowance method recognizes bad debts expense at the end of each period, when adjusting entries are made, and provides an allowance for accounts that will be written off. Therefore, when writeoffs occur, they are debited to the allowance account rather than to the expense account.

▶ Remember that the percentage of credit sales approach applies the estimated percentage to the credit sales to determine the appropriate amount of bad debts expense. When the adjusting journal entry is made to record this, the existing balance in Allowance for Doubtful Accounts is ignored.

▶ In the aging of accounts receivable approach, the aging analysis indicates the appropriate amount of allowance for doubtful accounts. The existing balance in Allowance for Doubtful Accounts must be considered to determine the correct amount for the adjusting journal entry.

| EXHIBIT 6-10A | BIG ROCK BREWERY INC.'S 2013 CONSOLIDATED STATEMENTS OF COMPREHENSIVE INCOME |

BIG ROCK BREWERY INC.
Consolidated Statements of Comprehensive Income
(In thousands of Canadian dollars, except per share amounts)

FINANCIAL
STATEMENTS

	Year ended	
	December 30, 2013	December 30, 2013
Net revenue (Notes 3.2 and 4)	$41,587	$46,057
Cost of sales (Notes 5 and 24)	20,260	21,149
Gross profit	21,327	24,908
Expenses		
Selling expenses (Notes 6 and 23)	12,910	13,987
General and administrative (Notes 7 and 24)	4,821	4,945
Depreciation and amortization	314	358
Operating expenses	18,045	19,290
Operating profit	3,282	5,618
Finance costs (Note 8)	9	93
Other income	286	351
Other expenses	109	147
Income before income taxes	3,450	5,729
Current income tax expense (Note 9)	2,485	426
Deferred income tax expense (recovery) (Note 9)	(1,586)	1,168
Net income and comprehensive income for the period	$ 2,551	$ 4,135

| EXHIBIT 6-10B | BIG ROCK BREWERY INC.'S 2013 CONSOLIDATED STATEMENTS OF FINANCIAL POSITION |

BIG ROCK BREWERY INC.
Consolidated Statements of Financial Position
(In thousands of Canadian dollars)

FINANCIAL
STATEMENTS

	December 30, 2013	December 30, 2012
ASSETS		
Non-current assets		
Property, plant and equipment (Note 11)	$ 35,142	$ 35,277
Intangible assets (Note 12)	108	128
	35,250	35,405
Current		
Inventories (Note 13)	2,983	3,892
Accounts receivable (Notes 14 and 22)	1,353	2,358
Prepaid expenses and other (Note 15)	754	364
Cash	2,317	4,281
	7,407	10,895
Total assets	$ 42,657	$ 46,300
LIABILITIES AND SHAREHOLDERS' EQUITY		
EQUITY		
Shareholders' capital (Note 16)	$100,109	$ 100,109
Contributed surplus (Notes 16 and 17)	892	701
Accumulated deficit	(71,043)	(68,739)
	29,958	32,071

continued

EXHIBIT 6-10B	BIG ROCK BREWERY INC.'S 2013 CONSOLIDATED STATEMENTS OF FINANCIAL POSITION (continued)

BIG ROCK BREWERY INC.
Consolidated Statements of Financial Position
(In thousands of Canadian dollars)

	December 30, 2013	December 30, 2012
LIABILITIES		
Non-current		
Long term debt (Notes 18 and 22)	—	1,342
Share-based payments (Note 17)	687	238
Deferred income taxes (Note 9)	4,745	6,331
	5,432	7,911
Current		
Accounts payable and accrued liabilities (Notes 19 and 22)	4,100	3,978
Dividends payable (Notes 20 and 22)	1,214	1,214
Current portion of long-term debt (Notes 18 and 22)	—	700
Current taxes payable (Note 9)	1,953	426
	7,267	6,318
Commitments (Note 26)		
Total liabilities and shareholders' equity	$ 42,657	$ 46,300

Suggested Solution to Chapter End Review Problem 1

a. The following journal entries would be made during the year by Kumar Company:

Accounts Receivable	150,000	
Sales Revenue		150,000
Cash	135,000	
Accounts Receivable		135,000
Allowance for Doubtful Accounts	2,725	
Accounts Receivable		2,725
Bad Debts Expense	3,000	
Allowance for Doubtful Accounts		3,000
(150,000 × 2% = 3,000)		

b. The statement of financial position at the end of 2016 would show the following:

Accounts receivable	$27,275*
Less: Allowance for doubtful accounts	725**
Net carrying value of accounts receivable	$26,550
Or	
Accounts receivable (net)	$26,550

*Beginning balance $15,000 + Credit sales $150,000 − Cash collections $135,000 − Writeoffs $2,725

**Beginning balance $450 − Writeoffs $2,725 + Adjustment $3,000

c. The first three journal entries would not be affected; they would be exactly the same as shown above. The calculation of the bad debts expense would differ, though, and requires that you first determine the balance in Allowance for Doubtful Accounts before adjustment, as follows:

Beginning balance $450 (credit) − Write-offs $2,725 (debit) = Balance before adjustment $2,275 (debit)

This must then be compared with the required allowance, as estimated by the aging analysis of the accounts receivable outstanding at year end. As stated in the problem, this indicated that an allowance of $1,000 was required. In order to adjust the existing balance in the allowance account (a debit of $2,275) to the required balance (a credit of $1,000), an adjustment must be made that credits the allowance account by $3,275 and debits Bad Debts Expense by the same amount. The year-end adjustment would therefore be as follows:

Bad Debts Expense	3,275	
Allowance for Doubtful Accounts		3,275

The statement of financial position at the end of 2016 would show the following:

Accounts receivable	$27,275
Less: Allowance for doubtful accounts	1,000
Net carrying value of accounts receivable	$26,275
Or	
Accounts receivable (net)	$26,275

Suggested Solution to Chapter End Review Problem 2

Current ratio:

2013: $\dfrac{7,407}{7,267} = 1.02$

2012: $\dfrac{10,895}{6,318} = 1.72$

Big Rock's current ratio has decreased significantly in 2013, as the company has $1.02 in current assets for every $1 in current liabilities, which is down from $1.72 in the prior year. Based on this, the company can meet its current liabilities as they come due.

Quick ratio:

2013: $\dfrac{7,407 - 2,983 - 754}{7,267} = 0.51$

2012: $\dfrac{10,895 - 3,892 - 364}{6,318} = 1.05$

Big Rock's quick ratio has decreased significantly in 2013, as the company has $0.51 in quick assets for every $1 in current liabilities, which is down from $1.05 in the prior year. Based on this information, it is critical for the company to sell its inventory and collect its receivables to meet current liabilities.

Accounts receivable turnover ratio:

2013: $\dfrac{41,587}{(2,358 + 1,353)/2} = 22.4$

2012: $\dfrac{46,057}{(2,788 + 2,358)/2} = 17.9$

Big Rock's A/R turnover ratio improved in 2013, as the company turned over its receivables 22.4 times during the year, which is up from 17.9 in 2012. This means that cash is being collected quicker than in the prior year.

Average collection period for accounts receivable:

2013: $\dfrac{365}{22.4} = 16.3$ days

2012: $\dfrac{365}{17.9} = 20.4$ days

Big Rock's average collection period was 20.4 days in 2013, which is four days quicker than in the prior year, so this was an improvement. From this, we can see that the company's customers normally pay their accounts just over two weeks from the date of sale.

STRATEGIES FOR SUCCESS

▶ Remember that the quick ratio includes only the most liquid current assets. Inventories and prepaid expenses should be excluded.

▶ In any ratio that involves a comparison between amounts from the statement of income and amounts from the statement of financial position (such as the accounts receivable turnover ratio), the statement of financial position amounts should, if possible, be averages.

ASSIGNMENT MATERIAL

Discussion Questions

DQ6-1 Explain why internal control is so important, especially for cash. Describe three types of internal control measures that organizations can put in place.

DQ6-2 Identify the special challenge that small organizations face when implementing effective internal control systems.

DQ6-3 Identify three of the common principles of internal control discussed in the chapter. Using a pharmacy as an example, give one example of how a pharmacy applies each of the three principles you have identified.

DQ6-4 Using a movie theatre as an example, identify three of the five principles of internal control. For each internal control principle you identify, give one example of a control that a movie theatre uses.

DQ6-5 Identify three of the common principles of internal control discussed in the chapter. Using your campus bookstore as an example, give one example of how it applies each of the three principles you have identified.

DQ6-6 Explain the purpose of a bank reconciliation and how it relates to internal control.

DQ6-7 Explain, in your own words, why there might be a difference between the cash balance per a company's general ledger and the closing balance on its monthly bank statement for the same account.

DQ6-8 When a company is thinking about making sales on account, what are some of the additional costs it needs to consider?

DQ6-9 Explain, in your own words, why a company may decide to accept credit cards rather than extend credit directly to its customers.

DQ6-10 Explain, in your own words, why a company needs to use the Allowance for Doubtful Accounts account when recording its bad debts expense each period.

DQ6-11 What is an "allowance for doubtful accounts"? Your explanation should include what type of account it is, why it is created, and how it is used.

DQ6-12 Identify two methods for estimating uncollectible accounts under the allowance method of accounting for bad debts. Outline how to implement each of these methods.

DQ6-13 Describe and compare the allowance method and the direct writeoff method for determining bad debts expense.

DQ6-14 Why is the allowance method of accounting for bad debts more consistent with accounting standards than the direct writeoff method? Under what circumstances is the direct writeoff method acceptable?

DQ6-15 Explain what it means if Allowance for Doubtful Accounts has a debit balance prior to the year-end bad debts entry.

DQ6-16 Identify and explain two ways that companies can shorten their cash-to-cash cycle related to accounts receivable.

DQ6-17 Describe two ratios that measure current liquidity, and compare the information they provide. Which measure is more likely to produce the lowest result for most companies? Why is this the case?

DQ6-18 Describe a ratio that can be used to assess the management of accounts receivable, and explain what information it provides.

DQ6-19 When calculating the accounts receivable turnover ratio, is a higher number generally better than a lower number? Explain your rationale.

Application Problems

AP6-1 (Preparation of bank reconciliation)

On May 31, 2016, JB Games Ltd. received its bank statement from the East Coast Savings Bank showing that JB had a balance of $12,200. The company's general ledger showed a cash balance of $8,600 at that date. A comparison of the bank statement and the accounting records revealed the following information:

1. A cheque from one of JB's customers in the amount of $1,120 that had been deposited during the last week of May was returned with the bank statement as NSF.
2. Bank service charges for the month were $55.
3. The company had written and mailed out cheques with a value of $4,235 that had not yet cleared the bank.
4. Cheque #791, which was a payment for advertising expenses of $230, was incorrectly recorded in the general ledger as $320.
5. During the month, the bank collected a $2,000 note receivable plus the outstanding interest on behalf of JB. The note was interest-bearing at 5% per annum and had been outstanding for one year.
6. The cash receipts for May 31 amounted to $1,650 and had been deposited in the night drop slot at the bank on the evening of May 31. These were not reflected on the bank statement for May.

Required:
    a. Prepare the bank reconciliation for JB at May 31, 2016.
    b. Prepare any journal entries necessary as a result of the bank reconciliation prepared in part "a."

AP6-2 (Preparation of bank reconciliation)

Infinity Emporium Company received the monthly statement for its bank account, showing a balance of $66,744 on August 31. The balance in the Cash account in the company's accounting system at that date was $71,952. The company's accountant reviewed the statement and the company's accounting records and noted the following.

1. After comparing the cheques written by the company and those deducted from the bank account in August, the accountant determined that all six cheques (totalling $6,180) that had been outstanding at the end of July were processed by the bank in August. However, five cheques written in August, totalling $4,560, were outstanding on August 31.
2. A review of the deposits showed that a deposit made by the company on July 31 for $11,532 was recorded by the bank on August 1, and an August 31 deposit of $12,240 was recorded in the company's accounting system but had not yet been recorded by the bank.
3. The August bank statement also showed:
   - a service fee of $24,
   - a customer's cheque in the amount of $204 that had been returned NSF,

- a bank loan payment of $900, which included interest of $130, that the bank had deducted automatically, and
- a customer's note for $3,500 plus $100 interest on the note that the bank had collected for Infinity Emporium and deposited in its account.

Required:

a. Prepare a bank reconciliation as at August 31. (Hint: Items that were outstanding last month but have been processed this month should no longer affect the bank reconciliation, since both the company and the bank now have them recorded.)

b. How much cash does Infinity Emporium actually have available as at August 31?

c. Explain how the adjusted (corrected) balance of cash, as determined by the bank reconciliation, could be higher than both the balance shown on the bank statement and the balance shown in the company's Cash account.

d. Prepare adjusting journal entries to record all the necessary adjustments to bring the Cash account to its correct balance.

AP6-3 (Placement of items on bank reconciliation)

Henri Heinzl is preparing a bank reconciliation for his business, Heinzl Company.

Required:

Indicate whether each of the following items would be added to the bank balance, deducted from the bank balance, added to the cash account balance in the general ledger (G/L), or deducted from the cash account balance in the general ledger (G/L). If any of the items do not have to be included in the bank reconciliation, explain why.

a. A deposit of $2,310 at the end of the previous month was processed by the bank on the first day of this month.

b. A $683 cheque written by Heinzl Company was erroneously processed through its account as $638 by the bookkeeper.

c. The bank statement showed a service charge of $15 for the month. Heinzl Company has not yet recorded this charge in its cash account.

d. A customer deposited an amount owed to Heinzl Company directly into its bank account. Henri had not recorded it yet.

e. Three cheques written by Heinzl Company totalling $6,842 have not yet been processed by the bank.

f. The bank lists a customer cheque that was received by Heinzl and deposited in the company's bank account as NSF.

g. A deposit of $1,280 made by Heinzl Company was recorded by the bank as $1,290. Heinzl Company had made an error in counting the money before making the deposit.

h. Three cheques that were outstanding at the end of the previous month are shown on the bank statement as having been processed by the bank this month.

i. Cash received by Heinzl Company on the last day of the month and deposited that evening is not shown on the bank statement.

j. An automatic payment for the company's electricity bill was processed by the bank. Heinzl Company had received notification from the electrical company, and recorded the amount as a payment earlier in the month.

k. A loan to Heinzl Company from the bank became due on the 21st of the month and the bank deducted the payment from the company's account. Henri had forgotten about the loan coming due.

AP6-4 (Placement of items on bank reconciliation)

You are preparing the bank reconciliation for your company, Hanneson Holdings Ltd., as at October 31.

Required:

Indicate whether each of the following items would be added to the bank balance, deducted from the bank balance, added to the cash account balance in the general ledger (G/L), or deducted from the cash account balance in the general ledger (G/L). If any of the items do not have to be included in the bank reconciliation, explain why.

a. Service charges of $35 were charged by the credit union during the month.

b. Cheques that Hanneson Holdings had written and mailed out that had not yet cleared the credit union amounted to $1,600.

c. One of your customers made an electronic payment to your account at the credit union in the amount of $1,050.

d. The cash receipts for October 31 amounted to $2,750 and had been deposited in the night drop slot at the credit union on the evening of October 31. These were not reflected on the bank statement for October.

e. A cheque from one of your customers in the amount of $270 that had been deposited during the last week of October was returned with the bank statement as NSF.

f. One deposit, for a receipt from a customer paying off its account, was incorrectly recorded by your bookkeeper. The correct amount of the receipt was $230, but the bookkeeper had recorded it as $320.

AP6-5 (Preparation of bank reconciliation)

Kinte Products Limited had a balance in its cash account of $38,755 on October 31, 2016. This included $2,650 of cash receipts from October 31, which had not yet been deposited in the bank. On the same date, its bank account had a balance of $42,301. Comparing the bank statement with the company's records indicated that the following cheques were outstanding on October 31:

#1224	$1,991
#1230	1,336
#1232	2,286
	$5,613

The following were shown on the bank statement and not yet recorded by the company:
- $376 deducted for a customer's cheque that was returned to Kinte Products marked NSF
- $420 added as a result of the direct deposit of an income tax refund from the Canada Revenue Agency
- $1,200 added as a result of a note collected by the bank and deposited in the company's account, representing $1,000 of principal and $200 of interest
- $34 deducted for service charges for the month

While preparing the data for its bank reconciliation, the company discovered that it had made an error in recording one of its deposits for cash sales during the month. The actual amount deposited was $2,282, but Kinte Products had recorded it as $2,882. The bank had also made an error in recording one of the company's cheques that was a payment to a supplier on account. The cheque had been issued in the amount of $336, but the bank processed it as $363.

Required:
    a. Prepare a bank reconciliation for Kinte Products Limited as at October 31, 2016.
    b. Prepare any journal entries required to adjust the cash account as at October 31, 2016.

AP6-6 (Preparation of bank reconciliation)

The April 30, 2016, bank statement for Comet Company showed a cash balance of $7,582. The cash account in the company's general ledger (G/L), according to the company's records on April 30, had a balance of $4,643. The following additional data were revealed during the reconciliation process:
1. A deposit of $652 that had been made by the company on March 31 was processed by the bank in April, and a deposit of $1,531 made on April 30 had not yet been processed by the bank.
2. The bank statement listed a deposit for $360 that was mistakenly put in Comet Company's bank account; it should have gone to Comment Company's account.
3. Comet Company determined that there were three cheques that had not yet been processed by the bank: #466 for $1,250, #467 for $520, and #470 for $1,350.
4. The bank had collected a note receivable for $1,000 from one of Comet Company's customers. An additional $15 in interest had been added to its account.
5. The bank service charge for the month was $25.

Required:
    a. Prepare a bank reconciliation for Comet Company as at April 30, 2016.
    b. What cash balance should Comet Company report on its statement of financial position as at April 30, 2016?
    c. Prepare the journal entries that are required to bring Comet Company's cash account to its correct balance.

AP6-7 (Preparation of bank reconciliation)

Catalina Holdings Ltd. (CHL), a Calgary-based property management company, is owned by Leslie Smeal. Leslie is trying to prepare a bank reconciliation for CHL's bank account for October 31, 2016. A review of CHL's bank statement and accounting records showed the following:
1. The cash balance per the bank statement was $26,936.89.
2. The accounting records showed a balance in the cash account of $21,260.16.
3. Two cheques that had been written and mailed by CHL had not been cashed. These were cheques #5109 for $10,505.10 and #5112 for $5,303.07.
4. CHL was paid $19.99 in interest by the bank during October.
5. A cheque for $1,125.58 that had been part of CHL's deposit on October 23 was not honoured by the bank because the client had insufficient funds.
6. Bank service charges for the month were $92.
7. Cheque #5101, which was for a utility payment, was incorrectly recorded by CHL's bookkeeper as $960 when the actual cheque was for $690 (which was the correct amount owing by CHL).
8. The bank had collected $3,110.25 on behalf of CHL related to a note receivable from one of CHL's clients. This included $110.25 in interest.
9. A deposit for $12,314.10 was made through the night deposit slot late on the evening of October 31.

Required:
    a. Prepare a bank reconciliation at October 31, 2016.
    b. Prepare the journal entries necessary as a result of the bank reconciliation

AP6-8 (Accounts receivable and uncollectible accounts—percentage of credit sales method)

Dundee Company started business on January 1 of the current year. The company made total sales of $900,000 during the year, of which $150,000 were cash sales. By the end of the year, Dundee had received payments of $675,000 from its customers on account. It also wrote off as uncollectible $10,000 of its receivables when it learned that the customer who owed this amount had filed for bankruptcy. That was Dundee Company's only entry related to bad debts for the period.

Dundee uses the allowance method of accounting for bad debts. Since Dundee is a new company and does not have past experience to base its own estimates on, it decides to use 3% of credit sales as an estimate for its bad debts expense, which is the average percentage for its industry.

Required:
   a. What amount of Bad Debts Expense would Dundee Company report on its statement of income for the year?
   b. Record the journal entry to write off the account of the customer who declared bankruptcy.
   c. What Allowance for Doubtful Accounts balance would be reported on the statement of financial position at the end of the year?
   d. What Accounts Receivable balance would be reported on the statement of financial position at the end of the year?
   e. Evaluate the reasonableness of the balance in Allowance for Doubtful Accounts at the end of the year.

AP6-9 (Accounts receivable and uncollectible accounts—percentage of credit sales method)

Majestic Equipment Sales Company, which sells only on account, had a $120,000 balance in its Accounts Receivable and a $4,200 balance in its Allowance for Doubtful Accounts on December 31, 2015. During 2016, the company's sales of equipment were $820,000 and its total cash collections from customers were $780,000.

During the year, the company concluded that customers with accounts totalling $6,000 would be unable to pay, and wrote these receivables off. However, one of these customers subsequently made a payment of $850 (note that this amount is not included in the cash collections noted above). At the end of 2016, management decided that it would use an estimate for bad debts of 1% of its credit sales.

Required:
   a. Prepare the journal entries to record all the 2016 transactions, including the adjustment for bad debts expense at year end.
   b. Show how the accounts receivable section of the statement of financial position at December 31, 2016, would be presented.
   c. What amount of bad debts expense would appear in the statement of income for the year ended December 31, 2016?

AP6-10 (Accounts receivable and uncollectible accounts—percentage of credit sales method)

The trial balance of M&D Inc. shows a $50,000 outstanding balance in Accounts Receivable at the end of the first year of operations, December 31, 2015. During the fiscal year, 75% of the total credit sales were collected and no accounts were written off as uncollectible. The company estimated that 1.5% of the credit sales would be uncollectible. During the following year, 2016, M&D had sales, all on account, totaling $250,000. It collected 80% of these sales, together with 95% of the outstanding receivables from 2015. During 2016, the accounts of seven customers who owed a total of $3,800, were judged uncollectible and were written off. During the year, the company recovered $1,500 from customers whose accounts had previously been written off (note that this amount was not included in the collection figures given above). The company estimated its bad debt expense to be 1% of its credit sales.

Required:
   a. Prepare the necessary journal entries for recording all the preceding transactions in the accounting system of M&D Inc. for 2015 and 2016.
   b. Show the accounts receivable section of the statement of financial position at December 31, 2016.

AP6-11 (Accounts receivable and uncollectible accounts—percentage of credit sales method)

A large corporation recently reported the following amounts on its year-end statements of financial position:

	2016	2015
Accounts receivable	$8,800,000	$8,400,000
Allowance for doubtful accounts	105,000	95,000

A footnote to these statements indicated that the company uses a percentage of its credit sales to determine its bad debts expense, that $60,000 of uncollectible accounts were written off during 2015 and $80,000 of uncollectible accounts were written off in 2016, and that there were no recoveries of accounts written off.

Required:
   a. Determine the amount of bad debts expense that must have been recorded by the company for 2016.
   b. How were the company's net receivables affected by the writeoff of the $80,000 of accounts in 2016?
   c. How was the company's net earnings affected by the $80,000 writeoff of accounts in 2016?

AP6-12 (Accounts receivable and uncollectible accounts—aging of receivables method)

The following is an aging schedule for a company's accounts receivable as at December 31, 2016:

Customer's name	Total amount owed	Current (not yet due)	1–30	31–60	61–90	Over 90
Aber	$ 20,000		$ 9,000	$11,000		
Bohr	30,000	$ 30,000				
Chow	35,000	15,000	5,000		$15,000	
Datz	18,000					$18,000
Others	158,000	95,000	15,000	13,000	15,000	20,000
	$261,000	$140,000	$29,000	$24,000	$30,000	$38,000
Estimated percentage that will be uncollectible		3%	6%	10%	25%	50%
Estimated value of uncollectibles	$ 34,840	$ 4,200	$ 1,740	$ 2,400	$ 7,500	$19,000

On December 31, 2016, the unadjusted balance in the Allowance for Doubtful Accounts (prior to the aging analysis) was a credit of $9,000.

Required:
 a. Journalize the adjusting entry for bad debts on December 31, 2016.
 b. Journalize the following selected events and transactions in 2017:
   i. On March 1, an $800 customer account that originated in 2017 is judged uncollectible.
   ii. On September 1, an $800 cheque is received from the customer whose account was written off as uncollectible on March 1.
 c. Journalize the adjusting entry for bad debts on December 31, 2017, assuming that the unadjusted balance in Allowance for Doubtful Accounts at that time is a *debit* of $1,000 and an aging schedule indicates that the estimated value of uncollectibles is $33,500.

AP6-13 (Accounts receivable and uncollectible accounts—aging of receivables method)

Xanadu Ltd. has accounts receivable totalling $142,800 and a $3,640 credit balance in its Allowance for Doubtful Accounts prior to adjustment on December 31, 2016. The company uses an aging analysis of its receivables to estimate its uncollectible accounts.
   The aging analysis shows the following:

Month of Sale	Accounts Receivable on December 31st
December	$ 91,000
November	26,040
September and October	16,800
July and August	8,960
	$142,800

The company's estimates of bad debts are as follows:

Age of Accounts	Estimated % Uncollectible
Current	2%
1–30 days past due	10%
31–90 days past due	25%
Over 90 days past due	40%

Required:
 a. Determine the total estimated uncollectibles as at December 31, 2016.
 b. Prepare the adjusting entry for the expected Bad Debts Expense as at December 31, 2016.

AP6-14 (Accounts receivable and uncollectible accounts—aging of receivables method)

On December 31, 2015, Ajacks Company reported the following information in its financial statements:

Accounts receivable	$1,193,400
Allowance for doubtful accounts	81,648
Bad debt expense	80,448

During 2016, the company had the following transactions related to receivables:
1. Sales were $10,560,000, of which $8,448,000 were on account.
2. Collections of accounts receivable were $7,284,000.
3. Writeoffs of accounts receivable were $78,000.
4. Recoveries of accounts previously written off as uncollectible were $8,100 (note that this amount is not included in the collections referred to in note 2 above).

Required:
a. Prepare the journal entries to record each of the four items above.
b. Set up T accounts for the Accounts Receivable and the Allowance for Doubtful Accounts and enter their January 1, 2016, balances. Then post the entries from part "a" and calculate the new balances in these accounts.
c. Prepare the journal entry to record the bad debts expense for 2016. Ajacks Company uses the aging of accounts receivable method and has prepared an aging schedule, which indicates that the estimated value of the uncollectible accounts as at the end of 2016 is $93,000.
d. Show what would be presented on the statement of financial position as at December 31, 2016, related to accounts receivable.

AP6-15 (Accounts receivable and uncollectible accounts—aging of receivables method)

The following information relates to Bedford Company's accounts receivable:

Accounts receivable balance on December 31, 2015	$ 900,000
Allowance for doubtful accounts balance on December 31, 2015	55,000
Credit sales made in 2016	5,800,000
Collections from customers on account in 2016	4,900,000
Accounts receivable written off in 2016	70,000
Accounts previously written off that were recovered in 2016 (not included in the collections above)	6,000

An aging analysis estimates the uncollectible receivables on December 31, 2016, to be $80,000. The allowance account is to be adjusted accordingly.

Required:
a. Calculate the ending balance in Accounts Receivable, as at December 31, 2016.
b. Calculate the Allowance for Doubtful Accounts balance, before adjustment, as at December 31, 2016.
c. Calculate the bad debts expense for the year 2016.

AP6-16 (Percentage of credit sales and aging of accounts receivable methods)

Clean Sweep Ltd. manufactures several different brands of vacuum cleaners, from hand-held models to built-in central vacuums. It sells its products to distributors on credit, giving customers 30 days to pay. During the year ending June 30, 2016, Clean Sweep recorded sales of $1,550,000. At June 30, the company prepared the following aging schedule:

Receivable Amount	Number of Days Outstanding	Estimated Percentage that Will Be Collected
$150,000	Less than 30	96%
50,000	31 to 45	93%
75,000	46 to 90	90%
100,000	More than 90	75%

The Allowance for Doubtful Accounts had a credit balance of $19,000 before the year-end adjustment was made.

Required:
a. Prepare the adjusting entry to bring Allowance for Doubtful Accounts to the desired level.
b. Clean Sweep's sales manager thinks the company would increase sales if it extended its normal collection cycle to 60 days from its current 30 days. Should the president accept or reject this recommendation? Why? What factors should be considered in making this decision?
c. What suggestions would you make regarding Clean Sweep's management of its accounts receivable?

AP6-17 (Comparison of all methods of accounting for uncollectible accounts)

DejaVu Company has been in business for several years and has the following information for its operations in the current year:

Total credit sales	$3,000,000
Bad debts written off in the year	60,000
Accounts receivable balance on December 31 (after writing off the bad debts above)	500,000

Required:

    a. Assume that DejaVu Company decides to estimate its bad debts expense at 2% of credit sales.

        i. What amount of bad debts expense will the company record if it has a *credit* balance (before adjustment) of $5,000 in its Allowance for Doubtful Accounts on December 31?

        ii. What amount of bad debts expense will it record if there is a *debit* balance (before adjustment) of $5,000 in its Allowance for Doubtful Accounts on December 31?

    b. Assume that DejaVu Company estimates its bad debts based on an aging analysis of its year-end accounts receivable, which indicates that a provision for uncollectible accounts of $40,000 is required.

        i. What amount of bad debts expense will the company record if it has a *credit* balance (before adjustment) of $5,000 in its Allowance for Doubtful Accounts on December 31?

        ii. What amount of bad debts expense will it record if there is a *debit* balance (before adjustment) of $5,000 in its Allowance for Doubtful Accounts on December 31?

    c. What amount of bad debts expense will DejaVu report if it uses the direct writeoff method of accounting for bad debts?

    d. State the two main reasons for using the allowance method to account for bad debts, rather than the direct writeoff method.

AP6-18 (Comparison of all methods of accounting for uncollectible accounts)

Crystal Lights Company manufactures and sells light fixtures for homes, businesses, and institutions. All of its sales are made on credit to wholesale distributors. Information for Crystal Lights for the current year follows:

Total credit sales	$3,500,000
Accounts receivable at December 31 (after writing off uncollectible accounts)	450,000

Required:

Assume that Crystal Lights estimates its bad debts based on an aging analysis of its year-end accounts receivable, which indicates that a provision for uncollectible accounts of $34,000 is required.

    a. If there is a *debit* balance of $6,000 in its Allowance for Doubtful Accounts on December 31, before adjustment:

        i. What amount will the company report on its statement of income as bad debts expense?

        ii. What amount will it report on its statement of financial position as the net value of its accounts receivable?

    b. If there is a $6,000 *credit* balance in the Allowance for Doubtful Accounts on December 31, before adjustment:

        i. What amount will the company report on its statement of income as bad debts expense?

        ii. What amount will it report on its statement of financial position as the net value of its accounts receivable?

Assume that Crystal Lights decides to estimate its bad debts expense at 1% of credit sales.

    c. If there is a *debit* balance of $6,000 in its Allowance for Doubtful Accounts on December 31, before adjustment:

        i. What amount will the company report on its statement of income as bad debts expense?

        ii. What amount will it report on its statement of financial position as the net value of its accounts receivable?

    d. If there is a $6,000 *credit* balance in the Allowance for Doubtful Accounts on December 31, before adjustment:

        i. What amount will the company report on its statement of income as bad debts expense?

        ii. What amount will it report on its statement of financial position as the net value of its accounts receivable?

Assume that Crystal Lights uses the direct writeoff method of accounting for bad debts and that the company wrote off accounts totalling $17,500 as uncollectible during the year.

    e. What amount will the company report on its statement of income as bad debts expense?

    f. What amount will it report on its statement of financial position as the net value of its accounts receivable?

Recall the discussion in the chapter on the allowance method.

    g. Briefly outline the main advantages of the allowance method of accounting for bad debts.

AP6-19 (Current and quick ratios)

The following amounts were reported by Liquid Company in its most recent statement of financial position:

Cash	$ 40,000
Accounts receivable	130,000
Short-term investments	18,000
Inventory	390,000
Prepaid insurance	35,000
Capital assets (net)	960,000
Accounts payable	85,000
Wages and salaries payable	37,000
Income tax payable	45,000
Sales tax payable	10,000
Short-term notes payable	90,000
Five-year bank loan	50,000

Required:
a. Calculate the current ratio and quick ratio for Liquid Company.
b. Based on a review of other companies in its industry, the management of Liquid Company thinks it should maintain a current ratio of 2.2 or more, and a quick ratio of 0.9 or more. Its current and quick ratios at the end of the prior year were 2.1 and 0.8, respectively. How successful has the company been in achieving the desired results this year?
c. How could the company improve its current position? What risks, if any, may be associated with the strategy you have suggested?

AP6-20 (Current and quick ratios)

The following amounts were reported by Moksh Ltd. in its most recent statement of financial position:

	2016	2015
Cash and cash equivalents	$ 50,000	$ 79,000
Accounts receivable (net)	170,000	120,000
Inventory	480,000	280,000
Prepaid expenses	11,000	5,000
Property, plant, and equipment (net)	420,000	360,000
Accounts payable	230,000	135,000
Wages and salaries payable	46,000	32,000
Income tax payable	23,000	18,000
Long-term bank loan payable	380,000	260,000
Common shares	220,000	220,000
Retained earnings	232,000	179,000

The company had sales of $860,000 in 2016 and $740,000 in 2015. All sales were on account.

Required:
a. Calculate the current ratio and quick ratio for Moksh Ltd. for the current and preceding year. Comment on whether the ratios have improved or worsened.
b. If Moksh's bank loan includes covenants that the company must maintain a minimum current ratio of 1.5 and a minimum quick ratio of 1.0, what would you advise Moksh's management to do?
c. Calculate Moksh's accounts receivable turnover ratio and average collection period for the current and preceding years. For the accounts receivable turnover ratio, use the balance of accounts receivable at each year end for this calculation, rather than average balances. Comment on whether these ratios have improved or worsened.
d. If Moksh's normal credit terms are "n/30," assess the company's collection experience for the current and preceding years.

AP6-21 (Liquidity evaluation)

The following statement of financial position accounts and amounts were for Classic Ltd. on October 31:

	2016	2015
Equipment	$350,000	$343,000
Bank loan payable (long-term)	322,000	336,000
Prepaid expenses	2,800	4,200
Accumulated depreciation, equipment	123,200	117,600
Income taxes payable	19,600	16,800
Inventory	315,000	322,000
Wages payable	36,400	33,600
Accounts receivable	64,400	51,800
Unearned revenue	67,200	56,000
Retained earnings	84,000	72,800
Common shares	70,000	70,000
Cash	67,200	50,400
Accounts payable	77,000	68,600

Required:
   a. Prepare a classified comparative statement of financial position for Classic Ltd. as at October 31, 2016.
   b. Calculate the amount of Classic's working capital (current assets minus current liabilities) at the end of its fiscal years 2016 and 2015. Has the company's working capital position improved or deteriorated during this period?
   c. Calculate Classic's current ratios at the end of its fiscal years 2016 and 2015. Has its current ratio improved or deteriorated during this period?
   d. Calculate Classic's quick ratios at the end of its fiscal years 2016 and 2015. Has the company's quick ratio improved or deteriorated during this period?
   e. Based on the results from parts "b," "c," and "d," do you think Classic's overall liquidity position improved or deteriorated during this period?
   f. How might Classic evaluate whether its overall liquidity is adequate?

User Perspective Problems

UP6-1 (Bank reconciliation and cash management)

Your friend, who owns a small landscaping business, asks you the following questions:

   "Someone told me that I should be preparing bank reconciliations for my business account. Why do I need to do this? If I want to know how much cash I have in the business, can't I just look at my bank balance online?"

Required:
Respond to your friend's questions.

UP6-2 (Bank reconciliation and cash management)

Required:
As a manager of a company, explain why a bank reconciliation would be important to your cash management.

UP6-3 (Bank reconciliation)

You own a small plumbing company that has an in-house bookkeeper. Since you are busy at the various job sites, the bookkeeper's responsibilities include billing and collections. She sends out invoices and statements to customers and processes payments received in person and by mail. She also prepares the monthly bank reconciliations.

Required:
   a. Why is it important that you review the bank reconciliation each month?
   b. What kind of information should you be looking at when you do this?

UP6-4 (Estimation of uncollectible accounts receivable)

There is a management compensation plan at See Saw Company that includes bonuses for managers when the company achieves a certain level of reported net income.

Required:

What incentives might this create for management to influence the estimate of the uncollectible portion of the accounts receivable?

UP6-5 (Accounts receivable and uncollectible accounts)

Ontario Company manufactures and sells high-quality racing and mountain bicycles. At the end of 2015, Ontario's statement of financial position reported total Accounts Receivable of $250,000 and an Allowance for Doubtful Accounts of $18,000. During 2016, the following events occurred:

1. Credit sales in the amount of $2,300,000 were made.
2. Collections of $2,250,000 were received on account.
3. Customers with total debts to Ontario Company of $38,000 were declared bankrupt and those accounts receivable were written off.
4. Bad debts expense for 2016 was recorded as 2% of credit sales.

Required:

As the chief financial officer for Ontario Company, you have been asked by a member of the executive committee to do the following things.

   a. Explain the effects of each of the above transactions on the company's financial statements.
   b. Show how the accounts receivable will be reported on Ontario's statement of financial position as at December 31, 2016.
   c. Evaluate the adequacy of the amount in the company's Allowance for Doubtful Accounts account as at December 31, 2016.

Fulfill the executive committee member's request.

UP6-6 (Accounts receivable and uncollectible accounts)

Lowrate Communications is in the cellular telephone industry. The following selected information has been compiled for the company (in thousands of dollars):

	2016	2015	2014
Accounts receivable (net)	$ 1,469.8	$ 1,230.6	$ 1,044.8
Allowance for doubtful accounts	128.9	121.9	118.0
Accounts written off	305.4	267.6	296.8
Bad debts expense	312.4	271.5	267.0
Sales revenue (all on account)	12,661.8	11,367.8	10,420.0

Required:

   a. In each of the three years presented, what percentage of the company's total accounts receivable is estimated to be uncollectible?
   b. In each of the three years presented, what percentage of the sales revenue is the bad debts expense?
   c. Did Lowrate's collection of accounts receivable improve or deteriorate over this three-year period?
   d. What was Lowrate's average collection period for 2016? Has this improved over the prior year?

Reading and Interpreting Published Financial Statements

RI6-1 (Accounts receivable and credit risk)

Big Rock Brewery Inc., which is based in Calgary, Alberta, is a publicly listed company. The company's products are sold across the country in nine provinces and three territories as well as being exported to Korea.

One of the reporting requirements for financial instruments is that a company must disclose if it has a high concentration of receivables from certain customers or categories of customers, because this may increase the company's level of credit risk as it depends greatly on the ability of those customers to pay their accounts. In accordance with this requirement, in its 2013 annual report, Big Rock disclosed the following:

> Big Rock has a concentration of credit risk because a majority of its accounts receivable are from provincial liquor boards, under provincially regulated industry sale and payment terms. The Corporation is not exposed to significant credit risk as payment in full is typically collected by provincial liquor boards at the time of sale and receivables are with government agencies. While substantially all of Big Rock's accounts receivable are from provincial government liquor authorities, the timing of receipts of large balances may vary significantly from period to period. The majority of product sold outside of Canada, which is included in GST and other receivables, is done so on a 'Cash on Delivery' basis with no credit risk.

Required:

How would this disclosure affect your assessment of Big Rock's level of credit risk?

RI6-2 (Analysis of accounts receivable)

According to its 2013 annual report, **RONA Inc.** is the largest Canadian distributor and retailer of hardware, home renovation, and gardening products. RONA's 2013 financial statements contained the following information, in thousands of Canadian dollars:

	2013	2012
Sales	$4,192,192	$4,444,175
Trade receivables (net)	$240,086	$354,482
Allowance for doubtful accounts	$12,231	$14,748

Required:

    a. What percentages of RONA Inc.'s accounts receivable were considered uncollectible in each of 2013 and 2012? Is the trend favourable or unfavourable?

    b. Calculate RONA's accounts receivable turnover rates for 2013 and 2012 using the ending balances of the receivables for each year rather than the average receivables. Is the trend favourable or unfavourable?

    c. What was the average number of days taken by RONA to collect its accounts receivable in 2013? In 2012? Do these figures provide insights beyond what the results in part "b" showed? Explain.

RI6-3 (Analysis of accounts receivable)

According to the company's 2013 annual review, **Finning International Inc.** is "the world's largest Caterpillar equipment dealer." The company is headquartered in Vancouver, but has operations in Western Canada, South America, and the United Kingdom and Ireland. The following information is taken from Note 4 of the financial statements in Finning's 2013 financial report:

December 31	2013		2012	
($ thousands)	Gross	Allowance	Gross	Allowance
Not past due	$619,839	$ 2	$548,989	$ —
Past due 1–30 days	156,644	1	160,844	—
Past due 31–90 days	80,998	299	73,470	872
Past due 91–120 days	8,956	883	15,264	820
Past due greater than 120 days	55,822	24,161	50,464	28,005
Total	$922,259	$25,346	$ 849,031	$29,697

The movement in the allowance for doubtful accounts in respect of trade receivables during the period was as follows:

For years ended December 31 ($ thousands)	2013	2012
Balance, beginning of year	$29,697	$20,737
Additional allowance	5,849	19,994
Receivables written off	(10,540)	(11,134)
Foreign exchange translation adjustment	340	100
Balance, end of year	$25,346	$29,697

The allowance amounts in respect of trade receivables are used to record possible impairment losses unless the Company is satisfied that no recovery of the amount owing is possible; at that point the amount is considered not recoverable and the financial asset is written off.

Required:

    a. Based on the above information, what is the trend of the collectibility of the company's receivables? Did the amount of accounts being written off increase in 2013?

    b. Calculate the percentage the allowance represents of each of the age groupings in 2013. Have these percentages changed from 2012? What do these percentages tell you about Finning's receivables after they are more than 120 days overdue?

    c. Based on the above information, what was Finning's bad debts expense for 2013?

RI6-4 (Current ratio, quick ratio, and accounts receivable turnover)

High Liner Foods Incorporated processes and markets prepared frozen seafood throughout Canada, the United States, and Mexico under the High Liner and Fisher Boy brands. It also produces private label products, and supplies restaurants and institutions.

Exhibit 6-11 contains financial statements that were included in the company's 2013 annual report:

EXHIBIT 6-11A   HIGH LINER FOODS INCORPORATED'S 2013 CONSOLIDATED STATEMENT OF INCOME

CONSOLIDATED STATEMENT OF INCOME

| | | Fifty-two weeks ended | |
| | | December 28, | December 29, |
(in thousands of U.S. dollars, except per share amounts)	Notes	2013	2012
Revenues		$ 947,301	$ 942,631
Cost of sales		731,884	735,970
Gross profit		215,417	206,661
Distribution expenses		53,368	44,511
Selling, general and administrative expenses		98,902	100,862
Impairment of property, plant and equipment		—	13,230
Business acquisition, integration and other expenses		3,256	10,741
Results from operating activities		59,891	37,317
Finance costs		16,329	36,585
(Income) loss from equity accounted investee, net of income tax		(86)	196
Income before income taxes		43,648	536
Income taxes			
Current	20	12,378	5,442
Deferred	20	(86)	(7,109)
Total income tax expense (recovery)		12,292	(1,667)
Net income		$ 31,356	$ 2,203

EXHIBIT 6-11B   HIGH LINER FOODS INCORPORATED'S 2013 CONSOLIDATED STATEMENT OF FINANCIAL POSITION

CONSOLIDATED STATEMENT OF FINANCIAL POSITION

| | | December 28, | December 29, |
(in thousands of U.S. dollars)	Notes	2013	2012
ASSETS			
Current:			
Cash		$ 1,206	$ 65
Accounts receivable	9	91,334	73,947
Income taxes receivable		3,509	5,145
Other financial assets	22	1,524	533
Inventories	8	254,072	222,313
Prepaid expenses		2,952	2,991
Total current assets		354,597	304,994
Non-current:			
Property, plant and equipment	6	97,503	89,268
Deferred income taxes	20	4,656	7,207
Other receivables and miscellaneous assets		1,906	2,035
Intangible assets	5	105,253	110,631
Goodwill	5	111,999	112,873
Total non-current assets		321,317	322,014
Assets classified as held for sale	7	542	4,819
Total assets		$ 676,456	$ 631,827

continued

EXHIBIT 6-11B	HIGH LINER FOODS INCORPORATED'S 2013 CONSOLIDATED STATEMENT OF FINANCIAL POSITION (continued)

(in thousands of U.S. dollars)	Notes	December 28, 2013	December 29, 2012
LIABILITIES AND SHAREHOLDERS' EQUITY			
Current:			
Bank loans	12	$ 97,227	$ 59,704
Accounts payable and accrued liabilities	10	103,215	101,441
Provisions	11	240	1,614
Other current financial liabilities	22	459	550
Income taxes payable		2,543	1,165
Current portion of long-term debt	13	–	34,237
Current portion of finance lease obligations	13	979	1,039
Total current liabilities		204,663	199,750
Non-current:			
Long-term debt	13	226,929	213,359
Other long-term financial liabilities	22	5,597	1,130
Other long-term liabilities		1,044	1,532
Long-term finance lease obligations	13	1,647	2,181
Deferred income taxes	20	43,998	45,126
Future employee benefits	14	7,929	13,791
Total non-current liabilities		287,144	277,119
Liabilities directly associated with the assets held for sale	7	–	1,604
Total liabilities		491,807	478,473
Shareholders' equity:			
Common shares	16	80,260	75,169
Contributed surplus		13,781	7,719
Retained earnings		90,792	66,373
Accumulated other comprehensive (loss) income		(184)	4,093
Total shareholders' equity		184,649	153,354
Total liabilities and shareholders' equity		$ 676,456	$ 631,827

Required:

a. Calculate High Liner's following ratios for both 2013 and 2012:
   i. Current ratio
   ii. Quick ratio
   iii. Accounts receivable turnover (use the balance of accounts receivable at each year end for this calculation, rather than average balances)
   iv. Average collection period
b. Comment on the results of the above ratio calculations and any significant trends they reveal.

RI6-5 (Current ratio, quick ratio, and accounts receivable turnover)

Saputo Inc. is a Montreal-based producer and distributor of dairy products, including cheese and yogurt products. According to the company's website, it is "one of the top ten dairy processors in the world."

Exhibit 6-12 shows the company's statement of financial position for the year ended March 31, 2014.

EXHIBIT 6-12A	SAPUTO INC.'S 2014 CONSOLIDATED BALANCE SHEETS

CONSOLIDATED BALANCE SHEETS

(in thousands of CDN dollars)

As at	March 31, 2014	March 31, 2013
ASSETS		
Current assets		
Cash and cash equivalents	$ 39,346	$ 43,177
Receivables	807,409	624,553
Inventories (Note 4)	933,232	770,158
Income taxes (Note 14)	30,867	2,786
Prepaid expenses and other assets	84,992	71,882
	1,895,846	1,512,556
Property, plant and equipment (Note 6)	1,928,761	1,617,195
Goodwill (Note 7)	1,954,691	1,569,592
Trademarks and other intangibles (Note 7)	484,830	454,876
Other assets (Note 8)	79,968	29,962
Deferred income taxes (Note 14)	12,796	9,459
Total assets	$ 6,356,892	$ 5,193,640
LIABILITIES		
Current liabilities		
Bank loans (Note 9)	$ 310,066	$ 181,865
Accounts payable and accrued liabilities	897,222	748,318
Income taxes (Note 14)	124,206	144,064
Current portion of long-term debt (Note 10)	393,600	152,400
	1,725,094	1,226,647
Long-term debt (Note 10)	1,395,694	1,395,900
Other liabilities (Note 11)	48,396	74,101
Deferred income taxes (Note 14)	348,548	191,320
Total liabilities	$ 3,517,732	$ 2,887,968
EQUITY		
Share capital	703,111	663,275
Reserves	242,282	38,049
Retained earnings	1,830,911	1,604,348
Equity attributable to shareholders of Saputo Inc.	2,776,304	2,305,672
Non-controlling interest (Note 16)	62,856	—
Total equity	$ 2,839,160	$ 2,305,672
Total liabilities and equity	$ 6,356,892	$ 5,193,640

The company's revenues for the year ended March 31, 2014, were as shown in Exhibit 6-12B.

EXHIBIT 6-12B	EXTRACT FROM SAPUTO INC.'S 2014 CONSOLIDATED STATEMENTS OF EARNINGS

CONSOLIDATED STATEMENTS OF EARNINGS

(in thousands of CDN dollars, except per share amounts)

Years ended March 31	2014	2013
Revenues	$ 9,232,889	$ 7,297,677

Required:

    a. Calculate Saputo's following ratios for both 2014 and 2013:
- i. Current ratio
- ii. Quick ratio
- iii. Accounts receivable turnover (use the balance of accounts receivable at each year end for this calculation, rather than average balances)
- iv. Average collection period

    b. Comment on the results of the above ratio calculations and any significant trends they reveal.

RI6-6 (Current ratio, quick ratio, and accounts receivable turnover)

Exhibit 6-13 is from the **Vancouver Fraser Port Authority's** 2013 financial report.

EXHIBIT 6-13A	VANCOUVER FRASER PORT AUTHORITY'S 2013 CONSOLIDATED STATEMENT OF FINANCIAL POSITION

(Expressed in thousands of dollars)
As at December 31

	2013	2012
Assets		
Current		
Cash and cash equivalents (notes 8 and 11)	$ 121,783	$ 160,042
Short-term investments (note 9)	501	600
Accounts receivable and other assets (notes 8 and 10)	79,102	40,932
Total current assets	201,386	201,574
Investments in securities (note 9)	2,523	1,997
Investment in joint venture (note 7)	7	—
Long-term receivables (note 10)	6,399	5,237
Deferred charges	1,541	1,247
Intangible assets (note 15)	2,771	2,521
Property and equipment (note 6)	1,146,996	1,023,199
	$1,361,623	$1,235,775
Liabilities and Equity of Canada		
Current		
Accounts payable and accrued liabilities (note 12)	$ 76,394	$ 40,270
Provisions (note 19)	12,932	13,006
Provision for investments in joint venture held for sale (note 7)	—	69
Short-term borrowing (note 13)	1,600	1,700
Payments in lieu of taxes	400	2,422
Deferred revenue	13,468	11,876
Current portion of long-term obligations (note 13)	45	43
Total current liabilities	104,839	69,386
Other employee benefits	1,280	1,483
Accrued benefit liability (note 14)	11,754	13,205
Deferred revenue	27,598	28,312
Provisions (note 19)	3,836	4,020
Other deferred amounts	3,267	3,214
Long-term obligations (note 13)	99,699	99,667
Total liabilities	252,273	219,287
Commitments and contingent liabilities (notes 17 and 18)		
Equity of Canada		
Contributed capital	150,259	150,259
Retained earnings	959,091	866,229
Total equity of Canada	1,109,350	1,016,488
	$1,361,623	$1,235,775

EXHIBIT 6-13B	NOTE 10 TO VANCOUVER FRASER PORT AUTHORITY'S 2013 CONSOLIDATED FINANCIAL STATEMENTS

10. ACCOUNTS RECEIVABLE AND OTHER ASSETS

(a) Accounts receivable and other assets

	2013	2012
Trade receivables	$ 12,995	$ 5,734
Provision for impairment	(3,326)	(3,113)
Restricted funds	7,698	3,125
Federal Government accrued grants	24,795	6,713
Other project partners accrued recoveries	9,270	2,615
Property rent related accrued revenues	12,906	11,861
Port related accrued revenues	6,279	7,090
Other	8,485	6,907
	$ 79,102	$ 40,932

At December 31, 2013, accounts receivable and other assets includes $7,697,585 in restricted funds (2012 – $3,124,409). Restricted funds are project related deposits, provincial share of lease revenue, and foreshore property owner deposits. Once information has been submitted to the VFPA's satisfaction, project related deposits are refunded in full plus interest. Provincial share of lease revenue is paid semi-annually. The foreshore property owner deposits are held to guarantee that the dykes on such properties will be maintained by the owners.

The single largest amount of the restricted funds is $3,724,766 of government funding to promote best practices for marine transportation of liquid bulk commodities (2012 – $757,498 was held for the replacement of a pile wall and a protection system at a terminal).

As of December 31, 2013, accounts receivables of $7,901,639 (2012 – $1,073,631) were past due but not impaired. These relate to a number of customers for whom there is no recent history of default. The ageing analysis of these trade receivables is as follows:

	2013	2012
Up to 90 days	$ 7,461	$ 691
91 to 120 days	88	68
Over 120 days	353	315
	$ 7,902	$ 1,074

As of December 31, 2013, trade receivables of $3,656,190 (2012 – $3,533,837) were provided for. The amount of the provision was $3,325,932 as of December 31, 2013 (2012 – $3,112,631). The individually impaired receivables mainly relate to customers disputing lease terms and conditions. The ageing of these receivables is as follows:

	2013	2012
Up to 90 days	$ 171	$ 227
91 to 120 days	2	52
Over 120 days	3,483	3,255
	$3,656	$3,534

Movements on the provision for impairment of accounts receivables are as follows:

	2013	2012
Balance, January 1	$ 3,113	$ 3,358
Provision for receivables impairment	232	238
Receivable written off during the year as uncollectable	(19)	(36)
Unused amounts reversed	–	(447)
Balance, December 31	$ 3,326	$ 3,113

Required:

a. Calculate the following ratios for both the current and preceding year:
   i. Current ratio
   ii. Quick ratio
   How do they compare with each other? Why is this the case?

b. Calculate the Port's allowance for doubtful accounts as a percentage of its accounts receivable for the current and preceding years. Also calculate the percentage of the Port's accounts receivable that were past due for both years. Comment on the trend.

c. What would the Port's allowance and writeoff entries have been for 2013?

RI6-7 (Accounts receivable and doubtful accounts)

BlackBerry Limited (formerly Research In Motion Ltd.) is known for its BlackBerry hand-held devices and the Playbook tablet. Based in Waterloo, Ontario, its shares trade on the Toronto Stock Exchange and the NASDAQ. The following information was taken from the 2014 annual report (in U.S. $ millions):

	2014	2013
Revenues	$ 6,813	$11,073
Accounts receivable, net of allowance for doubtful accounts of $17 in 2014 and $17 in 2013	$ 972	$ 2,352

Required:
   a. Is the balance in BlackBerry's accounts receivable at the end of 2014 significantly higher or lower than it was at the end of 2013? Quantify your answer and ensure that you consider the company's sales trends.
   b. Has the company's accounts receivable turnover and average collection periods changed significantly over the prior year? Use the balance of accounts receivable at each year end for the account receivable turnover calculation, rather than average balances.
   c. What possible explanations can you suggest for the change in accounts receivable turnover?

RI6-8 (Examine and analyze company's financial statements)

Required:
Follow your instructor's guidelines for choosing a company and do the following:
   a. Prepare an analysis of the company's cash (and cash equivalents, if applicable), gross accounts receivable, and allowance for doubtful accounts, by doing the following:
      i. List the beginning and ending balances in these accounts.
      ii. Calculate the net change, in both dollar and percentage terms, for the most recent year.
   b. If any of the accounts in part "a" has changed more than 10%, suggest an explanation for this change.
   c. Calculate the following ratios for the most recent two years and then comment on both their reasonableness and any significant changes in them:
      i.   Current ratio
      ii. Quick ratio
      iii. Allowance for doubtful accounts divided by gross accounts receivable
      iv. Accounts receivable turnover rate and average collection period (in days)

Cases

C6-1 Versa Tools Inc.

Versa Tools Inc. is a small tool and die manufacturing shop located in southwestern Ontario. The company's main shareholder, Arthur Eshelman, is becoming increasingly concerned about the safety and security of the company assets and, in particular, its cash. In the past, Arthur handled all the cash transactions. However, with increasing production levels and plans to expand into a plastics division, he has been too busy to continue with this hands-on approach.

Currently, there is only one person in the accounting department, a clerk who is responsible for recording all the cash receipts and disbursements and for depositing all the cash. Because she is so busy, cash is usually deposited in the bank only once a week. Until it is deposited, all cash collected is locked in a desk drawer in the main office.

The accounting clerk has no formal accounting education. In fact, she is a graduate of a local art school and is working at Versa only to earn enough money to move to Toronto and begin a career as a graphic artist. She often notes the cash receipts on slips of paper until she has time to enter them into the computer system several days later.

Finally, Arthur has not been preparing bank reconciliations. When asked about the bank reconciliations, he replied, "I'm so busy running the business that I don't have time to check every item on the bank statement each month. Besides, with the high fees that it charges us each month, shouldn't I be able to rely on the bank to keep an accurate record of the balance in our account?"

Required:
Prepare a memo to Arthur outlining the basic cash controls that should be put into place at Versa Tools Inc. to ensure the proper management and protection of its cash.

C6-2 Slackur Company

Slackur Company is a very profitable small business. However, it has not given much consideration to internal controls. For example, in an attempt to keep its clerical and office expenses to a minimum, the company has combined the jobs of cashier and bookkeeper. As a result, Rob Rowe handles all the cash receipts, keeps the accounting records, and prepares the monthly bank reconciliations.

On November 30, 2016, the balance on the company's bank statement was $18,380.00. The outstanding cheques on that date were #143 for $241.75, #284 for $258.25, #862 for $190.71, #863 for $226.80, and #864 for $165.28. Included with the statement was a bank credit memorandum in the amount of $300.00, indicating the bank's collection of a note receivable for Slackur on November 25, and a debit memorandum in the amount of $50.00 for the bank's service charges for the month. Neither of these transactions had been recorded by Slackur Company.

The company's Cash account had a balance of $21,892.72 on November 30, 2016, which included a substantial amount of undeposited cash on hand. Because he needed cash for holiday shopping and knew that the company's internal controls were weak, Rob decided to take some of the undeposited cash for his personal use and report undeposited cash of only $3,845.51. In an effort to conceal his theft, he then prepared the following bank reconciliation:

Balance per bank statement, November 30		$18,380.00
Add: Undeposited receipts		3,845.51
Less: Outstanding cheques		
No. 862	$190.71	
No. 863	226.80	
No. 864	165.28	(582.79)
Add: Note collected by bank		300.00
Less: Bank service charges		(50.00)
Corrected bank balance, November 30		$21,892.72
Cash balance per books, November 30		$21,892.72

When he presented this to the general manager, she called the bank to determine whether the undeposited receipts on November 30 had since been deposited, and was happy to hear the bank confirm that Rob Rowe had made a cash deposit of $3,845.51 on the morning of December 1. She then reviewed the bank reconciliation to satisfy herself that the items on it seemed reasonable, and that it was balanced. Assuming that everything must be in order, she then thanked Rob for his good work and made a mental note to herself that he should be given a $500 year-end bonus.

Required:
  a. Determine the amount of cash stolen by Rob Rowe. (Hint: Prepare a corrected bank reconciliation, treating the true amount of undeposited cash as an unknown. Then solve for this unknown, and compare the reported amount of undeposited cash with the true amount.)
  b. Explain what Rob Rowe did in the bank reconciliation that he prepared to try to conceal his theft. (Hint: You should be able to identify items whose combined effects match the amount of the discrepancy that you calculated in part "a.")
  c. What should Slackur Company do differently to prevent this type of occurrence?

C6-3 Sanjay Supplies Limited

Sanjay Supplies Limited is concerned about its ability to pay its debts. Selected financial information follows.

Sanjay Supplies Limited Selected Financial Information (in thousands)			
Years ended October 31	2016	2015	2014
Sales on credit	$17,100	$16,300	$12,700
Cash	20	60	210
Short-term investments (cashable on demand)	—	—	40
Accounts receivable	2,130	1,510	1,180
Inventories	1,730	1,250	940
Short-term bank loans (payable on demand)	560	140	—
Accounts payable	340	490	610
Other short-term liabilities	80	80	80

Required:

Analyze the information and explain why Sanjay is experiencing problems with its cash balance. What could Sanjay do to reduce these problems?

C6-4 Heritage Mill Works

Heritage Mill Works sells finished lumber and mouldings to a variety of housing contractors. Given the nature of the business, most of its sales are on credit, and careful management of credit and bad debts is critical for success. The normal credit period is 60 days.

The company's owners significantly emphasize the operating results as they appear on the statement of income. They believe that accurate net earnings are the best indicator of any business's success. The owners are currently looking at revising their credit-granting policies in light of a number of large writeoffs that were made in the past year. They are also wondering whether interest-bearing notes receivable with longer credit terms should be used in the future for certain types of customers and for very large sales.

The controller has asked you to estimate bad debts expense for the company, to be used in preparing the annual financial statements. The company had sales of $3,450,000 during the year, of which 90% were on credit. Historically, the percentage of bad debts has varied from 2% to 4% of credit sales. Bad debts are usually higher in times of economic downturns. Business has been strong this year for the entire industry, since interest rate reductions have led to a boom in new housing starts.

The balance in the Accounts Receivable account on December 31 is $330,000. During the year, the company had written off $73,400 of accounts receivable as uncollectible.

Required:

a. Provide the controller with an estimate of the bad debts expense for the current period. Be prepared to justify your recommendation to the controller. Be sure to comment on the magnitude of the accounts receivable that were written off as uncollectible during the year.
b. Discuss the trade-offs that must be considered when deciding credit-granting policies.
c. Explain why it might be appropriate to use notes receivable for certain types of customers or very large sales.
d. What other steps could this company take to reduce the risk of not collecting its receivables in the future?

C6-5 MegaMax Theatre

The MegaMax Theatre is located in the MetroMall and employs six cashiers. Two of them work from 12:30 to 6:00 p.m., and the other four from 6:00 to 11:30 p.m. The cashiers receive payments from customers and operate machines that eject serially numbered tickets. Some customers use debit or credit cards, but most payments are cash. The rolls of admission tickets are inserted and locked into the machines by the theatre manager at the beginning of each cashier's shift.

The cashiers' booths are located just inside the entrance to the lobby of the theatre. After purchasing their tickets, customers take them to a doorperson stationed at the entrance to the theatre, about 10 metres from the cashiers' booths. The doorperson tears each ticket in half and drops the ticket stub into a locked box. The other half of the ticket is returned to the customer.

At the end of each cashier's shift, the theatre manager removes the ticket rolls from each cashier's machine, counts the cash, and then totals it with the debit card and credit card transactions. Each cash count sheet is initialled by the cashier involved. The cash receipts from the first shift are stored in a safe located in the manager's office until the end of the day.

At the end of the day, the manager deposits the cash receipts from both shifts in a bank night deposit vault located in the mall. In addition, the theatre manager sends copies of the cash count sheets and the deposit slip to the company controller to be verified, and to the accounting department to be recorded.

Finally, the manager compares the total amount received by each of the cashiers with the number of tickets they issued, and notes any discrepancies, which are then discussed with the cashiers before their next shift.

Required:

a. Outline the main internal control considerations for cash receipts generally, and briefly discuss how they apply to MegaMax Theatre's cash receipts procedures.
b. Discuss any weaknesses in the current internal control system that could enable a cashier and/or doorperson to misappropriate cash.

ENDNOTES

1. Nicolas Van Praet, "Gildan Activewear Inc Moves into Women's Intimate Apparel with $110-million Doris Inc Acquisition," *Financial Post*, June 19, 2014; Gildan Activewear Inc. 2013 annual report; Gildan corporate website, www.gildan.com.
2. Canadian Tire Corporation's 2013 annual report.
3. New Flyer Industries Inc. 2013 annual report.
4. PotashCorp. 2013 annual integrated report.
5. RONA Inc.'s 2013 annual report, Note 26.

CHAPTER

7 Inventory

CORE QUESTIONS

If you are able to answer the following questions, then you have achieved the related learning objectives.

LEARNING OBJECTIVES

After studying this chapter, you should be able to:

⬤⬤⬤ INTRODUCTION

- What is inventory?
- Why is inventory of significance to users?

1 Discuss the importance of inventory to a company's overall success.

⬤⬤⬤ TYPES OF INVENTORY

- What are the major classifications of inventory?
- What goods are included in a company's inventory?

2 Distinguish between the different inventory classifications and determine which goods should be included in a company's inventory.

⬤⬤⬤ INVENTORY SYSTEMS

- What is a periodic inventory system?
- What is a perpetual inventory system?
- What are the key distinctions between periodic and perpetual inventory systems?
- How does management decide which inventory system to use?

3 Explain the differences between perpetual inventory systems and periodic inventory systems.

⬤⬤⬤ COST FORMULAS

- What costs are included in inventory?
- What are cost formulas and why are they necessary?
- How are cost of goods sold and ending inventory determined using the specific identification, weighted-average, and first-in, first-out cost formulas?
- How do companies determine which cost formula to use?

4 Explain why cost formulas are necessary and calculate the cost of goods sold and ending inventory under the specific identification, weighted-average, and first-in, first-out cost formulas.

⬤⬤⬤ INVENTORY VALUATION

- At what value is inventory reflected on the statement of financial position?
- How is the lower of cost or net realizable value applied to inventory?

5 Explain the value at which inventory is carried on the statement of financial position.

⬤⬤⬤ GROSS MARGIN

- What is gross margin and why is it a key measure?

6 Explain how a company's gross margin is determined and why it is an important measure.

⬤⬤⬤ INTERNAL CONTROLS AND INVENTORY

- What principles of internal control can be applied to inventory?

7 Describe management's responsibility for internal control measures related to inventory.

⬤⬤⬤ FINANCIAL STATEMENT ANALYSIS

- How often does the company sell through its inventory?
- How many days did it take to sell through the company's inventory?
- How can inventory amounts be estimated?

8 Calculate the inventory turnover ratio and the days to sell inventory ratio and explain how they can be interpreted by users.

●●● Mini Cars; Maxi Inventories

With annual sales of more than U.S. $34.8 billion, billions of dollars of inventory flow through Canadian-based auto parts supplier Magna International each year. Managing and accounting for this inventory as accurately as possible are critical to Magna's success, and key to delivering on its contracts with many of the world's largest auto manufacturers.

Magna is ranked as Canada's second-largest company by revenue. It has more than 300 plants in 29 countries, including 46 manufacturing operations in Canada, and has more than 125,000 employees worldwide. Magna produces parts for virtually every automaker in the world, making everything from side mirrors to electronic door latches to seats. It also has contracts to manufacture complete automobiles, such as the Mini for BMW Group, and provides tooling and engineering services for companies such as Ford and Jeep.

Each component manufactured by the company can require many inventory items. For example, Magna manufactures seats for the Ford Escape and each four-seat set includes 100–120 individual parts. When different fabric and colour combinations are taken into account, Magna actually has to stock about 250 individual parts in inventory. Every item used in the manufacturing process, along with its cost, must be accounted for so that the company's inventory records remain current and that its billings to companies such as Ford are accurate.

The U.S. $2.6 billion in inventory that Magna had on hand at the end of 2013 included raw materials and supplies valued at U.S. $947 million, work-in-process inventory valued at U.S. $273 million, finished goods valued at U.S. $339 million, and tooling and engineering valued at U.S. $1,078 million.

Having that much inventory on hand is costly for any company. Armed with inventory valuation numbers, Magna is working to find ways to eliminate waste in terms of reducing overproduction and gaining efficiencies in its warehouse floor space.

But having lots of inventory is not necessarily a bad thing. Magna's inventories increased by U.S. $125 million from 2012 for some good reasons. "The increase in inventories was primarily due to increased production inventory to support higher sales activities and for upcoming launches," the company noted in its 2013 annual report.[1]

INTRODUCTION

For a manufacturer, such as **Magna International**, or a retailer, inventory is generally its most important asset. Management must be very careful to buy or make the right items, at the right cost, and in the right quantities to make enough profit to cover expenditures. This chapter shows how companies account for this important asset.

■ **LEARNING OBJECTIVE 1**
Discuss the importance of inventory to a company's overall success.

What is inventory?

Inventory is any item purchased by a company for resale to customers or to be used in the manufacture of a product that is then sold to customers. All companies with the exception of service businesses have inventory. For example, the inventory of your local bookstore includes books, stationery, maps, and many other goods. Your local grocery store has hundreds of items in its inventory in numerous categories, such as fresh goods, frozen goods, canned goods, and dry goods. Companies such as the bookstore or grocery store are known as **merchandisers** or **retailers**. They purchase their inventory from publishers and food processors with the objective of selling it to you, the customer, at a profit.

Companies that make products are known as **manufacturers**. They, too, have inventory. Your smartphone or tablet is a good example of a manufactured product. Manufacturers such as **BlackBerry** and **Apple** have inventories that include components that are assembled at the factory. The company may purchase some of the components from other manufacturers or make all of them in one of its own factories.

While manufacturers and retailers are the first companies we think of when discussing inventory, they are not the only companies that have inventory. **Brookfield Asset Management Inc.**, a Canadian property development and management company, reported $6,291 million of inventory at December 31, 2013. Its inventory included residential properties under development and land held for development. **Canfor Corporation**, a Canadian forest products company, reported $471.9 million of inventory at December 31, 2013. This included finished products, raw logs, and residual fibre.

Why is inventory of significance to users?

For retailers and manufacturers, inventory is often the most significant current asset; that is, the largest asset that will be converted to cash over the next year. It's also often the most significant asset on the company's statement of financial position. Thus it is a critical asset for a company to manage and an important piece of information for investors and creditors to understand. Each company will have its own processes for purchasing, selling, and accounting for inventory.

For Example

A quick look at the annual financial statements of the following major Canadian manufacturers and retailers demonstrates the significance of inventory.

Company	Inventory (in thousands of $)	Percentage of Current Assets	Percentage of Total Assets	Year End
Bombardier Inc.	U.S. $8,234,000	56.2%	28.0%	Dec. 31, 2013
Gildan Activewear Inc.	U.S. $595,794	60.8%	29.2%	Sept. 29, 2013
Le Château Inc.	C $124,878	91.0%	59.2%	Jan. 25, 2014
RONA Inc.	C $738,752	71.3%	31.5%	Dec. 29, 2013
Finning International Inc.	C $1,755,808	54.0%	34.7%	Dec. 31, 2013
High Liner Foods Incorporated	U.S. $254,072	71.6%	37.6%	Dec. 28, 2013

Management's objective for inventory is to sell it to customers at a higher price than the company purchased it for. This sounds basic, but there are many steps that a company must take in order to achieve this objective.

First, the company needs to select suppliers: companies that can provide the required items on a timely basis. Location of the supplier can be an important consideration because of the amount of time required between the order date and the delivery date.

Second, management must decide how much inventory it wants to purchase from the supplier. Managers need to estimate how much product they think their customers will buy and also consider the price charged by the supplier. Companies must plan carefully because they do not want to have too much inventory on hand because it costs money to store the inventory. Also, the longer inventory remains unsold, the higher the risk that it will spoil, be damaged, or, in the case of technology companies, become obsolete. On the other hand, management wants to purchase a sufficient quantity of goods to meet customer demand. They do not want to run out of a particular item (called a **stockout**). Customers become frustrated if a company does not have a product in inventory when they order it. In the case of retail, the customer can either wait until a store has the required product or shop elsewhere.

Next, management needs to set the sale price so that it is high enough to provide a profit for the company while remaining competitive with other companies selling the same or similar products.

Finally, management needs to implement safeguards to prevent damage and loss due to theft.

The entire process is further complicated by the number of items a company has in its inventory. As an example, according to **Canadian Tire Corporation**'s 2013 annual information form, the company's stores "offer consumers over 136,000 Stock Keeping Units in Living, Fixing, Playing, Automotive and Seasonal & Gardening categories." With 136,000 different types of items in inventory, you can understand how critical inventory management is to Canadian Tire!

For Example

Target Canada opened 124 stores in Canada during 2013, promoting its Canadian expansion with the slogan "Expect more. Pay less." Since opening its first Canadian store in March, Target Canada management has experienced several challenges related to inventory. Many customers who had shopped at Target's U.S. stores were looking for the same low prices and specific inventory items in the Canadian stores. They did not find either low prices or the products. What they often found were empty shelves, caused by high demand for a product or delivery issues. At the same time, Target overestimated demand for some items of apparel and home goods and offered deep discounts on these overstocked inventory items. As a result, Target Canada's gross margin was significantly lower than expected.[2]

TYPES OF INVENTORY

What are the major classifications of inventory?

■ **LEARNING OBJECTIVE 2**
Distinguish between the different inventory classifications and determine which goods should be included in a company's inventory.

There are different types or classifications of inventory. Retailers and merchandisers buy products from many different suppliers. When the products arrive at stores, employees record the receipt of the products, price the products, and put them on the shelves for sale. These products are all classified as *inventory*.

On the other hand, manufacturers have multiple classes of inventory. At any point in time, a manufacturer's inventory will include **raw materials, work-in-process**, and **finished goods**.

Raw materials are all of the items required to make the product. For example, the raw materials category at a furniture manufacturer would include the wood, plastic, fabric, nails, glue, and other items needed to make the furniture.

Work-in-process is used to record the costs of products that have been started but have not been completed at the end of the accounting period. The category includes the costs of raw materials plus labour costs and **overhead** costs (other manufacturing costs such as utilities and depreciation of the manufacturing facility) that are incurred as the product is being made. Continuing with the furniture manufacturing company example, this category would include chairs and tables that are partially assembled but are not yet complete.

Finished goods represents the completed products such as chairs and tables. Once the manufacturing process is complete and the product is ready for sale, the full cost of making the product is transferred from the Work-in-Process account to the Finished Goods account.

Meal preparation in a restaurant is a good example of the flow of physical goods and costs in an inventory system. Your order is sent to the kitchen. First the chef gathers all of the items (raw materials) that are needed to make your meal. The next step is preparing and cooking the food to make the finished meal. In the second step, the chef's labour and overhead (electricity) costs are incurred. During the time the chef is making the meal, it is a work in process. When the dinner is prepared, it is delivered to your table in the restaurant (finished goods).

Exhibit 7-1 shows how the costs of raw materials, labour, and overhead items used in the manufacturing process flow through the three inventory categories. Note that these are the same categories of inventory shown in Magna International's financial statements in the opening story.

Exhibit 7-1 The Flow of Inventory at a Manufacturer

Raw Materials Inventory		Work-in-Process Inventory		Finished Goods Inventory		Cost of Goods Sold	
1	2	2	3	3	4	4	

There are four transactions as inventory moves through a manufacturer:

1. Raw materials are purchased.
2. Raw materials are used and incorporated into the manufacture of products. These are known as work-in-process until the manufacturing process has been completed.
3. The manufacturing process is completed and the goods move from work-in-process to finished goods.
4. The goods are sold and move from finished goods to cost of goods sold.

For Example

Danier Leather Inc. designs, manufactures, and retails leather apparel and accessories. At June 28, 2014, the company reported the following inventory balances:[3]

5 INVENTORIES

	(in thousands of Canadian dollars)	
	June 28, 2014	June 29, 2013
Raw materials	$ 1,026	$ 2,594
Work-in-process	198	222
Finished goods	20,497	19,994
	$21,721	$22,810

FINANCIAL STATEMENTS

What goods are included in a company's inventory?

The inventory of a retailer includes the products it has purchased to sell to its customers, while the inventory of a manufacturer includes raw materials, work-in-process, and finished goods. While this sounds pretty straightforward, determining whether or not goods should be included in inventory can be a little bit more complicated. The key criterion for making this determination is ownership: who has title to the goods? In this section, we will look at two common arrangements that are important to understand when trying to assess ownership.

First, we will look at the shipping terms (or transportation terms) associated with the purchase of the goods. The most commonly used shipping terms are **FOB shipping point** and **FOB destination**. FOB means *free on board*, which is a historical shipping term used when goods were transported by ship. It is now used for all forms of shipment (ship, truck, and rail). Let's look at what each of these terms means.

FOB shipping point means that the buyer is responsible for paying shipping and any other costs incurred while the goods are in transit from the seller's premises to the buyer's premises. Therefore, the buyer owns the inventory when it leaves the *seller's* premises (the shipping point) and the buyer includes these goods in its inventory even though they have not yet arrived.

FOB destination means that the seller is responsible for paying shipping and any other costs incurred while the goods are in transit from the seller's premises to the buyer's premises. Therefore, the buyer does not own the inventory until it reaches the *buyer's* premises (its destination) and the buyer does not record the inventory until it arrives. Exhibit 7-2 illustrates the difference between FOB shipping point and FOB destination in terms of when the goods would be included in the inventory of the buyer and be accounted as cost of goods sold by the seller.

Exhibit 7-2 FOB Shipping Point and FOB Destination

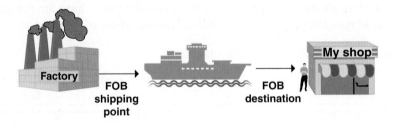

The Conceptual Framework
REVENUE RECOGNITION

Recall the revenue recognition criteria discussed in Chapter 4. A company recognizes revenue when performance has occurred or substantially all of the risks and rewards have transferred to the buyer. It makes sense, then, that when the seller recognizes revenue from the sale, ownership of the products has been transferred to the buyer and the goods are no longer inventory of the seller.

Consignment arrangements are the other situation that needs to be considered in relation to determining the ownership of goods held at the company's premises. You may be familiar with consignment stores and may have used one either as a seller or buyer. For example, some student unions operate consignment arrangements for used textbooks. The student (the owner or **consignor**) leaves their used textbook with the student union office (the **consignee**). When the book sells, the student union collects the full payment. It keeps its commission and gives the balance to the student who was selling the book. The student union would not report the books it is holding to sell as part of its inventory because these are not its goods. They would be the inventory of each student.

For Example

Vancouver-based **Ritchie Bros. Auctioneers Incorporated** is the world's largest auctioneer of used industrial equipment. During the year ended December 31, 2013, the company sold equipment that generated gross auction proceeds of $3.8 billion. From this, the company earned auction revenues of $467 million. The vast majority of the equipment auctioned by the company is held on consignment by the company pending the auction. While Ritchie Bros. takes possession of the used equipment prior to auctioning it off, it is on a consignment basis and is not recorded as inventory of the company. In other words, Ritchie Bros. is the consignee. As such, when the equipment is sold, there is no cost of goods sold. The difference between the gross auction proceeds of $3.8 billion and the auction revenues of $467 million is the amount due to the owner of the used equipment (the consignor) from the sale.[4]

INVENTORY SYSTEMS

■ **LEARNING OBJECTIVE 3**
Explain the differences between perpetual inventory systems and periodic inventory systems.

It is important that companies track inventory in order to know the quantities of product on hand and the quantities sold. Management uses this information to make decisions about pricing, production, and reordering. Before we discuss the two types of inventory systems, it is important for you to understand how inventory flows through inventory systems.

A company starts each accounting period with the inventory that it had at the end of the previous period. Because Inventory is a permanent account, the account balance carries over from one period to the next. This is referred to as *opening inventory* or *beginning inventory*. The quantity and costs are known because they were determined at the end of the prior year. The number of units purchased during the period and the cost of those purchases can be obtained from the related invoices. The cost of the opening inventory plus the cost of purchases is known as the **cost of goods available for sale (COGAS)**. This is the cost of all of the goods that the company had available to sell to its customers during the period. Companies must then determine how to allocate COGAS between the cost of goods sold and the cost of goods remaining in inventory. This decision will be affected by the type of inventory system used by the company.

The type of inventory system used depends on the nature and amount (both in terms of dollars and number of units) of inventory involved, as well as the cost of implementing the system. In the next section, we will discuss two types of inventory systems: periodic inventory systems and perpetual inventory systems.

KEY POINT
Opening Inventory
+ Purchases
COGAS

What is a periodic inventory system?

As the name implies, **periodic inventory systems** are systems that only update a company's inventory information *periodically* (once in a while). These updates only happen when the company has physically counted its inventory, which may be done only at the end of each month, each quarter, or even each year. Until a physical count is conducted, companies operating periodic inventory systems will not know their cost of the inventory on hand nor the cost of goods sold in the period. Companies using periodic inventory systems will use the cost of goods sold model as follows:

Opening Inventory	(Last period's ending inventory)
+ Purchases	(Based on invoices during the period)
Cost of Goods Available for Sale	
− Ending Inventory (EI)	(Based on a physical inventory count)
Cost of Goods Sold (COGS)	(Whatever goods are not on hand are assumed to have been sold)

Periodic inventory systems have the advantage of being easy to operate, but they have a significant disadvantage in that they do not provide management with up-to-date information about inventory quantities or costs. They are often manual systems and do not require the use of computer hardware or software. This makes the upfront costs of these systems less expensive than perpetual inventory systems. However, companies using periodic systems must have regular inventory counts conducted, which requires additional wage costs for staff or payments to outside contractors. Companies may also have to close for business to conduct counts, which can result in lost sales.

Companies that use periodic systems record all inventory purchases in a Purchases account (rather than updating the Inventory account). When goods are sold, an entry is made to record the sale to the customer, but no entries are made to the Inventory or Cost of Goods Sold accounts until the end of the accounting period when a physical count of inventory has been performed. In a retail store, for example, clerks know an item's retail price because it is written on the sales tag or comes up on the cash register when the item is scanned. However, they are unlikely to know what that item cost the company and this information is not available from the company's accounting software if it is operating a periodic inventory system.

Aside from the challenges created by the lack of timely inventory information, there are other weaknesses with periodic inventory systems. One of these is that companies using periodic inventory systems are unable to quantify the theft of inventory. This is because periodic inventory systems assume that whatever items are not remaining in ending inventory were sold. This may not always be the case, as goods may have been stolen rather than sold.

Exhibit 7-3 illustrates an example of a periodic inventory system.

Exhibit 7-3 Example of a Periodic Inventory System

When Tech Ltd. counted its inventory at December 31, 2016, it determined that goods with a total cost of $15,000 were still on hand. The company had started the year with inventory costing $9,000 and the company had made purchases totalling $27,000 during the year. Tech Ltd.'s cost of goods sold for 2016 would be determined as follows:

Opening Inventory	$ 9,000
+ Purchases	27,000
Cost of Goods Available for Sale	36,000
– Ending Inventory	15,000
Cost of Goods Sold	$21,000

Under the periodic inventory system, Tech Ltd.'s cost of goods sold would be $21,000, the residual amount after the cost of the goods still on hand is removed from the cost of all of the goods the company had available to sell during the period.

Another weakness with periodic inventory systems is the fact that the company does not have up-to-date inventory information during the period. As a result, management must develop other methods of determining when goods need to be reordered to avoid stockouts. These methods may require additional wage costs, due to having employees walk through the stores looking at inventory levels on the store shelves or actually counting the goods to determine if an order is necessary. These methods may also result in over- or understocking if the reordering is based on time (such as ordering a fixed number of goods every week).

What is a perpetual inventory system?

Again, the name of the inventory system provides an indication as to how it works. With **perpetual inventory systems**, a company's inventory information is updated *perpetually* (continuously or all the time). As such, inventory and cost of goods sold information is updated after every transaction (after each purchase or sale of goods) and a company does not have to wait for the results of a physical count to be able to determine it. These systems are computerized and generally require the use of bar code scanners. Some perpetual inventory systems track the physical flow of goods and their costs: the system has details on the specific goods sold or still on hand, along with their costs. Other perpetual inventory systems only track the physical flow of goods: the system has details on the specific goods sold or still on hand, but does not track the cost information.

It is important to note that, while inventory counts are not required for companies using perpetual inventory systems, they are still conducted at least once per year (at year end). They are necessary in order for companies to determine if the actual amount of physical goods on hand is equal to the ending inventory information according to the computer. It is virtually certain that these two amounts will not correspond due to the theft of goods. This difference is known as **inventory shrinkage**. Being able to quantify this is another advantage of using a perpetual inventory system.

Companies using perpetual inventory systems will use the cost of goods sold model as follows:

Opening Inventory	(Last period's ending inventory)
+ Purchases	(Based on invoices during the period)
Cost of Goods Available for Sale	
− Cost of Goods Sold	(Updated after each sale)
Ending Inventory	(Ending inventory that should be on hand)
− Actual Ending Inventory per Count	(Actual ending inventory on hand)
Shrinkage (or Theft)	

For Example

Inventory shrinkage is the term used to describe the loss of inventory due to theft, damage, or obsolescence. While management should be concerned about all three causes of shrinkage, theft, and specifically employee theft, can result in significant losses. Just how significant? Take small and medium-sized enterprises (SMEs), for example. The Certified General Accountants Association of Canada estimated the annual cost of employee fraud in Canada at $3.2 billion based on its survey of SMEs in 2011. The most frequently reported type of employee fraud was the misappropriation (theft) of inventory and non-cash assets. Fifty-four percent of the 800 companies participating in the survey reported loss of inventory as a result of employee theft.

In 2012, PricewaterhouseCoopers reported that Canadian retailers lose, on average, $10.8 million a day to theft. Theft by employees (internal theft) accounts for about one third of the total or approximately $3.6 million per day. Asset misappropriation was also identified in 87% of reported cases in the Association of Certified Fraud Examiners' global fraud survey. Companies reported losses, on average, of 5% of total revenues in 2012.

These are significant numbers and illustrate the importance of managing inventory in order to reduce or eliminate inventory shrinkage due to theft. We will return to inventory shrinkage and the use of internal controls later in the chapter.[5]

Exhibit 7-4 shows an example of a perpetual inventory system.

Exhibit 7-4 Example of a Perpetual Inventory System

When Tech Ltd. counted its inventory at December 31, 2016, it determined that goods with a total cost of $16,000 were still on hand. The company had started the year with inventory costing $9,000 and the company had made purchases totalling $27,000 during the year. According to Tech Ltd.'s perpetual inventory system, the cost of goods sold for 2016 was $19,000. The amount of shrinkage would be determined as follows:

Opening Inventory	$ 9,000
+ Purchases	27,000
Cost of Goods Available for Sale	36,000
− Cost of Goods Sold	19,000
Ending Inventory (per system)	17,000
Ending Inventory (per inventory count)	16,000
Shrinkage	$ 1,000

Under the perpetual inventory system, Tech Ltd. is able to quantify the amount of shrinkage. Under the periodic inventory system, this amount was included in the company's cost of goods sold. Being able to quantify this amount allows management to assess the strength of its internal controls over inventory.

What are the key distinctions between periodic and perpetual inventory systems?

Exhibit 7-5 outlines the key distinctions between the periodic and perpetual inventory systems, while Exhibit 7-6 outlines the primary advantages of each system.

Exhibit 7-5 Key Distinctions Between Inventory Systems

	Perpetual Inventory System	Periodic Inventory System
Timing of accounting entries	• Continuously • Every time inventory is purchased or sold	• Only purchase information is recorded • All other entries are made at the end of each accounting period
Accounting entries:		

When inventory purchased	DR Inventory
	  CR Cash or Accounts Payable
		DR Purchases
		  CR Cash or Accounts Payable

At time of sale	DR Cash or Accounts Receivable
	  CR Sales Revenue
	DR Cost of Goods Sold
	  CR Inventory
		DR Cash or Accounts Receivable
		  CR Sales Revenue

Additional closing entry required?	No year-end entry unless there is theft or shrinkage to record	DR Inventory (ending)
		DR Cost of Goods Sold
		  CR Purchases
		  CR Inventory (opening)

Inventory counts	Yes, they are required on an annual basis for internal control purposes, but are not required to calculate cost of goods sold and ending inventory	Yes, they are required at the end of each accounting period to calculate cost of goods sold and ending inventory

Exhibit 7-6 Advantages of Each Type of Inventory System

Perpetual Inventory System	Periodic Inventory System
• Provides up-to-date information on ending inventory and therefore cost of goods sold is always available. • Enables companies to automatically reorder when inventory amounts reach pre-established levels. • Enables companies to quantify the amount of shrinkage or theft. • Eliminates the need for frequent inventory counts.	• Cheaper in terms of initial costs.

How does management decide which inventory system to use?

There are several factors management considers when deciding whether to use a periodic or perpetual inventory system. First, it must assess the importance of having complete, timely inventory information for managing the business. The use of a perpetual system provides managers with the information to make better business decisions in a timely manner. At any point in time, managers can see what items are selling and how many units they still have on hand. Further, they can determine what items to reorder and when to place the order. This information is particularly useful for goods with a short shelf life or for inventory items that are in high demand or subject to seasonal fluctuations. Management does not want to experience stockouts related to high-demand items, such as the newest model of a smartphone, or have to reorder a large quantity of a seasonal item, such as snow blowers or beach umbrellas, at the end of the season. Having up-to-date inventory information also enables management to determine the profits that have been made from the sale of goods. This helps management monitor its pricing strategies.

Up-to-date inventory information is critical to many businesses. For example, with car dealerships, every car or truck at the dealership is unique. There are different features or options, different colour schemes, and therefore different costs. The sales personnel must know the cars and trucks on hand in order to intelligently interact with customers. In addition, because selling prices are negotiated and the costs of different cars can vary dramatically, the cost of a specific car must be known at the time of sale so that an appropriate price can be negotiated. As you can see, the dealer's profitability depends on the availability of up-to-date inventory information.

In a periodic system, complete inventory information is not available on a timely basis. Managers of companies using periodic inventory systems must develop other techniques to determine information that would be readily available from a perpetual system. For example, rather than having automated reordering, a card may be placed near the bottom of a stack of merchandise. When merchandise is sold and the card becomes visible, it is a signal that it is time to reorder. This is a very crude system that depends on the card not being removed and on someone noticing it when it becomes visible. Alternatively, employees could count a selection of items every day to determine quantities on hand. Canadian retailer **Dollarama Inc.** used this method until very recently. Because the company has hundreds of items in inventory, it took staff approximately 27 days to count all the items in a store.[6] Arrangements like this are not an effective use of staff resources and do not always prevent stockouts.

Another factor that should be considered when deciding which type of inventory system to implement relates to the identification of inventory shrinkage. As noted, the use of a periodic system makes it very challenging to identify shrinkage during the year. Management has no information about the quantities of inventory on hand until an inventory count is done. If inventory is missing or identified as damaged during the count, it is included in the cost of goods sold calculation. The costs of shrinkage can be significant and management will not necessarily know how much has been lost. Perpetual systems provide continuous information about the quantity of inventory that should be on hand, which makes it is easier for management to identify the costs associated with shrinkage. Management can compare the quantity counted during the annual count with the perpetual inventory records. Any difference between the inventory record and the physical inventory is shrinkage.

Finally, management must assess the costs of purchasing and maintaining the inventory system. While perpetual systems provide better, more current information about the quantity and costs of inventory on hand, they do so at a higher cost to the company. A small business, such as a neighbourhood convenience store, may not want to make a significant investment in the necessary technology. For example, does the convenience store owner need to install a bar code scanner to track inventory or use **electronic data interchange (EDI)** to automatically generate orders when inventory levels fall below a specified point? While convenience stores stock many different products, the quantities of each product are usually small. The owner knows which products sell quickly, such as milk, and she can monitor the quantities available for sale by walking around the store. Therefore, a perpetual inventory system may not be necessary for a convenience store.

To summarize, the costs of an inventory system must be balanced against the benefits of the information it provides. The main benefit of perpetual systems is the availability of complete, timely information. When this information is required for pricing, reordering, and other important business decisions, the benefits of the perpetual system may be greater than the costs required to acquire and maintain the system.

COST FORMULAS

What costs are included in inventory?

■ **LEARNING OBJECTIVE 4**
Explain why cost formulas are necessary and calculate the cost of goods sold and ending inventory using the specific identification, weighted-average, and first-in, first-out cost formulas.

Before we can explain what cost formulas are and why they are necessary, we must first discuss what costs are included in inventory. The general principle is that the cost amount originally assigned to inventory should contain all costs incurred by the company to purchase the goods, make them ready for sale, and get them to the place where they will be sold. Exhibit 7-7 outlines the various costs that are included in the cost of inventory.

As a practical matter, it is often difficult to assign a dollar amount of shipping costs to a specific item of inventory. For example, when grocery stores receive shipments of inventory, they often include many

Exhibit 7-7 Items Included in the "Cost" of Inventory

"Cost" includes...	
For a retailer:	**For a manufacturer:**
• Purchase price of item	• Purchase price of raw materials
• Non-refundable taxes	• Non-refundable taxes
• Shipping or transportation-in	• Shipping or transportation-in
• Import duties	• Import duties
	• Labour costs
	• Overhead costs

different products, such as boxes of cereal, heads of lettuce, and bags of apples. It is not practical to assign shipping costs to a single box of cereal or a single head of lettuce. Therefore, many companies treat shipping costs as an expense in the period in which they are incurred. These costs become part of cost of goods sold.

What are cost formulas and why are they necessary?

KEY POINTS
• Cost formulas are necessary because inventory purchase costs change.
• COGAS is the same regardless of the cost formula used.
• The three cost formulas result in different allocations of COGAS between ending inventory and COGS.

Cost formulas are necessary because the prices a company pays to purchase or manufacture its inventory change. Different units of inventory will have different costs due to changes in raw material costs, volume purchase discounts, changes in shipping costs, and so on. As a result, companies need to determine which unit costs will be allocated to cost of goods sold and which will be allocated to ending inventory. As we have discussed, the sum of a company's opening inventory and the total inventory purchase costs is known as cost of goods available for sale (COGAS). This is then allocated between ending inventory (on the statement of financial position) and cost of goods sold (on the statement of income). This allocation is done using one of three inventory cost formulas: **specific identification (specific ID)**, **weighted-average (W/A)**, and **first-in, first-out (FIFO)**.

The choice of cost formula is a significant accounting policy and management must give the decision serious thought because the choice of cost formula will impact the company's reported gross profit, net income, and ending inventory in each accounting period. Once selected, the cost formula cannot be easily changed, because a change in accounting policy requires restatement of the financial statements and additional note disclosure. It is important to note that a company does not have to select a single cost formula for its entire inventory. The same cost formula must be used for all inventories of a similar nature and use, but different cost formulas can be selected for inventories with a different nature or use.

For Example

High Liner Foods Incorporated, based in Lunenburg, Nova Scotia, manufactures and markets prepared and packaged frozen seafood products. The company uses the first-in, first-out cost formula to determine the cost of its manufactured products. However, it uses the weighted-average cost formula to determine the cost of its raw materials inventory and the cost of finished goods that it has purchased from other manufacturers. This is a good example of a company using different cost formulas when the nature or use of various inventories is different.[7]

KEY POINTS
The decision to use a perpetual or periodic inventory system will:
• have no impact on cost allocation for the specific identification and FIFO cost formulas.
• result in different cost allocations under the weighted-average cost formula.

We will now look at how each of the cost formulas works. As many companies use perpetual inventory systems, we will look at the mechanics of the weighted-average and FIFO cost formulas within a perpetual inventory system. A discussion of how cost formulas work with periodic inventory systems is in an appendix at the end of the chapter. The cost formulas work the same way under both systems, but the frequency of the calculations differs significantly. With perpetual systems, calculations must be made with each purchase of inventory, as these systems constantly update cost of goods sold and inventory information. With periodic systems, calculations are made only at the end of each accounting period (each month, quarter, or year) after an inventory count has been completed. Regardless of whether a perpetual or periodic inventory system is used, the results will be the same for both the specific identification and FIFO cost formulas. However, if a company is using the weighted-average cost formula, the allocation of costs between ending inventory and cost of goods sold will be different depending upon whether a perpetual or periodic inventory system is being used. Later in the chapter, we will discuss how companies determine which cost formula to use.

Specific Identification

As the name suggests, with the specific identification cost formula, the company knows the specific cost of the items that have been sold because they are specifically identifiable. As such, these specific costs will be allocated to cost of goods sold. The use of this cost formula requires the company to track the purchase cost of each item. Companies that use specific identification generally have small quantities of high-priced, unique products in inventory, so the cost and effort required to track the cost of the items is not too onerous.

For example, imagine that a Vancouver art gallery purchased two paintings from a new artist. Painting A was a landscape of the Gulf Islands and cost the gallery $400. Painting B was an abstract of Stanley Park. It was a larger painting and cost the gallery $750. If the gallery subsequently sold the landscape to a customer for $650, the cost of goods sold would be $400 (which is what the art gallery paid the artist for the painting). Painting B remains in inventory at a cost of $750. Art galleries are an example of a situation where it would make sense to use the specific identification cost formula because each painting is unique and the gallery is aware of what it paid for each one.

Weighted-Average

Under the weighted-average cost formula, a company's inventory cost is recalculated every time additional goods are purchased. The weighting is based on the number of goods purchased relative to the number of goods on hand. When inventory is sold, the weighted-average cost per unit at that point is used to assign a cost to the products sold.

Exhibit 7-8 illustrates the use of the weighted-average cost formula. Think of the illustration as an underground fuel tank at the gas station. There is always some fuel in the tank because the station owner wants to avoid a stockout and never lets the tank empty completely before buying more fuel. Each time the station owner purchases additional fuel, it is at a different price. But when the truck delivers the additional fuel, it is simply added to the tank and, consequently, is mixed with the fuel already on hand. Because one litre of gas looks exactly the same as another (that is, gas is **homogeneous**), when a sale is made, the station owner does not know which litres were sold. Therefore, the cost of the gas sold must be calculated using the weighted-average formula.

Exhibit 7-8 Weighted-Average Illustration

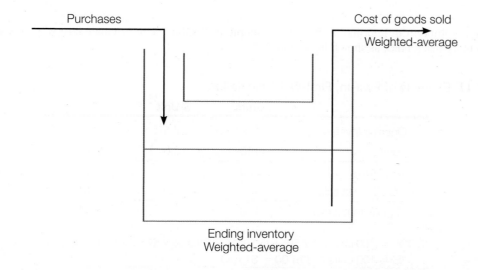

Purchases

Cost of goods sold
Weighted-average

Ending inventory
Weighted-average

Exhibit 7-9 shows an example of how to perform a weighted-average calculation.

Exhibit 7-9 Example of Weighted-Average Calculation

Rupert Co. had a beginning inventory of 100 units with a cost of $7.50 per unit. On April 3 it purchased 150 units for $16 per unit for a total cost of $2,400. On April 15 it sold 150 units. The cost of goods sold using the weighted-average cost is calculated as follows:

	Units	$/Unit	$
Opening Inventory	100	7.50	750
+ Purchases	150	16.00	2,400
COGAS	250		3,150
− COGS (units sold)	150		1,890[a]
EI (units remaining)	100		1,260[b]

COGAS/Total number of units = $3,150/250 = $12.60 (weighted-average cost per unit)

[a]COGS = 150 units × $12.60 = $1,890
[b]EI = 100 units × $12.60 = $1,260

First-In, First-Out (FIFO)

When a company uses the FIFO cost formula, the costs of the first units purchased are assigned to the first units sold and become cost of goods sold. The units remaining in inventory are assigned the costs from the last purchases. Exhibit 7-10 illustrates the use of the first-in, first-out cost formula. Think of the illustration as a pipeline, in which the costs of the first goods to enter the pipeline would be the costs assigned to the first goods out of the pipeline. In other words, the costs of the first goods in the pipeline (which are normally beginning inventory) would be used as the cost of goods sold for the first goods sold. Meanwhile, the costs of the last goods to enter the pipeline (the last goods purchased) would be assigned as the costs of ending inventory.

Exhibit 7-10 First-In, First-Out Illustration

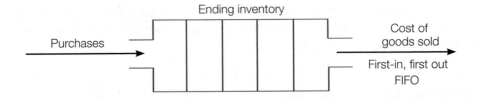

We can use the Rupert Co. information from the example in Exhibit 7-9 to calculate cost of goods sold and ending inventory using FIFO, as shown in Exhibit 7-11.

Exhibit 7-11 Example of First-In, First-Out Calculation

	Units	$/Unit	$
Opening Inventory	100	7.5	750
+ Purchases	150	16.0	2,400
COGAS	250		3,150
− COGS (units sold)	150		1,550[a]
EI (units remaining)	100		1,600[b]

[a]COGS = (100 units × $7.50) + (50 units × $16.00) = $750 + $800 = $1,550
[b]EI = 100 units × $16.00 = $1,600

The Rupert Co. example highlights the difference in allocation of COGAS between cost of goods sold and ending inventory that occurs when different cost formulas are used. The weighted-average formula resulted in a higher COGS ($1,890 versus $1,550) and a lower ending inventory ($1,260 versus $1,600) than the amounts calculated using FIFO. Management will consider the differences in allocation of costs when selecting an inventory cost formula.

How are cost of goods sold and ending inventory determined using the specific identification, weighted-average, and first-in, first-out cost formulas?

In this section, we will look at a slightly more complex example to reinforce our understanding of how the three cost formulas are used to allocate the cost of goods available (COGAS) between cost of goods sold (COGS) and ending inventory (EI). The calculations will be based on the information presented in Exhibit 7-12.

Exhibit 7-12 Data for Additional Cost Formula Example

The following information relates to inventory transactions made by Amon Ltd. during the month of September:

Sept. 1	Beginning inventory of 5 units at $65 each
Sept. 5	Purchased 10 units at $74 each
Sept. 15	Sold 9 units at $150 each
Sept. 27	Purchased 6 units at $81 each

Based on this information, we would first determine Amon's cost of goods available for sale (COGAS) because this is the starting point for all cost formulas:

	Units	$	Details
Beginning Inventory	5	$ 325	(5 × $65)
+ Purchases	16	1,226	(10 × $74) + (6 × $81)
COGAS	21	$1,551	

The various cost formulas will be used to allocate Amon's COGAS of $1,551 between the 9 units sold (the COGS) and the 12 units still on hand (the EI).

Specific Identification

With the specific identification cost formula, the company must be able to identify which goods were sold. In this case, let's assume that of the nine units sold on September 15, four were from beginning inventory and five were from the September 5 purchase. Exhibit 7-13 illustrates how the specific ID cost formula would be applied to the data in Exhibit 7-12.

Exhibit 7-13 Additional Specific Identication Illustration

COGS = (4 units × $65) + (5 units × $74) = $260 + $370 = $630

  EI = 12 units = COGAS − COGS = $1,551 − $630 = $921

   or

   = (1 unit × $65) + (5 units × $74) + (6 units × $81)

   = $65 + $370 + $486

   = $921

Weighted-Average

Recall that we need to calculate the weighted-average cost per unit every time new inventory is purchased. The weighted-average cost per unit is then used to calculate the cost of goods sold for the sales between the time it has been calculated and the next purchase of goods. This is shown in Exhibit 7-14.

Exhibit 7-14 Additional Weighted-Average Cost Formula Illustration

	A	B	= B/A	
	Total Units Available	COGAS	Weighted-Average Cost per Unit	Details
Sept. 1	5	$325	$65	COGAS = 5 × $65
Sept. 5	+10 — 15	+740 — 1,065	$71	COGAS = 5 × $65 + 10 × $74 = $1,065
Sept. 15	(9) — 6	(639) — 426	$71	COGS = 9 units × $71 = $639; EI = $1,065 − 639 = $426 [6 units]
Sept. 27	+6 — 12	+486 — $912	$76	COGAS = $426 + 6 × $81 = $912 (note this is also EI) Weighted-average cost = $912 ÷ 12 units = $76 per unit

TAKE**5**

First-In, First-Out (FIFO)

Recall that with the first-in, first-out inventory cost formula, we allocate the costs of the oldest items in inventory (those purchased first) to the first items sold. Conversely, the costs of the most recently purchased items are assigned to ending inventory.

Exhibit 7-15 shows another FIFO cost formula illustration.

Exhibit 7-15 Additional First-In, First-Out Cost Formula Illustration

	Total Units Available	COGAS	Details
Sept. 1	5	$325	COGAS = 5 × $65
Sept. 5	+10 — 15	+740 — 1,065	COGAS = (5 × $65) + (10 × $74) = $1,065
Sept. 15	(9) — 6	(621) — 444	COGS = (5 units × $65) + (4 units × $74) = $621 EI = 6 units × $74 = $444 (or $1,065 − $621)
Sept. 27	+6 — 12	+486 — $930	COGAS = $444 + 6 × $81 = $930 (note this is also EI)

We can see from the above exhibits that the choice of cost formula has an impact on the company's cost of goods sold and ending inventory balances. In this example, Amon Ltd. would have sales revenue of $1,350 (9 units × $150 per unit), but depending upon the cost formula adopted, the company would have had different gross margins and different ending inventory balances. Exhibit 7-16 presents the comparative results for the three cost formulas.

Exhibit 7-16 Comparative Results Across Cost Formulas

	Specific ID	Weighted-Average	FIFO
Sales Revenue	$1,350	$1,350	$1,350
− Cost of Goods Sold	630	639	621
Gross Margin	720	711	729
Ending Inventory	$ 921	$ 912	$ 930

While the numbers in this illustration are small, you can see the choice of cost formula does have an impact on gross margin and, therefore, on a company's net income. The decision also has an impact on the statement of financial position because the company's ending inventory balances are also affected. Imagine the financial statement impacts if the units in the illustration were in hundreds of thousands:

there would be a $1.8-million difference in net income and ending inventory between the results of the weighted-average and FIFO cost formulas!

How do companies determine which cost formula to use?

It is important to understand that, while there are three cost formulas, they are not all options that a company can choose to use. As illustrated in Exhibit 7-17, if a company's inventories are not interchangeable (that is, the goods are unique and each item can be identified), then the company is required to using the specific identification cost formula. If the goods are interchangeable (that is, they are homogeneous), then management has a decision to make, as they would have to choose between the weighted-average and the first-in, first-out cost formulas.

Exhibit 7-17 Cost Formula Decision Tree

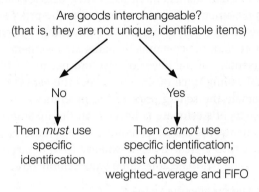

This means that the first decision when selecting a cost formula is based on the nature of the inventory. That is, does the company have small quantities of high-value, unique products in inventory? The art gallery previously discussed can use the specific identification cost formula. Car dealerships can also use specific identification because each vehicle has a unique vehicle identification number and individual characteristics such as the colour of the interior or type and size of the engine. For other businesses, it is not easy or even possible to specifically identify the costs of individual physical units. For example, can your bookstore identify one copy of a certain text from another of the same text?

If the product is interchangeable or homogeneous, then management may choose between the weighted-average and first-in, first-out cost formulas. They may base their decision on how the goods physically flow through inventory. Earlier, we discussed gas stations and how their fuel inventories are mixed together. In this case, the weighted-average cost formula would most closely align with the physical flow of goods. Alternatively, the FIFO cost formula would most closely align with the physical flow of goods in many businesses. For example, in grocery stores, new items are put behind old items on the shelf. Because customers usually select the item at the front of the shelf, the older items are sold first. If the grocery store did not rotate inventory in this way, some items would sit on the shelf for months, risking spoilage. The company in our feature story, Magna International, uses the FIFO cost formula to value the items it makes itself. This cost formula likely mirrors the physical flow of the goods that Magna produces for auto manufacturers.

Another major consideration for management when deciding whether to use weighted-average or FIFO is the impact that choice would have on the value of inventory and cost of goods sold. In Exhibit 7-16 above, we determined that the FIFO cost formula would result in a higher gross margin and therefore a higher net income than would be the case under weighted-average ($729 instead of $711). We also determined that FIFO would result in the company having a higher ending inventory balance than would be the case under weighted-average ($930 instead of $912). If management has an incentive to maximize earnings, (for example, if they have a bonus based on income), they would be inclined to select FIFO. If management was trying to minimize net income in order to minimize taxes, then they would be inclined to select the weighted-average method. This demonstrates the impact that the choice of accounting policies can have on a company's results.

INVENTORY VALUATION

At what value is inventory reflected on the statement of financial position?

Inventory is normally classified as a current asset because we assume that it will be sold within the next 12 months. We would also expect it to be sold for more that its cost. These are reasonable assumptions for many companies. However, they may not always be the case, as circumstances may arise that negatively affect the inventory's value. For example, changes in technology (such as computer processors) or in government regulations (such as changes in drug approvals that could affect pharmaceutical inventories) may significantly impact the value of inventory or render it obsolete. Inventory may also be damaged while on store shelves or in the warehouse. Management must consider all of these factors when preparing the company's financial statements. Damaged and obsolete inventory must be identified during the inventory count and management must then decide whether or not the inventory can be sold. If it can be sold, management will need to determine the price reduction that will be required.

KEY POINTS
• Inventory is carried at the lower of:
  - cost and
  - net realizable value (NRV).
• NRV = Selling Price – Estimated Costs to Make Sale

To ensure that the value of inventory presented on the company's statement of financial position reflects a value that is not more than the economic benefits management expects to flow from it, companies are required to carry inventory at the lower of cost and net realizable value. **Net realizable value (NRV)** is equal to the normal selling price of the goods less the estimated costs to make the sale. This requires management to estimate the selling price of the inventory item and the costs associated with selling the product. If management's estimate is lower than the inventory's cost (as determined by the cost formula) used by the company, the carrying amount of the inventory must be reduced. This is known as an **inventory writedown**, which is treated as an expense (part of cost of goods sold) in that period.

An illustration of determining net realizable value is in Exhibit 7-18.

Exhibit 7-18 Determining Net Realizable Value

Iqaluit Inc. has a product in its inventory with a cost of $100 per unit. To determine net realizable value, management must estimate the selling price and the selling costs.

a. If Iqaluit estimates a selling price of $150 and selling costs of $25, the net realizable value of this product is $125 ($150 − $25). In this case, the company would continue to carry the inventory at $100 per unit, because this is lower than the estimated NRV of $125 per unit.

b. If Iqaluit estimates a selling price of $120 and selling costs of $25, the net realizable value of the product is $95 ($120 − $25). In this case, the company would write the inventory down to the lesser amount (to $95 per unit). The $5 per unit writedown would be included in the company's cost of goods sold for the period.

The historical cost of inventory can be independently verified by looking at purchase orders and invoices. Net realizable value, however, relies on the reasonability of management's estimates because the selling price and associated selling costs are not certain until the product is actually sold. This is a situation where management's bias can impact the company's financial results.

FINANCIAL STATEMENTS

> **For Example**
>
> The following excerpt is taken from the significant accounting policy note in Canadian Tire Corporation's 2013 financial statements. It illustrates the way Canadian public companies value their inventories.
>
> **Merchandise inventories**
>
> Merchandise inventories are carried at the lower of cost and net realizable value. Net realizable value is the estimated selling price of inventory during the normal course of business less estimated selling expenses.[8]

How is the lower of cost or net realizable value applied to inventory?

As discussed in the previous section, a company will compare the cost of the inventory with its net realizable value and apply the lower of cost or net realizable value rule at the end of each accounting period.

Companies can apply this on an item-by-item basis, but more commonly it is done for groups of similar items, such as all of a certain type of computer processor. In Exhibit 7-19, there are three products in the company's inventory and we will compare the historical cost of each product with the estimated net realizable value.

Exhibit 7-19 Application of the Lower of Cost and NRV

Product	Historical Cost ($)	NRV ($)	Value Used in Inventory
A	2,000	1,500	1,500
B	750	900	750
C	1,800	1,900	1,800
Total	4,550	4,300	4,050

Note that the historical costs of Products B and C are less than the net realizable value, so no adjustment is required. However, the historical cost of Product A is higher than its net realizable value. Therefore, we need to make an entry as follows:

DR Cost of Goods Sold [2,000 − 1,500]   500
      CR Inventory   500

This entry has the effect of immediately reducing net income by the amount of the inventory writedown even though the inventory has yet to be sold. In other words, the loss in the value of the inventory is included in the cost of goods sold in the period in which it is realized rather than when the product is subsequently sold.

GROSS MARGIN

What is gross margin and why is it a key measure?

Gross margin was introduced in Chapter 4. We learned that it was the difference between sales revenue and the cost of goods sold. It tells the user the portion of sales revenue, after product costs, that is available to meet operating expenses and income taxes, and contribute to profit. The gross margin ratio is equal to gross margin divided by sales revenue. Both the gross margin and gross margin ratio can be used to analyze a company's performance over time. It is also a useful measure when comparing one company with others in the industry. Exhibit 7-20 illustrates how these ratios are calculated and interpreted.

■ LEARNING OBJECTIVE 6
Explain how a company's gross margin is determined and why it is an important measure.

KEY POINTS
- Sales Revenue
  − COGS
  = Gross Margin
- Gross margin is often expressed as a percentage of sales revenue.

Exhibit 7-20 Gross Margin and Gross Margin Ratio

The following table is selected financial information from Estevan Inc.'s statement of income for the years ended December 31.

		2016	2015	2014	2013
Sales revenue	A	$11,073	$18,423	$19,907	$14,953
Cost of goods sold	B	7,639	11,848	11,082	8,369
Gross margin	C = A − B	$ 3,434	$ 6,575	$ 8,825	$ 6,584
Gross margin ratio	D = C/A	31.0%	35.7%	44.3%	44.0%

What does the gross margin ratio tell us? In 2016 Estevan had 31% of sales ($3,434) available to cover expenses after covering the cost of products sold. If expenses were less than $3,434 in 2016, Estevan would report net income. If expenses were higher than $3,434, then the company would report a net loss.

We can see that there has been a significant decrease in Estevan's gross margin ratio in 2015 and 2016 when compared with 2013 and 2014. Possible reasons for this decrease may include:
- reduced selling prices in order to sell slow-moving inventory
- increasing prices for inventory that were not passed along to customers
- a large shrinkage cost from damaged and obsolete inventory included in COGS
- change in product mix; that is, high-volume, lower-margin products replaced low-volume, high-margin products

INTERNAL CONTROLS AND INVENTORY

■ LEARNING OBJECTIVE 7

Describe management's responsibility for internal control measures related to inventory.

What principles of internal control can be applied to inventory?

Recall the discussion of internal control principles from Chapter 6. The five key elements of internal control are (1) physical controls, (2) assignment of responsibility, (3) separation of duties, (4) independent verification, and (5) documentation. Since inventory is a significant asset in many businesses, effective management of it is critical to a company's success. Management will use internal control procedures to ensure that the inventory is not lost or stolen, that it is in the right place at the right time, that it does not spoil or get damaged prior to sale, and that it does not become obsolete.

Some common internal control procedures for managing inventory include:

- the use of electronic markers on items that sound an alarm when the item leaves the premises without being purchased;
- having different employees responsible for ordering the inventory, checking the inventory when it is received, and entering inventory information in the accounting system; and
- storing valuable goods in locked cabinets or behind counters.

The longer an item is stored, the greater the probability that it will be damaged, misplaced, or become obsolete. This, coupled with the fact that higher real estate costs have increased the expense of having large warehouses full of inventory, has placed increasing importance on inventory management. Companies have sought to develop ordering and delivery strategies that enable them to order, receive, and sell inventory as quickly as possible. The shorter the time the goods are on hand, the lower the company's costs. Some companies have moved to **just-in-time (JIT)** delivery strategies where the inventory is delivered as close as possible to the time when the customer will be ready to buy it. These arrangements require companies to have contractual agreements with their suppliers that include on-demand deliveries.

For Example

Walmart is an excellent illustration of the importance of inventory management. According to the company's website, the "company is continually seeking to improve (its) supply chain efficiency. Lack of supply chain reliability creates inefficiencies that drive up the cost of doing business, resulting in higher prices for the goods (the company) sell(s). These costs impede (Walmart) in providing . . . customers the everyday low prices they deserve." In order to best serve its customers, Walmart has a program that requires its suppliers to deliver the goods ordered to Walmart's distribution centres within a four-day window. Suppliers who fail to meet this target at least 90% of the time (measured monthly) have a 3% penalty applied to their invoices, which means they will only receive 97% of the invoice amount.[9]

A company's external auditors also play an important role with respect to inventory management. The auditors review the company's internal control systems to ensure that safeguards are in place to physically protect, record, and report inventory. During the annual audit, the auditors are normally present when the inventory is counted so that they can verify a sample of the company's inventory counts to ensure that the amount and valuation determined by the company are appropriate.

 Ethics in Accounting

The **Salvation Army** discovered several irregularities in the operations of a Toronto warehouse and distribution centre where donated toys were collected and distributed to needy children at Christmas. An internal audit conducted in August 2012 found that approximately 100,000 toys, worth about $2 million, were missing and believed stolen. At the time of the alleged theft, there were limited internal controls in place. The Salvation Army relied on manual count sheets and manually prepared spreadsheets to track the toys. A forensic accounting firm was engaged to investigate. Several charges of theft were subsequently laid.

Other charities, such as the **Daily Bread Food Bank**, have implemented several controls to safeguard the donated food and monitor the movement through distribution centres. These controls include the use of a food-weighing and tracking system and the use of bar codes.[10]

The counting and costing of ending inventory can be an expensive process, particularly for companies with large amounts of inventory. Companies often close their doors to customers during the counting process, which results in lost sales. Companies must also pay individuals to perform the count. Given these costs, it generally makes sense for most businesses to count inventory only once a year. However, in some industries, such as the food and beverage industry, companies count key items of inventory more frequently, sometimes daily or weekly.

FINANCIAL STATEMENT ANALYSIS

Before we calculate the inventory turnover ratio and determine the number of days sales in inventory, it is helpful to consider a challenge that arises when performing an analysis of inventory. As discussed, companies can use different cost formulas when calculating cost of goods sold and ending inventory balances. For example, one company may use weighted-average cost while another company in the same industry uses FIFO. While both formulas are acceptable, they can result in quite different inventory valuations, particularly if prices are increasing or decreasing frequently. Therefore, it is important to read the significant accounting policies note in the financial statements to be aware of such differences before doing ratio analysis.

■ **LEARNING OBJECTIVE 8**
Calculate the inventory turnover ratio and the days to sell inventory ratio and explain how they can be interpreted by users.

How often does the company sell through its inventory?

Companies purchase inventory with the intent of selling it to customers. When inventory is sitting on the company's store shelves or in its warehouse, it is not generating any return. Users are very interested in knowing how often the company is able to sell through or turn over its inventory. The **inventory turnover ratio** tells the user how fast inventory is sold or how long it is held before it is sold. It is calculated as follows:

$$\text{Inventory turnover ratio} = \frac{\text{Cost of Goods Sold}}{\text{Average Inventory*}}$$

*Average Inventory = (Opening Inventory + Ending Inventory)/2

Average inventory is used, where possible, rather than ending inventory because it represents a more appropriate measure of inventory levels if these have changed over the year.

A higher inventory turnover ratio is better than a lower one. A higher ratio means that the company has sold through its inventory (sold all of its products) more times than a company with a lower turnover ratio. This means that it has been more effective in managing its inventory and generating sales.

How many days did it take to sell through the company's inventory?

A second ratio that is helpful when analyzing inventory is the **days to sell inventory ratio**. This ratio tells us how many days, on average, that it took the company to sell through its inventory. It is calculated as follows:

$$\text{Days to Sell Inventory} = \frac{365 \text{ days}}{\text{Inventory Turnover Ratio}}$$

Generally, a lower number is considered to be better than a higher number. That is because selling inventories quickly is a good thing as it speeds up the cash-to-cash cycle we have discussed in previous chapters. However, if this ratio is too low, it could mean that the company will experience stockouts.

It is important to consider the nature of the company's business when interpreting this ratio. Questions that would need to be addressed as part of this analysis would include:
- Is the business seasonal?
- Does the company sell a few high-priced items or many low-priced items?
- Have new competitors entered the market?
- Has there been a change in economic conditions?

All of these factors can contribute to a change in the days to sell inventory ratio.

For Example

The following financial information is taken from the **Maple Leaf Foods** 2013 annual report:

($000's)	2013	2012	2011
Inventories (statement of financial position)	287,786	301,804	293,231
Cost of goods sold	3,920,652	3,878,219	4,126,460

$$\text{Inventory turnover ratio} = \frac{\text{Cost of Goods Sold}}{\text{Average Inventory}}$$

2013	2012
$\dfrac{3,920,652}{(301,804 + 287,786)/2}$	$\dfrac{3,878,219}{(293,231 + 301,804)/2}$
$\dfrac{3,920,652}{294,795}$	$\dfrac{3,878,219}{297,517}$
= 13.3 times	= 13.0 times

Days to sell inventory ratio = 365 days/13.3 = 27.4 days   365 days/13.0 = 28.1 days.

Given that Maple Leaf Foods operates in the food industry and many food products have short shelf lives, we would expect Maple Leaf to turn over its inventory fairly quickly. We can see that the company's turnover was slightly quicker compared with the prior year and that the company took about just over a half day less to sell through its inventories.[11]

How can inventory amounts be estimated?

There are times when management of a company with a periodic inventory system needs to know the cost of goods sold or the value of inventory but chooses not to count inventory because it would be too costly to close the business to do so. There are also cases where inventory cannot be counted, such as if it has been stolen or destroyed in a fire or flood. For example, estimates may be required to prepare interim financial statements to submit to a bank or make an insurance claim for inventory that was destroyed or lost. In these cases, management can attempt to estimate the cost of goods sold amount and inventory value. Management may also estimate the quantity of inventory on hand prior to the annual physical count if using the periodic inventory system. This allows them to get an approximation of the shrinkage that has occurred.

There are several inventory estimation techniques that can be used, but we will focus on the **gross margin estimation method**. This method estimates the cost of goods sold by multiplying the sales revenue for the period, a figure that is readily available, by the normal **cost-to-sales ratio**. The normal cost-to-sales ratio reflects the normal markup that the company applies to its products. For example, a company that normally marks up its products by 50% would price an item that costs $60 at $90. The cost-to-sales ratio then is 66.67% ($60 / $90). If the sales for a given month were $12,000, the estimated cost of goods sold would be $8,000 (66.67% × $12,000).

Once this company has estimated its cost of sales, it can subtract this amount from its cost of goods available for sale to arrive at an estimate for ending inventory. The company would be able to determine the cost of the goods available for sale by referring to the accounting records and finding the beginning inventory and the purchases for the period.

For example, if a company began the period with inventory of $2,000 and the purchases for the period were $9,000, then the goods available for sale would be $11,000 and the company's estimated ending inventory would be as follows:

TAKE**5**

Beginning Inventory	$ 2,000
+ Purchases	9,000
COGAS	11,000
– Estimated Cost of Goods Sold (see above)	8,000
Estimated Ending Inventory	$ 3,000

SUMMARY

1. **Discuss the importance of inventory to a company's overall success.**

   - Inventory includes any item purchased by a company for resale to customers or to be used in the manufacture of a product that is sold to customers.
   - Inventory is often a company's most significant current asset.
   - Management must source suppliers, determine order quantities (ensuring that the risks of obsolescence and stockouts are considered), establish selling prices, and implement safeguards to prevent damage and losses due to theft.

2. **Distinguish between the different inventory classifications and determine which goods should be included in a company's inventory.**

   - Manufacturers have three classes of inventory: (1) raw materials, (2) work-in-process, and (3) finished goods.
   - All of the goods that retailers and merchandisers have available for sale are included in a single class of inventory.
   - Goods that are purchased with shipping terms FOB shipping point become part of buyer's inventory when they leave the seller's premises. Goods purchased with shipping terms FOB destination become part of inventory when they are received at the buyer's premises.
   - Goods on consignment remain as part of the inventory of their owner (the consignor) and are not part of the inventory of the consignee (the business where the goods are being held for sale).

3. **Explain the differences between perpetual inventory systems and periodic inventory systems.**

   - Cost of goods available for sale (COGAS) is equal to opening inventory plus purchases. It is allocated between cost of goods sold and ending inventory. This allocation is affected by the type of inventory system in use.
   - Periodic inventory systems update a company's inventory information periodically (at the end of each month, quarter, or year) when inventory is physically counted. Until inventory is physically counted, a company using a periodic inventory system is unable to assign costs to cost of goods sold or ending inventory. It is also unaware of the number of units sold or that remain on hand.
   - Perpetual inventory systems constantly update a company's inventory information; it is updated with every purchase or sale of inventory. Companies always know their cost of goods sold and ending inventory amounts. Perpetual inventory systems often also track the physical flow of goods, enabling automatic reordering to occur. Perpetual inventory systems also enable companies to quantify shrinkage (theft) and eliminate the need for frequent inventory counts. An inventory count is still required at least annually in order to quantify shrinkage.

4. **Explain why cost formulas are necessary and calculate the cost of goods sold and ending inventory under the specific identification, weighted-average, and first-in, first-out cost formulas.**

   - The cost of inventory includes purchase price, non-refundable taxes, shipping or transportation costs, and import duties.
   - Cost formulas are necessary because inventory purchase costs change (that is, different units of inventory will have different costs) and companies need to determine which unit costs will be allocated to cost of goods sold and which will be allocated to ending inventory.
   - There are three cost formulas: (1) specific identification, (2) weighted-average, and (3) first-in, first-out.
   - If a company's goods are not interchangeable (in other words, the goods are unique and each item can be identified), then the specific identification cost formula must be used. If the goods are interchangeable, then the company can use either weighted-average or first-in, first-out.
   - The same cost formula must be used for all inventories of a similar nature or use, but different cost formulas can be selected for inventories with a different nature or use.
   - Specific identification assigns the specific costs of each item to either cost of goods sold or ending inventory depending upon whether it has been sold or remains on hand.
   - Under the weighted-average cost formula, a weighted-average cost per unit is determined each time additional goods are purchased. This is used to assign costs when goods are sold or when the value of ending inventory is determined.
   - When the first-in, first-out formula is used, the costs of the first units purchased are assigned to the first units sold. Ending inventory is valued using the costs of the most recent purchases.

5. **Explain the value at which inventory is carried on the statement of financial position.**

   - Inventory is carried on the statement of financial position at the lower of cost and net realizable value. Net realizable value is equal to selling price less the estimated costs to make the sale.
   - This ensures that inventory is being carried at a value that reflects the economic benefits expected to flow from it.
   - When the carrying amount of inventory is reduced to net realizable value, it is referred to as an *inventory writedown*.

6. **Explain how a company's gross margin is determined and why it is an important measure.**

   - Gross margin is equal to sales revenue less cost of goods sold. It is often expressed as a percentage of sales revenue.
   - It represents the portion of sales revenue, after product costs, available to meet operating expenses and income taxes.
   - Gross margin is commonly used to assess a company's performance in terms of its pricing strategies and controlling its product costs either period-to-period or relative to its competitors.

7. **Describe management's responsibility for internal control measures related to inventory.**

   - The five key elements of internal control are applied to inventory. These are:
     i. physical controls—use of locks, inventory behind counters, use of electronic alarm tags
     ii. assignment of responsibility—specific employees are responsible for different types of inventory
     iii. separation of duties—ordering and receiving are done by different employees
     iv. independent verification—use of independent count teams or external auditors
     v. documentation—use of purchase orders, receiving reports, and so on

8. **Calculate the inventory turnover ratio and the days to sell inventory ratio and explain how they can be interpreted by users.**

   - The inventory turnover ratio is determined by dividing cost of goods sold by average inventory. It is a measure of how fast inventory is sold or how long it is held before being sold.
   - The days to sell inventory ratio is calculated by dividing 365 days by the inventory turnover ratio. It measures the number of days, on average, that it took a company to sell through its inventory.

KEY TERMS

Consignee (320)
Consignment (320)
Consignor (320)
Cost formula (326)
Cost of goods available for sale
   (COGAS) (321)
Cost-to-sales ratio (336)
Days to sell inventory ratio (335)
Electronic data interchange (EDI) (325)
Finished goods (319)
First-in, first-out (FIFO) (326)

FOB destination (320)
FOB shipping point (320)
Gross margin (333)
Gross margin estimation method (336)
Homogeneous (327)
Inventory (317)
Inventory shrinkage (323)
Inventory turnover ratio (335)
Inventory writedown (332)
Just-in-time (JIT) (334)
Manufacturer (317)

Merchandiser (317)
Net realizable value (NRV) (332)
Overhead (319)
Periodic inventory system (321)
Perpetual inventory system (322)
Raw materials (319)
Retailer (317)
Specific identification (specific ID) (326)
Stockout (318)
Weighted-average (W/A) (326)
Work-in-process (319)

ABBREVIATIONS USED

COGAS	Cost of goods available for sale
COGS	Cost of goods sold
EDI	Electronic data interchange
EI	Ending inventory
FIFO	First-in, first-out
FOB	Free on board
JIT	Just in time
NRV	Net realizable value
SME	Small and medium-sized enterprise
W/A	Weighted-average

SYNONYMS

Cost formula | Cost flow assumption

CHAPTER END REVIEW PROBLEM 1

Matchett Manufacturing Ltd. (MML) uses a perpetual inventory system and had the following inventory transactions during the month of October:

		Units	Unit Cost	Total Cost
Oct. 1	Beginning inventory	2,000	$18.00	$36,000
Oct. 3	Purchased	3,000	$20.00	$60,000
Oct. 7	Sold	2,600		
Oct. 15	Sold	1,900		
Oct. 23	Purchased	3,000	$22.00	$66,000
Oct. 29	Sold	3,300		
Oct. 31	Purchased	1,800	$20.50	$36,900

Required:

a. Determine MML's cost of goods available for sale.
b. Calculate the cost of goods sold and ending inventory as at October 31 using a perpetual inventory system and the following cost flow assumptions:
   i. FIFO
   ii. Weighted-average

CHAPTER END REVIEW PROBLEM 2

You have been asked to assess the inventory turnover and days to sell inventory ratios for two leading Canadian fashion retailers: **Le Château Inc.** and **Reitmans (Canada) Ltd.** You have been provided with the following information, which was taken from the companies' financial statements:

	Le Château Inc.	Reitmans (Canada) Ltd.
	(in thousands of Canadian dollars)	(in thousands of Canadian dollars)
Year end	January 25, 2014	February 1, 2014
Beginning inventory	$111,440*	$ 93,317

Ending inventory	$113,915		$109,601
Cost of goods sold	$101,770		$377,913

*Excludes raw materials and work in process.

Specifically, you have been asked the following:
- a. Calculate the inventory turnover ratio for both companies.
- b. Calculate the days to sell inventory ratio for both companies.
- c. Comment on what the results of your calculations in parts "a" and "b" tell you about which company is doing the better job of managing its inventory.

Suggested Solution to Chapter End Review Problem 1

		Units	Unit Cost	Total Cost
Oct. 1	Beginning inventory	2,000	$18.00	$ 36,000
Oct. 3	Purchased	3,000	$20.00	$ 60,000
Oct. 7	Sold	2,600		
Oct. 15	Sold	1,900		
Oct. 23	Purchased	3,000	$22.00	$ 66,000
Oct. 29	Sold	3,300		
Oct. 31	Purchased	1,800	$20.50	$ 36,900
	Total units available	9,800 A		$198,900 ← COGAS D
	Total units sold	7,800 B		
	Total units remaining	2,000 C		

A = Beginning Inventory + Purchases = 2,000 + 3,000 + 3,000 + 1,800 = 9,800
B = Units Sold = 2,600 + 1,900 + 3,300 = 7,800 (Note: these units will make up COGS)
C = Units Remaining = Total Units Available − Total Units Sold = 9,800 − 7,800 = 2,000
  (Note: these units will make up EI)

a. **MML's cost of goods available for sale is $198,900 (see D above)**

b. **(i) First-in, first-out cost formula**

First sale, October 7:
Cost of goods sold (2,600 units)

2,000 units @ $18.00 (Beginning inventory)	$ 36,000	
600 units @ $20.00 (Oct. 3 purchase)	12,000	
2,600 units	48,000	A

Remaining inventory (5,000 − 2,600 = 2,400 units)

2,400 units @ $20.00 (Oct. 3 purchase)	$ 48,000

Second sale, October 15:
Cost of goods sold (1,900 units)

1,900 units @ $20.00 (Oct. 3 purchase)	$ 38,000	B

Remaining inventory (500 units)

500 units @ $20.00 (Oct. 3 purchase)	$ 10,000

Third sale, October 29:
Cost of goods sold (3,300 units)

500 units @ $20.00 (Oct. 3 purchase)	$ 10,000	
2,800 units @ $22.00 (Oct. 23 purchase)	61,600	
3,300 units	$ 71,600	C

Cost of goods sold (7,800 units):

A + B + C =	$157,600	

Ending inventory (2,000 units):

200 units @ $22.00 (Oct. 23 purchase)	$ 4,400
1,800 units @ $20.50 (Oct. 31 purchase)	36,900
2,000 units	$ 41,300

Proof: COGS + EI = $157,600 + $41,300 = $198,900 = COGAS

b. (ii) Weighted-average cost formula

	A	B	= B / A		
	Total Units Available	COGAS	Weighted-Average Cost per Unit	Details	COGS
Oct. 1	2,000	$36,000	$18.00	COGAS = 2,000 × $18.00	
Oct. 3	+3,000 / 5,000	+$60,000 / $96,000	$19.20	COGAS = 2,000 × $18.00 + 3,000 × $20 = $96,000	
Oct. 7	(2,600) / 2,400	$(49,920) / $46,080	$19.20	COGS = 2,600 units × $19.20 = $49,920 EI = $96,000 − $49,920 = $46,080 [2,400 units]	$49,920 A
Oct. 15	(1,900) / 500	$(36,480) / $9,600	$19.20	COGS = 1,900 units × $19.20 = $36,480 EI = $46,080 − $36,480 = $9,600 [500 units]	$36,480 B
Oct. 23	+3,000 / 3,500	+$66,000 / $75,600	$21.60	COGAS = 500 × $19.2 + 3,000 × $22 = $75,600	
Oct. 29	(3,300) / 200	$(71,280) / $4,320	$21.60	COGS = 3,300 units × $21.60 = $71,280 EI = $75,600 − $71,280 = $4,320 [200 units]	$71,280 C
Oct. 31	+1,800 / 2,000	+$36,900 / $41,220	$20.61	COGAS = $4,320 + (1,800 × $20.50) = $41,220 (note this is also EI)	

Cost of goods sold (7,800 units):

A + B + C = $157,680

Ending inventory (2,000 units): $ 41,220

Proof: COGS + EI = $157,680 + $41,220 = $198,900 = COGAS

Suggested Solution to Chapter End Review Problem 2

a. Inventory turnover ratio $\quad = \quad \dfrac{\text{Cost of Goods Sold}}{\text{Average Inventory}}$

	Le Château	Reitmans
	$\dfrac{101,770}{(111,440 + 113,915)/2}$	$\dfrac{377,913}{(93,317 + 109,601)/2}$
=	$\dfrac{101,770}{112,678}$	$\dfrac{377,913}{101,459}$
	0.90 times	3.72 times

b. Days to sell inventory ratio = 365 days/Inventory turnover ratio

   Le Château: 365 days / 0.90 = 405.6 days

   Reitmans: 365 days / 3.72 = 98.1 days

c. From the above analysis we can see that Reitmans was able to turn over its inventory four times more often than Le Château was able to. It took Reitmans just over 3 months (98.1 days) on average to sell through its inventory, while Le Château was unable to sell through its inventory once in a single year. Inventory turnover is a key measure for companies in the fashion industry as it is seasonal and trends change quickly. Investors and creditors look for a higher turnover ratio *or* a lower days to sell inventory ratio.

APPENDIX

Inventory Cost Formulas under the Periodic Inventory System

We discussed the weighted-average, first-in, first-out, and specific identification cost formulas using a perpetual inventory system earlier in the chapter. We will now discuss how these cost formulas are applied within periodic inventory systems. The good news is that the amounts that would be allocated to cost of goods sold and ending inventory under both the specific identification cost formula and the first-in, first-out cost formula are exactly the same regardless of whether a perpetual or periodic inventory system is used. As such, we do not need to revisit either of these cost formulas in detail.

Of course, one of the major differences between the two inventory systems is that inventory must be physically counted in the periodic inventory system in order to determine ending inventory. The value of ending inventory is then subtracted from cost of goods available for sale to determine the cost of goods sold for the period. As such, cost formulas are only applied when the goods are counted at the end of an accounting period (normally monthly or quarterly or annually).

KEY POINT
The allocation of COGAS to COGS and EI is the same under either the specific identification or first-in, first-out cost formulas regardless of which type of inventory system (periodic or perpetual) is used.

Weighted-Average

We illustrate the weighted-average cost formula under a periodic inventory system using the data for Amon Ltd. that was used earlier in the chapter, in Exhibit 7-21.

EXHIBIT 7-21	DATA FOR WEIGHTED-AVERAGE COST FORMULA/PERIODIC INVENTORY SYSTEM EXAMPLE

The following information relates to inventory transactions made by Amon Ltd. during the month of September:

Sept. 1	Beginning inventory of 5 units at $65 each
Sept. 5	Purchased 10 units at $74 each
Sept. 15	Sold 9 units at $150 each
Sept. 27	Purchased 6 units at $81 each

On September 28, Amon's staff counted inventory and there were 12 units still on hand. Based on this information, we would first determine Amon's cost of goods available for sale (COGAS) because this is the starting point for all cost formulas:

	Units	$	Details
Beginning Inventory	5	$ 325	(5 × $65)
+ Purchases	16	1,226	((10 × $74) + (6 × $81))
COGAS	21	$1,551	
− Ending Inventory	12		
COGS	9		

What Amon's management would not know at the time of the count is the cost (dollar value) assigned to the 12 units in ending inventory or the 9 units in cost of goods sold. These dollar values would depend upon the cost formula used.

If the company were using the weighted-average cost formula, they would need to:
1. Determine the weighted-average cost per unit.
2. Multiply the weighted-average cost per unit times the number of units in ending inventory (per the inventory count) to determine the cost of ending inventory.
3. Subtract the cost of ending inventory from the cost of goods available for sale to determine the cost of goods sold for the period.

1. Calculation of weighted-average cost per unit:

   COGAS ÷ number of units = average cost

   $1,551 ÷ 21 = $73.86 (rounded to the nearest two decimal places)

2. Calculation of ending inventory:

   EI = number of units in ending inventory × weighted-average cost per unit

   = 12 × $73.86 = $886.32

3. Calculation of cost of goods sold:

   COGS = cost of goods available for sale − ending inventory

   = $1,551 − $886.32 = $664.68

Note that the weighted-average cost per unit calculation ignored the various purchase dates because under the periodic inventory system, this analysis would be done at the end of the month (when inventory was counted). This is a major difference between the perpetual and periodic inventory systems. When we calculated the weighted-average cost per unit using a perpetual system, we recalculated a new weighted-average cost per unit each time there was a purchase.

When you use the weighted-average cost per unit to assign a cost to both the cost of goods sold and ending inventory, the sum of the two amounts may not add up to the cost of the goods available for sale due to rounding. To avoid this problem, you should calculate either the cost of goods sold or the ending inventory amount and then subtract that amount from the cost of goods available for sale to find the other amount.

First-In, First-Out (FIFO)

Under the periodic system, the cost of goods sold and ending inventory are not determined during an accounting period. Instead, at the end of each accounting period, the number of units left in inventory is determined either by a physical count or by an estimation method. Using this information, costs are then assigned to both the units sold and those remaining in ending inventory.

Cost of goods sold = 5 units × $65 per unit = $325
             = 4 units × $74 per unit = 296
               9 units $621
Ending inventory = COGAS − COGS
             = $1,551 − $621
             = $930

Note that the cost allocations under FIFO are the same as they were when a perpetual inventory system was used. It is a bit easier to do the calculations under a periodic inventory system because they can all be done at once, at the end of the accounting period.

ASSIGNMENT MATERIAL

Discussion Questions

DQ7-1 Explain why inventory is of significance to financial statement users.

DQ7-2 Describe the major classification(s) of inventory held by a retailer.

DQ7-3 Describe the major classifications of inventory held by a manufacturer.

DQ7-4 Describe the difference between the shipping terms *FOB destination* and *FOB shipping point*.

DQ7-5 Explain what it means if a company has some of its inventory out on consignment. Who owns the goods? In other words, whose inventory would they be part of?

DQ7-6 Explain which of the following goods, which were in transit at year end, would be included in the buyer's inventory at year end: (a) Goods costing $10,000 with terms FOB shipping point and (b) goods costing $12,000 with terms FOB destination.

DQ7-7 Describe a perpetual inventory system. Identify a type of company that might use it.

DQ7-8 Describe a periodic inventory system. Identify a type of company that might use it.

DQ7-9 Explain the basic differences between periodic and perpetual inventory systems.

DQ7-10 Discuss the advantages and disadvantages of the perpetual inventory system compared with a periodic inventory system.

DQ7-11 Explain why cost of goods sold is sometimes described as a residual amount. Under which type of inventory system would this description be more accurate?

DQ7-12 Explain whether or not the use of a perpetual inventory system eliminates the need for companies to conduct inventory counts.

DQ7-13 Explain why cost formulas are necessary.

DQ7-14 Describe the specific identification, FIFO, and weighted-average cost formulas.

DQ7-15 Explain when it is appropriate to use each of the three cost formulas.

DQ7-16 Identify the circumstances when it is appropriate for companies to use the specific identification cost formula. Explain why accounting standard setters may have taken this position.

DQ7-17 Explain how the statement of financial position and statement of income would compare if a company used FIFO instead of weighted-average when the prices of inventory were rising. How would this change if the prices of inventory were decreasing?

DQ7-18 Describe how the lower of cost and net realizable value is applied to inventory. Explain why this is done.

DQ7-19 What is gross margin? Explain why it is considered a key measure of a company's performance.

DQ7-20 Discuss the need for internal controls for inventory and describe the key controls that we expect to find.

DQ7-21 What are the two key ratios used to analyze inventory? Explain what each of the ratios tells us about a company's inventory.

DQ7-22 Discuss when a company might want or need to estimate the cost of goods sold or ending inventory.

DQ7-23 Explain what basic assumption is implicit in the gross margin inventory estimation method. Why would this assumption be a challenge to defend for many companies? Identify steps a company could take to overcome this challenge and strengthen the estimates made using this method.

Application Problems

AP7-1 (Calculation of ending inventory, cost of goods sold, and gross margin—perpetual system)

The Soft Touch Company sells leather furniture. The following schedule relates to the company's inventory for the month of April:

			Cost	Sales
April 1	Beginning inventory	75 units	$45,000	
3	Purchase	50 units	31,250	
5	Sale	30 units		$33,000
11	Purchase	25 units	16,250	
15	Sale	55 units		68,750
22	Sale	40 units		48,000
28	Purchase	50 units	33,750	

Soft Touch uses the perpetual inventory system.

Required:
a. Calculate Soft Touch Company's cost of goods sold, gross margin, and ending inventory using:
   i. FIFO
   ii. Weighted-average
b. Which cost formula produced the higher gross margin?

AP7-2 (Calculation of ending inventory, cost of goods sold, and gross margin—periodic system)

Required:
If your instructor has assigned the Appendix to this chapter, redo Problem AP7-1 assuming that the company uses the periodic inventory system.

AP7-3 (Calculation of ending inventory and cost of goods sold—perpetual system)

At the beginning of its operations in March 2016, Mastiff Supplies Ltd. began with 7,500 units of inventory that it purchased at a cost of $7.00 each. The company's purchases during March were as follows:

March 13	5,000 units @ $8.00

Sales during March:	
March 2	5,000 units
March 20	2,800 units

Mastiff Supplies uses a perpetual inventory system.

Required: (**Note: Round calculations to four decimal places.**)
    a. Calculate the cost of goods sold for March using the weighted-average cost formula.
    b. Calculate the cost of goods sold for March using the first-in, first-out cost formula.
    c. Which of the two inventory cost formulas results in the greater gross margin for March?
    d. Which of the two inventory cost formulas results in the larger inventory balance at the end of March?
    e. Compare your answers in parts "c" and "d" above and comment on the relationship between these items.

AP7-4 (Calculation of ending inventory and cost of goods sold—periodic system)

Required:
If your instructor has assigned the Appendix to this chapter, redo Problem AP7-3 assuming that the company uses a periodic inventory system.

AP7-5 (Calculation of ending inventory and cost of goods sold—perpetual system)

The following information relates to Glassworks Ltd.'s inventory transactions during the month of July.

		Units	Cost/Unit	Amount
July 1	Beginning inventory	4,000	$12.00	$48,000
4	Purchase	6,000	$12.50	75,000
8	Sale	6,000		
14	Sale	1,500		
22	Purchase	5,000	$12.75	63,750
28	Sale	3,500		

All of the units sold were priced at $20 per unit.

Required:
    a. Glassworks Ltd. uses the perpetual inventory system. Calculate Glassworks' cost of goods sold, gross margin, and ending inventory for the month of July using
        i. FIFO
       ii. weighted-average
    b. Which of the cost flow assumptions would produce the higher gross margin?

AP7-6 (Calculation of ending inventory and cost of goods sold—periodic system)

Required:
If your instructor has assigned the Appendix to this chapter, redo Problem AP7-5 assuming that the company uses a periodic inventory system.

AP7-7 (Calculation of ending inventory and cost of goods sold)

Exquisite Jewellers purchases chiming clocks from around the world for sale in Canada. According to its records, Exquisite Jewellers had no opening inventory, and had the following purchases and sales of clocks in the current year:

Clock No.	Date Purchased	Amount Paid	Date Sold	Sale Price
423	Jan. 5	$2,150	Mar. 8	$3,800
424	Mar. 15	4,500		
425	May 27	4,400	June 16	6,200
426	July 14	2,400	Aug. 9	3,350
427	Oct. 24	3,720		
428	Dec. 5	1,930	Dec. 24	2,640

Exquisite Jewellers uses the specific identification cost formula. The company uses a perpetual inventory system.

Required:

    a. Calculate Exquisite's cost of goods sold and ending inventory.

    b. What conditions generally must exist for specific identification to be used? Are these met in this case? Explain.

    c. Exquisite's management are wondering if they could use the weighted-average cost formula, as they figured it would be easier. Is this possible?

AP7-8 (Lower of cost and net realizable value)

Scott's Sporting Stores Inc. reported the following cost and net realizable value information for inventory at December 31:

Product Item	Units	Unit Cost	Unit NRV
Skates:			
Bauer	13	$259	$400
CCM	10	$412	$350
Running shoes:			
Adidas	5	$120	$120
Nike	8	$117	$110

Required:

    a. Calculate the ending inventory balance for skates and running shoes using the lower of cost and net realizable value for each item.

    b. Calculate the ending inventory balance for skates and running shoes using the historical unit costs provided.

    c. Compare the difference in the ending inventory amounts under the two approaches. Which method provides a more faithful representation of the inventory value?

AP7-9 (Lower of cost and net realizable value)

Canadian Paper Company (CPC) produces newsprint in its paper mills. At the end of 2016, CPC's chief financial officer noted that the international market price of newsprint had dropped significantly. The average cost of production for newsprint in 2016 was $520 per tonne. The average selling price for newsprint in January 2017 was $505 per tonne. CPC has also been working to reduce its production costs, hoping that they can be reduced to $495 per tonne in 2017.

Required:

    a. Why is the decline in the market price for newsprint relevant in this situation?

    b. If CPC has 1,250 tonnes of newsprint on hand on December 31, 2016, what amount should be reported for ending inventory on the statement of financial position?

    c. What other information would be relevant in determining the year-end reporting amount?

    d. Which accounting concepts are relevant in deciding the dollar amount of inventory to be reported? Explain why these concepts are important.

AP7-10 (Weighted-average, FIFO, and the lower of cost and net realizable value)

Grape Leaf Ltd. began operations in 2013. The following presentation relates to the inventory valuations of the company at the end of the year using different inventory methods.

Date	Weighted-Average	FIFO	NRV
Dec. 31, 2013	$120,000	$110,000	$105,000
Dec. 31, 2014	235,000	225,000	230,000
Dec. 31, 2015	235,000	245,000	235,000
Dec. 31, 2016	210,000	235,000	235,000

Required:

    a. If Grape Leaf uses the weighted-average cost formula, what is the value of ending inventory in each of the four years?

    b. If Grape Leaf uses the FIFO cost formula, what is the value of ending inventory in each of the four years?

    c. What cost formula would you recommend Grape Leaf use if the inventory prices are falling during the four-year period? Explain your answer.

AP7-11 (Inventory estimation)

Headstrong Hardware lost most of its inventory in an electrical fire that destroyed the company's warehouse and retail store in 2016. Fortunately, the accounting records were backed up on the owner's computer in her home office and could, therefore, be recovered. However, Headstrong uses the periodic inventory system. Therefore, it could not determine the amount of inventory that was lost in the fire because the inventory was destroyed. Headstrong's insurance company requires Headstrong to prepare a reasonable estimate of the lost inventory before it can process the insurance claim.

You are Headstrong's accountant. You review the accounting for 2015 and 2016 (to the date of the fire) and obtain the following information:

    1. Sales in 2015 were $963,000.

    2. Sales in 2016 up to the time of the fire amounted to $678,000.

    3. Cost of goods sold in 2015 was $597,060.

    4. 2016 inventory purchased to the date of the fire totalled $486,000.

    5. The ending inventory reported on the 2015 statement of financial position was $88,000.

Required:

Prepare an estimate of the amount of inventory lost in the fire.

AP7-12 (Inventory estimation)

On April 25, 2016, a flash flood destroyed one of High River Company's warehouses, including all of the inventory inside. The flood did not affect the inventory held at the company's other locations. The accounting records were kept at High River's head office in Canmore. A search through the records revealed the following information:

Purchases up to April 25	$742,500
Cost of inventory on hand, January 1	$137,200
Sales up to April 25	$1,028,000
Cost-to-sales ratio for 2016	65%

A count of inventory on hand at the other locations revealed that inventory costed at $121,300 was on hand.

Required:

Estimate the cost of the inventory that was destroyed in the flash flood.

AP7-13 (Inventory turnover)

The following information pertains to two competitors, Superior Inc. and Michigan Corp.

Company	Beginning Inventory	Ending Inventory	Cost of Goods Sold
Superior Inc.	$180,000	$150,000	$1,240,000
Michigan Corp.	$410,000	$460,000	$2,270,000

Superior Inc. reported sales revenues of $1,610,000 and Michigan Corp. reported sales revenue of $3,365,000.

Required:

    a. Calculate the inventory turnover ratio for Superior and Michigan.

    b. Calculate the gross margin and gross margin ratio for Superior and Michigan.

    c. On the basis of inventory turnover, which company is moving its inventory faster? Does that mean the inventory is better managed? Explain.

    d. On the basis of gross margin ratio, which company is earning a higher profit margin?

    e. Which company do you think is better managed? Explain your answer.

AP7-14 (Inventory turnover, gross margin, and shrinkage)

The following information was taken from the accounting records of Chicoutimi Ltée and Jonquière Ltée at December 31, 2016. The two companies are competitors.

	Chicoutimi Ltée	Jonquière Ltée
Ending inventory, Dec. 31, 2015	$ 395,000	$ 150,000
Ending inventory, Dec. 31, 2016	425,000	200,000
Cost of goods sold, 2016	2,460,000	962,500
Sales for 2016	6,150,000	2,406,250

Required:

a. Calculate the gross margin, gross margin ratio, and inventory turnover ratio at December 31, 2016, for:
  i. Chicoutimi Ltée.
  ii. Jonquière Ltée.
b. During the December 20, 2016, inventory count at Chicoutimi Ltée, $75,000 of inventory shrinkage was identified. It had not been recorded in the inventory account.
  i. Prepare the entry to record the inventory shrinkage of $75,000.
  ii. Recalculate Chicoutimi's gross margin, gross margin ratio, and inventory turnover ratio after the adjusting journal entry is made. (Hint: You need to adjust the ending inventory balance for 2016 and the cost of goods sold.)
  iii. Describe what happened to Chicoutimi's gross margin ratio and inventory turnover ratio after adjusting for the inventory shrinkage.
c. Which company do you think is better at managing inventory? Explain your answer.

AP7-15 (Evaluation of the inventory turnover ratio)

The following information was taken from the accounting records of three competitors for the 2016 fiscal year.

	Inventory Turnover Ratio	Days in Inventory
Company A	11.4	32.0
Company B	14.8	24.7
Company C	14.9	24.5

Required:

a. Explain how to calculate inventory turnover and the number of days sales in inventory.
b. What do the two ratios tell us about inventory?
c. Compare the ratios for the three companies and comment on the results. What might contribute to the lower turnover and higher number of days sales in inventory at Company A?

User Perspective Problems

UP7-1 (Inventory and internal controls)

You are a consultant who helps new entrepreneurs set up their accounting systems. You are frequently asked the following questions about inventory:

"What are internal controls?"
"Why do I need to implement internal controls for inventory?"
"What are some commonly used internal controls related to inventory?"

Required:
What is your response to these two questions?

UP7-2 (Use of ratio analysis)

An assignment in your accounting course requires that you prepare an analysis of two retail companies.

Required:
Which ratios would you find useful in analyzing inventory? Explain why the ratios are useful.

UP7-3 (Importance of inventory in loan considerations)

Suppose that you are a loan officer in a financial institution. A local retail store has applied for a loan.

Required:
Would you be interested in the cost of inventory reported on the statement of financial position? Explain. Are there other related account balances that you would be interested in? Explain. Are there other factors (qualitative and quantitative) that you might be interested in? If so, what are they? Explain the reasons for your interest.

UP7-4 (Inventory turnover and gross margin)

The following selected information has been compiled for Sherwood Park Inc. Sherwood Park owns a series of discount clothing stores in Western Canada.

	2016	2015	2014
Inventories	$1,410,000	$1,300,000	$ 800,000
Sales revenue	6,046,000	5,500,000	4,160,000
Cost of goods sold	4,970,000	4,490,000	3,300,000

You are the new accountant hired by Sherwood Park. The owner tells you that, based on sales growth, the company is doing so well that expansion plans are under discussion.

Required:

Calculate the:
   a. Inventory turnover for 2015 and 2016.
   b. Number of days sales in inventory for 2015 and 2016.
   c. Gross margin and gross margin ratio for 2014, 2015, and 2016.

Do you agree with the owner about the success of Sherwood Park? If not, what do your calculations show that contradicts the owner's opinion?

UP7-5 (Decision-making and inventory estimation)

Slick Snowboards Company reported sales of $700,000 in the first quarter of 2016. The company has never implemented an inventory system so the controller does not know how much inventory is actually on hand at the end of the quarter. The company is considering expansion; therefore, a complete set of financial reports for the first quarter of 2016 must be prepared for the bank loan application and shareholders. The company's accountant says Slick should count the inventory as part of the process, but management believes counting the inventory at the end of each quarter is too costly.

Therefore, the controller decides to estimate the value of inventory on hand. She determines that inventory on hand on January 1, 2016, was $100,000 based on the 2015 year-end financial statements, and she knows that an additional $400,000 of inventory was purchased during the first quarter. The company normally earns a 35% gross margin on sales. Based on this information, and using the gross margin estimation method, the controller arrives at what she thinks is a reasonable estimate of the cost of inventory on hand at the end of the first quarter of 2016.

Required:

   a. Calculate the ending inventory estimate at March 31, 2016. Explain how you arrived at your estimate.
   b. If the controller believes that the gross margin on sales is likely to be closer to 30% in 2016, recalculate the ending inventory estimate at March 31, 2016. Comment on the sensitivity of your estimate of the inventory on hand to changes in the gross profit on sales percentage.
   c. If the gross margin estimation method works reasonably well for interim estimates of inventory on hand, why not use it at year end as well and avoid altogether the cost of an annual inventory count?
   d. Based on your original estimate of Slick Snowboards' inventory at the end of the first quarter, what is your assessment of the company's inventory position? Does the amount seem reasonable? Why or why not? Why might inventory levels change from one quarter to the next?

UP7-6 (Inventory cost formulas)

Brandon's Bentwood Furniture Company designs, makes, and sells custom furniture. The cost of the special resin used to finish the furniture has been increasing over the past 12 to 18 months. For example, a litre of the resin cost $10 in January 2015 and $17 per litre in March 2016. The cost is expected to continue increasing over the next 12 months. Each piece of furniture requires approximately five litres of resin and it represents one of the most expensive components. The company typically makes 50 unique furniture pieces a year. The company's major investor informed Brandon that she requires annual financial statements that are prepared in accordance with generally accepted accounting principles. One of the outstanding items on Brandon's "to-do" list is to select an appropriate cost formula and accounting policy for inventory. Brandon hopes to increase the company's net profit over the next two years.

Required:

   a. Recommend an appropriate cost formula and accounting policy for inventory.
   b. Explain to Brandon and the major investor your reasons for the recommendation.
   c. If the cost of resin is decreasing over the period, would you recommend a different cost formula? Explain your reasons.

UP7-7 (Gross margin)

Required:

Explain how the Canada Revenue Agency might be able to use a company's gross margin to assess the possibility that the company might not be reporting all of its cash sales.

Reading and Interpreting Published Financial Statements

RI7-1 (The nature of inventory, inventory valuation, and gross margin)

CAE Inc. designs, manufactures, and sells simulation equipment services and develops training solutions for the civil aviation and defence industries. Its revenues are derived from the sale of simulation products, development and delivery of training solutions, in-service support, and crew sourcing.

The following selected financial information was taken from CAE's 2014 annual report.

(amounts in millions)	March 31	
	2014	**2013**
Inventories − total	219.5	176.2
Work-in-progress	129.7	103.1
Raw materials, supplies and manufactured products	89.8	73.1
Revenue	2,114.9	2,035.2
Cost of goods sold	1,518.0	1,450.4

Significant Accounting Policy Note:
Raw materials are valued at the lower of average cost and net realizable value. Spare parts to be used in the normal cost of business are valued at the lower of cost, determined on a specific identification basis, and net realizable value.

Work-in-progress is stated at the lower of cost, determined on a specific identification basis and net realizable value. The cost of work in progress includes materials, labour and an allocation of manufacturing overhead, which is based on normal operating capacity.

Required:
Using the above information, answer the following questions:
  a. Calculate the inventory turnover ratios for CAE Inc. for 2014 and 2013. Comment on any changes. Use the 2014 and 2013 inventory rather than the average inventory to calculate the ratios.
  b. Calculate the gross margin ratio for 2014 and 2013. Comment on any changes.
  c. CAE's statement of income reports revenue as one amount even though its operations include manufacturing and the delivery of services. How might this reporting format affect the analysis of the gross margin ratio?
  d. CAE uses the specific identification cost formula for spare parts and work in progress. Explain how and why specific identification is an appropriate cost formula for CAE.
  e. CAE uses average cost to value its raw materials inventories. Why would the specific item basis not be appropriate for this category of inventory?

RI7-2 (Inventory turnover and valuation)

Brick Brewing Co. Limited is a Canadian-owned brewery with its head office in Kitchener, Ontario. The company brews, sells, and markets its products under the Waterloo, Laker, Red Baron, Red Cap, and Formosa brand names. The company also produces, sells, markets, and distributes Seagram's Coolers across Canada. The information in Exhibit 7-22 was taken from the company's 2014 annual financial statements.

EXHIBIT 7-22A	BRICK BREWING CO. LIMITED'S STATEMENTS OF FINANCIAL POSITION

Statements of financial position
As at January 31, 2014 and January 31, 2013

	Notes	31-Jan-14	31-Jan-13
ASSETS			[Revised - note 27]
Non-current assets			
Property, plant and equipment	12	**$15,449,248**	$19,109,603
Intangible assets	13	**14,752,855**	14,259,612
Other assets		**−**	25,000
Deferred income tax assets	11	**2,548,732**	2,746,925
		32,750,835	36,141,140

continued

EXHIBIT 7-22A   BRICK BREWING CO. LIMITED'S STATEMENTS OF FINANCIAL POSITION (continued)

	Notes	31-Jan-14	31-Jan-13
Current assets			
Accounts receivable	14	5,865,024	5,187,785
Inventories	15	3,951,436	4,013,375
Assets held for sale	12	3,406,400	
Prepaid expenses		395,559	296,180
		13,618,419	9,497,340
TOTAL ASSETS		46,369,254	45,638,480
LIABILITIES AND EQUITY			
Equity			
Share capital	16	38,955,236	35,895,873
Share-based payments reserves	17	1,060,533	1,092,414
Deficit		(7,502,544)	(8,027,743)
TOTAL EQUITY		32,513,225	28,960,544
Non-current liabilities			
Provisions	19	289,083	326,646
Long-term debt and promissory note	20	4,265,018	6,078,719
		4,554,101	6,405,365
Current liabilities			
Bank indebtedness	21	1,694,178	2,310,809
Accounts payable and accrued liabilities	22	6,050,679	6,306,292
Current portion of long-term debt and promissory note	20	1,557,071	1,655,470
		9,301,928	10,272,571
TOTAL LIABILITIES		13,856,029	16,677,936
COMMITMENTS	24, 25		
TOTAL LIABILITIES AND EQUITY		$46,369,254	$45,638,480

EXHIBIT 7-22B   EXCERPT FROM NOTES TO BRICK BREWING CO. LIMITED'S 2014 FINANCIAL STATEMENTS

5.10 Inventories

Inventories are recorded at the lower of cost and net realizable value. Cost includes expenditures incurred in acquiring the inventories and bringing them to their existing location and condition. Net realizable value is the estimated selling price in the ordinary course of business, less the estimated costs to complete and sell the product.

The cost of raw materials, supplies and promotional items are determined on a first-in, first-out basis. The cost of finished goods and work-in-process are determined on an average cost basis and include raw materials, direct labour, and an allocation of fixed and variable overhead based on normal capacity.

Inventories are written down to net realizable value if that net realizable value is less than the carrying amount of the inventory item at the reporting date. If the net realizable value subsequently increases, a reversal of the loss initially recognized is applied to cost of sales.

EXHIBIT 7-22C   EXCERPT FROM NOTES TO BRICK BREWING CO. LIMITED'S 2014 FINANCIAL STATEMENTS

The inventories balance consists of the following:

	January 31, 2014	January 31, 2013
Promotional items	61,344	32,273
Raw materials and supplies	1,457,066	1,747,097
Work in progress and finished goods	2,433,026	2,234,005
	$3,951,436	$4,013,375

continued

EXHIBIT 7-22C	EXCERPT FROM NOTES TO BRICK BREWING CO. LIMITED'S 2014 FINANCIAL STATEMENTS (continued)

As at January 31, 2014, a provision of $154,036 (January 31, 2013 - $72,763) has been netted against inventory to account for obsolete materials.

The cost of inventories recognized as cost of sales during the year ended January 31, 2014 are $23,326,559 (January 31, 2013 - $22,339,768). Included in this amount are charges related to impairment caused by obsolescence. During the year ended January 31, 2014, these charges amounted to $152,820 (January 31, 2013 - $46,873).

Required:

a. Note 15, shown in Exhibit 7-22C, breaks down Brick's inventory into three categories. Which categories of inventory do you believe should be used in determining the inventory turnover ratio? Why?

b. Describe Brick Brewing's inventory valuation policies in your own words. Specifically, explain what Brick Brewing includes in inventory cost, what cost formula(s) the company uses, and how it values its inventory on the statement of financial position.

c. Calculate the inventory turnover ratio and days to sell inventory ratio for 2014 and 2013. Use the inventory values in 2014 and 2013 rather than the average inventory to calculate the ratios. Explain the amounts you selected from the financial statements to use in your calculation.

d. Calculate the current and quick ratios and comment on them.

RI7-3 (Inventory valuation, inventory turnover, and shrinkage)

Indigo Books & Music Inc. is Canada's largest book, gift, and specialty toy retailer. The company operates more than 200 stores under the Coles, Indigo, Indigospirit, SmithBooks, and The Book Company banners. The company also has a 50% interest in the Calendar Club of Canada Limited Partnership, which operates mall-based stores and seasonal kiosks. The financial information in Exhibit 7-23 is from the company's 2014 annual report.

EXHIBIT 7-23A	INDIGO BOOKS & MUSIC INC.'S 2014 CONSOLIDATED BALANCE SHEETS

(thousands of Canadian dollars)	As at March 29, 2014	As at March 30, 2013 restated (notes 4 and 22)	As at April 1, 2012 restated (notes 4 and 22)
ASSETS			
Current			
Cash and cash equivalents (note 6)	$157,578	$210,562	$206,718
Accounts receivable	5,582	7,126	12,810
Inventories (note 7)	218,979	216,533	229,199
Prepaid expenses	5,184	4,153	3,692
Total current assets	387,323	438,374	452,419
Property, plant and equipment (note 8)	58,476	58,903	66,928
Intangible assets (note 9)	21,587	22,164	22,810
Equity investment (note 20)	598	968	961
Deferred tax assets (note 10)	44,604	48,731	48,633
Total assets	512,588	569,140	591,751
LIABILITIES AND EQUITY			
Current			
Accounts payable and accrued liabilities (note 19)	136,428	150,177	173,416
Unredeemed gift card liability (note 19)	46,827	47,169	42,711
Provisions (note 11)	928	2,168	232
Deferred revenue	12,860	13,733	11,234
Income taxes payable	–	11	65
Current portion of long-term debt (notes 12 and 18)	584	773	1,060
Total current liabilities	197,627	214,031	228,718

continued

EXHIBIT 7-23A	INDIGO BOOKS & MUSIC INC.'S 2014 CONSOLIDATED BALANCE SHEETS (continued)		
(thousands of Canadian dollars)	As at March 29, 2014	As at March 30, 2013 restated (notes 4 and 22)	As at April 1, 2012 restated (notes 4 and 22)
Long-term accrued liabilities (note 19)	2,896	4,004	5,800
Long-term provisions (note 11)	164	78	460
Long-term debt (notes 12 and 18)	227	705	1,141
Total liabilities	**200,914**	**218,818**	**236,119**
Equity			
Share capital (note 13)	203,812	203,805	203,373
Contributed surplus (note 14)	8,820	8,128	7,039
Retained earnings	99,042	138,389	145,220
Total equity	**311,674**	**350,322**	**355,632**
Total liabilities and equity	**$512,588**	**$569,140**	**$591,751**

EXHIBIT 7-23B	EXCERPT FROM NOTES TO INDIGO BOOKS & MUSIC INC.'S 2014 FINANCIAL STATEMENTS

Inventories

The future realization of the carrying amount of inventory is affected by future sales demand, inventory levels, and product quality. At each balance sheet date, the Company reviews its on-hand inventory and uses historical trends and current inventory mix to determine a reserve for the impact of future markdowns which will take the net realizable value of inventory on-hand below cost. Inventory valuation also incorporates a write-down to reflect future losses on the disposition of obsolete merchandise. The Company reduces inventory for estimated shrinkage that has occurred between physical inventory counts and the end of the fiscal year based on historical experience as a percentage of sales. In addition, the Company records a vendor settlement accrual to cover any disputes between the Company and its vendors. The Company estimates this reserve based on historical experience of settlements with its vendors.

EXHIBIT 7-23C	EXCERPT FROM NOTES TO INDIGO BOOKS & MUSIC INC.'S 2014 FINANCIAL STATEMENTS

Inventories

Inventories are valued at the lower of cost, determined on a moving average cost basis, and market, being net realizable value. Costs include all direct and reasonable expenditures that are incurred in bringing inventories to their present location and condition. Net realizable value is the estimated selling price in the ordinary course of business. When the Company permanently reduces the retail price of an item and the markdown incurred brings the retail price below the cost of the item, there is a corresponding reduction in inventory recognized in the period. Vendor rebates are recorded as a reduction in the price of the products, and corresponding inventories are recorded net of vendor rebates.

EXHIBIT 7-23D	EXCERPT FROM NOTES TO INDIGO BOOKS & MUSIC INC.'S 2014 FINANCIAL STATEMENTS

7. Inventories

The cost of inventories recognized as an expense was $495.1 million in fiscal 2014 (2013 – $499.5 million). Inventories consist of the landed cost of goods sold and exclude online shipping costs, inventory shrink and damage reserve, and all vendor support programs. The amount of inventory write-downs as a result of net realizable value lower than cost was $8.6 million in fiscal 2014 (2013 – $3.9 million), and there were no reversals of inventory write-downs that were recognized in fiscal 2014 (2013 – nil). The amount of inventory with net realizable value equal to cost was $1.8 million as at March 29, 2014 (March 30, 2013 – $1.4 million; April 1, 2012 – $1.7 million).

Required:

a. Calculate Indigo's inventory turnover ratio and the days to sell inventory ratio for 2014 and 2013. Comment on the results.

b. Given the result of your analysis in part (a), would you expect Indigo to have significant payables to the publishing and distribution companies it purchases its inventory from? Was this the case?

c. Explain Indigo's inventory valuation polices in your own words. Specifically, explain what Indigo includes in inventory cost, what cost formula(s) the company uses, and how it values its inventory on the statement of financial position.

RI7-4 (Inventory turnover, gross margin ratio, and financial statement presentation)

Whistler Blackcomb Holdings Inc. has a 75% interest in Whistler Mountain Resort and Blackcomb Skiing Enterprise. The two companies operate a four-season mountain resort in Whistler, British Columbia. Exhibit 7-24 contains the statement of financial position and Notes 5 and 9 of the accompanying notes from the company's 2013 annual report.

EXHIBIT 7-24A   **WHISTLER BLACKCOMB HOLDINGS INC.'S 2013 CONSOLIDATED STATEMENTS OF FINANCIAL POSITION**

Consolidated Statements of Financial Position
As at September 30, 2013 and 2012
(in thousands)

	Note	2013	2012
			Recast (note 2)
Assets			
Current assets:			
Cash and cash equivalents	8	$41,353	$43,634
Accounts receivable		3,323	3,481
Income taxes receivable		–	240
Inventory	9	15,856	13,788
Prepaid expenses		2,727	3,104
Notes receivable	10	311	303
		63,570	64,550
Notes receivable	10	2,636	2,792
Property, buildings and equipment	11	322,316	328,414
Property held for development		9,244	9,244
Intangible assets	12	311,428	324,028
Goodwill		137,259	135,574
		846,453	864,602
Liabilities and Shareholders' Equity			
Current liabilities:			
Accounts payable and accrued liabilities		24,927	24,060
Income taxes payable		1,645	153
Provisions	13	2,858	2,903
Deferred revenue		22,347	20,718
		51,777	47,834
Long–term debt	14	258,042	256,800
Deferred income tax liability	7	20,690	15,489
Limited Partner's interest	2,3(f)	72,796	72,796
Total liabilities		403,305	392,919
Equity			
Whistler Blackcomb Holdings Inc. shareholders' equity		442,080	441,476
Common shares; no par value; unlimited number authorized; 37,958 outstanding (September 30, 2012 – 37,908)			
Additional paid–in capital		913	721
Deficit		(54,781)	(31,887)
Total Whistler Blackcomb Holdings Inc. shareholders' equity		388,212	410,310
Limited Partner's non–controlling interest	2, 3(f)	54,936	61,373
		443,148	471,683
		$846,453	$864,602

| EXHIBIT 7-24B | EXCERPT FROM NOTES TO WHISTLER BLACKCOMB HOLDINGS INC.'S 2013 FINANCIAL STATEMENTS |

5. Resort operations

Resort revenue, operating expenses (excluding depreciation and amortization) and selling, general and administrative are comprised of the following:

	2013	2012
Resort revenue:		
Lift	$123,289	$121,093
Retail and rental	40,332	39,747
Snow school	25,536	24,899
Food and beverage	30,155	29,815
Other	21,468	20,818
	$240,780	$236,372
Operating expenses:		
Operating labour and benefits	$ 61,092	$ 59,089
Retail and food services cost of sales	26,756	26,409
Property taxes, utilities, rent and insurance	18,956	18,682
Supplies, maintenance and other	19,869	20,045
	$126,673	$124,225
Selling, general and administrative expenses:		
Labour and benefits	$ 12,656	$ 12,647
Other	15,017	14,291
	$ 27,673	$ 26,938

| EXHIBIT 7-24C | EXCERPT FROM NOTES TO WHISTLER BLACKCOMB HOLDINGS INC.'S 2013 FINANCIAL STATEMENTS |

9. Inventory

	2013	2012
Retail goods	$14,056	$12,068
Food and beverage	245	200
Mountain operating supplies	1,555	1,520
	$15,856	$13,788

Required:

a. Calculate the inventory turnover ratio and the number of days sales in inventory for 2013 and 2012. Use the year-end inventory balances instead of the average inventory amounts. Comment on the results of your analysis.

b. Calculate Whistler Blackcomb's gross margin ratio for 2013 and 2012.

c. Comment on the challenges you encountered in calculating the gross margin ratio. For example, what amount of revenue did you use?

d. Based on your calculations in part "b" and the challenges identified in part "c," comment on the appropriateness of using the gross margin ratio to analyze Whistler Blackcomb's results.

e. Comment on the possible reasons for the revenue presentation format used by Whistler Blackcomb.

RI7-5 (Inventory classification, inventory turnover)

High Liner Foods Incorporated, which is headquartered in Lunenburg, Nova Scotia, operates in the North American packaged foods industry. The company's brands include High Liner, Fisher Boy, FPI, Sea Cuisine, Mirabel, and Royal Sea. The company also manufactures products for private labels. The information in Exhibit 7-25 was taken from the company's 2014 annual report.

EXHIBIT 7-25A	HIGH LINER FOODS INCORPORATED'S 2013 CONSOLIDATED STATEMENT OF FINANCIAL POSITION

CONSOLIDATED STATEMENT OF FINANCIAL POSITION

(in thousands of U.S. dollars)	Notes	28-Dec-13	29-Dec-12
ASSETS			*(note 27)*
Current:			
Cash		$ 1,206	$ 65
Accounts receivable	9	91,334	73,947
Income taxes receivable		3,509	5,145
Other financial assets	22	1,524	533
Inventories	8	254,072	222,313
Prepaid expenses		2,952	2,991
Total current assets		354,597	304,994
Non-current:			
Property, plant and equipment	6	97,503	89,268
Deferred income taxes	20	4,656	7,207
Other receivables and miscellaneous assets		1,906	2,035
Intangible assets	5	105,253	110,631
Goodwill	5	111,999	112,873
Total non-current assets		321,317	322,014
Assets classified as held for sale	7	542	4,819
Total assets		$ 676,456	$ 631,827
LIABILITIES AND SHAREHOLDERS' EQUITY			
Current:			
Bank loans	12	$ 97,227	$ 59,704
Accounts payable and accrued liabilities	10	103,215	101,441
Provisions	11	240	1,614
Other current financial liabilities	22	459	550
Income taxes payable		2,543	1,165
Current portion of long-term debt	13	—	34,237
Current portion of finance lease obligations	13	979	1,039
Total current liabilities		204,663	199,750
Non-current:			
Long-term debt	13	226,929	213,359
Other long-term financial liabilities	22	5,597	1,130
Other long-term liabilities		1,044	1,532
Long-term finance lease obligations	13	1,647	2,181
Deferred income taxes	20	43,998	45,126
Future employee benefits	14	7,929	13,791
Total non-current liabilities		287,144	277,119
Liabilities directly associated with the assets held for sale	7	—	1,604
Total liabilities		491,807	478,473
Shareholders' equity:			
Common shares	16	80,260	75,169
Contributed surplus		13,781	7,719
Retained earnings		90,792	66,373
Accumulated other comprehensive (loss) income		(184)	4,093
Total shareholders' equity		184,649	153,354
Total liabilities and shareholders' equity		$ 676,456	$ 631,827

EXHIBIT 7-25B	HIGH LINER FOODS INCORPORATED'S 2013 CONSOLIDATED STATEMENT OF INCOME

CONSOLIDATED STATEMENT OF INCOME

			Fifty-two weeks ended
(in thousands of U.S. dollars, except per share amounts)	Notes	28-Dec-13	29-Dec-12
Revenues		$ 947,301	$ 942,631
Cost of sales		731,884	735,970
Gross profit		215,417	206,661
Distribution expenses		53,368	44,511
Selling, general and administrative expenses		98,902	100,862
Impairment of property, plant and equipment		–	13,230
Business acquisition, integration and other expenses		3,256	10,741
Results from operating activities		59,891	37,317
Finance costs		16,329	36,585
(Income) loss from equity accounted investee, net of income tax		(86)	196
Income before income taxes		43,648	536
Income taxes			
Current	20	12,378	5,442
Deferred	20	(86)	(7,109)
Total income tax expense (recovery)		12,292	(1,667)
Net income		$ 31,356	$ 2,203

EXHIBIT 7-25C	EXCERPT FROM NOTES TO HIGH LINER FOODS INCORPORATED'S 2013 FINANCIAL STATEMENTS

Inventories

Inventories are measured at the lower of cost and net realizable value. The cost of manufactured inventories is based on the first-in first-out principle. The cost of procured finished goods and unprocessed raw material inventory is weighted average cost. Inventory includes expenditures incurred in acquiring the inventories, production or conversion costs and other costs incurred in bringing the inventories to their existing location and condition. In the case of manufactured inventories and work in progress, cost includes an appropriate share of production overheads based on normal operating capacity. Cost also may include transfers from OCI of any gain or loss on qualifying cash flow hedges of foreign currency related to purchases of inventories.

Net realizable value is the estimated selling price in the ordinary course of business, less the estimated costs of completion and selling expenses.

EXHIBIT 7-25D	EXCERPT FROM NOTES TO HIGH LINER FOODS INCORPORATED'S 2013 FINANCIAL STATEMENTS

Total inventories at the lower of cost and net realizable value on the statement of financial position are comprised of the following:

(Amounts in $000s)	28-Dec-13	29-Dec-12
Finished goods – procured	$ 76,396	$ 78,116
Finished goods – manufactured	78,515	70,762
Raw and semi-finished material	69,353	43,517
Supplies, repair parts and other	10,092	14,868
H&G[(1)], including H&G paid in advance	13,357	7,170
Inventory in transit, paid in advance	6,359	8,376
	254,072	222,809
Less: inventories held for sale (note 7)	–	(496)
	$ 254,072	$ 222,313

[(1)] Headless and gutted

Required:

a. Note 8 (Exhibit 7-25D) breaks down High Liner's inventory into numerous categories. Which categories of inventory do you believe should be used in determining the inventory turnover ratio? Why?

b. Describe High Liner's inventory valuation policies in your own words. Specifically, explain what High Liner includes in inventory cost, what cost formula(s) the company uses, and how it values its inventory on the statement of financial position.

c. Does High Liner use the same cost formula for all of its inventories? If not, explain what methods are used for which inventories and why this might be the case.

d. Calculate the inventory turnover ratio and days to sell inventory ratio for 2013 and 2012. Use the year-end inventory balances instead of the average inventory amounts.

RI7-6 (Examine and analyze a company's financial statements)

Required:

Follow your instructor's guidelines for choosing a company and do the following:

a. Identify the nature of inventory carried by the company. Does the company report more than one category of inventory?

b. Prepare an analysis of the company's inventory by listing the beginning and ending balances and calculating the net change, in both dollar and percentage terms, for the most recent year.

c. If the inventory balance in part "b" has changed by more than 10%, suggest an explanation for this change.

d. Calculate the inventory turnover and the number of days sales in inventory for each of the last two years, using the ending inventory balance for each instead of the average inventory. Report any difficulties that you had in finding the appropriate numbers to make this calculation.

e. Calculate the gross margin ratio for the last two years. Has there been any significant change? How is the change in gross margin ratio related to any change in inventory or cost of goods sold?

f. Calculate a current ratio for each of the last two years. Describe the significance that inventory has for this ratio in each year.

Cases

C7-1 Stanley Storage Systems

Peter Patel was recently hired as a new manager for Stanley Storage Systems. The company manufactures and assembles office storage systems. His compensation is composed of a base salary and a bonus based on gross profit. The bonuses are to be paid monthly, as determined by the gross profit for the preceding month.

Stanley Storage Systems currently uses a periodic inventory system, but Peter would like to see the company move to a perpetual system. The company's owners are willing to consider the change, provided that Peter prepares a written analysis outlining the two methods and detailing the benefits and costs of switching to the perpetual system.

Required:

Prepare a report that Peter could present to the owners of Stanley Storage Systems to support his request to change to a perpetual inventory system.

C7-2 Park Avenue Tire Company

Park Avenue Tire Company has been operating in Winnipeg for more than 30 years and has a very loyal customer base. The company sells and installs tires and the owners pride themselves on the excellent business relationships they have developed with both their customers and suppliers. The company often sells tires on credit, allowing customers to pay their balances within 30 days. Collection of accounts receivable has never been a problem, with most people paying their balances within 60 days.

Park Avenue purchases tires from most of the large national brands and, due to the nature of the business, generally maintains a fairly large inventory. It is essential that the company have the necessary tires on hand to meet customer needs due to increased competition from large retailers such as Canadian Tire and Walmart.

The company has always had sufficient cash to pay its suppliers immediately and take advantage of cash discounts. However, this month, for the first time ever, Park Avenue does not have sufficient cash in the bank to meet its supplier payments. Chris Park, son of the original owner, Ernest Park, is currently operating the business and is very concerned about the company's inability to maintain what he feels are adequate levels of cash.

Your firm has been the accountants for Park Avenue Tire Company for the past 20 years. Chris has approached the firm expressing his concerns and asking for advice on how to solve the cash flow problems. As part of your analysis, you review the company's financial statements for the past three years. Excerpts from the financial statements are presented below.

	Dec. 31, 2016	Dec. 31, 2015	Dec. 31, 2014
Current assets			
Cash	$ 10,000	$ 35,000	$ 31,500
Accounts receivable	15,000	12,000	9,000
Inventory	169,000	122,000	116,000
Prepaid expenses	6,000	8,000	6,500
Total current assets	$200,000	$177,000	$163,000
Current liabilities			
Accounts payable	$ 62,000	$ 47,000	33,000
Salaries payable	4,200	5,850	3,775
Income tax payable	1,200	1,150	1,950
Total current liabilities	$ 67,400	$ 54,000	$ 38,725

During 2016, credit sales and cost of goods sold were $160,000 and $97,000, respectively. The 2015 and 2014 credit sales were $175,000 and $177,000, and the cost of goods sold for the same periods were $93,000 and $95,000, respectively. The accounts receivable and inventory balances at the end of 2013 were $8,000 and $99,000, respectively.

Required:

Prepare a report for Chris Park detailing options that he can take to alleviate the company's cash problems. Remember that you are to present options, not recommendations. As a basis for the report, you should calculate and comment on the following ratios:

    a. Current ratio
    b. Quick ratio
    c. Receivables turnover ratio and average collection period
    d. Inventory turnover ratio and days in inventory

C7-3 Wascana Photography Services

Wascana Photography Services sells and services a variety of high-end photography equipment to professional photographers. An inventory count is conducted each year end to verify the information contained in the company's perpetual inventory system. Once counted, the inventory is valued for the purposes of preparing the financial statements. The following inventory items represent a cross-section of Wascana's inventory for the year ended June 30, 2016. Because computerized records are maintained and a specific identification method of inventory is applied, the historical cost of each inventory item can easily be determined.

In addition to the historical cost, the store management has also included information detailing net realizable value for each item.

Item	Quantity on hand June 30, 2016	Historical cost (per unit)	Net realizable value (per unit)
Nikon D3100 body	4	$ 400	$ 350
Nikon 5200 with zoom lens	2	$1,500	$1,600
Nikon 80-200mm/2.8 lens	2	$1,100	$1,150
Canon EOS 60 body	2	$1,600	$1,900
Canon EF 24-70mm/2.8 zoom lens	1	$2,500	$2,300
Olympus E5 body	3	$1,900	$1,700
Pentax K3 body	6	$1,050	$1,300

Aleksander Dudyk, the manager of Wascana, is confused about why there is a difference between historical cost and net realizable value. Aleksander is not an accountant and is unfamiliar with these terms. He is also wondering which number should be used to value the company's inventory on June 30, 2016.

Required:

For the purposes of this case, assume that the above items represent the total inventory of Wascana Photography Services on June 30, 2016.

    a. Explain the meaning of historical cost and net realizable value in the context of inventory valuation for Aleksander.
    b. Calculate the ending inventory value using the lower of cost and net realizable value.
    c. Explain the reasons for valuing ending inventory at the lower of cost and net realizable value to Aleksander.

C7-4 D'Souza Lesynski LLP

Jenna Scharmann has been a public accountant for the past 20 years and is now a partner in D'Souza Lesynski LLP, a prominent accounting firm based in Saskatoon, Saskatchewan. The local chamber of commerce asked Jenna to speak at its monthly meeting. Since many members of the chamber are small to mid-sized retailers, Jenna decided to prepare a talk on determining inventory values and inventory cost formulas.

It is now Friday afternoon and Jenna has just returned to her office following the presentation to the chamber. She is surprised to see messages from two clients who were at the meeting. The first message is from Sally French, who owns and operates the local Ford dealership. In addition to selling cars, the dealership has a large service department and maintains an extensive inventory of parts and accessories.

Sally is concerned about the large amount of parts inventory she maintains at the dealership. Other dealers have moved to a just-in-time approach for much of their parts inventory. They claim it has significantly reduced inventory costs and improved cash flow without hurting client service. Sally wants more information about just-in-time inventory; specifically, the effect of switching to JIT on accounting entries, cost formulas, and cash flow.

The second caller is Jason Mount, who manages his family's grocery store. Jason would like to know why his family is using the FIFO approach instead of weighted-average. From Jenna's chamber presentation, he learned that the weighted-average formula results in lower income in times of rising prices, and since lower income means less taxes, he is wondering why Jenna has not previously recommended switching to weighted-average.

Required:

    a. Determine which inventory cost formula would best suit the needs of each client. Be sure to provide support for your recommendation.

b. Prepare a draft response to Sally that addresses her questions about the use of a just-in-time inventory system and its possible effects on the dealership.

c. Prepare a draft response to Jason regarding his concerns about the use of weighted-average in his business. Do you think that the business should change to this method? Why or why not?

C7-5 Nikki's Gems

Nikki Obomsawin graduated from the Nova Scotia College of Art and Design (NSCAD) with a Master of Fine Arts in craft. While she was completing her degree, Nikki sold her jewellery designs at the Halifax Seaport Farmers Market on Saturdays. Nikki's designs are in great demand. Several of her customers suggested she open a combination retail store and design studio on the popular shopping street, Spring Garden Road, in Halifax so she would be more accessible to her customers and potential customers during the week. Nikki located suitable space and hopes to open Nikki's Gems in two weeks. Her friends have told her she needs to set up an inventory system to track the raw materials and finished pieces of jewellery. Someone suggested that she needs to count her inventory but Nikki thinks it is a waste of time. She would rather spend the time designing and crafting. Nikki's friends finally convinced her that she needs help with the inventory side of her business. During a recent meeting, Nikki provides you with the following information about the nature of her inventory.

1. Nikki attends the annual American Gem Trade Association trade show in Tucson, Arizona, where she buys precious and semi-precious gems for use in her designs. Prices for the gems range from $250 to over $1,000 depending upon the type, quality, and size of the stone. Nikki typically buys $25,000 of stones each trip.

2. Each gem is labelled as to cost, date of purchase, and relevant characteristics and is stored in a cardboard box on top of her design table in the new studio.

3. While moving into her new space, Nikki discovered that two of the turquoise stones in her inventory had small cracks. Total cost for the two stones was $495. Nikki thinks she can still use the stones but estimates the net realizable value is $350.

4. Nikki plans to hang the gold chains (14K and 18K) in a display case on top of the sales counter. During the move to her new space, Nikki discovered that she was missing three 18K gold chains.

5. There are several boxes of findings (small pieces required to assemble the jewellery) in the studio. Nikki normally buys the findings in bulk. The only distinguishing feature is the size of the finding.

Required:

Based on the information provided by Nikki, prepare a draft report that addresses the following questions:

a. Should Nikki's Gems use a periodic or perpetual inventory system? Consider the advantages and disadvantages of each one.

b. What inventory cost formula should Nikki use? Consider the nature of the inventory.

c. Explain the concept of net realizable value and how it applies to Nikki's business.

d. Discuss the importance of internal controls and provide suggestions for implementing appropriate controls in Nikki's new store and studio.

e. Explain why counting inventory is not a waste of time.

ENDNOTES

1. "Canada's 100 Biggest Companies by Revenue," *The Globe and Mail*, June 24, 2014; Matthew McClearn, "How Magna International Quietly Became a Powerhouse in China," *Canadian Business*, June 2, 2014; Magna International 2013 annual report; Magna International corporate website, www.magna.com. "Magna International Inc. Drives Business with Information Optimization," Datawatch newsletter, Datawatch corporate website. www.datawatch.com.

2. Marina Strauss, "Target's Canadian Woes Deepen," *The Globe and Mail*, November 22, 2013, B1; Hollie Shaw, "Target Corp Profit Drops Almost 50% as Costs of Expansion into Canada Weigh," *Financial Post*, November 21, 2013; Francine Kopun, "Target Canada Continues to Be a Drag on Earnings," *Toronto Star*, August 21, 2013.

3. Danier Leather Inc. 2014 annual financial statements.

4. Ritchie Bros. Auctioneers Incorporated, Annual Report 2013.

5. Association of Certified Fraud Examiners, *Report to the Nations on Occupational Fraud and Abuse, 2012 General Fraud Survey*, 2012; Certified General Accountants Association of Canada, *Does Canada Have a Problem with Occupational Fraud?* 2011; PricewaterhouseCoopers, *Securing the Bottom Line*, Canadian Retail Security Survey, 2012.

6. John Daly, "How Dollarama Turns Pocket Change into Billions," *The Globe and Mail*, March 29, 2012.

7. High Liner Foods Incorporated 2012 Annual Report, Note 3 to the financial statements.

8. Canadian Tire Corporation's 2013 Annual Report.

9. "Supplier Support Center," Walmart corporate website, http://corporate.walmart.com/suppliers/references-resources/supplier-support-center; Pradheep Sampath, "Wal-Mart Starts Enforcing 'Must Arrive By Date' Deductions," All About B2B, February 10, 2010, http://www.gxsblogs.com/sampathp/2010/02/wal-mart-starts-enforcing-must-arrive-by-date-deductions.html.

10. Chris Doucette, "Third Person Charged in Salvation Army Toy Theft," *Toronto Sun*, April 5, 2013; Canadian Press, "Police Charge Former Salvation Army Executive Director with Theft of 100,000 Toys," *National Post*, November 26, 2012; Rosie DiManno, "Theft Leaves Sally Ann Smarting," Toronto Star, November 22, 2012; Niamh Scallan, "Charities' Vulnerability Revealed," *Toronto Star*, November 24, 2012, GT6.

11. Maple Leaf Foods 2013 annual report.

CHAPTER 8

Long-Term Assets

CORE QUESTIONS
If you are able to answer the following questions, then you have achieved the related learning objectives.

LEARNING OBJECTIVES
After studying this chapter, you should be able to:

●●● INTRODUCTION

- What are the various types of long-term assets?
- Why are long-term assets of significance to users?

1 Identify and distinguish between the various types of long-term assets.

●●● VALUATION OF PROPERTY, PLANT, AND EQUIPMENT

- At what amount are property, plant, and equipment reflected on the statement of financial position?
- What is included in "cost"?
- What happens when a company purchases multiple assets for a single price?
- How do we account for costs subsequent to purchase?

2 Describe the valuation methods for property, plant, and equipment, including identifying costs that are usually capitalized.

●●● DEPRECIATION

- Why do we depreciate property, plant, and equipment?

3 Explain why property, plant, and equipment assets are depreciated.

●●● DEPRECIATION METHODS

- What are the methods used to depreciate property, plant, and equipment?
- How do we choose a depreciation method?
- How do we record depreciation expense?
- Does an asset's carrying amount tell me what it is worth?
- How do we determine depreciation for partial periods?

4 Identify the factors that influence the choice of depreciation method and implement the most common methods of depreciation.

●●● CHANGES IN DEPRECIATION METHODS

- Can we change depreciation estimates and methods?

5 Describe and implement changes in depreciation estimates and methods.

●●● IMPAIRMENT

- What does it mean if an asset is impaired?

6 Explain what it means if property, plant, and equipment assets are impaired.

●●● DISPOSAL OF PP&E

- How do we account for disposals of property, plant, and equipment?

7 Account for the disposal of property, plant, and equipment.

●●● DEPRECIATION AND INCOME TAXES

- Do depreciation decisions affect corporate income taxes?
- Can a company carry property, plant, and equipment at their fair values?

8 Explain the effect of depreciation on income taxes.

●●● A Canadian Icon's Long-Term Assets

More than 9 in 10 Canadians live within 15 minutes of a Canadian Tire store. Over the company's 90-year history, it has grown to 490 stores from coast to coast. The Canadian Tire Corporation Limited family of companies now includes the clothing retailer Mark's Work Wearhouse, acquired in 2001, and FGL Sports (formerly the Forzani Group Ltd.), which it bought in 2011. Mark's now has more than 380 stores, and FGL Sports, which includes Sport Chek and Sports Experts, has more than 400 stores across the country, making it Canada's largest sporting goods retailer.

All of these ventures have substantial long-term assets, which consist of property, plant, and equipment; intangible assets; and goodwill.

Canadian Tire's property, plant, and equipment includes land, store buildings, and fixtures and equipment. In 2013, the company had $3.5 billion in property and equipment on its consolidated balance sheets. Canadian Tire depreciates its buildings, fixtures, and equipment using the declining-balance method. (Land is never depreciated because its useful life is indefinite.)

Canadian Tire also has considerable intangible assets (those with no physical form) such as trademarks, including the iconic logo of a red triangle and green maple leaf, and the various banners and brands, including Mark's private-label brands. These

intangible assets are considered long-term assets. "The Company expects these assets to generate cash flows in perpetuity. Therefore, these intangible assets are considered to have indefinite useful lives," Canadian Tire said in its 2013 annual report.

The last type of long-term asset is goodwill, which companies like Canadian Tire acquire when purchasing other companies. Goodwill is the difference between what an acquiring company paid for the acquisition and what the acquired company's net assets are worth. Canadian Tire calculates the fair value of the assets it acquired on the transaction date, including trademarks and brands, whose value can only be estimated. When Canadian Tire acquired FGL Sports, for example, it recognized $308.4 million in goodwill, which it said was "attributable mainly to the expected future growth potential from the expanded customer base of FGL Sports' banners/brands, the network of stores which are predominantly mall-based and access to the important 18–35 year old customer segment." In fact, it was this expanded access that sealed the deal for Canadian Tire to buy FGL Sports. "By acquiring Forzani we gain access to a new set of customers—people at a point in their lives that typically don't shop our stores extensively today for sporting goods," Canadian Tire CEO Stephen Wetmore said at the time.[1]

INTRODUCTION

Our opening story describes some accounting issues associated with recording and reporting long-term assets at **Canadian Tire Corporation**, which has significant amounts invested in the assets that form its extensive retail network. This chapter will discuss the measurement, recording, and reporting issues that all companies encounter with their long-term assets.

What are the various types of long-term assets?

There are three main categories of long-term assets, also known as **capital assets**:

1. Property, plant, and equipment
2. Intangible assets
3. Goodwill

    Property, plant, and equipment (PP&E) are also known as **tangible assets** as they have a physical presence. This category includes such things as land, buildings, machinery, furniture, computer equipment,

■ **LEARNING OBJECTIVE 1**
Identify and distinguish between the various types of long-term assets.

A building:
- is purchased to generate revenues in future periods.
- has physical form.

A trademark:
- is purchased to generate revenues.
- lacks physical form.
- must be separable (that is, it could be sold or licensed).

Goodwill:
- results from a business combination.
- cannot be separated from the business and sold.

vehicles, planes, boats, and so on. Companies purchase these assets to use them to generate revenues over multiple future periods. Assets are used in a number of ways, such as to produce goods, to serve as the locations for the sale of goods, or to be the tools that enable companies to provide services. While these assets may be sold when the company has finished using them, these assets are *not* purchased for resale. (Otherwise, they would be considered to be inventory, as discussed in Chapter 7.)

Intangible assets are those long-term assets without physical form and include things such as trademarks, patents, copyrights, licences, franchise rights, and customer lists. Intangible assets must be separately identifiable from other assets, which means that they can be resold, licensed, or rented. Very often, intangible assets have legal or contractual rights associated with them. For technology companies such as Waterloo, Ontario–based **BlackBerry Limited**, intangible assets are the company's most significant assets. In BlackBerry's case, it had more than $1.4 billion of intangible assets on its statement of financial position at March 1, 2014, which represented more than 19% of the company's total assets.

Goodwill is a long-term asset that arises when two businesses are combined. It represents the expected future economic benefits that will arise from the combination that cannot be separately identified as either PP&E or an intangible asset. The easiest way to think about goodwill is that it is the premium or excess paid by one business when it is acquiring another that is related to factors such as management expertise, corporate reputation, or customer loyalty.

Why are long-term assets of significance to users?

As just mentioned, companies invest in long-term assets to generate future revenues. These assets generally have significant costs and will impact a company's operations for many years into the future. They are often critical to a company's future success and need to be understood by financial statement users.

Users will want to monitor the age of a company's long-term assets. They will want to understand the average age of these assets and also be able to anticipate when future outflows of cash will be required to replace them. They will also need to know the implications these assets will have on future costs by understanding the company's depreciation and amortization policies. As we learned in Chapter 2, depreciation and amortization refer to the allocation of the cost of these assets to the periods in which they are expected to help generate revenues for the company. This process is discussed later in the chapter.

Users will also want to know if the company has determined whether there have been any significant negative changes in the expected use of the asset. Finally, a user might also want to determine the extent to which the company's long-term assets have been pledged as security to creditors or the extent to which the company has chosen to lease its long-term assets rather than purchase them.

If you think back to our cash flow discussions, you will recall that the purchase and sale of long-term assets are often a company's most significant investing activities. The purchase of long-term assets represents an outflow of cash, while the proceeds from the sale of long-term assets represent an inflow (Exhibit 8-1). We would normally expect cash flows from investing activities to be negative (that is, a

Exhibit 8-1 Investing Activities – Common Transactions

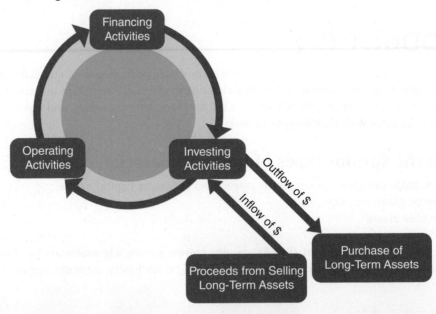

company is spending more by purchasing capital assets than it is generating from selling them). Understanding the cash flows related to capital assets is one way a user can quickly determine if the company is growing or shrinking.

This chapter will provide you with the necessary background information on long-term assets so that you can better understand the impact that these assets have on the financial statements.

VALUATION OF PROPERTY, PLANT, AND EQUIPMENT

At what amount are property, plant, and equipment reflected on the statement of financial position?

As we have discussed, an asset embodies or represents future economic benefits. In terms of PP&E, these future benefits include a company's ability to use them to generate revenues in the future, usually by producing products, facilitating sales, or providing services. It is important to recognize that normally PP&E assets do not produce revenues on their own. Instead, they are usually used in combination with other PP&E items, together with the efforts of employees, to produce revenues. PP&E assets also embody a secondary future benefit in that they may be sold in the future when they are no longer of use to the company.

Under IFRS, there are two models that can be considered when determining the amount at which PP&E will be reflected on the statement of financial position. These are the **cost model** and the **revaluation model**. Only the cost model is allowed under ASPE. The majority of both private and public corporations use the cost model. For now, we will assume that the cost model is being followed, but we will discuss the revaluation model toward the end of the chapter.

Under the **cost model**, PP&E assets are presented on the statement of financial position at their **carrying amount**, which is their **cost** less their **accumulated depreciation** and **accumulated impairment losses**. In Chapter 2, we learned that the costs of PP&E are allocated to the periods in which the asset generates revenues in a process known as **depreciation**. As a portion of the cost of the asset is expensed each period, the Accumulated Depreciation account is used to aggregate the depreciation recorded to date (Exhibit 8-2). Accumulated depreciation is a **contra-asset account**. This means that it is an asset account, but its normal balance will be a credit, which is contrary to what would normally be the case for an asset account. We will discuss accumulated impairment losses at the end of this chapter, so for now let's assume that there are none.

Regardless of whether the cost or revaluation model is adopted, all PP&E are initially recorded at cost. This sounds simple enough and has been in the examples we have seen so far. However, this can be a challenging area, so let's explore some of the issues.

■ **LEARNING OBJECTIVE 2**
Describe the valuation methods for property, plant and equipment, including identifying costs that are usually capitalized.

KEY POINTS
Carrying amount is:
- the portion of the asset's cost that has yet to be expensed.
- *not* what the asset is worth.

Exhibit 8-2 Carrying Amount

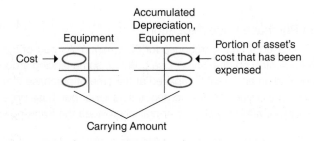

What is included in "cost"?

When PP&E is acquired, the company must decide which **costs** associated with the purchase of the asset should be **capitalized** (that is, included as a part of the asset's cost). The general guideline is that all of the costs necessary to acquire the asset and ready it for use should be capitalized. Any cost incurred that is not capitalized as part of the asset cost would be expensed in the period of the purchase. The following is a partial list of costs that would normally be capitalized (that is, included in the cost of a capital asset).

"COST" INCLUDES
• Purchase price (less any discounts or rebates) • Non-refundable taxes and import duties on the purchase price • Legal costs associated with the purchase • Shipping or transportation costs • Site preparation, installation, and set-up costs

For Example

When the **Port Authority** in Nanaimo, B.C., was looking for a container crane to use for loading barges several years ago, it was able to purchase an old crane from the Port of Vancouver for $1 (yes, $1). However, the Port Authority incurred costs in excess of $1 million to get the crane to Nanaimo and make it operational. This included transportation costs of $260,000 and installation costs of $750,000, which were capitalized as part of the cost of the crane. This illustrates how "cost" can be much more than just the purchase price of the asset.[2]

What happens when a company purchases multiple assets for a single price?

As you shop at the grocery store, you fill your cart or basket with a number of items. When you are finished shopping, you take it to the cash register where you pay a single price for all the goods in the basket. This same thing can occur when companies purchase PP&E. These kinds of purchases are called a **basket purchase** (or **lump-sum purchase**). The most common example is when a company purchases a warehouse or office building. At the same time, it would normally also acquire the land on which the building is situated. Just like at the grocery store, the warehouse purchase is completed for a single purchase price. It is important for the purchaser to be able to allocate this single purchase price between the building and the land because the building will need to be depreciated, while the land will not be.

The purchase price is allocated using the asset's **relative fair value** at the time of purchase, which can be determined in a number of ways. The most common way would be to have an appraisal completed that will provide the relative fair values of each asset. It is very common for the total purchase price and the total appraised value to differ. The purchaser may have received a good deal from a motivated seller or it may have paid a premium due to a number of factors such as superior location or the ability to complete the deal in a timely manner. It is important to remember that the company must record the purchase for what it paid, not what the appraised values are. Let's look at a simple example in Exhibit 8-3.

Exhibit 8-3 Example of Purchase Price Allocation

Assume that a company purchased a new warehouse for $2.4 million. As part of the purchase, it acquired the land that the warehouse was situated on, the warehouse building, some fencing around the property, and some storage racks. The company had an appraisal completed at the time of purchase that valued all components of the warehouse at $2.6 million. The buyer was able to negotiate a lower purchase price because the seller was in financial distress and was very motivated to sell. The appraisal provided the following values:

	Fair value	Percentage	Purchase price	Allocated cost
Land	$1,300,000	50%	$2,400,000	$1,200,000
Building	910,000	35%	$2,400,000	840,000
Storage racks	260,000	10%	$2,400,000	240,000
Fencing	130,000	5%	$2,400,000	120,000
	$2,600,000	100%		$2,400,000

Basket purchase scenarios can occur in other situations, including the purchase of an airplane or cargo vessel. In both these situations, IFRS requires companies to determine if there are separate depreciable components within the asset. For an airplane, it may be necessary to depreciate the fuselage (or body of the plane) on a different basis than the engines. For a cargo ship, the company may depreciate the hull differently from the propulsion system.

 Ethics in Accounting

If management's bias was for a higher net income, this could motivate them to allocate more of the overall cost to the land, and less to the building and other depreciable assets. Why is this so?

Since land is not depreciated, the company would incur less depreciation expense each year if the portion of the purchase price allocated to land was maximized. Alternatively, if management was motivated to minimize net income in order to minimize income-based bonuses to employees, then they could allocate a smaller portion of the total cost to the land and a larger portion to the building and other depreciable assets.

How do we account for costs subsequent to purchase?

After acquiring an asset, companies will continue to incur costs related to it. These would include ordinary repairs and maintenance, but could also include the costs of renovations or alterations to the asset. In determining whether these costs should be capitalized (that is, added to the cost of the asset) or **expensed** as period costs, management must consider whether or not these assets create a future economic benefit. In other words, will these costs extend the useful life of the asset (beyond the original estimate), will they reduce the asset's operating costs, or will they improve the asset's output either in terms of quantity or quality? If the answer to any of these questions is "yes," then a future economic benefit (an asset) has been created and the costs are capitalized. If no future economic benefit has been created, then these are period costs and should be expensed.

 The Conceptual Framework
CAPITALIZING VERSUS EXPENSING

Materiality is an element of the fundamental qualitative characteristic of **relevance**. Information is considered to be material if it would impact the decisions of a financial statement user. If it would not, it is considered to be immaterial and not relevant. If it would, then it is material and relevant. Materiality is considered by companies when they establish minimum thresholds for capitalizing PP&E. For example, companies often have policies that state that only PP&E with a cost in excess of $1,000 will be capitalized (that is, set up as an asset) and all purchases under that amount will be expensed as supplies because they are not material and therefore not relevant to financial statement users.

DEPRECIATION

Why do we depreciate property, plant, and equipment?

We depreciate PP&E in order to allocate a portion of the asset's cost to each of the periods in which the future economic benefits embodied in the asset are being used up or consumed as a result of its use (generally, PP&E can only be used to assist in the generation of revenue for a finite period). In other

■ **LEARNING OBJECTIVE 3**
Explain why property, plant, and equipment assets are depreciated.

words, a portion of the asset's cost is expensed and reported in the same period when the future benefits that it embodies are being used up.

In order to depreciate PP&E, we need to know three pieces of information:

Cost	Discussed in the previous section.
Estimated residual value	This is a management estimate and is the net amount that the company expects it would receive if the asset were sold in the condition it is expected to be in at the end of its useful life. This is the portion of the asset's cost that will never be an expense to the company as it expects to recover that cost when it is finished with the asset.
Estimated useful life	This is a management estimate and can be determined by **time** (such as years) or **usage** (such as units, hours, or kilometres). If time is used, then this is the period over which the asset is expected to be used by the company to generate revenue. If usage is used, then this is the total number of units that are expected to be obtained from the asset. Note that just because an asset has reached the end of its useful life for one company does not mean it can't be useful to another.

Once these amounts are known, the company can determine the asset's **depreciable amount**. This is the portion of the asset's cost that should be expensed over the periods in which the asset is expected to generate revenues and is determined as follows:

$$\text{Depreciable Amount} = \text{Cost} - \text{Estimated Residual Value}$$

Different assets will have different expected patterns of usage. In other words, the future benefits of some assets may be expected to be used up early in their useful life (such as information technology assets), some may be expected to be used up in a consistent manner over their useful life (such as buildings), while others may be expected to have fluctuating levels based on the asset's usage (such as a ski lift). As a result, there are a variety of acceptable depreciation methods and a company is expected to use the method that best reflects the pattern in which it expects the asset's future benefits to be used up. In addition, companies are required to review this decision annually to ensure that the depreciation method being used remains consistent with management's expectations for the asset.

Land is an exception to the requirement to depreciate PP&E. Even after it has been used by a company for several years, the land will still be there to be used indefinitely in the future. Therefore, unlike other capital assets, the cost of land is not depreciated. Consequently, assigning costs to land means that those costs will remain on the statement of financial position until such time as the land is sold and will never be expensed as depreciation.

We will now review three of the most commonly used depreciation methods.

DEPRECIATION METHODS

What are the methods used to depreciate property, plant, and equipment?

As accounting standards developed, rational and systematic methods of depreciating long-term assets were created. The simplest and most commonly used method (used by more than 50% of Canadian companies) is the **straight-line method** (illustrated in Chapter 2), which allocates the asset's depreciable cost evenly over its useful life. Many accountants have argued in favour of this method as it is a very simple method to apply.

A second type of depreciation method recognizes that the consumption of future economic benefits of some capital assets can be measured fairly specifically. This is the **units-of-production method** (also known as the units-of-activity method). Its use requires that the consumption of the asset's future economic benefits can be linked to the asset's use in terms of a measurable quantity. For example, a new truck might be expected to be used for a specific number of kilometres. If so, the depreciation cost per kilometre can be calculated and used to determine each period's depreciation expense, based on the number of kilometres driven during that accounting period.

For certain assets, more of their future economic benefits are used up early in the asset's useful life and less as time goes by (the consumption of the economic benefits does not occur evenly over time). In fact, many assets are of greater use in the early years of their useful lives. In later years, when these assets are wearing out, they require more maintenance, perhaps produce inferior products, or are used less and less. In this situation, it would be necessary to use a more rapid depreciation in the early years of the asset's life, when larger depreciation expenses could be recorded in the same period in which the asset is being used most extensively. The most common method that follows this pattern is known as the **diminishing-balance method** (also known as the declining-balance method), which is an **accelerated depreciation method**. That is, more of the asset's cost is depreciated early in its useful life and less as time goes by.

Exhibit 8-4 illustrates the pattern of depreciation expense under the three methods of depreciation: straight-line, units-of-production, and diminishing-balance. (The calculations used in these methods are discussed in detail later.) Exhibit 8-5 illustrates the pattern of decline in an asset's carrying amount under the same methods.

In Exhibit 8-4, you can see that, with the straight-line method, the depreciation expense for each period is the same; this produces the even (or straight-line) decline in the asset's carrying amount shown in Exhibit 8-5. With the units-of-production method, you can see in Exhibit 8-4 that the amount of depreciation expense will fluctuate each period depending upon the asset's actual usage (or production level) and in Exhibit 8-5 we see that there is no predictable pattern in terms of the asset's carrying amount. For the diminishing-balance method, Exhibit 8-4 shows that the annual depreciation expense is higher in the earlier years; this causes a faster decline in the carrying amount during the earlier years of the asset's life, as seen in Exhibit 8-5.

Exhibit 8-4 Annual Depreciation Expense

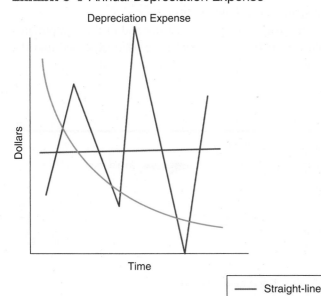

Exhibit 8-5 Asset Carrying Amount

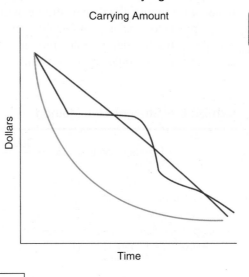

It is important to note that, although the pattern of expense recognition is different, the total amount of depreciation expense taken over the asset's life is the same for all methods. All of the methods start with the same cost amount and end with a carrying amount equal to that asset's estimated residual value.

To illustrate each of the depreciation methods, we will use the following example:

DATA FOR EXAMPLE DEPRECIATION CALCULATIONS
On January 1, 2016, a company buys equipment for $50,000. Management estimates that the equipment has an estimated useful life of five years and an estimated residual value of $5,000. The company has a December 31 year end.

Therefore, the depreciable amount would be:

$$\text{Depreciable Amount} = \text{Cost} - \text{Estimated Residual Value}$$
$$= \$50,000 - \$5,000 = \$45,000$$

This means that the company expects to ultimately expense $45,000 of the asset's $50,000 cost if the use of the asset is consistent with management's expectations. It also means that the company never expects to expense the remaining $5,000 as management expects to be able to recover this when it is finished with the asset.

Straight-Line Method

This is the most commonly used method of depreciation and assumes that the economic benefits embodied in the asset will be used up evenly over its useful life and, as such, its cost should also be allocated evenly over this same time frame. The **depreciation rate** under this method would be determined as follows:

$$\text{Depreciation Rate} = 1/\text{Estimated Useful Life}$$
$$= 1/5 \text{ years} = 0.2 \text{ or } 20\%$$

Using our example, the depreciation would be calculated as in Exhibit 8-6.

Depreciation expense of $9,000 is recorded each year for five years. At the end of the equipment's useful life, the full depreciable amount of $45,000 ($50,000 − 5,000) will have been expensed and the carrying amount would equal its estimated residual value of $5,000, as shown in Exhibit 8-6.

Exhibit 8-6 Straight-Line Method

$$\text{Depreciation Expense} = \frac{\text{Cost} - \text{Estimated Residual Value}}{\text{Estimated Useful Life}} \quad \longleftarrow \quad \text{In Years!}$$

$$= \frac{\$50,000 - \$5,000}{5 \text{ years}}$$

$$= \$9,000 \text{ per year}$$

Alternatively:

$$\text{Depreciation Expense} = \text{Depreciation Rate} \times \text{Depreciable Amount}$$

$$= 20\% \times (\$50,000 - \$5,000)$$

$$= \$9,000 \text{ per year}$$

Depreciation schedule:

Year	Beginning Carrying Amount		Depreciation Expense		Ending Carrying Amount
2016	$50,000	=	$ 9,000	=	$41,000
2017	41,000	=	9,000	=	32,000
2018	32,000	=	9,000	=	23,000
2019	23,000	=	9,000	=	14,000
2020	14,000	=	9,000	=	**5,000**
			$45,000		

Units-of-Production Method

This method assumes that the asset's useful life can be defined in terms of its units of output. If this is the case, then the asset's depreciable amount can be allocated or expensed on the basis of output. This method differs from the straight-line method, which assumes that output will not fluctuate significantly from period to period and that a constant expense allocation reflects the asset's expected use and, in turn, the consumption of its economic benefits. Because of its ability to allocate the asset's cost to each unit of output, the units-of-production method does the best job of allocating the asset's cost to the periods in which its economic benefits are consumed.

Under the units-of-production method, the asset's useful life is estimated in units of output or activity, rather than in years of service. For example, delivery trucks could be depreciated using this method if their expected useful lives can be expressed in kilometres driven. Machinery used in manufacturing products may have an expected useful life based on the total number of units of output. Other valid units of output include hours (in the aviation industry), cubic metres (in the forest industry), or tonnes (in the mining industry).

Under this method, the first step is to determine depreciation expense per unit as follows:

$$\text{Depreciation Expense per Unit} = \frac{\text{Cost} - \text{Estimated Residual Value}}{\text{Estimated Useful Life (in Units)}}$$

To calculate the depreciation expense for the period, the depreciation expense per unit is then multiplied by the total number of units produced or used during the period. Exhibit 8-7 illustrates this method using our previous example.

Exhibit 8-7 Units-of-Production Method

Estimated usage		
	2016	4,000 units
	2017	5,000 units
	2018	6,000 units
	2019	4,500 units
	2020	3,000 units
		22,500 units

$$\text{Depreciation Expense} = \frac{\text{Cost} - \text{Estimated Residual Value}}{\text{Estimated Useful Life}} \quad \longleftarrow \text{ In Units!}$$

$$= \frac{\$50,000 - \$5,000}{22,500 \text{ units}}$$

$$= \$2 \text{ per unit}$$

Depreciation schedule:

Year	Depreciation Expense per Unit		Units Produced		Depreciation Expense	Ending Carrying Amount
2016	$2	×	4,000	=	$ 8,000	$42,000
2017	2	×	5,000	=	10,000	32,000
2018	2	×	6,000	=	12,000	20,000
2019	2	×	4,500	=	9,000	11,000
2020	2	×	3,000	=	6,000	**5,000**
			22,500		**$45,000**	

The units-of-production method is the only depreciation method under which depreciation expense can be zero while an asset is held for use. This would be the case when the asset was idle and there would be no units produced and therefore no depreciation expense. Under both the straight-line and diminishing-balance methods, depreciation expense would be still be recorded even if the asset was idle as long as it was still held for use (that is, it was not being held for resale) and not fully depreciated.

Diminishing-Balance Method

The diminishing-balance method is an accelerated method of depreciation that assumes that a greater proportion of the asset's economic benefit will be consumed early in its useful life and less as time goes by. As a result, this method allocates more of the asset's cost to those earlier periods and less as time goes by. This is done by applying a constant rate of depreciation to the asset's carrying amount. As the carrying amount decreases with each year's depreciation charge, so does the amount of each year's depreciation expense.

The depreciation rate is determined on the basis of management's estimate of the asset's useful life. The shorter the useful life, the higher the depreciation rate. Different types of capital assets will be assigned different rates. A capital asset with a relatively long expected useful life (such as a building) would have a fairly low depreciation rate (such as 5% or 10%), while a capital asset with a relatively short expected useful life (such as equipment) would have a higher depreciation rate (such as 20% or 30%).

One of the most common accelerated methods is the **double-diminishing-balance method** (also known as the double-declining-balance method). With this method, the depreciation rate is *double* the **straight-line rate**. Thus, using the example shown in Exhibit 8-6, an asset with a five-year expected useful life would be depreciated using a straight-line rate of 20% (that is, 1/5 = 0.2 or 20%), but would be depreciated at 40% using the double-diminishing-balance method (that is, 2 × 20% = 40%).

It is important to note that under either the straight-line method or units-of-production method, it is *not* possible to depreciate an asset below its estimated residual value because this variable is removed from the calculation at the outset. This is not the case under the double-diminishing-balance method, so a step is added to the calculation process to ensure that the asset is not depreciated below its estimated residual value.

HELPFUL HINT

When using diminishing-balance depreciation, remember that you must ensure that you do not depreciate the asset below the estimated residual value. If you did, you would be recording an expense that will never be incurred because the company expects to recover the estimated residual amount when it has finished using the asset. Therefore, this portion of the asset's cost will never be an expense to the company.

THREE STEPS TO CALCULATING DOUBLE-DIMINISHING-BALANCE DEPRECIATION
STEP 1: Determine the depreciation rate.   (1 / Estimated Useful Life) × 2   STEP 2: Apply the rate to the asset's carrying amount.   STEP 3: Ensure that the asset's ending carrying amount is ≥ the asset's estimated residual value.   If not, then go back to STEP 2 and the depreciation expense for that period will be equal to the difference between the opening carrying amount and the estimated residual value.

Exhibit 8-8 shows the calculation under double-diminishing-balance depreciation using our ongoing example.

Exhibit 8-8 Double-Diminishing-Balance Method

Purchase cost	$50,000
Estimated residual value	$ 5,000
Estimated useful life	5 years

Remember the three steps:
1. Determine the depreciation rate.
2. Apply the rate to the asset's carrying amount.
3. Ensure the ending carrying amount is ≥ the asset's estimated residual value.

continued

Exhibit 8-8 Double-Diminishing-Balance Method (continued)

Determine rate:

$$= (1 / (\text{Estimated Useful Life})) \times 2$$
$$= (1 / 5) \times 2 = 0.4 \text{ or } 40\%$$

Depreciation schedule:

Year	Beginning Carrying Amount	Calculation of Expenses		Depreciation Expense	Ending Carrying Amount
2016	$50,000	40% × 50,000	=	$20,000	$30,000
2017	30,000	40% × 30,000	=	12,000	18,000
2018	18,000	40% × 18,000	=	7,200	10,800
2019	10,800	40% × 10,800	=	4,320	6,480
2020	6,480	40% × 6,480	=	~~2,592~~	~~3,888~~
				1,480[a]	**5,000**
				$45,000	

[a] In the final year, the depreciation expense is limited to whatever amount is needed to make the final carrying amount equal to the asset's residual value (in this case, 6,480 − 5,000 = 1,480).

Now that we have calculated depreciation expense and carrying amount under the three depreciation methods, let's revisit the graphs in Exhibit 8-4 (showing annual depreciation expense) and Exhibit 8-5 (showing asset carrying amount) using the numerical data from our example. Exhibits 8-9 and 8-10 show the annual depreciation expense and carrying amounts under the three methods for our ongoing example.

Exhibit 8-9 Annual Depreciation Expense: Three Methods

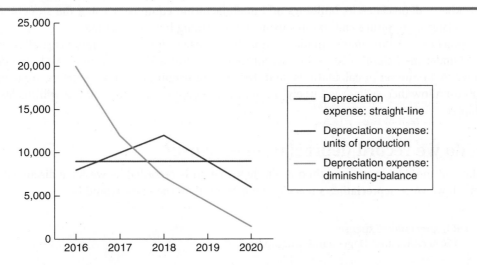

This graph reiterates the following:
- Under the straight-line method, depreciation expense remains constant each period.
- Under the units-of-production method, depreciation expense fluctuates depending upon the asset's usage.
- Under the diminishing-balance method, depreciation expense is greatest early in the asset's useful life and diminishes as time goes by.

Exhibit 8-10 Carrying Amount: Three Methods

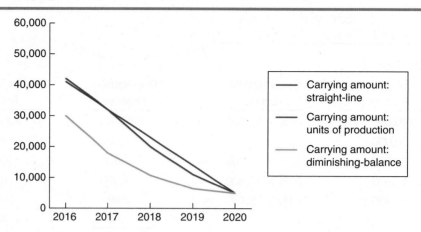

This graph reiterates the following:
- Under the straight-line method, the asset's carrying amount declines at an even rate over time.
- Under the units-of-production method, there is no regular pattern for the asset's carrying amount over time because this depends on the asset's usage.
- Under the diminishing-balance method, the asset's carrying amount declines most rapidly early in its useful life and diminishes as time goes by.

How do we choose a depreciation method?

Companies are expected to use the depreciation method that is most consistent with the manner in which management expects the asset's economic benefits to be consumed through usage. Any of the methods that have been discussed, or other systematic and rational methods that suit their circumstances, can be selected. Companies often use a number of different depreciation methods, selecting the straight-line method for certain types of PP&E and using the diminishing-balance method for other assets. For example, BlackBerry depreciates its buildings and manufacturing equipment using the straight-line method, but depreciates its furniture and fixtures using a diminishing-balance method.

For practical reasons, many smaller companies choose to follow the capital cost allowance method specified under the federal Income Tax Act for their accounting depreciation as well. By doing so, they only have to do one set of calculations, and their record keeping and tax reporting are simplified. The capital cost allowance system is largely a diminishing-balance system and we will discuss it later in the chapter.

How do we record depreciation expense?

Regardless of the depreciation method used, depreciation is recorded as we have discussed in previous chapters. If we were depreciating a piece of equipment, then the entry would be:

DR Depreciation Expense
    CR Accumulated Depreciation, Equipment

We use the contra-asset account, Accumulated Depreciation, Equipment, in order to preserve the original cost in the equipment account. This way, financial statement users can see what portion of the equipment's costs has been expensed and they are able to judge the relative age of the equipment. This enables them to make judgements about how soon the equipment will need to be replaced.

The financial statement effects of the depreciation entry are:
1. Statement of income: Expenses are increased and net income would be decreased.
2. Statement of financial position: The asset's carrying amount is decreased, thereby reducing total assets.
3. Statement of cash flows: No effect because depreciation is a non-cash transaction.

KEY POINT

Crediting Accumulated Depreciation rather than the equipment account keeps the original cost amount intact, allowing users to judge the asset's relative age.

KEY POINTS

Depreciation...
- does *not* involve cash.
- is a **non-cash expense**.

Ethics in Accounting

The estimates management makes about the useful life and residual value of PP&E provide them with opportunities to influence the net earnings on the income statement. For example, selecting a longer useful life or higher residual value would decrease depreciation expense and increase net income. If management received a bonus based on net income, these simple steps would increase the amount of the bonus. The choice of depreciation method (such as straight-line or diminishing-balance) provides a similar opportunity. For example, selecting the straight-line method would result in a lower depreciation expense early in the life of the asset relative to the double-diminishing-balance method. This would also increase the amount of the income-based bonus in the short term. Both of these management decisions provide the opportunity for what is known as **earnings management**, an unethical practice whereby revenue and expense methods are chosen in order to increase or decrease earnings in a particular period. Financial statement users can compare depreciation policies and estimates of useful lives across companies in similar industries as one way to identify if there are issues in this area.

Does an asset's carrying amount tell me what it is worth?

No! It is important to note that depreciation is a cost allocation process rather than an attempt to value PP&E. As such, the carrying amount of PP&E does *not* reflect what those assets could be sold for. Instead, carrying amount indicates the portion of the asset's cost that will be expensed in future periods when the asset generates revenues or the portion of the asset's cost that management expects to recover when the asset is disposed of (that is, its residual value).

How do we determine depreciation for partial periods?

Property, plant, and equipment assets are rarely acquired on the first day of a fiscal year. In reality, they are acquired at various times throughout the year. Since companies begin depreciating PP&E when they are available for use (when the asset's condition and location reflect management's intended use of it), they must determine the depreciation expense for the partial year by following one of a number of accounting conventions.

One simple way is to prorate the annual depreciation amount by using "the nearest whole month" rule or the "15-day rule." Accordingly, the company calculates depreciation for the full month if the asset was purchased in the first half of the month (in the first 15 days), because the asset was used for most of the month. If the asset was purchased in the last half of the month (after the 15th), then no depreciation is taken in that month, because the asset was used for less than half a month. The same would hold true in the year of disposal: depreciation expense for the month would be taken if the asset was sold after the 15th, but not if it was sold prior to the 15th.

$$\text{Depreciation Expense for Partial Period} = \text{Annual Depreciation Expense} \times \frac{\text{\# of Full Months}}{12}$$

Another convention is the "half-year" rule. This practice mirrors the rules specified under the Income Tax Act under which a half a year's depreciation is taken on the net acquisitions for the year (that is, acquisitions less disposals) no matter when the assets were acquired.

CHANGES IN DEPRECIATION METHODS

Can we change depreciation estimates and methods?

Yes! An asset's estimated useful life and estimated residual value are management estimates. The selection of the depreciation method is also based on management's expectations of how the economic benefits embodied in the asset will be consumed. These estimates and expectations can and do change over time. This is no different than the experience most of us have with the long-term assets we use in our day-to-day

■ **LEARNING OBJECTIVE 5**
Describe and implement changes in depreciation estimates and methods.

lives. Many of us have had a cellphone or computer that, when acquired, we thought we would use for a certain period or in a certain way only to have those expectations changed at some point down the road.

Companies are required to review annually the estimated residual values, estimated useful lives, and depreciation methods used (normally at each statement of financial position date). If there has been a significant change in any of these, then such changes must be reflected in the determination of the depreciation expense for the period in which the change(s) took place and for future periods. This is what is known as a **change in an accounting estimate**, which is treated prospectively (into the future) and not retrospectively (that is, we do not go back and change the depreciation amounts recorded in prior periods).

For Example

In 2011, **Danier Leather Inc.** changed the method it used to depreciate its property and equipment. The company switched from the diminishing-balance method to the straight-line method as management "believed (this) to more accurately reflect the usage…of property and equipment." This was accounted for prospectively as a change in estimate.[3]

KEY POINT
Whenever there is a change in its cost, estimated residual value, useful life, or depreciation method, you should determine the carrying amount at the time of the change. Then, you should carry on with this as the new "cost."

When there have been changes to the estimates related to depreciation, the key is to first determine the asset's carrying amount at the time of the change(s). This carrying amount is essentially treated as the new "cost" for the asset. The depreciation calculations are then made using the revised estimated residual value, the *remaining* estimated useful life, and the depreciation method that best reflects management's expectations of how the asset's economic benefits will be realized in the future.

To illustrate how changes in depreciation assumptions are handled, in Exhibits 8-11, 8-12, and 8-13 we will make a couple of changes to the data used in the example in Exhibit 8-6.

Exhibit 8-11 Example of Changes in Estimates of Useful Life and Residual Value under the Straight-Line Method

Assume that the equipment has been depreciated for three years. Management then decides that the equipment has four more years of useful life left (that is, it is now expected to have a useful life of seven rather than five years), and its residual value at the end of 2022 is expected to be $2,000.

Straight-line depreciation per year as originally determined	$ 9,000
Carrying amount at end of 2018 [$50,000 − (3 × $9,000)]	$23,000
Changes in estimates in 2019:	
Estimated remaining useful life	4 years
Estimated residual value	$ 2,000

Revised depreciation calculation:

$$\text{Depreciation Expense} = \frac{\text{Carrying Amount} - \text{Estimated Residual Value}}{\text{Remaining Estimated Useful Life}}$$

$$= \frac{\$23,000 - \$2,000}{4 \text{ years}} = \$5,250 \text{ per year}$$

Depreciation schedule:

Year	Beginning Carrying Amount	Depreciation Expense	Ending Carrying Amount
2016	$50,000	$ 9,000	$41,000
2017	41,000	9,000	32,000
2018	32,000	9,000	23,000
2019	23,000	5,250	17,750
2020	17,750	5,250	12,500
2021	12,500	5,250	7,250
2022	7,250	5,250	**2,000**
		$48,000	

Exhibit 8-12 Example of Changes in Estimates of Useful Life, Residual Value, and Depreciation Method

Assume that the equipment has been depreciated using the double-diminishing-balance method for three years. Management then decides that the equipment has four more years of useful life left (that is, it is now expected to have a useful life of seven rather than five years), its residual value at the end of 2022 is expected to be $2,000, and it should be depreciated using the straight-line method rather than the double-diminishing-balance method.

Double-diminishing-balance depreciation as originally determined:

2016 $20,000		
2017 $12,000	$39,200	
2018 $ 7,200		

Carrying amount at end of 2018 ($50,000 − $39,200)	$10,800
Changes in estimates in 2019:	
Estimated remaining useful life	4 years
Estimated residual value	$ 2,000

Revised depreciation calculation:

$$\text{Depreciation Expense} = \frac{\text{Carrying Amount} - \text{Estimated Residual Value}}{\text{Remaining Estimated Useful Life}}$$

$$= \frac{\$10,800 - \$2,000}{4 \text{ years}} = \$2,200 \text{ per year}$$

Depreciation schedule:

Year	Beginning Carrying Amount	Depreciation Expense	Ending Carrying Amount
2016	$50,000	$20,000	$30,000
2017	30,000	12,000	18,000
2018	18,000	7,200	10,800
Revised depreciation: (10,800 − 2,000) / 4 = 2,200			
2019	10,800	2,200	8,600
2020	8,600	2,200	6,400
2021	6,400	2,200	4,200
2022	4,200	2,200	**2,000**
		$48,000	

Exhibit 8-13 Example of Changes in Estimates of Useful Life and Residual Value under the Diminishing-Balance Method

Assume that the equipment has been depreciated using the double-diminishing-balance method for three years. Management then decides that the equipment has four more years of useful life left (that is, it is now expected to have a useful life of seven rather than five years), will have an expected residual value at the end of 2021 of $2,000, and should still be depreciated using the double-diminishing-balance method.

Double-diminishing-balance depreciation as originally determined:

2016 $20,000		
2017 $12,000	$39,200	
2018 $ 7,200		

Carrying amount at end of 2018 ($50,000 − $39,200)	$10,800
Changes in estimates in 2019:	
Estimated remaining useful life	4 years
Estimated residual value	$2,000

continued

Exhibit 8-13 Example of Changes in Estimates of Useful Life and Residual Value under the Diminishing-Balance Method (continued)

Revised depreciation calculation:

Determine rate:
$$= (1 / (\text{Estimated } \textbf{remaining} \text{ useful life})) \times 2$$
$$= (1 / 4) \times 2 = 0.5 \text{ or } 50\%$$

Depreciation schedule:

Year	Beginning Carrying Amount	Depreciation Expense	Ending Carrying Amount
2016	$50,000	$20,000	$30,000
2017	30,000	12,000	18,000
2018	18,000	7,200	10,800
Revised depreciation:			
2019	10,800	5,400	5,400
2020	5,400	2,700	2,700
2021	2,700	~~1,350~~ **700***	~~1,350~~ **2000**
2022	2,000	0	**2,000**
		$48,000	

*Depreciation expense is limited to $700 because we cannot depreciate the asset below its estimated residual value of $2,000. There will be no depreciation expense in 2022 because the asset will have been fully depreciated.

IMPAIRMENT

■ **LEARNING OBJECTIVE 6**
Explain what it means if property, plant, and equipment assets are impaired.

What does it mean if an asset is impaired?

Companies purchase PP&E to generate revenues in future periods. The total of these revenues would be expected to exceed the cost of the asset or else the company would not have purchased it in the first place. It is possible that circumstances change and management's expectations of the economic benefits that will flow from the asset in the future, either from its use or residual value, are reduced. If this is the case, then the asset is considered to be **impaired** and its carrying amount should be reduced accordingly.

These changing circumstances may arise as the result of external factors or internal factors. Changes in technology or in government regulations are examples of external factors that could result in significant changes in the manner in which an asset will be used in the future. Internal factors that would indicate a significant change in the manner in which an asset may be used in the future would include if the asset had been physically damaged or the business unit in which it operated was to be curtailed or shut down. Companies are required to consider whether there are any such factors present for all of their PP&E at each year end. This is known as assessing for indications of impairment or performing impairment testing. When indications of impairment are present, then management determines: (a) the future cash flows that are expected to be generated from the asset's use, and (b) the asset's fair value less any selling costs. The greater of these two amounts is known as the **recoverable amount**, as it would represent the best course of action that management could take with the asset. In other words, if the expected future cash flows from the asset exceed the amount that would be realized from selling it, then management will continue to use it or vice versa. Management then compares the asset's carrying amount with the recoverable amount. Any excess is an **impairment loss** (Exhibit 8-14).

Exhibit 8-14 Calculation of an Impairment Loss

Carrying amount	$ xxx
Less greater of:	
Recoverable Amount { (a) Expected future cash flows	
(b) Fair value-selling costs	xxx
Impairment loss	$ xxx

While impairment testing is beyond the scope of an introductory textbook, it is important for you to have a basic understanding of what is meant by an impairment loss and how it is determined.

For example, suppose that at the end of 2017, when the carrying amount of the asset in Exhibit 8-6 is $23,000, management determines that, as a result of damage to the equipment, the recoverable amount from its future use will be only $20,000. The following entry would be made to record the impairment loss:

Loss on Impairment	3,000	
Accumulated Impairment Losses, Equipment		3,000

In all likelihood, after this decline in value, the company would review the asset's estimated useful life and residual value so that changes could be made to the depreciation in future periods, if necessary.

The asset's carrying amount would be determined as shown in Exhibit 8-15 for future periods:

Exhibit 8-15 Determination of Carrying Amount

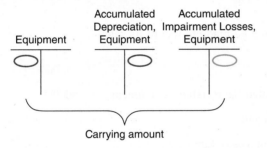

DISPOSAL OF PROPERTY, PLANT, AND EQUIPMENT

How do we account for disposals of property, plant, and equipment?

■ **LEARNING OBJECTIVE 7**
Account for the disposal of property, plant, and equipment.

Companies dispose of PP&E in a variety of circumstances. For example, the asset may have reached the end of its useful life or the company may have decided to replace it with another asset that uses more recent technology, can handle increased volumes, and so on. Companies may also dispose of PP&E if they are moving out of the line of business that the asset is related to. Assets may be sold if they still have value or scrapped if they have none. Whatever the circumstances, when PP&E is disposed of or scrapped, it is **derecognized** for accounting purposes. Two steps are necessary whenever PP&E is derecognized:

1. The asset should be depreciated up to the date of derecognition.
2. The asset and the related accumulated depreciation should be removed from the company's records and any resulting **gain** or **loss** be determined.

The first step is required in order to ensure that the portion of the asset's cost that generated economic benefits for the company has been expensed. The second step is required because the company no longer has the asset. We determine the amount of any gain or loss so that users are made aware of whether the company over- or under-expensed the asset during its useful life. Let's explore this further.

Recall that an asset's carrying amount is the asset's cost less accumulated depreciation. If the proceeds of sale exceed the carrying amount, then there is a gain on disposal. If the carrying amount is greater than the proceeds of sale, then there is a loss on disposal. If the proceeds of sale equal the asset's carrying amount, then there is neither a gain nor a loss. This is shown in Exhibit 8-16.

Exhibit 8-16 Determining the Gain/Loss on Disposal of PP&E

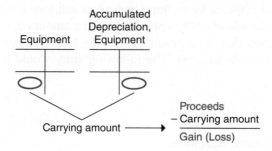

Using the information from Exhibit 8-6, assume that the equipment is sold at the end of its useful life for $6,000. This asset had an original cost of $50,000 and at the end of its useful life its accumulated depreciation would equal $45,000. This would result in a carrying amount equal to its estimated residual value of $5,000.

Proceeds of disposal	$6,000
Less: Carrying amount	5,000
Gain on sale	$1,000

The following entry would be made to record its sale:

Cash	6,000	
Accumulated Depreciation, Equipment	45,000	
Equipment		50,000
Gain on Sale of Equipment		1,000

When a company has a gain on the disposal of PP&E, we know that it claimed too much depreciation expense over the period in which it used the asset. In other words, the company's estimate of residual value was either too low or its estimate of the asset's useful life was too short. If the company has a loss on disposal, then the opposite is true. The company did not expense enough depreciation during the asset's useful life because the estimated residual value was too high or its estimate of the asset's useful life was too long.

If the asset is being scrapped rather than sold because it has no value at the end of its useful life, the accounting is exactly the same except that there would be no proceeds of sale to record and the loss would be equal to whatever the asset's carrying amount was at the time the asset was scrapped. This loss indicates that the company recorded an insufficient amount of depreciation expense while the asset was being used. Continuing with the previous example, if the equipment were scrapped at the end of its useful life, the following entry would result:

Accumulated Depreciation, Equipment	45,000	
Loss on Disposal of Equipment	5,000	
Equipment		50,000

DEPRECIATION AND INCOME TAXES

■ **LEARNING OBJECTIVE 8**
Explain the effect of depreciation on income taxes.

Do depreciation decisions affect corporate income taxes?

No! The Canada Revenue Agency (CRA) does not allow companies to deduct depreciation expense when calculating their taxable income. However, it does allow a similar type of deduction, called **capital cost allowance** (CCA). In other words, although accountants deduct depreciation expense when they calculate net earnings on the income statement, they have to use capital cost allowance instead of depreciation expense when they calculate the company's taxable income on its income tax return. CCA is calculated in a manner similar to accelerated depreciation, with a few exceptions.

While a detailed discussion of the CCA system is beyond the scope of an introductory financial accounting course, there are a few important differences between depreciation and CCA that you should understand.

1. When determining accounting depreciation, the company's management is able to determine the depreciation method (for example, straight-line or diminishing-balance). This is not the case for CCA because the Income Tax Act specifies the method that must be used. This is normally an accelerated method similar to the diminishing-balance method.

2. When determining accounting depreciation, the company's management is able to estimate the asset's useful life, which is then used to determine the depreciation rate. The Income Tax Act specifies the CCA rate that must be used.

3. When determining accounting depreciation, the company's management is able to estimate the residual value, which has an impact on the amount of the annual depreciation expense. Residual values are ignored within the CCA system.

4. While depreciation expense must be recorded annually on the income statement, the amount of CCA determined under the Income Tax Act only represents the *maximum* that can be claimed on the income tax return. Companies are free to claim any amount up to this maximum (therefore, it is possible for a company to claim no CCA). This is the only area where management's judgement can influence the CCA system.

From the above, it is easy to see that the CRA removes virtually all management judgement from the CCA system. While there is an opportunity for management bias to influence the determination of depreciation expense, there is little within the CCA system.

Can a company carry property, plant, and equipment at their fair values?

It depends! Earlier in the chapter we learned that, under IFRS, companies can choose between the **cost model** and the **revaluation model** in determining the amount at which PP&E will be reflected on the statement of financial position. We also learned that only the cost model is acceptable under ASPE. So far, we have discussed the cost model because this is the method used by the vast majority of both public and private Canadian companies. Given its very limited use, we will only briefly review the revaluation model. However, it is important that you be aware that this model is an option for public companies.

Under the **revaluation model**, PP&E assets are carried at their fair value (as determined at points of time known as the revaluation date) less any subsequent accumulated depreciation and any subsequent impairment losses. These revaluation dates may be annual for assets with rapidly changing values or every three to four years for assets whose values change slowly. It is also important to know that a company is not able to revalue only those assets whose values have increased. If a company is following the revaluation model for a class of assets, then *all* of the assets in that class must be revalued. (For example, all buildings or all land must be revalued, rather than just individual buildings or parcels of land.)

The Conceptual Framework
THE CARRYING AMOUNT OF PROPERTY, PLANT, AND EQUIPMENT

The choice between the cost model and the revaluation model is an excellent example of different perspectives on what is **relevant** to financial statement users. **Relevance** is one of the **fundamental qualitative characteristics** of the conceptual framework, with relevant information being information that is capable of making a difference to users in their decision-making.

One could argue that the fair value of PP&E is irrelevant to financial statement users because these assets are being held to use in the business and are not held for resale. Alternatively, it could be argued that for other users, such as creditors, the fair value of PP&E is very relevant in terms of any lending decisions they might be making that use these assets as collateral.

INTANGIBLE ASSETS

■ LEARNING OBJECTIVE 9
Explain the accounting treatment for intangible assets, including amortization.

What are intangible assets?

Intangible assets are long-term assets without physical form that are separately identifiable (that is, they can be resold or licensed). This category of long-term assets includes things such as the following:

1. **Intellectual property**
   - **Trademarks**

     Trademarks are words or designs that uniquely identify a company or organization. These could include organizational names (such as **Rona**), brand names (such as **President's Choice**), symbols (such as the **Hudson's Bay Company** crest), certification marks (such as that of the **Canadian Fair Trade Association**), or a unique way of packaging or wrapping goods (such as **French's** mustard bottle). In Canada, trademark registration provides the company with the exclusive right to use the mark within Canada for 15 years and is renewable every 15 years.

   - **Patents**

     Patents are legal rights to unique products or processes. They prevent others from making, using, or selling products that include the patented knowledge. In Canada, a patent provides the holder with legal protection for 20 years from the date of filing. Patents are a significant asset for many companies, especially those in the pharmaceutical, computer, and telecommunications industries.

   - **Copyrights**

     Copyrights are legal rights over literary, musical, artistic, and dramatic works. They provide the holder with the right to reproduce them. Copyrights extend to authors (creators of books, poems, and computer programs, for example), musicians (creators of songs), filmmakers (creators of films), playwrights (creators of scripts and plays), and artists (creators of paintings, photographs, drawings, maps, sculptures, and so on). In Canada, a copyright generally lasts for the life of the creator plus 50 years. Copyrights are significant assets in the publishing, media, music, and film industries.

For Example

In 2012, BlackBerry (then called Research In Motion) was part of a consortium of technology companies that paid $4.5 billion to purchase more than 6,000 patents and patent applications belonging to Nortel, which had been a leading Canadian telecommunications company prior to its bankruptcy in 2009. BlackBerry's share of the purchase price was $775 million.[4]

   - **Trade secrets**

     Trade secrets include recipes, chemical formulas, and processes. Canada has no legal registration system for trade secrets, so the only way companies can protect these assets is for the trade secret to be kept secret! Steps that can be taken to help protect these assets include asking employees to sign confidentiality agreements, restricting access to the secret information (for example, keeping the information in a safe or using secure passwords for computer access), and marking all documentation related to the secret "secret and confidential."

For Example

Canadian coffee giant **Tim Hortons** keeps the recipe for its famous coffee top secret. Only about five people in the world know the recipe and what blend of coffee beans is used in making it. Tim Hortons protects its coffee recipe with a high-tech security system.[5]

2. **Licences** (including fishing licences, broadcast licences, telecommunications licences, taxi licences, and aircraft landing rights).
3. **Customer lists** (including listing agreements in the real estate industry).
4. **Franchise rights** (that is, when a company, the "franchisor," grants another company, the "franchisee," the right to use its trademark, brand, and operating system). There is normally an upfront franchise fee and an ongoing royalty as part of the franchise agreement.

For Example

A Tim Hortons franchise costs between $480,000 and $510,000 and includes all of the restaurant equipment, furniture, display equipment, signage, a seven-week training program at Tim Hortons University, the right to use all company manuals, and the right to use Tim Hortons' trademarks and trade names. The franchise agreements are normally for a 10-year period with options to renew for up to an additional 10-year period. During the term of franchise agreement, franchisees also pay a franchise fee of approximately 20% of weekly gross sales to the franchisor.[6]

5. **Computer software** (including website development costs, as long as the site is used to generate revenues and enable customers to process orders rather than just to promote the company's products).
6. **Development costs**
   There is a distinction between research costs (the costs of investigating for new scientific or technical knowledge) and development costs (the cost of applying research findings to plan or design new products, materials, processes, and so on). Development costs can be capitalized as an intangible asset provided that six specific criteria have been met. A detailed discussion of these criteria is beyond the scope of an introductory accounting text. Essentially, the uncertainty around the future economic benefits of research costs precludes them being recognized as an asset, whereas if the specific criteria for development costs can be met, then there is sufficient certainty that the company will realize the future economic benefits from these outlays.

At what amount are intangible assets reflected on the statement of financial position?

Just like PP&E, intangible assets are initially recorded at cost (the amount paid to a third party for the asset). Similar to PP&E, IFRS allows companies to use the cost model or revaluation model (provided there is an active market for the asset that can be used in assessing fair value) for determining the carrying amount for intangible assets on the statement of financial position. Some intangibles such as licences (for example, taxi or commercial fishing licences) have active markets that can be used for assessing fair value, while other intangibles do not.

When intangible assets are acquired, management has to determine whether the asset has a **finite useful life** (that is, it will only generate economic benefits for a fixed period in the future) or an **indefinite useful life** (that is, there is no foreseeable limit to the period in which the asset will generate economic benefits for the company). The decision about an intangible asset's useful life is significant, as the costs of those assets with a finite useful life will have to be allocated to the periods in which the economic benefits of these assets are expected to be consumed by the company. This is achieved through a process similar to the depreciation of PP&E, except that it is known as **amortization**. Just as with depreciation, the cost of an intangible asset is allocated on a systematic basis to future periods in a manner that reflects management's expectations of how the future economic benefits will be consumed by the company. Normally, this systematic basis will be the straight-line method. The residual value of a finite life intangible asset is normally zero because, when the patent, licence, or franchise agreement expires, it has no value.

KEY POINTS
Intangible assets:
- are normally depreciated using the straight-line method.
- do *not* normally have a residual value.

For Example

Air Canada has recorded an intangible asset of $97 million related to international routes and slot rights at Tokyo's Narita International Airport, Washington's Reagan National Airport, and London's Heathrow Airport. (Slot rights are the rights granted by authorities to airlines to land and depart from airports at certain times.) Air Canada's management expects that the company will provide service to these international locations for an indefinite period and therefore these assets are not being amortized.[7]

KEY POINT
The legal life of most intangible assets *exceeds* their useful life.

Another important consideration with intangible assets is that management must assess the useful life relative to its legal life. Factors such as the potential for technological or commercial obsolescence, expected market demand for the related product or service, and the expected actions of competitors must be taken into consideration. Just because an IT company has a 20-year patent on some technology does not mean it is going to be able to realize economic benefits for that entire period. It is very likely that the patented technology will be superseded by advances in the field. If this is the case, then the asset should be amortized over its estimated useful life (that is, the shorter period).

Intangible assets with finite useful lives must be tested for impairment whenever the company becomes aware of something that may indicate a possible impairment. Intangible assets with indefinite useful lives must be tested for impairment annually. This is especially important because these assets are not being amortized.

Another aspect that is different when accounting for intangibles is that the accumulated amortization account is rarely used. Most companies simply reduce their intangible assets directly when they amortize them. Because of the uncertain valuation of intangibles and the fact that these assets normally cannot be replaced, it is not as important for users to know what the original costs were. As such, the journal entry to record the amortization of a patent would be as follows:

Amortization Expense	XXX	
Patents		XXX

How is accounting for intangible assets different than accounting for property, plant, and equipment?

Accounting for intangible assets differs from accounting for property, plant, and equipment in a number of ways:
1. A decision must be made for each intangible asset about whether it has a finite or indefinite useful life. In contrast, land is the only type of PP&E with an indefinite useful life.
2. Intangible assets with finite useful lives are normally amortized using the straight-line method. In contrast, PP&E items are often depreciated using the diminishing-balance and units-of-production methods.
3. Intangible assets normally have no residual values. In contrast, most items within PP&E have a residual value.
4. Generally, an accumulated amortization account is not used when amortizing intangible assets; instead, the intangible asset is reduced directly. In contrast, accumulated depreciation accounts are used to capture the cumulative depreciation expense for PP&E.

GOODWILL

LEARNING OBJECTIVE 10
Explain the accounting treatment for goodwill, including impairment.

What is goodwill?

Goodwill is a long-term asset that arises when two businesses are combined. It represents the expected future economic benefits that will arise from the combination that cannot be separately identified as either PP&E or an intangible asset. The easiest way to think about goodwill is that it is the premium or excess paid by one business when it is acquiring another that is related to factors such as management expertise, corporate reputation, or customer loyalty. In other words, it is the purchase price less the fair value of the PP&E and identifiable intangible assets being acquired plus the fair value of any liabilities being assumed as part of the purchase.

Exhibit 8-17 illustrates how goodwill would be determined in a simple business combination.

Exhibit 8-17 Determining Goodwill

Purchase price	$2,000,000
Less:	
Fair value of land	(900,000)
Fair value of building	(500,000)
Fair value of equipment	(300,000)
Fair value of inventory	(150,000)
Fair value of patent	(100,000)
Add:	
Fair value of mortgage assumed	350,000
Goodwill	$ 400,000

Goodwill is only recorded when a business combination has taken place (that is, there must be a transaction with a third party). Many companies have done a great job of developing their own goodwill. This can result from things like developing successful advertising campaigns, carrying out public service programs, making significant charitable gifts, or offering effective employee training programs. These actions can result in the company developing strong customer relationships or significant market share. They may also result in the company having a very skilled workforce. This kind of goodwill is known as internally generated goodwill and *cannot* be recognized as an asset under IFRS or ASPE. The rationale is that the company has no legal means of controlling its employees (because they are free to leave the company) or its customers (because they are free to take their business elsewhere) and, as a result, the amount of this goodwill cannot be reliably measured.

KEY POINTS
• Goodwill is only recognized when it has been purchased as part of a business combination.
• Internally generated goodwill cannot be recognized.

The Conceptual Framework
GOODWILL

Comparability is one of the **enhancing qualitative characteristics** of the conceptual framework. The accounting treatment of goodwill is an excellent example of how comparability is a challenge for financial statement users. If the company has developed goodwill on its own (that is, self-generated goodwill), it is not able to recognize it as an asset on its balance sheet under current accounting standards. However, if a company acquired goodwill by purchasing another business, it is able to record the goodwill as an asset. Users need to be aware of this when comparing companies.

For Example

As mentioned in the chapter-opening story, in 2011, Canadian Tire acquired control of FGL Sports (which owns a number a retail chains including Sport Chek, Sports Experts, Intersport, and Nevada Bob's Golf). The purchase price was $800.6 million. The notes to Canadian Tire's financial statements included the following information related to the purchase:

FINANCIAL STATEMENTS

(continued)

For Example (continued)

8.2.5 Fair value of identifiable assets acquired and liabilities assumed as at acquisition date

The fair values of identifiable assets acquired and liabilities assumed as at the acquisition date are as follows:

(C$ in millions)

Cash and cash equivalents	$ 25.3
Trade and other receivables[1]	111.1
Loans receivable	0.8
Merchandise inventories	455.9
Income taxes recoverable	3.4
Prepaid expenses and deposits	11.1
Long-term receivables and other assets	4.9
Intangible assets	382.3
Property and equipment	155.1
Trade and other payables	(288.9)
Short-term borrowings	(241.9)
Provisions	(31.0)
Deferred income taxes	(58.2)
Other long-term liabilities	(37.7)
Total net identifiable assets	$ 492.2

[1] *Gross trade and other receivables acquired is $112.4 million, of which $1.3 million was expected to be uncollectible as at the acquisition date.*

8.2.6 Goodwill arising on acquisition of FGL Sports

Goodwill was recognized as a result of the acquisition as follows:

(C$ in millions)

Total consideration transferred	$ 800.6
Less: Total net identifiable assets	492.2
Goodwill	$ 308.4

The goodwill recognized on acquisition of FGL Sports is attributable mainly to the expected future growth potential from the expanded customer base of FGL Sports banners and brands and the network of stores that are predominantly mall-based and provide access to the 18-to-35-year-old customer segment. None of the goodwill recognized is expected to be deductible for income tax purposes.

From this information, we can see that 38.5% ($308.4/$800.6) of the price paid to purchase FGL Sports was related to the company's goodwill. This $308-million asset was one of the most significant assets acquired by Canadian Tire when it made this purchase.[8]

At what amount is goodwill reflected on the statement of financial position?

Since goodwill is considered to have an indefinite useful life, it is not amortized. Instead, management is required to review the carrying amount of goodwill annually to determine whether there is evidence that it has been impaired. If it has, the goodwill should be written down (reduced in value) and an impairment loss recognized. Impairment testing for goodwill is beyond the scope of an introductory accounting text. There are many interesting facets to this issue because goodwill cannot be separated from the business it is related to and therefore cannot be tested for impairment on its own.

Purchased goodwill is carried on the statement of financial position at its cost less any accumulated impairment losses (Exhibit 8-18). The net amount is known as the "carrying amount."

Exhibit 8-18 Determining the Carrying Amount of Goodwill

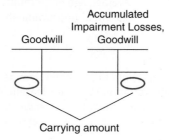

How is goodwill treated differently than other long-term assets?

There are a couple of ways in which goodwill is treated differently from other long-term assets:

1. Goodwill is not amortized (as it is considered to have an indefinite useful life).
2. Goodwill must be reviewed annually to determine whether there is evidence that it has been impaired.

FINANCIAL STATEMENT ANALYSIS

What is the relative age of the company's long-term assets?

■ **LEARNING OBJECTIVE 11**
Assess the average age of property, plant, and equipment; calculate the fixed asset turnover ratio; and assess the results.

Understanding the age of a company's long-term assets is useful to financial statement users. The newer the long-term asset base, the longer the company will be able to go without replacing these assets. Companies with older asset bases will need to reinvest in order to replace these assets and maintain their operating capacity. There are a couple of basic measures that can help users assess the relative age of a company's long-term assets: average age percentage and average age.

$$\text{Average Age } \% = \frac{\text{Total Accumulated Depreciation}}{\text{Total Property, Plant, and Equipment} - \text{Land}^*}$$

This ratio provides the user with information on the extent to which a company's PP&E assets have been depreciated.

*We remove land as it is not depreciated.

$$\text{Average Age} = \frac{\text{Total Accumulated Depreciation}}{\text{Depreciation Expense}}$$

This ratio provides the user with information on how long a company has been using its PP&E.

Let's compare the results of Danier Leather with **Le Château** to get a better understanding of these ratios. Specifically, we will analyze the leasehold improvements* of each company.

Danier's average age percentage:

$$= \frac{15,322}{22,679 - 0} = 0.676 \text{ or } 67.6\%$$

Le Château's average age percentage:

$$= \frac{39,716}{74,530 - 0} = 0.533 \text{ or } 53.3\%$$

This tells us that, on average, Danier's leasehold improvement assets are 67.6% or two thirds of the way through their useful lives whereas Le Château's leasehold improvement assets are 53.3% or about half of the way through their useful lives. This suggests that Danier will have to replace its leasehold assets sooner than Le Château.

*Leasehold improvements represent costs incurred by a company on space it has leased that will benefit multiple periods (new flooring, remodeling, and so on). These items become the property of the landlord at the end of the lease term.

Average age of Danier's leasehold improvements:	Average age of Le Château's leasehold improvements:
$= \dfrac{15,322}{1,699} = 9.02$	$= \dfrac{39,716}{7,900} = 5.0$

This tells us that, on average, Danier's leasehold improvement assets have been used for 9.02 years. When we compare this with Danier's depreciation policy for leaseholds, which is to depreciate them over the lease term not exceeding 10 years, we can see that, on average, the company's leaseholds are nearing the end of their useful lives. By comparison, Le Château's leaseholds are much newer, having been used for only 5.0 years.

How effectively has the company used its long-term assets?

Companies invest in long-term assets to help generate revenues. Financial statement users wanting to assess how effective the company has been in this area often use the fixed asset turnover ratio.

$$\text{Fixed Asset Turnover} = \frac{\text{Sales Revenue}}{\text{Average Net Property, Plant, and Equipment}^*}$$

This ratio provides the user with information on how effective the company has been in generating sales relative to its investment in PP&E.

*We use the average amount so that the effect of the timing of acquisitions is minimized.

Let's compare the results of Danier Leather with Le Château to get a better understanding of this ratio:

Danier's fixed asset turnover:	Le Château's fixed asset turnover:
$= \dfrac{154,995}{(16,034 + 15,012)/2} = 9.98$	$= \dfrac{274,840}{(69,870 + 83,315)/2} = 3.59$

This tells us that Danier was able to generate $9.98 in sales for every $1 in long-term assets. By comparison, Le Château only generated $3.59 in sales for every $1 in long-term assets. To assess the effectiveness of this, we would also need to compare this ratio with the results of prior periods. A low ratio would indicate a company that uses its PP&E inefficiently or that has unused capacity, whereas a high ratio may indicate very efficient use or that the company has old assets (as this would give a low average net PP&E amount).

SUMMARY

1. **Identify and distinguish between the various types of long-term assets.**

   - Property, plant, and equipment (PP&E) items: have physical substance and provide economic benefits to a company because they are used to generate revenues, usually in combination with other assets.

   - Intangible assets: have no physical substance, but provide economic benefits as a result of the rights they bestow on the company that owns them.

   - Goodwill: results from a business combination, has no physical substance, and cannot be separated from the business it is a part of. Provides economic benefits through the average earnings that are expected as a result of the acquisition.

2. **Describe the valuation methods for property, plant, and equipment, including identifying costs that are usually capitalized.**

   - PP&E items are reported on the statement of financial position at their carrying amount; that is, cost less accumulated depreciation and accumulated impairment losses.

- An asset's carrying amount is the portion of its cost that has yet to be expensed. It is *not* what the asset could be sold for.

- Cost includes purchase price, non-refundable taxes, legal costs, shipping costs, site preparation, and installation costs.

- When multiple PP&E assets are purchased for a single price (a basket purchase), the cost of each is determined using the assets' relative fair values.

- Costs incurred after the purchase of a PP&E asset are capitalized (added to the cost of the asset) if they will extend the useful life of the asset, reduce its operating costs, or improve its output in terms of quantity or quality. Otherwise, these costs are expensed as period costs (for example, repairs and maintenance expense).

3. **Explain why property, plant, and equipment assets are depreciated.**

- Depreciating PP&E allocates a portion of the cost of each asset to each period in which the asset's economic benefits are being used up or consumed.

- Only the depreciable amount (cost less estimated residual value) is expensed.

- The depreciable amount is allocated or expensed over the asset's estimated useful life.

4. **Identify the factors that influence the choice of depreciation method and implement the most common methods of depreciation.**

- The choice of depreciation method depends upon the pattern in which the PP&E asset's economic benefits are expected to be used up or consumed by the company.

- Common methods of depreciation:
  - straight-line: allocates the depreciable amount evenly over time (in equal amounts each period)
  - diminishing balance: allocates a greater portion of the depreciable amount early in the asset's life and less as time goes by (that is, there is a larger depreciation expense early in the asset's life, reducing over time)
  - units-of-production: allocates the depreciable amount on a per-unit basis (that is, depreciation expense varies with the asset's use)

- Companies are expected to select the method that is most consistent with the way in which they expect the asset's economic benefits will be used up or consumed.

- A contra-asset account, Accumulated Depreciation, is used to capture the portion of a PP&E asset's cost that has been depreciated.

- Depreciation should cease when the depreciable amount has been expensed; that is, when the asset's carrying amount is equal to the estimated residual value.

- Companies often use the "15-day rule" to determine depreciation for a partial period.

5. **Describe and implement changes in depreciation estimates and methods.**

- Depreciation expense is an estimate because the variables that go into its calculation are almost all estimates. Over time, if the estimates change materially, the periodic expense must also change. This is a *change in accounting estimate*, and is accounted for prospectively; in other words, in future periods, rather than going back and changing prior periods.

- Depreciation expense for future periods is based on the asset's carrying amount at the time of change, the revised estimate of

residual value, the remaining estimated useful life, and the pattern in which the asset's remaining economic benefits are expected to be used.

6. **Explain what it means if property, plant, and equipment assets are impaired.**

- With PP&E, management expects future economic benefits to flow from the use of the PP&E asset. These benefits should be at least equal to the asset's carrying amount.

- At year end, management must determine whether there are any internal or external factors that might indicate that their PP&E assets are impaired. That is, the expected future economic benefits are less than the asset's carrying amount.

- If such factors are present, the company will determine the amount of the asset's impairment loss, which is equal to the asset's carrying amount less the greater of the expected future cash flows and the asset's fair value less selling costs.

- Any impairment loss is recorded in the period in which it occurs. The asset's carrying amount is reduced through using Accumulated Impairment Losses, a contra-asset account.

7. **Account for the disposal of property, plant, and equipment.**

- Accounted for using a two-step approach:
  - Step one: The asset is depreciated to the disposal date so the correct expense from using it in the period is recognized and the relevant accumulated depreciation account is updated.
  - Step two: the carrying amount (balances in the asset and accumulated depreciation and impairment accounts) is removed from the records and the proceeds of sale (cash or other assets) are recognized. If the proceeds of sale exceed the carrying amount, a gain is recognized. If the proceeds of sale are less than the carrying amount, a loss is reported.

8. **Explain the effect of depreciation on income taxes.**

- The Income Tax Act does not allow depreciation expense as a deductible expense in calculating taxable income.

- Instead, the Income Tax Act allows *capital cost allowance (CCA)*, with specific rules about how the maximum amount of annual CCA is calculated.

9. **Explain the accounting treatment for intangible assets, including amortization.**

- Intangible assets are recorded only when purchased from a third party.

- Determining cost follows the same principles as used for PP&E.

- Intangible assets with a finite (limited) useful life are amortized (expensed) over this period, usually by the straight-line method. Amortization is similar to depreciation.

- The useful life of an intangible asset is often shorter than its legal life.

- Intangible assets with an indefinite useful life are not amortized, but are tested annually for impairment.

- An accumulated amortization account is not normally used. Instead the cost of the intangible asset is reduced directly.

10. **Explain the accounting treatment for goodwill, including impairment.**

- Recognition of goodwill:
  - happens only as a result of the acquisition of a business
  - is equal to the excess of the purchase cost over the fair values of the identifiable assets net of liabilities acquired,

because of the potential for above average earnings that are expected to result from the acquisition

- Internally generated goodwill cannot be recognized.
- After acquisition, goodwill is carried at cost and is not amortized. It is reviewed annually for evidence of impairment. If impaired, it is reported at cost less accumulated impairment losses.

11. **Assess the average age of property, plant, and equipment; calculate the fixed asset turnover ratio; and assess the results.**

- The *average age* of PP&E can be determined by dividing the company's accumulated depreciation by the annual depreciation expense.

- The *average age percentage* can be determined by dividing accumulated depreciation by total PP&E assets (excluding land).
- The older a company's PP&E assets, the more likely it will need cash for investing purposes in the near future.
- The *fixed asset turnover ratio* is equal to sales revenue divided by average net PP&E.
- Assessing the results of the fixed asset turnover ratio indicates how effective an entity has been in managing its investment in PP&E.

KEY TERMS

Accelerated depreciation method (367)	Depreciation (363)	Impairment loss (376)
Accumulated depreciation (363)	Depreciation rate (368)	Indefinite useful life (381)
Accumulated impairment losses (363)	Derecognized (377)	Intangible asset (362)
Amortization (381)	Diminishing-balance method (367)	Loss (377)
Basket purchase (364)	Double-diminishing-balance	Lump-sum purchase (364)
Capital assets (361)	method (370)	Recoverable amount (376)
Capital cost allowance (378)	Earnings management (373)	Relative fair value (364)
Capitalized (363)	Estimated residual value (366)	Revaluation model (379)
Carrying amount (363)	Estimated useful life (366)	Straight-line method (366)
Change in an accounting estimate (374)	Expensed (365)	Straight-line rate (370)
Contra-asset account (363)	Finite useful life (381)	Tangible asset (361)
Cost (363)	Gain (377)	Units-of-production
Cost model (363)	Goodwill (362)	method (366)
Depreciable amount (366)	Impaired (376)	

ABBREVIATIONS USED

CCA	Capital cost allowance
CRA	Canada Revenue Agency
PP&E	Property, plant, and equipment

SYNONYMS

Basket purchase | Lump-sum purchase
Cost | Original cost | Capitalized cost | Acquisition cost
Carrying amount | Net book value | Depreciated cost | Amortized cost
Depreciation | Amortization
Diminishing-balance method | Declining-balance method
Units-of-production method | Units-of-activity method | Production method | Usage method

CHAPTER END REVIEW PROBLEM

Pete's Trucking Company has a fleet of large trucks that cost a total of $1.5 million. The trucks have an estimated useful life of five years and an estimated residual value of $150,000. The trucks are expected to be driven a total of 5 million kilometres during their lives.

STRATEGIES FOR SUCCESS:

▶ For the units-of-production method, the "activity" in this case is measured in kilometres. Therefore, you need to calculate how much depreciation should be charged for each kilometre, and then multiply this rate by the number of kilometres driven each year.

▶ For the double-diminishing-balance method, remember to:
 a. Determine the depreciation rate (1 / estimated useful life) × 2.

Required:
 a. Calculate the annual straight-line depreciation that would be recorded over the lives of these trucks.
 b. Prepare a schedule showing depreciation on a units-of-production basis, if the following usage was expected.

Year 1	950,000 km
Year 2	1,050,000 km
Year 3	1,100,000 km
Year 4	1,000,000 km
Year 5	900,000 km

c. Prepare a schedule showing the depreciation that will result if Pete's Trucking uses the double-diminishing-balance method.

d. Assume that the trucks were sold at the end of the fourth year for a total of $250,000. Prepare journal entries to record the disposal of the trucks under each of the following assumptions about the depreciation method used by Pete's Trucking:
  i. straight-line depreciation
  ii. the units-of-production method of depreciation
  iii. double-diminishing-balance depreciation

e. Briefly explain why there is a gain or loss on the disposal of the trucks in each of these circumstances.

b. Apply the rate to the carrying amount each year (that is, cost − accumulated depreciation).
c. Ensure that the ending carrying amount is not less than the estimated residual value.

▶ When you record the disposal of a capital asset, you have two steps:
a. Depreciate the asset up to the date of disposal.
b. Remove the asset and the related accumulated depreciation and determine the amount of any gain or loss.

Suggested Solution to Chapter End Review Problem

a.

Straight-line method

$$\text{Depreciation Expense} = \frac{\text{Cost} - \text{Estimated Residual Value}}{\text{Estimated Useful Life}}$$

$$= \frac{\$1,500,000 - \$150,000}{5 \text{ years}} = \$270,000 \text{ per year}$$

b.

Units-of-production method

$$\text{Depreciation Expense} = \frac{\text{Cost} - \text{Estimated Residual Value}}{\text{Estimated Useful Life}}$$

$$= \frac{\$1,500,000 - \$150,000}{5,000,000 \text{ km}} = \$0.27 \text{ per km}$$

Depreciation Expense per Year

Year 1: $0.27 per km × 950,000 km = $256,500
Year 2: $0.27 per km × 1,050,000 km = $283,500
Year 3: $0.27 per km × 1,100,000 km = $297,000
Year 4: $0.27 per km × 1,000,000 km = $270,000
Year 5: $0.27 per km × 900,000 km = $243,000

c.

Double-diminishing-balance method

a. Determine rate: (1 / estimated useful life) × 2
   (1 / 5) × 2 = 0.40 or 40%

b. Apply rate to carrying amount

Year	Opening Carrying Amount	Calculation	Depreciation Expense	Ending Carrying Amount
1	$1,500,000	40% × $1,500,000	$600,000	$900,000
2	$ 900,000	40% × $ 900,000	$360,000	$540,000
3	$ 540,000	40% × $ 540,000	$216,000	$324,000
4	$ 324,000	40% × $ 324,000	$129,600	$194,400
5	$ 194,400	40% × $ 194,400	$~~77,760~~	$~~116,640~~
			$ 44,400	$150,000

Notice that, in the final year, the depreciation expense is the difference between the carrying amount at the beginning of the year and the estimated residual value that should be left in the asset account at the end of the year.

d. As the trucks have been depreciated up to the date of disposal, we can move straight to the second step and determine the amount of any gain or loss on disposal.

i. Straight-line method:

Cash	250,000	
Accumulated Depreciation, Trucks	1,080,000[a]	
Loss on Disposal	170,000	
Trucks		1,500,000

[a]4 years at $270,000 per year (from part "a")

ii. Units-of-production method:

Cash	250,000	
Accumulated Depreciation, Trucks	1,107,000[b]	
Loss on Disposal	143,000	
Trucks		1,500,000

[b]$256,500 + $283,500 + $297,000 + $270,000 (from part "b")

iii. Double-diminishing-balance method:

Cash	250,000	
Accumulated Depreciation, Trucks	1,305,600[c]	
Gain on Disposal		55,600
Trucks		1,500,000

[c]This is the sum of the depreciation expense from year 1 to year 4 (per table in part "c"), that is, $600,000 + $360,000 + $216,000 + $129,600

e. The actual life of the trucks was only four years, rather than the five years that had been expected; therefore, less of their cost was written off through depreciation, leaving them with higher net book values. In addition, the trucks were sold for $250,000 rather than the $150,000 residual value that had been expected. The combination of these factors creates a gain or loss on disposal.

As can be seen in the journal entry in part "d"(i), under straight-line depreciation, the trucks' carrying amount (acquisition cost − accumulated depreciation) had been reduced to $420,000 at the end of year 4 ($1,500,000 − $1,080,000 = $420,000). The trucks were sold for $250,000, which is $170,000 less than their carrying amount ($420,000 − $250,000 = $170,000). This shortfall is recorded as a loss on the disposal of the trucks.

Similarly, as shown in the journal entry in part "d"(ii), under the units-of-production method, the trucks' carrying amount (cost − accumulated depreciation) had been reduced to $393,000 at the end of year 4 ($1,500,000 − $1,107,000 = $393,000). The trucks were sold for $250,000, which is $143,000 less than their carrying amount ($393,000 − $250,000 = $143,000), which again results in a loss on the disposal.

As can be seen in the journal entry in part "d"(iii), under double-diminishing-balance depreciation, the trucks' carrying amount (cost − accumulated depreciation) had been reduced to $194,400 at the end of year 4 ($1,500,000 − $1,305,600 = $194,400). The trucks were sold for $250,000, which is $55,600 more than their carrying amount ($250,000 − $194,400 = $55,600). This excess is recorded as a gain on disposal of the trucks.

ASSIGNMENT MATERIAL

Discussion Questions

DQ8-1 Describe what is meant by "carrying amount" and explain how it differs from the asset's "cost."

DQ8-2 Explain why companies depreciate their property, plant, and equipment.

DQ8-3 Outline the types of costs that should be capitalized for a piece of equipment.

DQ8-4 Explain the implications of a cost being capitalized as part of property, plant, and equipment.

DQ8-5 Why is it necessary to allocate the cost of a basket purchase to the individual assets included in the purchase price?

DQ8-6 Describe the procedure that is used to allocate the cost of a basket purchase of assets to each asset that is acquired.

DQ8-7 Discuss the purpose of depreciating equipment and explain the possible patterns of depreciation.

DQ8-8 Explain why all companies do not use the straight-line method to depreciate their property, plant, and equipment.

DQ8-9 Discuss the factors that should be taken into consideration when choosing a depreciation method.

DQ8-10 Explain what is meant by "estimated residual value" and why it is important to take it into consideration when determining an asset's depreciation.

DQ8-11 Describe how estimated residual value and estimated useful life are used in the calculation of depreciation under the following methods: straight-line, units-of-production, and diminishing-balance.

DQ8-12 Explain when the units-of-production method of depreciation would be appropriate to use and what kind of "units" a company could consider using.

DQ8-13 Explain how a change in management's estimate of an asset's useful life and/or residual value is treated.

DQ8-14 Identify which depreciation method, straight-line or diminishing-balance, would result in the higher net income in the year that a piece of equipment is purchased.

DQ8-15 What does it mean if management determines that one piece of its manufacturing equipment is impaired?

DQ8-16 What do we know if a company records a gain on the disposal of a piece of equipment?

DQ8-17 Explain why the Canada Revenue Agency requires businesses to use the capital cost allowance (CCA) system for determining net income for tax purposes.

DQ8-18 Identify two key differences between the capital cost allowance (CCA) system and accounting depreciation.

DQ8-19 Describe the conditions under which intangible assets can be recorded in a company's accounting system, using patents and goodwill as examples.

DQ8-20 Explain how the accounting treatment of an intangible asset with indefinite useful life differs from the treatment of one with a finite useful life.

DQ8-21 Explain why the estimated useful life of a patent may differ from its legal life.

DQ8-22 Explain, in your own words, what goodwill is and how is it quantified.

DQ8-23 Explain why internally generated goodwill does not appear as an asset on the statement of financial position of the company that generated it.

Application Problems

AP8-1 (Capitalizing costs related to capital assets)

C & M Securities made several expenditures during the current fiscal year, including the following:

	Amount	Description of Expenditure
1.	$150,000	Acquisition of a piece of land to be used as a building site
2.	3,000	Demolition of a small building on the land, to make way for the new building
3.	7,500	Levelling of the land to prepare it for construction of the new building
4.	290,000	Construction of the new building
5.	12,000	Paving of a parking lot beside the building
6.	6,000	Addition of decorative landscaping around the building (such as planting flowers and ornamental shrubs)
7.	80,000	Purchase of a new piece of equipment
8.	6,000	Sales taxes on the new equipment
9.	3,000	Installation of the new equipment
10.	1,500	Testing and adjustment of the new equipment prior to its use
11.	1,000	Minor repairs to some old equipment
12.	7,000	Major overhaul of an old piece of equipment, extending its useful life by three years
13.	1,200	Routine maintenance of equipment
14.	2,000	Replacement of windows broken by disgruntled employees during a labour dispute

Required:

a. For each of the items listed above, indicate whether the cost should be debited to land, buildings, equipment, land improvements, or an expense account.

b. For each item that was expensed, explain why it was not appropriate to add the amount to an asset.

AP8-2 (Acquisition costs)

House Builders of Canada decided to expand its facilities and upgrade some of its log preparation equipment. The following events occurred during the year:

Date	Amount	Description of Expenditure
Jan. 2	$ 75,000	Purchased land adjacent to the company's existing property, to be used for the expansion
6	1,200	Paid legal fees and deed registration fees.
11	4,000	Paid its workers to clear the land on their days off.
15	120,000	Purchased equipment, which was delivered but not yet paid for.
17	900	Purchased building permit for construction of the addition.
20	2,500	Constructed temporary fencing as required by the building permit to enclose the construction site. Upon completion of the addition to the building, the fencing was to be removed.
22	400,000	Started construction of a new addition to the main building, which is estimated to cost $400,000.
25	3,500	Received bill for delivery of the equipment that was received on January 15.
Feb. 1		Paid the amounts owing on the equipment and its delivery.
28	11,000	Paid architect's fees for designing the building addition and supervising its construction.
May 9	380,000	Paid full amount to the construction company upon completion of the building.
11	800	Paid cost to remove temporary fencing.
14	2,500	Paid work crews to install the equipment.
24	1,200	Paid for party to celebrate the successful completion of the expansion.
June 7	700	Paid for set-up and adjustment of the new equipment so it would be ready to use.
10	700	Paid for an ad in the local paper to advertise that the company was hiring.

Required:
a. Determine the costs that should be capitalized as assets by Home Builders of Canada in its land, buildings, and equipment accounts.
b. State what should be done with any of the costs that are not capitalized.

AP8-3 (Acquisition costs; basket purchase)

Matchett Machinery Ltd. acquired a new site for its manufacturing operations. The company was able to find the ideal location in terms of lot size and highway access. Matchett paid $3.2 million to acquire the site. The bank, which was providing Matchett with the financing for the purchase, required that an appraisal be completed of the property. The appraisal report came back with the following estimated market values: land $1,800,000, building $1,080,000, and land improvements $120,000. Matchett explained, to the bank's satisfaction, that it paid the $200,000 premium because of the savings it would realize from minimizing transportation distances given the site's superior highway access.

Required:
Allocate the $3.2-million purchase price to the land, building, and land improvements. Also explain why this allocation process is necessary.

AP8-4 (Basket purchase and depreciation)

On March 20, 2016, FineTouch Corporation purchased two machines at auction for a combined total cost of $236,000. The machines were listed in the auction catalogue at $110,000 for machine X and $155,000 for machine Y. Immediately after the auction, FineTouch had the machines professionally appraised so it could increase its insurance coverage. The appraisal put a fair value of $105,000 on machine X and $160,000 on machine Y.

On March 24, FineTouch paid a total of $4,500 in transportation and installation charges for the two machines. No further expenditures were made for machine X, but $6,500 was paid on March 29 for improvements to machine Y. On March 31, 2016, both machines were ready to be used.

The company expects machine X to last five years and to have a residual value of $3,800 when it is removed from service, and it expects machine Y to be useful for eight more years and have a residual value of $14,600 at that time. Due to the different characteristics of the two machines, different depreciation methods will be used for them: machine X will be depreciated using the double-diminishing-balance method and machine Y using the straight-line method.

Required:

Prepare the journal entries to record the following:

a. The purchase of the machines, indicating the initial cost of each
b. The transportation, installation, and improvement costs for each machine
c. The depreciation expense to December 31, 2016, for each machine

AP8-5 (Depreciation calculations and journal entries; two methods)

Polar Company purchased a building with an expected useful life of 40 years for $600,000 on January 1, 2016. The building is expected to have a residual value of $40,000.

Required:

a. Give the journal entries that would be made by Polar to record the building purchase in 2016 and the depreciation expense for 2016 and 2017, assuming straight-line depreciation is used.
b. Repeat part "a," but now assume that the double-diminishing-balance is used.

AP8-6 (Calculation of depreciation; three methods)

On January 1, 2016, SugarBear Company acquired equipment costing $150,000, which will be depreciated on the assumption that the equipment will be useful for five years and have a residual value of $12,000. The estimated output from this equipment is as follows: 2016—15,000 units; 2017—24,000 units; 2018—30,000 units; 2019—28,000 units; 2020—18,000 units. The company is now considering possible methods of depreciation for this asset.

Required:

a. Calculate what the depreciation expense would be for each year of the asset's life, if the company chooses:
    i. The straight-line method
    ii. The units-of-production method
    iii. The double-diminishing-balance method
b. Briefly discuss the criteria that a company should consider when selecting a depreciation method.

AP8-7 (Calculation of depreciation; three methods)

Norika Company purchased a truck for $40,000. The company expected the truck to have a useful life of four years or 100,000 kilometres, with an estimated residual value of $4,000 at the end of that time. During the first and second years, the truck was driven 22,000 and 27,500 kilometres, respectively.

Required:

Calculate the depreciation expense for the *second year* under the straight-line, units-of-production, and double-diminishing-balance methods.

AP8-8 (Calculation of depreciation; three methods)

A machine that produces cellphone components is purchased on January 1, 2016, for $100,000. It is expected to have a useful life of four years and a residual value of $10,000. The machine is expected to produce a total of 200,000 components during its life, distributed as follows: 40,000 in 2016, 50,000 in 2017, 60,000 in 2018, and 50,000 in 2019. The company has a December 31 year end.

Required:

a. Calculate the amount of depreciation to be charged each year, using each of the following methods:
    i. Straight-line method
    ii. Units-of-production method
    iii. Double-diminishing-balance method
b. Which method results in the highest depreciation expense:
    i. during the first two years?
    ii. over all four years?

AP8-9 (Units-of-production depreciation and carrying amount calculations)

In August 2016, Heavy-lift Helicopters Ltd. purchased a new helicopter for its logging and heavy lift operations at a cost of $1.2 million. Based on past experience, management has determined that the helicopter will have a useful life of 14,000 flying hours, at which time it will have an estimated residual value of $150,000. During 2016, the helicopter was used for 1,400 flying hours and in 2017 it was used for 1,650 flying hours. Heavy-lift Helicopters has a December 31 year end and uses the units-of-production method of depreciation for its helicopters.

Required:

Determine the depreciation expense on this helicopter for 2017 and its carrying amount at December 31, 2017.

AP8-10 (Depreciation calculations and determination of gain or loss)

Prepare all necessary journal entries for 2016, 2017, and 2018 related to each of the following scenarios:

a. On January 1, 2016, Sustco Ltd. purchased a piece of equipment for $21,000. At the time, management determined that the equipment would have a residual value of $3,000 at the end of its five-year life. Sustco has a December 31 year end and uses the straight-line depreciation method.

b. Assume the same facts as in part "a" except that Sustco uses the double-diminishing-balance method for depreciation of equipment.

c. Assume the same facts as in part "a" except that Sustco purchased the equipment on September 30 rather than on January 1. Also assume that Sustco ended up selling the piece of equipment on June 30, 2018, for $13,000.

AP8-11 (Depreciation and determination of gain or loss)

SP Ltd. has a December 31 year end. On April 2, 2016, SP purchased a piece of equipment at a cost of $180,000. SP's management estimated that this piece of equipment would have a useful life of five years and a residual value of $30,000. SP uses the straight-line method for depreciating its manufacturing equipment.

Required:
If SP was to sell the piece of equipment on June 30, 2018, for $100,000, what would be the amount of the gain or loss that would have to be recorded?

AP8-12 (Depreciation and net income calculation)

On July 1, 2016, Silver Stone Company purchased equipment for a cost of $450,000 with an expected useful life of 10 years and an anticipated residual value of $30,000. For the year 2017 (the second year of the equipment's life), Silver Stone reported sales of $1,500,000 and operating expenses other than depreciation of $1,050,000. Silver Stone has a December 31 year end.

Required:
a. Assuming Silver Stone uses straight-line depreciation, what amount of income before income taxes will it report for 2017?

b. If Silver Stone had used double-diminishing-balance depreciation (in both 2016 and 2017), what amount of income before income taxes would it have reported for 2017?

c. For what type of assets is it appropriate to use double-diminishing-balance depreciation?

AP8-13 (Straight-line method depreciation with change in estimate)

Healthlabs Ltd. purchased lab equipment for $18,000 on January 1, 2016. At that time, management determined that the equipment would have a useful life of three years with no residual value and that the straight-line depreciation method would be used. On January 1, 2017, management revised its initial estimate and determined that the company would be able to use the lab equipment for a total of five years.

Required:
Determine the depreciation expense for 2017.

AP8-14 (Units-of-production method depreciation with change in estimate)

A company paid $66,000 for a machine and was depreciating it by the units-of-production method. The machine was expected to produce a total of 150,000 units of product, and to have a residual value of $6,000. During the first two years of use, the machine produced 45,000 units.

At the beginning of the machine's third year of life, its estimated lifetime production was revised from 150,000 to 120,000 units; its estimated residual value was unchanged.

Required:
Calculate the amount of depreciation that should be charged during the third year of the machine's life if 25,000 units are produced that year.

AP8-15 (Asset acquisition, subsequent expenditures, change in estimate, and depreciation)

South Seas Distributors completed the following transactions involving the purchase and operation of a delivery truck:

2015	Transaction Description
May 27	Paid $35,600 for a new truck. It was estimated that the truck would be sold for $15,000 after four years.
June 9	Paid $3,500 to have special racks installed in the truck. The racks did not increase the truck's estimated resale value, but were necessary to minimize the damage from products shifting during transit. The truck was put into service after the racks were installed.
Dec. 31	Recorded straight-line depreciation on the truck.
2016	
Apr. 5	Paid $650 for repairs to the truck's fender, which was damaged when the driver scraped a loading dock.
July 23	Paid $8,000 to have a refrigerating unit installed in the truck. This increased the truck's estimated resale value by $1,000.
Dec. 31	Recorded straight-line depreciation on the truck.

Required:
Prepare journal entries to record the above transactions.

AP8-16 (Asset expenditures)

Comfort Zone Housing paid $80,000 for a new air-conditioning system in an existing building.

Required:
Identify the account that should be debited and briefly explain your reasoning, in each of the following cases:
    a. The expected useful life of the air-conditioning system is the same as the remaining useful life of the building it was installed in.
    b. The air-conditioning system is expected to have a useful life of 15 years, while the building it was installed in is expected to have a remaining useful life of 30 years.

AP8-17 (Asset expenditures, changes in estimates, and depreciation)

Canada Canning Company owns processing equipment that had an initial cost of $106,000, expected useful life of eight years, and expected residual value of $10,000. Depreciation calculations are done to the nearest month using the straight-line method, and depreciation is recorded each December 31.

    During the equipment's fifth year of service, the following expenditures were made:

Jan. 7	Lubricated and adjusted the equipment to maintain optimum performance, at a cost of $500.
Mar. 13	Replaced belts, hoses, and other parts that were showing signs of wear on the equipment, at a cost of $350.
June 28	Completed a $14,000 overhaul of the equipment. The work included the installation of new computer controls to replace the original controls, which had become technologically obsolete. As a result of this work, the equipment's estimated useful life was increased to 10 years and the estimated residual value was increased to $11,000.

Required:
    a. Prepare journal entries to record each of the above transactions.
    b. Calculate the depreciation expense that should be recorded for this equipment in the fourth year of its life, in the fifth year of its life (the year in which the above transactions took place), and in the sixth year of its life.

AP8-18 (Asset refurbishment, changes in estimates, and depreciation)

At the end of 2016, Spindle Works Inc. owned a piece of equipment that had originally cost $21,000. It was being depreciated by the straight-line method, and had $8,500 of accumulated depreciation recorded as at the end of 2016 after the yearly depreciation was recorded.

    At the beginning of 2017, the equipment was extensively refurbished at a cost of $9,500. As a result of this work, the equipment's productivity was significantly improved, its total estimated useful life was increased from the initial 10 years to 14 years, and its residual value was increased from the initial estimate of $4,000 to $7,000.

Required:
    a. Calculate the age of the equipment at the end of 2016.
    b. Give the journal entry to record the refurbishment of the equipment at the beginning of 2017.
    c. Give the adjusting entry to record the depreciation of the equipment at the end of 2017.

AP8-19 (Acquisition, depreciation, disposal, and replacement)

Jijang Excavations Ltd. ("JEL") operates specialized equipment for installing natural gas pipelines. JEL, which has a December 31 year end, began 2016 with a single piece of equipment that had been purchased on January 1, 2013, for $40,000 and a truck that had been purchased on January 1, 2015, for $60,000. When the equipment was purchased, JEL's management had estimated that the equipment would have a residual value of $4,000 and a useful life of six years. When the truck was purchased, management determined that it would have a useful life of four years and a residual value of $5,000.

    On March 31, 2016, JEL sold this piece of equipment for $29,000 cash. On April 12, 2016, JEL purchased replacement equipment with double the capacity for $82,000 cash. JEL's management determined that this equipment would have a useful life of six years and a residual value of $10,000.

Required:
Prepare all necessary journal entries for the year ended December 31, 2016. Assume that JEL uses the straight-line depreciation method for its equipment and the double-diminishing-balance method for its trucks.

AP8-20 (Acquisition, change in estimates, depreciation, and disposal)

On July 1, 2012, Steelman Company acquired a new machine for $140,000 and estimated it would have a useful life of 10 years and residual value of $7,000. At the beginning of 2015, the company decided that the machine would be used for nine more years (including all of 2015), and at the end of this time its residual value would be only $1,000. On November 1, 2016, the machine was sold for $83,000. The company uses the straight-line method of depreciation and closes its books on December 31.

Required:
Give the necessary journal entries for the acquisition, depreciation, and disposal of this asset for the years 2012, 2015, and 2016.

AP8-21 (Straight-line depreciation with disposal)

On October 4, 2015, C and C Sandblasters Company purchased a new machine for $45,000. It estimated the machine's useful life at 12 years and the residual value at $4,000. On March 25, 2016, another machine was acquired for $70,000. Its useful life was estimated to be 15 years and its residual value $6,000. On May 24, 2017, the first machine was sold for $28,000. The company closes its books on December 31 each year, uses the straight-line method of depreciation, and calculates depreciation to the nearest month.

Required:
Give the necessary journal entries for the years 2015 through 2017 for both machines. Include the depreciation of the second machine on December 31, 2017.

AP8-22 (Straight-line and double-diminishing-balance depreciation with disposal)

On March 1, 2015, Zephur Winds Ltd. purchased a machine for $80,000 by paying $20,000 down and issuing a note for the balance. The machine had an estimated useful life of nine years and an estimated residual value of $8,000. Zephur Winds uses the straight-line-method of depreciation and has a December 31 year end. On October 30, 2017, the machine was sold for $62,000.

Required:
  a. Prepare the journal entry to record the acquisition of the machine.
  b. Assuming that the depreciation was correctly calculated and recorded in 2015 and 2016, prepare the journal entries to update the depreciation and record the sale of the machine on October 30, 2017.
  c. Assume instead that the company used the double-diminishing-balance method to depreciate the cost of the machine:
      i. What amount of depreciation would be recorded in 2015 and 2016?
      ii. What journal entries would be required to update the depreciation and record the sale of the machine on October 30, 2017?

AP8-23 (Intangibles and amortization)

Pinetree Manufacturing Company reports both equipment and patents on its statement of financial position.

Required:
  a. Explain how the amount reported on the statement of financial position for each of these types of asset is determined.
  b. The equipment and patents were both purchased three years ago for $40,000 each and were estimated to have 10 year useful lives. The equipment is expected to have a residual value of $2,000. The company uses the straight-line method to depreciate its equipment and amortize its patent. Based on this information, what amount would be reported for each of them on the statement of financial position at the end of the current period? Explain.
  c. Financial analysts sometimes ignore intangible assets when analyzing financial statements. Do you think this is appropriate? Explain.

AP8-24 (Intangibles and amortization)

Red Bear Ltd. purchased several intangible assets, as follows:

Asset	Purchase Cost
Licence	$ 80,000
Customer list	60,000
Patent	160,000
Copyright	250,000

The following information is also available:
  - In addition to the costs listed above, there were legal fees of $12,000 associated with the licence acquisitions. The licences are valid in perpetuity, and sales of the products produced under the licences have been strong and are expected to continue at the same level for many decades.
  - The customer lists are expected to be useful for the next six years.
  - The patent has a legal life of 20 years, but technological changes are expected to render it worthless after about eight years.
  - The copyright is good for another 40 years, but nearly all the related sales are expected to occur during the next 10 years.

Required:
   a. Calculate the annual amortization expense, if any, that should be recorded for each of these intangible assets assuming the straight-line method is appropriate.
   b. Show how the intangible assets section of the statement of financial position would be presented four years after acquisition of these assets, assuming that there has been no evidence that their values have been impaired. Assume that a full year of amortization was taken in the year of acquisition.

User Perspective Problems

UP8-1 (Expensing versus capitalizing the cost of tools)

During the current year, a large chain of auto mechanic shops adopted the policy of expensing small tools costing less than $100 as soon as they are acquired. In previous years, the company had carried an asset account, Small Tools, which it had depreciated over the average expected useful lives of the tools. The balance in the Small Tools account represented about 1% of the company's total capital assets, and the depreciation expense on the tools was 0.3% of its sales revenues. It is expected that the average annual purchases of small tools will be approximately the same amount as the depreciation that would have been charged on them.

   Is this in accordance with accounting standards? If so, briefly explain why. If not, identify the accounting principle or concept that has been violated and give a brief explanation of the nature of the violation.

UP8-2 (Capitalizing costs)

One of your co-workers, Dominique, asks you the following: "Can you briefly explain to me how a company determines whether it should capitalize or expense the cost of some work it had done on one of the buildings it owns?" Explain this to Dominique.

UP8-3 (Nature of depreciation charges)

While discussing the values reported on the statement of financial position for land and buildings, Jing Zhao, owner of Nobrex Ltd., said the following: "Land and buildings should not be recorded separately. They should be treated as a group of related assets. If you view them as a group, no depreciation should be charged on our buildings, because the increase in the value of our land each year more than makes up for any decline in the value of the buildings. Our company is located in a booming commercial area, and land values are rising all the time. In fact, even the value of our buildings has probably been increasing, rather than decreasing."

   Comment on the issues raised by Jing Zhao.

UP8-4 (Valuation of capital assets)

Many users of financial statements argue that, for most of the decisions that creditors, investors, analysts, and other users have to make, reporting the market values of companies' assets would be more relevant than other "values." Give two reasons why, despite the opportunity to report capital assets at fair value, companies usually continue to use historical costs as the basis for reporting these assets.

UP8-5 (Gains and losses)

You are in a meeting with Andrea Schwager, the new CEO of your company, discussing property, plant, and equipment, when she asks the following: "The accountants are telling me that, if we sell a piece of equipment for an amount in excess of its carrying amount on our statement of financial position, then we record a 'gain,' which increases net income. If it increases net income, then why don't we call it a 'revenue'? Wouldn't this be more understandable for financial statement users?"

   Answer Andrea Schwager's questions.

UP8-6 (Gains and losses)

During a discussion regarding the recent sale of a piece of equipment, your company president, Nanda Saloojee, stated: "I don't understand what it means to 'have a gain from the sale of equipment.' Why do we call it a 'gain' and not 'revenue'? Does the fact that we have a gain mean there was a problem with our prior years' financial statements? If so, please explain what that was."

   Prepare a brief response to the president's statement.

UP8-7 (Capital assets as collateral for loan)

As a lender, discuss whether you would be more comfortable with a company having long-term assets in the form of (a) property, plant, and equipment, or (b) goodwill, when you consider making a long-term loan to the company.

UP8-8 (Capital assets as collateral for loan)

As a lender, discuss whether you would prefer to see long-term assets reported at historical cost or fair value. What advantages and disadvantages would you see under each valuation?

UP8-9 (Auditing and valuation of capital assets)

As an auditor, discuss how you might evaluate a company's property, plant, and equipment to decide whether the value of these assets was impaired and should be written down.

UP8-10 (Goodwill's effect on financial statements)

In some countries, companies can write off goodwill at the date of acquisition by directly reducing their shareholders' equity; that is, the writeoff does not pass through net earnings. Suppose that a Canadian company and a company from a country that allows an immediate writeoff of goodwill agreed to purchase the same company for the same amount of money. As a stock analyst, describe how the statement of financial position and income statement would differ for the two companies after the acquisition. Discuss whether this would provide any advantage for either company.

UP8-11 (Impact of writedowns on remuneration)

Suppose that you are the accounting manager of a division in a large company and your remuneration is based partly on meeting an earnings target. In the current year, it seems certain that your division will not meet its target. You have some equipment that has been idle for a while but has not yet been written off. What incentives do you have to write off this asset during the current year? If you do write it off, how will this affect your future ability to meet the earnings targets for your division?

UP8-12 (Basket purchase price allocation)

Companies often face a basket purchase situation when they buy real estate, because the acquisition usually involves both the land that is purchased and the building that is located on the land. If you are the accounting manager, how would you go about allocating the real estate's purchase price between the land and the building? Why must you allocate the cost between these two assets? What incentives might you have to allocate a disproportionate amount to either the land or the building?

UP8-13 (Capital assets and company valuation)

Answer the following questions, assuming that you have been asked to analyze a potential acquisition by your company: (a) Which long-term assets on its financial statements are the most likely to be misstated by their carrying amounts? Explain your reasoning. (b) Is it possible that the company being considered for acquisition has some long-term assets that do not appear on its financial statements at all? Explain why or how this might occur.

Reading and Interpreting Published Financial Statements

RI8-1 (Financial statement analysis)

Reitmans (Canada) Limited is a leading Canadian retailer that operates more than 900 stores under the Reitmans, Smart Set, RW & Co., Thyme Maternity, Penningtons, and Addition Elle banners. The following information is an extract from Reitmans' annual report for its fiscal year ended February 1, 2014.

Property and Equipment (in thousands of Canadian dollars)

	Land	Building	Fixtures and Equipment	Leasehold Improvements	Total
Cost	5,860	48,598	147,762	164,540	366,760
Accumulated Depreciation	0	20,108	75,553	92,758	188,419
Net Carrying Amount	5,860	28,490	72,209	71,782	178,341
Depreciation Expense	0	2,459	24,026	24,691	51,176

Reitmans' depreciation policies for its property and equipment state that:

Depreciation is recognized in net earnings on a straight-line basis over the estimated useful lives of each component on an item of property and equipment. Land is not depreciated. Leasehold improvements are depreciated over the lesser of the estimated useful life of the asset and the lease term. Assets not in service include expenditures incurred to-date for equipment not yet available for use. Depreciation of assets not in service begins when they are ready for their intended use.

The estimated useful lives for the current and comparative periods are as follows:

Buildings	10 to 50 years
Fixtures and equipment	3 to 20 years
Leasehold improvements	6.7 to 10 years

Intangible assets are comprised of software and acquired trademarks and their useful lives are assessed to be either finite or indefinite.

Purchased software that is integral to the functionality of the related equipment is capitalized as part of that equipment.

Reitmans' trademarks were considered to have indefinite useful lives. During the year ended February 1, 2014, the full cost of $499 thousand of trademarks was subject to an impairment loss of $499 thousand.

Required:

a. Determine the average age percentage of Reitmans' property and equipment. Compare this with the ratio determined for Danier in the chapter and identify which company would be able to go longer without replacing its assets based on this ratio.

b. Determine the average age (in years) of Reitmans' leasehold improvements. Compare this with the ratio determined for Danier in the chapter and identify which company's leased stores are newer.

c. Given that Reitmans estimates that its fixtures and equipment will have useful lives between 3 and 20 years, determine the annual straight-line depreciation rate that Reitmans is using for its fixtures and equipment.

d. Explain, in your own words, why Reitmans does not begin depreciating assets until they are ready for their intended use.

e. Explain, in your own words, what Reitmans' management is saying with respect to purchased software being capitalized as part of equipment costs. What would be the alternative treatment?

f. Explain, in your own words, what Reitmans' management is saying about the company's trademarks.

g. If Reitmans' net carrying amount for property and equipment was $178,341 thousand for its year ended February 1, 2014, and $205,131 thousand for its year ended February 1, 2013, and its sales revenue was $960,397 thousand for fiscal year ended February 1, 2014, determine the company's fixed asset turnover ratio. Compare this with the ratio determined for Danier in the chapter and comment on which company did a better job of using its long-term assets to generate revenues.

RI8-2 (Accounting policies related to capital assets)

Metro Inc. owns and operates a network of 566 supermarkets and pharmacies in Quebec and Ontario under the Metro, MetroPlus, Super C, Food Basics, Adonis, Brunet, and Pharmacy and Drug Basics banners. Exhibit 8-19 shows Metro's notes on significant accounting policies for intangible assets and goodwill accompanying its 2013 financial statements.

EXHIBIT 8-19	METRO INC. 2013 ANNUAL FINANCIAL STATEMENTS; EXTRACT FROM NOTE 2

INTANGIBLE ASSETS

Intangible assets with finite useful lives are recorded at cost and are amortized on a straight-line basis over their useful lives. The amortization method and estimates of useful lives are reviewed annually.

Leasehold rights	20 to 40 years
Software	3 to 10 years
Improvements and development of retail network loyalty	5 to 30 years
Prescription files	10 years

The banners that the Corporation intends to keep and operate, the private labels for which it continues to develop new products and the loyalty programs it intends to maintain qualify as intangible assets with indefinite useful lives. They are recorded at cost and not amortized.

GOODWILL

Goodwill is recognized at cost measured as the excess of purchase prices over the fair value of the acquired enterprise's identifiable net assets at the date of acquisition. Goodwill is not amortized.

Required:

a. What major intangible assets does Metro own? Why does the company distinguish between the ones with definite lives and those with indefinite lives?

b. What method does Metro use to amortize its intangible assets? Are they amortized over their legal lives or useful lives? Explain why the treatment is appropriate.

c. Explain what the prescription files are. How are these related to Metro's major operations?

d. What is the source of the goodwill that Metro recognizes? Is the goodwill amortized? Explain how Metro determines and recognizes any impairment loss on the goodwill.

RI8-3 (Financial statement analysis)

Dollarama Inc. is Canada's largest dollar store operator. The following information is an extract from Dollarama's consolidated financial statements for the year ended February 2, 2014:

Property and Equipment (in thousands of Canadian dollars)

	Store and warehouse equipment	Computer equipment	Vehicles	Leasehold Improvements	Total
Cost	254,790	13,292	4,282	176,204	448,568
Accumulated Depreciation	129,059	5,593	1,453	61,851	197,956
Net Book Value	125,731	7,699	2,829	114,353	250,612
Depreciation Expense	25,564	1,564	781	16,594	44,503

Dollarama's depreciation policies for its property and equipment state that:

Property and equipment are carried at cost and depreciated on a straight-line basis over the estimated useful lives of the assets as follows:

Store and warehouse equipment	8 to 10 years
Vehicles	5 years
Leasehold improvements	Lease term
Computer equipment	5 years

Estimates of useful lives, residual values and methods of depreciation are reviewed annually. Any changes are accounted for prospectively as a change in accounting estimate. If the expected residual value of an asset is equal to or greater than its carrying value, depreciation on that asset is ceased. Depreciation is resumed when the expected residual value falls below the asset's carrying value. Gains and losses on disposal of an item of property and equipment are determined by comparing the proceeds from disposal with the carrying amount of the item and are recognized directly in the consolidated statement of comprehensive income.

Required:

    a. Determine the average age percentage of Dollarama's property and equipment. Compare this with the ratio determined for Danier in the chapter and identify which company would be able to go longer without replacing its assets based on this ratio.

    b. Determine the average age (in years) of Dollarama's leasehold improvements. Compare this with the ratio determined for Danier in the chapter and identify which company's leased stores are newer.

    c. Given that Dollarama estimates that its store and warehouse equipment will have useful lives between 8 and 10 years, determine the annual straight-line depreciation rate that Dollarama is using for its store and warehouse equipment.

    d. Explain, in your own words, how Dollarama treats changes in the estimated useful lives, residual values, and methods of depreciation for its property and equipment.

    e. Explain, in your own words, why Dollarama stops depreciating assets when their expected residual value is equal to or greater than their carrying amounts.

    f. If Dollarama's net carrying amount for property and equipment was $250,612 thousand at its 2014 year end and $197,494 thousand at its 2013 year end and its sales revenue was $2,064,676 thousand for the 2014 fiscal year, determine the company's fixed asset turnover ratio. Compare this with the ratio determined for Danier in the chapter and comment on which company did a better job of using its long-term assets to generate revenues.

RI8-4 (Financial statement analysis)

Contrans Group Inc. is a public company based in Woodstock, Ontario. The company provides freight transportation and waste collection services. The following information is an extract from Contrans' Consolidated Financial Statements for its year ended December 31, 2013.

Property and Equipment (in thousands of Canadian dollars)

	Land	Buildings	Rolling Stock and Other (Owned)	Rolling Stock and Other (Leased) Improvements	Total
Cost	21,608	45,478	202,676	61,630	331,392
Accumulated Depreciation	0	13,505	88,861	13,657	116,023
Net Carrying Amount	21,608	31,973	113,815	47,973	215,369
Depreciation Expense	0	1,201	19,638	6,249	27,088

Contrans' depreciation policies for its property and equipment state that:

The estimated useful lives and depreciation methods are as follows:

Description	Estimated useful life	Depreciation method	Recorded as
Buildings	15–40 years	Straight-line	General and administration expense
Rolling stock – highway tractors	25%	Declining balance	Direct operating expense
Rolling stock – waste trucks	8 years	Straight-line	Direct operating expense
Rolling stock – trailers	10–25 years	Straight-line	Direct operating expense
Waste bins	10 years	Straight-line	Direct operating expense
Service vehicles	20%–30%	Declining balance	General and administration expense
Other equipment	20%–30%	Declining balance	General and administration expense

Management reviews depreciation methods, residual values and the estimated useful lives of these assets annually and adjusts amortization accordingly on a prospective basis.

Required:

a. Determine the average age percentage of Contrans' rolling stock (highway tractors, waste trucks, and trailers), both owned and leased. Compare the average age percentage of the rolling stock owned by the company with that of the leased rolling stock. Which group is closer to being fully depreciated?

b. Determine the average age (in years) of Contrans' rolling stock (owned). Compare this with the ratio determined for the company's rolling stock (leased) and identify which group of rolling stock is newer.

c. Determine the annual straight-line depreciation rate that Contrans is using for its waste bins.

d. Compare the depreciation methods Contrans uses for its rolling stock. Explain, in your own words, what the company's management is saying about the pattern in which they expect the economic benefits of these assets will be consumed.

e. If Contrans' net carrying amount for property and equipment was $215,369 thousand at December 31, 2013, and $184,160 thousand at December 31, 2012, and its sales revenue was $572,331 thousand for the 2013 fiscal year, determine the company's fixed asset turnover ratio. Explain the result of this ratio.

RI8-5 (Financial statement disclosures)

Choose a company, as directed by your instructor.

Required:

a. Use the consolidated statements of financial position and the notes to the financial statements to prepare an analysis of property, plant, and equipment. First, list the beginning and ending amounts in the various property, plant, and equipment and accumulated depreciation accounts and then calculate the net change, in both dollar and percentage terms, for the most recent year.

b. If any of the amounts in part "a" have changed by more than 10%, provide an explanation for this change.

c. What percentage of the company's total assets is invested in property, plant, and equipment? Has this percentage changed significantly during the most recent year?

d. What depreciation method(s) does the company use?

e. Determine the following ratios for the company:
    i. average age percentage
    ii. average age
    iii. fixed asset turnover

Note: Remember that depreciation expense may not be separately disclosed in the statement of earnings but will usually appear in the statement of cash flows. Compare your results with any information disclosed in the notes. Do these results make sense?

f. Does the company have any significant intangible assets? If so, describe each of them and the company's amortization policies related to them.

Cases

C8-1 Manuel Manufacturing Company

Ramon Manuel, the president of Manuel Manufacturing Company, has e-mailed you to discuss the cost of a new machine that his company has just acquired.

The machine was purchased in Montreal for $150,000. Transporting it from Montreal to the company's factory in Hamilton, Ontario, and installing the machine were Manuel's responsibilities. Unfortunately, the machine was seriously damaged during this process and repairs costing $40,000 were required to restore it to its original condition.

Mr. Manuel wants to ensure that he can capitalize these repair costs as part of the cost of the machine, and has therefore consulted you on the following points as he understands them:

1. The cost of a capital asset should include all the costs that are necessary to get it in place and ready for use. The damaged machine was inoperative, so the repairs were definitely necessary.
2. All the other costs related to the transportation and installation of the machine are being capitalized.
3. An asset is expected to generate economic benefits in the future. Since the repairs have enhanced the machine's ability to help generate revenues in future period, they have increased the economic benefits that it will provide in future periods. Therefore, the repair costs should be capitalized.

Required:
Discuss how Manuel Manufacturing Company should account for the $40,000 cost of the repairs. Ensure that you explain your reasoning and address each of Mr. Manuel's arguments in your reply.

C8-2 Rolling Fields Retirement Homes

Rolling Fields Retirement Homes purchased land to use for a planned assisted-living community. As a condition of the sale, a title search had to be performed and a survey completed. Rolling Fields incurred both these costs. In order to prepare the land for new construction, a barn that was on the land when it was purchased had to be torn down, and a rocky hill in the middle of the property had to be levelled. A series of streets, sidewalks, water mains, storm drains, and sewers through the planned community also had to be constructed. Finally, street lighting had to be installed and green spaces for recreation and rest had to be landscaped.

The year after the land was purchased, construction of new homes began. The homes are to be owned by Rolling Fields and will be rented on a long-term basis to elderly residents who no longer feel they can live completely on their own but do not yet need nursing home care. Rolling Fields will be responsible for all the maintenance and repair costs associated with the properties. By the end of the year, Phase 1 was complete and 30 homes had been constructed and were occupied. The average cost of each home was $180,000.

In the first year, repair and maintenance costs averaged $1,200 per property. The company also borrowed $4 million to finance the construction of the homes. Interest on the loan for the year was $308,000.

Required:
a. Determine which of the above expenditures should be capitalized.
b. For the expenditures that should be capitalized, identify the appropriate account to which the costs should be charged.
c. For the expenditures that should be capitalized, discuss how each asset class should be depreciated.

C8-3 Maple Manufacturing Company

Maple Manufacturing Company recently purchased a property for use as a manufacturing facility. The company paid $850,000 for a building and four hectares of land. When recording the purchase, the company's accountant allocated $750,000 of the total cost to the building and the remaining $100,000 to the land.

After some investigation and an independent appraisal, you determine that the building is deemed to have a value of only $435,000. You also discover that the property is located near a major highway providing excellent access for shipping, and is therefore quite valuable. Similar properties in the area have been selling for $125,000 per hectare.

Maple Manufacturing is a very successful company and has traditionally reported very high net earnings. Last year, the company paid more than $200,000 in income taxes.

Required:
a. Determine the appropriate allocation between the buildings and land accounts for this basket purchase. (Remember that four hectares of land were purchased.)

b. Why would the company's accountant have wanted to allocate most of the purchase cost to the building rather than to the land?

C8-4 Preakness Consulting and Bellevue Services

Preakness Consulting and Bellevue Services are two petroleum engineering firms located in Calgary. Both companies are very successful and are looking to attract additional investors to provide them with an infusion of capital to expand. In the past year, both companies had consulting revenue of $1.5 million each.

On January 1, 2016, both companies purchased new computer systems. Currently, the only other asset owned by the companies is office equipment, which is fully depreciated. The computer systems, related hardware, and installation cost each company $660,000, and the systems have an expected life of five years. The residual value at the end of the five-year period is expected to be $30,000 in each case.

Preakness has chosen to depreciate the computer equipment using the straight-line method, while Bellevue has taken a more aggressive approach and is depreciating the system using the double-diminishing-balance method. Both companies have a December 31 year end and a tax rate of 25%. Information on their other expenses is as follows:

	Preakness	Bellevue
Salaries and wages	$750,250	$747,500
Rent	44,800	46,400
Other operating expenses	110,670	109,790

Required:

a. For each company, prepare a depreciation schedule showing the amount of depreciation expense to be charged each year for the computer system.
b. Prepare income statements for the current year for both companies.
c. How might an unsophisticated investor interpret the financial results from part "b"? Is one company really more profitable than the other?

C8-5 (Accounting for idle assets)

Conservative Company purchased a warehouse on January 1, 2011, for $400,000. At the time of purchase, Conservative anticipated that the warehouse would be used to facilitate the expansion of its product lines. The warehouse is being depreciated over 20 years and is expected to have a residual value of $50,000. At the beginning of 2016, the company decided that the warehouse would no longer be used and should be sold for its carrying amount. At the end of 2016, the warehouse still had not been sold and its net realizable value was estimated to be only $260,000.

Required:

a. Calculate the carrying amount of the warehouse on January 1, 2016.
b. Prepare all the journal entries that Conservative should make during 2016 related to the warehouse.
c. If Conservative sells the warehouse in 2017 for $220,000, what entry would be made for the sale?
d. During 2016, the financial vice-president expressed concern that, if Conservative put the building up for sale, the company might have to report a loss, and he did not want to reduce 2016 earnings. He wanted to continue treating the warehouse as an operating asset. How would the 2016 and 2017 financial statements be different if the warehouse were still treated as an operating asset during 2016? From a shareholder's perspective, do you think the treatment makes any difference? Explain.

ENDNOTES

1. Marina Strauss, "Canadian Tire Gets a Makeover," *The Globe and Mail*, March 26, 2014; Mario Toneguzzi, "FGL Sports Revenue Growth on Upward Trend since Canadian Tire Takeover," *Calgary Herald*, February 19, 2014; Canadian Tire 2013 annual report; "Canadian Tire Announces Third Quarter Results and Increases Quarterly Dividend," company news release, November 10, 2011; The Canadian Press, "Canadian Tire Buys Sport Chek, Athletes World Owner," *The Guardian* (Charlottetown), May 9, 2011; Canadian Tire corporate website, http://corp.canadiantire.ca.

2. Keith Norbury, "Port of Nanaimo Poised for Sea Changes," *Canadian Sailings*, August 14, 2013; "Celebrating a Half Century of Progress & Innovation...", Port of Nanaimo, 2011; Robert Barron, "NPA Crane Was Never Good Buy," *The Daily News* (Nanaimo), August 28, 2009.

3. Danier Leather Inc. Annual Report 2014.

4. Research In Motion Limited, Notes to the 2013 Consolidated Financial Statements, p. 22.

5. Jason Buckland, "The Secret to a Great Cup of Tim Hortons Coffee," MSNMoney.com, August 1, 2012; Karolyne Ellacott, "Ever Wonder Why Tim Hortons Coffee Tastes Like That? A Behind-the-Scenes Tour of their Roasting Plant," *Toronto Life*, July 5, 2012; "The Bean Is Key at Tim Hortons Coffee Roasting Plant," *Waterloo Region Record*, June 26, 2012.

6. "Franchising Program," Tim Hortons corporate website, retrieved from http://www.timhortons.com/ca/en/join/franchising-program-ca.html.

7. Air Canada Ltd. 2013 Annual Report.

8. Canadian Tire Ltd. 2012 Annual Report.

9 | Current Liabilities

CORE QUESTIONS

If you are able to answer the following questions, then you have achieved the related learning objectives.

LEARNING OBJECTIVES

After studying this chapter, you should be able to:

●●● INTRODUCTION

- Why is the distinction between current and non-current liabilities of significance to users?

> **1** Explain why current liabilities are of significance to users.

- At what amount are current liabilities reflected on the statement of financial position?

> **2** Describe the valuation methods for current liabilities.

●●● CURRENT LIABILITIES ARISING FROM TRANSACTIONS WITH LENDERS

- What current liabilities arise from transactions with lenders?

> **3** Identify the current liabilities that arise from transactions with lenders and explain how they are accounted for.

●●● CURRENT LIABILITIES ARISING FROM TRANSACTIONS WITH SUPPLIERS

- What current liabilities arise from transactions with suppliers?
- Why are accounts payable sometimes considered "free debt"?

> **4** Identify the current liabilities that arise from transactions with suppliers and explain how they are accounted for.

●●● CURRENT LIABILITIES ARISING FROM TRANSACTIONS WITH CUSTOMERS

- What current liabilities arise from transactions with customers?
- How are unearned revenues accounted for?
- How are the liabilities related to gift cards and loyalty programs accounted for?
- How are sales returns accounted for?
- How are warranties accounted for?

> **5** Identify the current liabilities that arise from transactions with customers and explain how they are accounted for.

●●● CURRENT LIABILITIES ARISING FROM TRANSACTIONS WITH EMPLOYEES

- What current liabilities arise from transactions with employees?
- How are payroll costs accounted for?
- Why are a company's wage costs greater than what it pays its employees?

> **6** Identify the current liabilities that arise from transactions with employees and explain how they are accounted for.

CORE QUESTIONS (continued)

●●● **CURRENT LIABILITIES ARISING FROM TRANSACTIONS WITH THE GOVERNMENT**

- What current liabilities arise from transactions with government?
- When are a company's taxes due?

LEARNING OBJECTIVES (continued)

7 Identify the current liabilities that arise from transactions with government and explain how they are accounted for.

●●● **CURRENT LIABILITIES ARISING FROM TRANSACTIONS WITH SHAREHOLDERS**

- What current liabilities arise from transactions with shareholders?

8 Identify the current liabilities that arise from transactions with shareholders and explain how they are accounted for.

●●● **FINANCIAL STATEMENT ANALYSIS**

- How do we determine how long a company takes to pay its suppliers?

9 Calculate the accounts payable turnover ratio and average payment period and assess the results.

●●● Customer Loyalty Is in the Books

More than 9 in 10 Canadians are a member of a loyalty program, carrying an average of eight such cards. Naturally, businesses like loyalty programs because they help increase customer loyalty and spending, and customers like loyalty programs because they get free merchandise or services. In addition, businesses are able to use loyalty cards to track customer information and spending habits, and to target special promotions to certain groups.

A recent loyalty program is Plum Rewards, a free program from Indigo Books & Music Inc. It awards points for almost all in-store purchases at Indigo, Chapters, and Coles book stores to be redeemed for discounts on future merchandise purchases. Launched in 2011, Plum Rewards and Indigo's existing irewards program had 6.7 million members at the end of Indigo's fiscal 2014 year.

Loyalty programs create deferred revenues, which are a liability because revenues have not been earned. There is a good chance that customers will redeem their points and the business will have to honour its obligation to provide something in return at a later date. In the case of Indigo, "When a Plum member purchases merchandise, the Company allocates the payment received between the merchandise and the points," it said in its 2014 annual report. "The payment is allocated based on the residual method, where the amount allocated to the

merchandise is the total payment less the fair value of the points. The portion of revenue attributed to the merchandise is recognized at the time of purchase. Revenue attributed to the points is recorded as deferred revenue and recognized when points are redeemed."

Indigo calculates the fair value of the points by multiplying the number of points issued by the estimated cost per point. "The estimated cost per point is based on many factors, including the expected future redemption patterns and associated costs," its annual report said. "On an ongoing basis, the Company monitors trends in redemption patterns (redemption at each reward level), historical redemption rates (points redeemed as a percentage of points issued) and net cost per point redeemed, adjusting the estimated cost per point based upon expected future activity."

How long should a company keep liabilities for loyalty programs on its books? It depends. Some loyalty programs have customer points expire at a certain time, after which the company would no longer carry that deferred revenue as a liability. But other loyalty programs, like Canadian Tire's paper "money," never expire, so those companies would have an indefinite obligation to provide rewards when points are redeemed.[1]

INTRODUCTION

Customer loyalty programs like the ones from **Indigo Books & Music Inc.** in the feature story are a current liability arising from a company's transactions with customers. They are part of the $12.8 million in deferred revenue reported as a current liability on the company's statement of financial position at March 29, 2014. Current liabilities are those that that the company expects to settle within the next 12 months. In this chapter, we'll look at not only how companies account for the current liabilities that arise from their transactions with customers, but also from transactions with lenders, suppliers, employees, governments, and shareholders.

■ **LEARNING OBJECTIVE 1**
Explain why current liabilities are of significance to users.

Why is the distinction between current and non-current liabilities of significance to users?

As we learned in Chapter 1, a simple definition of a liability is "an amount that the company owes to others." While this simple definition will work, accounting standard setters define a liability as an item that will require the outflow or sacrifice of economic resources in the future to settle an obligation that exists as a result of a transaction that has already taken place. In most cases, the economic resource that will be sacrificed is cash, but a company can also settle a liability by providing services or goods or even replacing it with another liability. We will see examples of all of these situations throughout the chapter.

Recall from Chapter 1 the characteristics of a liability, shown in the box below.

CHARACTERISTICS OF A LIABILITY
1. It is a present obligation of the entity.
2. The company expects to settle it through an outflow of resources that represent future economic benefits.
3. The obligation results from an event that has already happened.

In Chapter 1, we also introduced the concept of liquidity and discussed how liabilities could be classified as either current or non-current (that is, long-term). Current liabilities are expected to be settled within the next 12 months, while all other liabilities are considered to be long-term liabilities.

In Chapter 1, we also discussed the importance users place on working capital as a liquidity measure. Working capital was quantified as the difference between a company's current assets (those assets that are cash or will become cash within the next 12 months) and its current liabilities. We noted that users focus on it as a measure of a company's ability to meet its short-term obligations using its short-term assets. Since most current liabilities (such as accounts payable, wages payable, unearned revenue, and income taxes payable) will be settled with cash, identifying them as current liabilities helps users assess liquidity and enables them to determine how much cash will be required over the next year.

Assessing liquidity enables users, especially management and lenders, to determine whether the company will have sufficient cash available when its various liabilities come due. If the company's available cash is insufficient, the company will have to go to outside sources—taking on additional short-term or long-term debt, or issuing more shares—in order to raise additional cash. Understanding a company's short-term cash needs is essential to determining its current financial health and what may need to be done to ensure its long-term viability.

■ LEARNING OBJECTIVE 2
Describe the valuation methods for current liabilities.

At what amount are current liabilities reflected on the statement of financial position?

Theoretically, liabilities should initially be recorded at their fair value or at the present value of the payments that will be required to settle them. These present value amounts are discounted to take into account the **time value of money**, which recognizes that a dollar paid in the future is worth less than a dollar today. However, present value calculations are generally not used for most short-term liabilities, since the period until they must be settled is so short that the face value difference between their present value and their fair value (or face value) would not be material. Therefore, they are normally recorded at their face value.

The Conceptual Framework
THE ACCRUAL BASIS

As we discussed in Chapter 2, accounting standard setters have concluded that financial information prepared on the accrual basis provides users with information that is more relevant and representationally faithful than the information that results from the cash basis of accounting. All of the liabilities that we will discuss in this chapter are excellent examples of the accrual basis of accounting in action. Each of them is an attempt to capture and record the obligation and related expenses in the period in which they are incurred. You will see that a company's financial results, from the perspective of both earnings and financial position, can be significantly different as a result of using the accrual basis of accounting.

CURRENT LIABILITIES ARISING FROM TRANSACTIONS WITH LENDERS

What current liabilities arise from transactions with lenders?

■ **LEARNING OBJECTIVE 3**
Identify the current liabilities that arise from transactions with lenders and explain how they are accounted for.

Common current liabilities due to lenders include:

- Bank indebtedness
- Short-term loans
- Current portion of long-term debt

Let's explore each of these items in detail.

Bank Indebtedness (or Line of Credit)

Many companies have fluctuations in their cash flow throughout the year. These may be seasonal. For example, lawn and garden centres do not generate significant sales through the winter, but this is the time when they need to increase their inventory to be ready for the spring planting season. The fluctuations may also be related to the nature of the business. For example, contractors normally have more significant cash needs at the beginning of a large project than at the end of one. There can be other reasons for these cash shortages. Examples include a major customer failing to pay its receivable or an opportunity unexpectedly coming along to purchase additional equipment at an excellent price. Whatever the case, one way that companies plan to deal with temporary cash shortages is to arrange a **line of credit** with a bank.

When establishing a line of credit for a company, the bank assesses the company's ability to repay short-term debts and establishes a short-term loan limit that it feels is reasonable. If cheques written by the company exceed its cash balance in the bank, the bank covers the excess by immediately activating the line of credit and establishing a short-term loan. The bank uses subsequent cash deposits by the company to repay the loan. These are known as **revolving credit facilities** and are very similar to the overdraft feature you may have on your personal bank account. If you have this feature and need more money than you have available in your account, you can continue to write cheques and make withdrawals up to the amount of your overdraft.

A line of credit provides the company with greater flexibility and freedom to take advantage of business opportunities and/or to settle debts. If a company has made use of its line of credit, it is normally presented as **bank indebtedness** on the statement of financial position. This is normally presented as the first current liability because it will be repaid with the company's subsequent cash deposits.

For Example

Burnaby, British Columbia–based specialty coffee company, **Ten Peaks Coffee Company Inc.**, had one line of credit in place at December 31, 2013, against which it could draw a maximum of $14.5 million. As can be seen below, the company had drawn $4,786 thousand against it as at December 31, 2013.[2]

FINANCIAL STATEMENTS

12. BANK INDEBTEDNESS (amounts in thousands of $)

	December, 31 2013	December 31, 2012
Revolving operating line of credit	$4,786	$5,472
Swing line	–	497
Capital expenditure facilities	–	1,014
	$4,786	$6,983

On April 30, 2013, the Company repaid the previously outstanding capital expenditure facilities in full. In May 2013, the Company and the bank entered into a revised credit agreement, which reduced the total available credit (by eliminating the capital expenditure facilities), removed the fixed charge coverage covenant and added two new balance sheet-based financial covenants.

The Company had the following credit facilities as at December 31, 2013:
  a. a $14.5 million revolving operating line of credit which bears interest at the bank's prime lending rate plus 75 basis points; and
  b. a $1.5 million swing operating line of credit which bears interest at the bank's prime lending rate plus 75 basis points.

Note that the financial institutions that provide these revolving credit facilities generally charge **standby fees** on any unused portion of the credit facility. In other words, there is a cost to companies for having these funds available to them even if they don't use them.

Short-Term Loans (or Working Capital Loans)

Companies can also address cash shortfalls by arranging a **working capital loan** with a bank. As discussed in Chapter 1, working capital is the amount by which a company's current assets exceed its current liabilities. This type of short-term loan is often guaranteed (secured) by the company's accounts receivable, inventory, or both. The lender will agree to lend the company funds based on the amount of the company's receivables and inventory. For example, it may authorize a loan up to a maximum of 60% of receivables and 70% of inventory. As the company's receivable and inventory levels fluctuate, so will the maximum amount of the working capital loan.

Loans or other debts are said to be **secured** whenever specific assets have been pledged to guarantee repayment of the debt. Assets that have been pledged as security for debts are referred to as **collateral**. If the borrower defaults on a secured debt, the lender has the legal right to have the collateral seized and sold, and the proceeds used to repay the debt. If debts are **unsecured**, it means that no specific assets have been pledged as collateral to guarantee their repayment; in such cases, the creditors simply rely on the general creditworthiness of the company.

FINANCIAL STATEMENTS

For Example

High Liner Foods Incorporated, a Nova Scotia-based manufacturer and marketer of prepared and packaged frozen seafood products, has a $180-million working capital loan in place with the Royal Bank of Canada that enables the company to borrow funds as needed. These borrowings are secured by High Liner's inventory and accounts receivable. The lender also has a second charge on the company's plant and equipment. A second charge means that another lender has a first charge, or priority, over the Royal Bank of Canada in terms of being able to access these assets if the borrower were to default on its loan. At December 28, 2013, the company had borrowings of $97,227 thousand under these arrangements.[3]

In 2011 the Company replaced its existing working capital facility with a new five year $180 million working capital facility entered into with Royal Bank of Canada as Administrative and Collateral Agent expiring December 19, 2016 (the "facility"). This facility replaced all existing working capital debt facilities. The facility is asset-based and is collateralized by the Company's inventories and accounts receivable and other personal property in Canada and the U.S., subject to a first charge on brands and trade names and related intangibles under the long-term debt facilities. A second charge over the Company's plant and equipment is also in place. The facility was amended in February 2013, and allows the Company to borrow Canadian Prime Rate revolving loans, Canadian Base Rate revolving loans, and U.S. Prime Rate revolving loans plus 0.00% to 0.75%; BA Equivalent revolving loans, LIBOR revolving loans and letter of credit fees plus 1.75% to 2.25%. Standby fees are also required to be paid on the unutilized line.

Current Portion of Long-Term Debt

Some long-term loans have terms that require the borrower to repay a portion of the loan principal each year (but no interest), while others may require **blended instalment payments** (payments that include both principal and interest components) each month, quarter, or year. In these cases, even though the loan may be considered long term, such as a five-year term, not all of the principal is a long-term liability. The portion of the principal that is due within the next year would meet the definition of a current liability. This would also be the case for any long-term loan that is within a year of being due. These amounts are known as the **current portion of long-term debt**. Companies must ensure that these amounts are presented as current rather than as long-term liabilities. This is done by means of a **reclassification entry** as follows:

TAKE5

Long-Term Loan Payable	XXX	
Current Portion of Long-Term Debt		XXX

As you can see, both parts of the entry are to liability accounts, so there is no change to total liabilities. The only change is that the portion of the loan principal due within the next 12 months is now classified as a current liability rather than a long-term liability. This is why the entry is considered to be a reclassification entry.

Initially, this entry may not appear to be of significance because total liabilities remain unchanged, but this is an important entry. It enables users to estimate the expected outflow of cash during the following year. It can also have a significant effect on a company's current, quick, and other ratios. Without this reclassification entry, a company's current liabilities could be significantly understated, making their working capital position appear stronger than it actually is.

For Example

FINANCIAL STATEMENTS

The 2014 annual report of women's fashion retailer **Reitmans (Canada) Limited** included an excellent note that demonstrates how companies distinguish between the current and long-term portions of their debt. The company's debt consisted of a $7,003-thousand mortgage payable due in 2017, but the requirement for blended monthly instalment payments meant that $1,672 thousand of this would be repaid within 12 months of the reporting date and was a current liability.[4]

14 LONG-TERM DEBT (amounts in thousands of dollars)

	February 1, 2014	February 1, 2013
Mortgage payable	$7,003	$8,573
Less current portion	1,672	1,570
	$5,331	$7,003

The mortage, bearing interest at 6.04%, is payable in monthly instalments of principal and interest of $172. It is due November 2017 and is secured by the Company's distribution centre having a carrying value of $16,354 (February 2, 2013 − $17,330).

As at February 1, 2014, principal repayments on long-term debt are as follows:

Within 1 year	$1,672
Within 2 years	1,780
Within 3 years	1,896
Within 4 years	1,655
	$7,003

CURRENT LIABILITIES ARISING FROM TRANSACTIONS WITH SUPPLIERS

What current liabilities arise from transactions with suppliers?

■ **LEARNING OBJECTIVE 4**
Identify the current liabilities that arise from transactions with suppliers and explain how they are accounted for.

As you know from earlier chapters, accounts payable occur when a company buys goods or services on credit. They are often referred to as *trade accounts payable* (or **trade payables**). The requirement to pay them is generally deferred for a relatively short period of time, such as 30 to 60 days, although longer credit periods are allowed in some industries.

For Example

FINANCIAL STATEMENTS

Movie theatre operator **Cineplex Inc.** disclosed the following accounts payable and accrued liabilities in its financial statements for the year ended December 31, 2013 (in thousands of Canadian dollars):[5]

14 ACCOUNTS PAYABLE AND ACCRUED EXPENSES

Accounts payable and accrued expenses consist of:

	2013	2012
Accounts payable - trade	$ 46,178	$ 56,328
Film and advertising payables	59,164	32,124
Accrued salaries and benefits	19,974	17,710
Sales taxes payable	11,409	6,175
Accrued occupancy costs	3,304	3,251
Other payables and accrued expenses	17,304	13,911
	$157,333	$129,499

Why are accounts payable sometimes considered "free debt"?

Accounts payable generally do not carry explicit interest charges and are commonly thought of as "free debt" for the length of the credit period (usually 30 days). However, there is sometimes a provision for either a discount for early payment or a penalty for late payment. In such cases, not taking advantage of the discount, or paying a penalty for being late, can be viewed as equivalent to paying interest.

For Example

In its financial statements for the year ended December 28, 2013, **Canadian Tire Corporation, Limited** disclosed that the average term for its trade payables was between 5 and 120 days. This means that some suppliers required the company to pay within 5 days of receiving the goods, while others gave the company 120 days to settle their accounts.[6]

CURRENT LIABILITIES ARISING FROM TRANSACTIONS WITH CUSTOMERS

■ LEARNING OBJECTIVE 5
Identify the current liabilities that arise from transactions with customers and explain how they are accounted for.

What current liabilities arise from transactions with customers?

A number of current liabilities arise from ordinary transactions between a company and its customers or clients, including:

- **unearned revenue** (or **deferred revenue**)
- **gift card liability**
- **customer loyalty provision**
- **sales return provision**
- **provision for warranty claims**

You may be wondering why the word **provision** appears in the name of many of these current liability accounts. This word is used to indicate liabilities whose amounts have been determined using a significant degree of estimation or for which there is uncertainty with respect to the timing of settlement. For example, when determining its liability for warranty claims, a company has to estimate the likelihood of claims within the warranty period, estimate the amount of these claims, and so on. It is useful to just think of *provision* as another word for *liability*.

Now, let's explore how these liabilities arise and how they are normally settled.

How are unearned revenues accounted for?

KEY POINT
Unearned revenues only arise when a customer has made a *payment in advance* of receiving goods or services.

Many businesses require their customers to pay in advance of receiving the goods (such as on-line retailers) or service (such as insurance companies or airlines). Others require their customers to make deposits or down payments. For example, law and accounting firms often require new clients to pay a retainer before they will begin working on a case or file. Your university or college likely required you to pay your tuition for the entire semester before the start of the semester or within the first few weeks of it. These types of transactions create **partially executed contracts** between buyers and sellers. By paying, the buyers have done their part. However, since the sellers have not fulfilled their part of the contract, it would be inappropriate for them to recognize revenue at the time they receive the customer's payment. Instead, they defer the recognition of revenue from deposits and down payments until such time as the goods or services have been provided. These deferrals create liabilities that are known as *unearned revenues* or *deferred revenues*. Unearned revenue is a liability because the company receiving the payment has an obligation to provide the related goods or services (or, failing that, to return the money).

Fitness clubs that require members to pay their dues in 3-, 6-, or 12-month terms are an example of businesses that would have unearned revenue among their current liabilities. They receive money for memberships in advance and must initially record this as an asset (cash) offset by a liability (unearned revenue). They earn the revenue later, by providing the gym services over the period of the membership. Each month that the service is provided, they will reduce the liability account and record revenue. A sample entry for accounting for unearned revenue in a fitness club is shown below.

TAKE**5**

At the time of prepayment by the customer:		
Cash	XXX	
Unearned Revenue		XXX
At the time the service is provided by the company:		
Unearned Revenue	XXX	
Membership Revenue		XXX

For Example

VIA Rail Canada Inc.'s financial statements for the year ended March 31, 2013, reported deferred revenue from advanced ticket sales of $11.1 million. This represents payments received from customers in advance of rail services being provided by VIA.[7]

17 DEFERRED REVENUE

Deferred revenue is comprised of the following:

(IN MILLIONS OF DOLLARS)	2013	2012
Advanced ticket sales	**11.1**	9.4
Gift cards	**2.7**	2.5
Non-monetary transactions	**2.3**	1.6
VIA Préférence	**14.0**	13.6
Other	**0.7**	0.3
Total deferred revenue	**30.8**	27.4

For Example

WestJet Airlines Ltd. is an excellent example of a company that requires its customers to pay in advance of receiving services. These payments are recorded as a liability called *advance ticket sales*. This amounted to $551,022 thousand at December 31, 2013. The company's notes to the financial statements related to this were as follows:[8]

(d) Revenue recognition
  (i) Guest
Guest revenue, including the air component of vacation packages, are recognized when air transportation is provided. Tickets sold but not yet used are reported in the consolidated statement of financial position as advance ticket sales.

(b) Liabilities

	Note	2013	2012
Other current liabilities:			
Advance ticket sales		$551,022	$480,947

FINANCIAL STATEMENTS

How are the liabilities related to gift cards and loyalty programs accounted for?

The sale of gift certificates and prepaid cards is a major source of unearned revenue for many businesses. Gift cards remain a liability until such time as the cards are redeemed for goods or services. When a gift certificate or prepaid card is sold, the business records the cash received and an offsetting liability, representing its obligation to provide goods or services equal to the value of the card. Later, when the gift card is used, the liability is eliminated and revenue is recognized.

The popularity of gift cards is having a major effect on the sales patterns of many retail businesses. The November–December holiday shopping season is very important to most retailers. However, much of the money spent on gift cards late in the current year shows up in sales revenues early in the next year, when the gift cards

are redeemed. Thus, in terms of revenue recognition, selling gift cards during the holiday shopping period shifts revenues from December to January or February. In particular, gift card activations (when cards are purchased) drop off sharply after December. In contrast, January redemptions (when gift cards are used to purchase something) are very significant. As a result, the usual drop in sales from December to January has moderated. The recognition of December gift card sales as revenues in January has given the start of the new year a significant financial boost, in a time that has traditionally been a slow one for retail businesses.

There are two transactions that must be accounted for in relation to gift cards or prepaid cards: initial sale (purchase of the gift card) and redemption (usage of the gift card). The journal entries for these transactions are as follows:

1. Initial sale:		
Cash	XXX	
Unearned Revenue (or Gift Card Liability)		XXX
2. Redemption (for goods):		
Unearned Revenue (or Gift Card Liability)	XXX	
Sales Revenue		XXX
Cost of Goods Sold	XXX	
Inventory		XXX

For a variety of reasons, some gift cards will never be used by their owners. This is known as **breakage**. It is estimated that this is the case for between 10% and 15% of all gift cards purchased in Canada. Companies estimate the breakage rates on their outstanding gift cards. The portion that is estimated to remain unused is recognized as revenue and the unearned revenue/gift card liability is reduced.

FINANCIAL STATEMENTS

For Example

Indigo Books & Music Inc., our feature story company, reported an unredeemed gift card liability of $46,827 thousand in its financial statements at March 29, 2014. The company's accounting policy related to gift cards is as follows:[9]

Gift cards
The Company sells gift cards to its customers and recognizes the revenue as gift cards are redeemed. The Company also recognizes gift card breakage if the likelihood of gift card redemption by the customer is considered to be remote. The Company determines its average gift card breakage rate based on historical redemption rates. Once the breakage rate is determined, the resulting revenue is recognized over the estimated period of redemption based on historical redemption patterns, commencing when the gift cards are sold. Gift card breakage is included in revenues in the Company's consolidated statements of earnings (loss) and comprehensive earnings (loss).

For Example

A NEW "KIIND" OF GIVING

Like customer loyalty programs, prepaid gift cards are generally a win-win for consumers and businesses. That is, unless they languish in a drawer for years, and then everybody loses.

Obviously, if someone receives a gift card and loses it, forgets about it, or never gets around to using it, that person gets nothing. But unredeemed gift cards cause headaches for retailers, too. When they sell a card, they have to record a liability on their books because they owe the consumer the value of the gift card in goods or services. Because many governments in Canada have made it illegal for gift cards to expire, businesses have to carry these liabilities indefinitely.

Enter Victoria entrepreneur Leif Baradoy, who launched a start-up, Kiind, to help solve this conundrum. With traditional gift cards, "It doesn't mean 100 per cent in the pocket of the retailer," says Bartadoy. "It could mean a five-year accounting headache, and 50 per cent going to the government's pocket."

(continued)

For Example (continued)

Kiind.me lets North American vendors like Apple, Amazon, Cineplex, Home Depot, and Nike sell a digital gift card where the purchaser doesn't pay for it until the gift recipient redeems it. It's good for recipients because they are less likely to lose a digital card than a plastic one. It's good for the givers because they aren't out of pocket until the recipient redeems the card. And it's good for retailers because they aren't carrying a liability indefinitely; they only get paid—and record the revenue—when the gift card is activated and a good is purchased or a service is provided. A Kiind card expires if the recipient does not activate it within the time chosen by the giver, meaning that the vendor is off the hook for having an indefinite obligation to provide a good or service in the future.

One drawback for vendors is that Kiind estimates that up to 20% of traditional gift cards are never redeemed, which is money earned without expending any resources. With Kiind cards, that revenue stream would dry up. But retailers still feel the Kiind cards are worth it in order to reduce the accounting headaches related to these liabilities.[10]

Many businesses have customer loyalty programs to encourage their customers to buy from them. Under these programs, points (or other forms of credits) are awarded to customers when they make purchases, and these points can later be redeemed for free goods or services. Some companies participate in general rewards programs that are operated by independent entities, such as Air Miles from **LoyaltyOne, Inc.** In other cases, the loyalty programs are specific to particular companies, such as the Optimum rewards program operated by **Shoppers Drug Mart.**

Essentially, the accounting treatment for customer loyalty programs involves treating the original sale as a "bundle" consisting of two parts: the initial goods or services that are provided at that point, plus the additional goods or services that may be provided in the future under the rewards program. In other words, part of the amount that customers pay when they make a purchase is deemed to be for the rewards that will be provided later. Accordingly, the company allocates a portion of the sales revenue to the rewards program and treats it as unearned revenue until the rewards are delivered.

For Example

Shoppers Drug Mart's Optimum loyalty program is one of the largest in Canada, with over 10 million active cardholders. The company's note disclosure (below) related to this program provides a good example of how Canadian companies account for loyalty programs. When a customer makes a purchase at Shoppers and earns loyalty points, the company defers a portion of the sales revenue (and treats it as unearned revenue). It will recognize this revenue in the future when the customers redeem their points. Until that time, the deferred revenue is a current liability and is presented as part of accounts payable and accrued liabilities.[11]

FINANCIAL STATEMENTS

(c) Revenue

(i) Sale of Goods and Services

Revenue is comprised primarily of retail sales, including prescription sales. Retail sales are recognized as revenue when the goods are sold to the customer. Revenue is net of returns and amounts deferred related to the issuance of points under the Shoppers Optimum® Loyalty Card Program (the "Program") points. Where a sales transaction includes points awarded under the Program, revenue allocated to the Program points is deferred based on the fair value of the awards and recognized as revenue when the Program points are redeemed and the Company fulfills its obligations to supply the awards.

How are sales returns accounted for?

Most retailers have policies that enable customers to return goods within certain time frames. Accounting standards require the company to estimate the amount of expected returns based on a combination of past experience and current market conditions. A liability is then recorded, which reduces the related sales revenue. The entry is as follows:

Sales Returns and Allowances	XXX	
Sales Returns Provision		XXX

Sales Returns and Allowances is a **contra revenue account** because it reduces sales revenue. The advantage of using the Sales Returns and Allowances account, rather than just debiting Sales Revenue, is that it enables companies to track the amount of sales returns. Remember that the word *provision* is used to indicate a liability that has been estimated, so the Sales Returns Provision is another current liability account.

FINANCIAL STATEMENTS

For Example

From Note 10 of **Danier Leather Inc.**'s 2013 financial statements, we can see that customers returned merchandise in accordance with the company's return policy and received sales refunds of $2,001,000 in fiscal 2014. At June 28, 2014, the company's estimated liability for sales returns was $94,000.[12]

10. SALES RETURN PROVISION (amounts in thousands of dollars)

The provision for sales returns primarily relates to customer returns of unworn and undamaged purchases for a full refund within the time period provided by Danier's return policy, which is generally 14 days after the purchase date. Since the time period of the provision is of relatively short duration, all of the provision is classified as current. The following transactions occurred during the years ended June 28, 2014 and June 29, 2013, respectively, with respect to the sales return provision:

	Year Ended	
	June 28, 2014	**June 29, 2013**
Beginning of period	$ 99	$ 124
Amount provided during the period	1,996	2,049
Utilized or released during the period	(2,001)	(2,074)
End of period	**$ 94**	**$ 99**

How are warranties accounted for?

We will look at two different warranty scenarios in this section. In the first section, "Warranty Provisions," we will discuss warranties that are provided at no explicit additional charge. In other words, when products are sold with a warranty. The second section, "Warranty Sales," will cover scenarios where warranties are sold separately to customers.

Warranty Provision

When companies sell goods or services, there can be stated or implied guarantees, or warranties, to the buyers that are provided at no extra charge. If a product proves to be defective, the company that manufactured or sold it may have to provide warranty services to repair or replace it or refund the customer.

At the time of the product's sale, the company cannot know exactly how much the cost of the warranty services will ultimately be; however, it must estimate and accrue an estimate of these costs and establish a liability for them. Companies make these estimates each period based on their sales. They accrue a warranty expense and record a liability (**warranty provision**). If the company has been in business for a long time, this estimate will be based on historical warranty claims. For new products and new companies, estimating future costs will be more difficult, but information such as industry averages can be used.

The entry to record the warranty provision in the period of the sale would be as follows:

Warranty Expense	XXX
Warranty Provision	XXX

HELPFUL HINT

Warranty expense is estimated and recorded in the period when the sales revenue is recorded. At the same time, a liability account is created. When actual costs are subsequently incurred under the warranty, there is no expense recorded. Instead, the *Warranty Provision* account is reduced (or debited).

Note that the entire estimated warranty cost is recorded as an expense in the year of sale, regardless of the length of time covered by the warranty. The length of the warranty period is irrelevant for determining the expense to be reported on the statement of income. On the statement of financial position, the portion of the obligation that is expected to be settled within a year would be reported as a current liability and any portion that extends beyond one year would be reported as a non-current liability.

Warranties are especially interesting from an accounting perspective because they can be settled or extinguished in so many different ways. The following are some of the common outcomes when warranties are in place:

- Product replacement
- Product repair (which may include both parts and labour)
- Product returned/cash refund provided
- Product returned/store credit or gift card provided
- Warranty period expires without any claims

When a claim is made under the warranty, the entry would be as follows:

Warranty Provision		XXX	
	Inventory	XXX	If product replaced
or	Inventory and/or Wage Expense	XXX	If product repaired
or	Cash	XXX	If refund provided*
or	Unearned Revenue	XXX	If store credit provided
or	Miscellaneous Revenue	XXX	If warranty period expired

*This assumes that the product returned cannot be sold to another customer

As you can see, no expense is recorded when costs are incurred to honour the warranty. This is because the expense was accrued during the period in which the products were sold. So, instead of

For Example

FINANCIAL STATEMENTS

It is likely that you have flown on an aircraft or taken a trip on a train or subway car manufactured by the Canadian company, **Bombardier Inc.** As can be seen from the notes below, the company provides warranties on the products it manufactures for periods up to 20 years. It records the estimated warranty costs as part of cost of goods sold for the products sold each year and increases its provision for product warranties. As at December 31, 2013, the company had an $863-million provision for product warranties and incurred warranty claims of $356 million during the year. Of the $863-million provision, $715 million was considered to be a current liability, with the balance long-term.[13]

Product warranties – A provision for warranty cost is recorded in cost of sales when the revenue for the related product is recognized. The interest component associated with product warranties, when applicable, is recorded in financing expense. The cost is estimated based on a number of factors, including the historical warranty claims and cost experience, the type and duration of warranty coverage, the nature of products sold and in service and counter-warranty coverage available from the Corporation's suppliers. Claims for reimbursement from third parties are recorded if their realization is virtually certain. Product warranties typically range from one to five years, except for aircraft structural and bogie warranties that extend up to 20 years.

	Product warranties
Balance as at December 31, 2012	$ 907
Additions	369
Utilization	(356)
Reversals	(71)
Accretion expense	1
Effect of changes in discount rates	(1)
Effect of foreign currency exchange rate changes	14
Balance as at December 31, 2013	$ 863
Of which current	$ 715
Of which non-current	$ 148
	$ 863

debiting an expense, the Warranty Provision account is debited, to reflect the fact that a portion of the company's obligation has been satisfied.

By estimating its expected future obligation at the same time that it records the sale, the company records the warranty expense in the same accounting period as when the sales revenue is recorded. In this way, the statement of income provides a better indication of the profitability of that period's operations.

Warranty Sales

Some retailers, such as **Future Shop**, sell warranty coverage (either basic or extended warranties) on the products they sell. These warranties are essentially unearned revenue. When customers purchase these warranties, the company has to record the amount received as unearned revenue and carry this as a liability on its statement of financial position, until either the warranty services are provided or the warranty period expires.

CURRENT LIABILITIES ARISING FROM TRANSACTIONS WITH EMPLOYEES

▪ LEARNING OBJECTIVE 6
Identify the current liabilities that arise from transactions with lenders and explain how they are accounted for.

What current liabilities arise from transactions with employees?

Wages owed to employees can be another significant current liability. This liability is known as **wages payable**. The amount of the liability depends, in part, on how often the company pays its employees, because it reflects the wages that have been earned by employees since they were last paid.

In addition to the wages themselves, most companies provide *fringe benefits* for their employees. These costs—for medical insurance, pensions, vacation pay, and other benefits provided by the employer—must also be recognized as an expense in the periods in which they are incurred and a corresponding liability established.

Canadian companies are required to withhold taxes and other amounts from employee wages on behalf of the government. These amounts must then be remitted (paid) to the government. For example, companies must withhold income taxes from employees' wages. Companies must also withhold premiums that employees are required to pay to the Canada Pension Plan (or Quebec Pension Plan) and for Employment Insurance. These withholdings are known as **source deductions** because they are being deducted at the source of payment (the employer). They are a liability to the company because they are owed to the government. These main source deductions are described in more detail below.

Pensions

The **Canada Pension Plan (CPP)** and **Quebec Pension Plan (QPP)** programs are run by the federal government and the government of Quebec, respectively, and provide retirement benefits to retired workers based on the premiums they paid into the plan when they were working. The programs also provide disability payments and death benefits, including payments to surviving spouses and minor children. As of 2014, employees were required to pay CPP premiums of 4.95% of their wages subject to certain thresholds and limits. Employers are required to match the premiums paid by their employees. That is, they pay an equal amount as employees.

Employment Insurance

The **Employment Insurance (EI)** program is run by the federal government and provides assistance to unemployed individuals while they look for work or undertake education to upgrade or change their skills to improve their employment prospects. It also provides maternity and paternity benefits and payments to workers who are sick or who have to leave their job to care for a seriously ill family member. As of 2014, employees were required to pay EI premiums of 1.88% of their wages subject to certain thresholds and limits. Employers are required to pay 1.4 times (or 140%) the premiums paid by their employees.

Income Tax

The amount of income tax to be deducted from employees' earnings depends on many factors, including their expected annual earnings and their personal exemptions for income tax purposes.

How are payroll costs accounted for?

We will now show some examples of how payroll costs are accounted for. The examples and problems in this text will make the following assumptions.

1. Because the amount of income tax to be deducted from employees' earnings depends on many factors, we will simply state the amount of personal income tax that is to be withheld from the employees' pay.

2. The amount of CPP and EI premiums to be withheld from the employee's pay will also be stated. However, in some problems, you will be expected to calculate the employer's contributions. This means you need to know that employers match the employee's CPP premiums and pay 1.4 times their EI premiums.

3. We will assume that there are *no* other withholdings for things like medical or dental plans, group insurance, or company pension plans.

Accounting for a company's payroll costs involves the following four entries:

1. Employee Entry
   This entry accounts for the wages earned by the employees, the source deductions that had to be withheld, and wages due to the employee. The wages earned by the employee are known as the **gross wages**, while the wages that will be paid to the employee are known as the **net wages**.

EMPLOYEE ENTRY		
Wage Expense	XXX	
Employee Income Taxes Payable		XXX
CPP Payable		XXX
EI Payable		XXX
Wages Payable (or Cash if paid at this time)		XXX

2. Employer Entry
   This entry accounts for the employer's share of CPP and EI premiums.

EMPLOYER ENTRY		
Wage Expense	XXX	
CPP Payable (equal to amount in employee entry)		XXX
EI Payable (1.4 × amount in employee entry)		XXX

3. Payment of Wages
   This entry accounts for the payment of the net wages to the employees. It may not be necessary if the wages were paid as part of the first entry. As **pay periods** do not normally align with fiscal periods, it is common for companies to have wages payable at the end of each accounting period. These amounts represent the wages that have been accrued for employees working between the last pay date and the reporting date.

PAYMENT OF WAGES ENTRY		
Wages Payable	XXX	
Cash		XXX

4. Remittance of Source Deductions and Employer's Contributions
This entry accounts for the **remittance** (or payment) of the source deductions to the federal government. It is important to remember that the remittance includes both the employee's and employer's portions.

REMITTANCE ENTRY		
Employee Income Taxes Payable (from employee entry)	XXX	
CPP Payable (both employee and employer portions)	XXX	
EI Payable (both employee and employer portions)	XXX	
Cash		XXX

Most companies are required to remit the amounts owed related to their source deductions by the 15th of the month following the month in which they were withheld from employees. Large employers make their remittances weekly.

Let's assume that the employees of a company have earned wages of $10,000 and that the following totals of source deductions were withheld:

- Income tax: $2,500
- CPP premiums: $495 (4.95% of $10,000)
- EI premiums: $188 (1.88% of $10,000)

TAKE**5**

The company (the employer) is required to match the employee's CPP premiums and pay 1.4 times the employee's EI premiums. As such, the employer will have additional wage costs of $758 (CPP of $495 and EI of $263, which is $1.4 \times \$188$). Let's also assume that the net wages are paid to employees when the wages were recorded rather than at a later date. Based on the above, the journal entries to record the payroll would be as follows:

EMPLOYEE ENTRY			
Wage Expense	10,000		
Employee Income Taxes Payable		2,500	A
CPP Payable		495	B
EI Payable		188	C
Cash		6,817	

EMPLOYER ENTRY			
Wage Expense	758		
CPP Payable (equal to employee amount)		495	D
EI Payable (1.4 × 188)		263	E

REMITTANCE ENTRY			
Employee Income Taxes Payable	2,500		A
CPP Payable (495 + 495)	990		B + D
EI Payable (188 + 263)	451		C + E
Cash		3,941	

For Example

Open Text Corporation is a software company based in Waterloo, Ontario. The company develops and sells software products that enable its clients to manage their business information. As a technology company, wages are a significant cost. As at June 30, 2013, the company owed its employees U.S. $50,568 thousand for accrued salaries and commissions. This is a good example of how significant wage-related payables can be.[14]

Why are a company's wage costs greater than what it pays its employees?

The above discussion illustrates that an employer's total wage costs are more than the salary or wages earned by and paid to its employees. Employers are also required to match the CPP/QPP contributions of their employees and pay 1.4 times the EI contributions of their employees. In addition, companies are required to pay workers' compensation board (WCB) premiums based on their wage costs. The workers' compensation board uses these premiums to pay the medical and living costs of workers injured on the job. The rates vary depending upon the rates of injury experienced historically in each industry and occupation.

For Example

The 2014 WCB rates in British Columbia were are follows:
- Low-risk jobs: working in a movie theatre (0.88%) or large retail store (1.06%)
- High-risk jobs: working as a tree faller (9.45%) or in a fish packing plant (6.54%)[15]

Different provinces also impose other taxes on companies, including a number that are based on the corporation's payroll expenses rather than its net income.

As you can see, the company's total costs of paying an employee are more than the basic wage or salary.

 Ethics in Accounting

Companies with cash flow difficulties can be tempted to use their employees' source deductions as a type of financing. The company would withhold deductions as required, but not remit them or the employer's CPP and EI premiums to the Canada Revenue Agency (CRA). The company's employees would be unaware of this, as would the CRA. This is because there is no accounting for source deductions on an individual employee basis until the end of the year, when employers must provide to the employee and CRA the T4 slips that report each employee's income together with their income tax deductions, CPP/QPP premiums, EI premiums, and so on. As long as the source deductions are remitted by the end of the year, it is possible that no one would be aware of the company's failure to remit when required.

Actions like this constitute payroll fraud. Companies are charged interest and penalties in relation to late remittances of source deductions. Perhaps more significantly, company directors can also face fines and imprisonment in relation to this type of payroll fraud. The CRA conducts payroll audits that can identify such frauds.

For Example

The following are examples of provincial taxes that must be paid by corporations based on their payroll costs:
- Manitoba: Health and Post-Secondary Education Tax
- Ontario: Health Tax
- Quebec: Health Services Fund
- Newfoundland and Labrador: Health and Post-Secondary Education Tax[16]

CURRENT LIABILITIES ARISING FROM TRANSACTIONS WITH THE GOVERNMENT

What current liabilities arise from transactions with government?

Aside from any outstanding payroll source deductions, Canadian companies generally have liabilities to the federal and provincial governments for corporate income taxes. Companies may also be subject to taxation in other countries in which they operate. This liability results from the fact that, as discussed in Chapter 1, corporations are separate legal entities and are taxed separately from their shareholders.

In Canada, the combined federal and provincial corporate tax rates are different across many of the provinces and territories because each province or territory has different tax policies.

> ### For Example
>
> The combined federal and provincial tax rates for public companies ranged from 25% to 31% in 2013, while the rates for private companies ranged from 13% to 15%.[17]

FINANCIAL STATEMENTS

> ### For Example
>
> The mission of the **YMCA of Greater Toronto**, which is a charity, is to "offer opportunities for personal growth, community involvement and leadership." Note 13 of its financial statements provides a good overview of the types of transactions organizations can have with government that can create liabilities.[18]
>
> #### 13   GOVERNMENT REMITTANCES (amounts in thousands of dollars)
>
> Government remittances consist of property taxes, workplace safety insurance, sales taxes and payroll withholding taxes required to be paid to government authorities, and are recognized when the amounts come due. With respect to government remittances, $289 (2012 – $374) is included in accounts payable and accrued liabilities.

When are a company's taxes due?

The payment of corporate income taxes does not always coincide with when they are incurred. A corporation's income taxes are based on the company's income before tax (adjusted for a number of tax rules). This amount is not known until the end of the fiscal year, but the government is not prepared to wait until the end of the year to receive the company's income taxes. Instead, companies are generally required to make monthly income tax instalment payments, which are usually based on the taxes paid in the previous year. This provides the government with a steady flow of cash coming in during the year. At the end of their fiscal year, companies prepare their annual financial statements and are required to file a **corporate tax return** (which is known as a **T2**). This must be filed no later than six months after the company's fiscal year end, but the balance of any taxes owed for the year must generally be paid within two months of the year end, so this payment is sometimes based on an estimate of taxes owing.

Given the deadlines for paying outstanding income tax balances (that is, within two months), they are a current liability. This amount is presented as *income taxes payable* and is different from *deferred income taxes*, which may have portions that are current and non-current liabilities. We will discuss deferred income taxes in Chapter 10.

CURRENT LIABILITIES ARISING FROM TRANSACTIONS WITH SHAREHOLDERS

What current liabilities arise from transactions with shareholders?

Dividends payable is the most common liability that corporations have to their shareholders. This is because dividends are generally declared at the end of a quarter or year, once the net income for that period has been determined. Once the board declares dividends, the company has a liability to those shareholders holding shares of the class for which the dividend has been declared. Even if the board declares dividends on the last day of the fiscal year, most public companies will not pay these dividends until at least two weeks later, for reasons that will be discussed in Chapter 11. The result is that any dividends declared at the end of the year will remain outstanding until the next year.

When the board of directors declares dividends, the journal entry is as follows.

Dividends Declared	XXX	
Dividends Payable		XXX

For Example

Big Rock Brewery Inc. is a Calgary-based producer of craft beers and cider. Note 20 of the company's 2013 financial statements is a good example of dividends payable disclosure. The quarterly dividend that was declared on December 31, the company's year end, was not paid until January 15, so it was a liability at year end.[19]

20   DIVIDENDS PAYABLE

Big Rock declared dividends during the year ended December 30, 2013 in the amount of $4,855 ($0.80 per share) compared to $4,852 ($0.80 per unit) for the same period in 2012. Dividends were paid on April 15, July 15, and October 15 of 2013 and January 15, 2014.

FINANCIAL STATEMENTS

FINANCIAL STATEMENT ANALYSIS

Information on a company's total current liabilities and some of the specific liabilities is used in a number of different ratios. As was discussed in Chapter 6, current liabilities are a key component of both the current and quick ratios. In addition to these ratios, users may also calculate various turnover ratios related to current liabilities. The most common of these is the **accounts payable turnover** ratio, which measures the number of times per year that a company settles its trade payables. It is also used as a variable in determining a company's **average payment period**, which is the average number of days a company takes to pay its trade payables. In this section of the chapter, we will discuss each of these ratios further.

How do we determine how long a company takes to pay its suppliers?

■ LEARNING OBJECTIVE 9
Calculate the accounts payable turnover ratio and accounts payable payment period and assess the results.

Earlier in the chapter, we discussed how accounts payable are commonly considered to be "free debt." This stemmed from the fact that a company's suppliers will often provide it with 30 or more days to pay its account. During this period, the accounts payable are non–interest-bearing. As such, companies should take advantage of this free financing. However, abusing this and not paying suppliers on time will result in interest being charged on the account and can damage relationships with suppliers.

The accounts payable turnover ratio measures the number of times per year that a company settles its trade payables and is calculated as follows:

$$\text{Accounts Payable Turnover Ratio} = \frac{\text{Credit Purchases}}{\text{Average Accounts Payable*}}$$

*Average accounts payable = (Opening Accounts Payable + Ending Accounts Payable)/2

The amount of credit purchases is not usually reported directly in the financial statements. However, the cost of goods sold can be used as a starting point. Making an adjustment for the change in inventories during the period will convert the *cost of goods sold* to the *cost of goods purchased*. We will assume that all purchases were on account.

In Chapter 7, we learned about the cost of goods sold (COGS) model. Rearranging the elements in the model enables us to determine the amount of credit purchases as follows:

Cost of Goods Sold Model	Rearranged Model
Beginning Inventory	Cost of Goods Sold
+ Purchases	− Beginning Inventory
− Ending Inventory	+ Ending Inventory
= Cost of Goods Sold	= Purchases

Once the accounts payable turnover ratio has been calculated, it can be converted into days by determining the accounts payable payment period, which is calculated as follows:

$$\text{Accounts Payable Payment Period} = \frac{365 \text{ days}}{\text{Accounts Payable Turnover Ratio}}$$

To assess whether a company's accounts payable turnover ratio and accounts payable payment period are good or bad requires a comparison with the credit terms (payment period) of the company's creditors, with the results from previous years, and/or with the results for other companies in the same industry.

Let's look at these ratios over a two-year period for Canadian fashion retailer, **Le Château Inc.**

2014	2013
Accounts Payable Turnover Ratio:	**Accounts Payable Turnover Ratio:**

2014:

$$= \frac{103,430^a}{(11,250 + 10,290)/2} = \textbf{9.60}$$

	a		COGS	101,770
			Beg. Inventory	(123,218)
			End. Inventory	124,878
			Purchases	103,430

2013:

$$= \frac{96,458^b}{(12,505 + 11,250)/2} = \textbf{8.12}$$

	b		COGS	92,565
			Beg. Inventory	(119,325)
			End. Inventory	123,218
			Purchases	96,458

Accounts Payable Payment Period:	**Accounts Payable Payment Period:**
= 365/9.60 = **38 days**	= 365/8.12 = **45 days**

From this analysis, we can see that Le Château turned over its payables at a faster rate in 2014 than in 2013 (9.60 times versus 8.12 times). On average, Le Château took 38 days to pay its accounts payable in 2014, 7 days quicker than in 2013. While this change would be positive from the perspective of suppliers, it may also indicate that suppliers are tightening the payment terms they are offering the company (that is, requiring it to pay more quickly).

Now that you know how companies account for current liabilities, in the next chapter we'll look at how they account for long-term liabilities.

SUMMARY

1. Explain why current liabilities are of significance to users.

- Working capital is an important liquidity measure in assessing a company's ability to meet its short-term obligations and whether any additional financing is required. A company's current liabilities must be identified and measured in order to correctly determine working capital.

2. Describe the valuation methods for current liabilities.

- Current liabilities are carried at their fair value (or face value).
- They are not discounted to take into account the time value of money because the time period in which they will be settled is short (less than one year).

3. **Identify the current liabilities that arise from transactions with lenders and explain how they are accounted for.**

- Common current liabilities that arise from transactions with lenders include bank indebtedness, short-term loans, and the current portion of long-term debt.

- Bank indebtedness represents a company's use of a line of credit or revolving credit facility. It will normally be repaid with the company's subsequent cash deposits.

- Short-term loans (also known as working capital loans) are often secured by the company's accounts receivable and/or inventory, with the maximum amount of the loan changing as the level of the related security change.

- The current portion of long-term debt represents the principal portion of long-term loans that is due within the next year.

4. **Identify the current liabilities that arise from transactions with suppliers and explain how they are accounted for.**

- Accounts payable (or trade payables) are common current liabilities for all companies.

- They are sometimes considered "free debt" because payment to suppliers is not required for 30 or more days depending on the terms agreed to with the supplier.

5. **Identify the current liabilities that arise from transactions with customers and explain how they are accounted for.**

- Common current liabilities that arise from transactions between a company and its customers include unearned revenue, gift card liability, customer loyalty provision, sales return provision, and warranty provision.

- Unearned revenues (or deferred revenues) represent payments received from customers in advance of them receiving the goods or services being purchased.

- Gift card liabilities arise when customers purchase gift cards (or gift certificates) from a company. Until such time as the gift card is used, the company has a liability. Some gift cards will never be used or never fully used by their owners. This is known as *breakage* and companies record the estimated amount of breakage as revenue, reducing their gift card liability.

- Customer loyalty provisions are related to programs that enable customers to accumulate points or other credits when making purchases. These points can be subsequently redeemed for free goods or services. Companies offering such programs must estimate the value of the outstanding loyalty points and establish a liability for them.

- The sales return provision is established to record the estimated returns based on a company's past experience and market conditions. The Sales Returns and Allowances account, which is a contra revenue account (that is, it reduces sales revenue), is used to record this liability.

- The warranty provision is established to record the estimated costs of honouring any warranties offered by a company and is based on historical warranty claims or industry averages.

6. **Identify the current liabilities that arise from transactions with employees and explain how they are accounted for.**

- Common employee-related current liabilities include wages payable, CPP payable, EI payable, and employee income taxes payable.

- As employees normally work prior to being paid, a liability (wages payable) arises as employees work.

- Employers are responsible for withholding source deductions from the wages of their employees. These include CPP, EI, and income taxes. Employers are also required to pay CPP and EI based on the wages earned by their employees. These source deductions and employer portions result in current liabilities until they are remitted (sent in) to the government.

7. **Identify the current liabilities that arise from transactions with government and explain how they are accounted for.**

- Companies are required to file corporate tax returns (a T2). They must also make monthly income tax instalment payments, which are usually based on the taxes paid in the previous year, with any outstanding taxes due within two months of year end. Until it is paid, any outstanding income tax balance would be a current liability (income taxes payable).

8. **Identify the current liabilities that arise from transactions with shareholders and explain how they are accounted for.**

- The most common liability that companies have to their shareholders is in relation to dividends that have been declared but not yet paid. When dividends are declared, a company establishes a liability (dividends payable) that is extinguished when they are paid, which generally occurs within four to six weeks.

9. **Calculate the accounts payable turnover ratio and average payment period and assess the results.**

- The *accounts payable turnover ratio* can be determined by dividing a company's credit purchases by its average accounts payable. It measures the number of times per year that a company settles (or pays) its trade payables.

- The *average payment period* is equal to 365 days divided by the accounts payable turnover ratio. It measures the number of days on average a company took to pay its accounts payable.

- The results of the accounts payable turnover ratio and average payment period help users assess the extent of any change in the supplier payment portion of the cash-to-cash cycle from one period to another. It is ideally assessed in relation to the credit terms normally available in the industry in which the company operates.

KEY TERMS

Accounts payable turnover (421)
Average payment period (421)
Bank indebtedness (407)
Blended instalment payments (408)
Breakage (412)
Canada Pension Plan (CPP) (416)
Collateral (408)

Contra revenue account (414)
Corporate tax return (420)
Current portion of long-term debt (408)
Customer loyalty provision (410)
Deferred revenue (410)
Employment Insurance (EI) (416)
Gift card liability (410)

Gross wages (417)
Line of credit (407)
Net wages (417)
Partially executed contract (410)
Pay periods (417)
Provision (410)
Provision for warranty claims (410)

Quebec Pension Plan (QPP) (416)
Reclassification entry (408)
Remittance (418)
Revolving credit facilities (407)
Sales return provision (410)
Secured (408)

Source deductions (416)
Standby fees (408)
T2 (420)
Time value of money (406)
Trade payables (409)
Unearned revenue (410)

Unsecured (408)
Wages payable (416)
Warranty provision (414)
Working capital loan (408)

ABBREVIATIONS USED

CPP	Canada Pension Plan
EI	Employment Insurance
QPP	Quebec Pension Plan

SYNONYMS

Accounts payable | Trade accounts payable | Trade payables
Corporate tax return | T2
Unearned revenue | Deferred revenue
Warranty provision | Provision for warranty claims

CHAPTER END REVIEW PROBLEM 1

Answer each of the following questions related to various short-term liabilities.

a. A clothing store sells $5,000 worth of gift cards in December. In January, cards worth $4,000 are redeemed for merchandise that was purchased by the store in November and carried in its inventory at a cost of $2,500. Make summary journal entries for December and January.

b. A company has a payroll of $7,200 for its employees. Income tax of $1,080 is deducted from the employees, as well as $356 for CPP and $135 for EI. The company's CPP premiums matched the employees' CPP contributions and the company had EI premiums of $189. Calculate the total payroll expense for the company, the net amount that is payable to the employees, and the total amount that is payable to the government for this payroll.

c. Prepare all of the journal entries necessary to record the payroll transactions from part "b," including the remittance of the source deductions. Assume that the company pays its employees the same day as the payroll was recorded.

d. A manufacturing company offers a two-year warranty against failure of its products. The estimated cost of repairs and replacements under the warranty (as a percentage of the initial sales revenue) is 2% in the year of the sale and 4% in the following year. Sales and actual warranty costs for 2015 and 2016 (its first two years of operation) were:

	Sales	Actual Warranty Costs Incurred during Year
2015	$2,300,000	$ 45,000
2016	$2,500,000	$140,000

i. What amount of warranty expense should be reported on the statement of income for the year ended December 31, 2015?

ii. What amount of warranty obligation should be reported on the December 31, 2015, statement of financial position?

iii. What amount of warranty obligation should be reported on the December 31, 2016, statement of financial position?

CHAPTER END REVIEW PROBLEM 2

Dollarama Inc. is a Montreal-based company and is the leading operator of dollar stores in Canada, with more than 870 stores. All of the items in the company's stores are sold for $3 or less. The company purchases its merchandise from manufacturers, wholesalers, manufacturers' representatives, and importers. About half of the company's merchandise is purchased from North American vendors and half from suppliers overseas.

The company's financial statements included the following information:

(expressed in thousands of Canadian dollars)

	2014	2013	2012
Merchandise Inventories	364,680	338,385	315,873
Accounts Payable	58,937	50,786	30,751
Cost of Goods Sold	1,299,092	1,163,979	1,002,487

a. Calculate Dollarama's accounts payable turnover ratio for 2014 and 2103.

b. Calculate Dollarama's accounts payable payment period for 2014 and 2013.

c. Comment on whether the company's results have improved or worsened from 2013 to 2014. Why might the company turn over its payables so quickly?

Suggested Solution to Chapter End Review Problem 1

a.

December		
Cash	5,000	
Unearned Revenue (or Gift Card Liability)		5,000
January		
Unearned Revenue (or Gift Card Liability)	4,000	
Sales Revenue		4,000
Cost of Goods Sold	2,500	
Inventory		2,500

b.

Total payroll expense:	Gross Wages	$ 7,200
	+ Employer's CPP premiums	356
	+ Employer's EI premiums	189
		$ 7,745
Net pay:	Gross Wages	$ 7,200
	− Employee income taxes payable	(1,080)
	− Employee's CPP premiums	(356)
	− Employee's EI premiums	(135)
		$ 5,629
Remittance amount:	Employee income taxes payable	$ 1,080
	+ Employee's CPP premiums	356
	+ Employer's CPP premiums	356
	+ Employee's EI premiums	135
	+ Employer's EI premiums	189
		$ 2,116

c.

Employee Entry		
Wage Expense	7,200	
Employee Income Taxes Payable		1,080
CPP Payable		356
EI Payable		135
Cash		5,629

Employer Entry		
Wage Expense	545	
CPP Payable		356
EI Payable		189
Employee Entry		
Employee Income Taxes Payable	1,080	
CPP Payable	712	
EI Payable	324	
Cash		2,116

d. i. The expense that should be recognized in 2015 is calculated as follows: $(0.02 + 0.04) \times \$2,300,000 = \$138,000$. Note that the total expected warranty cost (6% of the sales revenue) should be reported as an expense in the year of the sale.

ii. The liability that should be reported at the end of 2015 is calculated as follows: $0 beginning balance + $138,000 accrued − $45,000 paid = $93,000 ending balance.

iii. The liability that should be reported at the end of 2016 is calculated as follows: $93,000 beginning balance + $([0.02 + 0.04] \times \$2,500,000)$ accrued − $140,000 paid = $103,000 ending balance.

Suggested Solution to Chapter End Review Problem 2

a.

2014				2013		
Accounts Payable Turnover Ratio:				**Accounts Payable Turnover Ratio:**		
$= \dfrac{1,325,387^{1}}{(50,786 + 58,937)/2} = \mathbf{24.2}$				$= \dfrac{1,186,491^{2}}{(30,751 + 50,786)/2} = \mathbf{29.1}$		
1	COGS	1,299,092	2	COGS	1,163,979	
	Beg. Inventory	(338,385)		Beg. Inventory	(315,873)	
	End. Inventory	364,680		End. Inventory	338,385	
	Purchases	1,325,387		Purchases	1,186,491	

b.

Accounts Payable Payment Period:	**Accounts Payable Payment Period:**
$= 365/24.2 = \mathbf{15.1}$ **days**	$= 365/29.1 = \mathbf{12.5}$ **days**

c. The company's accounts payable turnover ratio decreased and its payment period lengthened in 2014. The company took an average of 15.1 days to pay its payables in 2014, about two and half days longer than it took in 2012.

The company likely has a very fast turnover/average payment period because of the nature of its business. Given the low selling prices of their products, dollar stores have to keep their merchandise costs as low as possible. One of the ways to do this would be to take advantage of supplier sales discounts for prompt payment or to negotiate contracts with suppliers that do not require the supplier to finance Dollarama by providing lengthy payment periods.

ASSIGNMENT MATERIAL

Discussion Questions

DQ9-1 List three essential characteristics of a liability.

DQ9-2 Describe, in general terms, why it is appropriate for current liabilities to be carried at their face value.

DQ9-3 Explain the meaning of the terms *gross pay* and *net pay* in regard to employees' earnings.

DQ9-4 Why do you think employers often object when the government increases the rates for CPP, QPP, or EI?

DQ9-5 Explain the meaning of the term *source deductions*.

DQ9-6 Explain why an employer's wage expense will be more than the gross wages earned by its employees.

DQ9-7 Explain why warranty expenses and the actual costs incurred with respect to warranties often do not occur in the same period.

DQ9-8 If a product is sold at the beginning of year 1 with a three-year warranty, should the expected cost of honouring the warranty be spread over years 1, 2, and 3, or recognized entirely in year 1? Explain.

DQ9-9 Identify and explain three of the possible ways that companies can settle their estimated warranty obligations.

DQ9-10 Describe the nature of unearned revenues and provide an example.

DQ9-11 Why do companies use a contra revenue account when recording sales returns?

DQ9-12 Explain why accounts payable are considered to be "free debt."

DQ9-13 Identify and explain two current liabilities that can arise from a company's transactions with its customers.

DQ9-14 Outline what a line of credit is and how it operates.

DQ9-15 Differentiate between secured and unsecured liabilities.

DQ9-16 Explain what is meant by the term *working capital loan*. Is this considered to be a secured borrowing?

DQ9-17 What is meant by the *current portion of long-term debt*? Why is it recorded with the current liabilities?

DQ9-18 Why is the entry to recognize the current portion of long-term debt considered to be a reclassification entry? Why is this entry important in the context of determining a company's current ratio?

DQ9-19 Explain the meaning of the term *provisions*.

DQ9-20 Explain whether a company's suppliers would prefer the company to have a high accounts payable turnover or a low accounts payable turnover.

Application Problems

AP9-1 (Various current liabilities)

Joan's Golf Shop Ltd. had the following transactions involving current liabilities in its first year of operations:

1. The company ordered golf equipment from suppliers for $546,000, on credit. It paid $505,000 to suppliers during the year.
2. The shop has seven employees, who earn gross wages of $230,000 for the year. From this, the company deducted 22% for income taxes, $11,300 in CPP premiums, and $4,300 in EI premiums before distributing the cheques to the staff. As an employer, Joan was also required to match the employees' CPP premiums and pay $6,020 in EI premiums. Eleven-twelfths of the amounts due to the government (all except the last month) were paid before the end of the year.
3. The company gives customers a one-year warranty on golf clubs. Management estimated that warranty costs would total 2% of sales. Sales of golf clubs for the year were $1.1 million. During the year, the company spent $13,000 to replace faulty golf clubs under the warranty.
4. Some customers order very expensive, custom-made golf clubs. In these cases, the company requires them to pay a deposit of 50% of the selling price when the order is placed. During the year, deposits totalling $20,000 were received for custom orders. None of these orders have been delivered yet.

Required:
a. Prepare journal entries to record the transactions.
b. Prepare the current liabilities section of the statement of financial position as it would appear at the end of the year.

AP9-2 (Various current liabilities)

Shamsud Ltd. operates on a calendar-year basis. At the beginning of December 2016, the company had the following current liabilities on its books:

Accounts payable	$85,000
Rent payable	10,000
Warranty provision	12,000
Unearned revenue	14,000

In December, the following events occurred:

1. Shamsud purchased a new computer system on account at a cost of $28,000, payable on January 15, 2017. In addition to this, $4,000 was paid in cash to have the new system installed and customized to the company's requirements.
2. The company purchased inventory for $93,000 on account and made payments of $86,000 to its suppliers.
3. The rent that was payable at the beginning of December represented the payment that should have been made in November. In December, Shamsud paid the past rent owed, as well as the rent for December and January.
4. By December 31, the company had earned $5,000 of the service revenue that was received in advance from customers.
5. Shamsud's employees are paid a total of $2,000 per day. Three work days elapsed between the last payday and the end of the fiscal year. (Ignore deductions for income tax, CPP, and EI.)
6. The company's products are sold with a two-year warranty. Shamsud estimates its warranty expense for the year (not previously recorded) as $16,000. During December, it paid $1,200 in warranty claims.

Required:
a. Prepare the journal entries to record the December transactions and adjustments. (Ignore the amounts that the company pays for its share of CPP and EI.)
b. Prepare the current liability section of Shamsud's statement of financial position on December 31, 2016.

AP9-3 (Various current liabilities)

Required:
Answer each of the following questions related to various short-term liabilities:
a. On September 1, 2016, a company borrowed $100,000 from its bank and signed a nine-month note with 8% interest. The principal and interest on the loan are to be paid when the note matures. What is the total amount related to this loan that should be reported under current liabilities on the company's December 31, 2016, statement of financial position?
b. The balance in a company's long-term mortgage payable account on December 31, 2016, is $150,000. This is to be repaid at the rate of $25,000 per year for the next six years. How should this liability be reported on the company's statement of financial position on December 31, 2016?
c. During the spring and summer of 2016, the Prairie Predators hockey team sold 2,000 season tickets for the 2016–2017 hockey season. Each of the season tickets was sold for $500 and covered 20 games, with 8 to be played in the fall (October to December) and 12 in the winter (January to March). What is the effect on the team's financial statements when the season tickets are sold? What amount of liability (if any) related to the season tickets should be reported on the team's December 31, 2016, statement of financial position?
d. Bathurst Beverages Ltd. collects cash deposits on its returnable bottles and other containers. Past experience indicates that virtually all the bottles and containers will be returned and the deposits refunded. During the current year, the company received $150,000 in such deposits and it disbursed $140,000 for bottles and other containers that were returned. How would this information be reflected in the year-end statement of financial position for Bathurst Beverages?
e. During the current year, a company sold 10,000 units of a product that was covered by a two-year warranty. Past experience indicates that approximately 3% of the units sold will require warranty repairs, at an average cost of $50 per unit. The actual costs incurred during the year for repairs under the warranty totalled $7,000. What amount of liability (if any) should be reported on the company's statement of financial position at the end of the current year?

AP9-4 (Warranty obligations)

A manufacturing company sells its main product with a three-year warranty against defects. The company expects that 1% of the units sold will prove to be defective in the first year after they are sold, 2% will prove to be defective in the second year, and 3% will prove to be defective in the third year. The average cost to repair or replace a defective unit under the warranty is expected to be $60.

The company's sales and warranty costs incurred in its first three years were as follows:

	Units Sold	Actual Costs of Repairs and Replacements under the Warranty Plan
2014	9,000	$ 5,000
2015	12,000	$16,000
2016	17,000	$37,000

Required:
    a. Calculate the amount that should have appeared in the estimated warranty provision account at the end of 2014.
    b. Calculate the amount of warranty expense that should have been recognized in 2015.
    c. Considering the costs incurred to the end of 2016, do you think the company's estimates regarding the warranty costs were too high, too low, or just about right? Explain your reasoning.

AP9-5 (Two types of warranties)

Computers Galore Ltd. sells computers, computer accessories, and software. On its computer sales, the company provides a one-month warranty that is included in the cost of the computer. Claims under the warranties vary from replacing defective parts to providing customers with new computers if repairs cannot be made. During 2016, the estimated cost related to the one-month warranties was $40,000, of which $36,000 had been incurred before year end.

For an additional charge of $100, Computers Galore also offers extended warranty coverage for two years on its computers. This amount is expected to cover the costs associated with the extended warranties. During 2016, Computers Galore sold 800 two-year warranties. The costs incurred during the year for repairs and replacements under these warranties amounted to $31,000. Based on past experience, the company estimates that its total warranty costs over the two-year coverage period will be $60,000.

Required:
    a. Prepare journal entries to record the warranty transactions for 2016.
    b. Should Computers Galore classify its warranty provision as current or non-current? Explain.
    c. If the actual costs incurred by the company under the extended warranties are less than the amount charged for them, how should the company account for the difference?

AP9-6 (Revenues and current liabilities)

University Survival Magazine Ltd. is a small company run by two enterprising university students. They publish an issue of the magazine once a month from September through April. The magazine reports on various university activities and provides information such as how to get the best concert tickets, where the best pizza is sold for the best price, where the good study spots are located, and how to get library personnel to help you with your research assignments.

The magazine is sold either on a prepaid subscription basis for $12.00 for all eight issues, or for $2.00 per issue. During September, 2,000 subscriptions were sold. Up to the end of December, a total of 13,000 single copies were sold.

The company also pre-sells advertising space in the magazine to local businesses that focus on the student market. During July and August, the company signed up several businesses and collected $20,000 in advertising revenues. The advertisements are to be included in all eight issues of the magazine.

The cost of printing and distributing the first four issues of the magazine was $57,000, of which $46,000 was paid by the end of December. Miscellaneous other expenses totalling $2,000 were incurred and paid in cash.

Required:
    a. Journalize all the transactions to the end of December.
    b. Prepare any necessary adjusting entries on December 31.
    c. Prepare a simple statement of income for the magazine, for the period from July to December.
    d. Calculate the balance in the magazine's Cash account on December 31.
    e. Write a brief memo to the owners that explains why their net income is less than the net cash generated by their operations.

AP9-7 (Gift card sales and redemptions)

During the month of December, Emile's Electronics sells $7,000 of gift cards. In January, $5,000 of these cards are redeemed for merchandise with a cost of $3,000. In February, a further $1,500 of these cards are redeemed for merchandise with a cost of $1,000. The company uses a perpetual inventory system.

Required:
    a. Prepare journal entries to record the transactions for December, January, and February.
    b. How much income (if any) was earned in each of these months?
    c. What liability (if any) would appear on the company's statement of financial position at the end of each of these months?

AP9-8 (Payroll)

Hilton Ventures Ltd. had the following transactions:

Oct. 31	Recorded wages earned by the employees during the month, which amounted to $30,000. The source deductions on these wages were CPP of $1,485, EI of $565, and income taxes of $4,600.
Nov. 2	The company paid the wages recorded on October 31.
Nov. 15	Made the remittance to the government related to the October 31 payroll.

a. Determine the amount of the employees' net wages.

b. Prepare the journal entries necessary to record these transactions.

AP9-9 (Payroll, warranty costs, current portion of long-term debt, and interest payable)

Lyrtricks Ltd., which has a December 31 year end, had the following transactions in December 2016 and January 2017:

2016	
Dec. 1	The company borrowed $100,000 from a bank on a five-year loan payable. The terms of the loan stipulate that Lyrtricks must repay 1/5 of the principal every November 30 plus the interest accrued to that date. The loan bears interest at 9% per annum.
Dec. 31	Accrued warranty expense, which is estimated at 2% of sales for the month of $145,000.
Dec. 31	Recorded employee wages for December. The wages earned by employees amounted to $10,000 and the company withheld CPP of $576, EI of $486, and income taxes of $2,200. Lyrtricks' employer contributions were $576 for CPP and $680 for EI.
Dec. 31	Recorded the adjusting entry to record the interest incurred on the bank loan during December.
Dec. 31	Recorded the entry to reclassify the current portion of the bank loan.
2017	
Jan. 2	The company paid the wages recorded on December 31.
Jan. 10	A customer returned a defective product that was still under warranty. The product was not usable and the customer requested and received a full refund in the amount of $800.
Jan. 15	Made the remittance to the government related to the December 31 payroll.

Required:

Prepare all necessary journal entries related to the above transactions.

User Perspective Problems

UP9-1 (Effects of changes in CPP and EI rates)

Suppose you are the general manager of a company with approximately 100 employees and the government has just announced its new rates for contributions to the Canada Pension Plan and Employment Insurance. With respect to employee contributions, assume that the CPP rate is increasing from 4.95% to 5.20% and the EI rate is increasing from 1.88% to 1.98%. Assume that the company's required contributions for CPP and EI remain the same.

Required:

Assuming that gross wages amount to $6 million per year, calculate the financial impact that these changes will have on (a) the employees' net pay, and (b) the company's payroll costs.

UP9-2 (Accounting for customer loyalty program)

Suppose that you are the manager of a chain of coffee shops and you are planning to launch a loyalty program that will give one free coffee to customers who buy 10 cups of coffee. Customers will be given an electronic "Coffee Club" card, which will be swiped each time they make a purchase. Your computer system will keep track of how many cups each customer has purchased and will automatically award them a free cup when they have purchased 10.

Required:

Discuss the income measurement and liability recognition issues that are presented by this type of customer loyalty program. Your answer should explain how and when the revenues associated with the free cups of coffee should be reported. It should also outline some of the issues that will make it difficult to estimate the amount of the liability for future free coffees arising from current sales.

UP9-3 (Working capital loans)

You are negotiating financing with a commercial lender and it has proposed the following:

"The maximum amounts that can be drawn on the operating loan are subject to margin limitations based on the Company's trade receivables and inventory levels. The operating loan is repayable upon demand."

Required:

Explain what the lender is proposing and the implications these terms will have for the amount of the loan and its presentation for accounting purposes.

UP9-4 (Accounts payable turnover ratio and average payment period)

Your company's largest supplier has just notified you that it is changing its credit and payment terms. Previously, its standard terms were "n/30" and the company had no electronic payment option. Under its new policy, all customers (including your company) will have terms "2/10; n/30" and all payments must be by electronic funds transfer.

Required:

Explain the effect that these changes should have on your company's accounts payable turnover ratio and average payment period. Be sure your answer provides sufficient rationale for your position.

UP9-5 (Accounts payable turnover ratio and average payment period)

You are an analyst focused on the retail sector. In reviewing the financial statements of one of the companies you follow, you note that its accounts payable turnover ratio is significantly higher than those of all of the comparative companies in the sector.

Required:

Explain whether your report on this company for your firm's investing clients would note that this is a positive or a negative factor. Be sure that your response is somewhat balanced by providing some rationale for both perspectives.

Reading and Interpreting Published Financial Statements

RI9-1 (Deferred revenue)

Exhibit 9-1 is an extract from the **University of Saskatchewan**'s 2012/13 annual report. (Most post-secondary institutions in Canada have a fiscal year that ends on March 31, so it includes transactions from part of two calendar years.)

EXHIBIT 9-1	EXCERPT FROM THE UNIVERSITY OF SASKATCHEWAN'S 2012/13 ANNUAL REPORT

11. Deferred Revenue

	April 30		May 1
	2013	2012	2011
Student fees	$5,844	$6,177	$4,063
Unearned revenue-ancillary operations	629	553	387

Required:

a. Explain, in your own words, what deferred revenue represents in general. Also identify three types of transactions that could have given rise to the deferred revenue in Note 11 above.

b. Your own university's or college's most recent financial statements are generally available on-line through its website. Obtain a copy and determine the amount of the institution's deferred revenue.

RI9-2 (Line of credit, interest rates, and security)

Note 6 (Exhibit 9-2) of **Le Château**'s 2014 financial statements discusses the company's line of credit.

EXHIBIT 9-2	EXCERPT FROM LE CHÂTEAU INC.'S 2014 FINANCIAL STATEMENTS

6. CREDIT FACILITIES

On April 25, 2012, the Company entered into a Credit Agreement for an asset based credit facility of $70.0 million, replacing its previous banking facility. The revolving credit facility is collateralized by the Company's credit card accounts receivable and inventories, as defined in the agreement. The facility has a term of 3 years, and consists of revolving credit loans, which include both a swing line loan facility limited to $15.0 million and a letter of credit facility limited to $15.0 million. The available borrowings bear interest at a rate based on the Canadian prime rate, plus an applicable margin ranging from 0.75% to 1.50%, or a banker's acceptance rate, plus an applicable margin ranging from 2.00% to 2.75%. The Company is required to pay a standby fee ranging from 0.25% to 0.375% on the unused portion of the revolving credit. The Credit Agreement requires the Company to comply with certain covenants, including restrictions with respect to the payment of dividends and the purchase of the Company's shares under certain circumstances. As at January 25, 2014, the Company had drawn $30.6 million [2013 − $13.6 million] under this credit facility and had an outstanding standby letter of credit totaling $700,000 [2013 − $500,000] which reduced the availability under this credit facility.

Required:

a. What does it mean that the company has an operating line of credit of $70 million available? What kind of institution is the line of credit likely with?

b. The information regarding the interest rate on Le Château's line of credit refers to *Canadian prime rate*. What does this term mean? Is this a fixed interest rate?

c. Le Château is required to pay a standby fee ranging from 0.250% to 0.375% on unused portions of the revolving credit. What does this mean and why would an institution charge this type of fee?

d. Is Le Château's operating line of credit secured or unsecured? Explain what this means and why a company might prefer to have its debt secured.

RI9-3 (Line of credit, gift cards, and loyalty program)

Reitmans is a Canadian company that specializes in the sale of women's wear at retail. Exhibits 9-3A to C contain three notes from the company's 2014 annual report. All figures are expressed in thousands of dollars.

EXHIBIT 9-3A	EXCERPT FROM REITMANS' 2014 ANNUAL REPORT, MANAGEMENT DISCUSSION AND ANALYSIS

The Company has unsecured borrowing and working capital credit facilities available up to an amount of $125,000 or its U.S. dollar equivalent. As at February 1, 2014, $30,270 (February 2, 2013 – $46,792) of the operating lines of credit were committed for documentary and standby letters of credit. These credit facilities are used principally for U.S. dollar letters of credit to satisfy international third-party vendors which require such backing before confirming purchase orders issued by the Company and to support U.S. dollar foreign exchange forward contract purchases. The Company rarely uses such credit facilities for other purposes.

The Company has granted irrevocable standby letters of credit, issued by highly-rated financial institutions, to third parties to indemnify them in the event the Company does not perform its contractual obligations. As at February 1, 2014, the maximum potential liability under these guarantees was $5,019 (February 2, 2013 – $5,014). The standby letters of credit mature at various dates during fiscal 2015. The Company has recorded no liability with respect to these guarantees, as the Company does not expect to make any payments for these items.

EXHIBIT 9-3B	EXCERPT FROM REITMANS' 2014 ANNUAL REPORT, NOTE 12

12 Trade and other payables

	February 1, 2014	February 2, 2013
Trade payables	$ 49,593	$41,494
Non-trade payables due to related parties	55	74
Other non-trade payables	10,878	319
Personnel liabilities	25,566	24,443
Payables relating to premises	15,777	13,489
Provision for sales returns	707	756
	102,576	80,575
Less non-current portion	11,842	11,425
	$ 90,734	$69,150

The non-current portion of trade and other payables, which is included in payables relating to premises, represents the portion of deferred rent to be amortized and other payables beyond the next twelve months.

EXHIBIT 9-3C	EXCERPT FROM REITMANS' 2014 ANNUAL REPORT, NOTE 3(O)

O) REVENUE

Revenue is recognized from the sale of merchandise when a customer purchases and takes delivery of the merchandise. Reported sales are net of returns and estimated possible returns and exclude sales taxes.

Gift cards sold are recorded as deferred revenue and revenue is recognized when the gift cards are redeemed. An estimate is made of gift cards not expected to be redeemed based on the terms of the gift cards and historical redemption patterns.

Loyalty points and awards granted under customer loyalty programs are recognized as a separate component of revenue, and are deferred at the date of initial sale. Revenue is recognized when the loyalty points and awards are redeemed and the Company has fulfilled its obligation. The amount of revenue deferred is measured based on the fair value of loyalty points and awards granted, taking into consideration the estimated redemption percentage.

Required:
    a. Refer to Exhibit 9-3A. Explain why Reitmans uses letters of credit and how the working capital loan relates to them.
    b. Refer to Exhibit 9-3B. If Reitman's costs of goods sold for the year ending February 1, 2014, was $377,913, thousand and the company began the year with $93,317 thousand in inventory and ended with $109,601 thousand, calculate the accounts payable turnover ratio and average payment period.
    c. Refer to Exhibit 9-3C and explain in your own words how Reitmans accounts for deferred revenue.

RI9-4 (Sales returns and warranties/contingencies)

Canadian Tire Corporation, Limited is composed of two main business operations that offer a range of retail goods and services, including general merchandise, apparel, sporting goods, petroleum, and financial services. Exhibit 9-4 contains Note 3 setting out the accounting policies applied for sales and warranty returns and customer loyalty programs and Note 21 detailing Canadian Tire's provisions from the company's 2013 financial statements.

EXHIBIT 9-4	EXCERPT FROM CANADIAN TIRE CORPORATION, LIMITED'S 2013 ANNUAL REPORT

3. Significant accounting policies

Sales and warranty returns
The provision for sales and warranty returns relates to the Company's obligation for defective goods in current store inventories and defective goods sold to customers that have yet to be returned, as well as after sales service for replacement parts. Accruals for sales and warranty returns are estimated on the basis of historical returns and are recorded so as to allocate them to the same period the corresponding revenue is recognized. These accruals are reviewed regularly and updated to reflect management's best estimate; however, actual returns could vary from these estimates.

Customer loyalty
Provisions for the fair value of loyalty program redemptions are estimated on the basis of historical redemptions. The provisions are reviewed regularly and updated to reflect management's best estimate; however, actual redemptions could vary from these estimates.

21. Provisions

The following table presents the changes to the Company's provisions:

(C$ in millions)	Sales and Warranty Returns	Site Restoration and Decommissioning	Onerous Contracts	Customer Loyalty	Other	Total
Balance, beginning of year	$ 111.3	$ 34.6	$4.7	$ 73.2	$ 16.8	$ 240.6
Charges, net of reversals	234.9	7.6	0.5	131.8	8.6	383.4
Utilizations	(236.7)	(6.1)	(2.0)	(133.8)	(8.8)	(387.4)
Unwinding of discount	—	0.6	—	—	1.4	2.0
Change in discount rate	—	(4.3)	—	—	—	(4.3)
Balance, end of year	$ 109.5	$32.4	$3.2	$ 71.2	$ 18.0	$ 234.3
Current provisions	105.4	9.4	3.0	69.8	8.5	196.1
Long-term provisions	$ 4.1	$ 23.0	$0.2	$ 1.4	$ 9.5	$ 38.2

Required:
    a. Using the information from Notes 3 and 21 in Exhibit 9-4, explain how Canadian Tire accounts for its sales and warranty returns provision, including the financial impacts on the company's 2013 financial statements.
    b. The Canadian Tire "money" program is the company's most significant loyalty program. Using the information from Notes 3 and 21 in Exhibit 9-4, explain how the company accounts for its loyalty programs, including the financial impacts on the company's 2013 financial statements.

RI9-5 (Unearned revenue/gift card, accounts payable turnover ratio, and accounts payable payment period)

The Second Cup Ltd. is Canada's largest specialty coffee café franchisor (as measured by the number of cafés), with 360 cafés. Exhibits 9-5A to C contain Second Cup's statement of financial position, Note 12 detailing accounts payable and accrued liabilities, and Note 3(n).

| EXHIBIT 9-5A | THE SECOND CUP LTD.'S 2013 STATEMENTS OF FINANCIAL POSITION |

STATEMENTS OF FINANCIAL POSITION
As at December 28, 2013 and December 29, 2012
(Expressed in thousands of Canadian dollars)

	December 28, 2013	December 29, 2012
ASSETS		
Current assets		
Cash and cash equivalents	$ 6,501	$ 3,880
Trade and other receivables (note 7)	4,368	4,616
Notes and leases receivable (note 8)	220	265
Inventories (note 9)	123	137
Prepaid expenses and other assets	190	695
	11,402	9,593
Non-current assets		
Notes and leases receivable (note 8)	701	741
Property and equipment (note 10)	3,507	3,544
Intangible assets (note 11)	61,730	74,802
Total assets	$ 77,340	$ 88,680
LIABILITIES		
Current liabilities		
Accounts payable and accrued liabilities (note 12)	$ 4,586	$ 3,123
Provisions (note 13)	847	448
Other liabilities (note 14)	717	720
Income tax payable	138	318
Gift card liability	3,895	4,560
Deposits from franchise partners	878	1,480
	11,061	10,649
Non-current liabilities		
Provisions (note 13)	1,380	683
Other liabilities (note 14)	428	421
Long-term debt (note 15)	11,089	11,037
Deferred income taxes	7,418	9,190
Total liabilities	31,376	31,980
SHAREHOLDERS' EQUITY	45,964	56,700
Total liabilities and shareholders' equity	$ 77,340	$ 88,680

| EXHIBIT 9-5B | EXCERPT FROM THE SECOND CUP LTD.'S 2013 ANNUAL REPORT, NOTE 12 |

12. ACCOUNTS PAYABLE AND ACCRUED LIABILITIES

Accounts payable and accrued liabilities consist of:

	2013	2012
Accounts payable - trade	$ 1,953	$ 1,280
Accrued salaries, wages, benefits, and incentives	362	577
Sales tax payable	335	235
Accrued liabilities	1,936	1,031
	$ 4,586	$ 3,123

EXHIBIT 9-5C   **EXCERPT FROM THE SECOND CUP LTD.'S 2013 ANNUAL REPORT, NOTE 3(N)**

n. Gift card liability

Second Cup has a gift card program that allows customers to prepay for future purchases by loading a dollar value onto their gift cards through cash or credit/debit cards in the cafés or online through credit cards, when and as needed. The gift card liability represents liabilities related to unused balances on the Second Cup Café Card net of estimated breakage. These balances are included as sales from franchised cafés, or as revenue of Company-operated cafés, at the time the customer redeems the amount in a café for products.

The gift cards do not have an expiration date and the Company does not deduct non-usage fees from outstanding gift card balances. When the Company determines the likelihood of the gift card being redeemed by the customer is remote and there is not a legal obligation to remit the unredeemed gift cards to a relevant jurisdiction, this amount is recorded as breakage. The determination of the gift card breakage rate is based upon Company-specific historical load and redemption patterns. During 2013, the Company revised its estimated breakage rate from 2% to 3% of gift card sales. Gift card breakage is recognized on a pro rata basis based on historical gift card redemption patterns commencing after a reasonable period from the date of the gift card sale. Breakage is recognized in other operating expenses in the Statements of Operations and Comprehensive Loss and a portion is allocated to the Co-op Fund.

Required:

    a. Refer to Note 3(n) in Exhibit 9-5C. How does Second Cup account for gift card sales? Provide an explanation of breakage.

    b. Calculate the current ratio for 2013 and 2012. Comment on the company's ability to meet its current liabilities. Has it improved over the prior year?

    c. Calculate the accounts payable turnover ratio and accounts payable payment period. Second Cup's cost of goods sold was $4,054 thousand for its 2013 fiscal year. Comment on these ratios.

RI9-6 (Wages)

Gamehost Inc., a Calgary-based company, operates a number of hotels and casinos in Alberta. Exhibit 9-6 contains Note 5(a) from the company's financial statements for the year ended December 31, 2013. It outlines the company's human resource–related costs.

EXHIBIT 9-6   **EXCERPT FROM GAMEHOST INC.'S 2013 ANNUAL REPORT**

Human resources	twelve months ended December 31		three months ended December 31	
	2013	2012	2013	2012
Wages and salaries	17.1	16.9	4.6	4.4
Canada Pension Plan remittances	0.7	0.7	—	0.2
Employment Insurance remittances	0.5	0.4	0.3	0.1
Other human resource related expenses	1.2	1.3	0.3	0.3
	19.5	19.3	5.2	5.0

(in millions of dollars unless stated otherwise)

Required:

    a. Calculate Gamehost's CPP and EI remittances as a percentage of wages and salaries.

    b. Calculate other human resource–related expenses as a percentage of wages and salaries.

    c. Calculate the total additional CPP, EI, and other human resource–related expenses that Gamehost would be expected to incur if it expected salaries and wages cost to increase in 2014 by the same percentage it changed between 2012 and 2013.

RI9-7 (Deposits)

Big Rock Brewery Inc. is a regional producer of craft beers and cider that are sold in nine provinces and three territories in Canada. Exhibit 9-7 contains Note 3.10 detailing Big Rock's policy regarding keg deposits from the 2013 annual report.

| EXHIBIT 9-7 | **EXCERPT FROM BIG ROCK BREWERY INC.'S 2013 ANNUAL REPORT** |

3.10 Keg Deposits

Big Rock requires that customers pay deposits for kegs purchased which are reflected as a liability on the Corporation's consolidated statement of financial position. The deposits are subsequently refunded to customers via invoice credits or cash payments when kegs are returned. In the normal course of business, there are a percentage of kegs which are never returned for refund. As a result, Big Rock performs an analysis based on factors such as total kegs produced, current inventory rates and average keg turnover. In addition, return percentages are calculated and tracked to estimate an average keg turnover rate. Together, this information is used to estimate a keg deposit liability at each reporting date. Any adjustments required to the keg liability account are recorded through revenue.

Required:

Refer to Note 3.10 in Exhibit 9-7 and in your own words explain how Big Rock accounts for keg deposits.

RI9-8 (Financial statement analysis)

Ten Peaks Coffee Company Inc. is a Burnaby, British Columbia–based specialty coffee company. The company provides green coffee decaffeination services as well as green coffee handling and storage services. Exhibit 9-8 contains an excerpt from Ten Peaks' 2013 annual report.

| EXHIBIT 9-8 | **TEN PEAKS COFFEE COMPANY INC.'S 2013 CONSOLIDATED STATEMENTS OF FINANCIAL POSITION** |

TEN PEAKS COFFEE COMPANY INC.
Consolidated Statements of Financial Position
(Tabular amounts in thousands of Canadian dollars, except per share and number of shares figures) as at

	Note	December 31 2013	December 31 2012
Assets			
Current assets			
Inventories	6	$ 6,463	$ 9,494
Accounts receivable	7	4,972	3,962
Prepaid expenses and other receivables		236	169
Derivative assets	8	152	227
Cash		2,594	1,304
Total current assets		14,417	15,156
Non-current assets			
Plant and equipment	9	12,508	13,298
Intangible assets	10	2,465	2,724
Deferred tax assets	11	1,578	2,058
Derivative assets	8	-	37
Total non-current assets		16,551	18,117
Total assets		$ 30,968	$ 33,273
Liabilities and shareholders' equity			
Current liabilities			
Bank indebtedness	12	$ 4,786	$ 6,983
Accounts payable		916	1,559
Accrued liabilities		1,100	1,066
Dividend payable		417	417
Derivative liabilities	8	119	11
Current income tax liabilities	11	18	-
Current portion of other liabilities	13	219	-
Total current liabilities		7,575	10,036

continued

EXHIBIT 9-8	TEN PEAKS COFFEE COMPANY INC.'S 2013 CONSOLIDATED STATEMENTS OF FINANCIAL POSITION (continued)

	Note	December 31 2013	December 31 2012
Non-current liabilities			
Derivative liabilities	8	131	–
Other liabilities	13	28	69
Asset retirement obligation	14	725	705
Total non-current liabilities		884	774
Total liabilities		8,459	10,810
Shareholders' equity			
Share capital	15	24,631	24,631
Share-based compensation reserve		106	45
Deficit		(2,228)	(2,213)
Total equity		22,509	22,463
Total liabilities and shareholders' equity		$30,968	$33,273

Required:

a. Calculate the accounts payable turnover ratio and accounts payable payment period for Ten Peaks. The company's cost of goods sold for its 2013 fiscal year was $47,662 thousand.

b. Calculate the company's current and quick ratio for 2012 and 2013. Comment on the year-over-year trend.

RI9-9 (Financial statement analysis)

Gildan Activewear Inc. is principally in the business of manufacturing and selling activewear, socks, and underwear. Exhibits 9-9A and B contain the statements of financial position and statements of income and comprehensive income from Gildan's 2013 annual report.

EXHIBIT 9-9A	GILDAN ACTIVEWEAR INC.'S 2013 CONSOLIDATED STATEMENTS OF FINANCIAL POSITION

GILDAN ACTIVEWEAR INC.
CONSOLIDATED STATEMENTS OF FINANCIAL POSITION
(in thousands of U.S. dollars)

	September 29, 2013	September 30, 2012
Current assets:		
Cash and cash equivalents (note 6)	$ 97,368	$ 70,410
Trade accounts receivable (note 7)	255,018	257,595
Income taxes receivable	700	353
Inventories (note 8)	595,794	553,068
Prepaid expenses and deposits	14,959	14,451
Assets held for sale (note 18)	5,839	8,029
Other current assets	11,034	8,694
Total current assets	980,712	912,600
Non-current assets:		
Property, plant and equipment (note 9)	655,869	552,437
Intangible assets (note 10)	247,537	259,981
Goodwill (note 10)	150,099	143,833
Investment in joint venture	–	12,126
Deferred income taxes (note 19)	1,443	4,471
Other non-current assets	7,991	10,989
Total non-current assets	1,062,939	983,837
Total assets	$ 2,043,651	$ 1,896,437

continued

EXHIBIT 9-9A	GILDAN ACTIVEWEAR INC.'S 2013 CONSOLIDATED STATEMENTS OF FINANCIAL POSITION (continued)

	September 29, 2013	September 30, 2012
Current liabilities:		
Accounts payable and accrued liabilities	$ 289,414	$ 256,442
Total current liabilities	289,414	256,442
Non-current liabilities:		
Long-term debt (note 11)	-	181,000
Employee benefit obligations (note 12)	18,486	19,612
Provisions (note 13)	16,325	13,042
Total non-current liabilities	34,811	213,654
Total liabilities	324,225	470,096
Commitments, guarantees and contingent liabilities (note 24)		
Equity:		
Share capital	107,867	101,113
Contributed surplus	28,869	25,579
Retained earnings	1,583,346	1,306,724
Accumulated other comprehensive income	(656)	(7,075)
Total equity attributable to shareholders of the Company	1,719,426	1,426,341
Total liabilities and equity	$ 2,043,651	$ 1,896,437

EXHIBIT 9-9B	GILDAN ACTIVEWEAR INC.'S 2013 CONSOLIDATED STATEMENTS OF EARNINGS AND COMPREHENSIVE INCOME

GILDAN ACTIVEWEAR INC.
CONSOLIDATED STATEMENTS OF EARNINGS AND COMPREHENSIVE INCOME
Years ended September 29, 2013 and September 30, 2012
(in thousands of U.S. dollars, except per share data)

	2013	2012
Net sales	$ 2,184,303	$ 1,948,253
Cost of sales	1,550,266	1,552,128
Gross profit	634,037	396,125
Selling, general and administrative expenses (note 17(a))	282,563	226,035
Restructuring and acquisition-related costs (note 18)	8,788	14,962
Operating income	342,686	155,128
Financial expenses, net (note 15(c))	12,013	11,598
Equity earnings in investment in joint venture	(46)	(597)
Earnings before income taxes	330,719	144,127
Income tax expense (recovery) (note 19)	10,541	(4,337)
Net earnings	320,178	148,464
Other comprehensive income (loss), net of related income taxes (note 15(d)):		
Cash flow hedges	6,419	(6,399)
Actuarial gain on employee benefit obligations	436	323
	6,855	(6,076)
Comprehensive income	$ 327,033	$ 142,388

Required:
    a. Calculate the company's working capital for 2013 and 2012.
    b. Calculate the current and quick ratios for 2013 and 2012 and comment on any trends you noticed.
    c. Calculate the accounts payable turnover ratio and accounts payable payment period for the company.

Cases

C9-1 Greenway Medical Equipment Corporation

At a recent meeting of the board of directors of Greenway Medical Equipment Corporation, the company's chief financial officer, Robert Ables, presented a draft set of financial statements for the year. It is Greenway's corporate policy that the directors be allowed to review the financial statements before they are finalized.

    Following the meeting, Mr. Ables received a memo from Dr. Clarise Locklier that included questions about the draft financial statements. Dr. Locklier is a relatively new member of the board of directors and is not familiar with some of the accounting terms and concepts used in the statements. Before voting on approval of the financial statements at the next board meeting, she has several questions she would like to have answered.

MEMORANDUM

To: Robert Ables, CFO

From: Dr. Clarise Locklier, Director

Re: Draft financial statements

I have carefully reviewed the financial statements that you presented to the board last week. Being a physician, I do not have a lot of experience reading accounting information and I am confused about several items presented in the financial statements. I hope that you will clarify the following points for me.

1. I always thought that revenues are reported on the statement of income, so I was confused to see unearned revenues listed as a liability on the statement of financial position. How can revenues be reported on the statement of financial position? As well, if these revenues haven't been earned, shouldn't they be reported in a later period—when they have been earned—rather than in the current period?

2. In one of the notes to the financial statements, you state that the liability for warranty costs is based on an estimate, rather than on the actual warranty repair costs. If we know what our actual costs were for the year, why do we need to use an estimate?

3. I notice that in the current liabilities section of the statement of financial position you have listed an item called "current portion of long-term debt." How can debt be current and long-term at the same time? Also, since the long-term debt is also included as a liability on the statement of financial position, aren't we overstating our liabilities if we report the debt in this manner?

I would appreciate a response to these questions prior to our next board meeting, so that I can feel more comfortable approving the financial statements.

Thank you for your time in addressing these matters.

Required:
As Robert Ables, prepare a memo to Dr. Locklier addressing her concerns.

C9-2 Hanson Consulting

Jenny Ji, a recent business school graduate, is renegotiating her contract with her employer, Hanson Consulting Ltd., which offers business consulting services. Jenny knows it is important that she negotiate a good contract, because the amount of her raise will become a benchmark for the raises to be received by Hanson's 14 other staff consultants. Currently, Jenny and the other consultants are receiving payroll transfers into their personal bank accounts averaging $4,000 per month.

Under her existing contract, Jenny is allowed to review Hanson's annual financial statements. She is puzzled when she sees that Hanson is reporting over $900,000 in consulting salaries on its annual statement of earnings, because she knows that she and the other consultants are paid a total of $720,000 per year (that is, 15 consultants × $4,000 per month × 12 months). Jenny approaches you, the company controller, to see why the consulting salaries on the statement of earnings are higher than the amounts paid to the employees. She suspects that the company may have posted other expenses to the Consulting Salaries account, in order to improve its bargaining position for the contract negotiations.

Required:

Explain to Jenny why the company's payroll costs are significantly higher than the net amounts being received by the employees.

C9-3 Slip-n-Slide Water Park

It is July 31 and the Slip-n-Slide Water Park Ltd. has just completed its first three months of operations. The company's owners, Kelly and Derek Lurz, are very pleased with the results of operations and are trying to prepare the company's first set of financial statements. You have been controller for a local firm for several years and are good friends with Kelly and Derek, so the couple approaches you with some questions about how certain items should be recorded in their financial statements.

Kelly: To promote the park and encourage people to bring their kids to it, we gave away 1,000 coupons for free ice cream cones at our canteen, to be redeemed any time during the summer. We usually charge $1.50 for an ice cream, but the cost is only $0.50 per cone. Two hundred of these coupons have been redeemed already. What should we report about the coupons that have been redeemed, and do we need to report anything about the 800 coupons that haven't been used?

Derek: I can figure out how to record most revenues and expenses, but I don't know how to treat the revenues associated with the 300 season passes that we sold in May and June. They were sold for $60 each and are good for June, July, and August. Holders of season passes have unlimited access to the park for these three months.

Kelly: The other problem we have is that we just took out a $60,000 bank loan. The 10-year loan agreement requires us to repay $500 of the principal of the loan each month, plus interest at the rate of 8%. Since we'll be making payments on this loan in the next year, I think we should record the $60,000 as a current liability, but Derek thinks it should be recorded as a long-term liability, since it will be 10 years before it is fully repaid.

Required:

Provide the owners with advice on how each of these items should be recorded in the July 31 financial statements. Be sure to explain why they should report the items as you recommend.

ENDNOTES

1. Jennifer Horn, "Comparing Loyalty Programs in Canada," StrategyOnline.ca, August 13, 2013; "Indigo Celebrates Two Sweet Milestones with plum rewards," company news release, September 13, 2012; Alicia Androich and Kristin Laird, "Secrets of Canada's Top Loyalty Programs," *Marketing Magazine*, April 7, 2011; Indigo Books & Music Inc. 2013 annual report.
2. Ten Peaks Coffee Company Inc.'s 2013 annual report.
3. High Liner Foods Incorporated's 2013 annual report, Note 12.
4. Reitmans (Canada) Limited's 2014 annual report, Note 14.
5. Cineplex Inc.'s 2013 annual report, Note 14.
6. Canadian Tire Corporation, Limited's 2013 annual report, Note 20.
7. VIA Rail Canada Inc.'s 2013 annual report, Note 17.
8. WestJet Airlines Ltd.'s 2013 annual report, Notes 1 and 19.
9. Indigo Books & Music Inc.'s 2014 annual report, Notes 4 and 19.
10. Carolyn Nicander Mohr, "Kiind: A Different Kind of Gift Card," WonderOfTech.com, December 20, 2013; Ivor Tossell, "Buy Now, Pay-Later Gift Cards Come to Canada," *The Globe and Mail*, December 9, 2013; CBC News, "Pay-Later Gift Card Service Launched by B.C. Startup," July 10, 2013.

11. Shoppers Drug Mart Corporation's 2013 annual report, Note 3(c)(i).
12. Danier Leather Inc.'s 2014 annual report, Note 10.
13. Bombardier Inc.'s 2013 annual report, Notes 2 and 24.
14. Open Text Corporation's 2013 annual report, Note 9.
15. WorkSafeBC.com.
16. KPMG Provincial Payroll and Health Fund Taxes.
17. PwC Tax Facts and Figures Canada 2013.
18. YMCA of Greater Toronto's audited financial statements for year ending March 31, 2013.
19. Big Rock Brewery Inc.'s 2013 annual report, Note 20.

CORE QUESTIONS

If you are able to answer the following questions, then you have achieved the related learning objectives.

LEARNING OBJECTIVES

After studying this chapter, you should be able to:

●●● INTRODUCTION

- Why are long-term liabilities of significance to users?

1 Explain why long-term liabilities are of significance to users.

●●● LONG-TERM LIABILITIES ARISING FROM TRANSACTIONS WITH LENDERS

- What long-term liabilities arise from transactions with lenders?
- How are long-term loans and mortgages accounted for?
- What are bonds and how do they differ from long-term loans?
- How are bonds priced in the marketplace?
- How does the pricing of bonds affect a company's interest expense?

2 Identify the long-term liabilities that arise from transactions with lenders and explain how they are accounted for.

●●● LONG-TERM LIABILITIES ARISING FROM TRANSACTIONS WITH OTHER CREDITORS

- What long-term liabilities arise from transactions with other creditors?
- Why do companies lease capital assets?
- What are the differences between a finance lease and an operating lease? How are they accounted for?

3 Identify the long-term liabilities that arise from transactions with other creditors and explain how they are accounted for.

●●● LONG-TERM LIABILITIES ARISING FROM TRANSACTIONS WITH EMPLOYEES

- What long-term liabilities arise from transactions with employees?
- What are the differences between defined benefit, defined contribution, and hybrid pension plans?
- What are other post-employment benefits?

4 Identify the long-term liabilities that arise from transactions with employees and explain how they are accounted for.

●●● LONG-TERM LIABILITIES ARISING FROM DIFFERENCES BETWEEN ACCOUNTING STANDARDS AND THE INCOME TAX ACT

- What long-term liabilities arise as a result of differences between accounting standards and the Income Tax Act?

5 Identify the long-term liabilities that arise from differences between accounting standards and income tax regulations or law.

●●● COMMITMENTS AND CONTINGENCIES

- How are contractual commitments and guarantees reflected in the financial statements?

6 Explain what commitments and guarantees are and how they are treated.

- What are contingent liabilities and how are they accounted for?

7 Explain contingencies and how they are accounted for.

●●● FINANCIAL STATEMENT ANALYSIS

- How do users assess a company's degree of leverage?
- How do users assess a company's ability to service its long-term debt obligations?

8 Calculate leverage and coverage ratios and use the information from these ratios to assess a company's financial health.

●●● Avoiding Pension Turbulence

As you embark your career, retirement may be the last thing on your mind. But an understanding of pension basics can help you assess the compensation being offered by employers and will help you determine how much you'll have to save for retirement and how long you'll need to work.

A prolonged period of low interest rates, which resulted in poor returns for pension funds, and retirees living longer have contributed to the underfunding of many defined benefit pension funds, which are pensions that provide specific retirement benefits. In other words, the estimated pensions payable to retirees exceeded plan assets. All of this resulted in considerable discussion and debate regarding pensions and, in turn, to significant changes, including the emergence of a new type of plan, the hybrid plan. These changes have had consequences for both the employees who belong to these plans and their employers.

Air Canada is an example of a Canadian company that has experienced such changes. As of 2011, new employees in many areas of the company, including flight attendants, mechanics, and customer service agents, become members in a hybrid pension plan. This change means that, rather than belonging to a defined benefit plan, their plan is part defined benefit and part defined contribution. The result is that these new employees share more of the risk related to the amount of their eventual pensions than do their co-workers hired before these changes.

At the start of the 2013 fiscal year, Air Canada's pension plans had a $3.7-billion deficit. But as at January 1, 2014, the plans had a small surplus. Among other things, the airline credits a higher rate of return on investments in 2013 (at 13.8%), reductions to early-retirement benefits that lowered the plan's deficit by $970 million, and a $225-million company contribution to the plan.

"It is difficult to overstate the significance of this development," wrote President and CEO Calin Rovinescu in Air Canada's 2013 annual report. "It provides reassurance to our employees and retirees that their pensions are secure. Moreover, it provides encouragement to the investment community, which tended to regard the [pension] solvency deficit as some form of overhanging corporate debt which diminished Air Canada's market value."

According to Statistics Canada, fewer than 40% of Canadians were covered by an employer pension plan in 2011 and this proportion was shrinking. Understanding what, if any, pension exists in your workplace is important, as is understanding the implications of any proposed changes. This knowledge will help you plan for a secure retirement, as will knowledge of how to invest your other savings wisely—something this text can provide you with the tools to do.[1]

INTRODUCTION

Employee pension plans like **Air Canada**'s in our feature story are just one type of long-term liability that a company may have. Other common long-term liabilities include long-term loans, bonds payable, and future income taxes. This chapter will discuss how to evaluate a company's long-term liabilities, which can often be large amounts and last a long time.

■ **LEARNING OBJECTIVE 1**
Explain why long-term liabilities are of significance to users.

Why are long-term liabilities of significance to users?

Users of financial statement information need to understand a company's long-term liabilities. Whether they result from long-term borrowings (such as mortgages or bonds) or from pension plans offered to employees, these liabilities will affect the company for many years into the future. For example, bonds can have a term (length) of 20, 30, or even 40 years and, as our lifespans increase, retired employees can draw on their pensions over a similar number of years. It is equally important for users to have an awareness and understanding of potential liabilities such as contractual commitments or the possible outcomes of litigation against the company. These items may have significant impacts on the company's operating results well into the future.

In this chapter, we will build on our discussion of current liabilities from Chapter 9 and focus on some of the most common long-term (or *non-current*) liabilities, including:

- Long-term loans
- Bonds payable
- Lease liabilities
- Pension and other post-employment benefit liabilities
- Future income taxes

These are complex topics. In fact, most universities and colleges have a separate senior accounting course that focuses just on them. At an introductory level, it is important that you have a basic understanding of the main concepts, but the detailed accounting treatment is beyond the scope of the text. As such, the chapter's focus will be primarily conceptual as we move through each of these topics. We will also discuss contractual commitments and contingent liabilities and conclude the chapter by learning about three of the ratios commonly used in assessing a company's long-term debts.

LONG-TERM LIABILITIES ARISING FROM TRANSACTIONS WITH LENDERS

What long-term liabilities arise from transactions with lenders?

There are a number of long-term liabilities that can result from a company's transactions with its lenders. These transactions involve a company borrowing funds by taking out a loan or mortgage. Companies can also access debt funding through the issuance of notes or bonds. These borrowings are presented on a company's statement of financial position as long-term debt, long-term notes payable, loans payable, mortgages payable, notes payable, or bonds payable.

Most companies have some form of long-term debt due to lenders. The recorded liability represents the outstanding principal, as interest is normally paid in regular intervals, such as monthly, quarterly, semi-annually, or annually. Companies are required to disclose the details of their long-term loans in the notes to their financial statements. Such details include the term of loan, interest rate, and security and collateral provided. In the following sections, we will discuss the differences between these various forms of long-term debt and how they are accounted for.

How are long-term loans and mortgages accounted for?

In this section, we will be studying long-term loans and mortgages. A **mortgage** loan is simply a long-term debt with land, building or piece of equipment pledged as collateral or security for the loan. If the borrower fails to repay the loan according to the specified terms, the lender has the legal right to have the asset seized and sold, and the proceeds from the sale applied to the repayment of the debt.

At the time of borrowing, the company and its lender generally enter into a **financing agreement**. This agreement specifies the terms of the loan (such as the interest rate, payment dates, and length of the loan). Most long-term loans and mortgages are **instalment loans**. This means that loan principal repayments must be made periodically rather than only at the end of the loan term. These periodic payments are usually **blended payments**, consisting of both interest and principal components. The total amount of the payment is the same each period, but the portion of each payment that represents interest is reduced, as the outstanding loan principal is being repaid with each loan payment.

Companies must account for two basic transactions related to these debts. These are:

1. Initial borrowing

   At the time of borrowing, a company will simply record the receipt of the loan proceeds (the receipt of cash) and the corresponding loan liability. It is important to note that, while the loan will be interest-bearing, no interest is recorded at the time of borrowing. Interest expense will be incurred with the passage of time. In other words, each day the company has the borrowed funds, interest expense is accruing. The entry to record the initial borrowing is shown below.

Cash	XXX	
Long-Term Loan Payable/Mortgage Payable		XXX

2. Periodic loan payment

   This loan payment, to be made monthly, quarterly, or in other periods, will normally include both an interest component and a principal component. The entry to record the periodic loan payment is shown below.

Interest Expense	XXX	
Long-Term Loan Payable/Mortgage Payable	XXX	
Cash		XXX

Companies may receive a loan amortization schedule from their lender that allocates the amount of each loan payment between interest expense and loan principal or they will prepare one themselves. An example of how a loan amortization schedule is prepared is presented in Exhibit 10-1, along with the related entries for the first two monthly blended payments.

Exhibit 10-1 Accounting for a Loan with Blended Repayments

Assume that Atwal Ltd. enters into a three-year, $100,000 mortgage on September 30. The interest rate on the loan is 6% per year and the terms of the mortgage require that equal blended payments of $3,042.19 be made at the end of each month. As the company makes its loan payment each month, it needs to allocate each $3,042.19 payment between interest expense and principal repayment.

Let's look at the loan amortization table for the first two monthly payments.

Month	A Principal Outstanding at Beginning of Month	B Monthly Payment	$C = A \times 6\% \times 1/12$ Interest Expense	$D = B - C$ Principal Repayment	$E = A - D$ Principal Outstanding at End of Month
1	100,000.00	3,042.19	500.00[1]	2,542.19	97,457.81
2	97,457.81	3,042.19	487.29[2]	2,554.90	94,902.91

Notes:
1. $100,000.00 \times 6\% \times (1/12) = 500.00$
2. $97,457.81 \times 6\% \times (1/12) = 487.29$

This table would continue for the remaining 34 payments (for the balance of the term of the loan), at which point the $100,000 in principal would have been repaid.

At the time of initial borrowing:

Cash	100,000	
Long-Term Loan Payable/Mortgage Payable		100,000

When first monthly payment made:

Interest Expense	500.00	
Long-Term Loan Payable/Mortgage Payable	2,542.19	
Cash		3,042.19

When second monthly payment made:

Interest Expense	487.29	
Long-Term Loan Payable/Mortgage Payable	2,554.90	
Cash		3,042.19

It is very possible that a company's financial reporting period does not correspond with the loan payment schedule. For example, the company's loan payments may be due on the 18th of each month, but the company produces financial statements at the end of each month. When this is the case, companies must accrue the interest expense incurred between the date of the last loan payment and the reporting date. We have seen this entry earlier, in Chapter 3.

It is also possible that the financing agreement requires monthly interest payments but does not require any of the loan principal to be repaid until the end of the loan term. In this case, the monthly payment would be entirely interest expense and the Long-Term Loan Payable or Mortgage Payable account would not be adjusted until the end of loan term when the principal was repaid. Continuing with the example in Exhibit 10-1, the monthly payment for Atwal Ltd. would be $500.00 per month (loan principal $\times$ interest rate $\times$ 1/12 or $100,000 \times 6\% \times 1/12 = 500.00$).

It is also common for loan financing agreements to specify certain conditions that the borrower must meet during the loan period. These conditions or restrictions on the company are known as **covenants**.

The covenants may be financial or non-financial. Financial covenants may require the company to meet certain financial ratios or may include limits on the company's ability to borrow additional amounts, to sell or acquire assets, or to pay dividends. Non-financial covenants may include requirements to provide the lender with interim financial statements or to have an annual audit conducted. The restrictions specified in the covenants are intended to protect the lender against the borrower defaulting on the loan.

FINANCIAL STATEMENTS

For Example

Calgary-based **WestJet Airlines Ltd.** had a number of term loans outstanding at December 31, 2013. The loans were entered into to finance the purchase of aircraft. Note 10 to the company's 2013 financial statements outlines some of the terms of these loans, including the requirement for quarterly repayments of loan principal, together with interest.[2]

10 LONG-TERM DEBT

Amounts in thousands of $	2013	2012
Term loans – purchased aircraft[i]	$510,764	$669,859
Term loans – purchased aircraft[ii]	238,964	69,154
Term loans – purchased aircraft[iii]	128,667	—
Term loan – Calgary hangar facility	—	35
	878,395	739,048
Current portion	(189,191)	(164,909)
	$689,204	$574,139

(i)　52 individual term loans, amortized over a 12-year term, repayable in quarterly principal instalments totaling $40,676, at an effective weighted average fixed rate of 5.95%, maturing between 2014 and 2020. These facilities are guaranteed by Export-Import Bank of the United States (Ex-Im Bank) and secured by one 800-series aircraft, 38 700-series aircraft and 13 600-series aircraft.

(ii)　Seven individual term loans, amortized over a 12-year term, repayable in quarterly principal instalments totaling $5,576, in addition to a floating rate of interest at the three month Canadian Dealer Offered Rate plus a basis point spread, with an effective weighted average floating interest rate of 2.85% at December 31, 2013, maturing between 2024 and 2025. The Corporation has fixed the rate of interest on these seven term loans using interest rate swaps. These facilities are guaranteed by Ex-Im Bank and secured by seven 800-series aircraft.

(iii)　Eight individual term loans, amortized over a 12-year term, repayable in quarterly principal instalments totaling $2,231, at an effective weighted average fixed rate of 4.02%, maturing in 2025. Each term loan is secured by one Q400 aircraft.

Future scheduled repayments of long-term debt at December 31, 2013 are as follows:

Within 1 year	189,191
1–3 years	282,199
3–5 years	170,843
Over 5 years	236,162
	878,395

 ## Ethics in Accounting

Debt covenants usually include financial measures or tests, such as ratios, that the borrowers must satisfy; otherwise, the debt will become due and will be payable on demand. As a result, restrictive covenants can create environments that encourage bias in accounting and financial reporting. That is, debt covenants may put so much pressure on companies to achieve the required minimums and pass the tests that managers engage in aggressive accounting and business practices to satisfy the covenants.

Users of financial statements should therefore be aware of the existence and nature of key debt covenants, and be alert to the potential for manipulation of the financial statements to satisfy them.

What are bonds and how do they differ from long-term loans?

When a large company wants to borrow long-term funds to support its operations, it does not always have to take a loan from a specific lender such as a bank or other financial institution. Instead, it can borrow by issuing bonds. Bonds can be sold through a **public offering** or through a **private placement**. A public offering is open to all interested investors, both individual and institutional. A private placement is open only to specific **institutional investors** who have agreed to purchase the bonds in advance. Institutional investors include banks, insurance companies, and pension funds. These types of investors seek out long-term investments with stable rates of return, which we will see is exactly what bonds provide. Bonds sold through a public offering can continue to trade in public markets. That means the original purchaser can sell them to another investor.

A **bond** is a formal agreement between a borrower (the company that issues the bonds) and the lenders (the investors who buy the bonds) that specifies how the borrower is to pay back the lenders, as well as any conditions that the borrower must meet while the bonds are outstanding. The bond's terms, conditions, restrictions, and covenants are usually stated in a document called an **indenture agreement**.

Bonds that are traded in public markets are fairly standardized. The indenture agreement will state a **face value** or principal amount for the bonds, which is usually $1,000 per bond. The face value specifies the cash payment that the borrower will make to the lenders at the bond's **maturity date**. In other words, normally there is no repayment of principal prior to the maturity date. In addition to the cash payment at maturity, most bonds also include semi-annual (two times per year) interest payments to the lenders. The amount of these payments is determined by multiplying the **bond interest rate** (or **contract rate** or **coupon rate**) by the face value and dividing by two (because the interest payments are semi-annual). For reasons that we will explore shortly, it is common for the stated bond rate to be different from the **yield** (or **effective rate** or market rate of interest) that the bond will provide investors.

Another important item in the indenture agreement is the **collateral** (if any) that the company pledges as security to the lenders. If collateral is pledged, it means that if the company defaults on either the interest payments or the maturity payment, the bondholders can force the pledged assets to be sold in order to settle the debt.

A bond that carries no specific collateral but is backed by the company's general creditworthiness is known as a **debenture**. Debentures can be either **senior** or **subordinated**. The distinction between senior and subordinated is the order in which the bondholders (creditors) are paid in the event of bankruptcy: senior creditors are paid before subordinate claims.

Some indenture agreements contain special provisions that are designed to make the bonds more attractive to investors. **Convertible bonds**, for example, can be exchanged for, or converted to, a specified number of common shares in the company issuing them. This is a common feature of many of the short-term debentures issued by Canadian companies in recent years.

Generally, bonds are sold initially to institutional and individual investors through an **investment banker**. The investment banker sells the bonds to its clients before the bonds are traded in the open market, receiving a commission for handling the transaction. The investment banker first consults with the company about its objectives and helps design an issue that will both meet the company's objectives and attract investors. All the bond features that have been discussed in the previous sections will be considered when structuring the offering.

The investment banker is responsible for the initial sale of the issue to its clients. Because most issues involve larger amounts than one investment banker can easily sell, the investment banker usually forms a syndicate with other investment bankers, who will be jointly responsible for selling the issue. The syndicate members are sometimes known as the **underwriters** of the issue.

Once the bonds have been sold by the investment bankers, they can be freely traded between investors in the bond market—much as shares are traded on the stock market. At this point, any investors can buy or sell the bonds. The prices of the bonds will then fluctuate according to the forces of supply and demand, and with changes in economic conditions.

It should be noted that issuing bonds is an expensive process for companies, regardless of the amount raised. In order to mitigate these costs, companies generally only issue bonds when their borrowing requirements are significant, usually $100 million or more.

Bonds differ from loans and mortgages in a number of ways, including the following:

- Bonds are generally sold to a pool of investors (acting as lenders), whereas loans and mortgages are generally made by a single lender. Issuing bonds can enable a company to tap into a much larger pool of lenders than it would be able to when entering into loans or mortgages.
- Bonds normally have much longer terms than are available with loans and mortgages. It is not unusual for bonds to have a 40-year term, which is much longer than the usual terms of loans and mortgages.
- Bonds generally require semi-annual, interest-only payments, with the principal only repaid at the end of term. Loans often require blended repayments of principal and interest, with a monthly payment frequency.
- There is a secondary market for many corporate bonds, meaning they can be purchased through investment dealers or on major exchanges. This enables lenders to sell the debt to others rather than having to wait to collect it at maturity.
- Some corporate bonds are convertible into common shares at the option of the bondholder. The conversion price is specified in the indenture agreement.

The differences between bonds and loans and mortgages are summarized in Exhibit 10-2.

Exhibit 10-2 How Bonds Differ from Loans and Mortgages

	Bonds	Loans and Mortgages
Number of lenders	Multiple lenders	Single lender
Length of term	Generally longer than debt (5–40 years)	Generally shorter (1–5 years)
When interest is paid	Normally on a semi-annual basis (every 6 months)	Normally on a monthly basis
When principal is repaid	Normally at the end of the term (at maturity)	Not unusual to have a requirement for blended payments (each loan payment includes principal and interest)
Is there a secondary market?	Yes, there is an active secondary bond market	No, not normally
Is it convertible into shares?	Yes, this can be an option	No, not normally

FINANCIAL
STATEMENTS

For Example

Valeant Pharmaceuticals International, Inc., which is headquartered in Montreal, develops and markets prescription and non-prescription products primarily for the dermatology and neurology markets. At December 31, 2013, the company's total long-term debt was U.S. $17,162,946, which consisted of term loans and notes payable. There were a number of covenants related to these borrowings, which were detailed in Note 14 of the company's financial statements and include restrictions on activities such as selling assets, entering into mergers, and making certain investments.[3]

14. LONG-TERM DEBT

The Company's Senior Secured Credit Facilities and indentures related to its senior notes contain customary covenants, including, among other things, and subject to certain qualifications and exceptions, covenants that restrict the Company's ability and the ability of its subsidiaries to: incur or guarantee additional indebtedness; create or permit liens on assets; pay dividends on capital stock or redeem, repurchase or retire capital stock or subordinated indebtedness; make certain investments and other restricted payments; engage in mergers, acquisitions, consolidations and amalgamations; transfer and sell certain assets; and engage in transactions with affiliates.

The Company's Senior Secured Credit Facilities also contain specified financial covenants (consisting of a secured leverage ratio and an interest coverage ratio), various customary affirmative covenants and specified events of default. The Company's indentures also contain certain customary affirmative covenants and specified events of default.

How are bonds priced in the marketplace?

Bond prices are established in the marketplace by the economic forces of supply (from companies wanting to issue bonds) and demand (from investors wanting to buy them). The buyers determine the rate of return they want to earn, based on the risk of potential default by the company. Due to the extended length of time between the issuance and maturity of most bonds, investors also calculate the present value of the cash flows they will receive from the bonds, to determine the amount they are willing to pay for them.

Determining the present value of the bond's cash flows requires investors to determine a discount rate, which is known as the yield (or desired rate of return). This is done by considering the interest rates available from alternative investments with the same relative risks as the bond issue. The higher the level of risk, the higher the yield rate has to be. In other words, for buyers to accept a higher risk of default, they have to be compensated for that risk with a higher rate of return. Buyers also have to factor in any special features of the bonds, such as if they are convertible into shares.

Present value calculations are beyond the scope of this text. We will keep things as simple as possible by providing you with this value. This is consistent with the way in which bond values are quoted in the financial markets, in which bond prices are expressed on an index having a base of 100. A bond issued at 100 would have been issued at its face value (which is also known as being issued at **par**). For example, if a company issued bonds with a face value of $100 million at par, then investors would have paid $100 million for them.

As noted previously, underwriters work with the issuing company to determine the features of the bond that they believe are necessary to make the issue attractive to investors. Of course, one of the most critical features is the interest rate that will be paid on the bond, which is known as the *contract rate*. The contract rate will be determined after taking into account many factors, including the bond term, credit rating of the issuer, special features, rates on alternative investments, and economic conditions. In spite of the best efforts of the underwriters and management, the contract rate specified in the indenture agreement may not be equivalent to the rate demanded by investors by the time the bonds are finally issued because economic conditions may have changed in that time. Because the contract rate is fixed (it is specified in the indenture agreement), the only way that an investor can increase the return (or yield) they will receive on the bond would be to pay less than the face value of the bond. There are also circumstances where the investor may be willing to pay more than the face value of the bond. It is important to understand that regardless of whether the investors pay less or more than the face value of the bond on issuance, they will receive the full amount of the face value on maturity of the bonds.

Let's look at the case where the investors are seeking a yield that is higher than the contract rate offered on the bond. If they pay less than the face value of the bond, then on maturity they will be receiving more than they paid for the bond on issuance. This difference is additional income for the investor (and additional interest expense to the issuer) and would enable the investor to realize a yield that is higher than the contract rate. When bonds are issued for less than their face value, they have been issued at a **discount**. Bonds issued at a discount would be issued at less than the base index (that is, less than 100). For example, if the company issuing $100 million in bonds issued them at 98.4, investors would have paid $98,400,000 ($100,000,000 × [98.4/100]) for them. These investors would still receive $100 million on maturity, with the $1.6-million difference being additional interest income to the investors and additional interest expense to the issuing company.

Alternatively, it is possible that investors consider the terms of a company's bond issue to be very attractive. They may be willing to purchase these bonds for more than the face value of the bonds as they may still realize a yield greater than that available from alternative investments. In spite of the fact that they paid more than the face value of the bond, they only receive the face value of the bond on maturity. This difference reduces the investment income of the investor (and also reduces the interest expense of the issuer). The investor will realize a yield that is less than the contract rate. When bonds are issued for more than their face value, they have been issued at a **premium**. Bonds issued at a premium would be issued at more than the base index (that is, more than 100). For example, if the company issuing $100 million in bonds issued them at 101.5, investors would have paid $101,500,000 ($100,000,000 × [101.5/100]) for them. These investors would only receive $100 million on maturity, with the $1.5-million difference reducing the interest income of the investors and the interest expense of the issuing company.

Exhibit 10-3 outlines the possible scenarios of yields relative to contract rates and their implications for the amount investors will pay for the bonds and the issuer's interest expense.

TAKE5

Exhibit 10-3 Yield vs. Contract Rate

Investors' Required Yield vs. Contract Rate	Bonds will be Issued at...	Amount Received on Issuance vs. Face Value	Interest Expense vs. Contract Rate
Yield > Contract rate	Discount	< Face value	> Contract rate
Yield = Contract rate	Par	= Face value	= Contract rate
Yield < Contract rate	Premium	> Face value	< Contract rate

When a company issues bonds, it will record the long-term liability equal to the proceeds of issuance. This is also known as the **carrying value** of the bond. Using the case above where bonds were issued at a discount, the entry at the time of issuance would have been:

Cash	98,400,000	
Notes Payable[1]		98,400,000

[1] This textbook uses the term *notes payable* to refer to both notes payable and bonds payable because this is the terminology commonly used in public company financial statements. Historically, notes payable have had shorter terms than bonds payable, but today it is common for companies to issue notes with 20- or 30-year terms. Accounting for notes and bonds is the same, so this is only a terminology issue.

In the next section of the chapter, we will discuss the impact that discounts and premiums have on the issuing company's interest expense.

FINANCIAL
STATEMENTS

For Example

Many Canadian universities have gone to the bond market to raise long-term capital. This includes the University of Toronto, McGill, York, University of British Columbia, Concordia, Guelph, Brock, Laurier, Ottawa, and Lakehead. Most of these universities have used the funds from the bond issues to fund the construction of student residences and other revenue-generating commercial projects because these types of projects provide revenues that can be used to fund the bond interest and principal repayment. Note 11 from the **University of Toronto**'s 2013 financial statements reflects the type of bonds the various universities have issued, namely 40-year debentures. In this case, the University of Toronto was able to issue its bonds at a premium (at 102.6), which means that the investors' yield will be less than the 4.251% contract rate.[4]

11. SERIES E SENIOR UNSECURED DEBENTURE

On December 7, 2011, the University issued Series E senior unsecured debenture in the aggregate principal amount of $100.0 million at a unit price of $1,000 for proceeds of $100.0 million. On February 7, 2012, the University issued additional Series E senior unsecured debenture in the aggregate principal amount of $100.0 million at a unit price of $1,026 for proceeds of $102.6 million. The debenture bears interest at 4.251%, which is payable semi-annually on June 7 and December 7, with the principal amount to be repaid on December 7, 2051. To date, the University has spent $91.7 million of the proceeds on capital assets.

How does the pricing of bonds affect a company's interest expense?

Once a company has issued bonds, it is important to understand the impact that the contract rate and yield have on a company's accounting for the semi-annual interest payments. The contract rate will determine the amount of the cash payment that will be made to the bondholders, while the yield will determine the amount of the company's interest expense. The difference between these amounts will be known as the **amortization of the bond discount (or premium)**. This amount will be added to (or deducted from) the bonds' **carrying amount** so that by the time the bonds mature, their carrying value will be equal to their face value. The bondholders will receive the face value of the bonds at maturity, so this must be the amount of the company's liability at that time.

The steps in accounting for each semi-annual interest payment are as follows:

1. Determine the cash interest payment.
   Interest Payment = Face Value × Contract Rate × 6/12*

   (*if semi-annual payments)

2. Determine the interest expense.
   Interest Expense = Carrying Value × Yield × 6/12*

   (*if semi-annual payments)

3. Determine the amortization of the bond discount or premium.
   Amortization = Interest Expense − Interest Payment Discount (or Premium)

Let's look at an example. Assume that a company issues five-year bonds with a face value of $100,000 and a contract rate of 7%. The bonds were issued at 97.977, resulting in a yield of 7.5% for the investors. The entry would be as follows.

On issuance of the bonds:		
Cash	97,977	
Notes Payable		97,977*

*This is the bond's initial carrying amount; that is, the amount at which it will appear on the statement of financial position.

The discount of $2,023 ($100,000 − $97,977) will increase the company's interest expense because the company will pay the investors the full face value of the bonds ($100,000) in spite of only having received $97,977 when they were issued.

The company's semi-annual cash interest payment will be:

TAKE**5**

Interest Payment = Face Value × Contract Rate × Number of Months
$$= 100,000 \times 7\% \times (6/12)$$
$$= 3,500$$

This payment will be the same through the term of the bond.

The company's interest expense for the first interest payment would be:

Interest Expense = Carrying Value × Yield × Number of Months
$$= 97,977 \times 7.5\% \times (6/12)$$
$$= 3,674 \text{ (rounded to the nearest dollar)}$$

Therefore, the amount of the discount that the company would amortize would be:

Amortization = Interest Expense − Interest Payment
$$= 3,674 - 3,500$$
$$= 174$$

The journal entry would be as follows:

At time of first interest payment:		
Interest Expense	3,674	
Notes Payable		174
Cash		3,500

From this entry, we can see that the company's interest expense is higher than the amount of the cash payment. This reflects the fact that the effective interest rate on the bonds is 7.5% (the yield), not the contact rate of interest (7%). The carrying amount of the bond would rise by this amount, meaning that it would be $98,151 after this first interest payment.

The company's interest expense for the second interest payment would be:

$$\text{Interest Expense} = \text{Carrying Value} \times \text{Yield} \times \text{Number of Months}$$
$$= 98{,}151 \times 7.5\% \times 6/12$$
$$= 3{,}681 \text{ (rounded to the nearest dollar)}$$

Therefore, the amount of the discount that the company would amortize would be:

$$\text{Amortization} = \text{Interest Expense} - \text{Interest Payment}$$
$$= 3{,}681 - 3{,}500$$
$$= 181$$

The journal entry would be as follows:

At time of second interest payment:		
Interest Expense	3,681	
Notes Payable		181
Cash		3,500

The company would continue to amortize the bond discount with each semi-annual interest payment. With each amortization entry, the carrying value of the company's bonds would increase. By the time of maturity, the carrying value would have increased to the full amount of the face value ($100,000) and the company would record the following entry when it makes the payment required at maturity:

Notes Payable	100,000	
Cash		100,000

LONG-TERM LIABILITIES ARISING FROM TRANSACTIONS WITH OTHER CREDITORS

What long-term liabilities arise from transactions with other creditors?

Lenders (financial institutions and bondholders) are not the only creditors with whom companies have long-term liabilities. Many companies also enter into long-term leases for a variety of capital assets, such as equipment, vehicles, and buildings. While there is a multitude of different terms and conditions that can be built into leases, accountants classify a lease as either a finance lease or an operating lease. As we will discuss later in the chapter, the classification of a lease has a significant impact on the accounting treatment that will be used for it. First, let's think about why companies choose to lease capital assets in the first place.

Why do companies lease capital assets?

When a company needs a new capital asset, such as a piece of machinery, there are two ways it can obtain it. It can either purchase it or lease it. If it chooses to lease the asset, the company (the **lessee**) would enter into a **lease agreement** with another company (the **lessor**). The lease would specify the payments the lessee would be required to make to the lessor over the length of the lease (the lease term) in order to be able to use the asset. These payments may be required at the beginning of the lease, during the course of the lease, or at the end of the lease. The lease will also outline any maintenance requirements, usage limitations, and what happens to the leased asset at the end of the lease term. There are a number of reasons why a company may choose to lease an asset rather than purchase it. These include:

- It lacks the cash to be able to purchase it or it wants to use its cash for other purposes.
- It lacks the cash to be able to purchase it and is unwilling or unable to obtain a loan to finance the purchase of the asset.
- It only has a short-term need for the asset; that is, it will not need the asset for most of its useful life.
- The asset is expected to quickly become obsolete and the company wants to be able to have the newest model without having to sell the old asset and purchase the latest one. For example, some technology assets are quickly replaced with newer technology. If a company has short-term leases in place, then it can return the old equipment and lease the latest technology at the end of each lease term.

For Example

At December 31, 2013, WestJet Airlines Ltd. operated a fleet of 113 aircraft. The company owned 69 of these planes and was leasing the other 44 planes. This mix of owned and leased planes is fairly typical of the airline industry. By comparison, Air Canada had 193 aircraft in its fleet at December 31, 2013, of which 112 were leased.[5]

What are the differences between a finance lease and an operating lease? How are they accounted for?

Accounting standards classify leases into two categories: **finance leases** and **operating leases**. The classification has a major impact on the manner in which the lease and the capital assets being leased are accounted for. While accounting for leases, including the initial classification decision, is complex and beyond the scope of an introductory accounting text, it is important that you have an understanding of the basic differences between the two classifications and the resulting accounting impacts.

Accounting standard setters basically approach the lease classification decision by saying that any lease that does not meet the definition of a finance lease is an operating lease. In other words, the operating lease classification is a default position. Given this, we need to look at the definition of a finance lease. A finance lease is one in which the risks and rewards of ownership of the leased asset have been transferred from the lessor to the lessee. The lessee has essentially purchased the leased asset, with the lessor providing the financing. Accounting standard setters have laid out a number of factors that can be used to assess whether the risks and rewards of ownership have been transferred. These include:

- the ownership of the leased asset is transferred to the lessee by the end of the lease term,
- the lessee has the option to purchase the asset at less than fair value during the lease,
- the lease term represents most of the useful life of the leased asset,
- the present value of the minimum lease payments amounts represents substantially all of the fair value of the leased asset at the time the lease is entered into, or
- the leased asset is highly specialized and could not be used by others without major modifications.

It is important to understand that there is a significant amount of judgement involved in applying these criteria. Essentially, standard setters are saying that the lessee has effectively purchased the leased asset if:

- it will eventually own it,
- it is using the asset for most of its useful life,
- it is essentially paying for the asset through its lease payments, or
- it is an asset that is unique to the lessee's operations.

If a lease is classified as a finance lease, then the lessee will account for it in exactly the same way it would have if it had borrowed the money and purchased the asset, which is what it has done in substance. This means that the lessee will:

- record the asset as property, plant, and equipment (distinguishing it as being *under a finance lease*),
- record a related financing liability (called **obligations under finance lease**),
- depreciate the asset over its useful life, and
- allocate the lease payments between a repayment of the lease liability (equivalent to the repayment of loan principal) and interest expense.

KEY POINTS
- With a finance lease, the lessee's accounting is the same as if it had borrowed money and purchased the capital asset.
- With an operating lease, the lessee accounts for it as if it were simply renting the capital asset.

If the lease does not meet *any* of the criteria of a finance lease, then it will be classified as an operating lease. With operating leases, the lessee simply records each lease payment as rent expense. No asset or liability is recorded in relation to the lease. In terms of the financial statement effects, companies generally have a strong preference for treating leases as operating leases. This keeps the lease obligations off the statement of financial position, creating a situation often referred to as *off–balance sheet financing*. There is therefore no effect on the debt to total assets ratio, the debt to equity ratio, or the interest coverage ratios that we will be discussing later in the chapter.

The accounting for purchasing and leasing an asset are shown in Exhibit 10-4.

Exhibit 10-4 Accounting for Purchasing or Leasing An Asset

	Purchasing: Taking out a loan and purchasing the asset	Leasing: Entering into a finance lease for the asset	Leasing: Entering into an operating lease for the asset
Is the asset recorded on the statement of financial position?	Yes	Yes	No
Is a liability recorded on the statement of financial position?	Yes	Yes	No
Is depreciation expense recorded?	Yes	Yes	No
Are interest expense and repayment of principal recorded?	Yes	Yes	No
Is rent expense recorded?	No	No	Yes

LONG-TERM LIABILITIES ARISING FROM TRANSACTIONS WITH EMPLOYEES

■ LEARNING OBJECTIVE 4
Identify the long-term liabilities that arise from transactions with employees and explain how they are accounted for.

What long-term liabilities arise from transactions with employees?

While most employee wages and benefits are paid within or soon after the period in which the employees worked, some benefits are deferred until the employees have retired. The most common example of this is pension plans, but there are other post-employment benefits, including health care, dental benefits, and life insurance. These arrangements can result in significant long-term liabilities for employers. In the next section, we will focus on pensions because they are the most common long-term liability that results from transactions with employees.

A pension agreement between an employer and its employees results in the employer providing pension benefits (income) upon retirement. These pension benefits are a form of deferred compensation for work provided by the employees. That is, you work today, but receive part of your compensation

---

The Conceptual Framework
THE ACCRUAL BASIS OF ACCOUNTING AND PENSION COSTS

Accounting for pension and other post-retirement costs is an excellent example of the accrual basis of accounting in action. The conceptual framework notes that financial statement users are in a better position to assess a company's performance, including future operations, if the company accounts for transactions that will result in claims on economic resources in the period in which those claims arise even if the cash payments will occur in future periods. It may be years, or even decades, until a company's employees are entitled to receive pension and other post-employment benefit payments. However, companies are required to recognize an expense related to these in each period in which the employee works and earns the right to these future payments.

when you retire. In Chapter 9, we discussed how wages must be recorded in the period in which the employees have worked (that is, when the wage costs are incurred). This also holds true for the costs of any deferred compensation. As such, the employer should record its pension costs in the years when the company receives the benefits from the work of its employees. This also results in a long-term liability being recorded for any accrued pension benefits that have not been funded by the employer.

Pension accounting is complex and is another area that is beyond the scope of introductory accounting. However, it is important for you to have an understanding of the basic types of pension arrangements and some of the key provisions of each type of plan. Let's look at the major types of pension plans.

What are the differences between defined benefit, defined contribution, and hybrid pension plans?

Historically, there have been two kinds of pension plans commonly used by employers: defined contribution plans and defined benefit plans. While these are still the main types of plans, in recent years a third type of plan, hybrid pension plans, has been introduced. Let's explore each of these types of plans.

Defined Contribution Pension Plans

In a **defined contribution pension plan**, the employer agrees to make a specified (or defined) contribution to a retirement fund for the employees. The amount is usually set as a percentage of the employees' salaries. Employees often make their own contributions to the same fund, to add to the amounts invested. The amount of the pension benefits that will be paid to the employees in their retirement depends on how well the investments in the retirement fund perform. The employer satisfies its obligation to the employees when it makes the specified payments into the fund and, once this is done, it has no further liability due on its part. The fund is usually managed by a **trustee** (someone outside the company's employ and control). The assets are legally separated from the company's other assets, which means they are *not* reported on the company's statement of financial position.

The accounting for defined contribution plans is straightforward. The company accrues the amount of its obligation to the pension fund and then records a payment. Because payment settles the liability, no other recognition is necessary in the financial statements. The entries to recognize the pension expense and the related payment are as follows:

Pension Expense	XXX	
Pension Obligation		XXX
Pension Obligation	XXX	
Cash		XXX

Companies generally make cash payments that coincide with the accruals, because they cannot deduct the cost for tax purposes if the cash payment is not made. Therefore, with a defined contribution pension plan, there is usually no liability balance to report.

Defined Benefit Pension Plans

A **defined benefit pension plan** is similar to a defined contribution plan in that both the employee and employer generally contribute to the plan. However, these plans are much more complex in that they guarantee employees a certain pension in each year of their retirement. The formula used to calculate how much will be paid usually takes into consideration length of service (how long an employee has worked for the company), as well as an average of the highest salaries that the employee earned while working for the company. For example, a plan might specify that the employee will receive a pension equal to 2% of the average of the highest five years of salaries, multiplied by the number of years that the employee worked for the company. If the employee worked for the company for 25 years and had an average salary of $85,000 for the highest five years, the annual pension benefit would be $42,500 per year (2% × $85,000 × 25 years).

Of course, employees may leave the company at some point prior to their retirement. Most plans have **vested benefits**, meaning the benefits belong to the employees, even if they leave the company. However, in plans without vested benefits, employees can keep their portion of contributions, but the employer's share is forfeited and there is no obligation on the company's part to pay out pension benefits.

As the payments to retired employees will occur many years in the future, pensions represent an estimated future obligation. The challenge is that in estimating the cost of the future obligation (that is, the liability's present value), several estimates must be made relating to future events. These include:

- the length of time the employee will work for the company,
- the age at which the employee will retire,
- the employee's average salary during their highest salary years,
- the number of years the employee will live after retiring, and
- the investment returns that will be earned on the plan's assets until they are needed to fund pension payments.

Each of these factors will affect the amount and timing of the future cash flows (pension payments). For companies with many employees, the total obligation of the pension plan usually has to be estimated based on the characteristics of the average employee rather than on an employee-by-employee basis. In addition, the company must choose an appropriate interest rate to use for calculating the present value of the future pension payments.

Each year, as employees work for the company, they earn pension benefits that obligate the company to make cash payments at some point in the future. Calculating the present value of the future pension obligation generally requires the services of an **actuary**. An actuary is trained in the use of statistical procedures to make the types of estimates required for pension calculations.

While the amounts are more difficult to determine, the accounting entries for defined benefit pension plans are essentially the same as the preceding entry for defined contribution plans. The company must accrue the expense and the related obligation to provide pension benefits. The entry made to recognize the pension expense is called the **accrual entry**. Setting aside cash to pay for these future benefits is done by making a cash entry, which is sometimes called the **funding entry**. Many employee pension plan agreements have clauses that specify the funding policy for the plan, which outlines the targeted relationship of fund assets to pension obligations, meaning the level of funds the employer is required to set aside to cover the liability. Many companies with defined benefit plans have not fully funded their pension obligations. As we saw in our feature story, Air Canada's defined benefit and other pension plans went from a $3.7-billion deficit at the start of 2013 to a small surplus by the end of the fiscal year.

Because there is no accounting requirement that the amount expensed be the same as the amount funded, the amount of pension expense often differs from the amount of cash transferred to the trustee in a particular period. A net pension obligation will result if the accumulated pension expense exceeds the accumulated amount funded. The calculation of the pension expense to be recorded each period involves many complex factors and is beyond the scope of introductory accounting.

Pension funds are described as **underfunded** if the value of the pension fund assets is less than the present value of the future pension obligations. An extended period of low interest rates over the last 10 years coupled with an increase in average lifespans resulted in many corporate pension plans in Canada being underfunded. Pension plans in which the fund assets equal the present value of the future obligations are known as **fully funded**, while plans whose assets exceed the present value of the future pension obligations are described as **overfunded**.

The pension fund itself is usually handled by a trustee and contributions to the fund cannot be returned to the employer except under extraordinary circumstances. To provide sufficient funds to pay the pension benefits, the trustee invests the cash that is transferred to the fund. The trustee then pays benefits to the retired employees out of the assets of the pension fund.

For Example

Saputo Inc., which is based in St. Leonard, Quebec, is a major producer of dairy products, with operations in Canada, the United States, and Argentina. The company had 12,700 employees as at March 31, 2014. In Note 17 of the company's 2014 financial statements, it reported that 92% of its active employees (those still working for the company) were members of the company's defined contribution plan and that the company's pension expense for these employees amounted to $31.114 million for the year ended March 31, 2014. The remaining active workers and many retired employees belonged to the company's defined benefit plan. The company contributed $21.231 million to the plan during the year ended March 31, 2014, but the plan was underfunded by $22.4 million at the company's year end. This long-term liability was reported on the company's statement of financial position.[6]

Hybrid Pension Plans

Hybrid pension plans (also known as a **target benefit plans**) have emerged in recent years as an alternative to the traditional defined contribution and defined benefit plans. As the name suggests, hybrid plans combine features of both the traditional plans. Hybrid plans establish targeted benefit levels that are funded through *fixed* contributions by both the employer and employee. If these contributions and the return on them are insufficient to fund the targeted benefit levels, then the benefit levels are reduced. In other words, the targets are just that—targets—rather than the guaranteed benefits of defined benefit plans. The risk of failing to meet these targets would not fall solely on the employer, as is the case with defined benefit plans. Instead, depending upon the terms of the hybrid plan, the benefit levels could be reduced, the employer and employees could share the amount of the underfunding, and so on. The advantage over a defined contribution plan for employees is that they would be able to better understand the pension benefits that could be expected on retirement and plan their other retirement savings accordingly.

The differences between the three types of pension plans we've just covered are shown in Exhibit 10-5.

Exhibit 10-5 Differences Between Pension Plans

	Defined Contribution Plan	Defined Benefit Plan	Hybrid Plan or Target Benefit Plan
Do employees and the employer normally make contributions?	Yes	Yes	Yes
Are pension benefits fixed or predetermined?	No	Yes	Yes, but they can be changed if the return on plan assets is insufficient
Who bears the risk of an underfunded plan?	Employee	Employer	Depends, but can be shared
Is the pension expense reported each period?	Yes	Yes	Yes
Is a pension obligation reported on the statement of financial position?	Never	Yes, if the plan is underfunded	Perhaps; it depends on the plan arrangements

What are other post-employment benefits?

Employers sometimes offer other types of **post-employment benefits** to their retirees in addition to pensions. Health care benefits and life insurance are two of the most commonly offered benefits. Companies are required to account for these post-employment items in much the same way as they account for pensions. That is, they must record the estimated expense for them in the period in which the employees have worked, together with the related obligation.

For Example

As is detailed in the note below, **Canadian Tire Corporation, Limited** does not have a pension plan for its employees, but does provide post-retirement benefits for certain employees. These benefits are related to health care, dental, and insurance. The company has not set any funds aside to meet its obligations related to these benefits, which it estimated at $115.4 million as of December 28, 2013.[7]

FINANCIAL STATEMENTS

Defined Benefit Plan

The Company provides certain health care, dental care, life insurance and other benefits for certain retired employees pursuant to Company policy. The Company does not have a pension plan. Information about the Company's defined benefit plan is as follows:

(C$ in millions)	2013	2012
Change in the present value of defined benefit obligation		
Defined benefit obligation, beginning of year	$ 124.9	$ 107.4
Current service cost	2.2	2.5
Interest cost	4.9	4.9
Actuarial loss (gain) arising from changes in demographic assumptions	4.1	(0.6)
Actuarial (gain) loss arising from changes in financial assumptions	(17.4)	8.3
Actuarial (gain) loss arising from experience adjustments	(0.3)	5.7
Benefits paid	(3.0)	(3.3)
Defined benefit obligation, end of year*	$ 115.4	$ 124.9

*The accrued benefit obligation is not funded because funding is provided when benefits are paid. Accordingly, there are no plan assets.

LONG-TERM LIABILITIES ARISING FROM DIFFERENCES BETWEEN ACCOUNTING STANDARDS AND THE INCOME TAX ACT

■ **LEARNING OBJECTIVE 5**
Identify the long-term liabilities that arise from differences between accounting standards and income tax regulations or law.

What long-term liabilities arise as a result of differences between accounting standards and the Income Tax Act?

The topic of **deferred income taxes** (which are also known as **future income taxes**) is complex and beyond the scope of introductory accounting. However, we raise the topic here because significant deferred income tax balances are commonly found on the statements of financial position of Canadian public companies. We will briefly explore the concepts behind deferred income taxes, so that you can have a basic understanding of what they represent and, as importantly, what they do not.

To defer means to put off or delay something until some point in the future. Deferred income taxes are an accounting recognition of situations where a company's income taxes will be higher (or lower) in the future as a result of differences between accounting standards (IFRS or ASPE) and the Income Tax Act. These differences are temporary and will offset over time. However, in the period in which these differences arise and will result in higher income taxes in the future, companies recognize a deferred income tax liability. Alternatively, where these differences will result in lower income taxes in the future, a deferred income tax asset is recognized. It is important to note that we are talking about taxes that will come due *in the future, not now*. A company's deferred income tax liability is not due to the government at present, but will be, down the road, when these differences eventually offset.

Companies determine their *income tax expense* based on accounting income, which is the income determined following accounting standards. However, to determine the amount of income tax that must be paid to the government (*income taxes payable*), companies prepare a corporate tax return (which is called a T2). This is based on the requirements of the Income Tax Act. As we have discussed, accounting standards follow the accrual basis of accounting. This is not always the case with the Income Tax Act, which uses the cash basis of accounting for a number of items. For example, while a company's estimated warranty costs are expensed for accounting purposes in the period in which the sale of the related product took place, warranty costs are only deductible for tax purposes in the period in which they are paid. In other cases, the Income Tax Act may require a certain treatment to be followed for tax purposes that is inconsistent with what a company does for accounting purposes. For example, as discussed in Chapter 8, the Income Tax Act prescribes **capital cost allowance (CCA)** rates, which must be used instead of accounting depreciation when determining net income for tax purposes. It is common for these CCA rates to be different (either faster or slower) than the rates determined by management for depreciation purposes. These differences give rise to temporary differences between accounting income and income for tax purposes.

Let's assume that a company purchases a vehicle with a cost of $30,000. Management estimates that the vehicle has a useful life of five years, after which it will be sold. They estimate that it will have a residual value of $5,000 and they determine that the straight-line depreciation method best reflects their planned use of the vehicle. However, the Income Tax Act requires that companies claiming CCA on automobiles do so on a 30% declining-balance basis. (Note: we are ignoring the impact of the half-year rule in order to keep the example as simple as possible.)

As you can see from Exhibit 10-6, the CCA treatment would result in the vehicle being written off much quicker for tax purposes than it would be expensed for accounting purposes. This means that, in the first two years, income for tax purposes will be lower than income for accounting purposes. However, by year 3 this changes, with income for tax purposes being higher than income for accounting purposes. From this, you can see that the company's income taxes will be higher starting in year 3 as a result of the lower CCA deduction. In recognition of this, the company would record a deferred income tax liability in years 1 and 2. This would eventually be extinguished in years 3, 4, and 5.

In conclusion, it is important that you understand that deferred income taxes do *not* represent amounts due to the Canada Revenue Agency, but are the result of differences between accounting and

KEY POINTS
- Deferred income taxes are taxes that will come due in the future.
- These are not taxes that are payable to the government today.

Exhibit 10-6 Capital Cost Allowance vs. Depreciation Expense

While depreciation expense for this vehicle would be $5,000 per year ([$30,000 2 $5,000]/5 years), the CCA deduction would be as follows:

Year 1 – 9,000
Year 2 – 6,300
Year 3 – 4,410
Year 4 – 3,087
Year 5 – 2,161

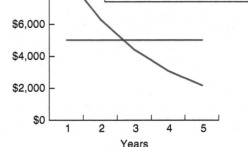

A comparison of the two methods would show:

taxation treatments. While they may not be due to the government at present, it is probable that these differences will result in higher taxes in the future (an outflow of economic benefits), the amount of which can be measured reliably. As such, the criteria for recognition of an expense (income tax expense) and the related liability (deferred income tax liability) have been met.

COMMITMENTS AND CONTINGENCIES

How are contractual commitments and guarantees reflected in the financial statements?

Corporations regularly enter into agreements committing them to future transactions. These can include commitments to purchase certain quantities of raw materials at certain prices, operating lease commitments, utility contracts, fixed labour rates on maintenance contracts, and the like. Contracts related to future transactions are known as **mutually unexecuted contracts** because neither party to the contact has done anything beyond entering into the contract. As such, no liability is recorded in relation to them. However, given the significance that these contracts can have for a company's operations in the future, information regarding material future contracts is presented in the notes to the financial statements as **commitments** (or **contractual commitments**).

An awareness of these commitments enables users to consider the impacts they will have on future operations. It also provides users with a basis for estimating the implications these arrangements will have for future cash flows.

■ **LEARNING OBJECTIVE 6**
Explain what commitments and guarantees are and how they are treated.

For Example

Note 26 of Calgary-based brewer **Big Rock Brewery Inc.** is a good example of the wide variety of contractual commitments that companies enter into.[8]

(amounts in thousands of Canadian dollars, unless stated otherwise)

26. COMMITMENTS FOR EXPENDITURE

As at December 30, 2013, the Corporation was a party to the following contracts:
• Effective July 1, 2011, the Corporation locked in an agreement with a natural gas retailer to provide natural gas at a fixed price of $4.83 per gigajoule for a period of two and one-half years, ending on December 31, 2013.
• In the third quarter of 2013, Big Rock entered into an agreement for the purchase of furniture for a total cost of approximately $59, of which $30 was payable at December 30. These materials, which will be used in the normal course of business, are expected to be received during the first quarter of 2014.
• In the fourth quarter of 2013, Big Rock entered into an agreement for the purchase of promotional materials for a total cost of approximately $127, of which $63 was payable at December 30. These materials, which will be used in the normal course of business, are expected to be received during the first quarter of 2014.

FINANCIAL
STATEMENTS

(continued)

For Example (continued)

- In the fourth quarter of 2013, Big Rock entered into an agreement for the purchase of machinery and equipment for Big Rock's new Vancouver brewery for a total cost of approximately $754, of which $403 was payable at December 30. This machinery and equipment, which will be used in the normal course of business, is expected to be received during the second quarter of 2014.
- Big Rock has a contract for the supply of malt barley through December 2015 at a fixed price of $545 per metric tonne. The barley will be used in the brewery's normal course of business, and delivered, as needed over a reasonable period of time, in quantities to ensure production targets are met.
- Big Rock has signed a contract for the supply of specialty malt through 2014 at a fixed price of $818 per metric tonne. The malt will be used in the brewery's normal course of business, and delivered, as needed over the calendar year 2014, in quantities to ensure production targets are met.
- In August 2010, Big Rock entered into an agreement with an electricity retailer to provide electricity for a period of five years beginning September 1, 2010 and ending August 31, 2015 at a fixed rate of $67.61 per megawatt hour.
- In December 2013, Big Rock renewed an operating lease for premises in Edmonton in the amount of $2 per month for a period of five years.

■ LEARNING OBJECTIVE 7
Explain contingencies and how they are accounted for.

What are contingent liabilities and how are they accounted for?

In Chapter 9, we noted that provisions are liabilities for which there is uncertainty with respect to timing or amount. They included arrangements such as estimated warranty claims, estimated sales returns, and customer loyalty arrangements. In spite of the uncertainties, these items met the definition of a liability and were recorded as such. That is, they were a present obligation of the company, were expected to be settled through an outflow of resources representing future economic benefits, and resulted from an event that had already occurred.

In this section, we will focus on other possible obligations that do not meet the definition of a liability because of one of the following reasons:

1. There is uncertainty about whether they are, in fact, an obligation of the company and this uncertainty will only be resolved when one or more future events occur and the event(s) is/are outside the control of the company;
2. It is not considered probable that an outflow of resources representing economic benefits will be required to settle the obligation; or,
3. The amount of the obligation cannot be reliably measured.

If any of these circumstances is present, then no liability can be recorded related to the obligation. Instead, these are considered to be **contingent liabilities**, meaning they may become liabilities, but that is contingent or dependent upon some future event. Given the impact that contingent liabilities can have on the future operations, accounting standards require companies to disclose them in the notes to the financial statements, including an estimate of the financial effect they may have, management's assessment of the uncertainties related to the amount, and timing of any economic outflows, and if there is any possibility for the company to be reimbursed for any portion of these as a result of insurance or joint liability.

The most common example of a contingent liability is when a company has been named in litigation. This could mean it is being sued by a customer for breach of contract, by a competitor for patent infringement, and so on. Let's take the example of a lawsuit against a company and review how each of the reasons outlined may result in it being considered a contingent liability rather than a liability for which a provision should be recorded:

Reason that no provision is established	How reason could apply to a lawsuit
1. There is uncertainty about whether there is, in fact, an obligation of the company and this uncertainty will only be resolved when one or more future events occur and the event(s) is/are outside the control of the company. **(Not a certain obligation)**	Whether or not the company will have a liability will depend upon the outcome of the litigation; it will depend on the judge's verdict or on the outcome of a negotiated settlement. A company's legal counsel (lawyer) would be consulted to determine their assessment regarding the likelihood of a liability based on the precedent established in related cases. If they assess it as unlikely or they are unable to provide an opinion, the uncertainty would preclude it from being treated as a liability.

2. It is not considered probable that an outflow of resources representing economic benefits will be required to settle the obligation.

   (Not a probable outflow of economic benefits)

A company's legal counsel may consider it unlikely that the lawsuit will result in any economic outflow, either because the company will win its case or the outcome is unlikely to result in material economic outflows.

3. The amount of the obligation cannot be reliably measured.

   (Cannot be reliably measured)

A company's legal counsel may be unable to estimate the potential outcome because there have been no precedents related to the subject of the lawsuit or because the range of possible settlements is very broad.

For Example

FINANCIAL STATEMENTS

Gildan Activewear Inc. is a manufacturer of activewear, socks, and underwear. Note 24 of the company's 2013 financial statements provides a good example of the type of contingent liabilities that may exist.[9]

24. COMMITMENTS, GUARANTEES, AND CONTINGENT LIABILITIES

(a) Claims and litigation

On October 12, 2012, Russell Brands, LLC, an affiliate of Fruit of the Loom, filed a lawsuit against the Company in the United States District Court of the Western District of Kentucky at Bowling Green, alleging trademark infringement and unfair competition and seeking injunctive relief and unspecified money damages. The litigation concerned labelling errors on certain inventory products shipped by Gildan to one of its customers. Upon being made aware of the error, the Company took immediate action to retrieve the disputed products. During the second quarter of fiscal 2013, the Company agreed to resolve the litigation by consenting to the entry of a final judgment providing for, among other things, the payment of $1.1 million.

The Company is a party to other claims and litigation arising in the normal course of operations. The Company does not expect the resolution of these matters to have a material adverse effect on the financial position or results of operations of the Company.

FINANCIAL STATEMENT ANALYSIS

How do users assess a company's degree of leverage?

■ **LEARNING OBJECTIVE 8**
Calculate leverage and coverage ratios and use the information from these ratios to assess a company's financial health.

As we have discussed previously, leverage is the extent to which a company is using the funds provided by creditors to generate returns for shareholders. In other words, it means a company is making money for its shareholders by using the creditors' money. When users are assessing the degree of leverage, they are essentially evaluating the company's capital structure to determine what portion of the company's capital has been provided by creditors versus shareholders. The greater the use of leverage (the more the company has made use of long-term debt), the greater the company's obligations are in terms of meeting the interest and principal repayments required by the related financing agreements. Recall that interest and principal repayments are not discretionary—they must be paid. So when a company takes on more debt, it increases its required interest and principal repayments. These ratios help assess a company's capital structure and the risk associated with the use of debt.

There are numerous ratios used to assess leverage and its related risks. We will focus on two ratios:
- Debt to equity ratio
- Net debt as a percentage of total capitalization ratio.

These ratios are measures commonly used by management and others in assessing a company's capital structure. You will see from the formulas for both of these ratios that they focus on **interest-bearing debt** (this refers to debt on which the company is required to pay interest, such as loans, mortgages and bonds payable) rather than on all the liabilities of a company. This is consistent with the approach generally taken by analysts, because they normally exclude short-term liabilities resulting from operations, such as accounts payable and wages payable. **Net debt** is the name given to the amount of interest-bearing debt less the amount of cash or cash equivalents that a company has available.

The **debt to equity ratio** measures the extent of debt relative to each dollar in equity. It is determined as follows:

$$\text{Debt to Equity} = \frac{\text{Net Debt}}{\text{Shareholders' Equity}}$$

$$\text{or} = \frac{\text{Interest-Bearing Debt}^1 - \text{Cash}}{\text{Shareholders' Equity}}$$

[1]Interest-bearing debt includes bank loans (both current and non-current) and notes payable.

This ratio measures the amount of debt relative to shareholders' equity. The resulting ratio is the amount of long-term debt that a company has for each dollar in shareholders' equity. The higher a company's debt load, the higher its debt to equity ratio will be. We can see in the "For Example..." box below that **Toromont Industries** had a debt to equity ratio of .11 at December 31, 2013. This means that the company had $0.11 in long-term debt for every dollar that it had in shareholders' equity. As such, it was not a highly leveraged company and most of the company's financing came from its shareholders. As with any ratio, it must be viewed in context, relative to prior years or to other companies. We can see that Toromont's debt to equity ratio has decreased from .33 in 2012, meaning that the company's degree of leverage has decreased. This change was the result of the company repaying some of its long-term debt in 2013 coupled with a significantly higher cash balance, and the $100,000 increase in shareholders' equity. The company's debt to equity ratio indicates that it is not a highly leveraged company.

The **net debt as a percentage of total capitalization ratio** measures the proportion that debt makes up of a company's total capitalization; that is, what percentage debt represents of the company's total financing. It is determined as follows:

$$\frac{\text{Net Debt as a Percentage}}{\text{of Total Capitalization}} = \frac{\text{Net Debt}}{\text{Total Capitalization}} = \frac{\text{Interest-Bearing Debt} - \text{Cash}}{\text{Shareholders' Equity} + \text{Interest-Bearing Debt} - \text{Cash}}$$

FINANCIAL STATEMENTS

For Example

Toromont Industries Ltd. is an Ontario-based company that operates a major Caterpillar equipment dealership. The company has more than 3,200 employees in more than 100 locations in North America. The following note from the company's financial statements outlines two of the ratios management uses in assessing its capital structure.[10]

20. CAPITAL MANAGEMENT

The Company defines capital as the aggregate of shareholders' equity and long-term debt less cash.

The Company's capital management framework is designed to maintain a flexible capital structure that allows for optimization of the cost of capital at acceptable risk while balancing the interests of both equity and debt holders.

The Company generally targets a net debt to total capitalization ratio of 33%, although there is a degree of variability associated with the timing of cash flows. Also, if appropriate opportunities are identified, the Company is prepared to significantly increase this ratio depending upon the opportunity.

The Company's capital management criteria can be illustrated as follows:

	2013	2012
Shareholders' equity	$ 576,557	$ 476,575
Long-term debt	132,418	159,767
Less cash	(70,769)	(2,383)
Total capitalization	$ 638,206	$ 633,959
Net debt as a % of total capitalization	10%	25%
Net debt to equity ratio	0.11:1	0.33:1

The Company is subject to minimum capital requirements relating to bank credit facilities and senior debentures. The Company has comfortably met these minimum requirements during the year.

There were no changes in the Company's approach to capital management during the year.

Again, the higher the level of a company's long-term debt, the higher this ratio will be. The higher the ratio, the more highly leveraged a company is. We can see in the "For Example..." box above that Toromont Industries' net debt as a percentage of total capitalization was 10%, meaning that a tenth of the company's total capital was from long-term debt and, therefore, 90% was from shareholders' equity. On a comparative basis, we can see that the company's net debt as a percentage of total capitalization decreased from 25% in the prior year and the percentage of capital provided by shareholders increased accordingly.

Different users will have different perspectives that must be taken into consideration when evaluating leverage analysis. If the assessment is being prepared from the perspective of a lender (or potential lender), then a lower degree of leverage is considered to be better than a higher one because the potential for the company to default on its debt obligations is reduced. In other words, it is more likely to be able to service the debt by making the required interest and principal repayments. A higher degree of leverage also exposes the company to greater risk resulting from increasing interest rates for those borrowings that have floating interest rates or that are nearing maturity and must be refinanced. From the perspective of a shareholder, a higher degree of leverage is normally preferable than a lower one. This is because it would mean that the company is using the capital of others (creditors) to generate higher returns for shareholders. There is, of course, a point where shareholders would consider a company to be over-leveraged, resulting in a heightened risk of the company defaulting on its debt obligations and being forced into bankruptcy.

Assessing the degree of leverage also requires consideration of the industry in which the company operates, the stability of the company's cash flows, and the nature of the company's assets. This type of contextual information is important when assessing whether a company's degree of leverage is too high or too low. Without this, our analysis will focus on determining how the degree of leverage has changed year over year and comparing the use of leverage by two or more companies within the same industry.

How do users assess a company's ability to service its long-term debt obligations?

In Chapter 1, we mentioned that when creditors lend money to a company, they are seeking to generate a return on those loans in the form of interest. The lenders also want to ensure that the monies they lend out will eventually be repaid; that is, that the principal is repaid. A borrower's ability to pay interest and return principal is often referred to as its ability to *service its debt*. While there are a number of ratios that are used by creditors and others to assess a company's ability to service its debt, we will focus on the interest coverage ratio.

The **interest coverage ratio** (which is also known as **times interest earned ratio**) measures a company's ability to meet its interest obligations through its earnings; that is, the company's ability to generate enough income from operations to pay its interest expense. This ratio uses **earnings before interest, taxes, depreciation, and amortization**, which is known by the acronym **EBITDA**, as the amount of a company's earnings. EBITDA is used in many financial analysis ratios. The interest coverage ratio is determined as follows:

$$\text{Interest Coverage} = \frac{\text{EBITDA}}{\text{Interest Expense}}$$

This ratio calculates the number of times a company's earnings could pay its interest expense. The higher the number, the less risk there is of the company being unable to meet its interest obligations through earnings. Conversely, the lower the number, the greater the risk. As we can see in the "For Example..." box below, **Maple Leaf Foods** had an interest coverage ratio of 1.8 in 2013. This meant that the company's EBITDA was sufficient to cover the company's interest expense almost twice over. This demonstrates that the risk of the company being unable to meet its interest obligations from future earnings was relatively low. We can also see that the ratio decreased significantly over the prior year, but that the company was still in a comfortable position in terms of being able to pay its interest expense through earnings.

There are a number of variations to the interest coverage ratio. Some companies and analysts will add annual lease payments and required principal repayments to the interest expense amount to determine a fixed-charge coverage ratio. Another common variation is to use cash flow from operating activities rather than EBITDA. This is known as the *cash coverage ratio* and recognizes that interest must be paid in cash, which is different from earnings. There are other variations, but they are beyond the scope of an introductory accounting text. It is important to recognize that there are many more ratios than the ones we will be exploring in this text.

For Example

Maple Leaf Foods Inc. is a packaged food company, headquartered in Toronto with operations across Canada and in the United States, United Kingdom, Asia, and Mexico. The company's brands include Maple Leaf, Schneiders, Dempsters, and Olivieri. The following note from the company's financial statements outlines two of the ratios the company's management uses in assessing its capital structure.[11]

18. FINANCIAL INSTRUMENTS AND RISK MANAGEMENT ACTIVITIES

Capital

The Company's objective is to maintain a cost effective capital structure that supports its long-term growth strategy and maximizes operating flexibility. In allocating capital to investments to support its earnings goals, the Company establishes internal hurdle return rates for capital initiatives. Capital projects are generally financed with senior debt and internal cash flows.

The Company uses leverage in its capital structure to reduce the cost of capital. The Company's goal is to maintain its primary credit ratios and leverage at levels that are designed to provide continued access to investment- grade credit pricing and terms. The Company measures its credit profile using a number of metrics, some of which are non-IFRS measures, primarily long-term debt and bank indebtedness, less cash and cash equivalents ("net debt") to adjusted earnings before interest, income taxes, depreciation, amortization, restructuring, and other related costs ("Adjusted EBITDA"), and interest coverage.

The following ratios are used by the Company to monitor its capital:

	2013	2012
		(Restated) (Note 32)
Interest coverage (Adjusted EBITDA to net interest expense)	1.8 x	5.3 x
Leverage ratio (Net debt to Adjusted EBITDA)	3.6 x	3.1 x

We have now seen how both short-term and long-term liabilities are accounted for. This completes our discussion of liabilities, one of the two sources of funding for companies. In the next chapter, we'll look at the other funding source, shareholders' equity, and learn about the accounting issues related to it.

SUMMARY

1. **Explain why long-term liabilities are of significance to users.**

   - Long-term liabilities will affect a company for many years. Some long-term liabilities, such as bonds or employee pensions, may not be settled for 30 or 40 years.

   - It is also important to be aware of the potential liabilities, such as contractual commitments or litigation involving the company.

2. **Identify the long-term liabilities that arise from transactions with lenders and explain how they are accounted for.**

   - Long-term liabilities involving lenders include loans payable, mortgages payable, notes payable, and bonds payable.

   - Mortgages are long-term debt for which a capital asset has been pledged as collateral.

   - Most loans and mortgages are instalment loans that require periodic loan payments. These are usually blended, meaning that they include both principal and interest components.

   - It is common for loan financing agreements to specify certain covenants, which are conditions or restrictions on the borrower.

   - The terms and conditions related to bonds (or notes) are specified in indenture agreements.

   - The bond rate (or contract rate) is used to determine the amount of the interest payment that will be made to the bondholders.

   - The yield (or effective rate) is used to determine the amount of the interest expense that will be recorded by the issuer.

   - Bonds may be issued at par (bond rate equals yield), at a premium (bond rate is greater than yield), or at a discount (bond rate is less than yield).

   - Bond premiums and discounts are amortized over the life of the bond, with the amortization amount for each period equal to the difference between the interest payment and the interest expense.

   - Debentures are bonds that are not backed by specific collateral.

3. **Identify the long-term liabilities that arise from transactions with other creditors and explain how they are accounted for.**

   - There are two types of leases: finance leases and operating leases.

   - With a finance lease, the company accounts for the transaction as if it had borrowed the money and purchased the asset (rather than leasing it). This is because one of five specific factors is present indicating that the risks and rewards of ownership of the asset being leased have been transferred. These conditions are: (1) ownership transfers by the end of the lease term; (2) there is an option to purchase the asset at less than fair value; (3) the lease term represents most of the asset's useful life; (4) the present value of the minimum lease payments represents all or substantially all of the asset's fair value; or (5) the asset is highly specialized and could not be used by others without major modifications.

- If a lease does not meet any of the five factors, then it is considered to be an operating lease. In this case, rent expense is recorded with each lease payment.

4. **Identify the long-term liabilities that arise from transactions with employees and explain how they are accounted for.**

- The most common type of long-term liability arising from transactions with employees is a pension plan. There are three types of pension plans: (1) defined contribution, (2) defined benefit, and (3) hybrid plans.

- With defined contribution plans, the employer is only responsible for funding its contribution and has no ongoing responsibility. The employee's pension will depend upon the investment returns realized on the funds in the plan.

- With defined benefit plans, the employer is responsible for providing employees with the agreed-upon benefit upon retirement. The employer bears the risk related to poor investment returns on the funds in the plan. If a defined benefit plan is fully funded, it means that the present value of the estimated future pension benefits is equal to the assets of the pension plan. Many defined benefit plans are underfunded, meaning that the present value of the estimated future pension benefits exceeds the plan's assets.

- Hybrid pension plans combine features of both defined contribution and defined benefit plans. Target benefit levels are established and funded through fixed contributions. If these are insufficient, then benefit levels can be reduced or contributions increased.

5. **Identify the long-term liabilities that arise from differences between accounting standards and income tax regulations or law.**

- Deferred income taxes result from differences between the accounting treatment followed by a company and the treatment specified by the Income Tax Act. A common difference is in how to depreciate capital assets, whereby a company would use accounting depreciation but the Income Tax Act requires using capital cost allowance for tax purposes.

- Deferred taxes are taxes that are expected to come due at some point in the future, but are not payable to the government at present.

6. **Explain what commitments and guarantees are and how they are treated.**

- Mutually unexecuted contracts are contracts in which neither party to the contract has done anything other than to enter into the contract. As neither party has done anything, no liability is recorded in relation to the contracts, but they are disclosed when they may have a material impact in future years.

7. **Explain contingencies and how they are accounted for.**

- Contingencies are potential liabilities for which there is uncertainty with respect to timing or amount. Their outcome depends upon some future event occurring.

- The most common type of contingency involves litigation against a company. The outcome of the litigation will depend upon a court decision or future settlement.

- Provisions are not established if there is uncertainty with respect to whether or not the company will have a liability, it is considered unlikely that the company will have a liability, or the amount of any obligation cannot be reliably measured.

8. **Calculate leverage and coverage ratios and use the information from these ratios to assess a company's financial health.**

- The *debt to equity ratio* can be determined by dividing net debt by shareholders' equity. Net debt is equal to a company's interest-bearing debt less its cash balance.

- The debt to equity ratio measures the amount of debt relative to shareholders' equity (that is, the amount of long-term debt a company has for each dollar of shareholders' equity). The higher a company's level of debt, the higher this ratio will be. Companies with a high debt to equity ratio are considered to be highly leveraged.

- The *net debt as a percentage of total capitalization ratio* can be determined by dividing net debt by total capitalization. Total capitalization is equal to a company's shareholders' equity plus its interest-bearing debt less its cash balance.

- The net debt as a percentage of total capitalization ratio measures the proportion that debt makes up of a company's total capitalization (that is, what percentage debt represents of the company's total financing). The higher a company's long-term debt, the higher this ratio will be. The higher the ratio, the more highly leveraged a company is considered to be.

- The *interest coverage ratio* can be determined by dividing earnings before interest, taxes, depreciation, and amortization (EBITDA) by interest expense.

- The interest coverage ratio measures the number of times a company's earnings could pay its interest expense. The higher the ratio, the less risk there is that the company will be unable to meet its interest obligations.

KEY TERMS

Accrual entry (456)	Capital cost allowance (CCA) (458)	Contractual commitments (459)
Actuary (456)	Carrying amount (451)	Convertible bonds (447)
Amortization of bond discount (or premium) (450)	Carrying value (450)	Coupon rate (447)
Blended payments (444)	Collateral (447)	Covenants (445)
Bond (447)	Commitments (459)	Debenture (447)
Bond interest rate (447)	Contingent liability (460)	Debt to equity ratio (461)
	Contract rate (447)	Deferred income taxes (458)

Defined benefit pension plan (455)

Defined contribution pension plan (455)

Discount (449)

Earnings before interest, taxes, depreciation, and amortization (EBITDA) (463)

Effective rate (447)

Face value (447)

Financing agreement (444)

Finance lease (453)

Fully funded (456)

Funding entry (456)

Future income taxes (458)

Hybrid pension plan (457)

Indenture agreement (447)

Instalment loans (444)

Institutional investors (447)

Interest-bearing debt (461)

Interest coverage ratio (463)

Investment banker (447)

Lease agreement (452)

Lessee (452)

Lessor (452)

Leverage (461)

Maturity date (447)

Mortgage (444)

Mutually unexecuted contract (459)

Net debt (461)

Net debt as a percentage of total capitalization ratio (462)

Obligations under finance lease (453)

Operating lease (453)

Overfunded (456)

Par (449)

Post-employment benefits (457)

Premium (449)

Private placement (447)

Public offering (447)

Senior debenture (447)

Subordinated debenture (447)

Target benefit plans (457)

Times interest earned ratio (463)

Trustee (455)

Underfunded (456)

Underwriters (447)

Vested benefits (455)

Yield (447)

ABBREVIATIONS USED

CCA   Capital cost allowance

EBITDA Earnings before interest, taxes, depreciation, and amortization

SYNONYMS

Bond interest rate | Contract rate | Coupon rate

Commitments | Contractual commitments

Carrying amount | Carrying value

Deferred income taxes | Future income taxes

Face value | Par value

Hybrid pension plans | Target benefit plans

Interest coverage ratio | Times interest earned ratio

Long-term liabilities | Non-current liabilities

Yield | Effective rate | Market rate of interest

STRATEGIES FOR SUCCESS

▶ Begin by calculating the amount that the company received on issuance of the bonds. This is the initial carrying value of the bonds and is equal to the face value of the bonds times the price paid by investors. This price is normally expressed relative to a base index of 100. This amount can be viewed as a percentage of face value.

▶ Next, calculate the amount of interest that will be paid to the bondholders every six months. Remember that this is based on the face value of the bonds using the contract rate.

▶ Calculate the interest expense for June 30 by multiplying the bond's carrying value by the yield rate. Because this is the first interest payment, the bond's carrying value is equal to its issue price. The difference between the amount of interest *paid* in cash and the amount of interest *expense* is the amount that the bond discount (or premium) will be amortized for the period. It is recorded as a debit or a credit to the Notes Payable account.

▶ Calculate the interest expense for December 31 by multiplying the carrying value of the bond by the yield rate. Remember that the carrying value reflects the amount of discount (or premium) that has already been amortized. In this case, the amortization from the June 30 entry must be taken into account. As before, the difference between the amount of interest *paid* and the amount of interest *expense* is recorded as a debit or a credit to the Notes Payable account.

▶ It can be useful to put together a table to calculate interest expense, amortization, and carrying value. Headings can include:

Opening Carrying Value	Yield Rate	Interest Expense	Cash Payment	Discount/Premium Amortization	Ending Carrying Value

CHAPTER END REVIEW PROBLEM 1

Carswell Ltd. issued bonds with a face value of $500,000 and a contract interest rate of 8% on January 1, 2016. The bonds mature in 10 years and pay interest semi-annually on June 30 and December 31. The bonds were issued at 93.496 to yield 9%.

Required: (Note: round all calculations to the nearest dollar)

a. How much did Carswell receive from investors on the issuance of these bonds (ignoring any underwriting fees)?

b. Prepare all of the journal entries that Carswell would make in 2016 in relation to the issuance of these bonds and the semi-annual interest payments.

c. At what amount would these bonds be carried on Carswell's statement of financial position at December 31, 2016?

d. If the market interest rate (or yield) for similar bonds was 7.5% (instead of 9%), investors would have been willing to purchase these bonds at 103.474. If the bonds had been issued at this price, prepare all of the journal entries that Carswell would make in 2016 in relation to the issuance of these bonds and the semi-annual interest payments.

e. Regardless of whether the bonds are issued at a discount (93.496) or a premium (103.474), what amount will the bondholders receive from Carswell at maturity?

CHAPTER END REVIEW PROBLEM 2

On January 1, 2016, Hannesson Technologies Ltd. enters into a three-year lease for a computer system for a new branch office it is opening in Charlottetown, P.E.I. The company had the option to purchase the system for $35,000, but decided to lease it to have more cash available for other costs related to opening the branch. At the end of the lease term, the system will be returned to the lessor, who estimates that it will have no residual value. The lease contract calls for payments of $988.07 at the end of each month and Hannesson's accounting office determined that the present value of these payments was $32,000 using the company's 7% borrowing rate. Hannesson uses similar technology, which it owns, in its other branch offices. It depreciates these assets on a declining-balance basis over their four-year estimated useful lives.

Required:

    a. Based on the above facts, explain how you think Hannesson should classify this lease.

    b. Explain the implications that your classification decision will have on:
       i. Hannesson's statement of financial position
       ii. Hannesson's statement of earnings

    c. Identify some reasons why Hannesson would choose to lease the computer system rather than buy it.

CHAPTER END REVIEW PROBLEM 3

Exhibit 10-7 shows excerpts from the pension-related notes to the financial statements of **Premium Brands Holdings Corporation**. The company is a food manufacturer and distributor, with Canadian operations from British Columbia to Quebec. The company also has U.S. operations in Nevada and Washington state. The company's brands include Duso's, Freybe, Pillers, Grimm's Fine Foods, and Maximum Seafoods.

EXHIBIT 10-7	EXCERPT FROM PREMIUM BRANDS HOLDING CORPORATION'S 2013 ANNUAL REPORT

(amounts in thousands of Canadian dollars)

15. PENSION OBLIGATION

The Company maintains a defined benefit pension plan (the Pension Plan) that covers certain salaried staff. Benefits under the Pension Plan are based on years of credited service and average compensation. The measurement date used to measure the plan assets and accrued benefit obligation is December 31 of each year. The most recent actuarial valuation of the Pension Plan for funding purposes was as of December 31, 2012.

Additional information on the Pension Plan is as follows:

	December 28, 2013	December 29, 2012
Funded status		
Defined benefit obligation	7,689	7,140
Fair value of plan assets	(7,036)	(5,267)
Pension obligation	653	1,873

FINANCIAL STATEMENTS

Required:

    a. What kind(s) of pension plan does Premium Brands have?

    b. At December 28, 2013, what was the funding status of the company's pension plan? Would this have had an implication for the company's statement of financial position at that date? Why or why not?

    c. Identify the factors that the company considers when determining its expected obligation under the pension plan. Why is it important that the company consider them?

Suggested Solution to Chapter End Review Problem 1

a. Amount received on issuance:

    $500,000 × (93.496/100) = $467,480 (that is, the bonds were issued at a discount)

b. Journal entries for initial issuance and first two interest payments:

    January 1, 2016: to record issuance of bonds

Cash	467,480	
Notes Payable		467,480

June 30, 2016: to record interest for the first six months

Interest Expense[1]	21,037	
Notes Payable		1,037
Cash[2]		20,000

December 31, 2016: to record interest for the second six months

Interest Expense[1]	21,083	
Notes Payable		1,083
Cash[2]		20,000

[1]See table below.
[2]Cash interest payment = Face Value × Contract Rate × Number of Months
= 500,000 × 8% × 6/12
= 20,000

	Opening Carrying Value	Yield	Interest Expense	Cash Payment	Discount/Premium Amortization	Ending Carrying Value
June 30, 2016	467,480	9%	21,037[3]	20,000	1,037	468,517
Dec. 31, 2016	468,517	9%	21,083[4]	20,000	1,083	469,600

[3]467,480 × 9% × 6/12 = 21,037
[4]468,517 × 9% × 6/12 = 21,083

c. The bonds would be carried at $469,600 on Carswell's statement of financial position at December 31, 2016.
d. If the bonds were issued at 103.474 to yield 7.5%, the entries for 2016 would have been as follows:
   January 1, 2016: to record issuance of bonds

Cash	517,370	
Notes Payable[5]		517,370

[5]500,000 × (103.474/100) = 517,370

June 30, 2016: to record interest for the first six months

Interest Expense[6]	19,401	
Notes Payable	599	
Cash[7]		20,000

December 31, 2016: to record interest for the second six months

Interest Expense[6]	19,379	
Notes Payable	621	
Cash[7]		20,000

[6]See table below.
[7]Cash interest payment = Face Value × Contract Rate × Number of Months
= 500,000 × 8% × 6/12
= 20,000

	Opening Carrying Value	Yield	Interest Expense	Cash Payment	Discount/Premium Amortization	Ending Carrying Value
June 30, 2016	517,370	7.5%	19,401[1]	20,000	599	516,771
Dec. 31, 2016	516,771	7.5%	19,379[2]	20,000	621	516,150

[1]517,370 × 7.5% × 6/12 = 19,401
[2]516,771 × 7.5% × 6/12 = 19,379

e. Regardless of whether these bonds were issued at a discount or premium, the bondholders will receive the face value of the bonds ($500,000 at maturity).

Suggested Solution to Chapter End Review Problem 2

a. Determining whether or not the lease is a finance lease requires us to look at the various finance lease criteria:

Criterion	How does it apply to Hannesson's lease?
Ownership transfers at the end of lease.	Does not apply.
Lessee has option to purchase the asset at the end of the lease for less than fair value.	Does not apply.
Lease term represents most of the useful life of the leased asset.	3-year lease term versus 4-year estimated useful life; therefore, it could be argued that this criterion is met.
Present value of the minimum lease payments represents substantially all of the fair value of the leased asset at the time the lease is entered into.	Present value of the minimum lease payments ($32,000) versus fair value ($35,000); therefore, it could be argued that this criterion is met.
Leased asset is highly specialized and could not be used by others without major modifications.	Does not apply.

Based on a review of the criteria, it would appear that the lease is a finance lease. This is due to the fact that the lease term covers most of the useful life of the computer system and the minimum lease payments represent substantially all of the fair value of the computer system.

b. If the lease is classified as a finance lease, it would have the following implications
   i. Hannesson's statement of financial position would include the leased capital asset and a corresponding liability. That is, it would be presented as "obligation under finance lease."
   ii. Hannesson's statement of earnings would include depreciation expense on the leased capital asset as well as interest expense; that is, a portion of each monthly lease payment.

c. Hannesson chose to lease rather than purchase the computer system so that it could preserve more of its cash to fund other costs associated with opening the new branch office. Other reasons it may have chosen to lease the computer system could have included:
   * The company was unable or unwilling to borrow funds to purchase the computer system.
   * The company wants to be able to replace its computer systems at the end of the lease term. In this case, it can just return the equipment to the lessor and get a new system at the end of the lease term.
   * The lessor may remain responsible if something major goes wrong with the system. The lease agreement would include clauses outlining the types of problems that the lessor agrees to fix and the types (if any) that are Hannesson's responsibility.

Suggested Solution to Chapter End Review Problem 3

a. Premium Brands has a defined benefit pension plan for its employees.
b. At December 28, 2013, Premium Brands' defined benefit pension plan was underfunded by $653 thousand. The fair value of the assets in the plan were $7,036 thousand relative to the estimated obligations of $7,869 thousand. This net liability of $653 thousand would have been presented as a long-term liability on the company's statement of financial position as at December 28, 2013.
c. Premium Brands indicated that management considers factors such as the expected return on plan assets, expected increases in employee wages, and the expected retirement age for the employees in the plan. The first factor has an impact on the assets that the company expects will be available within the plan to fund future pension benefit payments. The other two factors are important because the plan is a defined benefit plan. As such, these factors will affect the amount of the pension benefits that the employees will be entitled to upon retirement.

ASSIGNMENT MATERIAL

Discussion Questions

DQ10-1 Explain what a *mortgage* is.

DQ10-2 Explain what it means if a loan requires *blended payments*.

DQ10-3 Explain what loan covenants are and why they are used.

DQ10-4 Explain the difference between financial and non-financial covenants.

DQ10-5 Describe the following terms relating to a bond: *indenture agreement, collateral, face value, contract rate*, and *maturity date*.

DQ10-6 Identify and explain three typical ways in which bonds differ from loans.

DQ10-7 Explain what is meant by the yield rate of interest for a bond issue.

DQ10-8 Distinguish between the contract rate of interest on a bond and the yield (or effective rate).

DQ10-9 Discuss how bond prices are determined and how these prices are affected by changes in market interest rates.

DQ10-10 Describe the following terms as they relate to bond prices: *par*, *premium*, and *discount*.

DQ10-11 If bonds were issued at a discount, explain how the amount of cash received on issuance would compare with the face value of the bonds.

DQ10-12 If bonds were issued at a premium, explain how the amount of cash received on issuance would compare with the face value of the bonds.

DQ10-13 Explain why some bonds are issued at a discount, and what happens to the carrying value of these bonds between their issuance date and maturity date.

DQ10-14 Explain the effect that issuing bonds at a discount has on a company's interest expense relative to the contact rate of interest.

DQ10-15 Identify and discuss some of the common reasons companies lease capital assets.

DQ10-16 Identify and discuss the criteria that are used to distinguish finance leases from operating leases.

DQ10-17 Outline how finance leases are recorded and accounted for, including the impacts on the statement of financial position and statement of income.

DQ10-18 Differentiate between defined contribution pension plans and defined benefit pension plans.

DQ10-19 Explain how hybrid pension plans differ from defined benefit pension plans.

DQ10-20 As an employee, which of the three main types of pension plans would you prefer to belong to? Why? Would your thinking change if you owned the company and were considering a pension plan for your employees?

DQ10-21 Explain why vesting of the pension benefits and full funding of the pension plan would be important to employees.

DQ10-22 Identify and explain some of the reasons why defined benefit pension plans create accounting challenges for companies that offer them.

DQ10-23 Explain the nature of deferred income taxes, including how they arise and what they represent.

DQ10-24 Explain whether deferred income taxes are amounts a company currently owes to the government. If they are not, explain why they are considered a liability.

DQ10-25 Explain the difference between a contingent liability and a liability. How do contingent liabilities affect a company's statement of financial position and statement of income?

DQ10-26 Explain why a financial statement user would want to review a company's contractual commitment note.

DQ10-27 Explain what the following ratios tell you about a company's financial health: debt to equity ratio and interest coverage ratio.

Application Problems

AP10-1 (Journal entries for a loan)

A company takes out a five-year, $1-million mortgage on October 1. The interest rate on the loan is 6% per year, and blended payments of $19,333 (including both interest and principal) are to be made at the end of each month. The following is an extract from the loan amortization table the bank provided the company:

	Beginning Loan Balance	Payment	Interest	Principal	Ending Loan Balance
Payment 1	1,000,000	19,333	5,000	14,333	985,667
Payment 2	985,667	19,333	4,928	14,405	971,262
Payment 3	971,262	19,333	4,856	14,477	956,785
Payment 4	956,785	19,333	4,784	14,549	942,236

Required:
a. The monthly payments will be the same amount each month, throughout the entire term of the loan. From the loan amortization table, we can see that the portion of the payment related to interest is decreasing each payment. Prepare a brief explanation for why this is happening.
b. Prepare the journal entries to record the inception of the loan and the first two monthly payments.

AP10-2 (Journal entries for a loan)

A company takes out a four-year, $800,000 mortgage on May 1. The interest rate on the loan is 5% per year, and blended payments of $18,423 (including both interest and principal) are to be made at the end of each month. The following is an extract from the loan amortization table the bank provided the company:

	Beginning Loan Balance	Payment	Interest	Principal	Ending Loan Balance
Payment 1	800,000	18,423	3,333	15,090	784,910
Payment 2	784,910	18,423	3,270	15,153	769,757
Payment 3	769,757	18,423	3,207	15,216	754,541
Payment 4	754,541	18,423	3,144	15,279	739,262

Required:
  a. The monthly payments will be the same amount each month, throughout the entire term of the loan. From the loan amortization table, we can see that the portion of the payment related to interest is decreasing each payment. Prepare a brief explanation for why this is happening.
  b. Prepare the journal entries to record the inception of the loan and the first two monthly payments.

AP10-3 (Bond journal entries and financial statement effects)

Spring Water Company Ltd. needed to raise $50 million of additional capital to finance the expansion of its bottled water facility. After consulting an investment banker, it decided to issue bonds. The bonds had a face value of $50 million and an annual interest rate of 4.5%, paid semi-annually on June 30 and December 31, and will reach maturity on December 31, 2026. The bonds were issued at 96.1 on January 1, 2016, for $48,050,000, which represented a yield of 5%.

Required:
  a. Spring Water Company issued bonds with a face value of $50 million because it wanted to raise $50 million. However, it succeeded in raising only $48,050,000. Identify and explain two possible reasons why investors were not willing to pay $50 million for the bonds.
  b. Show the journal entry to record the issuance of the bonds.
  c. Show the journal entries to record the first two interest payments.
  d. What amount will be reported on the statement of financial position at the end of the first year related to these bonds?

AP10-4 (Bonds issued at par—journal entries)

Deleau Equipment Ltd. issued 10%, five-year bonds with a face value of $80 million on October 1, 2016. The bonds were issued at par and pay interest on March 31 and September 30 each year. Deleau's year end is December 31.

Required:
  a. Prepare the journal entry for the issuance of the bonds.
  b. Prepare the journal entry required at December 31, 2016, and the entries for the interest payments on March 31 and September 30, 2017.

AP10-5 (Bond issuance price, carrying value, and journal entries)

Sawada Insurance Ltd. issues bonds with a face value of $100 million that mature in 12 years. The bonds carry a 6% interest rate and are sold at 104.35 to yield 5.5%. They pay interest semi-annually.

Required:
  a. Calculate the proceeds on issuance of the bonds, and show the journal entry to record the issuance.
  b. Explain why the issuance price of the bonds is not the same as their face value.
  c. Will the carrying value of the liability for these bonds increase over time, or decrease? Explain briefly.
  d. Show the journal entries to record the first two interest payments on these bonds.

AP10-6 (Amount of bond issuance, journal entries, and carrying value)

Pacific Organics Ltd. has a number of commercial greenhouse operations in British Columbia's Fraser Valley. To finance the additional real estate and greenhouses necessary to meet the increasing demand for the company's products, the company decided to issue bonds. On January 1, it issued five-year, semi-annual bonds with a face value of $80 million. The contract rate on the bonds was 4.5% and the bonds were issued at 97.8 to yield 5%. Interest payments are to be made each June 30 and December 31.

Required:
  a. Determine the proceeds on issuance of the bonds and prepare the journal entry to record the bonds' sale on January 1.
  b. Provide the journal entries to record the first two interest payments.
  c. What amount will be reported for the bond liability on the company's statement of financial position at December 31 of the first year?

AP10-7 (Amount of bond issuance, journal entries, and carrying value)

On August 1, 2016, Tra Vinh Corporation issued $120 million 5% bonds, with interest payable on January 31 and July 31 each year. The market yield rate for these bonds on the date of issuance was 4.5% and they were issued at 103.99. The bonds had a maturity date of April 1, 2026. The company's fiscal year end is July 31.

Required:

    a. Calculate the cash proceeds from the issuance of these bonds.

    b. Prepare the journal entry made by the company on issuance.

    c. Provide the journal entries to record the first two interest payments.

    d. Determine the carrying amount these bonds would be reported at on the company's statement of financial position at July 31, 2017.

AP10-8 (Amount of bond issuance and journal entries at various yields)

Can-Ed University, which is owned by a group of Canadian universities and colleges, issued bonds to finance the construction of an overseas campus in China. Can-Ed issued 6% 20-year bonds with a face value of $100 million. The bonds will pay interest semi-annually.

Required:

    a. Calculate the amount of cash Can-Ed will receive if the bonds are sold at a yield rate of:

        i. 6% (issued at par)

        ii. 6.5% (issued at 94.448)

        iii. 5.5% (issued at 106.02)

    b. Prepare the journal entry Can-Ed would record at the time of the issuance of the bonds under each of the alternative yields. Also prepare the journal entries to record the interest expense for the first two periods under each alternative.

AP10-9 (Amount on bond issuance, journal entries, and carrying value)

Haulem Equipment Inc. issued $75 million 20-year bonds to finance the expansion of its school bus manufacturing operations in Winnipeg, Manitoba. The bonds pay 6% interest semi-annually and were issued at 89.322 to yield 7%.

Required:

    a. Calculate the amount of cash Haulem received on issuance of the bonds and prepare the related journal entry.

    b. Prepare the journal entries to record the first two interest payments.

    c. Calculate the carrying value of the bonds one year after issuance (that is, after the second semi-annual payment).

AP10-10 (Finance leases)

On January 1, 2016, Bountee Ltd. leased a machine from Vector Equipment Ltd. The machine had cost Vector $480,000 to manufacture, and would normally have sold for about $600,000. The lease was for 10 years and requires equal semi-annual payments of $40,000 to be made each June 30 and December 31, which reflects an annual interest rate of 10%. While the machine is expected to have a total useful life of 12 years, Bountee's management plans to return it to Vector at the end of the 10-year lease. Bountee's management has also determined that the present value of the minimum lease payments was $498,500 at the time the lease was entered into.

Required:

    a. Prepare and complete a table based on the one below. Conclude on whether the lease should be classified as an operating or finance lease.

Criterion	How does it apply?
Ownership transfers at the end of the lease.	
Lessee has the option to purchase the asset at the end of the lease for less than fair value.	
Lease term represents most of the useful life of the leased asset.	
Present value of the minimum lease payments represents substantially all of the fair value of the leased asset at the time the lease is entered into.	
Leased asset is highly specialized and could not be used by others without major modifications.	

b. Would your assessment in part "a" change if the lease term was two years longer? What if it was two years shorter?

c. If the annual interest rate was changed to 8%, then the present value of the minimum lease payments would have been $458,800. Would this change your assessment in part "a"? Explain.

User Perspective Problems

UP10-1 (Blended payments)

Required:

From a *management* perspective, what is the advantage of having long-term loans such as mortgages structured to be repaid through equal, blended monthly payments?

UP10-2 (Blended payments)

Required:

From a *lender's* perspective, what is the advantage of having long-term loans such as mortgages structured to be repaid through equal, blended monthly payments?

UP10-3 (Collateral for long-term debt)

Required:

As a potential lender considering making a long-term loan to a company, discuss how much comfort you might get from knowing what long-term assets the company has, specifically in the form of (1) property, plant, and equipment and (2) goodwill. As well as the existence of these assets, what else would you like to know?

UP10-4 (Seniority of liabilities)

Required:

Suppose you are considering investing in a particular bond. In assessing the riskiness of the bond, discuss the importance of being aware of the seniority of various company liabilities.

UP10-5 (Bond covenants)

Required:

Why do bond investors like to see restrictive covenants included in bond indenture agreements? Give two examples of common bond covenants, and explain why each would be beneficial to bond investors.

UP10-6 (Operating leases)

Suppose that you are a stock analyst and you are evaluating a company that has a significant number of operating leases.

Required:

a. Discuss the potential misstatement of the financial statements that may occur because of this treatment. Specifically, address the impact of this type of accounting on the debt to total assets ratio and return on total assets ratio.

b. Using disclosures provided in the notes to the financial statements, explain how you could adjust the statements to address the issues discussed in part "a."

UP10-7 (Finance leases)

A shareholder recently charged that the financial statements of a company in which he owned shares were false and misleading because a large amount of computer equipment, which the company leased from a financial institution and did not actually own, was included among the company's capital assets.

Required:

Is the company's treatment appropriate? Explain.

UP10-8 (Lease classification criteria)

"If two separate companies were each to lease identical capital assets under identical lease terms, the finance lease criteria used under International Financial Reporting Standards will ensure that each company reports the transaction in the same way."

Required:

As a financial statement analyst, would you agree or disagree with this statement? Explain.

UP10-9 (Impact of lease classification on earnings)

Suppose that your company leases a valuable asset and you are a manager whose compensation partially depends on the company meeting a particular earnings target.

Required:
- a. How is your ability to meet the earnings target affected by the decision to record the lease transaction as either an operating lease or finance lease?
- b. Which accounting treatment would you prefer? Does your answer depend on whether you are in the early years of the lease rather than the later years?

UP10-10 (Pension plan alternatives)

Required:
- a. Describe the three main types of pension plans.
- b. As a manager, which type of plan would you recommend to the company's senior executives? Explain.
- c. As an employee, which plan would you prefer? Explain.

UP10-11 (Pension plans)

Assume you are a member of your company's senior management team, which is recommending that the company implement a hybrid pension plan for its employees.

Required:
- a. Prepare a memo to be provided to the company's board of directors explaining why it could be beneficial for the board to authorize a pension plan for its employees.
- b. Explain why you are recommending that the company go with a hybrid plan if the board decides to proceed with implementing a pension plan.

UP10-12 (Post-employment benefits)

Companies have to accrue the cost and record the present obligation for post-employment benefits. In the past, the cost of these benefits was simply recorded as it was incurred, which was known as the pay-as-you-go approach.

Required:
- a. As a manager, explain why you would prefer to continue to use the pay-as-you-go method.
- b. What accounting concepts support the change in accounting method from the pay-as-you-go approach to recognizing the future obligation before the employees retire?

UP10-13 (Potential liabilities)

In assessing the risk of investing in a company, stock analysts are often very concerned that there may be potential liabilities that do not appear on the company's statement of financial position.

Required:
- a. Discuss the major types of potential liabilities that do not appear on the statement of financial position.
- b. Describe the information about these potential liabilities that may be included in the notes to the financial statements.

UP10-14 (Deferred income taxes as liabilities)

Some users of financial statements do not believe that deferred income tax liabilities meet the criteria for recognition as liabilities.

Required:
Discuss deferred income tax liabilities in terms of the criteria for recognizing liabilities, and provide your own arguments about whether they satisfy the criteria.

UP10-15 (Deferred income taxes and lending decisions)

Required:
As a potential lender, discuss how you might view the nature of a deferred income tax liability on a company's statement of financial position, and whether you would treat it in the same way as you would a long-term bank loan.

Reading and Interpreting Published Financial Statements

RI10-1 (Long-term debt)

Metro Inc. is one of Canada's leading food retailers and distributors and operates a network of supermarkets, discount stores, and drugstores. Exhibits 10-8A and B include the company's statement of financial position and Note 20 to the company's 2013 financial statements, which provides details of Metro's debt.

| EXHIBIT 10-8A | METRO INC.'S 2013 CONSOLIDATED STATEMENTS OF FINANCIAL POSITION |

metro

Consolidated statements of financial position

As at September 28, 2013 and September 29, 2012

(Millions of dollars)

	2013	2012
ASSETS		
Current assets		
Cash and cash equivalents	80.8	73.3
Accounts receivable *(notes 13 and 27)*	300.2	329.1
Inventories *(note 10)*	781.3	784.4
Prepaid expenses	15.3	6.6
Current taxes	10.9	13.9
	1,188.5	1,207.3
Assets held for sale *(note 11)*	0.9	0.6
	1,189.4	1,207.9
Non-current assets		
Investment in an associate *(note 12)*	206.4	324.5
Other financial assets *(note 13)*	27.5	25.8
Fixed assets *(note 14)*	1,328.4	1,280.3
Investment properties *(note 15)*	20.7	22.1
Intangible assets *(note 16)*	365.1	373.1
Goodwill *(note 17)*	1,855.6	1,859.5
Deferred taxes *(note 7)*	53.9	56.3
Defined benefit assets *(note 24)*	14.5	1.4
	5,061.5	5,150.9
LIABILITIES AND EQUITY		
Current liabilities		
Bank loans *(note 18)*	2.0	0.3
Accounts payable *(note 27)*	1,004.9	1,086.9
Current taxes	147.3	60.5
Provisions *(note 19)*	39.7	11.2
Current portion of debt *(note 20)*	12.4	12.1
	1,206.30	1,171.0
Non-current liabilities		
Debt *(note 20)*	650.0	973.9
Defined benefit liabilities *(note 24)*	69.8	156.9
Provisions *(note 19)*	4.5	3.1
Deferred taxes *(note 7)*	148.9	147.7
Other liabilities *(note 21)*	14.1	13.9
Non-controlling interest *(note 29)*	160.5	139.3
	2,254.1	2,605.8
Equity		
Capital stock *(note 22)*	640.4	666.3
Treasury shares *(note 22)*	(14.4)	(12.2)
Contributed surplus	14.6	16.2
Retained earnings	2,165.9	1,874.4
Accumulated other comprehensive income	(0.4)	(0.4)
Equity attributable to equity holders of the parent	2,806.1	2,544.3
Non-controlling interests	1.3	0.8
	2,807.4	2,545.1
	5,061.5	5,150.9

EXHIBIT 10-8B	**EXCERPT FROM METRO INC.'S 2013 ANNUAL REPORT**

20. DEBT

	2013	2012
Revolving Credit Facility, bearing interest at a weighted average rate of 2.47% (2.48% in 2012), repayable on November 3, 2017 or earlier	—	315.4
Series A Notes, bearing interest at a fixed nominal rate of 4.98%, maturing on October 15, 2015 and redeemable at the issuer's option at fair value at any time prior to maturity	**200.0**	200.0
Series B Notes, bearing interest at a fixed nominal rate of 5.97%, maturing on October 15, 2035 and redeemable at the issuer's option at fair value at any time prior to maturity	**400.0**	400.0
Loans, maturing on various dates through 2027, bearing interest at an average rate of 3.16% (3.06% in 2012)	**28.1**	32.6
Obligations under finance leases, bearing interest at an effective rate of 8.6% (8.6% in 2012)	**39.0**	43.2
Deferred financing costs	**(4.7)**	(5.2)
	662.4	986.0
Current portion	**12.4**	12.1
	650.0	973.9

The revolving credit facility with a maximum of $600.0 bears interest at rates that fluctuate with changes in bankers' acceptance rates and is unsecured. As at September 28, 2013, the unused authorized revolving credit facility was $600.0 ($284.6 as at September 29, 2012). Given that the Corporation frequently increases and decreases this loan through bankers' acceptances with a minimum of 30 days and to simplify its presentation, the Corporation found that it is preferable for the understanding of its financing activities to present the consolidated statement of cash flows solely with net annual changes.

Minimum required payments on debt in the upcoming fiscal years will be as follows:

	Loans	Notes	Obligations Under Finance Leases	Total
2014	8.6	—	6.8	15.4
2015	1.7	—	5.7	7.4
2016	1.1	200.0	6.0	207.1
2017	0.8	—	5.8	6.6
2018	0.4	—	5.4	5.8
2019 and thereafter	15.5	400.0	30.1	445.6
	28.1	600.0	59.8	687.9

The minimum payments in respect of the obligations under finance leases included interest amounting to $20.8 on these obligations in 2013 ($24.1 in 2012).

On October 1, 2013, the maturity of the revolving credit facility was extended to November 3, 2018 and this change is not taken into consideration in the present note tables.

Required:

a. Metro Inc. had a $600-million revolving credit facility in place at September 28, 2013. What is a revolving credit facility?

b. The revolving credit facility is described as *unsecured*. What does this mean?

c. The company also had $600 million in notes outstanding (Series A and Series B notes) at September 28, 2013. When do these notes have to be repaid to the note holders?

d. What is the annual interest expense that Metro Inc. incurs on the $600 million in outstanding notes?

e. Metro Inc. has a number of objectives in relation to its management of capital. One of these corporate objectives is to have a percentage of interest-bearing, non-current debt to total combined interest-bearing, non-current debt and equity (non-current debt/total capital ratio) of less than 50%. Did the company meet this in 2013? Explain why Metro may have this objective.

RI10-2 (Long-term debt)

Open Text Corporation provides a suite of business information software products. Exhibit 10-9 contains Note 10 from the company's 2013 annual report detailing long-term debt.

EXHIBIT 10-9	EXCERPT FROM OPEN TEXT CORPORATION'S 2013 ANNUAL REPORT

Long-term debt

Long-term debt is comprised of the following:

	As of June 30, 2013	As of June 30, 2012
Long-term debt		
Term Loan	$555,000	$585,000
Mortgage	10,492	11,374
	565,492	596,374
Less:		
Current portion of long-term debt		
Term Loan	41,250	30,000
Mortgage	10,492	11,374
	51,742	41,374
Non current portion of long-term debt	$513,750	$555,000

Term Loan and Revolver

Our credit facility consists of a $600 million term loan facility (the Term Loan) and a $100 million committed revolving credit facility (the Revolver). Borrowings under the credit agreement are secured by a first charge over substantially all of our assets. We entered into and borrowed the full amount under the Term Loan from this credit agreement on November 9, 2011.

The Term Loan has a five year term and repayments made under the Term Loan are equal to 1.25% of the original principal amount at each quarter for the first 2 years, 1.88% for years 3 and 4 and 2.5% for year 5. The Term Loan bears interest at a floating rate of LIBOR plus 2.25% starting in the last quarter of Fiscal 2013. For Fiscal 2012 and the first nine months of Fiscal 2013 interest was at a floating rate of LIBOR plus 2.5%. For the year ended June 30, 2013, we recorded interest expense of $15.5 million relating to the Term Loan (June 30, 2012—$10.9 million).

For the year ended June 30, 2012, we recorded interest expense of $2.7 million relating to our previously outstanding term loan (June 30, 2011—$7.3 million).

The Revolver has a five year term with no fixed repayment date prior to the end of the term. As of June 30, 2013, we have not drawn any amounts on the Revolver.

Mortgage

We currently have an "open" mortgage with a bank where we can pay all or a portion of the mortgage on or before August 1, 2014. The original principal amount of the mortgage was Canadian $15.0 million and interest accrues monthly at a variable rate of Canadian prime plus 0.50%. Principal and interest are payable in monthly installments of Canadian $0.1 million with a final lump sum principal payment due on maturity. The mortgage is secured by a lien on our headquarters in Waterloo, Ontario, Canada. We first entered into this mortgage in December 2005.

As of June 30, 2013, the carrying value of the mortgage was $10.5 million (June 30, 2012—$11.4 million).

As of June 30, 2013, the carrying value of the Waterloo building that secures the mortgage was $16.1 million (June 30, 2012—$16.3 million).

For the year ended June 30, 2013, we recorded interest expense of $0.4 million relating to the mortgage (June 30, 2012—$0.4 million, June 30, 2011—$0.6 million).

Required:

a. Open Text had a U.S. $100-million revolving credit facility in place at June 30, 2013, which the company referred to as "the Revolver" in the notes to its financial statements. What is a revolving credit facility?

b. What amount of "the Revolver" had been used at June 30, 2013? What is the maximum amount Open Text could access through "the Revolver"?

c. Open Text also had a U.S. $600-million term loan facility in place at June 30, 2013. What was the amount of the principal outstanding?

d. The term loan had a five-year term, so why did the company present a portion of the term loan as a current liability?

e. The company also had an outstanding mortgage at June 30, 2013. Was this mortgage secured? Did it require blended repayments?

RI10-3 (Long-term debt)

Exhibits 10-10A and B contain excerpts from the University of Toronto's annual report for its 2012/13 fiscal year.

EXHIBIT 10-10A	UNIVERSITY OF TORONTO'S 2012/13 CONSOLIDATED BALANCE SHEETS

UNIVERSITY OF TORONTO
CONSOLIDATED BALANCE SHEETS
(millions of dollars)

	April 30, 2013	April 30, 2012	May 1, 2011
			(note 2B)
ASSETS			
Current			
Cash and cash equivalents	104.1	121.0	99.3
Short-term investments (note 3)	645.1	663.9	535.1
Accounts receivable (notes 3 and 22)	82.7	84.7	104.8
Inventories and prepaid expenses	18.6	23.5	16.9
	850.5	893.1	756.1
Long-term accounts receivable	46.4	45.2	36.8
Investments (note 3)	2,403.6	2,095.6	2,085.7
Capital assets, net (note 4)	4,018.8	3,921.9	3,837.1
	7,319.3	6,955.8	6,715.7
LIABILITIES			
Current			
Accounts payable and accrued liabilities (notes 3, 6 and 12)	298.4	278.1	248.0
Deferred contributions (note 13)	372.7	371.2	370.3
	671.1	649.3	618.3
Accrued pension liability (note 5)	1,122.9	1,250.2	1,040.3
Employee future benefit obligation other than pension (note 5)	734.7	616.8	506.9
Series A senior unsecured debenture (note 7)	158.9	158.9	158.9
Series B senior unsecured debenture (note 8)	199.1	199.1	199.1
Series C senior unsecured debenture (note 9)	74.7	74.7	74.7
Series D senior unsecured debenture (note 10)	74.4	74.4	74.4
Series E senior unsecured debenture (note 11)	201.6	201.5	
Other long-term debt (note 12)	17.3	19.1	19.7
Deferred capital contributions (note 14)	1,076.4	1,018.3	986.3
	4,331.1	4,262.3	3,678.6
NET ASSETS (Statement 3)			
Unrestricted deficit	(129.7)	(134.9)	(173.6)
Internally restricted (note 15)	1,454.2	1,310.3	1,670.6
Endowments (notes 16, 17 and 18)	1,663.7	1,518.1	1,540.1
	2,988.2	2,693.5	3,037.1
	7,319.3	6,955.8	6,715.7

Contingencies and commitments (notes 3, 24 and 25)
(See accompanying notes)

| EXHIBIT 10-10B | EXCERPT FROM UNIVERSITY OF TORONTO'S 2012/13 ANNUAL REPORT |

11. SERIES E SENIOR UNSECURED DEBENTURE

On December 7, 2011, the University issued Series E senior unsecured debenture in the aggregate principal amount of $100.0 million at a unit price of $1,000 for proceeds of $100.0 million. On February 7, 2012, the University issued additional Series E senior unsecured debenture in the aggregate principal amount of $100.0 million at a unit price of $1,026 for proceeds of $102.6 million. The debenture bears interest at 4.251%, which is payable semi-annually on June 7 and December 7, with the principal amount to be repaid on December 7, 2051. To date, the University has spent $91.7 million of the proceeds on capital assets.

Required:

a. Refer to Note 11 in Exhibit 10-10B. Explain what it means when it states that the Series E debentures are "senior unsecured debentures"?

b. How much cash did the university raise through the two issuances of series E debentures? How does this compare with the face value of these debentures?

c. At what amount are these debentures carried on the University of Toronto's balance sheet (statement of financial position) in Exhibit 10-10A? Explain the amount these debentures will be carried at just prior to their maturing in 2051.

d. Note 11 states that the debentures bear interest at 4.251%, but given the amount that the university received at the time of issuance, will their interest costs be more, less, or equal to this rate?

RI10-4 (Long-term debt)

Alimentation Couche-Tard Inc. operates over 8,000 convenience stores in North America, Scandinavia, Poland, the Baltics, and Russia. The Laval, Quebec–based company generates income primarily from the sale of tobacco products, grocery items, beverages, fresh food, including quick service restaurants, other retail products and services, and road transportation fuels, among other chemicals. It operates in Canada mainly under the Mac's and Couche-Tard brands. Note 19(b) from the company's 2013 annual report in Exhibit 10-11 details Couche-Tard's senior unsecured notes (in millions).

| EXHIBIT 10-11 | EXCERPT FROM ALIMENTATION COUCHE-TARD INC.'S 2013 ANNUAL REPORT |

(b) Canadian dollar denominated senior unsecured notes

On November 1st, 2012, the Corporation issued Canadian dollar denominated senior unsecured notes totalling CA$ 1.0 billion, divided into three tranches:

	Notional amount	Maturity	Coupon rate	Effective rate as at April 28, 2013
Tranche 1	CA$300.0	November 1st, 2017	2.861%	3.0%
Tranche 2	CA$450.0	November 1st, 2019	3.319%	3.4%
Tranche 3	CA$250.0	November 1st, 2022	3.899%	4.0%

Required:

a. Looking at Couche-Tard's three tranches (which are portions of a bond issue that have different maturity dates, interest rates, etc.) of senior unsecured notes, comment on the relationship between the interest rates and the length of time to maturity of the notes. As an investor, explain why this relationship would be important to you.

b. Explain why Couche-Tard may have wanted to spread this borrowing across three tranches with different maturities.

c. What do we know about these notes given that the effective rates of interest are higher than the coupon rates for all three tranches?

RI10-5 (Leases)

Cineplex Inc. is the largest motion picture exhibitor in Canada and owns, leases, or has joint-venture interests in over 161 theatres with 1,630 screens. Exhibits 10-12A and B contain Notes 18 and 25 from the company's 2013 annual report detailing Cineplex's lease arrangements.

EXHIBIT 10-12A   EXCERPT FROM CINEPLEX INC.'S 2013 ANNUAL REPORT, NOTE 18

18 FINANCE LEASE OBLIGATIONS

Cineplex has two non-cancellable finance leases for theatres and a number of small equipment leases for various periods, including renewal options. Future minimum payments, by year and in the aggregate, under non-cancellable finance leases are as follows:

2013	$ 3,779
2014	3,894
2015	3,973
2016	3,961
2017	3,955
Thereafter	5,793
	25,355
Less: Amount representing interest (average rate of 7.3%)	5,239
	20,116
Less: Current portion	2,394
	$ 17,722

Until 2012, Cineplex had eight finance leases for theatre equipment. In the first quarter of 2012, Cineplex entered into agreements with the lessor of the theatre equipment to purchase new equipment in 2012 for seven of the leases, replacing the leased equipment. In the third quarter of 2013, the remaining finance lease was settled through the same agreement.

Interest expense related to finance lease obligations was $1,576 for the year ended December 31, 2013 (2012 – $1,790).

EXHIBIT 10-12B   EXCERPT FROM CINEPLEX INC.'S 2013 ANNUAL REPORT, NOTE 25

25 LEASES

Cineplex conducts a significant part of its operations in leased premises. Leases generally provide for minimum rentals and, in certain situations, percentage rentals based on sales volume or other identifiable targets; may include escalation clauses and certain other restrictions; and may require the tenant to pay a portion of realty taxes and other property operating expenses. Lease terms generally range from 15 to 20 years and contain various renewal options, generally, in intervals of five to ten years. Certain theatre assets are pledged as security to landlords for rental commitments, subordinated to the Credit Facilities.

Cineplex's minimum rental commitments at December 31, 2013 under the above-mentioned operating leases are set forth as follows:

2014	$ 141,669
2015	143,776
2016	144,974
2017	141,601
2018	131,481
Thereafter	708,705
	$ 1,412,206

Minimum rent expense relating to operating leases on a straight-line basis in 2013 was $135,490 (2012 – $123,639). In addition to the minimum rent expense, in 2013 Cineplex incurred percentage rent charges of $2,072 (2012 – $2,455).

Required:

a. Read Note 18 in Exhibit 10-12A and explain, in your own words, how Cineplex accounts for the theatres and theatre equipment under finance leases. Be sure to discuss the impacts, if any, that this treatment would have on the company's statement of financial position and statement of income.

b. After reading Note 25, consider where Cineplex operates its theatres, perhaps thinking about a theatre in your own city. Explain why it is reasonable that most of the company's leases would be operating leases rather than finance leases.

c. Explain, in your own words, how Cineplex accounts for leases. Be sure to discuss the impacts, if any, that this treatment would have on the company's statement of financial position and statement of income.

RI10-6 (Employee future benefits)

Note 19 to the 2013 financial statements of Cineplex Inc., dealing with employee future benefits, is presented in Exhibit 10-13 (amounts in thousands of dollars).

EXHIBIT 10-13	EXCERPT FROM CINEPLEX INC.'S 2013 ANNUAL REPORT

19 POST-EMPLOYMENT BENEFIT OBLIGATIONS

Pension and other retirement benefit plans

Cineplex sponsors the Defined Contribution Pension Plan for Employees of Cineplex Entertainment Limited Partnership ("Cineplex Entertainment Plan"), covering substantially all full-time employees. Effective December 31, 2013, the defined contribution plan has been converted to a group registered retirement plan. In addition, Cineplex sponsors a defined benefit supplementary executive retirement plan.

Cineplex also sponsors the Retirement Plan for Salaried Employees of Famous Players Limited Partnership, a defined benefit pension plan, and the Famous Players Retirement Excess Plan (collectively known as the "Famous Players Plans"). Effective October 23, 2005, Cineplex elected to freeze future accrual of defined benefits under the Famous Players Plans and move continuing employees into the Cineplex Entertainment Plan for future accrual. Effective December 31, 2007, Cineplex declared a full windup of the Retirement Plan for Salaried Employees of Famous Players Limited Partnership. Regulatory approval was granted in December 2008 and all defined benefit pension entitlements were settled and recognized in 2009.

In addition, Cineplex has assumed sponsorship of certain post-retirement health care benefits for a closed group of grandfathered Famous Players retirees.

Reconciliation of the unfunded status of the defined benefit provisions

	2013	2012
Fair value of plan assets	$ 180	$ 128
Accrued benefit obligations	(6,702)	(6,402)
Accrued pension benefit liability	$(6,522)	$(6,274)

Required:

a. What types of pension plans and other long-term benefit plans does Cineplex have?

b. What was the total plan obligation for Cineplex's defined benefit plans as at December 31, 2013?

c. What was the fair value of the defined benefit plan assets for Cineplex as at December 31, 2013?

d. Were Cineplex's defined benefit plans underfunded, overfunded, or fully funded? If they were underfunded or overfunded, by what amount?

e. Which type of pension plan do new employees of Cineplex become a member of? Is this the same for a new member of the company's executive team?

RI10-7 (Income tax disclosures)

Rogers Sugar Inc. is headquartered in Vancouver, but has operations in Alberta, Ontario, Quebec, and New Brunswick. The company is the largest producer of refined sugar in Canada and also packages and markets sugar products. Exhibits 10-14A to C contain extracts from the company's 2013 annual report.

EXHIBIT 10-14A ROGERS SUGAR INC.'S 2013 CONSOLIDATED STATEMENTS OF FINANCIAL POSITION

CONSOLIDATED STATEMENTS OF FINANCIAL POSITION
(In thousands of dollars)

	September 28, 2013	September 29, 2012
	$	$
Assets		
Current assets:		
Cash and cash equivalents	3,204	27,895
Trade and other receivables (note 7)	50,126	51,071
Income taxes recoverable	663	760
Inventories (note 8)	72,374	78,286
Prepaid expenses	2,047	1,689
Derivative financial instruments (note 9)	129	–
Total current assets	128,543	159,701
Non-current assets:		
Property, plant and equipment (note 10)	177,382	180,132
Intangible assets (note 11)	2,117	2,347
Other assets (note 12)	544	142
Deferred tax assets (note 13)	14,629	21,778
Derivative financial instruments (note 9)	432	15
Goodwill (note 14)	229,952	229,952
Total non-current assets	425,056	434,366
Total assets	553,599	594,067
Liabilities and Shareholders' Equity		
Current liabilities:		
Revolving credit facility (note 15)	25,000	60,000
Trade and other payables (note 16)	37,659	46,795
Income taxes payable	1,304	2,824
Provisions (note 17)	1,150	1,363
Finance lease obligations (note 18)	39	69
Derivative financial instruments (note 9)	3,670	7,922
Total current liabilities	68,822	118,973
Non-current liabilities:		
Revolving credit facility (note 15)	50,000	–
Employee benefits (note 19)	44,345	57,857
Provisions (note 17)	2,273	2,899
Derivative financial instruments (note 9)	623	2,283
Finance lease obligations (note 18)	7	46
Convertible unsecured subordinated debentures (note 20)	105,857	104,988
Deferred tax liabilities (note 13)	26,799	29,676
Total non-current liabilities	229,904	197,749
Total liabilities	298,726	316,722
Shareholders' equity:		
Share capital (note 21)	133,833	133,737
Contributed surplus	200,135	200,143
Equity portion of convertible unsecured subordinated debentures (note 20)	1,188	1,188
Deficit	(80,283)	(57,723)
Total shareholders' equity	254,873	277,345
Commitments (notes 23 and 24)		
Contingencies (note 25)		
Total liabilities and shareholders' equity	553,599	594,067

EXHIBIT 10-14B	ROGERS SUGAR INC.'S 2013 CONSOLIDATED STATEMENTS OF EARNINGS AND COMPREHENSIVE INCOME

CONSOLIDATED STATEMENTS OF EARNINGS AND COMPREHENSIVE INCOME

(In thousands of dollars except per share amounts)

	For the years ended	
Consolidated statements of earnings	September 28, 2013	September 29, 2012
	$	$
Revenues (note 31)	558,438	618,093
Cost of sales	472,785	540,232
Gross margin	85,653	77,861
Administration and selling expenses	18,005	18,923
Distribution expenses	8,110	8,334
	26,115	27,257
Results from operating activities	59,538	50,604
Net finance costs (note 5)	9,127	9,695
Earnings before income taxes	50,411	40,909
Income tax expense (note 6):		
Current	11,659	10,141
Deferred	1,487	507
	13,146	10,648
Net earnings	37,265	30,261

EXHIBIT 10-14C	EXCERPT FROM ROGERS SUGAR INC.'S 2013 ANNUAL REPORT

13. DEFERRED TAX ASSETS AND LIABILITIES:

The deferred tax assets (liabilities) comprise the following temporary differences:

	September 28, 2013	September 29, 2012
	$	$
Assets:		
Employee benefits	11,530	14,918
Derivative financial instruments	717	2,563
Losses carried forward	509	2,222
Provisions	890	1,099
Other	983	976
	14,629	21,778
Liabilities:		
Property, plant and equipment	(23,463)	(26,494)
Derivative financial instruments	(529)	(510)
Goodwill	(2,142)	(2,061)
Deferred financing charges	(290)	(205)
Other	(375)	(406)
	(26,799)	(29,676)
Net assets (liabilities):		
Property, plant and equipment	(23,463)	(26,494)
Employee benefits	11,530	14,918
Derivative financial instruments	188	2,053
Losses carried forward	509	2,222
Goodwill	(2,142)	(2,061)
Provisions	890	1,099
Deferred financing charges	(290)	(205)
Other	608	570
	(12,170)	(7,898)

Required:

a. For the year ended September 28, 2013, determine Rogers' total income tax expense. Also, determine how much of this was for current tax and how much was related to deferred taxes.

b. Rogers reported income taxes recoverable and income taxes payable on its statement of financial position. Quantify those amounts and explain how it would be possible to have a recoverable amount and a payable amount at the same time. *Hint:* These are the company's consolidated financial statements.

c. Rogers also reported deferred tax assets and deferred tax liabilities on its statement of financial position. Of the $26,799 in deferred tax liabilities, $23,463 related to property, plant, and equipment. Given that significant deferred tax liabilities exist, what do we know about how the company's depreciation expense related to its property, plant, and equipment compares with the capital cost allowance being claimed on these assets for tax purposes?

RI10-8 (Debt to total assets and times interest earned ratios)

ZoomerMedia Limited is a multimedia company that serves the 45-plus "Zoomer" demographic through television, radio, magazine, Internet, conferences, and tradeshows. Exhibits 10-15A and B contain excerpts from ZoomerMedia's 2013 annual report.

EXHIBIT 10-15A	ZOOMERMEDIA LIMITED'S 2013 CONSOLIDATED STATEMENTS OF INCOME (LOSS) AND COMPREHENSIVE INCOME (LOSS)

ZOOMERMEDIA LIMITED
Consolidated Statements of Income (Loss) and Comprehensive Income (Loss)
For the years ended June 30, 2013 and 2012

	2013	2012 (revised - Note 7)
Revenue	$ 56,424,047	$ 55,976,785
Operating expenses (Note 14)	47,949,596	48,921,614
Depreciation	1,909,597	3,446,938
Amortization of the other intangible assets	1,076,365	1,010,787
Impairment of goodwill and broadcast licenses	2,820,881	5,450,796
Operating income (loss)	2,667,608	(2,853,350)
Interest income	(79,391)	(2,183)
Interest expense	2,561,431	2,179,649
Net interest expense	2,482,040	2,177,466
Net income (loss) before income taxes	185,568	(5,030,816)
Income tax recovery (Note 12)	(5,122,516)	(1,471,428)
Net income (loss) and comprehensive income (loss) for the year	5,308,084	(3,559,388)
Net income (loss) per share (basic and diluted) (Note 16)	$ 0.01	$ (0.01)
Weighted average number of shares outstanding	655,247,197	655,116,857

EXHIBIT 10-15B	ZOOMERMEDIA LIMITED'S 2013 CONSOLIDATED STATEMENTS OF FINANCIAL POSITION

	June 30, 2013	June 30, 2012 (revised - Note 7)
ASSETS		
Current assets		
Cash	$ 2,829,733	$ 5,069,754
Restricted cash and investments (Note 5)	5,921,642	—
Trade and other receivables (Note 4)	13,227,045	13,876,209
Prepaid expenses	538,751	523,101
	22,517,171	19,469,064

continued

EXHIBIT 10-15B	ZOOMERMEDIA LIMITED'S 2013 CONSOLIDATED STATEMENTS OF FINANCIAL POSITION (continued)

	June 30, 2013	June 30, 2012
		(revised - Note 7)
Non-current assets		
Restricted cash and investments (Note 5)	—	6,420,758
Property and equipment (Note 6)	22,851,545	21,585,161
Deferred tax assets (Note 12)	6,817,751	777,967
Intangible assets (Note 7)	31,332,207	36,321,291
Goodwill (Note 7)	2,574,758	2,574,758
TOTAL ASSETS	$86,093,432	$87,148,999
LIABILITIES		
Current liabilities		
Trade and other payables (Note 23)	$ 7,071,876	$ 7,433,607
Deferred revenue (Note 8)	2,171,731	2,142,306
Income tax liabilities (Note 12)	802,387	160,996
Current portion of debt (Notes 9 and 23)	10,921,518	1,895,200
Current portion of other liabilities (Note 10)	2,472,870	6,747,779
Current portion of provisions (Note 11)	567,940	619,310
	24,008,322	18,999,198
Non-current liabilities		
Deferred revenue (Note 8)	1,064,453	1,224,496
Deferred tax liabilities (Note 12)	238,500	439,316
Debt (Note 9)	22,538,372	33,403,709
Other liabilities (Note 10)	332,762	471,936
Provisions (Note 11)	146,749	403,540
	48,329,158	54,942,195
EQUITY		
Equity attributable to owners of the parent		
Share capital	63,491,613	63,411,344
Contributed surplus	2,205,372	2,036,255
Deficit	(27,932,711)	(33,240,795)
Total equity	37,764,274	32,206,804
TOTAL LIABILITIES AND EQUITY	$86,093,432	$87,148,999

Commitments and contingencies (Note 21)

Required:

a. Calculate the debt to equity ratio, the net debts as a percentage of total capitalization ratio, and the interest coverage ratio for the years ending June 30, 2013 and 2012. *Note:* Impairment charges should be treated like amortization when determining EBITDA.

b. Identify the major factors that caused the changes in these ratios.

c. Write a short report commenting on the results of the ratio calculations in part "a." Be sure to comment from the perspectives of an existing shareholder and a potential lender of long-term debt.

RI10-9 (Debt to total assets and times interest earned ratios)

Fortress Paper Ltd. operates internationally in three distinct business segments: dissolving pulp, specialty papers, and security paper products. The statement of financial position and statement of income (statement of operations) from Fortress's 2013 annual report are presented in Exhibits 10-16A and B.

EXHIBIT 10-16A	FORTRESS PAPER LTD.'S 2013 CONSOLIDATED STATEMENTS OF FINANCIAL POSITION

FORTRESS PAPER LTD.
CONSOLIDATED STATEMENTS OF FINANCIAL POSITION
(Canadian dollars, amounts in thousands)

	Note	December 31, 2013 $	December 31, 2012 $
ASSETS			
Current			
Cash and cash equivalents		61,888	31,491
Restricted cash	5	14,934	2,600
Trade accounts receivable	6	12,446	13,835
Other accounts receivable	7	8,751	28,403
Inventories	8	62,390	53,064
Prepaid expenses	13	8,486	8,334
		168,895	137,727
Property, plant and equipment	10	412,949	440,227
Total assets		581,844	577,954
LIABILITIES AND SHAREHOLDERS' EQUITY			
Current			
Accounts payable and accrued liabilities	11	34,044	79,806
Income taxes payable	12	–	3,123
Current portion of long-term debt	13	14,572	7,761
		48,616	90,690
Long-term debt	13	213,558	248,140
Deferred income taxes	12	4,734	2,154
Provisions and other long-term liabilities	14	7,921	5,528
Employee future benefits	15	4,737	1,773
Total liabilities		279,566	348,285
Shareholders' equity			
Share capital	16	180,040	178,052
Contributed surplus		25,950	26,078
Retained earnings		75,368	23,387
Accumulated other comprehensive income		20,920	2,152
Total shareholders' equity		302,278	229,669
Total liabilities and shareholders' equity		581,844	577,954

| EXHIBIT 10-16B | FORTRESS PAPER LTD.'S 2013 CONSOLIDATED STATEMENTS OF OPERATIONS |

FORTRESS PAPER LTD.
CONSOLIDATED STATEMENTS OF OPERATIONS
For the years ended
(Canadian dollars, amounts in thousands)

	Note	December 31, 2013 $	December 31, 2012 $
Sales		207,785	163,923
Costs and expenses			
Manufacturing and product costs		(202,980)	(178,036)
Freight and other distribution costs		(3,750)	(1,674)
Amortization	10	(19,732)	(15,669)
Selling, general and administration		(41,180)	(29,208)
Stock-based compensation	17	(1,905)	(3,516)
Operating loss		(61,762)	(64,180)
Other income (expense)			
Finance expense	18	(16,970)	(11,153)
Finance income	18	298	326
Gain on sale of property, plant and equipment	10	5,242	19,297
Impairment of property plant and equipment	10	(32,907)	–
Foreign exchange (loss)		(138)	(66)
Net loss from continuing operations before income taxes		(106,237)	(55,776)
Income tax (expense) recovery	12	(1,586)	13,439
Net loss from continuing operations		(107,823)	(42,337)
Net income from discontinued operations	9	162,408	20,669
Net income (loss)		54,585	(21,668)

Required:
a. Calculate the debt to equity ratio, the net debt as a percentage of total capitalization ratio, and the interest coverage ratio for 2013 and 2012.
b. Identify the major factors that contributed to the changes in these ratios.
c. Write a short report commenting on the results of the ratio calculations that you did in part "a." Be sure to comment from the perspectives of an existing shareholder and a potential lender of long-term debt.

RI10-10 (Financial statement analysis)

Big Rock Brewery Inc. is a regional producer of craft beers and cider. The company's products are sold in nine provinces and territories in Canada. Exhibits 10-17A to C contain extracts from Big Rock's 2013 annual report.

EXHIBIT 10-17A	BIG ROCK BREWERY INC.'S 2013 CONSOLIDATED STATEMENTS OF FINANCIAL POSITION

BIG ROCK BREWERY INC.
Consolidated Statements of Financial Position
(In thousands of Canadian dollars)

	December 30, 2013	December 30, 2012
ASSETS		
Non-current assets		
Property, plant and equipment (Note 11)	$ 35,142	$ 35,277
Intangible assets (Note 12)	108	128
	35,250	35,405
Current		
Inventories (Note 13)	2,983	3,892
Accounts receivable (Notes 14 and 22)	1,353	2,358
Prepaid expenses and other (Note 15)	754	364
Cash	2,317	4,281
	7,407	10,895
Total assets	$ 42,657	$ 46,300
LIABILITIES AND SHAREHOLDERS' EQUITY		
EQUITY		
Shareholders' capital (Note 16)	$100,109	$100,109
Contributed surplus (Notes 16 and 17)	892	701
Accumulated deficit	(71,043)	(68,739)
	29,958	32,071
LIABILITIES		
Non-current		
Long term debt (Notes 18 and 22)	—	1,342
Share-based payments (Note 17)	687	238
Deferred income taxes (Note 9)	4,745	6,331
	5,432	7,911
Current		
Accounts payable and accrued liabilities (Notes 19 and 22)	4,100	3,978
Dividends payable (Notes 20 and 22)	1,214	1,214
Current portion of long-term debt (Notes 18 and 22)	—	700
Current taxes payable (Note 9)	1,953	426
	7,267	6,318
Commitments (Note 26)		
Total liabilities and shareholders' equity	$ 42,657	$ 46,300

| EXHIBIT 10-17B | BIG ROCK BREWERY INC.'S 2013 CONSOLIDATED STATEMENTS OF COMPREHENSIVE INCOME |

BIG ROCK BREWERY INC.
Consolidated Statements of Comprehensive Income
(In thousands of Canadian dollars, except per share amounts)

	Year ended	
	December 30, 2013	December 30, 2012
Net revenue (Notes 3.2 and 4)	41,587	46,057
Cost of sales (Notes 5 and 24)	20,260	21,149
Gross profit	21,327	24,908
Expenses		
Selling expenses (Notes 6 and 23)	12,910	13,987
General and administrative (Notes 7 and 24)	4,821	4,945
Depreciation and amortization	314	358
Operating expenses	18,045	19,290
Operating profit	3,282	5,618
Finance costs (Note 8)	9	93
Other income	286	351
Other expenses	109	147
Income before income taxes	3,450	5,729
Current income tax expense (Note 9)	2,485	426
Deferred income tax expense (recovery) (Note 9)	(1,586)	1,168
Net income and comprehensive income for the period	2,551	4,135

| EXHIBIT 10-17C | BIG ROCK BREWERY INC.'S 2013 CONSOLIDATED STATEMENTS OF CASH FLOWS |

BIG ROCK BREWERY INC.
Consolidated Statements of Cash Flows
(In thousands of Canadian dollars)

	Year ended	
	December 30, 2013	December 30, 2012
OPERATING ACTIVITIES		
Net income for the period	$ 2,551	$ 4,135
Items not affecting cash:		
Depreciation and amortization	3,157	3,228
Gain on sale of assets	(13)	(19)
Stock-based compensation	640	446
Deferred income tax expense (recovery)	(1,586)	1,168
Net change in non-cash working capital related to operations (note 25)	3,148	1,496
Cash provided by operating activities	7,897	10,454

continued

EXHIBIT 10-17C	BIG ROCK BREWERY INC.'S 2013 CONSOLIDATED STATEMENTS OF CASH FLOWS (continued)

	Year ended	
	December 30, 2013	December 30, 2012
FINANCING ACTIVITIES		
Dividend payments	(4,855)	(4,850)
Principal repayments of long-term debt	(2,042)	(641)
Cash received on exercise of options	—	131
Cash used in financing activities	(6,897)	(5,360)
INVESTING ACTIVITIES		
Purchase of property, plant and equipment	(2,992)	(1,487)
Purchase of intangibles	(6)	—
Proceeds from sale of equipment	34	19
Cash used in investing activities	(2,964)	(1,468)
Net increase (decrease) in cash	(1,964)	3,626
Cash, beginning of year	4,281	655
Cash, end of year	$ 2,317	$ 4,281

EXHIBIT 10-17D	EXCERPT FROM BIG ROCK BREWERY INC.'S 2013 ANNUAL REPORT

21. CAPITAL RISK MANAGEMENT

The Corporation includes as capital its common shares plus short-term and long-term debt, net of cash balances, and has no externally imposed capital requirements. The Corporation's objectives are to safeguard the Corporation's ability to continue as a going concern, in order to support the Corporation's normal operating requirements and to maintain a flexible capital structure which optimizes the costs of capital at an acceptable risk. This allows management to maximize the profitability of its existing assets and create long-term value and enhance returns for its shareholders.

	Dec. 30, 2013	Dec. 30, 2012
Bank indebtedness (cash)	$ (2,317)	$ (4,281)
Total debt	—	2,042
Shareholders' equity:		
Shareholders' capital	100,109	100,109
Contributed surplus	892	701
Accumulated deficit	(71,043)	(68,739)
Total shareholders' equity	29,958	32,071
Total capitalization (total debt plus shareholders' equity, net of cash balances)	$ 27,641	$29,832

The Corporation manages the capital structure through prudent levels of borrowing, cash-flow forecasting, and working capital management, and makes adjustments to it in light of changes in economic conditions and the risk characteristics of the underlying assets. In order to maintain or adjust the capital structure, the Corporation may issue new shares, issue new debt, acquire or dispose of assets or adjust the amount of cash and cash equivalents. In order to facilitate the management of its capital requirements, the Corporation prepares annual expenditure budgets, which are approved by the Board of Directors. These budgets are updated as necessary depending on various factors, including capital deployment, results from operations, and general industry conditions.

continued

| EXHIBIT 10-17D | **EXCERPT FROM BIG ROCK BREWERY INC.'S 2013 ANNUAL REPORT (continued)** |

In addition, the Corporation monitors its capital using ratios of (i) earnings before interest, taxes, depreciation and amortization ("EBITDA") to long-term debt and (ii) EBITDA to interest, debt repayments and dividends. EBITDA to interest, debt repayments and dividends is calculated by dividing the combined interest, debt repayments and dividend amounts by EBITDA and EBITDA to long-term debt is calculated by dividing long-term debt by EBITDA.

These capital policies, which remain unchanged from prior periods, provide Big Rock with access to capital at a reasonable cost.

Required:
  a. Calculate the ratios that the management of Big Rock Brewery have indicated they monitor in relation to their management of capital.
  b. Write a short report commenting on the results of the ratio calculations in part "a."

RI10-11 (Commitments)

The Second Cup Ltd. is Canada's largest specialty coffee café franchisor (as measured by number of cafés) with 365 cafés operating under the trade name Second Cup. Exhibit 10-18 is an excerpt from Note 21 from the company's 2013 annual report detailing Second Cup's commitments.

| EXHIBIT 10-18 | **EXCERPT FROM THE SECOND CUP LTD.'S 2013 ANNUAL REPORT** |

22. CONTINGENCIES, COMMITMENTS AND GUARANTEES

The Coffee "C" contract is the world benchmark for Arabica coffee. The contract prices physical delivery of exchange grade green beans from one of 19 countries of origin in a licensed warehouse to one of several ports in the U.S. and Europe, with stated premiums/discounts. Second Cup sources high altitude Arabica coffee which tends to trade at a premium above the "C" coffee commodity price. Second Cup has contracts with third party companies to purchase the coffee that is sold in all Second Cup cafés. In terms of these supply agreements, Second Cup has guaranteed a minimum volume of coffee purchases of $5,621 USD (2012 – $4,421 USD) during fiscal 2014. The coffee purchase commitment is comprised of three components: unapplied futures commitment contracts, fixed price physical contracts and flat price physical contracts.

Required:
Explain this note in your own words. Be sure to discuss the financial statement impacts, if any, of this roasting contract and the financial statement impacts it will have in future years.

RI10-12 (Contingencies)

Bombardier Inc. is a Canadian manufacturer of aircraft and rail transportation equipment and systems. Exhibit 10-19 contains an excerpt from Note 39 of the company's 2013 annual report detailing Bombardier's contingencies.

| EXHIBIT 10-19 | **EXCERPT FROM BOMBARDIER INC.'S 2013 ANNUAL REPORT** |

39. COMMITMENTS AND CONTINGENCIES (amounts in thousands of US dollars)

Litigation

In the normal course of operations, the Corporation is a defendant in certain legal proceedings currently pending before various courts in relation to product liability and contract disputes with customers and other third parties. The Corporation intends to vigorously defend its position in these matters.

While the Corporation cannot predict the final outcome of legal proceedings pending as at December 31, 2013, based on information currently available, management believes that the resolution of these legal proceedings will not have a material adverse effect on its financial position.

continued

| EXHIBIT 10-19 | EXCERPT FROM BOMBARDIER INC.'S 2013 ANNUAL REPORT (continued) |

S-Bahn claim

On March 4, 2013, S-Bahn Berlin GMBH ("SB") filed a claim against Bombardier Transportation GmbH, a wholly owned subsidiary of the Corporation, in the Berlin District Court ("Landgericht Berlin"), concerning the trains of the 481 Series delivered to SB between 1996 and 2004.

This lawsuit alleges damages of an aggregate value of €348 million ($480 million) related to allegedly defective wheels and braking systems. The claim is for payment of €241 million ($332 million) and also for a declaratory judgment obliging the Corporation to compensate SB for further damages. SB currently alleges such further damages to be €107 million ($148 million).

It is the Corporation's position that this claim i) is filed in absence of any defect, ii) is not founded on any enforceable warranty, iii) is filed after the expiry of any statute of limitations and iv) is based on inapplicable standards. The lawsuit contains allegations against the Corporation which the Corporation rejects as unfounded and defamatory.

The Corporation intends to vigorously defend its position and will undertake all actions necessary to protect its reputation. While the Corporation cannot predict the final outcome of this claim pending as at December 31, 2013, based on information currently available, management believes the resolution of this claim will not have a material adverse effect on its financial position.

Required:

Explain, in your own words, what Bombardier is saying in this note disclosure. Be sure to discuss the financial impacts this litigation could have on the company if a future judgement went against the company.

RII0-13 (Analysis of a company's liabilities)

Required:

Choose a company as directed by your instructor and do the following:

a. Prepare a quick analysis of the non-current liability accounts by listing the beginning and ending amounts in these accounts and calculating the net change, in both dollar and percentage terms, for the most recent year.

b. If any of the accounts changed by more than 10%, try to give an explanation for the change.

c. What percentage of the company's total liabilities is in the form of long-term bank loans? Long-term bonds? Have these percentages changed significantly over the last year?

d. What interest rates is the company paying on its long-term debt? (Hint: You will probably need to look in the notes to the financial statements to find the answer to this question.)

e. Calculate the company's debt to equity ratio and its times interest earned ratio. To the extent that you can, based on this limited analysis, comment on the company's financial health in terms of its level of debt and interest expense.

f. Read the company's note on income taxes and identify whether the company has a deferred income tax liability or asset.

g. Read the company's note on contractual commitments and identify the nature and amount of any commitments.

Cases

C10-1 Regal Cars

Regal Cars Ltd. has been manufacturing exotic automobiles for more than 50 years. It has always prided itself on its top-quality products and high levels of customer satisfaction. All Regal Cars are hand-built to the purchasers' individual specifications. In the past year, the popularity of Regal Cars has increased dramatically following a promotional campaign in which Regal provided complimentary cars to star members of the local NHL team. To meet the increasing demand, Mark Quaid, the president and largest shareholder of Regal Cars, is considering partially automating the production line.

To finance the conversion of the manual production line to a highly specialized robotic system, Mark will have to raise more than $1 million in capital. The company has been in the Quaid family for more than 50 years and Mark is unwilling to sell shares and risk diluting his family's equity in the business. As an alternative to equity financing, he has identified three potential sources of debt financing and has asked you to explain how each option would affect the company's financial statements.

Option 1—Bank loan

A national bank has offered to lend Regal the necessary funds in the form of a 10-year, 12% bank loan. Annual payments of $100,000 plus interest will be required. Because of the loan's size, the bank would require Mark Quaid to personally guarantee the loan with a mortgage on the family estate.

Option 2—Bond issue

Regal can issue 10-year, 10% bonds for the amount required. Currently, similar bonds in the market are providing a return of 10%.

Option 3—Lease

Regal can lease the equipment. The lease would require annual payments of $104,000 over a 10-year lease period. The present value of these payments, at an annual interest rate of 8%, would be $697,850. The equipment is expected to have a useful life of 12 years and to be worth about $100,000 at the end of the 10 years.

Required:

Prepare a memo to Mark Quaid discussing how each of these options would affect the company's financial statements. You should also include in your memo any other pertinent observations that could influence the financing decision he has to make.

C10-2 Jonah Fitzpatrick

Jonah Fitzpatrick would like to start investing and is considering purchasing some of the bonds being issued by Jennings Financial. Details of the bond issue were outlined in a recent article in *Financial Times Magazine*. The following is an excerpt from the article:

> Jennings Financial is planning to issue a series of bonds to help finance the acquisition of a large manufacturing facility. In consultation with its investment bankers, the company has decided to issue $100 million of 8%, five-year bonds. Each bond will be denominated at $1,000. The bonds will be classified as senior debenture bonds and will be sold to yield a return of 10%. Because this is such a large issue, the investment banker is required to underwrite the issue. However, given the company's historical performance and financial strength, a syndicate is willing to guarantee the entire issue.

Jonah is unfamiliar with bond issues and approaches Mike Scullino, his stockbroker, with some basic questions.

Jonah: I've always invested in equity securities, Mike, but I want to consider investing in the bonds being issued by Jennings Financial. I know very little about bonds, though, so I have a few questions.

Mike: Sure thing, Jonah. Just e-mail your questions and I'll get back to you later today.

Required:

Jonah has just sent Mike the following e-mail. Draft an appropriate response.

Mike, here are my questions on the Jennings bonds. I look forward to hearing from you.

1. The advertisement for the bond issue states that the bonds will be 8% bonds but will yield 10%. Why are there two interest rates? Which interest rate should I use to determine how much I'll earn on the bonds?
2. What are debenture bonds? Will I have any security if the company defaults on these bonds?
3. What is the role of the investment banker? What does it mean to use a syndicate?
4. What if I need my money back before the end of the five-year period? Does the five-year term mean that I would be locked into this investment for five years?

C10-3 Wasselec's Moving and Storage

Wasselec's Moving and Storage Ltd. is a small company based in Hamilton, Ontario. It operates in both the residential and commercial markets. To serve its various clients, Wasselec's owns two large moving trucks (tractor-trailer units), six medium-sized cartage trucks, two large vans, and two cars. Because its business relies on its vehicles, it has always been the company's policy to purchase new vehicles on a regular rotation basis. Its accountant and vehicle service manager have established guidelines that trigger the purchase of a new vehicle. For example, the large vans are replaced every 200,000 kilometres, the tractors every 10 years, and the trailers every 15 years.

The president of the company, Sylvia Wasselec, recently read an article about the increasing trend toward leasing. She wonders if Wasselec's should start leasing its vehicles instead of buying them, and has asked

Dogan Yilmaz, the chief financial officer (CFO), for guidance in this matter. In turn, the CFO has asked you, a recent addition to the company's staff, to prepare a summary of the advantages and disadvantages of ownership versus leasing.

Required:

Draft a memo to Dogan Yilmaz summarizing the advantages and disadvantages of ownership and leasing, with reference to the types of assets currently owned by Wasselec's Moving and Storage. The CFO is very busy, so your memo should be concise.

C10-4 Grant's Ice Cream Shop

Jack and Gillian Grant, owners of Grant's Ice Cream Shop Ltd., have recently expanded their business by moving into a second location in a nearby town. To open the second location, the company had to obtain three large ice cream machines. To buy the machines would have cost over $15,000, so Jack and Gillian decided to lease them instead.

The lease term is for five years and the machines are expected to have a useful life of eight to 10 years. According to the lease contract, the present value of the lease payments over the lease term is $12,000 and the Grants will have the option to purchase the leased machines for $1,000 at the end of the five-year lease term. Their fair market value is expected to be approximately $4,000 at the end of the lease.

Jack Grant is thrilled with the arrangement. "Not only do we get the machines that we need without a large initial cash outlay, but we don't have to record any liability on the statement of financial position; we can just report the annual lease payments as equipment rental expense on the statement of income."

Required:

Is Jack correct in assuming that the lease payments will be recorded as an expense and that no debt will have to be reported on the statement of financial position as a result of this transaction? Explain your answer fully, by referring to the criteria for lease classification and the appropriate accounting treatment for this type of lease.

C10-5 Peterson Corporation

As part of recent contract negotiations, Peterson Corporation has presented two pension plan options to its employees. The employees are to vote on which plan they would like the company to implement. Peterson Corporation owns and operates a chain of grocery stores throughout western Canada and employs more than 3,000 people. Most employees have a very limited accounting knowledge. Your cousin, Karen Rosolowski, is a cashier at a Peterson store located in Kamloops, British Columbia, and she has asked you for help in determining which pension option to vote for. She is confused over the terminology used in the proposal and would like you to explain the two alternatives in simpler terms, so that she can make an informed decision.

Option 1

The company will establish a defined contribution pension plan. The company will contribute 10% of the employee's gross wages to the pension plan each pay period. Vesting will occur immediately and the funds will be placed with an independent trustee to be invested. Employees will have the option of contributing additional funds to the plan.

Option 2

The company will establish a defined benefit plan. The plan will guarantee that each employee will receive 2% of the average of their highest five years of salary multiplied by the number of years the employee works for the company. The plan will be fully employer-funded and the pension entitlement will vest after five years of continuous service.

Required:

Briefly explain to Karen the difference between the two pension plan options. You should remember that Karen is unfamiliar with pension terminology and you therefore have to explain some of the terms used in the plan descriptions.

ENDNOTES

1. François Shalom, "How Air Canada Eliminated a $3.6-Billion Pension Deficit in under a Year," *The Gazette* (Montreal), January 27, 2014; The Canadian Press, "Air Canada $3.7B Pension Deficit Eliminated," CBC News, January 22, 2014; Statistics Canada, "Pension Plans in Canada, as of January 1, 2012," *The Daily*, December 1, 2013; Air Canada 2013 annual report.
2. WestJet Airlines Ltd.'s 2013 annual report, Note 10.
3. Valeant Pharmaceuticals International, Inc.'s 2013 annual report, Note 14.
4. University of Toronto's 2013 financial statements, Note 11.
5. WestJet Airlines Ltd.'s 2013 annual report; Air Canada's 2013 annual report, Note 8.
6. Saputo Inc.'s 2014 annual report, Note 17.
7. Canadian Tire Corporation, Limited's 2013 annual report, Note 27.
8. Big Rock Brewery Inc.'s 2013 annual report, Note 26.
9. Gildan Activewear Inc.'s 2013 annual report, Note 24.
10. Toromont Industries Ltd.'s 2013 annual report, Note 20.
11. Maple Leaf Foods Inc.'s 2013 annual report, Note 18.

CORE QUESTIONS

If you are able to answer the following questions, then you have achieved the related learning objectives

LEARNING OBJECTIVES

After studying this chapter, you should be able to:

●●● INTRODUCTION

- Why is shareholders' equity of significance to users?

1 Explain why the shareholders' equity section is significant to users.

- What is included in the shareholders' equity section of the statement of financial position?

2 Explain the components of the shareholders' equity section of the statement of financial position.

●●● TYPES OF SHARES

- What types of shares is a company allowed to issue?
- What is the difference between authorized, issued, and outstanding shares?
- Why would a company repurchase its own shares?
- What are the differences between common shares and preferred shares?

3 Describe the different types of shares and explain why corporations choose to issue a variety of share types.

●●● DIVIDENDS

- Do companies have to pay dividends?
- What are the different dates involved in declaring and paying a dividend?
- How are the declaration and payment of dividends recorded?
- What is the difference between a cash dividend and a stock dividend?

4 Describe the types of dividends, explain why one type of dividend may be used rather than another, and describe how dividends are recorded.

●●● STOCK SPLITS

- What is a stock split?
- Why would a company split its shares?

5 Describe what a stock split is and explain how it is accounted for.

●●● FINANCIAL STATEMENT ANALYSIS

- What is the price/earnings ratio?
- Which other ratios measure the return shareholders are earning?

6 Calculate and interpret the price/earnings ratio, dividend payout ratio, dividend yield, and return on shareholders' equity ratio.

●●● FINANCING WITH EQUITY

- What are the advantages and disadvantages of financing with equity?

7 Identify the advantages and disadvantages of using equity financing.

●●● Shareholders Get More than Small Change

When Salim Rossy opened a general store in Montreal in 1910, he financed it with his earnings from peddling items like brooms and dishcloths in the countryside around Montreal. By the time his grandson Larry took charge in 1973, S. Rossy Inc. had grown into a chain of 20 five-and-dime stores, with most items priced at either 5 or 10 cents. In 1992, the company opened its first Dollarama store, selling all items for $1. Today, the business, now called Dollarama Inc., is Canada's largest dollar store chain. It operates more than 870 stores across the country and now sells goods at between $1 and $3.

The company's rapid expansion between 1992 and 2009 was financed using a combination of debt and earnings. In 2009, approximately 92.5% of Dollarama's financing was debt-related. That same year, the company went public, issuing more than 17 million shares on the Toronto Stock Exchange, which raised $300 million. These proceeds were used to repay long-term debt and the promissory notes (formal agreements representing amounts owed to a creditor) owed to its founding shareholders. This significantly altered the company's financing structure, resulting in approximately 46% of the company's overall financing coming from shareholders. At the time, Larry Rossy noted, "As a result of our successful $300 million initial public offering . . . we have reduced our net debt and we are in a strong position to continue growing the business."

The company's share prices have mirrored its growth, increasing from $17.50 when Dollarama went public to $88.00 in June 2014—a 400% return in just six years! The increase in share price is just one of the ways that Dollarama's shareholders have benefited. They have also received regular quarterly dividends since June 2011, which have increased each year from $0.09 per share to $0.16 per share in 2014.

In 2013, the company decided that a portion of its cash balances was surplus to its requirements and used it to return some equity to shareholders. In fiscal 2013, it repurchased just over 3.7 million shares, returning $293.2 million to shareholders. This reduced Dollarama's share capital by $26.5 million and retained earnings by $266.7 million.

While Dollarama is publicly owned, the Rossy family remains involved. Entities controlled by the Rossy family continue to own about 6% of the company's shares, Larry Rossy remains the CEO, while his son Neil is a senior manager. The company's growth story is one Larry Rossy sees continuing. "From the experience I have, we're far from saturated," he said. "Every time I think we're saturated in an area, I open 10 more stores there."[1]

INTRODUCTION

■ **LEARNING OBJECTIVE 1**
Explain why the shareholders' equity section is significant to users.

As the chapter-opening feature article shows, companies like **Dollarama Inc.** issue shares to investors, but can also repurchase these shares if the company has cash that is surplus to its needs. This chapter discusses how publicly traded companies like Dollarama account for these changes in shareholders' equity.

Why is shareholders' equity of significance to users?

Most people will purchase shares of companies at some point in their lives. These share purchases are commonly made by individuals as part of their investment portfolios, either directly (by purchasing shares from the company or from other investors) or indirectly (by investing in mutual funds which, in turn, own shares of various companies). Individuals may also purchase shares in their role as an employee or an entrepreneur. In the first case, sometimes employers offer employees the opportunity to buy shares in the company. In the second case, an entrepreneur starting their own business would purchase shares on the incorporation of their company. Finally, most pension plans include the shares of companies among their investments.

No doubt you will find yourself in one or more of these situations in the future. Whatever the scenario, it will be important for you to understand how your ownership interest is measured and disclosed in the financial statements. You should also understand why companies choose to finance with equity and what the advantages and disadvantages of equity financing are. Finally, you will also want to understand the impact of a company's earnings on how shares are valued in the market and how you can assess the return on your investment.

So far in this book, we have talked about only one kind of shares: common shares. While all companies have at least one class of common shares, most have several different classes and types of shares. With the help of financial experts, companies design and create classes and types of shares that have a variety of features to provide investors with different levels of risk and return. This is achieved by varying the rights and privileges associated with these shares. Understanding them will enable you to more accurately assess the opportunities and risks they represent. In addition, when a company raises more capital by issuing new shares, you need to be aware of how that new issuance affects your ownership position.

As you can see, there are lots of reasons why you will want to understand shareholders' equity. Let's now take a brief look at what is included in the shareholders' equity section of the statement of financial position.

What is included in the shareholders' equity section of the statement of financial position?

■ **LEARNING OBJECTIVE 2**
Explain the components of the shareholders' equity section of the statement of financial position.

In Chapter 1, you were introduced to the two main components of the shareholders' equity section of the statement of financial position: share capital and retained earnings. Share capital represents the amount that investors paid for the shares when they were initially issued by the company. Retained earnings represents the assets generated from the accumulated earnings of the company that have not been distributed as dividends to shareholders. Up to this point, our discussion of share capital has focused on common shares. In the next section of this chapter, we will discuss different types of shares that a company could issue and how that affects the company's share capital. Later, we will briefly review retained earnings.

There are other accounts that may also be reported in the shareholders' equity section: Accumulated Other Comprehensive Income and Contributed Surplus. While the transactions involving these accounts are beyond the scope of an introductory textbook, it is useful for you as a financial statement user to have a basic understanding of them because you will come across them in the financial statements of most public companies.

Accumulated Other Comprehensive Income

When other comprehensive income was introduced in Chapter 4, we learned that accounting standards specify that certain gains and losses incurred by a company must be reported in other comprehensive income rather than net income. These gains and losses normally arise from transactions that revalue certain financial statement items. These transactions include the revaluation of certain types of investments to fair value or the revaluation of items denominated in foreign currencies into the reporting currency, such as the Canadian dollar. The gains and losses that result from these revaluations are considered to be unrealized because they did not result from transactions with third parties and are, therefore, excluded from net income. They are reported after net income as **other comprehensive income**. Just as they are excluded from net income, they are also excluded from retained earnings. Instead, other comprehensive income is usually aggregated in an account known as **accumulated other comprehensive income (AOCI)**, which is part of shareholders' equity. Accumulated other comprehensive income is like a separate type of retained earnings. Essentially, it is the "retained earnings" account for other comprehensive income. Some of the gains or losses reported in accumulated other comprehensive income are eventually transferred to net income or retained earnings, but that discussion is best left for more advanced accounting courses.

You might wonder why it is necessary to keep the other comprehensive income in a separate account in the shareholders' equity section instead of including it in retained earnings. This is to highlight the fact that the transactions that give rise to these gains and losses are unrealized. That is, they did not result from transactions with third parties. For example, let's say a company's other comprehensive income resulted from an increase in the market value of certain short-term investments. While the securities may have increased in value at the statement of financial position date, resulting in other comprehensive income, the company has yet to sell the securities; that is, the gain is unrealized. When the company does sell the securities, the final gain may be higher or lower, or a loss may even result. Given this uncertainty, it is important to exclude such gains (and losses) from retained earnings. Doing so ensures that shareholders can be made aware of the financial effects of such revaluations, but excludes the resulting gains (and losses) from retained earnings. This means that they have no effect on the earnings available for distribution as dividends until they have actually been realized.

Contributed Surplus

Contributed surplus arises from certain transactions with shareholders involving the sale or repurchase of a company's shares or the issuance of stock options. Sometimes parts of those transactions do not fit the definitions of share capital or retained earnings and are recorded in the Contributed Surplus account. For example, as we will discuss later in the chapter, companies (such as Dollarama in our feature story) sometimes repurchase their own shares. If the company repurchases these shares for less than they were originally issued for, the difference is considered contributed surplus.

For example, let's say the company had initially issued shares at $10.00 per share but was able to repurchase some of them at a market price that is lower, say $8.00. In that case, the $2.00 per share difference would be credited to Contributed Surplus. It is not reported as a gain on the statement of income because that statement only reports transactions with external parties and not those with owners.

Exhibit 11-1 illustrates the statement of changes in shareholders' equity, which provides the shareholders' equity account balances that are reported on the statement of financial position. The statement of changes in shareholders' equity provides the opening and ending balance for each of the accounts that are included

Exhibit 11-1 Contents of the Statement of Changes in Shareholders' Equity

Statement of Changes in Shareholders' Equity

	Share Capital	Contributed Surplus	Retained Earnings	AOCI	Total
Opening Balance	✓	✓	✓	✓	✓
+ Net Income			+		✓
+ Other Comprehensive Income				+	✓
− Dividends Declared			−		✓
+ Shares Issued	+				✓
− Shares Repurchased	−	+			✓
+ Share-Based Payments		+			✓
Ending Balance	✓	✓	✓	✓	✓

in shareholders' equity, and explains the reason for any changes in the account balance. For example, if new shares were issued, then the Share Capital account balance would increase. If the company generated net income or paid dividends, the Retained Earnings account would be affected. Other comprehensive income would increase the Accumulated Other Comprehensive Income account.

TYPES OF SHARES

What types of shares is a company allowed to issue?

When a business operates as a corporation (as opposed to a proprietorship or partnership), the company is incorporated either under federal legislation, the Canada Business Corporations Act, or under similar provincial or territorial acts. The shareholders incorporating the company work with their legal counsel to prepare the company's **articles of incorporation**. This document includes important details on what type of business the company will conduct, how the board of directors will be organized, who the management will be, and what kinds of shares can be issued, as well as other information. The exact content of the articles will depend on the decisions of the incorporating shareholders. Once the company has been incorporated, the articles of incorporation can generally be amended only by a unanimous shareholder vote, so it is important that the articles be carefully considered at the time of incorporation.

For accounting purposes, the most important section a company's articles of incorporation is the section outlining the various types and classes of shares that the company is authorized to issue. These are referred to as the **authorized shares**.

There are two main types of shares: common shares and preferred shares. There can be different classes of each type of share (class A common, class B common, class A preferred, class B preferred, etc.). Within each class of shares, there can also be one or more series of shares (class A preferred, series A).

All companies are required to have at least one class of common shares. However, most companies have articles of incorporation that authorize them to issue multiple classes of common shares, such as Class A or Class B. Most companies are also authorized to issue multiple classes of preferred shares, such as Class A preferred or Class B preferred. Later in the chapter, we will discuss some of the key differences between common and preferred shares and why a company may wish to have different classes of shares. For now, it is important to understand that companies can issue a variety of shares.

The articles of incorporation may specify a maximum number of shares that the company can issue or it may state that the amount is unlimited. If a company's articles limit the number of authorized shares, the company may face the risk that, over time, it will issue all of the authorized shares. If it wanted to issue additional shares, then the company would have to change its articles of incorporation. While this can be done, it may not be easy because all shareholders would have to agree to any changes. Setting the authorized shares at an unlimited amount gives companies the greatest flexibility and allows the board of directors to issue shares as necessary as a means for raising capital.

■ **LEARNING OBJECTIVE 3**
Describe the different types of shares and explain why corporations choose to issue a variety of share types.

What is the difference between authorized, issued, and outstanding shares?

Three terms are used to refer to the number of company shares: authorized shares, issued shares, and outstanding shares. Shares that have been issued (sold) by the company are known as **issued shares**. As long as the shares remain in the possession of shareholders outside the company, they are also considered to be **outstanding shares**. As discussed in the next section, sometimes a company repurchases some of its own shares. If the company cancels these shares, they will cease to be issued and will revert to the status of only being authorized. If the company continues to hold these shares, they are known as **treasury shares**. These shares are considered issued but are no longer outstanding. Therefore, outstanding shares are the issued shares excluding any that the company has repurchased and is holding for potential reissue. This distinction is important because dividends are only paid on shares that are issued *and* outstanding. The number of shares that are issued and outstanding is also used to calculate earnings per share (EPS), an important measure that will be discussed later in the chapter.

When a company issues shares, the amount it receives on issuance is called the **legal capital**. This amount must be kept intact and cannot be paid out as dividends or returned to shareholders, except under specific circumstances. This protects creditors by ensuring that shareholders continue to have their own capital invested and "at risk" within the company.

PAR VALUE SHARES

In the past, a company's articles of incorporation could assign a specific dollar value to each share. This was known as the share's **par value**. When the shares were issued, the par value of each share was credited to the Common Shares account and any excess was credited to an account called Contributed Surplus. The amount credited to the Common Shares or Share Capital account (in this case, the par value of the shares) is referred to as the legal capital and must be kept intact. Except under specific circumstances, it cannot be paid out as dividends. This provides protection for creditors.

Under most jurisdictions in Canada, par value shares are no longer permitted. Instead, most companies issue **no par value shares**. When no par value shares are issued, the total amount received for the shares is credited to the Common Shares or Share Capital account. This results in a larger amount of legal capital that must be maintained in the company, and thus provides greater protection for creditors.

Although seldom seen in Canada now, the use of par values for shares is still common internationally.

Why would a company repurchase its own shares?

As we saw with Dollarama in our feature story, companies can decide to repurchase some of the shares they have previously issued. A company might do this when it has cash that is surplus to its needs. Repurchasing shares reduces the number of shares outstanding. Fewer outstanding shares results in an increase in the company's earnings per share, which may, in turn, increase the share price. Alternatively, if a company has a stock option plan that enables its employees to purchase shares in the company, it may repurchase shares in the market and then use them to meet its obligations under the plan rather than issue new shares. Finally, as we will see in the discussion on preferred shares, sometimes the company repurchases or redeems its shares as a way of retiring them, similar to repaying principal when paying off debt.

The repurchase of shares that are then cancelled (that is, they are not held as treasury shares) reduces the share capital account by the amount that the shares were originally issued for. In addition, if the company buys them back at a higher or lower price than it issued them for, there is a form of gain or loss on the repurchase. The gain or loss is not considered part of the company's earnings. Instead, it is recorded in either the Contributed Surplus account or the Retained Earnings account.

What are the differences between common and preferred shares?

As previously mentioned, a company's articles of incorporation specify the types and classes of shares that can be issued. A company's articles may also allow it to issue different series within a specific type and class of share, such as class A preferred shares, series A, B, or C. Being able to issue different types

of shares (that is, common versus preferred shares) with multiple classes gives the company flexibility to attract different kinds of investors as it raises share capital. Different classes or types of shares can have different rights that accrue to their holders, resulting in different risk and return characteristics. These include:

- whether it can vote and, if so, the number of votes per share
- whether it pays regular dividends
- how large the dividend is
- whether it gets priority on liquidation
- whether it can be redeemed (bought back by the company)

By offering securities that provide different levels of risk and return, companies can attract a wider group of investors, which may make it easier to raise capital. Financial statement users can find information about the different types of shares a company is authorized to issue in the share capital note in the financial statements. Users can also see the number of each share type that has been issued.

Exhibit 11-2 provides an example of this disclosure, using **Gildan Activewear Inc.**'s share capital note. Gildan manufactures branded basic activewear such as T-shirts, sport shirts, and sweatshirts. The company sells its products as blanks, which are subsequently decorated with designs and logos for sale to consumers. You may own a T-shirt or hoodie with a Gildan label in it.

Gildan is a medium-sized Canadian company, with an interesting history regarding its equity. We will use the company to illustrate the concepts of shareholders' equity in a Canadian context. Note that the excerpts used in this chapter are from the 2013 annual report. When reading the report, we will be focusing on numbers in the 2013 column, which covers the 12 months from October 1, 2012, to September 29, 2013.

As you can see from Exhibit 11-2, Gildan has one class of common shares and two classes of preferred shares (which can be issued in series). As at September 29, 2013, there were 121,626,076 common shares issued and outstanding, but no preferred shares had been issued.

Exhibit 11-2 Excerpt from Excerpt from Note 14 on Equity—Gildan Activewear Inc. 2013 Annual Report

> **(c) Share capital:**
>
> *Authorized:*
>
> Common shares, authorized without limit as to number and without par value. First preferred shares, without limit as to number and without par value, issuable in series and non-voting. Second preferred shares, without limit as to number and without par value, issuable in series and non-voting. As at September 29, 2013 and September 30, 2012 none of the first and second preferred shares were issued.
>
> *Issued:*
>
> As at September 29, 2013, there were 121,626,076 common shares (September 30, 2012 – 121,386,090) issued and outstanding, which are net of 282,761 common shares (September 30, 2012 – 210,400) that have been purchased and are held in trust as described in note 14(e).

FINANCIAL STATEMENTS

Corporations generally issue shares through a firm of investment bankers, known as underwriters, in much the same way that bonds are issued. (See Chapter 10 for a discussion of the bond issuance process.) When common or preferred shares are issued, the details and features of the shares being issued are discussed in a legal document called a **prospectus**. The prospectus is distributed to potential investors prior to the shares being sold. The first time a company issues shares on a public stock exchange is known as an **initial public offering** (or **IPO**).

Common Shares

As previously noted, every corporation must have one class of shares that represents the company's basic voting ownership rights. These shares are normally referred to as **common shares** (or, outside of

HELPFUL HINT

A company must have common shares and can, but doesn't have to, have preferred shares. Each type of share can also have different classes. The types and classes have differing rights to meet different investors' objectives.

North America, **ordinary shares**). At least one class of a company's common shares must have *all three* of the following rights:

1. the right to vote at meetings of the company's shareholders;
2. the right to receive dividends, if declared; and
3. the right to a share of the company's net assets upon liquidation of the company.

These rights are shared proportionately, based on the number of shares held relative to the total number of shares that are issued and outstanding. Let's explore each of these rights in more detail.

The Right to Vote at Meetings of the Company's Shareholders

Common shareholders have the right to vote at shareholder meetings. Public companies must have at least one meeting per year, which is known as the **annual meeting**. One of the most important things that happens at this meeting is the selection of the corporation's board of directors. The standard rule for voting is one share equals one vote; so the more shares an individual owns, the greater the influence that individual has. The board of directors then represents the shareholders and most decisions are made by a vote of the board of directors rather than a vote of all shareholders. Canadian public companies must have at least three independent directors. A director is considered to be independent if they meet a number of conditions, including that they are not an employee of the company, not related to members of senior management, and not an employee of the company's external auditor. Most Canadian public companies have more than three independent directors in order to ensure that the board has all of the necessary skills (such as finance, accounting, and legal knowledge) among its members. Having a majority of independent directors helps to ensure that the board meets its responsibility of acting in the best interests of the company and *all* of its shareholders.

One of the board's key responsibilities is hiring (and firing) the company's senior management team. The board oversees senior management, including establishing performance targets and approving budgets, but the company's day-to-day operations are the responsibility of management. Other key responsibilities of the board include determining whether or not dividends should be declared and being ultimately responsible for the financial information that is prepared by management and examined by the company's external auditors.

The Right to Receive Dividends, if Declared

A company is not obligated to declare dividends. However, if a company's board does declare dividends, different types or classes of shares may be entitled to different dividend amounts. Normally, preferred shares are restricted to the stated dividend amount for their class of preferred shares. Common shares normally have no restrictions on the amount of dividends they can receive, once the preferred shareholders have received their dividends. Lenders may restrict the level of dividends that can be distributed to common shareholders through debt covenants, as was discussed in Chapter 10.

If a company has different classes of common shares, then dividends may be declared on a different basis to each class. This would mean that the holders of the different classes of common shares would receive different amounts of dividends. However, each outstanding share within that class of shares will receive the same dividend per share.

The Right to a Share of the Company's Net Assets upon Liquidation of the Company

Common shareholders have the right to share in the company's net assets upon liquidation. If a company goes bankrupt or otherwise liquidates, there is an established order in which creditors and shareholders are paid. The proceeds from liquidating the company's assets must first be used to settle the company's liabilities to its creditors. Any balance remaining is then paid to preferred shareholders up to the amount of their share capital. Any remaining balance is then available for distribution to the common shareholders and is divided proportionately among them, based on their relative number of shares. This means that common shareholders come last and bear the highest risk, since there may be nothing left for them. On the other hand, they could reap the largest benefit if there is a substantial sum left over.

Other Common Shareholder Rights

There are two other rights that *may* exist for a company's common shareholders: the right to purchase subsequent issues of shares and special voting rights. Whether or not these rights exist depends upon the company's articles of incorporation. Since both are seen in Canadian public companies, we will explain each of them.

1. **Right to purchase subsequent issues of shares.** Common shareholders may have the right to share proportionately in any new issuance of shares. This is what is known as a **pre-emptive right**. Pre-emptive rights are not automatic. They must be explicitly stated in the articles of incorporation. If present, this right allows current shareholders to retain their proportionate interest in the company when new shares are issued. This ensures that the ownership interest of existing shareholders will not be diluted by future share issuances. It is important to note that the existing shareholders are not obligated to purchase additional shares, but they have the option to do so. It is often called an **anti-dilution provision**.

   For example, if a company's articles include an anti-dilution provision, a shareholder owning 20% of a company's shares has the pre-emptive right to purchase 20% of any new shares of that class that may be issued. Anti-dilution provisions provide the greatest protection for shareholders who have a **minority interest** or **non-controlling interest** in a company. Pre-emptive rights prevent their ownership interests from being diluted.

2. **Special voting rights.** A number of Canadian companies have what are known as dual-class share structures. These provide holders of a certain class of common shares with special voting rights. These are also known as **multiple voting shares**. The holder of one of the multiple voting common shares is entitled to more than one vote for each of the common shares owned. The multiple voting shares are normally owned by the founding shareholder(s) (or their families) and are used to maintain control of the company in spite of additional common shares being issued by the company. Normally the issuance of additional common shares would dilute the control of the existing common shareholders, but the presence of special voting rights enables the existing shareholders to maintain control in spite of owning less than 50% of the shares of a company.

   Multiple voting share structures have been under scrutiny over the last few years because they are not considered to reflect good corporate governance practices. Concerns about these structures have been raised by shareholder rights advocates because the voting rights are not proportional to the amount of capital invested. Usually the majority of the financing has been provided by investors who do not hold shares with special voting rights. However, because the founders hold shares with special voting rights, these other investors are unable to have a vote or voice regarding the operation of the company that is commensurate with the proportion of the company's capital that has been provided by them. Institutional investors such as pension and mutual funds have been especially active in trying to enhance the rights of shareholders by eliminating multiple voting share arrangements.

For Example

Bombardier Inc. is an example of a Canadian company that still has multiple voting common shares in its share structure. The company has Class A and Class B common shares. Each of the Class A shares, which are owned by the Bombardier family, has special voting rights that give the shareholder the right to 10 votes for each share owned. The Class B shareholders are entitled to the normal one vote per share. As a result of this dual-class share structure, the Class A shareholders are able to control about 69% of the votes in spite of owning just over 18% of the company's common shares.[2]

For Example

DIFFERENT PERSPECTIVES ON DUAL-CLASS OR MULTIPLE VOTING SHARE STRUCTURES

In September 2013, the Canadian Coalition for Good Governance, a coalition of major institutional investors, pension funds, and mutual funds, issued a statement "calling on companies with dual-class shares to voluntarily limit the power of their controlling shareholders with measures that include caps on the number of directors they can elect." The CCGG wanted to ensure that public shareholders (those not holding the multiple voting shares) are able to elect directors to a company's board. The CCGG noted that there were 77 companies with dual-class share structures listed on the TSX in September 2013.

However, the news related to multiple voting shares was not all negative. In June 2013, the Clarkson Centre for Board Effectiveness at the University of Toronto released a study demonstrating that family-controlled companies outperformed the rest of the TSX index. Over the 15-year period ending in 2012, the family-controlled companies had 25% better returns than the rest of the companies that comprise the TSX index. Many of these family-controlled companies are controlled by founding families holding multiple voting shares; however, the other shareholders in these companies have also benefited from these better returns.[3]

FINANCIAL
STATEMENTS

Preferred Shares

Preferred shares (or, outside North America, **preference shares**) are shares that have preferences over common shares in one or more areas. The most common preference is related to dividends whereby, if dividends are declared, preferred shareholders receive them before common shareholders do. This does not mean that preferred shareholders are guaranteed to receive dividends, because the board may choose not to declare any dividends. However, if dividends are declared, then preferred shareholders receive theirs ahead of common shareholders. Another preference is that preferred shareholders are entitled to receive a return of their share capital, from the net assets, if any, when a company is liquidated. This means that, if a company is liquidated and its creditors have been paid, the preferred shareholders will be entitled to a return of their share capital before any of the net assets are returned to the common shareholders. In exchange for these preferences, preferred shareholders give up certain rights. For example, preferred shares are normally non-voting, meaning that these shareholders have no say in electing the company's board of directors. Also, preferred shares normally have a **fixed dividend rate** (or **stated dividend rate**). This may be stated as a dollar amount per share (a quarterly or annual dividend rate per share per year) or as a percentage of the share's issue price.

FINANCIAL STATEMENTS

For Example

In 2012, the **National Bank of Canada**'s issued and outstanding preferred shares included the following features:

Series 20
Redeemable in cash at the Bank's option, subject to prior approval of OSFI, on or after May 15, 2013, in whole or in part, at a price equal to $26.00 per share if redeemed before May 15, 2014, at a price equal to $25.75 per share if redeemed during the 12-month period preceding May 15, 2015, at a price equal to $25.50 per share if redeemed during the 12-month period preceding May 15, 2016, at a price equal to $25.25 per share if redeemed during the 12-month period preceding May 15, 2017, and at a price equal to $25.00 per share if redeemed on or after May 15, 2017, plus, in all cases, all declared and unpaid dividends at the date fixed for redemption. These shares carry a non-cumulative quarterly dividend of $0.375.

Series 24
Redeemable in cash at the Bank's option, subject to prior approval of OSFI, on or after February 15, 2014 and February 15 every five years thereafter, in whole or in part, at a price equal to $25.00 per share, plus all declared and unpaid dividends at the date fixed for redemption. Convertible into floating-rate non-cumulative Series 25 First Preferred Shares of the Bank, subject to certain conditions, on February 15, 2014 and on February 15 every five years thereafter. These shares carry a non-cumulative quarterly dividend of $0.4125 for the initial period ending February 15, 2014. Thereafter, these shares carry a non-cumulative quarterly fixed dividend in an amount per share determined by multiplying the interest rate, equal to the sum of the Government of Canada yield on the calculation date of the applicable fixed rate plus 4.63%, by $25.00.[4]

Series 20 first preferred shares pay dividends of $0.375 quarterly, or $1.50 annually. Fixed dividend rates create risks for both the company issuing the preferred shares and the investors purchasing them. If economic circumstances change and interest rates rise, the fixed dividend rate may not provide investors with an adequate rate of return. Alternatively, if rates decline, the fixed dividend rate may end up being expensive financing for the company. To protect against this risk, some companies now issue preferred shares with dividend rates that reset periodically. These are known as *rate reset* preferred shares and are discussed further below.

Series 24 preferred shares have what is known as a **floating rate**. It's called *floating* because the dividend changes when interest rates change. In this case, the shares pay a quarterly dividend based on the Government of Canada interest rate plus 4.63% times a value of $25.00.

In addition to fixed rate and floating rate preferred shares, there are also **rate reset** preferred shares. Rate reset preferred shares pay a fixed dividend from their issuance until a pre-established **reset date**. At the reset date, a new fixed rate is established by the issuing company and remains in effect until the next reset date. This new fixed rate reflects the economic conditions and borrowing rates at that time. The rate reset feature helps to mitigate some of the risks associated with fixed dividend rates.

According to research conducted by BMO Capital Markets, rate reset was the most common type of dividend feature for preferred shares in Canada as at September 30, 2012.[5]

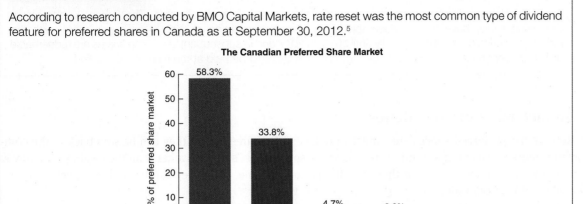

Aside from the dividend rate, there are a number of other features of preferred shares that are important to understand, which we will discuss here further.

Cumulative vs. Non-cumulative Preferred Shares

Cumulative preferred shares have a feature whereby dividends that are not declared in one year carry over to the next year. These undeclared dividends are known as **dividends in arrears**. Each year that dividends are not declared, the amount of dividends in arrears grows. When dividends are eventually declared by the company's board, all dividends in arrears on the preferred shares must be paid, together with the preferred dividend for the current year, before any dividends can be paid to the common shareholders. This feature provides some assurance to the preferred shareholders that they will receive their annual dividends at some point, as it is likely that the common shareholders will ultimately wish to receive dividends and any dividends in arrears would have to be cleared first. In contrast, if the preferred shares are **non-cumulative** and the company's board does not declare dividends in a year, then the preferred shareholders' right to any dividend is lost for that year.

The Conceptual Framework
WHY DIVIDENDS IN ARREARS ARE *NOT* A LIABILITY

When a company has dividends in arrears, they are not recorded as a liability on the statement of financial position. This is because they do not meet the definition of a liability, which states that "an essential characteristic of a liability is that the entity has a present obligation." In the case of dividends in arrears, there is no present obligation until the company's board of directors actually declares dividends. Until that time, the company has no obligation to the holders of the cumulative preferred shares.[6]

Redeemable Preferred Shares

Redeemable preferred shares have a feature that enables the issuing company to repurchase them from the shareholder at a price and time specified in the articles of incorporation. The redemption is at the issuing company's option. Potential investors in preferred shares must read the issuing company's articles of incorporation very carefully to ensure that they are aware of all of the shares' features, including dividend rates and redemption terms.

For Example

All of the National Bank of Canada's preferred share issues are redeemable. The Series 20 shares we discussed earlier have been redeemable since May 2013 starting at $26.00 cash per share, with the redemption price decreasing annually until 2017. In 2017 and in subsequent years, the shares are redeemable at $25.00 per share. Any declared but unpaid dividends must be paid at the time of redemption.[7]

Retractable Preferred Shares

Retractable preferred shares are similar to redeemable shares in that they can be sold back to the company (retired), except that in this case, it is at the shareholder's option rather than the issuing company's. The price that must be paid for them and the periods of time when they can be sold are specified in the articles of incorporation.

Convertible Preferred Shares

Convertible preferred shares can be converted, at the shareholder's option, into other types of preferred shares based on a ratio stated in the articles of incorporation. While it is uncommon, some preferred shares are convertible into common shares.

Participating Preferred Shares

Participating preferred shares are preferred shares that not only have a preference with regard to dividends, but, if dividends are declared to common shareholders beyond the level declared to the preferred shareholders, the preferred shareholders also share in the excess dividends. Again, this is an uncommon feature as most preferred shares are non-participating.

As noted earlier, the variety of features and different types of shares provide investors with different levels of risk and return. This allows companies to raise financing from different types of investors—those who might prefer the steady dividends of preferred shares, or others who are willing to forgo dividends and assume more risk in the hope of higher returns. Targeting different types of investors increases the pool of capital available to the company.

Exhibit 11-3 lists the major differences between common and preferred shares. While the features of various classes of shares differ, the accounting issues related to all of them are basically the same. Therefore, in the sections that follow, we limit the discussion to common shares.

Exhibit 11-3 Comparison of Major Differences Between Common and Preferred Shares

TAKE5

	Common Shares	Preferred Shares
Receive dividends?	Only when declared by the board and only after any preferred dividends have been paid (including any dividends in arrears)	Only when declared by the board
		Amount of dividend is normally fixed (as stated in the articles of incorporation)
	Generally, no limit on the amount of dividends they can receive	If participating shares, may receive additional dividends
		Dividends can be cumulative or non-cumulative
Right to vote for the board of directors?	Yes, at least one class must be voting	No, usually non-voting
	Different classes could have different voting rights or none at all	
Priority on liquidation?	Last after creditors and all preferred shareholders are satisfied	After creditors, but before common shareholders

DIVIDENDS

Do companies have to pay dividends?

No. Companies are *not* required to pay dividends. One of the responsibilities of the board of directors is to determine what portion of the company's profits should be retained and reinvested to help grow the company. The board may decide that it is necessary to retain all of the profits or that a portion of them should be distributed as dividends to shareholders. Some companies have never paid any dividends while others have regular dividend distribution programs. As we saw in the feature story to Chapter 3, the **Hudson's Bay Company** paid dividends for 249 of the 314 years between its inception in 1670 and 1984! Once a company starts to pay out dividends, it is best if the dividends can be maintained. If the company has to stop distributing dividends or has to cut them back, it normally has a negative effect on the company's stock price. Investors in the stock market prefer predictability. If there is uncertainty regarding dividends, investors will perceive the stock to be riskier and the share price will usually fall.

Early-stage or growing companies do not normally pay dividends because they need to retain any profits in the organization to finance growth and expansion. As growth opportunities diminish or earnings become more predictable, these companies will often start a dividend program.

Generally, a company must meet two conditions to be able to declare dividends. The first condition is that the company must have retained earnings (past profits) greater than or equal to the amount of the dividend. The second condition is that the company must have enough cash to be able to fund the dividend.

Most companies that pay dividends do so quarterly. When first starting to pay dividends, a company might declare and pay a **special dividend** or *one-time dividend*. This move indicates that they would like to return some of the company's profits to the shareholders, but it does not send any signals to the market that regular dividends can be expected. A special dividend is also used if the company has benefited from an unusual gain, such as selling off a division, and has excess cash available.

■ **LEARNING OBJECTIVE 4**
Describe the different types of dividends, explain why one type of dividend may be used rather than another, and describe how dividends are accounted for.

KEY POINTS
To declare dividends, a company must have:
• retained earnings and
• sufficient cash.

> ### For Example
>
> Gildan Activewear Inc. introduced a dividend program only in December 2010 despite going public in 1998. The following excerpt from Gildan's 2013 annual report illustrates the factors it considers in its dividend policy:
>
> *While the Board of Directors of the Company wishes to retain some of the Company's earnings to take advantage of opportunities to develop and expand its business, the Company aims to declare and pay cash dividends on a quarterly basis. The Board of Directors will consider several factors when reviewing dividend payments, including the Company's present and future earnings, cash flows, capital requirements and future regulatory restrictions, while complying with laws governing the Company. There can be no assurance as to the amount or timing of dividends in the future.*[8]

FINANCIAL STATEMENTS

What are the different dates involved in declaring and paying a dividend?

There are four key dates in the **dividend declaration** process:
1. The date of declaration
2. The ex-dividend date
3. The date of record
4. The date of payment

Date of Declaration

The **date of declaration** is the date on which the board of directors votes to declare a dividend. Once the board has declared dividends, the company has a liability to pay them to shareholders. Note that public companies are not able to pay the dividends on the date of declaration. Because the shares of public companies are continuously changing hands, the company may not know who its shareholders are on the date of declaration. Instead, the company sets a date, normally at least two weeks into the future, which is known as the **date of record**. Shareholders on that date are entitled to receive the dividend payment.

This delay allows investors to make informed decisions about buying and selling the stock relative to whether or not they will receive the dividend. If a shareholder sells shares before the ex-dividend date, which is defined below, the new owner of the shares will then be entitled to receive the dividend.

Ex-dividend Date

The **ex-dividend date** is two business days *prior* to the date of record. Because it takes three business days for share trades to be completed, trades made in the two business days prior to the date of record will not be completed until after the date of record. As such, investors purchasing shares on or after this date will not own the shares on the date of record and will not be entitled to receive the dividend. The dividend would be paid to the previous owner of the shares. As you would expect, the value of shares normally decreases on the ex-dividend date, with the decrease approximating the amount of the dividend.

Date of Record

As previously mentioned, shareholders on the date of record will be entitled to receive the dividend payment.

Date of Payment

The **date of payment** is the date that the dividend payment is made to shareholders and the company's liability for the dividends is settled, or *extinguished*. The date of payment is normally at least two weeks after the date of record. Again, a delay is needed so that the company can update its list of shareholders and calculate the total amount of dividends owed to each.

How are the declaration and payment of dividends recorded?

We learned how the declaration and payment of dividends were recorded in Chapter 3, but it is useful to review it. We will also see how the ex-dividend date and date of record affect this process. Exhibit 11-4 outlines what happens on the four key dates, including any necessary journal entries.

Exhibit 11-4 An Overview of the Four Key Dates Related to the Declaration and Payment of Dividends

Date	Journal Entry	Explanation
Date of declaration	DR Dividends Declared CR Dividends Payable	In Chapter 3, we learned that the Dividends Declared account is a temporary account. It is closed to the Retained Earnings account at the end of the accounting period. Not all companies use a Dividends Declared account. Some prefer to debit dividends directly to Retained Earnings.
Ex-dividend date	No journal entry required	There is no accounting entry required. This date is used in the marketplace to indicate the date on which a purchaser of the shares would not be entitled to receive the dividend.
Date of record	No journal entry required	There is no accounting entry required. This date is used by the company to determine who the dividend payments will be made to.
Date of payment	DR Dividends Payable CR Cash	This company settles or extinguishes its liability on this date.

What is the difference between a cash dividend and a stock dividend?

Cash Dividends

Dividends are paid to shareholders only if the board of directors has voted to declare a dividend. Dividends are normally cash dividends; that is, the shareholder receives a cash payment from the company.

For Example

On November 20, 2013, Gildan's board of directors declared a quarterly cash dividend payable to its common shareholders. The details, which were presented in the investor information section of the company's website, were as follows:

Dividend Information

Declaration	Record	Payment	Amount of Dividends*
November 20, 2013	December 12, 2013	January 6, 2014	$0.108

In this case, the ex-dividend date was December 10, 2013.

The company announced the declaration of the dividend in a news release on November 21, 2013, which included the following information:

Increase in Quarterly Dividend
Although the Company is continuing to focus on pursuing its growth strategies, as a result of the Company's continuing positive outlook for earnings growth and free cash flow generation the Board of Directors has approved a 20% increase in the amount of the current quarterly dividend and has declared a cash dividend of U.S. $0.108 per share, payable on January 6, 2014 to shareholders of record on December 12, 2013. This dividend is an "eligible dividend" for the purposes of the Income Tax Act (Canada) and any other applicable provincial legislation pertaining to eligible dividends.[9]

Stock Dividends

Not all dividends are cash dividends. If a company declares **stock dividends** rather than cash dividends, then shareholders will receive additional shares instead of cash. Stock dividends can be used when the company wishes to declare a dividend but does not want to use, or is not in a position to use, cash. Stock dividends allow the company to capitalize a portion of its earnings because the effect of a stock dividend is to transfer a portion of the company's retained earnings into share capital. This means that those earnings are no longer part of retained earnings and, therefore, are no longer available for distribution to shareholders. Creditors will likely view this step favourably because it increases the amount of the shareholders' capital in the company. Shareholders who receive stock dividends have the option of keeping the new shares or selling them in the market for cash.

Stock dividends are normally declared as a percentage of the total shares outstanding. For example, if a company declared a 10% stock dividend, then shareholders would receive additional shares equal to 10% of the shares they held when the stock dividend was declared. So, if a shareholder owned 100 common shares when the dividend was declared, they would receive another 10 common shares as a result of the stock dividend (100 × 10% = 10). While the shareholder owns more shares as a result of the stock dividend, their percentage ownership of the company remains unchanged. They would still own 10% of the company's common shares.

For accounting purposes, companies must determine a value for the new shares being issued as a result of the stock dividend. This is done using the market value (the value that the shares were trading at) on the date the stock dividend was declared.

It is helpful to use a two-step approach when recording the effects of a stock dividend. The two steps are as follows:

STEP 1: Determine the number of new shares being issued as a result of the stock dividend.

STEP 2: Determine the value of the new shares being issued.

Once these two steps have been completed, the company can account for the dividend. While the accounting is similar to that used for cash dividends, there are a couple of important differences. Let's look at the entries at the date of declaration and the date that new shares are issued.

Date of declaration	DR Stock Dividends Declared
	CR Stock Dividends Issuable

The declaration of cash dividends results in a liability because the company will have to sacrifice an asset (cash). This is not the case when stock dividends are declared, because no asset will be given up. Instead, additional company shares will be distributed. This is why the credit is to the account Stock Dividends Issuable rather than to a payable account. Just like the Dividends Declared account, Stock Dividends Declared is a temporary account that is closed to Retained Earnings at the end of each accounting period. Both Stock Dividends Declared and Stock Dividends Issuable are shareholders' equity accounts.

Date new shares are issued	DR Stock Dividends Issuable
	CR Common Shares

It is important to remember that stock dividends result in common shares being distributed rather than cash.

Exhibits 11-5 and 11-6 illustrate the effects of stock dividends both on the company and on an individual investor.

Exhibit 11-5 Illustration of the Effect of a Stock Dividend on the Company

TAKE5

Let's consider the effects of a company, which has 100,000 common shares outstanding, declaring a 10% common stock dividend. At the date of declaration, the market price of the company's shares was $15. Assume that the company's common shares had originally been issued for $2 per share, giving the company share capital (common shares) of $200,000. Also assume that it had retained earnings of $500,000.

To record the stock dividend, we will perform the following steps.

Step 1: Determine the number of new shares being issued as a result of the stock dividend.

= Dividend percentage × Number of shares outstanding
= 10% × 100,000
= 10,000 new shares

Step 2: Determine the value of the new shares being issued.

= Number of new shares × Market price at date of declaration
= 10,000 shares × $15
= $150,000

Date of declaration	DR Stock Dividends Declared	150,000	
	CR Stock Dividends Issuable		150,000
Date new shares issued	DR Stock Dividends Issuable	150,000	
	CR Common Shares		150,000

The effect of this stock dividend would be to "capitalize" $150,000 of the company's retained earnings, as the stock dividends declared account would be closed to retained earnings at the end of the period, reducing retained earnings, while the balance in the common shares account would increase by the same amount. The impact on shareholders' equity would be as follows:

Shareholders' equity section	Before stock dividend	After stock dividend
Common shares	$200,000	$350,000
Retained earnings	500,000	350,000
Total shareholders' equity	$700,000	$700,000

Exhibit 11-6 Illustration of the Effect of a Stock Dividend on an Individual Investor

Let's use the same scenario; that is, a company with 100,000 common shares outstanding declares a 10% common stock dividend. Now let's look at the effect on an individual investor who owned 2,000 shares when the stock dividend was declared.

At the time the stock dividend was declared, the investor owned 2% of the company's common shares (2,000 ÷ 100,000). The dividend would result in the investor receiving an additional 200 shares (10% × 2,000) of the 10,000 additional shares (10% × 100,000). Note that the investor would still own 2% of the common shares (2,200 ÷ 110,000).

While stock dividends have no effect on the ownership percentage of individual shareholders, they do have an effect on share values. The additional shares issued as a result of the stock dividend are expected to result in a decrease in the shares' market price. This is due to the market value for the company as a whole being allocated across a greater number of shares.

Staying with our example, at the time the stock dividend was declared, the market price of the company's common shares was $15 per share. The company had 100,000 outstanding common shares at that time, which means that the market valuation for the company was $1.5 million ($15 × 100,000). After the 10% stock dividend, the company had 110,000 common shares and the $1.5 million market value would now be allocated across this greater number of shares. As a result, we expect the market price of an individual common share to drop from $15 to $13.636 ($1,500,000 ÷ 110,000). However, this may not be the reaction of the market. If that were the case, shareholders would be better off to the extent that the market price of the common shares does not drop to this amount, as this would be equivalent to an increase in the market price of the shares.

Coming back to our individual investor, we can see that if the market reacts as expected, the total value of the investor's common share holdings would remain unchanged. It was $30,000 ($15 × 2,000 shares) before the stock dividend and remains $30,000 ($13.636 × 2,200 shares) after the stock dividend.

If shareholders are expected to be no better off after a stock dividend than they were before, why would a company issue such a dividend? There are a couple of good reasons.

1. Stock dividends allow the company to capitalize a portion of its retained earnings. As explained above, stock dividends have the effect of transferring a portion of the company's retained earnings to its Share Capital account. This reduces the amount of retained earnings available for dividends to shareholders and increases share capital. Share capital represents stated or legal capital, meaning that it cannot be used to issue dividends. Thus, the company has capitalized some of its past earnings. This amount is now permanently invested in the company, which provides increased security for the creditors. Companies that have a substantial amount of retained earnings but do not have cash available for dividends will sometimes issue stock dividends to reduce the retained earnings amount.

2. As noted above, it is also possible that the shareholders are better off after a stock dividend. Often the market price does not fully compensate for the increase in the number of shares.

Finally, let's take a minute to compare the effect of paying a stock dividend and a cash dividend on the investor and the company. With a cash dividend, the investor receives cash and therefore their wealth, or personal net assets, increases. With a stock dividend, they received more shares of the company but, if the share price falls by an amount proportionate to the dividend, there is no net change in their wealth.

For the company, both a cash dividend and a stock dividend cause retained earnings to decrease. With cash dividends, cash leaves the company, so both assets and shareholders' equity have decreased and the company's net assets are reduced. There has been a transfer of wealth from the company to the investor as the company has distributed retained earnings to the shareholder. With stock dividends, while retained earnings have decreased, share capital increased by the same amount: the retained earnings have been capitalized. There is no net decrease in either assets or shareholders' equity. The wealth of the company did not change. Again, this is consistent with the effect on the investor: their wealth did not change either.

STOCK SPLITS

What is a stock split?

A **stock split** involves a company issuing additional shares to shareholders based on a specified ratio, such as two-for-one or five-for-one. For example, with a two-for-one stock split, the number of outstanding shares would double: each shareholder would have two shares for every one share they had prior to

■ **LEARNING OBJECTIVE 5**
Describe what a stock split is and explain how it is accounted for.

KEY POINTS
Stock splits:
• increase the number
  of outstanding shares.
• have no effect on
  retained earnings.

the split. Stock splits can involve shareholders exchanging their existing shares for new shares. Alternatively, shareholders may keep their current shares and receive additional shares for each share they own. Stock splits are similar to stock dividends in that the number of outstanding shares increases, but they differ in that they have no effect on retained earnings, because no dividend has been declared. As with stock dividends, the increase in the number of outstanding shares reduces the market price per share. A two-for-one stock split, which doubles the number of outstanding shares, should have the effect of cutting the market price per share in half.

Why would a company split its shares?

The effect that stock splits have on share prices is the primary reason that companies use them. It may sound odd to think that a company would take steps to reduce the market price of its shares. Normally, increasing share prices is one of the objectives of management. However, there are circumstances when share prices have increased to an amount that makes the shares seem unaffordable to certain types of investors. A share split can alleviate this issue, meaning that a broader group of investors are able to purchase shares of the company. This increased base of investors may actually increase demand for the shares, which can result in an increase in the market price of the shares. Stock splits are normally associated with profitable growing companies and a stock split can reinforce this perception.

There is no accounting entry necessary to record a stock split because there is no change in either share capital or retained earnings. The change in the number of shares issued and outstanding is made with an informal or **memorandum entry** in the accounting system. That is, a notation is made about the details of the stock split and the new numbers of shares, but no accounts are debited or credited.

For Example

There's another good reason for companies to use stock splits: to make their share prices more accessible to individual shareholders. That's particularly the case with Canada's big banks, whose shares have been trading well above $50 for some time. The desire to lower share price for individual investors is partly what prompted the National Bank of Canada to announce a two-for-one stock split in late 2013. As *The Globe and Mail* noted, "companies want to encourage retail investors to buy their shares, and they figure that more people will be interested if the price is low . . . they think it's important to keep their share prices from surging to levels that might turn off some retail investors." Stock splits are also a signal to the market that a company is doing well, which is why their share prices have risen, and that management expects the prosperity to continue.[10]

There can also be **reverse stock splits** (also known as **consolidations**), which have the opposite effect of a stock split. Reverse stock splits decrease the number of outstanding shares and have the effect of increasing share prices. Reverse stock splits are done based on a specified ratio, such as one-for-two or one-for-five. They are used by companies whose low share price:
• puts the company at risk of being delisted from a stock exchange as a result of its share price being barely above the minimum threshold for listing on the exchange;
• makes them ineligible investments for certain institutional investors (for example, some pension funds are not allowed to invest in stocks trading at less than $1.00 per share); or
• prevents them from listing on a public exchange.

Exhibit 11-7 summarizes the effects of different types of dividends on the financial statements.

Exhibit 11-7 Comparison of Different Types of Dividends and Stock Splits

Effect on:	Cash Dividend	Stock Dividend	Stock Split
Total assets	Cash decreases	No effect	No effect
Share capital	No effect	Increases	No effect
Retained earnings	Decreases	Decreases	No effect
Total shareholders' equity	Decreases	No effect	No effect
Number of shares outstanding	No effect	Increases	Increases

FINANCIAL STATEMENT ANALYSIS

When analyzing the shareholders' equity section of the financial statements, we normally assume the investor's perspective. Investors monitor their investment's value to assess company performance and their rate of return. In Chapter 1, we discussed the two ways that shareholders can realize a return when investing in corporations: the receipt of dividends and capital appreciation (an increase in the value of their shares). We will look at four different measures that investors and analysts use when assessing investment performance. These are: the price/earnings ratio, the dividend payout ratio, the dividend yield, and the return on shareholders' equity ratio. Let's look at each of these in detail.

■ **LEARNING OBJECTIVE 6**
Calculate and interpret the price/earnings ratio, dividend payout ratio, dividend yield, and return on shareholders' equity ratio.

What is the price/earnings ratio?

The **price/earnings ratio** (also known as the **P/E ratio**) is a key ratio. To quantify it, we will first need to determine the company's **earnings per share (EPS)**, which was introduced in Chapter 4. Earnings per share provides a measure of the earnings relative to the number of common shares outstanding. It is useful for tracking the return per share earned by the company over time. The price/earnings ratio relates EPS to the current market price per share. The P/E ratio is calculated as follows:

$$\text{P/E ratio} = \frac{\text{Market price per share}}{\text{Earnings per share}}$$

The price/earnings ratio relates the accounting earnings to the market price at which the shares trade. If two companies in the same industry had the same earnings per share of $5, and Company A's shares were selling for $25 and Company B's shares were selling for $50, the price/earnings ratios would be different. Company A's price/earnings ratio would be 5 ($25 ÷ $5) and Company B's would be 10 ($50 ÷ $5). This indicates that the market is placing a higher value on Company B's shares. Looking at it another way, investors are willing to pay more for the earnings of Company B ($10.00 for every $1.00 of earnings) than they are for the earnings of Company A ($5.00 per $1.00 of earnings). There are many possible reasons for the higher valuation, such as an assessment of higher earning potential in the future, a lower risk with respect to debt repayment, or an assessment of the company's future competitive position.

Gildan's year-end price/earnings ratios on its common shares for its 2012 and 2013 year ends were as follows:

September 29, 2013	$47.01 ÷ $2.64 = 17.8 times
September 28, 2012	$31.68 ÷ $1.22 = 25.9 times

Note that Gildan's year end differs by a few days each year because it selects its year end to always fall on a Sunday. Because the stock markets are not open on Sunday, the previous Friday's closing market price is used.

Gildan's price/earnings ratio fell in the year ending September 29, 2013, meaning the share price was lower in relation to the company's earnings per share. When evaluating a company's price/earnings ratio, it is important to compare it with those of other companies in the same industry. This comparison gives the user information about how the market is valuing the company in relation to others.

For Example

The financial media regularly feature analysts' perspectives on identifying companies that may be good investment prospects. The analysis supporting these assessments generally includes the price/earnings ratio as one of the tools used to screen investments. Usually, a low P/E ratio could mean that a company is undervalued in the market. Companies in established, lower-growth industries also tend to have a lower P/E ratio.

Writer and portfolio manager Michael Bowman analyzed the results of Canada's six largest banks for *The Globe and Mail*. He determined the following price/earnings ratios:

- TD Bank   13.29
- Royal Bank of Canada   13.05
- Bank of Nova Scotia   12.48
- Bank of Montreal   11.33
- CIBC   10.83
- National Bank of Canada   9.43

From this analysis, we can see that all of the banks were trading at values within a relatively narrow range of earnings multiples. Strictly based on this analysis, the shares of National Bank of Canada would be the least expensive relative to historic earnings of the major banks.[11]

What other ratios measure the return the shareholders are earning?

Dividend Payout Ratio and Dividend Yield

There are two ratios related to dividend payments that are commonly used by investors: the dividend payout ratio and the dividend yield. The **dividend payout ratio** measures the portion of a company's earnings that is distributed as dividends. More mature or stable companies generally pay out a higher portion of their earnings as dividends, as they have fewer growth opportunities and less need to retain funds inside the company to finance growth. Young companies need to finance their growth from internal sources and generally distribute little, if any, of their earnings as dividends. The dividend payout ratio can be determined on a per share basis, as shown below, or by comparing total dividends paid to net income.

$$\text{Dividend payout ratio} = \frac{\text{Dividends per share}}{\text{Earnings per share}}$$

The **dividend yield** measures the dividends an investor will receive relative to the share price. As noted earlier, a shareholder earns returns from receiving dividends and/or capital appreciation. The dividend yield measures the return provided by dividends. Mature companies tend to be low-growth stocks (their share prices do not increase dramatically) and pay out a larger portion of their earnings as dividends. As such, a larger portion of an investor's total return will come from dividends rather than from capital appreciation. The opposite is true of young companies. As their operations grow and expand, so can their share price. These companies normally pay out little or no dividends, choosing instead to use any profits to finance future growth.

$$\text{Dividend yield} = \frac{\text{Dividends per share}}{\text{Price per share}}$$

The two measures for Gildan in 2013 and 2012 are:

	2013	**2012**
Dividend payout	$0.36 ÷ $2.64 = 13.6%	$0.30 ÷ $1.22 = 24.6%
Dividend yield	$0.36 ÷ $47.01 = 0.77%	$0.30 ÷ $31.68 = 0.95%

From the dividend payout ratio, you can see that Gildan's earnings per share increased from 2012 and the company also increased the amount paid out as dividends. However, the percentage of the company's earnings that was paid out as dividends decreased from 24.6% to 13.6%. This means that Gildan retained a larger portion of its earnings to reinvest in the company. The dividend yield shows that very little of an investor's return on their shares in Gildan results from the dividends. However, an investor would have earned a 48.4% return from the increase in the share price over the year (($47.01 − $31.68) ÷ $31.68 = 48.4%).

Return on Shareholders' Equity Ratio

Another useful indicator of profitability is the return on shareholders' equity, or simply the **return on equity (ROE) ratio**. This is a more general measure than earnings per share because it relates the earnings available to common shares to total common shareholders' equity. It is calculated as follows:

$$\text{Return on equity ratio} = \frac{\text{Net income} - \text{Preferred dividends}}{\text{Average common shareholders' equity*}}$$

*Average common shareholders' equity = (Opening common shareholders' equity + Ending common shareholders' equity)/2

Preferred dividends need to be subtracted from net income because preferred dividends must be declared and paid before any dividends can be paid on common shares and we are using this ratio to determine the return on the common shares. Common shareholders' equity is the total shareholders' equity less any amounts that owners other than common shareholders (that is, preferred shareholders) are entitled to.

This ratio tells you the rate of return that the common shareholders are earning on the amount that they have invested in the company, which includes assets represented by undistributed retained earnings. Obviously, from an investor's perspective, a higher ratio is better than a lower one. Investors can compare this rate of return to that available from other investment opportunities to help them decide whether they should stay invested (or invest if they are not already a shareholder).

The following are the rates of return for Gildan in 2013 and 2012 (all figures in thousands):

$$\frac{2013}{ROE} \quad \frac{\text{Net income}}{\text{Average shareholders' equity}} = \frac{\$327,033}{(1,719,426 + \$1,426,341)/2} = 20.8\%$$

$$\frac{2012}{ROE} \quad \frac{\text{Net income}}{\text{Average shareholders' equity}} = \frac{\$142,388}{(\$1,426,341 + \$1,311,090)/2} = 10.4\%$$

Gildan has no preferred shares issued, so all the net income accrues to the common shareholders. From the calculations, we can see that the return on common shareholders' equity increased in 2013 consistent with the increase in the company's net income. Gildan's shareholders earned a very respectable 20.8% return on their investment in Gildan in 2013.

Chapter 12 includes a more detailed discussion of other types of analysis that involve shareholders' equity.

What are the advantages and disadvantages of financing with equity?

■ LEARNING OBJECTIVE 7
Identify the advantages and disadvantages of using equity financing.

When a company issues additional shares, it is using equity to finance growth, such as expanding facilities, purchasing competitors, stocking additional product lines, or opening new locations.

The advantages of financing with equity instead of debt are:

1. *Equity financing does not have to be repaid.*

   Equity financing is considered to be permanent capital: it does not have to be returned to shareholders unless the company is being liquidated. This is a significant difference from debt financing, which requires that the principal borrowed be repaid by a specific date.

2. *Dividends are optional.*

   Unlike interest, which must be paid on borrowed money, dividends are at the discretion of the board. This ensures that, if needed, the company can reinvest all of its profits to grow and support the business, instead of using a portion of profits to pay interest to creditors.

KEY POINTS
The advantages of using equity financing are:
• It does not have to be repaid.
• Dividends are optional.

The disadvantages of using equity financing instead of debt are:

1. *Ownership interests may be diluted.*

   Issuing additional common shares may dilute the ownership interest of existing shareholders because existing shareholders will own a lower percentage of the company's voting shares. Of course, this would not be the case if the existing shareholders purchased all of the new shares, but that is very unlikely for a public company.

2. *Dividends are not deductible for tax purposes.*

   Interest paid on borrowed funds is an expense to the borrower and is deductible for tax purposes. This is not the case with dividends paid because these are not expenses, but a distribution of profits. As such, dividends do not reduce a company's income for tax purposes.

KEY POINTS
The disadvantages of using equity financing are:
• Ownership interests may be diluted.
• Dividends are not tax deductible.

SUMMARY

1. **Explain why the shareholders' equity section is significant to users.**

   • Share ownership is common in a wide variety of circumstances, such as among individuals, companies, and pension funds.

   • It is important for shareholders to understand how shareholders' equity is measured and disclosed in the financial statements, so they can assess their return on investment, have an awareness of the various types and classes of shares a company can issue, and understand the reasons for changes in a company's equity.

2. **Explain the components of the shareholders' equity section of the statement of financial position.**

   • The components of shareholders' equity are (1) share capital, (2) retained earnings, (3) accumulated other comprehensive income, and (4) contributed surplus.

     ▪ Share capital is the amount received from investors on the initial issuance of a company's shares.

     ▪ Retained earnings represents the company's accumulated earnings that have not been distributed as dividends.

- Accumulated other comprehensive income includes unrealized gains and losses resulting from revaluations rather than from transactions with third parties.
- Contributed surplus results from the sale or repurchase of a company's shares or from the issuance of stock options.

3. **Describe the different types of shares and explain why corporations choose to issue a variety of share types.**

- A company's articles of incorporation outline the various types and classes of shares that it can issue.
  - The types and classes of shares that a company can issue are referred to as the *authorized shares*.
  - Shares that have been issued (sold) to shareholders are referred to as *issued and outstanding*.
  - If a company repurchases shares from shareholders and does not cancel them, then they are considered to be issued but not outstanding and are referred to as *treasury shares*. These shares are not entitled to any dividends.
- There are two types of shares: (1) common and (2) preferred.
- Being able to issue different types of shares (that is, common versus preferred shares), with multiple classes providing differing levels of risk and return, enables companies to appeal to a wider group of investors, making it easier to raise capital.
- Every company must have at least one class of common shares, but can have multiple classes (such as Class A, Class B). Common shares come with the right to vote at shareholder meetings, the right to receive dividends (if declared), and the right to a share of the company's net assets upon liquidation of the company.
  - Common shares can also include an anti-dilution provision, which enables shareholders to maintain their proportionate ownership in future shares issuances.
  - There can also be multiple voting common shares, which enable their owner to more than one vote for each share owned.
- Preferred shares are typically non-voting, but are normally entitled to receive dividends (the amount of which is normally fixed) ahead of common shareholders in the event that dividends are declared. They are also entitled to receive a return of their capital upon liquidation of the company before common shareholders. Preferred shares may be:
  - redeemable—the issuing company can repurchase them;
  - retractable—the shareholder can require the company to repurchase them;
  - convertible—they may be converted into common shares;
  - cumulative—if dividends are not declared in one year, the right to receive them accumulates until dividends are eventually declared; or
  - participating—preferred shareholders share with common shareholders in any dividends declared that are in excess of the fixed rate on the preferred shares.

4. **Describe the types of dividends, explain why one type of dividend may be used rather than another, and describe how dividends are recorded.**

- Companies are not required to declare dividends.
- In order to declare dividends, a company must have retained earnings and sufficient cash.
- There are different types of dividends. The two most common forms of dividends are (1) cash dividends, and (2) stock dividends.

- Cash dividends entitle shareholders to cash payments and are the most common type of dividend.
- Stock dividends entitle shareholders to receive additional shares rather than cash. A company can declare stock dividends when it wants to declare dividends, but also wants to preserve its cash.

Both cash and stock dividends reduce retained earnings.

- The recording of the declaration and payment of dividends is affected by the four key dates in the dividend declaration process:
  - the date of declaration—creates a liability
  - the ex-dividend date—used in the marketplace to determine who will receive the dividend
  - the date of record—used by the company to determine who the dividend payments will be made to
  - the date of payment—the date the company pays the dividends

5. **Describe what a stock split is and explain how it is accounted for.**

- A stock split occurs when the company issues additional shares to existing shareholders at a specified ratio (such as two-for-one) without any effect on retained earnings. Stock splits lower the share price in the market.
- Companies may also have reverse stock splits (known as consolidations), which decrease the number of outstanding shares at a specified ratio (such as one-for-two). This increases the share's market price.
- There is no accounting entry necessary to record a stock split because there is no change in either share capital or retained earnings.

6. **Calculate and interpret the price/earnings ratio, dividend payout ratio, dividend yield, and return on shareholders' equity ratio.**

- The price/earnings ratio is determined by dividing the market price per share by earnings per share. It is used by investors to assess a company's share price relative to earnings and relative to the share prices of other companies.
- The dividend payout ratio is calculated by dividing dividends per share by earnings per share. It measures the portion of a company's earnings that are distributed as dividends.
- The dividend yield is determined by dividing dividends per share by price per share. It measures the return provided to investors from dividends.
- The return on shareholders' equity ratio is calculated by dividing net income (after deducting preferred dividends) by average common shareholders' equity. It measures the rate of return that common shareholders are earning on the equity they have invested in the company.

7. **Identify the advantages and disadvantages of using equity financing.**

- The advantages of using equity financing are that it does not have to be repaid (whereas loan principal must be repaid) and dividends are at the option of the company's board (whereas interest must be paid).
- The disadvantages of using equity financing are that it can result in a dilution of ownership and dividends are not tax-deductible (whereas interest is).

KEY TERMS

Accumulated other comprehensive income (AOCI) (498)
Annual meeting (502)
Anti-dilution provision (503)
Articles of incorporation (499)
Authorized shares (499)
Common shares (501)
Consolidations (512)
Contributed surplus (498)
Convertible preferred shares (506)
Cumulative preferred shares (505)
Date of declaration (507)
Date of payment (508)
Date of record (507)
Dividend declaration (507)
Dividend payout ratio (514)
Dividend yield (514)

Dividends in arrears (505)
Earnings per share (EPS) (513)
Ex-dividend date (508)
Fixed dividend rate (504)
Floating rate (504)
Initial public offering (IPO) (501)
Issued shares (500)
Legal capital (500)
Memorandum entry (512)
Minority interest (503)
Multiple voting shares (503)
Non-controlling interest (503)
No par value shares (500)
Ordinary shares (502)
Other comprehensive income (498)
Outstanding shares (500)
Par value shares (500)

Participating preferred shares (506)
Pre-emptive right (503)
Preference shares (504)
Preferred shares (504)
Price/earnings (P/E) ratio (513)
Prospectus (501)
Rate reset (504)
Redeemable preferred shares (505)
Reset date (504)
Retractable preferred shares (506)
Return on equity (ROE) ratio (514)
Reverse stock splits (512)
Special dividend (507)
Stated dividend rate (504)
Stock dividend (509)
Stock split (511)
Treasury shares (500)

ABBREVIATIONS USED

AOCI	Accumulated other comprehensive income
EPS	Earnings per share
IPO	Initial public offering
P/E	Price/earnings ratio
ROE	Return on equity

SYNONYMS

Common shares | Ordinary shares
Fixed dividend rate | Stated dividend rate
Minority interest | Non-controlling interest
Preferred shares | Preference shares
Reverse stock splits | Consolidations

CHAPTER END REVIEW PROBLEM 1

Gillis Equipment Ltd. (GEL) had the following shareholders' equity section balances at December 31, 2015:

Share capital	$4,700,000
(Unlimited number of common shares authorized; 240,000 issued)	
Retained earnings	4,000,000
Total shareholders' equity	$8,700,000

During 2016, the company had the following transactions:

1. On January 2, 2016, GEL declared a cash dividend of $1.50 per share to the shareholders of record on January 27, 2016, payable February 15, 2016.
2. On March 15, 2016, GEL issued 10,000 new shares and received proceeds of $40 per share.
3. On June 29, 2016, GEL declared and paid a 10% stock dividend. The market price of GEL's shares on June 29, 2016, was $45 per share.
4. On June 30, 2016, GEL declared a cash dividend of $1.50 per share to the shareholders of record on July 15, 2016, payable on July 31, 2016.
5. On September 1, 2016, GEL issued 100,000 new shares at $50 per share.
6. On December 31, 2016, GEL declared a four-for-one stock split.

Additional information:

7. Net income for 2016 was $1.5 million.
8. The market price of the shares on December 31, 2016, was $13.00.

Required:

a. Prepare the journal entries necessary to record each of the above transactions. If a transaction does not require a journal entry, state why.
b. Determine GEL's retained earnings balance as at December 31, 2016.
c. Determine the number of shares GEL had issued and outstanding at December 31, 2016.

CHAPTER END REVIEW PROBLEM 2

The Northwest Company Inc. is a Winnipeg, Manitoba–based retailer serving markets in Northern Canada, rural Alaska, the South Pacific Islands, and the Caribbean. The company's operations include 121 Northern stores, 31 Giant Tiger discount stores, 13 Quickstop convenience stores, 2 fur-marketing outlets, and The Inuit Art Marketing Service, which is Canada's largest distributor of Inuit art. The following information has been extracted from the company's 2013 annual report:

	2013	2012	2011
Market price per share	$25.42	$23.14	$19.40
Earnings per share	$1.33	$1.32	$1.20
Dividends per share	$1.12	$1.04	$1.05
Net income (in thousands)	$64,263	$63,888	$57,961
Shareholders' equity (in thousands)	$322,440	$296,250	$283,709

Required:

a. Calculate Northwest's price/earnings ratio for 2011 through 2013. Comment on whether the ratio's trend over this period reflects the market having a positive outlook regarding the company's future.

b. Calculate Northwest's dividend payout ratio and dividend yield for 2012 and 2013. What do the results of these ratios tell us about Northwest?

c. Calculate Northwest's return on equity ratio for 2012 and 2013. Note that Northwest's articles of incorporation authorize only common shares. Comment on how effectively Northwest's management has been able to use the equity of its shareholders to generate returns.

Suggested Solution to Chapter End Review Problem 1

EXHIBIT 11-8   SPREADSHEET TO ACCOMPANY THE PRACTICE PROBLEM

Date and event	Number of Common Shares	Common Shares Account	Retained Earnings Account
Opening	240,000	$ 4,700,000	$4,000,000
Jan. 2: Dividends (cash) 240,000 × $1.50 = 360,000			(360,000)
March 15: Issued shares 10,000 × $40.00	10,000	400,000	
June 29: Dividends (stock)[a] 250,000 shares × 10% × $45	25,000	1,125,000	(1,125,000)
June 30: Dividends (cash) 275,000 × $1.50			(412,500)
Sept. 1: Issued shares 100,000 × 50.00	100,000	5,000,000	
Dec. 31: Stock split (4:1) 375,000 × 4 = 1,500,000 shares outstanding afterwards	1,125,000		
+ Net income			1,500,000
Ending balance	1,500,000	$11,225,000	$3,602,500

a. Step 0: Determine the number of shares outstanding = 240,000 + 10,000 = 250,000 shares
   Step 1: Determine the number of new shares to be issued: 250,000 shares × 10% = 25,000
   Step 2: Determine the value of the new shares being issued: 25,000 × $45 per share = $1,125,000
Journal entries: See Exhibit 11-8 above for calculations

January 2, 2016: Declaration of a cash dividend		
Dividends Declared—Common Shares	360,000	
Dividend Payable		360,000
February 15, 2016: Payment of dividend to shareholders		
Dividends Payable	360,000	
Cash		360,000

March 15, 2016: Common share issuance entry (10,000 shares)

Cash	400,000	
Common Shares		400,000

June 29, 2016: Stock dividend entries

Declaration

Stock Dividends Declared	1,125,000	
Stock Dividends Issuable		1,125,000

Issuance

Stock Dividends Issuable	1,125,000	
Common Shares		1,125,000

June 30, 2016: Declaration of dividend

Dividends Declared—Common Shares	412,500	
Dividends Payable		412,500

July 31, 2016: Payment of dividend to shareholders

Dividends Payable	412,500	
Cash		412,500

September 1, 2016: Issuance of new shares (100,000 shares)

Cash	5,000,000	
Common Shares		5,000,000

December 31, 2016: No entry is needed. However, a memorandum entry could be made to indicate that the number of shares outstanding has changed from 375,000 (275,000 + 100,000) to 1,500,000 (375,000 × 4 = 1,500,000). During a stock split, the number of shares increases but the company's value does not change. The purpose of the stock split is to lower the current market price of the company's shares. In the four-for-one split that was used in the practice problem, the market price would immediately drop to one quarter of the price before the split. The lower price would make the shares accessible to more investors.

b. The balance in the Retained Earnings account will be:

Opening balance	$4,000,000
+ Net income	1,500,000
− Dividends (cash)	(360,000)
− Dividends (stock)	(1,125,000)
− Dividends (cash)	(412,500)
Ending balance	$3,602,500

c. GEL would have 1.5 million common shares issued and outstanding at December 31, 2016. (See the Exhibit 11-8 for detailed calculations.)

Suggested Solution to Chapter End Review Problem 2

a.

		2013	2012	2011
Price/earnings ratio =	Market price per share	25.42	23.14	19.40
	Earnings per share	1.33	1.32	1.20
		= 19.1	= 17.5	= 16.2

Northwest's price/earnings ratio has increased in the period between 2011 through 2013. This increase means that the amount investors have been willing to pay on an annual earnings basis has continued to grow. Based on this, the market appears to have a positive outlook regarding Northwest's future.

b.

		2013	2012
Dividend payout ratio =	Dividends per share	1.12	1.04
	Earnings per share	1.33	1.32
		= 84.2%	= 78.8%

		2013	2012
Dividend yield =	Dividends per share	1.12	1.04
	Price per share	25.42	23.14
		= 4.41%	= 4.49%

Northwest's dividend payout ratio is very high. In other words, the company pays out a large portion of its earnings as dividends and retains a small portion to reinvest in its operations. Based on this, it is likely that the company is either mature (that is, not growing, opening new locations, and so on) or is growing with borrowed funds.

Northwest's dividend yields for 2012 and 2013 were relatively low. These returns were boosted by capital appreciation because the share price rose by $2.28 (or 9.8%).

c.

$$\text{Return on equity} = \frac{\text{Net income} - \text{Preferred Dividends}}{\text{Average Common Shareholders' Equity}}$$

$$2013 \text{ ROE} = \frac{64,263}{(296,250 + 322,440)/2} = \frac{64,263}{309,345} = 20.8\%$$

$$2012 \text{ ROE} = \frac{63,888}{(283,709 + 296,250)/2} = \frac{63,888}{289,979.5} = 22.0\%$$

This ratio shows that Northwest's management has been effective at using the equity of its shareholders to generate returns. For every dollar in shareholders' equity, the company has been able to generate annual returns in excess of $0.20.

ASSIGNMENT MATERIAL

Discussion Questions

DQ11-1 Explain why understanding the shareholders' equity section is important to an investor.

DQ11-2 Identify four different accounts that could be found in the shareholders' equity section of the statement of financial position. Briefly explain what each represents.

DQ11-3 Explain what the term *IPO* means and how that is related to the form of the organization.

DQ11-4 Describe what is contained in a company's articles of incorporation and what significance the articles have for the accounting system.

DQ11-5 Briefly describe each of the following terms: *authorized shares*, *issued shares*, and *outstanding shares*.

DQ11-6 Discuss why a company might want to repurchase its shares.

DQ11-7 Explain why it is important that companies distinguish treasury shares from other issued shares.

DQ11-8 List and briefly describe the three rights that common shareholders typically have in a corporation.

DQ11-9 Discuss how preferred shares differ from common shares.

DQ11-10 Briefly describe what each of the following features means in a preferred share issue: participating, cumulative, convertible, and redeemable.

DQ11-11 Describe the process of declaring and paying a cash dividend, including information about the declaration date, date of record, and payment date.

DQ11-12 Discuss why a company might pay a special dividend and how that differs from a regular dividend.

DQ11-13 Explain why companies might declare a stock dividend rather than a cash dividend.

DQ11-14 Differentiate between a stock dividend and a stock split.

DQ11-15 When a company declares stock dividends, it is sometimes said that it has "capitalized a portion of its retained earnings." Explain why.

DQ11-16 Explain why a company might want to split its shares.

DQ11-17 What are the advantages to a company of financing growth with equity?

DQ11-18 Describe what the price/earnings ratio is intended to tell users about a company.

DQ11-19 Differentiate between the dividend yield and the dividend payout ratio.

DQ11-20 Explain why the return on shareholders' equity provides information on the rate of return to common shareholders only.

Application Problems

AP11-1 (Shareholders' equity section)

The following information is available for Beauvalon Inc. for the preparation of its September 30, 2016, financial statements:

Income before taxes	$ 265,400
Income tax expense	$ 62,600
Other comprehensive income (loss)	$ (12,300)
Earnings per share	$ 1.878
Dividends declared, common	$ 40,000
Dividends declared, preferred	$ 15,000
Retained earnings, October 1, 2015	$1,457,850
Accumulated other comprehensive income, October 1, 2015	$ 43,700
Share capital, common shares, October 1, 2015	$2,000,000
Share capital, preferred shares, October 1, 2015	$ 500,000

Beauvalon did not issue or buy back any shares during the year.

Required:

a. Prepare the shareholders' equity section of the statement of financial position as at September 30, 2016. (Hint: Identify which accounts will appear in the equity section and then calculate the year-end balances in those accounts.)

b. How many common shares does Beauvalon have outstanding?

AP11-2 (Distribution on liquidation)

HighTech Inc. was a small company started by four entrepreneurs a few years ago. They each initially invested $200,000 and sold $1 million in preferred shares to a wealthy private investor. The company did not earn much profit during its operations but was able to pay the promised annual dividend of $100,000 on the preferred shares. The company did successfully develop several patents, some of which it sold and some it still holds. The four shareholders are planning to sell the remaining patents and all other assets and wind up the company to allow them to move on to other ventures. A summary of the company's statement of financial position is as follows:

HIGHTECH INC. Statement of Financial Position as at April 30, 2016	
Total assets	$2,110,700
Total liabilities	85,000
Preferred shares	1,000,000
Common shares	800,000
Retained earnings	225,700
Total liabilities and equity	$2,110,700

Required:

a. How much will each group of shareholders receive on the windup if HighTech is able to sell its assets for:
   i. $2,110,700?
   ii. $5,000,000?
   iii. $1,800,000?

b. Why is it unlikely that HighTech would be able to sell its assets for $2,110,700?

c. If HighTech had never paid dividends to the common shareholders, what would be the total rate of return the common shareholders earned on their venture for each of the three prices given in part "a"?

AP11-3 (Entries for dividend payments)

Massawippi Co. has 10 million authorized common shares. The company has issued 4.4 million but due to some share repurchases and cancellations, only 4.2 million were outstanding at the beginning of 2016. Massawippi pays dividends of $0.25 per quarter on March 31, June 30, September 30, and December 31 each year. The dividends are declared at the monthly board meeting in the same month that they are paid. The board meets on the 1st of each month. The date of record is the 15th of the month and the shares trade ex-dividend on the 13th.

Required:

Prepare all journal entries, including dates, related to the dividends for Massawippi for 2016.

AP11-4 (Multiple share classes and participating dividends)

The following information is available about the capital structure for MacTavish Corporation:

- Common shares, Class A: 1 million authorized and outstanding. The Class A common shares are entitled to five votes per share and to receive dividends as declared by the board of directors.
- Total share capital for Class A common shares as at the end of the year was $1.5 million.
- Preferred shares: unlimited authorized, 2.2 million issued and outstanding. The preferred shares are entitled to one vote per share and to receive a preferential cumulative dividend of $0.20 per share per year. After the Class A common shares are paid the same return, the preferred shares are entitled to participate equally with the Class A common shares in any further dividends.
- Total share capital for the preferred shares as at the end of the year was $25.3 million.

Required:

a. What is the minimum dividend payment the company should make each year to avoid being in arrears in its dividend obligations?
b. Assume that MacTavish has $2 million available for dividend payments this year and there are no dividend arrears at the beginning of the current year. What will be the total dividend paid to each of the preferred and Class A common shareholders individually and as a class?
c. Why might MacTavish have the share structure it does?
d. On average, what did each class of shareholder pay (or invest) per share originally?
e. When electing the board of directors, or voting on other corporate issues, what portion of the total available vote does each class of shares have? Prepare a table comparing the voting rights with the capital invested. Comment briefly.

AP11-5 (Types of dividend and dividend policy)

D'Ambrosio Ltd. has been operating for 10 years. The company's net income and other information since inception are shown below.

Year	Net income (loss) ($)	Retained earnings ($)	Cash ($)
2007	(150,000)	(150,000)	-
2008	(25,000)	(175,000)	2,500
2009	35,000	(140,000)	3,000
2010	(5,000)	(145,000)	2,000
2011	50,000	(95,000)	2,800
2012	125,000	30,000	12,000
2013	140,000	170,000	12,500
2014	160,000	330,000	15,000
2015	170,000	500,000	14,200
2016	200,000	700,000	22,000

Required:

a. Which year would have been the first year D'Ambrosio could have legally paid out dividends?
b. Would you recommend that the company pay out dividends at that time? Explain briefly.
c. In 2015, the board of directors was starting to believe the company was becoming more stable. Directors began discussing the options for rewarding the shareholders for the company's success but they were hesitant to commit the company to any long-term payments. What options would you suggest to the board?
d. In 2016, the board felt more comfortable that the company was on the road to long-term success. What dividend policy could the company consider now? If the company wanted to preserve its cash, what other option could it consider?

AP11-6 (Equity transactions)

Southern Exposure Ltd. begins operations on January 2, 2016. During the year, the following transactions affect shareholders' equity:

1. Southern Exposure's articles of incorporation authorizes the issuance of 1 million common shares, and the issuance of 100,000 preferred shares, which pay an annual dividend of $2 per share.
2. A total of 240,000 common shares are issued for $5 a share.

3. A total of 15,000 preferred shares are issued for $14 per share.
4. The full annual dividend on the preferred shares is declared.
5. The dividend on the preferred shares is paid.
6. A dividend of $0.10 per share is declared on the common shares but is not yet paid.
7. The company has net income of $150,000 for the year. (Assume sales of $750,000 and total operating expenses of $600,000.)
8. The dividends on the common shares are paid.
9. The closing entry for the dividends declared accounts is prepared.

Required:

a. Prepare journal entries to record the above transactions, including the closing entries for net income and dividends declared mentioned in items 3 through 6 above.
b. Prepare the shareholders' equity section of the statement of financial position as at December 31, 2016.
c. Why would an investor choose to purchase the common shares rather than the preferred shares? Or vice versa?

AP11-7 (Share issuance, dividends, financial statement preparation)

The Equitee Corporation was incorporated on January 2, 2015, with two classes of share capital: an unlimited number of common shares and $3 cumulative non-voting preferred shares with an authorized limit of 50,000.

During the first year of operations, the following transactions occurred:

1. The company issued 3,000 preferred shares for a total of $75,000 cash, and 10,000 common shares for $20 per share.
2. It issued 4,000 common shares in exchange for a parcel of land with an estimated fair market value of $120,000.
3. The company had sales of $1,050,000 and incurred operating expenses of $925,000 during the year.
4. No dividends were declared during the first year of operations.

During the second year of operations, the following transactions occurred:

5. In November, the company's board of directors declared cash dividends sufficient to pay a dividend of $4 on each common share. The dividends were payable on December 14. (Hint: Remember that no dividends can be paid on the common shares until the dividends in arrears and the current dividends on the preferred shares are paid.)
6. In December, the cash dividends from November were paid.
7. In December, the board of directors declared and distributed a 10% stock dividend on the common shares. The estimated market value of the common shares at the time was $24 per share.
8. The company had sales of $1,200,000 and incurred $1,025,000 in operating expenses during the second year.

Required:

a. Prepare journal entries to record the above transactions, including closing entries for net income and dividends declared in transactions 3, 5, 7 and 8. Use a spreadsheet or table format like the one in the first practice problem to track the changes in all of the shareholders' equity accounts over the two-year period. Prepare the shareholders' equity section of the statement of financial position at the end of the second year.
b. Why would the owners have designated the preferred shares as non-voting?

AP11-8 (Equity transactions, financial statement preparation)

Pharma Shop Ltd. was a mid-sized public company that had been in operation for many years. On December 31, 2015, it had an unlimited number of common shares authorized and 5.2 million shares issued at an average value of $25 per share. As well, there were 5 million preferred shares authorized, with 250,000 of them issued at $20 per share. The balance in retained earnings was $26,610,000. The balance in accumulated other comprehensive income was $525,000. The preferred shares pay an annual dividend of $2 per share. During 2016, the following transactions affected shareholders' equity:

1 In total, 200,000 new common shares were issued at $30 per share.
2. The preferred dividend for the year was declared and paid.
3. A 10% common stock dividend was declared when the market price was $33 per share. The shares were distributed one month after the declaration.
4. In early December 2016, a dividend of $1.50 per share was declared on the common shares. The date of record was December 15, 2014. The dividend will be paid the following year.
5. The company earned a net income of $14,820,000 and had an other comprehensive loss of $145,000.
6. On December 31, 2016, the company declared a two-for-one stock split on common shares.

Required:

a. Use a spreadsheet or table format like the one in the first practice problem to track all of the changes in the shareholders' equity accounts in 2016.
b. Prepare the statement of changes in shareholders' equity for 2016 and the shareholders' equity section of the statement of financial position as at the end of 2016. (Hint: The statement of changes in shareholders' equity will be similar to the table from part "a" but similar transactions, such as dividends, will be grouped into one line.)

AP11-9 (Share issuance, types of shares, dividends, and stock splits)

Eastwood Inc. had the following shares authorized in its articles of incorporation and issued on December 31, 2015:

- 100,000 preferred shares, no par, $4 semi-annual dividend, non-voting, redeemable at $103, none issued
- Unlimited number of common shares authorized, 500,000 shares issued for $4.4 million

On December 31, 2015, the company had the following balances in other equity accounts:

Retained Earnings	$5,120,000
Accumulated Other Comprehensive Income	$ 345,000

During 2016, the following events occurred:

1. On January 2, Eastwood decided to raise more capital and issued 30,000 preferred shares for $100 per share.
2. The company declared and paid the dividend on the preferred shares for the first half of the year.
3. The company declared and distributed a 5% common stock dividend when the market price of the common shares was $46 per share.
4. In November, the share price of the common shares had risen to $100 per share, so the board of directors voted to split the shares five-for-one.
5. Late in December, the company declared and paid the dividend on the preferred shares for the second half of the year and declared a cash dividend on the common shares of $0.50 per share payable in early January 2016. In past years, the dividend had generally been about $2.00 per share.
6. The company earned a net income of $720,000 for 2015 and reported other comprehensive income of $85,000.

Required:

a. Use a spreadsheet or table format like the one in the first practice problem to track all of the changes in the shareholders' equity accounts in 2016. Use the table to prepare the statement of changes in shareholders' equity for 2016.
b. Prepare the shareholders' equity section of the statement of financial position as at the end of 2016.
c. What reasons might the company have for issuing preferred shares instead of common shares at the start of the year?
d. If you owned 50,000 common shares on January 1, 2016, and did not buy or sell any shares during the year, how has your ability to influence the management of the company changed over the year? Did you need to consider the existence of preferred shares on January 1, 2016? Explain briefly.
e. What effect did each dividend (stock dividend and cash dividend) have on the financial statements?
f. What reason might the company have for declaring a stock dividend?
g. What reason might the company have for splitting the shares?
h. If you were a common shareholder, would you be happy or unhappy with the stock dividend and stock split? Explain briefly.
i. What do you think about the reduction in the cash dividend from $2.00 to $0.50? Explain.
j. Why would an investor purchase common shares rather than preferred shares? Or vice versa?

AP11-10 (Share classes, statement of changes in shareholders' equity)

The following information was available for The Gibson Group Inc. (TGGI) for 2016:

1. Class A common shares, 10 votes per share, unlimited authorized, 7,530,000 issued and outstanding on January 1, 2016, for $18,825,000. Class B common shares, 1 vote per share, unlimited authorized, 25,432,000 issued and outstanding for $216,172,000.
2. January 1, 2016, balance of $252,475,000 in retained earnings and $674,000 in accumulated other comprehensive income.
3. In December, TGGI paid dividends of $1.50 on all shares outstanding.
4. Net income for 2016 was $85,993,000 and other comprehensive income reported was $43,000.

Required:

a. What was the average amount per share originally invested by each class of shareholder?
b. How many total votes are there available on TGGI's common shares?
c. What portion of the voting rights does each class of shareholder control?
d. Explain why the company might have the two classes of shares that it does.
e. Prepare TGGI's statement of changes in shareholders' equity for 2016.
f. What portion of net income did TGGI pay out in dividends?

AP11-11 (Stock dividends)

Sealand Company has 100,000 common shares outstanding. Because it wants to retain its cash flow to use for other purposes, the company has decided to issue stock dividends to its shareholders. The market price of each Sealand Company share is $22.

Required:
   a. Prepare the journal entries if the company decides to declare and issue a 10% stock dividend.
   b. Prepare the journal entry if instead of declaring the stock dividend the company decides to split its shares two-for-one.
   c. What should happen to the market price of the company's shares in part "a"? In part "b"?
   d. Based on the current share price, do you think it is likely the company would split its shares? Why or why not?

AP11-12 (Change in shareholders' equity)

The shareholders' equity of Deer Ltd. at the end of 2016 and 2015 appeared as follows:

	2016	2015
Share capital, preferred shares, $2 cumulative, 2,000,000 shares authorized, 25,000 shares issued	$ 200,000	$ 200,000
Share capital, 5,000,000 common shares authorized, 1,200,000 common shares issued (2015—1,000,000 shares)	5,000,000	4,000,000
Retained earnings	3,920,000	3,160,000
Total shareholders' equity	$9,120,000	$7,360,000

During 2016, Deer paid a total of $125,000 in cash dividends.

Required:
   a. Assume the preferred shares were not in arrears at December 31, 2015. How was the $125,000 in cash dividends distributed between the two types of shares in 2016?
   b. Assume the preferred share dividends were in arrears for one year; that is, the dividends were not paid in 2015. How was the $125,000 in cash dividends distributed between the two classes of shares?
   c. Both common shares and retained earnings changed during the year. Provide journal entries that would account for the changes.

AP11-13 (Dividend distributions)

Flatfish Limited reported the following items in shareholders' equity on December 31, 2016:

Share capital: Preferred shares, $5 cumulative dividend, 150,000 shares issued and outstanding	$15,000,000
Share capital: Common shares, 750,000 issued and outstanding	30,000,000
Retained earnings	25,000,000

Required:
   a. No dividends were declared in 2014 or 2015; however, in 2016 cash dividends of $5 million were declared. Calculate how much would be paid to each class of shares.
   b. Assuming that the number of common shares remained constant throughout 2016, what was the cash dividend per share distributed to the common shareholders?
   c. Early in 2017, when its common shares were selling at $59 per share, the company declared and distributed a 10% stock dividend. Describe the impact that this declaration will have on the shareholders' equity accounts. (Hint: It may be helpful to prepare the journal entry and closing entry related to this transaction.)
   d. Explain why a company would choose to issue a stock dividend rather than a cash dividend.

AP11-14 (Dividend distributions)

Holt Company paid out cash dividends at the end of each year as follows:

Year	Dividends
2014	$250,000
2015	$325,000
2016	$400,000

Required:
   a. Assume that Holt had 250,000 common shares and 10,000, $7, non-cumulative preferred shares. How much cash would be paid out in 2014, 2015, and 2016 to each class of shares?
   b. Assume that Holt had 100,000 common shares, and 5,000, $4, cumulative preferred shares that were three years in arrears as at January 1, 2014. How much cash would be paid out in 2014, 2015, and 2016 to each class of shares?

AP11-15 (Book value, market value, EPS)

Woods Inc. is a provincially incorporated company working in software development. The company was initially owned by a group of 40 investors that included the four original founders, their friends and families, and employees. The company is authorized to issue 50 million common shares. At the beginning of 2016, there were 1 million common shares outstanding which had been issued for $2.5 million, all of these shares were owned by the initial group. Due to the company's rapid success, management decided to raise funds for further growth by issuing more shares. In 2016, the company went public with an initial public offering (IPO) that sold 5 million shares and raised $50 million. Other information is as follows:

1. After losses in the early years, the company recently had positive earnings. The opening balance of retained earnings on January 1, 2016, was $1.2 million.
2. In 2016, net income was $2.5 million.
3. On December 31, 2016, the shares were trading at $10.50.

Required:

a. What percentage of the company does the original group of investors own after the IPO? How could the group have maintained their control of the company? How would that have likely influenced the price of the shares sold?
b. What was the EPS amount for 2016 based on the end-of-year number of shares outstanding?
c. If you were an investor who bought shares in the IPO, would you be surprised that dividends were not paid in 2016? Why or why not?

AP11-16 (Statement of income and statement of changes in shareholders' equity)

The following are selected account balances from Eastern Shore Ltd.'s trial balance on December 31, 2016:

	Debits	Credits
Accumulated other comprehensive income		$ 17,250
Assets	$21,390,000	
Liabilities		6,712,500
Depreciation expense	105,000	
Dividends declared—common shares	225,000	
Common shares		6,885,000
Cost of goods sold	1,020,000	
Interest expense	90,000	
Operating expenses	300,000	
Other comprehensive income		5,000
Dividends declared—preferred shares	69,000	
Preferred shares		3,750,000
Retained earnings		3,892,750
Sales revenue		2,326,500
Wages expense	390,000	
	$23,589,000	$23,589,000

Required:

a. Prepare Eastern Shore's statement of income and comprehensive income and statement of changes in shareholders' equity in good form for the year ended December 31, 2016. Assume there have been no share issues or redemptions during 2016. (Hint: At what date is the retained earnings balance of $3,892,750 measured? How can you tell?)
b. Prepare the shareholders' equity section of the statement of financial position as at December 31, 2016.
c. Based on this information, does it appear likely that Eastern Shore will be able to continue paying common and preferred dividends at similar levels in the future? Explain.
d. Why might viewing Eastern Shore's statements of income for the previous few years help you in answering part "c"? What other information would you find helpful in reaching a conclusion?
e. Considering both common and preferred shares, what was Eastern Shore's dividend payout ratio in 2016?

User Perspective Problems

UP11-1 (New share issuance)

As a loan officer at a bank, six months ago you helped Cedar Ltd. arrange a $1.5-million, 20-year mortgage. Cedar Ltd. has just announced an issuance of new shares from which it intends to raise $5 million.

Required:
How do you think this new issuance will affect the bank's outstanding loan? Identify some positive and negative outcomes.

UP11-2 (Dividends and stock splits)

You own 10,000 shares (1%) of the outstanding shares of Yangtze Inc. You paid $5.00 per share shortly after the company went public. The company's most recent statement of financial position is summarized below. The current market price of Yangtze shares is $15.00 and the company has never paid dividends. Yangtze is considering either paying a one-time special dividend of $1.50 per share or declaring a 10% stock dividend.

YANGTZE INC. Summarized Statement of Financial Position As at December 31, 2016	
Cash	$ 1,700,000
Other current assets	1,600,000
Non-current assets	6,800,000
Total assets	$10,100,000
Current liabilities	$ 450,000
Long-term bank loan	2,550,000
Share capital (1 million shares outstanding)	3,000,000
Retained earnings	4,100,000
Total liabilities and equity	$10,100,000

Required:
a. Assume that Yangtze decides to pay a cash dividend.
   i. Compare your personal financial position (investment and any cash received) before and after the payment of the dividend.
   ii. Compare Yangtze's financial position before and after the payment of the dividend.
   iii. Contrast the change in your financial position with that in Yangtze's.
b. Assume that Yangtze decides to issue a stock dividend.
   i. Compare your personal financial position (investment and any cash received) before and after the payment of the stock dividend.
   ii. Compare Yangtze's financial position before and after the payment of the stock dividend.
   iii. Contrast the change in your financial position with that in Yangtze's.
c. From your personal point of view, which of the two types of dividends would you prefer to receive?
d. From Yangtze's point of view, which type of dividend would you recommend that it declare?
e. Which type of dividend do you think the creditor who has provided the long-term bank loan would prefer that Yangtze pay? Why?
f. Yangtze managers have heard that several other companies have recently declared 100% stock splits and they wonder if they should do so too to keep up with the trend.
   i. Based on the reasons for stock splits discussed in the chapter, do you think Yangtze is a good candidate for a stock split? Why or why not?
   ii. What would be the effect of a stock split on your personal financial position? On Yangtze's?

UP11-3 (Stock splits and dividends)

Gildan Activewear Inc. is a Montreal-based manufacturer of branded activewear. Since going public in 1998, Gildan's common shares have been split as follows:

Stock Split	Date Declared	Type
First split	February 7, 2001	Two-for-one
Second split	May 4, 2005	Two-for-one
Third split	May 2, 2007	Two-for-one

Gildan announced in December 2010 that it would introduce a quarterly dividend. It has paid the following dividends up to January 2014:

Payment month	Dividends per share
March, June, and September 2011	$0.075
January, March, June, and September 2012	$0.075
January, March, June, and September 2013	$0.090
January 2014	$0.108

Required:

    a. If you had purchased 100 shares of Gildan when the company went public in 1998 and not bought or sold any shares since, how many shares would you currently own?

    b. What is the total amount of dividends you would have received by the end of January 2014?

    c. What can you infer about the growth of Gildan from the frequency of stock splits and its decision to introduce a quarterly dividend in December 2010?

UP11-4 (Stock dividends)

The shareholders' equity section of Carswell Corporation's comparative statement of financial position at the end of 2016 and 2015 was presented as follows at a recent shareholders' meeting:

	Dec. 31, 2016	Dec. 31, 2015
Share capital, common shares, no par value, 500,000 shares authorized, 290,000 shares issued and outstanding	$4,720,000	$4,000,000
Retained earnings	2,066,000	2,555,000
Total shareholders' equity	$6,786,000	$6,555,000

The following items were also disclosed at the shareholders' meeting:

- Net income for 2016 was $666,000.
- A 16% stock dividend was issued on December 14, 2016, when the market value was $18 per share.
- The market value per share on December 31, 2016, was $16.
- Management has put aside $900,000 and plans to borrow $200,000 to help finance a new plant addition, which is expected to cost a total of $1 million.
- The customary $1.74 per share cash dividend was revised to $1.50 for the cash dividend declared and paid in the last week of December 2016.

As part of their shareholders' goodwill program, management asked shareholders to write down any questions they might have concerning the company's operations or finances. As assistant controller, you are given the shareholders' questions.

Required:

Prepare brief but reasonably complete answers to the following questions from shareholders.

    a. What did Carswell do with the cash proceeds from the stock dividend issued in December?

    b. I owned 5,000 shares of Carswell in 2015 and have not sold any shares. How much more or less of the corporation do I own on December 31, 2016? What happened to the market value of my interest in the company?

    c. I heard someone say that stock dividends don't give me anything I didn't already have. Are you trying to fool us? Why did you issue one?

    d. Instead of a stock dividend, why didn't you declare a cash dividend and let us buy the new shares that were issued?

    e. Why are you cutting back on the dividends I receive?

    f. If you have $900,000 put aside for the new plant addition that will cost $1 million, why are you borrowing $200,000 instead of just the missing $100,000?

UP11-5 (Cash dividends)

You have been considering buying some common shares of Sherlock Ltd., which has 1.5 million common shares outstanding. While the company has been through difficult times, it is now doing better and your main concern is whether you will receive cash dividends. In addition to the common shares, the company has 50,000 no par, $8, Class A preferred shares outstanding that are non-cumulative and non-participating. The company also has 10,000, $7.50, Class B preferred shares outstanding. These shares are non-participating but are cumulative. The normal dividend was paid on both classes of preferred shares until last year, when no dividends were paid. This year, however, Sherlock is doing well and is expecting net income of $2.1 million. The company has not yet declared its annual dividends but has indicated that it plans to pay total dividends equal to 35% of net income.

Required:

  a. If you were to immediately buy 100 shares of Sherlock Ltd., what amount of common dividend would you expect to receive?
  b. If you were to immediately buy 100 shares of Sherlock Ltd., what amount of common dividend would you expect to receive if the Class B preferred shares were non-cumulative?

UP11-6 (Stock dividends and splits)

Peninsula Minerals Ltd.'s authorized share capital consists of an unlimited number of common shares, with 9.3 million outstanding. After some early successes, the company has failed to locate new mineral deposits and has also decreased its estimates of the amount of minerals in existing mines. As a result, earnings per share and the share price have been declining and are currently $0.17 and $0.68 per share, respectively. Peninsula Minerals is considering a reverse stock split (one that decreases the number of shares outstanding instead of increasing them) of one-for-three.

Required:

  a. What is the current price/earnings ratio?
  b. What is the current market value of the company?
  c. Why would any company want to reverse split its shares? What would be the likely effect of the reverse split on the EPS and share price?
  d. Would repurchasing shares achieve the same result as a reverse split? What is the likely reason that management prefers a reverse split over repurchasing shares?
  e. If the board of directors approves the reverse split, how many shares will be outstanding?
  f. Assuming the price/earnings ratio is the same after the reverse split as it was before the split, what will Peninsula Minerals' share price be after the reverse split?

UP11-7 (Retained earnings and dividends)

You are considering purchasing some Stanley Ltd. common shares. Although Stanley recently had to incur significant expenditures for new capital assets, the company has been relatively profitable over the years and its future prospects look good. The summarized statement of financial position at the end of 2016 is as follows:

Cash	$ 137,500
Other current assets	640,500
Capital assets (net)	4,702,000
Total	$5,480,000
Current liabilities	$ 414,000
Long-term debt	2,000,000
Share capital, common shares	1,000,000
Retained earnings	2,066,000
Total	$5,480,000

The company has 150,000 common shares outstanding, and its earnings per share have increased by at least 10% in each of the last 10 years. In several recent years, earnings per share increased by more than 14%. Given the company's earnings and the amount of retained earnings, you judge that it could easily pay cash dividends of $3 or $4 per share, without reducing its retained earnings.

Required:

  a. Discuss whether it is likely that you would receive a cash dividend from Stanley during the next year if you were to purchase its shares.
  b. Discuss whether it is likely that you would receive a cash dividend from Stanley during the next five years if you were to purchase its shares.
  c. In making an investment decision, would it help you to know whether Stanley has paid dividends in the past? Explain.
  d. Suppose Stanley borrowed $2 million cash on a five-year bank loan to provide working capital and additional operating flexibility. While no collateral would be required, the loan would stipulate that no dividends be paid in any year in which the ratio of long-term debt to equity was greater than 60%.
    i. If Stanley were to enter into the loan agreement, would you be likely to receive a dividend next year?
    ii. Would you be likely to receive a dividend at some point in the next five years? (Hint: What would you expect to happen to the statement of financial position values for long-term debt and for equity?)

UP11-8 (Return on investment)

Windmere Corporation's statement of financial position at December 31, 2016, appears as follows:

Cash	$ 63,000
Other current assets	1,106,000
Capital assets (net)	7,140,000
Total	$8,309,000
Current liabilities	$ 546,000
Long-term debt	1,400,000
Preferred shares	700,000
Share capital—common shares	2,100,000
Retained earnings	3,563,000
Total	$8,309,000

For the year just ended, Windmere reported net income of $540,000. During the year, the company declared preferred dividends of $50,000 and common dividends of $300,000.

Required:
  a. Calculate the following ratios for Windmere:
     i.   Return on assets, using net income in the calculation
     ii. Dividend payout ratio
     iii. Return on common shareholders' equity
  b. Assume that the company issued $1.4 million of common shares at the beginning of 2016 and paid off the long-term debt. By repaying the long-term debt and not incurring any interest expense, the company's net income increased by $70,000.
     i.   What would the return on common shareholders' equity be? (Hint: Remember that shareholders' equity is affected by net income.)
     ii. Would common shareholders be better or worse off?
     iii. Does switching from debt to equity financing always have this effect on the return on common shareholders' equity? Explain.
  c. Assume that the long-term debt remains as shown on the statement of financial position and that the company issued an additional $700,000 of common shares at the beginning of 2016. The company used the proceeds to redeem and cancel the preferred shares.
     i.   What would the return on common shareholders' equity be?
     ii. Would shareholders be better or worse off?
     iii. Does switching from preferred equity financing to common equity financing always have this effect on the return on common shareholders' equity? Explain.

Reading and Interpreting Published Financial Statements

RI11-1 (Capital stock)

Note 13 to the January 25, 2014, financial statements of **Le Château Inc.** is shown in Exhibit 11-9. All dollar amounts are in thousands.

EXHIBIT 11-9	EXCERPT FROM LE CHÂTEAU INC. 2013 ANNUAL REPORT

13. SHARE CAPITAL

Authorized
An unlimited number of non-voting first, second and third preferred shares issuable in series, without par value
An unlimited number of Class A subordinate voting shares, without par value
An unlimited number of Class B voting shares, without par value

Principal features
[a] With respect to the payment of dividends and the return of capital, the shares rank as follows:
     First preferred
     Second preferred
     Third preferred
     Class A subordinate voting and Class B voting.
[b] Subject to the rights of the preferred shareholders, the Class A subordinate voting shareholders are entitled to a non-cumulative preferential dividend of $0.0125 per share, after which the Class B voting shareholders are entitled to a non-cumulative dividend of $0.0125 per share; any further dividends declared in a fiscal year must

continued

| EXHIBIT 11-9 | **EXCERPT FROM LE CHÂTEAU INC. 2013 ANNUAL REPORT (continued)** |

be declared and paid in equal amounts per share on all the Class A subordinate voting and Class B voting shares then outstanding without preference or distinction.

[c] Subject to the foregoing, the Class A subordinate voting and Class B voting shares rank equally, share for share, in earnings.

[d] The Class A subordinate voting shares carry one vote per share and the Class B voting shares carry 10 votes per share.

[e] The Articles of the Company provide that if there is an accepted or completed offer for more than 20% of the Class B voting shares or an accepted or completed offer to more than 14 holders there of at a price in excess of 115% of their market value [as defined in the Articles of the Corporation], each Class A subordinate voting share will be, at the option of the holder, converted into one Class B voting share for the purposes of accepting such offer, unless at the same time an offer is made to all holders of the Class A subordinate voting shares for a percentage of such shares at least equal to the percentage of Class B voting shares which are the subject of the offer and otherwise on terms and conditions not less favourable. In addition, each Class A subordinate voting share shall be converted into one Class B voting share if at any time the principal shareholder of the Company or any corporation controlled directly or indirectly by him ceases to be the beneficial owner, directly or indirectly, and with full power to exercise in all circumstances the voting rights attached to such shares, of shares of the Company having attached thereto more than 50% of the votes attached to all outstanding shares of the Company.

Issued and outstanding

	January 25, 2014		January 26, 2013	
	Number of shares	$	Number of shares	$
Class A subordinate voting shares				
Balance – beginning of year	22,682,961	42,338	20,228,864	37,327
Issuance of subordinate voting shares upon conversion of long-term debt	—	—	2,454,097	5,011
Issuance of subordinate voting shares upon exercise of options	99,500	159	—	—
Reclassification from contributed surplus due to exercise of share options	—	61	—	—
Balance, end of year	22,782,461	42,558	22,682,961	42,338
Class B voting shares	4,560,000	402	4,560,000	402
Balance, end of year	27,342,461	42,960	27,242,961	42,740

All issued shares are fully paid.

During the year ended January 26, 2013, a $5.0 million loan payable to a company that is directly controlled by a director was converted into 2,454,097 Class A subordinate voting shares [note 19].

Required:

a. Describe the differences between the Class A subordinate voting shares and Class B voting shares with respect to the following:
   i. their ability to influence the selection of management and to influence company decision-making and
   ii. the amount and priority of expected dividends.

b. If you owned 100,000 Class A subordinate voting shares at January 25, 2014, what proportion of total votes would you control? If you owned 100,000 Class B voting shares, what proportion of total votes would you control?

c. Why would investors choose to purchase the Class A rather than the Class B shares? Or vice versa?

d. Why might Class A shareholders choose to convert their shareholdings into Class B shares, as described in Principal features part [e]?

RI11-2 (Capital stock, dividends equity analysis)

Required:

Use the 2014 financial statements for **Danier Leather Inc.** in Appendix A to answer the following questions:

a. In your own words describe the share capital of Danier. Why do you think the company has the share structure that it does?

b. Based on the statement of financial position, does Danier appear to be in a financial position to pay out dividends? What about based on the statement of income? What amount of dividends did the company pay out?

c. Danier calculates its EPS using both the multiple voting shares and the subordinated voting shares. Do you agree with this method of calculation? Why or why not?

d. Calculate Danier's return on equity ratio for 2014 and 2013 and comment on your findings. (For the 2013 ratio, you can find the 2012 balances in the statement of changes in shareholders' equity.)

e. Calculate Danier's dividend payout ratio for 2014.

f. On June 29, 2014, Danier's share price was $9.41. Calculate the price/earnings ratio as at that date.

RI11-3 (Types of shares, statement of changes in shareholders' equity)

With corporate offices in Quebec, **RONA Inc.** operates approximately 800 stores of various sizes and formats across Canada and is the largest Canadian distributor and retailer of hardware, renovation, and gardening products. Exhibit 11-10 presents the shareholders' equity section of the statement of financial position and excerpts from Note 23 to RONA's consolidated financial statements for 2013. All amounts are in thousands.

EXHIBIT 11-10A   EXCERPT FROM RONA INC. 2013 ANNUAL REPORT

CONSOLIDATED FINANCIAL STATEMENTS

December 29, 2013 and December 30, 2012

(In thousands of dollars)	2013	2012
Equity		
Share capital (Note 23)	$ 765,203	$ 765,443
Retained earnings	879,415	1,071,426
Contributed surplus	12,972	12,521
Accumulated other comprehensive income	(2,158)	(3,643)
Total equity attributable to owners of RONA inc.	1,655,432	1,845,747

EXHIBIT 11-10B   EXCERPT FROM RONA INC. 2013 ANNUAL REPORT

23. Share capital

Authorized

Unlimited number of shares

        Common without par value

        Class A preferred shares, without par value, issuable in series

                Series 5, non-cumulative dividend equal to 70% of prime rate, redeemable at the Corporation's option at their issuance price

                Series 6, cumulative dividend of 5.25%, subject to approval by the Board of Directors, fixed for the first five years, redeemable at the Corporation's option at their issuance price

                Series 7, annual cumulative dividend at variable rate, redeemable at the Corporation's option at their issuance price

        Class B preferred shares, 6% non-cumulative dividend, redeemable at the Corporation's option at their par value of $1 each

        Class C preferred shares, issuable in series

                Series 1, non-cumulative dividend equal to 70% of prime rate, redeemable at the Corporation's option at their par value of $1,000 each

        Class D preferred shares, without par value, 4% cumulative dividend, redeemable at their issuance price over a maximum of ten years from the sixth anniversary of their date of issuance, on the basis of 10% per year.

Issued and fully paid:

The following tables present changes in the number of outstanding shares and their carrying amounts:

	Common shares		Preferred shares [b]		Deposits on common share subscriptions [a]		Share capital	
	Number of shares	Amount	Number of shares	Amount	Number of shares	Amount	Number of shares	Amount
Balance, December 30, 2012 – Restated (Note 32)	121,408,037	$590,763	6,900,000	$172,500	–	$2,180	128,308,037	$765,443
Issuance of share capital in exchange of cash	34,121	409	–	–	–	–	34,121	409
Issuance of share capital under stock option plans	279,900	3,647	–	–	–	–	279,900	3,647
Issuance in exchange of common share subscription deposits	199,078	2,118	–	–	–	(2,118)	199,078	–
Repurchase of common shares for cancellation	(1,177,300)	(5,764)	–	–	–	–	(1,177,300)	(5,764)
Deposits on common share subscriptions received	–	–	–	–	–	1,595	–	1,595
Deposits on common share subscriptions refunded	–	–	–	–	–	(127)	–	(127)
Balance, December 29, 2013	120,743,836	$591,173	6,900,000	$172,500	–	$1,530	127,643,836	$765,203

continued

| EXHIBIT 11-10B | EXCERPT FROM RONA INC. 2013 ANNUAL REPORT (continued) |

(a) Deposits on common share subscriptions represent amounts received during the year from affiliated and franchised merchants in accordance with commercial agreements. These deposits are exchanged for common shares on an annual basis. If the subscription deposits had been exchanged for common shares as at December 29, 2013, the number of outstanding common shares would have increased by 117,084.

(b) Class A preferred shares, Series 6 (Note 25).

Required:
a. i. How many types of shares does RONA have authorized?
   ii. What are the main differences in the types?
   iii. Why would a company have different types of shares authorized?
b. Are there any preferred shares outstanding? If so, how many?
c. Compare the information included in the tables in Note 23 with a statement of changes in equity. How are the two tables similar? How are they different?
d. RONA Inc. had a net loss of $153,014 thousand for the year ended December 29, 2013, yet the company still declared dividends of $17,043 thousand on its common shares and $9,288 thousand on its preferred shares. How was it able to do this?

RI11-4 (Ratios)

Using the consolidated statement of earnings for **Cineplex Inc.** to the financial statements in Exhibit 11-11, calculate the ratios below. The market price of Cineplex's shares on December 31, 2013, was $44.06.

| EXHIBIT 11-11 | EXCERPT FROM CINEPLEX INC. 2013 ANNUAL REPORT |

Consolidated statements of operations
For the years ended December 31, 2013 and 2012
(expressed in thousands of Canadian dollars, except per share amounts)

	2013	2012 (note 2)
Revenues		
Box office	$ 665,306	$ 638,296
Concessions	350,353	329,332
Other	155,608	124,873
	1,171,267	1,092,501
Expenses		
Film cost	346,373	331,281
Cost of concessions	74,693	68,398
Depreciation and amortization	70,890	62,163
Loss (gain) on disposal of assets	4,372	(−2,352)
(Gain) on acquisition of business (note 3 d)	—	(−24,752)
Other costs (note 23)	551,819	495,537
Share of income of joint ventures	(−3,850)	(−3,263)
Interest expense	10,743	12,585
Interest income	(−307)	(−205)
	1,054,733	939,392
Income before income taxes	116,534	153,109
Provision for income taxes		
Current (note 10)	3,608	31,436
Deferred (note 10)	29,369	1,189
	32,977	32,625
Net Income	$ 83,557	$ 120,484
Basic net income per share (note 24)	$ 1.33	$ 1.98
Diluted net income per share (note 24)	$ 1.32	$ 1.97

continued

EXHIBIT 11-11	EXCERPT FROM CINEPLEX INC. 2013 ANNUAL REPORT (continued)

16. Dividends payable

Cineplex has declared the following dividends during the years:

	2013		2012	
Record date	Amount	Amount per share	Amount	Amount per share
January	$7,063	$0.1125	$6,279	$0.1075
February	7,065	0.1125	6,303	0.1075
March	7,070	0.1125	6,558	0.1075
April	7,070	0.1125	6,561	0.1075
May	7,541	0.1200	6,945	0.1125
June	7,542	0.1200	6,955	0.1125
July	7,542	0.1200	6,974	0.1125
August	7,542	0.1200	6,979	0.1125
September	7,542	0.1200	6,982	0.1125
October	7,542	0.1200	6,983	0.1125
November	7,548	0.1200	6,990	0.1125
December	7,552	0.1200	7,063	0.1125

Required:
   a. Calculate Cineplex's price/earnings ratio.
   b. Calculate the dividend payout ratio for 2013.
   c. Calculate the return on common shareholders' equity for 2012 and 2013 and comment on your findings. (Total shareholders' equity was $748,272 thousand at December 31, 2103; $747,314 thousand at December 31, 2012; and $621,609 at December 31, 2011.)

RI11-5 (Shares, ratios)

Finning International Inc., headquartered in Vancouver, describes itself as "the world's largest Caterpillar equipment dealer," with operations in Western Canada, South America, and the United Kingdom and Ireland.

As at December 31, 2013, the company had a straightforward share capital structure described in Note 7 to the financial statements as:

The Company is authorized to issue an unlimited number of preferred shares without par value, of which 4.4 million are designated as cumulative redeemable preferred shares. The Company had no preferred shares outstanding for the years ended December 31, 2013 and 2012.

The Company is authorized to issue an unlimited number of common shares.

Exhibit 11-12 contains the 2013 consolidated statement of shareholders' equity. All amounts are in thousands.

EXHIBIT 11-12	EXCERPT FROM FINNING INTERNATIONAL INC. 2013 ANNUAL REPORT

(Canadian $ thousands, except share amounts)	Share Capital			Accumulated Other Comprehensive Income (Loss)			
	Shares	Amount	Contributed Surplus	Foreign Currency Translation and Gain/ (Loss) on Net Investment Hedges	Gain/ (Loss) on Cash Flow Hedges	Retained Earnings	Total
Balance, January 1, 2012	171,573,752	$566,452	$35,812	−$28,758	−$9,435	$780,883	$1,344,954
Net income (restated – Note 1t)	—	—	—	—	—	326,774	326,774
Other comprehensive income (loss) (restated – Note 1t)	—	—	—	(−15,110)	2,829	(−3,248)	(−15,529)
Total comprehensive income (loss)	—	—	—	(−15,110)	2,829	323,526	311,245

continued

EXHIBIT 11-12	EXCERPT FROM FINNING INTERNATIONAL INC. 2013 ANNUAL REPORT (continued)

Issued on exercise of share options	336,006	4,648	(−4,393)	—	—	—	255
Share option expense	—	—	4,627	—	—	—	4,627
Dividends on common shares	—	—	—	—	—	(−94,527)	(−94,527)
Balance, December 31, 2012	171,909,758	571,100	36,046	(−43,868)	(−6,606)	1,009,882	1,566,554
Net income	—	—	—	—	—	335,255	335,255
Other comprehensive income (loss)	—	—	—	71,971	(−7,694)	(−11,874)	52,403
Total comprehensive income (loss)	—	—	—	71,971	(−7,694)	323,381	387,658
Issued on exercise of share options	104,472	2,065	(−2,002)	—	—	—	63
Share option expense	—	—	6,252	—	—	—	6,252
Dividends on common shares	—	—	—	—	—	(−102,763)	(−102,763)
Balance, December 31, 2013	172,014,230	$573,165	$40,296	$28,103	(−$14,300)	$1,230,500	$1,857,764

Required:

a. Finning has an unlimited number of authorized shares on each class of shares. Why do many companies today prefer to have an unlimited authorized number of shares?

b. How many common shares were outstanding on December 31, 2013? What was the average issue value of those shares?

c. What was Finning's reported net income for 2013? How much did it pay out in dividends? What was its dividend payout ratio?

d. Using only the statement of shareholders' equity, calculate the return on equity for Finning for 2013 and 2012.

RI11-6 (Share structures, initial stock offerings, ratios)

Quebec-based **BRP Inc.** designs, develops, manufactures, distributes, and markets a diversified group of products including Ski-Doo snowmobiles, Sea-Doo watercraft, Can-Am motorcycles, and Evinrude engines. The share capital note (Note 16) from the company's financial statements for the year ended January 31, 2014, is presented in Exhibit 11–13. Exhibit 11-13 also includes an extract from BRP's annual information form that outlines the multiple-voting share structure.

EXHIBIT 11-13A	EXCERPT FROM BRP INC. 2014 ANNUAL REPORT

16. CAPITAL STOCK

Prior to the closing of the IPO, the Company's authorized capital stock was comprised of an unlimited number of Class A voting Common Shares, an unlimited number of Class A.1 voting Common Shares, an unlimited number of Class B non-voting Common Shares, an unlimited number of Super B non-voting Common Shares and an unlimited number of non-voting preferred shares.

a) Share Reorganization

The Company's authorized capital stock was amended prior to the closing of the IPO and all the classes of shares included in the authorized capital stock of the Company prior to the amendment were repealed and replaced by an unlimited number of multiple voting shares and subordinate voting shares with no par value and an unlimited number of preferred shares issuable in series with no par value.

Also, following the amendment of the authorized capital stock and prior to the closing of the IPO, the Company consolidated its outstanding shares on a 3.765 to one basis.

b) Initial Public Offering

On May 29, 2013, the Company completed the initial public offering of its subordinate voting shares with the securities regulatory authorities in each of the provinces and territories of Canada. The Company issued 12.2 million subordinate voting shares and received gross proceeds of $262.3 million from the issuance ($246.1 million net of related fees and expenses of $22.1 million and income taxes recovery of $5.9 million).

continued

EXHIBIT 11-13A   **EXCERPT FROM BRP INC. 2014 ANNUAL REPORT (continued)**

On June 27, 2013, the Company issued 1.8 million subordinate voting shares following the exercise of the over-allotment option granted to the underwriters in connection with the IPO. The Company received gross proceeds of $39.3 million from the issuance ($37.7 million net of related fees and expenses of $2.1 million and income taxes recovery of $0.5 million).

c) Secondary Offerings

During the year ended January 31, 2014, Bain Capital and CDPQ completed two secondary offerings for a total of 18,000,000 subordinate voting shares of the Company to a syndicate of underwriters. Prior to such transactions, Bain Capital and CDPQ converted an aggregate of 18,000,000 multiple voting shares into an equivalent number of subordinate voting shares. The Company did not receive any of the proceeds of these secondary offerings. In accordance with the terms of the registration rights agreement entered into in connection with its initial public offering, the Company incurred approximately $0.9 million of fees and expenses related to these secondary offerings.

16. CAPITAL STOCK [CONTINUED]

The changes in capital stock issued and outstanding and classified in liabilities were as follows:

	Number of shares	Carrying Amount
Class A Common Shares		
Balance at February 1, 2012	229,387,717	$32.70
Balance at January 31, 2013	229,387,717	32.7
Repurchased	(−9)	−
Reduction of stated capital	−	(−27.5)
Exchanged for multiple voting shares	(−229,387,708)	(−5.2)
Balance at January 31, 2014	−	−
Class A.1 Common Shares		
Balance at February 1, 2012	123,516,460	17.3
Balance at January 31, 2013	123,516,460	17.3
Reduction of stated capital	−	(−14.8)
Exchanged for multiple voting shares	(−123,516,460)	(−2.5)
Balance at January 31, 2014	−	−
Class B Common Shares		
Balance at February 1, 2012	20,310,623	2.2
Issued upon exercise of stock options	792,800	0.3
Repurchased	(−289,800)	(−0.3)
Balance at January 31, 2013	20,813,623	2.2
Issued upon exercise of stock options	9,103,750	15.1
Repurchased	(−368,844)	(−0.1)
Reduction of stated capital	−	(−2.6)
Exchanged for multiple voting shares	(−12,388,723)	(−0.2)
Exchanged for subordinate voting shares	(−17,159,806)	(−14.4)
Balance at January 31, 2014	−	−
Multiple voting shares		
Balance at January 31, 2013	−	−
Issued in exchange of Class A Common Shares	229,387,708	5.2
Issued in exchange of Class A.1 Common Shares	123,516,460	2.5
Issued in exchange of Class B Common Shares	12,388,723	0.2
Share consolidation	(−268,269,547)	−
Exchanged for subordinate voting shares	(−18,000,000)	(−1.5)
Balance at January 31, 2014	79,023,344	6.4
Subordinate voting shares		
Balance at January 31, 2013	−	−
Issued in exchange of Class B Common Shares	23,009,339	47.8
Issued in exchange of Class Super B Common Shares	3,621,327	20.7
Share consolidation	(−19,557,447)	−
Issued following the IPO	12,200,000	246.1
Issued following the exercise of the over-allotment option	1,830,000	37.7
Issued upon exercise of stock options	32,504	0.2
Issued in exchange of multiple voting shares	18,000,000	1.5
Balance at January 31, 2014	39,135,723	$354.00
Total outstanding at January 31, 2014	118,159,067	$360.40

EXHIBIT 11-13B	BRP INC. 2014 ANNUAL INFORMATION FORM

Voting Rights

Under the Company's articles, the Subordinate Voting Shares carry one vote per share and Multiple Voting Shares carry six votes per share. Based on the number of shares issued and outstanding as at March 26, 2014, the Subordinate Voting Shares represented 33.1% of the Company's total issued and outstanding Shares and 7.6% of the voting power attached to all of the Shares.

Required:
  a. Describe the changes that the company made to its capital structure when it went public.
  b. How much money did BRP raise through its IPO? On a percentage basis, how much were the total fees and expenses incurred as part of the IPO relative to the funds raised though the IPO?
  c. Note 16(b) states that prior to the IPO, the company consolidated its outstanding shares on a 3.765-to-1 basis. Explain what this means and what effect this step would have on share value.
  d. The extract from the company's 2014 annual information form explains that the subordinate voting shares represent 33.1% of the company's total issued capital and 7.6% of the voting power attached to all shares. Rephrase this in terms of the company's multiple voting shares. Also, quantify the relationship between voting power and the capital invested.

RI11-7 (Examination of shareholders' equity for real company)

Required:
Choose a company as directed by your instructor and answer the following questions.
  a. Prepare a quick analysis of the shareholders' equity accounts by doing the following.
    i. List their beginning and ending amounts.
    ii. Calculate the net change for the most recent year in both dollar and percentage terms.
    iii. If any of the accounts changed by more than 10%, explain why.
  b. For each type of share authorized by the company, list the following:
    i. the nature of the issue
    ii. the number of shares (authorized, issued, and outstanding)
    iii. whether it is par value or no par value
    iv. the market price at the end of the year
    v. any special features of the issue.
  c. What was the company's market value at the end of the most recent year? Compare this with the company's book value and discuss why these amounts are different. Be as specific as possible.
  d. Did the company pay dividends in the most recent year? If so, what was the dividend per share and has this amount changed over the past three years?
  e. Did the company declare any stock dividends or have a stock split during the most recent year? If so, describe the nature of the event and the effects on the shareholders' equity section.

Cases

C11-1 Manonta Sales Company

Manonta Sales Company's summary statement of financial position and income statement as at December 31, 2015, follow.

Statement of Financial Position (in thousands)	
Current assets	$150,000
Net property, plant, and equipment	75,000
Total assets	$225,000
Current liabilities	$ 95,000
Long-term debt	90,000
Shareholders' equity	40,000
Total liabilities and shareholders' equity	$225,000

Statement of Income (in thousands)	
Sales revenue	$460,000
Cost of goods sold, operating, and other expenses	420,000
Income before income taxes	40,000
Income taxes	14,000
Net income	$ 26,000
Earnings per share	$ 1.30

The long-term debt has an interest rate of 6% and is convertible into 9 million common shares. After carefully analyzing all available information about Manonta, you decide the following events are likely to happen.
1. Manonta will increase its income before income taxes by 10% next year because of increased sales.
2. The effective tax rate will stay the same.
3. The holders of long-term debt will convert it into shares on January 1, 2016.
4. The current price/earnings of 20 will increase to 24 if the debt is converted, because of the reduced risk.

You own 100 common shares of Manonta and are trying to decide whether you should keep or sell them. You decide you will sell the shares if you think their market price is not likely to increase by at least 10% next year.

Required:
Based on the information available, should you keep the shares or sell them? Support your answer with a detailed analysis.

C11-2 Tribec Wireless Inc.

Tribec Wireless Inc. had the following shareholders' equity section as at December 31, 2016:

Common shares, no par value, unlimited number authorized, 2 million issued and outstanding	$4,000,000
Retained earnings	1,958,476
Total shareholders' equity	$5,958,476

In 2013 and 2014, Tribec paid a cash dividend of $0.75 per share. In 2015, the company expanded operations significantly and the board of directors decided to retain the assets generated by its earnings in the business rather than pay them out as a cash dividend. In lieu of the cash dividend, the board voted to distribute a 10% stock dividend. In December 2016, the company returned to its previous dividend policy and again paid a $0.75 cash dividend.

In 2013, you inherited 5,000 shares of Tribec Wireless. At that time, the shares were trading at $5 per share. Given the tremendous growth in the wireless market, by 2015, when the stock dividend was distributed, the company's shares were trading at $80 per share. After the stock dividend, the share price dropped slightly but has since risen again. As at December 31, 2016, they were trading at $82 per share.

Required:
a. From Tribec's perspective, how would the accounting for the stock dividend distributed in 2015 differ from the accounting for the cash dividends paid in the other years?
b. Immediately after the stock dividend, the price of the Tribec shares dropped slightly. Does this mean the value of the company (and your investment) decreased due to the payment of the stock dividend? Explain.
c. Prepare a schedule illustrating the total amount of cash dividends you have received since inheriting the Tribec shares. What is the value of your investment on December 31, 2016? How does this compare to the value of the shares when you inherited them?

C11-3 Blooming Valley Custom Landscaping

Blooming Valley Custom Landscaping provides landscaping services to a variety of clients in southern Ontario. The company's services include planting lawns and shrubs and installing outdoor lighting and irrigation systems, as well as constructing decks and gazebos. The company also remains very busy in the winter by using its trucks for snow removal. Blooming Valley would like to extend its operations into the northern United States, but Jack Langer, the owner, feels that the company would require at least $2 million in new capital before such a venture could be successful. Mr. Langer is excited about the prospects of expanding because his projections indicate that the company could earn an additional $750,000 in income before interest and taxes.

Currently, Blooming Valley has no long-term debt and is entirely owned by the Langer family, with 300,000 common shares outstanding. The company's current income before tax is $900,000, with a tax rate of 25% that is not expected to change if the expansion goes ahead. As the family does not have enough money to finance the expansion, it needs to obtain outside financing. Mr. Langer is considering three financing options:

Option 1
The first option is to borrow, using a conventional bank loan. Interest on the loan would be 9% annually with an annual payment of principal and interest required on the anniversary date of the loan.

Option 2

The second possibility is to issue 100,000 common shares to a local venture capitalist. As part of the plan, the venture capitalist would be given a seat on the board of directors and would also have a say in the day-to-day running of the company.

Option 3

The final option is to sell 100,000 non-voting cumulative preferred shares. The preferred shares would have an annual dividend of $2.85. A number of investors have expressed interest in purchasing these shares.

Required:

a. Calculate the effect of each financing option on the company's earnings per share. Which option will result in the highest earnings per share?

b. Recommend an option to Mr. Langer and explain your reasoning. Be sure to consider both quantitative and qualitative factors as part of your analysis.

C11-4 Teed's Manufacturing Corporation

Teed's Manufacturing Corporation has the following shareholders' equity at December 1, 2016:

Shareholders' Equity	
Share capital	
$2 preferred shares, no par value, cumulative, 20,000 shares authorized, 16,000 shares issued	360,000
Common shares, no par value, unlimited number of shares authorized, 60,000 shares issued	600,000
Total share capital	960,000
Retained earnings	687,500
Total shareholders' equity	$1,647,500

The company was formed in January 2014 and there has been no change in share capital since that time. It is now December 1, 2016, and after a very strong year, the company has just declared a $160,000 cash dividend to shareholders of record as at February 10, 2017. The dividend payment date is February 28, 2017. Teed's has always used business earnings for further expansion and has never paid a dividend before.

Jan Barangé owns 500 shares of Teed's Manufacturing common stock and is curious to know how much of a dividend she will receive. She is confused about the difference between preferred and common shares and wonders why the preferred shareholders would purchase shares in a company without having the right to vote. Finally, she is confused about the differences between the declaration date, date of record, and payment date. She wants to know when she will actually receive her dividend.

Required:

a. Determine how much of the dividend will be paid to the preferred shareholders and how much to the common shareholders.

b. Prepare a memo addressing Jan's questions.

ENDNOTES

1. "Fab 30: Larry Rossy, CEO, Dollarama Inc.," *Profit Guide*, July 18, 2012; Boyd Erman, "Dollarama Would Pay Top Dollar in Buyback," *The Globe and Mail*, June 3, 2012; John Daly, "How Dollarama Turns Pocket Change into Billions," *The Globe and Mail*, March 29, 2012; "Dollarama Records Strong Sales and Earnings Growth in Initial Financial Report Following IPO," Dollarama news release, December 10, 2009; "Dollarama Shares Soar after IPO," CBC News, October 9, 2009; Dollarama 2014 and 2009 Annual Reports; Dollarama corporate website, www.dollarama.com.

2. Bombardier Inc. 2013 Annual Report.

3. Janet McFarland, "Group Pushes for New Rules on Dual-Class Shares," *The Globe and Mail*, September 24, 2013; "The Impact of Family Control on the Share Price Performance of Large Canadian Publicly-Listed Firms (1998–2012)," Clarkson Centre for Board Effectiveness, University of Toronto, June 2013.

4. National Bank of Canada; Annual Report 2013.

5. Based on data from "Understanding Preferred Shares," BMO Exchange Traded Funds, www.bmo.com/pdf/Understanding%20Preferred%20Shares_E_FINAL.pdf

6. IFRS: The Conceptual Framework for Financial Reporting.

7. National Bank of Canada 2013 Annual Report.

8. Gildan Activewear Inc. Annual Report 2013.

9. Gildan Activewear Inc. website, www.gildan.com.

10. John Heinzl, "Why More Companies Are Doing the Splits," *The Globe and Mail*, December 6, 2013; "National Bank of Canada Announces Two-for-One Share Split by Way of a Share Dividend," National Bank of Canada news release, December 4, 2013; Jonathan Ratner, "Stock Splits – Coming to a Bank Near You," *Financial Post*, October 25, 2013.

11. Michael Bowman, "Building the Straight 'A' Portfolio," *The Globe and Mail*, February 25, 2014; Michelle Cerone, "Is a Low P/E Ratio Always a Steal?," *Forbes*, March 9, 2011; John Shmeul, "National Bank 'Undervalued and Underappreciated' Says Analyst," *Financial Post*, March 10, 2011.

CHAPTER 12 Financial Statement Analysis

CORE QUESTIONS
If you are able to answer the following questions, then you have achieved the related learning objectives.

LEARNING OBJECTIVES
After studying this chapter, you should be able to:

●●● INTRODUCTION

- What is financial statement analysis?
- What is the process for analyzing financial statements?

1 Understand and explain the process of financial analysis.

●●● THE CONTEXTS FOR FINANCIAL STATEMENT ANALYSIS

- What are the common contexts for financial statement analysis?
- Why is an understanding of context essential to the analysis?

2 Identify the common contexts for financial statement analysis and explain why an awareness of context is essential to the analysis.

●●● BUSINESS INFORMATION

- Why is it essential to understand the business being analyzed?

3 Explain why knowledge of the business is important when analyzing a company's financial statements.

- What information is the financial statement analysis based on and where is it found?

4 Identify the types of information used when analyzing financial statements and where it is found.

●●● FINANCIAL STATEMENT ANALYSIS PERSPECTIVES

- What is the difference between retrospective and prospective analysis?
- What is the difference between trend analysis and cross-sectional analysis?

5 Explain the various perspectives used in financial statement analysis, including retrospective, prospective, trend, and cross-sectional analysis.

●●● FINANCIAL STATEMENT ANALYSIS TECHNIQUES

- What is common-size analysis?
- How is ratio analysis used to analyze financial statements?
- What are the common categories of ratios?

6 Identify the different metrics used in financial analysis, including common-size analysis and ratio analysis, and explain how they are used.

●●● RATIO ANALYSIS

- What liquidity ratios are commonly used?
- What activity ratios are commonly used?
- What solvency ratios are commonly used?
- What profitability ratios are commonly used?
- What equity analysis ratios are commonly used?

7 Identify, calculate, and interpret specific ratios that are used to analyze the liquidity, activity, solvency, profitability, and equity of a company.

●●● LIMITATIONS OF RATIO ANALYSIS

- What are the limitations of ratio analysis?

8 Identify and explain the limitations of ratio analysis.

●●● Student Stock Analysts Try to "Beat the Street"

Every campus has a number of clubs—from sports teams to the student newspaper. But a growing number of Canadian universities have investment clubs in which students are investing and managing funds. While some clubs run simulations, a number of clubs invest real money, often cash that has been donated to their universities' endowment and scholarship funds.

The students, usually studying finance or business at the undergraduate or graduate level, apply what they've learned about analyzing the financial statements of public companies to try to pick winning stocks. Some investment clubs run simulations which do not involve actual cash. In these, students invest in certain stocks and see whether the stocks appreciate at a higher rate than various stock indexes, or see who among the club members "makes" the most money from trading the stocks.

There are a handful of investment clubs where students invest real money. Among them are Brock University, Concordia University, the University of British Columbia, the University of New Brunswick, Queen's University, and McGill University.

At Queen's University, some MBA and Master of Finance students participate in the Queen's University Alternative Asset Fund (QUAAF), a notional company with a corporate structure that is a fund of hedge funds, which are funds with investments in stocks and other vehicles that are not sold to the public. Started by eight MBA students who each put up $6,000 of their own money, QUAAF subsequently received an amount, reported to be in the six figures, from the university's endowment fund to manage.

In Montreal, all the students in the Honours Investment Management program at McGill University's Desautels Faculty of Management work for Desautels Capital Management Inc., Canada's first university-owned, student-run registered investment firm. It has two funds: an equity fund of stocks and a fixed income fund, which includes foreign currency and mortgage assets. Students with the equity fund can work as analysts, analyzing the financial statements of companies in a certain sector. Twelve teams each manage $250,000 in assets. Student analysts meet twice a week to discuss market conditions and, based on their analysis of the companies' financial performance, recommend which stocks to buy, sell, or hold. In early 2012, Desautels Capital Management owned stocks of companies as diverse as TELUS, Metro Inc., Canadian Tire Corporation, and Canadian National Railway.

"We look for undervalued stocks and bonds that the street overlooks. Our edge is that we are young and diverse, and often we find the 'next big thing' before [Bay] Street does," said Ivan Di, Bachelor of Commerce student and a Desautels equity strategist. Typically, stock analysts use data in companies' financial statements to calculate ratios measuring profitability, liquidity, activity, and other things that indicate performance.

How did Desautels student analysts do in analyzing financial statements and picking winners? When the firm was launched in 2008, it had $1 million in donations that had been made to the business school some 20 years earlier. By late 2012, it had grown to about $3 million in assets. The funds consistently match the performance of indexes—an excellent return for paying attention in class.[1]

INTRODUCTION

In each chapter of this book, we have sought to enhance your understanding of financial accounting information and you should now be able to read financial statements with understanding, just like the students in the campus investment clubs in our feature story. Now that you have this perspective, it is time to step back, put the pieces from each chapter together, and discuss how financial statements are analyzed as a whole.

■ **LEARNING OBJECTIVE 1**
Understand and explain the process of financial analysis.

What is financial statement analysis?

In Chapter 1, we discussed how the primary goal of this book was to help you become an intelligent user of accounting information by enhancing your ability to read and understand corporate financial statements. We also identified many circumstances and career paths in which these skills would be necessary.

Through the various chapters, you have been introduced to a number of ratios, each related to the topic(s) under discussion in that chapter. In this chapter, these will be organized cohesively, enabling you to think about analysis as a structured activity.

In this chapter, we will use the term *analyst* to describe the person doing the analysis. It is important to understand that this analysis could be undertaken from the perspective of any of the financial statement users we discussed in Chapter 1. These included existing shareholders, potential investors, creditors, securities analysts, and credit rating agencies. When necessary, we will identify the perspective(s) being used in the analysis.

Financial statement analysis is the process of evaluating a company's performance based on an analysis of their financial statements: the statement of financial position, statement of income, statement of changes in equity, statement of cash flows, and the notes to the financial statements. The analysis would include calculating ratios, looking at relationships within the financial statements, and comparing the results with historical or industry benchmarks.

Analysts use financial statement analysis to help them evaluate corporate performance and the risks related to investment or lending decisions involving the company. These decisions are supported by other information, including an industry analysis, site visits, interviews with management, or other steps the analysts believe will assist in their decision-making. Financial statement analysis does not provide all of the answers, but it does provide signals about financial health, cash flows, and operating efficiency. Equally importantly, financial statement analysis will generate additional questions and point to areas that require further analysis.

This chapter provides an overview of financial statement analysis and a discussion of the basic techniques involved. However, financial statement analysis is a large and complex area, so this is intended to serve only as an introduction to the topic. It is also important that you understand that each financial statement analysis is unique and the techniques used will often differ from analysis to analysis. Each needs to be tailored to fit the context, including the nature of the company and its industry.

In this chapter, we will use the financial statements of **Saputo Inc.** to illustrate the analysis process. Saputo is headquartered in Montreal and is Canada's largest dairy processor and one of the 10 largest in the world. The company's products are sold in 40 countries under brand names including Saputo, Neilson, Nutrilait, and Frigo Cheese Heads. Saputo sells its cheese and milk products, including yogourt and creams, to supermarket chains, retailers such as convenience stores and specialty cheese stores, restaurants, distributors, and mass merchandisers. The company also has a small grocery products division that produces and distributes snack cakes. The information presented in this chapter comes from Saputo's 2014 annual report, which covers the year that ended on March 31, 2014.

What is the process for analyzing financial statements?

While the context for performing a financial analysis can vary and different analysts will structure their analysis in different ways, it is possible to use a general framework when performing an analysis. The following five-step process, adapted from the Chartered Financial Analyst Institute's financial statement analysis framework, will help you approach financial statement analysis in a logical manner.

The steps in the process are as follows:
1. Determine the purpose and context of the analysis.
2. Collect the information needed for the analysis.
3. Prepare common-size analysis and calculate ratios or other metrics.
4. Analyze and interpret the metrics from Step 3.
5. Develop conclusions and recommendations.

Let's discuss each step in turn.

1. **Determine the purpose and context of the analysis.**

   From the outset, it is critical that you understand the purpose or context for the analysis. One way of doing this is to determine the questions that the analysis will assist in answering. For example, should we extend credit to this company? Should we invest in this company? Knowing the context for the analysis or the type of questions you are trying to answer will help you make decisions regarding the type(s) of information that you will need to gather and determine the tools or techniques that would best support this analysis.

2. **Collect the information needed for the analysis.**

   Having completed Step 1, the analyst can then focus on obtaining the necessary data. Sources of data will be discussed later in the chapter, but certainly include the company's annual report, which includes the annual financial statements and management's discussion and analysis (MD&A). Industry data (including industry ratios and trends) and other economic data (such as inflation rates and exchange rates) may also be gathered. It is important to understand that the analyst must move beyond the four financial statements and use information from the notes to the financial statements. The notes contain important information that is not available on the face of the financial statements. The analyst will also attend the quarterly conference call and webcast for analysts in which company officials review quarterly and annual results, and are available to answer questions.

3. **Prepare common-size analysis and calculate ratios or other metrics.**

   In this step, the analyst will prepare common-size financial statements and calculate the ratios or other metrics identified in Step 1. Caution must be exercised in this step. It is easy to program an Excel file to calculate dozens and dozens of ratios, not all of which will be meaningful. The challenge is to ensure the right data are being used and the metrics being calculated make sense given the purpose of the analysis.

4. **Analyze and interpret the metrics from Step 3.**

Using the ratios or metrics calculated in Step 3, combined with the knowledge of the company and other information gathered, the analyst analyzes the information and interprets the results. This might involve comparing the ratios with those from previous years, or with industry averages to help form opinions. This step is where the analyst adds the most value to the analysis. For example, instead of looking at individual ratio results in isolation, they can be assessed collectively, compared with common-size analysis for consistency, and so on.

5. **Develop conclusions and recommendations.**

In this final step, conclusions and recommendations are made based on the analysis performed in Step 4. These are answers to the questions established in Step 1. When developing conclusions, it is important that the analysis differentiate between factual results and the analyst's opinion(s).

THE CONTEXTS FOR FINANCIAL STATEMENT ANALYSIS

What are the common contexts for financial statement analysis?

There are a wide variety of contexts that commonly require the analysis of financial statements. These include:

- An investment analyst or stockbroker may undertake an analysis in order to make a recommendation to clients to buy, sell, or continue to hold shares of a particular company.
- A commercial lender may undertake an analysis to assess the creditworthiness of a loan applicant or analyze the financial statements of an existing borrower to determine whether they have complied with any loan covenants.
- A company's credit department may analyze the financial statements of customers seeking credit terms.
- A company may analyze the financial statements of companies that may be potential acquisition targets.
- A pension fund may analyze the financial statements of companies it is considering as potential investments or of the companies it is currently invested in.

■ **LEARNING OBJECTIVE 2**
Identify the common contexts for financial statement analysis and explain why an awareness of context is essential to the analysis.

Why is an understanding of context essential to the analysis?

Understanding the context for the analysis is essential because it will determine the type of information and data that will be required. It will also drive decisions regarding the techniques that will be used to complete the analysis. Given the wide variety of available information and potential techniques, understanding the context provides focus to both areas.

Each analyst will tailor the analysis to the demands of the decision to be made. For example, a banker trying to decide whether to make a short-term loan will likely use the company's historic results, in addition to comparing these with other companies in the same or similar industries. The historic results are important because they will help the lender determine the company's ability to service the debt. A banker would also consider the client's financial projections, especially its cash flow projections, as part of this assessment. The lender must also be aware of industry trends in order to get an overall assessment of how well a particular company performs relative to its competitors.

An investment analyst, on the other hand, will analyze the company's results relative to other companies. Analysts must consider the return versus risk trade-off across many companies. They must, therefore, directly compare companies in different industries and, often, in different countries. While the investment analyst would also look at the company's historic results, they would focus on the potential for growth and returns to the shareholders.

In this chapter, we take a general approach to financial statement analysis. In order to provide a broad understanding of the possible techniques, we will discuss a wide variety of ratios, without focusing on a particular context. However, we will identify contexts where one particular ratio may be more helpful than others.

BUSINESS INFORMATION

Why is it essential to understand the business being analyzed?

Understanding the business means more than understanding a company's financial statements. It means having a grasp of the operating activities of the business, the underlying economics, the risks involved, and the external economic factors that are crucial to the company's long-term and short-term health. It means having an understanding of the various types of businesses that the company is in.

For example, a major company such as **Canadian Tire Corporation, Limited** is involved in more than auto parts, tires, and auto service. The company is a major retailer of hardware and sporting goods, and is one of Canada's largest independent retailers of gasoline. In addition, the company owns FGL Sports, which is Canada's largest sporting goods retailer. The company's banners include Sport Chek, Sport Mart, Atmosphere, and Intersport. The company also operates Mark's, a leading Canadian clothing retailer, whose banners include Mark's, Mark's Work Wearhouse, and L'Équipeur. Finally, Canadian Tire also operates a significant financial services division. In fact, the company is a regulated financial institution (similar to a bank) and more than 4 million Canadians hold a Canadian Tire MasterCard. Given the range of the company's operations, it's essential for an analyst to understand the various businesses when performing analysis and assessing the risks related to the company.

When analyzing companies that have diverse business activities like Canadian Tire Corporation, analysts rely on segmented information. For example, while Canadian Tire's annual report presents the results of all of its operations summarized in a single set of consolidated financial statements, it also includes financial information broken down for its retail segment, its real estate segment, and its financial services segment. In accounting terms, we describe different business activities within a company, or different geographic regions in which it operates, as **operating segments**. If a company has more than one distinctive operating segment and meets certain quantitative thresholds, it is required to disclose information related to the segments in a note to the financial statements. Segments can differ significantly with regard to risk and are affected in different ways by such economic factors as commodity prices, inflation, exchange rates, and interest rates. Segmented information allows users to better assess the overall risks facing the company and the success of the different segments in which the company operates. An overall assessment of the company must take into consideration the relative significance of each segment.

Returning to Saputo, it reports two segments, which it refers to as sectors: the dairy products sector and the grocery products sector. When discussing the results of the operations, it further breaks the dairy products sector into two regions: Canada, Argentina, and Europe; and the United States.

Understanding a company's business also requires an analyst to understand the corporation's strategies because companies follow different strategies to achieve success. While a detailed discussion of corporate strategy is beyond the scope of this book, you should be familiar with a few basic strategies that companies follow. The two most common strategies are:

- being a low-cost producer, and
- following a product differentiation strategy.

A low-cost producer focuses on providing goods or services at the lowest possible cost and selling at low prices. To be successful, these companies need to sell a high volume of goods at the lower prices. This strategy works best when competing products are similar and price is the most important decision factor for customers. Discount grocery chains or discount retailers usually follow this strategy.

The product differentiation strategy is to sell products that are specialized or to provide superior service that customers are willing to pay a premium for. If the company can make a higher profit margin on the goods or services provided, it does not need to sell as many goods to make the same level of total profit as a company that sells more for less—it can succeed with a lower volume. Gourmet grocery or specialty stores and high-end retailers usually follow this strategy.

Understanding the company's strategy will help you interpret the financial results and explain differences if, for example, you are trying to compare a discount retailer with a specialty store and are wondering why the results are so different.

The products Saputo produces and sells are closer to commodity-type products. There is little to distinguish its cheeses or other products from competitors. Consumers often choose based on price. This means that Saputo needs to follow a strategy closer to low-cost producer than product differentiation. In the overview to its annual report, Saputo refers to the goals of improving overall efficiencies and it has been consolidating production and distribution facilities.

What information is the financial statement analysis based on and where is it found?

■ **LEARNING OBJECTIVE 4**
Identify the types of information used when analyzing financial statements and where it is found.

The primary source of information is the company's annual report. You will recall from Chapter 1 that the annual report contains several sections, including the **management discussion and analysis (MD&A)**, the auditors' report, the financial statements, and the notes to the financial statements. The financial statements have been discussed at length throughout this book, so we will not repeat those here. We will, however, discuss the MD&A and the auditors' report a bit more to enhance your understanding of these two important sections.

Management Discussion and Analysis

You can usually gain a basic understanding of the company's range of business activities, including its recent achievements and management's future expectations, by reading the first section of the company's annual report and the MD&A. The first section contains the description of the company, some general highlights of the year, and letters to the shareholders from the CEO and the chief financial officer. Annual reports may also contain data other than strictly financial data, such as numbers of employees or sales volumes expressed in physical units rather than dollars, which can be useful for the analyst.

The MD&A is a very important section for an analyst to read. In it, management discusses many aspects of the company's financial performance in greater detail. It includes a discussion of past results, but also of management's expectations for the future and the risks the company is facing. The objective of the MD&A is to allow the user to see the company through the eyes of management. Although this descriptive section of most annual reports does not explain everything you need to know about the company, it does provide some insight into what the company does and the types of risks it faces.

From Saputo's MD&A, we can learn that the company's strategy is to provide high-quality food products to customers and develop new platforms and new markets primarily through acquisition. As noted earlier, the company is also focused on improving operational efficiency. At the beginning of October 2013, Saputo made a bid to take over Warrnambool Cheese and Butter Factory Company Holdings Limited, a large Australian dairy processor. Warrnambool produces a line of dairy products similar to Saputo's and this acquisition provided the company with access to the Australian market as well as a base for exports to Asia and Oceania. By January 21, 2014, Saputo had acquired enough shares to have a controlling interest. By February 14, 2014, the date the takeover bid ended, the company was ultimately able to acquire 88% of the outstanding shares of Warrnambool. The Warrnambool acquisition cost approximately $450 million, of which $390 million was financed by new long-term debt. This explains the increase in total assets and debt that we will see in subsequent trend analysis. Because the acquisition occurred close to the year end, the effect on the statement of income was not significant because only the revenues and expenses for the period between January 21, 2014 (the date when control of the company was achieved) and the March 31, 2014, year end are included. The acquisition did have a significant impact on the company's statement of financial position because the assets and liabilities of Warrnambool are included in the year-end balances. We will see that the size and timing of the acquisition were significant enough to affect some of the ratios we calculate.

The Auditors' Report

Another item of interest to analysts is the auditors' report. It provides the opinion of the external auditor appointed by the company's board of directors, on behalf of the company's shareholders, regarding whether the company's financial results are fairly presented. Financial statement users, including analysts, value this opinion because the auditor is an independent third party.

TAKE**5**

It is important to understand that the auditor's report does not guarantee the accuracy of the information contained in the financial statements. Financial statements are prepared by management, and management has primary responsibility for them. Auditors express their opinion on whether the financial statements present the information fairly according to accounting standards, which are IFRS in the case of most Canadian public companies. The auditor's report does not indicate whether the information contained in the financial statements is positive or negative. It remains the reader's responsibility to interpret the information provided.

The vast majority of auditors' reports will be *unqualified* opinions. This means that the auditor is of the opinion that the financial statements are fairly presented. In other words, the auditor has no qualifications to make on the information. Canadian auditors use a standardized opinion, meaning they all use the same wording. This makes it easy for a user to understand the auditors' opinion. An unqualified (or "clean") audit opinion is one in which the auditors do not express any concerns, reservations, or qualifications regarding the financial statements. Deloitte LLP in their auditor's report provide a typical *unqualified* auditor's opinion for the 2014 financial statements of Saputo.

> In our opinion, the consolidated financial statements present fairly, in all material respects, the financial position of Saputo Inc. as at March 31, 2013 and 2012, and its financial performance and its cash flows for the years then ended in accordance with International Financial Reporting Standards.

The above paragraph states that without any exceptions, in their professional opinion, the financial statements fairly present the company's financial position and the results of its operations in accordance with the applicable accounting standards (IFRS in the case of Saputo). This is what the users of the financial statements want to see; any other type of audit opinion warrants very careful consideration. An unqualified audit report for Danier Leather is reproduced in Appendix A of this text.

FINANCIAL STATEMENT ANALYSIS PERSPECTIVES

What is the difference between retrospective and prospective analysis?

As discussed earlier, financial statement analysis is done to help decision-makers with investment or lending decisions. Normally those decisions have future consequences. For example, lenders try to forecast companies' future cash flows to ensure that the borrower will be able to service the loan; that is, pay interest and repay principal. When the analyst is trying to determine what the future results of the company may be, it is known as **prospective analysis**, which is forward-looking.

The challenge with prospective analysis is that the world is an uncertain place; no one can predict the future with complete accuracy. In trying to predict future outcomes, generally the most reliable source of data available is the company's historical results. To the extent that an analyst expects the future to follow past trends, they can use **retrospective analysis**, which is historical, as the basis for predicting future outcomes. For example, if the company had a 7% growth rate historically and we expect that to continue, then we can build prospective numbers based on these expectations. If the analyst is to rely on retrospective analysis, they must be confident that past results are a suitable predictor of future outcomes. This requires them to be aware of any significant changes in either the company's operations or in the industry in which it operates that would make it likely that future outcomes will differ from past results. When this is considered likely, the information being used as a basis for the analysis must be adjusted or an alternative source found.

In many cases, a company's historic results provide a solid foundation for predicting future outcomes. When this is the case, an analysis of the historic results is in order. There are two major types of retrospective analyses: trend analysis and cross-sectional analysis.

What is the difference between trend analysis and cross-sectional analysis?

With **trend analysis**, the analyst examines a company's information from multiple periods (normally years) to look for any patterns in the data over time. For example, examining the sales data over a five-year period would enable the analyst to determine whether sales are increasing, decreasing, or remaining stable. If no significant changes have occurred within the company or the industry in which it operates, the trend observed would provide a basis for predicting the company's future sales. If changes have taken place or are expected to that would negate this assumption, there is no reason to perform trend analysis.

Many companies recognize the importance of trend analysis and provide five-year or 10-year summaries to help users make this analysis. In the first part of its annual report, Saputo prepares a review covering a three-year period. Because this is not adequate for the purpose of a trend analysis, Exhibit 12-1 extracts some of the key accounts from Saputo's analysis and has extended the summary to five years using data obtained from earlier annual reports. From this, we can see that net revenues have increased significantly, though not exactly steadily, from 2010 to 2014. Net earnings increased from 2010 to 2011, and then fell in 2012 before recovering in 2013 and increasing in 2014. This should lead the analyst to question what occurred in 2012 and whether it is something that could occur again in future periods.

KEY POINTS

Trend analysis:

- compares results of the same company over a period of time (such as 3–10 years), and
- is useful for identifying patterns and changes.

Exhibit 12-1 Saputo Inc. Comparison of Key Figures

(in $ thousands)

	2014	2013	2012	2011	2010
Statement of earnings data					
Net revenues	9,232,889	7,297,677	6,930,370	6,002,932	5,810,582
Operating costs excluding depreciation, amortization, acquisition, and restructuring	8,212,544	6,436,905	6,099,439	5,214,651	5,118,511
EBITDAR	1,020,345	860,772	830,931	788,281	692,071
Depreciation and amortization	146,607	116,629	101,943	105,981	113,506
Acquisition, restructuring, impairment costs	45,663	42,277	125,000	13,600	
Interest costs and financial charges	69,085	34,099	24,650	23,874	35,062
Net earnings	533,966	481,921	380,840	450,051	382,714
Selected balance sheet (statement of financial position) data					
Total assets	6,356,892	5,193,640	3,599,120	3,578,331	3,253,451
Interest-bearing debt	2,099,360	1,730,165	546,506	549,069	442,362
Shareholders' equity	2,839,160	2,305,672	2,105,686	2,072,635	2,028,598
Statement of cash flows data					
Net cash generated from operations	656,310	645,792	522,987	588,520	583,615
Additions to property, plant, and equipment, net of proceeds on disposal	223,371	177,336	105,716	105,822	106,334

FINANCIAL STATEMENTS

Note: The 2010 financial statements were prepared under the former Canadian "generally accepted accounting principles" standards while the 2011 to 2014 financial statements were prepared under IFRS. If 2010 were to be restated for comparative purposes, there would be small differences in some numbers. The effect of the adjustments is not considered material enough to change the discussion in this chapter.

Saputo reports a figure for **EBITDAR** (earnings before interest, taxes, depreciation, acquisition, and restructuring) on its financial statements. It is the metric the company uses to evaluate recurring operating performance. EBITDAR grew steadily throughout the five-year period. Therefore, the drop in net earnings in 2012 must have come from other costs, such as acquisition and restructuring costs. Learning to spot figures or trends is a useful skill for an analyst. Between 2010 and 2104, EBITDAR has normally been between 11% and 12% of net revenues, but in 2011 it was 13.1%. A more detailed analysis of these costs could be prepared using additional data that Saputo discloses in the notes to its financial statements, including changes in raw materials costs and selling costs. Saputo has been growing through an aggressive acquisition program. Since 1997, it has acquired more than 20 other companies. We will discuss the effect of that strategy on other parts of the financial statements as we work through our analysis.

A review of the statement of financial position items presented shows that assets grew substantially between 2010 and 2014 (from $3,253,451 thousand to $6,356,892 thousand). You would expect assets

HELPFUL HINT

As you are performing your analysis, keep track of questions as they arise. You may find the answers to them later in your analysis, or they may help you refine your analysis and help you think of other ratios that should be calculated. In the end, if you are still not satisfied, you may want to ask further questions of management or research other sources.

to increase to support the increased sales as a result of the acquisitions. It appears that the acquisitions were financed primarily by interest-bearing debt because this grew from $442,362 thousand to $2,099,360 thousand, and to a lesser extent through equity. From the statement of cash flows, we can see that cash from operations has increased steadily (with the exception of 2012), which is useful for servicing the increase in long-term debt, including interest charges, which grew from $34,953 thousand in 2013 to $65,837 thousand in 2014.

Saputo's full financial statements upon which two of the five years of data in Exhibit 12-1 were based are in Exhibits 12-2A to C. These statements provide additional details in support of the key figure data presented above. The level of detail also illustrates why analysts pull out these key figures, making it easier to focus on them without getting lost in the detail of the financial statements. The information from these statements will be used to prepare a variety of analyses in the remainder of this chapter.

Cross-sectional analysis compares the data from one company with those of another company over the same time period. Normally, the companies should operate in the same industry, perhaps as competitors. Cross-sectional analysis may also compare one company with an average of the other companies in the same industry. For example, you might compare the growth in sales for **Groupe Danone**, the France-based producer of dairy and yogourt products, with Saputo. However, any cross-sectional comparisons must consider that different companies use different accounting methods; for example, different depreciation methods or different inventory cost formulas. In addition, different companies in different countries may use different accounting principles. Fortunately, both Saputo in Canada and Groupe Danone in France use IFRS. Comparing across countries has been greatly facilitated with the growing use of IFRS around the world, resulting in fewer accounting differences and, therefore, easier and more meaningful international comparisons.

KEY POINTS

Cross-sectional analysis compares the results of two or more companies, normally operating in the same industry.

Exhibit 12-2A Saputo Inc.'s 2014 Consolidated Balance Sheets

CONSOLIDATED **BALANCE SHEETS**

(in thousands of CDN dollars)

FINANCIAL
STATEMENTS

As at	March 31, 2014	March 31, 2013
ASSETS		
Current assets		
Cash and cash equivalents	$ 39,346	$ 43,177
Receivables	807,409	624,553
Inventories (Note 4)	933,232	770,158
Income taxes (Note 14)	30,867	2,786
Prepaid expenses and other assets	84,992	71,882
	1,895,846	1,512,556
Property, plant and equipment (Note 6)	1,928,761	1,617,195
Goodwill (Note 7)	1,954,691	1,569,592
Trademarks and other intangibles (Note 7)	484,830	454,876
Other assets (Note 8)	79,968	29,962
Deferred income taxes (Note 14)	12,796	9,459
Total assets	$6,356,892	$5,193,640
LIABILITIES		
Current liabilities		
Bank loans (Note 9)	$ 310,066	$ 181,865
Accounts payable and accrued liabilities	897,222	748,318
Income taxes (Note 14)	124,206	144,064
Current portion of long-term debt (Note 10)	393,600	152,400
	1,725,094	1,226,647

continued

Exhibit 12-2A Saputo Inc.'s 2014 Consolidated Balance Sheets (continued)

As at	March 31, 2014	March 31, 2013
Long-term debt (Note 10)	1,395,694	1,395,900
Other liabilities (Note 11)	48,396	74,101
Deferred income taxes (Note 14)	348,548	191,320
Total liabilities	$3,517,732	$2,887,968
EQUITY		
Share capital	703,111	663,275
Reserves	242,282	38,049
Retained earnings	1,830,911	1,604,348
Equity attributable to shareholders of Saputo Inc.	2,776,304	2,305,672
Non-controlling interest (Note 16)	62,856	—
Total equity	$2,839,160	$2,305,672
Total liabilities and equity	$6,356,892	$5,193,640

Exhibit 12-2B Saputo Inc.'s 2014 Consolidated Statements of Earnings

CONSOLIDATED STATEMENTS OF **EARNINGS**

(in thousands of CDN dollars, except per share amounts)

FINANCIAL
STATEMENTS

Years ended March 31	2014	2013
Revenues	$9,232,889	$7,297,677
Operating costs excluding depreciation, amortization, acquisition, restructuring and other costs (Note 5)	8,212,544	6,436,905
Earnings before interest, depreciation, amortization, acquisition, restructuring, other costs and income taxes	1,020,345	860,772
Depreciation and amortization (Notes 6 and 7)	146,607	116,629
Acquisition, restructuring and other costs (Note 22)	45,663	42,277
Interest on long-term debt	53,239	29,896
Other financial charges (Note 13)	15,846	4,203
Earnings before income taxes	758,990	667,767
Income taxes (Note 14)	225,024	185,846
Net earnings	$ 533,966	$ 481,921
Attributable to:		
Shareholders of Saputo Inc.	533,097	481,921
Non-controlling interest (Note 16)	869	—
	$ 533,966	$ 481,921
Earnings per share (Note 15)		
Net earnings		
Basic	$ 2.73	$ 2.44
Diluted	$ 2.70	$ 2.41

HELPFUL HINT

A word of caution: Most companies, like Saputo, present their financial information with the most recent year closest to the account titles. But occasionally a company might present its information the other way, with the earliest year closest to the account titles. When you are reading financial statements, be careful to observe the format used or you may end up thinking sales are falling when they are, in fact, growing!

Exhibit 12-2C Saputo Inc.'s 2014 Consolidated Statements of Cash Flows

CONSOLIDATED STATEMENTS OF CASH FLOWS

(in thousands of CDN dollars)

Years ended March 31	2014	2013
Cash flows related to the following activities:		
Operating		
Net earnings	$ 533,966	$ 481,921
Adjustments for:		
Stock-based compensation	22,084	17,537
Interest and other financial charges	69,085	34,099
Income tax expense	225,024	185,846
Depreciation and amortization	146,607	116,629
Gain on disposal of property, plant and equipment	(122)	(53)
Restructuring charges related to plant closures	22,096	23,820
Share of joint venture earnings	(1,406)	—
Funding of employee plans in excess of costs	(6,486)	(12,485)
	1,010,848	847,314
Changes in non-cash operating working capital items	(129,363)	(4,425)
Cash generated from operating activities	881,485	842,889
Interest and other financial charges paid	(65,837)	(34,953)
Income taxes paid	(159,338)	(162,144)
Net cash generated from operating activities	656,310	645,792
Investing		
Business acquisition	(449,578)	(1,433,945)
Additions to property, plant and equipment	(223,624)	(178,237)
Proceeds on disposal of property, plant and equipment	253	901
Other	803	(13,719)
	(672,146)	(1,625,000)
Financing		
Bank loans	77,810	21,884
Proceeds from issuance of long-term debt	390,000	1,198,565
Repayment of long-term debt	(175,045)	(38,100)
Issuance of share capital	41,861	38,468
Repurchase of share capital	(154,371)	(190,404)
Dividends	(175,321)	(161,651)
	4,934	868,762
Decrease in cash and cash equivalents	(10,902)	(110,446)
Effect of exchange rate changes on cash and cash equivalents	7,071	9,486
Cash and cash equivalents, beginning of year	43,177	144,137
Cash and cash equivalents, end of year	$ 39,346	$ 43,177

FINANCIAL STATEMENT ANALYSIS TECHNIQUES

What is common-size analysis?

Although a company's financial data can reveal much about its performance, certain relationships are more easily understood when some elements of the data are compared with other elements. This is where **common-size analysis** comes in. It involves converting the dollar values in the financial statements into percentages of a specific base amount. For example, when preparing common-size analysis of a statement of financial position, the base used is normally total assets. When preparing common-size analysis of a statement of income, the base is normally total revenues. This means that each item on a **common-size statement of financial position** is determined as a percentage of total assets, while each item on a **common-size statement of income** is expressed as a percentage of total revenues. This presentation format makes it much easier for an analyst to quickly understand the degree of change.

In Exhibit 12-3, we have applied common-size analysis to Saputo's statements of income for three years, expressing each item as a percentage of total revenues; that is, the amount of each item on the statement of income ÷ total revenues for that year.

■ **LEARNING OBJECTIVE 6**
Identify the different metrics used in financial analysis, including common-size analysis and ratio analysis, and explain how they are used.

KEY POINTS
• A common-size statement of financial position uses total assets as the base.
• A common-size statement of income uses total revenues as the base.

Exhibit 12-3 Common-Size Statement of Income: Saputo Inc.

	2014	2013	2012
Revenues	100.0%	100.0%	100.0%
Operating costs excluding those below	88.9%	88.2%	88.0%
EBITDAR	11.1%	11.8%	12.0%
Depreciation and amortization	1.6%	1.6%	1.5%
Acquisition, restructuring, and impairment costs	0.5%	0.6%	1.8%
Interest on long-term debt and other financial charges	0.7%	0.5%	0.4%
Earnings before taxes	8.2%	9.2%	8.4%
Income tax expense	2.4%	2.5%	2.9%
Net earnings[1]	5.8%	6.6%	5.5%

TAKE**5**

FINANCIAL
STATEMENTS

(1) Note: Some numbers do not appear to add due to rounding differences.

We observed from Exhibit 12-1 that revenues, operating profit (EBITDAR), and net earnings have been increasing for Saputo but in 2012 net earnings had experienced a decline. This common-size statement of earnings gives us a better understanding of those changes for the past three years, but you could also do a longer series using previous years' financial statements. It shows that Saputo's net earnings as a proportion of revenues have fallen from 6.6% in 2013 to 5.8% in 2014, but that this percentage is above the level achieved in 2012. Because operating costs are the largest expense on the statement, it makes sense to look more closely at these costs. Saputo's operating costs as a proportion of sales have been increasing over the three-year period, from 88.0% of sales in 2012 to 88.9% in 2014, a 0.9-percentage-point increase. It is costing Saputo more to produce the goods it sells. This has caused the operating profit (EBITDAR) to fall from 12.0% to 11.1% and signals to the user that, despite its goal to improve cost efficiencies, Saputo has not been able to keep its major operating costs in check.

Changes in operating profit (EBITDAR) could reflect a shift to selling more products that are more expensive to produce, or perhaps price cuts were required due to competitive or economic conditions, or perhaps cost control has just been ineffective. An analyst would want to try to find out more information about the cause of the change, either from management or by performing additional analysis. Most of Saputo's products require raw milk or cheese as inputs and its MD&A discusses the price fluctuations of those inputs and the effect on its results. An analyst will examine a company's financial statements carefully when sales are rising or falling. If sales are rising and the cost of those sales rises proportionately more than the sales themselves, the new sales are costing the company more and management should be looking for ways to control the costs. As a percentage of sales, when all other costs remain the same, an increase in the operating costs results in an identical decrease in net income. Imagine if you sell an item for $1.00 and it now costs you $0.03 more to make or acquire the item than it did last year. This means there will be $0.03 less to spend on other items or left over as net income. Let's try to look for more interesting relationships on the statement of income for Saputo:

- Net earnings as a percentage of sales actually increased by 0.3 percentage points from 2012 to 2014, from 5.5% of sales to 5.8%. As Saputo's major operating costs as a percentage of sales increased by 0.9 percentage points (from 88.0% to 88.9%), the company must have been able to control other costs well enough to prevent net earnings from declining by the amount of the increase in its operating costs. Many of the items between its operating profit (EBITDAR) and the net earnings are unusual or non-recurring costs such as the restructuring and goodwill impairment charges shown on its statement of earnings.

- Income tax as a proportion of sales decreased, which could explain why net earnings did not decrease as much as operating profit (EBITDAR), but income tax expense is generally not under management's control. A more useful margin might be the earnings before tax margin, which decreased by 0.2 percentage points, from 8.4% to 8.2%.

- It is difficult to draw strong conclusions in this case without additional information. For example, although Saputo discloses its cost of sales in the notes to the financial statements, it is combined with other operating costs on the statement of income. Consequently, our common-size statement does not break down this information for our analysis. The signals on this common-size statement of income are mixed: the major operating costs are increasing but overall, the effect on net earnings is smaller. The analyst would want to discuss unusual expenses such as goodwill impairment and restructuring with management to determine how much weight should be given to their impact.

Common-size statements could also be prepared for the statement of financial position and the statement of cash flows. The common-size data could then be used in a trend analysis, as we have done for the statement of income, or they could be used in a cross-sectional analysis of different companies. In fact, common-size statements are particularly useful in cross-sectional analysis because they allow you to compare companies of different sizes.

How is ratio analysis used to analyze financial statements?

As we have seen throughout the preceding chapters, ratio analysis can be used to compare a company's results from period to period, or to compare one company with others. It also enables users to compare companies of different sizes more easily.

The ratios compare the relationships between various elements in the financial statements, such as:

- an amount from one statement, such as the statement of income, and an amount from another, such as the statement of financial position (for example, cost of goods sold relative to inventory);
- amounts from the statement of financial position (such as current assets relative to current liabilities); or
- amounts from the statement of income (such as cost of goods sold relative to total sales revenue).

HELPFUL HINT
When commenting on ratios and trends, be sure to use evaluative or interpretive terms. Do not simply make superficial, mathematical observations; show that you understand what the figures *mean*.

For example, do not simply say that a ratio or percentage is higher/lower or increasing/decreasing. Instead, try to use terms such as *stronger/weaker*, *better/worse*, and *improving/deteriorating*, when you describe the numeric results.

Although ratios tell you about the relationship between two figures and changes in that relationship from year to year, or compared with another company, they do not tell you the reason for the changes. That is, ratios will tell you *what* happened but not *why*. For example, if inventory turnover slowed, is it a problem with not being able to sell existing inventory or has the company introduced new product lines that have a longer selling or manufacturing period? As such, interpreting the results of ratio analysis requires the user to apply judgement. Often ratios raise as many questions as they answer. They are more often attention-directing—highlighting areas that should be explored further—than conclusive. As such, interpreting the ratio results, rather than simply calculating them, is the most important job of an analyst.

When interpreting ratios, you should state more than whether the ratio simply increased or decreased. You should recall, from the ratios looked at earlier in the book, that some ratios are considered to have improved if they increase, while the opposite is true for others. It may also be possible for a small increase in a ratio to indicate improvement, but too large an increase to indicate a concern. For example, an increase in the current ratio may indicate improved liquidity, but if it is too high there may be problems with excessive inventory levels or with the collection of accounts receivable.

You will usually need to do further research and analysis to understand the reasons for the changes. Sometimes changes in ratios are referred to as **red flags**—they identify areas that the user needs to investigate further.

You should also be careful not to draw conclusions too readily from limited amounts of data. In this chapter, due to time and space constraints, we are limited to only three years of ratios for Saputo and no cross-sectional comparisons with other companies or the industry. Looking at longer time series and cross-sectional comparisons with other companies or industry data would greatly improve the analysis. In a complete analysis of our sample company, Saputo, an analyst would seek more information before making any decisions.

What are the common categories of ratios?

You have already been introduced to ratios that related to the specific content of each chapter in this book. In fact, 24 different ratios have been discussed throughout the book. While this may seem like a large number, it is important to note that there are many other ratios used in business. The 24 ratios we have focused on include many of the most commonly used ratios and will provide you with the tools to undertake meaningful ratio analysis of most companies.

The 24 ratios we have studied can be organized into common categories. Let's take a minute and think about the way golf clubs are organized in a golf bag. Are they just put into the bag randomly or are they organized in some way? Normally, most golfers try to organize them. For example, all the drivers are placed in a section of the bag, as are the irons and putters. That way, when the golfer needs to select a club, they can quickly find the one that best suits their need without having to look through them all. Analysts do a very similar thing with ratios, bundling them into common categories according to the broad measure they can be used to assess. That way, when an analyst needs a ratio to assess a certain measure, they can select one from the relevant category rather than having to consider all of them. We will use five common categories of ratios: **liquidity ratios**, **activity ratios**, **solvency ratios**, **profitability ratios**, and **equity analysis ratios**. Exhibit 12-4 presents the five common categories of ratios and identifies where the ratios that we have studied fit.

Exhibit 12-4 Common Categories of Ratios

Category and Description	Common Ratios in the Category	Chapter
1. Liquidity Ratios – used to assess a company's ability to meet its obligations in the near future	Current Ratio	6
	Quick Ratio	6
2. Activity Ratios – used to assess how efficiently a company manages its operations	Accounts Receivable Turnover	6
	Average Collection Period	6
	Inventory Turnover	7
	Days to Sell Inventory	7
	Accounts Payable Turnover	9
	Accounts Payable Payment Period	9
3. Solvency Ratios – used to assess a company's ability to meet its long-term obligations	Debt to Equity	10
	Net Debt as a Percentage of Total Capitalization	10
	Interest Coverage	10
	Cash Flows to Total Liabilities	5
4. Profitability Ratios – used to assess a company's ability to generate profits	Gross Profit Margin	7
	Net Profit Margin	2
	Return on Equity	2
	Return on Assets	2
5. Equity Analysis Ratios – used to assess shareholder returns	Basic Earnings per Share (EPS)	4
	Price/Earnings (P/E) Ratio	11
	Dividend Payout	11
	Dividend Yield	11
	Net Free Cash Flow	5

Note: Only 21 of the 24 ratios presented in the text are included in this table. The other three are unique to the analysis of property, plant, and equipment and do not fit within the five common categories. These are: Average Age, Average Age Percentage, and Fixed Asset Turnover, all from Chapter 8.

Before completing ratio analysis for Saputo, let's review the ratio formulas for the 21 ratios discussed above. These are presented in Exhibit 12-5.

Exhibit 12-5 Ratio Summary

	Ratio	Formula	Result
Liquidity	Current Ratio	$\dfrac{\text{Current Assets}}{\text{Current Liabilities}}$	Ability to meet current obligations with current assets
	Quick Ratio	$\dfrac{\text{Current Assets} - \text{Inventory} - \text{Prepaid Expenses}}{\text{Current Liabilities}}$	Ability to meet current obligations with most liquid assets
Activity	Accounts Receivable Turnover	$\dfrac{\text{Credit Sales}}{\text{Average Accounts Receivable}}$	Efficiency of receivables collection
	Average Collection Period	$\dfrac{365 \text{ days}}{\text{Accounts Receivable Turnover}}$	Number of days to collect receivables
	Inventory Turnover	$\dfrac{\text{Cost of Goods Sold}}{\text{Average Inventory}}$	How frequently inventory is turned over during period
	Days to Sell Inventory	$\dfrac{365 \text{ days}}{\text{Inventory Turnover}}$	Number of days to sell through inventory
	Accounts Payable Turnover	$\dfrac{\text{Credit Purchases}}{\text{Average Accounts Payable}}$	How frequently creditors are paid
	Accounts Payable Payment Period	$\dfrac{365 \text{ days}}{\text{Accounts Payable Turnover}}$	Number of days to pay suppliers
Solvency	Debt to Equity	$\dfrac{\text{Net Debt}}{\text{Shareholders' Equity}}$	Amount of debt relative to shareholders' equity
	Net Debt as a Percentage of Total Capitalization	$\dfrac{\text{Net Debt}}{\text{Shareholders' Equity} + \text{Net Debt}}$	Portion of total financing represented by debt
	Interest Coverage	$\dfrac{\text{EBITDA (Earnings before Interest, Taxes, Depreciation, and Amortization)}}{\text{Interest Expense}}$	Ability to cover interest expense from earnings
	Cash Flows to Total Liabilities	$\dfrac{\text{Cash Flows from Operating Activities}}{\text{Total Liabilities}}$	Portion of total obligations that could be met with operating cash flows
Profitability	Gross Profit Margin	$\dfrac{\text{Gross Margin}}{\text{Sales Revenue}}$	Profit after product costs to cover other operating costs
	Net Profit Margin	$\dfrac{\text{Net Income}}{\text{Sales Revenue}}$	Net profit earned on each $1 of sales
	Return on Equity	$\dfrac{\text{Net Income}}{\text{Average Total Shareholders' Equity}}$	Rate of return on resources provided by investors
	Return on Assets	$\dfrac{\text{Net Income}}{\text{Average Total Assets}}$	Rate of return on assets used
Equity Analysis	Basic Earnings per Share	$\dfrac{\text{Net Income} - \text{Preferred Dividends}}{\text{Weighted Average Number of Common Shares Outstanding}}$	Profit earned on each common share
	Price/Earnings	$\dfrac{\text{Market Price per Share}}{\text{Earnings per Share}}$	Multiple of EPS represented by current share price
	Dividend Payout	$\dfrac{\text{Dividends per Share}}{\text{Earnings per Share}}$	Proportion of income paid out as dividends
	Dividend Yield	$\dfrac{\text{Dividends per Share}}{\text{Price per Share}}$	Rate of return provided by dividends relative to current share price
	Net Free Cash Flow	Cash Flows from Operating Activities $-$ Net Capital Expenditures $-$ Dividends on Preferred Shares	Cash flow generated from operating activities that would be available to common shareholders

RATIO ANALYSIS

What liquidity ratios are commonly used?

As discussed in Chapters 1 and 6, when assessing a company's liquidity, we are focused on determining a company's ability to convert assets into cash so that liabilities can be paid. An important part of liquidity analysis considers the company's ability to meet its short-term obligations with its short-term assets. Two ratios that are commonly used are the **current ratio** and the **quick ratio**.

■ **LEARNING OBJECTIVE 7**
Identify, calculate, and interpret specific ratios that are used to analyze the liquidity, activity, solvency, profitability, and equity of a company.

Current Ratio

Current Ratio	$\dfrac{\text{Current Assets}}{\text{Current Liabilities}}$	Ability to meet current obligations with current assets
2014	$\dfrac{\$1,895,846}{\$1,725,094} = 1.10$	
2013	$\dfrac{\$1,512,556}{\$1,226,647} = 1.23$	
2012	$\dfrac{\$1,399,464}{\$902,441} = 1.55$	

Note: All of the dollar amounts in the ratio calculations are in thousands of Canadian dollars.

Based on the above, Saputo had $1.10 of current assets for every $1 in current liabilities in 2014. While the company's current ratio declined during the year, it is still greater than 1.0, indicating that there are more than enough current assets with which to settle current liabilities. Upon reviewing the current assets, we can see that cash and cash equivalents decreased (the company used some cash in an acquisition), while accounts receivable, inventory, income taxes, and prepaids all increased, also likely due to the acquisition. While Saputo's total current assets increased, the growth in current liabilities, especially in the current portion of its long-term debt, was greater, which decreased liquidity and lowered the current ratio.

One rule of thumb for the current ratio is that for most industries, it should be 1.0 or more, but it is not uncommon to see companies with current ratios of less than 1.0. The size of this ratio depends on the type of business and the types of assets and liabilities that are considered current. For example, a company that sells primarily on a cash basis and does not have any accounts receivable, like a grocery store, normally has a low current ratio.

It is important to note that it is possible for a company to be *too liquid*—to have too much money invested in assets such as cash and accounts receivable that do not generate any returns for the company.

You should also realize that different users may have different perceptions about liquidity. A creditor or banker would prefer high levels of liquidity because that reduces the risk that the company may not be able to repay the debt. However, a shareholder or investor does not want a company to have too much money in cash or cash equivalents because there is an opportunity cost of having money tied up in low-earning assets.

Quick Ratio

Quick Ratio	$\dfrac{\text{Current Assets} - \text{Inventory} - \text{Prepaid Expenses}}{\text{Current Liabilities}}$	Ability to meet current obligations with most liquid assets
2014	$\dfrac{\$1,895,846 - \$933,232 - \$84,992}{\$1,725,094} = 0.51$	
2013	$\dfrac{\$1,512,556 - \$770,158 - \$71,882}{\$1,226,647} = 0.55$	
2012	$\dfrac{\$1,399,464 - \$712,885 - \$54,576}{\$902,441} = 0.70$	

Based on the above, the quick ratio of 0.51 in 2014 is lower than the quick ratio of 0.55 in 2013, which should not be surprising. Remember that when we discussed the current ratio we noted increases in Saputo's current liabilities and a decrease in its cash balance.

Like the current ratio, the desirable level for this ratio depends on the type of industry. The rule of thumb for this ratio is that it should be approximately 1.0 or more but industries without accounts receivable may have a very low quick ratio.

Taken together, the current ratio and quick ratio indicate that Saputo's liquidity position is solid and there are no working capital concerns. However, the company's liquidity has declined and additional information on the reasons for this would be useful. Developing meaningful analysis is a challenge when there is ratio information for only a few years, and especially when major acquisitions have occurred during that time period. This illustrates the importance of trend analyses, because having ratios beyond just two or three years would enable you to see broader patterns. Cross-sectional analyses should also be undertaken with other companies in the food-processing industry.

What activity ratios are commonly used?

The activity ratios provide additional insight into how efficiently the company manages its operations and are sometimes called **operating efficiency ratios**. We looked at a number of asset-related activity ratios in Chapters 6 and 7 involving accounts receivable and inventory. We also looked at two liability-related activity ratios in Chapter 9 involving accounts payable. These activity ratios help the analyst assess the company's management of its working capital.

Accounts Receivable Turnover and Average Collection Period

Accounts Receivable Turnover	$\dfrac{\text{Credit Sales}}{\text{Average Accounts Receivable}}$	Efficiency of receivables collection

$$2014 \quad \frac{\$9,232,889}{(\$624,553 + \$807,409)/2} = 12.9$$

$$2013 \quad \frac{\$7,297,677}{(\$487,502 + \$624,553)/2} = 13.1$$

$$2012 \quad \frac{\$6,930,370}{(\$460,807 + \$487,502)/2} = 14.6$$

When the **accounts receivable turnover** ratio is calculated based on information from the financial statements, the assumption is usually made that all sales revenues were on account. This is necessary because no information is normally provided indicating the percentage of credit sales (or sales on account) versus cash sales. If the turnover ratio were being prepared for internal use by management, this type of information would be available and only credit sales would be used when calculating it. In this case, it is probable that most of Saputo's sales are credit sales, since it sells its products to retailers and wholesale distributors. Companies that sell directly to the public, like grocery stores, tend to sell primarily on a cash basis and hence have few (if any) credit sales.

Note that average accounts receivable should only include receivables related to credit sales (trade receivables). It should not include other miscellaneous receivables (such as income tax receivable or advances to employees). We have assumed that the receivables on Saputo's balance sheet are all related to credit sales.

Finally, although we have included only two years of financial information in Exhibits 12-2A, B, and C, we have obtained additional information for the fiscal year ended March 31, 2011, and included it in the calculation of the average accounts receivable shown above, as well as in other ratios that use average rather than year-end figures. While we recommend you trace the amounts used in the calculations in these ratios back to Exhibits 12-2A, B, and C as appropriate, you will not be able to trace the figures shown for 2012 because they have not been included in the chapter. You could trace them if you obtained the company's 2012 financial statements from the company's website or through SEDAR (www.sedar.com).

Average Collection Period		$\dfrac{365 \text{ days}}{\text{Accounts Receivable Turnover}}$	Number of days to collect receivables
	2014	$\dfrac{365}{12.9} = 28.3$ days	
	2013	$\dfrac{365}{13.1} = 27.9$ days	
	2012	$\dfrac{365}{14.6} = 25.0$ days	

The accounts receivable turnover can also be used to determine the **average collection period**. Users may find that average collection period is easier to interpret than accounts receivable turnover. Although companies probably do not sell goods or collect receivables every day of the year, the convention is to calculate it based on a 365-day period.

To determine how effectively a company is at collecting its receivables, its accounts receivable turnover must be compared with the company's credit terms. For example, companies that normally allow customers 30 days to pay, would be expected to have an accounts receivable turnover of 12 (365 days/30 days = 12). An accounts receivable turnover higher than 12 would mean that the company is collecting its receivables faster, speeding the flow of cash from the company's customers.

With an accounts receivable turnover of 12.9 times, it appears that Saputo is collecting its receivables, on average, in 28.3 days. Since we have no information on Saputo's credit terms, we will assume that the company's normal credit terms are 30 days. If you were working for a financial institution considering lending the company funds, you would be able to obtain this information from the company. Assuming the company provides 30-day credit terms, the company is collecting its receivables on a timely basis. Its customers are, on average, paying slightly faster than the terms given and Saputo is benefitting from the earlier cash inflows. The 2014 turnover is lower (worse) than in 2013 (13.1 times) and 2012 (14.6 times), indicating that the collection rate for its receivables has been slowing. This could be related to the acquisition of Warrnambool in 2014 and U.S.-based dairy producer Morningstar in 2013. Only two months of sales for Warrnambool are included in revenues, which understates the revenues (numerator) relative to the accounts receivable. However, overall collection of accounts seems strong for the company.

A decrease in the accounts receivable turnover or a higher average collection period can indicate that the company is having difficulty collecting its accounts receivable. Alternatively, the company may be selling to customers with higher credit risk or may have old accounts receivable requiring writeoff.

Inventory Turnover and Days to Sell Inventory Ratios

Inventory Turnover		$\dfrac{\text{Cost of Goods Sold}}{\text{Average Inventory}}$	How frequently inventory is turned over during period
	2014	$\dfrac{\$7,419,529}{(\$770,158 + \$933,232)/2} = 8.7$	
	2013	$\dfrac{\$5,816,940}{(\$712,885 + \$770,158)/2} = 7.8$	
	2012	$\dfrac{\$5,523,298}{(\$662,194 + \$712,885)/2} = 8.0$	

The **inventory turnover ratio**, introduced in Chapter 7, gives the analyst some idea of how fast inventory is sold or, alternatively, how long the inventory is held prior to sale.

All companies are required to disclose the amount of their cost of goods sold. Some companies include this information directly on the statement of income, while others disclose information about it in the notes to their financial statements, as was the case with Saputo. Exhibit 12-6 shows how cost of sales was disclosed in Note 4 to the company's financial statements.

Exhibit 12-6 Excerpt from Saputo Inc.'s 2014 Annual Report: Calculation of Cost of Sales

FINANCIAL
STATEMENTS

NOTE 4 INVENTORIES

in 000s	March 31, 2014	March 31, 2013
Finished goods	$ 651,660	$ 551,733
Raw materials, work in progress and supplies	281,572	220,971
Inventory write-down	—	(2,546)
Total	$ 933,232	$ 770,158

The amount of inventories recognized as an expense in operating costs for the year ended March 31, 2014 is $7,419,529,000 ($5,816,940,000 for the year ended March 31, 2013).

For fiscal 2014, no write-down ($2,546,000 at March 31, 2013) was included as an expense in "Operating costs excluding depreciation, amortization, acquisition, restructuring and other costs" under the caption "Changes in inventories of finished goods and work in process" in Note 5.

Days to Sell Inventory	$\dfrac{365 \text{ days}}{\text{Inventory Turnover}}$	Number of days to sell through inventory

$$2014 \qquad \frac{365}{8.7} = 41.9 \text{ days}$$

$$2013 \qquad \frac{365}{7.8} = 46.8 \text{ days}$$

$$2012 \qquad \frac{365}{8.0} = 45.6 \text{ days}$$

The **days to sell inventory ratio** tells us how many days, on average, that it took the company to sell through its average inventory.

The average number of days that inventory is held depends on the type of inventory produced, used, or sold. In Saputo's case, its major operations are the sale of food products to both retailers and wholesalers. The 41.9 days, therefore, is the average length of time that costs remain in inventory, from original processing to sale of the products to customers. Because the product is perishable, you would expect a reasonably quick turnover, but remember this is an average of all products: some dairy products (yogourt or cream) would require a quicker turnover than some cheeses that might be aged. You would want to review this turnover ratio over time and compare it with the inventory turnover ratios of other companies producing and selling similar products. Saputo's inventory turnover is the highest it has been in three years, which means it has done well at turning over its inventories and the ratio is fairly constant between the two years, which is also a positive sign. We can see that, on average, the company took just under 42 days to sell through its inventory, which is just about 5 days quicker than it did in 2013; this should improve or shorten the company's cash-to-cash cycle as the time it took the company to collect its receivables was consistent from 2013 to 2014 (about 28 days).

Saputo is a processing company, and the inventory turnover ratio that we calculated used all types of its inventory, including raw materials, work in process, finished goods, and supplies. A more appropriate inventory turnover measure could be to use only the finished goods amounts, which could be done as Saputo discloses the components of its inventory in Note 4 (Exhibit 12-6). To simplify the calculation, we have just used total ending inventory.

An inventory turnover ratio that has changed significantly from one period to the next or that is significantly different from that of others in the industry may be a warning sign. If the ratio is lower, it could indicate that the company is having trouble selling its inventory, or perhaps has obsolete inventory on hand that overstates the company's current ratio and levels of liquidity, similar to a low accounts receivable turnover. If the inventory turnover ratio is too high, there is a risk the company's inventory level might be too low—it might be losing sales if it does not have enough items on hand to meet orders.

Accounts Payable Turnover and Accounts Payable Payment Period Ratios

Accounts Payable Turnover	$\dfrac{\text{Credit Purchases}}{\text{Average Accounts Payable}}$	How frequently creditors are paid

$$2014 \quad \frac{\$7,582,603}{(\$748,318 + \$897,222)/2} = 9.2$$

$$2013 \quad \frac{\$5,874,213}{(\$571,814 + \$748,318)/2} = 8.9$$

$$2012 \quad \frac{\$5,573,989}{(\$573,779 + \$571,814)/2} = 9.7$$

The challenge with the **accounts payable turnover** ratio is that a company's credit purchases do not appear directly in the financial statements. An alternative is to use the cost of goods sold in place of credit purchases, because the cost of goods sold is more readily available either in the statement of income or in the accompanying notes. If the level of inventories did not change dramatically during the period, this would be a good approximation.

Recall that in Chapter 9, we learned how rearranging the elements in the cost of goods sold (COGS) model enabled us to determine the amount of credit purchases as follows:

COGS Model	Rearranged Model	2014	2013	2012
Beginning Inventory	Cost of Goods Sold	$7,419,529	$5,816,940	$5,523,298
+ Purchases	− Beginning Inventory	− 770,158	− 712,885	− 662,194
− Ending Inventory	+ Ending Inventory	+ 933,232	+ 770,158	+ 712,885
= Cost of Goods Sold	= Purchases	$7,582,603	$5,874,213	$5,573,989

Accounts Payable Payment Period	$\dfrac{365 \text{ days}}{\text{Accounts Payable Turnover}}$	Number of days to pay suppliers

$$2014 \quad \frac{365}{9.2} = 39.7 \text{ days}$$

$$2013 \quad \frac{365}{8.9} = 41.0 \text{ days}$$

$$2012 \quad \frac{365}{9.7} = 37.6 \text{ days}$$

With an accounts payable turnover of 9.2, Saputo's **accounts payable payment period** was 39.7 days in 2014. This indicates, on average, how long it takes Saputo to pay its payables. Interpreting this ratio depends on the credit terms of the company's suppliers. If the terms are 30 days, Saputo appears to be exceeding them; if the terms are 60 days, Saputo appears to be paying too quickly. If a company is paying too quickly, it is not taking advantage of the fact that accounts payable normally do not charge interest and hence are "free" credit. However, if the company is paying too slowly, there may be interest charges for late payments. Additional information on the payment terms would enhance this analysis. In addition, cross-sectional and trend analysis should be undertaken.

What solvency ratios are commonly used?

Solvency is the company's ability to pay its obligations in the long term (more than one year into the future). Analysts use it as a key indicator of a company's level of risk. A trend analysis of the statement of cash flows and the company's cash flow patterns over time should provide much of the insight you need to assess a company's abilities to service its long-term debt. Two dimensions are used to assess solvency: (1) risk, based on the level of **leverage** in the company, and (2) **coverage**, based on the company's ability to meet its interest and debt payments. We will look at four ratios that are commonly used in the assessment of long-term solvency: the **debt to equity ratio**, **net debt as a percentage of total capitalization**, the **interest coverage ratio**, and the **cash flows to total liabilities ratio**. The first two are often referred to as **leverage ratios**, and the latter two as **coverage ratios**.

Leverage Ratios

Debt to Equity	$\dfrac{\text{Net Debt}}{\text{Shareholders' Equity}}$	Amount of debt relative to shareholders' equity

2014	$\dfrac{\$2,060,014}{\$2,839,160} = 0.73$	
2013	$\dfrac{\$1,686,988}{\$2,305,672} = 0.73$	
2012	$\dfrac{\$ 402,369}{\$2,105,686} = 0.19$	

In Chapter 10, we learned that net debt was equal to a company's interest-bearing debt less cash and cash equivalents. Saputo's net debt for 2014, 2013, and 2012 was as follows:

2014	Bank loans	$ 310,066
	+ Current portion of long-term debt	393,600
	+ Long-term debt	1,395,694
	− Cash and cash equivalents	(39,346)
	= Net debt	$2,060,014
2013	Bank loans	$ 181,865
	+ Current portion of long-term debt	152,400
	+ Long-term debt	1,395,900
	− Cash and cash equivalents	(43,177)
	= Net debt	$1,686,988
2012	Bank loans	$ 166,631
	+ Current portion of long-term debt	–
	+ Long-term debt	379,875
	− Cash and cash equivalents	(144,137)
	= Net debt	$ 402,369

The debt to equity ratio measures the amount of debt the company has relative to shareholders' equity. The result is the amount of debt the company has for each dollar in shareholders' equity. The higher a company's debt load, the higher (worse) its debt to equity ratio will be. In Chapter 10, we also discussed leverage and learned that leverage means the company uses debt to finance some of its assets. We also noted that the more leverage a company has, the riskier its position and the higher its fixed commitments to pay interest are. Comparing the amount of debt with the amount of equity, as is done with the debt to equity ratio, is one way of assessing this risk.

A variety of formulas are used to calculate the debt to equity ratio. Some use total liabilities rather than net debt, while others use interest-bearing short-term and long-term debt without taking a company's cash balance into account. Since the ratio results will differ depending upon the formula used, it is important that you be aware of how the various ratios have been calculated when analyzing them and especially when comparing them with those that have been determined by someone else for a comparable company.

The debt to equity ratio illustrates that the amount of debt Saputo uses in its financing has increased from $0.19 for every dollar in shareholders' equity in 2012 to $0.73 in 2013 and 2014. The ratio is almost four times higher in 2013 and 2014 and is a result of the company's two significant acquisitions (Warrnambool and Morningstar), which were largely financed using long-term debt.

Net Debt as a Percentage of Total Capitalization	$\dfrac{\text{Net Debt}}{\text{Shareholders' Equity + Net Debt}}$	Portion of total financing represented by debt
2014	$\dfrac{\$2,060,014}{\$2,839,160 + \$2,060,014} = 0.42 \text{ or } 42\%$	
2013	$\dfrac{\$1,686,988}{\$2,305,672 + \$1,686,988} = 0.42 \text{ or } 42\%$	
2012	$\dfrac{\$402,369}{\$2,105,686 + \$402,369} = 0.16 \text{ or } 16\%$	

From the net debt as a percentage of total capitalization ratio, we can see that debt represented 42% of total capitalization in 2014 and 2013, up from 17% in 2012. In other words, the mix of debt and equity used to finance the company's assets changed significantly in 2013. Saputo added debt to finance major acquisitions in 2013 (Morningstar) and again in 2014 (Warrnambool). In the MD&A, management stated that they wanted to increase the company's use of leverage, which is consistent with the results of these ratios.

The two leverage ratios have sent consistent messages to the user. Based on these results, the user would want to consider whether the level of debt is appropriate for Saputo. Again, a cross-sectional analysis could reveal whether the company has excessive debt compared with other companies. As a general guide, however, the average corporate debt on the books of non-financial companies in Canada was approximately 36% of total assets at the end of 2013.[2] With a ratio of 42% in 2014, Saputo is just above that average.

Coverage Ratios

Interest Coverage	$\dfrac{\text{EBITDA}}{\text{Interest Expense}}$	Ability to cover interest expense from earnings
2014	$\dfrac{\$1,020,345}{\$53,239} = 19.2$	
2013	$\dfrac{\$860,772}{\$29,896} = 28.8$	
2012	$\dfrac{\$830,931}{\$23,081} = 36.0$	

The interest coverage ratio calculates the number of times a company's earnings could pay its interest expense. The higher the number, the less risk there is of the company being unable to meet its interest obligations through earnings. We can see from the results of this ratio that Saputo appears to have no concerns with meeting its interest expense through earnings because earnings were 19.2 times interest charges in 2014. This is down from 28.8 times in 2013 and 36.0 times in 2012, but this decrease is consistent with our expectations from the company's increased debt load. Because the coverage is still high, it is not of concern.

Cash Flows to Total Liabilities		$\dfrac{\text{Cash Flows from Operating Activities}}{\text{Total Liabilities}}$	Portion of total obligations that could be met with operating cash flows
	2014	$\dfrac{\$656,310}{\$3,517,732} = 0.19$	
	2013	$\dfrac{\$645,792}{\$2,887,968} = 0.22$	
	2012	$\dfrac{\$522,987}{\$1,493,434} = 0.35$	

In addition to determining the level of risk that a company is exposed to through its use of debt to finance its assets, users want to assess the company's ability to meet the interest and principal payments that arise from the debt obligations. We will assess this using the cash flows to total liabilities ratio. This ratio measures the percentage of a company's total liabilities that could be met with one year's operating cash flows. It is important to note that total liabilities include both current and non-current liabilities and that only the current liabilities are due within the next year. In addition, some of the liabilities will not be paid in cash. For example, unearned revenues are often settled by providing services to customers. The company may also have other assets that could be used to settle liabilities, such as investments in the shares of other companies. As such, this ratio can safely be less than 1.0.

Saputo's ratio has fallen from 35% in 2012 to 22% in 2013 and again to 19% in 2014. This means that in 2014 just under one fifth of Saputo's total liabilities could be paid off with the current levels of operating cash flow. Dividing this ratio into 1, we can determine how many years of operating cash flow would be required to pay off the company's liabilities. Based on the operating cash flows generated in 2014, it would take 5.3 years (1/0.19) to generate enough cash to pay off the liabilities that existed at year end in 2014.

What profitability ratios are commonly used?

Profitability measures help analysts assess the potential return. The profitability ratios such as **gross profit margin** and **net profit margin**, introduced in Chapters 7 and 2, can be combined with the return ratios, return on assets, and return on equity to assess a company's overall performance.

Gross Profit Margin

Gross Profit Margin		$\dfrac{\text{Gross Margin}}{\text{Sales Revenue}}$	Profit after product costs to cover other operating costs
	2014	$\dfrac{\$1,813,360}{\$9,232,889} = 0.196 \text{ or } 19.6\%$	
	2013	$\dfrac{\$1,480,737}{\$7,297,677} = 0.203 \text{ or } 20.3\%$	
	2012	$\dfrac{\$1,407,072}{\$6,930,370} = 0.203 \text{ or } 20.3\%$	

For most companies, cost of goods sold is the largest single expense. Companies need to closely monitor their gross profit margin to ensure that gross profit will be sufficient to cover all other expenses. Changes in a company's gross profit margin would indicate a change in the product's profitability, indicating changes in the cost structure or pricing policy.

Using the sales revenue as reported on the statement of earnings and the cost of goods sold information from Note 4 to its financial statements, we can quantify the company's gross margin as follows:

Revenues − Cost of Sales = Gross Margin

2014: $9,232,889 − $7,419,529 = $1,813,360

2013: $7,297,677 − $5,816,940 = $1,480,737

2012: $6,930,370 − $5,523,298 = $1,407,072

We can see that Saputo's gross profit margin dropped slightly in 2014 to 19.6% after remaining unchanged from 2012 to 2013. In other words, in 2014, for each $1.00 in sales, the company had $0.196 remaining after product costs to cover its other costs (down from $0.203 in 2013 and 2012). The fact that the company gross profit margin stayed constant tells us that the company was able to control its costs or was able to pass these additional costs along to its customers in the form of higher prices. Either way, the company was able to hold its margins, which is a positive signal.

Net Profit Margin

Net Profit Margin	$\dfrac{\text{Net Income}}{\text{Sales Revenue}}$	Net profit earned on each $1 of sales
2014	$\dfrac{\$533,966}{\$9,232,889} = 0.058$ or 5.8%	
2013	$\dfrac{\$481,921}{\$7,297,677} = 0.066$ or 6.6%	
2012	$\dfrac{\$380,840}{\$6,930,370} = 0.055$ or 5.5%	

While net profit margin indicates the overall profitability of the company, it does not provide any information about how that profit was achieved. When it is analyzed together with the gross profit margin, a more complete picture comes to light. Earlier, we saw that Saputo's gross profit margin decreased by 0.7 percentage points from 20.3% in 2013 to 19.6% in 2014. When analyzing the company's net profit margin, we can see that it decreased 0.8 percentage points from 2013 to 2014. As such, we know that most of this was the result of a lower gross margin and not the result of increases in other costs (depreciation, acquisition costs, restructuring costs, impairment charges, interest, or income taxes).

In addition to the profitability of earnings relative to revenues, it is important to examine the earnings relative to the amount invested to earn them. If two companies generate the same amount of net earnings, but one company requires twice as many assets to do so, that company would clearly be a less desirable investment. In Chapter 2, we discussed two profitability ratios related to the amounts invested to generate earnings: **return on equity** and **return on assets**. Return on equity measures the return generated by a company on the equity invested by shareholders (return from the perspective of investors). Return on assets measures return from the perspective of management. Management obtains resources from both shareholders and creditors and invests them in assets. The return generated on this investment in assets is then used to repay creditors and provide returns to shareholders.

Return on Equity Ratio

Return on Equity	$\dfrac{\text{Net Income}}{\text{Average Total Shareholders' Equity}}$	Rate of return on resources provided by investors
2014	$\dfrac{\$533,966}{(\$2,305,672 + \$2,839,160)/2} = 0.208$ or 20.8%	
2013	$\dfrac{\$481,921}{(\$2,105,686 + \$2,305,672)/2} = 0.218$ or 21.8%	
2012	$\dfrac{\$380,840}{(\$2,072,635 + \$2,105,686)/2} = 0.182$ or 18.2%	

The return on equity (ROE) ratio shows that Saputo earned a 20.8% ROE in 2014. This is a 1.0 percentage point decrease from the previous year's ROE of 21.8%, but still 2.6 percentage points higher than in 2012. This ROE of 20.8% should be compared with the ROE of other similar companies or with the results of Saputo over time. Cross-sectional comparisons of ROE are difficult in that differences in the risks involved should result in differences in returns. Differences in the risks cannot, however, always explain large differences in returns, because there are many factors that affect ROE.

Return on Assets Ratio

Return on Assets	$\dfrac{\text{Net Income}}{\text{Average Total Assets}}$	Rate of return on assets used
2014	$\dfrac{\$533,966}{(\$5,193,640 + \$6,356,892)/2} = 0.092 \text{ or } 9.2\%$	
2013	$\dfrac{\$481,921}{(\$3,599,120 + \$5,193,640)/2} = 0.110 \text{ or } 11.0\%$	
2012	$\dfrac{\$380,840}{(\$3,578,331 + \$3,599,120)/2} = 0.106 \text{ or } 10.6\%$	

We can see that Saputo's return on assets (ROA) decreased by 1.8 percentage points from 2013 to 2014. The return on assets ratio is useful in measuring the overall profitability of the funds invested in the company's assets. However, comparisons of ROAs across industries must be made with care. The level of ROA reflects, to some extent, the risk that is inherent in the type of assets that the company invests in. Investors trade off risk for return. The more risk investors take, the higher the return they demand. If the company invested its assets in a bank account, which is a very low-risk investment, it would expect a lower return than if it invested in oil exploration equipment, which is a high-risk business. Although this factor cannot explain all the variations in ROA between companies, it must be kept in mind. It may be useful to perform a trend analysis of this ratio and to look at the changes in the elements used to determine the ratio, such as the growth in net income relative to the change in net assets.

What equity analysis ratios are commonly used?

Equity analysts are interested in the long-term risk and return of the company, as measured by many of the ratios discussed so far. But equity analysts and investors are uniquely interested in the relative value of the company's shares. This is assessed using the equity analysis ratios.

Basic Earnings per Share

Basic Earnings per Share	$\dfrac{\text{Net Income} - \text{Preferred Dividends}}{\substack{\text{Weighted Average Number} \\ \text{of Common Shares Outstanding}}}$	Profit earned on each common share

In Chapter 4, we learned how to calculate **basic earnings per share (EPS)**, including how to determine the weighted average number of common shares outstanding. The weighted average calculation requires us to know the date when shares were either issued or repurchased. This information is not typically available to an analyst outside the company because it is not required to be disclosed in the annual report. Financial statement users are told the number of shares issued and repurchased, but not the specific dates. However, since accounting standards require EPS to be reported on the statement of income or in a note accompanying the financial statements, we can rely on the company to prepare the calculation for us.

In the case of Saputo, the company had only common shares outstanding, so we do not need to worry about any preferred dividends. The company had 195,068,912 common shares issued and outstanding at the end of 2014, down from 196,619,440 common shares that were issued and outstanding at the end of 2013. This net reduction resulted from the company issuing 1,701,272 common shares under its share option plan, but also repurchasing 3,251,800 common shares. Exhibit 12-7 presents the note from Saputo's financial statements related to EPS.

Exhibit 12-7 Excerpt from Saputo Inc.'s 2014 Annual Report: Earnings Per Share Note

NOTE 15 EARNINGS PER SHARE

	2014	2013
Net earnings attributable to shareholders of Saputo Inc.	$ 533,097	$ 481,921
Weighted average number of common shares outstanding	195,123,232	197,589,714
Dilutive options	2,551,443	2,731,407
Weighted average diluted number of common shares outstanding	197,674,675	200,321,121
Basic earnings per share	$ 2.73	$ 2.44
Diluted earnings per share	$ 2.70	$ 2.41

FINANCIAL
STATEMENTS

From Exhibit 12-7, we can see that Saputo's basic EPS was $2.73 in 2014, up 11.9% from the EPS of $2.44 in 2013. This increase in EPS is considered a positive signal.

The major problem with using EPS as a measure of performance is that it ignores the level of investment. Companies with the same earnings per share might have very different rates of return, depending on their investment in net assets. Because of this, the best use of the EPS figure is in a trend analysis, determining how it has changed within the same company over time, rather than in a cross-sectional analysis, determining how one company's EPS compares with another's.

A detailed discussion of **diluted earnings per share** and how it is calculated is beyond the scope of this book. However, it is important that you understand the difference between basic EPS and diluted EPS. The reason the diluted EPS measure is presented is that companies may issue securities that are convertible into common shares. Examples of these types of securities are convertible debt, convertible preferred shares, and stock options. The key feature of these securities is that they are all convertible into common shares under certain conditions. If additional common shares are issued upon their conversion, the earnings per share number could decrease because of the larger number of shares that are outstanding. This is called the *potential dilution of earnings per share*. A diluted EPS figure is determined to reflect what EPS would have been if all of these securities had been converted into common shares. As you would expect, diluted EPS will be less than basic EPS whenever dilutive securities exist.

P/E Ratio

Price/Earnings	$\dfrac{\text{Market Price per Share}}{\text{Earnings per Share}}$	Multiple of EPS represented by current share price
	2014	$\dfrac{\$55.69^3}{\$2.73} = 20.4$
	2013	$\dfrac{\$51.58}{\$2.44} = 21.1$
	2012	$\dfrac{\$43.21}{\$1.89} = 22.9$

Note: Market price per share data was the closing share price on the last trading day closest to year end. This information can be obtained from various financial websites.

The **price/earnings (P/E) ratio**, or **P/E multiple**, was introduced in Chapter 11 and relates the market price of a company's shares with its earnings per share. This ratio is thought of by many analysts as the amount investors are willing to pay for a dollar's worth of earnings. The interpretation of this ratio is somewhat difficult because stock market share prices are affected by many factors and are not well understood. It might help to think of the multiple in terms of its inverse. If a company is earning $1 per common share and its shares are selling for $20 on the stock market, this indicates that the current multiple is 20, meaning the current price of the stock is 20 times the current earnings per share. The inverse of this multiple is 1/20, or 5%. This indicates that the shares are returning 5% in the form of earnings per share when compared with the market price.

On March 31, 2014, the company's year end, Saputo's common shares were trading on the Toronto Stock Exchange (TSX) at approximately $55.69 per share. Its P/E ratio on that date was 20.4 ($55.69/$2.73).

Remember that the earnings per share is the portion of the earnings that is attributable to an individual share: it is not the amount that the company normally pays out as a dividend to each shareholder. A shareholder earns a return both from receiving dividends and from the change in the price of the share. Therefore, the return calculated from the P/E ratio will differ from the actual return. Many factors affect the level of stock market prices, including the prevailing interest rates and the company's future prospects. It is sometimes useful to think that the market price reflects the present value of all of the company's future expected earnings. Companies with a low growth potential or higher levels of risk tend to have lower P/E ratios, because investors are not willing to pay as much per dollar of earnings if the earnings are not expected to grow much or are more risky. Conversely, companies with high growth potential or lower levels of risk tend to have higher P/E ratios. Many factors ultimately affect the P/E ratio, but the earnings per share figure serves as an important link between the accounting numbers in the financial statements and the stock market price of the company's shares.

Dividend Payout Ratio

Dividend Payout	$\dfrac{\text{Dividends per Share}}{\text{Earnings per Share}}$	Proportion of income paid out as dividends
2014	$\dfrac{\$0.92}{\$2.73} = 0.337 \text{ or } 33.7\%$	
2013	$\dfrac{\$0.84}{\$2.44} = 0.344 \text{ or } 34.4\%$	
2012	$\dfrac{\$0.76}{\$1.89} = 0.402 \text{ or } 40.2\%$	

In Chapter 11, we also learned about the **dividend payout ratio**. This ratio measures the portion of a company's earnings that is distributed as dividends.

From the calculations above, we can see that Saputo's dividend payout ratio was 33.7% in 2014, down from 34.4% in 2013. This percentage is consistent with the company's goal, which is stated in its MD&A, of returning approximately 30% of its net earnings to shareholders through the declaration and payment of dividends. In Note 24 on dividends in Exhibit 12-8, we can see that the total amount of dividends paid per share increased from $0.84 per share in 2013 to $0.92 per share in 2014, a 9.5% increase. So, while Saputo paid out a lower portion of its earnings as dividends, the total dividends paid to shareholders did increase. Trend analysis should be used to analyze the dividend payout ratio, in order to have a broad picture of the company's dividend practices.

Exhibit 12-8 Excerpt from Saputo Inc.'s 2014 Annual Report: Dividends Note

FINANCIAL
STATEMENTS

NOTE 24 DIVIDENDS

During the year ended March 31, 2014, the Company paid dividends totalling $175,321,820, or $0.92 per share ($161,651,170, or $0.84 per share for the year ended March 31, 2013).

Dividend Yield Ratio

Dividend Yield	$\dfrac{\text{Dividends per Share}}{\text{Price per Share}}$	Rate of return provided by dividends relative to current share price
2014	$\dfrac{\$0.92}{\$55.69} = 0.0165 \text{ or } 1.65\%$	
2013	$\dfrac{\$0.84}{\$51.58} = 0.0163 \text{ or } 1.63\%$	
2012	$\dfrac{\$0.76}{\$43.21} = 0.0176 \text{ or } 1.76\%$	

The **dividend yield ratio** was also presented in Chapter 11. It measures the dividends an investor will receive relative to the price per share. The yield measures the return provided to shareholders as dividends, but does not factor in any returns resulting from capital appreciation (an increase in share price).

Throughout the text, we have discussed the two ways in which shareholders realize returns: through the receipt of dividends and through capital appreciation (growth in share price). The dividend yield ratio measures the return from the first of these. From the calculations above, we can see that Saputo's shareholders realized a dividend yield of 1.65% in 2014, up slightly from 1.63% in 2013. That being said, it is important to consider the variable on which the yield is based. Both the amount of dividends per share and the price per share increased in 2014. These increases are positive for investors who have continued to hold shares. New investors would need to consider the 1.65% yield relative to other possible investments. They would also need to factor in the potential for future increases in share price.

Net Free Cash Flow

Net Free Cash Flow	Cash Flows from Operating Activities	− Net Capital Expenditures	− Dividends on Preferred Shares	Cash flow generated from operating activities that would be available to common shareholders
2014	$656,310 − $223,371 − $0 = $432,939			
2013	$645,792 − $177,336 − $0 = $468,456			
2012	$522,987 − $105,716 − $0 = $417,271			

In Chapter 5, we learned that **net free cash flow** is considered to be the cash flow generated from a company's operating activities that would be available to the company's common shareholders. We also mentioned that it is unlikely that the entire amount would be distributed to shareholders. Instead, portions of it are used to repay debt, finance expansion plans, repurchase company shares, and so on.

The ratio analysis above illustrates that the net free cash flow generated by Saputo decreased by 7.6% in 2014, falling from $468,456 in 2013 to $432,939 in 2014. While the decrease is not a positive sign, we can see that the company continues to generate significant net free cash flow, which provides it with additional financial flexibility.

LIMITATIONS OF RATIO ANALYSIS

What are the limitations of ratio analysis?

■ **LEARNING OBJECTIVE 8**
Identify and explain the limitations of ratio analysis.

It is important to be aware of a number of limitations inherent in ratio analysis. These must be considered when performing ratio analysis or interpreting its results. These limitations include:

1. **Accounting policies**

   As we have discussed throughout the text, a company's accounting policies will affect its results. Public companies in Canada use IFRS, but some also use U.S. accounting standards. You must be aware of significant differences in accounting treatment if you are analyzing the results of companies using different accounting policies. This is also an issue even if the companies being compared both use IFRS, because it allows for some choices and requires assumptions and estimates. For example, some assets and liabilities are carried at historical cost values while others are at market values. Some companies may depreciate their capital assets using the straight-line method, while others may use an accelerated or production-based method. These choices will affect the financial statements and, in turn, the ratios determined based on them.

2. **Definitions of ratios**

There are often several ways to calculate a given ratio or different names given to the same ratio. Therefore, if you are trying to interpret a ratio that has been calculated by the company and presented in its annual report or is from some other source, it is important that you understand how it was determined before you attempt to interpret it.

3. **Diversity of operations**

The degree of diversity in a company's operations will affect your ability to interpret ratios related to it. For example, it will be easier to interpret the ratios of a company that operates in one industry, or in one country, than it will be for a multinational company with highly diverse operations. Data on a company's operating segments can help to reduce this concern. While diversity of operations can make it difficult to compare companies, it does not normally affect trend analysis for the same company unless the company's mix of operations has also changed over time, such as if it has acquired or divested of major segments.

4. **Seasonality**

Companies normally choose to have their financial year end at the end of their business cycle. For example, fashion retailers **Reitmans (Canada) Limited** and **Le Château Inc.** have year ends of January 31, which is after the holiday sales period. Choosing such a year end means that there is less inventory on hand to count; it is easier to make estimates for things like sales returns, bad debts, and warranties; and staff is less busy. It follows that the balances on the statement of financial position may be lower than the average balances for the year and that ratios based on those values will be affected. The effects of seasonality can be somewhat mitigated by using the quarterly financial information that public companies are required to report.

5. **Potential for manipulation**

Certain ratios, like the current and quick ratios, are based on figures at one point in time. This makes it possible for a company to manipulate them. This can be done by either undertaking or postponing transactions that affect the balances used to calculate the ratio in order to produce a more desirable number. This is sometimes referred to as **window dressing**. For example, a company could choose to delay inventory purchases to enhance its current and quick ratios.

Everything you learned in the previous chapters built up to this one, giving you the knowledge to use various tools, including common financial ratios, to analyze and interpret financial statements. You should now have a solid foundation in financial accounting knowledge that will help you use accounting information to make good decisions in a variety of circumstances.

SUMMARY

1. **Understand and explain the process of financial analysis.**

- Financial analysis involves evaluating a company's performance based on the information in its financial statements, MD&A, and so on.

- A basic five-step analysis process includes: (1) determining the purpose or context for the analysis, (2) collecting the required information, (3) preparing common-size analysis and calculating ratios, (4) analyzing and interpreting the common-size analysis and ratios, and (5) developing conclusions and recommendations.

2. **Identify the common contexts for financial statement analysis and explain why an awareness of context is essential to the analysis.**

- Financial statement analysis is conducted in a variety of contexts, including share purchase/hold/sale decisions,

lending decisions, credit application decisions, and corporate acquisitions analysis.

- The context for the analysis is important in determining the most appropriate tools for the analysis, such as trend analysis (the same company's results over time) or cross-sectional analysis (one company's results relative to another's).

3. **Explain why knowledge of the business is important when analyzing a company's financial statements.**

- Interpreting the results of ratios and other analysis requires the analyst to have an understanding of the business, including the various activities the company is engaged in and any significant changes to the company's operations during the period being analyzed.

- Companies present information on any distinct operating segments that meet certain thresholds. These segments can be based on different types of businesses the company is involved in or the different geographic regions it operates in, if applicable.

- Understanding a company's strategies is also essential to being able to interpret financial statement analysis correctly.

4. Identify the types of information used when analyzing financial statements and where it is found.

- The primary source of the information used in the analysis is a company's annual report. It includes the company's comparative financial statements, management's discussion and analysis of the most recent results, and the auditors' report.

5. Explain the various perspectives used in financial statement analysis, including retrospective, prospective, trend, and cross-sectional analysis.

- Retrospective analysis is historical analysis (assessing past results), while prospective analysis is forward-looking analysis (trying to determine what the future results may be).

- There are two major types of retrospective analysis: trend analysis and cross-sectional analysis.

- Trend analysis involves assessing results over a period of time, such as 3 to 10 years, and looking for patterns or changes over time.

- Cross-sectional analysis normally involves comparing the results of one company with other companies in the same industry, including competitors. In certain contexts, cross-sectional analysis can also involve comparisons with companies in other industries.

6. Identify the different metrics used in financial analysis, including common-size analysis and ratio analysis, and explain how they are used.

- Common-size analysis involves restating the various amounts in the financial statements into percentages of a specific base amount. For example, statements of income can be restated so that each amount is a percentage of total revenues or statements of financial position can be restated so that each amount is a percentage of total assets. Common-size statements make it easy to identify the degree of changes from period to period.

- Ratio analysis is also commonly used to assess a company's results from one period to the next or to compare one company with others.

- Ratios are useful for identifying issues that require further investigation, but do not provide the reason for the changes.

- There are five common categories of ratios: liquidity, activity, solvency, profitability, and equity analysis ratios.

- The formulas for the various ratios in each category are presented in Exhibit 12-5.

7. Identify, calculate, and interpret specific ratios that are used to analyze the liquidity, activity, solvency, profitability, and equity of a company.

- The current and quick ratios are used to analyze liquidity.

- The ratios commonly used to assess activity include accounts receivable turnover, average collection period, inventory turnover, days to sell inventory, accounts payable turnover, and accounts payable payment period ratio.

- The debt to equity, net debt as a percentage of total capitalization, interest coverage, and cash flows to total liabilities ratios are used to analyze solvency.

- Profitability is assessed using the gross profit margin, net profit margin, return on equity, and return on assets ratios.

- Equity analysis uses the basic earnings per share, price/earnings, dividend payout, dividend yield, and net free cash flow ratios.

8. Identify and explain the limitations of ratio analysis.

- The limitations of ratio analysis include companies using different accounting policies or estimates, the existence of different ratio definitions, the challenge of comparing diverse operations, the impacts of seasonality in terms of when ratio analysis is conducted, and the potential for manipulation by management.

KEY TERMS

Accounts payable payment period (560)
Accounts payable turnover (559)
Accounts receivable turnover (556)
Activity ratios (553)
Average collection period (557)
Basic earnings per share (EPS) (564)
Cash flows to total liabilities ratio (560)
Common-size analysis (551)
Common-size statement of financial position (551)
Common-size statement of income (551)
Coverage (560)
Coverage ratios (560)
Cross-sectional analysis (548)
Current ratio (555)

Days to sell inventory ratio (558)
Debt to equity ratio (560)
Diluted earnings per share (565)
Dividend payout ratio (566)
Dividend yield ratio (567)
EBITDAR (547)
Equity analysis ratios (553)
Gross profit margin (562)
Interest coverage ratio (560)
Inventory turnover ratio (558)
Leverage (560)
Leverage ratios (560)
Liquidity ratios (553)
Management discussion and analysis (MD&A) (545)
Net debt as a percentage of total capitalization (560)

Net free cash flow (567)
Net profit margin (562)
Operating efficiency ratios (556)
Operating segments (544)
P/E multiple (565)
Price/earnings (P/E) ratio (565)
Profitability ratios (553)
Prospective analysis (546)
Quick ratio (555)
Red flags (552)
Retrospective analysis (546)
Return on assets (ROA) (563)
Return on equity (ROE) (563)
Solvency ratios (553)
Trend analysis (546)
Window dressing (568)

ABBREVIATIONS USED

EBITDA	Earnings before interest, taxes, depreciation, and amortization
EBITDAR	Earnings before interest, taxes, depreciation, amortization, acquisition, and restructuring
EPS	Earnings per share
MD&A	Management discussion and analysis
P/E ratio	Price/earnings ratio
ROA	Return on assets
ROE	Return on equity

SYNONYMS

Activity ratios | Operating efficiency ratios
Price/earnings (P/E) ratio | P/E multiple

CHAPTER END REVIEW PROBLEM

The consolidated statements of financial position, net earnings and comprehensive income, and cash flows for **Dollarama Inc.** are presented in Exhibits 12-9A to C. Dollarama is Canada's largest operator of dollar stores. The company's headquarters are in Montreal, and it operates stores in every province.

EXHIBIT 12-9A	DOLLARAMA INC.'S 2014 CONSOLIDATED STATEMENT OF FINANCIAL POSITION

Dollarama Inc.
Consolidated Statement of Financial Position as at
(Expressed in thousands of Canadian dollars)

	Note	February 2, 2014 $	February 3, 2013 $
Assets			
Current assets			
Cash and cash equivalents		71,470	52,566
Accounts receivable		5,963	5,798
Deposits and prepaid expenses		5,382	5,756
Merchandise inventories		364,680	338,385
Derivative financial instruments	15	11,455	3,710
		458,950	406,215
Non-current assets			
Property and equipment	7	250,612	197,494
Intangible assets	8	129,436	122,201
Goodwill	8	727,782	727,782
Total assets		1,566,780	1,453,692
Liabilities and shareholders' equity			
Current liabilities			
Accounts payable and accrued liabilities	9	128,857	101,286
Dividend payable		9,823	8,099
Income taxes payable		22,102	23,636
Derivative financial instruments	15	—	185
Current portion of finance lease obligations	11	1,022	604
Current portion of long-term debt	10	3,017	—
		164,821	133,810

continued

| EXHIBIT 12-9A | **DOLLARAMA INC.'S 2014 CONSOLIDATED STATEMENT OF FINANCIAL POSITION (continued)** |

	Note	February 2, 2014 $	February 3, 2013 $
Non-current liabilities			
Long-term debt	10	395,446	262,071
Finance lease obligations	11	1,484	—
Deferred rent and tenant inducements	12	51,592	45,327
Deferred income taxes	14	89,271	80,994
Total liabilities		702,614	522,202
Commitments	11		
Shareholders' equity			
Share capital	13	493,602	517,306
Contributed surplus		10,884	8,157
Retained earnings		346,478	403,266
Accumulated other comprehensive income	13	13,202	2,761
Total shareholders' equity		864,166	931,490
Total liabilities and shareholders' equity		1,566,780	1,453,692

| EXHIBIT 12-9B | **DOLLARAMA INC.'S 2014 CONSOLIDATED STATEMENT OF NET EARNINGS AND COMPREHENSIVE INCOME** |

Dollarama Inc.
Consolidated Statement of Net Earnings and Comprehensive Income for the years ended
(Expressed in thousands of Canadian dollars, except share and per share amounts)

	Note	52-weeks February 2, 2014 $	53-weeks February 3, 2013 $
Sales		2,064,676	1,858,818
Cost of sales		1,299,092	1,163,979
Gross profit		765,584	694,839
General, administrative and store operating expenses		363,182	339,662
Depreciation and amortization	18	47,898	39,284
Operating income		354,504	315,893
Net financing costs	18	11,673	10,839
Earnings before income taxes		342,831	305,054
Provision for income taxes	14	92,737	84,069
Net earnings for the year		250,094	220,985

continued

EXHIBIT 12-9B	DOLLARAMA INC.'S 2014 CONSOLIDATED STATEMENT OF NET EARNINGS AND COMPREHENSIVE INCOME (continued)

	Note	52-weeks February 2, 2014 $	53-weeks February 3, 2013 $
Other comprehensive income			
Items to be reclassified subsequently to net earnings			
Unrealized gain on derivative financial instruments, net of reclassification adjustment		14,249	1,093
Income taxes relating to component of other comprehensive income		(3,808)	(308)
Total other comprehensive income, net of income taxes		10,441	785
Total comprehensive income for the year		260,535	221,770
Earnings per share			
Basic net earnings per common share	17	$3.48	$3.00
Diluted net earnings per common share	17	$3.47	$2.94
Weighted average number of common shares outstanding during the year (*thousands*)	17	71,838	73,660
Weighted average number of diluted common shares outstanding during the year (*thousands*)	17	72,046	75,190

EXHIBIT 12-9C	DOLLARAMA INC.'S 2014 CONSOLIDATED STATEMENT OF CASH FLOWS

Dollarama Inc.
Consolidated Statements of Cash Flows for the years ended
(Expressed in thousands of Canadian dollars)

	Note	52-weeks February 2, 2014 $	53-weeks February 3, 2013 $
Cash flows			
Operating activities			
Net earnings for the year		250,094	220,985
Adjustments for:			
Depreciation and amortization	18	47,898	39,284
Interest accrual long-term debt	10	3,017	(216)
Amortization of debt issue costs		592	1,133
Excess of receipts over amount recognized on derivative financial instruments	15	6,319	1,272
Recognition of deferred leasing costs		465	295
Recognition of deferred tenant allowances	12	(3,543)	(2,871)
Deferred lease inducements	12	3,750	5,328
Deferred tenant allowances	12	6,058	6,832
Share-based compensation	13	4,053	1,558
Deferred income taxes	14	4,469	6,921
Loss on disposal of assets		1,017	716
		324,189	281,237

continued

EXHIBIT 12-9C	DOLLARAMA INC.'S 2014 CONSOLIDATED STATEMENT OF CASH FLOWS (continued)

		52-weeks	53-weeks
		February 2,	February 3,
	Note	2014	2013
		$	$
Changes in non-cash working capital components	19	(15,811)	(24,198)
Net cash generated from operating activities		308,378	257,039
Investing activities			
Additions to property and equipment	7	(96,303)	(69,577)
Additions to intangible assets	8	(11,095)	(8,210)
Proceeds on disposal of property and equipment		552	256
Net cash used by investing activities		(106,846)	(77,531)
Financing activities			
Proceeds from senior unsecured notes	10	400,000	—
Disbursements on long-term debt		(264,420)	(10,361)
Proceeds from bank indebtedness		166,000	—
Repayment of bank indebtedness		(166,000)	—
Payment of debt issue costs		(2,797)	(837)
Repayment of finance leases		(985)	(695)
Dividends paid		(38,418)	(30,972)
Repurchase and cancellation of shares	13	(277,438)	(155,942)
Issuance of common shares		1,430	1,594
Net cash used by financing activities		(182,628)	(197,213)
Increase (decrease) in cash and cash equivalents		18,904	(17,705)
Cash and cash equivalents – Beginning of year		52,566	70,271
Cash and cash equivalents – End of year		71,470	52,566
Cash payment of interest		6,025	7,639
Cash payment of income taxes		89,801	75,090

Required:

Calculate the following ratios for the year ending February 2, 2014, based on the data provided in Exhibits 12-9A to C. Comment on what the ratios tell you about the company, providing your comments for each of the five categories of ratios (liquidity, activity, solvency, performance, and equity). Also identify any further analysis that should be undertaken.

Short-Term Liquidity Ratios

    a. Current ratio
    b. Quick ratio

Activity Ratios

    c. Accounts receivable turnover and average collection period: because Dollarama does not extend credit to its customers, these ratios are not applicable
    d. Inventory turnover and days to sell inventory
    e. Accounts payable turnover and accounts payable payment period (assume that trade payables were $58,937 in 2014 and $50,786 in 2013)

Solvency Ratios

    f. Debt to equity ratio
    g. Net debt as a percentage of total capitalization
    h. Interest coverage (assume cash interest payments are equal to interest expense)
    i. Cash flow to total liabilities

Performance Ratios

j. Gross profit margin
k. Net profit margin
l. Return on equity
m. Return on assets

Equity Analysis Ratios

n. Price/earnings ratio (assume a share price of $84, nearest closing price to year end)
o. Dividend payout ratio (assume that dividends of $0.56 per share were paid during the year)
p. Dividend yield
q. Net free cash flow (assume that there are no preferred shares outstanding)

Suggested Solution to Chapter End Review Problem

Ratios for Dollarama Inc. for the year ending February 2, 2014:

(Amounts used in the ratios are in thousands of dollars.)

Liquidity Ratios

a.	Current Ratio	$\dfrac{\text{Current Assets}}{\text{Current Liabilities}}$	
		$\dfrac{\$458,950}{\$164,821}$	2.78
b.	Quick Ratio	$\dfrac{\text{Current Assets} - \text{Inventory} - \text{Prepaid Expenses}}{\text{Current Liabilities}}$	
		$\dfrac{\$458,950 - \$364,680 - \$5,382}{\$164,821}$	0.54

Activity Ratios

c1.	Accounts Receivable Turnover	$\dfrac{\text{Credit Sales}}{\text{Average Accounts Receivable}}$	
		N/A – Dollarama does not extend credit	N/A
c2.	Average Collection Period	$\dfrac{365 \text{ days}}{\text{Accounts Receivable Turnover}}$	
		N/A – Dollarama does not extend credit	N/A
d1.	Inventory Turnover	$\dfrac{\text{Cost of Goods Sold}}{\text{Average Inventory}}$	
		$\dfrac{\$1,299,092}{(\$338,385 + \$364,680)/2}$	3.70
d2.	Days to Sell Inventory	$\dfrac{365 \text{ days}}{\text{Inventory Turnover}}$	
		$\dfrac{365}{3.70}$	98.6 days
e1.	Accounts Payable Turnover	$\dfrac{\text{Credit Purchases}}{\text{Average Accounts Payable}}$	
		$\dfrac{\$1,325,387^{1}}{(\$50,786 + \$58,937)/2}$ [1]Credit Purchases = COGS − Beginning Inventory + Ending Inventory = $1,299,092 − $338,385 + $364,680	24.2
e2.	Accounts Payable Payment Period	$\dfrac{365 \text{ days}}{\text{Accounts Payable Turnover}}$	
		$\dfrac{365}{24.2}$	15.1 days

Solvency Ratios

f.	Debt to Equity	$$\frac{\text{Net Debt}}{\text{Shareholders' Equity}}$$	
		$$\frac{\$702{,}614 - \$71{,}470}{\$864{,}166}$$	0.73
g.	Net Debt as a Percentage of Total Capitalization	$$\frac{\text{Net Debt}}{\text{Shareholders' Equity} + \text{Net Debt}}$$	
		$$\frac{\$702{,}614 - \$71{,}470}{\$864{,}166 + \$702{,}614 + \$71{,}470}$$	0.422
h.	Interest Coverage	$$\frac{\text{EBITDA}}{\text{Interest Expense}}$$	
		$$\frac{\$342{,}831 + \$47{,}898}{\$6{,}025}$$	64.8
i.	Cash Flows to Total Liabilities	$$\frac{\text{Cash Flows from Operating Activities}}{\text{Total Liabilities}}$$	
		$$\frac{\$308{,}378}{\$702{,}614}$$	0.439

Profitability Ratios

j.	Gross Profit Margin	$$\frac{\text{Gross Margin}}{\text{Sales Revenue}}$$	
		$$\frac{\$765{,}584}{\$2{,}064{,}676}$$	0.371
k.	Net Profit Margin	$$\frac{\text{Net Income}}{\text{Sales Revenue}}$$	
		$$\frac{\$250{,}094}{\$2{,}064{,}676}$$	0.121
l.	Return on Equity	$$\frac{\text{Net Income}}{\text{Average Total Shareholders' Equity}}$$	
		$$\frac{\$250{,}094}{(\$931{,}490 + \$864{,}166)/2}$$	0.279
m.	Return on Assets	$$\frac{\text{Net Income}}{\text{Average Total Assets}}$$	
		$$\frac{\$250{,}094}{(\$1{,}453{,}692 + \$1{,}566{,}780)/2}$$	0.166

Equity Analysis Ratios

n.	Price/Earnings	$$\frac{\text{Market Price per Share}}{\text{Earnings per Share}}$$	
		$$\frac{\$84.00}{\$3.48}$$	24.14
o.	Dividend Payout	$$\frac{\text{Dividends per Share}}{\text{Earnings per Share}}$$	
		$$\frac{\$0.56}{\$3.48}$$	0.161
p.	Dividend Yield	$$\frac{\text{Dividends per Share}}{\text{Price per Share}}$$	
		$$\frac{\$0.56}{\$84.00}$$	0.007
q.	Net Free Cash Flow	Cash Flows from Operating Activities − Net Capital Expenditures − Dividends on Preferred Shares	
		$\$308{,}378 - \$107{,}398 - \$0$	$200,980

Liquidity Ratios

The current ratio of 2.78 is considered on the high side and indicates that Dollarama has $2.78 in current assets for each $1 in current liabilities. The much lower quick ratio (0.54) indicates that Dollarama has large amounts of current assets invested in inventories. (Almost 80% of current assets are composed of inventories.) From the statement of financial position, we can see that 78% of the company's current liabilities are related to accounts payable and accrued liabilities. Of these, about half represent trade payables. Assuming that the company can continue to sell its inventory, it should have no difficulty in meeting its current obligations. Overall there appear to be no liquidity concerns for Dollarama.

Activity Ratios

The inventory turnover of 3.7 times indicates that there is enough inventory on hand to cover 98.6 days of sales. This appears a bit slow given the nature of Dollarama's business, but trend analysis and cross-sectional analysis would be needed to substantiate whether there are concerns in this area.

The accounts payable turnover of 24.2 times indicates that the company pays its suppliers an average of 15.1 days after incurring the obligation. To interpret this correctly, you would need to know the terms that Dollarama's suppliers offer. If their terms are net/30 days, then the company is paying too quickly, but we would need to determine if the company receives purchase discounts for quick payment.

The activity ratios paint a picture that is consistent with what we saw from the liquidity analysis: Dollarama is a company that carries considerable inventory, yet pays its suppliers quickly.

Solvency Ratios

Dollarama's debt to equity ratio is 73%, which indicates that the company uses $0.73 in debt financing for every $1 in equity. The net debt to total capitalization ratio indicates that 42.2% of the company's financing is provided by debt. The company had total long-term debt of $398,463 ($3,017 + $395,446), with less than 1% of this due within the next 12 months. We would want to look at the notes to the financial statements to get a sense of when the rest of the long-term debt will be due.

The interest coverage ratio of 64.8 indicates that Dollarama has no issues generating sufficient earnings to cover the interest expense on its debt. The cash flows to total liabilities ratio of 0.439 indicates that the company could repay its entire debt in under two and a half years (1/0.439 = 2.28 years) from operating cash flows. Overall, Dollarama's solvency appears to be sufficient. Its debt levels are supported by strong cash flows.

Profitability Ratios

In analyzing the performance of any company, one of the first things to consider is the net earnings and its trend. Dollarama had net earnings of $250,094 in 2014, which is up 13.2% from 2013. This is a positive trend. The company's net profit margin was 12.1% in 2014, meaning that there was $0.12 in net profit for every $1 in sales. The company's gross profit margin was 37.1% in 2014. Some trend analysis and cross-sectional analysis on gross profit would be very useful in helping us to reach a meaningful conclusion regarding trends and comparative results on this key ratio.

Dollarama had a return of equity of 27.9%, demonstrating that the company did a good job of using leverage to generate returns for shareholders. The company's return on assets was 16.6%. Again, some trend analysis would help us reach conclusions in this area.

Equity Analysis Ratios

Dollarama's P/E ratio of 24.14 shows that its shares are relatively expensive and that the potential for significant capital appreciation may be limited. The company is paying 16.1% of its earnings out to shareholders as dividends, providing them with a limited yield of only 0.7%. The company is generating a significant amount of net free cash flow ($200,980 in 2014), meaning that it has significant internally generated capital to repay debt, pursue additional growth opportunities, or possibly increase its dividends to shareholders.

In conclusion, Dollarama's liquidity, activity, solvency, performance, and equity analysis ratios do not raise any significant concerns. Ratios for more than one year, which would allow for additional trend analysis, and cross-sectional analysis would better support this conclusion and could identify other potential concerns.

ASSIGNMENT MATERIAL

Discussion Questions

DQ12-1 Explain what is meant by the term *financial statement analysis*. What analysis or information might an analyst use in their decision-making process?

DQ12-2 Identify and explain some common contexts in which financial statement analysis is used.

DQ12-3 Briefly describe the steps followed in preparing a financial statement analysis.

DQ12-4 Explain the link between retrospective and prospective analysis. Describe two types of retrospective analysis.

DQ12-5 Explain how the analysis of a company might be different for an investor than a creditor.

DQ12-6 Explain why knowledge of a business is important when using ratio analysis. What aspects of the business should you learn more about?

DQ12-7 What information other than the financial statements would be of interest to an analyst in a company's annual report? Describe how an analyst would use it.

DQ12-8 Explain what an analyst might determine from preparing a common-size statement of income.

DQ12-9 Explain what an analyst might determine from preparing a common-size statement of financial position.

DQ12-10 Explain the difference between trend analysis and cross-sectional analysis and provide an example of when each might be used.

DQ12-11 Identify the five main types of ratios used in this chapter to analyze a company. What does each group of ratios attempt to measure?

DQ12-12 Briefly explain, in your own words, what each of the following ratios helps the analyst to assess and whether the analyst would generally perceive an increase in the ratio as a positive change.
a. Current ratio
b. Quick ratio
c. Accounts receivable turnover
d. Inventory turnover
e. Accounts payable turnover

DQ12-13 Briefly explain, in your own words, what each of the following ratios helps the analyst to assess and whether the

analyst would generally perceive an increase in the ratio as a positive change.
a. Debt to equity ratio
b. Net debt as a percentage of total capitalization
c. Interest coverage
d. Cash flows to total liabilities
e. Gross profit margin
f. Net profit margin
g. Return on equity
h. Return on assets

DQ12-14 Briefly explain, in your own words, what each of the following ratios helps the analyst to assess and whether the analyst would generally perceive an increase in the ratio as a positive change.
a. Basic earnings per share
b. Price/earnings
c. Dividend payout
d. Dividend yield
e. Net free cash flow

DQ12-15 Contrast liquidity and solvency ratios in terms of what each category is used to assess.

DQ12-16 Briefly explain the difference between basic EPS and diluted EPS.

DQ12-17 Briefly explain why the dividend yield does not fully capture the return realized by a shareholder during the period.

DQ12-18 Explain how the accounts receivable and inventory turnover ratios can be useful in assessing a company's liquidity, especially when considered together with the current ratio.

DQ12-19 Why are ratios that use cash flows useful under accrual-based accounting?

DQ12-20 Explain how two companies in the same business (use retail clothing stores as an example) can earn the same profit (or net income), yet have very different operating strategies and different net profit margin ratios.

DQ12-21 Explain how the current ratio can be manipulated as a measure of liquidity.

DQ12-22 Explain the limitations of ratio analysis.

Application Problems

AP12-1 (Common-size analysis and differences in profitability)

Comparative financial statement data for First Ltd. and Foremost Ltd., two competitors, follow:

	First Ltd.		Foremost Ltd.	
	2016	2015	2016	2015
Net sales	$337,500		$1,950,000	
Cost of goods sold	202,500		1,092,000	
Operating expenses	68,250		468,000	
Interest expense	3,375		37,800	
Income tax expense	17,400		70,500	
Current assets	165,000	$142,500	1,020,000	$ 780,000
Capital assets (net)	420,000	367,500	1,530,000	1,425,000
Current liabilities	52,500	42,750	225,000	2,400,000
Long-term liabilities	67,500	95,250	630,000	540,000
Share capital	345,000	270,000	1,200,000	1,125,000
Retained earnings	120,000	102,000	495,000	300,000

Required:
   a. Prepare a common-size analysis of the 2016 statement of income data for First Ltd. and Foremost Ltd.
   b. Calculate the return on assets and the return on shareholders' equity for both companies.
   c. Comment on the relative profitability of these companies.
   d. Based on your calculations above, identify two main reasons for the difference in their profitability.

AP12-2 (Common-size analysis and differences in profitability and leverage)

Comparative financial statement data for Cool Brewery Ltd. and Northern Beer Ltd., two competitors, follow (amounts in thousands):

	Cool Brewery Ltd.		Northern Beer Ltd.	
	2016	2015	2016	2015
Net sales	$206,700		$40,500	
Cost of goods sold	100,500		15,300	
Operating expenses	85,400		17,190	
Interest expense	7,800		370	
Income tax expense	4,700		1,130	
Cash	12,000	$ 10,000	4,500	$ 2,500
Other current assets	86,000	80,500	8,200	7,400
Long-term assets (net)	210,000	209,600	29,100	30,700
Current liabilities	71,900	60,800	3,900	4,000
Long-term liabilities	103,900	117,500	8,000	7,400
Share capital	51,200	48,500	17,800	16,700
Retained earnings	81,000	73,300	12,100	12,500

Required:
   a. Prepare a common-size analysis for 2016 for Cool Brewery Ltd. and Northern Beer Ltd.
   b. Calculate the return on assets and the return on shareholders' equity for both companies.
   c. Comment on the relative profitability of these companies.
   d. Based on your calculations above, identify two main reasons for the difference in their profitability.

e. Calculate the debt to equity ratio for both companies at the end of 2016.

f. Calculate the net debt as a percentage of total capitalization for both companies.

g. Compare the use of leverage by these companies based on the ratios calculated in parts "e" and "f."

AP12-3 (Liquidity and profitability analysis)

Cathy's Cuisine Ltd. is a small restaurant and catering business started three years ago by Cathy Crosby. Initially the company's operations consisted of a small diner. In 2015, the company added the catering services as a way to expand sales without having to add space for seats. As the catering side of the business grew in 2016, the company purchased a used vehicle for deliveries. All sales in the diner are cash, debit, or credit card, but for catering jobs, customers are invoiced after the event. Most of the company's suppliers offer terms of 30 days. Selected financial information for Cathy's Cuisine Ltd. follows.

	2016	2015
Assets		
Cash	$ 8,600	$ 3,200
Accounts receivable	15,500	10,000
Inventory	10,900	6,000
Land	15,000	15,000
Building and equipment	30,000	25,000
Total assets	$ 80,000	$ 59,200
Liabilities and Equity		
Accounts payable	$ 9,500	$ 8,000
Short-term note payable	1,800	0
Mortgage payable current	2,500	2,500
Mortgage payable	22,500	25,000
Share capital	12,000	12,000
Retained earnings	31,700	11,700
Total liabilities and equity	$ 80,000	$ 59,200
Other information		
Sales	$180,000	$150,000
Cost of goods sold	80,000	75,000
Net income	20,000	5,500

Required:

a. Assume the growth in sales in 2016 is primarily from the catering business. Calculate the gross profit margins and the net profit margins and comment on whether you think the company should be focusing on the catering business or the diner.

b. Calculate the company's current ratio and quick ratio for both years and comment on the company's liquidity. Do you think the company is more liquid or less in 2016? What items on the statement of financial position support your position?

c. Calculate the company's accounts receivable turnover ratio for 2016. How quickly is the company collecting its receivables? Do you think it is doing a good job of managing its receivables?

d. Assume that 50% of the sales come from the catering business and recalculate the accounts receivable turnover for 2016. How does that affect your assessment of how receivables are being managed?

e. Calculate the company's inventory turnover ratio for 2016.

f. Calculate the company's accounts payable turnover ratio for 2016. Are suppliers being paid on time?

g. Using your analysis of the company's receivables and payables, what would you recommend be done to improve the management of those accounts?

h. Prepare a brief memo to Cathy outlining why it may be useful to break out the company's financial results by segment (diner and catering).

AP12-4 (Liquidity ratios)

The financial data for Alouette Resources Ltd. are as follows (amounts in thousands):

	2013	2014	2015	2016
Current assets				
Cash	$ 240	$ 160	$ 280	$ 320
Accounts receivable	800	1,040	960	860
Inventories	1,300	1,840	2,480	3,620
Prepaid expenses	200	200	300	200
	$2,540	$3,240	$4,020	$5,000
Current liabilities				
Accounts payable	$1,200	$1,320	$1,560	$1,640
Accrued salaries	140	200	240	300
Other current liabilities	200	300	320	600
	$1,540	$1,820	$2,120	$2,540

Required:

a. Calculate the current and quick ratios for 2013 through 2016.
b. Comment on the short-term liquidity position of Alouette.
c. Is your analysis is part "a" a trend analysis or a cross-sectional analysis? What is this type of analysis most useful for?
d. Which ratio do you think is the better measure of short-term liquidity for Alouette? Can you tell? Explain. What would your answer depend on?

AP12-5 (Basic strategies)

You are considering investing in the retail sector and have identified two companies for further analysis. Financial information for the two companies is as follows:

(in thousands)	Company A	Company B
Sales	$1,250,000	$1,400,000
Cost of goods sold	687,500	980,000
Net income	100,000	63,000
Average inventory	215,800	150,600
Average total assets	833,333	525,555

Required:

a. Calculate and compare the following ratios for the two companies:
   i. Return on assets
   ii. Gross margin
   iii. Net profit margin
   iv. Inventory turnover
   v. Days to sell inventory
b. Which company is likely following a low-cost producer strategy? Support your conclusion with reference to the ratios in part "a." What strategy might the other company be following?

AP12-6 (Accounts receivable turnover)

The financial data for Michaels' Foods Inc. and Sunshine Enterprises Ltd. for the current year are as follows (amounts in thousands):

	Annual Sales	Accounts Receivable Jan. 1	Accounts Receivable Dec. 31
Michaels' Foods	$60,600	$6,200	$8,100
Sunshine Enterprises	30,100	1,800	2,050

Required:
   a. Calculate the accounts receivable turnover for each company assuming that all sales are on account.
   b. Calculate the average number of days required by each company to collect its receivables.
   c. Which company appears to be more efficient at handling its accounts receivable?
   d. What additional information would be helpful in evaluating management's handling of the collection of accounts receivable?

AP12-7 (Inventory turnover)

Information on the activities of Novel-T Toys Ltd. is as follows:

	2012	2013	2014	2015	2016
Cost of goods sold	$893,100	$1,002,700	$1,174,500	$1,326,300	$1,391,780
Average inventory	128,450	157,100	206,310	323,420	442,990

Required:
   a. Do a trend analysis of the inventory turnover for each year. Also calculate the days to sell inventory ratio for the respective years.
   b. Is Novel-T Toy Ltd. managing its inventories efficiently? Do you have enough information to answer this question? If not, what else do you need to know?
   c. Provide an example of a situation where management may deliberately reduce inventory turnover, but still be operating in the company's best long-term interests.

AP12-8 (Inventory turnover)

The financial data for Ken's Fresh Fruits Incorporated and Al's Supermarket Ltd. for the current year are as follows:

	Annual Cost of Goods Sold	Inventory Jan. 1	Inventory Dec. 31
Ken's Fresh Fruits	$ 9,875,600	$ 695,000	$ 695,600
Al's Supermarket	53,885,000	4,776,500	1,040,500

Required:
   a. Calculate the inventory turnover for each company.
   b. Calculate the days to sell inventory ratio for each company.
   c. Knowing the type of inventory these companies sell, comment on the reasonableness of the inventory turnover. Which company manages its inventory more efficiently?
   d. Which company would be a more profitable investment? Can we tell? Explain.
   e. What are the potential problems with fast inventory turnovers? Would these be a concern for Ken's Fresh Fruits?

AP12-9 (Liquidity ratios and limitations)

Manitoba Manufacturing Inc. (MMI) has a loan from the Canadian National Bank to help finance its working capital. The terms of the loan are that the bank will lend MMI an amount up to 33% of its inventory balance and 50% of its accounts receivable. One of the loan covenants requires that MMI maintain a current ratio greater than 2.0. Information related to MMI's current assets and current liabilities is shown in the following table:

In thousands	2016	2015
Cash	$ 115	$ 160
Accounts receivable	875	870
Inventory	1,930	1,650
Other current assets	240	280
Bank loan, current	400	200
Accounts payable	995	950
Other current liabilities	40	80

Required:

    a. Does MMI satisfy the loan covenant in both years?

    b. Based on the loan size requirement only of the loan covenant, what is the maximum amount of loan MMI could borrow in each year?

    c. Based on a review of the accounts receivable balances, do you think sales have grown for MMI in 2016 over 2015?

    d. Identify three different ways management could have "managed" the statement of financial position to ensure that MMI met the loan covenant in 2016.

AP12-10 (Analysis using selected ratios)

The following ratios and other information are based on a company's comparative financial statements for a two-year period:

	2016	2015
Current ratio	1.84	2.20
Quick ratio	1.07	0.89
Net debt as a percentage of total capitalization ratio	0.43	0.58
Debt to equity ratio	0.75	1.38
Earnings per share	$ 0.24	$ 0.15
Gross profit margin	42.3%	45.6%
Total assets	$2,143,702	$3,574,825
Current assets	$ 965,118	$1,462,763

Required:

    a. What is the amount of current liabilities at the end of 2016?

    b. What is the amount of total debt at the end of 2016?

    c. What is the total shareholders' equity at the end of 2016?

    d. Do you think this company is a retail company, a financial institution, or a service organization? Explain.

    e. If the company has 1,650,200 common shares outstanding during 2016 and has issued no other shares, what was its net income for 2016?

    f. Based on the information available, what is your assessment of the company's liquidity? Explain.

    g. Given the limited information, what is your assessment of the company's overall financial position? Explain, identifying what changes you see between 2015 and 2016 that appear particularly significant.

    h. What changes do you see between 2015 and 2016 that appear particularly significant? What explanations might there be for the changes identified in "g"?

AP12-11 (Analysis using selected ratios)

HomeStar Ltd. is a chain of retail hardware stores with total assets of $2.5 billion. Selected financial ratios for HomeStar are as follows:

	2016	2015	2014
Current ratio	2.35	2.38	2.39
Quick ratio	0.56	0.51	0.58
Inventory turnover	5.57	5.33	5.27
Debt to equity ratio	0.68	0.87	0.86
Return on assets	7.3%	9.0%	9.8%
Gross profit margin	7.71%	8.36%	8.73%
Net profit margin	3.28%	3.87%	4.19%
Return on equity	11.4%	15.1%	16.8%

In 2014, HomeStar was affected by a decline in the demand for home hardware items and the entry of a major U.S. chain into the market.

Required:
  a. Briefly discuss what these financial ratios indicate about how HomeStar was affected by the events of 2014.
  b. Which measures have deteriorated during the subsequent periods?
  c. Which ratios indicate positive action taken by HomeStar during the subsequent periods?

AP12-12 (Activity ratios)

The following financial information is for Ambroise Industries Inc.:

	2016	2015
Sales	$5,000,000	$4,500,000
Cost of goods sold	2,250,000	2,025,000
Accounts receivable	585,500	558,800
Inventory	770,800	707,400
Accounts payable	200,750	195,250
Total assets	1,875,200	1,690,500

Ambroise is a distributor of auto parts operating in eastern Ontario that offers 30-day terms and has all sales on credit. The company has a large inventory due to the number of parts it stocks for different makes and models of cars. Most of its suppliers offer terms of 30 days, and Ambroise tries to stay on good terms with its suppliers by paying on time.

Required:
  a. What is the average time it takes Ambroise to collect its accounts receivable? How does that compare with the credit terms that the company offers?
  b. What is the average length of time that it takes Ambroise to sell through its inventory?
  c. What is the average length of time that it takes Ambroise to pay its payables? How does that compare with the credit terms it is offered?
  d. The cash-to-cash cycle is the length of time from when a company purchases an item of inventory to when it collects cash from its sale, reduced by the days it takes to pay the related accounts payable. How long is Ambroise's cash-to-cash cycle?
  e. Assume that Ambroise finances its inventory with a working capital loan from the bank. If Ambroise could improve its inventory management system and reduce the days to sell inventory to an average of 50 days, how much lower would the company's bank loan be?

AP12-13 (ROE, ROA, and gross profit)

The following financial information relates to Smooth Suds Brewery Ltd. (amounts in thousands):

	2014	2015	2016
Sales	$18,360	$25,840	$36,120
Average total assets	23,715	31,965	47,340
Average shareholders' equity	14,664	22,415	31,515
Net income	715	1,845	3,580
Gross profit	9,180	13,954	19,866

Required:
For each year:
  a. Calculate the return on equity. Comment on the trend in this ratio.
  b. Calculate the return on assets. Comment on the trend in this ratio.
  c. Calculate the company's gross profit margin. Comment on the trend in this ratio.
  d. Comment on the profitability of Smooth Suds Brewery Ltd.

AP12-14 (Debt to equity, debt as a percentage of total capitalization, and interest coverage)

Artscan Enterprises' financial data are as follows:

	2014	2015	2016
Income before depreciation, amortization, interest, and taxes	$1,650	$2,625	$3,300
Interest expense	150	340	435
Cash	50	115	225
Current liabilities (does not include any debt)	600	800	1,200
Bank loan payable (all long-term)	2,000	4,000	4,500
Shareholders' equity	4,250	5,500	7,250

Required:
a. Calculate the debt to equity, net debt as a percentage of total capitalization, and interest coverage ratios.
b. Comment on the solvency position of Artscan Enterprises.

AP12-15 (Debt to equity, debt as a percentage of total capitalization, and interest coverage)

Silver City Ltd.'s financial data are as follows:

	2014	2015	2016
Income before depreciation, amortization, interest, and taxes	$6,900	$7,200	$5,700
Interest expense	380	340	280
Cash	200	260	310
Current liabilities (does not include any debt)	1,010	1,900	2,700
Bank loan payable (all long-term)	5,500	6,100	5,200
Shareholders' equity	6,500	6,900	7,600

Required:
a. Calculate the debt to equity, debt as a percentage of total capitalization, and interest coverage ratios.
b. Comment on the solvency position of Silver City Ltd.

AP12-16 (Transaction effects on ratios)

Two lists follow: one for ratios (including the ratio prior to the transactions) and another for transactions.

Ratios:
1. Current ratio, 1.2:1
2. Quick ratio, 0.6:1
3. Accounts receivable turnover, 12 times
4. Inventory turnover, 6 times
5. Return on assets, 10%
6. Return on equity, 15%

Transactions:
1. Goods costing $200,000 are sold to customers on credit for $380,000.
2. Accounts receivable of $140,000 are collected.
3. Inventory costing $110,000 is purchased from suppliers.
4. A long-term bank loan for $500,000 is arranged with the bank, and the company receives the cash at the beginning of the year.
5. The bank loan carries an interest rate of 18% and the interest payment is made at the end of the year. Assume no interest expense had previously been recognized.
6. The company uses $40,000 to buy short-term investments.
7. New common shares are issued for $250,000.

Required:
State the immediate effect (increase, decrease, or no effect) of each transaction on each ratio. You may want to format your answer in a table with the ratios across the top, and the transactions down the left side.

AP12-17 (Asset investment effect on ratios)

Beachwood Manufacturing Inc., a manufacturer of wood furniture in Nova Scotia, has approached you to make a private equity investment in the company. The owner has provided you with financial statements for the years ended December 31 and other relevant information. Selected data for the past three years are as follows:

In thousands $	2016	2015	2014
Cash	$ 5,900	$ 3,200	$ 1,450
Accounts receivable	8,800	6,800	6,200
Inventory	9,500	7,000	6,850
Property, plant, and equipment	20,300	15,000	15,500
Total assets	44,500	32,000	30,000
Current liabilities (does not include any debt)	14,000	13,000	12,500
Long-term debt	18,000	8,000	8,000
Total shareholders' equity	12,500	11,000	9,500
Sales revenue	50,000	48,000	45,000
Cost of goods sold	30,000	28,800	27,450
Earnings before interest and taxes	6,953	6,245	6,030
Interest expense	1,620	1,245	1,230
Earnings before taxes	5,333	5,000	4,800
Net income	4,000	3,750	3,600

Other information:
On December 30, 2016, Beachwood purchased the assets of another small furniture manufacturer as part of an expansion plan. Beachwood paid $10 million for the assets and financed them entirely by borrowing. Beachwood is seeking a private equity investor to invest $8 million and will use the proceeds to reduce the debt from the purchase. The $10 million purchase consisted of $2 million of accounts receivable, $2.2 million of inventory, and $5.8 million of property, plant, and equipment.

Required:
a. Start your analysis by reviewing the company's historical performance. Calculate and comment on the receivables and inventory turnover ratios for the three years. For 2014, use year-end values, not averages, for the assets in your calculations.
b. Next, review the solvency and profitability of the company. Calculate and comment on the debt to equity, interest coverage, return on assets, and return on equity for the company. For 2014, use year-end values, not averages, for the assets and equity in your calculations.
c. You realize that Beachwood bought a large amount of assets right at the year end and that those assets are included on the 2016 statement of financial position, but that the company has not used them yet to generate any sales. Therefore, including the assets in your values distorts your analysis. You decide to recalculate the turnover ratios and return on assets excluding the new assets. Comment on your results.
d. Finally, adjust the liability and equity side of the 2016 statement of financial position to see what it will look like once the company obtains the new equity financing and pays down the debt. Recalculate the debt to equity ratio and return on equity under the new capital structure. Comment on your results.
e. Assume that, as a result of the acquisition, Beachwood expects its sales revenue to grow at 1.3 times the growth experienced in 2016, while its gross margin percentage will remain constant. What impact would this have on the company's 2017 gross margin?
f. Comment on the usefulness of retrospective analysis and of using the financial statements alone to make investment decisions.

AP12-18 (Equity analysis ratios)

Two companies in the transportation industry had the following information:

	Company 1	Company 2
Basic earnings per share	$ 0.87	$ 0.67
Market price per share	$ 11.82	$ 25.26
Dividends per share	$ 0.475	$ 0.535
Cash flows from operating activities ($ thousands)	$64,621	$235,786
Net capital expenditures ($ thousands)	$ 6,155	$ 75,042

Required:
a. Calculate the P/E ratios for both companies and comment on which is more affordable from that perspective.
b. Calculate the dividend payout ratio and dividend yield for both companies and comment on the results.

c. Determine the net free cash flows of both companies. Comment on what these amounts represent.

d. What picture do you have of each company based on the financial information provided and the ratios you have calculated?

AP12-19 (Analysis of assets)

You have inherited money from your grandparents and a friend suggests that you consider buying shares in Galena Ski Products, which manufactures skis and bindings. Because you may need to sell the shares within the next two years to finance your university education, you start your analysis of the company data by calculating (1) working capital, (2) the current ratio, and (3) the quick ratio. Galena's statement of financial position is as follows:

Current assets	
Cash	$154,000
Inventory	185,000
Prepaid expenses	21,000
Non-current assets	
Land	50,000
Building and equipment	145,000
Other	15,000
Total	$570,000
Current liabilities	$165,000
Long-term debt	190,000
Share capital	80,000
Retained earnings	135,000
Total	$570,000

Required:

a. What amount of working capital is currently maintained? Comment on the adequacy of this amount.

b. Your preference is to have a quick ratio of at least 0.80 and a current ratio of at least 2.00. How do the existing ratios compare with your criteria? Based on these two ratios, how would you evaluate the company's current asset position?

c. The company currently sells only on a cash basis and had sales of $900,000 this past year. How would you expect a change from cash to credit sales to affect the current and quick ratios?

d. Galena's statement of financial position is presented just before the company begins making shipments to retailers for its fall and winter season. How would your evaluation change if these balances existed in late February, following completion of its primary business for the skiing season?

e. How would Galena's situation as either a public company or private company affect your decision to invest?

AP12-20 (Ratio analysis over time)

The following information comes from the accounting records of Hercep Ltd. for the first three years of its existence:

	2014	2015	2016
Statement of Financial Position			
Assets			
Cash	$ 22,500	$ 20,000	$ 25,000
Accounts receivable	67,500	50,000	145,000
Inventory	110,000	130,000	220,000
Capital assets (net)	430,000	450,000	500,000
Other assets	232,000	210,000	266,400
	$862,000	$860,000	$1,156,400
Liabilities and equity			
Accounts payable	$100,000	$ 50,000	$ 100,000
Long-term debt	200,000	250,000	500,000
Common shares	525,000	525,000	525,000
Retained earnings	37,000	35,000	31,400
	$862,000	$860,000	$1,156,400

	2014	2015	2016
Statement of Earnings			
Sales	$ 700,000	$ 800,000	$ 900,000
Cost of goods sold	(420,000)	(540,000)	(630,000)
Other expenses	(170,000)	(220,000)	(218,000)
	110,000	40,000	52,000
Income tax	(33,000)	(12,000)	(15,600)
Net income	$ 77,000	$ 28,000	$ 36,400

Required:
a. Based on above information, analyze and comment on the changes in the company's profitability and liquidity, in addition to the management of accounts receivable and inventory from 2014 to 2016.
b. Based on the above information, analyze and comment on the company's use of leverage from 2014 to 2016.

AP12-21 (Ratio analysis of two companies)

You have obtained the financial statements of A-Tec and Bi-Sci, two new companies in the high-tech industry. Both companies have just completed their second full year of operations. You have acquired the following information for an analysis of the companies (amounts in thousands):

	A-Tec		Bi-Sci	
	2016	2015	2016	2015
Cash	$ 10	$ 0	$ 25	$ 25
Accounts receivable	195	140	120	100
Inventory	130	100	110	100
Prepaid expenses	5	5	5	5
Capital assets (net)	350	300	230	160
Current liabilities	110	125	50	50
Long-term debt	200	220	0	0
Share capital—common shares	100	100	220	220
Retained earnings	280	100	220	120
Sales (all credit sales)	1,900	1,300	1,250	1,200
Cost of goods sold	1,250	900	910	900
Interest expense	20	22	–	–
Taxes (30%)	77	56	64	56
Net income	180	130	150	130

Required:
a. Calculate the following ratios for the two companies for the two years:
   i. Current ratio
   ii. Accounts receivable turnover
   iii. Inventory turnover
   iv. Debt to equity
   v. Interest coverage
   vi. Gross margin ratio
   vii. Net profit margin
   viii. Return on assets
   ix. Return on equity
b. Write a brief analysis of the two companies based on the information given and the ratios calculated. Be sure to discuss issues of short-term liquidity, activity, solvency, and profitability. Which company appears to be the better investment for the shareholder? Explain. Which company appears to be the better credit risk for the lender? Explain. Is there any other information you would like to have to complete your analysis?

AP12-22 (Compare ratios and comment on results)

Selected financial data for two intense competitors in a recent year follow (amounts in millions):

	Zeus Corporation	Mars Company
Statement of income data:		
Net sales	$3,350	$ 6,810
Cost of goods sold	2,980	5,740
Selling and administrative expenses	95	410
Interest expense	130	175
Other expenses	8	0
Income taxes	62	110
Net income	$ 75	$ 375
Statement of cash flows data:		
Net cash inflow from operating activities	$ 125	$ 260
Net increase in cash during the year	10	37
Statement of financial position data:		
End-of-year balances:		
Current assets	$1,020	$1,620
Property, plant, and equipment (net)	1,865	2,940
Other assets	720	1,020
Total assets	$3,605	$5,580
Current liabilities	$ 575	$ 830
Long-term debt	2,220	3,130
Total shareholders' equity	810	1,620
Total liabilities and shareholders' equity	$3,605	$5,580
Beginning-of-year balances:		
Total assets	$3,250	$5,160
Total shareholders' equity	750	1,245
Other data:		
Average net receivables	$ 350	$ 790
Average inventory	290	575

Required:

    a. For each company, calculate the following ratios:

        i. Average collection period for receivables
       ii. Days to sell inventory
      iii. Current ratio
      iv. Net debt as a percentage of total capitalization
       v. Interest coverage
      vi. Return on assets
     vii. Return on equity

    b. Compare the financial position and performance of the two companies, and comment on their relative strengths and weaknesses.

User Perspective Problems

UP12-1 (Use of ratios in debt restrictions)

Contracts with lenders typically place restrictions on a company's activities in an attempt to ensure that the company will be able to repay both the interest and the principal on the debt owed to the lenders. These restrictions are frequently stated in terms of ratios. For instance, a restriction could be that the debt to equity ratio cannot exceed 1.0. If it does exceed 1.0, the debt covered by the restrictions becomes due immediately. The other commonly used ratio is the current ratio.

Required:
Explain why the debt to equity and current ratios might be used as restrictions. How do they protect the lender?

UP12-2 (Cross-sectional analysis)

Required:
In using cross-sectional analysis to evaluate performance, what factors should an investor match in choosing companies for comparison? Why are these factors important?

UP12-3 (Understanding the business)

Understanding the nature of the business is important for analysts. It helps them interpret the results but it also helps them focus their analysis on the ratios that are key for the industry or strategy being pursued.

Required:
a. From the ratios discussed in the chapter, identify three ratios you think would be key measures of performance for a retail clothing business that operates inside malls.
b. Which ratios would be key measures of performance or efficiency for a hydroelectric utility?

UP12-4 (Use of ROA in performance measurement)

Management compensation plans typically specify performance criteria in terms of financial statement ratios. For instance, a plan might specify that management must achieve a certain level of return on investment—for example, ROA.

Required:
If managers were trying to maximize their compensation, how could they manipulate the ROA ratio to achieve this goal?

UP12-5 (Use of cash flow ratios)

There is judgement involved in preparing financial statements. For example, management must often estimate warranty expense and bad debts expense. Management may also need to select an accounting policy if accounting standards allow a choice. Ultimately, these estimates and decisions affect the determination of net income.

Required:
Do you believe that financial statement ratios using cash flows are more reliable than measures of performance that use net income? Discuss.

UP12-6 (Types of information)

A friend of yours has received a scholarship and wants to invest the funds for a year, because she earned enough money in her summer job to pay for her current academic year. She explains to you that she went to an on-line investing site that had lots of ratios calculated for companies and has selected the company with the highest ROE to invest in. She has asked your advice on if there is any information other than ratios she should be considering and what you think of her decision to select based on ROE.

Required:
a. Explain to your friend that, although ratio analysis provides a good indication as to a company's financial strength, there is much more information available that an informed investor should consider before making any investment decisions. Provide her with several examples of additional information to consider.
b. Comment on your friend's choice of ROE as the sole criterion.

UP12-7 (Using ratios to evaluate creditworthiness)

You are the lending officer in a bank and a new customer has approached you for a working capital loan. A working capital loan is intended to help a business finance the fluctuations in daily cash flows that arise from long cash-to-cash cycles in operating a business.

Required:
Explain how you would use the accounts receivable turnover ratio, inventory turnover ratio, and accounts payable turnover ratio to assist you in your analysis.

UP12-8 (Use of ratios in decision-making)

Managers, investors, and creditors usually have a specific focus when making decisions about a business.

Required:
Each of the following independent cases asks one or more questions. Identify the ratio or ratios that would help the user answer the question and/or identify areas for further analysis:

    a. A company's net income has declined. Is the decrease in net income due to:
       i. a decrease in sales or an increase in cost of goods sold?
       ii. an increase in total operating expenses?
       iii. an increase in a specific expense, such as tax expense?
    b. Is the company collecting its accounts receivable on a timely basis?
    c. Does the company rely more heavily on long-term debt financing than other companies in the same industry?
    d. In a comparison of two companies, which company is using its assets more effectively?
    e. In a comparison of two companies, which company has used the capital invested in it more profitably?
    f. Has the decline in the economy affected the company's ability to pay its accounts payable?
    g. Has the company been successful in reducing its investment in inventories as a result of installing a new ordering system?

UP12-9 (Discuss value of comparability)

One enhancing qualitative characteristic that underlies financial accounting is comparability. As you will recall, comparability is the similarities of financial information between different companies, and consistency of the financial information produced by a company over time, that allows financial statement users to make meaningful and equal comparisons. Two of the many ways of achieving comparability for users are by limiting the number of different ways transactions may be recorded, and by specifying how assets, liabilities, equities, revenues, and expenses will be reported in the financial statements.

    One argument against comparability is that it limits companies' ability to choose among accounting methods, and thus may result in financial reports that may not be agreeable to management or best suited to the particular circumstances.

Required:
Discuss the pros and cons of limiting accounting choices, with reference to the analysis of financial statements.

Reading and Interpreting Published Financial Statements

RI12-1 (Ratio analysis for public company)

The financial statements for **Danier Leather Inc.** are in Appendix A.

Required:
Use the financial statements to answer the following questions:

    a. Calculate the following ratios for 2014 and 2013. For the 2013 ratios, use the year-end balance sheet amounts, rather than an average for the year.
       i. Gross profit margin
       ii. Net profit margin
       iii. Inventory turnover
       iv. Debt to equity and net debt as a percentage of total capitalization
       v. Return on assets and return on equity

    b. Comment on Danier's profitability and use of leverage over the period.
    c. Calculate and comment on Danier's current ratio and quick ratio for both years. What factor leads these ratios to be high for Danier? Why might your interpretation of its current ratio depend on if you were an investor or a creditor?

RI12-2 (Comparison of two companies in same industry)

The balance sheets and statements of earnings and loss for **Le Château Inc.** are in Exhibits 12-11A and B. In Canada, Le Château and Danier Leather are both in the fashion industry. Both companies manufacture and retail goods, although they sell in different segments of the fashion market. Danier operates in the niche segment of quality leather goods, primarily coats and accessories, whereas Le Château sells a wide range of clothing and accessories targeted to the young adult market.

EXHIBIT 12-11A	LE CHÂTEAU INC.'S 2014 CONSOLIDATED BALANCE SHEETS

CONSOLIDATED BALANCE SHEETS

As at January 25, 2014 and January 26, 2013
[In thousands of Canadian dollars]

	2014 $	2013 $
ASSETS		
Current assets		
Cash	1,446	1,783
Accounts receivable [note 6]	1,476	1,906
Income taxes refundable	6,663	3,211
Derivative financial instruments	418	215
Inventories [notes 6 and 7]	124,878	123,218
Prepaid expenses	2,292	1,890
Total current assets	137,173	132,223
Property and equipment [notes 8 and 12]	69,870	83,315
Intangible assets [note 9]	3,815	4,672
	210,858	220,210
LIABILITIES AND SHAREHOLDERS' EQUITY		
Current liabilities		
Bank indebtedness [note 6]	30,767	13,034
Trade and other payables [note 10]	19,553	20,718
Deferred revenue	3,712	3,558
Current portion of provisions [note 11]	265	228
Current portion of long-term debt [note 12]	7,987	9,844
Total current liabilities	62,284	47,382
Long-term debt [note 12]	7,843	14,290
Provisions [note 11]	391	530
Deferred income taxes [note 14]	1,829	2,298
Deferred lease credits	13,412	15,912
Total liabilities	85,759	80,412
Shareholders' equity		
Share capital [note 13]	42,960	42,740
Contributed surplus	3,581	2,664
Retained earnings	78,253	94,239
Accumulated other comprehensive income	305	155
Total shareholders' equity	125,099	139,798
	210,858	220,210

EXHIBIT 12-11B	LE CHÂTEAU INC.'S 2014 CONSOLIDATED STATEMENTS OF LOSS

CONSOLIDATED STATEMENTS OF LOSS

Years ended January 25, 2014 and January 26, 2013
[in thousands of Canadian dollars, except per share information]

	2014 $	2013 $
Sales [note 20]	274,840	274,827
Cost of sales and expenses		
Cost of sales [note 7]	101,770	92,565
Selling [note 8]	155,859	155,561
General and administrative [notes 8 and 9]	36,218	35,847
	293,847	283,973
Results from operating activities	(19,007)	(9,146)
Finance costs	2,714	3,063
Finance income	(13)	(23)
Loss before income taxes	(21,708)	(12,186)
Income tax recovery [note 14]	(5,722)	(3,469)
Net loss	(15,986)	(8,717)
Net loss per share [note 17]		
Basic	(0.59)	(0.34)
Diluted	(0.59)	(0.34)
Weighted average number of shares outstanding	27,288,766	25,658,585

Required:

Use the information provided, the ratios you calculated for Danier Leather in problem RI12-1, and Le Château's financial statements to answer the following questions:

    a. Prepare a common-size analysis of the statements of income (loss) for the two companies for both years. Why do you think the cost of sales percentages are so different for the two companies? In which areas does Le Château seem to have an advantage? In which areas does Danier have an advantage?

    b. Compare the current and quick ratios for the two companies. Which company is more liquid? Are you surprised by the large difference between the current ratio and the quick ratio for the companies? Why or why not?

    c. Compare the inventory turnover of the two companies.

RI12-3 (Ratio analysis for public company)

Big Rock Brewery Inc. is Calgary-based public company. The company is a producer of all-natural craft beers and cider. Its products are sold in nine provinces and three territories in Canada. The 2013 consolidated statements of income, financial position, and cash flows are shown in Exhibits 12-12A to C (amounts in thousands).

EXHIBIT 12-12A	BIG ROCK BREWERY INC.'S 2013 CONSOLIDATED STATEMENTS OF COMPREHENSIVE INCOME

BIG ROCK BREWERY INC.
Consolidated Statements of Comprehensive Income
(In thousands of Canadian dollars, except per share amounts)

	Year ended	
	December 30, 2013	December 30, 2012
Net revenue (Notes 3.2 and 4)	$ 41,587	$ 46,057
Cost of sales (Notes 5 and 24)	20,260	21,149
Gross profit	21,327	24,908
Expenses		
Selling expenses (Notes 6 and 23)	12,910	13,987
General and administrative (Notes 7 and 24)	4,821	4,945
Depreciation and amortization	314	358
Operating expenses	18,045	19,290

continued

| EXHIBIT 12-12A | **BIG ROCK BREWERY INC.'S 2013 CONSOLIDATED STATEMENTS OF COMPREHENSIVE INCOME (continued)** |

	Year ended	
	December 30, 2013	December 30, 2012
Operating profit	3,282	5,618
Finance costs (Note 8)	9	93
Other income	286	351
Other expenses	109	147
Income before income taxes	3,450	5,729
Current income tax expense (Note 9)	2,485	426
Deferred income tax expense (recovery) (Note 9)	(1,586)	1,168
Net income and comprehensive income for the period	$ 2,551	$ 4,135
Net income per share (Note 10)		
Basic and diluted	$ 0.42	$ 0.68

| EXHIBIT 12-12B | **BIG ROCK BREWERY INC.'S 2013 CONSOLIDATED STATEMENTS OF FINANCIAL POSITION** |

BIG ROCK BREWERY INC.
Consolidated Statements of Financial Position
(In thousands of Canadian dollars)

	December 30, 2013	December 30, 2012
ASSETS		
Non-current assets		
Property, plant and equipment (Note 11)	$ 35,142	$ 35,277
Intangible assets (Note 12)	108	128
	35,250	35,405
Current		
Inventories (Note 13)	2,983	3,892
Accounts receivable (Notes 14 and 22)	1,353	2,358
Prepaid expenses and other (Note 15)	754	364
Cash	2,317	4,281
	7,407	10,895
Total assets	$ 42,657	$ 46,300
LIABILITIES AND SHAREHOLDERS' EQUITY		
EQUITY		
Shareholders' capital (Note 16)	$ 100,109	$ 100,109
Contributed surplus (Notes 16 and 17)	892	701
Accumulated deficit	(71,043)	(68,739)
	29,958	32,071
LIABILITIES		
Non-current		
Long term debt (Notes 18 and 22)	—	1,342
Share-based payments (Note 17)	687	238
Deferred income taxes (Note 9)	4,745	6,331
	5,432	7,911
Current		
Accounts payable and accrued liabilities (Notes 19 and 22)	4,100	3,978
Dividends payable (Notes 20 and 22)	1,214	1,214
Current portion of long-term debt (Notes 18 and 22)	—	700
Current taxes payable (Note 9)	1,953	426
	7,267	6,318
Commitments (Note 26)		
Total liabilities and shareholders' equity	$ 42,657	$ 46,300

EXHIBIT 12-12C	BIG ROCK BREWERY INC.'S 2013 CONSOLIDATED STATEMENTS OF CASH FLOWS

BIG ROCK BREWERY INC.
Consolidated Statements of Cash Flows
(*in thousands of Canadian dollars*)

	Year ended	
	December 30, 2013	December 30, 2012
OPERATING ACTIVITIES		
Net income for the period	$ 2,551	$ 4,135
Items not affecting cash:		
Depreciation and amortization	3,157	3,228
Gain on sale of assets	(13)	(19)
Stock-based compensation	640	446
Deferred income tax expense (recovery)	(1,586)	1,168
Net change in non-cash working capital related to operations (note 25)	3,148	1,496
Cash provided by operating activities	7,897	10,454
FINANCING ACTIVITIES		
Dividend payments	(4,855)	(4,850)
Principal repayments of long-term debt	(2,042)	(641)
Cash received on exercise of options	—	131
Cash used in financing activities	(6,897)	(5,360)
INVESTING ACTIVITIES		
Purchase of property, plant and equipment	(2,992)	(1,487)
Purchase of intangibles	(6)	—
Proceeds from sale of equipment	34	19
Cash used in investing activities	(2,964)	(1,468)
Net increase (decrease) in cash	(1,964)	3,626
Cash, beginning of year	4,281	655
Cash, end of year	$ 2,317	$ 4,281
Supplemental cash-flow information		
Cash interest paid	$ 52	$ 103
Cash taxes paid	958	—

Required:
Based on the financial statements in Exhibits 12-12A to C, answer each of the following questions:
   a. Calculate the following ratios for both 2013 and 2012:
      i. Current ratio
      ii. Quick ratio
      iii. Inventory turnover
      iv. Days to sell inventory
   b. Comment on Big Rock's liquidity.
   c. Calculate the following ratios for both 2013 and 2012, and comment on the changes:
      i. Return on assets
      ii. Return on equity
   d. Comment on the use of leverage by Big Rock, using appropriate ratios to support your analysis.
   e. Calculate Big Rock's net free cash flow for 2013 and 2012. What does this tell us about the company's financial flexibility?
   f. What do you know about Big Rock given that its basic and diluted earnings per share amounts are the same?

RI12-4 (Ratio analysis for public company)

Cineplex Inc. is the largest movie exhibition company in Canada. It operates theatres in 10 provinces across Canada. The company's financial statements are presented in Exhibits 12-13A to C.

EXHIBIT 12-13A	CINEPLEX INC.'S 2013 CONSOLIDATED BALANCE SHEETS

Cineplex Inc.
Consolidated Balance Sheets

(expressed in thousands of Canadian dollars)	December 31, 2013	December 31, 2012 (note 2)	January 1, 2012 (note 2)
Assets			
Current assets			
Cash and cash equivalents (note 6)	$ 44,140	$ 48,665	$ 50,145
Trade and other receivables (note 7)	100,891	77,278	70,473
Inventories (note 8)	7,234	5,193	4,124
Prepaid expenses and other current assets	6,838	3,047	3,727
	159,103	134,183	128,469
Non-current assets			
Property, equipment and leaseholds (note 9)	459,112	418,498	389,674
Deferred income taxes (note 10)	17,635	53,528	12,052
Fair value of interest rate swap agreements (note 4)	92	–	–
Interests in joint ventures (note 11)	44,359	41,623	26,163
Intangible assets (note 12)	113,601	78,460	84,379
Goodwill (note 13)	797,476	608,929	608,929
	$ 1,591,378	$ 1,335,221	$ 1,249,666
Liabilities			
Current liabilities			
Accounts payable and accrued expenses (note 14)	$ 157,333	$ 129,499	$ 115,076
Share-based compensation (note 15)	12,151	–	1,331
Dividends payable (note 16)	7,552	7,063	6,285
Income taxes payable (note 10)	2,656	13,654	17,485
Deferred revenue	136,373	106,253	93,955
Finance lease obligations (note 18)	2,394	2,222	2,411
Fair value of interest rate swap agreements (note 4)	635	513	565
Convertible debentures (note 21)	–	–	76,864
	319,094	259,204	313,972
Non-current liabilities			
Share-based compensation (note 15)	15,622	12,223	9,466
Long-term debt (note 17)	217,151	148,066	167,531
Fair value of interest rate swap agreements (note 4)	–	273	1,199
Finance lease obligations (note 18)	17,722	20,548	26,474
Post-employment benefit obligations (note 19)	6,522	6,274	5,688
Other liabilities (note 20)	170,125	141,319	103,727
Convertible debentures (note 21)	96,870	–	–
	524,012	328,703	314,085
Total liabilities	843,106	587,907	628,057
Equity			
Share capital (note 22)	853,411	847,235	764,801
Deficit	(107,323)	(102,547)	(140,469)
Accumulated other comprehensive loss	(1,715)	(1,142)	(2,723)
Contributed surplus	3,899	3,768	–
	748,272	747,314	621,609
	$ 1,591,378	$ 1,335,221	$ 1,249,666

EXHIBIT 12-13B   **CINEPLEX INC.'S 2013 CONSOLIDATED STATEMENTS OF OPERATIONS**

Cineplex Inc.
Consolidated Statements of Operations

(expressed in thousands of Canadian dollars)

	2013	2012 (note 2)
Revenues		
Box office	$ 665,306	$ 638,296
Concessions	350,353	329,332
Other	155,608	124,873
	1,171,267	1,092,501
Expenses		
Film cost	346,373	331,281
Cost of concessions	74,693	68,398
Depreciation and amortization	70,890	62,163
Loss (gain) on disposal of assets	4,372	(2,352)
(Gain) on acquisition of business (note 3 d)	—	(24,752)
Other costs (note 23)	551,819	495,537
Share of income of joint ventures	(3,850)	(3,263)
Interest expense	10,743	12,585
Interest income	(307)	(205)
	1,054,733	939,392
Income before income taxes	116,534	153,109
Provision for income taxes		
Current (note 10)	3,608	31,436
Deferred (note 10)	29,369	1,189
	32,977	32,625
Net income	$ 83,557	$ 120,484
Basic net income per share (note 24)	$ 1.33	$ 1.98
Diluted net income per share (note 24)	$ 1.32	$ 1.97

EXHIBIT 12-13C   **CINEPLEX INC.'S 2013 CONSOLIDATED STATEMENTS OF CASH FLOWS**

Cineplex Inc.
Consolidated Statements of Cash Flows
For the years ended December 31, 2013 and 2012

(expressed in thousands of Canadian dollars)

	2013	2012 (note 2)
Cash provided by (used in)		
Operating activities		
Net income	$ 83,557	$120,484
Adjustments to reconcile net income to net cash provided by operating activities		
Depreciation and amortization of property, equipment and leaseholds, and intangible assets	70,890	62,163
Amortization of tenant inducements, rent averaging liabilities and fair value lease contract liabilities	(6,735)	(5,033)
Accretion of debt issuance costs and other non-cash interest	2,001	562
Loss (gain) on disposal of assets	4,372	(2,352)
(Gain) on acquisition of business	—	(24,752)
Deferred income taxes	29,369	1,189
Interest rate swap agreements – non-cash interest	(939)	1,485
Non-cash share-based compensation	1,826	2,108
Accretion of convertible debentures	274	323
Net change in interests in joint ventures	(2,686)	4,356
Tenant inducements	5,417	7,615
Changes in operating assets and liabilities (note 26)	37,302	7,486
Net cash provided by operating activities	224,648	175,634

continued

EXHIBIT 12-13C	CINEPLEX INC.'S 2013 CONSOLIDATED STATEMENTS OF CASH FLOWS (continued)		
		2013	**2012** (note 2)
Investing activities			
Proceeds from sale of assets		3,573	3,683
Purchases of property, equipment and leaseholds		(62,410)	(72,242)
Acquisition of business, net of cash acquired (note 3)		(238,338)	(2,811)
Net cash invested in CDCP		(50)	(438)
Net cash used in investing activities		(297,225)	(71,808)
Financing activities			
Dividends paid		(88,130)	(80,794)
Borrowings (repayments) under credit facility, net		70,000	(20,000)
Repayment of debt acquired with business (note 3)		(12,875)	—
Payments under finance leases		(2,277)	(2,104)
Proceeds from issuance of shares		—	501
Net proceeds from issuance of convertible debentures (note 21)		103,469	—
Deferred financing fees (notes 17 and 21)		(2,135)	—
Shares repurchased and cancelled		—	(1,786)
Repayment of convertible debentures at maturity		—	(1,123)
Net cash provided by (used in) financing activities		68,052	(105,306)
Decrease in cash and cash equivalents		(4,525)	(1,480)
Cash and cash equivalents – Beginning of year		48,665	50,145
Cash and cash equivalents – End of year		$ 44,140	$ 48,665
Supplemental information			
Cash paid for interest		$ 9,421	$ 10,293
Cash paid for income taxes		$ 14,148	$ 35,268

Required:

a. Assess the company's operating effectiveness by calculating and comparing the activity ratios for Cineplex for 2012 and 2013. (Note: use other revenues for the accounts receivable turnover ratio; use cost of concessions as cost of goods sold.)

    i. Based on those ratios, do you think Cineplex is operating more effectively in 2013? Support your conclusion.

    ii. What other information would you like to have to assess its management of receivables, inventory, and payables?

b. Assess the financial riskiness of the company by calculating and comparing the following ratios. Based on those ratios, do you think the financial risk on the company has decreased in 2013? Support your conclusion.

    i. Current ratio

    ii. Quick ratio

    iii. Debt to equity

    iv. Interest coverage

c. Calculate the company's profitability by determining the following ratios and comment on them:

    i. Net profit margin

    ii. Return on equity

    iii. Return on assets

d. Determine the company's net free cash flow for 2012 and 2013. Has this improved or worsened?

RI12-5 (Ratio analysis of a public company)

Required:

Choose a company as directed by your instructor and answer the following questions:

a. Using the ratios given in the text, prepare an analysis of the company for the past two years with respect to profitability, liquidity, activity, solvency, and equity analysis ratios.

b. Even though the ratios calculated in part "a" do not span a long period of time, discuss the company's financial health. Would you invest in it? Why or why not?

Cases

C12-1 Cedar Appliance Sales and Service Ltd.

Cedar Appliance Sales and Service Ltd. owns several retail and service centres in northern British Columbia. Financial ratios for the company for the years ended December 31, 2016 and 2015, are provided below. For comparative purposes, industry averages have also been provided.

Ratio	2016	2015	Industry Average
Current ratio	1.6:1	1.7:1	2:1
Quick ratio	0.75:1	0.80:1	1:1
Accounts receivable turnover	8 times	7.75 times	12 times
Inventory turnover	4.0 times	3.8 times	7.0 times

The company is in the process of opening two new retail outlets and will need to obtain a line of credit to finance receivables and inventory. To receive a competitive interest rate on its line of credit, it needs to ensure that its liquidity ratios are close to the average for the industry. In particular, the company would like to see the current ratio at 2:1. The company has hired you, an independent consultant, to suggest how it might improve its liquidity ratios.

In preparing your report, you have gathered the following additional information:
1. The company's credit terms to its customers are net 45 days; no discounts are provided for early payment.
2. The company policy is to pay accounts payable every 45 days regardless of the credit terms. Many supplier invoices offer discounts for payments within 30 days.
3. Cedar's policy is to keep high amounts of inventory on hand to ensure that customers will have maximum selection.

Required:
Propose several steps that Cedar Appliance Sales and Service Ltd. might take to improve its liquidity. All suggestions must be ethical.

C12-2 Christine's Yogourt Venture

Christine Wilde is considering opening a frozen yogourt store. One option is to purchase an existing independent store that is available for sale. The seller, Mark Preradovic, has operated the store for three years and has assured Christine that his location, although smaller than the average store, is an above-average performer for the industry. Mark has provided the financial data shown below for his outlet.

Mark's Yogourt Plus Store Selected Financial Results			
	Year 1	Year 2	Year 3
Store size: 1,200 square feet (110 square metres)			
Sales	$240,000	$280,000	$330,000
Gross margin	168,000	196,000	231,000
Other expenses	160,000	180,000	200,000
Net income	$ 8,000	$ 16,000	$ 31,000

Christine has approached you to help her decide. You find the following information on the website of Yogourt Yogourt, a franchisor of similar outlets:
- The average store is 1,500 square feet (140 square metres) and contains six yogourt machines, a topping bar, and seating for 20.
- Sales in the first year average $400,000 and $650,000 for a mature store. It usually takes three years for a store to mature.
- Gross margins on start-up average 70% and normally increase to 75% for established locations.
- Operating costs start at 50% and drop to 43% of sales for mature stores as the fixed costs are spread out.
- The initial investment for a 1,500-square-foot store is $350,000 for machines, franchise fees, and other capital costs, plus $50,000 for liquid assets including inventory.
- Franchisees are expected to invest two thirds of the required investment in equity and arrange to borrow the remaining one third.

You recall that in retail, a key statistic is sales per square foot and you make a note to yourself to factor the different store sizes into your analysis.

Mark is asking $400,000 for his store and explained to Christine: "I am offering you a great deal by just asking for the carrying value of the total assets. I just want to recoup my initial investment plus a little bit more for the time and sweat equity I have put in. I have done all the hard work getting the store established; it should be easy for you now."

Required:

   a. Use financial statement analysis to evaluate the performance of Mark's store compared with the average Yogourt Yogourt franchise.
   b. Based on Mark's most recent financial results and Christine's investment if she pays Mark's asking price, what would be her ROA and ROE compared with a start-up franchise?
   c. What other factors would you want to consider before buying the store?
   d. Do you recommend Christine purchase Mark's store? Why or why not?

C12-3 Hencky Corporation

The management of Hencky Corporation is developing a loan proposal to present to a local investor. The company is looking for a $1-million loan to finance the research and development costs of producing a revolutionary new wearable computer. Most of the loan proceeds will be spent on intangible costs, such as research salaries, and this will therefore be a very risky investment. Because of the risk associated with the project, the investor is requiring some assurance that the company is currently solvent and operating as a going concern.

As the accountant for Hencky Corporation, you have used the most recent financial statements to calculate the following ratios:

	2016	2015
Current ratio	1.8:1	1.7:1
Quick ratio	1.10:1	1.08:1
Accounts receivable turnover	10 times	11 times
Inventory turnover	6 times	5 times
Debt to equity ratio	25.2%	35.8%

Required:

Provide an explanation of how each of the above ratios should be interpreted and what they specifically tell you about Hencky's solvency and ability to continue as a going concern.

ENDNOTES

1. Adam Stanley, "Investing Clubs Put Real Money on the Line," *The Globe and Mail*, November 5, 2013; "MBA Students: Head of the (Asset) Class," *Canadian Business*, November 6, 2012; "The Desautels Capital Management Inc. Unearthed," *The Bull & Bear*, March 31, 2012; Paul Dalby, "MBA Students Start Fund with Their Own Money and Queen's Cash to Do Battle on Bay Street," *Toronto Star*, February 11, 2012; McGill University website, www.mcgill.ca; Queen's University website, www.queensu.ca.
2. Statistics Canada, "National Balance Sheet and Financial Flow Accounts, Fourth Quarter 2013," *The Daily*, March 14, 2014.
3. The market share information in this analysis was obtained from the historic prices section of Yahoo Finance's website (http://ca.finance.yahoo.com) and Stockhouse's price history website (www.stockhouse.com).

Specimen Financial Statements: Danier Leather Incorporated

This appendix includes a number of extracts from the 2014 annual report of **Danier Leather Inc.** These extracts provide an example of the financial reporting of a Canadian public company and are referred to throughout the text. The extracts include:

- management's statement of responsibility for the financial statements
- independent auditor's report to shareholders
- consolidated financial statements
- notes to the consolidated financial statements

Students are encouraged to refer to these financial statement extracts as they move through the text. These extracts provide additional context to help students develop an understanding of the material.

We thank Danier Leather Inc. for granting us permission to include these extracts in the text. The complete annual report of Danier Leather Inc. can be found on the company's website (www.danier.com) or on the Canadian Securities Administrators' SEDAR (System for Electronic Document Analysis and Retrieval) site (www.sedar.com) as well on the companion site for this text and in *WileyPLUS*.

MANAGEMENT'S RESPONSIBILITY FOR FINANCIAL STATEMENTS

The accompanying financial statements and other financial information contained in this Annual Report are the responsibility of management and have been approved by the Board of Directors of Danier Leather Inc. The financial statements have been prepared by management in conformity with International Financial Reporting Standards using management's best estimates and judgments based on currently available information, where appropriate. The financial information contained elsewhere in this Annual Report has been reviewed to ensure consistency with that in the financial statements.

Management is also responsible for a system of internal controls which is designed to provide reasonable assurance that assets are safeguarded, liabilities are recognized and that financial records are properly maintained to provide timely and accurate financial reports.

The Board of Directors is responsible for ensuring that management fulfills its responsibility in respect of financial reporting and internal control. The Audit Committee of the Board, which is comprised solely of unrelated and outside directors, meets regularly to review significant accounting and auditing matters with management and the independent auditors and to review the interim and annual financial statements.

The financial statements have been audited by PricewaterhouseCoopers LLP, the independent auditors, in accordance with Canadian generally accepted auditing standards on behalf of the shareholders. The Auditor's Report outlines the nature of their examination and their opinion on the financial statements. PricewaterhouseCoopers LLP have full and unrestricted access to the Audit Committee to discuss their audit and related findings as to the integrity of the financial reporting.

Jeffrey Wortsman
President and CEO

Bryan Tatoff, CPA, CA
Executive Vice-President, CFO and Secretary

INDEPENDENT AUDITOR'S REPORT TO SHAREHOLDERS

To the Shareholders of Danier Leather Inc.

We have audited the accompanying consolidated financial statements of Danier Leather Inc. and its subsidiaries, which comprise the consolidated balance sheets as at June 28, 2014 and June 29, 2013 and the consolidated statements of earnings (loss) and comprehensive earnings (loss), cash flow, and changes in shareholders' equity for the 52-week period ended June 28, 2014 and 52-week period ended June 29, 2013, and the related notes, which comprise a summary of the significant accounting policies and other explanatory information.

Management's responsibility for the consolidated financial statements

Management is responsible for the preparation and fair presentation of these consolidated financial statements in accordance with International Financial Reporting Standards, and for such internal control as management determines is necessary to enable the preparation of consolidated financial statements that are free from material misstatement, whether due to fraud or error.

Auditor's responsibility

Our responsibility is to express an opinion on these consolidated financial statements based on our audits. We conducted our audits in accordance with Canadian generally accepted auditing standards. Those standards require that we comply with ethical requirements and plan and perform the audits to obtain reasonable assurance about whether the consolidated financial statements are free from material misstatement.

An audit involves performing procedures to obtain audit evidence about the amounts and disclosures in the consolidated financial statements. The procedures selected depend on the auditor's judgment, including the assessment of the risks of material misstatement of the consolidated financial statements, whether due to fraud or error. In making those risk assessments, the auditor considers internal control relevant to the entity's preparation and fair presentation of the consolidated financial statements in order to design audit procedures that are appropriate in the circumstances, but not for the purpose of expressing an opinion on the effectiveness of the entity's internal control. An audit also includes evaluating the appropriateness of accounting policies used and the reasonableness of accounting estimates made by management, as well as evaluating the overall presentation of the consolidated financial statements.

We believe that the audit evidence we have obtained in our audits is sufficient and appropriate to provide a basis for our audit opinion.

Opinion

In our opinion, the consolidated financial statements present fairly, in all material respects, the financial position of Danier Leather Inc. and its subsidiaries as at June 28, 2014 and June 29, 2013 and their financial performance and their cash flows for the 52-week period ended June 28, 2014 and the 52-week period ended June 29, 2013 in accordance with International Financial Reporting Standards.

PricewaterhouseCoopers LLP

Chartered Professional Accountants, Licensed Public Accountants
Toronto, Ontario
August 13, 2014

CONSOLIDATED STATEMENTS OF EARNINGS (LOSS) & COMPREHENSIVE EARNINGS (LOSS)

(thousands of Canadian dollars, except per share amounts and number of shares)

	Years Ended	
	June 28, 2014	June 29, 2013
	52 weeks	52 weeks
Revenue	$141,930	$154,995
Cost of Sales (Note 13)	73,697	76,579
Gross profit	68,233	78,416
Selling, general and administrative expenses (Note 13)	79,086	76,620
Interest income	(118)	(236)
Interest expense	59	51
Earnings (loss) before income taxes	(10,794)	1,981
Provision for (recovery of) income taxes (Note 14)	(3,131)	570
Net earnings (loss) and comprehensive earnings	($7,663)	$1,411
Net earnings (loss) per share:		
Basic	($2.00)	$0.34
Diluted	($2.00)	$0.33
Weighted average number of shares outstanding:		
Basic	3,840,319	4,180,829
Diluted	3,948,336	4,323,619
Number of shares outstanding at period end	3,854,168	3,832,168

See accompanying notes to the consolidated financial statements

CONSOLIDATED BALANCE SHEETS

(thousands of Canadian dollars)

	June 28, 2014	June 29, 2013
Assets		
Current Assets		
Cash	$ 13,507	$ 24,541
Accounts receivable	638	1,197
Income taxes recoverable	3,461	358
Inventories (Note 5)	21,721	22,810
Prepaid expenses	643	803
	39,970	49,709
Non-current Assets		
Property and equipment (Note 6)	16,826	16,034
Computer software (Note 7)	1,459	1,143
Deferred income tax asset (Note 14)	2,374	2,163
	$ 60,629	$ 69,049
Liabilities		
Current Liabilities		
Payables and accruals (Note 9)	$ 9,185	$ 10,101
Deferred revenue	1,511	1,548
Sales return provision (Note 10)	94	99
	10,790	11,748
Non-current Liabilities		
Deferred lease inducements and rent liability	1,432	1,392
	12,222	13,140
Shareholders' Equity		
Share capital (Note 11)	11,772	11,533
Contributed surplus	1,040	954
Retained earnings	35,595	43,422
	48,407	55,909
	$ 60,629	$ 69,049

Contingencies, Guarantees and Commitments (Notes 16 and 17)

Approved by the Board of Directors
August 13, 2014

Jeffrey Wortsman

Jeffrey Wortsman, Director

Edwin F. Hawken, Chairman

Edwin F. Hawken, Chairman

See accompanying notes to the consolidated financial statements

CONSOLIDATED STATEMENTS OF CASH FLOW (thousands of Canadian dollars)

	Years Ended	
	June 28, 2014	June 29, 2013
	52 weeks	*52 weeks*

Cash provided by (used in)
Operating Activities

Net earnings (loss)	($7,663)	$1,411
Adjustments for:		
Amortization of property and equipment	3,517	3,149
Amortization of computer software	791	412
Impairment loss on property and equipment	663	327
Amortization of deferred lease inducement	(75)	(100)
Straight line rent expense	115	121
Stock-based compensation	209	131
Interest income	(118)	(236)
Interest expense	59	51
Provision for (refund of) income taxes	(3,131)	570
Changes in working capital (Note 15)	883	1,348
Interest paid	(107)	(12)
Interest received	133	244
Income taxes (paid) recovered	(183)	(664)
Net cash generated from (used in) operating activities	**(4,907)**	**6,752**

Financing Activities

Subordinate voting shares issued	227	183
Subordinate voting shares repurchased (Note 11)	(275)	(11,399)
Net cash used in financing activities	**(48)**	**(11,216)**

Investing Activities

Acquisition of property and equipment	(4,972)	(4,498)
Acquisition of computer software	(1,107)	(829)
Net cash used in investing activities	**(6,079)**	**(5,327)**

Decrease in cash	(11,034)	(9,791)
Cash, beginning of period	24,541	34,332
Cash, end of period	**$13,507**	**$24,541**

See accompanying notes to the consolidated financial statements

CONSOLIDATED STATEMENTS OF CHANGES IN SHAREHOLDERS' EQUITY

(thousands of Canadian dollars)

	Share Capital	Contributed Surplus	Accumulated Other Comprehensive Income	Retained Earnings	Total
Balance - June 29, 2013	$11,533	$954	$ -	$43,422	$55,909
Net loss	-	-	-	(7,663)	(7,663)
Stock based compensation related to stock options	-	209	-	-	209
Exercise of stock options	350	(123)	-	-	227
Share repurchases (net of tax)	(111)	-	-	(164)	(275)
Balance - June 28, 2014	$11,772	$1,040	$ -	$35,595	$48,407

	Share Capital	Contributed Surplus	Accumulated Other Comprehensive Income	Retained Earnings	Total
Balance - June 30, 2012	$15,040	$925	$-	$49,526	$65,491
Net earnings	-	-	-	1,411	1,411
Stock based compensation related to stock options	-	131	-	-	131
Exercise of stock options	285	(102)	-	-	183
Share repurchases	(3,792)	-	-	(7,515)	(11,307)
Balance - June 29, 2013	$11,533	$954	$-	$43,422	$55,909

See accompanying notes to the consolidated financial statements

NOTES TO CONSOLIDATED FINANCIAL STATEMENTS

For the Years Ended June 28, 2014 and June 29, 2013
(unless otherwise stated, all amounts are in thousands of Canadian dollars)

1.   GENERAL INFORMATION:

Danier Leather Inc. and its subsidiaries ("Danier" or the "Company") comprise a vertically integrated designer, manufacturer, distributor and retailer of leather apparel and accessories. Danier Leather Inc. is a corporation existing under the Business Corporations Act (Ontario) and is domiciled in Canada. The Company's subordinate voting shares (the "Subordinate Voting Shares") are listed on the Toronto Stock Exchange (the "TSX") under the symbol "DL". The address of its registered head office is 2650 St. Clair Avenue West, Toronto, Ontario, M6N 1M2, Canada.

The Company's operations are focused on the design, manufacture, distribution and retail of leather apparel and accessories in Canada. As such, the Company presents one operating segment in its consolidated financial statements.

Due to the seasonal nature of the retail business and the Company's product line, the results of operation for any interim period are not necessarily indicative of the results of operations to be expected for the fiscal year. A significant portion of the Company's sales and earnings are typically generated during the second fiscal quarter, which includes the holiday selling season. Sales are usually lowest and losses are typically experienced during the period from April to September.

2.   BASIS OF PREPARATION:

(a)   Statement of Compliance

These consolidated financial statements have been prepared in accordance with International Financial Reporting Standards ("IFRS") as issued by the International Accounting Standards Board ("IASB") and using the accounting policies described herein. These consolidated financial statements were approved by the Board of Directors of the Company on August 13, 2014.

(b)   Basis of Presentation

These consolidated financial statements have been prepared on a going concern basis, under the historical cost convention, except for the following items which are measured at fair value:

- Financial instruments at fair value through profit and loss; and
- Liabilities for cash-settled share-based compensation plans.

(c)   Functional and Presentation Currency

These consolidated financial statements are presented in Canadian dollars ("CC$"), the Company's functional currency. All financial information is presented in thousands, except per share amounts, which are presented in whole dollars, and number of shares, which are presented as whole numbers.

(d)   Use of Estimates, Judgments and Assumptions

The preparation of these consolidated financial statements in accordance with IFRS requires management to make certain judgments, estimates and assumptions that affect the application of accounting policies and the reported amounts of assets and liabilities and disclosure of contingent liabilities at the date of the consolidated financial statements, and the reported amounts of revenues and expenses during the period.

Judgment is commonly used in determining whether a balance or transaction should be recognized in the consolidated financial statements, and estimates and assumptions are more commonly used in determining the measurement of recognized transactions and balances. However, judgments and estimates are often interrelated.

Management has applied its judgment in its assessment of the classification of leases and financial instruments, the recognition of tax provisions, determining the tax rates used for measuring deferred taxes, and identifying the indicators of impairment of property and equipment.

Estimates are used when estimating the useful lives of property and equipment and computer software for the purposes of depreciation and amortization, when determining the number of share-based payments that will ultimately vest, when accounting for or measuring items such as inventory provisions, gift card breakage, assumptions underlying income taxes, sales and use taxes and sales return provisions, certain fair value measures including those related to the valuation of share-based payments and financial instruments and when testing assets for impairment. These estimates depend upon subjective and complex judgments about matters that may be uncertain, and changes in those estimates could materially impact the consolidated financial statements. Volatile equity, foreign currency and energy markets, the potential illiquidity of credit markets and unpredictable changes in consumer spending have combined to increase the uncertainty inherent in such estimates and assumptions. As future events and their effects cannot be determined with precision, actual results may differ significantly from such estimates and assumptions.

Estimates and underlying assumptions are reviewed on an ongoing basis. Revisions to accounting estimates are recognized in the period in which the estimates are revised and in any future periods affected.

3.   SIGNIFICANT ACCOUNTING POLICIES:

The accounting policies described below have been applied consistently to all periods presented in these consolidated financial statements.

(a)   Basis of Measurement:

The consolidated financial statements have been prepared on a going concern basis, under the historical cost convention as modified by the revaluation of certain financial assets and financial liabilities (including derivative instruments) at fair value through profit and loss.

(b)   Basis of Consolidation:

The consolidated financial statements include the accounts of Danier Leather Inc. consolidated with those of its wholly-owned subsidiaries, 1331677 Ontario Inc., Danier International Corporation and Danier Leather (USA), Inc. 1331677 Ontario Inc. was incorporated in Ontario, Canada on December 22, 1998 to hold vacant land next to the Company's Toronto head office. Danier International Corporation was incorporated in Barbados on April 7, 2006 to hold the international intellectual property of Danier. Danier Leather (USA), Inc. is currently inactive and was incorporated in Delaware, U.S.A. on September 8, 1998 to operate Danier stores in the United States, which operations have since been discontinued. On consolidation, all intercompany transactions, balances, revenue and expenses have been eliminated.

(c)   Year-End:

The fiscal year end of the Company consists of a 52 or 53 week period ending on the last Saturday in June each year. The current fiscal year for the consolidated financial statements is the 52-week period ended June 28, 2014 and, comparably, the 52-week period ended June 29, 2013.

(d)   Foreign Currency Translation:

Items included in the financial statements of each wholly-owned consolidated entity in the Danier Leather Inc. group are measured using the currency of the primary economic environment in which the entity operates (the "functional currency"). The consolidated financial statements are presented in Canadian dollars, which is the Company's presentation currency.

Accounts in foreign currencies are translated into Canadian dollars. Monetary financial position items are translated at the foreign currency exchange rate in effect at the balance sheet date and non-monetary items are measured at historical cost and are translated into Canadian dollars at foreign currency exchange rates that approximate the rates in effect at the dates when such items are transacted. Revenues and expenses are translated at the foreign currency exchange rate in effect on the transaction dates or at the average foreign currency exchange rate for the reporting period. The resulting net gain or loss is included as part of selling, general and administrative expenses ("SG&A") in the consolidated statement of earnings (loss).

(e)   Revenue Recognition:

Revenue comprises the fair value of the consideration received or receivable for the sale of merchandise and services in the ordinary course of the Company's activities inclusive of amounts invoiced for alteration services and shipping. Revenue is shown net of sales tax and estimated returns.

The Company recognizes revenue when the amount can be reliably measured, it is probable that future economic benefits will flow to the Company and when specific criteria have been met for each of the Company's activities as described below. The Company bases estimates on historical results, taking into consideration the type of activity and the specifics of each arrangement.

Retail Sales

Revenue for merchandise sold to customers through the Company's stores is recognized at the time of purchase. Alteration revenue is recorded at the time the buyer takes possession of the merchandise.

Online Sales

Revenue for online customers is recognized upon estimated receipt of the merchandise by the customer.

Third Party Distributor

Revenue for merchandise sold through a third party distributor is recognized when the significant risks and rewards of ownership have been transferred to the buyer, which is at the time the distributor ships the merchandise to their customer.

Gift Cards

Gift cards sold are recorded as deferred revenue and revenue is recognized at the time of redemption or in accordance with the Company's accounting policy for breakage. Breakage income represents the estimated value of gift cards that are not expected to be redeemed by customers where the unredeemed balance is more than two years old from the date of issuance. Historically, breakage has not been material.

(f)   Share-Based Compensation Plans:

The Company maintains an equity-settled Stock Option Plan and cash-settled Restricted Share Unit ("RSU") and Deferred Share Unit ("DSU") share-based compensation plans.

For the equity-settled Stock Option Plan, where options to purchase Subordinate Voting Shares are issued to directors, officers, employees or service providers (further details of which are described in Note 12(a)), the expense is based on the fair value of the awards granted, excluding the impact of any non-market service conditions (for example, continued employment over a specified time period). Non-market vesting conditions are considered in making assumptions about the number of awards that are expected to vest. The fair value of options granted is estimated at the date of grant using the Black-Scholes Option Pricing Model. The expense is recognized on a graded vesting basis over the vesting period of the stock options, which is generally three years.

When stock options are subsequently exercised, share capital is increased by the sum of the consideration paid together with the related portion previously added to contributed surplus when compensation costs were charged against income.

For the cash-settled RSU plan, where RSUs are issued to eligible directors, officers or employees and vest over a period of up to three years (further details of which are described in Note 12(c)), the expense is recognized on a graded vesting schedule and is determined based on the fair value of the liability incurred at each balance sheet date until the award is settled. The fair value of the liability is measured at each balance sheet date by applying the Black-Scholes Option Pricing Model, taking into account the extent to which participants have rendered services to date.

For the cash-settled DSU plan, where DSUs are issued to directors and vest immediately and can only be redeemed once the director leaves the Board of Directors of the Company (further details of which are described in Note 12(b)), the expense is recognized on the grant date based on the fair value of the award by applying the Black-Scholes Option Pricing Model. The fair value of the liability is measured at each balance sheet date by applying the Black-Scholes Option Pricing Model until the award is settled.

At each balance sheet date, the Company reassesses its estimates of the number of awards that are expected to vest and recognizes the impact of any revisions in the statement of earnings (loss) with a corresponding adjustment to equity or liabilities, as appropriate.

(g) Cash:

Cash consists of cash on hand and bank balances.

(h) Financial Instruments:

(i) Classification of Financial Instruments

Financial instruments are classified into one of the following three categories: fair value through profit and loss, loans and receivables or financial liabilities at amortized cost. The classification determines the accounting treatment of the instrument. The classification is determined by the Company when the financial instrument is initially recorded, based on the underlying purpose of the instrument.

The Company's financial instruments are classified and measured as follows:

Financial Asset/Liability	Category	Measurement
Cash	Loans and receivables	Amortized cost
Accounts receivable	Loans and receivables	Amortized cost
Payables and accruals	Financial liabilities	Amortized cost
Sales return provision	Financial liabilities	Amortized cost
Foreign currency option contract derivatives[1]	Fair value through profit and loss	Fair value through profit and loss

[1] The carrying value of the Company's derivatives are included in the consolidated balance sheet as accounts receivable (if the fair value is an unrealized gain) or payables and accruals (if the fair value is an unrealized loss).

Loans and receivables are initially recognized at fair value and then subsequently at amortized cost using the effective interest method, less any impairment losses recognized in the statement of earnings (loss) in the period in which the impairment is recognized. Financial liabilities are initially recognized at the amount required to be paid less, when material, a discount to reduce the payables to fair value. Subsequently, financial liabilities are recorded measured at amortized cost using the effective interest method. Changes in fair value of financial instruments classified as held for trading are recorded in the statement of earnings (loss) in the period of change.

The Company categorizes its financial assets and financial liabilities that are recognized in the balance sheets at fair value using the fair value hierarchy. The fair value hierarchy has the following levels:

- Level 1 – quoted market prices in active markets for identical assets or liabilities;
- Level 2 – inputs other than quoted market prices included in Level 1 that are observable for the asset or liability, either directly (as prices) or indirectly (derived from prices); and
- Level 3 – unobservable inputs such as inputs for the asset or liability that are not based on observable market data.

The level in the fair value hierarchy within which the fair value measurement is categorized in its entirety is determined on the basis of the lowest level input that is significant to the fair value measurement in its entirety.

(ii) Transaction Costs

Transaction costs are added to the initial fair value of financial assets and liabilities when those financial assets and liabilities are not measured at fair value subsequent to initial measurement. Transaction costs are recorded in SG&A using the effective interest method.

(iii) Derivative Financial Instruments

The Company uses derivatives in the form of foreign currency option contracts and forwards, which are used to manage risks related to its inventory purchases, which are primarily denominated in United States dollars. All derivatives have been classified as fair value through profit and loss, are not designated as hedges, are included in the balance sheets as accounts receivable or payables and accruals, and are classified as current or non-current based on the contractual terms specific to the instrument. Gains and losses on re-measurement are included in SG&A.

(iv) Fair Value

The fair value of a financial instrument is the estimated amount that the Company would receive to sell an asset or pay to transfer a liability in an orderly transaction between market participants at the measurement date. These estimates are subjective in nature, often involve uncertainties and the exercise of significant judgment and are made at a specific point in time using available information about the financial instrument and may not reflect fair value in the future. The estimated fair value amounts can be materially affected by the use of different assumptions or methodologies.

The methods and assumptions used in estimating the fair value of the Company's financial instruments are as follows:

- The derivative financial instruments, which consist of foreign currency option contracts and forwards, have been marked-to-market and are categorized as Level 2 in the fair value hierarchy. Factors included in the determination of fair value include the spot rate, forward rates, estimates of volatility, present value factor, strike prices, credit risk of the Company and credit risk of counterparties. As at June 28, 2014, a $364 unrealized loss (June 29, 2013 – $822 unrealized gain) was recorded in SG&A for the contracts outstanding.
- Given their short-term maturity, the fair value of cash, accounts receivable, payables and accruals and sales return provision approximates their carrying values.

(i) Impairment of Financial Assets:

At each reporting date, the Company assesses whether there is objective evidence that a financial asset is impaired. Evidence of impairment may include: indications that a debtor or a group of debtors are experiencing significant financial difficulty; default or delinquency in interest or principal payments; and observable data indicating that there is a measurable decrease in the estimated future cash flows. If such evidence exists, the Company recognizes an impairment loss.

For financial assets carried at amortized cost, the loss is the difference between the amortized cost of the receivable and the present value of the estimated future cash flows, discounted using the instrument's original effective interest rate. The carrying amount of the asset is reduced by this amount either directly or indirectly through the use of an allowance account. Impairment losses on financial assets carried at amortized cost are reversed in subsequent periods if the amount of the loss decreases and the decrease can be related objectively to an event occurring after the impairment was recognized.

(j) Inventories:

Merchandise inventories are valued at the lower of cost, using the weighted average cost method, and net realizable value. For inventories manufactured by the Company, cost includes direct labour, raw materials, manufacturing and distribution centre costs related to inventories and transportation costs that are directly incurred to bring inventories to their present location and condition. For inventories purchased from third party vendors, cost includes the cost of purchase, duty and brokerage, quality assurance costs, distribution centre costs related to inventories and transportation costs that are directly incurred to bring inventories to their present location and condition.

The Company estimates the net realizable value as the amount at which inventories are expected to be sold, taking into account fluctuations in retail prices due to seasonality, age, excess quantities, condition of the inventory, nature of the inventory and the estimated variable costs necessary to make the sale. Inventories are written down to net realizable value when the cost of inventories is not estimated to be recoverable due to obsolescence, damage or declining selling prices. When circumstances that previously caused inventories to be written down below cost no longer exist, the amount of the write-down previously recorded is reversed.

Storage costs, administrative overheads and selling costs related to the inventories are expensed in the period in which the costs are incurred.

(k) Property and Equipment:

Property and equipment are recorded at cost less accumulated amortization and accumulated impairment losses, if any. Cost includes expenditures that are directly attributable to the acquisition of the asset. Borrowing costs attributable to the acquisition, construction or production of qualifying assets are added to the cost of those assets, until such time as the assets are substantially ready for their intended use. Qualifying assets are those assets that take longer than nine months to be substantially ready for their intended use. All other borrowing costs are recognized as interest expense in the statement of earnings (loss) in the period in which they are incurred.

Subsequent costs are included in the asset's carrying amount or recognized as a separate asset, as appropriate, only when it is probable that future economic benefits can be measured reliably. The carrying amount of a replaced asset is de-recognized when replaced. Repair and maintenance costs are charged to the statement of earnings (loss) during the period in which they are incurred.

Depreciation of an asset begins once it is available for use. The Company allocates the amount initially recognized in respect of an item of property and equipment to its significant parts and depreciates each such part separately. The depreciable amount of an asset, being the cost of an asset less the residual value, if any, is allocated on a straight-line basis over the estimated useful life of the asset. Residual value is estimated to be zero unless the Company expects to dispose of the asset at a value that exceeds the estimated disposal costs. Gains and losses on disposals of property and equipment, if any, are determined by comparing the proceeds with the carrying amount of the asset and are included as part of SG&A in the statement of earnings (loss).

The major categories of property and equipment, their methods of amortization and useful lives for the fiscal years ended June 28, 2014 and June 29, 2013 are as follows:

Building	25 years straight-line
Roof	20 years straight-line
HVAC equipment	5 to 15 years straight-line
Computer hardware	4 to 7 years straight-line
Furniture and equipment (non-retail)	5 to 7 years straight-line
Leasehold improvements, furniture and fixtures (retail locations)	Term of lease not to exceed 10 years

The residual values, useful lives and amortization methods applied to assets are reviewed annually based on relevant market information and management considerations.

Property and equipment is derecognized either upon disposal or when no future economic benefits are expected from their use. Any gain or loss arising on derecognition is included as part of SG&A in the statement of earnings (loss).

(l) Computer Software:

Computer software is recorded at cost less accumulated amortization and accumulated impairment losses, if any. Amortization commences when the computer software application is available for its intended use. Residual value is estimated to be zero unless the Company expects to dispose of the asset at a value that exceeds the estimated disposal costs. The residual values, useful lives and amortization methods applied to computer software are reviewed annually based on relevant market information and management considerations. Computer software costs are capitalized and amortized on a straight line basis over the period of its expected useful life which ranges from 4 to 7 years. The assets are reviewed for impairment whenever events or circumstances indicate that the carrying amount may not be recoverable.

Computer software is derecognized either upon disposal or when no future economic benefit is expected from its use. Any gain or loss arising on derecognition is included as part of SG&A in the statement of earnings (loss).

(m) Impairment of Non-Financial Assets:

Property and equipment and computer software with finite lives are tested for impairment at each reporting date and whenever events or changes in circumstances indicate that the carrying amount may not be recoverable. Events or changes in circumstances which may indicate impairment include: a significant change to the Company's operations, a significant decline in performance or a change in market conditions which adversely affects the Company.

An impairment loss is recognized for the amount by which the asset's carrying amount exceeds its recoverable amount. For purposes of measuring recoverable amounts, assets are grouped at the lowest levels for which there are separately identifiable cash flows (cash-generating units or CGUs), which is at the individual store level for the Company. The recoverable amount is the greater of an asset's fair value less costs to sell and value in use (being the present value of the expected future cash flows of the relevant asset or CGU). The Company evaluates impairment losses for potential reversals when events or circumstances warrant such consideration.

(n) Leased Assets:

Leases are classified as either operating or finance, based on the substance of the transaction at inception of the lease. Classification is re-assessed if the terms of the lease are changed.

Leases in which a significant portion of the risks and rewards of ownership are not assumed by the Company are classified as operating leases. The Company enters into leases of varying terms for the operation of its stores, which are accounted for as operating leases. Payments under an operating lease are recognized in SG&A on the statement of earnings (loss) on a straight-line basis over the term of the lease. When a lease contains a predetermined fixed escalation of the minimum rent, the Company recognizes the related rent expense on a straight-line basis and records the difference between the recognized rental expense and the amount payable under the lease as deferred rent, which is included in deferred lease inducements and rent liability on the balance sheet. Contingent rentals (rent as a percentage of sales above a predetermined sales threshold) are recognized in SG&A in the period in which they are incurred.

Tenant allowances are recorded as deferred lease inducements and amortized as a reduction of rent expense over the term of the related leases.

(o) Provisions:

Provisions represent liabilities to the Company for which the amount or timing is uncertain. Provisions are recognized when the Company has a present legal or constructive obligation as a result of past events, it is probable that an outflow of resources will be required to settle the obligation and the amount can be reliably estimated. The sales return provision primarily comprises customer returns of unworn and undamaged purchases for a full refund within the time period provided by Danier's return policy, which is generally 14 days after the purchase date. The sales return provision is estimated based on historical experience and, since the time period of the provision is of relatively short duration, the present value of the expenditure expected to be required to settle the obligation approximates the actual provision estimate. The provision is reviewed at each balance sheet date and updated to reflect management's latest best estimate. However, actual returns could vary from these estimates.

(p) Deferred Lease Inducements and Rent Liability:

Deferred lease inducements represent cash benefits received from landlords pursuant to store lease agreements. These lease inducements are amortized against rent expense over the term of the lease, not exceeding 10 years.

Rent liability represents the difference between minimum rent as specified in the lease and rent calculated on a straight-line basis.

(q) Income Taxes:

Income tax comprises current and deferred tax. The Company's income tax expense is based on tax rules and regulations that are subject to interpretation and require estimates and assumptions that may be challenged by taxation authorities.

Current income tax is the expected tax payable on the taxable income for the year using tax rates enacted or substantially enacted at the end of the reporting period and any adjustments to tax payable in respect of previous years. A weighted average of rates across provinces or categories of income is used if it is a reasonable approximation of the effect of using more specific rates. The Company's estimates of current income tax are periodically reviewed and adjusted as circumstances warrant, such as for changes to tax laws and administrative guidance and the resolution of uncertainties through either the conclusion of tax audits or expiration of prescribed time limits within the relevant statutes. The final results of government tax audits and other events may vary materially compared to estimates and assumptions used by management in determining income tax expense and in measuring current income tax.

In general, deferred tax is recognized in respect of temporary differences arising between the tax bases of assets and liabilities and their carrying amounts in the consolidated financial statements. Deferred income tax is determined on a non-discounted basis using tax rates and laws that have been enacted or substantially enacted at the balance sheet date and are expected to apply when the deferred tax asset or liability is settled. The effect on deferred income tax assets and liabilities of a change in tax rates are included in net earnings in the period that the laws have been enacted or substantially enacted. Deferred tax assets are recognized to the extent that it is probable that the assets can be recovered.

Estimation of income taxes includes evaluating the recoverability of deferred tax assets based on an assessment of the Company's ability to utilize the underlying future tax deductions against future taxable income before they expire. As described above, the Company's assessment is based upon substantially enacted tax rates and laws that are expected to apply when the assets are expected to be realized, as well as on estimates of future taxable income. If the assessment of the Company's ability to utilize the underlying future tax deductions changes, the Company would be required to recognize more or fewer of the tax deductions or assets, which would decrease or increase (respectively) the income tax expense in the period in which this is determined. Deferred income tax assets are recognized on the balance sheet under non-current assets, irrespective of the expected date of realization or settlement.

Significant judgment is required in determining the provision for taxation. There are many transactions and calculations for which the ultimate tax determination is uncertain during the ordinary course of business. The Company assesses the need for provisions for uncertain tax positions using best estimates of the amounts that would be expected to be paid based on a qualitative assessment of all relevant factors. However, it is possible that at some future date an additional liability could result from audits by taxation authorities. Where the final outcome of these matters is different from the amounts that were initially recorded, such differences will affect the tax provisions in the period in which such determination is made.

(r) Earnings Per Share:

Basic earnings per share is calculated by dividing the net earnings available to shareholders by the weighted average number of shares outstanding during the year (see Note 11(c)). Diluted earnings per share is calculated using the treasury stock method, which assumes that all outstanding stock options with an exercise price below the average monthly market price of the Subordinate Voting Shares on the TSX are exercised and the assumed proceeds are used to purchase the Company's Subordinate Voting Shares at the average monthly market price on the TSX during the fiscal year.

(s) Share Capital:

Subordinate Voting Shares are classified as equity. When Subordinate Voting Shares are purchased for cancellation, the carrying amount of the Subordinate Voting Shares is recognized as a deduction from share capital. The excess of the purchase price over the carrying amount of the Subordinate Voting Shares is charged to retained earnings.

5. INVENTORIES:

	June 28, 2014	June 29, 2013
Raw materials	$ 1,026	$ 2,594
Work-in-process	198	222
Finished goods	20,497	19,994
	$ 21,721	$ 22,810

	Year Ended	
	June 28, 2014	June 29, 2013
Cost of inventory recognized as an expense	$ 73,084	$ 75,805
Write-downs of inventory due to net realizable value being lower than cost	$ 2,589	$ 1,632
Write-downs recognized in previous periods that were reversed	$ 9	$ 30

6. PROPERTY AND EQUIPMENT:

	Year Ended June 28, 2014							
	Land	Building	Roof	HVAC	Leasehold Improvements	Furniture & Equipment	Computer Hardware	Total
Cost								
At June 29, 2013	$ 1,000	$ 6,063	$ 308	$ 840	$ 22,679	$ 9,957	$ 3,348	$44,195
Additions	-	-	-	-	3,078	1,671	223	4,972
Disposals	-	-	-	-	(2,451)	(270)	(280)	(3,001)
At June 28, 2014	$ 1,000	$ 6,063	$ 308	$ 840	$ 23,306	$ 11,358	$3,291	$46,166
Accumulated amortization and impairment losses								
At June 29, 2013	-	$2,508	$216	$625	$15,322	$6,754	$2,736	$28,161
Amortization for the period	-	154	16	49	1,865	1,005	428	3,517
Impairment losses	-	-	-	-	661	2	-	663
Disposals	-	-	-	-	(2,451)	(270)	(280)	(3,001)
At June 28, 2014	-	$2,662	$232	$674	$15,397	$7,491	$2,884	$29,340
Net carrying value								
At June 28, 2014	$1,000	$3,401	$76	$166	$7,909	$3,867	$407	$16,826
Capital work in progress included above								
At June 28, 2014					$56		$81	$137

(c)   Accounting Standards Implemented During Fiscal 2014:

The Company adopted the following new accounting standards in preparing these annual consolidated financial statements:

(i) Financial Instruments – Offsetting Financial Assets and Financial Liabilities: The IASB issued an amendment to IFRS 7, Financial Instruments: Offsetting Financial Assets and Financial Liabilities ("IFRS 7") which was effective for annual periods beginning on or after January 1, 2013 and was adopted by the Company on June 30, 2013. Amendments to IFRS 7 increased the disclosure requirement related to offsetting of financial assets and liabilities. The implementation of IFRS 7 did not have a significant impact on the Company.

(ii) Fair Value Measurement: The IASB issued a new standard, IFRS 13, Fair Value Measurement ("IFRS 13"), which was required to be adopted for annual periods beginning on or after January 1, 2013 and was prospectively adopted by the Company on June 30, 2013. IFRS 13 provides a standard definition of fair value, sets out a framework for measuring fair value and provides for specific disclosures about fair value. IFRS 13 defines fair value as the price that would be received to sell an asset, or paid to transfer a liability, in an orderly transaction between market participants at the measurement date. The Company determined that the adoption of IFRS 13 had no measurement impact on the Company's consolidated financial statements. The Company has included the disclosures required by this standard in Note 18.

4. FUTURE ACCOUNTING STANDARDS:

A number of new standards, and amendments to standards and interpretations, are not yet effective for the year ended June 28, 2014 and have not been applied in preparing these annual consolidated financial statements. New standards and amendments to standards and interpretations that are currently under review include:

IFRS 9 – Financial Instruments

On November 12, 2009, the IASB issued a new standard, IFRS 9, Financial Instruments ("IFRS 9"), which will ultimately replace IAS 39, Financial Instruments: Recognition and Measurement ("IAS 39"). The replacement of IAS 39 is a multi-phase project with the objective of improving and simplifying the reporting for financial instruments and the issuance of IFRS 9 is a part of the first phase.

On November 19, 2013, the IASB published IFRS 9, Hedge Accounting, which is a part of the third phase of its replacement of IAS 39. The new requirements allow entities to better reflect their risk management activities in the financial statements. As part of the amendments, entities may change the accounting for liabilities that they have elected to measure at fair value before applying any of the requirements in IFRS 9. This change in accounting would mean that gains caused by a worsening in an entity's own credit risk on such liabilities would no longer be recognized in profit or loss.

Because the impairment phase of the IFRS 9 project is not yet completed, the IASB decided that a mandatory effective date of January 1, 2015 would not allow sufficient time for entities to prepare to apply IFRS 9. Accordingly, the IASB determined to apply a later mandatory effective date, which will be determined when IFRS 9 is closer to completion. However, entities may still choose to apply IFRS 9 immediately. IFRS 9 must be applied retrospectively; however, hedge accounting is to be applied prospectively (with some exceptions). At the present time, Danier does not expect to apply IFRS 9 earlier than the date required by the IASB. The Company is assessing the potential impact of IFRS 9.

IAS 32 – Financial Instruments: Presentation ("IAS 32")

The IASB issued an amendment to IAS 32 which provides further guidance on the requirements for offsetting financial instruments. The amendments to IAS 32 are effective for annual periods beginning on or after January 1, 2014 and must be applied retrospectively. The Company will apply IAS 32 beginning in the first quarter of fiscal 2015 and no significant impact on the consolidated financial statements is expected.

IAS 36 – Impairment of Assets: Recoverable Amount Disclosures for Non-Financial Assets ("IAS 36")

The IASB issued amendments to IAS 36 which reduces the circumstances in which the recoverable amount of assets or cash generating units is required to be disclosed, clarifies the disclosure required and introduces an explicit requirement to disclose the discount rate in determining impairment or reversals where the recoverable amount (based on fair value less costs of disposal) is determined using a present value technique. The amendments to IAS 36 are effective for annual periods beginning on or after January 1, 2014 and must be applied retrospectively. The Company will apply IAS 36 beginning in the first quarter of fiscal 2015 and no significant impact on the consolidated financial statements is expected.

IFRIC 21 – Levies ("IFRIC 21")

The IFRS Interpretations Committee ("IFRIC") of the IASB issued IFRIC 21 which addresses the accounting for a liability to pay a levy to a government. IFRIC applies to levy liabilities within the scope of IAS 37 – Provisions, Contingent Liabilities and Contingent Assets, and to levy liabilities when the timing and amount is uncertain. IFRIC 21 is effective for years beginning on or after January 1, 2014 and must be applied retrospectively. The Company will apply IFRIC 21 beginning in the first quarter of fiscal 2015 and no significant impact on the consolidated financial statements is expected.

A number of other standards have been adopted by the IASB but currently have no impact on the Company.

Property and Equipment

					Year Ended June 29, 2013			
	Land	Building	Roof	HVAC	Leasehold Improvements	Furniture & Equipment	Computer Hardware	Total
Cost								
At June 30, 2012	$1,000	$6,063	$508	$793	$22,208	$9,088	$3,386	$42,846
Additions	-	-	-	47	2,970	1,333	148	4,498
Disposals	-	-	-	-	(2,499)	(464)	(186)	(3,149)
At June 29, 2013	$1,000	$6,063	$508	$840	$22,679	$9,957	$3,348	$44,195
Accumulated amortization and impairment losses								
At June 30, 2012	-	$2,354	$201	$578	$15,875	$6,321	$2,505	$27,834
Amortization for the period	-	154	15	47	1,669	847	417	3,149
Impairment losses	-	-	-	-	277	50	-	327
Disposals	-	-	-	-	(2,499)	(464)	(186)	(3,149)
At June 29, 2013	-	$2,508	$216	$625	$15,322	$6,754	$2,736	$28,161
Net carrying value								
At June 29, 2013	$1,000	$3,555	$92	$215	$7,357	$3,203	$612	$16,034
Capital work in progress included above								
At June 29, 2013	-	-	-	-	$299	$19	-	$318

The Company conducted an impairment test for its property and equipment and determined that there were impairments at some non-performing stores in the amount of $663 for the year ended June 28, 2014 ($327 for the year ended June 29, 2013) and recorded in SG&A during the third and fourth quarters of fiscal 2014. The recoverable amount of the CGU was estimated based on value-in-use calculations as this was determined to be higher than fair value less costs to sell. These calculations use cash flow projections based on actual performance during the past 12 months which are then extrapolated over each CGU's remaining lease term and then discounted using an estimated discount rate. The key assumptions for the value-in-use calculations include discount rates, growth rates and expected cash flows. Management estimates discount rates using pre-tax rates that reflect a current market assessment of the time value of money and the risks specific to the CGUs. Changes in revenues and direct costs are based on past experience and expectations of future changes in the market.

The pre-tax discount rate used to calculate the value-in-use range is 12% (11% during the year ended June 29, 2013) and is dependent on the specific risks in relation to the CGU. The discount rate is derived from retail industry comparable post-tax weighted average cost of capital.

If management's cash flow estimate were to decrease by 10%, the impairment would have increased by $128 (unchanged for the year ended June 29, 2013). Similarly, if the discount rate were to increase by 100 basis points, the impairment would have increased by $36 (unchanged for the year ended June 29, 2013).

7. COMPUTER SOFTWARE:

	Year Ended	
	June 28, 2014	June 29, 2013
Cost		
Beginning of fiscal year	$4,684	$3,994
Additions	1,107	829
Disposals	(752)	(139)
End of Period	5,039	4,684
Accumulated amortization		
Beginning of fiscal year	$3,541	$3,268
Amortization for the period	791	412
Disposals	(752)	(139)
End of Period	$3,580	$3,541
Net carrying value		
End of period	$1,459	$1,143
Beginning of fiscal year	$1,143	$726
Capital work in progress include at end of period	$2	$702

8. BANK FACILITIES:

The Company has an operating credit facility for working capital and for general corporate purposes to a maximum amount of $25 million that is committed until June 25, 2016 and bears interest at prime plus 0.75%. The Company also has a revolving term credit facility ("Term capex facility") to be used exclusively for capital expenditures in the amount of $4 million that is committed until June 25, 2016 and bears interest at prime plus 0.75%. At the end of each quarter, repayments equal to 6.25% of the aggregate principal amount of all borrowings under the term capex facility must be paid.

Standby fees of 0.50% are paid on a quarterly basis for any unused portion of the operating credit facility and term capex facility. The operating credit facility and term capex facility are subject to certain covenants and other limitations that, if breached, could cause a default and may result in a requirement for immediate repayment of amounts outstanding. Security provided includes a security interest over all personal property of the Company's business and a mortgage over the land and building comprising the Company's head office/distribution facility.

The Company also has an uncommitted letter of credit facility to a maximum amount of $10 million and an uncommitted demand overdraft facility in the amount of $0.5 million to be used exclusively for issuance of letters of credit for the purchase of inventory. Any amounts outstanding under the overdraft facility will bear interest at the bank's prime rate. In addition, the Company has a US$4.05 million foreign exchange line available to hedge foreign currency exposure not exceeding 12 months. The foregoing facilities and exchange line are secured by the Company's personal property from time to time financed with the proceeds drawn thereunder.

9. PAYABLES AND ACCRUALS:

	June 28, 2014	June 29, 2013
Trade payables	$ 1,250	$ 1,840
Accruals	5,089	4,981
RSU/DSU liability	1,591	2,516
Commodity and capital taxes	891	764
Derivative financial instruments	364	-
	$ 9,185	$ 10,101

10. SALES RETURN PROVISION:

The provision for sales returns primarily relates to customer returns of unworn and undamaged purchases for a full refund within the time period provided by Danier's return policy, which is generally 14 days after the purchase date. Since the time period of the provision is of relatively short duration, all of the provision is classified as current. The following transactions occurred during the years ended June 28, 2014 and June 29, 2013, respectively, with respect to the sales return provision:

	Year Ended	
	June 28, 2014	June 29, 2013
Beginning of period	$99	$124
Amount provided during the period	1,996	2,049
Utilized or released during the period	(2,001)	(2,074)
End of period	$94	$99

11. SHARE CAPITAL:

(a) Authorized

1,224,329 Multiple Voting Shares

Unlimited Subordinate Voting Shares

Unlimited Class A and B Preference Shares

(a) *(continued)*

	Fiscal Year Ended	
	June 28, 2014	June 29, 2013
Number of shares repurchased under Offer		787,404
Number of shares repurchased under NCIBs	25,000	75,400
Amount charged to share capital	$111	$3,792
Amount charged to retained earnings representing the excess over the average paid-in value	$164	$7,515
Total cash consideration	**$275**	**$11,307**
Income tax related to Offer that was recorded directly to Shareholders' Equity		$92

12. SHARE-BASED COMPENSATION:

The Company's net share-based compensation expense recognized in SG&A related to its stock option, RSU and DSU plans is presented below:

	Fiscal Year Ended	
	June 28, 2014	June 29, 2013
Stock option plan expense	$209	$131
RSU plan expense	296	693
DSU plan expense	(157)	75
	$348	**$899**

The carrying amount of the Company's share-based compensation arrangements including stock option, RSU and DSU plans are recorded on the consolidated balance sheet as follows:

	Fiscal Year Ended	
	June 28, 2014	June 29, 2013
Payables and accruals	$1,591	$2,516
Contributed surplus	1,040	954
	$2,631	**$3,470**

(a) Stock Option Plan

The Company maintains a Stock Option Plan, as amended, for the benefit of directors, officers, employees and service providers, pursuant to which granted options are exercisable for Subordinate Voting Shares. As at June 28, 2014, the Company has reserved 525,100 Subordinate Voting Shares for issuance under its Stock Option Plan. The granting of options and the related vesting periods are at the discretion of the Board of Directors, on the advice of the Governance, Compensation, Human Resources and Nominating Committee of the Board (the "Committee"), at exercise prices determined as the weighted average of the trading prices of the Company's Subordinate Voting Shares on the TSX for the five trading days preceding the effective date of the grant. In general, options granted to officers, employees and service providers under the Stock Option Plan typically vest over a period of three years from the grant date and expire no later than the tenth anniversary of the date of grant (subject to extension in accordance with the Stock Option Plan if the options would otherwise expire during a black-out period).

A summary of the status of the Company's Stock Option Plan as of June 28, 2014 and June 29, 2013 and changes during the fiscal years ended on those dates is presented below:

	June 28, 2014		June 29, 2013	
Stock Option	Shares	Weighted Average Exercise Price	Shares	Weighted Average Exercise Price
Outstanding at beginning of year	277,900	$6.45	357,767	$7.14
Granted	85,000	$11.29	26,200	$12.97
Exercised	(47,000)	$4.83	(48,067)	$3.80
Forfeited	(28,100)	$10.68	(58,000)	$15.85
Outstanding at end of year	287,800	$7.73	277,900	$6.45
Options exercisable at end of year	185,332	$5.60	232,966	$5.37

(b) Issued

Multiple Voting Shares	Number	Consideration
Balance June 30, 2012	1,224,329	Nominal
Balance June 29, 2013	1,224,329	Nominal
Balance June 28, 2014	1,224,329	Nominal

Subordinate Voting Shares	Number	Consideration
Balance June 30, 2012	3,422,573	$15,040
Shares repurchased	(862,801)	(3,792)
Shares issued upon exercising of stock options	48,067	285
Balance June 29, 2013	2,607,839	$11,533
Shares repurchased	(25,000)	(111)
Shares issued upon exercising of stock options	47,000	350
Balance June 28, 2014	2,629,839	$11,772

The Multiple Voting Shares and Subordinate Voting Shares have identical attributes except that the Multiple Voting Shares entitle the holder to 10 votes per share and the Subordinate Voting Shares entitle the holder to one vote per share. Each Multiple Voting Share is convertible at any time, at the holder's option, into one fully paid and non-assessable Subordinate Voting Share. The Multiple Voting Shares are subject to provisions whereby, if a triggering event occurs, then each Multiple Voting Share is converted into one fully paid and non-assessable Subordinate Voting Share. A triggering event may occur if, among other things, Mr. Jeffrey Wortsman, President and Chief Executive Officer: (i) dies; (ii) ceases to be a senior officer of the Company; (iii) ceases to own 5% or more of the aggregate number of Multiple Voting Shares and Subordinate Voting Shares outstanding; or (iv) owns less than 918,247 Multiple Voting Shares and Subordinate Voting Shares combined.

(c) Earnings Per Share

Basic and diluted per share amounts are based on the following weighted average number of shares outstanding:

	Fiscal Year Ended	
	June 28, 2014	June 29, 2013
Weighted average number of shares for basic earnings per share calculations	3,840,319	4,180,829
Effect of dilutive options outstanding	108,017	142,790
Weighted average number of shares for diluted earnings per share calculations	3,948,336	4,323,619

The computation of dilutive options outstanding only includes those options having exercise prices below the average market price of Subordinate Voting Shares on the TSX during the period. The number of options excluded was 111,200 as at June 28, 2014 and 26,200 as at June 29, 2013.

(d) Issuer Bids

During the fiscal year ended June 29, 2013, the Company announced its intention to commence a substantial issuer bid (the "Offer"). The Offer was formally commenced on October 24, 2012 by filing and mailing a formal offer to purchase and accompanying circular, pursuant to which the Company offered to purchase for cancellation up to $10 million in value of its Subordinate Voting Shares from shareholders for cash by way of a "modified Dutch Auction" at a range of Offer prices between $12.55 and $13.30 per share. The Offer expired on November 28, 2012 and a total of 1,748,470 Subordinate Voting Shares were validly deposited and not withdrawn under the Offer. Pursuant to the terms of the Offer, the Company determined the purchase price to be $12.70 per share. As the aggregate value of Subordinate Voting Shares deposited under the Offer exceeded the $10 million maximum value of consideration payable by the Company pursuant to the Offer, a pro-ration factor of 0.9852 was applied to deposited Subordinate Voting Shares (except for odd lot deposits, which were not subject to pro-ration), and the Company repurchased for cancellation 787,401 Subordinate Voting Shares at a purchase price of $12.70 per share. Approximately $3,460 of the purchase price, representing the average paid-in value of the shares, was charged to share capital, and approximately $6,913, which included the excess paid-in value of the shares as well as the transaction costs (net of tax) associated with the Offer, was charged to retained earnings.

During the past several years, the Company has from time to time received approval from the TSX to commence various normal course issuer bids ("NCIBs"). On February 12, 2014, the Company announced that the TSX had accepted a notice of its intention to proceed with its seventh NCIB (the "2014 NCIB"). Pursuant to the 2014 NCIB, the Company may purchase for cancellation up to a maximum of 145,496 Subordinate Voting Shares. The maximum number of Subordinate Voting Shares that may be purchased pursuant to the 2014 NCIB represents approximately 10% of the "public float" of the Subordinate Voting Shares outstanding as at the date of the notice of its intention to proceed with the 2014 NCIB. The 2014 NCIB commenced on February 14, 2014 and will terminate on February 13, 2015, or on such earlier date as the Company may complete its purchases under the 2014 NCIB.

The following Subordinate Voting Shares were repurchased for cancellation under the Offer and NCIBs then in effect during the years ended June 28, 2014 and June 29, 2013, respectively:

The following table summarizes the distribution of these options and the remaining contractual life as at June 28, 2014;

	Options Outstanding			Options Exercisable	
Exercise Prices	# Outstanding	Weighted Average Remaining Contractual Life	Weighted Average Exercise Price	Shares	Weighted Average Exercise Price
$3.15	83,600	4.3 years	$3.15	83,600	$3.15
$6.25	50,000	4.0 years	$6.25	50,000	$6.25
$7.80	28,000	2.6 years	$7.80	28,000	$7.80
$8.68	15,000	2.8 years	$8.68	15,000	$8.68
$10.99	25,000	9.6 years	$10.99	-	$10.99
$11.21	25,000	9.6 years	$11.21	-	$11.21
$11.56	35,000	9.3 years	$11.56	-	$11.56
$12.97	26,200	8.6 years	$12.97	8,732	$12.97
	287,800	5.9 years	$7.73	185,332	$5.60

During the year ended June 28, 2014, the Company granted an aggregate of 85,000 stock options with exercise prices ranging from $10.99 to $11.56 per stock option (June 29, 2013 – 26,200 stock options were granted with an exercise price of $12.97 per stock option). The estimated fair value at the date of grant for the options granted during the year ended June 28, 2014 was between $3.74 and $4.10 per stock option (June 29, 2013 – $6.57 per stock option). The fair value of each option granted was estimated on the date of grant using the Black-Scholes Options Pricing Model with the following assumptions:

	Year Ended			Year Ended	
	June 28, 2014			June 29, 2013	
Grant date	Oct 30, 2013	Feb 7, 2014	Feb 12, 2014	Feb 7, 2013
Number of options granted	35,000	25,000	25,000	26,200
Expected option life	5 years	5 years	5 years	10 years
Risk free rate	1.7%	1.6%	1.6%	2.0%
Expected stock price volatility	36%	36%	36%	38%
Dividend yield	0%	0%	0%	0%
Estimated forfeiture rate	$11.56	$11.21	$10.99	$12.97
Share price at grant date	$4.10	$3.82	$3.74	$6.57
Weighted average fair value of options granted				

The risk free rate was based on the Government of Canada benchmark bond yield on the date of grant for a term equal to the expected life of the options. Expected volatility was determined by calculating the historical volatility of the Company's share price over a period equal to the expected life of the options. The expected contractual life was based on the contractual life of the awards and adjusted, based on management's best estimate and historical redemption rates. The estimated forfeiture rate was estimated based on forfeiture rates for options granted between January 2007 and December 2013.

The Black-Scholes Option Pricing Model was developed for use in estimating the fair value of traded options, which have no black-out or vesting restrictions and are fully transferable. In addition, the Black-Scholes Option Pricing Model requires the use of subjective assumptions, including the expected stock price volatility. As a result of the Company's Stock Option Plan having characteristics different from those of traded options, and because changes in the subjective assumptions can have a material effect on the fair value estimate, the Black-Scholes Option Pricing Model does not necessarily provide a reliable single measure of the fair value of options granted.

(b)   Deferred Share Unit Plan

The cash-settled DSU Plan, as amended, was established for non-management directors. Under the DSU Plan, non-management directors of the Company may receive an annual grant of DSUs at the discretion of the Board of Directors on the advice of the Committee, and can also elect to receive their annual retainers and meeting fees in DSUs. A DSU is a notional unit equivalent in value to one Subordinate Voting Share of the Company based on the five-day average high and low board lot trading prices of the Company's Subordinate Voting Shares on the TSX immediately prior to the date on which the value of the DSU is determined.

Upon retirement from the Board of Directors, a participant in the DSU Plan receives a cash payment equal to the market value of the accumulated DSUs in their account. The fair value of the liability is measured at each balance sheet date by applying the Black-Scholes Option Pricing Model until the award is settled.

The following transactions occurred during each of the years ended June 28, 2014 and June 29, 2013, respectively, with respect to the DSU Plan:

	Year Ended	
	June 28, 2014	June 29, 2013
Outstanding at beginning of year	83,136	103,920
Granted	-	-
Redeemed	-	(20,784)
Outstanding at end of period	83,136	83,136
Danier stock price at end of period	$9.41	$11.31
Liability at end of period	$782	$940

(c)   Restricted Share Unit Plan

The Company has established a cash-settled RSU Plan, as amended, as part of its overall compensation plan. An RSU is a notional unit equivalent in value to one Subordinate Voting Share of the Company. The RSU Plan is administered by the Board of Directors, with the advice of the Committee. Under the RSU Plan, certain eligible officers, employees and directors of the Company are eligible to receive a grant of RSUs that generally vest over periods not exceeding three years, as determined by the Committee. Upon the exercise of the vested RSUs, a cash payment equal to the market value of the exercised vested RSUs will be paid to the participant. The market value is based on the average daily closing prices of the Subordinate Voting Shares on the TSX immediately prior to the applicable payment date. RSU expense is recognized on a graded vesting schedule and is determined based on the fair value of the liability incurred at each balance sheet date until the award is settled. The fair value of the liability is measured by applying the Black-Scholes Option Pricing Model, taking into account the extent to which participants have rendered services to date.

The following transactions occurred during each of the years ended June 28, 2014 and June 29, 2013, respectively, with respect to the RSU Plan:

	Year Ended	
	June 28, 2014	June 29, 2013
Outstanding at beginning of period	174,605	167,536
Granted	45,000	46,600
Redeemed	(91,647)	(36,063)
Forfeited	(4,569)	(3,468)
Outstanding at end of period	123,389	174,605
RSUs vested at end of period	14,785	39,331
Liability at end of period	$809	$1,576

13.   AMORTIZATION AND IMPAIRMENT LOSS:

Amortization of property and equipment and computer software and impairment loss on property and equipment, included in cost of sales and SG&A is summarized as follows:

	Year Ended	
	June 28, 2014	June 29, 2013
Cost of sales	$165	$168
SG&A	4,806	3,720
End of period	$4,971	$3,888

14. INCOME TAXES:

The Company's income tax expense is comprised as follows:

	Year Ended	
	June 28, 2014	June 29, 2013
Current tax expense		
Current period	(2,856)	746
Adjustment for prior years	(64)	(14)
Current tax expense	(2,920)	732
Deferred tax expense		
Recognition and reversal of temporary differences	(158)	(156)
Changes in tax rates	(6)	(7)
Adjustment for prior years and other	(47)	1
Deferred tax expense	(211)	(162)
Total income tax expense	**(3,131)**	**570**

The Company's effective income tax rate consists of the following:

	June 28, 2014	June 29, 2013
Combined basic federal and provincial average statutory rate	26.5%	26.4%
Current year losses applied to prior year	2.6%	4.2%
Non-deductible expenses	(1.1%)	(0.3%)
Future federal and provincial rate changes	0.1%	(0.7%)
Adjustment for prior years	1.1%	(0.8%)
Other	(0.2%)	
	29.0%	28.8%

Deferred income tax asset is summarized as follows:

	June 28, 2014	June 29, 2013
Amortization	1,190	1,041
Stock based compensation	421	667
Deferred lease inducements and rent liability	380	369
Federal and provincial tax credits	308	
Other deferred expenses	75	86
	2,374	2,163

15. CHANGES IN WORKING CAPITAL ITEMS:

	Year Ended	
	June 28, 2014	June 29, 2013
Decrease (increase) in:		
Accounts receivable	559	(680)
Inventories	1,089	2,081
Prepaid expenses	193	(53)
Increase (decrease) in:		
Payables and accruals	(916)	(60)
Deferred revenue	(37)	85
Sales return provision	(5)	(25)
	883	1,348

16. CONTINGENCIES AND GUARANTEES:

(a) Legal proceedings

In the course of its business, the Company from time to time becomes involved in various claims and legal proceedings. In the opinion of management, all such claims and suits are adequately covered by insurance, or if not so covered, the results are not expected to materially affect the Company's financial position.

(b) Guarantees

The Company has provided the following guarantees to third parties and no amounts have been accrued in the consolidated financial statements for these guarantees:

(i) In the ordinary course of business, the Company has agreed to indemnify its lenders under its credit facilities against certain costs or losses resulting from changes in laws and regulations or from a default in repaying a borrowing. These indemnifications extend for the term of the credit facilities and do not provide any limit on the maximum potential liability. Historically, the Company has not made any indemnification payments under such agreements.

(ii) In the ordinary course of business, the Company has provided indemnification commitments to certain counterparties in matters such as real estate leasing transactions, director and officer indemnification agreements and certain purchases of non-inventory assets and services. These indemnification agreements generally require the Company to compensate the counterparties for costs or losses resulting from legal action brought against the counterparties related to the actions of the Company. The terms of these indemnification agreements will vary based on the contract and generally do not provide any limit on the maximum potential liability.

17. COMMITMENTS:

(a) Operating leases:

The Company leases various store locations, a distribution warehouse and equipment under non-cancellable operating lease agreements. The leases are classified as operating leases since there is no transfer of risks and rewards inherent to ownership.

The leases have varying terms, escalation clauses and renewal rights. Minimum lease payments are recognized on a straight-line basis. Leases run for varying terms that generally do not exceed 10 years, with options to renew (if any) that do not exceed five years. The majority of real estate leases are net leases, which require additional payments for the cost of insurance, taxes, common area maintenance and utilities. Certain rental agreements include contingent rent, which is based on revenue exceeding a minimum amount. Minimum rentals, excluding rentals based upon revenue, are as follows:

Not later than one year	10,978
Later than one year and not later than five years	30,740
Later than five years	14,793
Total	56,511

Minimum lease payments and contingent rentals recognized as an expense are summarized as follows:

	Year Ended	
	June 28, 2014	June 29, 2013
Minimum lease payments	11,875	11,550
Contingent rentals	289	292

(b) Letters of credit:

As at June 28, 2014, the Company had outstanding letters of credit in the amount of $7,746 (June 29, 2013 – $8,743) for the importation of finished goods inventories to be received.

18. FINANCIAL INSTRUMENTS:

(a) Fair value disclosure

The following table presents the carrying amount and the fair value of the Company's financial instruments:

			June 28, 2014		June 29, 2013	
	Classification	Maturity	Carrying Value	Fair Value	Carrying Value	Fair Value
Cash	Loans and receivables	Short-term	$13,507	$13,507	$24,541	$24,541
Accounts receivable	Loans and receivables	Short-term	$638	$638	$375	$375
Payables and accruals	Financial liabilities	Short-term	$8,821	$8,821	$10,101	$10,101
Sales return provision	Financial liabilities	Short-term	$94	$94	$99	$99
Derivative financial instruments(1)	Fair value through profit and loss	Short-term	($364)	($364)	$822	$822

(1) Included in payables and accruals for the fiscal year ended June 28, 2014 and included in accounts receivable for the fiscal year ended June 29, 2013.

The fair value of a financial instrument is the estimated amount that the Company would receive to sell an asset or pay to transfer a liability in an orderly transaction between market participants at the measurement date. These estimates are subjective in nature, often involve uncertainties and the exercise of significant judgment and are made at a specific point in time using available information about the financial instrument and may not reflect fair value in the future. The estimated fair value amounts can be materially affected by the use of different assumptions or methodologies.

The principal methodologies and assumptions used in estimating the fair value of the Company's financial instruments are as follows:

- The derivative financial instruments, which consist of foreign exchange contracts, have been marked-to-market and are categorized as Level 2 in the fair value hierarchy. Factors included in the determination of fair value include the spot rate, forward rates, estimates of volatility, present value factor, strike prices, credit risk of the Company and credit risk of counterparties. As at June 28, 2014, a $364 unrealized loss (June 29, 2013 – $822 unrealized gain) was recorded in SG&A for the foreign exchange contracts outstanding.
- Given their short-term maturity, the fair value of cash, accounts receivable, payables and accruals and sales return provision approximate their carrying values. There were no transfers between Level 1 and 2 during the year.

(b) Financial instrument risk management

Foreign Currency Risk

Foreign currency risk is the risk that the fair value or future cash flows of a financial instrument will fluctuate because of changes in foreign currency exchange rates. The Company purchases a significant portion of its leather and finished goods inventory from foreign vendors with payment terms in U.S. dollars. The Company uses a combination of foreign exchange contracts and spot purchases to manage its foreign exchange exposure on cash flows related to these purchases. A foreign exchange contract represents an option with a counterparty to buy or sell a foreign currency to meet its obligations. Credit risk exists in the event of a failure by a counterparty to fulfill its obligations. The Company reduces this risk by mainly dealing with highly-rated counterparties such as major Canadian financial institutions.

During the years ended June 28, 2014 and June 29, 2013, the Company entered into foreign exchange contracts with Canadian financial institutions as counterparties with U.S. dollar notional amounts as listed below. Foreign exchange contracts outstanding as at June 28, 2014 expired or will expire at various times between July 3, 2014 and April 24, 2015 and the foreign exchange contracts that were outstanding as at June 29, 2013 expired or will expire between July 8, 2013 and August 29, 2014.

	Year Ended	
	June 28, 2014	June 29, 2013
Notional amount outstanding at beginning of period (US$000)	$32,700	$21,000
Notional amount of foreign exchange contracts entered into during the period (US$000)	21,800	38,200
Notional amount of foreign exchange contracts expired during the period (US$000)	(29,000)	(26,500)
Notional amount outstanding at end of period (US$000)	$25,500	$32,700
Maturing in less than 1 year (US$000)	$25,500	$29,000
Maturing from 1 to 2 years (US$000)	-	$3,700
Fair value of foreign exchange contracts — gain/(loss) – (CDN$000)	($364)	$822

As at June 28, 2014, a sensitivity analysis was performed on the Company's U.S. dollar denominated financial instruments, which principally consist of US$1.7 million of cash, to determine how a change in the U.S. dollar exchange rate would impact net earnings. A 500 basis point rise or fall in the Canadian dollar against the U.S. dollar, assuming that all other variables, in particular interest rates, remain the same, would have resulted in a $62 decrease or increase in the Company's net loss for the year ended June 28, 2014.

Liquidity Risk

Liquidity risk is the risk that the Company will not be able to meet its financial obligations as they become due. The Company's approach to managing liquidity risk is to ensure, to the extent possible, that it will have sufficient liquidity to meet its liabilities when due. As at June 28, 2014, the Company had $13.5 million of cash; an operating credit facility of $25 million and term capex facility of $4 million that are committed until June 25, 2016; and a $10 million uncommitted letter of credit facility which includes an uncommitted demand overdraft facility in the amount of $0.5 million and an uncommitted foreign exchange credit line in the amount of US$4.05 million related thereto. The credit facilities are used to finance seasonal working capital requirements for merchandise purchases and other corporate purposes. The Company expects that the majority of its payables and accruals and deferred revenue will be discharged within 90 days.

Interest Rate Risk

Interest rate risk is the risk that the fair value or future cash flows of a financial instrument will fluctuate because of changes in market interest rates. The Company's exposure to interest rate fluctuations is primarily related to cash borrowings under its existing credit facility, which bears interest at floating rates, and interest earned on its cash balances. The Company has performed a sensitivity analysis on interest rate risk at June 28, 2014 to determine how a change in interest rates would have impacted net loss. As at June 28, 2014, the Company's cash available for investment was approximately $13.5 million. A 100 basis point change in interest rates would have increased or decreased net loss by approximately $0.1 million for the year ended June 28, 2014. This analysis assumes that all other variables, in particular foreign currency exchange rates, remain constant.

Equity Price Risk

Equity price risk is the risk that the fair value or future cash flows of a financial instrument will fluctuate because of changes in market equity prices. The Company's exposure to equity price fluctuations is primarily related to the RSU and DSU liability included in payables and accruals. The value of the vested DSU and RSU liability is adjusted to reflect changes in the market value of the Company's Subordinate Voting Shares on the TSX. The Company has performed a sensitivity analysis on equity price risk as at June 28, 2014 to determine how a change in the price of the Company's Subordinate Voting Shares would have impacted net loss. As at June 28, 2014, a total of 123,389 RSUs and 83,136 DSUs have been granted and are outstanding. An increase or decrease of $1.00 in the market price of the Company's Subordinate Voting Shares would have increased or decreased net loss by approximately $0.2 million for the year ended June 28, 2014. This analysis assumes that all RSUs and DSUs were fully vested and all other variables remain constant.

Credit Risk

Credit risk is the risk that a customer or counterparty to a financial instrument will cause a financial loss to the Company by failing to meet its obligations. The Company's financial instruments that are exposed to concentrations of credit risk are primarily cash, accounts receivable and foreign exchange option contracts. The Company limits its exposure to credit risk with respect to cash by investing in short-term deposits with major Canadian financial institutions. The Company's accounts receivable, excluding derivative financial instruments, consist primarily of credit card receivables from the last few days of the fiscal period end, which are settled within the first few days of the new fiscal period. Accounts receivable also consist of accounts receivable from distributors and corporate customers. Accounts receivable are net of applicable allowance for doubtful accounts, which is established based on the specific credit risks associated with the distributor and each corporate customer and other relevant information. The allowance for doubtful accounts is assessed on a quarterly basis. Concentration of credit risk with respect to accounts receivable from distributors and corporate customers is limited due to the relatively insignificant balances outstanding and the number of different customers comprising the Company's customer base. Credit risk for foreign exchange option contracts exists in the event of a failure by a counterparty to fulfill its obligations. The Company reduces this risk by mainly dealing with highly-rated counterparties such as major Canadian financial institutions.

As at June 28, 2014, the Company's exposure to credit risk for these financial instruments was cash of $13.5 million, accounts receivable of $0.6 million and foreign exchange option contracts that had a notional value of US$25.5 million.

19. CAPITAL DISCLOSURE:

The Company defines its capital as shareholders' equity. The Company's objectives in managing capital are to:

- Ensure sufficient liquidity to support its current operations and execute its business plans;
- Enable the internal financing of capital projects; and
- Maintain a strong capital base so as to maintain investor, creditor and market confidence.

The Company's primary uses of capital are to finance non-cash working capital along with capital expenditures for new store additions, existing store renovation or relocation projects, information technology software and hardware purchases and production machinery and equipment purchases. The Company maintains a $25 million operating credit facility, a $4 million term capex facility and a $10 million uncommitted letter of credit facility which includes an uncommitted demand overdraft facility in the amount of $0.5 million and an uncommitted foreign exchange line in the amount of US$4.05 million related thereto, that it uses to finance seasonal working capital requirements for merchandise purchases and other corporate purposes. The Company does not have any long-term debt and therefore net earnings generated from operations are available for reinvestment in the Company.

The Board of Directors does not establish quantitative return on capital criteria for management, but rather promotes year-over-year sustainable profitable growth. On a quarterly basis, the Board of Directors monitors share repurchase program activities. Decisions on whether to repurchase shares are made on a specific transaction basis and depend on the Company's cash position, estimates of future cash requirements, market prices and regulatory restrictions, among other things. The Company does not currently pay dividends.

Externally imposed capital requirements include a debt-to-equity ratio covenant as part of the operating credit facility. The Company was in compliance with this covenant as at June 28, 2014 and June 29, 2013. There has been no change with respect to the overall capital risk management strategy during the year ended June 28, 2014.

20. RELATED PARTIES:

Key management personnel are those individuals having authority and responsibility for planning, directing and controlling the activities of the Company, including members of the Company's Board of Directors. The Company considers key management to be the Company's Board of Directors and its five most highly compensated executive officers. Compensation awarded to key management included:

	Year Ended	
	June 28, 2014	June 29, 2013
Salaries and short-term benefits	$2,090	$2,000
Termination benefits	457	-
Share-based compensation	249	810
	$2,796	$2,810

The Company's subsidiaries are described in Note 3(b).

21. EXPENSE ANALYSIS:

Selling, general and administrative expenses include the following:

	Year Ended	
	June 28, 2014	June 29, 2013
Selling expense	$60,168	$60,464
General and administrative expense	18,918	16,156
	$79,086	$76,620

Selling expense comprises costs incurred to operate the Company's stores including wages and benefits for store management and staff, rent and occupancy, advertising, credit card fees, amortization of store property and equipment and computer software and other store operating expenses.

General and administrative expense includes the cost of design, merchandising, sourcing, merchandise planning, marketing, store administrative support, finance, loss prevention, information technology, human resource and executive functions.

22. EMPLOYEE BENEFITS EXPENSE:

Selling, general and administrative expenses include the following:

	Year Ended	
	June 28, 2014	June 29, 2013
Wages, salaries and bonus	$27,523	$27,783
Short-term benefits expense	4,125	4,295
Termination benefits	783	237
Share-based compensation	348	898
	$32,779	$33,213

GLOSSARY

A

Accelerated depreciation method A method of depreciation that allocates a higher portion of an asset's cost to the earlier years of its life than to the later years. (p. 367)

Accounting cycle The sequence of steps that occurs in the recording, summarizing, and reporting of events in the accounting system. (p. 120)

Accounting equation The equation that provides structure to the financial statements, in which assets = liabilities + shareholders' equity. (p. 16)

Accounting Standards for Private Enterprises (ASPE) Accounting standards that Canadian private companies may follow, unless they elect to use International Financial Reporting Standards. (p. 52)

Accounts Elements of a company's financial records that group transactions of a similar nature and are given a title, such as Cash, or Equipment, or Retained Earnings. (p. 58)

Accounts payable payment period A measure of the number of days, on average, it takes a company to pay suppliers, calculated as 365 days divided by the accounts payable turnover. (p. 560)

Accounts payable turnover The number of times per year that a company settles (pays) its accounts payable. It is calculated as the credit purchases divided by the average accounts payable. (pp. 421, 559)

Accounts receivable Assets of a seller that represent the promise made by buyers to pay the seller at some date in the future. (p. 269)

Accounts receivable turnover The number of times that accounts receivable are turned over, or how often they are collected in full and replaced by new accounts. It is calculated as the credit sales divided by the average accounts receivable. (pp. 289, 556)

Accrual basis of accounting The accounting basis, used by almost all companies, that recognizes revenues in the period when they are earned and expenses in the period in which they are incurred, and not necessarily in the period when the related cash inflows and outflows occur. (p. 55)

Accrual entry In the context of pension accounting, the journal entry to record the pension expense and create the pension obligation. (p. 456)

Accruals Adjusting journal entries required when a company needs to recognize a revenue before the receipt of cash or an expense prior to the payment of cash. (p. 133)

Accumulated depreciation The total amount of depreciation expense that has been taken on an asset, up to a particular point in time. (pp. 129, 363)

Accumulated impairment losses A contra-asset account representing all of the impairment charges recorded on property, plant, and equipment. (p. 363)

Accumulated other comprehensive income (AOCI) A component of shareholders' equity representing the cumulative amount of unrealized increases and decreases in the values of an entity's net assets. (p. 498)

Acid test ratio Synonym for *quick ratio*. (p. 288)

Activity ratios Ratios used to assess how efficiently a company manages its operations. Synonym for *operating efficiency ratios*. (p. 553)

Actuary A professional, trained in statistical methods, who can make detailed estimates of pension costs. (p. 456)

Adjusted trial balance A listing of the accounts and their balances after the adjusting entries have been made, but before the closing entries have been made. (p. 134)

Adjusting entries Journal entries made at the end of the accounting period to record an event or transaction that was not recorded during the period. Events or transactions that are not signalled in any other way are recorded through adjusting entries. The entries do not involve the Cash account. (p. 133)

Aging of accounts receivable method The process of analyzing customers' accounts and categorizing them by how long they have been outstanding. Usually done as a basis for estimating what amounts may be uncollectible. Also known as the statement of financial position method. (p. 281)

Allowance for doubtful accounts A contra account to accounts receivable, reflecting the estimated amount of accounts receivable that will be uncollectible and eventually have to be written off. (p. 277)

Allowance method A method used to value accounts receivable by estimating the amount of accounts receivable that will not be collected in the future. Makes it possible to recognize bad debts expense in the period of the sale rather than waiting until specific non-paying customers can be identified. (p. 277)

Amortization The depreciation of intangible assets that are not natural resources. (p. 381)

Amortization of bond discount (or premium) Difference between the contract rate and yield rate on bonds a company issues. (p. 450)

Annual meeting Meeting of shareholders required to be held every year by public companies during which shareholders elect the corporation's board of directors, among other things. (p. 502)

Annual report An annual document prepared and published by a corporation in which it reports on its business activities during the year. The report includes the corporation's annual financial statements. (p. 4)

Anti-dilution provision Synonym for *pre-emptive right*. (p. 503)

Articles of incorporation A document filed with federal or provincial regulatory authorities when a business incorporates under that jurisdiction. The articles include, among other items, the authorized number of shares and dividend preferences for each class of shares that is to be issued. (p. 499)

Assets Elements of the statement of financial position that have probable future benefits that can be measured, are owned or controlled by a company, and are the result of a past transaction. (p. 16)

Auditor A professionally trained accountant who examines a company's accounting records and financial statements and provides an opinion regarding whether they fairly present the company's financial position and operating results in accordance with accounting standards. (p. 23)

Audit trail Sequence of transactions and events as traced by an auditor or company official through source documents. (p. 271)

Authorized shares The maximum number of shares that a company is authorized to issue under its articles of incorporation. (p. 499)

Average collection period Average length of time, in days, that it takes a company to collect its receivables, calculated as 365 days divided by the accounts receivable turnover. (pp. 290, 557)

Average payment period The average number of days that a company takes to pay for its credit purchases. (p. 421)

B

Bad debts expense Bad debts resulting from customers who fail to pay their accounts, as a result of selling on account. (p. 276)

Bank indebtedness The amount that a company has borrowed on its line of credit from its bank. (p. 407)

Bank overdraft facility A pre-arranged short-term loan that a company can draw upon as required. (p. 214)

Bank reconciliation The procedure that is used to identify the differences between the cash balance recorded in a company's accounting records and the balance per its bank statement. This enables the company to ensure that everything is correctly recorded and to determine the correct amount of cash available. (p. 271)

Basic earnings per share A measure of a company's performance, calculated by dividing the net income for the period, less preferred dividends, by the weighted average number of common shares that were outstanding during the period. Determines the profit earned on each common share. (pp. 188, 564)

Basket purchase A purchase of assets in which more than one asset is acquired for a single purchase price. Synonym for *lump-sum purchase*. (p. 364)

Blended instalment payments Loan payments that consist of both interest and principal, with the total amount remaining constant but the portion for interest becoming smaller as each payment is made and the outstanding loan principal is reduced. (pp. 408, 444)

Board of directors The governing body of a company elected by the shareholders to represent their ownership interests. (p. 6)

Bond A corporation's long-term borrowing that is evidenced by a bond certificate. The borrowing is characterized by a face value, interest rate, and maturity date. (p. 447)

Bond interest rate An interest rate that is specified in a bond contract and used to determine the interest payments that are made on the bond. Synonym for *contract rate* and *coupon rate*. (p. 447)

Breakage The estimate of the amount of gift cards that will not be redeemed by their holders. (p. 412)

Bundling A practice by some companies, such as telecommunications companies, of selling services and/or goods together at a discount. (p. 179)

C

Canada Pension Plan (CPP) The federal government program providing retirement benefits to retired workers based on the premiums they and their employers paid into the plan when they were working. (p. 416)

Canada Revenue Agency The federal taxing authority in Canada, which is responsible for federal tax collection. (p. 7)

Capital appreciation The gain or increase in value in a company's share price. (p. 10)

Capital assets Long-lived assets that are normally used by a company in generating revenues and providing services (such as buildings and equipment). (p. 361)

Capital cost allowance (CCA) The deduction permitted by the Canada Revenue Agency for tax purposes, instead of depreciation. (pp. 378, 458)

Capitalized Characteristic of a cost that has been recorded as an asset, rather than an expense. (p. 363)

Carrying amount The full value of all of a company's accounts receivable less the allowance for doubtful accounts. In the context of long-term assets, carrying amount or carrying value is equal to the asset's cost, less accumulated depreciation, less accumulated impairment losses. It represents the portion of the asset's cost that has yet to be expensed. Synonym for *net book value*. (pp. 74, 277, 363, 451)

Cash Amounts of money a company has on hand, plus balances in chequing and savings accounts, plus cash equivalents. (pp. 213, 269)

Cash basis of accounting The accounting basis, used by some entities, that recognizes revenues whenever cash is received and expenses when cash is paid, regardless of whether the revenues have been earned or expenses incurred. (p. 55)

Cash equivalents Current assets that are very liquid and readily convertible into cash, or current liabilities that may require the immediate use of cash. Examples are short-term investments and bank overdrafts or lines of credit. (pp. 213, 270)

Cash flow The net change in cash that occurs from the beginning of an accounting period to the end of the period. (p. 209)

Cash flow pattern The direction (positive or negative) of cash flows in three categories: operating, investing, and financing. (p. 227)

Cash flows to total liabilities ratio The portion of total obligations that could be met with operating cash flows, calculated by dividing cash flows from operating activities by total liabilities. (pp. 228, 560)

Cash-to-cash cycle The period of time between when cash is disbursed for the purchase of inventory and when cash is received from selling the inventory and collecting the accounts receivable. (p. 225)

Change in an accounting estimate Any change to an estimate made by management for accounting purposes, including an asset's useful life or residual value, the percentage of receivables considered to be uncollectible, the extent of warranty claims, and so on. (p. 374)

Chart of accounts A listing of the names of the accounts used in a particular accounting system. (p. 121)

Classified statement of financial position A statement of financial position in which the assets and liabilities are listed in liquidity order and are categorized into current (or short-term) and non-current (or long-term) sections. (pp. 16, 73)

Closing entries Entries made at the end of the accounting period to transfer the balances from the temporary revenue, expense, and dividend declared accounts into the retained earnings account. Resets the balance of all temporary accounts to zero. (p. 137)

Collateral An asset that has been pledged as security for a debt. If the borrower defaults on the debt, the lender can have the collateral seized and sold, with the proceeds used to repay the debt. (pp. 408, 447)

Collusion What occurs when two or more employees work together to commit theft, fraud, or another crime, and conceal it. (p. 271)

Commitments Obligations that a company has undertaken that do not yet meet the recognition criteria for liabilities. Significant commitments are disclosed in the notes to the financial statements. Synonym for *contractual commitments*. (p. 459)

Common shares Certificates that represent portions of ownership in a corporation. These shares usually carry a right to vote. (pp. 8, 501)

Common-size analysis Analysis performed by converting the dollar values in a company's financial statements into percentages of a specific base amount. (p. 551)

Common-size statement of financial position Statement of financial position in which each item is determined as a percentage of total assets. (p. 551)

Common-size statement of income Statement of income in which each item is expressed as a percentage of total revenues. (p. 551)

Comparability An enhancing qualitative characteristic that states that accounting information has when financial statement readers are able to compare different sets of financial statements over time and across like companies. (p. 53)

Comparative information Financial information showing the results of both the current period and preceding period. (p. 13)

Complete An element of the fundamental qualitative characteristic of faithful representation that states that financial statements should provide users with all of the information needed to understand what is being presented in the statements, including any necessary explanations. (p. 54)

Compound journal entry A journal entry with more than two parts (that is, multiple debits and/or multiple credits). As with any journal entry, the total amount debited must equal the total amount credited. (p. 127)

Comprehensive income The total change in the shareholders' equity (net assets) of the entity from non-owner sources. Includes net income as well as other components, which generally represent unrealized gains and losses. (p. 184)

Conceptual framework A framework that provides the underlying set of objectives and concepts that guide accounting standard-setting bodies and assists accountants in determining how to account for items for which no specific standards have been developed. (p. 52)

Confirmatory value An element of the fundamental qualitative characteristic of relevance that states that accounting information is relevant to decision makers if it provides feedback on their previous decisions. (p. 53)

Consignee An entity that sells goods on consignment on behalf of consignors, receiving a commission when the goods are sold. (p. 320)

Consignment The selling of goods on behalf of another party, usually for a commission. (p. 320)

Consignor The owner of goods sold on consignment by a consignee.(p. 320)

Consolidated financial statements Financial statements that represent the combined financial results of a parent company and its subsidiaries. (p. 12)

Consolidation Synonym for *reverse stock split*. (p. 512)

Contingent liability A liability that is not recorded in the accounts, because it depends on a future event that is not considered probable and/or cannot be estimated reliably. Significant contingent liabilities are disclosed in the notes. (p. 460)

Contra-asset account An account used to record reductions in a related asset account. An example is accumulated depreciation. (pp. 129, 363)

Contra-revenue account An account that is offset against (reduces) a revenue account on the statement of income. Examples include sales returns and allowances and sales discounts. (pp. 180, 414)

Contract rate Synonym for *bond interest rate* and *coupon rate*. (p. 447)

Contractual commitments Synonym for *commitments*. (p. 459)

Contributed Surplus The account that records a surplus arising from certain transactions with shareholders involving the sale or repurchase of a company's shares or the issuance of stock options and that do not fit the definitions of share capital or retained earnings. (p. 498)

Control account An account that contains the overall amounts related to a particular item in the financial statements, with the details recorded in a subledger. For example, Accounts Receivable is a control account, containing the total balance for all of a company's receivables, while the Accounts Receivable subledger would contain the balances for each of the individual customers. The balance in the control account should equal the sum of all the balances in the related subledger. (p. 277)

Convertible bond A bond that is convertible into common shares under certain conditions. (p. 447)

Convertible preferred shares Preferred shares that are exchangeable or convertible into a specified number of common shares. (p. 506)

Corporate tax return An annual filing required of corporations by the federal government to determine the amount of corporate income tax owed. Synonym for *T2*. (p. 420)

Cost The price paid to acquire goods (such as property, plant, and equipment) and services. (p. 363)

Cost constraint A constraint within the conceptual framework that states that, when preparing financial statements, the benefits of reporting financial information must exceed the costs of doing so. (p. 54)

Cost formula Method of allocating cost of goods available for sale to cost of goods sold and ending inventory. (p. 326)

Cost model A model under which property, plant, and equipment are reflected on the statement of financial position at their carrying amount. (p. 363)

Cost of goods available for sale (COGAS) The cost of all of the goods that a company had available to sell to its customers during the period, calculated as the cost of the opening inventory plus the cost of purchases. (p. 321)

Cost of goods sold The expense that records the cost to the selling company of the inventory that was sold during the period. (p. 63)

Cost-to-sales ratio Ratio reflecting the normal markup that a company applies to its products, calculated as the product's cost price divided by its marked-up selling price. (p. 336)

Coupon rate Synonym for *bond interest rate* and *contract rate*. (p. 447)

Covenants Conditions or restrictions placed on a company that borrows money. The covenants usually require the company to maintain certain minimum ratios and may restrict its ability to pay dividends. (pp. 289, 445)

Coverage A company's ability to meet future obligations, including interest expense or total liabilities. Also known as solvency. (p. 560)

Coverage ratios   Ratios that can be used to assess a company's ability to meet future obligations. Examples include the interest coverage ratio and the cash flows to total liabilities ratio. (p. 560)

Credit   The right side of a T account, or an entry made to the right side of a T account. (p. 118)

Credit card discount   Fee charged by credit card companies to merchants making sales. (p. 286)

Creditors   Individuals or entities that are owed something by a company. (p. 3)

Credit sale   Synonym for a sale *on account*. (p. 63)

Cross-sectional analysis   A type of financial statement analysis in which one company is compared with other companies, either within the same industry or across industries, for the same time period. (p. 548)

Cumulative preferred shares   Preferred shares that accumulate dividends in periods even if there are no dividends declared. These accumulated undeclared dividends, called dividends in arrears, must be paid before a dividend can be declared for common shareholders. (p. 505)

Current   An asset or a liability that will be received, realized, or consumed, or else settled or paid within 12 months from year end. (p. 16)

Current asset   An asset that will be turned into cash or consumed in the next year or operating cycle of a company. (p. 16)

Current liability   A liability that will require the use of cash or the rendering of a service, or will be replaced by another current liability, within the next year or operating cycle of the company. (p. 16)

Current portion of long-term debt   The portion of long-term debt that is due within one year (or one operating cycle). (p. 408)

Current ratio   A ratio that is calculated by dividing the total current assets by the total current liabilities and is a measure of short-term liquidity. Synonym for *working capital ratio*. (pp. 287, 555)

Customer loyalty provision   A current liability arising when a company has loyalty programs that enable customers to accumulate points or other credits when making purchases and redeem them for free goods or services. Companies offering such programs must estimate the value of the outstanding loyalty points and establish a liability for them. (p. 410)

D

Date of declaration   The date on which the board of directors votes to declare a dividend. On this date, the dividend becomes legally payable to shareholders and a liability to the company. (p. 507)

Date of payment   The date on which a dividend is paid to shareholders. (p. 508)

Date of record   The date on which a shareholder must own the shares in order to receive the dividend from a share. (p. 507)

Days to sell inventory ratio   The number of days, on average, that it took a company to sell through its inventory, calculated as 365 days divided by the inventory turnover ratio. (pp. 335, 558)

Debenture   A bond that is issued with no specific collateral. (p. 447)

Debit   The left side of a T account, or an entry made to the left side of a T account. (p. 118)

Debt to equity ratio   A measure of a company's leverage (the amount of debt relative to shareholders' equity), calculated as net debt divided by shareholders' equity. (pp. 461, 560)

Deferrals   Adjusting journal entries required when a company needs to recognize a revenue in an accounting period after the cash has been received or an expense in an accounting period after the cash has been paid. (p. 133)

Deferred income taxes   An asset or liability representing tax on the difference between the accounting balance of assets/liabilities at a given point in time and the tax balance of the same assets/liabilities. These differences arise when a company uses one method for accounting purposes and a different method for tax purposes. Synonym for *future income taxes*. (p. 458)

Deferred revenues   A liability representing cash receipts from customers that have not yet met the criteria for revenue recognition. Synonym for *unearned revenues*. (p. 410)

Defined benefit pension plan   A pension plan that specifies the benefits that employees will receive in their retirement. The benefits are usually determined based on the number of years of service and the highest salary earned by the employee. (p. 455)

Defined contribution pension plan   A pension plan that specifies how much a company will contribute to its employees' pension fund. No guarantee is made of the amount that will be available to the employees upon retirement. (p. 455)

Demand deposits   Amounts in chequing and savings accounts with banks and other financial institutions. (p. 213)

Depreciable amount   The portion of an asset's cost that should be expensed over the periods in which the asset is expected to help generate revenues, calculated by the cost minus the estimated residual value. (p. 366)

Depreciation   The allocation of the cost of capital assets to expense over their estimated useful lives. (pp. 68, 363)

Depreciation rate   A percentage that describes the amount of depreciation to be recorded during a given period. For straight-line depreciation, the rate is equal to one divided by the number of years of the asset's useful life. (p. 368)

Derecognized   The removal of a long-lived asset from the accounts upon its disposal or when it no longer provides any future benefits. (p. 377)

Diluted earnings per share   A type of earnings per share calculation whose purpose is to provide the lowest possible earnings per share figure under the assumption that all of a company's convertible securities and options have been converted into common shares. It measures the maximum potential dilution in earnings per share that would occur under these assumed conversions. (p. 565)

Diminishing-balance method   An accelerated method of depreciation that assumes that a greater proportion of the asset's economic benefits will be consumed early in its useful life and less as time goes by. (p. 367)

Direct method   A method of presenting the cash flow from operations that shows the direct gross amounts of cash receipts from revenues and cash payments for expenses. (p. 214)

Direct writeoff method   A method that only recognizes bad debts when the accounts receivable of specific customers are written off. No estimates of future writeoffs are made, and the allowance for doubtful accounts is not required. (p. 285)

Discount   In the context of bond prices, a term used to indicate that a bond is sold or issued at an amount below its face value. (p. 449)

Dividend declaration   An action by a corporation's board of directors that legally obliges the corporation to pay a dividend. (p. 507)

Dividend payout ratio   A measure of the portion of a company's earnings that are distributed as dividends, calculated by dividing dividends per share by earnings per share. (pp. 514, 566)

Dividend yield ratio   A measure of the dividends an investor will receive relative to the share price, calculated by dividing dividends per share by price per share. (p. 514)

Dividends   Payments made to shareholders that represent a portion of a company's net income that is being distributed to shareholders. Dividends are paid only after they are declared by the board of directors. (p. 10)

Dividends in arrears   Dividends on cumulative preferred shares that have not yet been declared from a prior year. (p. 505)

Double-diminishing-balance method   A particular type of diminishing-balance depreciation method that is calculated by using a percentage rate that is double the rate that would be used for straight-line depreciation. Also known as the double-declining-balance method. (p. 370)

Double-entry accounting system   An accounting system that maintains the equality of the basic accounting equation by requiring that each entry have equal amounts of debits and credits. (pp. 57, 117)

E

Earned   What occurs when a company has provided goods or services to customers and it is probable that measurable economic benefits will flow to a company. (p. 56)

Earnings   Synonym for *net income, net earnings*, and *profit*. (p. 12)

Earnings before interest, taxes, depreciation, and amortization (EBITDA)   The amount of a company's earnings before interest, taxes, depreciation, and amortization are deducted. (p. 463)

Earnings management   The practice of choosing revenue and expense methods so that earnings are increased or decreased in particular accounting periods, or smoothed over time. (pp. 14, 373)

Earnings per share (EPS)   A ratio calculated by dividing the earnings for the period by the average number of shares outstanding during the period. (pp. 14, 188, 513)

EBITDAR   Earnings before interest, taxes, depreciation, acquisition, and restructuring. (p. 547)

Effective rate   The interest rate that reflects the rate of return earned by investors when they purchase a bond, and the real interest cost to the issuer of the bond. It reflects the competitive market rate for similar bonds, and is used in determining the selling price of the bond. Synonym for *yield*. (p. 447)

Electronic data interchange (EDI)   A link between two companies with computers allowing inventory to be ordered directly over the computer connection. (p. 325)

Electronic funds transfer (EFT)   Receipts or payments made directly between two bank accounts through computer networks. (p. 271)

Employment Insurance (EI)   The federal government program that provides benefits to unemployed individuals looking for work or undergoing retraining, maternity and paternity benefits to parents, and payments to workers who are sick or who have to leave their job to care for a seriously ill family member. (p. 416)

Enhancing qualitative characteristics Qualitative characteristics of financial statements that enhance the usefulness of information. (p. 53)

Equity The net assets of a company (its assets less its liabilities), representing the interest of shareholders in the company. It is the sum of a company's share capital and retained earnings. It is also sometimes used to refer simply to the shareholders' equity section of the statement of financial position. (p. 15)

Equity analysis ratios Ratios used to assess shareholder returns. (p. 553)

Estimated residual value The amount a company estimates it may be able to recover from the disposal of an asset when the company is finished using it. The amount is equal to the estimate of the amount that the company would receive today if it disposed of the asset in the age and condition it is expected to be in at the time of disposal. (pp. 68, 366)

Estimated useful life The amount of time a company estimates an asset will be used to generate revenue. (pp. 68, 366)

Ex-dividend date The date on which shares are sold in the market without the most recently declared dividend. (p. 508)

Expensed The practice of classifying a cost, such as repairs to an item of property, plant, and equipment, as a cost in a certain period rather than capitalizing it. (p. 365)

Expenses The decrease in economic benefit that results from resources that flow out of the company in the course of it generating its revenues. (p. 12)

F

Face value A value in a bond contract that specifies the cash payment that will be made on the bond's maturity date. The face value is also used to determine the periodic interest payments made on the bond. (pp. 179, 447)

Factor A company purchasing the accounts receivable of another company. (p. 287)

Factoring The process whereby a company sells its accounts receivable to another company, typically a financial institution (known as the factor). Often done to shorten the cash-to-cash cycle. (p. 287)

Finance lease A lease arrangement that the lessee must treat as the acquisition of an asset and a related long-term liability, as if the transaction represented a purchase of the asset with financing. (p. 453)

Financial accounting The study of the accounting concepts and principles that are used to prepare financial statements for external users. (p. 3)

Financial statement users Decision makers who utilize a company's financial statements, which include the owners (shareholders) and those who have lent money to the organization. (p. 3)

Financial statements Reports prepared by the management of a company for its shareholders, creditors, and others summarizing how the company performed during a particular period. Includes the statement of financial position, the statement of income, the statement of changes in equity, the statement of cash flows, and the notes to the financial statements. (p. 4)

Financing activities A company's activities that involve raising funds to support the other activities of the company or represent a return of these funds. The two major ways to raise funds are to issue new shares or borrow money. Funds can be returned via debt repayment, dividend payments, or the repurchase of shares. (pp. 9, 210)

Financing agreement A lending agreement between a lender and a borrower which specifies the terms and conditions of the loan. These include loan term, interest rate, repayment provisions, and so on. (p. 444)

Finished goods Products completed by a manufacturer and ready for sale to customers. (p. 319)

Finite useful life The characteristic of an asset that will generate economic benefits for a fixed period in the future. (p. 381)

First-in, first-out (FIFO) The cost flow formula that assigns the cost of the first unit into the inventory to the first unit sold. (p. 326)

Fiscal year The one-year period that represents a company's operating year. (p. 13)

Fixed dividend rate Stated amount of dividends paid on preferred shares, stated as either a dollar amount per share (a quarterly or annual dividend rate per share per year) or as a percentage of the share's issue price. Synonym for *stated dividend rate*. (p. 504)

Floating rate Amount of dividend paid on preferred shares that changes as interest rates change. (p. 504)

FOB destination Shipping term signifying that the seller is responsible for paying shipping and any other costs incurred while the goods are in transit from the seller's premises to the buyer's premises. (p. 320)

FOB shipping point Shipping term signifying that the buyer is responsible for paying shipping and any other costs incurred while the goods are in transit from the seller's premises to the buyer's premises. (p. 320)

Free cash flow The amount of cash that a company generates from its operations that is in excess of the cash required to maintain the company's productive capacity. (p. 229)

Free from error An element of the fundamental qualitative characteristic of faithful representation that states that financial information should be determined based on the best information available, using the correct process and with an adequate explanation provided. (p. 54)

Fully funded A pension plan in which the value of the plan assets equals the amount of the projected benefit obligation. (p. 456)

Function A method of organizing expenses on the statement of income by way of the activity (business function) for which they were incurred (such as cost of goods sold, administrative, and selling). (p. 185)

Fundamental qualitative characteristics Qualitative characteristics of financial statements that are essential if financial information is to be considered useful and, without them, the information is useless. Relevance and representational faithfulness are both fundamental qualitative characteristics. (p. 53)

Funding entry The journal entry made to show the cash payment made to the trustee of a pension plan to fund the obligation. (p. 456)

Future income taxes Synonym for *deferred income taxes*. (p. 458)

G

Gains Increases in income resulting from the sale of investments; property, plant, and equipment; or intangible assets at amounts in excess of their carrying amounts. (pp. 12, 377)

General journal A chronological listing of all the events that are recorded in a company's accounting system. (p. 123)

General ledger (G/L) The financial records containing details on a company's asset, liability, and shareholders' equity, revenue, and expense accounts. (p. 119)

General ledger account An account in the general ledger. (p. 119)

General revenue recognition criteria Criteria established by accounting standard setters to help management and other financial statement users determine when revenue is earned. (p. 174)

Gift card liability A current liability arising when customers purchase gift cards (or gift certificates) from a company. Until such time as the gift card is used, the company has a liability. (p. 410)

Goodwill An intangible asset that represents a company's above-average earning capacity as a result of

reputation, advantageous location, superior sales staff, expertise of employees, and so on. It is only recorded when a company acquires another company and pays more for it than the fair market value of its identifiable net assets. (p. 362)

Gross margin Sales revenue minus cost of goods sold. Synonym for *gross profit*. (p. 333)

Gross margin estimation method A method for estimating the cost of ending inventory by converting the sales amount to cost of goods sold using the gross margin ratio. The calculated cost of goods sold amount is subtracted from the goods available for sale to determine the ending inventory cost. (p. 336)

Gross profit Synonym for *gross margin*. (p. 13)

Gross profit margin A profitability ratio that compares the gross profit with a company's sales. It measures what portion of each sales dollar is available to cover other expenses after covering the cost of goods sold. (p. 562)

Gross wages Wages earned by employees before source deductions. (p. 417)

H

Homogenous Characteristic of inventory that is interchangeable (that is, where one unit of inventory cannot be distinguished from another), such as litres of fuel. (p. 327)

Hybrid pension plan Pension plan combining features of defined contribution and defined benefit plans, which establishes targeted benefit levels that are funded through fixed contributions by both the employer and employee. Synonym for *target benefit plan*. (p. 457)

I

Immaterial The characteristic of information in financial statements that would not affect the user's decisions. (p. 53)

Impaired The characteristic of an asset whose expected future economic benefits are estimated to be less than its carrying amount as a result of a change in circumstance. This results in its carrying amount being reduced accordingly. (p. 376)

Impairment loss The decline in the recoverable value of an asset below its current carrying value. It is recognized as a loss on the statement of income. (p. 376)

Income The inflow of resources that increase shareholders' equity but are not the result of shareholder activities. Income includes revenues and gains. (p. 12)

Income Summary account An optional account that is often used when closing the books, to summarize all the temporary statement of income accounts (revenues and expenses) before transferring the net income to retained earnings. (p. 137)

Incorporation The process of organizing a business as a separate legal entity having ownership divided into transferable shares held by shareholders. (p. 59)

Incurred What occurs when an expense needs to be recorded in the period in which it has helped to generate revenue. (p. 56)

Indefinite useful life The characteristic of an asset for which there is no foreseeable limit to the period in which it will generate economic benefits. (p. 381)

Indenture agreement An agreement that accompanies the issuance of a bond and specifies all the borrowing terms and restrictions, or covenants. (p. 447)

Indirect method A method of presenting the cash flow from operations in which the amount of net income is adjusted for all the non-cash revenues or expenses, to convert net income from an accrual-basis amount to its cash-basis equivalent. (p. 214)

Initial public offering (IPO) The initial offering of a corporation's shares to the public. (p. 501)

Instalment loan A type of loan in which payments (including both interest and a portion of the principal) are made periodically, rather than only at the end of the loan. (p. 444)

Institutional investors Banks, insurance companies, pension funds, and other institutions that purchase corporate bonds or shares. (p. 447)

Intangible asset A non-physical capital asset that usually involves a legal right, which will provide future economic benefits to the organization. (p. 362)

Interest An expense incurred on money borrowed from creditors that is incurred with the passage of time. (p. 7)

Interest-bearing debt Debt on which a company is required to pay interest, such as loans, mortgages, and bonds payable. (p. 461)

Interest coverage ratio A measure of a company's ability to meet its interest obligations through its earnings; that is, the company's ability to generate enough income from operations to pay its interest expense. It is calculated as the earnings before interest, taxes, depreciation, and amortization (EBITDA) divided by interest expense. Synonym for *times interest earned ratio*. (pp. 463, 560)

Internal control system The set of policies and procedures established by an enterprise to safeguard its assets and ensure the integrity of its accounting system. (p. 270)

International Financial Reporting Standards   (IFRS) The accounting standards that must be followed by Canadian public companies and that private companies may elect to adopt. (pp. 22, 52)

Inventory Any item purchased by a company for resale to customers or to be used in the manufacture of a product that is then sold to customers. (p. 317)

Inventory shrinkage The losses of inventory due to spoilage, damage, theft, or waste. (p. 323)

Inventory turnover ratio A ratio that measures how fast inventory is sold and how long it is held before it is sold. It is calculated as cost of goods sold divided by average inventory. (pp. 335, 558)

Inventory writedown The reduction of an inventory item's carrying amount when its estimated net realizable value is less than its cost. A writedown is treated as an expense (part of cost of goods sold) in that period. (p. 332)

Investing activities Company activities involving long-term investments. Primarily investments in property, plant, and equipment, and in the shares of other companies. (p. 9, 210)

Investment banker The intermediary who arranges the issuance of bonds in the public debt market on behalf of others. The investment banker sells the bonds to its clients before the bonds are traded in the open market. (p. 447)

Investors Individuals or entities that acquire shares of a company as an investment. (p. 3)

Issued shares The shares of a corporation that have been issued. (p. 500)

J

Journal entry An entry made in the general journal to record a transaction or event. (p. 123)

Just-in-time (JIT) A delivery strategy where the inventory is delivered as close as possible to the time when the customer will be ready to buy it. (p. 334)

L

Lease agreement An agreement between a lessee and a lessor (in the case of an operating lease) for the rental of or (in the case of a finance lease) the effective purchase of an asset. (p. 452)

Legal capital The amount that is recorded in the common share account when the shares are first issued. (p. 500)

Lessee The party or entity that is renting or effectively purchasing the asset in a lease arrangement. (p. 452)

Lessor   The owner of an asset that is rented or effectively sold to a lessee under a lease arrangement. (p. 452)

Leverage   A company's use of debt to improve the return to shareholders. (pp. 461, 560)

Leverage ratios   Ratios used to assess a company's level of leverage. (p. 560)

Liability   An element of the statement of financial position that leads to a probable future sacrifice of a company's resources. (p. 16)

Line of credit   An arrangement with a financial institution that allows a company to overdraw its bank account. The overdrawn amounts become a loan that must be repaid. (pp. 214, 407)

Liquidity   An organization's short-term ability to convert its assets into cash to be able to meet its obligations and pay its liabilities. (pp. 16, 119, 269)

Liquidity ratios   Ratios used to assess a company's ability to meet its obligations in the near future. (p. 553)

Loss   A decrease in income resulting from the sale of investments; property, plant, and equipment; or intangible assets at amounts less than their carrying amounts. (pp. 12, 377)

Lump-sum purchase   Synonym for *basket purchase*. (p. 364)

M

Management   The individuals responsible for running (managing) a company. (p. 3)

Management discussion and analysis (MD&A)   Section of a company's annual report where management provides their perspective and analysis of the financial statements. The information is meant to complement or supplement the financial statements and be forward-looking. (pp. 4, 229, 545)

Managerial accounting   The study of the preparation and uses of accounting information by a company's management. (p. 3)

Manufacturer   A company that makes products. (p. 317)

Market value   The amount that an item would generate if it were sold in a transaction between independent parties. (p. 19)

Material   The characteristic of information in financial statements that is relevant to the user's decisions. (p. 53)

Materiality   An element of the fundamental qualitative characteristic of relevance that states that information is material, if it would affect the decision-making of financial statement users. (p. 53)

Maturity date   The date in a bond contract that specifies when the principal amount borrowed must be repaid. (p. 447)

Memorandum entry   An entry made to record a stock split. No general ledger accounts are affected; only the record of the number of shares issued is affected. (p. 512)

Merchandiser   A company that purchases goods from manufacturers or suppliers and sells them to customers. Synonym for *retailer*. (p. 317)

Minority interest   A block of shares owed by an investor that represents less that 50% of the outstanding shares. Synonym for *non-controlling interest*. (p. 503)

Mortgage   A debt for which some type of property, plant, and equipment is pledged as collateral in the event of default by a company. (p. 444)

Multi-step statement of income   A statement of income in which revenues and expenses from different sources are shown in separate sections. (p. 182)

Multiple voting shares   A class of common shares granting special voting rights so that the holder is entitled to more than one vote for each of the common shares owned. (p. 503)

Mutually unexecuted contract   A contract between two entities in which neither entity has performed its part of the agreement. (p. 459)

N

Nature   A method of organizing expenses on the statement of income by way of their natural classification (such as salaries, transportation, depreciation, and advertising). (p. 185)

Net assets   Assets minus liabilities. Net assets are equal to shareholders' equity. Also known as shareholders' equity. (p. 19)

Net book value   Synonym for *carrying amount*. (p. 74)

Net debt   The amount of interest-bearing debt less the amount of cash or cash equivalents that a company has available. (p. 461)

Net debt as a percentage of total capitalization ratio   A measure of the proportion that debt makes up of a company's total capitalization; that is, what percentage debt represents of the company's total financing. It is calculated as net debt (interest-bearing debt minus cash) divided by total capitalization (shareholders' equity plus interest-bearing debt minus cash). (pp. 462, 560)

Net earnings   Synonym for *earnings, net income,* and *profit.* (p. 12)

Net free cash flow The cash flow generated from a company's operating activities that would be available to the company's common shareholders, calculated as cash flows from operating activities less net capital expenditures and dividends on preferred shares. (pp. 229, 567)

Net income A company's total revenues less its total expenses, plus gains, less losses. Synonym for *earnings, net earnings,* and *profit.* (p. 12)

Net loss What results when expenses for a period exceed the income earned. (p. 12)

Net profit margin A profitability measure that compares a company's net income to its total revenues. It measures what portion of each sales dollar is left after covering all the expenses. Synonym for *profit margin ratio.* (p. 562)

Net realizable value (NRV) The selling price of a unit of inventory less any costs necessary to complete and sell the unit. (p. 332)

Net sales Gross sales less sales returns and allowances and sales discounts. (p. 180)

Net wages Wages that will be paid to employees after source deductions. (p. 417)

Neutral An element of the fundamental qualitative characteristic of faithful representation that states that financial information should be unbiased: neither optimistic nor overly conservative. (p. 54)

No par value shares Shares that have no par value assigned to them in the articles of incorporation. (p. 500)

Non-controlling interest Synonym for *minority interest.* (p. 503)

Non-current An asset or liability presented in financial statements that will not be received, realized, consumed, or settled or paid within 12 months from the fiscal year end. (p. 16)

Non-IFRS financial measure A measure that has not been defined by accounting standard setters as part of the International Financial Reporting Standards. (p. 229)

Normal balance The balance (debit or credit) that an account is normally expected to have. Assets, expenses and losses normally have debit balances. Liabilities, shareholders' equity, revenues and gains normally have credit balances. It is also used to indicate how the account is increased in a journal entry. The opposite of an account's normal balance is used to record a decrease to the account. (p. 118)

Notes to the financial statements Section of a company's financial statements where management provides more details about specific items, such as significant accounting policies, the types of inventory and assets held, and so on. (p. 21)

O

Obligations under finance lease A financing liability recorded when a lease is classified as a finance lease. (p. 453)

On account A transaction to purchase goods or services to be paid for at a later date, which creates an account receivable on the seller's books and an account payable on the purchaser's books. Synonym for *credit sale.* (p. 63)

Operating activities The activities of a company that are related to selling goods and services to customers, and other basic day-to-day activities related to operating the business. (pp. 9, 173, 210)

Operating efficiency ratios Synonym for *activity ratios.* (p. 556)

Operating lease A lease in which the lessee does not record an asset and related obligation but treats the lease as a mutually unexecuted contract. Lease expense or rent expense is then simply recognized as payments are made. (p. 453)

Operating segments The various businesses activities within a company, or various geographic regions in which a company operates. (p. 544)

Ordinary shares A term, used primarily outside North America, for common shares. (p. 502)

Other comprehensive income Changes in net asset values representing unrealized gains and losses, which are not included in net earnings but are included in comprehensive income. (pp. 184, 498)

Outstanding shares The number of shares that are held by individuals or entities outside the corporation (that is, it excludes treasury shares). (p. 500)

Overfunded A pension plan in which the value of the plan assets exceeds the amount of the projected benefit obligation. (p. 456)

Overhead Manufacturing costs other than the costs of raw materials and labour, such as utilities and depreciation of the manufacturing facility. (p. 319)

P

Par In the context of bond prices, a term used to indicate that a bond is sold or issued at its face value. (p. 449)

Par value shares Common shares for which a value per share is set in the articles of incorporation. (p. 500)

Parent company A company that owns and controls other companies, known as subsidiaries. (p. 12)

Partially executed contract A contract between two entities in which one or both of the parties has performed a portion of its part of the agreement. (p. 410)

Participating preferred shares Preferred shares with a feature that increases the dividend rate on the shares so that it results in dividends equivalent to those being paid to common shareholders. (p. 506)

Pay periods The time frames for which employees are paid. Normally these are two weeks in duration, with employees being paid 26 times each calendar year. (p. 417)

P/E multiple Synonym for *price/earnings (P/E) ratio*. (p. 565)

Percentage of completion method A method of revenue recognition used in the construction industry in which a percentage of the profits that are expected to be realized from a given project are recognized in a given period, based on the percentage of the project's completion. The percentage completed is typically measured as the fraction of costs incurred to date relative to the total estimated costs to complete the project. (p. 177)

Percentage of credit sales method A method of estimating bad debts expense by using a percentage of the credit sales for the period. Also known as the statement of income method. (p. 281)

Periodic inventory system An inventory system in which cost of goods sold is determined by counting ending inventory, assigning costs to these units, and then subtracting the ending inventory value from cost of goods available for sale (that is, the sum of the beginning inventory plus purchases for the period). (p. 321)

Permanent accounts Accounts whose balances carry over from one period to the next. All statement of financial position accounts are permanent accounts. (p. 122)

Perpetual inventory system An inventory system in which the cost of goods sold is determined at the time a unit is sold and ending inventory is always known, in both units and dollars. (p. 322)

Post-employment benefits Benefits other than pensions provided to retirees. These benefits are typically health care or life insurance benefits. (p. 457)

Posting The process of transferring the information from the journal entries in the general journal to the ledger accounts in the general ledger. (p. 131)

Predictive value An element of the fundamental qualitative characteristic of relevance that states that accounting information is relevant to decision makers when it helps predict future outcomes. (p. 53)

Pre-emptive right The right of shareholders to share proportionately in new issuances of shares so that their ownership interest will not be diluted by future share issuances. Synonym for *anti-dilution provision*. (p. 503)

Preference shares A term, used primarily outside North America, for preferred shares. (p. 504)

Preferred shares An ownership right in which the shareholder has some preference over common shareholders as to dividends; that is, if dividends are declared, the preferred shareholders receive them first. Other rights that are normally held by common shareholders may also be changed in preferred shares; for example, most preferred shares are non-voting. (p. 504)

Premium In the context of bond prices, a term used to indicate that a bond is sold or issued at an amount above its face value. (p. 449)

Price/earnings (P/E) ratio A performance ratio that compares the market price per share with the earnings per share. It is calculated as market price per share divided by earnings per share. Synonym for *P/E multiple*. (pp. 513, 565)

Principal The initial amount lent or borrowed. (p. 7)

Private company Company whose shares do not trade on a public stock exchange. (p. 6)

Private placement The offering of corporate bonds for sale only to specific institutional investors, such as banks, insurance companies, and pension funds, that have agreed to purchase the bonds in advance. (p. 447)

Profit Synonym for *earnings*, *net earnings*, or *net income*. (p. 12)

Profit margin ratio A ratio that compares the net income (or profit or earnings) during an accounting period with the related revenues. Synonym for *net profit margin*. (p. 76)

Profitability ratios Ratios used to assess a company's ability to generate profits. (p. 553)

Prospective analysis A financial statement analysis of a company that attempts to look forward in time to predict future results. (p. 546)

Prospectus A document filed with a securities commission by a corporation when it wants to issue public debt or shares to the pubic. (p. 501)

Provision for warranty claims Synonym for *warranty provision*. (p. 410)

Provisions Liabilities where there is uncertainty about the timing or the amount of the future expenditures. (p. 410)

Public company   Company whose shares trade on a public stock exchange. (p. 6)

Public offering   The offering of corporate bonds for sale to the public, both individuals and institutions. (p. 447)

Q

Quantity discount   A price reduction that reduces the purchase price and is given to the buyer for volume purchases. (p. 179)

Quebec Pension Plan (QPP)   The Quebec government program providing retirement benefits to retired workers based on the premiums they and their employers paid into the plan when they were working. (p. 416)

Quick assets   A company's current assets less inventory and prepaid expenses. (p. 288)

Quick ratio   A measure of a company's short-term liquidity, calculated by dividing the most liquid current assets (primarily cash, short-term investments, and accounts receivable) by the total current liabilities. Synonym for *acid test ratio*. (pp. 288, 555)

R

Rate reset   Characteristic of preferred shares by which they pay a fixed dividend from their issuance until a pre-established reset date when a new fixed rate will be established. (p. 504)

Raw materials   All of the items required to manufacture a product. (p. 319)

Reclassification entry   Journal entry to reclassify an item, such as a non-current item becoming current. (p. 408)

Recoverable amount   Amount used when there are indications that an item of property, plant, and equipment may be impaired. The impairment amount is equal to carrying amount less the recoverable amount, which is the greater of the future cash flows that are expected to be generated from an asset's use, and the asset's fair value less any selling costs. (p. 376)

Recovery   The reinstatement and collection of an account receivable that was previously written off. (p. 280)

Redeemable preferred shares   Preferred shares with a feature that gives the issuer the right to repurchase (or redeem) them from shareholders at specified future dates and amounts. (p. 505)

Red flags   Changes in ratios that identify areas for analysts to investigate further. (p. 552)

Relative fair value   The proportion that an asset's fair value represents of the total fair value of a group of assets

purchased in a single transaction (that is, a basket purchase), which is used to allocate the purchase price. (p. 364)

Relevant   A fundamental qualitative characteristic of useful financial information that states that useful financial information must matter to users' decision-making. (p. 53)

Remittance   The payment of employee source deductions, together with the employer's share, to the federal or other government. (p. 418)

Representationally faithful   A fundamental qualitative characteristic of useful financial information, stating that the information in the financial statements should represent events and transactions as they actually took place or are at present. (p. 53)

Reset date   Date on which the fixed dividend paid on rate reset preferred shares is set at a new fixed rate reflecting the economic conditions and borrowing rates at that time. (p. 504)

Retailer   Synonym for *merchandiser*. (p. 317)

Retained earnings   Earnings that are kept within a company and reinvested, rather than being paid out to shareholders in the form of dividends. (p. 10)

Retractable preferred shares   Shares that can be sold back to a company (retired) at the shareholder's option. The price that must be paid for them and the periods of time within which they can be sold are specified in the articles of incorporation. (p. 506)

Retrospective analysis   A financial statement analysis of a company that looks only at historical data. (p. 546)

Return on assets (ROA)   A measure of profitability that measures the return on the investment in assets. It is calculated by dividing net income by the average total assets. (pp. 77, 563)

Return on equity (ROE)   A measure of profitability that measures the return on the investment made by common shareholders. It is calculated by dividing net income by the average common shareholders' equity. (pp. 76, 563)

Revaluation model   A model used to determine the amount at which property, plant, and equipment will be reflected on the statement of financial position, by which assets are carried at their fair value less any subsequent accumulated depreciation and any subsequent accumulated impairment losses. (p. 379)

Revenue recognition criteria   Conditions that must be satisfied for revenues to be recognized according to accrual accounting. (p. 56)

Revenues   Inflows of resources to a company that result from the sale of goods and/or services. (p. 12)

Reverse stock split   A stock split that decreases the number of outstanding shares and has the effect of increasing share prices. Reverse stock splits are done based on a specified ratio, such as one-for-two or one-for-five. Synonym for *consolidation*. (p. 512)

Revolving credit facilities   An agreement a company enters into with its bank, enabling it to borrow up to a negotiated limit. The company can use the credit facility as needed and repay it as funds are available. (p. 407)

S

Sales discount   A price reduction that is based on the invoice price less any returns and allowances and is given by a seller for early payment of a credit sale (for example, 2/10; n/30). (pp. 180, 286)

Sales return provision   A provision established for the current liability to record the estimated returns based on a company's past experience and market conditions and recorded in the Sales Returns and Allowances account. (p. 410)

Sales returns   Returns of goods. (p. 180)

Sales returns and allowances   A contra revenue account used to record the estimate for returned goods or reduction in price for unsatisfactory merchandise. (p. 181)

Secured   Characteristic of loans or other debts for which specific assets have been pledged to guarantee repayment of the debt. (p. 408)

Senior debenture   A general borrowing of a company that has priority over other types of long-term borrowing in the event of bankruptcy. (p. 447)

Share capital   The shares issued by a company to its owners. Shares represent the ownership interest in the company. (p. 15)

Shareholders   The individuals or entities that own shares in a company. (p. 6)

Shareholders' equity   The shareholders' claim on total assets, represented by the investment of the shareholders (share capital) and undistributed earnings (retained earnings) generated by the company. (p. 10)

Single-step statement of income   A statement of income in which all revenues are listed in one section and all expenses (except income tax, perhaps) are listed in a second section. (p. 182)

Solvency ratios   Ratios used to assess a company's ability to meet its long-term obligations. (p. 553)

Source deductions   Amounts withheld from employee wages and remitted to the government by the employer to pay for such things as income taxes and Employment Insurance and government pension premiums. (p. 416)

Special dividend   A dividend declared and paid by a company periodically without any regularity. Also known as a one-time dividend. (p. 507)

Specific identification (specific ID)   A cost formula of assigning costs to units of inventory in which the cost of a unit can be specifically identified from company records. (p. 326)

Specific revenue recognition criteria   Criteria developed that specify the conditions under which revenue should be recognized for the sale of goods, the provision of services, and the receipt of interest, royalties, and dividends. (p. 175)

Standby fees   Fees or interest charged by financial institutions for any unused portion of revolving credit facilities such as a line of credit, as the cost of having funds available when needed. (p. 408)

Stated dividend rate   Synonym for *fixed dividend rate*. (p. 504)

Statement of cash flows   Financial statement that summarizes the cash flows of a company during the accounting period, categorized into operating, investing, and financing activities. (pp. 20, 209)

Statement of changes in equity   Financial statement that measures the changes in the equity of a company over a period of time, differentiating between changes that result from transactions with shareholders and those resulting from the company's operations. Also known as the statement of changes in shareholders' equity, statement of shareholders' equity, and statement of equity. (p. 15)

Statement of comprehensive income   Financial statement showing net income plus other components of other comprehensive income, combined to produce the total comprehensive income. (p. 184)

Statement of financial position   Financial statement that indicates the resources controlled by a company (assets) and the claims on those resources (by creditors and investors) at a given point in time. Also known as the balance sheet. (p. 16)

Statement of income   Financial statement showing a company's revenues and expenses, indicating the operating performance over a period of time. Also known as the income statement, the statement of operations, statement of earnings, and statement of profit or loss. (p. 12)

Stock dividend   A distribution of additional common shares to shareholders. Existing shareholders receive shares in proportion to the number of shares they already own. (p. 509)

Stock split A distribution of new shares to shareholders. The new shares take the place of existing shares, and existing shareholders receive new shares in proportion to the number of old shares they already own. (p. 511)

Stockout A situation arising when a company sells all of a specific item of inventory and has no more available (in stock). (p. 318)

Straight-line depreciation A method of calculating depreciation in which the amount of expense for each period is found by dividing an asset's depreciable amount (equal to cost less estimated residual value) by its estimated useful life. Synonym for *straight-line method*. (p. 68)

Straight-line method Synonym for *straight-line depreciation*. (p. 366)

Straight-line rate The depreciation rate for the straight-line method, determined by dividing one by the estimated useful life of an asset. (p. 370)

Subledger Ledger that contains the details of information included in a general ledger account; for example, with accounts receivable, all of the account details for each customer are specified in the accounts receivable subledger. The total of all accounts in the subledger must equal the total in the related general ledger account, which is known as the control account. Synonym for *subsidiary ledger*. (p. 277)

Subordinated debenture A general borrowing of a company that has a lower priority than senior debentures in the event of bankruptcy. (p. 447)

Subsidiary company A company that is owned and controlled by a parent company. (p. 12)

Subsidiary ledger Synonym for *subledger*. (p. 277)

Synoptic approach Synonym for *template approach*. (p. 57)

T

T2 The corporate tax return document required to be filed by corporations with the federal government to indicate the amount of corporate income tax owed. Synonym for *corporate tax return*. (p. 420)

Tangible asset An asset that has physical substance. (p. 361)

Target benefit plan Synonym for *hybrid pension plan*. (p. 457)

Template approach The most basic of accounting systems, which uses the accounting equation for transaction analysis and recording. Synonym for *synoptic approach*. (p. 57)

Temporary accounts Accounts used to keep track of information temporarily during each accounting period. The balances in these accounts are eventually transferred to a permanent account (Retained Earnings) at the end of the period by making closing entries. (p. 122)

Time value of money The concept that a specified sum of money is worth more if it is paid or received now rather than later (because money received now can be invested to grow to a larger amount later). More generally stated, the value of a specified amount of money decreases as the time until it is paid or received increases. (p. 406)

Timeliness An enhancing qualitative characteristic that states that the information in financial statements must be timely to be useful. (p. 53)

Times interest earned ratio Synonym for *interest coverage ratio*. (p. 463)

Trade discount A negotiated or posted reduction to the selling price of a good or service. (p. 179)

Trade payables Amount of goods or services a company has purchased on credit from suppliers. (p. 409)

Treasury shares Shares that are repurchased by a corporation and held internally. Repurchased shares are normally cancelled immediately upon purchase. (p. 500)

Trend analysis The examination of a company's information from multiple periods (normally years) to look for any patterns in the data over time. (p. 546)

Trial balance A listing of all the general ledger accounts and their balances. Used to check whether the total of the debit balances is equal to the total of the credit balances. (p. 132)

Trustee In the context of pension plans, an independent party that holds and invests the pension plan assets on behalf of a company and its employees. (p. 455)

U

Uncollectible accounts Accounts receivable that are deemed to be bad debts. The point at which they are deemed uncollectible is generally established by company policy. (p. 269)

Underfunded A pension plan in which the value of the plan assets is less than the amount of the projected benefit obligation. (p. 456)

Understandability An enhancing qualitative characteristic that states that accounting information is useful when it is prepared with enough information and in a clear enough format for users to comprehend it. (p. 53)

Underwriter   An investment bank that arranges and agrees to sell the initial issuance of bonds or other securities. (p. 447)

Unearned revenues   Synonym for *deferred revenues*. (p. 410)

Units-of-production method   A method of depreciation that allocates an asset's depreciable cost to the years of its useful life as a function of the amount of its usage or production each period. Also known as the units-of-output method. (p. 366)

Unsecured   Characteristic of loans or other debts when no specific assets have been pledged to guarantee repayment of the debt. (p. 408)

Useful life   The period of time that management estimates a capital asset (such as equipment) is expected to be used. (p. 68)

V

Verifiability   An enhancing qualitative characteristic that states that useful financial information is such that a third party, with sufficient understanding, would arrive at a similar result to that determined by management. (p. 53)

Vested benefits   Employer contributions to a company pension plan that belong to the employees, even if they leave the company. (p. 455)

W

Wages payable   A current liability representing the amount of wages earned by employees since they were last paid. (p. 416)

Warranty provision   A liability representing the estimated cost of providing warranty services on goods sold in each period. Synonym for *provision for warranty claim*. (p. 410)

Weighted-average (W/A)   A cost formula for assigning costs to units of inventory in which each unit is assigned the weighted-average cost of the units available for sale at that point. (p. 326)

Window dressing   The manipulation of certain ratios, such as current and quick ratios, by undertaking or postponing transactions to produce a more desirable number. (p. 568)

With recourse   Characteristic of a company's receivables purchased by a factor whereby the factor can go back to the seller for payment if it is unable to collect the receivable. (p. 287)

Without recourse   Characteristic of a company's receivables purchased by a factor whereby the factor will bear the loss of any receivable it is unable to collect. (p. 287)

Work-in-process   A class of inventory used to record the costs of products that have been started but have not been completed at the end of the accounting period. (p. 319)

Working capital   The liquid funds available for use in a company, calculated as current assets minus current liabilities. (p. 16)

Working capital loan   A short-term loan, often on a demand basis, that is arranged with a bank to cover a company's short-term cash shortages. (p. 408)

Working capital ratio   Synonym for *current ratio*. (p. 287)

Writeoff   The process of removing an account receivable from a company's books when the account is deemed uncollectible. (p. 279)

Y

Yield   Synonym for *effective rate*. (p. 447)

COMPANY INDEX

SUBJECT INDEX

PHOTO CREDITS

KEY EXHIBITS

KEY DISTINCTIONS BETWEEN THE FORMS OF BUSINESS (Chapter 1)

Distinguishing Feature	Corporation	Proprietorship	Partnership
Number of owners	Can be a single owner or multiple owners	Single owner	Multiple owners
Separate legal entity?	Yes, personal assets of shareholders *are not* at risk in the event of legal action against company	No, personal assets of owner *are* at risk in the event of legal action	No, partners' personal assets *are* at risk in the event of legal action
Owner(s) responsible for debts of the business?	Only to extent of investment	Yes	Yes
Taxed?	Yes, taxed separately	No, profits taxed in hands of owner	No, profits taxed in hands of owners
Costs to establish	Most expensive	Least expensive	Moderately expensive
Cost to maintain	Most expensive	Least expensive	Moderately expensive

CATEGORIES OF BUSINESS ACTIVITIES (Chapter 1)

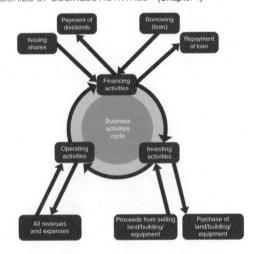

INFORMATION FLOWS BETWEEN THE THREE F/S (Chapter 1)

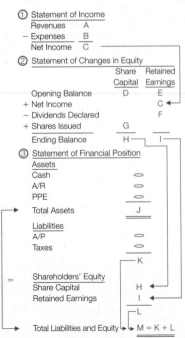

① Statement of Income

Revenues	A
– Expenses	B
Net Income	C

② Statement of Changes in Equity

	Share Capital	Retained Earnings
Opening Balance	D	E
+ Net Income		C
– Dividends Declared		F
+ Shares Issued	G	
Ending Balance	H	I

③ Statement of Financial Position

Assets
- Cash
- A/R
- PPE
- Total Assets   J

Liabilities
- A/P
- Taxes
  K

= Shareholders' Equity
- Share Capital   H
- Retained Earnings   I
  L

Total Liabilities and Equity   M = K + L

QUALITATIVE CHARACTERISTICS GRAPHIC (Chapter 2)

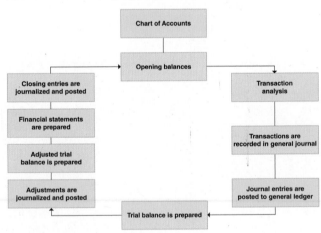

NORMAL BALANCES (Chapter 3)

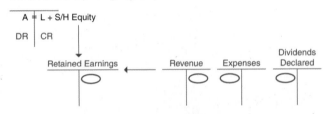

ACCOUNTING CYCLE (Chapter 3)

- Chart of Accounts
- Opening balances
- Transaction analysis
- Transactions are recorded in general journal
- Journal entries are posted to general ledger
- Trial balance is prepared
- Adjustments are journalized and posted
- Adjusted trial balance is prepared
- Financial statements are prepared
- Closing entries are journalized and posted

CLOSING ENTRIES (Chapter 3)

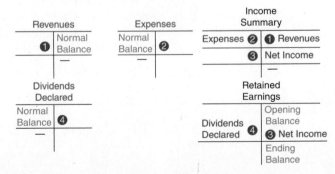

REVENUE RECOGNITION CRITERIA BY CATEGORY (Chapter 4)

	Revenue is earned from the:		
Criteria	**Sale of Goods**	**Provision of Services**	**Receipt of Interest, Royalties, and Dividends**
1. The significant risks and rewards of ownership of the goods have been transferred to the buyer.	Yes	Not applicable	Not applicable
2. The seller has no continuing involvement or control over the goods.	Yes	Not applicable	Not applicable
3. The amount of the revenue can be reliably measured.	Yes	Yes	Yes
4. It is probable that the economic benefits from the transaction will flow to the seller.	Yes	Yes	Yes
5. The costs incurred or that will be incurred to complete the transaction can be reliably measured.	Yes	Yes	Not applicable
6. The portion of the total services completed can be reliably measured (if services are ongoing).	Not applicable	Yes	Not applicable

TYPICAL TRANSACTIONS BY CASH FLOW CATEGORY (Chapter 5)

Typical Operating Activities	Inflows:	• Cash sales to customers • Collections of amounts owed by customers
	Outflows:	• Purchases of inventory • Payments of amounts owed to suppliers • Payments of expenses such as wages, rent, and interest • Payments of taxes owed to the government
Typical Investing Activities	Inflows:	• Proceeds from the sale of property, plant, and equipment • Proceeds from the sale of shares of other companies
	Outflows:	• Purchases of property, plant, and equipment • Purchases of shares of other companies
Typical Financing Activities	Inflows:	• Borrowing money • Issuing shares
	Outflows:	• Repaying loan principal • Paying dividends

DIRECT METHOD – COMMON CATEGORIES (Chapter 5)

Category	Starting Point (from Statement of Income)	Adjustments (from Statement of Financial Position)
Receipts from Customers	Sales Revenue	+/– Change in Accounts Receivable
Payments to Suppliers	Expenses other than:	+/– Change in Inventory
	• Wage Expense	+/– Change in Prepaid Expenses
	• Interest Expense	+/– Change in Accounts Payable
	• Income Tax Expense	
	• Depreciation and Amortization Expense	
Payments to Employees	Wage Expense	+/– Change in Wages Payable
Payment of Interest	Interest Expense	+/– Change in Interest Payable
Payment of Income Taxes	Income Tax Expense	+/– Change in Income Taxes Payable

CASH FLOW PATTERNS (Chapter 5)

Cash Flow from Operating Activities	Cash Flow from Investing Activities	Cash Flow from Financing Activities	Pattern Number and Company Profile
+	+	+	1. Successful, but actively repositioning or relocating using financing from operations together with cash from creditors and shareholders
+	+	–	2. Successful, mature company that is downsizing and returning capital to shareholders or repaying debt
+	–	+	3. Successful and growing, with growth partially financed by creditors and shareholders
+	–	–	4. Successful, with operating activities providing sufficient cash to finance growth and repay debt or pay dividends
–	+	+	5. Struggling, but using cash inflows from the sale of property, plant, and equipment and new borrowings to remain in operation
–	+	–	6. Struggling and using cash from the sale of property, plant, and equipment to repay creditors
–	–	+	7. A start-up or a struggling company that is able to attract financing for growth or reorganization
–	–	–	8. Struggling, but using existing cash balances to cover losses, purchase property, plant, and equipment, and repay creditors

FORMAT OF A BANK RECONCILIATION (Chapter 6)

Things we know, but the bank does not
- Bank Balance
  - add: Outstanding Deposits
  - less: Outstanding Cheques

Things the bank knows, but we don't until bank statement received
- G/L Balance
  - add: Interest / EFT Receipts
  - less: Bank Charges / EFT Payments / NSF Cheques

Reconciled Balance = Reconciled Balance

ACCOUNTS RECEIVABLE AND ALLOWANCE FOR D/A (Chapter 6)

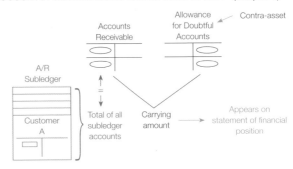

CASH-TO-CASH CYCLE (Chapter 6)

① Goods may be on hand for 30–90 days

② Customer may have 30 or more days of free credit

KEY DISTINCTIONS BETWEEN INVENTORY SYSTEMS (Chapter 7)

	Perpetual Inventory System	Periodic Inventory System
Timing of accounting entries	• Continuously • Every time inventory is purchased or sold	• Only purchase information is recorded • All other entries are made at the end of each accounting period

Accounting entries:

When inventory purchased	DR Inventory
	   CR Cash or Accounts Payable
		DR Purchases
		   CR Cash or Accounts Payable

At time of sale	DR Cash or Accounts Receivable
	   CR Sales Revenue
	DR Cost of Goods Sold
	   CR Inventory
		DR Cash or Accounts Receivable
		   CR Sales Revenue

Additional closing entry required?	No year-end entry unless there is theft or shrinkage to record	DR Inventory (ending)
		DR Cost of Goods Sold
		   CR Purchases
		   CR Inventory (opening)

Inventory counts	Yes, they are required on an annual basis for internal control purposes, but are not required to calculate cost of goods sold and ending inventory	Yes, they are required at the end of each accounting period to calculate cost of goods sold and ending inventory

COST FORMULA DECISION TREE (Chapter 7)

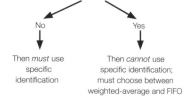

Are goods interchangeable?
(that is, they are not unique, identifiable items)

No → Then *must* use specific identification

Yes → Then *cannot* use specific identification; must choose between weighted-average and FIFO

CARRYING AMOUNT (Chapter 8)

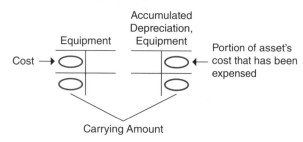

Cost → Equipment

Accumulated Depreciation, Equipment → Portion of asset's cost that has been expensed

Carrying Amount

ANNUAL DEPRECIATION EXPENSE / ASSET CARRYING AMOUNT (Chapter 8)

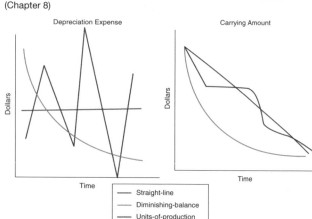

Depreciation Expense — Dollars / Time

Carrying Amount — Dollars / Time

— Straight-line
— Diminishing-balance
— Units-of-production

DETERMINATION OF GAINS/LOSSES (Chapter 8)

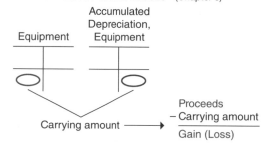

Equipment

Accumulated Depreciation, Equipment

Carrying amount →

Proceeds
− Carrying amount
Gain (Loss)

DIFFERENCES BETWEEN BONDS AND LOANS (Chapter 10)

	Bonds	Loans and Mortgages
Number of lenders	Multiple lenders	Single lender
Length of term	Generally longer than debt (5–40 years)	Generally shorter (1–5 years)
When interest is paid	Normally on a semi-annual basis (every 6 months)	Normally on a monthly basis
When principal is repaid	Normally at the end of the term (at maturity)	Not unusual to have a requirement for blended payments (each loan payment includes principal and interest)
Is there a secondary market?	Yes, there is an active secondary bond market	No, not normally
Is it convertible into shares?	Yes, this can be an option	No, not normally

YIELD VS. CONTRACT RATE (Chapter 10)

Investors' Required Yield vs. Contract Rate	Bonds will be Issued at…	Amount Received on Issuance vs. Face Value	Interest Expense vs. Contract Rate
Yield > Contract rate	Discount	< Face value	> Contract rate
Yield = Contract rate	Par	= Face value	= Contract rate
Yield < Contract rate	Premium	> Face value	< Contract rate

PURCHASING VS. LEASING (Chapter 10)

	Purchasing: Taking out a loan and purchasing the asset	Leasing: Entering into a finance lease for the asset	Leasing: Entering into an operating lease for the asset
Is the asset recorded on the statement of financial position?	Yes	Yes	No
Is a liability recorded on the statement of financial position?	Yes	Yes	No
Is depreciation expense recorded?	Yes	Yes	No
Are interest expense and repayment of principal recorded?	Yes	Yes	No
Is rent expense recorded?	No	No	Yes